【山海经濮语解读】中英对照

SHANHAIJING: a Bilingual Text

张小蓉　译　张明友　著

竹和松出版社

出版：竹和松出版社（Zhu & Song Press）

Zhu & Song Press, LLC

North Potomac, MD 20878

书名：【山海经濮语解读】中英对照

著者：张小蓉 张明友

责任编辑：朱晓红

责编信箱：editor@zhuandsongpress.com

封面设计：竹和松传媒

出版社网址：www.zhuandsongpress.com

印刷地：美国，英国

开本：8.5 inch x 11 inch

字数：372 千字

印次：2025 年第 1 版

发行：全球（中国大陆除外）

ISBN-13：978-1-950797-61-5

电子版 ISBN-13：978-1-950797-62-2

前言

《山海经》是一部以商周文化之前的夏文化濮文编写的地理丛书，尽管战国时期及汉代对该书籍进行过翻译、汇总整理，但《山海经》的原书分册成书年代却是在夏末商初时期，《山经》的成书是在夏朝，《海经》的成书是在商朝。区别两者的依据是“可以”一词，这个词汇在《山经》中有，《海经》中没有，“可以”在濮语中是指“夏国的”。书中表达的基本概念是濮文化概念。笔者在研究夜郎文化的过程中，得到一个粗浅的认识，即商周文化之前的夏文化是已经很成熟的濮文化，这个阶段的濮文文字称为六划文，文字的笔划不能超过六划，这个规定说明，夏朝的濮文不能像甲骨文那样用原始的象形图形来表达。所以濮文与甲骨文之间反映出一个因战争和政权的变故出现的文化否定与倒退现象。这一现象促使夏王朝通行的濮语与濮文被边缘化，从而也使《山海经》不能让人读懂，甚至被译为风马牛不相及的奇形异物。如开篇的“狌狌”，原是指面部刺青的氏族，被译成了野生动物；江西峡江南段有个峡阳国，被译成在一万年前就绝迹于江南与两广地区的红毛猩猩。由于语言系统不同，后人用汉文化去解读濮文化的语言，就会出现偏差，以至生成怪象，表示种粮氏族的饶族饶夷被译成八足八尾，表示有“九”概念的九夷或共工氏族被译为有九个头，表示大城山地区的缴夷牧民被译为青丘九尾狐。

晋朝记室参军郭璞说：“物不自异，待我而异，异果在我，非物异也”。又说司马迁因张骞从西域回来，对西域的地理民风了解甚详，也未见到西王母，所以对《山海经》中的所有怪物不敢评论。其实司马迁之所以不敢评论，是因为他不知道汉文化对濮文化做了些什么。《山海经》就其书名而言已经说得很明白，是地理人文书籍，而不是《神异经》，我们有责任还原《山海经》的本来面目。

《山海经》在夏商时期成书，为我们提供了一些人们已经忘却的历史资料，如“二负杀窫窳”将夜郎国兴起的历史推至于商朝早期；“鲧窃息壤”记录了夏启北上收复失地的事件；“有易杀王亥”记录了黑龙江双鸭山地区部落兼并的事件；“东海夔牛”记录了夏族的北僚支系开辟流球群岛的事件；“九丘建木”记录了黄帝统一华夏后将国家划分为九个管理区的事件等等。

综观《山海经》全书，其内容表述的语言，至今仍包含在仡佬语、凉山彝语、阿坝羌语、布衣语、苗语、壮语、越闽语、粤语、古印度语、阿拉伯语、北非语、古希腊语、拉丁语、通古斯语、日语和雅利安语中。这些语言或多或少存在于夜郎文化的语言系统中，也存在于全国各族的地区方言中。如印度的“雅利安”，德国的“宝马”、“雪福莱”，法国的“嘎纳”，瑞士的“维也纳”，英国的“不列颠”、“出行”、“枪炮”，日本的“山”、“阿基姆族”、“樱花”，利比亚的“的里亳里”、“班加西”，两河流域的“汉莫拉比”，红海湾的“索马里”、“莫桑比克”等等都是用濮语表达的。我们可以用濮文来解读古希腊神话，可以用濮文来读印度河流域出土的陶制印章，也可以通过濮文了解德国和英国所保持的十字太阳崇拜的传统。在我国北方，蒙古语的“索额济纳”、赫哲族、满族的狩猎概念“腊博”、狩猎氏族“拉拉”、渔业氏族“赫哲”与仡佬语的表达相同，所以南方也有拉拉氏族和赫哲氏族。凉山彝族的语言与贵州的布衣族、仡佬族的语言基本相同，他们都以“阿”作否定语，以“灭蒙”表示母亲，所以“凉山”原是指“娘山”，凉山的彝族，《山海经》记录为“灭蒙僚”（汉译为灭蒙鸟）。这些民族的语言在新石器时代就已经融合、并普及为夏朝行政濮语语言。《山海经》就是一部用濮文编写的书籍。

笔者以濮文对汉译《山海经》进行还原和解读，除了尽可能恢复《山海经》作为地理、人文和历史读本的原貌外，还想证明“夜郎自司马相如进入后才有文化”的观点是不正确的。文化的概念不是以某种语言、文字试图覆盖其它的语言、文字而称其所有所无，商周文化之所以未能盖住《山海经》的传承，其原因就是人们希望读懂它隐藏的奥秘。

《山海经》的记述范围涵盖整个亚洲板块，东北至白令海峡的楚科奇山，东至日本列姑射岛，东南至菲律宾棉兰佬岛，西北至高加索山，西至土耳其阿菲永地区，西南至波斯湾霍尔姆斯海峡，南至我国的海南岛南端，北至西伯利亚北端的泰梅尔半岛。从记述的范围来看，在远古时期地理资料欠缺的情况下，《山海经》这部书，或《山经》、《海经》、《大荒经》、《海内经》这类书籍非一两个人能够编著完成，它应是夏王朝和商王朝的国家行为，是由一个聚各方经商而来的智者的写作班子集体编纂而成。写作的成员包括阿基姆人（汉语称倭奴）、棉兰人、通古斯人、丁零人、犬戎人、突厥人，鞑靼人、俄罗斯人、氐羌人、百濮人和中原的妥鲁则柯人。这些人从自己的家乡带来了他们所熟知的地理知识，将其汇总编纂成为夏王朝和商王朝的地理书籍，分为《山经》、《海经》、《大荒经》、《海内经》四个部分。这些书籍原本并无重复的记述，后人将其合编为《山海经》后就出现了重复之处，但记述的内容还是各有侧重。本人采用濮语解读，尽最大可能还原古书的原意，对一些大的神话还原，采用地理图片支持，比如三个表达西王母的地理举用昆仑山和乔戈里峰来说明;"钟山烛阴"附"天山草原"图片来说明;"狌狌"附面部刺青的黎族的图片来说明。因本人能力有限，不可能收集到所有的地理人文图片，书中所用图片，皆为借用各位摄影作者的图片，为参与诠释华夏古濮文化，望各位作者给予支持。读者在阅读《山海经濮语解读》时，可参照《中国地图册》和《世界地图册》，能够形成较为清晰的地理映像。

Introduction:

【Shanhaijing】 is an ethnogeographical compilation based on the Pu speech and graphs during the Xia period before the Shang and Zhou Dynasties。Although during the Warring times and Han Dynasty, Shanhaijing had gone through retranslation, editing and rearrangement, it is obvious that the original text had already been organized into different Juans (卷 volumes） by the end of Xia and early years of the Shang Dynasty。The volumes of Shan (山经 Mountains) are completed during the Xia Dynasty。The volumes of Hai (海经 Regions) are completed during the Shang Dynasty。 The telltale term is Keyi (可以）, which can be found in the first 5 volumes of Shan （山经五卷）, but not in the rest of the volumes。"keyi" is a Pu term to refer to Xia Guo （夏国 Xia Nation） and of the Xia Guo （夏国的）。 The basic terms throughout the pages are Pu concepts。 During my investigation and research of the Yelang culture （夜郎文化）, I have come to the basic understanding that the Xia culture that flourished before Shang and Zhou Dynasties had already developed to a mature stage。The writing system employs graphs which are called "liuhuawen"(六划文 six stroke graph） meaning each graph can only be made with no more than six strokes。This rule implies that the Pu script is no longer created in the same way the bone script is made by pictographs, which is a more primitive way of visualizing semantic information。 This shows a gap between the Pu script and Bone script, a reflection of a backward movement, a denial and return from the more advanced Pu writing system to the more primitive writing system。This is due to the wars and change of powers between different dynasties。 This regression had caused the Pu language and script to be marginalized and the writing system available during the Xia Dynasty to decline。Therefore, the Classical book of Shanhaijing is no longer intelligible to the following generations and suffers the fate of being translated into nonrelated terms descriptive of the grotesque and the strange。For instance, there is the mention of a "shengsheng"(translated by Anne Birrell as live-lively, a long-tailed ape)。 In Chinese it is a two-parts compound, on the left is an animal sign。The original meaning of Shengsheng refers to the clans that tattoo their faces (blue ink tattoo on the faces 面部刺青)。In this way, the clans have come to be identified as wild animals。 There is also a Xiayang Guo (峡阳国） on the southern stretch of the Xiajiang River (峡江)in today's Jiangxi （江西） province。This human group is written in Chinese characters as red-haired apes, which as a species had died out 10,000 years ago from the land south of Yangtze River, Guangdong, and Guangxi provinces。 Because of the information is registered in two different systems of linguistic import, the readers of later generation take it for granted that the classical book of Shanhaijing was written in Chinese and based their interpretation on Chinese rather than on the Pu language。This totally misleads the understanding and translation of the text and created a picture of the grotesque and the strange, its true meaning not accessible to its readers。 For instance, the Rao clans (饶族) of the crop growers are termed to have eight feet and eight tails。The Pu concept of Nine, originally a term for Jiu Yi (九夷 nine Yi) and Gonggong Shi （共工氏 the Shu Shi), are translated as having nine heads。 Also, the Jiao Yi (缴夷游牧民） nomadic clans from the Dachengshan （大城山）region are translated as a fox with nine tails perching on the green mount (qing qiu jiu wei hu 青丘九尾狐)。

The commentator Mr. Guo Pu, a secretary to the Record department of the Jin Dynasty(晋朝), said the following: "wu bu zi yi (物不自异 objects --things and beings-- are not differentiated of their own sake,) da wo er yi (待我而

异 they become different because I term them differently); Yi guo zai wo (异果在我 the different namings are the results of my mind,) fei yi wu ye (非异物也 not the results of their own provenance)。
It is also said that after Zhang Qian (张骞) returned from the West, he became well acquainted with the geography and social life there, yet he did not find the Queen Mother of the West, therefore Sima Qian (司马迁) kept his mouth shut about all the strange animals。The reason why Mr. Si Maqian kept his mouth shut is that he was not able to judge what the Chinese scribes and cultural environment had done to the Pu culture。The book 's title is obviously self-revealing, it is a compilation of geo- and ethno-information, not one of fantastic fictional objects。 It is our duty to restore this classic book to its true significance and true linguistic imports。

Shanhaijing was completed during the times of later Xia and early Shang, some historical events or information lost to later memory are still available on its pages。For instance, er fu sha ya yu【二负杀窫窳】: has pushed the rise of the Yelang Guo 【夜郎国】 further back to the earlier period of the Shang Dynasty。Gun qie xi rang【鲧窃息壤】 is a record of Qi【夏启】, the Xia leader, who led a military campaign to the north and reclaimed lost territory。 You yi sha wang hai【有易杀王亥】: records the event of the tribal annexation in Shuangyashan【双鸭山】 area, in today's Heilongjiang province。Dong hai kui niu【东海夔牛】 records the event of Beiliao branch 's exploration of the Kyoto Islands。 Jiu qiu jian mu【九丘建木】 records the event that Yellow Emperor had divided the territory of a unified Huaxia nation into nine administrative units。

In sum, Shanhaijing is a linguistic enterprise with inputs from different languages of Gelao, Liangshan Yi, Qiang from Aba, Buyi, Miao, Zhong, Yuemin, Yue, ancient Indian, Arabian, Northern Africa, ancient Greek, Latin, Tunguska, Japanese and Aryan。Those languages can still be found in the linguistic data bank of Yelang culture。 There are relics also in the many local dialects in the provinces all over China。 For instance, the following words:
Aryan from India,
Logo of BMW and Chevron from Germany,
Cana (Portu Canus) from France,
Vienna from Austria,
Bryton, canon from England,
Yama, Ajimu, Sakura from Japan,
Tripoli, Benghazi from Libya,
Hammurabi from Mesopotamia,
Somalia and Mozambique from Red Sea are all traceable to the Pu language。 We can explain and decode the Greek mythology, and read the clay seals from Indus River Valley, also gain insights into the tradition of sun cross worship in German and English cultures。In the northern parts of our country, the concept of Suoejina （索额济纳） from Mongolian, share the same roots with Hezhe, Bola, Lala from the hunting clans and the Man(满) people。The term of Hezhe（赫哲） is the same in Gelao speech, therefore one finds Lala tribes and Hezhe tribes both in the northern and in the southern parts of China。 The Yi people's(彝族) speech from Liangshan, is similar to the speech of Buyi people（布衣） and Gelao（仡佬） people from Guizhou（贵州）, they all use A as a negative marker, and they all call mother Miemeng（灭蒙）。Thus, we know the present Liangshan is originally called Niangshan, (mother mount 娘山) 。 And the Yi people from Liangshan is written down in Chinese as "Miemengliao" translated into Chinese as Miemeng bird(灭蒙鸟)。Bird in Chinese reads as niao, a close phonetic match to liao, N/L being interchangeable。Those tribal-nation speeches had gone through the process of assimilation during the Neolithic stages, and popularized into a common lingua franca as an administrative tool during the Xia dynasty and Shanhaijing is written in the Pu language and script。

This author has presented a translation of Shanghaijing 's old text into a new translation in present day Chinese, tracing the terms in the old text back to their roots in the Pu speech。 Besides restoring the historical information of geography and ethnology to their roots, and doing my best in decoding the text, I wish to make a statement that the long-held opinion that Yelang Guo(夜郎国) only started to become cultured after Si Ma Xiangru(司马相如) arrived is not valid。The concept of culture is not decided on whether Chinese language or script had arrived。The reason why the cultures of Shang and Zhou dynasties failed to block the transmission of Shanhaijing is because the desire of the following generations of readers to know what secret information it contains between its lines。

The territories covered by Shanhaijing is the entire Asian part of the Eurasian continent, with Chukchi mountain by the Bering Strait in the northeast; Japanese Islands in the east, Mindanao in Philippines in the southeast , the Great Caucasus mountains in the northwest, Afyon region in Turkey in the west, Hormoz Strait in Persian Gulf in Southwest, Hainan Island in the south in China and Taymyr Peninsula in the northern tip of Siberia in the north。Judging from the scope of its geological description, withstanding the lack of geological information in ancient times, the enterprise of compiling Shanhaijing, or its volumes of Shan（山经）, Hai（海经）, Dahua（大荒经） and Hainei（海内经）, far surpasses the abilities of one or two individual compilers。 It should have been a national enterprise sponsored by the courts of Shang and Zhou Dynasties, with contributors made up of traders and literary persons from four corners of the world。Its members include Ajimu (倭奴 Wonu in Chinese), Mindanao（棉兰人）, Tunguska（通古斯人）, Dingling（丁零人）, Dogrong（犬戎人）, Turkish（突厥人）, Dadarian（鞑靼人）, Russian（俄罗斯人）, Diqiang（氐羌人）, Baipu（百濮人）, and Tuoluzeke（妥鲁则柯） from Zhongyuan (中原 middle plains)。Those people brought their familiar information of their homelands to this center, and those pieces of information were compiled into a set of geographical volumes as Shanjin(山经), Haijing（海经）, Dahuajing（大荒经） and Haineijing （海内经）, a total of 4 parts。 In the beginning, there are no repetitions。However, later compilers put the four parts into a whole book and named it Shanhaijing。Therefore, some repetitions occur, withstanding the emphasis in each part is different。 I am now offering a new reading of the Chinese text through my knowledge of the Pu speech and doing my best to restore the original linguistic imports to my Chinese text。 For a number of major mythological narratives, I offer my narratives and support my claims with pictures of geography。 For instance, the three instances of reference to the Queen Mother of the West (西王母)are shown together with photos of Kunlun Mountains and K2。Zhongshanzhuyin（钟山烛阴） are explained with a picture of the Tianshan Steppe。Shengsheng (狌狌)is aided with a picture of a woman from the Li tribe who has her face tattooed with blue ink。Taken into consideration of my limited access to graphic data of geography and ethnology, I have made use of photos by various photographers, as an aid to the elucidation and explanation of the ancient Huaxia (华夏) history recorded mainly in Pu speech。Readers of my re-translation of Shanhaijing through Pu speech will be best served by the aid of maps of China and the World, to form concrete ideas of its geographical information。

“龙”的起源与《山海经》的关系提示

《山海经》是濮文书籍，没有龙的概念与读音表达。“龙”的读音在《山海经》中主要是记写如“僚”（liao/lao）音，意思是“人”与“河流”。而龙的概念的产生起源于红山文化的“天空王”概念，“天空王”在濮语中读为“幕古瓦muguwa”，“幕古”是指天空，“瓦”是指猪，濮文化的“王”是由猪概念演绎而成的，原因是一猪二熊三老虎，猪是老大。“天”字在濮文中写为“丁”，而且横笔划一般写成波浪形，“空”字在濮文中写为反“C”字，可以与“丁”字合形，就成了“玉猪龙”的形像，以猪头代替“王”字既形像，又有美感。但这个造型饰品产生时并不读“龙”，只读“慕古瓦”，简称“古瓦”，主要用作对上苍的祭祀，再后来，成为部落姜央宫闱的专用玉勾以显示其王者的身份。龙的概念的真正产生，是黄帝族“燕僚”被谐音解读为应龙，王者古瓦的概念同时被移植到应龙身上，此时王者古瓦的文化意识才开始显现在“僚”的谐音“龙”的概念上，而且，商周甲骨文对此有明确的注释，说明古瓦为龙是商周时期才开始拟定的。虽然夏王朝已有初步的龙凤概念，但这个概念是以东西方位的汾洛概念来表达的，只是代替男女阴阳关系，而并不表达王者意识。因为人类社会的发展进程是从濮到僚，从母系到父系，所以用方位概念与用濮僚概念一样，都是对阴阳概念的一种比拟。而商王朝的以阳性表达天王的意识还来源于他们的太阳崇拜，“古瓦”同时也谐音为“寡”，所以从商王朝开始，那些自比至高无上的王者们总以“寡人”自称。在继承燕僚为龙的王者概念的基础上，商族这个狼崇拜的氏族开始将猪龙的形象修改为狼龙的形象，而且还给龙加了两只前脚。到了周朝晚期，龙才开始有了四只脚可以腾云驾雾。那么在此之前的夏文化和商初文化中，我们根本找不到成熟的龙文化概念，所以《山海经》的汉译本的龙的牵强附会是可想而知的，我们在阅读《山海经》时，应当注意这个问题。

The Creation of Dragon concept and its relationship to Shanhaijing

Shanhaijing is a classic based on Pu speech, and there is no concept of dragon and its vocalization in Pu language。Loong(dragon) is a phonetic rendering of the concept of Liao（lao 僚） in Shanhaijing, which mainly refers to people or rivers。The germination of the concept of dragon Liao only came through the Hongshan (红山文化)culture's concept of the Lord of sky。 In the Pu speech, "the lord of sky" is vocalized as Muguwa, in it, mugu means sky, wa means pig。In Pu culture, the concept of Lord comes from the concept of pig。This is because during the Hongshan period, the hierarchy of power is shown with pig as the greatest, bear the second and tiger the third。Pig is number One。In the Pu script, the graph for sky （tian 天） is written as 丁。 The top horizontal stroke is written as a waving line。 The graph for empty (kong 空 or the big void) is written as C turned into its mirror image。 The combination of these two graphs makes a compound, which is the picture image of the Jade pig dragon（玉猪龙）。 The pig head is a graphic sign for the Lord which is a visual construction of the image and pleasing to the eyes。However, this image does not read as Loong（龙, it is read only as Muguwa, or shortened to Guwa, a term mostly used for ritual to the High Above。Later, the design has become a functional hook of jade decorating the handrails of the tribal palace to show the standing of the Lord。 The real coming of age of the concept of dragon /Loong is during the Huangdi tribes time, when their identity of "Yanliao" （燕僚）was shifted to a phonetic rendering of Yingloong （应龙）。The Lordship carried by the Guwa concept is also shifted to Yingloong。 Only till then, the Lord of Guwa as a culture concept has been added to the Liao/Loong term。This term is defined by the Bone script of the Shang and Zhou dynasties, which shows that only during the Shang and Zhou period, did the concept of Guwa being replaced by Loong completed。Although there is the priliminary conception of the Dragon Loong and Bird Phoenix during the Xia dynasty, the concept is signified by the cardinal terms of east and west through the river names of Luo(洛) and Fen（汾）, Luo being the west and Fen being the east in reference of Yellow River。 Even so, the conception is only a metaphor for male and female, or Yin and Yang relatedness, not for the ideology of Lord or King。The early thoughts concerning the stage of human development is described as from the Pu to Liao, from matrilocal to patrilocal, therefore the concept of cardinal direction is the same as growth from Pu to Liao, both sets of concepts are based on the metaphor of Yin and Yang。The Shang people express their Yang essence (masculinity) in the form of the Sky lord in religious worship of the sun。The term Guwa is also conjugated into the term Gua (寡)。 This is why since the Shang dynasty, all the supreme leaders always use the epithet of Gua to address themselves to show their highest standing above everyone else。After inheriting this Guwa/loong (dragon) /Lord concept from the Yanliao, the Shang people, a wolf worshipping race started to attribute some of the features of Guwa/Pig-dragon to the Wolf-dragon by adding two front legs to the dragon。 It was only till the Zhou dynasty that the dragon thus acquired four legs and feet to be able to fly in the sky, riding the clouds。Yet before this point in history, we fail to find any concept of dragon which only came to maturity in the Xia and Shang cultures。 Therefore, it is not surprising to find rather compelled and far-fetched explanations of the concept and motif of dragon in the Chinese text of Shanhaijing。 This point deserves special attention。

《山海经解译》作者简介 :About the author and the translator

张明友，1957 年生于贵州省贵阳市，1980 年毕业于昆明地质学校探矿工程专业。曾就职于贵州地矿局第二水文工程勘察院、中化贵州地质勘查院，任工程师、高级工程师。业余爱好古濮文研究、夜郎文化研究，对贵州红崖碑文、青海柳湾遗址彩绘文、姜寨、大溪、台西、半坡、仰韶文化刻文、安徽蚌埠刻文、良渚和龙山文化刻文有详细的濮文化解读，对夜郎文化有独立的见解，对《山海经》的解读更为详细、真实。

Zhang Mingyou: born in 1957, Guiyang city, Guizhou province。A graduate of Kunming Dizhixuexiao, he has worked as a senior engineer in geo-sciences company in prospecting。An independent researcher in Pu and Yelang culture, Zhang Mingyou has presented detailed interpretations in Redcliff rock glyphs in Guizhou; of Pottery glyphs at Liuwan site, Qinghai province; at Jiangzhai, Daxi, Taixi, Banpo, Yangshao, as well as at Bengbu, Anhui province; and of glyphs at Liangzhu site and at Longshan site。 Furthermore, he offers his independent insight into the reinterpretation of Yelang culture and Shanhaijing based on his knowledge of Pu language。

《山海经解译》英译者 English translator

张小蓉 1952 年生于青海省西宁市，中国社会科学院研究生院新闻采编专业毕业，现旅居美国。

Zhang Xiaorong : born in 1952 in Xining city, Qinghai province, a graduate of English News Writing, graduate school, China's Institute of Social Sciences, now lives in Santa Rosa, California, USA。

英译者说明：

1. 【山海经濮语解读】原书的图片插图，本书未予以复制。
   All the pictures from the Chinese book are not reproduced。
2. 【山海经】一书的英译名，采用汉语拼音 SHANHAIJING, 书名中的【海】字，根据全书的语境，本译者认为译为英文 Seas , 是不妥的。因而对海外四经，海内四经， 海内经的各卷译名皆采用汉语拼音 Haiwai, Hainei 表达，而避免使用 beyond the seas, within the seas 的译法。
   The title of the book keeps the Pinyin version 【SHANHAIJING】。The word Hai 海 is not translated into 【sea】 or 【seas】 since this translator does not think Hai 海 means 【Seas】 in the context of the book。 Therefore, in the titles of book 6,7,8,9,10,11,12, 13,18, 【Haiwai 海外】 and 【Hainei 海内】 are used to avoid using terms of 【beyond the seas 】 or 【within the seas】。
3. 本文的汉字拼音记写使用的是汉语普通话的读音拼写。
   All the spellings of Chinese characters are based on Putonghua。

《山海经》常用濮语词例

A vocabulary list :
缩写说明：notes:

CS: Chinese sign 汉字
PTHPY: Putonghua Pinyin 普通话汉语拼音
EM: English meaning 英语语义
ET: English translation 英译
PC: Pu concept 濮语概念
PP: Pu Pronunciation 濮语读音

序号 汉字 普通话读音 英语语义 濮概念的汉语义和英译文 濮语读音
CS PTH Pinyin EM Pu concept in CM and ET PP

1 鸟 Niao bird 人，人群，河流 People，ethno-group，rivers Nao
2. 兽 Shou beast 属，族，氏族，Ethno belonging to, tribe, clan Shu
3. 鱼 Yu fish 夷，哲氏族，Yi, zhe, the zhe tribe, fishing tribes Yi, zhe,
4. 虫 chong worm 移民，草，人，Migrants, grass, people Chuo
5. 蛇 She snake 塞族，集市，夷 Saka, market town, yi people Sai
6. 蝮虫 Fuchong Worms moving on their stomach 濮族 Pu people, Pu clan, Pu tribes. Fucu
7. 水 Shui Water, river 族属 Affiliated to a tribe, or a clan Shui, shu
8. 虎 Hu tiger 濮族，胡族，牧业：Pu people, Hu people, husbandry. Fu, hu,
9. 豹 Bao leopard 僰，农业：bo people, agriculture Bo
10. 熊 xiong bear 肃慎族，狩猎业，华胥氏，sushen tribe, hunting, Huaxu Shi Su, xu,
11. 罴 Pi A kind of bear 蚂蚁，手工业，工业，河：Ants, handicrafts, industry, river. Bi
12. 鸾 luan A kind rare bird 西，西方，west, western Luo (洛)
13. 凤 feng Phoenix东，东方，east, eastern, Fu
14. 歌 ge Singing, song 城，皋，city, poli Go
15. 帝 Di Emperor 狄，北，北方：northern tribes，north, northern Di
16. 无 wu no，void， 做，部落，北方，to do，to make, tribes, northern part Wu
17. 巫 wu Witch, witchcrafts 部落：tribes, clans, Wu
18. 人 ren human 惹，永，定居，聚落，集镇
Re, lasting, settlement, inhabitation, townships Re
19. 婴儿 Ying'er baby 阴阿，北面 shady side, northern, north Ying e
20. 舞 wu dance，mime 部落，北：tribes, clans, northern, Wu
21. 草 cao grass 移民：immigrants, migrants Chuo
22. 木 mu tree 中心：center， Mu
23. 建木 jianmu Raise a tree 管理中心：administration center。 Jiemu
24. 可以 Keyi can，able 夏国的：of the Xia nation Ko e
25. 其音如 qiyinru Its voice is like-- 歇脚在，住在，stop over at, live at, Qiyinre

26. 尸 shi corpse 肆，集市，bazaar, marketplace, mart Si
27. 舜葬 Shun zang God Shun's burial 纹身氏族疆域：the territory of tribes who tattoo themselves. Sengzang
28. 夸父 Kua fu Boast father 北胡，卓资联盟：northern Hu, Zhuozi confederacy Kuohu
29. 豕 Shi pig 插，种植，planting, growing She
30. 马 ma horse 莽，蒙，苗：Mang, meng, Miao ethno-groups. Ma. mang
31. 马腹 mafu Horse belly 莽山濮：pu tribes from Mangshan Mountain Mangfu
32. 比 bi compare 河：river Bi
33. 臂 bi arm 河：river Bi
34. 首 shou Head，chieftain 族，属：Tribe, belong to, shu，shou.
35. 窫窳 yayi Notch flaw (Anne Birrell) 大河，大河边，big river, big river bank, by the big river Yeyi
36. 二负，贰负 Er fu Twain load 能洪鲁（mountain name）阿富 afghan, Afghanistan Lehu
37. 杀 sha Kill, murder Se: 入侵：invade,
Sa: 外边，旁边，远：outside, by the side, faraway Se, sa
38. 八 ba Eight 饶，粮食，种植：abundance，grain, growing Rao
39. 食 shi Food, eat 始，古老的, beginning, ancient, old, Si
40. 毒 du Poison, poisonous 古老的：ancient, old，Du
41. 毒鱼 duyu Poisonous fish 古老的夷人，ancient Yi people Duyi
42. 此 ci this，移民，迁徙，游：migrants，migrate，nomads, roam Ci
43. 黄帝 huangdiYellow emperor 黄帝，北山，北胡，大自然：yellow emperor, northern mountain northern Hu, nature. Hudi
44. 帝俊 dijun God handsome 世间，大自然，北方，北方部落：existence, nature, north, northern tribes. Dijin
45. 太昊 Tai hao Supreme brightness 宇宙，世间，大自然 Cosmos, existence, nature Tohou
46. 嘎 ga A sound imitation 外边，旁边，outside, by the side Ga
47. 西王母 xiwangmu West queen mother 雪域高原：snowcapped plateau Xiwumu
48. 开明兽 kaimingshou Enlightened beast 丝绸族：silk making tribes, Kemieshu
49. 共工 gonggong Common work 共和，索额羲，数底羲，叔德羲，republic, suo'exi, shudixi, shudexi Shudixi
50. 颛顼 zhuanxu God benevolent 长河，贤德，贤明者，照羲，long river, Enlightened, benevolent, zhaoxi Zhongxi
51. 奚仲 xizhong 贤德，贤明者，Enlightened, benevolent, Xizhong
52. 鸟鼠同穴 niaoshutongxue Bird rat share cave 俄罗斯，（罗斯妥羲）大草滩国：Russia, Russ, big steppe nation. Luosituoxi
53. 轩辕 Xuan yuan Cart shaft 大的，首脑的，主席；of the big, of the head, chairman, first seat, Xieye
54. 珥践 Er jian Earlop bugged，管理 Management,
55. 四蛇 Si she Four snakes 四夷，四方百姓：branches of major clan, people from four corners. Buyi
56. 一足 Yi zu One-foot 崇拜虎，大支系，tiger worship, major lineage. Yezhu
57. 使四鸟 Shi si niao Employ 4 birds 从事四种劳动：engaged in four kinds of labour, bird/niao/liao; 鸟，僚，Shibulao
58. 见则 jianze When seen --then--- 那里，那个：there, that Jinjio

59. 佩之 peizhi Wear it 经常，常用于：often， often used in Peize
60. 瘕疾 Jiaji Belly illness 首饰，jewlery
decoration, headdress, Jiaoji
61. 据比 Jubi Rely compare 清河，clear water river Jibi
62. 龙身鸟首 Longshenniaoshou Dragon body bird head 普通僚族 average Liao branches
Lusenglaosu
63. 鸟身龙首 niaoshenlongshou Bird body dragon head 僚族的普通人 average member of the
Liao tribes Laosenglusu
64. 人面马身 renmianmashen Human face horse body 定居的蒙族，定居的胡族 settled Meng
tribes, settled Hu tribes Remimengseng
65. 羊身人面 yangshenrenmian Goat body human face 牧羊的居民: shepherds' residents
Hosengremi
66. 人身龙首 Renshen longshou Human body dragon head 定居的牧族 settled herders
Resengleshu
67. 兽首人面 Shoushou renmian Beast head human face 狩猎的居民 hunters' residents Susuremi
68. 人身羊角 Renshen yangjiao Human body ram horns 定居的东部氏族，定居的东夏族：
settled eastern tribes, settled Eastern Xia tribes: dongxia tribes. Resengcigo
69. 人面兽身 renmianshoushen Human face beast body 定居的狩猎氏族：settled hunting tribes
Remisuseng
70. 马身龙首 mashenlongshou Horse body dragon head 苗族僚属 liao branch of the Miao
tribe. Mangsenglaoshu

目录：Contents

第一卷南山经(Mountains in the South)

南山经第一山系

Book 1 Nanshanjing; Chapter 1

01-01-01 鹊山 招摇山
Queshan Zhaoyaoshan
（105,6759E；23,61161N）

南山经之首曰鹊山[1]。其首曰招摇[2]之山，临于西海之上，多[3]桂，多金玉。有草[4]焉，其状如韭而青花[5]，其名曰祝余[6]，食之不饥[7]。有木[8]焉，其状如穀而黑理[9]，其花四照[10]，其名曰迷穀[11]，佩之不迷[12]。有兽[13]焉，其状如禺而白耳[14]，伏行人走[15]，其名曰狌狌[16]，食之善走[17]。丽麂（ji）之水出焉，而西流注于海[18]，其中多育沛[19]，佩之无瘕疾[20]。

注释：[1]鹊：指向阳之方、南边、最南边。在此指最南边。
Notes: [1] que（magpie）
Tr: towards the sunny direction; south, the southmost, here it refers to the southmost area。

[2] 招摇：指瑶山，在此指上瑶山，音译为六诏瑶，简称六诏，今广西六诏山。
[2] zhao yao (wave shake),
Tr: it refers to Yaoshan, the Shangyaoshan (Upper Yao Mountain) 。It is a Phonetic rendering into Chinese Liuzhaoyao, shortened to Liu Zhao, today's Liuzhaoshan in Guangxi province。

[3]多：指多、生长着、生活着、出产。
[3] duo（many, a lot}
Tr:1: many, a great quantity, plenty，(Chinese)
2: dwell，growing, living, producing, (Pu concept)

[4]草：指移民氏族。
[4] cao（grass）
Tr:1：grass；(Chinese)
2：migrant tribes, tribes of immigrants (Pu concept)

[5] 韭而青花：指广原的稌禾支系。广原即广西。
[5] jiu er qing hua:（leek with green flowers）。

Tr: refers to the Jihe [Panicum miliaceum /millet planters] branch from Guangyuan area, Guangyuan refers to the present Guangxi province。

[6] 祝余：指僮（zhong) 夷，濮族的支系氏族，今称壮族。

[6] zhu yu（pray extra）

Tr: it refers to the Zhuang ethnic group, a Pu branch, known today as the Zhuang people。

[7] 食之不饥：古老的广原氏族。

[7] shi zhi bu ji（eat it never hungry）

Tr: it refers to the ancient Guangyuan clan.

Shi(食，始)

1: eat, food, (Chinese)

2: beginning, (Chinese)

3: ancient, age-old, (Pu concept)

Eat 食: shi, a phonetic match to shi 始 (beginning) which means very old tribes。

[8]木：指苗瑶氏族。

[8]mu (wood, tree)

Tr: it refers to the Miaoyao （Hmong–Mien） clan。

[9] 榖而黑理：唱歌的能手。

[9]gu er hei li（paper mulberry bark with dark markings）

Tr: great singers。gu: a close phonetic match to Chinese term singing or songs 。 榖/歌 gu/ge 歌: songs or singing, is read as gu in Pu language。

[10] 其花四照：才华是天生的。

[10] qi hua si zhao（its flowers shine four corners）

Tr: their talents are naturally born。

[11] 迷榖：迷指舞，榖指歌；迷榖指歌舞氏族。

[11]mi gu: （lost paper mulberry）

Tr: mi: dance, gu: singing, migu refers to clans famous for their singing and dancing talents。

[12] 佩之不迷：经常跳舞。

[12] pei zhi bu mi（wearing this never get lost）

Tr: often dance。mi: mime

[13]兽：指氏族。

[13] shou (beast)

Tr: a term refers to clans， a close phonetic match to shou(兽)， a Chinese term for beast, animal。

[14] 禺而白耳：水边的部落氏族。白耳即“巴莱”、部落。

[14]yu er bai er（monkey with white ears)

Tr: it refers to the clans by the riverbank。【White ear】reads as 【bai er】in Chinese， reads as 【Balai】 in Pu speech, which means tribes。

[15] 伏行人走：善于织花。

[15] fu xing ren zou（crouch move human walk）

Tr: skillful in weaving flowery patterns。

[16] 狌狌：指舜舜，即纹身氏族和刺绣氏族，在此指二者兼备的氏族。

[16] sheng sheng（ape-like animal),

Tr: a close phonetic match to Shunshun clans。Shunshun refers to clans that tattoo themselves and are skillful in needle work(embroidery), here the term Shunshun refers to tribes with both features。

[17] 食之善走：古老的纹身氏族。

[17] shi zhi shan zou (eat it good at walking)

Tr: ancient clans that tattoo their bodies。

[18] 丽麂（ji) 之水出焉，而西流注于海：驮娘江发源于这座山，向东流入大海。濮语“东” 的读音为 xi。
[18]li ji zhi shui chu yan (Liji River rises out of here), er xi liu zhu yu hai (flows west into sea) 。
Tr: Tuoniangjiang (carry mother river) rises out of this mountain and goes east into the sea。 East in Pu speech reads as 【xi】, an accidental phonetic punning to Chinese concept of west【西】。

[19] 育沛：指水晶。
[19]yu pei (breed energetic)
Tr：it refers to shui jing—crystal。

[20] 佩之无瘕疾：常用于做首饰。无，指舞弄、做；瘕疾，指首饰。
[20] pei zhi wu jia ji (wear it no growing lumps in belly) 。 Jiaji：（lumps in the belly）
Tr: wu:
1: Pu concept: make or play with
2: Chinese concepts: void 无,
瘕疾 Jiaji： a Pu concept for jewelry , a close phonetic match to Chinese concept: lumps in the belly。

译文：南山经的第一山系称为鹊山山系，鹊山最西边的山叫六诏山，临于西部的边缘，出产桂树、金矿和玉石。那里有一个移民氏族，是广原的穄禾支系，名叫僮夷，是古老的广原氏族。那里有一个苗瑶氏族，是著名的唱歌能手，才华是天生的，称为歌舞氏族，他们经常跳舞。那里还有一个氏族，是水边的部落氏族，善于织花，名叫舜舜，是古老的纹身氏族。驮娘江发源于这座山，向东流入大海，驮娘江中有许多水晶，常用于做首饰。
Translation:
The 1st list of mountains in the South (Nanshanjing) is called Queshan Mountains 。 Its westmost mountain is the Liuzhaoshan, which sits on the western boundary。 Chinese cinnamon trees, deposits of gold and jade are found there。There lives a clan of migrants, who are known as Millet (Jihe 穄禾) branches of Guangyuan。 They are called Zhuang people, an ancient clan from Guangyuan。Another Miaoyao clan lives there, who are famous for singing, a talent they are born with。 They are called clans of singers and dancers。They often dance。There is another clan by the riverbank, whose people are most skilled in weaving flowery patterns。They are called Shunshun, a very ancient clan whose members keep a tradition of tattooing their bodies。 Tuoniangjiang River rises from this mountain and flows east into the sea。Crystals are found in the river and often made into jewelry。

01-01-02 堂庭山
Tangtingshan
（107,14334E；23,08145N)

又东三百里，曰堂庭之山[1]，多棪木[2]，多白猿[3]，多水玉[4]，多黄金[5]。

注释：[1]堂庭山：指天地山，今称天等山，今广西崇左市天等县城。
Notes:[1] tang ting shan (hall court mountain)
Tr: it refers to Tiandishan (sky earth mount), also known today as the Tiandengshan (sky wait mount), in the Tiandeng county seat, Chongzuo City, Guangxi province。Tingtang, Tiandi and Tiandeng are close phonetic matches。

[2] 多棪木：住着丽川氏族。多，指住着；棪，读 you，指丽；木，读 me，指川。
[2]duo yan mu (plenty Yan tree)
Tr: it refers to the Lichuan clans。 duo 多: live, yan 棪: reads as 【you】 in Pu speech, meaning li 丽:(pretty), mu 木(tree) reads as me, meaning river, chuan 川 (river, water) 。

[3] 白猿：指百灵氏族。猿，读琊，指灵。
[3] bai yuan (white ape)

Tr: it refers to the Bailing clans。
Tr：yuan 猿(ape) reads as xia in Pu language, which means clever, spirited。 Bailing 百灵（clever in a hundred ways), the name of the local clan: the Bailing clan。
[4] 水玉：指虽夷，即青云夷，今称水族。
[4] shui yu (water jade)
Tr: it refers to Sui Yi 虽夷, also known as the Qingyun 青云夷（blue cloud yi）, today is listed as a Shui ethnic group 水族。shui(water); shui/sui, close phonetic matches。
[5] 黄金：指放更氏族，今称更放氏族。
[5] huang jin (yellow gold)
Tr: it refers to the Fanggeng 放更 (release change) clan, known today as the Gengfang 更放 clan。 The name is in reversed word order。

译文：由六诏山往东三百里，有座山叫天地山，那里住着丽川氏族，住着百灵氏族，住着水族，住着放更氏族。
Translation:
Three hundred li further east from Liuzhaoshan there stands Tiandishan。On the mountain there live the Lichuan clan, the Bailing clan, the Shui clan and the Fanggeng clan。

01-01-03 猨翼山
Yuanyishan
（108,47848E；22,74757N）

又东三百八十里，曰猨翼之山[1]，其中多怪兽[2]，多怪鱼[3]，多白玉[4]，多蝮虫[5]，多怪蛇[6]，多怪木[7]，不可以上[8]。

注释：[1]猨翼山：指大堂山，汉译为堂俞山，今谐音称为铜鱼山。实际指南宁地区。
Notes：[1] yuan yi shan (monkey wing mount)
Tr: it refers to Datangshan 大堂山 (Big court mountain)，the Chinese translation is Tangyushan 堂俞山, a close phonetic match to its present name Tongyushan 铜鱼山 (bronze fish mountain), which refers to the present Nanning 南宁 area in Guangxi province。
[2] 怪兽：南宁古称蓝舍，濮语读为灌舍，灌舍的氏族谐音称为怪兽。
[2] guai shou (grotesque beast)
Tr: it refers to the present Nanning Area in Guangxi province, its ancient name is Lanshe 蓝舍 (blue house) 。In Pu concept，Lanshe reads as guan she 灌舍（flood house）, a close phonetic match to guai shou 怪兽。
[3] 怪鱼：蓝舍夷。
[3] guai yu (grotesque fish)
Tr: the term refers to the Lanshe Yi (blue house Yi) (蓝舍夷)
[4] 白玉：百越氏族。
[4] bai yu (white jade),
Tr: it refers to the Baiyue 百越 clans--the Hundred Yue clans。
[5] 蝮虫：濮族。
[5] fu chong:（snake /or worms moving on their bellies)
Tr: it refers to the Pu 濮 ethnic people。
[6] 怪蛇：蓝舍。
[6] guai she (grotesque snake)
Tr: it refers to the Lanshe Yi, (the blue house people) 。
She:

1. Snake 蛇
2. House 舍

[7] 怪木：蓝舍苗。
[7] guai mu (grotesque wood)
Tr: it refers to the Lanshe Miao。

[8] 不可以上：夏族以外的氏族。
[8] bu ke yi shang (cannot go up there),
Tr: it refers to the clans and tribes other than the Xia (夏)ethnic people。

译文：由天地山往东三百八十里，有座山叫铜鱼山。这里生活着蓝舍氏族: 分别是蓝舍夷、百越人、濮族和蓝舍的苗瑶氏族，是夏族以外的氏族。
Translation:
Three hundred and eighty li further east from Tiandishan there stands the Tongyushan (bronze fish mount) 。The Lanshe clans live there, they are the Lanshe Yi, Baiyue people (Hundred Yue people), Pu people, Hmong Mien clans of the Lanshe。They are the outsider ethnic groups other than the Xia 夏 people 。

01-01-04 杻阳山
Niuyangshan
（109,2695E；22,41536N）

又东三百七十里，曰杻阳之山[1]，其阳多赤金，其阴多白金。有兽焉，其状如马而白首[2]，其文如虎而赤尾[3]，其音如谣[4]，其名曰鹿蜀[5]，佩之宜子孙[6]。怪水[7] 出焉，而东流注于宪翼之水 [8] 。其中多玄龟 [9] ，其状如龟，鸟首虺尾 [10] ，其名曰旋龟 [11] 。其音如判木[12] 。佩之不聋[13]，可以为底[14]。

注释：[1]杻阳山：指罗阳山。
Notes： [1] niu yang shan (niuwood sun mount) refers to Luoyanshan。

[2] 马而白首：苗族的山区氏族。
[2]ma er bai shou (horse with white head),
Tr: it refers to the mountain clans of the Miao people。

[3] 其文如虎而赤尾：服饰像胡族犬戎的服饰。
[3] qi wen ru hu er chi wei (its markings like tiger's, with red tail)
Tr： the tribal dresses with patterns and decors like that of the Dogrong 犬戎 people--the Hu tribes。

[4] 其音如谣：住在乐民镇。
[4] qi yin ru yao (its voice like a lullaby）
Tr: living in Leminzhen （happy people town）。

[5] 鹿蜀：指罗族。
[5]lu shu (deer shu) refers to the Luo tribe。

[6] 佩之宜子孙：常用家支标记纹身。
[6] pei zhi yi zi sun (wearing these benefits one's descendants)
Tr: often tattoo their bodies with the totem patterns of their branches。

[7] 怪水：指北水，濮语称北为阔和武，怪是阔的谐音，今称武思江。
[7] guai shui (grotesque water）
Tr: Beishui (northern water), north is read in Pu speech as Kuo 阔 (broad, rich) and Wu 武(militant, warlike), guai and kuo are close phonetic matches, referring to the present Wusijiang 武思江(Wusi River)。

[8] 宪翼：指长江，在此指珠江。
[8] xian yi (constitution wings)

Tr: refers to the Yangtze 长江 river (also written as Changjiang, Yangzi River), here it refers to the Pearl 珠江 River, or the Zhujiang 珠江 River 。

[9] 玄龟：指东蓝舍濮，读音邪灌。

[9] xuan gui (black turtle)

Tr: refers to the east Lanshe （blue house） Pu people, xuan-gui(玄龟) and xie-guan (邪灌 evil fill in) a near phonetic match。

[10] 鸟首虺尾：僚族的贵族。

[10] niao shou hui wei (yi), (bird head poisonous snake tail),

Tr： it refers to the noble lineage of the Lao/Liao tribes。

[11] 旋龟：同玄龟，指东蓝舍濮，读音邪灌。

[11] xuan gui (rotating turtle)

Tr: another name for the black turtle, xuan 旋, 玄, (a pair of close phonetic matches to xie guan, a Pu concept for the East Lanshe Pu) 。

Tr: refers to the east Lanshe Pu people, (玄龟, 旋龟, 邪灌)

[12] 判木：帕木镇，今称木梓镇。

[12] pan mu (split wood, or judgment wood),

Tr: it refers to Pamuzhen, the present Muzizhen, pan/pa are close phonetic matches。

[13] 佩之不聋：经常打猎。

[13] pei zhi bu long (wear this never deaf)

Tr： often go hunting。

[14] 可以为底：夏国的南方少数民族。可以，指夏国的；为，指南方；底，指少、少数。

[14]ke yi wei di (can be the bottom)

Tr： refers to the minority ethnic peoples in the south of the Xia 夏 country, ke-yi/of Xia 夏 country; wei/ south; di： minority, smaller in number。

译文：由铜鱼山往东三百七十里，有座山叫罗阳山，山的南坡出产赤金，北坡出产白金。有一个氏族，是苗瑶的山区氏族，服饰像胡族犬戎的服饰，住在乐民镇，名叫罗族，常用家支标记纹身。武思江发源于这座山，向东北流入珠江。武思江畔生活着东蓝舍濮，是僚族的贵族，名叫邪灌，住在木梓镇，他们经常打猎，是夏国的南方少数民族。

Translation:

Three hundred and seventy li further east from the Tongyushan there stands the Luoyangshan。 On its southern slope, there is red gold, on its northern slope, there is white gold。 A clan lives there, they are the mountain tribes of the Miaoyao people。Their dresses resemble the outfit of the Hu tribe's Dogrong。They live in Leminzhen。Known as the Luo tribe, those people tattoo their bodies with the totem patterns of their branches。 The Wusi River rises from this mountain and goes northeast into the Pearl River。The east Lanshe Pu people along the riverbank are the noble lineage of the Liao tribe, whose name is Xieguan。They live in Muzizhen。 They often go hunting and are the ethnic minority in the Xia nation's southern part。

01-01-05 柢山

Dishan

（110,8419E；22,98104N）

又东三百里，曰柢山[1]，多水，无草木[2]。有鱼[3]焉，其状如牛 [4]，陵居 [5]，蛇尾有翼 [6]，其羽在魼下 [7]，其音如留牛 [8]，其名曰鯥 [9]，冬死而夏生[10]，食之无肿疾[11]。

注释：[1]柢山：待山的谐音，指云开大山。

Notes: [1] di shan /dai shan; di/dai: phonetic match, refers to Yunkaidashan，（clouds open big mountain）。

[2] 多水，无草木：隶属于苍梧。
[2] duo shui, wu cao mu:(much water, no grass wood)
Tr: belongs to the Cangwu land or the Cangwu country。
[3]鱼：指渔民氏族。
[3]yu(fish): fishing clans。
[4]牛：指勾漏国。
[4] niu (bull, ox): the Goulou Guo （hook leak) country。
[5] 陵居：中心部落。
[5] ling ju:(higher ground residence)
Tr： refers to the central tribes。
[6] 蛇尾有翼：黄华河的瑶夷。
[6] she yi you yi (snake tail with wings)
Tr: it refers to the Yao Yi from the Huanghua （yellow blossom) River。
[7] 其羽在鲑下：住在棋象，也称象棋。
[7] qi yu zai qu xia (its feathers under que fish), allegedly the flatfish,
Tr: living in Qixiang, also written as Xiangqi (in reverse word order), qi(chess), xiang(elephant)。
[8] 其音如留牛：住在漏良，今称自良。
[8] qi yin ru liu niu; (its voice like remaining bull) 。
Tr: living in a place called Louliang, lou 漏(leaking), liang 良(good), its present name is Ziliang 自良。
[9]鯥：指漏瑶。
[9]lu4: 鱼，坴，blue fish, refers to the Louyao tribe,
[10] 冬死而夏生：家支建在象肆（即象棋）。
[10] dong si er xia sheng:(winter die summer come alive):
Tr: its home branch has established their living quarters in Xiangsi, Xiangsi and Xiangqi refer to the same location。
[11] 食之无肿疾：古老的贵族部落氏族。
[11] shi zhi wu zhong ji: (eat it will stop swelling)
Tr: the royal lineage of ancient clans。

译文：由罗阳山往东三百里，有座山叫云开大山，位于苍梧部落之地。有一个渔业氏族，是勾漏国的中心部落氏族，是黄华河的瑶夷，住在象棋和漏良，名叫漏瑶，家支建在象棋，是古老的贵族部落氏族。
Translation:
Three hundred li further east from the Luoyangshan there stands the Yunkaidashan。It is situated in where the Cangwu tribes live。 A fishing clan--the central branch of Goulou 勾漏 Guo(国), the Yao tribe from the Huanghua River, lives in Xiangqi, and Louliang。Known as Louyao, with their home branch center in Xiangqi， they are of the noble lineage of that ancient clan。

01-01-06 亶爰山
Danyuanshan
（112,03683E；22,92595N）

又东四百里，曰亶爰之山[1]，多水，无草木[2]，不可以上[3]。有兽焉，其状如狸而有髦[4]，其名曰类[5]，自为牝牡[6]，食之不妒[7]。

注释：[1]亶爰山：指云雾山。
Notes： [1] dan yuan shan: refers to Yunwushan (clouds mist mount) 。
[2] 多水，无草木：隶属于苍梧部落之地。
[2] duo shui, wu cao mu (plenty water, no grass wood)

Tr: belong to the land of the Cangwu tribes。

[3] 不可以上：夏国的外夷地区。

[3] bu ke yi shan（cannot go up)

Tr: ke yi (ko e)，a Pu term meaning the Xia 夏 country, it refers to the area where the outsider Yi 外夷 lives in the Xia country。

[4] 狸而有髦：山区的瑶苗。狸，指山区。

[4]li er you mao:（fox have hair)

Tr: li/fox；refers to mountainous area where the Yao-miao tribes live。

[5]类：指过山瑶。

[5] lei(category); refers to Guoshanyao (cross mountain yao)。

[6] 自为牝牡：自为，指江南，这里指珠江南岸；牝牡，指河岸边。

[6] zi wei pin mu:(self is female and male)

Tr：zi wei: south of the river, e.g., south of the Pearl River。pin mu：the bank of the river。

[7] 食之不妒：食之，始之，古老的；不妒，樊笃，农耕民。

[7] shi zhi bu du:(eat it not jealous),

Tr: shi zhi: ancient，the beginning；Bu du: agricultural people, who till the land。

译文：由云开大山往东四百里，有座山叫云雾山，位于苍梧部落之地，是夏国的外夷地区。那里有一个氏族，是山区的瑶苗，名叫过山瑶，住在珠江南岸的河岸边，是古老的农耕民族。

Translation:

Four hundred li further east from Yunkaidashan there stands Yunwushan, which is in the territory of the Cangwu tribe, where all the Xia country's outsider Yi tribes live。A tribe known as the mountain Yao-Miao tribe lives there。Their name is Guoshanyao。The Guoshanyao lives along the south bank of the Pearl River and are very ancient agricultural people。

01-01-07 基山

Jishan

（113,24699E；23,12203N）

又东三百里，曰基山[1]，其阳多玉，其阴多怪木[2]。有兽焉，其状如羊[3]，九尾四耳[4]，其目在背[5]，其名曰猼訑[6]，佩之不畏[7]。有鸟焉[8]，其状如鸡而三首[9]，六目、六足、三翼[10]，其名曰【尚鸟】【付鸟】[11]，食之无卧[12]。

注释：[1]基山：指棘山，即广山，今广州地区，又称为 bəRas（稻米）山，今谐音称为白云山，属九连山南麓。

Notes: [1] ji shan:(base mount)

Tr：refers to guang shan（(broad mount），present Guangzhou area, also known as rice mountain。bəRas (rice), is a close phonetic match to Baiyunshan (white clouds mountain), the south part of the Jiulianshan (nine link mountain)。

[2] 怪木：指棘勉族，南方读音为广勉、桂勉。

[2] guai mu (strange wood)

Tr: refers to the Jimian Zu (族，ethnic group)。In southern speech, it is read as guangmian, or guimian。

[3]羊（chi)：指东部的。

[3] yang (sheep)

Tr: yang is read as 【chi】 in Pu speech, means east part, of the east。

[4] 九尾四耳：指棘夷部落。四耳，在此读巴勒。

[4] jiu yi si er:（nine tail four ears)。

Tr: refers to the tribes of Ji Yi, or Ji people。Si er(四耳)：reads as bale。

[5] 其目在背：指溪蒙江南边，今流溪河南边。

[5] qi mu zai bei (its eyes on its back)

Tr: south side of the Ximeng River, present Liuxi River's south side。

[6] 猼訑：指 bəRas（稻米）族，音译为补粤、布衣。

[6]bo yi, bəRas, (rice planting tribes)

Tr: buyue, buyi, a close phonetic match to bəRas, the rice tribe。(布依文：Buxqyaix，国际音标：/pu˧ ʔjai˧ /；壮文：Bouxyaej；越南语：Bố Y)

[7] 佩之不畏：佩杰博维，指稻城，广州的古称谓，也称番禺。得名自 pajəy（水稻）。

[7] pei zhi bu wei:(wear it no fear)

Tr: close phonetic rendering of Peijiebowei 佩杰博维, a Pu term for rice city, the ancient name for Guangzhou city, which is also known as Panyu 番禺。The Chinese name comes from the term pajəy (water rice, paddy rice)。

[8] 有鸟焉：有一群人。

[8] you niao yan (have birds)

Tr: there is a group of people。

[9] 鸡而三首：棘山之外的氏族。

[9] ji er san shou:(chicken with three heads)

Tr: Refers to the tribes outside the Jishan。

[10] 六目、六足、三翼：指大城中心外边之夷，即乡村夷。六目六足，指大城中心。

[10] liu-mu,（six eyes）；liu-zu（six feet）；san-yi（three wings）：

Tr： refers to the outsider tribal people who live outside the major town centers。They are known as the countryside Yi 乡村夷。Liumu 六目 liuzu 六足: refers to the big town center。

[11] 【尚乌】【付乌】：指从濮。

[11] shang niao, fu niao: refers to Cong Pu。

[12] 无卧：从化部落，从化部落氏族。

[12] wu wo（no lying down）, refers to the Conghua tribe, and their clans。

译文：由云雾山往东三百里，有座山叫棘山，山的南面住着稻濮，北面住着棘勉族群。那里有一个氏族，是东部的棘夷部落氏族，住在溪蒙江南边的佩杰博维，名叫布衣。有一群人，是棘山之外的氏族，属乡村夷，名叫从濮，是古老的从化氏族。

Translation:

Three hundred li further east from Yunwushan there stands Jishan。The Rice grower Pu tribes live on its south side; the Jimian tribes live on its north side。 There lives a clan, they are the East Jiyi tribes。The Jiyi tribes live in Peijie(zhe)bowei, on the south side of the Ximeng River。They are known as Buyi people。 Another group of people， an outsider tribe to Jishan, is the countryside Yi, the Cong Pu。They are the ancient Conghua clans。

01-01-08 青丘山

Qingqiushan

（114,70405E；23,75711N）

又东三百里，曰青丘之山[1]，其阳多玉，其阴多青雘[2]。有兽焉，其状如狐而九尾[3]，其音如婴儿[4]，能食人[5]，食者不蛊[6]。有鸟焉，其状如鸠[7]，其音若呵[8]，名曰灌灌[9]，佩之不惑[10]。英水出焉[11]，南流注于翼之泽[12]。其中多赤鱬[13]，其状如鱼而人面[14]，其音如鸳鸯[15]，食之不疥[16]。

注释：[1]青丘山：濮语中青丘指东城，也读洛敷，今称罗浮，东城山即罗浮山。

Notes：[1] qing qiu shan (green mound)

Tr: qing qiu also read in Pu speech as luofu, referring to Dongcheng （east city), Dongchengshan, or Luofushan。

[2]玉、青雘：玉指粤濮，青雘指东濮。

[2]yu（jade），qing(green) hu(dyestuff)

Tr: refers to Yue Pu people; qinghu refers to east Pu people。

[3] 狐而九尾：濮族的棘夷。即濮族的南方夷。

[3]hu er jiu yi;(fox with nine tails)

Tr: refers to the Ji Yi of the Pu people, they are the southern Yi of the Pu ethnic people。

[4] 婴儿：指阴阿，即北边、北面。

[4] ying er: （infant baby）

Tr: refers to shady side, northern, or north side。

[5] 能食人：中心集镇。

[5] neng shi ren （can eat people）

Tr: refers to the market town in the central location。

[6] 食者不蛊：须浙博谷，即东江博谷，今称东源。

[6] shi zhi bu gu: （eat it not bewitched)

Tr: it is a phonetic rendering of the Pu concept: xu-zhe-bo-gu, (east river profound gully), e.g., Dongjiangbogu, present name is Dongguan, place name, dong (east), yuan(origin)。

[7]鸠：濮族九夷。

[7] jiu（pigeons），refers to the Jiu Yi（nine branches) of Pu people。

[8] 若呵：指若呵镇，今称回龙镇。

[8] ruo ke; Ruokezhen, the present Huilongzhen (returning dragon town) 。

[9] 灌灌：指蓝濮。

[９] guanguan (fill fill)

Tr: it refers to the Lan Pu tribe, the Blue Pu。

[10] 佩之不惑：指水稻的种植氏族。不惑，指僰禾，即种植。

[10] pei zhi bu huo (wear it never confused),

Tr: refers to paddy rice planting tribes。 bohe 僰禾, planting, a phonetic match to buhuo 不惑 (not confused) 。

Bo: broadcast seeds, sowing and planting。

[11] 英水：指东江。

[11] yin shui (yin river)

Tr: it refers to Dongjiang: East River,

[12] 翼之泽：指伊枝江。

[12] yi zhi ze (wings of big water），refers to Yizhijiang River。

[13] 赤鱬：指移民，（蚩鲁）。

[13] chi ru (red fish) refers to the immigrants, migrating people, written as chi lu。In Pu speech, r/l is interchangeable 。

[14] 鱼而人面：水边的定居氏族。

[14]yu er ren mian (fish with human face)

Tr: refers to the tribal people who settled by the water。

[15] 鸳鸯：指河源。

[15] yuanyang （love birds），refers to a place name Heyuan（river origin）

[16] 食之不疥：始之补哲，古老的渔民氏族。

[16] shi zhi bu jie (eat, no skin complains)

Tr: it is a close phonetic match to shi-zhi-bu-zhe: refers to the ancient fishing tribes。

译文：由棘山往东三百里，有座山叫罗浮山，山的南面生活着粤濮，北面生活着东濮。那里有一个氏族，是濮族的棘夷氏族，住在北部地区的中心集镇东源镇。有一群人，也是濮越的棘夷支系，住在回龙镇 名叫蓝濮，是水稻的种植氏族。英水发源于这座山，向南流入伊枝江。那里还生活着移民的族群，他们是水边的定居氏族，住在河源，是古老的渔民氏族。
Translation:
Three hundred li further east from Jishan there stands Luofushan。 On its south side there live the Yue Pu people, on its northern side there live the East Pu people。A Ji tribe of the Pu people lives in the central market town known as Danyuanzhen, in the northern part。Another group of people, also the Ji tribe branch of the Pu Yue, lives in Huilongzhen。They are called Lan Pu--the paddy rice cultivators。 The Ying River rises from this mountain and flows southward into the Yizhi River。Other migrant people now have settled down by the water source, they belong to an ancient fisherman clan。

01-01-09 箕尾山
Jiweishan
(116,18228E；23,74882N)

又东三百五十里，曰箕尾之山[1]，其尾踆[2]于东海，多沙石。汸水[3] 出焉，而南流注于淯 [4]，其中多白玉。
凡鹊山之首自招摇之山，以至箕尾之山，凡十（实际是九）山，二千九百五十里。其神状皆鸟身而龙首 [5] 。其祠之礼：毛 [6] 用一璋玉瘗 [7] ，糈 [8] 用稌米 [9] ，一璧，稻米，白菅为席 [10] 。

注释：[1]箕尾：指莲花。箕尾山指莲花山。
Notes:[1] ji wei： refers to lotus, therefore the Lianhuashan （lotus mountain）。
[2]踆（chui）：濮语指依着、紧挨着。
[2] chui, a Pu concept: seating on, lying close to, next to。
[3] 汸水：指丰顺水。
[3] Pang shui: the present Fengshunshui, or Fengshun River。
[4] 淯水：指榕江。
[4] Yu shui:(Yu River), the present Rongjiang River, (Rong River) 。
[5] 鸟身龙首：指种稻的僚族人形像。
[5] niao shen long shou（bird body with dragon head）
Tr: a set phrase for images of the rice planting tribes, which refers to the Liao/Lao people。
[6]毛：闻、祭词，代替祭词的玉。
[6] mao (fur, hair)
Tr: meaning 1. Hear； 2. votive speech。
Here it refers to a piece of jade as representing the votive speech。
[7]瘗：掩埋。
[7] yi, to bury, to cover。
[8]糈：指食物。
[8] xu3, food, (for sacrificial ceremony),
[9] 稌米：指荞麦米。濮语 "稌" 指荞，对于种稻的民族来说，荞是稀罕之物。
[9] tu2, refers to buckwheat in Pu language; the buckwheat is a rarity to the rice growing people。
[10] 白菅为席：用白茅草扎草人。席，指席儒，意为草人。
[10] Bai jian wei xi (white rush as mat), making strawman with white rush grass。mat: xiru, （mat scholar） straw figure made of white rush。

译文：由罗浮山往东三百五十里，有座山叫莲花山，紧挨着东海，多沙石。丰顺水从山间流出，向南流入榕江，这里住着布衣（稻米）氏族。

综观鹊山山系，自六诏山至莲花山，凡十山（实际只记录了九座山），蜿蜒二千九百五十里。这些山的山神，皆为种稻的僚族人的形象。祭祀之礼：祭词的玉用一璋玉埋入地下，供奉食品是荞米，用白茅草扎草人。

Translation:

Three hundred and fifty li further east from Luofushan there stands Lianhuashan, next to the East China Sea。There is a lot of sand and stone。 The Fengshun River flows out from the mountain, and goes south into the Rongjiang River, where the rice growing Buyi clans live。

In sum, the Queshan mountain list, from the Liuzhaoshan to the Lianhuashan, records 10 mountains in total, (in fact, there are only nine mountains), covering a distance of 2,950 li。All the Deities of the mountains are in the images of the rice growing tribes of the Liao Zu people。 The rite of sacrifice is as follows: bury underground a piece of Jade called Zhang, as representing the votive speech。 Sacrificial food is buckwheat, the messenger is a strawman made of white rush。

南山经第二山系

Book 1 Nanshanjing; chapter 2

01-02-01 柜山

Guishan/Kushan

（112,10267E；25,40507N）

南次二经之首，曰柜山[1]，西临流黄[2]，北望诸毗[3]，东望长右[4]。英水出焉[5]，西南流注于赤水[6]，其中多白玉，多丹粟[7]。有兽焉，其状如豚[8]，有距[9]，其音如狗吠[10]，其名曰狸力[11]，见则其县多土功[12]。有鸟焉，其状如鸱而人手[13]，其音如痺[14]，其名曰鴸[15]，其名自号也，见则多放士[16]。

注释：[1]柜（ku)山:指九山，濮语读苦狸，汉译为九嶷，后来又加了一个"山"字，成了九嶷山。

Notes： [1] ku shan（jiu shan： nine mount）。It reads as Gui in PTH (Putonghua, the common Chinese speech 普通话)， however reads as Ku in Pu language。

Tr： reads in Pu language as ku li (bitter leopard), Chinese transcribes it into jiu yi, and the classifier Mountain 山 is added to it, it is now known as Jiuyishan。

[2] 流黄：指江华镇。

[2] liu huang (flow yellow)

Tr： it refers to Jianghuazhen。

[3] 诸毗：指北面相邻的集镇。

[3] zhu pi（various neighbouring towns)

Tr: market towns near the north, pi: adjoin to 。

[4] 长右：指昌乐，今称乐昌。

[4] chang you (long right)

Tr: it refers to Changle, today's Lechang (pinyin: Lèchāng; historically Lokchong) 。

[5] 英水：连江，濮语读白(be)液，又称英水。

[5] ying shui: now known as Lianjiang, is read in Pu language as Beye (white liquid) also known as Yingshui (Ying River) 。

[6] 赤水：指珠江。

[6] chi shui（red water), refers to the Pearl River。

[7] 多白玉、多丹粟：住着连江集镇氏族。白玉，指连江；丹粟，指集镇氏族。

[7]duo bai yu、duo dan su (plenty white jade, plenty red Millet)

Tr: The Lianjiangzhen clans live here。baiyu; white jade -- Lianjiang River, dansu: red millet-- refers to township clans。

[8]豚：指土家族。

[8] tun (young pig), here refers to the Tujia people。

[9] 有距：指部落。

[9] you ju (having distance): refers to tribes。

[10] 狗吠：指蓝莞，今称蓝山县。

[10] gou fei (dog barking) refers to Languan (a kind of blue grass), today known as Lanshan County（blue mountain) 。

[11] 狸力：指嶷黎，即山里人。

[11]li li（leopard strength): refers to Yili：the mountain people。

[12] 见则其县多土功：那里的百姓较贫穷。土功，即吐躬，指贫穷。

[12] jian ze qi xian duo tu gong (seen, those counties are doing earth projects)

Tr: people there are rather poor。 tugong; Pu concept: being poor。

[13] 鴟而人手：靛江的纺织氏族。鴟，在此读 di 音，与靛谐音。

[13] di er ren shou (owl with human hands):

Tr: the textile clan by the Dian (blue color) River。鴟 chi/鴟 di, a kind of owls, di/dian, close phonetic match。

[14]痺：指沘，即河边，又称临澳，今称临武县。

[14] pi（numbness);

Tr: refers to a river, riverside, or over by the river. It refers to Linwu county (also as Lin'ao) 。

[15]鴸：指僮夷，今称壮族。

[15] zhu (a bird): refers to the Zhuang people, previously known as the Tóng Yi, the Zhuàng people。

[16] 见则其县多放士：那里的人们都对歌。

[16] jian ze qi xian duo fang shi（seen, counties more release scholar)

Tr：when they meet, people always sing to each other。

译文：南次二经的第一座山叫九嶷山。这座山西临江华镇，北望诸毗，东望昌乐（yue)。英水发源于这座山，向东南流入珠江，那里住着连江集镇氏族。那里有一个氏族，是土家部落氏族，住在蓝莞镇，名叫嶷黎，那里的百姓较贫穷。那里有一群人，是靛江的纺织氏族，住在临武镇，名叫僮（zhong)，他们自己也这样称呼，那里的人们都对歌。

Translation:

The first mountain of the 2nd mountain list in the Southern area is Jiuyishan。 The mountain looks onto Jianghuazhen to its west, the market towns to its north, and Changyue/Changle county to its east。 Originating from this mountain, the Ying River flows southeast to empty itself into the Pearl River。 The Tujia people live in Languan zhen, they are known as Yi Li。 People there are rather poor。 Another group of people known as the textile Zhuang along the Dian River live in Linwuzhen。 They address themselves as the Zhong。 When those people meet, they call and respond to each other in songs, a local tradition known as [dui ge] 。

01-02-02 长右山

Changyoushan

（113,35127E；25,13071N）

东南四百五十里，曰长右之山[1]，无草木，多水。有兽焉，其状如禺而四耳[2]，其名曰长右，其音如吟[3]，见则郡县大水[4]。

注释：[1]长右山：指昌乐（yue)山，今称乐昌山。
Notes：[1] chang you shan (long right mount)
Tr: chang：长/昌，乐：yue, le, today known as the Lechangshan。
[2] 禺而四耳：指水边的部落。
[2]yu er si er (animal with four ears)
Tr: tribes living close to the water。
[3] 其音如吟：住在乳源。
[3] qi yin ru yin (its voice like humming)
Tr: lives in Ruyuan (milk source) town。
[4] 见则郡县大水：那里的百姓都放牧。
[4] jian ze jun xian da shui (seen this animal, whole county be flooded)
Tr： the people there are herders。

译文：由九嶷往东南四百五十里，有座山叫乐昌山，那里是移民部落，住着云氏族。有一个氏族，是水边的部落氏族，名叫昌乐氏，住在乳源，那里的百姓都放牧。
Translation：
Four hundred and fifty li further southeast from the Jiuyishan there stands the Lechangshan where the Yun clan, a migrant people live。 A clan lives there, they are the riverside clan, known as the Changyue clan。 They live in a place called Ruyuan town, where people make a living herding animal。

01-02-03 尧光山
Yaoguangshan
（113,94849E；26,07693N）

又东三百四十里，曰尧光之山[1]，其阳多玉[2]，其阴多金[3]。有兽焉，其状如人而彘鬣[4]，穴居而冬蛰[5]，其名曰猾褢[6]，其音如斫木[7]，见则县有大繇[8]。

注释：[1]尧光山：指饶拱山，意为八门山，汉译为八面山。
Notes：[1] yao guang shan (rao light mount)
Tr: refers to the Raogongshan, the present Bamianshan（eight door mount or eight-sided mount）。
[2]玉：指河畔氏族。
[2]yu(jade) refers to riverbank clans。
[3]金：指横岭氏族。
[3] jin(gold) refers to the Hengling clan，Hengling (horizontal range) 。
[4] 彘鬣：指支那族，东夷苗族的统称。
[4] zhi lie (boar bristle) refers to the Zhina Zu (China/sina), an umbrella name for the Miao ethnic groups of Dong Yi (Eastern Yi) 。
[5] 穴居而冬蛰：且舍部落的支系。
[5] xue ju er dong zhe (cave live hibernate in winter)
Tr: the branches of Qieshe tribes。
[6] 猾褢（gui）：沤桂苗。
[6] hua gui: refers to the Ougui Miao people。

[7] 斫木：渣蒙，今称桂东，旁边有遗存名传承为龙渣。
[7] zhuo mu (split wood)
Tr: refers to Zhameng, a place in east Gui country, a relic place name Longzha remains。
[8] 大繇：指都有，即物产丰富。
[8] da yao (big kite)
Tr: it means abundance, rich in everything。

译文：从昌乐山往东北三百四十里，有座山叫八面山。山的南面住着河畔氏族，北面住着横岭氏族。有一个氏族，是定居的支那氏族，是且舍部落的支系，称为沤桂氏，他们住在桂东，那里物产丰富。
Translation:
Three hundred and forty li further northeast from Changyueshan there stands Bamianshan。 On its south side there live the riverbank clans, and on its northern side, lives the Hengling clan。 A sedentary clan called Chi-na lives there, they are a Qieshe branch, known as the Ougui Shi (氏)。 They live in the east of the Gui country, which is a place of abundance。

01-02-04 羽山
Yushan
（115,33384E；26,08484N）

又东三百五十里，曰羽山[1]，其下多水[2]，其上多雨[3]，无草木[4]，多蝮虫[5]。

注释：[1]羽山：今称于山。
Notes:[1]yu shan (feather mount), today's Yushan。
[2] 其下多水：东面生活着瑞氏族。
[2] qi xia duo shui (beneath it plenty water)
Tr：On its east side lives the Rui clan。
[3] 其上多雨：西面生活着于氏族。
[3] qi shang duo yu (above it lot rain)
Tr: On its west side lives the Yu clan。
[4] 无草木：没有迁徙的苗民。
[4] wu cao mu (no grass wood)
Tr: no migrant Miao people。
[5] 多蝮虫：都是濮族。
[5] duo fu chong (many belly moving snakes)
Tr: all the people living there belong to the Pu ethnic people。

译文：由八面山往东三百五十里，有座山叫于山，山的东边生活着瑞氏族，山的西边生活着于氏族，没有外来移民，都是濮族。
Translation:
Three hundred and fifty li further east from the Bamianshan there stands the Yushan。 The Rui clan lives on the east side of the mountain while the Yu clan lives on the west side。 There are no outside migrants, all the people belong to the Pu Zu。

01-02-05 瞿父山
Qufushan
（116,38005E；27,28904N）

又东三百七十里，曰瞿父之山[1]，无草木[2]，多金玉[3]。

注释：[1]瞿父山：指军峰山，实际是在于山的东北面。
Notes： [1] Qu fu shan (Qu father mount)
Tr: it refers to the Junfengshan (army peak mount), it lies to the northeast of Yushan。
[2] 无草木：没有移民。
[2] wu cao mu (no grass wood)
Tr: Having no migrants。
[3] 金玉：指黎夷。"金"的读音，濮语指人丁，黎也指人。（有黎川为证）
[3] jin yu (gold jade)
Tr: refers to the Li Yi。In Pu pronunciation, Jin refers to person, Li(黎)also refers to people， (as evidenced by Li Chuan, Li River, 黎川)。

译文：由于山往东北三百七十里，有座山叫军峰山，那里没有移民，只有黎夷。
Translation：
Three hundred and seventy li further northeast from Yushan there stands Junfengshan, a place without migrants but only the Li Yi。

01-02-06 句余山
Gouyushan
（116,65532E；27,88041N）

又东四百里，曰句余之山[1]，无草木[2]，多金玉[3]。

注释：[1]句余山：指虎龙山。濮语虎读 go 音，与"句"（gou）谐音。
Notes： [1] gou yu shan: refers to Hulongshan, Hu/tiger, Long/dragon, Pu speech for tiger is [go]， a close phonetic match to gou。
[2] 无草木：没有移民。
[2] wu cao mu (no grass wood): no migrants。
[3] 多金玉：生活着黎夷。
[3] duo jin yu (plenty gold jade): the Li Yi lives here。

译文：由军峰山往东北四百里，有座山叫虎龙山，那里没有移民，只有黎夷。
Translation:
Four hundred li further northeast from the Junfengshan there stands the Hulongshan, no migrants, only the Li people live there。

01-02-07 浮玉山
Fuyushan
（117,9962E；28,8104N）

又东五百里，曰浮玉之山[1]，北望具区[2]，东望诸毗[3]。有兽焉，其状如虎而牛尾[4]，其音如吠犬[5]，其名曰彘[6]，是食人[7]。苕水[8] 出于其阴，北流注于具区。其中多鮆鱼 [9] 。

注释：[1]浮玉山：指怀玉山。
Notes: [1] fu yu shan（float jade mount)
Tr: refers to Huaiyushan: huai: holding to the bosom, yu: jade。

[2] 具区：指大水，这里指长江。
[2] ju qu (big water), here refers to the Yangtze River。
[3] 诸毗：这里指具枝诸毗，即浙江诸毗邻集镇。
[3] zhu pi (various neighbours)
Tr: refers to the neighbouring townships in Zhejiang。
[4] 虎而牛尾：濮族的稻夷，牛尾，指稻夷。
[4]hu er niu yi (tiger with bull's tail)
Tr: the rice growers of the Pu Zu, Bull's tail: rice growing Yi。
[5] 吠犬：读音 hu qi，是尝山的倒装句，今称常山。Hu，指山；qi，指尝、赏。
[5] fei quan (barking dog) reads as hu qi
Tr: today's Changshan, a reverse word order, Hu: mountain, qi; taste, gift。
[6]彘：指种植夷。
[6] zhi (swine, male pig): refers to growers of crops。
[7] 是食人：古老的定居氏族。
[7] shi shi ren (thus eating human)
Tr: ancient, settled clans。
[8] 苕水：指洛苕水，读音 luo tiao en，意为西流水，今称乐安江。
[8] tiao shui（reed water) reads as Luo Tian En。
Tr: Luoitaoen: Xiliushui (west flowing river), it refers to today's Le 'an River。
[9] 鮆鱼：指香屯夷。
[9]ci yu (ci/sword fish) refers to the Xiangtun Yi (sweet village people) 。

译文：由虎龙山往东五百里有座山，叫怀玉山。怀玉山北望长江，东望浙江诸毗邻集镇。有一个氏族，是濮族的僚夷，住在常山，称为种植夷，是古老的定居氏族。乐安江发源于山的北面，向北流入长江。那里住着香屯夷。

Translation:
Five hundred li further east from the Hulongshan, there stands the Huaiyushan。 It looks to the Yangtze River to its north, to the townships in Juzhi to its east。 A clan from Lao Yi of the Pu Zu lives in Changshan。 They are the long-settled clans of crop growers。The Le'an River rises from the north side of the mountain and goes north into the Yangtze River。The Xiangtun Yi lives there。

01-02-08 成山
Chengshan
（119,27984E；29,47036N)

又东五百里，曰成山[1]，四方而三坛[2]，其上多金玉，其下多青雘。闟（du）水[3]出焉，而南流注于虖勺[4]，其中多黄金[5]。

注释：[1]成山：指千山，今称千里岗。成，濮语读音 du。
Notes: [1] cheng shan（fulfill mount）
Tr: Pu concept: du shan, refers to Qianshan, today's Qianligang Mountain (thousand-mile range) 。
[2] 四方而三坛：指私那的边缘地区。私那是东夏国的濮语读音。
[2]si fang er san tan (four sides and three terrace-altars)
Tr: the outlying area of Sina, Sina being the Pu concept of the Eastern Xia (夏) state/nation。
[3] 闟水：指千水，新安江的支流。
[3] du shui: refers to the Qian Shui (thousand water) River, a tributary of Xin'an River。

[4] 虖勺：指东边的江，今称为富春江。
[4]hu shao, refers to the river to the east, known today as Fuchun (rich spring) River。
[5] 黄金：虖己，指东部的部落氏族。
[5] huang jin (yellow gold)
Tr: in Pu concept huang jin reads as hu ji, close phonetic match, referring to the tribes and people of the East。

译文：由怀玉山往东五百里，有座山叫千里岗，是私那的边缘地区，西边生活着黎夷，东边生活着穄禾氏族。千水发源于这座山，向南流入富春江，那里生活着东部的部落氏族。
Translation：
Five hundred li further east from Huaiyushan there stands the Qianligang Mountain。 It belongs to the outlying areas of Sina, the Xia state。To its west lives the Li Yi。 To its east live the rice growing tribes。Qianshui River originates from this mountain, and flows south into the Fuchun River, where the tribal clans from the East live。

01-02-09 会稽山
Kuaijishan
（120,57485E；29,99505N）

又东五百里，曰会稽之山[1]，四方[2]，其上多金玉[3]，其下多砆石[4]。勺水[5] 出焉，而南流注于湨 [6] 。

注释：[1]会稽山：指南具枝山，后演绎为会稽山。
Notes：[1] kuai ji shan, refers to Nanjuzhi-- south Juzhishan, later known as Kuaijishan。
[2] 四方：指私那地区。
[2]si fang (four areas), refers to the Si-na area。
[3] 金玉：指穄夷，种稻夷。
[3] jin yu (gold jade), refers to the Ji Yi, the Pu concept for the rice growers。
[4] 砆石：指房奉氏。砆，只能译为房，而不能译为防。
[4] fu shi（fu stone), refers to the tribal people bearing the surname of Fangfeng, Fang/房（house) 防（protect), the surname should only be written with the first Chinese fang(house)。
[5] 勺水：指沙溪。
[5] shao shui (spoon river), refers to Sha River (sand river), sha/sand（沙）
[6]湨：指曹娥江。
[6] ju: refers to the Cao'e River。

译文：由千里岗往东五百里，有座山叫会稽山，是私那地区，山的西边生活着穄禾氏族，山的东边生活着房奉氏。沙溪发源于这座山，向东南流入曹娥江。
Translation：
Five hundred li further east from the Qianligang Mountain there stands Kuaijishan, the area known as Si-na area。On the west mountain side live the rice growing clans bearing the surname of Jihe 。 On its east side, live the tribes bearing the surname of Fangfeng。 Shaxi River originates from this mountain and flows southeast into the Cao'ejiang River。

01-02-10 夷山
Yishan
（117,48725E；27,33666N）

又东五百里，曰夷山[1]。无草木[2]，多沙石 [3] 。湨水 [4] 出焉，而南流注于列涂 [5] 。

注释：[1]夷山：指武夷山，武夷山地区。从江西军峰山起算距离。
Notes: [1] yi shan, refers to the Wuyishan, or the Wuyishan area, its distance starts from Junfengshan in Jiangxi province。

[2] 无草木：这里的“无”是指部落，“草木”是指崇氏族，也称崇濮、从濮。
[2] wu cao mu (no grass wood)
Tr: wu: a Pu concept of tribe, here refers to the Chong clan, also known as Chong Pu, or Cong Pu。 chong: 崇, cong 从，a phonetic match to caomu (grass wood) 。

[3] 多沙石：生活着杉黎氏族。濮语“石”，读音为 li。
[3] duo sha shi （a lot of sand and stone）
Tr: here lives the Shan Li clan。In Pu concept stone is Li, sha: 沙/shan; 杉，close in pronunciation, Pu concept stone reads as Li, phonetic match to Chinese shi(stone)。

[4] 湨水：指崇阳溪。
[4] ju shui, refers to Chongyangxi River, (sun worshipping water) 。

[5] 列涂：指富屯溪。
[5] lie tu, refers to Futunxi River, (rich village river) 。

译文：由军峰山往东五百里，有座山叫武夷山，是崇濮部落和杉黎部落的生活地区。崇阳溪发源于这座山，向南流入富屯溪。
Translation:
Five hundred li from Junfengshan further east there stands Wuyishan, an area settled by the Chongpu tribes and the Shanli tribes。 Chongyangxi River originates from this mountain and flows southward to empty into the Futonxi River。

01-02-11 仆勾山
Pugoushan
（118,53247E；27,92018N）

又东五百里，曰仆勾之山[1]。其上多金玉[2]，其下多草木 [3]，无鸟兽 [4] 无水 [5] 。

注释：[1]仆勾山：指濮城山，今称浦城山，主峰在东侧的三天子都山。
Notes: [1] bu gou shan, or pu gou shan, refers to Puchengshan, its main peak is on its east side, known as the “san tian zi du shan” (three heavenly princes capital mountain) 。

[2] 金玉：指广丰夷。金，指具、广。
[2] jin yu (gold jade),
Tr: it refers to the Guangfeng Yi。jin/ju, close phonetic match, meaning big, broad。

[3] 草木：指崇濮氏族。
[3] cao mu (grass wood), refers to the Chongpu clans。

[4] 无鸟兽：北部的僚族。
[4] wu niao shou (no bird beast)
Tr: it refers to the northern Liao people, Liao is read as Lao。L/N phonetic shift。

[5] 无水：九夷部落氏族。
[5] wu shui (no water)
Tr: it refers to the Jiuyi clans, known as the Nine Yi clans。

译文：由武夷山往东五百里，有座山叫浦城山。西边生活着广丰氏族，东面生活着崇濮、北部的僚族和九夷部落氏族。

Translation:
Five hundred li further east from Wuyishan, there stands Puchengshan。 On its west side lives the Guangfeng clan。 On its east side live the Chongpu clans, the Northern Liao Zu and the Jiuyi clans。

01-02-12 咸阴山
Xianyinshan
（119,92965E；28,46171N）

又东五百里，曰咸阴之山[1]。无草木[2]， 无水 [3] 。

注释：[1]咸阴山：指绚溢山，今称丽水市。
Notes: [1] xian yin shan (salty shady mount)
Tr: refers to Xuan yi shan, today's Lishui （pretty water） City。
[2] 无草木：指崇濮部落氏族。
[2] wu cao mu, (no grass wood), refers to the Chongpu clans。
[3] 无水：指九夷部落。
[3] wu shui, (having no water) refers to the Jiuyi tribes。

译文：由浦城山往东五百里，有座山叫绚溢山。那里是崇濮部落和九夷部落氏族生活的地方。
Translation:
Five hundred li further east from Puchengshan there stands Xuanyishan。 This is the area where the Chongpu tribes and the Jiuyi clans live。

01-02-13 洵山
Xunshan
（121,13368E；28,84794N）

又东四百里，曰洵山[1]，其阳多金[2]，其阴多玉[3]。有兽焉，其状如羊而无口[4]，不可杀也[5]，其名曰䍺[6]。洵水出焉，而南流注于阏之泽[7]，其中多芘蠃[8]。

注释：[1]洵山：指沿海岸的山，今称临海山。洵水指沿海岸的水，简称沿水。
Notes: [1] xun shan, refers to mountains along the seashore, it is known today as the Linhaishan。Xunshui: refers to the rivers along the seashore, also known as Yanshui (rivers following the sealine) 。
[2]金：山头、岭上氏族，这里指屿头氏族。
[2] jin, (gold) meaning mountain top, here refers to the clans on the mountain top, Lingshang clans, also known as Yutou（isles head) clans。
[3]玉：指天台氏族。
[3]yu, (jade) refers to Tiantai clans, tian(sky)tai(terrace)。
[4]羊（chi) 而无口：东部的夏部落。
[4] chi(lamb), chi er wu kou, (lamb has no mouth)
Tr: refers to the Xia tribes living in the east。
[5] 不可杀也：夏族的边远夷。
[5] bu ke sha ye (can't kill) refers to the outlying areas Yi of the Xia ethnicity。
[6]䍺：指隔水氏族，"隔水"，濮语读 he en，谐音䍺。
[6] huan/he en: close phonetic match, refers to the Geshui clan。
[7] 阏之泽：指台州湾。
[7]yu zhi ze; refers to Taizhou Bay。

[8] 芘嬴：指灵江氏族。
[8]bi/pi ying：refers to the Lingjiang clans。

译文：由绚溢山往东四百里，有座山叫临海山。山的南面住着屿头氏族，山的北面住着天台氏族。有一个氏族，是东部的夏部落氏族，是夏族的边远夷，名叫隔水氏。沿水发源于这座山，向南流入台州湾，那里生活着灵江氏族。
Translation:
Four hundred li further east from the Xuanyishan, there stands the Linhaishan。 On its south side lives the Yutou clan, on its north side lives the Tiantai clan。 Another clan of the Xia from the east, living in outlying areas, is known as the Geshui clan。 Yanshui River originates from this mountain and flows south into Taizhou Bay。The Linjiang clan lives around the Taizhou Bay area。

01-02-14 虖勺山
Hushaoshan
（116,62659E；25,36231N）

又东四百里，曰虖勺之山[1]，其上多梓枏[2]，其下多荆杞[3]。滂水[4] 出焉，而东流注于海。

注释：[1]虖勺山：松山的倒装句，又称玳瑁山。距离由于山算起，实际是向东南。
Notes：[1]hu shao shan; refers to Songshan, also known as Daimaoshan。 Its distance starts from Yushan， going southeast。
[2] 梓枏：指羊古河氏族，今称汀江氏族。
[2] zi nán （kind of wood）
Tr: it refers to the Yangguhe clan, now known as the Tingjiang clan。
[3] 荆杞：指沙石溪氏族，今称石溪氏族。
[3] jing ji (thorny twigs)
Tr: it refers to the Shashixi clan, known today as the Shixi clan。
[4] 滂水：指朋水，今称旧县河。
[4] pang shui (overflowing water)
Tr: it refers to Peng River, known today as Jiuxian River (old county river) 。

译文：由于山往东南四百里，有座山叫松山。山的西面住着羊古河氏族，山的东面住着沙石溪氏族。朋水发源于这座山，向东流入东海中。
Translation:
Four hundred li further southeast from Yushan there stands Songshan (pine mountain) 。 On its west side lives the Yangguhe clan, while on its east side lives the Shashixi clan。Pangshui River originates from this mountain and flows east to empty itself into the East China Sea。

01-02-15 区吴山
Quwushan
（117,68196E；24,50431N）

又东五百里，曰区吴之山[1]，无草木[2]，多沙石[3]。鹿水[4] 出焉，而南流注于滂水 [5] 。

注释：[1]区吴山：指瓯部落山，包括厦门、漳州及北部的华安地区。实际是向东南。

Notes: [1] qu wu shan, refers to the mountains of the Ou tribe, including Xiamen, Zhangzhou, and the Hua'an area to the North. The direction is in fact to the southeast。

[2] 无草木：指高车部落。

[2] wu cao mu (no grass wood) 。

Tr: it refers to the Gaoche tribe, gaoche, (high carriage)

[3] 沙石：绍氏，指庄灶氏族。

[3] sha shi, (sand and stone)

Tr: it refers to Shao Shi, the Zhuangzao (village hearth) clan， bearing the surname of Shao。

[4] 鹿水：指龙水，今称九龙江。

[4]lu shui, (deer river)

Tr: it refers to the Long River (dragon river), known today as the Jiulong River (nine dragon river) 。

[5] 滂水：滂，在此读 bang 音，指海。滂水即海中。

[5] pang shui, pang/bang: sea (as in Pontus, refers to the sea) means in the sea。

译文：由松山往东南五百里，有座山叫瓯部落山，那里有高车部落，住着庄灶氏族。龙水从那里流出，向南流入海中。

Translation:

Five hundred li further southeast from Songshan stands the Oubuluo Mountain (Ou tribe mountain), the land of the Gaoche people, where the Zhuangzao clan lives。The Long River flows out of the mountain and goes south into the sea。

01-02-16 鹿吴山

Luwushan

（119,00975E；25,43118N）

又东五百里，曰鹿吴之山[1]。上无草木[2]，多金石 [3] 。泽更之水 [4] 出焉，而南流注于滂水 [5] 。水有兽焉，名曰蛊雕 [6]，其状如雕而有角 [7]，其音如婴儿之音 [8]，是食人 [9] 。

注释：[1]鹿吴山：指莆部落山，今称莆田市。鹿、鲁，是脯和莆的濮语读音。

Notes:[1]lu wu shan, refers to Pu tribe mountain, known today as Putian city。In Pu language, lu, reads as fu, or pu, a p/f phonetic shift。

[2] 上无草木：边远的仙游部落。无，指部落；草木，仙游的倒装句。

[2] shan wu cao mu (up no grass wood)

Tr: refers to the Xianyou tribe in the outlying area, wu: tribe, caomu (grass wood): xianyou tribe， Xian you (fairy travel, in a reversed order) 。

[3] 多金石：住着盖氏族。金在此读 gen 音，与盖谐音。

[3] duo jin shi (plenty gold stone)

Tr: Gai clan lives here, jin/gen/gai, phonetically close。

[4] 泽更：指盖江，今称木兰溪。

[4] ze geng（bigwater change）

Tr: refers to Gai River, today's Mulanxi River。

[5] 滂水：指海水，即指海中。

[5] pang shui/bang shui,

Tr: refers to sea water, meaning in the middle of the sea。

[6] 蛊雕：指平岛氏族。

[6]gu diao, (evil force eagle)

Tr: refers to the Pingdao (flat island) clan。

[7] 雕而有角（gu): 平潭的岛屿氏族。
[7] diao er you gu (eagle has horns)
Tr: refers to the Daoyu (Island) clan in Pingtan。
[8] 婴儿之音：化川的北面，即今兴化湾的北面。
[8]in er zhi yin (infant voice)
Tr: north to Huachuan, today's Xinghua Wan (Xinghua Bay) 。
[9] 是食人：是古老的定居氏族。
[9] shi shi ren (yes eat human)
Tr: refers to the old sedentary clan。

译文：由瓯部落山往东北五百里，有座山叫莆部落山，是边远的仙游部落区域，住着盖氏族。盖江之水从这里流出，向南流入海中。海水中有一个氏族，名叫平岛氏，是平潭的岛屿氏族，住在兴化湾的北面，是古老的定居氏族。
Translation:
Five hundred li further northeast from Oubuluoshan stands the Pubuluo Mountain。 This is the Xianyou tribe's outlying area, where the Gai clan lives。 The Gai River originates from here and flows south into the Sea。 In the middle of the East China Sea lives the Pingdao Shi。The Daoyu clans of the Pingtan area live to the north of the Xinghua Bay, they are a very ancient sedentary clan。

01-02-17 漆吴山
Qiwushan
（119,53176E；26,65883N）

又东五百里，曰漆吴之山[1]。无草木[2]，多博石 [3], 无玉 [4] 。处于东海，望丘山 [5]，其光载出载入 [6]，是惟日次 [7] 。

凡南次二经之首，自柜山至于漆吴之山。凡十七山，七千二百里。其神状皆龙身而鸟首[8] 。其祠：毛用一璧瘗，糈用稌。

注释：[1]漆吴山：指东部落山，又称且部落山，今称太姥山，实际介绍福建临德。
Notes：[1] qi wu shan: refers to the east tribe mountain, also known as the Qiebuluo mountain。 It is known today as the Tianlaoshan (Great grandma), in fact this is about the Linde County in Fujian province。
[2] 无草木：且苗部落。
[2] wu cao mu (no grass wood): refers to Qiemiao tribe, qie/east。
[3] 多博石：住着黄湾氏族。
[3] duo bo shi: (a lot of Bo stone)
Tr： there lives the Huangwan clan, Huangwan: yellow bay,
[4] 无玉：白港夷。
[4] wu yu (no jade) refers to Baigang people, Baigang:(white port)
[5] 丘山：指星仔岛。
[5] qiu shan (mound mount): refers to the Xingzai Island: xingzai: starlets。
[6] 载出载入：若隐若现。
[6] zai ru zai chu: lurking in the waves, now appear, now disappear。
[7] 日次：指游龙。
[7] ri ci（Sun order）
Tr: refers to a floating dragon, the string of islands appears like a swimming dragon, in and out of the waves。
[8] 龙身而鸟首：种稻的僚族形像。

[8] long shen er niao shou:(dragon body with bird head) in the image of the Lao people who are rice growers。

译文：由莆部落山往东北五百里，有座山叫东部落山。那里是且舍部落的疆域，住着黄湾氏族和白港夷。站在东海岸，可以看见星仔岛若隐若现，像一条游龙。

综观南山第二列山系，从九嶷到东部落山，共有十七座山，蜿蜒七千二百里。这些山的山神的形像，皆为种稻的僚族人的形像。祭祀礼为：代替祭词的玉，用一璧埋入地下；供奉的食品用荞饭。

Translation:

Five hundred li further northeast from the Pubuluo Mountain, stands the Dongbuluo Mountain。The Qiemiao clans, as well as the Huangwan clan and the Baigang Yi live there。 Standing from the east seashore, one can see the Xingzai Island group in and out of the wave like a dragon。

In sum, the 2nd list of mountains in the south, from Jiuyishan to Dongbuluo Mountain, records 17 mountains, covering a total distance of 7,200 li。 The mountain deities are in the image of the local Liao Zu clans who are the rice growers。When performing sacrificial rite, a piece of jade is buried representing the votive speech。 The sacrificial food is cooked buckwheat。

南山经第三山系

Book1 Nanshanjing； chapter 3

01-03-01 天下虞山

Tianxiayushan

（108,07851E； 26,38432N）

南次三经之首，曰天下虞山[1]，其下多水[2]，不可以上[3]。

注释：[1]天下虞山：指雷公山。天下读 tyxie, 指雷公，虞，指嶷。今贵州雷山县。

Notes： [1] tian xia yu shan (heaven under yu mount)

Tr: refers to Leigongshan (thunder father mount) Tianxia reads as tyxie (thunder father) yu/yi, today's Leishan county in Guizhou Province。

[2] 其下多水：指且舍民的氏族。且舍民即苗民，由山东地区迁徙而来。

[2] qi xia duo shui (under it plenty water)

Tr: refers to the Qieshe Min clan, also known as the Miao Min ethnic people, they migrate from Shandong Province in east China。

[3] 不可以上：夏族的边远地区。

[3] bu ke yi shang (can't go up)

Tr: the outlying areas of the Xia Zu。

译文：南山经第三系列最西边的山是雷公山，是且舍氏族生活的地区，是夏族的边远地区。

Translation：

The westmost mountain of the 3rd system of Mountains in the south is the Leigong Mountain。 This is the land of the Qieshe clans, the outlying areas of the Xia Zu people。

01-03-02 祷过山
Daoguoshan
（109,78252E；26,15915N）

东五百里，曰祷过之山[1]。其上多金玉[2]，其下多犀、兕，多象 [3] 。有鸟焉，其状如鵁而白首 [4]，三足、人面 [5]，其名曰瞿如 [6]，其鸣自号也。浪水 [7] 出焉，而南流注于海。其中有虎蛟 [8]，其状鱼身而蛇尾 [9]，其音如鸳鸯 [10]，食者不肿 [11]，可以已痔 [12]。

注释：[1]祷过山：指通道山，又称八十里大南山。
Notes:[1] dao guo shan (pray pass mount)
Tr: refers to the Tongdaoshan (passage mount), also known as the eighty-li big south mountain, Bashili-Danan Mountain。
[2] 其上多金玉：西边生活着菁夷。
[2] qi shang duo jin yu (up there plenty gold jade)
Tr: on its west side, lives the Qing Yi。
[3]犀、兕，多象：寻江氏族、私黎江氏族、都柳江氏族。这些氏族实际居住在南边。
[3] xi, si， duo， xiang (rhinoceros, black rhino-like animal, elephant)
Tr: refers to the Xunjiang clan, the Silijiang clan and the Duliujiang clan。In fact those clans live in the southern part。
[4] 鵁而白首：东边的城步氏族。
[4] jiao er bai shou (duck with white head)
Tr： it refers to the Chengbu (city step) clan from the east side。
[5] 三足、人面：外来的定居氏族。
[5] san zu (three feet) 、 ren mian (human face)
Tr: tribes of immigrants who settled down locally。
[6] 瞿如：指且奴，即且舍民。由山东迁徙而来的苗民。
[6] qu ru: a phonetic match to qie nu (the Qieshe people) who are the Miao people having migrated from Shandong Province。
[7] 浪水：指融江。
[7] yin shui: refers to Rongjiang (melt)River。
[8] 虎蛟：指濮族。
[8]hu jiao (tiger salamander) refers to the Pu Zu。
[9] 鱼（zhe) 身而蛇尾： 江边的氏族。
[9] zhe shen er she yi (fish body snake tail)
Tr: clans having settled along the river 。
[10] 鸳鸯：融江河畔。
[10] yuan yang (water bird) refers to the banks along the Rongjiang River。
[11] 食之不肿：古老的僮族。
[11] shi zhi bu zhong (eat it cures swelling)
Tr: it refers to the ancient Zhong people。
[12] 可以已痔：夏国夷人的大支系。
[12] ke yi yi zhi (can cure Hemorrhoids)
Tr; the leading branch of the Yi people of the Xia nation。

译文：由雷公山往东五百里，有座山叫通道山。山的西边生活着菁夷氏族，南边生活着寻江氏族、私黎江氏族和都柳江氏族。有一群人，是东边的城步氏族，是外来的居民，名叫且舍民，他们也这样称呼自己。

融江发源于这座山，向南流入海中。那里生活着濮族群体，是江边的氏族，住在融江河畔，是古老的僮夷，是夏国夷人的大支系。
Translation:
Five hundred li further east from Leigongshan there stands Tongdaoshan。 On its west side lives the Qingyi clan。 On its south side live the Xunjiang clan, the Silijiang clan and the Duliujiang clan。 One group of immigrants, known as the Chengbu clan from the east side, are outsiders。 They are called Qieshe people。 They also address themselves as such。 The Rongjiang River originates from this mountain and goes south into the sea。A group of Pu tribal people lives there; they are the riverbank people along the Rongjiang River。 They are the very ancient Zhong Yi, a leading branch of the Yi people of the Xia nation。

01-03-03 丹穴山
Danxueshan
（110,86746E；26,17034N）

又东五百里，曰丹穴之山[1]，其上多金玉[2]。丹水[3] 出焉，而南流注于渤海 [4] 。有鸟焉，其状如鸡[5]，五采而文[6]，名曰凤皇[7]，首文曰德[8]，翼文曰义[9]，背文曰礼[10]，膺文曰仁[11]，腹文曰信[12]。是鸟也，饮食自然[13]，自歌自舞[14]，见则天下安宁[15]。

注释：[1]丹穴山：指真顶山，今称真宝顶。
Notes:[1] dan xue shan (cinnabar cave mount)
Tr: refers to Zhendingshan (true top mount), known today as Zhenbaoding (Mountain)。
[2] 其上多金玉：西边住着资夷。今称资源夷。
[2] qi shang duo jin yu (up plenty gold jade)
Tr: The Zi Yi lives on its west side, Zi Yi is known today as the Ziyuan Yi。
[3] 丹水：指真水。
[3] dan shui (cinnabar water) refers to the Zhenshui (true water) River。
[4] 渤海：指湘江。湘江，濮语读沘湘（hang），被谐音译为渤海了。
[4]bo hai (rush sea) refers to the Xiangjiang River。In Pu concept, the river is read as pihang, a close phonetic match to bohai。
[5]鸡：指广原，即广西。
[5]ji(chicken) refers to Guangyuan, today's Guangxi province。
[6] 五采而文：指东北部水源地。五即武，指北方；采即且，指东方；文即汶，指水。
[6] wu cai er wen (five color with markings)
Tr: the water source of the northeast areas。 five;(wu, north), color: cai (qie, east), marking; wen(water)。
[7] 凤皇：指润泽之乡。
[7] feng huang (phoenix emperor) refers to well-watered land。
[8] 首文曰德：东边的河叫英德, 今称连江。
[8] shou wen yue de (head markings spell virtue)
Tr： the river on the east is Yingde River, known today as the Lianjiang River。
[9] 翼文曰义：北边的河叫营水, 今称潇水。
[9] yi wen yue yi;(wing markings spell rightness)
Tr: the river on the north is Yingshui River, known today as the Xiaoshui River。
[10] 背文曰礼：南边的河叫嶷（li) 水, 今称贝江。
[10] bei wen yue li (back markings spell rite)
Tr： the river in the south is the Lishui River, known today as the Beijiang River。
[11] 膺文曰仁：永水叫惹水, 今称永明河。

[11] ying wen yue ren (chest markings spell benevolence), refers to the Yongshui River, known today as the Yongming (forever bright) River。

[12] 腹文曰信：富水叫信江。

[12] fu wen yue xin (belly markings spell trust) refers to Fushui River, known today as the Xinjiang River。

[13] 是鸟也，饮食自然：这些河流都发源于江永。自然，指浙惹，即江永。

[13] shi niao ye (are birds), yin shi zi ran (drink eat naturally):
Tr: all those danao(waters) originate from Jiangyong。Jiangyong is a Pu concept for Nature, also read as zhere. Ziran, zhere, Jiangyong, phonetic matches。

[14] 自歌自舞：自歌，指道县的古名江城；自舞，指江华。

[14] zi ge zi wu (self-sings self-dances)
Tr: zige: refers to Jiangcheng, the ancient name for Daoxian。 ziwu: refers to Jianghua。

[15] 见则天下安宁：那里还有一条较长的宁河。（指宁远河）。天下，指较长的。

[15] jian ze tian xia an ning (seen under heaven peace)
Tr: another longer river there is called Ning River, also known as the Ningyuan (peace far) River。 Tianxia (under heaven): means longer。

译文：由通道山往东五百里，有座山叫真顶山，西边生活着资源夷。真水发源于这座山，向南流入湘江。那里有许多河流，是广原东北部的水源地，称为润泽之乡。东边的一条河叫英德；北边的一条河叫营水；南边的一条河叫嶷水；永水又叫惹江；富水又叫信江。这些河流，大多发源于江永、江城、和江华。那里还有一条较长的河流叫宁水。

Translation:
Five hundred li further east from Tongdaoshan there stands Zhendingshan。 On its west side lives the Ziyuan Yi。 Zhenshui River originates from this mountain and goes south into the Xiangjiang River。 There are a lot of rivers, a land known as the well-watered areas, water source for the northeast part of Guangyuan。The river to its east is the Yingde River。The river to its north is the Yingshui River。 The river to its south is the Lishui River。The Yongshui River is also called Rejiang River, while the Fushui River is also called Xinjiang River。 Most of the rivers originate from locations known as the Jiangyong, Jiangcheng, and Jianghua。There is another longer river known as the Ningshui River。

01-03-04 发爽山
Fashuangshan
(111,83113E; 26,17084N)

又东五百里，曰发爽之山[1]，无草木，多水[2]，多白猿[3]。汎水[4] 出焉，而南流注于渤海[5]。

注释：[1]发爽山：指天明山，今称阳明山。
Notes:[1] fa shuang shan (hair cool mount)
Tr: refers to the Tianmingshan (skydawn mount)， today's Yangmingshan (sun bright mount)。

[2] 无草木，多水：移民部落氏族生活的地区。

[2] wu cao mu (no grass wood)， duo shui (plenty water)
Tr: refers to areas settled by the migrant tribes and clans。

[3] 多白猿：生活着土家氏族。"白"读音为"土"，猿，"夷"的谐音。

[3] duo bai yuan (lot white apes)
Tr: the Tujia clans live here. bai(white) a Pu concept, read as tu (soil, earth),yuan/yi, phonetic match。

[4] 汎水：指天水。实际为东南流。

[4] fan shui: refers to Tian shui (sky water),in fact it flows southeast。

[5] 渤海：指湘江。

[5]bo hai: refers to the Xiangjiang River。

译文：由真顶山往东五百里，有座山叫阳明山。那里是移民部落氏族生活的地区，生活着土家氏族。天水发源于这座山，向东南流入湘江。
Translation:
Five hundred li further east from Zhendingshan there stands Yangmingshan。 This is the area where migrant tribes and clans settled down, among them the Tujia clan。 Tianshui River originates from this mountain and goes southeast into the Xiangjiang River。

01-03-05 旄山
Maoshan
（112,8513E；26,41417N）

又东四百里，至于旄山之尾[1]。其南有谷[2]，曰育遗[3]，多怪鸟[4]，凯风自是出[5]。

注释：[1]旄山之尾：指冠山之南。即今耒阳。
Notes:[1] mao shan zhi yi (mao mount tail); refers to the south of the Guanshan (mount crown), today's Leiyang county。
[2]谷：指国家。
[2]gu(grain), a Pu concept for nation, country, or state。
[3] 育遗：指钺阳国，后称耒阳国。钺是种田工具，又称耒耜。
[3]yu yi (care remain)
Tr: it refers to the Yueyang Guo, later known as the Leiyang Guo。 Yue, a field tool for working the soil, also known as lei si。
[4] 怪鸟：指桂僚。
[4] guai niao (strange bird) refers to the Liao people from Gui—Guangxi。
[5] 凯风自是出：衡山南面的平坦区域。
[5] kai feng zi shi chu (south wind self-blow out)
Tr: refers to the flatland areas south of Hengshan 。

译文：由阳明山往东四百里，到达冠山之南，那里有一个国家，叫耒阳国，住着桂僚氏族，是衡山南面的平坦区域。
Translation:
Four hundred li further east from the Yangmingshan one arrives at the south part of Guanshan。There is a nation called Leiyang Guo, where the Guiliao clans live。 This nation is situated in the flatland to the south of Hengshan。

02-03-06 非山
Feishan
（113,84028E；27,63919N）

又东四百里，至于非山[1]之首，其上多金玉[2]，无水[3]，其下多蝮虫[4]。

注释：[1]非山：指屏山、屏门山，武功山。实际介绍山边的屏乡，今称萍乡市。
Notes:[1] fei shan (fei 非, in Chinese means the opposite of yes 是)。

Tr： refers to Pingshan, Pingmenshan, Ping 屏 (screen) men 门 (door) today's Wugongshan (marshal art mount) 。It is in fact a description of the township Pingxiang (screen village), today's Pingxiang city at the foot of the mountain。

[2] 金玉：指龙台夷。

[2] jin yu (gold jade)

Tr: refers to the Longtai (dragon terrace) Yi。

[3] 无水：指屏乡氏族。

[3] wu shui (no water), refers to the Pingxiang (screen village) clan。

[4] 蝮虫：指濮族。

[4] fu chong (snake moves on belly)， refers to the Pu Zu people。

译文：由冠山往东四百里，到武功山的西面，西面住着龙台夷和屏乡氏族，东面住着濮族。

Translation:

Four hundred li further east from Guanshan, one arrives at the west side of Wugongshan。 On its west side live the Longtai Yi and the Pingxiang clan。On its east side live the Pu Zu people。

01-03-07 阳夹山

Yangjiashan

（114,92564E；28,23564N）

又东五百里，曰阳夹之山[1]，无草木[2]，多水[3]。

注释：[1]阳夹山：耶且山的音译，指大高山，今称上高县。

Notes:[1] yang jia shan (sun pinch mount)

Tr: it is a phonetic rendering of Yeqieshan, the Dagaoshan (big high mount), today's Shanggao county。

[2] 无草木：移民部落区域。

[2] wu cao mu (no grass wood)

Tr: it refers to the areas settled by tribes of immigrants。

[3] 多水：住着青云濮。

[3] duo shui (lot water)

Tr: there live the Qingyun (blue clouds) Pu people。

译文：由武功山往东五百里，有座山叫大高山。那里是移民部落区域，住着青云濮。

Translation:

Five hundred li further east from Wugongshan there stands the Dagaoshan。 This area is settled by tribes of immigrants。 The Qingyun Pu people live there。

01-03-08 灌湘山

Guanxiangshan

(115,86942E；28,68741N)

又东五百里，曰灌湘之山[1]，上多木[2]，无草[3]；多怪鸟[4]，无兽[5]。

注释：[1]灌湘山：指赣湘山，实际指南昌市。赣湘指鄱阳湖。

Notes: [1] guan xiang shan (fill xiang mount)

Tr： it refers to the Ganxiangshan, in fact it is about Nanchang City, Jiangxi province。Ganxiang refers to the Poyang Lake。

[2] 多木：住着梅岭氏族。
[2] duo mu (plenty wood)
Tr: there lives the Meiling (plum range) clan。
[3] 无草：移民部落氏族。
[3] wu cao (no grass): clans of immigrants。
[4] 多怪鸟：住着赣僚。
[4] duo guai niao (many strange birds) the Gan Liao tribes live here。
[5] 无兽：指云部落氏族，实际指青云部落氏族。兽，谐音虽，指云。
[5] wu shou (no beast)
Tr: it refers to the Yun (clouds)clan, specifically the Qingyun (blue cloud) clan。 shou(beast) sui(cloud), close phonetic matches。

译文：由大高山往东北五百里，有座山名叫赣湘山。那里住着梅岭氏族、移民部落氏族；住着赣湘僚和青云部落氏族。
Translation:
Five hundred li further northeast from Dagaoshan there stands Ganxiangshan。The Meiling clans, and tribes of immigrants live there。 Also, the Ganxiang Liao people and the Qingyun tribes and clans live there。

01-03-09 鸡山
Jishan
（116,67303E；28,98914N）

又东五百里，曰鸡山[1]，其上多金[2]，其下多丹雘[3]。黑水[4] 出焉，而南流注于海 [5] 。其中多鱄（tan) 鱼[6]，其状如鲋而彘毛[7]，其音如豚[8]，见则天下大旱[9]。

注释：[1]鸡山：指角山，原读音为 qi,被译为 ji 音。今鄱阳县城。
Notes: [1] ji shan (chicken mount)
Tr: reads as qi, rendered as ji, refers to Jiaoshan (horn mount), today's Poyang County seat。
[2]金：指场镇氏族。
[2] jin(gold) refers to the Changzhen (field town) clan。
[3] 丹雘：指塘湖氏族。
[3] dan hu: refers to the Tanghu (pond lake) clan。
[4] 黑水：指桂江，读为赫水和黑水，今称长江。
[4] hei shui (black water)
Tr: it refers to Guijiang River, which reads as Heshui, or Heishui, today known as the Yangtze River。
[5]海：指鄱阳湖。
[5] hai(sea) refers to the Poyang Lake。
[6] 鱄鱼：指团夷。团，指水塘。
[6] tuan yu (tuan fish) refers to the Tuan Yi, tuan 团: pond。
[7] 鲋而彘毛：湖区的种植苗族。
[7] fu er zhi mao (sturgeon with pig bristle)
Tr: it refers to the planter Miao people from the lake area。
[8] 其音如豚：住在团林。
[8] qi yin ru tun (its voice like piglet's)
Tr： lives in a place called Tuanlin。
[9] 见则天下大旱：是那个地区的王族。大旱，即达罕，指王。
[9] jian ze tian xia da han (when seen, big draughts under heaven)

Tr: they are the king tribe of that area. dahan:(big drought) a phonetic rendering of Da Khan, meaning king, or lord。

译文：由赣湘山往东五百里，有座山叫角山。山的西边住着场镇氏族，山的东面住着塘湖氏族。桂水从这里流出，向南流入鄱阳湖。那里生活着团夷，是湖区的种植苗，住在团林，是那个地区的王族。
Translation:
Five hundred li further east from Guanxiangshan there stands Jiaoshan。 On its west lives the Changzhen clan。 On its east lives the Tanghu clan。 Guishui River flows out of this mountain and goes south into the Poyang Lake, where the Tuan Yi lives。 They are the planter Miao tribes from the lake area, living in Tuanlin。 They are the King lineage of that area。

01-03-10 令丘山
Lingqiushan
（117,25175E；29,37253N）

又东四百里，曰令丘之山[1]。无草木，多火[2]。其南有谷[3]焉，曰中谷 [4]，条风 [5] 自是出。有鸟焉，其状如枭 [6]，人面四目而有耳[7]，其名曰颙[8]，其名自号也，见则天下大旱[9]。

注释：[1]令丘山：指稻梗山，又称禾杆岭，今景德镇浮梁县城。令，读 liu 音，指稻。
Notes:[1] ling qiu shan (order mound mount)
Tr： it refers to the Daogengshan (rice stalk mount), also known as the Heganling (crop stalk range)， today 's Fuliang (float beam) county seat, in Jingde township, Jiangxi province。令： ling, reads as liu, meaning rice。
[2] 无草木，多火：苗族部落，住着禾杆岭氏族。
[2] wu cao mu (no grass wood) duo huo (many fire)
Tr: refers to the Miao tribes, the Heganling clans live here 。
[3]谷：指国家。
[3]gu(grain) means country, nation, state。
[4] 中谷：指陶国。中，在此按濮语语音读为 to, 指陶。
[4] zhong gu (middle grain)
Tr: it refers to Tao Guo (china /pottery country) Pu concept zhong 中 reads as to 陶, refers to clay pottery。
[5] 条风：读 to fei，指陶盘，在此指所有陶器。
[5] tiao feng (strip wind)
Tr: it reads as to fei; refers to Potter's wheel, a term stands for all the pottery。
[6]枭：指谢人，这里将其归为苗族。
[6] xiao(owl)
Tr： it refers to the Xie people, which is identified as part of the Miao ethnic people。
[7] 人面四目而有耳：定居的苗族部落。四目读补蒙，有耳读巴莱。
[7] ren mian si mu er you er (human face four eyes with ears)
Tr: referring to the settled Miao tribes。 simu (four eyes) reads as bumeng(miao) you-er (with ears) reads as balai。
[8]颙：指罗姓氏族。
[8]yu: refers to the clan bearing the surname of Luo。
[9] 大旱：指达罕，即王族。
[9] da han (big drought) refers to the Da Khan, king clan, or the Lord lineage。

译文：由角山往东四百里，有座山叫禾杆岭。那里是苗族部落，住着禾杆岭氏族。南面有一个国家，叫陶国，这里出产陶器。有一群人，是谢人定居的苗族部落氏族，称为罗姓氏族，他们自己也这样称呼，是那个地区的王族。
Translation:

Four hundred li further east from Jiaoshan there stands the Heganling Mountain。 This is the land of the Miao tribes, the Heganling clan lives here。 To its south, there is a nation called Taoguo, a pottery producing nation。A group of settled Miao people is known as the Xie people, bearing the surname of Luo。 They thus address themselves。 They are the King lineage of that area。

01-03-11 仑者山
Lunzheshan
（117,85892E；29,25885N）

又东三百七十里，曰仑者之山[1]。其上多金玉[2]，其下多青雘 [3] 。有木焉 [4]，其状如穀而赤理 [5]，其汗如漆 [6]，其味如饴[7]，食者不饥[8]，可以释劳[9]，其名曰白咎[10]，可以血玉[11]。

注释：[1]仑者山：指星江山，今称婺源。实际往东北。
Notes:[1] lun zhe shan: refers to Xingjiangshan: known today as Maoyuan, in the northeast direction。
[2] 金玉：指漫岭氏族。
[2] jin yu (gold jade) refers to the Manling clan。
[3] 青雘：指东山氏族。今称东升氏族。
[3] qing hu refers to the Dongshan (east mount) clan, today's Dongsheng (east rising) clan。
[4]木：指苗民。
[4]mu(wood) refers to Miao people。
[5] 穀而赤理：这个国家的星江黎。
[5]gu er chi li (bark with red markings)
Tr: this nation's Xingjiang Li。 Li- people。
[6] 汗如漆：称雄于东部。
[6] han ru qi (sweat like lacquer), in control of the east。
[7] 其味如饴：东南诸邑。
[7] qi wei ru yi （its flavor as sweet)
Tr: the various local communities in the southeast。
[8] 食者不饥：古老的首脑氏族。不饥，指博贾、首脑氏族。
[8] shi zhe bu ji (eat it cures hunger)
Tr: the ancient leading clan, buji (bojia): head or leading clan。
[9] 可以释劳：夏国的私那氏族。
[9]ke yi shi lao (can relieve fatigue)
Tr: The Si-na clan of the Xia Nation。
[10] 白咎：指白苗，读音为婺纠。
[10] bai jiu (white mistake) refers to the Baimiao (white miao) which reads as Mao Jiu。
[11] 可以血玉：夏国的谢夷。
[11]ke yi xue yu (can blood wash jade)
Tr: the Xie Yi of the Xia Nation。

译文：由禾杆岭往东北三百七十里，有座山叫星江山。西边住着漫岭氏族，东边住着东山氏族。那里有一支苗族，是这个国家的星江黎，称雄于东部、东南诸邑，是古老的首脑氏族，是夏国的私那氏族，名叫婺纠，是夏国的谢夷。
Translation:
Three hundred and seventy li further northeast from Heganling Mountain there stands the Xingjiangshan。 On its west side lives the Manling clan。 On its east side lives the Dongshan clan. A Miao branch is known as the

Xingjiang Li of this nation。 It is in control of the east part, and the various local communities in southeast。They are the ancient leading head clan, Xia Nation's Sina clan。 They are known as Maojiu, the Xie people of the Xia Nation。

01-03-12 禺稾山
Yugaoshan
（119,08427E；29,56204N）

又东五百八十里，曰禺稾之山[1]。多怪兽[2]，多大蛇 [3] 。

注释：[1]禺稾山：指阴康，又称北强、武强。后称淳安，遗址已淹没在水中。
Notes: [1]yu gao shan (yu high mount)
Tr： it refers to Yinkang, also as Beiqiang (north strong, wu strong), later as Chun'an , this location is now under water。
[2] 怪兽：指阴康氏族，属夏族的阴康部落支系。怪，指北。
[2] guai shou (strange beast)
Tr: it refers to the Yinkang ethnic group, part of the Yinkang branch of the Xia ethnic people。guai(strange), means north。
[3] 大蛇：指泰氏族，指泰州移民。
[3] da she (big snake)
Tr: it refers to the Tai clan, the immigrants from Taizhou。

译文：由星江山往东五百八十里，有座山叫武强山。那里住着阴康氏族，住着泰氏族。
Translation:
Five hundred and eighty li further east from Xingjiangshan there stands the Wuqiangshan。 The Yinkang clan lives there, so does the Tai clan。

01-03-13 南禺山
Nanyushan
（119,99028E；30,39278N）

又东五百八十里，曰南禺之山[1]。其上多金玉[2]，其下多水 [3] 。有穴焉，水出耳入[4]，夏乃出，冬则闭[5]。佐水[6]出焉，而南流注于海，有凤皇[7]，鹓雏[8]。
凡南次三经之首，自天下虞山以至南禺之山，凡一十四山(13)，六千五百三十里。其神皆龙身而人面。其祠皆一白狗[9]祈，糈用稌。
右南经之山志，大小凡四十山，万六千三百八十里。

注释：[1]南禺山：指良渚川，音译为南诸夭，简称南夭，谐音南禺。
Notes:[1] nan yu shan (south yu mount) refers to the Liangzhuchuan， phonetically close to Nanzhuwo, shortened to Nanwo, near phonetic rendering to Nanyu。
[2] 金玉：指渚岭夷。
[2] jin yu (gold jade) refers to the Zhuling Yi。
[3]水：指畲姓氏族。畲姓是东南特有的姓氏。
[3] shui(water) refers to the clans bearing the surname of She 畲, a family name unique to southeast China。
[4] 有穴焉，水出耳入：由轩辕畲族治理，即畲族的轩辕治理。轩辕，指大主席。

[4] you xue yan (have cave), shui chu yi ru (water out noise yin)
Tr:(state affairs) run by the Xuanyuan branch of the She clan, in another word, the Xuanyuan of She Zu runs the affairs of the clan。 Xuanyuan: big leader, chieftain, chairman。

[5] 夏乃出，冬则闭：属夏僚建立的分支部落。闭，属于；冬则，分支部落。

[5] xia na chu, dong ze bi (summer, venture out, winter therefore shut)
Tr: refers to the branches of the Xia nation's Liao tribes。 bi(shut): belong to, dong ze (winter therefore): tribal branches。

[6] 佐水：指良渚水。简称渚水。

[6] zuo shui (aid water) refers to the liangzhushui, shortened to Zhushui。

[7] 凤皇：指灌溉。

[7] feng huang(phoenix) refers to irrigation。

[8] 鹓雏：指水渠网络。

[8] yuan chu （phoenix type bird）
Tr: refers to the water irrigation network。

[9] 白狗：指香猪，一种只能长到一百多斤的小种猪。今苗文写为 Nbuat Ghangb。

[9] bai gou (white dog)
Tr: it refers to a pig called Xiangzhu (delicious piglet), a small size pig growing only up to about 50 kg。 In Miao script the pig's name is written as Nbuat Ghangb。

译文：由武强山往东五百八十里，有个地方叫良渚川。西面住着渚岭夷，东面住着畲姓夷，由畲族的轩辕治理，属夏僚建立的分支部落。良渚水从这里流出，向东南流注于海。这里有用于灌溉的水渠网络。

Translation:
Five hundred and eighty li further east from the Wuqiangshan there is a place called Liangzhuchuan。 On its west side lives the Zhuling Yi。On its east side lives the She Yi, run by its Xuanyuan branch。The She Yi belongs to the branch established by the Xia Liao people。 The Liangzhu River flows from here, goes southeast into the sea。 This place is provided with an irrigation system。

综观南山第三系列，从雷公山到良渚川，共有十四座山（实际十三山），蜿蜒六千五百三十里。这些山的山神皆为僚族居民的形象。祭祀这些山神时，用香猪和荞饭祭祀。

所有南经的山系，大小共四十座山头，共一万六千三百八十里。

In sum, the 3rd list of the mountains in the south, from Leigongshan to Liangzhuchuan, records 14 （in fact 13） mountains covering a distance of 6,530 li。The mountain deities are in the images of the Liao residents。When sacrificing to the deities, Xiang pig and cooked buckwheat are used。

The full lists of mountains in the south – 40 (actually 39) in total, large or small-- covers a distance of 16,380 li。

第二卷西山经(Mountains in the West)

西山经第一山系

Book 2 Xishanjing; chapter 1

02-01-01 华山 钱来山
Huashan Qianlaishan
（110,8933E；34,5292N）

西山经华山之首，曰钱来之山[1]。其上多松[2]，其下多洗石 [3] 。有兽焉，其状如羊而马尾 [4]，名曰羬羊（qian chi) [5]，其脂可以已腊(xi)[6] 。

注释：[1]钱来山：指契那山，即东边的山。属亚武山东麓，又称荆山。在灵宝市阳平镇。
Notes: [1] qian lai shan (money come mount)
Tr: refers to Chi-na-shan（mountain in the east）。 It belongs to the east part of Yawushan, which is also known as Jingshan。 The mountain is situated in Lingbao city's Yangping town。

[2]松：数，指共工国氏族，又称数国氏族。
[2] song (pine) phonetic match to shu (number)
Tr: refers to the Gonggong clans, also known as the Shuguo clans。

[3] 洗石：指羲氏族，王族之意。
[3] xi shi (wash stone)
Tr: refers to the Xi clan, the ruling clan. Xi 洗(wash), xi 羲 (east, king) a phonetic match。

[4]羊（chi) 而马尾：指东边的莽夷。莽夷指荆莽夷，又称荆夷。
[4] chi er ma yi (sheep with horse tail)
Tr: refers to the Mang Yi from the east part。Mang Yi is also known as Jingmang Yi, Jing Yi。

[5] 羬羊（qian chi)：指阳平氏。
[5] qian chi (east sheep/goat) refers to the Yangping Shi。

[6] 其脂可以已腊（xi)：这个支系是夏国的羲夷，即王族。
[6] qi zhi ke yi yi xi (its fat can cure meat)
Tr: refers to the Xi Yi, a royal lineage of the Xia nation, the ruling clan。

译文：西山第一列山系为华山山系，最东边的山叫契那山。山的西边生活着共工国氏族，山的东边生活着羲氏族。有一个氏族，是东边的荆莽夷，名叫阳平氏，这个支系是夏族的王族。
Translation:
The first list of the west mountains is headed by Chinashan (Qinashan) at its east most end。 On its west side lives the Gonggong Guo clan。 On its east side lives the Xi clan. Another people known as the Jingmang Yi from the east also live there。They bear the surname of Yangping。 They are the royal lineage of the Xia people。

02-01-02 松果山
Songguoshan
（110,39161E；34,46746N）

西四十五里，曰松果之山[1]。濩水出焉[2]，北流注于渭，其中多铜 [3] 。有鸟焉，其名曰螐渠 [4] ，其状如山鸡[5]，黑身赤足[6]，可以已【月暴】[7]。

注释：[1]松果山：指亚武山，实际介绍山脚的豫灵镇和太要镇。松，指雌、亚。果，读 gou，指武。
Notes： [1] song guo shan (pinecone mount)
Tr: refers to Yawushan, it is in fact, descriptive of the Yulingzhen and the Taiyaozhen by the foot of the mountain。 song(pine)means female, secondary; guo：Pu concept， reads as gou, means wu（warlike）。
[2] 濩水：指峪水，实际流入黄河。
[2] huo shui (roof rain drops)
Tr: it refers to the Yushui River, it flows in fact into the Yellow River。
[3]铜：指太氏族，即太要氏。
[3] tong (copper)
Tr: it refers to the Tai clan, also known as Taiyao Shi。
[4] 螐渠：读 te ts'i，指太要氏。
[4] tong qu（a pheasant-like bird canal）
Tr: a Pu concept reads te ts'i, refers to the Taiyao Shi。
[5] 山鸡：读 so ji，指亚部落，全称是亚武部落。
[5] shan ji (mountain chicken)
Tr: A Pu concept reads as: so ji, refers to the Ya tribe, whose full name is Yawu tribe。
[6] 黑身赤足：贵族的太要支系。
[6] hei shen chi zu (black body red feet)
Tr: the royal lineage, the Taiyao branch。
[7] 可以已【月暴】：夏国的农业夷。
[7]ke yi yi bao (can cure skin disease)
Tr: the agriculture Yi of the Xia nation。

译文：由契那山往西四十五里，有座山叫亚武山。峪水从山间流出，向北流入黄河，那里生活着太要氏族。有一个氏族群体，叫太要氏，是亚部落贵族的太要支系，是夏国的农业夷。
Translation：
Forty-five li further west from Chinashan there stands Yawushan。 Yushui River originates from this mountain and goes north into the Yellow River, where the Taiyao clan lives。 Known as the Taiyao Shi, they are the Taiyao branch of the royal lineage of the Ya clan, the agriculture Yi of the Xia nation。

02-01-03 太华山
Taihuashan

（110,08416E；34,48076N）

又西六十里，曰太华之山[1]，削成而四方[2]，其高五千仞，其广十里，鸟兽莫居[3]。有蛇焉[4]，名曰肥【虫遗】[5]，六足四翼 [6]，见则天下大旱 [7] 。

注释：[1]太华山：华山。又称云华山，是华山主峰。
Notes: [1] tai hua shan (grand blossom mount)
Tr: refers to Huashan, also known as Yunhuashan (clouds blossom mount)， the main peak of the Huashan。
[2] 削成而四方：指华山的主峰。削成，读胥照，指华山。四方，读布法，指主峰。
[2] xiao cheng er si fang (cut it become four sides)
Tr: refers to the peak of the Huashan。 Xiaocheng (cut into) reads in Pu concept as xu zhao, (the Huashan) 。si fang reads in Pu concept as bufa, meaning main peak。
[3] 鸟兽莫居：指人们很难上去。
[3] niao shou mo ju (bird beast can't stay)
Tr: a very difficult place for human to get to。
[4] 有蛇焉：有一个氏族。
[4] you she yan (has snake):
Tr: there is a clan。
[5]肥【虫遗】：指夫水氏族。濮语称夫溢，即夫水之意。谐音成了肥遗。
[5] fei yi（fat remain）
Tr: refers to the Fushui clan。In Pu concept Fushui read as fuyi, a close phonetic match to fei yi, fu shui--fu yi--fei yi。
[6] 六足四翼：指母系氏族。
[6] liu zu si yi (six feet four wings)
Tr: refers to the matrilineal clans。
[7] 见则天下大旱：是那个地方的牧羊氏族。大旱，在此指鞑贺。
[7] jian ze tian xia da han (seeing it causes the world big drought),
Tr: they are the sheep/goat herders, refers to the Dahe clan。Dahan 大旱/dahe 鞑贺 a close phonetic match。

译文：由亚武山往西六十里，有座山叫太华山，是华山的主峰。这座山高五千仞，延绵十里，人们很难上去。山下有一个氏族，名叫夫水氏，是母系氏族，是那个地方的牧羊氏族。
Translation:
Sixty li further west from Yawushan there stands Taihuashan, the main peak of Huashan。 This mountain rises as high as five thousand Ren, stretches for an area of ten square li, a very difficult place for people to get to 。 A clan bearing the name of Fushui is a matrilineal people。 They are the shepherd's clan of that place。

02-01-04 小华山
Xiaohuashan
（109,7664E；34,50652N）

又西八十里，曰小华之山[1]。其木多荆杞[2]，其兽多㸲牛 [3]，其阴多磬石 [4]，其阳多㻬琈之玉 [5] 。鸟多赤鷩 [6]，可以御火 [7] 。其草多萆荔 [8]，状如乌韭，而生于石上 [9]，亦缘木而生[10]，食之已心痛[11]。

注释：[1]小华山：指少华山。这里实际指华县地区。
Notes：[1] xiao hua shan (lesser blossom mount)
Tr: it refers to the Shaohuashan, a description of the Hua County area in Shaanxi province。
[2] 其木多荆杞：在管理中心生活着井氏族。木，指检目。

[2] qi mu duo jing qi (its wood plenty thorny twigs)
Tr: at the management center lives the Jin (water well) clan, mu(wood 木) (eyes 目) refers to the administrative township。

[3] 其兽多牸牛：在西边生活着柞水氏族。牸牛，即柞流、柞河，柞水。

[3] qi shou duo zuo niu (among beast, plenty mountain cattle)
Tr: it refers to the Zuoshui clan living on the west side of the mountain。 Zuo niu: zuo liu-- zuo water, zuo river, zuo rio。

[4] 其阴多磬石：在北边生活着骞姓氏族。

[4] qi yin duo qing shi (its shady side, plenty music stone)
Tr: it refers to the Qian clan living on the north side of the area。

[5] 其阳多瑦琈之玉：南边生活着白石堡氏族。濮语读为“吐放夷”。

[5] qi yang duo tu fu zhi yu (on sunny side, plenty tufu jade) refers to the Baishipu people who live on the south side of the area。 In Pu concept, Baishipu reads as Tufang Yi, a phonetic play on tufu jade。

[6] 鸟多赤鷩：还有赤水氏族。赤鷩，指赤沘。

[6] niao duo chi bi (plenty red bird)
Tr: there is also the Chishui(chibi) clan, chibi, red bird（鷩） or red river（沘）, a pun on bi。

[7] 可以御火：夏国的延贺氏族。即牧羊氏族。

[7]ke yi yu huo (can protect from fire)
Tr: Xia nation's Yanhe clan, the shepherd clan。

[8] 其草多萆荔：移民有呗黎。呗黎，即火粟人。

[8] qi cao duo bi li (its grass plenty bili)
Tr: migrants are the Bei Li, known as the Huosu (fire millet) people。Bili/beili: phonetic close match。

[9] 乌韭而生于石上：华州的富饶的胥夷。石上，指富饶。生于，指胥夷、华胥氏。

[9] wu jiu er sheng yu shi shang (dark leek grows on the stone)
Tr: it refers to the rich Xu Yi from the Huazhou (zhou: Prefecture) 。 Shi shang (on stone) means rich, sheng yu (grows on) refers to the Xu Yi, also known as the Huaxu Shi。

[10] 缘木而生：织绸的氏族。

[10] yuan mu er sheng: (climb trees to live)
Tr: it refers to the silk making clan。

[11] 食之已心痛：古老的华胥中心支系氏族。

[11] shi zhi yi xin tong (eat to cure heart pain)
Tr: the ancient Huaxu clans' central branches。

译文：由太华山往西八十里，是少华山地区。在管理中心生活着井氏族，在西边生活着柞水人氏族，在北边生活着骞姓氏族，在南边生活着白石堡氏族。还有赤水人，是夏国的延贺氏族。还有移民的呗黎，是华州富饶胥夷的织绸氏族，是古老的华胥中心支系氏族。

Translation:
Eighty li further west from the Taihuashan is the Shaohuashan area。In the center of its management township lives the Jing clan。 On its west side lives the Zuoshui clan。 On its north side lives the Qian clan, and on its south side lives the Baishipu clan。There is also the Yanhe clan--the Chishui people from the Xia nation。 The migrants of Beili are the silk making branches from the rich Xu Yi of the Hua Prefecture。 They are the ancient central branch of the Huaxu clan。

02-01-05 符禺山
Fuyushan
（109,50204E；34,5004N）

又西八十里，曰符禺之山[1]。其阳多铜[2]，其阴多铁 [3] 。其上有木焉 [4]，名曰文茎 [5]，其实如枣[6]，可以已聋[7]。其草多条[8]，其状如葵[9]，而赤华黄实[10]，如婴舌[11]，食之使人不惑[12]。符禺之水[13]出焉，而北流注于渭。其兽多葱聋[14]，其状如羊而赤鬣[15]。其鸟多鴖[16]，其状如翠而赤喙[17]，可以御火。

注释：[1]符禺山：指华渭地区，今称渭南市。
Notes:[1] fu yu shan: refers to the Huawei area, in today's Weinan city。(south of Wei River)
[2]铜：指临潼氏族。
[2] tong (copper)
Tr: it refers to the Lintong clan。
[3]铁：指油坊氏族。
[3] tie (iron)
Tr: it refers to the Youfang clan。 (oil press mill)
[4] 其上有木：西边有一支蒙族。
[4] qi shang you mu (upon it has wood)
Tr: a branch of Mongolians in the west side of the mountain。
[5] 文茎：指泾河。
[5] wen jing (culture stalk)
Tr: refers to the Jing River。
[6]枣：指草市。
[6] zao(date)
Tr: refers to Caoshi: grass market。
[7] 已聋：指河边夷。
[7] yi long (cure deaf)
Tr: refers to the Hebian Yi, (river side branch) 。
[8]条：指喊族，即呼麦氏族。
[8] tiao(stripe)
Tr: refers to Hanzu (yell branch) known as the Humai clan。 Humai: humming, throat singing。
[9]葵：指北方。
[9] kui (sunflower) refers to the north。
[10] 赤华而黄实：游牧的胡族。
[10] chi hua er huang shi (red flower with yellow fruit)
Tr: refers to the Hu branch of the nomadic clans。
[11] 婴舌：阴山氏族。
[11] ying she (baby tongue) refers to the Yinshan clan (shady mount) 。
[12] 食之使人不惑：古老的草原牧羊氏族。
[12] shi zhi shi ren bu huo (eat it won't get confused)
Tr: refers to the ancient shepherd clans of the steppes。
[13] 符禺水：指沋河。
[13] fu yu shui: refers to You River。
[14] 葱聋：指岔河氏族。沋河、赤水都称岔河。
[14] cong long (lush green)
Tr: refers to the Chahe clan, Chahe (fork river) refers to You River and the Chishui River。
[15] 羊而赤鬣：东部的赤水氏族。
[15] yang er chi lie (lamb with red mane)
Tr: refers to the Chishui clan from the east。 chishui: red water。
[16]鴖：指蒙族。

[16] wen/man/(bird): refers to the Mongolian clans。

[17] 翠而赤喙：草原的牧羊氏族。

[17] cui er chi hui (green feather and red beak)
Tr: refers to the shepherds' clans from the steppe。

译文：由少华山地区往西八十里，到达华渭地区。它的南面生活着临潼氏族，北面生活着油坊氏族。西边有一支蒙族，叫泾河氏族，其实是草市的河边夷。有一支呼麦氏族，是北方的游牧胡族，是阴山古老的草原牧羊氏族。氿河发源于这座山，向北流入渭河。这里的氏族还有岔河氏族，是东部的赤水氏。还有一些蒙族人，是草原的牧羊氏族，是夏国的延贺氏。

Translation:
Eighty li further west from Shaohuashan area, there is the Huawei region。 To its south lives the Lintong clan, to its north lives the Youfang clan。 On the west is a Mongolian branch, the Jinghe clan。 They are in fact the Hebian Yi from Caoshi。 Another branch is called Humai clan, a nomadic Hu tribe from the north。They are the ancient steppe shepherds clans from Yinshan。 You River rises from this mountain and flows north into Wei River。There also live other clans such as the Chahe clan, known otherwise as the Chishui Shi from the east。 There also live the Mongolians, the steppe shepherd's clan-- the Yanhe Shi of the Xia nation。

02-01-06 石脆山
Shicuishan
（109,32249E；34,15121N）

又西六十里，曰石脆之山[1]。其木多棕枏[2]，其草多条 [3]，其状如韭而白华黑实 [4]，食之已疥 [5]。其阳多㻬琈之玉 [6]，其阴多铜。灌水 [7] 出焉，而北流注于禺水 [8]。其中有流赭 [9]，以涂牛马无病 [10]。

注释：[1]石脆山：指草链岭，实际指西南部的蓝田地区。
Notes [1] shi cui shan (stone breakable mount)
Tr: refers to the Caolianling mountains (grass chain range), a description of the Lantian (blue field) area in the southwest。

[2] 棕枏：指贵族。

[2] zong nan (palm machilus nanmu)
Tr: it refers to the royal or the noble clan。

[3]条：此处与铜读音相同，指临潼。

[3] tiao(strip)
Tr: a phonetic Pu concept to tong(copper); referring to the Lintong area， Shaanxi province。

[4] 韭而白华黑实：管理层的博恒氏贵族。

[4] jiu er bai hua hei shi (leek with white flowers black fruits)
Tr: refers to the management level of the tribe—the noble lineage of the Boheng Shi。

[5] 已疥：管理夷。

[5] yi jie (cure skin disease） refers to the management Yi。

[6] 㻬琈之玉：此处指银川夷。

[6] tu fu zhi yu (tufu jade)
Tr: it refers to the Yinchuan Yi, yin(silver)chuan(gully)

[7] 灌水：蓝水，发源于草链岭。

[7] guan shui: lan shui (blue water)
Tr: refers to the Lanshui River, it originates from the Caolianling Mountains。

[8] 禺水：指玉水，今称灞河。

[8]yu shui，（jade water) today is known as the Ba River。

[9] 流赭：指兒竹氏，今称竹娃。濮语“兒”，指幼儿。
[9] liu zhe (flowing ochre)
Tr: refers to the Erzhu (baby bamboo) people, today known as zhuwa (bamboo baby) 。Er: a Pu concept for 'baby', refers to very small kids。

[10] 涂牛马无病：属白兒蒙部落。无，指部落；病，指属。
[10] tu niu ma wu bing (smear ox horse no illness)
Tr: belong to the Bai'ermeng tribe. wu(no)refers to tribes, bing(illness) means belong to。

译文：由华渭地区往西南六十里，到达草链岭。那里的管理贵族，是来自于临潼的管理层的博恒氏贵族，是古老的管理夷。山的南面生活着银川氏族，北面生活着临潼氏族。蓝水发源于草链岭，向北流入灞河。蓝水河畔有一个叫兒竹的氏族，属于白兒蒙部落氏族。
Translation:
Sixty li further southwest from the Huawei area, one arrives at the Caolianling Mountain。The management nobles are from the ancient Boheng elite group, who come from Lintong area。 On the south of the mountain lives the Yinchuan clan。 In the north lives the Lintong clan。 Lanshui River originates from Caolianling Mountains and goes north into the Ba River。 On the Lanshui River's bank, a tribe known as the Erzhu clan lives there, they belong to the Bai'ermeng tribal clans。

02-01-07 英山
Yingshan
（108,6033E；34,10799N）

又西七十里，曰英山[1]。其上多杻橿[2]，其阴多铁 [3[]，其阳多赤金[4]。禺水[5]出焉，北流注于招水[6]，其中多鲜鱼[7]，其状如鳖[8]，其音如羊[9]。其阳多箭䉋[10]，其兽多𤙖牛[11]、䍮羊[12]。有鸟焉，其音如鹑[13]，黄身而赤喙[14]，其名曰肥遗[15]，食之已疠[16]，可以杀虫[17]。

注释：[1]英山：指户山，户与家在濮语中读 yin,今陕西西安鄠邑区。
Notes: [1] ying shan: refers to Hushan (household mount), in Pu concepts, household and home all read as Yin, a close phonetic match to Ying, refers to today 's Huyi district in Xi'an city, Shaanxi province。

[2] 杻橿：指延祖氏，今称庵祖。
[2] niu jiang (plant niu and oak) refers to the Yanzu Shi, today known as Anzu。

[3]铁：指苍游氏，游音通油。
[3] tie(iron) refers to the Cangyou Shi, you，游，油： a phonetic match.

[4] 赤金：指石井氏。
[4] chi jin (red gold) refers to the Shijing (stone well) Shi。

[5] 禺水：指涝峪河。
[5] Czegledy1983 shui: refers to the Laoyu（flood valley） River。

[6] 招水：指王者之水，即渭河。
[6] zhao shui (summon water)
Tr: refers to the King's water, the Wei River。

[7]鲜（feng) 鱼：指沣水夷。
[7] feng yu (feng fish) refers to the Fengshui Yi。

[8]鳖：指博恒氏。
[8] bie(turtle): refers to the Boheng Shi。

[9]羊（chi)：指东边。

[9] chi/yang(sheep) refers to the east。

[10] 箭䉋：指五竹氏。

[10] jian mei: refers to the Five bamboo Shi。

[11] 犲牛：指卓黎氏，今演绎为张良、张良寨。

[11] zuo niu (legendary mountain bull)

Tr: refers to Zhuoli Shi, today the name becomes Zhangliang/ the Zhangliang village. zuo/zhuo/zhang a close Pu phonetic match。

[12] 羬羊：指流沙氏，后称东沙氏。

[12] chi yang:(chi goat)

Tr: refers to Liusha (moving sands) Shi, later known as the Dongsha (east sands) Shi。

[13]鶉：指漾，鄠邑的小地名为漾陂。

[13] chun(bird) refers to Yang（ripple）, the nickname for Huyi, known as Yangbo。

[14] 黄身而赤喙：华族的游牧胡。

[14] huang shen er chi hui (yellow body and red beak)

Tr: the nomadic Hu from the Hua ethnic clan。

[15] 肥遗：在此指鄠 hu4 夷。

[15] fei yi（fat remains）: refers to the Hu Yi。

[16] 已疠：指小月氏，疠指小。

[16] yi li (cure leprosy) refers to the Xiaoyuezhi (minor rouzhi) Li: small。

[17] 可以杀虫：夏国的外来移民。

[17]ke yi sha chong (can kill worms)

Tr: it refers to the outsider migrants to the Xia nation。

译文：由草链岭往西七十里，到达户山。它的西面住着延祖氏，北面住着苍游氏，南面住着石井氏。涝峪河从山间流出，向北流入渭河。这里生活着沣水夷，是博恒氏族，住在东边。南面还住着五竹氏、卓黎氏、流沙氏。有一群人，住在漾陂，是华族的游牧胡，名叫鄠夷，是古老的小月氏夷，是夏国的外来移民。

Translation:

Seventy li further west from the Caolianling Mountain there stands the Hushan。 On its west side lives the Yanzu Shi, on its north, the Cangyou Shi。 In its south lives the Shijing Shi。 The Laoyu River originates from the mountain and goes north into the Wei River。 The Fengshui Yi, who belong to the Boheng tribe, lives in the east side。 In the south side, live the Wuzhu Shi, Zhuoli Shi, Liusha Shi。 Another group of people lives at Yangpo。 They are called Hu Yi from the Hua nomadic tribe, they are the ancient Xiaoyuezhi Yi, an outsider migrant tribe to the Xia nation。

02-01-08 竹山

Zhushan

（108,22208E；34,16357N）

又西五十二里，曰竹山[1]。其上多乔木[2]，其阴多铁 [3]。有草焉，其名曰黄雚[4]，其状如樗[5]，其叶如麻[6]，白华而赤实[7]，其状如赭，浴之已疥[8]，又可以已胕[9]。竹水[10]出焉，北流注于渭，其阳多竹箭[11]，多苍玉[12]。丹水[13]出焉，东南流注于洛水，其中多水玉[14]，多人鱼[15]。有兽焉，其状如豚而白毛，大如笄而黑端[16]。名曰豪彘[17]。

注释：[1]竹山：指卓资山，是周至的古称谓，周至是卓资夷南下至渭河边的音译。

Notes:[1] zhu shan（bamboo hill)

Tr: refers to Zhuozishan, an old name for Zhouzhi. Zhou zi, zhuozhi, phonetic matches。 When the Zhuozi Yi moved down south to the Wei River, they give their tribe’s name to the place。

[2] 其上多乔木：西边住着凉水和五泉氏族。

[2] qi shang duo qiao mu (on it many tall trees)
Tr: on its westside lives the Liangshui (cold water) clan and the Wuquan (five springs) clan。

[3] 其阴多铁：北面住着潭堡氏族。潭，通谈，读音为 tie。

[3] qi yin duo tie (its shady side more iron)
Tr: on its north lives the Tanbao clan。 Tan, tie, phonetic shift。

[4] 黄雚：指伏辛氏，又称伏恒氏。

[4] huang huan (yellow grass) refers to the Fuxin Shi, also known as the Fuheng Shi。

[5]樗：在此指草原氏族。

[5] chu (useless wood) refers to the steppe clans。

[6]麻：指蒙族。

[6]ma(hemp): refers to the Mongolian ethnic people。

[7] 白华而赤实：巴彦胡的移民氏族。

[7] bai hua er chi shi (white flowers with red fruit)
Tr: it refers to the migrant clan of the Bayan Hu's。

[8] 赭浴之已疥：卓资夷的管理夷。

[8] zhe yu zhi yi jie (ochre shower cure skin disease)
Tr: it refers to the management branch （Yi） of the Zhuozi Yi。

[9] 可以已胕：夏国的北夷。胕，音 zhou, 指北。

[9]ke yi yi zhou (can cure foot illness)
Tr: it refers to the northern Yi of the Xia nation. zhou, means north。

[10] 竹水：即卓水，今称黑河。

[10] zhu shui (bamboo water)
Tr: it refers to the Zhuoshui River, known today as Hei River (black river) 。

[10] 竹箭：卓资族的管理夷。

[10] zhu jian (bamboo arrows)
Tr: it refers to the management branch of the Zhuozi clan。

[11] 苍玉：指草原夷。

[11] cang yu (dark jade)
Tr: it refers to the steppe Yi。

[12] 丹水：指光头水，读音岱羲水。又称薄水、薄江，读音薄蒙。洛水：汉水的古名称。

[12] dan shui (red water)
Tr: it refers to the Guangtou shui (bald head water) reads as Daixishui, also as Bo Shui, Bo Jiang， Bojiang, reads as bo meng。 Luoshui, the old name for Hanshui, the Han River。

[13] 水玉：指熊姓夷，即有熊氏。

[13] shui yu (water jade)
Tr: refers to the Xiong Yi, Xiong (bear)the Youxiong Shi。

[14] 人鱼：指孔姓夷，即孔家湾氏族。

[14] ren yu (human fish)
Tr: it refers to the Yi bearing the family name of Kong, the people and tribes from the Kongjiawan clan。

[15] 豚而白毛：薄江的管理氏族。

[15] tun er bai mao (baby pig with white hair)
Tr: it refers to the management branches of Bojiang。

[16] 大如笄而黑端：鞑鲁部落的牧羊坪。黑，读贺，指羊。端，指坪。

[16] da ru ji er hei duan (big as hairpin with black ends)

Tr: it refers to the Shepherds town, Muyangping, of the Dalu tribe。 Hei(black): reads as he, refers to goats/sheep shepherds' tribes, duan(ends)refers to ping--a township。

[17] 豪彘：指贺坪，牧羊坪；今谐音称为石猴子。

[17] hao zhi (big swine)

Tr: refers to the Heping, shepherds town, today known as Shihouzi (stone monkey)。 haozhi, houzi: a phonetic match。

译文：由户山往西五十二里，到达卓资山。它的西边住着凉水、五泉氏族，北面住着潭堡氏族。有一个移民氏族，名叫伏辛氏，是草原蒙族，是巴彦胡的移民，是卓资夷的管理夷，是夏国的北夷。竹水发源于这座山，向北流入渭河，竹山的南面住着卓资族的管理夷和草原夷。薄水发源于这座山，向南流入汉水。这里住着熊姓夷，住着孔姓夷。这里有一个氏族，是薄江的管理氏族，是鞑鲁部落的牧羊坪氏族，名叫贺坪氏。

Translation:

Fifty-two li further west from Hushan stands Zhuozishan。 On its west live the Liangshui clan and the Wuquan clan。 To its north lives the Tanbao clan。 A migrant tribe known as the Fuxin Shi is of the steppe Mongolians。They are part of the Bayan Hu, a management branch of the Zhuozi people, the northern Yi of the Xia nation。Zhushui River originates from this mountain, flows north into the Wei River。On its south side of the Zhushan live the Zhuozi management tribe and the steppe people。Boshui River originates from this mountain and flows south into Hanshui River。 The Xiong clan lives here, so does the Kong Yi。 One management clan from Bo River, the Dalu tribe's shepherds from Muyangping, are called Heping Shi。

02-01-09 浮山

Fushan

（107,75138E；34,2738N）

又西百二十里，曰浮山[1]。多盼木[2]，枳叶而无伤 [3]，木虫居之 [4] 。有草焉，名曰薰草 [5]，麻叶而方茎 [6]，赤华而黑实[7]，臭如蘼芜[8]，佩之可以已疠[9]。

注释：[1]浮山：指王族山，在陕西眉县地区。

[1] fu shan (floating mount)

Tr: it refers to the King tribe mount, (Wangzushan), in today's Mei county (eyebrow county), Shaanxi province。

[2] 盼木：指河岸氏族。

[2] pan mu (expectation wood)

Tr: it refers to the riverbank clan。 Pan(盼，畔): a phonetic match 。

[3] 枳叶而无伤：清水河（在内蒙古）的乌善部落。乌指头、首。

[3]： zhi ye er wu shang (citrus leaf and no wound)

Tr： refers to the Qingshui (clear water) River's Wushan tribe。 Wu, head, wu shan/wu shang（乌善，无伤）, a close phonetic match。

[4] 木虫居之：指内迁部落支系。

[4]mu chong ju zhi (wood worm stay in it) refers to the outside tribes that migrated to this place。

[5] 薰草：指匈奴移民。

[5] xun cao (scented grass) refers to the Xiongnu immigrants。

[6] 麻叶而方茎：蒙夷的王族。这里将匈奴、鞑靼、东胡都称为蒙族。

[6]ma ye er fang jing (hemp leaf and square stalk)

Tr： refers to the king house of the Meng Yi，Meng Yi being an umbrella term for the various ethnic groups of Xiongnu, Dadan, Donghu people。

[7] 赤华而黑实：游牧胡的贵族。
[7] chi hua er hei shi (red flower with black fruit)
Tr: it refers to the noble lineage of the nomadic Hu people。
[8] 臭如蘼芜：分支的眉部落氏族。臭，指分岔。
[8] chou ru fei wu (smells like miwu grass),
Tr: it refers to the branches of the Mei tribal people, chou; branch, fork。
[9] 佩之可以已疠：常称为夏国的伊吾人。
[9] pei zhi ke yi yi li (wear it can cure sore)
Tr: (they are) often addressed as the Yiwu people of the Xia nation。

译文：由卓资山往西一百二十里，就到了王族山。那里住着河畔氏族，是清水河的乌善氏族内迁的部落支系。还有一群人，是匈奴移民，是蒙夷的王族，是游牧胡贵族分支的眉部落支系，常称为夏国的伊吾人。
Translation:
One hundred and twenty li further west from Zhouzishan stands Wangzushan。 The riverbank tribes live there, they are the Wushan tribes' immigrants from the Qingshui River。 Another group is the Xiongnu immigrants, they are the noble lineage of the Meng (Mongolian)people, they are the Mei tribe's branches of the nomadic Hu's elite class。 They are often being addressed as the Yiwu people of the Xia nation。

02-01-10 羭次山
Yucishan
（107,4691E；34,30535N）

又西七十里，曰羭次之山[1]。漆水出焉[2]，北流注于渭。其上多棫橿 [3]，其下多竹箭 [4]，其阴多赤铜 [5]，其阳多婴恒之玉 [6] 。有兽焉，其状如禺而长臂 [7]，善投 [8]，其名曰嚣[9]。有鸟焉，其状如枭[10]，人面而一足[11]，曰橐𩇯[12]，冬见夏蛰[13]，服之不为雷[14]。

注释：[1]羭次山：指游龙山，今称龙王山。主要介绍山下的天王镇地区。
[1]yu ci shan; refers to the Youlongshan (swimming dragon mount), known today as the Longwangshan (dragon king mount), this is a description mainly about the Tianwang (heavenly Lord) township at the foot of the mountain。
[2] 漆水：指岔河水，流到山下后又汇合在一起。
[2] qi shui (lacquer water)
Tr: refers to the Cha(forked) River, it first forks, and then joins together when coming down from the mountain。
[3] 棫橿：指践河氏族，今称剑家沟人。
[3]yu jiang (thorny shrub and oak)
Tr: refers to the Jianhe clan （Jian River people）, today known as the Jianjiagou people, jian(sword), jia(home) gou(gully)。
[4] 竹箭：指梁渚氏族，今称梁崖、梁家崖。
[4] zhu jian (bamboo arrows)
Tr： refers to the Liangzhu people, (not to be confused with 良渚 Liangzhu in the east), today is called Liangyan, or Liangjiayan。Yan(rock, cliff) 。
[5] 赤铜：渭河北岸的阳平氏。
[5] chi tong (red copper)
Tr: refers to the Yangping people who live on the north bank of the Wei River。
[6] 婴恒之玉：指阏塬夷。
[6] ying heng zhi yu (baby longlasting jade) refers to the Yanyuan Yi。
[7] 禺而长臂：岔河源头的。
[7]yu er chang pi (yu with long arm) refers to the source of the Cha River。

[8] 善投：东岭氏族。
[8] shan tou (good at hurling)
Tr: refers to the Dongling clan。 dong(east), ling(range)
[9]嚣：东岭氏。读为羲氏。
[9] xiao (noisy) refers to the Dongling people, in Pu concept reads as Xi people, xi(east)。
[10]枭：东边。
[10] xiao(owl) refers to the east。
[11] 人面而一足：定居的虎崇拜氏族、尚武氏族。
[11] ren mian er yi zu (human face and one foot) refers to the tribes that worship tigers, the people who are militant。
[12] 橐𩇯：指老堡子氏族。在阳平镇的东边。
[12] tuo fei: refers to the Laopuzi/Laobaozi clan, they are situated to the east side of Yangpingzhen。
[13] 冬见夏蛰：阳平部落东部支系。
[13] dong jian xia zhe (winter appear, summer hibernate) 。
Tr: refers to the east branch of the Yangping tribe。
[14] 服之不畏雷：胡坪博维人。胡坪博维曾经是一个古城池。
[14] fu/hu zi bu wei lei (eat it not to fear thunder)
Tr： refers to the Hupingbowei people, Hupingbowei used to be an ancient township。

译文：由王族山往西七十里，有座山叫龙王山。岔河发源于这座山，向北流入渭河。它的西边住着践河氏族，东边住着梁崖氏族，北面住着阳平氏族，南面住着阏塬之夷。有一个氏族，是岔河源头的东岭氏族，名叫羲氏。有一群人，是东部定居的尚武氏族，叫老堡子氏族，是阳平部落东部支系的胡坪博维人。
Translation:
Seventy li further west from Wangzushan there stands Longwangshan。Cha River originates from the mountain and flows north into Wei River。On its west side lives the Jianhe clan, on its east side lives the Liangyan clan。The Yangping clan lives on the north side, and the Yuyuan Yi lives on the south side。 One tribe is the Dongling tribe at the water source area of the Cha River。 They bear the surname of Xi。 Another group of people is the warlike tribe from the east who settled down here, they are called the Laopuzi clan。 They are the Hupingbowei people of the east branch of the Yangping tribes。

02-01-11 时山
Shishan
(107,22584E；34,34205N)

又西百五十里，曰时山[1]，无草木[2]。逐水出焉[3]，北流注于渭，其中多水玉 [4] 。

注释：[1]时（she)山：指凤凰山。时读奢音，指凤凰。实际指凤凰山下的宝鸡地区。
Notes:[1] shi(time)(she) shan: time mount
Tr: refers to Fenghuangshan, shi reads as she/refers to phoenix, here is about the Baoji area at the foot of Fenghuangshan。
[2] 无草木：移民部落。
[2] wu cao mu (no grass wood)
Tr： refers to the tribes of immigrants。
[3] 逐水：指茹（zhue) 水。今称洁江河。
[3] zhu shui (chase water)
Tr： refers to the Zhue River, today's Jiejiang River。jie(clean)
[4] 水玉：指共工氏。

[4] shui yu (water jade) refers to the Gonggong Shi。

译文：由龙王山往西一百五十里，有座山叫凤凰山。那里是移民部落的区域。茹水发源于这座山，向北流入渭河，那里生活着共工氏族。
Translation:
One hundred and fifty li further west from Longwangshan, there stands Fenghuangshan。The migrant tribes live there。 Rushui River originates from the mountain, goes north into Wei River, where the Gonggong people live on the bank of the rivers。

02-01-12 南山
Nanshan
（105,89983E；34,55416N）

又西百七十里，曰南山[1]。上多丹粟[2] 。丹水 [3] 出焉，北流注于渭。兽多猛豹 [4] ，鸟多尸鳩 [5] 。

注释：[1]南山：指麦积山。濮语称麦为僚（lao)，僚、南谐音。
Notes： [1] nan shan (south mount)
Tr: refers to the Maijishan。 In Pu concept, mai reads as liao; liao/nan are close phonetic match。
[2] 丹粟：丹指集镇，丹粟指集镇氏族。
[2] dan su (red millets)
Tr： dan/red refers to town, dansu: township clan。
[3] 丹水：指岭子河，发源于麦积山主峰。
[3] dan shui (red water)
Tr： refers to the Lingzi (mountain ridge) River, originates from the main peak of the Maijishan。
[4] 猛豹：指柴部落氏族。今称伯阳镇人。
[4] meng bao (vicious leopard)
Tr: refers to the Chai(firewood) clan, known today as the Boyangzhen people。
[5]尸（she) 鳩：指腰舍，腰巴氏族。濮语读腰为 jiao 音，与鳩谐音。
[5] shi jiu (corpse pigeon)
Tr: shi/she, a close phonetic match to refer to the Yaoshe, also known as the Yaoba clan。 In Pu concept, yao/jiao/jiu are close phonetic matches。

译文：由凤凰山往西一百七十里，有座山叫麦积山。它的西边生活着集镇氏族。岭子水从山上流出，向北流入渭河。这里还生活着柴部落氏族和腰巴人。
Translation:
One hundred and seventy li further west from Fenghuangshan stands Maijishan。 On its west side lives the township clan。Lingzi River comes from the mountain and goes north into Wei River。 This is the area where the Chai tribes and the Yaoba people live。

02-01-13 大时山
Dashishan
（104,18605E；34,74838N）

又西四百八十里，曰大时之山[1]。上多榖柞[2] ，下多杻橿 [3] ，阴多银 [4] ，阳多白玉 [5] 。涔水 [6] 出焉，北流注于渭。清水 [7] 出焉，南流注于汉水。

注释：[1]大时山：指大草滩，今甘肃省漳县大草滩镇。

Notes: [1] da shi shan (big time grass swamp)
Tr: refers to the Dacaotan township in Zhang County, Gansu Province。

[2] 穀柞：读 go tso，指中寨氏族，今王旗乡中寨、中寨沟、下中寨。

[2] go tso (grain wood)
Tr: refers to the Zhongzhai clan, today known as Zhongzhai, Zhongzhaigou, Xiuzhongshan in Wangqi township。
wang qi: king banner, zhong(middle) zhai(village) gou(gully), xia (lower)。

[3] 杻橿：读 liao jiang，指乌马氏族，今马泉乡氏族。

[3] liao jiang:
Tr: refers to the Wuma (black horse) clan, today known as the Maquanxiang (horse spring village) clan。

[4]银：指遮阳山氏族。

[4] yin(silver) refers to the Zheyangshan (block sun mount) clan。

[5] 白玉：指摆夷，即店子夷，今老幼店子村夷。

[5] bai yu (white jade) refers to the Bai Yi, bai(wave), today known as Dianzi Yi, Laoyoudianzicun Yi。 Lao(aged); you(young); dianzi(shop); cun(village); yi(people)。

[6] 涔水：指漳河。

[6] cen shui (continuous water) refers to Zhanghe River。

[7] 清水：指卜子水，实际流入洮河。青，音译词，指占卜的巫术。

[7] qing shui (clear water) refers to the Bozishui River, which flows into Taohe River。 qing (to divine) a close phonetic match to qing (clear)。

译文：由麦积山往西四百八十里，有座山叫大草滩，西边住着中寨氏族，东边住着乌马氏族，北边住着遮阳山氏族，南边住着店子氏族。漳河发源于这座山，向北流入渭河；卜子水发源于这座山，向南流入洮河。

Translation:
Four hundred and eighty li further west from the Maijishan, there stands a mountain called Dacaotan 。 On its west lives the Zhongzhai clan, on its east side lives the Wuma clan, on its north lives the Zheyangshan clan, and on its south lives the Dianzi clan。 Zhanghe River originates from this mountain and goes north into the Wei River; while Bozishui River, also originating from the same mountain, goes south into the Tao River。

02-01-14 嶓冢山
Bozhongshan
（102,07692E；33,99754N）

又西三百二十里，曰嶓冢之山[1]。汉水[2] 出焉，而东南流注于沔 [3] 。嚣水 [4] 出焉，北流注于汤水 [5] 。其上多桃枝钩端 [6] ，兽多犀兕熊罴 [7] ，鸟多白翰赤鷩 [8] 。有草焉，其叶如蕙[9] ，其木如桔梗[10]，黑华而不实[11]，名曰蓇蓉[12]。食之使人无子[13]。

注释：[1]嶓冢山：指扎尔加佐瑞山，也称樊尔加佐瑞山。简称樊佐山，谐音嶓冢山。这里介绍山下的玛曲集镇的情况。

Notes: [1]bo zhong shan: refers to the Zha’erjiazuorui Mountain, also known as Boerjiazuorui Mountain, shortened to Bozuoshan, a phonetic match for Bozhongshan, zuo/zhong。 This is a description of the Maqu town at the mountain foot。

[2] 汉水：指憨水，今称白龙江。

[2] han shui: a phonetic match of Han(dumb)shui, known today as Bailong Jiang (white dragon river) 。

[3]沔：指岷江，其实是白龙江的一条支流。古时两江汇合后，下游就以岷江为名，直至与嘉陵江汇合。

[3] mian: refers to Minjiang River。In fact, the Minjiang is a tributary of Bailongjiang。In ancient times, after the two rivers join, the lower water is named Minjiang River, until it joins Jialing River。

[4] 嚣水：嶓冢西部的扎尔加沃干峰东沟水。

[4] xiao shui (noisy water): refers to Donggou River from the Zharjiawoganfeng, on the west side of the Bozhong。

[5] 汤水：指洮河。

[5] tang shui (hot water): refers to Tao River。

[6] 其上多桃枝钩端：北面是洮江的源头。其上，在此指北面。枝，指江，在此指河。

[6] qi shang duo tao zhi gou duan (upon it plenty peach branch hook end)
Tr: to the north is the headwater of Tao River, qi shang（upon it）meaning north; zhi/ branch, means jiang/river。

[7] 犀兕熊罴：犀，指齐哈玛部落；兕，指卓格尼玛部落；熊，指叟契柯部落；罴，即制陶的手工业族群，指奥拉部落。

[7] xi si xiong pi (rhinoceros, rhino like beast, bear, brown bear) refers to the Qihama tribe(xi), Zhuogenima tribe(si); Suoqike tribe(xiong); Aola tribe, the potter's tribe(pi)。

[8] 白翰赤鷩：指黄河边的牧羊族。白翰，指补贺，即牧羊族；赤鷩，指赤泚，即黄河。

[8] bai han chi bi: refers to the sheep/goat herders along the Yellow River banks。 Baihan, a phonetic match for Buhe, the sheep/goat shepherd's tribe; chibi/red water, refers to the Yellow River。

[9]蕙：指环木卡尔人。

[9] Hui, refers to the Huanmukar people。

[10] 其木如桔梗：其支系为勾部落。即焉犁巩部落。

[10] qi mu ru ju geng (its wood like citrus twig) its branches are the Gou tribes, which refers to the Yanligong tribe, gou/gong a phonetic match。

[11] 黑华而不实：环木卡尔峰下的布若氏。

[11] hei hua er bu shi (black flower yet no fruit) refers to the Bunuo tribe at the foot of the Huanmukar peak。

[12] 菅蓉：勾戎。

[12]gu rong (kind grass): refers to Gou Rong, rong: the nomads。

[13] 食之使人无子：古老的北方草原氏族。使人无子，在此指北方草原。

[13] shi zhi shi ren wu zi (eaten to stop having babies) refers to the ancient northern steppes' tribes。 Shi ren wu zi (stop from having descendants) a code term for the northern steppes。

译文：由大草滩往西三百二十里，有座山叫樊佐山。白龙江发源于这座山，向东南与岷江汇合。东沟水发源于这座山，向北流入洮河。山的北部是洮河的源头。这里的氏族是齐、卓、叟、泚四大部落氏族，人群都是黄河岸边的牧羊族群。有一个移民氏族，是环木卡尔人，其支系为勾部落支系，是环木卡尔峰下的布若氏，名叫勾戎。是古老的北方草原氏族。

Translation:

Three hundred twenty li further west from the Dacaotan stands the Bozuoshan。 Bailongjiang River originates from this mountain and goes southeast to join Mingjiang River。Donggou River originates from this mountain and goes north into the Tao River。On the west of the mountain, many headwaters of the Tao River flow out。The clans living here are the four major ones bearing the surnames of Qi, Zuo, Sou, Bi; their people are the sheep/goats' keepers from the banks of Yellow River。One group of migrants is the Huanmukaer people, one of their branches is the Gou tribal branch, they are the Bunuo people from the foot of the Huanmukaer peak。This clan is known as the Gourong, a very ancient northern steppe people。

02-01-15 天帝山

Tiandishan

（99,90391E；33,96678N）

又西三百里，曰天帝之山[1]。上多椶枏[2]，下多菅蕙 [3] 。有兽焉，其状如狗[4]，名曰谿边[5]，席其皮者不蛊[6]。有鸟焉，其状如鹑[7]，黑文而赤翁[8]，名曰栎[9]，食之已痔[10]。有草焉，其状如葵[11]，其臭如芜蘼[12]，名曰杜衡[13]，可以走马[14]，食之已瘿[15]。

注释：[1]天帝山：指甘德山，今青海省甘德县城东侧。甘德，即 god，指天帝。
Notes：[1] tian di shan (sky god mount)
Tr: it refers to Gandeshan, the east part of Gande county in Qinghai Province。 Gande： e.g., God, meaning sky god。

[2] 椶枏：指查郎氏族。
[2] zong nan: tree,
Tr: it refers to the Chalang clan。

[3] 菅蕙：指东山部落，今有东吾遗存。
[3] jian hui (rush flower)
Tr: it refers to the Dongshan tribe, a relic name Dongwu still exists。

[4]狗：指柯曲氏族。
[4] gou(dog)
Tr: it refers to the Kequ clan。

[5] 谿边：东柯曲又称羲沘，谐音谿边。
[5] xi bian (creek side)
Tr: it refers to the Dong Kequ, also known as xibi, a phonetic match to xibian。

[6] 席其皮者不蛊：羲沘的柯氏族。
[6] xi qi pi zhe bu gu (seat on its skin won't be bewitched)
Tr: it refers to the Ke clan of Xibi。

[7]鹑：指滩涂。这里指东吉滩。
[7] chun(quail)
Tr: it refers to swamp, the Dongjitan: east lucky swamp。

[8] 黑文而赤翁：贵族的支系。
[8] hei wen er chi weng (black marking and red oldman)
Tr: it refers to the noble lineage。

[9]栎：指吾勒氏，即勒部落氏族。
[9] le (kind of tree)
Tr: it refers to Wule Shi, also known as Le tribal clans。

[10] 已痔：指平原夷
[10] yi zhi (cure hemorrhoids)
Tr: it refers to Pingyuan Yi, pingyuan(plain)。

[11]葵：北部的氏族。
[11] kui(sunflower)
Tr: it refers to the northern clans。

[12] 芜蘼：羁蘼部落。
[12] wumi (a kind flower)
Tr: it refers to the Jimi tribe。Jimi: a loose or long rein control of non-Chinese areas with self-administrative system。

[13] 杜衡：指德山氏，今称德里氏。
[13] du heng(flower)
Tr: it refers to Deshan Shi, also known as Deli Shi。

[14] 走马：指花苗氏族。
[14] zou ma (walk horse)
Tr: refers to the Huamiao (flower Miao) clans。

[15] 已瘿：北部夷。
[15] yi jing (cure skin disease)
Tr: it refers to the Beibu Yi (the northern Yi) 。

译文:由僰佐山往西三百五十里，有座山叫甘德山。它的西边住着查郎氏族，东边住着东山氏族。有一个氏族，是柯曲氏族的支系，名叫羲沘氏，是羲沘的柯氏族。有一群人，是东吉滩的贵族支系，名叫勒氏。是古老的平原夷。有一个移民氏族，是北部的罽靡支系，名叫德山氏，是夏国的花苗，古老的北部氏族。
Translation:
Three hundred and fifty li further west from Bozuoshan there stands Gandeshan。 On its west side lives the Chalang clan。 On its east side lives the Dongshan clan。 There is a clan, a branch of the Kequ clan, which is called Xibi Shi, also known as the Ke clan of the Xibi。 Another group of people, a noble lineage of Dongjitan, is called Le Shi. They are the ancient Pingyuan Yi。 Another migrant clan is the Jimi branch from the north, they are called Deshan Shi。 They are the Huamiao from the Xia nation, a very ancient northern clan。

02-01-16 皋涂山
Gaotushan
（97,45691E；33,69612N）

西南三百八十里，曰皋涂之山[1]。蔷水[2]出焉，西流注于诸资之水[3]；涂水[4]出焉，南流注于集获之水[5]。其阳多丹粟[6]，其阴多银、黄金[7]，其上多桂木[8]。有白石[9]焉，其名曰礜[10]，可以毒鼠[11]。有草焉，其状如藁茇[12]，其叶如葵而赤背[13]，名曰无条[14]，可以都鼠。有兽焉，其状如鹿而白尾[15]，马足人手而四角[16]，名曰【犭婴】如[17]。有鸟焉，其状如鸱而人足[18]，名曰数斯[19]，食之已瘿[20]。

注释：[1]皋涂山：指白鹤山，在青海称多县东北面，主峰海拔 5,088 米。这里主要介绍称多。
Notes: [1] gao tu shan: refers to the Baiheshan (white crane mount), in the northeast part of Chengduo county, Qinghai province。Its main peak is 5,088 m. above sea level。 This chiefly describes the Chengduo area。
[2] 蔷水：指稍扔水。
[2] qiang shui: the Shaoreng River。
[3] 诸资水：指清江水，是扎曲的上游。
[3] zhu zi shui: refers to the Qingjiang River, the upper tributary of Zhaqu River。
[4] 涂水：皋涂山主峰的溪流。汉语称白水。
[4] tu shui: the brook and stream from the main peak of the Gaotushan。 In Chinese, the River is called Bai(white)water。
[5] 集获水：指扎曲。
[5] ji huo shui；refers to Zhaqu River。(Tibetan: rdza chu)
[6] 丹粟：指多弥部落和苏毗部落，简称多素，已成为玉树的古名称。
[6] dan su (red millet) refers to the Duomi tribe and the Subi tribe, the names are shortened to Duosu, a phonetic match, an old name for the Yushu (jade tree) county， its full name :Yushu Tibetan Autonomous Prefecture。
[7]银、黄金：指靠巴阳硬部落和俄佳部落。
[7] yin, huangjin (silver, yellow gold)
Tr: refers to the Kaobayangying tribe and the Ejia tribe。
[8] 桂木：指更倾扎谷部落和蒙策同部落。
[8] gui mu refers to the Gengqingzhagu tribe and the Mengcetong tribe。
[9] 白石：指部落氏族。
[9] bai shi (white stone) refers to the tribes and clans。
[10]礜：指云达部落。也称吾云达。吾，指部落。

[10]yu (mineral) refers to the Yunda tribe, also known as the Wuyunda, wu being the phonetic notation for tribe。

[11] 毒鼠：古老的共工氏。

[11] du shu (poisonous rat) refers to the ancient Gonggong Shi。

[12] 藁茇：尕朵部落。简称尕巴。

[12] hao ba (Ligusticum sinense)
Tr：refers to the Gaduo tribe，its name is shortened to Gaba。

[13] 葵而赤背：北部的黄河流域。

[13] kui er chi bei (sunflower and red back)
Tr：refers to the Yellow River basin to the north。

[14] 无条：武汤氏，今称阴尔汤氏。

[14] wu tiao: refers to the Wutang Shi, known today as the Yin'ertang Shi。

[15] 鹿而白尾：山区的巴彦夷。

[15]lu er bai wei/yi (deer with white tail)
Tr: refers to the Bayan Yi from the mountain area。

[16] 马足人手而四角：蒙族集镇的补苦氏。四角，读 bu go，是补苦的谐音。

[16]ma zu ren shou er si jiao (horse foot human hands with four horns)
Tr: The Buku/Bugo tribe from the Mongolian towns, si jiao (bu go /four horns) is a phonetic match。

[17] 【犭婴】如：补苦氏族，又称燕奴。

[17] ying ru: refers to the Bugo people, also known as Yannu。

[18] 鴟而人足：东边的定居族。

[18] di er ren zu (owl with human feet)
Tr: refers to the tribes that come from the east and settled down。

[19] 数斯：共工氏。

[19] shu si: Gonggong Shi。

[20] 已瘿：指益日埃部落。

[20] yi yin refers to the Yire'ai tribes。

译文：由甘德山往西南三百八十里，有座山叫白鹤山。稍扔水发源于这座山，向西流入清江水；白水发源于这座山，向南流入扎曲。它的南面住着多、苏两个部落，北面住着靠巴阳硬、俄佳两个部落，西面住着更、蒙两个部落。有个部落氏族，名叫云达，是夏国古老的共工氏族。有个移民氏族，是尕巴北部的黄河流域的氏族，名叫武汤氏，是夏国古老的共工氏族。有一个氏族，是山区的巴彦蒙族的补苦氏，名叫燕奴。有一群人，是来自东部的定居氏族，名叫共工氏，是古老的益日埃部落氏族.

Translation：

Three hundred and eighty li further southwest from Gandeshan there stands Baiheshan。Shaoreng River originates from the mountain and goes west into Qingjiang River; Baishui River originates from this mountain and goes south into Zhaqu River。 On its south side live the Duo tribe and the Su tribe。 On the north side live the Kaobayangyin tribe and the Ejia tribe。 On its west side live the Geng tribe and Meng tribe。 One tribe known as the Yunda tribe is the ancient Gonggong people of the Xia nation。 Another clan, known as Wutang Shi, the Buku people of the Bayan Meng Shi from the mountains, is called Yannu, belongs to the ancient Gonggong Shi of the Xia nation。 There is also the Yiri'ai clan of the Gonggong Shi, who came from the east and settled down in the west。

02-01-17 黄山

Huangshan

（96,13958E；34,4456N）

又西百八十里，曰黄山[1]，无草木[2]，多竹箭[3]。盼水[4] 出焉，西流注于赤水 [5]，其中多玉[6]，有兽焉，其状如牛[7]，而苍黑大目[8]，其名曰【敏/牛】[9]。有鸟焉，其状如鸮[10]，青羽赤喙，人舌能言[11]，名曰鹦䳇[12]。

注释：[1]黄山：指翁意加陇，汉语称鄂（wo)山、黄山，在称多县塔鄂惹的西北面。
Notes:[1] huang shan (yellow mount)
Tr： refers to Wengyijialong。 In Chinese, it is called Woshan/huangshan, situated in the northwest part to Ta'e-re, of today's Chengduo county。

[2] 无草木：游牧民族地区。
[2] wu cao mu (no grass wood)
Tr: refers to the nomadic nations' area。

[3] 竹箭：指诸加部落群。如加巧岗、加巧折西那、加巧年扎、加核松卡、查人穷小、加塔龙让等。
[3] zhu jian (bamboo arrows) refers to a group of various tribes that have prefixes of Jia in their tribal names, such as the Jiaqiaogang, Jiaqiaozhexina, Jiaqiaonianzha, Jiahesongka, Charenqiongxiao, Jiatalongrang。zhu jia 竹箭, a phonetic match for zhu jia 诸加。

[4] 盼水：指弱水，又称瘦水（邹曲）、小水（尕曲），是黄河的源头。
[4] pan shui (expect water)
Tr: refers to Ruoshui (weak water), also known as Shoushui (lean water， Zouqu），Xiaoshui(small water, Gaqu),is the headwater of Yellow River。

[5] 西流注于赤水：向东流入黄河。赤水，指黄河。
[5] xi liu zhu yu chi shui (west flow into the red water)
Tr: flows east into the Yellow River, Chishui (red water) means Yellow River。

[6] 多玉：指有人烟。
[6] duo yu (more jade)
Tr: humans live there。

[7]牛: 指河边的。
[7] niu(ox): of the riverbanks。

[8] 苍黑大目：指措合朵姆部落氏族，也读措合达，是制作土陶的氏族。
[8] cang hei da mu (dark black big eyes)
Tr: refers to the Cuoheduomu tribes, shortened to Cuoheda, a clay potters' tribe。

[9] 【敏/牛】: 指牟氏族，也称母氏族。
[9] min(ox)refers to the Mou clan, also means the matrilineal clan, min/mou/mu: phonetic matches。

[10]鸮：指东边的。
[10] xiao(owl)
Tr： it refers to the east, or from the east。

[11] 青羽赤喙人舌能言：卡里卡维惹舍能彝。能彝，指中心氏族。
[11] qing yu chi hui ren she neng yan (black feather red beak human tongue can speak) 。
Tr: Kalikaweireshe Neng Yi: Neng Yi: central clan。

[12] 鹦䳇：指缨姆氏，又称纵(直)目氏族，指佩饰帽缨的氏族和留额发髻的氏族。
[12] yin mu (bird)refers to the Yingmu Shi or the Zongmu (vertical /straight eyes) clan。
Tr: tribes wearing hats with tassels and with hair knot over their foreheads。

译文：由白鹤山往西北一百八十里，有座山叫鄂山, 是游牧族的地区，生活着诸加部落群。弱水发源于这座山，向东流入黄河，弱水河边有人烟，有一个氏族，是河边的措合朵姆部落氏族，名叫牟氏。有一群人，是卡里卡维惹舍的能彝，名叫纵（直）目氏(即古彝人)。
Translation:

One hundred and eighty li further northwest from the Baiheshan stands the Woshan。On this land of the nomads, live the various Jia tribal groups。 The Ruoshui River originates from this mountain and flows east into the Yellow River, with people living on its banks。 One clan, bearing the surname of Mou, is the Cuoheduomu clan along the riverbanks。 Another group is the Kalikaweireshe Neng Yi, they are called Zongmu （Zhimu）Shi（ancient Yi people）。

02-01-18 翠山
Cuishan
（95,26514E；34,9546N）

又西二百里，曰翠山[1]。其上多椶枏[2]，其下多竹箭[3]，其阳多黄金玉[4]，其阴多牦牛、麢、麝[5]。其鸟多鸓[6]，其状如鹊[7]，赤黑而两首四足[8]，可以御火[9]。

注释：[1]翠山：指措池雅陇，汉语称措池山。
Notes： [1] cui shan (green mount) refers to the Cuochiyalong, known today in Chinese as Cuochishan, the name is a close phonetic match。
[2] 椶枏：指扎年、扎拉依部落区域。
[2] zong nan refers to the areas where the Zhanian tribe and the Zhalayi tribe live。
[3] 竹箭：指者纳查纳部落区域。简称者查。
[3] jian zhu (bamboo arrows) refers to the areas where the Zhena tribe and the Chana tribe live。 The names are combined to a shorter version of Zhecha。
[4] 黄金玉：指合乒康哟惹区域。
[4] huang jin yu（yellow gold jade) refers to the Hebingkangyoure area。
[5] 牦牛、麢、麝：指汶莱（热水）、阿拉克湖、沙尔陶勒盖区域。
[5] maoniu, ling, she (yak, deer, musk deer)
Tr: refers to the Wenlai(reshui/hotwater), Alaq Lake 35° 34′ 21.36″ N, 97° 7′ 23.88″ E, and the Sha'er taolegai areas。(Shaer Tolgoi， Shar Tolgoi, Zavkhan Soum, Uvs Aimag, Mongolia)
[6]鸓：指扎陵湖区域。
[6] lei(rodent) refers to the Zhaling Lake area。
[7]鹊：东边的。
[7] que(sparrow) east, oriental。
[8] 赤黑而两首四（bu) 足：黄河流域的鸟俗氏族。
[8] chi hei er liang shou si/bu zu (red, black with two heads four feet)
Tr: The Niaosu (bird habit) clan from the Yellow River drainage area。
[9] 可以御火：夏国的延贺氏族。即牧羊氏族。
[9]ke yi yu huo: the Yanhe clan, the sheep/goat husbandry clans of the Xia nation。

译文：由鄂山往西北二百里，有座山叫错池山。山的西面住着扎年地区的部落氏族，山的东面住着者查地区的部落氏族，山的南面住着合乒康哟惹的部落氏族，山的北面住着汶莱、阿拉克湖、沙尔陶勒盖的部落氏族。有一群扎陵湖人，是东边的黄河流域的鸟俗氏，是夏国的延贺氏族。
Translation：
Two hundred li further northwest from Woshan stands the Cuochishan。 On its west side live the clans from the Zhanian area。 On the east side, live the clans from the Zhecha area。 On the south side live the Hebingkangyoure tribes, on the north side live the tribes from Wenlai, Alaq Lake, Shar Tolgoi。 A group of Zhaling Lake people, the Niaosu Shi from the Yellow River drainage area to the east, is the Yanhe clan of the Xia nation。

02-01-19 騩山
Guishan
（93,5533E；35,71969N）

又西二百五十里，曰騩山[1]。是錞于西海，无草木[2]，多玉[3]。淒水[4]出焉，西流注于海[5]，其中多采石[6]、黄金[7]，多丹粟[8]。
凡西经之首，自钱来之山至于騩山，凡十九山，二千九百五十七里。华山冢也[9]，其祠之礼：太牢[10]。羭山神也[11]，祠之用烛，斋百日以百牺，瘗用百瑜，汤其酒百樽，婴[12]以百珪百璧。其馀十七山之属，皆毛牷[13]用一羊祠之。烛者，百草之未灰[14]，白席采等纯之[15]。

注释：[1]騩山：指昆仑山。这里指昆仑山东麓黑海地区。
Notes:[1] gui shan: refers to the Kunlunshan。
Tr: it refers to Heihai（black sea) area on the east part of Kunlunshan。
[2] 无草木：指没有人烟。
[2] wu cao mu (no grass wood)
Tr: no human inhabitation。
[3] 多玉：指多水。
[3] duo yu:(more jade)
Tr: a lot of water。
[4]淒（xi) 水：指楚玛尔水。（曲麻莱河/曲玛河）
[4] xi/qi shui: refers to the Chumar River。
[5]海：指东海。（西流注于海：东流注于东海）
[5] hai(sea) refers to the East China Sea。Flowing west into sea here means flowing east into the East Sea。
[6] 采石：指楚肆，即冰丘。
[6] cai shi (mining stone) refers to Chusi: glaciers。
[7] 黄金：指劃脊，即峭壁。
[7] huang jin (yellow gold); refers to Huji: cliff,
[8] 丹粟：在此指雪峰。
[8] dan su (red millet): refers to the snowcapped peaks。
[9]冢：指宗山。
[9] zhong (tomb mount) refers to the ancestor's mountains。
[10] 太牢：猪、牛、羊三牲俱全的祭祀礼。
[10] tai lao: the highest rite of sacrifice with pig, ox and sheep。
[11] 神也：指社祭山。神，指氏族；也，指祭坛，即社。
[11] shen ye (deity or God) refers to the community sacrificial mountain。 shen: clan, ye, shrine, also means she（community， society）。
[12]婴：指佩饰。
[12] yin(infant): refers to the body ornaments。
[13]牷：指璩，即玉环，这里实际指瑗。
[13] shuan: a kind of jade ring，here referring to the Yuan。 yuan/huan, phonetic close match。
[14] 百草之未灰：采用香苇绒。百草，指采用；之未灰，指香苇绒。
[14] bai cao zhi wei hui (hundred grass ashes)
Tr: uses fragrant reed flowers。baicao（to use），zhi wei hui（fragant reed flowers）。
[15] 白席，采等纯之：白席，指再以；采等纯之，指羊油浇制。
[15] bai xi, cai deng chun zhi;(white mat, pick purify)
Tr: after that, use lamb butter to mix in the making。

译文：由错池山往西二百五十里，有座山叫昆仑山。这里紧靠西海，没有人烟，有很多水源。楚玛尔河从这里流出，向东流入东海。这里有很多冰丘峭壁，有很多雪峰。

Translation:

Two hundred and fifty li westward from Cuochishan there stands Kunlunshan。 It is close to the west sea(region), with no humans but a lot of water sources。 The Chumar River rises out of here, goes east into the East China Sea。 There are a lot of glacier cliffs and many snowcapped peaks。

综观西山第一列山系，从契那山到昆仑山，共十九座山，延绵二千九百五十七里。华山是众山的宗山，祭祀时，要用太牢礼。羭山是社祭山，祭祀时要用烛，以百牺斋祭百日，并埋一百块美玉，温酒一百樽，并佩以百珪百璧。其余十七座山，皆用瑗代替祭词，用羊祭祀。祭祀用的烛，采用香苇绒，再以羊油浇制。

In sum， of the first list of mountains in the west: from Qinashan to Kunlunshan, there are a total of 19 mountains, covering a distance of 2,957 li。 Huashan is the Mountain Superior above all the mountains。 When sacrificing to this mountain, the Tailao rite is observed 。 Yushan is a community sacrifice site。Ceremony lasts for one hundred days, candles are used 。 One hundred sacrificial animals are used, and one hundred pieces of beautiful jade are buried。One hundred pots of warm wines are used, together with another one hundred Gui jade pieces and one hundred Bi jade pieces。As for the rest of the 17 mountains, Yuan jade pieces are used in place of the votive speech。 And lambs are sacrificed。 The candles are made of fragrant reed flowers, and lamb butter is poured over it。

西山经第二山系：

book2 Xishanjing; chapter 2

02-02-01 铃山

Qianshan

(110,26588E； 36,33497N)

西山二经之首，曰铃山[1]。其上多铜[2]，其下多玉 [3] 。其木多杻橿 [4]。

注释：[1]铃山：指嶷（lei)且，今音译为雷池。主峰斗咀峰，古称布嘎嶷，“布嘎嶷是嶷且主峰”读为“博嘎嶷嶷且额博”，今演绎为“不敢越雷池一步”。

Notes： [1] qian shan (lei qie ; Mount seal) Pu concept Lei qie, Chinese concept Yi qie。

Tr: a phonetic match of Leichi (thunder pond), its main peak is Douzuifeng; its old name: Bugalei, the concept “Bugalei is the chief peak of Leiqie mountain” in Pu language reads as: bogaleileiqie’ebo, a phonetic match to-- bu gan yue lei chi yi bu (dare not to go one step beyond the Thunder Pond) 。

[2]铜：在此指史姓氏族。

[2] tong(copper) refers to the tribes bearing the surname of Shi。

[3]玉：在此指原姓氏族。

[3]yu(jade) refers to the tribes bearing the surname of Yuan。

[4] 其木多杻橿：那里的牧民主要是延祖氏。

[4] qi mu duo chou jiang (its wood many Holm oak) 。

Tr: the chief herders are the Yanhe Shi。

译文：西山第二系列最东边的一座山叫巇且(山)。山的西边住着史氏族，山的东边住着原氏族。那里的牧民主要是延祖氏。

Translation:

The eastmost mountain heading the second list of mountains in the west is the Leiqie Mountain。 On its west side live the tribes bearing the surname of Shi。 On the east side of the mountain live the tribes bearing the surname of Yuan。 The chief herdsmen are the Yanzu Shi。

02-02-02 泰冒山

Taimaoshan

（110,12834E；35,68059N）

西二百里，曰泰冒之山[1]。其阳多金[2]，其阴多铁 [3] 。浴水[4] 出焉，东流注于河[5]，其中多藻玉[6]，多白蛇[7]。

注释：[1]泰冒山：指云高山，今称大岭，在陕西省黄龙县东北面。

Notes:[1] tai mao shan: refers to the Yungao (clouds high) Mountain, today known as the Daling Mountain, situated to the northeast of Huanglong (yellow dragon) county, Shaanxi province。

[2]金：在此指沙河氏族。

[2] jin(gold) refers to the Shahe (sand river) tribes。

[3]铁：在此指崾崄氏族。

[3] tie (iron) refers to the Yaoxian tribe。

[4] 浴水：指龙曲水。

[4]yu shui (bathing water) refers to the Longqu River (dragon twists) 。

[5]河：指黄河。

[5] he refers to the Yellow River。

[6] 藻玉：指赵姓夷。

[6] cao yu: refers to the people bearing the surname of Zhao。

[7] 白蛇：指黄龙山氏族，因黄读蛇音，今谐音称桑岭氏族。

[7] bai she (white snake) refers to the Huanglong Mountain (yellow dragon mount) tribe. Yellow/she/ huang/snake are phonetic matches and semantic shifts。【she】 yellow in Pu concept, 【snake】 in Chinese. Refers to the Sangling tribe, sang/she。

译文：由巇且往西南二百里，有座山叫大岭。山的南面住着沙河氏族，北面住着崾崄氏族。龙曲水发源于这座山，向东流入黄河，那里住着赵夷和桑岭氏族。

Translation:

Two hundred li further southwest from Leiqie Mountain, stands the Daling Mountain。On its south side live the Shahe tribe, on its north the Yaoxian tribe。 The Longqu River originates from this mountain, goes east into the Yellow River。The Zhao Yi and the Sangling tribes live there。

02-02-03 数历山

Shulishan

(110,12834E,35,68059N)

又西一百七十里，曰数历之山[1]。其山多黄金[2]，其下多银 [3]，其木多杻橿 [4]，其鸟多鹦姆 [5] 。楚水 [6] 出焉，而南流注于渭，其中多白珠 [7] 。

注释：[1]数历山：指数衙山，是共工氏族的府衙，也称彭衙山，在今陕西省白水县史官镇。
Notes： [1] shu li shan: refers to Shuyashan, which is the administration center of the Gonggong tribes, also known as the Pengyashan。 It is situated in today's Shiguan township, Baishui county, Shaanxi province。
[2] 黄金：在此指东崾崄氏族，简称东崄氏族。
[2] huang jin (yellow gold) here refers to the Dongyaoxian tribe, shortened to the Dongxian tribe。
[3]银：读音 nei，在此指春立氏族。
[3] yin(silver)reads as nei, refers to the Chunli tribe。
[4] 杻橿：读麟角，指鹿角坡，在此指鹿角坡氏族。
[4] chou jiang: reads as linjiao, refers to the Lujiaopo (deer horn slope) tribe。
[5] 鹦姆：读缨姆，原读音纵目，指佩饰帽缨的氏族和留额发髻的氏族。
[5] ying mu reads as zong mu (vertical eyes)， refers to the tribes sporting the tassels caps and the tribe sporting hair knots over foreheads。
[6] 楚水：指白水。
[6] chu shui: refers to Baishui (white water)， the Bai River。
[7] 白珠：指蚌埠氏，也称彭祖氏。
[7] bai zhu (white pearl) refers to the Bengbu Shi, also known as the Pengzu Shi。 Bai, bang, peng, as phonetic close matches。

译文：由大岭往西南一百七十里，有座山叫数衙山。山的西面住着东崾崄氏族，山的东面住着春立氏族。这里还住着鹿角坡氏牧民，住着僚人的北纵目氏族。白水从这里流出，向南汇入洛水后流入渭河，白水河畔住着彭祖氏族。
Translation:
One hundred and seventy li further southwest from Dalingshan, stands Shuyashan。 On its west side lives the Dongyaoxian tribe。 On its east side lives the Chunli tribe。 The Lujiaopo herdsmen tribe also live here, so does the Beizongmu tribe of the Lao people。 Baishui River flows out of here and goes south first into the Luo River and then into the Wei River。The Pengzu tribes live along the Baishui Riverbanks。

02-02-04 高山
Gaoshan
(109,40408E,35,13106N)

又西百五十里，曰高山[1]。其上多银[2]，其下多青碧 [3] 、雄黄 [4]，其木多棕[5]，其草多竹[6]。泾水[7]出焉，而东流注于渭，其中多磬石[8]、青碧。

注释：[1]高山：指林皋山。在陕西白水县林皋镇西侧。
Notes: [1] gao shan (high mount) refers to the Lingaoshan。It is situated in the west part of Lingao township in the Baishui county, Shaanxi province。
[2]银：在此指阴台氏族，今谐音称印台氏族。
[2] yin(silver) refers to the Yintai tribe, yin, a phonetic match。
[3] 青碧：指白水氏族。（读泾泚）。

[3] qing bi (green clear); refers to the Baishui (white water) tribe, reads as Jingbi。qingbi/jingbi: close phonetic match。

[4] 雄黄：指索冯氏，即冯雷氏族。

[4] xiong huang (male yellow): refers to the Suofeng Shi, also known as the Fenglei tribe。

[5]棕：指贵族、王族。今演绎为王益。

[5] zong(palm): refers to the nobles or the king clan. Today, the name is transmitted as Wangyi, (king benefit) 。

[6]竹：指卓资夷，即夸父族。

[6] zhu （bamboo），refers to the Zhuozi Yi, also known as the Kuafu tribe。

[7] 泾水：指白水河。

[7] jing shui: refers to the Baishui River。

[8] 磬石：指庆兴氏族。

[8] qing shi（sound stone): refers to the Qingsheng tribe。 Qingshi/qingxing, close phonetic matches。

译文：由数衙山往西一百五十里，有座山叫林皋山。山的西面住着印台氏，东面住着白水氏族和冯雷氏族。那里的牧民多为贵族和王族，移民多为卓资夷。白水发源于这座山，向东汇入洛水后流入渭河，河岸边住着庆兴氏族。

Translation:

One hundred and fifty li further west from Shuyashan stands Lingaoshan。 On its west side the Yintai people live, on its east side, the Baishui people and the Fenglei people live。 The herdsman tribal people mostly belong to the King clan or the nobles, immigrants are mostly the Zhuozi people。Baishui River originates from this mountain, goes east into the Luo River, and then to the Wei River。 On the riverbanks live the Qingxing tribes。

02-02-05 女床山

Nvchuangshan

（107,7952E；34,67793N）

西南三百里，曰女床之山[1]。其阳多赤铜[2]，其阴多石涅 [3]，其兽多虎豹犀兕 [4] 。有鸟焉，其状如翟而五采文 [5]，名曰鸾鸟 [6]，见则天下安宁 [7] 。

注释：[1]女床山：在此指定居农民与游牧民族共同居住的山。今称麟游山，麟指令、固定，游指牧民。

Notes: [1] nv chuang mount (female bed mount)

Tr: refers to the mountain where the agriculture settlers and nomads co-inhabit。It is called Linyou Mountain。Lin/ling: order/settle; you: nomads, herdsman。

[2] 赤铜：指游牧区。

[2] chi tong (red copper) refers to the nomadic husbandry area。

[3] 石涅：指畲黎、种植。

[3] shi nie（stone black): refers to the She Yi, planters, growers。

[4] 虎豹犀兕：虎豹犀指牧业、农业、狩猎业，兕指氏族。

[4]hu bao xi si: tiger(husbandry)leopard(agriculture)；rhinos (hunting)；si(tribes)。

[5] 翟而五采文：北方的东胡部落氏族。

[5] di er wu cai wen（bird with five-color markings) refers to the Donghu people from the north。

[6] 鸾鸟：指石僚氏，即石姓氏族。

[6] luan niao (long tail bird) refers to the Shiliao people, the people bearing surname of shi(stone)。

[7] 安宁：在此指头领氏族、统治氏族。

[7]an ning (settled peaceful) refers to the leader tribes or the leading clans。

译文：由林皋山往西南三百里，有座山叫麟游山。山的南边是游牧区，山的北边是种植区，氏族为牧业、农业和狩猎氏族。有一群人，是北方的东胡部落氏族，名叫石僚氏，是那个地区的统治氏族。
Translation：
Three hundred li further southwest from the Lingaoshan, stands the Linyoushan。 Its southern part is the nomads' region, on its northern part it is the planter's region, where the tribes are making a living on husbandry, agriculture and hunting。 A group of people are the Donghu tribes from the North, known as the Shiliao people, they are the ruling people。

02-02-06 龙首山
Longshoushan
（106,85736E；34,8929N）

又西二百里，曰龙首之山[1]。其阳多黄金[2]，其阴多铁 [3] 。苕水 [4] 出焉，东南注于泾水[5]，其中多美玉[6]。

注释：[1]龙首山：指陇苕（tiao), 又称陇苕（shao),今称枣岭。实际介绍陇镇。
Notes: [1] long shou shan (dragon head mount)
Tr： refers to Longtiao, also read as Longshao, known today as the Zaoling （date range) Mountain。 It in fact describes the Longzhen township。
[2] 黄金：在此指堡子山部落氏族。
[2] huang jin (yellow gold) here refers to the tribes from the Bao/Pu-zishan。
[3]铁：指苕部落氏族。
[3] tie(iron) refers to the Tiao tribe。
[4] 苕水：今称达溪河。
[4] Tiao shui: refers to today's Daxi River 。
[5] 泾水：今称泾河。
[5] jing shui: the Jing River。
[6] 美玉：指五举夷。也称五林夷。
[6] mei yu (beautiful jade) refers to the Wuju Yi, also known as the Wulin (five wood) people, mei/may/five。

注释：由麟游山往西二百里，有座山叫枣岭。山的南面住着堡子山部落氏族，北面住着苕部落氏族。达溪河从山间流出，向东南流入泾河，达溪河畔住着五举夷。
Translation:
Two hundred li further west from Linyoushan, stands Zaolingshan。 On its south side lives the Baozi tribe， on its north lives the Tiao tribe。 The Daxi River flows out of the mountain, goes eastward into the Jing River。On the Daxi River's banks live the Wuju tribe。

02-02-07 鹿台山
Lutaishan
（105,67104E；34,86049N）

又西二百里，曰鹿台之山[1]。其上多白玉[2]，其下多银 [3]，其首多㸲牛 [4] 、羬羊 [5] 、白豪 [6] 。有鸟焉，其状如雄鸡而人面 [7]，名曰凫徯 [8]，其名自叫也，见则有兵 [9] 。

注释：[1]鹿台山：指葫芦部落中心的山，即天水秦安县城。鹿台即葫芦中心。

Notes: [1]lu tai shan (deer terrace mount) refers to the Hulu(calabash) tribes' central mountain, which is today 's Qin'an county seat in Tianshui city, Gansu Province。Lutai is the Hulu center。

[2] 白玉：指伯益氏，今称雨伯。属大月氏支系。

[2] bai yu (white jade) refers to the Boyi Shi, reads as yubo (rain uncle) belongs to the Dayuezhi (darouzhi)， also known as Great Yuezhi。

[3]银：即嬴氏，属小月氏中心支系。

[3] yin(silver) refers to the Ying Shi, it belongs to the central branch of the Xiao Yuezhi, also known as the Lesser/Little Yuezhi。

[4] 牪牛：指偬河氏族，今称黑河、黑龙河氏族。

[4] zuo niu （big mountain cattle)

Tr: refers to the Zong River tribe, known today as the Heihe (black river), as well as the Heilonghe (black dragon river) tribe。

[5] 羬羊：指东阳部落氏族。

[5] qian yang refers to the Dongyang tribe。Yang; with two different meanings in Chinese, yang(sun) or (sheep)。

[6] 白豪：指博恒氏。

[6] bai/bo hao (white hair) refers to the Boheng tribe， a close phonetic match to bohao。

[7] 雄鸡而人面：华胥氏的定居氏族。

[7] xiong ji er ren mian （rooster with human face)

Tr： settled tribes of the Huaxu Shi。

[8] 凫徯：指伏羲氏族。

[8] fu xi: refers to the Fuxi people。

译文：由枣岭往西二百里，有座山叫葫芦台。山的西面住着伯益氏，东面住着嬴氏族。这里的氏族还有黑河、东阳氏族和博恒氏。有一个族群，是华胥氏的定居氏族，名叫伏羲氏，他们也这样称呼自己，是那里的统治氏族。

Translation:

Two hundred li further west from Zaolingshan, there stands the Hulutai Mountain。 On its west side lives the Boyi tribe, on its east side lives the Ying tribe。 Also around here are the Heihe River tribe, the Donggyang tribe and the Boheng tribe。 Another tribe by the settled people from the Huaxu Shi, is the Fuxi people。 They also address themselves thus, they are the ruling tribes there。

02-02-08 鸟危山

Niaoweishan

（105,04235E；35,34164N）

西南二百里，曰鸟危之山[1]。其阳多磬石[2]，其阴多檀楮 [3]，其中多女床 [4] 。鸟危水出焉，西流注于赤水 [5]，其中多丹粟 [6]。

注释：[1]鸟危山：指嚎马山，又称辽坡，在甘肃通渭县马营镇北面。鸟，指马；危，指嚎。

Notes:[1] niao wei shan (bird danger mount)

Tr: refers to Mount Haoma (neighing horse mount) also known as Liaopo, situated to the north of the Maying township, Tongwei county， Gansu Province。 niao(bird/horse), wei(danger/yelling) horse neighing。

[2] 磬石：指店肆氏族。店肆，是马营镇的古称谓。

[2] qing shi (music stone)

Tr: refers to the Diansi tribe。 Diansi, an old name for Mayingzhen town。 Maying (horse camp) 。

[3] 檀楮：指中央氏，这里指华族的中央氏，今华家岭氏族。

[3] tan zhu (hard wood)

Tr: refers to the Zhongyang (center)Shi, the Zhongyang Shi of Hua tribes, today's Huajialing tribe，(hua family range) 。

[4] 女床：这里指牛棚子氏族。

[4] nv chuang (female bed) refers to the Niupengzi (cattle shed) tribe。

[5] 鸟危水：指嚎马水，今称牛谷河。实际向北流。

[5] niao wei shui (bird danger water) refers to the Haomashui River, today's Niugu (cattle valley) River, it flows to the north in fact。

[6] 赤水：黄河。

[6] chi shui (red water) refers to the Yellow River。

[7] 丹粟：读 dai su，指柴门氏族。门，读 dai 音。

[7] dan su (red grain) read as dai su, refers to the Chaimen (firewood gate) tribe。 gate(men) reads as dai。

译文：由葫芦台往西北二百里，有座山叫嚎马山。山的南面住着店肆氏族，北面住着华族的中央氏，住着牛棚子氏族。嚎马水发源于这座山，向北汇入祖厉河后流入黄河，河边住着柴门氏族。

Translation:

Two hundred and twenty li further northwest from the Hulutai Mountain, stands the Haoma Mountain。 On its south side lives the Diansi tribe, on its north side live the Zhongyang tribe of the Hua ethnic people, and the Niupengzi tribe。 Haoma River rises out of this mountain and flows north to join the Zuli River before emptying into the Yellow River。 On the riverbanks live the Chaimen tribe。

02-02-09 小次山

Xiaocishan

（103,83881E；36,05389N）

又西四百里，曰小次之山[1]。其上多白玉[2]，其下多赤铜 [3] 。有首焉，其状如猿，而白首[4] 赤足[5]，名曰朱厌[6]，见则有兵[7]。

注释：[1]小次山：指小茨山，意为比较平缓的山，这里指兰州盆地。

Notes: [1] xiao ci shan: refers to Xiaozishan, a term for a rather smooth flat mountainous area, here it refers to the Lanzhou Basin。

[2] 白玉：指元峁夷。

[2] bai yu (white jade) refers to the Yuanmao Yi。

[3] 赤铜：指紫堡川氏族。

[3] chi tong (red copper) refers to the Zibaochuan tribes。Bao/pu。

[4] 猿而白首：指裕固族的巴苏氏。

[4] yuan er bai shou (ape with white head) refers to the Basu Shi of the Yugu people。

[5] 赤足：指支系。

[5] chi zu (bare feet) refers to the tribes' branches。

[6] 朱厌：指渚夭，即低地。朱厌氏，即低地氏族。

[6] zhu yan: reads as zhuwo, refers to the low land, the Zhuyan Shi is a lowland tribe。

[7] 见则有兵：那里的统治氏族。

[7] jian ze you bing (when seen, there will be wars)： refers to the ruling tribes 。

译文：由嚎马山往西四百里，有座山叫小茨山。山的西面住着元峁夷，东面住着紫堡川氏族。有一个氏族，是裕固族的巴苏氏支系，名叫低地氏族，是那里的统治氏族。

Translation:

Four hundred li further west from Haomashan, stands the Xiaozishan。 On its west side live the Yuanmao people, on its east side the Zibaochuan people。 One tribe is the Basu branch from the Yugu people。 They are known as the lowland people; they are the ruling tribes there。

02-02-10 大次山
Dacishan
（103,83881E；36,05389N）

又西三百里，曰大次之山[1]。其阳多垩[2]，其阴多碧 [3]，其兽多牸牛[4] 、麢羊[5]。

注释：[1]大次山：指拉脊山，这里介绍拉脊山边的西宁。
Notes: [1] da ci shan: refers to the Lajishan, here it describes the area of Xining city by the Lajishan。
[2]垩：指湟水氏族。垩读 wo 音，湟也读 wo 音。
[2] wo refers to the Woshui people. Wo also reads as huang in Chinese。
[3]碧：指大有氏族。【有】读 bei 音，与碧谐音。
[3]bi: refers to the Dayou people, you, reads as bei, a phonetic match to the bi， bei/bi。
[4] 牸牛：在此指草原人。
[4] zuo niu: refers to the grassland people。
[5] 麢羊（le chi): 指乐东氏族，今称海东氏族。
[5] le chi: refers to the Ledong tribes, known today as the Haidong (sea east) tribes。

译文：由小茨山往西三百里，有座山叫拉脊山，山的南面住着湟水氏族，北面住着大有氏族。这里的氏族还有草原人和乐东氏族。
Translation:
Three hundred li further west from Xiaozishan, stands Lajishan。 On its south side live the Woshui people, on its north side live the Dabei people。 On this land also live the grassland tribes and the Ledong tribes。

02-02-11 熏吴山
Xunwushan
(99.77592E,36,73066N)

又西四百里，曰熏吴之山[1],无草木[2]，多金玉[3]。

注释：[1]薰吴山：指象湖山。青海湖被称为王者之湖，曾以象湖称谓，旁边的山也称为象湖山，今称象皮山。
Notes: [1] xun wu shan (scent wu mount)
Tr: it refers to Xianghushan (elephant lake mount) 。 Qinghai Lake is viewed as the Lake of the Lord, in another word, Lake of Elephant。 The mountain nearby is called Xianghushan, today, it is called Xiangpishan (elephant skin mount) 。
[2] 无草木：指游牧部落。
[2] wu cao mu (no grass wood) refers to the nomadic tribes。
[3] 金玉：指加卜隆夷和直却呼夷。
[3] jin yu (gold jade)
Tr: it refers to the Jiapulong Yi and the Zhiquehu Yi。

译文：由拉脊山往西四百里，有座山叫象皮山，是游牧族的部落，住着加卜隆夷和直却呼夷。

Translation:
Four hundred li further west from Lajishan there stands the Xiangpishan, a place of the nomadic tribes。 The Jiapulong Yi and Zhiquehu Yi live there。

02-02-12 底阳山
Diyangshan
（97,3603E；37,39016N）

又西四百里，曰底阳之山[1]。其木多椶[2] 、枏 [3] 、豫章[4]，其兽多犀兕[5]、虎豹[6]、牲牛[7]。

注释：[1]底（di）阳山：指德令哈。
Notes： [1] di yang shan: Delingha, Delhi city, romanization of Mongolian: Delhi hot in Mongolian : the golden world。
[2]椶：指戈壁，即苏亥戈壁。
[2] zong: refers to the Govi, the Suhai Gobi Desert。
[3]枏：指淖尔，今称尕海。
[3] nan: nuur, today known as the Gahai lake。 Hai: means lake in Chinese。
[4] 豫章：指鄂照，即鄂博氏族。照和博都是指“山”。
[4]yu zhang： e zhao, refers to the Ebo tribe, Zhao/bo： Pu concepts meaning mountain。
[5] 犀兕：指蓄肆，今称蓄集。
[5] xi si: xu si, refers to Xu ji, a close phonetic match。
[6] 虎豹：指敷博，即东山氏族。
[6]hu bao: a phonetic match to Fu bo, refers to the Dongshan tribe。
[7] 牲牛：指卓僚，即乌察汗氏族。卓与乌都指北部，乌又指部落。
[7] zuo niu: refers to zhuo lao/liao: the Wuchahan tribe。 Both zhuo and wu refer to the north, wu also means tribe。

译文：由象皮山往西北四百里，有座山叫德令哈。那里的牧民有苏亥戈壁氏族、尕海氏族、鄂博氏族，还有蓄集氏族、东山氏族和乌察汗氏族。
Translation:
Four hundred li further northwest from the Xiangpishan, stands the Dehli hot Mountain (Delingha)。The grassland tribes are Suhai Govi tribe, Gahai tribe, Ebo tribe, as well as the Xuji tribe, Dongshan tribe and the Wuchahan tribe。

02-02-13 众兽山
Zhongshoushan
（95,55253E；37,31751N）

又西二百五十里，曰众兽之山[1]。其上多㻬琈之玉[2]，其下多檀楮[3]，多黄金[4]，其兽多犀兕[5]。

注释：[1]众兽山：指像铁一样的山，今称锡铁山。
Notes: [1] zhong shou shan (many beasts mount) refers to the iron like mountain, today's Xitieshan, xitie(tin iron)。
[2] 㻬琈之玉：指拉他萨尔哈夷，简称他哈夷，谐音㻬琈玉。
[2] tu fu zhi yu: refers to the Latasarha Yi, shortened to Taha Yi, a near phonetic match to tufuyu。
[3] 檀楮：指特门口尊部落。
[3] tan zhu: refers to the Temenkouzun tribes.
[4] 黄金：指浩日格力金乌，简称浩金，谐音黄金。今已迁至西边。

[4] huang jin (yellow gold) refers to Haorigelijinwu tribe, shortened to the Haojin, a phonetic match to Huangjin, now migrated to the west。

[5] 犀兕：指铅肆，也称锡肆，今称锡铁山镇。

[5] xi si refers to the Qian (lead) si (town), also known as Xi(tin) si(town), today's Xitieshan (tin iron mount) township。

译文：由德令哈往西二百五十里，有座山叫锡铁山。山的西面住着拉他萨尔哈夷，东面住着特门口尊夷、浩日格力金乌夷，那里还住着锡肆氏族。

Translation:

Two hundred and fifty li further west from Delingha Mountain, there stands the Xitieshan。 On its west side live the Latasarha Yi, on its east side the Temenkouzun Yi, the Haorigelijinwu tribe and the Xisi tribe。

02-02-14 皇人山

Huangrenshan

（101,6133E；37,37554N）

又西五百里，曰皇人之山[1]，其上多金玉[2]，其下多青雄黄[3]。皇水[4] 出焉，西流注于赤水 [5]，其中多丹粟 [6] 。

注释：[1]皇人山：指大浩山，这里介绍大浩山下的门源镇。到达这里的距离由小茨山算起。

Notes: [1] huang ren shan (emperor people mount) refers to the Dahaoshan, this is a description of the Menyuan town at the foot of the mountain。Its distance starts from the Xiaozishan。

[2] 金玉：指金尖夷。

[2] jin yu (gold jade) refers to the Jinjian (gold tip) people。

[3] 青雄黄：指东胥胡。

[3] qing (green) xiong(male) huang(yellow) refers to the Dongxu Hu people。

[4] 皇水：指浩水，今称大通河。

[4] huang shui (royal water) refers to the Haoshui River, known today as the Datong (big through) River。

[5] 赤水：指黄河。西流指东流，濮语的"东" 读 xi 音。

[5] chi shui (red water) refers to the Yellow River, xiliu (west flowing) a misconcept。 The Pu concept means flowing east, xi/east 。

[6] 丹粟：指鞑属，即游牧民族。

[6] dan su (red millets) refers to the Darda people, the nomads。

译文：由小茨山往西北五百里，有座山叫大浩山。山的西面住着金尖夷，东面住着东胥胡。大通河从这里流出，向东流入黄河，大通河畔住着游牧民族。

Translation:

Five hundred li further northwest from the Xiaozishan, stands the Dahaoshan。 On its west side lives the Jinjian Yi, on its east side live the Dongxu Hu people 。 The Datong River flows out from here, goes east into the Yellow River。 On the banks of the Datong River, live the nomads。

02-02-15 中皇山

Zhonghuangshan

（100,25138E；38,17625N）

又西三百里，曰中皇之山[1]，其山多金[2]，其下多蕙[3]、棠[4]。

注释：[1]中皇山：指托勒南山，这里指山下的祁连城。
Notes: [1] zhong huang shan (middle emperor mount) refers to the Tuolenanshan, here it is a description of the Qilian city at the foot of the mountain。

[2]金：指鹿场氏族。"场"读音为 jin。
[2] jin(gold) refers to the Luchang people。 chang/jin, lu/deer。

[3]蕙：指峨堡岭氏族。
[3] hui (plant): refers to the Ebaoling tribe。

[4]棠：指白石崖氏族。
[4] tang(fruits): refers to the Baishiyan (white stone cliff) tribe。

译文：由大浩山往西北三百里，有座山叫托勒南山，山的西面住着鹿场氏族，东面住着峨堡岭氏族和白石崖氏族。
Translation:
Three hundred li further northwest from the Dahaoshan, stands the Tuolenanshan。 On its west side live the Luchang tribe, on its east side live the Ebaoling tribe and the Baishiyan tribe。

02-02-16 西皇山
Xihuangshan
（99,12931E；38,1374N）

又西三百里，曰西皇之山[1]，其阳多金[2]，其阴多铁[3]，其兽多麋[4]、鹿[5]、牸牛[6]。

译文：[1]西皇山：指疏勒南山，主峰是岗则吾结。这里介绍山下的木里镇。
Notes: [1] xi huang shan (west emperor mount)
Tr: refers to the Shulenanshan, its main peak is Gangzewujie。 This is a description of the Muli town at the foot of the mountain。

[2]金：指扎玛东村。
[2] jin(gold) refers to Zhamadong village。

[3]铁：指唐莫日氏族。
[3] tie(iron)refers to the Tangmori tribe。

[4]麋：指木里。
[4]mi(deer) a phonetic match for Muli town。

[5]鹿：指尕尔当。"鹿"的濮语读音为 gong，与尕谐音。
[5]lu(deer) refers to the Gaerdang。Lu/deer reads in Pu concept as gong, a close phonetic match to ga, ga/gong。

[6] 牸牛：在此指佐陇氏族。
[6] zuo niu（zuo ox): refers to the Zuolong tribe。 Zuo, a phonetic match。

译文：由托勒南山往西三百里，有座山叫疏勒南山。山的南面住着扎玛氏族，北面住着唐莫日氏族，这里的氏族还有木里氏族、尕尔当氏族和佐陇氏族。
Translation:
Three hundred li westward from the Tuolenanshan, stands the Shulenanshan。On its south side live the Zhama tribe, on its north, the Tangmori tribe。 Other tribes also live here, they are the Muli tribe, Gaerdang tribe, and the Zuolong tribe。

02-02-17 莱山
Laishan
（96,02076E；39,81006N）

又西三百五十里，曰莱山[1]，其木多檀楮[2]，其鸟多罗罗[3]，是食人[4]。

凡西次二经之首，自钤山至于莱山，凡十七山，四千一百四十里。其十神者，皆人面马身[5]。其七神皆人面牛身[6]，四足而一臂[7]，操以行[8]，是为飞兽之神[9]，其祠之，毛用少牢[10]，白菅为席。其十輩神者，其祠之毛一雄鸡[11]，钤而不糈[12]：毛采[13]。

注释：[1]莱山：指放牧山，又称野马山，在今甘肃石包城一带。
Notes: [1] lai shan: refers to the Fangmushan (grazing mount), also known as the Yemashan (wild horses mount), in today's Shibaocheng area, Gansu province。

[2] 檀楮：指鹰咀山氏族和龚岔氏族。
[2] tan zhe: refers to the Yingzuishan (eagle beak mount) clan, and the Gongcha clan。

[3] 罗罗：指石城，后期建立的城镇称石包城。
[3] luoluo refers to stone city, the city was built later here and was named Shibao city。

[4] 食人：古老的集镇氏族。
[4] shi ren (eat human) refers to the ancient Jizhen (township) clan。

[5] 人面马身：胡族居民。
[5] ren mian ma shen (human face horse body) refers to the Hu settlers。

[6] 人面牛身：农业氏族居民。
[6] ren mian niu shen (human face ox body) refers to the agricultural settlers。

[7] 四足而一臂：大河的支系。一臂指榆沘，即大河；四足读 bu ze，指支系。
[7]si zu er yi bi (four feet with one arm)
Tr: it refers to the big river's tributaries。 Here, yi bi (one arm) refers to Yubi (big river), si zu/bu ze, refers to branches。

[8] 操以行：旁边的贵族。
[8] cao yi xing: the nobles who are living nearby。

[9] 飞兽之神：指管理氏族。
[9] fei shou zhi shen (flying beast's god) refers to the managerial clan。

[10] 毛用少牢：毛和用都是少牢礼。少牢指有猪羊的祭祀礼和掩埋两件以上玉器的祭祀礼。
[10] mao yong shao lao： mao and yong are smaller rite(shaolao)。 Shaolaoli refers to the sacrificing rite with pig, lamb, and burial of more than two jade pieces。

[11] 毛一雄鸡：代替祭词的玉是一块华胥玉。华胥玉即和田玉，用以象征祥和。
[11] mao yi xiong ji (rite with one rooster)
Tr: using Huaxu jade piece in place of the votive speech, Huaxu jade is the Hetian jade, a token of benevolence and peace。

[12] 钤而不糈：只祈祷而不供奉食物。
[1] qian er bu xu (stamp but no food)
Tr: only offer prayers but not to offer food。

[13] 毛采：祭文，这里指只读祭文。
[13] mao cai: votive speech, here means only reading the speech。

译文：由疏勒南山往西北三百五十里，有座山叫野马山。那里的牧民主要是鹰咀山氏族和龚岔氏族，人群主要生活在石城，他们是那里的原住居民。

Translation

Three hundred and fifty li further northwest from Shulenanshan there stands the Yemashan。 The herders living there are mostly of the Yinzuishan clan and the Gongcha clan。 People are living mainly in the Shicheng city, they are the original settlers。

综观西山第二列山系，从嶷且山到野马山，共计十七座山，延绵四千一百四十里。其中有十座山的山神是牧民的形像。另外有七座山的山神是农民的形像，是以农业的大支系的贵族形像塑造，称为管理之神，以少牢礼祭祀，以茅草人为通灵命官。其余十座山的山神的祭祀，用一和田玉，祈祷而不供奉食物，只读祭文。

In sum, the second list of mountains in the west, from Yiqieshan to Yemashan, there are a total of 17 mountains, covering 4,140 li in distance。 Ten of the mountain deities are in the images of the husbandry people。 Another 7 mountain deities are in the images of the peasants， of the major local clans' nobles， who are known as the Management deities。The rite for sacrificing to those deities are called Shaolao rite。A straw man is used for the massager envoy。The rest of the ten mountain deities are offered a piece of Hetian jade。No food is offered, only a speech is read。

西山经第三山系

Book 2 Xishanjing; chapter 3

02-03-01 崇吾山
Chongwushan
（105,29297E；36,81006N）

西次三经之首，曰崇吾之山[1]。在河[2] 之南，北望冢遂 [3]，南望罃之泽[4]，西望帝之搏兽之山[5]，东望焉渊[6]。有木焉，员叶而白柎[7]，赤华而黑理[8]，其实如枳[9]，食之宜子孙[10]。有兽焉，其状如禺而文臂[11]，豹虎而善投[12]，名曰举父[13]。有鸟焉，其状如凫，而一翼一目[14]，相得乃飞[15]，名曰蛮蛮[16]，见则天下大水[17]。

注释：[1]崇吾山：指盐部落的山，今称盐池山，在甘肃白银市平川区东侧。37° 46′ 59.88″ N, 107° 24′ 25.92″ E
Notes:[1] chong wu shan (worship me mount)
Tr: it refers to the mountain of the Yanbuluo (salt tribe) 。 Today it is known as Yanchishan（salt pool mount), situated on the east side of the Pingchuan district, Baiyin (white silver) city， Gansu province。
[2]河：指黄河。
[2] he（river): refers to Yellow River。
[3] 冢遂：指喊叫山。今称香山。
[3] zhong sui （burial follows）
Tr: refers to the Hanjiaoshan (shout yell mount)， known today as Xiangshan (fragrant mount)。
[4] 罃之泽：指大沟河，属祖厉河的支系。
[4] yao zhi ze（earthware 's water)
Tr： it refers to Dagou (big gully) River, a tributary of Zuli River。

[5] 帝之搏兽之山：吊沙山氏族之所。帝之搏，指吊沙山。吊、钓在濮语中指小。
[5] di zhi bo shou zhi shan (God fight off beasts' mount)
Tr: it refers to the place the Diaoshashan clan occupies。Di zhi bo (God fight off) refers to the Diaoshashan。 Diao (1. hanging, 2. fishing) here it means junior, small as a Pu concept。

[6] 焉渊：指惹安，即安镇老城。
[6] yan yuan (yan gulf): refers to Re'an, the old part of Anzhen。

[7] 员叶而白柎：指阴黄水的山区胡族。
[7] yuan ye er bai fu （round leaves and white calyx)
Tr： refers to the mountain Hu tribes from Yihuangshui River。

[8] 赤华而黑理：指东山的赫胥黎。今称面梨子人。
[8] chi hua er hei li (red flowers with black markings)
Tr; refers to the Hexuli from Dongshan, known today as the Mianlizi （face/soft, pear） people。

[9] 其实如枳：指东流水人。
[9] qi shi ru zhi （its fruits like Poncirus)
Tr: it refers to Dongliushui (east flowing water) people。

[10] 食之宜子孙：指神江水支系氏族。食之宜，指神江水，在盐池山东侧。
[10] shi zhi yi zi sun (eat it, benefits the descendants)
Tr： refers to the branches of the Shenjiangshui clan。 Shi zhi yi: Shenjiang River, on the east side of Yanchishan。

[11] 禺而文臂：指河门河。文臂，读汶丙，指河门。
[11]yu er wen bi (yu with marked arms)
Tr: it refers to the Hemen (river gate) River。wen bi: wen bing, refers to the river gate/hemen。

[12] 豹虎而善投：山区胡族的外地支系。
[12] bao hu er shan tou (leopard tiger good throw)
Tr： refers to the outsider branches of the mountain Hu 。

[13] 举父：指林胡, 又称东胡，原籍在赤峰即辽河流域。
[13] ju fu （lift father)
Tr: refers to Lin Hu, also known as Dong Hu, its original home is at Chifeng （red cliff）, in the Liao River basin。

[14] 凫而一翼一目：胡族的裕固夷支系。
[14] fu er yi yi yi mu (waterbird one wing one eye)
Tr: the Yugur Yi of the Hu ethnic tribes。

[15] 相得乃飞：谢家河的管理氏族。
[15] xiang de nai fei (have so can fly)
Tr: the administration tribe of the Xiejia River area。

[16] 蛮蛮：裕固夷又称蛮蛮，今称维吾尔族。
[16] man man (wild wild-barbarous)
Tr: another name for the Yugur Yi, today known as the Uyghurs。

[17] 见则天下大水：是那个地方的达罕氏族。达罕，即王。
[17] jian ze tian xia da shui (seeing it world under sky be flooded)
Tr: they are the leading king clan of that place。 dahan, a phonetic match to king, khan, or lord。

译文：西山经第三系列最东边的山，名叫盐池山。这座山位于黄河的南岸，北望喊叫山，南望大沟河，西望吊沙山氏族之所，东望惹安。这里的牧民有阴黄水的山区胡族，有东山的赫胥黎，有东流水人，有神江水支系氏族。有一个氏族，是河门河山区胡族的外地支系，名叫林胡。有一群人，是胡族的裕固夷支系，是谢家河的管理氏族，名叫蛮蛮，是那个地区的达罕氏族。
Translation:

The east most mountain of the third list of mountains in the west is known as Yanchishan。 It is situated on the south bank of the Yellow River。To its north, it faces the Hanjiaoshan, to its south, the Dagou River, to its west, the settlement of the Diaoshashan clan, and to its east, the town of Re'an。 The herdsmen living here are the mountain Hu people from the Yinhuangshui River, the Hexuli from the Dongshan, the people of Dongliushui tribe, and the branch of the Shenjiangshui tribe。 One tribe, the outsider branch from the Hemen River's Mountain Hu people, is known as the Lin Hu。 Another group of people are the Hu's Yughur （Urghur) branch, known as Manman, they are the administration tribe of the Xiejiahe River, they are the ruling Da Khan clan of that region。

02-03-02 长沙山
Changshashan
（102,18504E；38,52199N)

西北三百里，曰长沙之山[1]。泚水[2] 出焉，北流注于泑水 [3]，无草木[4]，多青雄黄[5]。

注释：[1]长沙山：指昌奢山。今译为汉语称金昌山。奢，指黄色，指金。
Notes： [1] chang sha shan (long sand mount)
Tr: it refers to the Changsheshan, a phonetic match to today's Jinchangshan。 In Pu concept, she means yellow color or gold。
[2] 泚水：指羊河。已消失。只遗存南泚水，今称石羊河。
[2]ci shui:(goat river)
Tr: it refers to Yang River， which has disappeared。Only the Nancishui still flows, today it is called the Shiyang (stone sheep) River。
[3] 泑水：指弱水湖，今称东湖。
[3] you shui: refers to the Ruoshui (weak water) Lake, known today as the Dong Lake, the East Lake。
[4] 无草木：游牧部落。无，指部落。
[4] wu cao mu (no grass wood) refers to the nomadic tribes， wu(no): tribe。
[5] 青雄黄：指东煦湖。今称金水湖。那里的氏族称东胥湖氏族。
[5] qing xiong huang (green male yellow) refers to the Dongxu Lake， known as the Jinshui (gold water) Lake。 The clans there are called the Dongxu Lake clans。

译文:由盐池山往西北三百里，有座山叫金昌山。羊河水从山间流出，向东北流入弱水湖，这里是游牧部落，住着东胥湖氏族。
Translation:
Three hundred li further northwest from Yanchishan there stands the Jinchangshan。 The Yang River flows out of the mountain and goes northeast into the Ruoshui Lake。 This is the land of nomadic tribes, the Dongxu Lake clans live here。

02-03-03 不周山
Buzhoushan
（101,06024E；41,95765N)

又西北三百七十里，曰不周之山[1]。北望诸毗之山，临彼岳崇之山[2]，东望泑泽[3]，河水所潜也，其源浑浑泡泡[4]。爰有嘉果[5]，其实如涛[6]，其叶如枣[7]，黄华而赤柎[8]，食之不劳[9]。

注释：[1]不周山：指补照山，今称包尔乌拉山。实际介绍山下的索额济纳。

Notes: [1] bu zhou shan: (not surround mount)
Tr: refers to the Buzhaoshan, today's Baoer Ula (bor ul shan) Mountain 41° 30′ 0″ N, 98° 36′ 0″ E. It is a description of Ejina at the foot of the mountain。

[2] 岳崇山：指大戈撮壁山，今称戈壁阿尔泰山。

[2] yue chong shan (mighty lofty mount)
Tr: it refers to the big Gocuobishan, today's Govi (Gobi) Altai Mountain。

[3] 泑泽：即弱水，又称额济纳、索额济纳。

[3] you ze: Ruo shui (weak water) also known as Ejina, Suo-e-ji-na。

[4] 其源浑浑泡泡：河水走走停停，即断断续续。

[4] qi yuan hun hun pao pao (its source, muddy, bubbly)
Tr: its water flows and stops, on and off it goes。

[5] 嘉果：指吉格德, 即吉格镇。

[5] jia guo (best fruit) refers to Jigede，the Jigede town。

[6] 其实如桃：指陶莱尚德, 即陶莱尚镇。

[6] qi shi ru tao (its fruits like peaches) refers to Taolaishangde，the Taolaishang town。

[7] 其叶如枣：指补照氏。周族，古称补照。

[7] qi ye ru zao (its leaves like dates)
Tr: refers to the Buzhao Shi, also known as the Zhou people/Zhouzu, its ancient name is Buzhao。

[8] 黄华而赤柎：胡区农业的东胡氏族。

[8] huang hua er chi fu (yellow flowers and red calyx)
Tr: refers to the Dong Hu clans of the Hu agriculture regions。

[9] 食之不劳：古老的农业氏族。

[9] shi zhi bu lao (eat without labor)
Tr: refers to the ancient agriculture clans。

译文：由金昌山往西北三百七十里，有座山叫包尔乌拉山。这里向北可以眺望相邻的山和戈壁阿尔泰山，向东可以眺望弱水，河水常潜入地下，断断续续。那里有吉格德、陶莱尚德氏族，有补照夷，是古老的农业氏族。

Translation:
Three hundred and seventy li further northwest from the Jinchangshan there stands the Bur ul Mountain。 From here looking to its north are the adjoining mountains and the Govi Altai mountain。To its east, the Ruoshui River flows or goes underground, off and on。There live the Jigede clans and the Taolaishangde clans。 Also living there are the clans known as the Buzhao Yi, an ancient agriculture people。

02-03-04 峚山
Mishan
（93,51194E；42,81824N）

又西北四百二十里，曰峚山[1]。其上多丹木[2]，员叶而赤茎[3]，黄华而赤实[4]，其味如饴[5]，食之不饥[6]。丹水[7]出焉，西流注于稷泽[8]，其中多白玉[9]。是有玉膏[10]，其源沸沸汤汤[11]，黄帝[12]是食是飨[13]。是生玄玉[14]，玉膏所出，以灌丹木，丹木五岁[15]，五色乃清[16]，五味乃馨[17]。黄帝乃取峚山之玉荣[18]，而投之钟山之阳。瑾瑜之玉为良[19]，坚粟精密[20]，浊泽而有光[21]。五色发作[22]，以柔和刚[23]。天地鬼神，是食是飨，君子服之，以御不祥。自峚山至于钟山，四百六十里，其间尽泽也[24]。是多奇鸟、怪兽、奇鱼[25]，皆异物焉[26]。

注释：[1]峚山：指木提山，又称密山，主峰托木尔提山。在新疆哈密。木提指天的区域。

Notes： [1]mi shan: refers to the Muti Mountain, also known as the Mishan, its peak is the Tomur(ti) Mountain 42° 2′ 15″ N, 80° 7′ 30″ E。It is situated in the Hami area in Xinjiang Province。 Muti; the region of Sky area, refers to highlands。

[2] 丹木：指托木尔提牧民.

[2] dan mu (red wood) refers to the herdsmen from Tomurti。

[3] 员叶而赤茎：指草原的犬戎部落。

[3] yuan ye er chi jing (round leaf with red stem) refers to the Dog Rong tribes。

[4] 黄华而赤实：胡族山区的犬戎氏族。黄华，指胡族山区，简称胡山。

[4] huang hua er chi shi (yellow flowers and red fruits)

Tr: refers to the Dogrong clan from the mountainous region of Hu clans。 huanghua (yellow flowers) refers to the mountain areas controlled by the Hu, shortened to Hushan。 (Hu Mountain)。

[5] 其味如饴：东回鹘夷。

[5] qi wei ru yi (it tastes like candy) eastern Uyghur Yi。 luo

[6] 食之不饥：古老的贝加尔湖人。

[6] shi zhi bu ji (eat and feel no hunger)

Tr: refers to the ancient people from the Baikal Lake。

[7] 丹水：指托木尔提河。

[7] dan shui (red water) refers to the Tomurti River。

[8] 稷泽：指馍淖尔，今称淖毛湖。稷和馍都是指粮食。

[8] ji ze (millet sea):

Tr: refers to the Mo-nuur, today known as the Naomao Lake, ji/mo all refers to grain。

[9] 白玉：指伊山氏族，又称伊吾氏族。

[9] bai yu (white jade) refers to the Yishan clan, also known as the Yiwu clan。

[10] 玉膏：指泉水。

[10]yu gao (jade ointment) refers to spring water。

[11] 沸沸汤汤：指泉水涌出的状态。

[11] fei fei tang tang (bubbly and steaming) describes the movement of the springs。

[12] 黄帝：在此有两种含义，一是指北方牧民，一是指北王。

[12] huang di (yellow emperor)

Tr: Huangdi has two meanings, it refers first to the herdsmen from the north, also it refers secondly to Bei Wang (northern lord) 。

[13] 是食是飨：一直依赖这股水生存。

[13] shi shi shi xiang (for food for livelihood) has always relied on the spring water for existence。

[14] 是生玄玉：这里出美女。玄玉，指荣伊，即美女之意。

[14] shi sheng xuan yu (is born with black jade)

Tr: this place is famous for the beautiful women。xuanyu: close phonetic match to rongyi (beauties, pretty girls) 。

[15] 丹木五岁：托木尔提部落的包容。五岁，指部落的包容。

[15] dan mu wu sui (red wood five years old)

Tr: the inclusive policy by the Tomurti tribes。 wusui (five years old)means the policy of inclusiveness by the tribes。

[16] 五色乃清：长安之道。五色，指长安；清，指术、道。

[16] wu se nei qing (five colors are clear)

Tr: the way to achieve long term peace, wuse (five color) means long term peace, qing(clear) refers to the way or the policies, the Tao。

[17] 五味乃馨：兴盛之举。五味，指兴盛；馨，指制作、举动。

[17] wu wei nai sheng (five tastes are spreading)

Tr: policies for prosperity, wu wei(prosperity); sheng (produce, gestures)

[18] 取峚山之玉荣，而投之钟山之阳：将密山的美女嫁到天山之南。
[18] qu mi shan zhi yu rong (get Mishan's beautiful jade), er tou zhi zhongshan zhi yang (drop to the sunny side of Bellshan)
Tr: arrange for the pretty girls from Mishan to be married to the south of Tianshan。
[19] 瑾瑜之玉为良：使公主瑾和瑜成为那里的首领。
[19] jin yu zhi yu wei liang (jin and yu jade the best) make princess Jin, and Princess Yu the chieftains of that place。
[20] 坚粟精密：将粟进贡给峚山。
[20] jian su jing mi (solid millets and refined packed) send as tributes the millets to Mishan。
[21] 浊泽而有光：这是造泽福佑的方法。浊泽，指造泽；而有，指福佑；光，指门，法门。
[21] zhuo ze er you guang (muddy sea with lights)
Tr: this is a way to benefit the people and the following generations, zhuo zi: provide benefits, er you: protection for prosperity, lights: refers to the door, the passage or initiation to the doctrine。
[22] 五色发作：是振兴部落的国策。
[22] wu se fa zuo (five color effect results)
Tr: a nation's policy to rejuvenize the clans。
[23] 以和柔刚：以和亲消除战争。刚，指勾，即战争。
[23] yi he rou gang (use peace softens hard confrontation)
Tr: use inter-tribal or racial marriages to eliminate wars。 Gang: gou, hook, refers to the warfare。
[24] 其间尽泽也：其间有很多支系氏族。
[24] qi jian jin ze ye (in this place lot water)
Tr: with many tribal branches living in the places between。
[25] 奇鸟、怪兽、奇鱼：奇鸟指乌鲁木克齐人；怪兽，指古尔班通人；奇鱼，指奇台人。
[25] qi niao, guai shou, qi yu (strange bird, grotesque beast, weird fish)
Tr: the Urumqi people, the Gurbantung people and the Qitai people。Guerbantong: N44°15′ ~ 46°50′, E84° 50′ ~ 91°20′。
[26] 皆异物焉：都是伊吾国的臣民。异物，即伊吾。
[26] jie yi wu yan (all strange stuff)
Tr: they are all the subjects of the Yiwu nation。Strange stuff: a phonetic match for yi wu。

译文：由包尔乌拉山往西北四百二十里，有座山叫密山。山的西面住着托木尔提牧民，是草原的犬戎部落夷，是胡族山区的犬戎氏族，是东回鹘夷，是古老的贝加尔湖人。托木尔提水从山间流出，向东北流入淖毛湖，河畔住着伊吾部落氏族。这里有一股泉水，沸沸汤汤地涌出，北部的牧民一直依靠着股泉水生存。这里出美女。泉水所出，以滋养托木尔提人，托木尔提部落的包容，是长安之道，是兴盛之举。北王将密山的美女嫁到天山之南。公主瑾和公主瑜成为那里的首领，将粟米进贡给密山，这是造泽福佑的方法。振兴部落的策略是以和亲消除战争。天地鬼神都享受着这样的安宁。君子用此以御不祥。从密山到天山，四百六十里，其间有许多氏族。他们是乌鲁木克齐、古尔班通和奇台人，都是伊吾部落的臣民。
Translation:
Four hundred and twenty li further northwest from the Bor ula Mountain there stands Mishan。 On its west live the herdsmen from Tomurti. They are the steppe Dog Rong tribes from the Hu mountains。 They are the Dong Uyghurs, ancient people from the Baikal Lake。The Tomurti River rises from this mountain, and goes east into the Naomao Lake, on its banks live the Yiwu clans。 A spring bubbles out, the local herdsmen from the northern parts depend on the spring。This is a land of beautiful girls。The spring nurtures and benefits the Tomurti people。 The Tomurti's policy of inclusiveness is a guarantee for long term peace and prosperity。 The Northern Lord marry the beautiful girls from Mishan to the south part of Tianshan。 Princess Jin and Princess Yu are made chieftains of those clans。 Also, millets are brought in as tributes to Mishan。 Inter-racial marriages as a policy can dissolve the war to vitalize the clans。 All the ghosts and deities enjoy such peaceful coexistence under the Heaven。

Gentlemen use such policy against misfortune。 From Mishan to Tianshan, there is a distance of 460 li long, many tribes live on this land between the two mountains。They are the Urumqi people, the Gurtongban people and the Qitai people, all those people are the subjects of the Yiwu tribal nation。

02-03-05 钟山
Zhongshan
（87,6131E；43,8264N）

又西北四百二十里，曰钟山[1]。其子曰鼓[2]，其状如人面而龙身[3]，是与钦䲹杀葆江[4]于昆仑之阳[5]，帝乃戮（chuo)之[6]。钟山之东曰瑶崖[7]。钦䲹化为大鹗[8]，其状如雕而黑文白首[9]，赤喙而虎爪[10]，其音如晨鹄（gao)[11]，见则有大兵[12]；鼓亦化为鵕鸟[13]，其状如鸱（di)，赤足而直喙[14]，黄文而白首[15]，其音如鹄（gao)，见则其邑大旱[16]。

注释：[1]钟山：指天山。又叫齐城山。
Notes: [1] zhong shan (bell mount) also known as Tianshan, (sky mount),another name is Qichengshan。
[2] 其子曰鼓：主峰叫格达。濮语“博”是指山，博格达是倒装句。
[2] qi zi yue gu (its son name drum)
Tr: the main peak is called Geda, in Pu concept, Bo means mountain, Bogeda, a reversed order of Gedabo。
[3] 人面而龙身：西部氏族的定居地。龙，指洛，即西方、西部。
[3] ren mian er long shen (human face with dragon body)
Tr: a place where the western clans settled, long/luo(dragon) west, or occidental。
[4] 钦䲹杀葆江：指齐城外的首府。齐城，指乌鲁木克齐，意为蜘蛛城。杀，指外边，之外。葆江，指博贾，即首府、政治中心，牧民有住帐包的习俗，首府是可以移动的。
[4] qin pei sha bao jiang:(qin pei kill baojiang)
Tr: the capital residence outside the Qicheng。 Qicheng: Urumqi, meaning the spider city, sha(kill): outside, beyond the city proper。Baojiang: bojia means capital residence, political center。The herdsmen live in tents, and they can relocate their capital seat around。
[5] 昆仑之阳：指高山的南坡。
[5] kunlun zhi yan (kun lun ‘s sunny side)
Tr: refers to the southern slope of the high mountains。
[6] 帝乃戮之：北方的游牧支系。
[6] di nai chuo zhi (God therefore spear it)
Tr: the nomadic branches of the north region。
[7] 钟山之东曰瑶崖：天山的支系叫雅利安亚希库都氏，简称雅亚氏。东，指栋，即支系。
[7] zhong shan zhi dong yue yao yan (bell mount east is Yao cliff)
Tr: refers to the Tianshan branch, the Aryan Yaxikudu Shi, shortened to Yaya Shi。Dong(east): column, means branches。
[8] 钦邳化为大鹗：齐城山南面的农牧民。大鹗，指农牧兼顾的氏族。
[8] qin pi hua wei da e(qin pi becomes big Osprey)
Tr: the herdsmen and agriculturists on the southern side of the Qichengshan。 Da e refers to the clans involved in both animal husbandry and agriculture。
[9] 雕而黑文白首：鞑鲁的直系僰族。
[9] diao er hei wen bai shou (eagle with black marking and white head)
Tr: The Bo ethnic group, the direct descendent branch from the Dalu, the nomads。
[10] 赤喙而虎爪：犬戎的胡族支系。
[10] chi hui er hu zhua (red beak and tiger claw)
Tr: The Hu branches of the Dog rong。

[11] 晨鹄：指盆地，这里指齐城。第二个“鹄”字指交河古城。
[11] chen hu (morning bird) refers to the basin, here it points to Qicheng, the second word hu refers to the ancient city of Jiaohe。 Yar City, Yarkhoto：42° 56′ 59″ N, 89° 3′ 55″ E。

[12] 见则有大兵：是那里的统治氏族。
[12] jian ze you da bing (seeing will lead to big warfare)
Tr: the ruling clan in that region。

[13] 鼓亦化为鵔鸟：格达山南面的交河氏族。鵔鸟，指交河，这里指交河古城。
[13]gu yi hua wei jun niao (drum will turn into a jun bird)
Tr: refers to the Jiaohe (Yarkhoto) clan on the south side of the Gedashan (Bogeda), Jun niao (jun bird) refers to the Jiaohe （connected rivers) ancient city。 42° 57′ 2″ N, 89° 3′ 50″ E Yarnaz Valley。

[14]鴖（di）赤足而直喙：氐羌北迁的直目人支系。赤足，指北迁。
[14] di chi zu er zhi hui (di-bird red foot straight beak)
Tr: refers to the Zhimuren (vertical eyes) tribe of the Diqiang, who had moved to the north。 Chi zu (red feet, or bare feet) refers to the move of migration to the north。

[15] 黄文而白首：胡杨水的农业氏族。黄文，指胡杨水，今称艾丁湖。
[15] huang wen er bai shou (yellow marking with white head)
Tr: refers to the agricultural clans by the Huyangshui River。 Huang wen: Huyangshui, Huyang （Populus euphratica）river, today's Ayding Lake：42° 39′ 27″ N, 89° 16′ 14″ E

[16] 见则其邑大旱：是那个地方的达罕氏族。
[16] jian ze qi yi da han (seeing it the town will have a big drought) they are the Khan tribe in that area。

译文：由密山往西北四百二十里，有座山叫天山。天山的主峰叫格达山，这里是西部氏族的定居地，是乌鲁木克齐城外的南山首府，这里住着北方游牧支系的天山支系，叫雅利安亚希库都氏。齐城山南面的农牧民是鞑鲁的直系僰族；犬戎的胡族支系，住在齐城，是那里的统治氏族；格达山南面的交河氏族，是氐羌北迁的直目人支系，是胡杨水区域的农业氏族，住在交河古城，是那个城镇的达罕氏族。
Translation:
Four hundred and twenty li further northwest from Mishan there stands the Tianshan Mountain。 The peak of Tianshan is Gedashan, the settlement region of the western clans。 It is also the south mountain residence capital outside the Urumqi city, where the northern nomadic tribe's Tianshan branch live。 They are called the Aryan Yaxikudou Shi。 On the south side of the Qichengshan (Urumqi)live the direct descendent clan of the Dalu people, the Bo Yi。 The Hu branch of the Dog Rong people live in the Qi city, they are the ruling clans there。 The Jiaohe （Yar city，Yarkhoto）clan, who live on the south side of the Gedashan, are the Zhimu branch of the Diqiang clans who migrated to the North。 They are the agriculture clans from the Huyangshui area。They live in the Jiaohe old town and are the ruling clan in that town。

02-03-06 泰器山
Taiqishan
（90,3796E；46,67493N）

又西百八十里，曰泰器之山[1]。观水[2] 出焉，西流注于流沙 [3] 。是多文鳐鱼 [4] ，状如鲤鱼[5] ，鱼身而鸟翼[6]，苍文而白首赤喙[7]，常行西海[8]，游于东海，以夜飞[9]。其音如鸾鸡（lue gai)[10], 其味酸甘[11]，食之已狂[12]，见则天下大穰（hang)[13]。

注释：[1]泰器山：指阿尔泰东山。即阿尔泰山的东南麓。
Notes： [1] tai qi shan（big instrument mount)
Tr: it refers to the Altai Mountain's southeast part, the Altai Dongshan。

[2] 观水：指布尔干河，简称干河、干水。

[2] guan shui (watch water)
Tr: refers to the Bulgan River, shortened to Gan River, or the Ganshui。

[3] 流沙：指福海和乌伦湖。

[3] liu sha (moving sands)
Tr： refers to the Fuhai Lake 47° 6′ 42.84″ N, 87° 29′ 12.12″ E and the Wulun Lake。

[4] 文鳐鱼：指蕴戎夷。戎，在濮语中读雍，与鳐谐音。蕴，指越，即客居的。

[4] wen yao yu (marking yao fish)
Tr： refers to the Yunrong Yi。 In Pu concept, rong reads as yong, a close phonetic match to yao, Yun refers to crossover, meaning a guest tribe。

[5] 鲤鱼：指尼溢，即青河。

[5]li yu (carp) refers to Ni yi， the Qing (green) River。

[6] 鱼身而鸟翼：青河夷的西部支系。鸟，读洛音，指西部。

[6]yu shen er niao/luo yi (fish body with bird wings)
Tr: refers to the western branches of the Qinghe （green river） Yi. Niao/luo, west, occidental。

[7] 苍文而白首赤喙：青河的山区犬戎支系。苍文，指青河。

[7] cang wen er bai shou chi hui (black marking and white head red beak)
Tr: The Dogrong's mountainous branch from the Qinghe River; cang wen refers to Qinghe River。

[8] 常行西海：由西海迁移。西海，指哈萨克斯坦地区。

[8] chang xing xi hai (often moves from west sea), migrates from Xihai, west sea refers to the Kazakhstan region。

[9] 游于东海以夜飞：进入东海的富蕴。夜飞，指外来之系、客家支系，今称富蕴。

[9] you yu dong hai yi ye fei (swim in east sea to nightly fly)
Tr: enter the Fuyon area in Donghai （east region）, ye fei (nightly fly) refers to the outside branches, the guest branches, known as Fuyon tribes。

[10] 鸾鸡：指列盖镇，与北部的乌列盖镇相对应。今称阿尕什。（阔克阿尕什，福海）杰勒阿尕什。

[10] luan ji (luan bird)
Tr： refers to Liegai, today known as Agashi （46° 36′ 3.42″ N, 83° 55′ 12.86″ E） a close phonetic match, a corresponding place name is the northern Olgii, in Mongolia。

[11] 其味如酸甘：南面的索干。索干，指喀斯克尔索干。

[11] qi wei ru suan gan (it taste like sour sweet)
Tr: refers to the Suogan to the South, suogan: today's kirskirsuogan。

[12] 食之已狂：古老的北部夷。

[12] shi zhi yi kuan (eat to cure craziness) refers to the ancient northern Yi。

[13] 大穰：读达罕，指王、王族。

[13] da xiang: reads as dahan, refers to the king tribe, the lord, DaKhan (great khan) 。

译文：由天山往西北一百八十里，有座山叫阿尔泰东山。布尔干河从山间流出，向西流入乌伦湖。那里住着蕴戎夷，是青河夷的西部支系，是青河的山区犬戎族，由西海迁至东海的富蕴镇；他们住在列盖镇南面的喀斯克尔索干，是古老的北部夷，是那个地区的达罕氏族。

Translation：

One hundred and eighty li further northwest from the Tianshan there stands the Altai Dongshan。 Burgan River flows out from the mountain and goes west into Ulun Lake。 The Yunrong Yi, the west branch of the Qing River people lives there, they are the mountainous Dogrong from the Qing River。 Having migrated from Xihai in the west to Fuyonzhen in Donghai in the east, they live in Kaskesuogan in the south side of Liegai （Olgii）。They are the ancient northern Yi, the ruling clan in that area。

02-03-07 槐江山
Huaijiangshan
（87,43979E；48,571N）

又西三百二十里，曰槐江之山[1]。丘时之水[2]出焉，而北流注于泑水[3]。其中多蠃母[4]。其上多青雄黄[5]，多藏琅玕[6]、黄金、玉[7]，其阳多丹粟[8]，其阴多采黄金、银[9]。实为帝之平圃[10]，神英招司之[11]，其状马身而人面，虎文而鸟翼[12]，徇于四海，其音如榴[13]。南望昆仑，其光熊熊[14]，其气魂魂[15]。西望大泽，后稷所潜也[16]。其中多玉[17]，其阴多榣木之有若[18]。北望诸毗，槐鬼离仑居之[19]，鹰鹯之所宅也[20]。东望恒山四成[21]，有穷鬼居之[22]，各在一搏[23]。爰有淫水[24]，其清洛洛[25]。有天神[26]焉，其状如牛[27]，而八足二首马尾[28]，其音如勃皇[29]，见则其邑有兵[30]。

注释：[1]槐江山：槐江，指西山，这里指阿尔泰西山。
Notes:[1] hui jiang shan: refers to the mountain on the west, the west part of the Altay/Altai, Altaixishan。
[2] 丘时水：指齐斯水，即额尔齐斯河。这里包括额尔齐斯河的支流喀纳斯河。
[2] qiu shi shui: Qisishui/Qisi River, the Irtysh River 61°05′24″N，68°49′15.60″E。It includes the tributary Kanasi River 48° 48′ 54″ N, 87° 2′ 24″ E。
[3] 泑水：指鄂毕河。
[3] you shui: Ob River。
[4] 蠃母：指牧民。
[4] ying mu (winner mother) refers to the herdsmen。
[5] 青雄黄：指东锡勒克。
[5] qing xiong huang (green male yellow) refers to Dong-xileke (east xileke)。
[6] 藏琅玕：指铁勒沙干。铁，在濮语中读 ze 音。
[6] cang lang gan:(legendary tree) refers to the Tiele/tele-shagan 。 In Pu concept, Iron/tie reads as ze.
[7] 黄金玉：指赛勒廷夷。
[7] huang jin yu (yellow gold jade) refers to the Saileting Yi。
[8] 丹粟：这里指屯得沙拉。屯读 den 音。
[8] dan su (red millet) refers to the Dendeshala。tun/den, a phonetic shift。
[9] 采黄金银：指他乌部落夷。他，濮语读为采。
[9] cai huang jin yin (mine yellow gold silver) refers to the Tawu tribe Yi。 Ta/cai, in Pu concept。
[10] 帝之平圃：北方的宗山。平圃，指祖宗。
[10] di zhi ping pu（ god's flat garden）
Tr; refers to the Ancestor's Mountain in the North； pingpu, refers to the ancestors。
[11] 神英招司之：北斋桑氏族的发源地。
[11] shen ying zhao si zhi (God Yingzhao manage it):
Tr: it refers to the birthplace of the Northern Zhaisang (Zaysan kole48° 0′ 0″ N, 84° 0′ 0″ E) clans。
[12] 虎文而鸟翼：富蕴的西部支系。
[12]hu wen er niao yi (tiger markings with bird wings)
Tr: the west branches of the Fuyon people。
[13]榴：指阿勒泰镇。
[13] liu (pomegranate)refers to the Aletaizhen。
[14] 其光熊熊：指昆仑丘的孔塔普坎峰像一根竹签样的小柱子。
[14] qi guang xiong xiong（its lights blazing)
Tr: The Kongtapucan peak of Kunlunqiu Mountain looks like a toothpick column。
[15] 其气魂魂：指昆仑丘的噻尔山像一个小圆点。
[15] qi qi hunhun（its Qi mighty)

Tr: The Sauershan of Kunlunqiu Mountain looks like a little dot。

[16] 大泽，后稷所潜也：斋桑泊、哈萨克国东部的平原。

[16] da ze(big water) hou ji suo qian ye (hou ji retreat to)

Tr: refers to the Zaysan Kole, and the plain in the east part of Kazakhstan。

[17]玉：伊哈氏族，即北哈萨克氏族。

[17]yu(jade) refers to the Yiha clan, the Northern Kazakh clans。

[18] 榣木之有若：北卡缅氏族的城池。

[18] yao mu zhi you ruo （yao wood has it)

Tr: the township establishment of the Northern Kamian clan。

[19] 槐鬼离仑居之：北山的谊峰最高。槐指山，鬼指北。

[19] huai gui li lun ju zhi: （Huai ghost Lilun resides here)

Tr: Beishan/North Mountain 's Yifeng (friendship peak) is the highest, Huai: mountain, gui (ghost） refers to North。

[20] 鹰鹯之所宅也：鹰鹯，即英招，全句为：北斋桑地区的主峰。

[20] ying tan zhi suo zhai ye (eagle 's nest)

Tr: ying tan/ying zhao; refers to the main peak of the Northern Zaysang region。

[21] 恒山四成：指杭爱山科布多地区。四成，濮语读布都。

[21] heng shan si cheng （stable mount four complete)

Tr: refers to the Kebuduo (Kobdo) region of the Hanggai (khangai 47° 30′ 0″ N, 100° 0′ 0″ E) Mountains。 Si cheng: in Pu concept reads bu du. Budu is a close phonetic match for Kebuduo。

[22] 穷鬼居之：指戈壁阿尔泰最高。穷鬼读撮戈，即戈撮壁。

[22] qiong gui ju zhi (poor devil resides here)

Tr: refers to the highest Govi Altai. Qiong gui: reads in Pu concept as cuo ge, a close phonetic match, refers to the Gecuobi, (govi, gobi)

[23] 各在一搏：是戈撮壁地区的大山。

[23]ge zai yi bo (each has its fight), is the big mountain in Gecuobi region.

[24] 淫水：指耶水，全称为大塔米尔水，鄂尔浑河的上游。

[24] yin shui: refers to the Yeshui, also known as the Datamireshui（Greater Tamir River), the upper arm of Orkhon River。

[25] 其清洛洛：向东流去。

[25] qi qing luo luo (its clear water) flows east,

[26] 天神：指勒泰梅族。岩画表达为勒泰梅补。

[26] tian shen (heavenly deity)

Tr: it refers to the Letaimay tribe。The local rock glyphs read as Letaimaybu。

[27]牛：指阿勒泰地区。

[27] niu(ox) refers to the Altai region。

[28] 八足二首马尾：粮食种植氏族的胡夷。八足，读饶阻，指粮食；二，读畬，指种植。

[28]ba zu er shou ma wei/yi (eight feet two heads horse tail)

Tr: it refers to the grain planter clans of Hu Yi。Ba zu: reads in Pu concept as raozu(grain) er/two/she, means planting，growing。

[29] 勃皇：指巴哈，也称哈巴。在今哈巴河县。

[29]bo huang: refers to Baha, or in reversed word order as Haba, in today's Haba county。

[30] 见则其邑有兵。

[30] jian ze qi yi you bing (seeing it, the town will have war) 。

译文：由阿尔泰东山往西北三百二十里，有座山叫阿尔泰西山。额尔齐斯水从这里流出，向北流入鄂毕河。这里住着牧民。山的西面住着东锡勒克人、铁勒沙干人和赛勒廷夷，南面住着屯得沙拉人，北面住着他乌部落夷。这座山实际是北方的宗山，是北斋桑氏族的发源地，他们是胡族的居民，是富蕴的西部支系，游牧于四方，住在阿勒泰。从这里南望昆仑，孔塔普坎峰像一根小柱子，噻尔山像一个小圆点。西望斋桑泊地区，那里是哈萨克国东部的平原，有伊哈氏族和北卡缅氏族的城池。北望诸毗之峰，北山的谊峰最高，是北斋桑地区的主峰。东望杭爱山的科布多地区，戈壁阿尔泰山最高，是戈撮壁地区的大山。那里还有大塔米尔水，源源不断地向东流去。有一个勒泰梅族，是阿勒泰的粮食种植胡夷，住在巴哈，是那个集镇的统治氏族。

Translation：

Three hundred and twenty li further northwest from the Altai-dongshan there stands the Altai-xishan。 Irtysh River flows out of here and goes north into Ob River。 The nomads live here。 On the west side of the mountain live the Dong Xileke people, the Tieleshagan people and the Saileting people。On the south side live the Dendeshala people。On the north live the Tawu tribal Yi。 This Mountain is the 'Ancestor's Mount in the north, a birthplace of the Northern Zaysan clans。 They are the Hu tribes' denizens, a west branch of the Fuyon tribes, they roam around and stay in Altai。 From here looking to the south, one sees the Kunlunshan, its peak Kongtapucan looks like a toothpick, the Sauershan ¬like a dot。 Looking to the west, to the Zaysan Kole region, one sees the east plain of the Kazakhstan nation, the Yiha clan and the North Kamian clan have their townships there。 Looking north to various mountain peaks, the Yifeng（Friendship ） Peak is the highest, the chief peak of the Northern Zaysan area。 Looking to the east, is the Kobdo(kebuduo)region of the Khangai Mountain, the highest point of the Govi Altai Mountain, a big massif in Govi region。 The Greater Tamir River flows out of here, keeps flowing to the east。 The Letaimay tribe, an Altai grain growing Hu clan, lives in Baha (Haba county) town, they are the ruling clans there。

02-03-08 昆仑丘

Kunlunqiu

（82,98196E；46,20204N）

西南四百里，曰昆仑之丘[1]。是实惟帝之下都[2]，神陆吾司之[3]。其神状虎身而九尾[4]，人面而虎爪[5]；是神也，司天之九部及帝之囿时[6]。有兽焉，其状如羊而四角[7]，名曰土蝼[8]，是食人。有鸟焉，其状如蜂，大如鸳鸯[9]，名曰钦原[10]，蠚鸟兽则死[11]，蠚木则枯[12]。有鸟焉，其名曰鹑鸟[13]，是司帝之百服[14]。有木焉，其状如棠[15]，黄华赤实[16]，其味如李而无核[17]，名曰沙棠[18]，可以御水[19]，食之使人不溺[20]。有草焉，名曰蘋草[21]，其状如葵[22]，其味如葱[23]，食之已劳[24]。河水[25]出焉，而南流注于无达[26]。赤水[27]出焉，而东南流注于氾天之水[28]。洋水[29]出焉，而西南流注于丑涂之水[30]。黑水[31]出焉，而西流注于大杅[32]，是多怪鸟兽[33]。

注释：[1]昆仑丘：指孔塔普坎山。也包括东北面的噻尔山(萨吾尔山)。

Notes: [1] kunlun qiu (kunlun mount) refers to the Kongtapucan Mountain, which includes the Saurshan on the northeast side 。

[2] 帝之下都：北方的边缘地区。

[2] di zhi xia du（god's lower capital）

Tr: it refers to the outlying region of the North。

[3] 神陆吾司之：游牧氏族部落的统治区域。

[3] shen luwu si zhi (God Luwu controls it)

Tr: it refers to places ruled by the nomadic tribes。

[4] 其神状虎身而九尾：氏族是西部的胡族。九尾，读姜夷，指西部夷。

[4] qi shen zhuang hu shen er jiu wei/yi (its god tiger body with nine tails)
Tr: the tribes are the Hu people from the west, jiuyi (nine tails) reads as jiang yi, close phonetic match with jiangyi, referring to the western Yi。

[5] 人面而虎爪：定居的胡族支系。

[5] ren mian er hu zhua (human face with tiger claws): meaning settled Hu branches。

[6] 司天之九部及帝之囿时：建立天山西部及北部的裕固氏族部落。天，指南天山。

[6]si tian zhi jiu bu ji di zhi you shi (controls sky's nine parts and god's garden)
Tr: set up the Yugu clans on the west and north side of the Tianshan, Tian refers to the South Tianshan。

[7] 羊而四角：指东边的白碱滩地区。

[7] yang er si jiao (sheep with four horns)
Tr: it refers to the salt swamps in the east part of the place。

[8] 土蝼：指白城，今称克拉玛依。

[8] tu lou (earth ants)
Tr: it refers to Baicheng (white city) today's Kalamay, a city in China now。45° 34′ 47.64″ N, 84° 53′ 21.12″ E。

[9]蜂，大如鸳鸯：山区的塔鲁耶西克人。

[9] feng(bee)， da ru yuanyang (as big as water birds) refers to the Taluyexike people from the mountains。

[10] 钦原：东耶西克。今称托里县。

[10] qin yuan: east Yexike, today's Tuoli county。45° 55′ 52.82″ N, 83° 36′ 13.97″ E

[11] 蠚鸟兽则死：牧羊族的支系。

[11] he niao shou ze si (stings birds and beast dead)
Tr: it refers to the branches of the sheep/goat herders。

[12] 蠚木则枯：贺蒙则柯氏。也称塔塔尔人。

[12] he mu ze ku （worm eaten wood，wither) Hemengzeke Shi, known also as Tatar （Tartar） people。

[13] 鹑鸟：指哈萨克人。濮语读哈为吹，吹、鹑谐音。

[13] chun niao（quail） refers to the Kazakhs, in Pu concept, ha reads as chui, chui/chun a close phonetic match。

[14] 司帝之百服：统治北方的王族。百服，读补冯，指王族。

[14]si di zhi bai fu (control god's hundred subjects)
Tr: the ruling king lineage over the north。 baifu, bufeng, refers to the king lineage。

[15]棠：指陶唐，又指中原。

[15] tang: refers to Taotang, as well as to the central region of China—Zhongyuan(Central Plain)。

[16] 黄华赤实：华山地区的迁徙氏族。

[16] huang hua chi shi (yellow flowers red fruits)
Tr： refers to the clans who have migrated from the Huashan to settle here。

[17] 其味如李而无核：车围子人的乌苏部落。核，指熟，熟、苏谐音。

[17] qi wei ru li er wu he (it tastes like plum without stone)
Tr: The Wusu tribes from Cheweizi people。 Stone: reads in Pu concept as shu(ripen), a phonetic match with su, su/shu。

[18] 沙棠：指远唐氏族。

[18] sha tang（sand fruit)
Tr： refers to the Yuantang (far away in China) clans。

[19] 可以御水：夏国的客家氏族。客家，指某中心氏族到远处的其他民族地区生活。

[19]ke yi yu shui (can stop flood)
Tr: refers to the guest clans of Xia nation, which migrate to settle as guests in a faraway place , where other ethnic peoples live。

[20] 食之使人不溺：古老的乌苏镇的令狐氏。使人，指苏惹、苏镇。

[20] shi zhi shi ren bu ni (eat one will not drown)

Tr: refers to the ancient Linghu Shi from Wusuzhen。Shi ren (make people) reads as su re, refers to Suzhen。

[21] 蘋草：指艾比湖边的移民。

[21]bin cao (bin grass)： refers to the immigrants on the bank of Aybi Lake 44° 53′ 0″ N, 83° 0′ 0″ E。

[22]葵：指奎屯。

[22] kui (sun flowers) refers to Kuitun (Khuiten) township, kui a phonetic match。

[23] 其味如葱：指奎屯的车围子人的分支、支系。

[23] qi wei ru cong (its smell like onion)

Tr: refers to the branches, lineages of the Cheweizi people from Kuitun。

[24] 食之已劳：古老的河滨夷。

[24] shi zi yi lao (eat relax fatigue)

Tr: refers to the ancient riverbank people known as the Hebing Yi。

[25] 河水：指贺水。

[25] he shui (river water) refers to the He River, a phonetic match。

[26] 乌达：今称艾比湖。

[26] wu da: today's Aybi Lake.

[27] 赤水：指东河。

[27] chi shui (red water) refers to the Donghe, the East River。

[28] 汜天之水：指苏屯河，流经乌苏和奎屯。

[28]si tian zhi shui (waves up to heaven)

Tr: refers to the Sutun River, which flows through Wusu（Usu) and Kuitun (Kuyton) town。

[29] 洋水：指裕固水。

[29] yang shui （ocean water）, refers to the Yugu River。

[30] 丑涂水：今称多斯特克河。

[30] chou tu shui (ugly smear water): today's Dostyk River。

[31] 黑水：指额敏河

[31] hei shui (black water) refers to Emin River。

[32] 大杅：指阿拉湖。

[32] da yu:(big water basin) refers to Ala Lake (Lake Alakol) 46° 10′ 0″ N, 81° 35′ 0″ E。

[33] 怪鸟兽：指克鲁氏族

[33] guai niao shou: （grotesque bird and beast）: refers to the Kelu clan。

译文：由阿尔泰西山往西南四百里，有座山叫孔塔普坎山。这里实际是北方的边缘地区，是游牧氏族部落的统治区域。这里的氏族是西部的胡族定居的支系；这个氏族统治着南天山西部及北部的裕固氏族。有一个氏族，是东部的白碱滩氏族，名叫白城氏族，是古老的集镇氏族。有一群人，是山区的塔鲁耶西克人，名叫东耶西克，是牧羊氏族支系的贺蒙则柯氏。有一群人，名叫哈萨克人，是统治北方的王族。有一群牧民，是中原华山地区的迁徙氏族，是车围子人的乌苏支系，名叫远唐人，是夏国的客家人，是古老的乌苏镇的令狐氏。有一个移民氏族，名叫滨绰，是奎屯的车围子支系，是古老的河滨夷。贺水从山间流出，向南流入艾比湖。东河水从山间流出，向东南流入苏屯河。裕固水从山间流出，向西南流入多斯特克河。额敏水从山间流出，向西流入阿拉湖。那里住着克鲁氏族。

Translation：

Four hundred li further southwest from Altai-xisha stands the Kongtapucan Mountain。This is in fact the border area of the north, a place controlled by the Nomadic herders' clans。 One clan is the settled branch of the West Hu people, this clan controls the Yugur people on both the west and the north part of South Tianshan。 A clan, a Baijiantan people from the east, is called Baicheng clan。 They are the ancient township clan。 Another group, the Taluyexike people from the mountains is known as the Dongyexike people, they are the Hemengzeke Shi of the sheep/goat herding branch。 Another group of people are the Kazakhs, they are the king lineage who controls the north。 Another group of herders are the migrant clan from Huashan from central plain of China, known as the Wusu branch of the Cheweizi people, called Yuantang people。 They are the guest (Hakha) clans from the Xia nation, the Linghu Shi from the ancient Wusuzhen。 A migrant clan is known as Bingchuo, the ancient riverside Cheweizi branch from Kuitun。 The He River flows out of the mountain and goes southwest into Aybi Lake。 Donghe River rises from the mountains and flows southeast into Sutun River。 Yugushui River rises from the mountains and flows southwest into the Duositeke River。Emin River flows out of the mountains, goes west into the Ala Lake where the Keru clans live。

02-03-09 乐游山
Leyoushan
（80,2625E；41,16946N）

又西三百七十里，曰乐游之山[1]。桃水[2] 出焉，西流注于稷泽[3]，是多白玉[4]，其中多滑鱼[5]，其状如蛇而四足[6]，是食鱼[7]。

注释：[1]乐游山：指西南山，即天山西山与南山交界处的山，有汗腾格里峰和托木尔峰两个山峰，主峰为托木尔峰。
Notes： [1]le you shan(happy stroll mount) refers to the Xinanshan, which is situated on the place where the West Tianshan meets the South Tianshan 。Two peaks rise, the Khantengeri Feng and Tuomu'er Feng, with Tuomu'er being the chief peak。In Uyghur, it is called Tömür (Pik Pobeda (Tumor Feng) 42° 2′ 15″ N, 80° 7′ 30″ E 。
[2] 桃水：指托盖博水，今称托盖博依，实际向东流。
[2] tao shui (peach water)
Tr: refers to the Tuogaibo River, known today as the Tuogaiboyi, which in fact flows east。
[3] 稷泽：指馍扎提河，今称木扎提河。馍字在濮语中也读稷。
[3] ji ze (millet pond)
Tr: refers to Mozhati River, known today as the Muzhati River。 Mo, a Pu concept reads as Ji。
[4] 白玉：指博孜墩夷，即博孜镇夷。41° 43′ 25.57″ N, 80° 41′ 59.64″ E。
[4] bai yu (white jade)
Tr: refers to the Bozdun Yi, also known as the Boz-zhen Yi, zhen(township), today's Bozdun Kyrgyz Township。
[5] 滑鱼：指温巴肆夷，即温巴集市夷，今称温巴什乡夷。"滑"（wo）与"温"谐音。
[5] hua yu (slippery fish)
Tr: refers to the Ombash Yi, known as the people from the Ombash market town 41° 39′ 58.68″ N, 81° 45′ 1.44″ E, today's Ombash township Yi（Ombash）。 wun, a phonetic match to Hua (reads as wo), wun/wo/hua。
[6] 蛇而四足：塞族人的氏族。
[6] she er si zu (snake with four feet)
Tr： refers to the Saka clans。
[7] 是食鱼：是古老的夷人。
[7] shi yu (yes, eat fish)
Tr: refers to the ancient Yi people。

译文：从孔塔普坎山向西南三百七十里有座山，名叫西南山，主峰为托木尔峰。托盖博水从山间流出，向东流入馍扎提河。这里生活着博孜镇夷和温巴肆夷，他们是塞人的氏族，是古老的夷人。
Translation:

Three hundred and seventy li further southwest from the Kongtapucan Mountain, stands Xinanshan。 Its chief peak is the Tuomuer Feng. Tuogaibo River flows out of the mountains and goes east into Mozhati River 。 The Bozizhen Yi and Wobasi Yi live here, they are the Sakas, and of very ancient Yi people。

02-03-10 羸母山
Luomushan
（75,3288E；38,46175N）

西水行四百里，曰流沙[1]，二百里至于羸母之山[2]。神长乘[3] 司之，是天之九德也 [4] 。其神状如人而犳尾 [5] 。其上多玉 [6] ，其下多青石而无水[7]。

注释：[1]流沙：指疏勒。倒装句为勒疏。
Notes: [1] liu sha (moving sands) a close phonetic match, in reversed word order for Shule/leshu/liusha。
[2] 羸母山：指游牧山，是天山南脉山的东南麓，也称南脉山。主峰公格尔峰。
[2] luo mu shan (wasp mother mount)
Tr： refers to Youmushan (nomads' mount), the southeast side of the Nanmaishan, a part of Tianshan, its main peak is the Gonggur Feng。 (Kongur Tagh, Kongkoerh)
[3] 神长乘：指乌孜别克氏族。乌与长同意，皆指辽阔的。
[3] shen chang cheng (God long ride)
Tr: refers to Uzbek clans, wu/chang both mean broad and wide。
[4] 天之九德也：天山山口之乡。九德，指纠塔门，即天门，今称乌孜别里山口。
[4] tian zhi jiu de ye: (sky's nine virtues)
Tr： refers to the Shankouxiang of Tianshan。 Jiu-de （nine virtues) means Jiutamen (heavenly gate), or pass, today's Uzbieli Pass。 38° 39′ 13.7″ N, 73° 48′ 8.61″ E
[5] 人而犳(zhuo)尾：定居的草原夷。
[5] ren er zhuo yi (human with animal tail)
Tr: refers to the Steppe Yi who settled down。
[6]玉：指吉木河氏族。濮语读玉为珏，珏、吉谐音。
[6]yu(jade) refers to the Jimuhe clan. In Pu concept, yu/jade/reads as ji, ji/jade/yu phonetic match。
[7] 青石而无水：叶尔羌河的北部氏族。无，指北部；水，指氏族。
[7] qing shi er wu shui (black stone without water)
Tr: refers to the northern clans from the Yarkand River: 40° 27′ 32.4″ N, 80° 51′ 57.6″ E， wu/north, shui/tribe。

译文：由西南山往西南水行四百里，到达疏勒，再走旱路二百里到达南脉山。这里是乌孜别克氏族统治的地区，是天山山口之乡。这里的氏族是定居的草原夷，山的西面住着吉木河氏族，山的东面住着叶尔羌河的北部氏族。
Translation:
Four hundred li by water further southwest from the Xinanshan, one arrives at Shule, then for another two hundred li by land, comes to Nanmaishan 。 This place is controlled by the Uzbek clans, known as the land of Tianshan Pass 。 The clans here are the settled steppe Yi。On the west side of it, live the Jimu River clan, on its east side live the northern clans of the Yerqiang River. (Yarkand River, Yarkent River, Yeh-erh-ch'iang Ho)

02-03-11 玉山
Yushan
（76,57395E；35,61512N）

又西三百五十里，曰玉山[1]，是西王母所居也[2]。西王母其状如人[3]，豹尾虎齿而善啸[4]，蓬发戴胜[5]，是司天之厉及五残[6]。有兽焉，其状如犬而豹文[7]，其角如牛[8]，其名如狡[9]，其音如吠犬[10]，见则其国大穰[11]。有鸟焉，其状如翟而赤[12]，名曰胜遇[13]，是食鱼[14]，其音如录[15]，见则其国大水[16]。

注释：[1]玉山：指最大的山，又称羲乌姆、乔戈里峰。羲乌姆，意为雪域峰，谐音西王母。
Notes:[1] yu shan (jade mount);
Tr: it refers to the biggest mountain; also known as Xiwumu, a.k.a. Qiaogeli (Chhogori, K2), Xiwumu: a phonetic match for Xiwangmu (western goddess), meaning snowcapped Peak。

[2] 是为西王母所居也：这里是雪域高峰之最。实际在慕士塔格峰的东南面。
[2] shi wei xi wang mu suo ju ye (is western Goddess 's residence) 。
Tr: here is the highest point of the snowy mountain massif. It is situated to the southeast of the Mushitage Feng（Muztag）。

[3]人：指柱子。可译为人才、巨人。
[3] ren(human)
Tr: it refers to column, beam, pole, meaning human talents, or giant。

[4] 豹尾虎齿而善啸：山南护卫着边疆。
[4] bao yi hu chi er shan xiao (leopard tail tiger teeth and good at shouting)
Tr: its south side protects the border frontier land。

[5] 蓬发戴胜：山峰伸向云端。
[5] peng fa dai sheng (flowing hair with hairdressers)
Tr: the mountain peaks thrusting above the clouds。

[6] 是司天之厉及五残：在云中生长着雪莲。
[6] shi si tian zhi li ji wu can (is managing heaven's punitive force and five disabilities)
Tr: snow lotus grows above the clouds。

[7] 犬而豹文：羌而啵汶，即叶尔羌的源头。
[7] quan er bao wen (dog with leopard markings)
Tr: a phonetic match to Qiang er bo wen, (yarkent river 's source) bao/leopard/bowen。

[8] 其角如牛：乔戈里河。
[8] qi jiao ru niu (its horns like ox) 。
Tr: refers to the Qiaogeli (Chogori/Qogir) River。

[9]狡：突厥族。
[9] jiao（cunning）: Turks

[10] 吠犬：指东岔口。
[10] fei quan (barking dog)
Tr: refers to the east fork pass--the Dongchakou。

[11] 大穰：统治氏族。
[11] da rang ruling clans。

[12] 翟而赤：北部的游牧氏族。
[12] di er chi: （bird red)
Tr: it refers to the nomads from the North。

[13] 胜遇：罕萨夷。
[13] sheng yu (victory encounter)
Tr: refers to the Hunza Yi。

[14] 是食鱼：是古老的民族。
[14] shi yu (is eats fish) the age-old nation of clans。

[15]录：指塔土鲁，今塔土鲁沟。(帕米尔高原上塔什库尔干塔吉克自治县境内)
[15]lu(record) refers to the Tatulu: today's Tatulu Gully。37° 20′ 33.83″ N, 75° 24′ 23.62″ E。

[16] 大水：指达罕氏族。
[16] da shui (big water) refers to the Khan clan。

译文：由南脉山往东南三百五十里，有座山叫乔戈里峰，这里是雪域高峰之最。雪域峰像一个巨人，在山南护卫着边疆，山峰伸向云端，在云中生长着雪莲。有一个氏族，是叶尔羌河源的乔戈里河边的氏族，名叫突厥，住在东岔口，是那里的统治氏族。有一群人，是北部的游牧民，名叫罕萨夷，是古老的民族，住在塔土鲁沟，是那里的达罕氏族。

Translation:
Three hundred and fifty li further southeast from Nanmaishan, stands the Qiaogeli feng (K2), the highest point on the snowcapped plateau。The snowcapped peak stands like a giant, protects the border frontier land from the south side。Its peak thrusts above the clouds, the snow lotus grows above the clouds。 A clan, known as the Turks, live on the banks of Qiaogeli River at the Yarkent River source。They live at Dongchakou, they are the ruling clan there。 Another group of people, the northern nomads, is known as the Hunza Yi 。They are an age-old ethnic people, living in Tatulu gully, and are the Khan clan 。

02-03-12 轩辕丘
Xuanyuanqiu
（71,83335E；36,26278N）

又西四百八十里，曰轩辕之丘[1]。无草木[2] 。洵水出焉 [3] ，南流注于黑水[4]，其中多丹粟[5]，多青雄黄[6]。

注释：[1]轩辕丘：指兴都大山、又称身（juan）毒大山，简称兴耶山，谐音轩辕。今称兴都库什山。主峰蒂里奇米尔峰。
Notes: [1] xuan yuan qiu（cart shaft mound)
Tr：it refers to the Xingdu Mountain (the Shendu Mountain, the Hindu Kush Mountains) a phonetic match to Xing Ye, to Xuan Yuan, today known as the Hindu Kush Mountain, its main peak is the Tirich Mir (Khowar Language) (alternatively Terich Mir, Terichmir and Turch Mir)36° 15′ 15″ N, 71° 50′ 36″ E。

[2] 无草木：游牧部落地区。
[2] wu cao mu (no grass wood)
Tr: it refers to the Nomadic tribe's region。

[3] 洵水：兴耶水。印度河的源头。
[3] xun shui (run through water)
Tr: it refers to xing ye shui, the headwater of Indus River。

[4] 黑水：指霍斯特水，今称喀布尔河。
[4] hei shui (black water)
Tr：it refers to the Huoste River, today's Khabur (Khabul, Kabul) River。

[5] 丹粟：达里族，是雅利安人的支系氏族。
[5] dan su (red millets)
Tr：it refers to the Dari clan, a branch of the Aryan people。

[6] 青雄黄：东身(juan)毒胡，又称东胥度胡。
[6] qing xiong huang (green male yellow)
Tr: refers to the eastern Hsingdu Hu, also known as the East Xudu Hu。

译文：由乔戈里峰往西四百八十里，有座山叫兴都库什山，是游牧部落地区。兴耶水从山间流出，向南流入喀布尔河。那里住着达里族，住着东身毒胡。
Translation:
Four hundred and eighty li further west from the Chogori Peak (K2) there stands the Hindu Kush Mountain, the land of the nomads。 Hinye River flows out of the mountain and goes south into the Kabul River。 The Dari clans and the east Juandu (Hindu) Hu live in this region。

02-03-13 积石山
Jishishan
（66,13163E；34,25736N）

又西三百里，曰积石之山[1]。其下有石门[2]，河水冒以西流 [3] 。是山也，万物无不有焉 [4]。

注释：[1]积石山：指土尔其斯坦山。
Notes: [1] ji shi shan (pile stone mount) refers to the Turkestan Range。
[2] 石门：指萨、桑部落。
[2] shi men (stone gate) refers to the Sa tribe and the Sang tribe。
[3] 河水冒以：指贺硕穆溢。今称穆尔加布河。
[3] he shui mao yi (river water bubble)
Tr: a phonetic match for He shuo mu yi, refers to the present Murghāb River。（36° 26′ 47″ N, 62° 38′ 6″ E）
[4] 万物无不有焉：大宛部落的北山氏族乡。有焉，读补耶，指氏族乡。
[4] wan wu wu bu you yan (everything it has)
Tr： it refers to the Beishan (northern mountain) clans' land， of the Dayuan （Tayuan,) tribe。you yan: reads as bu ye, refers to the land of the clans。

译文：由兴都库什山往西三百里，有座山叫土尔其斯坦山。山的东面住着萨、桑部落氏族。穆尔加布河发源于这座山，向西边流去。这座山是大宛部落的北山氏族乡。
Translation：
Three hundred li further west from the Hindu Kush Mountain there stands the Turkestan Range。 On its east side live the Sa clan and the Sang clan 。 The Murghāb River originates from this mountain and flows westward。 This mountain is the home of the Beishan clan of the Dayuan people。

02-03-14 长留山
Changliushan
（63,13297E；34,98708N）

又西二百里，曰长留之山[1]，其神白帝少昊居之[2]。其兽皆文尾[3]，其鸟皆文首[4]。是多文玉石[5]。实惟员神磈氏之宫[6]。是神也，主司反景[7]。

注释：[1]长留山：指乌孜山，又称班迪突厥斯坦山。
Notes: [1] chang liu shan:(long remain mount)
Tr: it refers to the Uz Mountain, also known as the Bandi-turkestan Mountain。
[2] 白帝少昊居之：班迪萨胡的部落。
[2] bai di shao gao ju zhi (white god shao gao resides here)
Tr: it is a close phonetic match of Band-i/Bend-i; shaogao/sahu, refers to the Band-i Sar Hu tribes。
[3] 文尾：宛夷。
[3] wen wei/yi: (marking tail) refers to the Yuan Yi。

[4] 文首：宛族。
[4] wen shou (marking head) refers to the Yuan ethnic people。
[5] 文玉石：宛夷氏族。
[5] wen yu shi (marking jade stone) refers to the Yuan Yi clans。
[6] 员神魂氏之宫：宛氏族凯萨尔氏之门（应是南大门）。
[6] yuan shen kui shi zhi gong (Yuan god gui 's palace)
Tr: The Kaisar Shi's gate, （the south gate）, of the Yuan clans。
[7] 反景：读"胡吉"，指吉良马，即汗血马。
[7] fan jing (opposite image)
Tr： reads as Huji： fan/hu, jing/ji, huji means the Jiliang horse, the Hanxuema （sweat blood horse) --the Ferghana horse (Nisean Horse）。

译文：由土尔其斯坦山往西二百里，有座山叫乌孜山，是班迪萨胡部落氏族的区域。那里的氏族皆为宛夷，人群皆为宛族，有很多宛夷氏族。实际是宛族凯萨尔氏的南大门。这些氏族，主要饲养汗血马。
Translation:
Two hundred li further west from the Turkestan Range there stands the Uz (Wuzi) Mountain, the region where the Band-i-Sa-Hu clans live。 The clans belong to the Yuan people， many Yuan clans live here。The place is the South Gate of the Kaisar Shi of the Yuan clans。Those clans are mainly engaged in raising the Ferghana horses。

02-03-15 章莪山
Zhang'eshan
（60,26502E；33,72973N）

又西二百八十里，曰章莪之山[1]，无草木[2]，多瑶碧[3]。所为甚怪[4] 。有兽焉，其状如赤豹[5]，五尾一角[6]，其音如击石[7]，其名如狰[8]。有鸟焉，其状如鹤，一足[9]，赤文青质而白喙[10]，名曰毕方[11]，其鸣自叫也，见则其邑有譌火[12]。

注释：[1]章莪山：指贾恩山，在伊朗东部。
Notes: [1] zhang e shan (chapter grass mount)
Tr: it refers to Jia'en Mountain in the east part of Iran。
[2] 无草木：游牧部落。
[2] wu cao mu (no grass wood)
Tr: refers to the nomadic tribes。
[3] 瑶碧：伊马目河氏族。
[3] yao bi (jade green)
Tr： refers to Imams River clans。
[4] 所为甚怪：萨维信国。
[4] suo wei shen guai (its behaviors very strange)
Tr: refers to the Saweixin (Savi) nation。
[5] 赤豹：东波斯。
[5] chi bao (red leopard)
Tr: refers to the Eastern Persia。
[6] 五尾一角：部落夷的大支系。
[6] wu yi yi jiao (five tails one horn)
Tr: refers to the big branches of the tribal people。
[7] 击石：贝杰斯坦，今称马什哈德。
[7] ji shi (strike stone)

Tr: refers to Bajestan, today's Mashhad in Iran。

[8]狰：指俾尔詹氏。

[8] zheng(fierce)

Tr: refers to the Baloch (Birjand Shi)

[9]鹌，一足：指马什哈的大支系。

[9] he, yi zu (crane, one foot)

Tr: refers to the big branch of the Mashhad tribes。

[10] 赤文青质而白喙：莫兹杜兰【马扎德兰，马赞达兰】的山区支系。

[10] chi wen qing zhe er bai hui (red marking green texture white beak)

Tr: the mountain branches of the Mazanderani people。

[11] 毕方：俾胡，即俾路支胡。

[11]bi fang (finish square)

Tr: refers to Bi Hu, also known as the Balochi Hu。

[12] 譌火：埃兰胡。埃兰，伊朗远古的国名。

[12]e huo (false fire)

Tr: refers to Alan Hu, Alan （Elam）, the ancient name of Iran。

译文：由班迪突厥斯坦山往西二百八十里，有座山叫贾恩山，是游牧部落地区，住着伊玛目河氏族。称为萨维信国。有一个氏族，是东波斯部落的大氏族，住在马什哈德，名叫俾尔詹氏。有一群人，是马什哈大支系的莫兹杜兰山区支系，名叫俾胡，他们自己也这样称呼，是那个集镇的埃兰胡。

Translation:

Two hundred and eighty li further west from the Bandi-turkestan Mountain, stands the Jia 'en Mountain, a region where the nomads roam。 The Imams River clans live here, known as the Saweixin nation。 Another clan, the east Farsian clan live in Mashhad, and are known as Baluchians。 Another group of people, the Mozduland branch of the Mashhad people, is called Balochi Hu。 They also address themselves so, they are the Alan Hu of that town。

02-03-16 阴山

Yinshan

（57,09546E；30,29788N）

又西三百里，曰阴山[1]。浊浴之水[2] 出焉，而南流注于蕃泽 [3]，其中多文贝 [4] 。有兽焉，其状如狸而白首[5]，名曰天狗[6]，其音如榴榴[7]，可以御凶[8]。

注释：[1]阴山：指伊鲁德山，在伊朗中南部。在贾恩山的西南面。

Notes: [1] yin shan (shade mount)

Tr: it refers to Yilude Mountain, in the middle south part of Iran, to the southwest of Jia'en Mountain。

[2] 浊浴水：指扎兰河。

[2] zhu yu shui (dirty bath water)

Tr: refers to Zhanland River。（Jarahi River)

[3] 蕃泽：波泽，即波斯湾。

[3] pan ze (foreign sea)

Tr: The Persian Gulf。pan, po, per are phonetic matches。

[4] 文贝：维俾，即南俾路支人。

[4] wen bei (marked shell)

Tr: wei pi, it refers to the south Balochi people。

[5] 狸而白首：山区的农业氏族。

[5]li er bai shou (leopard with white head)
Tr: refers to the agriculture clans from the mountains。
[6] 天狗：达尔格布里支系。
[6] tian gou (sky dog)
Tr: it refers to the Dargabli tribe。
[7] 榴榴：伊鲁河。
[7] liu liu: refers to the Yilu River (Erud river) 。
[8] 可以御凶：克尔曼伊斯，今称克尔曼。
[8]ke yi yu xiong (can prevent brutality)
Tr: refers to Kerman-is （Carmania), known today as the Kerman。

译文：由贾恩山往西南三百里，有座山叫伊鲁德山。扎兰河发源于这座山，向南流入波斯湾，这里住着南俾路支氏族。有一个氏族，是山区的农业氏族，名叫达尔格布里氏，住在伊鲁河北岸的克尔曼（伊斯）。
Translation:
Three hundred li further southwest from Jia 'en Mountain there stands the Yilude Mountain. Zaran-rud originates from this mountain and goes south into the Persian Gulf。The south Balochi people live here。 An agricultural tribe from the mountains called Dargabli Shi lives in Kerman （-is) on the north bank of Erud River。

02-03-17 符惕山
Futishan
（51,64624E；32,65871N）

又西二百里，曰符惕之山[1]，其上多棪枏[2]，其下多金玉[3]。神江疑居之[4] 。是山也，多怪雨 [5] ，风云之所出也[6]。

注释：[1]符惕山：指洪萨尔特山。属扎格罗斯山北麓。实际介绍伊斯法罕城。
Notes: [1] fu ti shan (code anxiety mount)
Tr: refers to the Zardkooh (Kuh Zard, Zard-Kuh) mountain, on the northern section of the Zagros Mountain, in fact, it is a description of the Isfahan city。
[2] 棪枏：指扎兰氏族，又称杰耶氏族、纳杰法氏族，属俾路支的卢尔人支系。
[2] zong nan:
Tr: refers to the Zaran clan, also known as the Jieye, or Najiefa （Najaf）clan, a Lur branch of the Balochi （Baluchi） people 。
[3] 金玉：指库赫帕耶氏族，属俾路支的卢尔人支系。
[3] jin yu (gold jade)
Tr: refers to the kuhpayeh clan, a branch of the Lur people, a Baluchian branch。
[4] 神江疑居之：杰耶氏族部落的区域，杰耶氏族又称纳杰法 (夫）氏族。
[4] shen jiang yi ju zhi (God Jiangyi lives here)
Tr: refers to the Jieye clans' territory, Jieye is also known as the Najiefa (Najaf)clan。
[5] 怪雨：指北方夷，北方氏族。
[5] guai yu (strange rain):
Tr: refers to the northern Yi, the northern clans。
[6] 风云之所出也：洪萨尔夷建立的行宫。
[6] feng yun zhi suo chu ye(wind clouds come from here)
Tr: refers to the seasonal palace of the Kuh-Zar Yi。

译文：由伊鲁德山往西北二百里，有座山叫洪萨尔特山，山的西面住着杰耶氏族，东面住着库赫帕耶氏族。这里是杰耶氏族部落的区域。这座山实际是北方氏族洪萨尔夷建立的行宫。
Translation:
Two hundred li further northwest from the Yilude Mountain there stands the Kuh-e Zard Mountain。 On the west side of it live the Jieye clan, on its east side, live the Kuhepaye clan。 Here is the region of the Jieye tribe。The mountain serves as the seasonal palace location, setup by the Northern clans--the Kuh-zar Yi。

02-03-18 三危山
Sanweishan
（47,06495E；34,33518N）

又西二百二十里，曰三危之山[1]，三青鸟居之[2]。是山也，广员百里[3]。其上有兽焉，其状如牛，白身而四角[4]，其豪如披蓑[5]，其名【彳敖彳因】[6]，是食人[7]。有鸟焉，一首三身[8]，其状如鸈[9]，其名曰鴟[10]。

注释：[1]三危山：克尔曼沙阿山，简称沙阿山，实际介绍克尔曼沙阿城。
Notes: [1] san wei shan (three danger mount)
Tr: refers to the Kermanshar Mountain, shortened to Sharshan, this is a description of the city Kermanshahr。
[2] 三青鸟居之：萨吉勒部落区域，又称萨尔波勒部落区域。
[2] san qing niao ju zhi (three green birds reside here)
Tr: refers to the region of the Sajile tribes, also known as the Sarpol-e （Zahab 扎哈卜） tribes' region。34.46111°N 45.86278°E。
[3] 广员百里：克尔曼人的都城。当"曼"由粤濮语译为汉语时，就读为员。
[3] guang yuan bai li (as wide as 100 li)
Tr： bai li (hundred li): the capital city of the Kermanians。 In Pu concept Man is read as Yuan, as in the Yue language。Yuan, man, wan are interchangeable。
[4]牛，白身而四角：卢尔人的农业氏族。
[4] niu, bai shen er si jiao (ox, white body four horns)
Tr: refers to the agriculturist clans of the Lur people。
[5] 其豪如披蓑：霍鲁沘族，今称喀克河族。
[5] qi hao ru pei suo (its hair like grass mat)
Tr： refers to the Huolubi tribe, known today as the Karkheh River (33° 5′ 46″ N, 47° 31′ 34″ E 33.096111, 47.526111) tribes。
[6] 【彳敖彳因】(wo yuan)：农业氏族名，与此相同的有馍里苑氏。
[6] wo yuan: name of the agriculturist tribes, another people sharing the same naming practice is the Moliyuan Shi。
[7] 是食人：是古老的定居氏族。
[7] shi shi ren (is eats human)
Tr: they are the age-old settled clans。
[8] 一首三身：大氏族的沙阿氏。
[8] yi shou san shen (one head three bodies)
Tr: refers to the leading major lineage of the big Shahr clans。
[9]鸈(luo)：阿洛古达氏。
[9] luo:
Tr: refers to the Aluoguda（Aliguda） Shi。
[10]鴟：兹支系。鸈，鴟联译为：阿洛古达尔兹。

[10] di; the Zi branch, Luo di is compounded into the name: Aluogudarz。

译文：由洪萨尔特山往西北二百二十里，有座山叫克尔曼沙阿，是萨尔波勒部落区域。是克尔曼人的都城。这里有一个氏族，是卢尔人的农业氏族，是喀克河族群的【亻敖 亻因】支系，是古老的定居氏族。有一群人，是大氏族沙阿氏的阿洛古达尔兹支系，简称兹氏族。
Translation:
Two hundred and twenty li further northwest from the Kuh-sarte Mountain, stands the Kermanshar, a region belonging to the Sarpol-e tribes, as the capital city of the Kermanians。 Here live the agriculturist clan of Lur, the Keke River tribes' Wo Yuan branch, a very ancient, settled people。 Another group of people is the Aluogudarzi branch of the chief clan, the Shahr people, shortened to the Zi clan。

02-03-19 䰠山
Guishan
（47,69578E；38,28648N）

又西一百九十里，曰䰠山[1]，其上多玉而无石[2]，神耆童居之[3]，其音长如钟磬[4]。其下多积蛇[5] 。

注释：[1]䰠山：指北山，又称萨巴兰山。实际在克尔曼阿沙的北面。
Notes: [1] gui shan (mount gui)
Tr: refers to Beishan (the mountain on the north）, the Savalan （Sabalan) Mountain, to the north of Kermanshahr。
[2] 玉而无石：指大不里士（城镇名）。玉与耶谐音，无与不同意，石与士谐音。
[2]yu er wu shi (jade but no stone)
Tr: refers to Tabliz township, phonetic matches in Jade: yu/ye, wu/bu, shi/stone （staff）。
[3] 神耆童居之：指东托罗斯氏族部落的区域。
[3] shen shi tong ju zhi (God old child lives here)
Tr： refers to the region where the east Taurus clans live。
[4] 长如钟磬：指乌鲁米湖东岸。长如，读乌鲁。
[4] chang ru zhong qing (long as bell stone)
Tr： refers to the Urmia Lake's east bank, changru, reads in Pu concept as wulu。 wulu/uru/changru。
[5] 积蛇：指盖杰氏族。住在今天的阿尔达比勒地区。
[5] ji she (collect snakes)
Tr: refers to the Gaijie clan， in today's Ardabil area。 (As in Hajie Firuz Tepe: 36° 59′ 39.84″ N, 45° 28′ 27.84″ E or 36.9944, 45.4744)

译文：由克尔曼阿沙往北一百九十里，有座山叫萨巴兰山，山的西面是大不里士的东托罗斯氏族部落的区域，人们住在乌鲁米湖的东岸。山的东面住着盖杰氏族。
Translation：
One hundred and ninety li further north from Kermanshahr there stands the Sabalan Mountain。 On its west is the region settled by the Tabliz's east Taurus clans。They live on the east bank of Urumia Lake。 On the east side of the mountain there live the Gaijie clans。

02-03-20 天山
Tianshan
（41,94274E；38,92846N）

又西三百五十里，曰天山[1]，多金玉[2]，有青雄黄[3]。英水[4] 出焉，而南流注于汤谷[5]。有神焉，其状如黄囊[6]，赤如丹火[7]，六足四翼[8]，浑敦无面目[9]，是识歌舞[10]，实惟帝江也[11]。

注释：[1]天山：指托罗斯山，在土尔其东部。
Notes： [1] tian shan (celestial mount)
Tr: refers to the Taurus Mountain in east Turkey。
[2] 金玉：指基伊氏族。
[2] jin yu (gold jade) refers to the Jiyi clan。
[3] 青雄黄：指东锡尔万氏族。
[3] qing xiong huang (green male yellow)
Tr: refers to the eastern Silvan clan (38° 8′ 32″ N, 41° 0′ 5″ E) 。
[4] 英水：比赫坦河的北支流。
[4] ying shui: refers to the Buhtan Deresi's northern tributary。 (Bühtan Deresi)
[5] 汤谷：指比赫坦河。
[5] tang gu (hotwater valley)
Tr: refers to the Buhtan Deresi 37°56′N 42°14′E。
[6] 黄囊：指凡湖。
[6] huang nang (yellow bag) refers to Lake Van。
[7] 赤如丹火：游牧集镇胡。
[7] chi ru dan huo (red as red fire)
Tr: refers to the township Hu tribes of the nomads。
[8] 六足四翼：母系氏族。
[8] liu zu si yi (six feet four wings) refers to the Matrilineal clans。
[9] 浑敦无面目：凡镇北面的穆什镇。
[9] hun dun wu mian mu (undifferentiated without face)
Tr： refers to the Mushi (Muş) township 穆什镇 (北纬 38.7 度，东经 41.5 度） on the north of Van city。
[10] 是识歌舞：是什城的部落氏族。什城，即穆什镇。
[10] shi shi ge wu (surely knows singing dancing)
Tr: refers to the tribal people in Shicheng town, the present Mush township。
[11] 帝江也：指泰尔詹夷。属闪族的支系氏族。
[11] di jiang ye （God River)
Tr: refers to the Taierzhan (Tercan)Yi, belonging to the Semitic people。

译文：由萨巴兰山往西三百五十里，有座山叫托罗斯山，那里住着基伊氏族和东锡尔万氏族。英水从山间流出，向南流入比赫坦河。有一个氏族，是凡湖的游牧集镇胡，属母系氏族，在凡城北面的穆什镇，是穆什城的部落氏族，实际是泰尔詹夷。
Translation:
Three hundred and fifty li further west from the Sabalan Mountain, stands the Taurus Mountain。 The Jiyi clan and the east Silvan clan live there。 Ying River flows out of the mountain and goes south into Buhtan Deresi 。 One clan is the township Hu of the nomads from Van Lake。 They are a matrilineal clan, living in the Mushizhen (Mus) on the north side of Van city, they are the tribal residents of Mush city, a Semitic Tercan people。

02-03-21 泑山
Youshan
（32,84744E；39,93867N）

又西二百九十里，曰泑山[1]，神蓐收居之[2]。其上多婴短之玉[3]，其阳多瑾瑜之玉[4]，其阴多青雄黄[5]。是山也，西望日之所入，其气员[6]，神红光之所司也[7]。

注释：[1]泑山：克尔奥罗山，简称奥山、泑山。实际介绍乌鲁斯古城。
Notes:[1] you shan: keraolus Mountain, shortened to Aoshan, Youshan, a description of Ulus old city quarter。
[2] 神蓐收居之：鲁斯部落氏族的区域。鲁斯部落，又称乌鲁斯，今属安卡拉的古城区。
[2] shen rushou ju zhi (God harvest lives here)
Tr: refers to the region where the Lus tribes reside。Lus, also known as Ulus， it is today's Ankara's old city quarter。
[3] 婴短之玉：埃斯基谢尔镇之夷，简称埃顿之夷。
[3] ying duan zhi yu (infant short 's jade)
Tr: refers to the Eskişehir township's people, shortened to the E'tun Yi。
[4] 瑾瑜之玉：格尔巴舍夷和耶尼杰夷，简称格耶之夷。
[4] jin yu zhi yu (Princess jin and Yu 's jade)
Tr: refers to the Kerbashe Yi and the Jiernijie Yi, shortened to Geye Yi。
[5] 青雄黄：东锡尔万氏族区，今称其地为丘布克镇。
[5] qing xiong huang (green male yellow)
Tr: refers to the east Silvan clans' region, today known as the Qiubuke town, written in English as Çubuk， 40° 14′ 19″ N, 33° 1′ 59″ E。
[6] 西望日之所入，气员：锡尔万人统治的克尔奥罗。克也读柒、气。
[6] xi wang ri zhi suo ru (west look sun sink in here)
Tr: qi yuan: refers to the Keraoluo ruled by the Silvan （38° 8′ 32″ N, 41° 0′ 5″ E） people。ker: reads as Qia,qi。
[7] 神红光之所司也：养鹿氏族的西部大肆。神红光，指养鹿氏族。
[7] shen hong guan zhi suo si ye(god Redlight 's sovereign)
Tr: refers to the deer keeping clans' west big city, shen hongguang (God redlight) refers to the deer keeping clans。

译文：由托罗斯山往西二百九十里，有座山叫克尔奥罗山，这里是鲁斯部落的区域。山的西面住着埃顿之夷，南面住着格耶之夷，北面住着东锡尔万氏族。这个地方是锡尔万人统治的克尔奥罗养鹿氏族的西部大肆。

Translation：
Two hundred and ninety li further west from the Taurus Mountain there stands the Keraoluo Mountain, the area of the Lusi tribes。On the west live the Aidun Yi, on its south live the Geye Yi。 on the north live the east Silvan clans。This is the west big city center of the deer keeping Keraoluo clans which are controlled by the Silvan people。

02-03-22 翼望山
Yiwangshan
（30,5387E；38,75693N）

西水行百里，至于翼望之山[1]，无草木[2]，多金玉[3]。有兽焉，其状如狸[4]，一目而三尾[5]，名曰讙[6]，其音奪百声[7]，是可以御凶[8]，服之已瘅[9]。有鸟焉，其状如乌[10]，三首六尾而善笑[11]，名曰鵸鵌[12]，服之使人不厌[13]，又可以御凶。

凡西次三经之首，崇吾之山至于翼望之山，凡二十三山（实际 22 山），六千七百四十四里。其神状皆羊身人面[14]，其祠之礼，用一吉玉瘗[15]，糈用稷米[16]。

注释：[1]翼望山：指永王山，永久管理的山，今阿菲永地区。
Notes： [1] yi wang shan (wing look mount)

Tr: refers to Yong Wang (forever king) Mountain, the mountain under permanent control, today's Afyon region in Turkey。

[2] 无草木：游牧部落地区。

[2] wu cao mu (no grass wood)

Tr： refers to the nomadic regions。

[3] 金玉：指恰伊氏族。(chay, Karachay, 地名和族名, 来自高加索的古老山里人)

[3] jin yu (gold jade) refers to the Qiayi （Chay) clan。 (Old mountain people from the Caucasus)

[4]狸：指山区的。

[4]li (leopard) refers to the mountain area。

[5] 一目而三尾：一目人的塞夷，即雅利安人。

[5] yi mu er san yi (one eye and three tails)

Tr: the Saka of the One-eyed tribes, refers to the Aryans。

[6]讙：指萨利赫利人。

[6] huan: refers to the Saliholi (Salhalli) people。

[7] 奪百声：丹布尔森，今称布尔丹。

[7] duo bai sheng (snatch hundred voice)

Tr: refers to Danbuersen, known today as the Buldan people, a close phonetic match in Duobaisheng to Danbulsen。

[8] 可以御凶：阿柯伊河的匈奴。阿柯伊河，今称大门德雷斯河。

[8] ke yi yu xiong (can protect from danger)

Tr: refers to the Xiongnu (Huns) from the Akkoy River。Akkoy River known today as the Büyük Menderes River, Akkoy is today's Pamukkale。

[9] 服之已瘅：胡族的布尔丹夷。

[9] fu zi yi dan（take it cure disease）: Hu tribes' Buldan Yi。

[10]乌：乌沙克人。

[10] wu (bird) refers to Wushake【Usak】 people。 38° 40′ 40″ N, 29° 24′ 15″ E Usak。

[11] 三首六尾而善笑：塞族能夷的边缘夷。能夷，指中心氏族。

[11] san shou liu yi er shan xiao (three heads six tails and best laughing)

Tr: the border people of the Saka's Neng Yi-- the central clans。

[12] 鵸鵌：指奇吐人，又称奇夫里尔人。

[12] qi tu(bird) refers to the Qitu people, known today as the Qifulier （Çivril ） people。

[13] 服之使人不厌：胡族古老的河滨氏族。

[13] fu zhi shi ren bu yan(eaten will make you not disgusted)。

Tr： refers to the old riverside clans of the Hu people。

[14] 羊身人面：牧羊氏族的居民形象。

[14] yang shen ren mian (sheep body human face)

Tr: refers to the resident's images of the herd keeping clans。

[15] 吉玉：指上等品质的玉。濮语、彝语都称第一等级为吉。

[15] ji yu (luck jade) first class jade

Tr: in Pu and Yi languages, the first class is referred to as the Ji class。

[16] 稷米：指黄米，比粟米的颗粒稍大一些。

[16] ji mi (proso millet) bigger in size than the yellow millets and Su millets。

译文：由克尔奥罗山向西南水行百里，到达阿菲永山，那里是游牧氏族的部落，住着恰伊氏族。有一个氏族，是山区的雅利安人，名叫赫利氏，住在布尔丹，是阿柯伊河的匈奴，是古老的布尔丹夷。有一群人，是乌沙克塞族能夷的边缘氏族，名叫奇夫里尔人，是胡族古老的河滨夷，也是阿柯伊河的匈奴。

Translation:

About one hundred li further southwest by water from Keraolou Mountain, stands the Afyon Mountain。 This is the nomadic tribe's area, the Koy tribes live here。 One clan of the mountain Aryans is known as the Houli people, they live in Burdan。 A Xiongnu clan from the Akkoy River are the ancient Burdan people。Another group of people are the border tribes from the Usak, the Saka central clans。 They are called Cilriv people, the old riverside Hu Yi, also one of the Xiongnu clans from Akkoy River 。

综观西山第三系列，从盐池山到阿菲永山，共有二十三（实际22）座山，延绵六千七百四十四里。这些山神的形象皆为牧羊氏族的居民形象，祭祀之礼，用一块上等的玉埋入地下，食物用黄米食品。

In sum: the 3rd list of mountains in the west describes a total of 22 mountains starting with Yanchishan and ending with Afyon Mountain (Afyonkarahisar), covering a total distance of 6,744 li。 All the mountain deities are in the image of the herd keeping tribal people。 When sacrificing to the deities, a first-class jade piece is buried under the ground and food made of yellow millet is offered。

西山经第四山系

Book 2 Xishanjing; Chapter 4

02-04-01 阴山
Yinshan
（109,37996E；35,98843N）

西次四经之首，曰阴山[1]，上多穀[2]，无石[3]，其草多茆、蕃[4]。阴水[5]出焉，西流注于洛。

注释：[1]阴山：指英山，在陕西境内，属黄龙山北麓洪福梁。
Notes:[1] yin shan (shade mount)
Tr: refers to Yinshan in Shaanxi province。 Yinshan belongs to the northern face of Huanglongshan (yellow dragon mount), known as the Hongfuliang (big luck ridge) 。

[2]穀：指道姓氏族。濮语读"道"为工，与穀谐音。
[2]gu (grain)
Tr： refers to the clans bearing the surname of Dao。 In the Pu concept, dao(way)is read as Gong, Gong/gu, a close phonetic match。

[3] 无石：指阿氏，今有地名阿党。
[3] wu shi (no stone)
Tr: refers to the surname Ah, today this surname is retained in the local place name Ahdang。

[4] 茆蕃：指富堡，今陕西富县县城。
[4] mao fan (mao foreign)
Tr: refers to Fubao (rich town), it is today's Fuxian city's seat in Shaanxi province。

[5] 阴水：指英水。
[5] yin shui (shadowy water) refers to the Ying River。

译文：西山经第四列山系的第一座山，名叫英山。山的西面住着道姓氏族和阿姓氏族，这里的移民为富堡氏族。英水发源于这座山，向西流入洛河。
Translation:
The first mountain heading the 4th list of mountains in the west is Yingshan。 On its west side live the Dao clan and the Ah clan, the migrants here belong to the Fubao clan。 The Ying River originates from here and goes west into the Luo River。

02-04-02 劳山
Laoshan
（109,06325E；36,59596N）

北五十里，曰劳山[1]，多茈草[2]。弱水[3] 出焉，而西流注于洛。

注释：[1]劳山：指陕西崂山。
Notes: [1] lao shan (labor mount) refers to the Laoshan in Shaanxi province。
[2] 茈草：指卓资移民，即夸父族移民。
[2]ci cao (a plant)
Tr： refers to the Zhuozi migrants, the Kuafu people。 (Legendary figure of Kuafu who chases the sun shadow) 。
[3] 弱水：今称周水。
[3] ruo shui (weak water) known today as the Zhou River。

译文：由英山向北五十里，有座山叫崂山，这里住着卓资移民。弱水从这里流出，向西流入洛河。
Translation:
Fifty li northwards from Yingshan there stands the Laoshan。 The Zhuozi migrants live here。The Ruo River flows out of here and goes west into the Luo River。

02-04-03 罢父山
Bafushan
(108,50432E；37,1781N)

西五十里，曰罢父之山[1]，洱水[2]出焉，而西流注于洛，其中多茈、碧[3]。

注释：[1]罢父山：指巴彦胡的山，今谐音称白于山，在陕西境内。
Notes:[1]ba fu shan (stop father mount)
Tr: refers to the mountain controlled by the Bayan Hu people, a close phonetic match to today's Baiyushan in Shaanxi province。
[2] 洱水：又称资水、资沘。今称周河。
[2]er shui（er water）
Tr: it is also known as Zishui, Zibi, which refers to today's Zhou River。
[3] 茈碧：指资沘，因夸父族而得名。资沘氏族即卓资夷。
[3] zi bi （plant green）
Tr： refers to Zibi, derived from the Kuafu tribe, zibi /zuozi /kuafu, all refer to the Zhuozi Yi。

译文：由崂山向西北五十里，有座山叫白于山，洱水发源于这座山，向西流入洛河。这里住着卓资夷。
Translation:

Fifty li further northwest from Laoshan there stands Baiyushan。The Ershui River originates from this mountain and goes west into the Luo River。 Zhuozi Yi lives here。

02-04-04 申山
Shenshan
（108,83253E；38,59729N）

北七十里，曰申山[1]，其上多穀柞[2]，其下多杻橿[3]，其阳多金玉[4]。区水[5] 出焉，而东流注于河。

注释：[1]申山：指经线走向的山，汉语称横山；这里指乌审山，今称乌审旗。在内蒙古鄂尔多斯南面。
Notes： [1] shen shan (stretch mount)
Tr: it refers to the mountain of horizontal direction, in Chinese it is called Heng mountain。 It refers to the Wushenshan, known as today's Wushen Banner (Uxin banner) in southern Ordos, Inner Mongolia。
[2] 穀柞(paper mulberry green shrub)：指草原氏族。穀柞读仡卓，指草类。
[2]gu zuo: refers to the steppe clans, guzuo reads in Pu concept as Gazhuo/gazou, meaning grass。
[3] 杻橿（oak, holmoak）：在此指榆林氏族。杻橿读杻举，指榆林。
[3] niu jiang: refers to the Yulin clan, Niujiang reads as Niuju, a close phonetic match。
[4] 金玉：指岭夷，即横岭夷。
[4] jin yu (gold jade) refers to the Ling(ridge) Yi, the Hengling (horizontal ridge) Yi。
[5] 区水：指无定河。
[5] ou shui: refers to the Wuding (no definite course) River。

译文：由白于山向北七十里，有座山叫乌审山。山的西面住着草原氏族，东面住着榆林氏族，南面住着横岭夷。无定水从这里流出，向东流入黄河。
Translation:
Seventy li further north from Baiyushan there stands Wushenshan。 On its west side live the steppe clans, on its east side, the Yulin clans， and on its south side, the Hengling Yi。 The Wuding River flows out of here and goes east into the Yellow River。

02-04-05 鸟山
Niaoshan
（109,83366E；40,66059N）

北二百里，曰鸟山[1]，其上多桑[2]，其下多楮[3]，其阴多铁[4]，其阳多玉[5]。辱水[6] 出焉，而东流注于河。

注释：[1]鸟山：指乌拉山。濮语乌、拉都指鸟。
Notes: [1] niao shan (birds mount)
Tr: it refers to Wulashan (ura/ula mountain), in Pu concepts, both wu and la refer to birds。
[2]桑：指桑根达莱氏族。
[2] sang（paper mulberry）
Tr： refers to the Sanggendalai clan。
[3]楮：指卓资氏族。
[3] zhu: refers to the Zhuozi clan。
[4]铁：指查干氏族。
[4] tie(iron) refers to the Chagan clan。

[5]玉：指伊金霍洛氏族。
[5]yu(jade) refers to the Ejin Horo clan。(Ejin Horo Banner)
[6] 辱水：指乌加河。
[6]ru shui (shame water) refers to the Wujia River。

译文：由乌审山往北二百里，有座山叫乌拉山。山的西面住着桑根达来氏族，东面住着卓资氏族，北面住着查干氏族，南面住着伊金霍洛氏族。乌加河水发源于这座山，向东流入黄河。
Translation:
Two hundred li further north from Wushenshan there stands the Ula Mountain。On its west side lives the Sanggendalai clan, on its east side lives the Zhuozi clan。 The Chagan clan lives on the north side, and the Ejinhoro clan lives on the south side。Wujia River originates from this mountain and goes east into the Yellow River。

02-04-06 上申山
Shangshenshan
(109,35164E；42,23051N)

又北百二十里，曰上申山[1]。上无草木[2]，而多硌石[3]，下多榛楛[4]，兽多白鹿[5]。其鸟多当扈[6]，其状如雉[7]，以其髯飞[8]，食之不眴目[9]。汤水[10]出焉，东流注于河。

注释：[1]上申山：指桑根达莱山，今称阴山。
Notes： [1] shang shen shan(upper shen mount)
Tr: refers to the Sangendalai Mountain, known today as the Yinshan 。
[2] 上无草木：西面是游牧部落地区，
[2] shang wu cao mu (upon it no grass wood)
Tr: the west face of the mountain is the nomadic area。
[3]硌(luo)石：指西部的氏族。
[3]ge/luo shi (luo stone) refers to the clans in the west。
[4] 榛楛：指查干氏族。
[4] zhen ku: refers to the Chagan clan。
[5] 白鹿：指白陇氏族，今白云鄂博氏族。
[5] bai lu (white deer)
Tr： refers to the Bailong clan， known today as the Baiyun'ebo /Bayan Obo clan。
[6] 当扈：指当胡，又称达尔罕胡。
[6] dang hu: to the Danghu, or Darkhan Hu。
[7]雉：指雉鸡场山地区的通古斯氏族。
[7] zhui (longtail bird)
Tr: refers to the Tungus clans from the Zhuijichang Mountain area。
[8] 其髯飞：犬戎胡。
[8] qi ran fei (his beard flying)
Tr: refers to the Dog rong Hu。
[9] 食之不眴：古老的匈奴。不眴，读补胥，匈奴、华胥氏都称补胥。
[9] shi zhi bu shun (eat it not dizzy)
Tr: refers to the ancient Xiongnu, bu xun: a phonetic match to the Pu concepts of buxu: which refers to Buxu, Xiongnu， Huaxushi。
[10] 汤水：指陶木格水，先汇入乌加河（五加河Үжяхө 41'N, 107'E），再向东流入黄河。
[10] tang shui (hot water)

Tr: refers to the Taomuge River, which flows into Wujia River and then flows eastwards into the Yellow River。

译文：由乌拉山往北一百二十里，有座山叫桑根达莱山。山的西面是游牧部落，住着西部的氏族，东面住着查干氏族和白云鄂博氏族。有一群当胡人，是通古斯族的犬戎胡，是古老的匈奴支系。陶木格水从山间流出，向东流入黄河。
Translation:
One hundred and twenty li further north from the Ula Mountain, stands the Sangendalai Mountain。 On its west side live the steppe herding clans, they are the western clans。On the east side live the Chagan clans and the Bayan Obo clan。 Another group of people are the Danghu, the Dog rong clan of the Tungus people, they are the ancient Xiongnu branch。 The Taomuge River flows out of the mountains and goes east into the Yellow River。

02-04-07 诸次山
Zhucishan
（106,26919E；45,76345N）

又北百八十里，曰诸次之山[1]，诸次之水出焉，而东流注于河[2]。是山也，多木无草[3]，鸟兽莫居[4]，是多众蛇[5]。

注释：[1]诸次山：指曼达勒低地牧区。简称低放山，诸次是低放的音译。
Notes： [1] zhu ci shan: refers to the Mandal lowland grazing ground, shortened to Difangshan (low grazing mount), Zhuci is the phonetic transliteration of Low grazing (the Great Lake Depression) 。
[2]河：指哈尔艾拉格沼泽。
[2] he refers to the Harailage （Har Airag） swamps。
[3] 木无草：指曼达勒游牧部落。
[3]mu wu cao:(wood no grass)
Tr: refers to the Mandal nomadic tribes。
[4] 鸟兽莫居：勒属蒙纪，牧民的蒙族部落。
[4] niao shou mo ju (birds beasts don't stay)
Tr: a phonetic match for Leshumengji, refers to the Mongolian tribes of the herdsmen。
[5] 众蛇：指牂氏族，即牧羊氏族。
[5] zhong she (group snake)
Tr: refers to the Zang clan, the shepherd clans。

译文：由桑根达来山往北一百八十里，到达曼达勒低地牧区，低地之水从这里流出，向东流入哈尔艾拉格沼泽。这个地方住着曼达勒游牧部落氏族，他们是蒙族部落的牧民，是牧羊氏族。
Translation:
One hundred and eighty li further north from Sangendalai Mountain there stands the Mandal lowland grazing ground。 Didi （lowland） River flows out of here and goes east into the Har-airag swamps。 The Mandal nomadic clans live here, they are the shepherd clans of the Mongolian ethnicity。

02-04-08 号山
Haoshan
（101,09866E；46,91304N）

又北百八十里，曰号山[1]。其木多漆[2]、椶[3]，其草多药[4]、虈[5]、芎䓖[6]。多汵石[7]。端水[8]出焉，而东流注于河[9]。

注释：[1]号山：指杭爱山，在蒙古国。
Notes: [1] hao shan（yell mount): Hanggay Uul in Mongolia 。
[2]漆：指克列人，属突厥的一个大支系。
[2] qi(lacquered) refers to the Kelie （Keraites）people， a major branch of the Turks。
[3]椶：指赫雷人，属克列支系。
[3] zong(palm): refers to the Helei people, a branch that belongs to the Kelie。
[4]药：指大塔米尔人，属克列支系。
[4] yao(medicine)refers to the Datamir people, a branch of the Kelie。
[5]藭：指居图人，属克列支系。
[5] ju(herbs): refers to the Jutu people, a branch of the Kelie。
[6] 芎藭：洪丘，指洪戈尔人，属克列支系。
[6] gong qiong(herbs):
Tr： refers to Hongqiu, the Hongger (Khongir) people, a branch of the Kelie。
[7] 汵石：戈壁阿尔泰氏族。
[7] gan shi (water seeping stone) the Altai clan of the Gobi。
[8] 端水：指塔米尔水，鄂尔浑河的支流。
[8] duan shui: refers to the Tamir River, a tributary of Orkhon River。
[9]河：指鄂尔浑河。
[9] he; refers to the Orkhon river。

译文：从曼达勒戈壁往西北一百八十里，有座山叫杭爱山。这里的牧民是克列人的赫雷、大塔米尔、居图、洪戈尔等戈壁阿尔泰支系。塔米尔水从山间流出，向东流入鄂尔浑河。
Translation:
One hundred and eighty li further northwest from the Mandal Govi there stands the Khangai Mountains。The herdsmen clans here are the Kelie (Keraites) branches such as the Helei, Datamir, Jutu, and Khongir, they are the Altai Gobi branches。 Tamir River rises out of the mountains and goes east into Orkhon River。

02-04-09 盂山
Yushan
（103,29044E；50,39829N）

又北二百二十里，曰盂山[1]。其阴多铁[2]，其阳多铜[3]，其兽多白狼白虎[4]，其鸟多白雉白翟[5]。生水[6]出焉，而东流注于河[7]。

注释：[1]盂山：指伊赫山，在俄罗斯贝加尔湖南岸。
Notes： [1]yu shan (water basin mount)
Tr: refers to the Yihe Mountain, on today's south bank of the Baikal Lake in Russia。
[2]铁：濮语 "油" 的音译，氐羌语读 "柳"音。这里指斯柳江卡。
[2] tie(iron)
Tr： a phonetic match for the Pu concept of Oil, in Diqiang language it is read as Liu, hereby refers to the Siliujiangka (Slyudyanka)town in Russia。
[3]铜：指呼塔格，在蒙古境内。
[3] tong(copper) refers to Hutage in Mongolia。
[4] 白狼白虎：读吐拉吐乌，指麦拉氏族和乌克钦氏族，属突厥氏族。吐指突。

[4] bai lang bai hu （white wolf white tiger)

Tr: reads as tulatuwu; a phonetic rendering: la/lang/wolf, hu/wu/tiger, in Pu concept, bai, reads as tu, a phonetic match to turk, tu/turk. Here it refers to the Maila clan and the Wukechin (Okiptchi) clan。 They belong to the Turkish ethnicity。

[5] 白雉白翟：读吐卓吐德，指普卓氏和德兹氏族，属突厥氏族。

[5] bai zhui bai di: (white bird, white pheasant)

Tr: reads as tuzhuotude, refers to Puzhuo Shi and the Dezi Shi (Dzhida), both belong to the Turkish clans。

[6] 生水：指德兹水。濮语读"生"为叨，叨、德谐音。

[6] sheng shui (raw water)

Tr：refers to the Dzhida River, in Pu concept sheng/raw is read as dao, dao /de are phonetic matches。

[7]河：指色楞河。

[7] he(water) refers to the Selenge River。

译文：由杭爱山往北二百二十里，有座山叫伊赫山。山的北面住着斯柳江卡氏族，山的南面住着呼塔格氏族。这座山的氏族还有麦拉、乌克钦、普卓和德兹等突厥氏族。德兹水从山间流出，向东流入色愣河。

Translation:

Two hundred and twenty li northward from the Khangkai Mountains, stands the Yihe Mountain。 On its north side live the Syluyanka (Slujanka) clan, on its south live the Hotage clan。 Also living here are the Maila clan, the Wukechin clan, the Puzuo clan and the Dzhida clan。 They all belong to the Turkish people。Dzhida River rises from the mountains and goes east into Selenge River。

02-04-10 白於山

Baiyushan

（101,19694E；53,68425N）

西二百五十里，曰白於之山[1]。上多松柏[2]，下多栎檀 [3]，其兽多柞牛[4] 、羬羊[5]，其鸟多鸮[6]。洛水[7]出于其阳，而东流注于渭[8]；夹水出于其阴[9]，东流注于生水[10]。

注释：[1]白於山：读博伊尔库特，指伊尔库特山，在伊尔库茨克西侧。实际往西北。

Notes：[1] bai yu shan (white by mount)

Tr: it reads as BoYirkute, refers to Yirkut mountain, to the west of Irkutsk, in a northwest direction。

[2] 松柏：指索西博尔人，也称索西比尔人。(lesosibirsk)

[2] song bo (pine poplar)

Tr: refers to the Sosibor people, also called Sosibir people。

[3] 栎檀：指伊利姆族。

[3] le tan (hard wood)

Tr: refers to the Ilim tribes。

[4] 柞牛：指扎姆佐尔人。

[4] zuo niu (mountain bull)

Tr: refers to the Zamzor people。

[5] 羬羊：指卡勒人，也称卡赖人。羊，读 ci 音，意同勒，指牧。

[5] qian yang (sheep with horse tail)

Tr: refers to Kale people, also known as Kaly people, yang; reads as Chi, shares the same meaning with Le, both mean herding。

[6]鸮：指下乌金斯克人。

[6] xiao (owl)

Tr: refers to Nizhneudinsk (Нижнеудинск)people。

[7] 洛水：指博罗格勒，今称波罗格河。
[7] luo shui (luo water)
Tr: refers to Bologol, known today as Bologe River。
[8] 渭水：指奥克河。
[8] wei shui: refers to Ok River,
[9] 夹水：指阿嘎拉，今称安加拉河。实际向西流。
[9] jia shui (pinch water)
Tr: refers to Agara, aka: Angara River, in fact, the river flows west。
[10] 生水：指叶尼塞河。
[10] sheng shui (raw water)
Tr: refers to Yenisei River。

译文：由伊赫山往西北二百五十里，有座山叫伊尔库特山。山的西边住着索西博尔人，东边住着伊利姆族，狩猎氏族有扎姆佐尔族和卡赖族等氏族。波罗格河从山的南面流出，向东流入奥卡河；安加拉河从山的北面流出，向西流入叶尼塞河。
Translation:
Two hundred and fifty li further northwest from Yihe Mountain there stands the Irkut Mountain。On its west side live the Sosibir people, on its east side live the Ilim people, the hunting clans such as the Zamzor people and Kaly people。Bratak River rises from the south face of the mountain and flows east into Oka River。Angara River rises from the north face of the mountain and flows west into Yenisei River。

02-04-11 申首山
Shenshoushan
（95,76695E；54,2401N）

西北三百里，曰申首之山[1]，无草木[2]，东夏有雪[3]。申水[4] 出于其上，潜[5]于其下，是多白玉[6]。

注释：[1]申首山：指大阴山，谐音称萨彦山。
Notes： [1] shen shou shan (appeal head mount)
Tr: refers to the Big Yin Shan, a phonetic match to Sayan Mountains。
[2] 无草木：游牧部落地区。
[2] wu cao mu (no grass wood)
Tr: refers to the nomadic regions。
[3] 东夏有雪：指东萨彦岭。东，在此不是指方位，而是濮语"屏障"的音译。
[3] dong xia you xue (east summer has snow)
Tr: refers to the east Sayanling Mountains, east/dong, does not refer to the direction East as in Chinese but a Pu concept as a screen, a block, a phonetic match。
[4] 申水：指萨彦水。
[4] shen shui: refers to the Sayan River。
[5]潜：指迁，流向。
[5] qian（submerge）： migrant, flows to 。
[6] 白玉：在此指白夷，即突厥人。又称奥尔利柯人。
[6] bai yu (white jade)
Tr: refers to the white people, the turkish people, also known as the Orliq people。

译文：由伊尔库特山往西北三百里，有座山叫萨彦山，是游牧部落地区，又称东萨彦岭。萨彦水发源于山的西面，流向山的东面，这里生活着突厥人。
Translation:
Three hundred li further northwest from the Irkut Mountains stands the Sayan mountain, a place inhabited by the herdsmen clans。It is also known as the Dong(east) Sayanling mountain。Sayan River rises from this mountain's west flank and flows to the east of the mountain。 The Turkish people live here。

02-04-12 泾谷山
Jinggushan
（88,34843E；54,55191N）

又西百五十五里，曰泾谷之山[1]。泾水[2] 出焉，东南注于渭[3]，是多白金白玉[4]。

注释：[1]泾谷山：指卡拉戈尔山, 在萨亚诺戈尔斯克南面(53° 3′ 0″ N, 91° 27′ 0″ E) 53.05, 91.45(Temir Tau)Gorno Altay。
Notes: [1] jing gu shan: refers to the Karagor Mountains, to the south of Sayanogorsk。
[2] 泾水：指卡拉戈尔水，今称阿拉斯水。
[2] jing shui: refers to the Karagor River, known today as the Alas River。
[3]渭：指南河，是叶尼塞河的支流，今称赫奇克河。
[3] wei: refers to the Nan(south) River, a tributary of the Yenisei River, known today as the Keqike (Khemchik) River。The Khemchik 51° 44′ 7.08″ N, 92° 11′ 30.48″ E --51.7353, 92.1918。
[4] 白金白玉：指突厥部落和突厥人。
[4] bai jin bai yu (white gold white jade)
Tr: refers to the Turkish tribes and Turkish people。

译文：由东萨彦岭往西一百五十五里，有座山叫卡拉戈尔山。阿拉斯水从这里流出，向东南流入赫奇克河，这里住着突厥部落和突厥人。
Translation:
One hundred and fifty-five li further west from the east Sayanling Mountain, stands the Karagor Mountain。 The Alas River rises from this mountain and goes southeast into the Hechik River。 The Turkish tribes and Turkish people live here。

02-04-13 刚山
Gangshan
（85,95066E；51,96939N）

又西百二十里，曰刚山[1]，多柒木[2]，多㻬琈之玉[3]。刚水出焉[4]，北流注于渭[5]。是多神【光鬼】[6]，其状人面鸟身[7]，一足一手[8]，其音如钦[9]。

注释：[1]刚山：指戈尔诺山，在戈尔诺阿尔泰斯克西面。
Notes:[1] gang shan (strong mount) refers to the Gorno Mountain, which is to the west of Gorno Altaisk。
[2] 柒木：指克列牧民氏族。
[2] qi mu（lacquer wood）： refers to the Kelie herdsmen clans。
[3] 㻬琈之玉：指突胡夷，即突厥人。
[3] wu fu zhi yu (jade) refers to the turkish Hu Yi, the Turkish people。

[4] 刚水：指戈尔诺水，今称比斯克拉亚河。

[4] gang shui (strong water) refers to the Gorno River, known today as the Biyskraya （Biya） River。

[5]渭：指鄂毕河。

[5] wei (wei water) refers to the Ob River。

[6]神【光鬼】(wo)：指农业氏族。

[6] shen wo; refers to the agricultural clans。

[7] 人面鸟身：定居的僚族。

[7] ren mian niao shen (human face bird body) refers to the settled Lao/Liao people。

[8] 一足一手：指伊尔古族, 又称巴尔虎族, 既从事游牧业，也从事农业。

[8] yi zu yi shou (one foot one hand)

Tr: refers to the Yirgu tribe, also known as the Barhu (Barga Mogolian) tribe。 They are engaged in both nomadic husbandry and agriculture。

[9]钦：指乌怯列，今称戈尔诺阿尔泰斯克。

[9] qin: refers to Wuquelie （Ulala, Ulalu), known today as the Gorno Altaysk。

译文：由卡拉戈尔山往西一百二十里，有座山叫戈尔诺山，住着克列氏族，住着突厥人。戈尔诺水从这座山流出，向北流入鄂毕河。这里住着农业氏族，是定居的僚族伊尔古氏，住在乌怯列。

Translation:

One hundred and twenty li further west from Karagir[karagor] Mountain stands the Gorno Mountain。 The Kelie clan, a turkish people, live here。 The Gorno River flows out of the mountain and flows north into the Ob River。 An agricultural clan, the Irgu clan, a settled Lao people, lives in Wuquelie。

02-04-14 刚山尾

Gangshanwei

（78,93864E；52,56649N）

又西二百里，至刚山之尾[1]。洛水[2] 出焉，而北流注于河[3]。其中多蛮蛮[4]，其状鼠身而鳖首[5]，其音若吠犬[6]。

注释：[1]刚山之尾：指库隆达山，山体呈多列排列为狭长型，犹如匈奴人的发辨，故得名库隆达，意为象发辨样的山体。汉文化则视发辨为小尾巴，就将“达”译成“尾”。

Notes: [1] gang shan zhi wei/yi (strong mount's tail)

Tr: refers to the Kulunda Mountain。 The shape of the mountain's body looks like closely braided hair of the Xiongnu, hereby the name; a mountain resembles braided hair。 In Chinese, braided hair is usually compared to the tail, thus the word da, which is translated into 'tail', a transliteration of the meaning 。

[2] 洛水：指库隆达西面的河流，今称布拉河。实际向东北流。

[2] luo shui: refers to the water channel west of Kulunda Mountain, known today as the Bula River, which in fact flows in a northeast direction。

[3]河：指鄂毕河。

[3] he(river) refers to the Ob River。

[4] 蛮蛮：匈奴人苏克族的一个支系，善于饲养鹿。蛮蛮，意为回鹘。

[4] man-man: a branch of the Suke tribe of the Xiongnu people。 They are good at keeping deer herds。 Man-man means Huigu, a Chinese term for Uighur， huigu, weiwuer, 维吾尔，hui/wei, gu/ge/

[5] 鼠身而鳖首：苏克族的直系。

[5] shu shen er bie shou (rat body with turtle head)

Tr: refers to the direct descendants of the Suk tribe。

[6] 吠犬：指费斯怯卡，也称维斯怯卡，今称布拉哥斯维斯怯卡。
[6] fei quan (barking dog) refers to Feisiqueka, or Weisiqueka。Vischaqa or Wischaqa known today as Pragsvischaqa。

译文：由戈尔诺山往西二百里，有座山叫库隆达山。布拉河水从这里流出，向东北流入鄂毕河。这里生活着蛮蛮氏族，是苏克族的直系氏族，住在维斯怯卡。
Translation:
Two hundred li further west from Gorno Mountain there stands the Khulunda Mountain。Bula River rises out of the mountain and flows northeast into Ob River。 The Manman tribes, the direct descendants of the Suk tribes, live in Vischaqa。

02-04-15 英鞮山
Yingtishan
(71,46519E；51,16573N)

又西三百五十里，曰英鞮之山[1]，上多漆木[2]，下多金玉[3]，鸟兽尽白[4]。涴水[5]出焉，而北流注于陵羊之泽[6]，是多冉遗之鱼[7]，鱼身蛇首而六足[8]，其目如马耳[9]，食之使人不眯[10]，可以御凶[11]。

注释：[1]英鞮山：指伊铁米尔山，音译为英鞮山，后称埃斯塔纳或阿斯塔纳。
Notes: [1] ying ti shan(outstanding leather shoes mount)
Tr: refers to Yitemir Mountain, a phonetic match， known previously as Astana, today known as Nur Sultan。
[2] 漆木：指克吾卡人。
[2] qi mu (lacquered wood) refers to the Kheuka people。
[3] 金玉：指加拉干达人，今已发展至南面。
[3] jin yu (gold jade) refers to the Qaraganda （Karaganda, Karagandy) people who have further moved to the south。
[4] 鸟兽尽白：族群皆突厥人。
[4] niao shou jin bai (birds beasts all white) all the tribes are turkish。
[5] 涴水：指涴克特雅布尔水。
[5] wan shui: Wanketejiabur River。（Uakt yarbul river ）
[6] 陵羊之泽：今称斯马勘德湖
[6] ling yang zhi ze (ling goat's waterhole) refers to the Symkant (Shyamkant)Lake。
[7] 冉遗之鱼：指冉斯浦布里夷。冉斯浦布里是湖边的一个村镇。
[7] ran yi zhi yu (ran left the fish)
Tr: refers to the Ransipubli Yi, Ransipubli is a village town by the lake。
[8] 鱼身蛇首而六足：渔民塞族的母系氏族。
[8]yu shen she shou er liu zu (fish body snake head and six feet)
Tr: fishing clans of the Saka's matrilineal lineages。
[9] 其目如马耳：支系为缅纳支系。(Mayna) 53° 0′ 1″ N, 91° 28′ 56″ E； 53.000278, 91.482222
[9] qi mu ru ma er (its eyes like horse ears)
Tr: its branches are the Miana branch。
[10] 食之使人不眯：古老的定居缅族。
[10] shi zhi shi ren bu mi (eat it your eyes will not blur)
Tr: ancient Mian sedentary people。
[11] 可以御凶：哈萨克的匈奴人。
[11]ke yi yu xiong (can defend against brutality)

Tr： refers to the Kazakh Xiongnu people。

译文：由库隆达山往西三百五十里，有座山叫伊铁米尔山。山的西面住着克吾卡人，东面住着加拉干达人，这里的氏族皆为突厥人。涴克特雅布尔水发源于这座山，向北流入陵羊之泽。湖边住着冉斯浦布里渔民，是渔民塞族的母系氏族，其支系为缅纳支系，是古老的定居缅族，是哈萨克的匈奴。

Translation:

Three hundred and fifty li further west from the Khulunda Mountain there stands the Yitemir Mountain。 On its west side live the Khouka people, on its east side live the Jialaganda people。 All the people here are of the Turkish ethnicity。 Wanketeyabuer River rises out of this mountain and goes north into Lingyang Lake。 The Ransipubuli fishing population lives there on the lake side, they are the Saka's （Sarts） matrilineal branches。 Its branch is the Miana tribe, an ancient, settled Miana people。 They are the Kazakh's Xiongnu。

02-04-16 中曲山

Zhongqushan

（63,49598E；49,65268N）

又西三百里，曰中曲之山[1]。其阳多玉[2]，其阴多雄黄、白玉即金[3]。有兽焉，其状如马而白身黑尾[4]，一角，虎牙爪[5]，音如鼓音[6]，其名曰駮[7]，是食虎豹[8]，可以御兵[9]。有木焉，其状如棠[10]，而员叶赤实[11]，实大如木瓜[12]，名曰櫰木[13]，食之多力[14]。

注释：[1]中曲山：指哈萨克斯坦图尔盖高原。"图尔盖"、"图撮"都是指突厥的草原之意。图也与托谐音，指中部，此处将北部草原的"图撮"译为中曲，就是这个原因。

Notes： [1] zhong qu shan (middle music mount)

Tr: refers to the Tolgai plateau， Turlgai， tucuo all refer to the Turkish steppe。 Tu/tuo/means middle section, a phonetic close match， the reason to be translated into middle (zhong)， which is in the Northern steppe。

[2]玉：指伊尔吉兹氏族。

[2]yu (jade) refers to the Irgiz clan。

[3] 雄黄、白玉、金：指绍拉克赛、图尔盖、杰尔温三个部落氏族。

[3] xiong huang, bai yu, jin (male yellow, white jade, gold)

Tr： refer to the Shulaksy clan, Turgai (also spelled Turgay or Turgaj) clan and Jirvn clan。

[4] 马而白身黑尾：指胡族的突厥贵族。

[4]ma er bai shen hei yi (horse with white body black tail)

Tr: refers to the elite Turkish nobles of the Hu people。

[5] 一角虎牙爪：伊科夫河支系氏族。伊科夫河是托博尔河的东侧支流。

[5] yi jiao hu ya zhua (one horn tiger teeth claw)

Tr: refers to the Yikev River clan. Yikev river is the east tributary of Tobol River。

[6] 鼓音：指科伊，今称博罗夫斯科伊。

[6]gu yin (drum sound)

Tr: refers to Koy, today known as the Bolovskoy。(Borovsy)

[7]駮：指博罗夫氏。

[7] jiao: refers to the Bolov Shi。

[8] 是食虎豹：是古老的胡人农业氏族。

[8] shi shi hu bao (is eats tiger leopard)

Tr: the ancient agricultural clans of the Hu people。

[9] 可以御兵：哈萨克的直系夷。兵，读比，指直系。

[9] ke yi yu bing (can defend against soldiers)

Tr： refers to the Kazakh's direct lineages, bing(soldier) reads as bi, which means direct lineage。

[10]棠：指图尔盖。
[10] tang: Turgai plateau。
[11] 员叶赤实：草原游牧氏族。
[11] yuan ye chi shi (member leaf red fruit)
Tr: refers to the steppe nomadic clans。
[12] 实大如木瓜：科斯塔奈牧城人。
[12] shi da ru mu gua (fruit big as wood melon)
Tr： refers to the Kustana herdsman's township people。
[13] 櫰木：指贺蒙则柯氏。
[13] huai mu: （huai/gui wood）
Tr： refers to the Hemengzeke people， (shepherd clans) 。
[14] 食之多力：古老的德内人。德内人，即丁伶人。
[14] shi zhi duo li :(eat it more energy)
Tr: the ancient Dene people, also known as the Dingling people。

译文：由伊铁山往西三百里，有座山叫图尔盖山。山的南面住着伊尔吉兹氏族，北面住着绍拉克赛、图尔盖和杰尔温氏族。有一个氏族，是胡族的突厥贵族支系的伊科夫河支系氏族，住在博罗夫斯科伊，名叫博罗夫氏，是古老的胡人农业氏族，是哈萨克的直系氏族。有一群牧民，是图尔盖草原的游牧氏族，是科斯塔奈牧城人，名叫贺蒙则柯氏，是古老的德内人。
Translation：
Three hundred li further west from the Yitemir Mountain (伊铁米尔山） stands the Turgai plateau。 In its south lives the Irgiz clan, in its north lives the Shaolakesai clan, the Tolgai clan, and the Jerwen clan。 One clan is from the Hu 's Turkish noble lineage, they are the Yikev river clan, living at Bolovskoy。 They are the Bolov people, the ancient agricultural clan of the Hu people。 They are the direct lineage of the Kazakhs。One group of herders are from the nomadic Tulgai steppes, they are the Kustana herder's town people, known as the Hemengzeke people, they are the ancient Dene people。

02-04-17 邽山
Guishan
(58,91606E；49,42007N)

又西二百六十里，曰邽山[1]。其上有兽焉，其状如牛，蝟毛[2]，名曰穷奇[3]，音如獋狗[4]，是食人[5]。濛水[6] 出焉，南流注于洋水 [7] ，其中多黄贝；蠃鱼 [8] ，鱼身而鸟翼[9]，音如鸳鸯[10]，见则其邑大水[11]。

注释：[1]邽山：指穆戈贾尔山。简称戈山，谐音邽山。
Notes:[1] gui shan, refers to the Mugodzhar Hills 48° 38′ 38″ N, 58° 32′ 47″ E, shortened to Gorshan, a phonetic match to Guishan 。
[2]牛，蝟毛：应为牛蝟毛，指赫罗姆人。也称罗姆人。
[2] niu, wei mao (ox, porcupine hair) should be niu-wei-mao:
Tr: refers to the Huorom people， which is also known as the Rom people。
[3] 穷奇：克列托盖氏族译为汉语，即为穷奇。也称克列人，属突厥族。
[3] qiong qi (poor strange)
Tr: A Chinese translation for the Kelie-tuogai tribe。 Also known as the Kelie （Keri） people， they are of the Turkish ethnicity。
[4] 獋狗：指赫罗姆城，今称阿克托别城。

[4] gao gou: refers to the Huoluomu city, today's Aktyubinsky city, (Aqtübä) 54° 49′ 0″ N, 52° 48′ 0″ E。

[5] 是食人：是古老的定居氏族。

[5] shi shi ren (is eats humans) refers to the ancient, settled people。

[6] 濛水：指穆戈贾尔水。

[6] meng shui: Mugodzhar River。

[7] 洋水：指里海。

[7] yang shui（big water): refers to the Caspian Sea。

[8] 黄贝嬴鱼：指北贝什诺伊氏族。黄，是"北" 概念 "武" 的音译。

[8] huang bei ying yu (yellow back win fish) refers to the northern Byshinuoy tribe。Huang/wu/north。

[9] 鱼身而鸟翼：渔民氏族的诺伊氏。鸟，读诺音。

[9] yu shen er niao yi (fish body and bird wings)
Tr: refers to the Nuoy Shi of the fishing tribes, Niao/nuo。

[10] 鸳鸯：指恩巴城。

[10] yuanyang: water fowl, refers to the Emba city。

[11] 大水：指达罕氏族，即统治氏族。

[11] da shui (big water) refers to the great Khan clan, the ruling tribes。

译文：由图尔盖山往西南二百六十里，有座山叫穆戈贾尔山。山的西面有一个氏族，是赫罗姆人，名叫克列托盖氏，住在赫罗姆城，是古老的定居氏族。穆戈贾尔水从山间流出，向南流入里海，这里生活着北贝什诺伊氏族，是渔民氏族的诺伊氏，住在恩巴城，是那里的达罕氏族。
Translation:
Two hundred and sixty li further southwest from the Turgay Mountain stands the Mugodzhar Hills。 On its west side live the Hor-roma people。 They are also known as the Kelie turgay people, who live in the Horom city。 They are the settled township people。Mugodzhar River flows out of the mountain and goes south into the Caspian Sea。The northern Byshinuoy clans live here。The fishing clan of the Nuoy Shi live in Emba city, they are the Khan lineage there。

02-04-18 鸟鼠同穴山
Niaoshutongxue Mountain
（56,91998E；57,43215N）

又西二百二十里，曰鸟鼠同穴之山[1]。其上多白虎、白玉[2]。渭水[3] 出焉，而东流注于河[4]。其中多鳋鱼[5]，其状如鳣鱼[6]，动则其邑有大兵[7]。滥水[8]出于其西，西流注于汉水[9]。多【如/鱼】(ru)魮之鱼[10]，其状如覆銚[11]，鸟首而鱼翼[12]，音如磬石之声[13]，是生珠玉[14]。

注释：[1]鸟鼠同穴山：指罗斯妥羲山，又称乌拉尔山。罗斯妥羲，俄罗斯的古称谓。实际指乌拉尔山南麓以及哈萨克斯坦的乌拉尔地区。
Notes:[1] niao shu tong xue shan (bird rat in same cave mount)
Tr: refers to the Russ Tuoxi Mountain, known today as the Ural Mountain, Russ Tuoxi being an ancient name for Russia。This is a description of the south part of the Ural Mountain and the Ural area in Kazakhstan。

[2] 白虎、白玉：指吐胡吐夷，即突厥族群。

[2] bai hu, bai yu (white tiger, white jade)
Tr： refers to the Tu Hu, Tu Yi, the turkish clans。

[3] 渭水：指别廖佐沃水，简称沃水，谐音渭水。

[3] wei shui: a coded name for Byliuzuov (Beryozovo) River, shortened to Uo River, a phonetic match for Wei。

[4]河：指鄂毕河。
[4] he: Ob River。
[5] 鳋鱼：索利卡姆夷，简称索夷，谐音鳋鱼。
[5] sao yu（sao fish）: refers to Sulykam/Соликáмск/Solikam people, shortened to Suo Yi, a phonetic match to Sao Yu, suoyi/saoyu。
[6] 鳣鱼：朝拉夷，简称朝夷，谐音鳣鱼。
[6] zhan1 yu(sturgeon)
Tr: refers to Chaola (Chora, Pechora River) people, shortened to Chao/Cho yi, a phonetic match to zhan yu, shao/zhan, yi/yu。
[7] 动则其邑有大兵：塔吉尔地区属于他管辖。塔吉尔，又称西塔吉尔。与表示东塔吉尔的下塔吉尔对应。
[7] dong ze qi yi you da bing (move so its city see big soldier)
Tr: Tajil area belongs to his sovereign。 Tajil, also known as West Tajil, corresponding to the Nizhny Tagil（Нижний Тагил） East Tajil or the lower Tajil; in Pu concept, west is up,(higher), east is down (lower)。
[8] 滥水：指切尔内水。(车尔尼？车尔臣河，且末河：Qiemo river)
[8] jian shui: qie-er-nei, refers to Chelyn River。
[9] 汉水：指阿斯特拉罕河，简称罕河。今称伏尔加河。
[9] han shui (han river)
Tr: refers to Astrakhan River, shortened to Han River, known today as the Volga River。 Han/khan a close phonetic match。
[10] 【如/鱼】(ru)魮之鱼：指乌法河渔民，简称乌沘渔。乌沘是切尔内河的支流。
[10] ru bi zhi yu (ru bi zhi fish)
Tr: refers to the fishing people on Ufa River, simply as Wubiyu.Ufa River is a tributary of the Chelny River。
[11] 覆銚：指东塔吉尔人。
[11] fu tiao (overturn pot)
Tr: it refers to eastern Tajil people。
[12] 鸟兽而鱼翼：俄罗斯族的大支系。
[12] niao shou er yu yi(bird beast with fish wings)
Tr: the major branch of the Russian ethnic people。
[13] 磬石之声：切尔内之所。
[13] pan shi zhi sheng (pan music stone voice) Chelny 's place。
[14] 是生珠玉：是两岔河地区的渔民。乌法河与切尔内河交汇处，称两岔河地区。
[14] shi sheng zhu yu (is born pearl jade)
Tr: the fishing people on the two rivers' confluence, known as the place on the two rivers。

译文：由穆戈贾尔山往西北二百二十里，有座山叫乌拉尔山。这里住着白胡白夷，别廖佐沃水从山间流出，向东流入鄂毕河。这里住着索利卡姆夷，是朝拉支系氏族，塔吉尔地区都属于他管辖。切尔内水从山的西面流出，向西流入伏尔加河。这里住着乌法河渔民，是东塔吉尔氏族，是俄罗斯的大支系氏族，住在切尔内之所，是两岔河地区的渔民。

Translation:

Two hundred and twenty li further northwest from the Mugodzhar Hills (Mugodzhar Mountain), stands the Ural Mountain。 The white Hu, white Yi live here。Beryozovo River rises from the mountain and goes east into Ob River。 The Suolikam people live there, they are the Chaola (Chora)branch, the ruling tribe of the Tajil area。 Chelny River flows out of the west part of the mountain and flows westwards into the Volga River。 The Ufa River fishermen live here, they are known as the East Tajil tribe, a major branch of the Russian people。They live in what is known as Chelny 's place, they are fishermen at a place where two rivers meet。

02-04-19 崦嵫山
Yanzishan
(44,65924E；43,02943N)

西南三百六十里，曰崦嵫之山[1]。其上多丹木[2]，其叶如榖[3]，其实大如瓜[4]，赤符而黑理[5]，食之已瘅[6]，可以御火[7]。其阳多龟[8]，其阴多玉[9]。苕水[10]出焉，而西流注于海[11]，其中多砥砺[12]。有兽焉，其状马身而鸟翼[13]，人面蛇尾[14]，是好举人[15]，名曰孰湖[16]。有鸟焉，其状如鸮而人面，蜼身犬尾[17]，其名自号也，见则其邑大旱[18]。

凡西次四经自阴山以下至于崦嵫之山，凡十九山，三千六百八十里。其神祠：皆用一白鸡[19]祈，糈以稻米，白菅为席[20]。

右《西经》之山，凡七十七山，(实际 76 山)一万七千五百一十七里。

注释：[1]崦嵫山：指大高加索山。
Notes: [1] yan zi shan: it refers to the Greater Caucasus Mountain。
[2] 丹木：指鞑牧，即游牧氏族。
[2] dan mu (red wood)
Tr: it refers to the Nomadic Tartar, the nomadic herdsman clans。
[3] 其叶如榖：支系为高加索支系。
[3] qi ye ru gu (its leaves like grain),
Tr: it refers to the branches belonging to the Caucasus clan。
[4] 其实大如瓜：克拉斯达尔国。
[4] qi shi da ru gua (its fruits big as melon)
Tr: it refers to the Klasdar nation。
[5] 赤符而黑理：契费人的贵族支系。
[5] chi fu er hei li (red marking and black stripes)
Tr: it refers to the noble clan of the Qifei people 。
[6] 食之已瘅：古老的达尔夷。
[6] shi zhi yi dan (eat can cure fatigue)
Tr: it refers to the ancient Dar Yi。
[7] 可以御火：高加索的牧羊族。御火，即延贺，指牧羊。
[7] ke yi yu huo (can protect from fire)
Tr: it refers to the shepherd clans from the Caucasus, Yuhuo--yanhe, a phonetic match for herders –sheep keeping 。
[8]龟：指格鲁吉亚人。
[8] gui(turtle)
Tr: a phonetic match for the Gerogians.in Pinyin: gelujiya, gelu/gui/Georgian。
[9]玉：指杰尔沘氏族。
[9]yu(jade) refers to Jierbi clans。
[10] 苕水：指向西北或东北方向流的河流，这里指杰尔沘。
[10] tiao shui: refers to rivers flowing towards northwest or northeast, here it refers to the Jierbi River。
[11]海：指亚速海。
[11] hai: the Azov Sea
[12] 砥砺：指符拉迪克人。
[12] di li: refers to the Vladik people。
[13] 马身而鸟翼：胡族的俄罗斯支系。
[13]ma shen er niao yi (horse body and bird wings)

Tr: it refers to the Hu people's Russian branch。

[14] 人面蛇尾：定居的塞夷。（实际是定居的高加索雅利安人而非塞夷）

[14] ren mian she yi (human face snake tail)

Tr: it refers to the Saka people who settled down as township people。 (Refers to the settled Caucasus Aryans, not the Saka people) 。

[15] 是好举人：是奥克兹居民。

[15] shi hao ju ren (is good lift people)

Tr: it refers to the Avkaz residents.

[16] 孰湖：指高加索胡，简称索胡。

[16] shu hu (which lake)

Tr: it refers to the Caucasus' Hu people, shortened to Sou Hu。

[17] 鸮而人面蜼身犬尾：东部定居的阿塞拜疆犬戎。

[17] xiao er ren mian zhui shen quan ye (owl with human face worm body dog tail)

Tr: it refers to the settled Azerbaijan Dogrong people in the east part。

[18] 大旱：达罕氏族。

[18] da han (big drought)

Tr: a phonetic match of drought in Chinese; han/khan, refers to the king clan。

[19] 白鸡：指白璧。

[19] bai ji (white chicken) refers to white jade Bi 。

[20] 白菅为席：茅草人为通灵命官。

[20] bai qian wei xi (white reeds mattress)

Tr: use straw made manikins for messenger in rite。

译文：由乌拉尔山往西南三百六十里，有座山叫大高加索山。这里住着游牧民族，支系为高加索克拉斯达尔国契费人的贵族支系，是古老的达尔夷，是高加索的牧羊氏族。山的南面住着格鲁吉亚人，北面住着杰尔沘氏族。苕水（杰尔沘）从这里流出，向西北流入亚速海，河边住着符拉迪克人。有一个氏族，是胡族的俄罗斯支系定居的塞夷，是奥克兹居民，名叫索胡。有一群人，是东部定居的阿塞拜疆犬戎，他们自己也这样称呼，是那个地区的达罕氏族。

Translation:

Three hundred and sixty li further southwest from the Ural Mountains stands the Great Caucasus Mountain。 The nomads live here, one is the ancient Dar Yi, the noble branch of the Qifei people of the Klasdar nation of the Caucasus' shepherd clans。 On the south side live the Georgians。 On the north side live the Jierbi clans。 Tiao （Jierbi ） River flows out of here and goes northwest into the Azov Sea. On the bank of the river live the Vladic people 。One tribe, the settled Saka people from the Russ Hu people, is the Avkaz people, they are known as the Suo Hu。 Another group of people, Azerbaijan's Dogrong who settled in the east part, address themselves as such and are the Khan clan in that area。

In sum, the 4th list of the mountains in the west between the Ying Mountain and the Great Caucasus Mountains, records a total of 19 mountains, covering a distance of 3,680 li。 When offering sacrifice to those mountain deities, a white jade Bi is used。Rice is also used, and one straw man acts as the messenger。 Hereby, the total number of the mountains in Book Two is 77, covering a distance of 17,517 li。

第三卷北山经 （Mountains in the North）

北山第一山系

Book 3 Beishanjing; chapter 1

03-01-01 单狐山
Danhushan
（110,71247E；35,59367N）

北山经之首，曰单狐之山[1]，多机木[2]，其上多华草[3]。逢水[4] 出焉，而西流注于泑水 [5]，其中多茈石文石 [6] 。

注释：[1]单狐山：指汾河口的山，一般译为"当汾山"，在山西运城河津市、稷山市北面。
Notes:[1] dan hu shan (single fox mount)
Tr: it refers to the mountain at the river mouth of Fen River, usually termed as Dangfenshan, Dan/Dang: phonetic shift。 Danhushan is situated in Hejin city, Yuncheng County, in Shanxi (west of mountain) province, north of Jishan city。 35° 1′ 35.04″ N, 111° 0′ 27.36″ E。

[2] 机木：指稷峰镇牧民。
[2] ji mu (machine wood)
Tr： it refers to the Herders from Jifeng town, 35° 36′ 14.18″ N, 110° 58′ 42.06″ E。

[3] 华草：指化裕氏移民。
[3] hua cao（vibrant grass)
Tr: it refers to the migrants who bear the surname of Huayu。

[4] 逢水：指汾水。
[4] feng shi (feng water)
Tr: it refers to Fen River, fen/feng， a phonetic shifting。

[5] 泑水：指黄河。
[5] you shui (you water)
Tr: it refers to the Yellow River/Huanghe River。

[6] 茈石文石：指河津氏族和泉镇氏族。

[6]bi shi wen shi (bi stone wen stone)
Tr: it refers to Hejin(riverside)clans and Quanzhen (spring town) clans。

译文：北山经第一山系最南端的山，叫当汾山，这里住着稷峰牧民，西面住着化裕氏移民。汾水从这里流过，向西流入黄河，河畔住着河津氏族和泉镇氏族。
Translation:
The southmost mountain of the 1st list of mountains in the North is called Dangfenshan。 The Jifeng herders live here。 On its west side live the Huayu Shi migrants。 Fen River flows through here and goes west into the Yellow River。 On its riverbanks live the Hejin clans and Quanzhen clans。

03-01-02 求如山
Qiurushan
（110,68255E；36,09869N）

又北二百五十里，曰求如之山[1]。其上多铜[2]，其下多玉 [3]，无草木 [4] 。滑水[5] 出焉，而西流注于诸毗之水[6]。其中多滑鱼[7]，其状如鱓(shan)[8]，赤背[9]，其音如梧[10]，食之已疣[11]。其中多水马[12]，其状如马，文臂牛尾[13]，其音如呼[14]。

注释：[1]求如山：指管坡山，今称管头山。实际介绍整个吉县。
Notes:[1] qiu ru shan（seek likewise mount）
Tr: it refers to Guanposhan, known today as Guantoushan。 This segment is in fact about the whole Ji County (36° 5′ 48.12″ N, 110° 40′ 50.16″ E) 。
[2]铜：指教岭氏族。今称文城氏族。
[2] tong(copper)
Tr： it refers to the Jiaoling clan, today known as the Wencheng clan。
[3]玉：指舆氏族。今称车城氏族。
[3]yu (jade)
Tr: it refers to the Yu clan, known today as the Che(car)cheng clan。Yu（玉、舆-车）che, car, cart。
[4] 无草木：游牧部落。
[4] wu cao mu (no grass wood)
Tr： it refers to nomadic tribes。
[5] 滑水：指南水。今称兰家河。
[5] hua shui (slippery water)
Tr： it refers to Nan(south) River, known today as Lanjia River。
[6] 诸毗之水：指州川河，是兰家河的下游。
[6] zhu bi zhi shui（various neighboring waters）
Tr: it refers to Zhouchuan River, a lower tributary of the Lanjia River。
[7] 滑鱼：指南部夷，今称鄂夷。
[7] hua yu (slipper fish)
Tr： it refers to Nanbu Yi--people from south, known today as E Yi。
[8]鱓：指中垛和桐柏氏族。
[8] shan (powerful fish)
Tr: it refers to Zhongduo clan and Tongbai clan。
[9] 赤背：指赤沘，即黄河支系。
[9] chi bei (bare back)
Tr： it refers to Chibi-- chi, red, bi water, refers to the Yellow River's tributary。
[10]梧：指崖头。今称吉昌镇

[10] wu (Chinese parasol tree)
Tr： it refers to Yantou (cliff head), known today as Jichangzhen (36° 5′ 52.12″ N, 110° 40′ 45.05″ E) 。
[11] 食之已疣：古老的阳夷。疣，指阳。
[11] shi zhi yi you （eat it cure worts）
Tr：it refers to the ancient Yang Yi。You (sunny, yang) 。
[12] 水马：指教岭苗族。水，濮语 "教" 的不同读音。
[12] shui ma (water horse)
Tr：it refers to Jiaoling Miao clans; Pu concept jiao/teach, reads as shui, one of the pronunciations。
[13] 文臂牛尾：指文河僚夷。
[13] wen bi niu yi (script arm ox tail)
Tr: it refers to the Liao Yi from Wen River。
[14]呼：指马城。今称文城。
[14]hu(shout)
Tr: it refers to Macheng (horse city) known today as Wencheng city。

译文：由当汾山往东北二百五十里，有座山叫管头山。山的西面住着教岭氏族，山的东面住着车城氏族。兰家河水从这里流出，向西流入州川河。这里住着鄂夷，是中垛和桐柏氏族的黄河支系，住在吉昌镇，是古老的阳夷。这里还住着教岭苗，是苗族的文河僚夷，住在文城。

Translation:

Two hundred and fifty li further northeast from Dangfenshan there stands the Guantoushan。 On its west side lives the Jiaoling clan, on its east side, the Checheng clan。Lanjia River flows out of this mountain and goes west into Zhouchuan River。 The E 'clan lives here, it belongs to the Yellow River branch of Zhongduo and Tongbai clans。They live in Jichangzhen, an ancient people known as Yang Yi。The Jiaoling Miao people also live here, they are the Liao people from Wen River, living in Wencheng city。

03-01-03 带山

Daishan

（111,18257E； 36,98229N）

又北三百里，曰带山[1]。其上多玉[2]， 其下多青碧 [3] 。有兽焉，其状如马 [4]， 一角有错 [5]， 其名曰臛(guan)疏 [6], 可以辟火 [7] 。有鸟焉，其状如乌[8]，五采而赤文[9]，名曰鵸鵌[10]，是自为牝牡[11]，食之不疽[12]。彭水[13]出焉，而西流注于芘湖之水[14]，其中多儵鱼[15]，其状如鸡而赤毛[16]。三尾六足四首[17]，其音如鹊[18]，食之可以已忧[19]。

注释：[1]带山：指交口山，在山西吕梁市交口县。
Notes:[1] dai shan （belt mount）
Tr：it refers to Jiaokoushan, in Jiaokou county, Luliang city, Shanxi province (36° 55′ 0″ N, 111° 20′ 0″ E) 。
[2]玉：指西卫氏族。
[2]yu(jade)
Tr：it refers to Xiwei clan。Xiwei: west guard。
[3] 青碧：指红桃坡氏族。
[3] qing bi (green clear blue)
Tr: it refers to the Hongtaopo (red peach slope) clan。
[4]马：指胡族。
[4]ma(horse)refers to the Hu ethnic people。
[5] 一角有错：大支系的迁徙氏族。
[5] yi jiao you cuo (one horn have mistake)

Tr: it refers to the migrant clans of the major branches。

[6]朧(guan)蔬：手工艺师的称谓。作为群体称为朧输氏，也称公输氏，是著名的手工业和工匠氏族。

[6] guan shu (guan vegetable)

Tr： it refers to the title of handicrafts masters。 As a group of handicraftsmen, this community is known as Guanshushi, or Gongshushi, a clan famous for tool masters and their craftsmanship。

[7] 可以辟火：夏国的手工业胡。火，胡的谐音。

[7]ke yi bi huo (can avoid fire)

Tr: it refers to the Xia nation's famous handicrafts Hu。Fire (huo) and hu is a pun in Chinese, huo/hu。

[8]乌：指北方的。

[8] wu (bird)， refers to north, or northern。

[9] 五采而赤文：千山部落的移民。采，指豺山，今称千山。

[9] wu cai er chi wen (five color and red markings)

Tr： refers to the migrants from the Qianshan (thousand mountains) tribes, cai(采，豺，千) close in sound, refers to Qianshan。

[10] 鵸鵌：指千山夷。

[10] qi tu(bird) refers to Qianshan Yi。

[11] 自为牝牡：芝水河畔。

[11] zi wei qin mu(hermaphrodite)

Tr: it refers to Zhi River banks。

[12] 食之不疽：古老的林胡。不疽，指补举，即林胡。

[12] shi zhi bu ju (eaten to stop swallow)

Tr： it refers to the ancient Lin Hu people, bu ju—Linhu。

[13] 彭水：指交水又称交口河。今称城川河。

[13] peng shui: refers to Jiaoshui River, or Jiaokou River, known today as Chengchuan River。

[14] 芘湖之水：指陡坡水。

[14]bi hu zhi shui (bi lake water) refers to Doupo River。

[15]儵(shu)鱼：即肃夷，指狩猎夷。

[15] shu yu (shu fish) refers to Su Yi, a hunting Yi。

[16] 鸡而赤毛：指雉鸡场山的移民。雉鸡场山在伊勒呼里山西北面。

[16] ji er shi mao (rooster with red feathers)

Tr: refers to the migrants from Zhijichang Mountain, which is on the northwest side of Yilehuli Mountain (51°19′14″N 124°04′04″E) 。

[17] 三尾六足四首：三岔河的母系氏族。三岔河，今称午城。

[17] san wei/yi, liu zu si shou (three tails, six feet, four heads)

Tr： it refers to the Matrilineal clans at Sancha (three fork) river, today the place is known as Wu(noon) city。

[18]鹊：指南面。

[18] que(sparrow) refers to the south.

[19] 食之可以已忧：古老的夏国的奥洛奇夷。奥是多音字，也读 you 音。

[19] shi zhi ke yi yi you (eat this to cure worries)

Tr: it refers to the ancient Oluoqi Yi of the Xia nation。 Ao, O, You, all registered by one Chinese graph: ao 奥。

译文：由管头山往北三百里，有座山叫交口山。山的西面住着西卫氏族，东面住着红桃坡氏族。有一个氏族，是胡族大支系的迁徙氏族，名叫公输氏，是夏国的手工业胡。有一群人，是北方的千山部落的移民，叫千山夷，住芝水河畔，是古老的林胡。交口水从山间流出，向西流入陡坡河，这里住着狩猎夷，是雉鸡场山的移民，是三岔河的母系氏族，住在南面，是夏国古老的奥洛奇夷。

Translation:

Three hundred li further north from Guantoushan there stands Jiaokoushan。 On its west side live the Xiwei (west guard) clans, on its east side, the Hongtaopo (red peach slope) clans。 A Hu tribe, a major migrant people is called Gongshu Shi。 They are the handicraftsman group from the Qianshan clans from the North。 The Qianshan people live on the Zhi Riverbank, they are the Lin Hu people with a long history。 Jiaokou river flows out of the mountain and goes westward into Doupo River。 The hunting Yi lives here, they are a matrilineal people from Sancha River, they are the immigrants from Zhuijichang Mountain, living on the south side of the mountain。 They are the ancient Aoluoqi Yi of the Xia nation。

03-01-04 谯明山
Qiaomingshan
（111,11631E；38,17119N）

又北四百里，曰谯明之山[1]。谯水[2] 出焉，西流注于河 [3] 。其中多何罗之鱼 [4] ，一首十身[5] ，其音如吠犬[6]，食之已痈[7]。有兽焉，其状如貆而赤豪[8]，其音如榴榴[9]，名曰孟槐[10]，可以御凶[11]。是山也，无草木[12]，多青雄黄[13]。

注释：[1]谯明山：指湫明山。今称黑茶山。实际介绍山南的湫河流域。
Notes:[1] qiao ming shan: refers to Qiumingshan, a rebus, today known as Heichashan (black tea mount) 。This segment is about the Qiu River basin on the south side of the mountain。

[2] 谯水：指湫水。
[2] qiao shui (watch water) refers to Qiu River。

[3]河：指黄河。
[3] he: Yellow River。

[4] 何罗之鱼：指碛石之夷，在此指碛口之夷。
[4] he luo zhi yu (how net the fish)
Tr: it refers to the Qishi Yi。 Qishi, here refers to the Qikou Yi。

[5] 一首十身：大氏族的博恒氏。
[5] yi shou shi shen (one head ten bodies)
Tr: refers to the Boheng Shi, they form a big clan。

[6] 吠犬：指东碛，也称东岐。
[6] fei quan (barking dog)
Tr: it refers to Dongqi (east stony river side) also known as Dongqi, east fork。

[7] 食之已痈：古老的雍夷，雍，指丛罗。
[7] shi zhi yi yon (eaten to get rid of swollenness) refers to the ancient Yong people, Yong, refers to Congluo, a relic placename。

[8] 貆而赤豪：山区的游胡。
[8] huan er chi hao (young racoon dog with red brittles)
Tr: it refers to the nomadic Hu from the mountains。

[9] 榴榴：临县县城古称迎湄，读音 liuliu。
[9] liu liu: ancient name for Lin County seat, called Yingmei, in Pu concept, it reads Liuliu。

[10] 孟槐：临县县城西侧的靠山称为孟山，读音孟槐。
[10] meng huai: Styphnolobium japonicum Schott
Tr: it refers to the Kaoshan, which is also known as Mengshan in the west side of the county, reads in Pu as Menghuai。 Huai/shan/mountain。

[11] 可以御凶：夏国的匈奴夷。
[11]ke yi yu xun (can defend from viscous ones)

Tr: it refers to the Xiongnu (Hun Yi) of the Xia nation。

[12] 无草木：游牧部落。

[12] wu cao mu (no grass wood)

Tr: it refers to the nomads。

[13] 青雄黄：东部的匈奴胡。

[13] qing xiong huang（green male yellow)

Tr: refers to the eastern Huns (Xiongnu) qing/east, xiong/xiong, huang/hu。

译文：由交口山往北四百里，有座山叫湫明山，湫水从山上流出，向西流入黄河。这里住着碛口夷，是大氏族的博恒氏，住在东碛，是古老的雍夷。有一个氏族，是山区的游牧胡，住在迎湄，名叫孟山氏，是夏国的匈奴夷。这座山是游牧地区，住着东部的匈奴胡。

Translation:

Four hundred li further north from Jiaokoushan there stands Qiumingshan. Qiu River flows down from the mountain and goes west into the Yellow River。 The Qikou Yi, the Boheng Shi of the major clan live in Dongqi, and they are age-old nomadic Hu from the mountains。They live in Yingmei, known as Mengshan Shi, also known as the Xiongnu Yi from the Xia nation。 This mountain is the place of the nomads, the Xiongnu Hu from the east live here。

03-01-05 涿光山

Zhuguangshan

（111,08167E；39,02103N）

又北三百五十里，有座山叫涿光之山[1]。嚣水[2] 出焉，而西流注于河 [3] 。其中多鳛鳛之鱼 [4] ，其状如鹊而十翼[5] ，鳞皆在羽端[6]，其音如鹊，可以御火[7]，食之不瘅[8]。其上多松柏[9]，其下多棳橿[10]，其兽多麢羊[11]，其鸟多蕃[12]。

注释：[1]涿光山：指洼窖。后称保德。今山西保德县有窖洼乡。

Notes:[1] zhuo guang shan (dripping light mount)

Tr: it refers to Wajiao, later known as Baode, today's Baode county, where there is a Jiaowa village in Baode county, Shanxi Province, but the word order is reversed。

[2] 嚣水：朱家川又称赵水，古音为勺水，谐音嚣水。

[2] xiao shui (noisy water)

Tr: it refers to Zhujiachuan River, also known as Zhao River。 Its ancient name reads as Shao(spoon) River, a pun on Xiao, shao/xiao/zhao。

[3]河：指黄河。

[3] he(river) refers to the Yellow River。

[4] 鳛鳛之鱼：指零散的、少量的人。

[4] xi xi zhi yu (loach)

Tr: it refers to a small number of people, few and scattered。

[5] 鹊而十翼：南面的山区夷。十，读博，指山。

[5] que er shi yi (sparrow with ten wings)

Tr: it refers to the mountainous Yi in the south side, shi; reads in Pu as bo, means mountain。

[6] 鳞皆在羽端：定居在河口。

[6] lin jie zai yu duan (scales on the tip of the feathers)

Tr: settled by the river mouth (Ust)。

[7] 可以御火：夏国的延贺氏族，即牧羊氏族。

[7]ke yi yu huo (can stop fire)

Tr: it refers to the Yanhe clan, a sheep keeping clan of Xia nation。

[8] 食之不瘅：古老的补鞑。即古老的游牧氏族。

[8] shi zhi bu dan (eat to stop fatigue)

Tr: it refers to ancient Buda （鞑族）, an age-old nomadic clan。

[9] 松柏：指深洼氏族。

[9] song bai (pine poplar)

Tr: it refers to the Shenwa (deep low land) clan。

[10] 椶橿：指山梁氏族。

[10] zong jiang (palm tree, nan wood)

Tr： it refers to the Shanliang (mountain range) clans。

[11] 麢羊：读鬲秧，指府谷氏族。

[11] ling yang(sheep)

Tr: Pu concept reads as 【li yang】, a pun on yang: sheep, grain shoots, refers to the Fugu clan。 Fu, big house, gu, grain。

[12]蕃：指东关。

[12] fan(foreign) refers to East pass, Dong Guan。

译文：由湫明山往北三百五十里，有座山叫洼窖山。赵水从山间流出，向西流入黄河。这里住着少量的居民，是南岸的山区夷，定居在河口，住在南岸，是夏国的牧羊氏族，是古老的牧民。洼窖的西边住着深洼氏族，东边住着山梁氏族。有些氏族住在府谷，有的人住在东关。

Translation:

Three hundred and fifty li further north from Qiumingshan there stands Wajiaoshan。 Zhao River flows out of the mountain and goes west into the Yellow River。 This area is inhabited by a small number of people。 They are the mountainous Yi on the south bank, having settled on the river mouth。They are the sheep keepers of Xia nation, an age-old shepherd clan。 On the west side of Wajiao live the Shenwa clan, on the east side live the Shanliang clan。 Some clans live at Fugu area, some live at Dongguan area。

03-01-06 虢山

Guoshan

（111,66938E；39,91582N）

又北三百八十里，曰虢山[1]，其上多漆[2]，其下多桐椐[3]。其阳多玉[4]，其阴多铁 [5] 。伊水 [6] 出焉，西流注于河 [7] 。其兽多橐驼 [8] ，其鸟多寓[9]，状如鼠而鸟翼[10]，其音如羊[11]，可以御兵[12]。

注释：[1]虢山：指通道山，简称道山，读音虢山。今内蒙古清水河县城。

Notes:[1] guo shan (guo mount)

Tr: refers to Tongdaoshan (through pass mount), shortened to Daoshan, reads as Guoshan。 It is in the Qingshui River county seat in Inner Mongolia。

[2]漆：指高姓氏族。

[2] qi(lacquer) refers to clans bearing the surname of Gao。

[3] 桐据：指通道部落氏族。桐，指通。

[3] tong ju: refers to Tongdao clan， tong: tree /through, a pun。

[4]玉：指台子梁氏族。

[4]yu(jade) refers to Taiziliang clan。

[5]铁：指泡子氏族。

[5] tie(iron) refers to Paozi clan。

[6] 伊水：指小河水。
[6] yi shui: small river。
[7]河：指黄河。
[7] he refers to the Yellow River 。
[8] 橐驼：指通卡氏族。
[8] tuo tuo:(bellow camel)
Tr：it refers to Tongka clan。
[9]寓：指河滨氏族。
[9]yu （housing）
Tr：it refers to Riverside clan (Hebin)。
[10] 鼠而鸟翼：凉城的僚夷。
[10] shu er niao yi (rat with bird wings)
Tr：it refers to the Liao people from Liangchen (cool city) 。
[11]羊：指杨家窑。
[11] yang(sheep)
Tr: it refers to Yangjiayao。
[12] 可以御兵：夏国的河滨夷。
[12]ke yi yu bing (can resist soldiers)
Tr: it refers to the Riverside Yi from the Xia nation。

译文：由洼窖山往北三百八十里，有座山叫通道山，山的西面住着高姓氏族，东面住着通道部落氏族。南面住着台子梁氏族，北面住着泡子氏族。小河水从山间流出，向西流入黄河。这里的氏族还有通卡氏族，人群还有河滨夷，是来自凉城的僚夷，是夏国的河滨夷。

Translation:

Three hundred and eighty li further north from Wajiaoshan there stands Tongdaoshan。 On the west side lives the Gao clan, on its east side lives the Tongdao clan。 On the south side lives the Taiziliang clan, and on its north lives the Paozi clan。Xiaohe River flows out of this mountain and goes west into the Yellow River。 Other clans living here are the Tongka clan, the Hebin Yi。Hebin Yi is part of the Liao Yi from Liang city, they belong to the Hebin Yi of the Xia nation。

03-01-07 虢山尾
Guoshanwei
（111,6885E；40,82606N）

又北四百里，至于虢山之尾[1]，其上多玉而无石[2]。鱼水[3] 出焉，西流注于河 [4]，其中多文贝 [5]。

注释：[1]虢山尾：指通道的尾端，即今呼和浩特。
Notes:[1] guo shan wei: refers to the end of Tongdao, aka today's Hohhot city, Inner Mongolia, China。
[2] 玉而无石：指河滨的部落氏族。这里的其上是指卓资水的西面。
[2]yu er wu shi (jade but no stone)
Tr: it refers to the tribal clans of the riverside (Hebin)。Here the term Qishan (above it) refers to the west side of Zhuozi River。
[3] 鱼水：指卓资水，今称大、小黑河。濮文"鱼"读 zhu、zhe 两个读音。
[3]yu shui (fish river)
Tr: it refers to the Zhuozi River, known today as the Greater Black River and the Lesser Black River。 In Pu concept, the term Yu/Fish reads as zhu and zhe。
[4]河：指黄河。

[4] he: the Yellow River。

[5] 文贝：指水湾氏族。

[5] wen bei (marked shell)
Tr: it refers to the Shuiwan clan, shuiwan/bay。

译文：由通道山往北四百里，到达通道尾，卓资水的西面住着河滨部落氏族。卓资水从山间流出，向西流入黄河，这里住着水湾氏族。

Translation:
Four hundred li further north from Tongdaoshan, one arrives at Tongdaowei (mountain)。 To the west of Zhuozi River lives the Hebin tribal clan。 Zhuozi River flows out of the mountain and goes west into Yellow River。 Here the Shuiwan clan lives。

03-01-08 丹熏山
Danxunshan
（111,30861E；41,18596N）

又北二百里，曰丹熏之山[1]。其上多樗柏[2]，其草多韭薤 [3]，多丹臒 [4] 。熏水[5] 出焉，而西流注于棠水[6]。有兽焉，其状如鼠，而菟首麋身[7]，其音如獆犬，以其尾飞[8]，名曰耳鼠[9]，食之不脎[10]，又可以御百毒[11]。

注释：[1]丹熏山：指秃亥山，即今内蒙古武川县上秃亥乡。
Notes:[1] dan xun shan (red smoky mount)
Tr: refers to Tuhaishan, aka today's Tuhai village in Wuchuan county, Inner Mongolia。

[2] 樗柏：指马莲窊氏族。

[2] chubai:（wood） refers to Malianwa clan。

[3] 韭薤：指梁盖氏族。

[3] jiu xie (leek Chinese onion) refers to Lianggai clan。

[4] 丹臒：指秃亥胡。

[4] dan hu (red clay) refers to Tuhai Hu。

[5] 熏水：指秃亥水。

[5] xun shui (smoked water) refers to Tuhai River。

[6] 棠水：指土城河。濮语读土、泥为棠。

[6] tang shui: refers to Tucheng (dirt city) River, Pu concept for dirt, earth, mud reads as tang。

[7] 鼠而菟首麋身：农耕的吐苏密支系。吐苏密支系即贵族支系。

[7] shu er tu shou mi shen (rat with rabbit head, elk body)
Tr: it refers to the agricultural Tusumi branch， which is the noble branch。

[8] 獆犬以其尾飞：布连的东南治区。今碌碡梁子。

[8] gao quan yi qi wei fei (ao dog fly on its tail)
Tr: Bulian's southeast district, known today as Luduliangzi。

[9] 耳鼠：指碌碡氏。碌碡，是一种石辊子农具，用于代指农耕民族。

[9]er shu (ear rat)
Tr: it refers to Ludu Shi。Ludu, a stone grinding tool, a term to refer to agriculture people。

[10] 食之不脎：古老的外来氏族。

[10] shi zhi bu cai (eaten, not to grow big belly)
Tr: ancient outside clans。

[11] 又可以御百毒：阴康氏的碌毒部落夷。

[11] you ke yi yu bai du (can also defeat 100 poisons)
Tr: it refers to the Ludu tribal Yi from Yinkang Shi。

译文：由通道尾往北二百里，有座山叫秃亥山。山的西面住着马莲窊氏族，住着梁盖游牧民和秃亥胡。秃亥水从这里流出，向西流入土城河。有一个氏族，是农耕的贵族支系，住在布连的东南治区，名叫碌磚氏，是古老的外来氏族，实际是阴康氏的碌毒部落夷。
Translation：
Two hundred li further north from Tongdaowei (mountain) there stands the Tuhaishan。 On its west side live the Malianwa clan, the Gailiang nomads, and the Tuhai Hu。 Tuhai River comes out of here and goes west into Tucheng (dirt city) River。 One clan, an agriculture people of noble lineage, the Ludu Shi live in the southeast district。They are the ancient immigrants。 They are in fact the Ludu tribal Yi of the
Yinkang Shi。

03-01-09 石者山
Shizheshan
（111,70477E；41,52208N）

又北二百八十里，曰石者之山[1]，其上无草木[2]，多瑶碧[3]。泚水[4] 出焉，西流注于河 [5] 。有兽焉，其状如豹，而文题白身 [6] ，名曰孟极 [7] ，是善伏[8]，其名自呼。

注释：[1]石者山：指什颗碌磚山，简称什磚，今谐音称四子山，在内蒙古四子王旗。
Notes: [1] shi zhe shan (stone person mount)
Tr： it refers to Shenkeludu Mountain, shortened to Shendu, a close phonetic match with Sizishan, known today as Siziwang Banner (four son king banner) in Inner Mongolia。

[2] 无草木：指游牧部落。
[2] wu cao mu (no grass wood)
Tr: it refers to the nomadic tribes。

[3] 瑶碧：指河川氏族。
[3] yao bi (jade blue)
Tr： it refers to Hechuan clans。

[4] 泚水：指塔莲水，又称大黑水。
[4]ci shui. refers to Talian (tower lotus) River, also known as Daheishui（big black) River。

[5]河：指伊和河。
[5] he(river) refers to Yihe River。

[6] 豹而文题白身：指从事农业的梧桐不浪氏族。
[6] bao er wen ti bai shen (leopard with marking on its forehead and with white body)
Tr： it refers to the agriculture clans, the Wutongbulang clans。

[7] 孟极：指牧纪氏，又称胡纪氏、忽鸡氏。
[7] meng ji refers to Muji Shi, who are also known as Huji Shi, huji is also a pun with Hu rooster, therefor Huji Shi。

[8] 善伏：指外来胡。
[8] shan fu（good lurking）
Tr： refers to outside Hu tribes。

译文：由秃亥山往北二百八十里，有座山叫什磚山，山的西边是游牧部落，住着河川氏族。塔莲水从这里流出，向西流入伊和河。这里有一个氏族，是从事农业的梧桐不浪氏族，牧纪氏，是外来胡，他们自己也这样称呼。
Translation:

Two hundred and eighty li further northward from Tuhaishan there stands Shenlushan。 On its west side live the nomads, the Hechuan clan。 Talian River flows out of here and goes west into Yihe River。 One clan, an agriculture people of Wutongbulang, also known as Muji Shi, are outsider Hu。 They also address themselves thus。

03-01-10 边春山
Bianchunshan
（111,69502E；41,75835N）

又北百一十里，曰边春之山[1]，多葱[2]、葵[3]、韭[4]、桃[5]、李[6]。杠水[7] 出焉，而西流注于泑泽[8] 。有兽焉，其状如禺而文身[9]，善笑[10]，见人卧则卧[11]，名曰幽鴳[12]，其名自呼。

注释：[1]边春山：指满莲梁子，读音笨且纠。今称马莲梁子。
Notes： [1] bian chun shan（edge spring mount)
Tr: it refers to Manlianliangzi, Pu reads benqiejiu。 Today's name: Malianliangzi。
[2]葱：指岔口氏族。
[2] cong(onion) refers to Chakou clans。
[3]葵：指北格少氏族。
[3] kui(sunflower) refers to Beigeshao clans。
[4]韭：指梁子氏氏族。
[4] jiu(leek) refers to Liangzi Shi clans。
[5]桃：指中义恒氏族。
[5] tao(peach) refers to Zhongyiheng clans。
[6]李：指府壕子氏族。
[6]li(plum)refers to Fuhaozi clans。
[7] 杠水：指公合水，简称公水，谐音杠水。
[7] gang shui (stick water) refers to Gonghe River, shortened to Gongshui, a close phonetic match to 'gangshui', gong/gang。
[8] 泑泽：指伊和河。
[8] you ze; refers to Yihe River。
[9] 禺而文身：指水边的温都花氏族。
[9]yu er wen shen (yu with tattoos)
Tr： it refers to the Wenduhua clans by the river side。
[10] 善笑：指外匈奴氏族。
[10] shan xiao (laugh a lot)
Tr: it refers to the Outer Xiongnu clans。
[11] 见人卧则卧：定居出水口处。见人指定居；则卧，指出水口。
[11] jian ren wo ze wo (lay down when seeing human lay down)
Tr: settled at the water mouth place。Jian ren (seeing human) means settle down, ze wo,
Lay down too, means water outlet。
[12] 幽鴳：指伊和氏。和，濮语读音 han、an。
[12] you an (shady bird)
Tr: it refers to Yihe clan。 He (and or harmony) in Pu concept reads han/an。

译文：由什礴山往北一百一十里，有座山叫满莲梁子。这里住着岔口氏族、北格少氏族、梁子氏族、中义恒氏族、府壕子氏族。公合水从这里流出，向西流入伊和河。有一个氏族，是水边的温都花氏族，是外匈奴，定居在出水口处，名叫伊和氏，他们也这样介绍自己。

Translation:
One hundred and ten li further north from Shenlushan there stands the Manliangzi Mountain。 The Chakou clan, the Beigeshao clan, the Liangzi clan, the Zhongyiheng clan, and the Fuhaozi clan live here。 Gonghe River flows out of here and goes west into the Yihe River。 One clan, the Wenduhua clan by the riverbank belongs to the Outer Xiongnu。They settle down at the water outlet place, they are call Yihe Shi。They also address themselves thus。

03-01-11 蔓联山
Manlianshan
（112,56278E；42,20739N）

又北二百里，曰蔓联之山[1]，其山无草木[2]。有兽焉，其状如禺而有鬣[3]，牛尾、文臂，马蹄[4]，见人则呼[5]，名曰足訾[6]，其名自呼。有鸟焉，群居而朋飞[7]，其毛如雌雉[8]，名曰䴔(bo)[9]，其鸣自呼，食之已风[10]。

注释：[1]蔓联山：指忙軨山，意思是无鹿的地方。今称忙可图山。
Notes： [1] man lian shan: refers to Mangling Mountain, (a place without deers), today known as Mangketu Mountain。

[2] 无草木：游牧部落。
[2] wu cao mu (no grass wood)
Tr: it refers to the nomadic tribes。

[3] 有鬣：指游牧氏族、游牧民。
[3] you lie (have horse mane)
Tr： it refers to nomadic clans, the herders。

[4] 牛尾、文臂，马蹄：指怒青水河的马尼特人。
[4] niu wei/yi, (ox tail,) wen bi （tattooed arm), ma ti (horse hoof)
Tr: it refers to the Manite people from Nuqingshui River (angry green water river) 。

[5] 见人则呼：定居的胡族支系。
[5] jian ren ze hu (when seeing people, it yells) refers to the settled Hu branches。

[6] 足訾：指低地人。
[6] zu zi (foot edge)
Tr: it refers to the low land dwellers。

[7] 群居而朋飞：指桑廷巴润治区。
[7] qun ju er peng fei (live in group, fly in two)
Tr： it refers to the Sangtingbarun district。

[8] 其毛如雌雉：支系为游牧支系。雌雉，在此指游牧支系。
[8] qi mao ru ci zhi (its feathers are like that of the female bird)
Tr: its branches are the nomads, chizhi means nomadic branches。

[9]䴔：指勃日和氏族。
[9] jiao(bird), refers to the Borihe clan。

[10] 已风：读夷冯，指山区夷。
[10] yi feng （cure illness from wind）
Tr: reads yifeng in Pu concept, refers to the mountain Yi。

译文：由满莲梁子往北二百里，有座山叫忙軨山，山的西面是游牧部落。有一个氏族，是水边的牧民，是怒青水河的马尼特人，是定居的胡族支系，称为低地人，他们也这样介绍自己。有一群人，是桑廷巴润治区的游牧支系，名叫勃日和氏，他们也这样称呼自己，是古老的山区夷。
Translation:
Two hundred li further north from Manlianliangzi there stands the Manglingshan。 On its west side live the nomads。 One tribe of herders is from the Nuqingshui River。They are the Manites of settled Hu people, also known as the low land people, they also introduce themselves as such。 Another group is the herding branch, the Borihe Shi from the Sangtingbarun district。 They address themselves thus, they are an ancient mountain Yi。

03-01-12 单张山
Danzhangshan
（112,65488E；42,74541N）

又北百八十里，曰单张之山[1]，其上无草木[2]。有兽焉，其状如豹而长尾[3]，人首而牛耳，一目[4]，名曰诸犍[5]，善吒[6]，行则衔其尾[7]，居则蟠其尾[8]。有鸟焉，其状如雉，而文首、白翼、黄足[9]，名曰白鵺[10]，食之已嗌（yi）痛[11]，可以已痸[12]。栎水出焉[13]，而南流注于杠水[14]。

注释：[1]单张山：指平疆山，蒙语称达奇扎哈山。今苏尼特右旗。
Notes:[1] dan zhang shan (single page mount)
Tr: it refers to Pingjiangshan, read Daqizhaha in Mongolian，known today as Sunite (Sonite) Right Banner。42° 44′ 49″ N, 112° 39′ 36″ E。
[2] 无草木：游牧部落。
[2] wu cao mu (no grass wood) refers to the Nomads。
[3] 豹而长尾：指宝拉格迁徙夷。
[3] bao er chang wei (leopard with long tail)
Tr: refers to the migrant Baolage Yi。
[4] 人首而牛耳，一目：惹苏淖尔的大支系。惹苏淖尔，苏尼特右旗城的古称谓。
[4] ren shou er niu er (human head with ox ears), yi mu (one eye)
Tr: big branch from Resunaoer, an old name for Sonite Right Banner。
[5] 诸犍：指低坡。
[5] zhu jian(various ox) refers to low slope。
[6] 善吒：指森吉图氏。
[6] shan cha (good yelling) refers to Senjitu Shi 41.887106, 116.564644。
[7] 行则衔其尾：指森吉汗其夷。
[7] xing ze xian qi wei (moving with its tail in its month)refers to Senjihanqi Yi。
[8] 居则蟠其尾：吉呼帕其夷。
[8] ju ze pan qi wei (stay with its tail in coil) refers to Jihupaqi Yi。
[9] 雉而文首、白翼、黄足：指平原蒙族富饶的胡族。
[9] zhui er wen shou, (bird with patterned head) bai yi (white wings), huang zu(yellow feet)
Tr: the rich Hu people of the Mongolian plain (flat land) 。
[10] 白鵺：指巴彦氏。
[10] bai ye (white bird) refers to Bayan Shi。
[11] 已嗌痛：指阴山族。
[11] yi yi tong (cure throat pain)
Tr: it refers to Yinshan tribes。
[12] 可以已痸：夏国的游牧夷。

[12]ke yi yi zhi (can cure retardedness)
Tr: refers to the nomads of the Xia nation。

[13] 栎水：指诺如水

[13]li shui: refers to Nuoru River。

[14] 杠水：指惹苏淖尔水。

[14] gang shui: refers to Resunuur River。

译文：由忙軡山往北一百八十里，有座山叫达奇扎哈山，山的西面是游牧部落。有一个氏族，是宝拉格迁徙夷，是惹苏淖尔的大支系，称为低坡的森吉图氏、森吉汗其夷、吉呼帕其夷。有一群人，是平原蒙族富饶的胡族，名叫巴彦氏，是古老的阴山夷，是夏国的游牧夷。诺如河水从山间流出，向南流入惹苏淖尔。

Translation:

One hundred and eighty li further north from Manglingshan there stands the Daqizhaha Mountain。 On its west side live the nomads。A migrant clan Baolage, the big branch from Resunuur, are known as the Senjitu Shi, the Senjihanqi Yi, the Jihupaqi Yi from the lower slopes。 Another group, the rich Hu people, the Bayan Shi from Mongolian plain, is the ancient Yinshan Yi。They are the nomads of Xia nation。 Nuoru River flows out of the mountains and goes south into Resu nuur。

03-01-13 灌题山

Guantishan

（112,12188E；43,47163N）

又北三百二十里，曰灌题之山[1]，其上多樗柘[2]，其下多流沙[3]，多砥[4]。有兽焉，其状如牛耳白尾[5]，其音如訆[6]，名曰那父[7]。有鸟焉，其状如雌雉而人面[8]，见人则跃[9]，名曰竦斯[10]，其鸣自呼也。匠韩之水[11] 出焉，而西流注于泑泽 [12]，其中多磁石[13]。

注释：[1]灌题山：指查干特格山，简称干特山，谐音灌题山。

Notes:[1] guan ti shan: refers to Chagantege Mountain, or simply Ganteshan, Guan ti/gan te, close phonetic match。

[2] 樗柘：指苏吉嘎查，简称苏吉，谐音樗柘。

[2] chu zhe (inferior wood)

Tr： it refers to Sujigacha, shortened to Suji, a close phonetic to chu zhi。

[3] 流沙：指包饶勒吉音，简称勒吉，释义流沙。

[3] liu sha (flowing sand)

Tr： it refers to Baoraolejiyin, shortened to Leji, meaning moving sand。

[4]砥：指坝子。泛指平原地区或平缓地区的氏族。

[4] di (whet stone)

Tr: it refers to bazi, a term for flat land or tribes living on plain。

[5] 牛而白尾：西边的查干夷。白，指查干。

[5] niu er bai wei/yi (ox with white tail)

Tr: the Chagan Yi on the west, bai(white) refers to Chagan。

[6]訆：指梁子上，实际是查干特格驻地。

[6] jiu:(yep) refers to Liangzi (mountain range), it is the campsite Chagantege。

[7] 那父：指那仁胡。

[7]na fu (na hu) refers to Naren Hu。

[8] 雌雉而人面：指雉鸡场山地区的迁入的定居氏族，也称雌雉山氏族。

[8]ci zhi er ren mian (female pheasant with human face) refers to the settled clans who migrated from Zhijichang Mountain area。Zhijichang clan is also called Cizhishan (female pheasant mount) clan。

[9] 见人则跃：包日呼吉日音浑迪，简称且日吉音，谐音见人则跃。包，读且音。

[9] jian ren ze yue (when seeing human, it jumps)
It refers to Baorihujiriyinhundi people, shortened to Qierijiyin, a pun with Jian ren ze yue 。 In Pu concept bao(wrap)reads as qie。

[10] 竦斯：指肃慎。

[10] shu si: refers to Sushen people。

[11] 匠韩水：指乔勒浩拉水。

[11] jiang han shui (craftsman Han water)
Tr: refers to Qiaolehaola River。

[12] 泑泽：在查干特格西侧。

[12] you ze: a lake on the west side of Chagantege。

[13] 磁石：指游牧氏族。

[13]ci shi (magnetic stone) refers to the nomadic clans。

译文：由达奇扎哈山往北三百二十里，有座山叫查干特格山。山的西面住着苏吉嘎查氏族，东面住着包饶勒吉音氏族以及平坝地区氏族。有一个氏族，是西边的查干夷，住在梁子上，名叫那仁胡。有一群人，是从雌雉山地区迁入的定居氏族，住在包日呼吉日音浑迪，名叫肃慎，他们也这样介绍自己。乔勒浩拉水从山间流出，向西流入泑泽，这里住着游牧氏族。

Translation:
Three hundred and twenty li further north from Daqizhaha Mountain stands the Chagantege Mountain。 On its west side live the Sujigacha clans, on its east side live the Baoraolejiyin clans and the clans from the flatland。One clan, known as Naren Hu, the Chagan people from the west, lives on the mountain range。 Another people settled here after migrating from Cizhishan area。 They live at Baorihujiriyinhundi, known as Sushen, they also address themselves thus。 Qiaolehaola River flows out of the mountain and goes westward into Youze Lake, there the nomads live。

03-01-14 潘侯山
Panhoushan
（112,10978E；43,84306N）

又北二百里，曰潘侯之山[1]。其上多松柏[2]，其下多榛楛[3]，其阳多玉[4]，其阴多铁[5]。有兽焉，其状如牛而四节生毛[6]，或曰旄牛[7]。边水[8]出焉，而南流注于栎泽[9]。

注释：[1]潘侯山：指巴日钦哈达山，简称巴哈山，谐音潘侯山。在二连浩特东北面。

Notes： [1] pan hou shan (Prince Pan's mount)
Tr: it refers to Bariqinhada Mountain, shortened to Bahashan, a close phonetic match to Panhoushan。 It is situated to the northeast side of Erlianhot (43° 39′ 0″ N, 111° 59′ 0″ E) 。

[2] 松柏：指绍日布格氏族。

[2] song bai (pine poplar)
Tr: it refers to the Shaoribuge clan。

[3] 榛楛：指党项人，属鲜卑族。今为何村落人不详。

[3] zhen ku (useless wood)
Tr: it refers to Dangxiang people, they belong to the Xianbeis。It is not sure what villages their descendants belong nowadays。

[4]玉：指巴音阿吉氏族。

[4]yu(jade) refers to Bayin 'aji clan。

[5]铁：指呼仍德勒氏族。

[5] tie(iron) refers to Hurengdele clan。

[6] 牛而四节生毛：指河边的聚落苏木。相同于劳庆根的氏族苏木。

[6] niu er si jie sheng mao (ox with four segments growing hair)

Tr: refers to the Sum that situates along the riverbank, like the Laoqinggen clan sum。

[7] 旄牛：指低地的牧民毛勒氏。旄，指朱、诸，即低地之意。

[7] mao niu(buffalo)

Tr： refers to the Maole Shi, a herders clan。 Mao refers to zhu, meaning low land。

[8] 边水：指巴润水。

[8] bian shui (edge water) refers to Barun River。

[9] 栎泽：额热恩达布森淖尔的古称谓。

[9]li ze (li lake) the old name for Ere 'endabusen Nuur， a Salt Lake, at Erlianhot。

译文：由查干特格山往北二百里，有座山叫巴日钦哈达山。山的西面住着绍日布格氏族，东面住着党项氏族，南面住着巴音阿吉氏族，北面住着呼仍德勒氏族。有一个氏族，是河边的聚落苏木人，叫毛勒氏。巴润水从山间流出，向南流入栎泽。

Translation:

Two hundred li further north from Chagantege Mountain there stands Bariqinhada Mountain。On its west side live the Shaoribuge clan, on its east side live the Tangut clan。 The Bayin 'aji clan live on the south side, the Hurengdele clan live on the north side。 A clan, a riverbank sum people, is called Maole Shi。Barun river flows out of the mountains and goes south into Lize。

03-01-15 小咸山

Xiaoxianshan

（110,13554E； 44,90518N）

又北二百三十里，曰小咸之山[1]，无草木[2]，冬夏有雪[3]。

注释：[1]小咸山：指赛音山达山。赛音山达，谐音小咸。

Notes:[1] xiao xian shan (small salty mount)

Tr: refers to Saiyinshanda (Sainted) Mountain, a close phonetic match to Xiaoxian,
44° 53′ 30.12″ N, 110° 8′ 12.12″ E。

[2] 无草木：游牧部落。

[2] wu cao mu (no grass wood)

Tr: refers to the nomadic tribes。

[3] 冬夏有雪：冬夏，指栋啥，即外国，外国的。古人以祭拜的栋柱为国。雪，指羲，即山峰。在夏朝时期，外蒙属于国外，所以才称栋啥。

[3] dong xia you xue (winter summer has snow)

Tr: dongxia is a close phonetic match to dong sha, meaning foreign, from abroad。 Ancient people worship columns as border landmark for their country, dong: column。 xue(snow) refers to xi, mountain top。 During Xia time, outer Mongolia is considered as foreign territory。This is the meaning for the term Dong sha。

译文：由巴日音哈达山往北二百三十里，有座山叫赛音山达山，是游牧部落地区，是外国的山峰。

Translation:

Two hundred thirty li further north from Bariyinhada Mountain there stands the Sainshand Mountain。 It is the land of the nomads; the mountains are in foreign territory。

03-01-16 大咸山

Daxianshan
（109,25071E；46,62997N）

北二百八十里，曰大咸之山[1]，无草木[2]，其下多玉[3]。是山也，四方[4]，不可以上[5]。有蛇名长蛇[6]，其毛如彘豪 [7]，其音如鼓柝 [8]。

注释：[1]大咸山：指达尔汗山。咸，在此读 han 音。
Notes:[1] da xian shan (big salty mount)
Tr: refers to Darkhan Mountain。 Xian reads as han。
[2] 无草木：游牧部落。
[2] wu cao mu (no grass wood) refers to nomads。
[3]玉：指河边的氏族。
[3]yu(jade) refers to riverbank clans。
[4] 也四方：读耶补伏，指大巫师。远古时期的部落以大巫师为酋长。
[4]ye bu fu (also four corner)
Tr: reads as yebufu, referring to the master priest。 In ancient time, the chieftain is usually the chief priest of the tribes。
[5] 不可以上：补苦以外的国家。补苦，指东胡，但也指夏国。在此指东胡。
[5] bu ke yi shan (cannot go up)
Tr: bu ke, close phonetic match for Bu ku, a term refers to Donghu, (east Hu) as well as Xia nation。 It means Dong Hu people here。
[6] 长蛇：蛇，指集肆；长蛇，指昌塞，实际就是达尔汗城。
[6] chang she (long snake)
Tr: she/snake refers to market towns, Chang she, a close phonetic match for Chang Sai, the great Khan's city--Darkhan city, 49° 28′ 8″ N, 105° 57′ 27″ E。
[7] 其毛如彘豪：支系为靺鞨支系。彘豪，指靺鞨。
[7] qi mao ru zhi hao (its hair is like that of the wild boar)
Tr: its branches are the Mohe clans, zhihao means Mohe。
[8] 鼓柝：指城中心。
[8]gu tuo (drumstick)
Tr: refers to the center district of the city。

译文：由赛音山达山往北二百八十里，有座山叫达尔汗山，是游牧部落地区，山的东面住着河边氏族。这座山是大巫师居住的地方，是补苦以外的联盟中心。这里有一个集肆叫昌塞，居民的支系为靺鞨支系，住在城中心。
Translation:
Two hundred and eighty li further north from Sainshand Mountain there stands the Darkhan Mountain. This is the land of the nomads。On its east side live the riverbank clans。 This is the place the chief priest lives, a center for confederacy outside the Buku proper。A market town is called Changsai, its inhabitants are the branches of the Mohe people, they live in the town center。

03-01-17 敦薨山
Donghongshan
（108,33129E；48,67088N）

又北三百二十里，曰敦薨之山[1]，其上多椶枏[2]，其下多茈草[3]。敦薨之水出焉[4]，而西流注于泑泽[5]。出于昆仑 [6] 之东北隅，实惟河 [7]源。其中多赤鲑 [8]，其兽多兕，旄牛[9]，其鸟多鸤鸠[10]。

注释：[1]敦薨山：指肯特洪山。
Notes:[1] dun hong shan; refers to Khentii Mountains in Mongolia。
[2] 椶枏：指美丽河，蒙语为巴彦高勒。
[2] zong nan (palm nanmu)
Tr: refers to Meili (beautiful) River, Bayan Gol in Mongolia。
[3] 茈草：指游牧的草原氏族，也称摆嘎氏族，今标注为巴嘎氏族。
[3]ci cao (purple grass)
Tr: refers to steppe's nomads, also known as the Baiga clan, today is registered as Baga clan。
[4] 敦薨水：指肯特洪水。
[4] dun hong shui: refers to Kenthong River。
[5] 泑泽：指鄂尔浑河。
[5] you ze: refers to Erhun (Orkhon) River。50° 15′ 0″ N, 106° 8′ 20″ E。
[6] 昆仑：指肯特洪山。仑、洪都是指山，肯特与昆谐音。
[6] kun lun: refers to Khentii Mountains。 Lun, hong, all means mountain, kent and kun are close phonetic matches。
[7]河：指鄂尔浑河。
[7] he(river) refers to Orkhon River。
[8] 赤鲑：指游牧的达里岗嘎人，蒙古族。
[8] chi gui (red chum salmon):
Tr: refers to the Daligangga people, they are Mongolian nomads。
[9]兕：指韶阿特人，又称明阿特人，蒙古族。
[9] si(unicorn)
Tr: it refers to the Shao'ate people, also known as Mingates, a Mongolian tribe。
[10] 鳲鸠：斯基泰人，匈奴。
[10] shi jiu (Cuculus canorus bakeri)
Tr: refers to Scythians, (aka Xiongnu) 。

译文：由达尔汗山往北三百二十里，有座山叫肯特洪山，山的西面住着巴彦高勒氏族，东面住着巴嘎氏族。肯特洪水从山间流出，向西流入鄂尔浑河。肯特洪水发源于这座山的东北隅，实际是鄂尔浑河的源头之一。这里住着游牧的达里岗嘎人、明阿特人等蒙族人，还住着斯基泰人。
Translation:
Three hundred and twenty li further north from the Darkhan Mountain there stands the Khentii Mountain。 On its west side live the Bayan Gol clan, on its east side live the Baga clan。 Khentiihong River flows out of the mountain and goes west to empty into the Orkhon River。 Khentiihong River originates from its northeast corner and is one source of the Orkhon River。 The Mongolian nomads, the Daligangga clan, the Mingate clan as well as Scythian clan live here。

03-01-18 少咸山
Shaoxianshan
（109,27475E；50,13102N）

又北二百里，曰少咸之山[1]。无草木[2]，多青碧 [3] 。有兽焉，其状如牛而赤身人面马足 [4]，名曰窫窳 [5]，其音如婴儿[6]，是食人[7]。敦水[8]出焉，东流注于雁门之水[9]，其中多鯆鯆之鱼[10]。食之杀人[11]。

注释：[1]少咸山：指苏赫山。
Notes:[1] shao han shan (young salty mount)

Tr: it refers to Suhe Mountain。

[2] 无草木：游牧部落地区。

[2] wu cao mu (no grass wood)
Tr: it refers to the territory of the steppe nomadic tribes。

[3] 青碧：即奇沘，指奇科伊氏族。伊，指河流。

[3] qing bi (green clear)
Tr：it refers to Qi Bi, the Qikeyi clan。 Yi refers to rivers。

[4] 牛而赤身人面马足：涅涅茨氏的定居胡族。牛而赤，指涅涅茨，意思为放鹿人。

[4] niu er chi shen ren mian ma zu (ox with naked body, human face, and horse feet)
Tr: refers to the Nenets' settled Hu people, niu er chi refers to Nenets, meaning reindeer keepers。

[5] 窫窳：读雅溢，指大河氏族，属涅涅茨人的支系。

[5]ya yu (Pu: ya yi)
Tr：it refers to big river clan， one branch of the Nenets。

[6] 婴儿：指阴阿，即北部地区。

[6] ying er (infant)
Tr：it refers to Yin a, the northern region。

[7] 是食人：是古老的定居氏族。人，读惹，指永居、定居。

[7] shi shi ren (yes eats human)
Tr: it refers to the ancient clans, ren: human, reads as re in Pu concept, means settlement, permanent residence。

[8] 敦水：指苏赫山南河北面的溪流，紧邻南河。

[8] dun shui: refers to the brooks to the north of Nan River, at the Suhe Mountain, close to Nan River。

[9] 雁门水：奇科伊西侧的支流。

[9] yan men shui (goose gate water)
Tr: it refers to the west tributary of Qikeyi(kikoy) River。

[10] 鲋鲋鱼：指贝沘夷，今称卡雅塔人。贝沘，即南河，流入色愣河。

[10] fei fei yu; refers to Beibi Yi, today known as Kayata people。 Beibi: Nan River, flows into Selenga River。

[11] 食之杀人：古老的塞族定居氏族。

[11] shi zhi sha ren (eat it kills you)
Tr: it refers to the ancient, settled clans of Saka。

译文：由肯特洪山往北二百里，有座山叫苏赫山。这里是游牧部落地区，住着奇科伊氏族。有一个氏族，是涅涅茨氏的定居胡族，名叫雅溢，住在北部地区，是古老的定居氏族。敦水从山间流出，向东流入雁门河，这里住着贝沘夷，是古老的塞族定居氏族。

Translation:
Two hundred li further north from Khentii Mountain there stands Suhe Mountain。This region belongs to the nomads, where the Kikoy clan live。 One Hu clan, the settled Nenets， live in the north。 They are called Yayies, they are ancient, settled clans。 Dun River flows out of the mountains and goes east into Yanmen River, where the Beibi Yi live。They are the Saka people who are ancient sedentary clans。

03-01-19 狱法山
Yufashan
（113,46946E；52,05702N）

又北二百里，曰狱法之山[1]。瀤泽之水[2] 出焉，而东流注于泰泽 [3] 。其中多鱳鱼 [4] ，其状如鲤而鸡足 [5] ，食之已疣[6]。有兽焉，其状如犬而人面，善投，见人则笑[7]，其名山[8]，其行如风[9]，见则天下大风[10]。

注释：[1]狱法山：指雅布洛夫山，简称雅夫山，谐音狱法山。以赤塔为中心。
Notes:[1]yu fa shan (prison law mount)
Tr: it refers to Yabulov Mountain, shortened to Yafushan, a close phonetic match to Yufashan。 It is centered at Chita, (red pagoda) 52° 3′ 0″ N, 113° 28′ 0″ E。

[2] 瀤泽水：指马河。
[2] huai ze shui: refers to Ma(horse)River.

[3] 泰泽：指塔卢马河。简称塔河，谐音泰河。
[3] tai ze （big water）
Tr: it refers to Taluma River, shortened to Tahe (Ta River), a close phonetic match to Taihe （Tai River）。

[4] 鱳鱼：指扎索尔卡夷。简称扎夷，谐音鱳鱼。
[4] zao yu (carp like fish)
Tr： it refers to Zasurka Yi, shortened to Zayi, a close phonetic match to Zaoyu。

[5] 鲤而鸡足：涅涅茨的部落支系。鸡，读纪，指部落。
[5]li er ji zu (carp with chicken feet)
Tr: it refers to Nenets branch。Ji refers to tribe, ji/chicken is a pun on tribe。

[6] 已疣：南部夷。对赤塔而言。
[6] yi you (cure warts) refer to Nanbu Yi， the tribes in the south region in reference to Chita。

[7] 犬而人面，善投，见人则笑：犬戎定居萨克萨镇的匈奴支系。赤塔城，古称萨克萨。
[7] quan er ren mian (dog with human face) shan tou (good at hurling), jian ren ze xiao (laugh when seeing people)
Tr： it refers to a branch of Xiongnu, the Dog Rong's branch who settled in Saksa town, Saksa being an old name for Chita。

[8]山【犬军】：读啥哼，指萨克萨人。
[8] shan hun: reads as shahe in Pu concept, refers to the Saksa people。

[9] 其行如风：早期为王族。风，指冯，即王族。
[9] qi xing ru feng (move like wind)
Tr: it means, in early time, it is the royal tribe。feng/wind, feng/von, royal tribe。

[10] 见则天下大风：是那个国家的统治氏族。这里的国家指部落国。
[10] jian ze tian xia da feng (seeing it there will be big winds under the heaven)
Tr: this branch is the ruling clan in that tribal nation。

译文：由苏赫山往北二百里，有座山叫雅布洛夫山。马河水从山间流出，向东北流入塔卢马河。这里住着扎索尔卡夷，是涅涅茨人的部落支系，是古老的南部夷。有一个氏族，是犬戎定居于萨克萨场镇的匈奴支系，名叫萨克萨人，早期为王族，是那个国家的统治氏族。
Translation:
Two hundred li further north from Suhe Mountain there stands the Yabulov Mountain。 Ma river flows out from the mountains and goes northeast into Taluma River。 The Zasurka Yi live here, they are the branches of Nenets, an ancient southern Yi。 Another clan, the Dog Rong people, a branch of Xiongnu, settled at the Saksa fieldtown。 They are the Saksas, an earlier royal clan, the ruling clan of that nation。

03-01-20 北岳山
Beiyueshan
（114,19525E； 57,85135N）

又北二百里，曰北岳之山[1]。多枳棘刚木[2] 。有兽焉，其状如牛，而四角人目彘耳 [3] ，其名曰诸怀 [4] ，其音如鸣雁[5]，是食人[6]。诸怀之水[7]出焉，而西流注于嚣水[8]，水中多鮨鱼[9]，鱼身而犬首[10]，其音如婴儿[11]，食之已狂[12]。

注释：[1]北岳山：贝加尔北山，也称博代托、博代博，简称贝阴山，谐音北岳山。
Notes:[1] bei yue shan (northern mount)
Tr: it refers to the Baikal Beishan, also knowns as Bodaituo, Bodaibo, shortened to Beiyinshan, a close phonetic match for Beiyueshan。

[2] 枳棘刚木：雉鸡岗蒙。
[2] zhi jin gang mu (citrus trifoliata branes hard wood)
Tr： it refers to the Zhijigangmeng (female pheasant range Mongolian) 。

[3] 牛而四角人目彘耳：柳伊斯克部落通古斯牧民。
[3] niu er si jiao (ox with four horns) ren mu zhi er (human eyes with pig ears)
Tr: The Tungusic nomads from Liuyisk tribes。(Vilyuysk) 63° 45′ 19″ N, 121° 37′ 29″ E 。

[4] 诸怀：指季姆维。今称维季姆。
[4] zhu huai (various bosoms)
Tr: it refers to Jimuwei (Timvi), today known as Settlement of Vitim 63° 45′ 0″ N, 121° 38′ 0″ E。

[5] 鸣雁：读蒙雁，指江北。
[5] ming yan (calling goose)
Tr: it reads as mengyan, refers to the north of the river。

[6] 是食人：是古老的居民，是原住居民。
[6] shi shi ren (yes eating human)
Tr: ancient settlers, original settlers。

[7] 诸怀水：今维季姆河。实际往东流。
[7] zhu huai shui (various bosom water)
Tr: refers to today's Vijim River, in fact it goes to east。

[8] 嚣水：指孙塔尔河。今称维柳伊河。
[8] xiao shui (noisy water)
Tr： it refers to Suntar River, today known as the Vilyuy River。

[9] 鮨鱼：指渔夷。即渔业氏族。
[9] zhi yu(fish) refers to Yuyi, the fishing clans。

[10] 鱼身而犬首：犬戎族渔民。
[10]yu shen er quan shou (fish body with dog heads)
Tr: fishing tribes of the Dog Rong people。

[11] 婴儿：指北岸。
[11] ying er (infant) refers to the north bank。

[12] 已狂：指北夷。
[12] yi kuan (already gone mad) refers to northern Yi。

译文：由雅布洛夫山往北二百里，有座山叫博代博。这里住着雉鸡岗蒙。有一个氏族，是柳伊斯克部落通古斯牧民，名叫季姆维人，住在江北，是原住居民。季姆维水从这里流出，向东流入孙塔尔河，河边住着渔业氏族，是犬戎族渔民，住在北岸，是古老的北夷。

Translation:

Two hundred li northward from Yabulov Mountain there stands the Bodaibo Mountain。 The Zhuijigang-meng live here。One clan, the Vilyuysk 's Tungusic nomads, known as the Timvi (Vitim) people， lives on the north bank。They are the original settlers here。Timvi (Vitim) River flows out of here and goes east into the Suntar River。 On the bank of this river there live the fishing tribes of the Dog Rong tribes。 They live on the north bank; they are the ancient northern people。

03-01-21 浑夕山
Hunxishan

（102,59188E；61,43261N）

又北百八十里，曰浑夕之山[1]。无草木[2]，多铜玉[3]。嚣水[4]出焉，而北流注于海[5]。有蛇一首两身[6]，名曰肥遗[7]，见则其国大旱[8]。

注释：[1]浑夕山：读恒羲山，意为王顶、主峰之山。又称伊吉尔山，濮语读为伊吉尔玛。
Notes:[1] hun xu shan (blur dusk mount)
Tr: reads as Hengxishan: The King Peak, highest, reads Yijierma in Pu speech, known as Yijier Mountain。
[2] 无草木：指游牧部落。
[2] wu cao mu (no grass wood)
Tr: it refers to the nomadic tribes。
[3] 铜玉：读同玉，是"伊吉尔"一词的汉译。
[3] tong yu (copper jade)
Tr: reads as tongyu (same jade) a close phonetic match， Chinese translation of Yijier。
[4] 嚣水：指下通古斯卡河。
[4] xiao shui (noisy water)
Tr: it refers to the Xia Tungus River –the Nizhnyaya Tunguska River, also the Lower Tunguska River。 [65°47′0″N, 87°57′ 20″E]
[5]海：指北冰洋的喀拉海。
[5] hai (sea, zee) refers to the Kara Sea in Arctic。
[6] 蛇一首两身：氏族，伊吉尔氏。是按谐音"一级二氏"译成的："一首两身"。
[6] she yi shou liang shen (snake one head two bodies)
Tr: it refers to clan, the Yijier Shi。A close phonetic makeover of "yi ji er shi" (one class two surnames) shou/ji, shi/shen。
[7] 肥遗：濮语的"东"概念常读成且、伏、希。而伏和希，常被译为肥和新。肥遗即新伊吉尔玛。
[7] fei yi (fat remain)
Tr： Pu concept East, Oriental reads as qie, fu, xi。 Fu /fei, xi/xin-- close phonetic matches, fei yi refers to New Yijierma。
[8] 大旱：指达罕氏族。
[8] da han （big drought)

译文：由博代博山往西北一百八十里，有座山叫恒羲山。这里是游牧部落地区，住着伊吉尔氏族。下通古斯河发源于这座山，向北流入喀拉海。这里的氏族是伊吉尔氏族，名叫东伊吉尔氏，是这个国家的达罕氏族。

Translation:
One hundred and eighty li further northwest from Bodaiboshan there stands the Hengxishan。This is the land of the nomads, where the Yijier clan live。 The Nizhnyana Tunguska originates from this mountain and goes north into the Kara Sea。 The Yijier clan bears the surname of Dongyijier Shi, they are the Da khan (ruling)clan of that nation。

03-01-22 北单山
Beidanshan
（100,31359E；63,03605N）

又北五十里，曰北单之山[1]，无草木[2]，多葱韭[3]。

注释：[1]北单山：指拜基特山。谐音拜德山、北单山。

[1] bei dan shan (north single mount)
Tr: refers to the Baijiteshan, a close phonetic match to baideshan, beidanshan, byjiteshan。

[2] 无草木：游牧部落地区。

[2] wu cao mu (no grass wood)
Tr: the land of nomads。

[3] 葱韭：指分水岭氏族。

[3] cong jiu (onion leek)
Tr: refers to the Fenshuiling clan, the watershed clan。

译文：由恒羲山往北五十里，有座山叫拜基特山，是游牧部落地区，住着分水岭氏族。

Translation:
Fifty li further north from Hengxishan there stands Byjiteshan。 This is the region of nomadic tribes。 The Fenshuiling clan lives there。

03-01-23 罴差山
Pichaishan
（100,33693E；67,55744N）

又北百里，曰罴差之山[1]，无草木[2]，多马[3]。

注释：[1]罴差山：指分水岭。
Notes:[1] pi chai shan: refers to Fenshuiling (watershed mountain)。

[2] 无草木：游牧部落地区。

[2] wu cao mu (no grass wood)
Tr: it refers to the region of the nomads。

[3]马：指穆鲁克氏族。

[3]ma(horse) refers to the Muruke clan。

译文：由拜基特山往北一百里，有座山叫分水岭，是游牧部落地区，住着穆鲁克氏族。

Translation:
One hundred li further north from Byjiteshan there stands the Fenshuiling。 This region is where the nomads roam, the Muluke clan lives here。

03-01-24 北鲜山
Beixianshan
（106,68703E；72,13958N）

又北百八十里，曰北鲜之山[1]，是多马[2]，鲜水[3]出焉，北流注入涂吾之水[4]。

注释：[1]北鲜山：指布纳亚东山，读布纳亚新雷。简称布新雷，译为北鲜山。
Notes:[1] bei xian shan (north fresh mount)
Tr: refers to Bunaya-Dongshan, reads as Bunayaxinlei, shortened to Buxinlei, a close phonetic match to Beixianshan。

[2]马：指穆鲁克氏族。

[2]ma(horse)refers to Muluke clan。

[3] 鲜水：东河水。

[3] xian shui (fresh water) refers to Donghe River。

[4] 涂吾水：指科图部落河，简称科图河、科图伊。

[4] tu wu shui (smear me river)
Tr: refers to the Ketu clan river, shortened to Ketu River or Ketuy。

译文：又北一百八十里，有座山叫布纳亚东山，这里住着穆鲁克氏族，东河水从山间流出，向北流入科图河。
Translation:
One hundred and eighty li further north there stands the Bunaya-Dongshan。 The Muruke clans live there。 Donghe River flows out of there and goes north into Ketu River。

03-01-25 隄山
Tishan
（95,15394E；75,26323N）

又北百七十里，曰隄山[1]，多马[2]。有兽焉，其状如豹而文首[3]，名于泑[4]。泑水[5]出焉，东流而注于泰泽[6]，其中多龙鱼[7]。

凡北山经之首，自单狐之山至于隄山，凡二十五山，五千四百九十里，其神皆人面蛇身[8]。其祠之，毛用一雄鸡彘瘗[9]，吉玉用一珪[10]，瘗而不糈，其山北人[11]，皆生食不火之物[12]。

注释：[1]隄山：指泰梅尔山。
Notes:[1] ti shan (dam mount) refers to Taymyr Mountain。
[2]马：指穆鲁克氏族。
[2]ma(horse) refers to Muluke clan。
[3] 豹而文首：山区的乌斯季氏族。
[3] bao er wen shou (leopard with patterned head)
Tr: it refers to the Wusiji 【Ust】 clans from the mountains。
[4]泑：指塔列亚人。
[4] you refer to Taleya people。
[5] 泑水：指塔列亚河。
[5] you shui: refers to Taleya River。
[6] 泰泽：指泰梅尔湖。
[6] tai ze: Taymyr Lake 74° 32′ 34″ N, 101° 38′ 39″ E。
[7] 龙鱼：指湖畔的渔民。仡佬语读“湖”为龙。
[7] long yu (dragon fish)
Tr： it refers to the fishing tribes at the lake side。In Gelao concept, lake is read as long, a phonetic match to Chinese Long, the dragon。
[8] 人面蛇身：指定居的塞族的形象。
[8] ren mian she shen (human face snake body)
Tr: it refers to the image of the Saka people who settled down here。
[9] 毛用一雄鸡彘：代替祭词的玉用一软苍玉。雄鸡彘，指软苍玉。
[9] mao yong yi xiong ji shi (fur use one male rooster pig)
Tr: offering one jade piece in place of votive speech。 xiong ji shi: soft dark jade。
[10] 吉玉用一珪：最好的玉用一珪。在此解读为：最好用一珪。
[10] ji yu yong yi gui (best jade use one gui) best to use a jade gui。
Tr: it is mostly desirable to use one gui, (tablette de jade, silicium) 。
[11] 其山北人：东边有集镇。其山读且啥，指东边；北人，读贝惹，指有集镇。
[11] qi shan bei ren (its mount north person)

Tr: there is market town on the east side, qi shan: in Pu concept, it reads as qie sha, referring to east side, beiren: reads beire, meaning there exists market town。

[12] 生食不火之物：肃慎胡族的部落。生食，读竦斯，指肃慎；不火，读补胡，即胡族；物，指部落。
[12] sheng shi bu huo zhi wu (raw eat food not cooked)
Tr: it refers to the Sushen Hu tribe, a Pu phonetic match: shengshi/susi/sushen, buhuo/buhu/huzu, wu/stuff, refers to tribe。

译文：由布纳亚东山往西北一百七十里，有座山叫泰梅尔山，住着穆鲁克氏族。有一个氏族，是山区的乌斯季氏族，名叫塔列亚人。塔列亚河水从山间流出，向北流入泰梅尔湖，这里住着湖畔的渔民。
Translation:
One hundred and seventy li further northwest from Bunaya-dongshan there stands the Taymyr Mountain, where the Muluke clan live。 A mountain Wusiji clan known as Tayleya people is one of them。Tayleya river rises from the mountains and flows north into Taymyr Lake, where the Lakeside fishermen live。

综观北山经第一列山系，从当汾山到泰梅尔山，共计二十五座山，延绵五千四百九十里。这些山的山神皆塞族人的形象，祭祀时用一软苍玉代替祭词，最好是用一珪埋入地下而不用食物。东边有集镇，都是肃慎胡族的部落。
In sum, of the 1st list of mountains in the north, from Dangfenshan to Taymyr Mountain, there are a total of 25 mountains covering a distance of 5,490 li。 The mountain deities are in the image of local Saka people。When offering votive speech, instead of using grain, a piece of jade is used in its place, best to use a dark jade gui, buried under ground。 On the east side of the mountain there are townships of the Sushen Hu clans。

北山经第二山系

Book 3 Beishanjing; Chapter 2

03-02-01 管涔山
Guancenshan
（112,07354E；38,94927N）

北次二经之首，在河[1]之东，其首枕汾[2]，其名曰管涔之山[3]。其上无木而多草[4]，其下多玉 [5]。汾水出焉，而西流注于河。

注释：[1]河：指黄河。
Notes:[1] he(river)refers to Yellow River 。
[2] 枕汾：头靠着汾河。
[2] zhen fen (pillow fen)
Tr: its first mountain rests next to Fen River。
[3] 管涔山：指管涔山脉主峰，在忻州宁武县西南侧。
[3] guan cen shan (manage leaking mount)
Tr: it refers to the Guancenshan's main peak, on the southwest of Ningwu county, Xinzhou city, 38° 24′ 57.6″ N, 112° 44′ 2.4″ E。

[4] 无木而多草：指北胡的部落民。北胡，今演变为虎北；草，指察，即部落.
[4] wu mu er duo cao (no wood but a lot of grass)
Tr: the tribal people of Northern Hu, beihu: the term now becomes Hubei (tiger north), grass: cao/cha, refers to tribes。

[5]玉：指余庄氏族。
[5]yu(jade)
Tr：it refers to Yuzhuang clan, zhuang(village)。

译文：北山第二列山系的第一座山，在黄河的东侧，头靠着汾河，名叫管涔山. 它的西面是北胡的部落民，东面住着余庄氏族。汾河水从这里流出，向西流入黄河。
Translation:
The first mountain of the 2nd list of mountains in the north is situated to the east side of Yellow River。 It rests next to Fen River, it is called Guancenshan。 On its west side live the tribal people of Bei Hu。 On its east side live the Yuzhuang clan。Fen River rises out of here and flows west into Yellow River。

03-02-02 少阳山
Shaoyangshan
（111,65555E；38,95588N）

又西二百五十里，曰少阳之山[1]。其上多玉[2]，其下多赤银 [3] 。酸水出焉[4]，而东流注于汾水，其中多美赭[5]。

注释：[1]少阳山：指杏阳山，又称杏岭。
Notes:[1] shao yang shan (young sun mount)
Tr: it refers to Xinyangshan, also known as Xingling, xing(apricot)。

[2]玉：指水峪氏族。
[2]yu(jade) refers to Shuiyu clan。

[3] 赤银：指涔嶷氏族。
[3] chi yin (red silver) refers to Cenyi clan。

[4] 酸水：指杏岭水，简称杏水。
[4] suan shui (sour water)
Tr: it refers to Xingling River, shortened to Xing River 。

[6] 美赭：指五寨氏族。
[6] mei zhe (beautiful ocher)
Tr: it refers to Wuzhai clan (five villages clan) 。

译文：由管涔山往西二百五十里，有座山叫杏岭。山的西面住着水峪氏族，东面住着涔嶷氏族。杏水从山间流出，向东流入汾河，河边住着五寨氏族。
Translation:
Two hundred and fifty li further west from Guancenshan there stands the Xingling。 On its west side there live the Shuiyu clan, on its east side there live the Cenyi clan。Xing River comes out of the mountains and goes east into Fen River。The Wuzhai clan lives on its bank。

03-02-03 县雍山
Xianyongshan
（111,62654E；39,16622N）

又北五十里，曰县雍之山[1]。其上多玉[2]，其下多铜 [3]，其兽多闾麋 [4]，其鸟多白翟白鶮[5] 。晋水[6]出焉，而东南流注于汾水。其中多鮆鱼[7]，其状如鯈而赤鳞[9]，其音如叱[10]，食之不骄[11]。

注释：[1]县雍山：指县川山，原意为长界山。
Notes:[1] xian you shan: refers to Xianchuanshan, original meaning is Changjieshan， chang(long), jie(boundary)。
[2]玉：指河川氏族。
[2]yu(jade) refers to Hechuan tribe, Hechuan (river gully) 。
[3]铜：指岩臂氏族。今称大严备氏族。
[3] tong(copper) refers Yanbi (cliff arms) tribe, known today as Dayanbei, (big strict readiness) tribe。
[4] 闾麋：指令庄氏族。今或称利民。
[4]lv mi (kind of deer) refers to Linzhuang (order village) tribe, might be named as Limin (benefit people) 。
[5] 白翟白鶮：指羽窊、峪窊。今无考。白，读摆，窊的濮语读音。
[5] bai di bai you:(white bird white wild bird): refers to Yuwa: yuwa: valley gully, bai2 bai 3, Pu concept of wa reads as bai3, a phonetic match, found no trace in local place names。
[6] 晋水：指界水或畛水，从神池流入汾河。
[6] jin shui: refers to Jie River or Zhen River, Jie/zhen, border, flows from Shenchi (holy pond) into Fen River。
[7] 鮆鱼：指移民氏族。
[7]ci yu (ci fish: Japanese grenadier anchovy, Coilia nasus) refers to tribes of migrants。
[8] 鯈而赤鳞：饕餮的移民。鳞，读黎，指人和民。
[8] tiao er chi lin (fish with red scales) Taotie tribe of migrants, Lin/li, refers to people。
[9]叱：指神池。
[9] cha(accuse) refers to Holy Pond (shen chi) chi/chi, close phonetic match。
[10] 不骄：指北方氏族。
[10] bu jiao (not arrogant) refers to the tribes from the Northern parts。

译文：由杏岭往北五十里，有座山叫县川山。山的西面住着河川氏族，东面住着岩臂氏族，还有令庄氏族和羽窊人、峪窊人。畛水从山间流出，向东流入汾河。河口处住着移民氏族，是饕餮的移民，住在神池，是古老的北方氏族。
Translation:
Fifty li further north from Xingling there stands the Xianchuanshan。 On its west side live the Hechuan tribe, on its east, the Yanbi tribe, Lingzhuang tribe, Yuwa people, and Yuwa people。 Zhen River comes out of the mountains, flowing east into the Fen River。 On its river mouth, live the migrants, the Taotie tribes。 They live in Shenchi, they are very ancient northern tribes。

03-02-04 狐岐山
Huqishan
（112,04009E；39,73261N）

又北二百里，曰狐岐之山[1]，无草木[2]，多青碧[3]。胜水[4] 出焉，而东流注于汾水 [5] 。其中多苍玉[6]。

注释：[1]狐岐山：指胡阻山。今称阻虎山，属山西朔州阻虎乡。
Notes:[1]hu qi shan (fox fork mount) refers to Huzu Mountain, today is reversed into Zuhu Mountain (stop tiger), belongs to the Zuhu Xiang, Suo Zhou39° 19′ 50.88″ N, 112° 25′ 55.2″ E, Shanxi province。
[2] 无草木：游牧部落地区。

[2] wu cao mu (no grass wood) refers to the region of the nomads。

[3] 青碧：指高姓氏族。碧，在此指属、姓。

[3] qing bi (green clear) refers to the tribe bearing the surname of Gao, bi, refers to belong to, surname。

[4] 胜水：指酸茨河。

[4] sheng shui (victory water) refers to Suanci River。

[5] 汾水：指东河。又称桑干河。

[5] fen shui (fen water)

Tr： it refers to Dong(east) River, also known as Sanggan River。 Also is transliterated into Sangkan River。

[6] 苍玉：读澄溢，指清水河氏族。

[6] cang yu (dark jade)

Tr： reads as Cheng yi, a close Pu concept of clear water river, here refers to the Qingshuihe clan。

译文：由县川山往东北二百里，有座山叫阻虎山。这里是游牧部落地区，住着高姓氏族。酸茨水从山间流出，向东流入桑干河。这里住着清水河氏族。

Translation:

Two hundred li northeastward from Xianchuanshan, stands the Zuhushan。 This is the region of nomads, the tribe bearing surname of Gao live here。 Suanci River comes out of here, going east into Sanggan River。 The Qingshuihe tribe live there。

03-02-05 白沙山

Baishashan

（112,49562E； 40,53169N）

又北三百五十里，曰白沙之山[1]，广员三百里，尽沙也[2]，无草木鸟兽[3]。鮪水[4] 出于其上，潜[5] 于其下，是多白玉[6]。

注释：[1]白沙山：指沙呼山，是内蒙古凉城的古称谓，今有沙呼村遗存。

Notes： [1] bai sha shan (white sand mount) refers to Shahu (sand yelling) Mountain, old name for Liangcheng (cool city) 40°29′ ~ 40°32′N， 112°28′ ~ 112°30′ E, in Inner Mongolia, today, shahu is retained in the village name: Shahu village。

[2] 尽沙也：沙乡部落。

[2] jin sha ye (full of sands) refers to the Shaxiang tribe。

[3] 无草木鸟兽：游牧僚族部落。

[3] wu cao mu niao shou (no grass wood bird beast) 。

Tr: Lao tribes of nomads。

[4] 鮪水：指小南河。

[4] you shui: refers to Lesser Nanhe River。

[5]潜：指迁、流向。

[5] qian: submerge,

Tr: moving, flowing。

[6] 白玉：指沙呼夷。

[6]: bai yu （ white jade）: refers to shahu Yi。

译文：由阻虎山往北三百五十里，有座山叫沙呼山。这里三百里开阔地，是沙乡部落，是游牧僚族的部落。小南河发源于西边，流向东边，这里住着沙呼夷。

Translation:

Three hundred and fifty li further north from Zuhushan there stands the Shahushan。 In this open land of three hundred li, there lives the Shaxiang clan, they are the Liao tribes of the nomads。 Xiao Nanhe River originates from the west and goes east; the Shahu Yi lives here。

03-02-06 尔是山
Ershishan
（112,59378E；41,14834N）

又北四百里，曰尔是之山[1]，无草木[2]，无水[3]。

注释：[1]尔是山：锡勒草原，也读锡尔蓍，谐音尔是。今察哈尔右翼中旗。
Notes: [1]er shi shan:
Tr: it refers to Xile steppe, also reads as Xi'ershi, a close phonetic match, known today as Chaha'er Right Middle Banner 41° 17′ 0″ N, 112° 38′ 0″ E。
[2] 无草木：游牧部落。
[2] wu cao mu (no grass wood) refers to the nomads。
[3] 无水：指苏部落。也称苏纪，今有地名苏计。
[3] wu shui (no water) refers to the Su tribe, Su/shui, a close phonetic match, also known as Su Ji, Ji: tribe, a relic place name is Su Ji。

译文：由沙呼山往北四百里，有座山叫锡尔蓍山，是游牧部落地区，是苏部落的居住地。
Translation:
Four hundred li further north from Shahushan, stands the Xiershishan。 It is the land of the nomads, where the Su tribes live。

03-02-07 狂山
Kuangshan
（112,66734E；41,8143N）

又北三百八十里，曰狂山[1]，无草木[2]。是山也，冬夏有雪[3]。狂水[4] 出焉，而西流注于浮水[5]，其中多美玉[6]。

注释：[1]狂山：指库仑山，今称库仑苏木。
Notes： [1] kuang shan(crazy mount) refers to Kulun Mountain, known today as Kulun Sum 41° 45′ 33.7″ N, 112° 39′ 55.55″ E。
[2] 无草木：游牧部落地区。
[2] wu cao mu (no grass wood) refers to the land of the nomads。
[3] 冬夏有雪：外部落国地区。
[3] dong xia you xue (winter summer have snow) refers to outside tribes' settlements。
[4] 狂水：指库仑水。
[4] kuang shui (crazy water); refers to the Kulun River。
[5] 浮水：指铁沙盖水。
[5] fu shui (floating water) refers to the Tieshagai (iron sand lid) River。
[6] 美玉：指巴音夷。巴音、白音的意思是"美"。
[6] mei yu (beautiful jade) refers to the Bayin tribe, Bayin, Baiyin, a Mongolian term for beautiful。

译文：由锡尔著山往北三百八十里，有座山叫库仑山，是游牧部落地区。这座山是外部落国地区。库仑水从山间流出，向西流入铁沙盖水，这里住着巴音夷。
Translation:
Three hundred and eighty li northward from the Xiershishan, stands the Kulun Mountain, the region where the nomads roam。This mountain is occupied by outside tribes。Kulun River comes out of the mountain, going west into Tieshagai River, where the Bayin tribes live。

03-02-08 诸余山
Zhuyushan
（112,9032E；42,4005N）

又北三百八十里，曰诸余之山[1]。其上多铜玉[2]，其下多松柏[3]，诸余之水出焉，而东流注于旄水[4]。

注释：[1]诸余山：指朱日山，今称朱日和。和，是山概念"洪"的谐音。
Notes: [1] zhu yu shan (various remaining mount)。
Tr: it refers to Zhurihe, meaning Zhurishan, he/hong, Pu concept of mountain, a phonetic match。
[2] 铜玉：指住在敖包边的人。
[2] tong yu (copper jade)
Tr: refers to the people who live around Aobao (pile of stones)。
[3] 松柏：读苏泊，指小的淖尔。这里指哈日淖尔居民
[3] song bai (pine poplar)
Tr: reads as su bo, meaning small nuur (lake) here it refers to the residents of Harinuur。118°27′E，49°51′N。
[4] 旄水：朱也读旄（mao），旄水实际为朱日水的下游。
[4] mao shui (banner water)
Tr: zhu is read as mao, here it refers to the lower branch of the Zhuri River。

译文：由库仑山往北三百八十里，有座山叫朱日山。山的西面住着敖包人，东面住着哈日淖尔人。朱日水从山间流出，向东流入旄水。
Translation：
Three hundred and eighty li further north from Kulunshan there stands the Zhurishan。On the west side of the mountain live the Aobao people。On the east side of the mountain live the Harinuur people。Zhuri River rises from the mountains and flows east into Maoshui River。

03-02-09 敦头山
Duntoushan
（113,65671E；43,8533N）

又北三百五十里，曰敦头之山[1]，其上多金玉[2]，无草木[3]。旄水出焉，而西流注于印泽[4]。其中多勃马[5]，牛尾而白身[6]，一角[7]，其音如呼[8]。

注释：[1]敦头山：指冈仡山，今称冈干山。实际介绍北麓的聚居区，今称苏尼特左旗。
Notes：[1] dun tou shan: refers to Gangga Mountain, known today as Ganggan Mountain。It is a description of the settlements in the north side of the Mountain, known today as Sunite Left Banner。
[2] 金玉：指冈干乌拉氏族。
[2] jin yu (gold jade) refers to the Ganggan Ula tribe。
[3] 无草木：游牧部落。
[3] wu cao mu (no grass wood) refers to the nomadic tribes。

[4] 印泽：指道布音泽。
[4] yin ze: refers to the Daobuyinze Lake。
[5] 勃马：指山区的忙勒族。
[5]bo ma (strong horse) refers to the Mangle tribe in the mountains。
[6] 牛尾而白身：僚夷的山区氏族。白，在此读 bo 音。
[6] niu wei er bai shen (ox tail and white body) refers to the mountain tribes of the Liao people。 Bai, in Pu concept reads as bo。
[7] 一角：大支系。
[7] yi jiao (one horn) big or major branch of the tribe。
[8]呼：指呼和德惹，苏尼特左旗的古称谓。
[8]hu(shout) refers to huhedere: the old name for Sunite Left Banner。

译文：由朱日山往北三百五十里，有座山叫冈干山，山的西面住着冈干乌拉夷，是游牧部落。旄水从这里流出，向西流入道布音泽。这里住着山区的忙勒族，是僚夷的山区氏族的大支系，住在呼和德惹。
Translation:
Three hundred and fifty li northward from Zhuri Mountain, stands the Ganggan Mountain。 On its west side live the Ganggan Ula tribe, they are the nomads。 Mao River flows out of here, goes west into Daobuyinze。 The mountain tribe Mangle people live there。 They are the big branch of the mountain tribes of the Liao people, living in Huhedere。

03-02-10 钩吾山
Gouwushan
（113,90837E；45,2398N）

又北三百五十里，曰钩吾之山[1]。其上多玉[2]，其下多铜[3]。有兽焉，其状如羊而人面[4]，其木在腋下[5]，虎齿人爪[6]，其音如婴儿[7]，名曰狍鸮[8]，是食人[9]。

注释：[1]钩吾山：指达里甘嘎部落山，简称甘吾山。
Notes: [1] gou wu shan (hook me mount) refers to Daligangga tribe Mountain, shortened to Ganwu Mountain。
[2]玉：指水门氏族。今称翁贡氏族。
[2]yu(jade) refers to Shuimen (water gate) tribe, today known as Wonggong tribe。
[3]铜：指通黎山氏族，也称输黎山氏族。今称斯林博德。
[3] tong(copper) refers to the Tonglishan tribe。 Also known as the Shulishan tribe, they are called today Silinbode。
[4] 羊身人面：牧羊氏族居民。
[4] yang shen ren mian (sheep body human face) refers to the shepherds' tribes。
[5] 腋下：耶湘，今称甘嘎湖。
[5]ye xia (armpit) close phonetic match for Yexiang, known today as Ganga Lake。
[6] 虎齿人爪：游牧的定居支系。
[6]hu chi ren zhua (tiger teeth human fingernails) refers to the settled tribe of the nomads。
[7] 婴儿：北面。
[7] yin er(infant) refers to the north。
[8] 狍鸮：指跑狼岭氏族。
[8] pao xiao (roe owl) refers to the Paolangling clan。 Pao(run) a close phonetic to Pao(roe)。
[9] 是食人：是原住居民。
[9] shi shi ren (yes eat human); refers to the original settlers。

译文：由冈干山往北三百五十里，有座山叫甘吾山。山的西面住着翁贡人，东面住着输黎山人。有一个氏族是牧羊氏族的居民，检目在耶湘，住在北面，名叫跑狼岭氏，是原住居民。

Translation：

Three hundred and fifty li northward from Ganggan Mountain stands the Ganwu Mountain。 On its west side, live the Wengong tribe, on its east side the Shulishan tribe。 A shepherd's tribe, with its center in Yexiang Lake, lives on the north, the Paolangling (running wolf range) tribe。 They are the original settlers。

03-02-11 北嚣山

Beixiaoshan

（115,78035E；49,14573N）

又北三百里，曰北嚣之山[1]。无石[2]，其阳多碧[3]，其阴多玉[4]。有兽焉，其状如虎，而白身犬首[5]，马尾彘鬣[6]，名曰独谷[7]。有鸟焉，其状如乌，人面[8]，名曰䳤鹛[9]，宵飞而昼伏[10]，食之已暍[11]。涔水出焉，而东流注于印泽[12]。

注释：[1]北嚣山：指跑狼岭。

Notes：[1] bei xiao shan (north noisy mount) refers to Paolangling (running wolf range) Mountain。

[2] 无石：沙尔部落的区域。

[2] wu shi (no stone) refers to the region where the Shar tribes live。

[3] 碧：指河滨夷，即克鲁伦河滨氏族。

[3]bi(clear) a Pu concept refers to river, here means Hebin Yi--the riverside tribes, the Kelulun riverside tribes。

[4] 玉：此处沙尔被以意译为 jue 音了，而 jue 又是"玉"的濮语读音。

[4]yu(jade),

Tr: jue: Pu concept for jade, refers to Shar, transliterated into Jue。

[5] 虎而白身人首：游牧的山区犬戎。

[5]hu er bai shen ren shou (tiger with white body human head) 。

Tr: it refers to the Dog Rong of the mountain nomads。

[6] 马尾彘鬣：通古斯胡夷。

[6]ma wei zhi zong (horse tail pig mane)

Tr: refers to the Tongus Hu people。

[7] 独谷：指吐谷浑。谷，读音 yu。

[7] du gu (lonely valley) refers to Tuyuhun, gu: yu。

[8]乌，人面：乌尔特的居民。

[8] wu, ren mian (bird, human face)

Tr: refers to Wu'erte settlers。

[9] 䳤鹛：指跑蒙，即跑狼岭蒙族。

[9] pan mao:

Tr: pan/po mao/meng, a close phonetic match for Paomeng; refers to the Mongolian tribes from the Paolangling Mountain。

[10] 宵飞而昼伏：跑狼岭东面的山胡。昼，读照音，指"山"之意。

[10] xiao fei er zhou fu (night fly but day sleep)

Tr: refers to the Mountain Hu tribe living on the east side of the Paolangling Mountain。 zhou(day) refers as zhao, a close Pu concept of Mountain。

[11] 已暍：指杭乌拉夷和辉尼特夷。毫、杭、辉，都读暍音。

[11] yi ye (cure heatstroke)

Tr: refers to Hang Ula Yi and Huinite Yi。 Hao, Hang, Hui, close phonetic match to ye。

[12] 印泽：指阿愣多尔莫湖。
[12] ang/yang ze; a body of water
Tr: refers to Aleduoermo Lake 117°08′E，48°58′N 。

译文：由甘吾山往北三百里，有座山叫跑狼岭，是沙尔部落的区域。山的南面住着河滨氏族，北面住着沙尔氏族。有一个氏族，是游牧的山区犬戎，是通古斯胡夷，名叫吐谷浑。有一群人是乌尔特居民，名叫跑蒙，是跑狼岭东面的山胡，是古老的杭乌拉夷和辉尼特夷。涔水从山间流出，向东流入阿愣多尔莫湖。
Translation:
Three hundred li further northward from Ganwushan, stands the Paolangling Mountain, a region where the Shar tribes live。On the south side lives the Lakeside clan, on its north side lives the Shar clan。 A mountain Dog Rong clan, the nomadic Tongus Hu, is called Tuyuhun。 A group of people belongs to the Mountain Hu, who live on the east part of the Paolangling Mountain, they are known as Pao mongolian, the settlers of Wu'erte, the ancient Hang Ula Yi and the Huiteni Yi。 Cen River comes out of the mountains and goes east into Alengduoermo Lake。

03-02-12 梁渠山
Liangqushan
（119,9052E；51,35479N）

又北三百五十里，曰梁渠之山[1]。无草木[2]，多金玉 [3] 。脩水[4] 出焉，而东流注于雁门[5]，其兽多居暨[6]，其状如彙而赤毛[7]，其音如豚[8]。有鸟焉，其状如夸父[9]，四翼一目犬尾[10]，名曰嚣[11]，其音如鹊[12]，食之已腹痛[13]，可以止衕[14]。

注释：[1]梁渠山：指洛奇山，今称奥洛奇山。48° 18′ 0″ N, 89° 30′ 0″ E
Notes： [1] liang qu shan (range ditch mount)
Notes [1] refers to Luoqi Mountain, known today as Oluoqi Mountain。
[2] 无草木：游牧部落地区。
[2] wu cao mu (no grass wood) refers to the land of the nomads。
[3] 金玉：指洛奇夷。濮语读金玉为涅吉，与洛奇谐音。
[3] jin yu (gold jade)
Tr: refers to Olgii Yi, Pu concept jinyu reads as nieji, a phonetic match for luoji。
[4] 脩水：指色勒布尔河。(色勒博河)
[4] xiu shui (tall water)
Tr: refers to Selebur River, xiu/see a close phonetic match, written in English as Selbe River。
[5] 雁门：指大江，在此指额尔古纳河。
[5] yan men: (goose gate)
Tr: refers to big river, here the Argun River。
[6] 居暨：指吉宝沟氏族。
[6] ju ji
Tr: refers to the Jibaogou tribe。 Jibao (best treasure) gou(gully)。
[7] 彙而赤毛：室韦的移民。
[7] hui er chi mao (gather and red hair) 。
Tr： refers to Shiwei migrants。
[8]豚：指集镇。
[8] tun(pig)
Tr： refers to township。
[9] 夸父：指北胡。在此是指广义的北胡，而非卓资夷。
[9] kua fu (boast father) refers to Northern Hu, an umbrella term for the Beihu, but no the Zhuozi Yi。

[10] 四翼一目犬尾：母系的雅利安犬戎夷。
[10]si yi yi mu quan wei（four wings one eye dog tail)
Tr: refers to the Dog Rong Yi from the matrilineal Aryans。
[11]嚣：指匈奴。
[11] xiao(noisy) refers to the Huns, or the Xiongnu。
[12]鹊：指洛奇镇。
[12] que(sparrow) refers to Olgii town。
[13] 已腹痛：指扎乌德夷。
[13] yi fu tong (cure belly ache) refers to Zhawude people。
[14] 可以止衕：指阿金斯科耶 51° 6′ 0″ N, 114° 30′ 0″ E 的支系。止衕，指支系。衕，应读为 dong。
[14]ke yi zhi tong/dong (can stop pain)
Tr: refers to the Aginskoye branch; zhidong: refers to branch, tong/dong, close phonetic match 。

译文：由跑狼岭往北三百五十里，有座山叫洛奇山，是游牧部落地区，住着洛奇氏族。色勒布尔水从山间流出，向东流入额尔古纳河。这里住着吉宝沟氏族，是室韦的移民，住在集镇上。有一群人，是北胡氏族，是母系的雅利安犬戎夷，名叫匈奴，住在洛奇镇，是古老的扎乌德夷，是阿金斯科耶的支系。
Translation：
Three hundred and fifty li further northward from Paolangling Mountain， stands the Olgii Mountain, a region of the nomads, where the Olgii clans live。Selber River comes from the mountain and goes east into Argun River。The Jibaogou, a migrant clan of Shiwei, lives in the town。Another group, the North Hu tribe, the matrilineal tribe of Ayan's Dog Rong, is called the Huns or the Xiongnu。They live in the Olgii town。They are the ancient Zhawude Yi, a branch of the Aginskoye clan。

03-02-13 姑灌山
Guguanshan
（124,68974E；56,67297N）

又北四百里，曰姑灌之山[1]，无草木[2]。是山也，冬夏有雪[3]。

注释：[1]姑灌山：指贾格德山，是外兴安岭的中心区。今称涅留恩格里。实际向东北。
Notes：[1]gu guan shan。
Tr: it refers to Jiagede Mountain, the central area of Waixinganling Mountains。 It is known today as Neryungr, in fact in a northeast direction。
[2] 无草木：游牧部落地区。
[2] wu cao mu (no grass wood)
Tr: refers to the territories of the nomadic clans and tribes。
[3] 冬夏有雪：外部落国的山峰。
[3] dong xia you xue (winter summer has snow)
Tr: the mountains and peaks of the foreign tribal nations。

译文：由洛奇山往东北四百里，有座山叫贾格德山，是游牧部落地区。这座山是外部落国的山峰。
Translation:
Four hundred li further northeast from Olgii Mountain there stands the Jiagede Mountain。 This is the territory of the nomads。This mountain is in the foreign tribal nation 's land。

03-02-14 湖灌山
Huguanshan

（129,74172E；62,03975N）

又北三百八十里，曰湖灌之山[1]。其阳多玉[2]，其阴多碧[3]，多马[4]。湖灌之水[5]出焉，而东流注于海[6]，其中多䱇[7]。有木[8]焉，其叶如柳而赤理[9]。

注释：[1]湖灌山：指乌古尔山。中心区在乌古尔，今称雅库茨克。
Notes：［1］hu guan shan (lake fill mount) refers to Wugur Mountain。 Its center is in Wugur, todays Yakutsk 62° 1′ 38″ N, 129° 43′ 55″ E。
[2]玉：指日利古尔氏族。日，多由“桔”音译成，而桔指玉。
[2]yu(jade) refers to Riligur tribe. ri/ju/yu close phonetic match 。
[3]碧：指河滨夷。有勒拿河滨的氏族，也有维柳河滨的氏族。
[3]bi (clear) refers to the riverside tribes including the tribes along the Lena River, as well as the Weiliu River (the Vilyuy River)。
[4]马：指胡族。
[4]ma(horse) refers to the Hu tribes。
[5] 湖灌水：指勒拿河的古尔部落段，实际是东北流向。
[5]hu guan shui: refers to the Gur tribe tributary of the Lena River, it goes in fact to the Northeast direction。
[6]海：指伯陵海，今称拉普捷夫海。
[6] hai (sea) refers to the Beling Sea, today's Laptev Sea。
[7]䱇：指萨内亚氏族。
[7] dan (snake like fish) refers to the Saneiya tribe。
[8]木：指氏族支系。
[8]mu(wood) refers to the tribe branches。
[9] 柳而赤理：维柳河边的车尔尼人。
[9] liu er chi li (willow with red marking) refers to the Chernites along the Vilyuy River。 chyorny/cherny) meaning "black"。

译文：由贾格德山往北三百八十里，有座山叫乌古尔山。山的南面住着日利古尔氏族，北面住着河滨夷及胡族。乌古尔水从这里流过，向东北流入伯陵海，这里住着萨内亚氏族。有一个氏族支系，是维柳河滨的车尔尼人。
Translation:
Three hundred and eighty li further north from Jagede Mountain, stands the Wugur Mountain。 On its south side live the Riligur clan, on its northern side, live the Riverside Yi and Hu Yi。 Wugur River flows through here and goes northeast into Beling Sea (the Laptev Sea) 。 The Saneiya clan lives here. Another clan is the Chernys, who lives along the Vilyuy River。

03-02-15 洹山
Huanshan
（147,08033E；65,16911N）

又北水行五百里，流沙[1]三百里，至于洹山[2]，其上多金玉[3]。三桑生之[4]，其树皆无枝[5]，其高百仞[6]。百果树生之[7]。其下多怪蛇[8]。

注释：[1]流沙：指行旱路。流读劳音，指旱；沙，指行。
Notes： [1] liu sha (moving sand) means travel by land; liu/lao-- to drought, sha/sand --to move。
[2] 洹山：指海厄尔山，今称切尔斯基山。部落中心在萨瑟尔。

[2] huan shan: Hainuoer Mountain, today known as Chersky Mountain。The tribal center is at Saser,

[3] 金玉：指埃利金夷。

[3] jin yu (gold jade) refers to the Elgin people。

[4] 三桑生之：萨瑟尔建立的。

[4] san sang sheng zhi (three mulberry produce it)
Tr: Saser establishes it。

[5] 其树皆无枝：属于因迪吉尔卡河部落支系。

[5] qi shu jie wu zhi (its tree has no branches)
Tr: belong to the Indigirka River tribal branches。

[6] 其高百仞：河边部落集镇。

[6] qi gao bai ren (its height hundred ren)
Tr: tribal township along the river。

[7] 百果树生之：巴格雷昌族建立的集镇。

[7] bai guo shu sheng zhi (hundred fruit tree produce it) 。
Tr: The Bageleichang tribe built those towns。

[8] 怪蛇：巴格雷昌氏族。

[8] guai she (strange snake) refers to the Bageleichang tribe。

译文：由乌古尔山往北水行五百里，旱行三百里，到达海厄尔山。山的西面住着埃利金夷，这里是萨瑟尔人建立的属于因迪吉尔卡河部落支系的河边部落集镇。这个国家的集镇，还有巴格雷昌族建立的集镇。在山的东面，住着巴格雷昌氏族。

Translation:
Five hundred li by water northward and then another three hundred li by land from the Wugur Mountain, stands the Hainuor Mountain。On its west side live the Egilli tribe, a riverside town is built by the Saser people who belong to the Indigirka River tribal branch。 The town established by Bageleichang is the nation's township。On its east side, the Bageleichang tribe live。

03-02-16 敦题山
Duntishan
（140,2283E；70,53719N）

又北三百里，曰敦题之山[1]，无草木[2]，多金玉[3]。是錞于北海。

凡北次二经之首，自管涔之山至于敦题之山，凡十七山，五千六百九十里。其神皆蛇身人面[4] 。其祠：毛用一雄鸡彘 [5]瘗，用一璧一珪，投 [6] 而不糈。

注释：[1]敦题山：指图马特山。
Notes: [1] dun ti shan: refers to Tumat Mountain。

[2] 无草木：游牧部落地区。

[2] wu cao mu (no grass wood) refers to the nomadic region。

[3] 金玉：指因迪吉尔卡夷。在海厄尔山西面的金玉族群也是因迪吉尔卡夷。

[3] jin yu (gold jade) refers to Indigirka tribe。 The Jinyu tribes on the west side of Hainuor Mountain also belong to the Indigirka Yi。

[4] 蛇身人面：指肃慎族居民的形象。肃慎族又称金，读音奢，谐音蛇。

[4] she shen ren mian (snake body human face)
Tr: the image of Sushen settlers, Sushen is also addressed by Jin, in Pu concept it is read as she1, a pun on snake, reads as she2 in Chinese。

[5] 雄鸡彘：指软苍玉。

[5] xiong ji shi (male chicken pig) refers to soft dark jade。

[6]投：指说、念、唱、辞。

[6] tou (throw) refers to speak, read, chanting and speech。

译文：由海厄尔山往北三百里，有座山叫图马特山，是游牧部落地区，住着因迪吉尔卡夷。这里紧邻北海。

Translation:

Three hundred li further northward from Hainuor Mountain, stands Tumat Mountain。 This is the region of the nomads; the Indigirka Yi lives here. It is close to North Sea。

综观北山第二列山系，从管涔山到图马特山，共十七座山（实际是 16 座），延绵五千六百九十里。这些山的山神都是肃慎族人的形象。祭祀这些山神时，用软苍玉代替祭词，用一璧一珪念一下祭词，不用食物。

In sum， the 2nd list of mountains in the north, from Guancenshan to Tumat Mountain, records a total of 17 mountains (in fact only 16), covering a distance of 5,690 li。 The mountain deities are in the images of the Sushen tribal men。When sacrificing to the deities, use a piece of soft dark jade in place of speech。One bi jade and one gui jade are offered, and votive speech is read, food is not offered。

北山经第三山系

Book 3 Beishanjing; chapter 3

03-03-01 归山

Guishan

(112,41385E，35,4863N)

北次三经之首，曰太行之山。其首曰归山[1]，其上有金玉 [2]，其下有碧[3]。有兽焉，其状如麢羊而四角[4]，马尾而有距[5]，其名曰驒，善还[6]，其名自訆。有鸟焉，其状如鹊，白身、赤尾、六足[7]，其名曰鷾，是善惊[8]，其名自詨。

注释：[1]归山：指沁河出口处的衙道山。归，读工音，指道路。今山西阳城。

Notes： [1] gui shan(return mount)refers to the Yadao Mountain at the water outlet of the Qin River。 gui(return) reads in Pu concept as gong, refers to way, road。 This is about the Yang City in Shanxi province。

[2] 金玉：指沁河夷。金玉，在此是沁溢的音译。

[2] jin yu (gold jade) refers to the Qin River tribe。 Jin yu, a close phonetic match for Qin Yi, yi Pu concept for river。

[3]碧：指罗河、柿河氏族。

[3]bi(clear) refers to the Luo River tribe and the Shi River tribe。

[4] 麢羊而四角：指犁川的氏族。

[4] ling yang er si jiao (deer with four horns) refers to the Lichuan tribe, Ling/li, a close phonetic match。

[5] 马尾而有距：指苗夷的部落氏族。有距，读补纪，指部落氏族。

[5]ma wei/yi er you ju:(horse tail with distance between) refers to the Miao tribes。 Ma yi: miao people, you ju/reads as bu ji, refers to tribes。

[6]驔，善还：驔和善还都是指凰头氏族，凰头苗。

[6] huan/xuan, shan huan: refers to the Miao people, the Fengtou Miao. Both huan and shan huan all refers to the Fengtou (phoenix head) miao people。

[7]鹊，白身、赤尾、六足：南面的红土岭游牧氏族。

[7] que(sparrow), bai shen (white body), chi yi (red tail), liu zu (six feet) refers to the Nomadic Hongtuling (red earth range)tribes to the south。

[8]鳻(fen)，是善惊：指盘氏，是尚部落氏族。今称盘爽。

[8] fen, shi shan jing (fen is easily scared) refers to Pan people, the Shang tribe。 Today they are called Panshuang。

译文：北山第三列山系为太行山系，第一座山名叫衙道山。山的西面有沁河氏族，东面有罗河、柿河氏族。有一个氏族，是犁川的部落氏族，是苗夷的部落氏族，名叫凰头苗，他们也这样介绍自己。有一群人，是南面的红土岭游牧氏族，名叫盘氏，是尚部落氏族，他们也这样介绍自己。

Translation:

The third system of the mountains in the north is the Taihang range。Its first mountain is the Yadao Mountain。On its west side live the Qinhe River tribe, on its east, the Luo River tribe, and the Shi River tribe。A tribe, the Lichuang Miao people is called Fengtou Miao, they thus introduce themselves so。A group people known as bearing the surname of Pan, the nomadic Hongtuling tribe live in the south。 They belong to the Shang people; they introduce themselves as such。

03-03-02 龙侯山
Longhoushan
(113,26856E， 35,54988N)

又东北二百里，曰龙侯之山[1]，无草木[2]，多金玉[3]。决决之水[4] 出焉，而东流注于河 [5] 。其中多人鱼 [6] ，其状如鳑鱼 [7] ，四足[8]，其音如婴儿[9]，食之无痴疾[10]。

注释：[1]龙侯山：指陇猴，即猴山。濮语读猴为夺，又称陇夺，今称夺火山。

Notes： [1] long hou shan: refers to Long Hou(monkey)thus, the Houshan (monkey mount) Pu concept read monkey as duo, therefore Longduo。Today it is known as Duohuo Mountain, duohuo (snatch fire) 。

[2] 无草木：游牧部落地区。

[2] wu cao mu (no grass wood) refers to the nomadic region。

[3] 金玉：指金掌夷。

[3] jin yu (gold jade) refers to Jinzhang (golden palm) people。

[4] 决决水：指夹沟水。

[4] jue jue shui: refers to Jiagou River。

[5]河：指关河。

[5] he(river) refers to the Guan River。

[6] 人鱼：定居夷。

[6] ren yu (human fish); refers to settlement people。

[7] 鳑鱼：指半坡夷。

[7] ti yu (big carp): refers to the Banpo (half slope) people。

[8] 四足：指支系。

[8]si zu (four feet) refers to tribal branches。

[9] 婴儿：指北面。

[9] yin er (infant) refers to the north。

[10] 无痴疾：指掌咀部落氏族，今称屋掌口人。

[10] wu chi ji (no retarded illness) refers to Zhangzui tribe, known today as Wuzhangkou people。 wu/house, zhang/palm, kou/mouth。

译文：由衙道山往东北二百里，有座山叫夺火山，是游牧部落地区，住着金掌夷。夹沟水从山间流出，向东南流入关河。这里住着定居之夷，是半坡夷的氏族，住在北面，是古老的掌咀部落夷。

Translation:

Two hundred li northeastward from Yadaoshan, stands the Duohuoshan, a nomadic region, where the Jinzhang tribe live。Jiagou River comes out of the mountain, goes southeast into Guan River。 A settled tribe, known as the Banpo people live in the north。They are the ancient Zhangzui tribal Yi。

03-03-03 马成山

Machengshan

(113,56456E，36,0314N)

又东北二百里，曰马成之山[1]，其上多文石[2]，其阴多金玉[3]。有兽焉，其状如白犬而黑头[4]，见人则飞[5]，其名曰天马[6]，其鸣自訆，有鸟焉，其状如乌[7]，首白而身青，足黄[8]，是名曰鶌鶋[9]。其名自詨，食之不饥[10]，可以已寓[11]。

注释：[1]马成山：指蒙且山，意为苗坪，又称恒坪、恒且，今称杏城。

Notes： [1]ma cheng mount refers to Mengqieshan, a close phonetic match, meaning the place of the Miao people。 It is also known as Hengping, Hengqie, or today's Xing(apricot) city, cheng/qie/xing, phonetic shifting。

[2] 文石：指水头沟氏族。

[2] wen shi: refers to Shuitougou tribe。

[3] 金玉：在此指圪丁夷。丁，在濮语中读金。

[3] jin yu (gold jade) refers to Gading Yi。ding, Pu concept, reads as jin(gold)。

[4] 白犬而黑头：山东面的杏陶氏。杏，读恒音，与黑谐音。

[4] bai quan er hei tou (white dog with black head); refers to the Xingtao tribe on the east side of the mountain. xing(apricot) in Pu concept reads heng, a close phonetic match for hei (black), thus black head。

[5] 见人则飞：是那个集镇的统治氏族。

[5] jian ren ze fei (seeing people fly away)

Tr: the ruling clan of that town。

[6] 天马：指陶蒙，即中心苗、红苗。

[6] tian ma (heavenly horse) refers to Taomeng, a close phonetic match to tian ma, meaning the central Miao, the Hong(red) miao。

[7]乌：在此指北方。

[7] wu(bird)refers to the North。

[8] 首白而身青，足黄：苏泊淖尔犬戎胡族。身青，指犬戎族；足黄，指胡族。

[8] shou bai er shen qing, zu huang (head white body green, feet yellow)

Tr: body green: Dog quan, quan/qing, a close phonetic match, feet yellow, refers to the Hu tribes。 Hu/huang, a close phonetic match。

[9] 鶌鶋：指玉峡关氏族。鶌鶋是玉峡的倒装句。

[9] qu ju (bird) refers to Yuxiaguan tribe, qu ju/ju qu, yu xia: phonetic shifting。

[10] 不饥：指部落氏族。

[10] bu ji (not hungry) refers to tribal people。

[11] 可以已寓：夏国的玉夷。
[11] ke yi yi yu (can self-housed) refers to the Yu people of the Xia nation。

译文：由夺火山往北二百里，有座山叫蒙且山。山的西面住着水头沟氏族，北面住着圪丁氏族。有一个氏族，是山东面的杏陶氏,是那个集镇的统治氏族，名叫陶蒙。他们自己也这样称呼。有一群人，是北方氏族，是苏泊淖尔的犬戎胡族，他们的名称叫玉峡氏，他们自己也这样解释，是古老的部落氏族，是夏国的玉夷。
Translation:
Two hundred li northward from Duohuoshan, stands the Mengqieshan。On its west live the Shuigou tribe, on its north the Gading tribe。A clan, the ruling people, the Xingtao tribe live in the east of the mountain, they are the Taomeng。They also address themselves thus。Another group, the northern tribe, the Dog Rong from Supanaor, are the Hu people, known as Yuxia tribe, they thus call themselves。 They are an ancient tribe, the Yu people of the Xia nation。

03-03-04 咸山
Xianshan
(113,52521E，36,24656N)

又东北七十里，曰咸山[1]，其上有玉[2]，其下多铜[3]，是多松柏[4]，草多茈草[5]。条菅之水[6] 出焉，而西南流注于长泽 [7] 。其中多器酸 [8] ，三岁一成 [9] ，食之已疠 [10] 。

注释：[1]咸山：指长岭，今称长寺岭。
Notes： [1] xian shan (salty mount) refers to Changling (long range) today's Changsi (long temple) ling (mount)。
[2]玉：指峪水氏族。
[2]yu(jade) refers to the Yushui tribe, Yu/yu a phonetic match。
[3]铜：指桃花洞氏族。
[3] tong(copper) refers to the Taohuadong tribe。Taohuadong (peach flower cave) a close phonetic match between tao /tong。
[4] 松柏：指西岭背氏族。
[4] song bai (pine poplar) refers to Xilingbei (west range back) tribe。
[5] 茈草：指羊坡、草庄氏族。
[5] zi cao: refers to Yangpo (goat slope) tribe and Caozhuang (grass village) tribe。
[6] 条菅水：指喊梁水，又称寒梁水。今谐音称天脊水。
[6] tiao guan shui: refers to Hanliang River, or Hanliang River, a close phonetic match, today known as the Tianji (heavenly spine) River。
[7] 西南流注于长泽：东南流入漕水。
[7] xi nan liu zhu yu chang ze (west south flows into the long lake) 。
Tr: flows southeast into the Cao River。 xi/west a Pu pun to east。
[8] 器酸：指且舍氏族，属苗族支系。
[8] qi suan: refers to Qieshe tribe, a branch of the Miao people。
[9] 三岁一成：指三家坪。三岁，读叟所；一，读伊，指家；成，读扯，指坪。
[9] san sui yi cheng (three years one yield) refers to the Sanjiaping. sansui: sousuo, yi: one, refers to househood, cheng: che, refers to Ping, flat land or level ground between the hills。
[10] 已疠：指石板夷。今地名用苗语表达为罗板，故又称罗板夷。
[10] yi li (cure diarrhea) refers to Shiban (stone slap)tribe, shi(stone)Pu concept reads as Li, a pun in Chinese and Pu phonetic。This place name is in Miao concept, written in Chinese sign, therefore the people is referred to Luoban Yi。

译文：由蒙且山往东北七十里，有座山叫长岭。山的西面有峪水氏族，东面住着桃花洞氏族，这里还住着西岭背氏族、羊坡氏族和草庄氏族。天脊水从山间流出，向东南流入漕水。天脊河畔住着且舍氏族和三家坪氏族，是古老的罗板夷。
Translation：
Seventy li northeastward from Mengqie Mountain stands the Changling Mountain。On its west, live the Yushui tribe, on its east side, the Taohuadong tribe。The Xilingbei tribe, Yangpo tribe and Caozhuang tribe also live here。Tianji River comes out of the mountain, goes southeast into Cao River。 Along the Tianji Riverbank, live the Qieshe tribe and Sanjiaping tribe。They are the ancient Luoban Yi。

03-03-05 天池山
Tianchishan
(113,78073E， 36,58442N)

又东北二百里，曰天池之山[1]，其上无草木[2]，多文石[3]。有兽焉，其状如兔而鼠首[4]，以其背飞[5]，其名曰飞鼠[6]。渑水[7] 出焉，潜于其下，其中多黄垩 [8] 。

注释：[1]天池山：指南天池山。又称九山、九峰山。
Notes： [1] tian chi shan (heavenly lake mount) refers to Nantianchi Mountain (south tianchi),also known as Jiushan(nine mountain)，Jiufengshan(nine peak mountain)。
[2] 无草木：游牧部落氏族。
[2] wu cao mu (no grass wood) refers to the nomads。
[3] 文石：读维氏，指南天池氏族，又称南池氏族。
[3] wen shi (patterned stone) Pu concept reads as weishi （southern tribe) wei/south, shi/stone/tribe。 Refers here to the Nantianchi tribe, or simply Nanchi tribe。
[4] 兔而鼠首：指台西氏族。鼠，指九，也指西。
[4] tu er shu shou (rabbit with rat head) refers to the Taixi (terrace west) tribe。 rat/shu/nine/west. Phonetic shift。shu is the Pu concept, Chinese shu/rat is a close phonetic match。
[5] 其背飞：伊耆泚山，即清漳河山。飞，读胡，指山。
[5] qi bei fei: refers to Yishibi Mountain, the Qingzhanghe Mountain。 fei/hu, refers to mount。 fei/fly/hui/hu, a phonetic shift。
[6] 飞鼠：指九山氏、九峰氏。
[6] fei shu (flying rat) refers to Jiushan Shi, or Jiufeng Shi。 jiu/nine/shu, fei/flying/hui/hu/mount。
[7] 渑水：指满肆水。
[7] min shui; refers to Mansi River。
[8] 黄垩：指山南氏族。
[8] huang e: refers to Shannan tribes， (mountain south) 。

译文：由长岭往东北二百里，有座山叫天池山。山的西边是游牧部落，住着南池氏族。有一个氏族，是台西氏族的清漳河山区氏族，名叫九山氏。满肆水从山间流出，流向东南而去，河畔住着山南氏族。
Translation:
Two hundred li northeastward from Changlingshan, stands the Tianchishan。On its west side live the nomadic tribes, the Nanchi tribe。 Another tribe is the Jiushan tribe, who belongs to the Taixi people。 From the Qingzhang River's mountainous region。The Mansi River comes out of the mountain, goes southeast, on its riverbank, lives the Nanshan tribe。

03-03-06 阳山
Yangshan
(114,45479E　36,83086N)

又东三百里，曰阳山[1]，其上多玉[2]，其下多金铜[3]。有兽焉，其状如牛而赤尾[4]，其颈肾[5]，其状如句瞿[6]，名曰领胡[7]，其鸣自詨，食之已狂[8]。有鸟焉，其状如赤雉，而五采以文[9]，是自为牝牡[10]，名曰象蛇[11]，其名自詨。留水[12] 出焉，而南流注于河 [13] 。其中有䱵父之鱼 [14] ，其状如鲋鱼，鱼首而彘身[15]，食之已呕[16]。

注释：[1]阳山：阳山，又称阳城山，即今沙河市。
Notes：[1] yang shan(sun mount) also known as Yangcheng Mountain, today it is the Shahe(sand river)city，36° 51′ 17.64″ N, 114° 30′ 11.88″ E。

[2]玉：指邑城氏族
[2]yu(jade) refers to Yicheng tribe。

[3] 金铜：指经台氏族，在城东北角。
[3] jin tong (gold copper) refers to the Jingtai people, who live in the northeast corner of the city。

[4] 牛而赤尾：指游牧的。
[4] niu er chi wei/yi(ox with red tail) a coded term for nomadic way of life。

[5] 颈肾：指井陉氏族。
[5] jing shen (neck kidney) refers to Jingxing people. jing(well) xing(trail)。

[6] 句瞿：指城东氏族。
[6] ju qu (sentence eagle vision) refers to the Chengdong (city east) tribe。

[7] 领胡：指东胡，领，读蚩音，指东。也称作林胡。
[7] ling hu (lead hu) refers to Dong Hu, (east hu people), ling/chi/east, also known as lin hu (forest hu)。

[8] 已狂：指北方夷。
[8] yi kuan (cure craziness) refers to Norther people.

[9] 赤雉，而五采以文：东部的北汪坪部落。采，在此读扯，指坪。以文读阴汶，指北汪。
[9] chi zhui (red bird), er wu cai yi wen(thus five colors to pattern)refers to the Beiwangping tribe in the east, cai/che/ping, yi wen/yin wen ,yin(north)wen(water) refers to Beiwang。

[10] 自为牝牡：东南连目。连目，古时的行政区划单位，也称目连。
[10] zi wei bin mu (male female in one body)
Tr: Lianmu in the Southeast, Lianmu (join eyes) an ancient administrative unit, also known as Mulian (reversed word order) a classifier, a term for administrative division。

[11] 象蛇：指象肆。
[11] xiang she (elephant snake) refers to Xiangsi, an administrative unit, a market town。

[12] 留水：指大油水。
[12] liu shui (remain water) refers to Dayou (big oil) River。

[13]河：指南澧河。
[13] he(river), refers to Nanfeng River, Nanfeng (south feng) 。

[14] 䱵父夷：指辛湖夷。辛湖已消失，今只遗存有辛家寨。
[14] xian fu yi: refers to Xin Lake tribe, the Xin Lake has disappeared, but a village name remains as Xinjiazhai (xin family village) xin/xian a close Pu phonetic match。

[15] 鱼首而彘身：通古斯的赫哲族。
[15]yu shou er shi shen (fish head with pig body) refers to Tongus Hezhe tribe。

[16] 已呕：指水上夷。
[6] yi ou (cure vomit) refers to Shuishang (on water) people。

译文：由天池山往东三百里，有座山叫阳山，山的西面住着邑城氏族，东面住着经台氏族。有一个氏族，是游牧的井陉氏族，是城东氏族，名叫林胡，他们自己也这样解释，是古老的北方夷。有一群人，是东部的北汪坪部落氏族，是东南连目的氏族，名叫象肆人，他们自己也这样解释。大油水从西边流出，向东南流入南澧河。这里住着辛湖渔民，是湖上的通古斯赫哲族，是古老的水上夷。
Translation:
Three hundred li eastward from the Tianchi Mountain, stands the Yang Mountain。 On its west side, the Yicheng people live; on its east, live the Jingtai people。A nomadic tribe, the Jingjing people live there, in the east of the city。They are called Lin Hu; they thus call themselves so。They are ancient northern people。 Another group belongs to the Beiwangping tribe from the East。 They have their Lianmu in the southeast, they are called Xiangsi people。They also address themselves thus. The Dayou River flows through the west, goes southeast into Nanfeng River。The fishing tribes from Xin Lake live here, they are lake people known as the Tongus Hezhe, ancient people who make their living by the water。

03-03-07 贲闻山
Penwenshan
（115,66692E；37,04362N）

又东三百五十里，曰贲闻之山[1]，其上多苍玉[2]，其下多黄垩[3]，多涅石[4]。

注释：[1]贲闻山：指沘渭山，今称卫河山。即今河北清河县。
Notes: [1] pen wen shan: refers to Biweishan, today known as Weiheshan, which is the Qinghe county, Hebei Province。
[2] 苍玉：指清河夷。
[2] cang yu (dark jade): refers to the Qinghe Yi。
[3] 黄垩：指胡族部落。
[3] huang e refers to the Hu tribes。
[4] 涅石：指金人氏族。即称为金人的肃慎族。
[4] nie shi (black stone) refers to the Jin ethnic people, the Sushen people, also known as Jin (gold)。

译文：由阳山往东三百五十里，有座山叫卫河山。山的西面住着清河夷，东面住着胡人部落和金人氏族。
Translation:
Three hundred and fifty li eastward from Yanshan there stands the Weiheshan。To its west live the Qinghe Yi, to its east live the Hu tribe and the Jin tribes。

03-03-08 王屋山
Wangwushan
(115,57455E，37,20861 N)

又北百里，曰王屋之山[1]，是多石[2]。联水[3] 出焉，而西流注于泰泽 [4] 。

注释：[1]王屋山：指王吴山，意思是迁入的地区，在河北衡水市地区。
Notes： [1] wang wu shan (wang house mount) refers to Wangwushan, which means an area to migrate to , refers to Hengshui city, Hebei province。
[2] 多石：指住着种植氏族， 石，读畲音，指种植。
[2] duo shi (many stone) refers to the planters’ tribe。 Shi reads as she, meaning planting, growing。
[3] 联水：指索泸河。濮语读东流为西流，此处实际指东北流。

[3] lian shui (joint water) refers to Suoluhe River。The Pu concept of east reads as xi, written in Chinese as xi(west), the river in fact flows in a northeast direction。

[4] 泰泽：指渤海。

[4] tai ze (big lake) refers to Bohai。

译文：由卫河山往北一百里，有个地方叫王吴山，这里住着种植氏族。索泸河从这里流过，向东流入渤海。

Translation:

One hundred li northward from the Weiheshan there is a place called Wangwushan。 The planter's tribe lives here。 Suolu River flows through here and goes eastward into Bohai。

03-03-09 教山

Jiaoshan

(115,68776E; 37,73285N)

又东北三百里，曰教山[1]。其上多玉而无石[2] 。教水 [3] 出焉，西流注于河，是水冬干而夏流 [4]，实惟干河。其中有两山[5]。是山也，广员三百步，其名曰发丸之山[6]，其山有金玉[7]。

注释：[1]教山：指衡漳河，后称衡水，在河北省衡水市城区。

Notes: [1] jiao shan (teaching mount) refers to Hengzhanghe River, later known as Hengshui ,in the city quarters of Hengshui city, Hebei province。

[2] 玉而无石：指水边的部落氏族。

[2] yue er wu shi (jade with no stone)

Tr: the riverbank tribes。

[3] 教水：指衡水，今称【氵釜】阳水。实际往东流。

[3] jiao shui (teaching water) refers to Fuyangshui River, which flows to the east。

[4]河：指滹沱河。

[4] he(river) refers to Hutuohe River。

[5] 两山：指凹地。

[5] liang shan (two hills) refers to the low land。

[6] 发丸之山：指藏水的地方。

[6] fa wan zhi shan (issue balls hill): refers to a place where a lot of water is stored。

[7] 金玉：指场镇夷，又称集贸夷。

[7] jin yu (gold jade): refers to the Zhenchang Yi, also called Jimao Yi。 Zhenchang (town field), Jimao (market trade) 。

译文：由王吴山往东北三百里，有个地方叫衡水。河的西面住着水边部落氏族，衡水从这里流出，向东流入滹沱河，这条河冬干而夏流，实际是干河。这里是一片凹地，有三百步长，是藏水的地方，这里生活着场镇氏族。

Translation:

Three hundred li northeastward from the Wangwushan, there is a place called Hengshui。 On the west side of the river live the riverbank tribes。Hengshui River flows out of here and goes east into Hutuohe River。 This river is a dry river in winter and flows in summer, known as the dry river。 This is also the low land, 300 feet long, a place to store water。 The Changzhen tribes live here。

03-03-10 景山

Jingshan
(116,25636E; 37,69162N)

又南三百里，曰景山[1]，南望盐贩之泽[2]，北望少泽[3]。其上多草[4]，藷䓨[5]，其草多秦椒[6]，其阴多赭[7]，其阳多玉[8]。有鸟焉，其状如蛇，而四翼六目三足[9]，名曰酸与[10]，其名自詨，见则其邑有恐[11]。

注释：[1]景山：指河北景县，古时称景山。
Notes: [1] jin shan: refers to Jing County, in Hebei Province, known in the ancient times as Jing Mountain。

[2] 盐贩泽：指吴桥的贩盐市场，读沙卧恩泽，后谐音演变为桑园河。
[2] yan fan ze (salt selling lake) refers to the salt market in Wu Qiao, in Pu concept reads Sha wo en ze, later shifted into phonetic match：san yuan he(mulberry garden river)。

[3] 少泽：指双河肆，在今洚河流镇。
[3] shao ze (young lake), refers to Shuanghesi, known today as Jiangheliu town。

[4]草：指移民。
[4] cao(grass); refers to migrants。

[5] 藷䓨：指明氏族和郁氏族。
[5] zhu yu: refers to the Ming tribe and the Yu tribe。

[6] 秦椒：指东店子。秦，指东；椒，指店子。
[6] qin jiao (qin pepper) refers to Dongdianzi, qin: east, jiao， shop。

[7]赭：指者，濮语表达为苏，即苏庄氏族。
[7] zhe : refers to Pu concept Su, the Su village tribe。

[8]玉：在此读伊，里伊族群，即带"小"字的族群。如小留屯、小青草河、小王庄等。
[8]yu(jade) Pu concept reads as yi, refers to the Liyi tribes, the names of which are prefixed with yi/xiao/small/junior: xiaoliutun, xiaoqingcao river, xiao wang village。

[9] 蛇而四翼六目三足：指谢人的母系氏族的外支系。
[9] she er si yi liu mu san zu (snake with four wings six eyes three feet) refers to the outside tribes married into the matrilineal tribes of Xie people。

[10] 酸与：指谢夷。
[10] suan yu: refers to the Xie people。

[11] 有恐：指阴康氏。
[11] you kong (have fears) refers to Yinkang people。 You kong/yin kang are close phonetic matches。

译文：由衡水往南三百里，有座山叫景山。从这里南望桑园河，北望双河肆。山的西面住着移民的明氏族和郁氏族，东面住着东店子氏族，北面住着苏氏族，南面住着里伊氏族。有一群人，是谢人的母系氏族的外支系，名叫谢夷，他们自己也这样解释，是那个集镇的阴康氏。
Translation:
Three hundred li southward from Zhiqiu, stands Jingshan。 Looking from here, southward flows the Sangyuan River, and northward stands the Shuanghe town。 On the west side of the mountain, live the Ming tribe and the Yu tribe, on the east side, the Dongdianzi tribe, and on the north side, the Su tribe, and the Liyi tribes are on the south side。A group of people, the outside branch of the matrilineal tribe of the Xie people, also thus explaining themselves, are the Yinkang tribe of that town。

03-03-11 孟门山
Mengmenshan
(117,37837E; 37,59643N)

又东南三百二十里，曰孟门之山[1]，其上多苍玉[2]，多金[3]，其下多黄垩[4]，多涅石[5]。

注释：[1]孟门山：在山东惠民县城西侧的孟北村。原名传承。
Notes: [1] meng men shan (meng door mount) at the west side of the Huimin county, Shandong province, in Mengbei village, its original name is still in use。
[2] 苍玉：指里伊氏族，即在名称前加“小”字的氏族。
[2] cang yu (black jade) refers to the Liyi tribes, who has junior, or xiao as a prefix in their tribal names。
[3]金：指场镇氏族。
[3] jin(gold) refers to Changzhen tribe。
[4] 黄垩：指后韩，南韩村落氏族。
[4] huang e (yellow clay) refers to the Houhan, Nanhan village tribes。
[5] 涅石：指孙姓氏族。濮语称“孙”为涅嘎拉。
[5] nie shi （black stone) refers to the Sun tribes, in Pu concept, sun, /grandson, reads as Niegala。

译文：由景山往东南三百二十里，有个集镇叫温店。集镇的西面住着里伊氏族和场镇氏族，在东面住着南韩村氏族和孙姓氏族。
Translation:
Three hundred and twenty li southeastward from Jingshan, stands the town Wendian。 On its west lives the Liyi tribe and Changzhen tribe。On its east live the Nanhan village tribe and the tribes bearing the surname of sun。

03-03-12 平山
Pingshan
(118,06267E; 36,81139N)

又东南三百二十里，曰平山[1]。平水出于其上，潜于其下，是多美玉[2]。

注释：[1]平山：指淄博，濮语读平山为“淄博”。
Notes: [1] ping shan (flat mount) refers to Zibo, in Pu concept, pingshan, is read as Zibo。
[2] 美玉：指蒙夷，苗族的古称谓。
[2] mei yu (beautiful jade) refers to the Meng Yi, an ancient name for the Hmong, the Miao。

译文：由温店往东南三百二十里，有座山叫淄博。淄水从西边流出，向东边流去，这里住着蒙夷。
Translation:
Three hundred and twenty li southeastward from Wendian stands the Zibo Mountain。Zi River flows from its west side, goes east。The Hmong, or the Miao Yi live here。

03-03-13 京山
Jingshan
(118,79023E; 36,85645N)

又东二百里，曰京山[1]，有美玉[2]，多漆[3]，多竹[4]，其阳多赤铜[5]，其阴有玄礵[6]。高水[7] 出焉，南流注于河 [8] 。

注释：[1]京山：指纪山，是纪国的山。
Notes: [1] jing shan: refers to Jishan, the Mountain of Ji nation。
[2] 美玉：指蒙夷。
[2] mei yu (beautiful jade) refers to Hmong or the Miao people。

[3]漆：指毛沙坨氏族，简称毛坨氏族。
[3] qi(lacquer) refers to Maoshatuo tribes, shortened to Maotuo tribe。
[4]竹：在此指组姓氏族。
[4] zhu(bamboo) refers to the tribe bearing the surname of Zhu (sacrifice meat) 。
[5] 赤铜：指纪台氏族。
[5] chi tong (red copper) refers to the Jitai tribe。
[6] 玄礵：指兴西氏族。
[6] xuan xiao (black stone) refers to the Xingxi tribe。
[7] 高水：指古水，今已消失，只有入河口处有一小段沟渠和地名遗存。
[7] gao shui (high water) refers to Gu(ancient)River。 It has since disappeared, only at its old river mouth, a small ditch and a place name remain。
[8]河：指弥河。
[8] he(river) refers to Mi River。

译文：由淄博往东二百里，有座山叫纪山，是蒙夷地区，住着毛沙坨氏族和组姓氏族。南面住着纪台氏族，北面住着兴西氏族。古水从高处流出，向南流入弥河。
Translation:
Two hundred li eastward from Zibo Mountain, stands the Jishan, a region of Meng or Hmong-Miao people live。They are the Maoshatuo tribe and the Ju tribe。On its south side live the Jitai tribe。 The Xingxi tribe lives on the north side。The Gu River flows down from the high place, goes south into the Mi River。

03-03-14 虫尾山
Chongweishan
(119,39259E；36,84577N)

又东二百里，曰虫尾之山[1]，其上多金玉[2]，其下多竹[3]、多青碧[4]。丹水[5] 出焉，南流注于河 [6]；薄水[7] 出焉，而东流注于黄泽[8]。

注释：[1]虫尾山：指昌邑山。
Notes: [1] chong wei shan (worm tail mount): refers to Changyishan。
[2] 金玉：指夹沟河族群。也称夹沟夷。
[2] jin yu (gold jade) refers to the Jiagouhe tribes, also known as Jiagou yi。
[3]竹：在此指郜部落氏族。原本读郊部落，但传承读音为郜。
[3] zhu (bamboo): refers to the Hao tribal clans. Known originally as Jiao tribes, now passed down phonetically as Hao。
[4] 青碧：指岔河氏族。
[4] qing bi (green blue) refers to the Chahe tribes。
[5] 丹水：指堤水，即今堤河。
[5] dan shui (red water): refers to the Dishui, known today as the Dihe river。
[6]河：指潍河。
[6] he(river): refers to Weihe。
[7] 薄水：指浦河。
[7]bo shui (thin water): refers to Pu River。
[8] 黄泽：今称胶莱河。
[8] huang ze (yellow zee): refers to todays' Jiaolai River。

译文：由纪山往东二百里，有座山叫昌邑山，山的西面住着夹沟夷，东面住着郜部落氏族和岔河氏族。堤水从高处流出，向南流入潍河；浦水从高处流出，向东流入胶莱河。
Translation:
Two hundred li further east from Jishan, there stands the Chayishan。 On its west side live the Jiagou Yi, on its east side live the Hao tribal clans and Chahe tribes。 Dishui river flows from high point and southward into Wei River; the Po River flows from high point and eastward into the Jiaolai River。

03-03-15 彭毗山
Pengbishan
(120,52016E; 36,88803N)

又东三百里，曰彭毗之山[1]，其上无草木[2]，其下多水[3]。蚤林之水[4] 出焉，东南流注于河 [5] 。肥水出焉 [6]，而南流注于床水[7]，其中多肥遗之蛇[8]。

注释：[1]彭毗山：指蚌埠山，耗河山，今莱西市城区。
Notes: [1] peng bi shan: refers to Bengbushan, Haoheshan, at Laixi city's west side，36° 52′ 0″ N, 120° 32′ 0″ E 。
[2] 无草木：游牧部落。
[2] wu cao mu (no grass wood) refers to the nomadic tribes。
[3]水：指莱西氏族。水，在此译为西。
[3] shui(water)refers to Laixi tribe, shui, transliterated into xi(west)。
[4] 蚤林水：指产芝水。濮语读产芝为者雷，谐音蚤林。
[4] zao lin shui (lice wood) refers to Chanzhi River, which is read as zhe lei, a close phonetic match to zao lin。
[5]河：指大沽河。
[5] he: river, refers to Dagu River。
[6] 肥水：指府水，又称府伊，谐音肥遗。
[6] fei shui (fat water) refers to Fu River, also reads as Fuyi, a close phonetic match to feiyi。
[7] 床水：小沽河，又称岔河。床，是岔的谐音。
[7] chuang shui (bed water) refers to Xiaogu River, which is also known as the Cha (fork)river, cha, fork, branched out。
[8] 肥遗之蛇：指府水氏族。今称云山镇氏族。
[8] fei yi zhi she (fat remains of snake) refers to the Fushui tribe, known today as the Yushan (clouds mount) township tribe。

译文：由昌邑山往东三百里，有座山叫蚌泚山，山的西面是游牧部落，东面住着莱西氏族。产芝水从山间流出，向东南流入大沽河。府水从山间流出，向南流入岔河。河滨住着府水氏族。
Translation:
Three hundred li eastward from Changyishan stands the Bengbishan。On its west live the nomadic tribes, on its east, the Laixi tribe。Chanzhi River flows out of the mountain, goes southeast to the Dagu River。 The Fu River flows out of the mountain, goes south into the Cha River。 On the river's bank live the Fushui tribes。

03-03-16 小侯山
Xiaohoushan
(120,99151E; 36,99871N)

又东百八十里，曰小侯之山[1]，明漳之水出焉[2]，南流注于黄泽[3]。有鸟焉，其状如乌而白文[4]，名曰鸪【習鸟】[5]，食之不灂[6]。

注释：[1]小侯山：指发创山，今称发城。濮语读“发创”为“修侯”，谐音小侯。
Notes: [1] xiao hou shan: refers to Fachuang Mountain, known today as Facheng (hair town) 。The Pu concept Fachuang, reads as xiuhou, a close phonetic match to xiao hou。

[2] 明漳水：明漳是发创的同意词，明漳水今称为昌水。
[2] ming zhang shui: the same meaning to Fachuang, known as Zhang River, today's Chang River; chang/prosper。

[3] 黄泽：今称富水。
[3] huang ze (yellow lake) known today as Fu River, Fu/rich。

[4] 乌而白文：指水湾部落，今称龙湾部落。白，读贝，指湾；文读汶，指水。
[4] wu er bai wen (bird with white markings) refers to the Shuiwan (bay area)tribe, known today as Longwan(dragon bay)tribe。In Pu concept, bai/white/bay, wen/water。

[5]鴣【習鸟】：指古羲氏，夏屋庄与古家兰都属古羲氏。
[5]gu xi: refers to people bearing the surname Guxi, the Xiawu village and Gujialan belong to Guxi Shi people。

[6] 不澊：指补纠，是苗族的称谓。
[6] bu jiu: bujiu, refers to Hmong Miao。

译文：由埠泚山往东一百八十里，有座山叫发城山。昌水发源于这里，向南流入富水。有一群人，是龙湾部落的氏族，名叫古羲氏，是古老的苗族。

Translation:

One hundred and eighty li eastward from the Bengbishan stands the Fachengshan。 The Chang River originates from here and goes south into the Fu River。 A group of people, the Guxi tribe, belong to the Longwan tribe, they are ancient Hmong Miao。

03-03-17 泰头山
Taitoushan
(122,04839E; 37,30226N)

又东三百七十里，曰泰头之山[1]。共水[2] 出焉，南流注于虖池 [3] 。其上多金玉 [4] 。其下多竹箭 [5] 。

注释：[1]泰头山：指泰博顶前面的山。头，即前面。中心在文登市岗山镇西侧。
Notes: [1]tai tou shan: the mountain before the Taiboding, you/head/ahead of , center is in the west side of Qingshan Township E121°54′53 ″ ~122°06′04 ″ ，N37°12′56 ″ ~37°21′33 ″ , in Wendeng city, Shandong province。

[2] 共水：指郭庄水，简称郭水。
[2] gong shui: refers to Guozhuang River, shortened to Guo River。

[3] 虖池：指泊子河。
[3]hu chi refers to Bozi River。

[4] 金玉：指西梁子夷。
[4] jin yu (gold jade) refers to Xiliangzi Yi people。

[5] 竹箭：指诸岗氏族。
[5] zhu jian (bamboo arrow) refers to the various Qing tribes。

译文：由发城山往东三百七十里，有座山叫泰头山。郭水从山间流出，向南流入泊子河。山的西面住着西梁子氏族，东面住着诸岗氏族。

Translation:

Three hundred and seventy li eastward from Fachengshan stands the Taitoushan。 Guo river flows out of the mountain, goes south into the Bozi River。On the west side of the mountain live the Xiliangzi tribe, on its east side the various Qing tribes。

03-03-18 轩辕山
Xuanyuan Mountain
(122,45752E; 37,15742N)

又东北二百里，曰轩辕之山[1]，其上多铜[2]，其下多竹[3]。有鸟焉，其状如枭而白首[4]，其名曰黄鸟[5]，其名自詨，食之不妒[6]。

注释：[1]轩辕山：指荣成山。濮语读“荣成”为“写耶”，谐音轩辕。
Notes: [1] xuan yuan shan: refers to the Rongcheng Mountain。 The Pu concept of Rongcheng reads as xie yie, a close phonetics match to xuan yuan。
[2]铜：在此指黄泥埠氏族。
[2] tong(copper) refers to Huangnipu tribe, Huangni (yellow clay) pu: higher ground。
[3]竹：在此指嘴，即松埠嘴氏族。
[3] zhu(bamboo) refers to zui(mouth), the Songpuzui tribes。
[4] 枭而白首：指东边的博霞山氏族。
[4] xiao er bai shou (owl with white head) refers to the Boxiashan tribe on the east。
[5] 黄鸟：指冯僚。
[5] huang niao (yellow bird) refers to Fengliao, a Pu phonetic match in which h/f is switched, l/n is switched。 liao/lao, refers to the Lao people。
[6] 不妒：指博霞氏族。不妒，读博堵，指博霞。
[6] bu du (not jealous) refers to the Boxia tribe, bu du/a close phonetic match to read as bu du, refers to Boxia。

译文：由泰头山往东北二百里，有座山叫荣成山，山的西面住着黄泥埠氏族，东面住着松埠嘴氏族。有一群人，是东边的博霞山氏族，名叫冯僚，他们自己也这样解释，是古老的博霞氏。
Translation:
Two hundred li northeastward from the Taitoushan stands the Rongchengshan。On its west side live the Huangnipu tribe, on its east side the Songpuzui tribe。A group of people, known as the Boxia tribe from the east, call themselves Feng Liao, they also thus describe themselves。They are very ancient tribes。

03-03-19 谒戾山
Yelishan
(120,42282E; 37,36413N)

又北二百里，曰谒戾之山[1]，其上多松柏[2]，有金玉[3]。沁水[4] 出焉，南流注于河 [5] 。其东有林焉，名曰丹林 [6] 。丹林之水出焉，南流注于河。婴侯之水[7] 出焉，北流注于汜水[8]。

注释：[1]谒戾山：指招远山。招远，濮语读为越莱，谐音谒戾。主要介绍招远集镇。招远的距离起点从蚌沘山算起。
Notes: [1]ye li shan: refers to the Zhaoyuanshan. In Pu concept, zhao yuan reads as yue lai, a pun phonetic on yeli。 This segment is a descriptive of the Zhaoyuan township 37° 21′ 40″ N, 120° 23′ 55.7″ E。 The distance in between starts from Bengbishan。
[2] 松柏：在此读数博，指西山氏族。
[2] song bo (pine poplar) In Pu concept it reads as shu bo, refers to the Xishan(west hill) tribes。

[3] 金玉：在此指岭上夷，今称山上夷。
[3] jin yu (gold jade) refers to the Lingshang Yi known today as the Shanshang Yi。
[4] 沁水：指曲水。今称九曲水。
[4] qin shui: refers to Qu River, known today as the Jiuqu (nine twists) River。
[5]河：指界河。
[5] he(river) refers to Jie (boundary) River。
[6] 丹林：指邓蓠，今称苇都、都苇子，是部落名。
[6] dan lin (red forest) refers to Dengli, known today as Weidu (reeds capital), the Duweizi, they are tribal names。
[7] 婴侯水：指乐后水。
[7] yin hou shui (infant prince water) refers to the Yuehou River, a close phonetic match of yin hou /yue hou。
[8] 氾水：指黄水。
[8]si shui (dead water，still water) refers to the Huangshui（yellow water）River, not to be confused with the Yellow River。

译文：由蚌沘山往北二百里，有座山叫招远山，山的西面住着西山氏族和岭上夷。九曲水从山间流出，向南流入界河。山的东边有个苇子部落，名叫都苇子。都苇子水从山间流出，向南流入界河。乐后水从山间流出，向北流入黄水。
Translation:
Two hundred li northward from Bengbishan stands Zhaoyuanshan。On its west side live the Xishan tribe and the Lingshang Yi。The Jiuqu River flows out of the mountain, goes south into the Jie River。 On the east side of the mountain, live the Weizi tribe, known as Duweizi tribe。The Duweizi River flows out of the mountain, goes south into Jie River。Yuehou River comes out from the mountain, goes north into Huang River。

03-03-20 沮洳山
Jurushan
(121,3951E; 37,51111N)

东三百里，曰沮洳之山[1]，无草木[2]，有金玉[3]。濝水[4] 出焉，南流注于河 [5]。

注释：[1]沮洳山：指芝罘山，在山东烟台市。
Notes: [1] ju ru shan: refers to Zhifushan in today's Yantai city 37° 27′ 51.84″ N, 121° 26′ 52.08″ E Shandong province。
[2] 无草木：游牧部落地区。
[2] wu cao mu (no grass wood) refers to the nomads' regions。
[3] 金玉：在此指夹河氏族。
[3] jin yu (gold jade) refers to the Jiahe tribe。
[4] 濝水：指芝水。
[4] qi shui: refers to Zhi shui, the Zhi River。
[5]河：指夹河。
[5] he (river) refers to Jia River。

译文：由招远山往东三百里，有座山叫芝罘山，是游牧部落地区，住着夹河氏族。芝水从山间流出，向南流入夹河。
Translation:
Three hundred li eastward from Zhaoyuanshan stands the Zhifushan, a nomad's region, where the Jia River tribe live。The Zhi River flows out of the mountain and goes south into Jia River。

03-03-21 神囷山
Shenqunshan
（114,50504E；37,44073N）

又北三百里，曰神囷之山[1]，其上有文石[2]，其下白蛇[3]，有飞虫[4]。黄水[5] 出焉，而东流注于洹[6]；滏水 [7] 出焉，而东流注于欧水 [8] 。

注释：[1]神囷山：指神角山，在河北临城西侧，今称嶂石岩。实际介绍山下的临城，在崆山旁边。到嶂石岩的距离由天池山算起。
Notes: [1] shen qun shan: refers to the Shenjiaoshan, to the west side of Lincheng, Hebei province, known today as the Zhangshiyan mountain。 It is a description of the town Lincheng at the foot of the mountain, next to the Kongshan。Its distance starts from Tianchishan。
[2] 文石：指翁城氏族。
[2] wen shi (markings stone) refers to the Wengcheng tribes。
[3] 白蛇：指瀑肆，今称北瀑水。也有地名演绎为盘石。
[3] bai she (white snake); refers to the Paosi, known as Beibaoshui, a place named after it becomes Panshi。
[4] 飞虫：指东部的游牧民族。
[4] fei chong（flying bugs）refers to the nomadic people from the East part。
[5] 黄水：指黄坪水。简称黄水。
[5] huang shui (yellow water): refers to Huangpingshui, shortened to Huangshui。
[6]洹：指槐水。
[6] huan: refers to Huaishui。
[7] 滏水：指灰山水。简称灰水。
[7] fu shui: refers to Huishanshui, shortened to Huishui。
[8]欧水：指菅等水。等，读湾音，与欧谐音。
[8]ou shui: refers to Jiandengshui, deng: reads as wan, a pun with ou。

译文：由天池山往北三百里，有座山叫嶂石岩，东侧有一座崆山。山的西面住着翁城氏族，东面住着北瀑水氏族。黄水从嶂石岩流出，向东流入槐水；灰水从嶂石岩流出，向东流入菅等水。
Translation:
Three hundred li further north from Tianchishan stands the Zhangshiyan Mountain, to its east, there is the Kongshan。On the mountain's west side live the Wengcheng tribes, on its east side live the Beibaoshui tribes。Huangshui flows out of Zhangshiyan Mountains and goes east into Huaishui; Huishui flows out of Zhangshiyan Mountains and goes east into Jiandengshui。

03-03-22 发鸠山
Fajiushan
(114,14433E; 38,03297N)

又北二百里，曰发鸠之山[1]，其上多柘木[2]。有鸟焉，其状如乌，文首，白喙，赤足[3]，名曰精卫[4]，其鸣自詨。是炎帝之少女[5]，名曰女娃 [6]，女娃游于东海 [7]，溺而不返 [8]，故为精卫 [9] 。常衔西山之木石 [10]，以堙东海[11]。漳水[12]出焉，东流注于河[13]。

注释：[1]发鸠山：指偏岩山，又称岩苍山、苍石岩。

Notes:[1] fa jiu shan (hair streptopelia) refers to Pianyan Mountain, also known as Yancang Mountain, or the Cangshiyan Mountain，Cang (black)；shi(stone)；yan(rock)。

[2] 柘木：指江畔夷。柘木，读浙陌，指江畔，也称江滨。

[2] zhe mu (Maclura tricuspidata) wood, refers to the Jiangpan Yi。 Zhe mu reads as zhe mo, meaning riverbank, or waterside，jiang(river)。

[3]乌，文首，白喙，赤足：山区游牧的水边部落氏族。

[3] wu(bird)wen shou (marking head) bai hui (white beak), chi zu(red feet) 。

Tr: the nomadic tribes from the mountains who live by the riverbanks。

[4] 精卫：指井陉 vei 氏族，谐音精卫氏。精，濮语读音 vei, 也称微。

[4] jing wei： refers to the Jingwei tribe, the name shortened to Jingwei, a close pun to Jingwei people， Jing reads as vei, or wei in Pu language。

[5] 炎帝之少女：指北方的草原游牧部落。炎帝，指北原、北方；少女，读蓍勒。

[5] yan di zhi shao nv (emperor Yan's youngest daughter)

Tr: the steppe nomadic tribes from the north。 Yandi: refers to north, the northern regions, shaonv (young girl /youngest daughter) reads as Shile, a Pu concept。

[6] 女娃：指勒瓦部落。勒瓦，即瓦伊勒，指草原。又称瓦剌。

[6] nv wa (female girl) refers to Lewa tribe。 Lewa: Wayile, refers to steppe, also known as Wala。

[7] 游于东海：迁徙于东海。此处的 "游" 按 "越" 解读。

[7] you yu dong hai (swimming in east sea)

Tr: migrate to the East Sea, swimming: you, meaning over to, across。

[8] 溺而不返：定居于发鸠山。溺，指定居；不返，指博发，即发鸠山。

[8]ni er bu fan (drown and never return)

Tr: settled in Fajiushan。ni/settle, bufan: bofa, refers to the Fajiushan, bufan/bofa are puns。

[9] 故为精卫：城池为井径（陉 xing)，今井陉县城。

[9]gu wei jing wei (there become elite guard)

Tr: the township is the Jingwei township， today's Jingxing county。

[10] 木石：指"瑪施"，即军备，军队。

[10]mu shi (wood stone) refers to Mashi, meaning war preparedness, arms--mu shi, mashi, a close phonetic match。

[11] 以堙东海：以战东海，即攻打东海地区。湮，指战。

[11] yan dong hai (flood east sea)

Tr: to attack the east sea region。Yan：attack。

[12] 漳水：即障水，因障城镇而得名，又称甘陶河。

[12] zhang shui: a river which got its name from the Zhangcheng town, the river also known as Gantao River。

[13]河：指冶河。

[13] he(river) refers to the Ye River。

译文：由嶂石岩往北二百里，有座山叫苍岩山，山的西面住着江滨氏族。有一群人，是山区游牧的水边部落氏族，名叫井径(陉)氏，他们也这样称呼自己。他们是北方的草原游牧部落，叫勒瓦部落。勒瓦部落迁徙到东海（地区），定居于苍岩山，城池为井径（陉）镇。他们常命西山的军队，去攻打东海地区。南甘陶河从山间流出，向东北流入冶河。

Translation：

Two hundred li northward from Zhangshiyan Mountain, stands the Cangyanshan。On its west side live the riverside tribes known as Jiangbin people。Another group of people are the mountainous nomadic tribes who live by the water, who are known Jingxing Shi。They also explain themselves thus。They are the nomads from the Northern steppe, known as Lewa tribe。The Lewa tribe migrated to the East Sea region, settled at Cangyanshan and established their township in Jingxing。They often ordered the army from the west hills to attack the Donghai area。The Nangantao River flows out of the mountain, goes northeastward into the Ye River。

03-03-23 少山
Shaoshan
(113,37827E; 37,07907N)

又东北百二十里，曰少山[1]。其上有金玉[2]，其下多铜 [3] 。清漳之水出焉，东流注于浊漳之水。

注释：[1]少山：指丰坡山，今山西省左权县城。到丰坡的距离从天池山算起，朝西北走向。
Notes: [1]shao shan(young mount) refers to the Fengposhan, today known as the Zuoquan township in Shanxi province。 The distance in between starts from Tianchishan, going northwest。

[2] 金玉：指大将山氏族。今称大江山氏族。
[2] jin yu:(gold jade) refers to the Dajiangshan tribe, also known as the Dajiangshan tribe, a pun in Chinese, first: big marshal mount, second: big river mount， jiang/jiang pun in Chinese。

[3]铜：指掌背氏族。
[3] tong(copper) refers to Zhangbei (hand back) tribe。

译文：由天池山往西北一百二十里，有座山叫丰坡山。山的西面住着大江山氏族，东面住着掌背氏族。清漳水从这里流出，向东流入浊漳河。
Translation:
One hundred and twenty li northwestward from the Tianchishan stands the Fengboshan。 On its west side, the Dajiangshan tribe live, on its east side, the Zhangbei tribe live。 The Qingzhang River flows out of here, goes eastward into Zhuzhang River。

03-03-24 锡山
Xishan
(113,70627E; 37,60868N)

又东北二百里，曰锡山[1]，其上多玉[2]，其下多砥[3]。牛首之水[4] 出焉，而东流注于滏水 [5] 。

注释：[1]锡山：指曦山。今称曦阳山，即山西昔阳县城。
Notes:[1]xi shan(tin mount) refers to xishan, today's Xiyangshan， the Xiyang county 37° 36′ 39.6″ N, 113° 42′ 25.2″ E in Shanxi province。 xi: dawn, xi: bygone, a Chinese pun。

[2]玉：在此指瑶湾氏族。
[2]yu: jade, refers to the Yaowan tribe。

[3]砥：指雪岭氏族。
[3] di: refers to the Xueling (snow range) tribe。

[4] 牛首水：指松溪水。松溪原读松河，倒装句的读音为 lao so，谐音牛首。
[4] niu shou shui (ox head water), refers to the Songxi River, its old name is Songxi, xi being small river。 In Pu concept, the word order is reversed, reads as lao so, a close phonetic match for niu shou。

[5] 滏水：指滹沱河。
[5] fu shui; refers to the Hutuo River. E122°16′--116°6′， N37°27′--39°25′。

译文：由丰坡山往东北二百里，有座山叫曦阳山。山的西面住着瑶湾氏族，东面住着雪岭氏族。松溪水从山间流出，向东流入滹沱河。

Translation:
Two hundred li northeastward from the Fengboshan stands the Xiyangshan。On its west side, the Yaowan tribe live。 On its east side, the Xueling tribe live。The Songxi River flows out of the mountain, goes eastward into the Hutuo River。

03-03-25 景山
Jingshan
(113,40835E; 38,08643N)

又北二百里，曰景山[1]，有美玉[2]。景水[3] 出焉，东南流入海泽 [4] 。

注释：[1]景山：指盂山。台字的濮语，既读景，又读盂。今山西盂县县城。
Notes: [1] jing shan (scenic mount) refers to Yushan。In Pu concept, tai reads as jing, as well as yu, this is about the Yu County seat 38° 5′ 17″ N, 113° 24′ 48″ E in Shanxi province。
[2] 有美玉：指南五台。
[2] you mei yu (have beautiful jade) refers to Nanwutai (mountain)。
[3] 景水：指盂水。
[3] jing shui: refers to Yu River。
[4] 海泽：指赛鱼河。今称桃河。
[4] hai ze (sea lake) refers to Saiyu (race fish) River, today known as the Tao River。

译文：由曦阳山往北二百里，有座山叫盂山，又称为南五台。盂水从山间流出，向东南流入赛鱼河。
Translation:
Two hundred li northward from Xiyangshan stands the Yushan, also known as the Nanwutai Mountain。 The Yu River flows out of the mountain, goes southeast into the Saiyu River。

03-03-26 题首山
Tishoushan
(113,36711E；38,38647N)

又北百里，曰题首之山[1]，有玉[2]焉，多石[3]，无水[4]。

注释：[1]题首山：指下社山，今山西盂县下社乡。题，指下方。
Notes: [1] ti shou shan: refers to the Xiasheshan, in Xiashexiang, Yu County, Shanxi province。Ti means lower side。
[2]玉：指夷、人群。
[2]yu(jade): refers to Yi, people groups。
[3]石：指桃峪氏族。
[3] shi(stone): refers to the Taoyu tribes。
[4] 无水：指细腰部落。
[4] wu shui (no water) refers to the Xiyao tribes。

译文：由盂山往北一百里，有座山叫下社山，这里有人烟，住着桃峪氏族，属细腰部落氏族。
Translation:
One hundred li further north from Yushan, there stands the Xiasheshan。 Peoples live there, they are the Taoyu tribes, belonging to the Xiyao tribes。

03-03-27 绣山

Xiushan
(113,25911E； 38,7227N)

又北百里，曰绣山[1]，其上有玉[2]、青碧[3]，其木多栒[4]，其草多芍药[5]、芎䓖[6]。洧水[7] 出焉，而东流住于河 [8]，其中有鳠 [9] 、黾 [10] 。

注释：[1]绣山：指富川山，简称富山。今山西五台县城。
Notes: [1] xiu shan: refers to the Fuchuanshan, shortened to Fushan。 It is the county seat of Wutai County, Shanxi province。
[2]玉：指走马岭氏族。
[2] yu(jade) refers to the Zoumaling tribes。
[3] 青碧：指河东氏族。
[3] qing bi (green blue): refers to the Hedong (river east) tribes。
[4]栒：指沿河氏族，即滤滹水的沿河氏族。
[4] xun: refers to the Yanhe (along the river) tribes, the Yanhe tribes along the Luhushui River。
[5] 芍药：指富川氏族。
[5] shao yao: refers to the Fuchuan tribes。
[6] 芎䓖：指匈奴移民。
[6] xiong qiong (a kind of herb) refers to the Xiongnu migrants。
[7] 洧水：指滤滤水。
[7] you shui: refers to the Luhushui River。
[8]河：指清水河，
[8] he refers to the Qingshui River。
[9]鳠、黾：指滤椿坪氏族。今称环椿坪氏族。黾，当读 mei 音。
[9]hu, mei: refers to the Huchunping tribes。It is known today as the Huanchunping tribes， Min/mei。

译文：由下社山往北一百里，有座山叫富山，山的西面有走马岭氏族、东河氏族，中部住着沿河氏族，住着富川匈奴移民。滤滤水从山间流出，向东流入清水河，河口住着滤椿坪氏族。
Translation:
One hundred li further north from Xiasheshan stands the Fushan。On its west live the Zoumaling tribes, Hedong tribe, in its middle part, live the Yanhe tribes, and the Xiongnu migrants from Fuchuan。 Luhushui flows out of the mountains, and goes east into Qingshui River, at its water mouth live the Huchunping tribes。

03-03-28 松山
Songshan
(113,59574E; 39,00065N)

又北百二十里，曰松山[1]。阳水出焉，东北流注于河[2]。

注释：[1]松山：指守银山，简称守山。又称五台山。今山西五台县台怀镇。
Notes: [1] song shan (pine mount) refers to Shouyin (keep silver) Mountain, shortened to Shoushan, also known as the Wutai Mountain, in today's Huai town, Wutai County, Shanxi province。
[2]河：指滹沱河。
[2] he(river); refers to the Hutuo River。

译文：由富川山往北一百二十里，有座山叫守山。阳水从山间流出，向东北流入滹沱河。
Translation:

One hundred and twenty li northward from Fuchuanshan stands Shoushan。 The Yang River comes out of the mountain, goes northeast into the Hutuo River。

03-03-29 敦与山
Dunyushan
(113,7651E; 39,29202N)

又北百二十里，曰敦与之山[1]，其上无草木[2]，有金玉[3]。溹水[4] 出于其阳，而东流注于泰陆之水[5]；泜水[6]出于其阴，而东流注于彭水[7]；槐水[8]出焉，东流注于泜泽[9]。

注释：[1]敦与山：指平川山，今称大营山。在山西繁峙县大营镇。
Notes: [1] dun yu shan: refers to Pingchuan (flat gully mount)mountain, known today as the Dayingshan(big camp), in today's Daying town, Fanshi County 39° 11′ 20.4″ N, 113° 15′ 57.6″ E, Shanxi Province。
[2] 无草木：指游牧部落。
[2] wu cao mu (no grass wood) refers to the nomadic tribes。
[3] 金玉：指金夷。
[3] jin yu (gold jade) refers to the Jin people。
[4] 溹水：指富溪、文溪等水系。
[4] suo shui: refers to the Fuxi, Wenxi, a few water systems。
[5] 泰陆水：指坦山水系，简称坦山河。
[5] tai lu shui: refers to the Tanshan water system。
[6] 泜水：指北跃溪、马牙河水系。简称北跃溪。
[6] di shui: refers to Beiyaoxi, Maya River system。
[7] 彭水：指盘沟、古之河水系，简称盘水。
[7] peng shui: refers to Pangou, Guzhihe water system, shortened to Panshui。
[8] 槐水：指西涧岔的洪水溪。
[8] huai shui: refers to the Hongshuixi, part of the Xijiancha。
[9] 泜泽：指小沼泽，今已成旱地，叫小淤地。
[9] di ze: small swamp, today is dryland, known as Xiaoyudi。

译文：由守山往北一百二十里，有个地方叫平川山。山的西面是游牧部落地区，住着金夷。富溪水从山的南面流出，向东流入坦山河；北跃溪之水从山的北面流出，向东北流入盘水。洪水溪发源于这里，向东流入小沼泽。
Translation:
One hundred and twenty li northward from Shoushan stands the Pingchuan Mountain。On the west side live the nomadic tribes, the Jin Yi。The Fuxishui River comes out of the south of the mountain, goes east into the Tanshan River。The Beiyuexi River comes out of the north of the Mountain, goes northeast into the Pan River。Hongshuixi River originates from here, goes eastward into the small swamps。

03-03-30 柘山
Zheshan
(114,27968E; 39,76474N)

又北百七十里，曰柘山[1]，其阳有金玉[2]，其阴有铁[3]。历聚之水[4] 出焉，而北流注于洧水 [5] 。

注释：[1]柘山：指宽广的山，谐音又称蕉山。今山西大同市广灵县城。

Notes: [1] zhe shan; meaning mountain with broad body, a close phonetic to Jiaoshan, in today's Guangling county seat, Hebei province。

[2] 金玉：指集兴曈夷。

[2] jin yu (gold jade) refers to the Jixingtong Yi， Tong: bright dawn 。

[3]铁：指泡子氏族。今称壶泉氏族。

[3] tie (iron) refers to the Paozi people, Paozi(lake), today known as the Huquan people， hu(pot)quan(spring)。

[4] 历聚水：指大沙河。今称沙河。

[4]li ju shui; refers to the Dasha (big sand) River, today known as Sha River。

[5] 洧水：指化稍营的河流。在此称化水。

[5] wei shui: refers to the river in Huashaoying, today known as the Hua River。

译文：由平川山往北一百七十里，有座山叫蕉山，山的南面住着集兴曈氏族，北面住着泡子氏族。大沙河水从山间流出，向北流入化水。

Translation:

One hundred and seventy li northward from Pingchuanshan stands the Jiaoshan。 On its south side live the Jixingtong tribes, on its north side, the Paozi tribes。 The Dashahe River flows out of the mountain, goes north into the Hua River。

03-03-31 维龙山

Weilongshan

(115, 24972E; 40,4859N)

又北三百里，曰维龙之山[1]。其上有碧玉[2]，其阳有金 [3]，其阴有铁 [4] 。肥水 [5] 出焉，而东流注于皋泽 [6]，其中多礨石[7]。敝铁之水[8]出焉，而北流注于大泽[9]。

注释：[1]维龙山：指花园山，今涿鹿县北侧的山。

Notes: [1] wei long shan: refers to the Huayuanshan (garden mount), in today' s Zhuolu country's northern part。 Zhuolu county: 40° 22′ 0″ N, 115° 13′ 0″ E。

[2] 碧玉：指蚌埠夷，彭姓氏族。

[2]bi yu (green jade) refers to the Bengbu Yi who bear the surname of Peng。

[3]金：指集镇氏族。

[3] jin (gold) refers to the township people。

[4]铁：指泡子氏族。泡子，指洋河泽。

[4] tie (iron) refers to the Paozi tribes, Paozi; the Yangheze, a lake。

[5] 肥水：指东沟水。

[5] fei shui (fat water) refers to the Donggou River, fei/east。

[6] 皋泽：指古城泽。今已扩建为官厅水库。

[6] gao ze: the Guchengze, today it has been turned into the Guanting Reservoir。

[7] 礨石：指游牧氏族。

[7] lei shi(stone) refers to the nomads。

[8] 敝铁水：指归泡水。

[8]bi tie shui: refers to the Guipaoshui, a river。

[9] 大泽：指洋河泽。

[9] da ze(big lake) refers to Yangheze Lake。

译文：由蕉山往北三百里，有座山叫花园山。山的西面住着蚌埠夷，南面住着集镇氏族，北面住着泡子氏族。东沟水从山间流出，向东流入古城泽。那里住着游牧氏族。归泡水从山间流出，向北流入洋河泽。
Translation:
Three hundred li northward from Jiaoshan stands the Huayuanshan。 On its west side live the Bengbu Yi, on its south, live the Township tribes。On its north, live the Paozi tribes。 Donggou River comes out of the mountain, goes east into the Guchengze Lake。The nomadic tribes live there。 The Guipaoshui River flows out of the mountain, goes north into the Yangheze Lake。

03-03-32 白马山
Baimashan
(115,83072E; 40,91265N)

又北百八十里，曰白马之山[1]，其阳多石玉[2]，其阴多铁[3]，多赤铜[4]。木马之水[5] 出焉，而东流注于虖沱 [6] 。

注释：[1]白马山：指百马山，即大马群山。实际介绍赤城。
Notes: [1] bai ma shan (white horse mount) refers to the Baimashan (hundred horses mountain), the Dama Mountains (dama/big horse), it describes Chicheng, the red city。
[2] 石玉：指榆树夷。
[2] shi yu (stone jade) refers to Yushu Yi。yushu (Ulmus pumila, the Siberian elm) 。
[3]铁：指泡子氏族。泡子，今已建为云州水库。
[3] tie (iron) refers to Paozi people, Paozi(lake) is now the Yunzhou reservoir。
[4] 赤铜：指游牧地区的氏族。今称赤城氏族。
[4] chi tong (red copper), refers to the nomadic tribes, known today as the Chicheng people。
[5] 木马水：指百马河，今称白河。
[5]mu ma shui (wood horse water) refers to the Baima River, known as today's Bai River, bai: hundred, or white, a pun in Chinese， mu/bai closer phonetic match。
[6] 滹沱：指滹沱河，今密云水库。
[6]hu tuo: refers to Hutuo River, today's Miyun Reservoir。

译文：由花园山往北百八十里，有座山叫大马群山。山的南面住着榆树氏族，北面住着泡子氏族和牧区氏族。白河水从山间流出，向东流入滹沱河。
Translation：
One hundred and eighty li northward from Huayuanshan。 On its south side, live the Yushu tribe, on its north side, the Paozi tribes and the grassland herders tribe。The Baihe River flows out of the mountain, and goes east into the Hutuo River。

03-03-33 空桑山
Kongsangshan
(116,4637E; 41,20834N)

又北二百里，曰空桑之山[1]，无草木[2]，冬夏有雪[3]。空桑之水出焉，东流注于虖沱[4]。

注释：[1]空桑山：指夏丰山，读音 ko sa，今丰宁县。因空桑的历史意义，对此山不作意译。
Notes: [1] kong sang shan: refers to Xiafeng Mountain。 In Pu concept xia(ko)feng(sa), is today's Fengning county, the name has historical significance, and author keeps its phonetic information, so not to translate it。
[2] 无草木：游牧部落地区。

[2] wu cao mu (no grass wood) refers to the nomadic region。

[3] 冬夏有雪：指外部落国的山峰。东读栋，夏读啥，栋啥指外国。

[3] dong xia you xue(winter summer has snow)refers to the mountain peaks of foreign countries, dong/column ,xia/sha dongsha refers to foreign countries。

[5] 虖沱：指虖沱河，今密云水库。

[5]hu tuo: refers to the Hutuo River, now known as the Miyun reservoir。

译文：由大马群山往北二百里，有座山叫空桑山，是游牧部落地区，是外部落国的山峰。空桑之水从山间流出，向东南流入虖沱河。

Translation：

Two hundred li northward from Damaqunshan stands the Kongsang Mountain, a region where the nomads roam。This is the foreign country's territory。 The Kongsang River flows out of the mountain, goes southeast into the Hutuo River。

03-03-34 泰戏山

Taixishan

(116,48564E; 42,20187N)

又北三百里，曰泰戏之山[1]，无草木[2]，多金玉[3]。有兽焉，其状如羊，一角一目[4]，目在耳后[5]，其名曰㸟㸟[6]，其名自訆。虖沱之水[7] 出焉东流注于溇水 [8] 。液女之水 [9] 出于其阳，南流注于沁水 [10] 。

注释：[1]泰戏山：指玛尼图羲山，简称图羲。今多仑县城。

Notes: [1] tai xi shan: refers to Manituxi Mountain, shortened to Tuxi, in today's Duolun county。

E115°30′-116°55′，N41°45′-42°39′ 。

[2] 无草木：游牧部落地区。

[2] wu cao mu (no grass wood) refers to the nomadic regions。

[3] 金玉：指集镇夷。

[3] jin yu (gold jade) refers to the township people, the Jizhen Yi。

[4]羊，一角一目：指羊场伊尔古支系。

[4] yang(sheep) yi jiao yi mu (one horn one eye) refers to the Yiergu branch of the Yangchang (sheep farm) 。

[5] 目在耳后：检目在大羊场。多仑县城，又称大羊场。

[5]mu zai er hou (eyes behind ears) township (Jianmu/administration) is at Dayangchang (big sheep farm), now the county seat of Duolun。

[6] 㸟㸟(dong)：氏族名，一个好斗的氏族的称谓。可按英语读为当当。

[6] dong dong: tribal name, refers to a warlike tribe read as dangdang。

[7] 虖沱水：指多伦城的水井河，又称八里子河。

[7]hu tuo shui: the Shuijing (water well) River in Duolun city, also known as Balizi River, Ba(eight) li(mile)。

[8] 溇水：指多仑城东面的闪电河。

[8] lou shui: refers to the Shandian(lightening) River in the east part of the Duolun city。

[9] 液女水：指页滦水。今称滦河。

[9]ye nv shui (liquid girl water) refers to Yeluan Rive, today's Luan River。

[10] 沁水：指磬丘河。

[10] qin shui: refers to Qingqiu River。

译文：由空桑山往北三百里，有座山叫图羲山，是游牧部落地区，住着集镇夷。有一个氏族，是羊场的伊尔古支系，检目在大羊场，名叫当当氏，他们自己也这样称呼。虖沱水从这里流出，向东流入闪电河。滦河水发源于山的南面，向南流入磬丘河。

Translation:

Three hundred li northward from the Kongsang Mountain, stands the Tuxi Mountain, a region of the nomadic tribes, where the Jizhen Yi live。One tribe is known as the Yiergu branch from the sheep farm, with their township at Dayangchang。They are called Dangdang Shi, and they address themselves thus。 The Hutuo River flows out of here, goes east into the Shandian River。The Luan River originates from the south side of the mountain, flows south into the Qinqiu River。

03-03-35 石山

Shishan

(118,17911E; 42,84236N)

又北三百里，曰石山[1]，多藏金玉[2]。濩濩之水[3] 出焉，而东流注于虖沱 [4]； 鲜于之水 [5]出焉，而南流注于虖沱。

注释：[1]石山：指始山，又称新开地乡，实际往东北方向。

Notes: [1] shi shan (stone mount) refers to Shishan, also known as Kinkaidi Township, the direction is toward the northeast。

[2] 藏金玉：指新兴的窝铺夷。

[2] cang jin yu (hide gold jade) refers to upcoming Wopu Yi。

[3] 濩濩水：指羊肠子水。

[3]hu hu shui: refers to Yangchangzi River, Yangchangzi (sheep's intestines) 。

[4] 虖沱：指老哈河。因是牧区重要的水源，所以称为虖沱。

[4]hu tuo: refers to Laoha River, the important water source for the grassland. Therefore, the name Hutuo。

[5] 鲜于水：指金阴河。今称阴河与英金河。

[5] xian yu shui: refers to Jinyin River, meaning the Yin River and the Yingjin River。

译文：由图羲山往东北三百里，有座山叫新开山，住着新兴的窝铺夷。羊肠子水从山间流出，向东流入老哈河；英金水从山间流出，向南流入老哈河。

Translation:

Three hundred li northeastward from Tuxishan stands Xinkaishan。 The upcoming Wopu Yi lives here。The Yangchangzi River flows out of the mountains, goes east into the Laoha River。 The Yingjin River goes out of the mountain and flows south into the Laoha River。

03-03-36 童戎山

Tongrongshan

(119,00403E；42,93449N)

又北二百里，曰童戎之山[1]，皋涂之水[2]出焉，而东流注于溇液水[3]。

注释：[1]童戎山：指白镇山，是白河镇的简称，蒙古语读为乌丹。今赤峰市翁牛特旗。实际走向为东北。

Notes: [1] tong rong shan: refers to Baizhenshan, a shorthand name for Baihezhen Township, reads as Wudan in Mongolian language。 It is today's Wengniute Banner in Chifeng city。 Its direction in fact is northeast。

[2] 皋涂水：指白鹤水，今称白河水。

[2] gao tu shui: refers to the Baiheshui (white crane river), known today as the Baiheshui River。

[3] 溇液水：指少郎水。
[3] lou ye shui: refers to the Shaolangshui River。

译文：由新开山往东北二百里，有座山叫乌丹山，白河水从山间流出，向东流入少郎水。
Translation:
Two hundred li northeast from Xinkaishan stands the Wudanshan, the Baiheshui River flows out of the mountain and goes east into the Shaolangshui River。

03-03-37 高是山
Gaoshishan
(119,55317E；43,25465N)

又北三百里，曰高是之山[1]，滋水[2]出焉，而南流注于虖沱[3]。其木多棕[4]，其草多条 [5] 。滱水 [6] 出焉，东流注于河 [7] 。

注释：[1]高是山：指高力罕草山，简称高蓍山，谐音高是山，今称海日苏，实际往东北。
Notes: [1] gao shi shan (high yes mount): refers to the Gaolihan grass mountain, which is shortened to Gaoshishan, known today as Hairisu. It in fact goes northeast。
[2] 滋水：指宽阔水，今称伊和诺尔水。
[2] zi shui: refers to the wide and broad water, known today as the Yihenuur River。
[3] 虖沱：指老哈河。
[3]hu tuo: refers to the Laoha River。
[4] 其木多棕：住在这里的牧民是牧羊氏族。
[4] qi mu duo zong (its wood lot palm): meaning the nomadic people live here are the sheep herder tribes。
[5] 其草多条：住在这里移民是种植氏族。
[5] qi cao duo tiao (its grass lot blades)； meaning the immigrants are the planters' tribes。
[6] 滱水：指喊叫水，这里实际指人工开凿用于灌溉的喊叫水支流。
[6] kou shui: refers to the Hanjiaoshui, which is a tributary of Hanjiaoshui, a manmade irrigation system。
[7]河：指西拉木伦河。
[7] he refers to the Xilamulun River。

译文：由乌丹山往东北三百里，有座山叫高蓍山，宽阔水从山间流出，向南流入老哈河。这里住着牧羊氏族和从事种植的移民。喊叫水的支流从灌区流过，向东流入西拉木伦河。
Translation：
Three hundred li further northeast from Wudanshan stands the Gaoshishan。 Kuankuoshui flows out of this mountain and goes south into the Laoha river。 Here live the sheep herding tribes and the immigrants who are the planters。 Hanjiaoshui's tributary flows through the irrigated areas and goes east into the Xilamulun River。

03-03-38 陆山
Lushan
(121,30927E; 43,60124N)

又北三百里，曰陆山[1]，多美玉[2]，姜阝水[3]出焉，而东流注于河[4]。

注释：[1]陆山：指鲁山，今称开鲁山，在内蒙古开鲁县。实际是往东北。
Notes: [1]lu shan (land mount) refers to Lushan, known today as the Kailushan。 It is in the Kailu county120°25′—121°52′E、43°9′—44°10′N, following a northeast direction。

[2] 美玉：指莫力达瓦夷。
[2] mei yu (beautiful jade) refers to the Molidawa Yi。
[3] 姜阝水：西辽河。姜阝，即姜，指西。西拉木伦河在这里被分为西辽河与新开河两部分。
[2] jiang shui: refers to Xiliao River, jiang(west)。 Xar Moron river is divided from here into the Xiliao River and the Xinkai River。
[4]河：指辽河。
[4] he(river), refers to the Liao River。

译文：由高蓍山往东北三百里，有座山叫开鲁山，住着莫力达瓦夷，西辽河从这里分出，向东流入辽河。
Translation:
Three hundred li northeastward from the Gaoshishan stands the Kailushan。 The Molidawa Yi lives here。 The Xiliao River branches out of here, goes east into the Liao River。

03-03-39 沂山
Yishan
(122,00501E；44,03578N)

又北二百里，曰沂山[1]，般水[2]出焉，东流注于河[3]。

注释：[1]沂山：指河山，濮语读奢伯。今称奢伯吐，即奢伯管理区。
Notes: [1] yi shan: refers to Heshan, in Pu language it is read as Shebo。It is known today as Shebotu, meaning the administration of Shebotu。
[2] 般水：指塔班水。
[2] ban shui: refers to Tabanshui, a river。
[3]河：指新开河。
[3] he: river, refers to the Xinkai River。

译文：由开鲁山往北两百里，有座山叫奢伯，塔班水从这里流出，向东流入新开河。
Translation:
Two hundred li further north from the Kailushan, there stands the Sheboshan。 Tabanshui flows out of here and goes east into the Xinkai River。

03-03-40 燕山
Yanshan
（122,05128E；44,43981N）

北百二十里，曰燕山[1]，多婴石[2]。燕水[3] 出焉，东流注于河 [4] 。

注释：[1]燕山：指好腰山，在奢伯吐北面。
Notes: [1]: yan shan (sparrow mount): refers to the Haoyaoshan (good waist mount), to the north of Shebotu。
[2] 婴石：指好腰氏族。"好腰"又读"窝勒"、"乌讷"。
[2] ying shi (infant stone) refers to the Haoyao tribe. Haoyao is read as Wole, as well as Wune。
[3] 燕水：指好腰水。
[3] yan shui (sparrow water) refers to the Haoyaoshui, a river。
[4]河：指乌訥格琴高勒。
[4] he(river): refers to the Wunageqin Kol。

译文：由奢伯往北一百二十里，有座山叫好腰山，住着好腰氏族。好腰水从这里流出，向东流入乌訥格琴高勒。
Translation:
One hundred and twenty li further north from Shebo stands the Haoyaoshan, where live the Haoyao tribe。The Haoyaoshui flows out of here and goes east into Wunageqin Kol。

03-03-41 饶山
Raoshan
(123,95749E; 47,31969N)

又北山行五百里，水行五百里，至于饶山[1]。是无草木[2]，多瑶碧[3]，其兽多橐驼[4]，其鸟多鹠[5]。历虢之水[6]出焉，而东流注于河[7]，其中多师鱼[8]，食之杀人[9]。

注释：[1]饶山：龙山，今称扎龙山，是齐齐哈尔的古称谓。饶，读 rue 音，指龙。
Notes: [1] rao shan: refers to Long (dragon) mountain, known today as the Zhalong Mountain, an ancient name for the city Qiqihar 47° 21′ 17.64″ N, 123° 55′ 5.52″ E 。 In Pu concept, rao reads as rue, meaning dragon, the Long in Chinese spelling, not to be confused with the English spelling。

[2] 无草木：游牧部落地区。
[2] wu cao mu (no grass wood) refers to the land of the nomads。

[3] 瑶碧：指昂沘氏族，今称昂昂溪氏族。
[3] yao bi (clear water) refers to the Anbi (a river) tribe, known today as the Ananxi tribe。

[4] 橐驼：指莫力达瓦达瀚尔氏族。因名称中有两个重音达字，便简称为橐驼。
[4] tuo tuo(camel) refers to the Molidawadawoer tribe Morin Dawa Daur. Its name has two da, therefore is shortened to tuo tuo。

[5]鹠：读勒音，指牧民。
[5] liu (kins of bird) reads: le, refers to herders。

[6] 历虢水：指嫩江。
[6]li hu shui: refers to the Nenjiang River, or the Nen River。

[7]河：指松花江。
[7] he(river); refers to the Songhua River。

[8] 师鱼：指水师夷。
[8] shi yu (teacher fish) refers to the Shuishi (water teacher) Yi。

[9] 食之杀人：古老的边远集镇氏族。
[9] shi zhi sha ren; (eat it starts killing people) refers to the ancient township people of outlying areas。

译文：由好腰山往北行山路五百里，再行水路五百里，就到了扎龙山。这里是游牧部落地区，住着昂昂溪部落氏族，称为莫力达瓦达瀚尔氏，人群都是牧民。嫩江水从这里流出，向东南流入松花江，这里还住着水师夷，是古老的边远集镇氏族。
Translation:
Five hundred li through mountain trails northward from the Haoyaoshan, one arrives at the Zhalong Mountain, the land of the nomads。The Ananxi tribe live here, they are called Morin Dawa Daur tribe, a group of herders。 The Nenjiang River flows out of here, goes southeast into the Songhua River。 The Shuishi people also live here, they are the ancient township tribes of outlying areas。

03-03-42 乾山
Qianshan
（121,47634E；45,05948N）

又北四百里，曰乾山[1]，无草木[2]。其阳有金玉[3]，其阴有铁而无水 [4] 。有兽焉，其状如牛而三足 [5]，其名曰獂 [6]，其名自詨。

注释：[1]乾山：指前德门山，是内蒙古科尔沁右中旗的古称谓。距离由开鲁山算起。
Notes: [1] qian shan: refers to Qiandemen Mountains, which is the ancient name for the Kelqin Right middle banner, Inner Mongolia, its distance starts from Kailushan。
[2] 无草木：游牧部落地区。
[2] wu cao mu (no grass wood), refers to the nomadic areas。
[3] 金玉：指佳木延艾夷。
[3] jin yu (gold jade) refers to the Jiamuyanai Yi。
[4] 铁而无水：指浑迪阿玛萨尔氏族。铁，译为浑；阿玛萨尔音意混译为无水。
[4] tie er wu shui (iron bu with water)
Tr: refers to the Hundi-armasar tribes。 Tie/iron: muddy/hun, Armasar is transliterated into Wushui。
[5] 牛而三足：指牧族的外来支系。
[5] niu er san zu (bull with three feet)： refers to the outsider nomadic tribes。
[6]獂：鹛：读勒音，指牧民，简称呼苏氏。
[6] yuan refers to the Bayan Husu Shi, simplified to Husu Shi。

译文：由开鲁山往北四百里，有座山叫前德门山，是游牧部落地区。山的南面住着佳木延艾夷，北面住着浑迪阿玛萨尔夷。有一个氏族，是牧族的外来支系，名叫呼苏氏，他们也这样称呼自己。
Translation:
Four hundred li northward from Kailu Mountain there stands the Qiandemen Mountain, a nomadic tribal area。 On its south live the Jiamuuyanai Yi, on its north live the Hundi-Armasar Yi。There lives a tribe, an outsider herders people known as Husu Shi。They thus address themselves。

03-03-43 伦山
Lunshan
（120,47775E; 45,97228N）

又北五百里，曰伦山[1]。伦水[2] 出焉，而东流注于河 [3] 。有兽焉，其状麋 [4]，其川在尾上[5]，其名曰罴[6]。

注释：[1]伦山：指中心的山，今称桃合木。桃，通陶，也指中心。
Notes: [1] lun shan: the mountain in the center, today known as Taohemu, tao/center。
[2] 伦水：指桃合木水。
[2] lun shui (lun river) refers to the Taohemu River。
[3]河：指阿其郎图嘎查河。
[3] he(river) refers to the Aqilangtu gacha River。
[4]麋：在此指五间房（地名）。麋通梅，指数序五。
[4]mi: refer to the place name wujianfang (five houses) mi: may, five。
[5] 其川在尾上：阿其郎图嘎查河西面。
[5] qi chuan zai wei shang (its gully on its tail), refers to the west side of the Aqilangtu gacha River。
[6]罴：指手工业氏族。
[6] pi (kind of bear),refers to the handicraftsman tribes。

译文：由前德门山往北五百里，有座山叫桃合木山。桃合木水从山间流出，向东流入阿其郎图嘎查河。有一个氏族，是五间房氏族在阿其郎图嘎查河西面的支系，叫手工业氏族。
Translation:
Five hundred li northward from the Qiandemen Mountain, stands the Taohemu Mountain。 The Taohemu River flows out of this mountain, goes eastward into Aqilangtu Gachar River。 A tribe, known as the Wujianfang people, who live on the west side of the Aqilangtu Gacha River, is called handicraftsman tribe。

03-03-44 碣石山
Jieshishan
(119,8742E; 47,30057N)

又北五百里，曰碣石之山[1]。绳水[2] 出焉，而东流注于河 [3]，其中多蒲夷之鱼 [4]。其上有玉 [5]，其下多青碧 [6]。

注释：[1]碣石山：指伊尔施山。伊尔施，谐音碣石。
Notes: [1] jie shi shan: refers to Yiershi Mountain, a phonetic match to Jieshi。
[2] 绳水：指森水，濮语读绰尔汶，今称绰尔河。
[2] sheng shui (rope water) refers to the Sen(forest) River。 In Pu concept, Sen shui reads as nuur wen, known today as the Nuur River。
[3]河：指嫩江。
[3] he refers to the Nenjiang River。
[4] 蒲夷之鱼：指胡尔勒夷。
[4] pu yi zhi yu (pu people the fish) refers to the Hurle Yi。
[5]玉：指伊尔施氏族。
[5]yu(jade) refers to the Yiershi tribe.47° 16′ 57.92″ N, 119° 48′ 51.7″ E。
[6] 青碧：指青沘氏族，今称根多河氏族。
[6] qing bi (green clear) refers to the Qingbi tribes, known today as the Genduo River tribes。

译文：由桃合木山往北五百里，有座山叫伊尔施山。绰尔水从山间流出，向东流入嫩江，河边住着胡尔勒夷。山的西面住着伊尔施氏族，东面住着根多河氏族。
Translation:
Five hundred li northward from the Taohemu Mountain, stands the Yiershi Mountain。The Nuur River flows out of the mountain, goes east into the Nenjiang River。On the bank of the river, live the Hurle tribes。On the west side of the mountain, live the Yiershi tribes, on its east side, the Genduo River tribes。

03-03-45 雁门山
Yanmenshan
(119,74957E; 49,22171N)

又北水行五百里，至于雁门之山[1]，无草木[2]。

注释：[1]雁门山：指伊敏山，今称呼伦贝尔。
Note: [1] yan men shan (sparrow gate mount) refers to the Yimin Mountain, known today as the Hulun Buir。49° 12′ 25.92″ N, 119° 46′ 15.96″ E。
[2] 无草木：指游牧部落地区。
[2] wu cao mu (no grass wood) refers to the region where the nomads roam。

译文：由伊尔施往北水行五百里，到达呼伦贝尔，这里是游牧部落地区。
Translation:
Five hundred li by water northward, one arrives at the Hulun Buir, a region where the nomads roam。

03-03-46 帝都山
Didoushan
(121,9697E; 50,99683N)

又北水行四百里，至于泰泽[1]。其中有山焉，曰帝都之山[2]，广员百里，无草木[3]，有金玉[4]。

注释：[1]泰泽：指额尔古纳河流域。
Notes: [1]tai ze: the Erguna (Argun River)river basin。
[2] 帝都山：指耳朵山，这里指得耳布尔山。
[2] di du shan (emperor capital mount) refers to Erduo(ears)Mountain, here refers to De'erbuer Mountain 。
[3] 无草木：指游牧部落地区。
[3] wu cao mu (no grass wood) refers to the regions of nomads。
[4] 金玉：指岭上夷。
[4] jin yu (gold jade); refers to the Lingshang Yi, lingshang (mountain range) 。

译文：由呼伦贝尔水行四百里，到达额尔古纳地区，这里有座山叫得耳布尔山，有近百里宽，是游牧部落区域，住着岭上夷。
Translation:
Four hundred li northward by water from the Hulun Buir, one arrives at the Erguna (Argun) area。Here stands the De'erbuer Mountain, almost one hundred li wide, a region for the nomads。 The Lingshang Yi live here。

03-03-47 錞于毋逢山
Mufeng Mountain
(124,1193E; 50,42516N)

又北五百里，曰錞于毋逢之山[1]，北望鸡号之山[2]，其风如飚[3]。西望幽都之山[4]，浴水 [5] 出焉。是有大蛇 [6]，赤首白身[7]，其音如牛[8]，见则其邑大旱[9]。

凡北次三经之首，自太行之山以至于毋逢之山，凡四十六山(47)，万二千三百五十里。其神皆马状而人面[10] 者廿神。其祠之，皆用一藻茝 [11] 瘗之。其十四神状皆彘身而载玉 [12] 。其祠之，皆玉，不瘗。其十神状皆彘身而八足蛇尾 [13] 。其祠之：皆用一璧瘗之。大凡四十四神，皆用稰米 [14] 祠之。此皆不火食。

右北经之山志，凡八十七山，二万三千二百三十里。

注释：[1]錞于毋逢：指鄂伦春夷的部落山。錞于，指鄂伦春的；毋，指部落；逢，指山。今称伊勒呼里山。
Notes: [1] chun yu mu feng: the tribal mountain of the Elunchun people, chun yu: elunchun, mu/tribe, feng/mount, known today as the Yilehuli Mountain。
[2] 鸡号山：指雉鸡场山。
[2] ji hao shan (rooster shout mount) refers to the Zhuijichang Mountain。
[3] 其风如飚：此山垂向于……，即此山垂向于伊勒呼里山。
[3] qi feng ru piao: this mount is facing the Yilelhuli Mountain。
[4] 幽都山：指奥洛奇山。
[4] you do shan (dark capital mount) refers to the Olgii Mountain。

[5] 浴水：指伊敏水，即额尔古纳河。
[5]yu shui (bath water) refers to Yimin River, the Erguna, Argun River。
[6] 大蛇：指加格达奇塞族，简称达塞。
[6] da she (big snake) refers to the Jiagedaqi Saka people, shortened to Dasai。
[7] 赤首白身：犬戎的山区氏族。
[7] chi shou bai shen (red head white body) refers to the mountain Dog rong people 。
[8] 其音如牛：住在嫩江边。
[8] qi yin ru niu (its voice like ox) lives by the Nenjiang River。
[9] 大旱：达罕氏族，王族。
[9] da han (big draught) refers to the chief branch, the king branch。
[10] 马状而人面：指胡族居民形象。
[11]ma zhuang er ren mian (horse look with human face) refers to the images of the Hu people。
[11] 藻茝：在此读璪珏，指璪玉。
[11] zao chen: zao yu, a kind of jade。
[12] 彘身而载玉：指通古斯的山区氏族形象。彘身在此作通古斯解；载，读照，指山区。
[12] zhi shen er zai yu (boar body with body jade) refers to the Tongus mountain tribe images。 Zhi shen: here refers to the Tongus, zai(carry) reads as zhao, refers to the mountainous areas。
[13] 彘身而八足蛇尾：指农业的粮食种植夷。彘身在此作农业解；八足，读饶则，作粮食解；蛇尾，指奢夷，即种植夷。
[13] zhi shen er ba zu she wei/yi (pig body with 8 feet snake tail) refers to the agriculture tribe of planters。 Zhi shen: agriculture, eight feet: reads as rao ze, meaning grain, snake tail: She Yi, the planter people。
[14] 糈米：指米类食物。食读 xie，与糈谐音。
[14] xu mi (seed grain type food),shi/xie a close phonetic match。

译文：由额尔古纳的得耳布尔山往东北五百里，有座山叫伊勒呼里山。从这里北望鸡号山，垂向于伊勒呼里；西望奥洛奇山，伊敏水向那里流去。这里有加格达奇塞族，是犬戎的山区氏族，住在嫩江边，是那个集镇的达罕氏族。

Translation:

Five hundred li northeastward from the De’erbuer Mountain in Erguna area, stands the Yilehuli Mountain。 To its north, stands the Jihao Mountain, facing Yilehuli Mountain。 To its west, stands the Olgii Mountain。 The Yimin River flows toward it。The Jiagedaqi Saka tribe live here, they are the mountain Dogrong people, by the Nenjiang River。 They are the ruling clan of that township。

综观北山经第三系列，自太行山到伊勒呼里山，共计四十六座山（实际 47 山），延绵一万二千三百五十里。这些山的山神中，有二十尊神是胡族居民的形象，祭祀他们时，用璪玉掩埋传达祭词。有十四神为通古斯的山区氏族形象，祭祀他们时，传达祭词皆用玉，但不掩埋。还有十尊神为农业的粮食种植夷的形象，祭祀皆用一璧掩埋。总共有四十四神，皆用米食生祭，不用熟食。

以上记载北方的山，共有八十七座，延绵二万三千二百三十里。塞种，肃慎，胡族，通古斯，农业粮食种植夷的形象

In sum， of the 3rd system of mountains in the Northern part, from the Taihang Mountain to the Yilehuli Mountain, there are a total 46 mountains (47 de facto) covering a distance of 12,350 li。Of the mountain deities, twenty of them are in the images of the Hu people。 When sacrificing to them, bury a jade piece called zao, to transmit the message。Another 14 deities are in the images of the Tongus mountain people, when sacrificing to them, uses jade in place of speech, but no need to bury the jade。Another ten deities are in the images of the agriculture planters。Use one jade Bi in sacrifice and votive speech。 For the total of 44 deities, all the sacrificial food are raw grains, no cooked food is allowed。 The above record registers the mountains in the north, a total of 87 mountains covering a total of 23,230 li。

第四卷东山经 (Mountains in the East)

东山经第一山系

Book 4 Dongshanjing; Chapter 1

04-01-01 樕螽山
Suzhushan
(136,9633E;50,56934N)

东山经之首，曰樕螽之山[1]，北临乾昧[2]。食水[3] 出焉，而东流注于海。其中多鳙鳙之鱼 [4]，其状如犁牛 [5]，其音如彘鸣 [6]。

注释：[1]樕螽山：指松江山。今称锡霍特山。
Notes: [1]su zhu shan: refers to Songjiang Mountain, known today as the Sikhote-Alin 45° 20′ 0″ N, 136° 10′ 0″ E。
[2] 乾昧：指切尔斯基山脉。
[2] qian mei: refers to Chersky Range 64° 44′ 0″ N, 142° 58′ 0″ E。
[3] 食水：指松花江。
[3] shi shui: refers to Songhua River 。
[4] 鳙鳙鱼：指戎戎夷，即鞑靼族。
[4] yong yong yu (yongyong fish) refers to Rongrong people, also known as Dadar tribes，Tatars，татарлар，татары, rong/戎， warrior, war loving, rebus, yong/rong， fish; yi/yu。
[5] 犁牛：指拉扎列人。
[5]li niu (plowing ox) refers to the Lazarev tribe。
[6] 彘鸣：枝米，共青城的古称谓。
[6] zhi ming (pig grunt), refers to Zhimi, 50° 33′ 0″ N, 137° 0′ 0″ E , today known as the Комсомо́льск-на-Аму́ре， Komsomolsk-na-Amure， known also as Gongqing City。 Gong (common, together, qing: young, former city built by the Communist Youth League members)。

译文：东山第一列山系最北端的山，名叫松江山。这座山与切尔斯基山相望。松花江水从这里流出，向东北流入大海。这里住着戎戎夷，是拉扎列人，住在枝米。
Translation:

The northmost Mountain of the first system in this chapter [Mountains in the East] is called Songjiang Mountain。It faces Chersky Mountain。Songhua River flows out of here, going northeast to empty into the sea。The Rongrong Yi/Tartars live here, they are the Lazarev tribe, settled in today's Komsomolsk-na-Amure。

04-01-02 藟山
Leishan
(113,52999E;46,84593N)

又南三百里，曰藟山[1]，其上有玉[2]，其下有金[3]。湖水[4]出焉，东流注于食水[5]，其中多活师[6]。

注释：[1]藟山：指勒山，即放牧之山。今称完达山。
Notes:[1] lei shan: refers to Leshan, the herder's mountain, known today as Wanda Mountains，45° 53′ 30″ N, 132° 13′ 30″ E。
[2]玉：指友谊氏族。"友谊"在此是音译词，指环泡水。
[2]yu(jade); refers to the Youyi tribe, youyi(friendship)a rebus, you: 有，友，yi; 谊，夷。
[3]金：指沘金氏族,今称比金氏族。
[3] jin(gold)refers to the Jinbi tribe, bi: 沘 water, gold water tribe。
[4] 湖水：指虎林水，穆林河的下游。
[4]hu shui (lake water) refers to Hulin River (tigerwood river) a tributary on the lower part of Mulin (Muling) River 。
[5] 食水：指松花江。
[5] shi shui (food water or eat the water), refers to the Songhua River, 47° 41′ 56.4″ N, 132° 31′ 3.36″ E。
[6] 活师：指贺氏，即牧羊氏族。
[6] huo shi (live teacher) a rebus for He Shi, the sheep herding tribes, Huo 活，he 贺。

译文：由松江山往南三百里，有座山叫勒山。山的西面住着友谊氏族，东面住着金沘氏族。虎林水从这里流出，向东流入松花江，这里住着牧羊氏族。
Translation:
Three hundred li southward from Songjiangshan, stands Leshan。 On its west side live the Youyi tribe, on its east, the Jinbi tribe。 Hulin River flows out of here, going eastward to join the Songhua River。 The sheep herder tribes live here。

04-01-03 栒状山
Xunzhuangshan
(130，96653E；45，29551N)

又南三百里，曰栒状之山[1]，其上多金玉[2]，其下多青碧石[3]。有兽焉，其状如犬，六足[4]，其名曰从从[5]，其鸣自詨。有鸟焉，其状如鸡而鼠毛[6]，其名曰蚩鼠[7]，见则其邑大旱[8]。【氵只】水[9]出焉，而北流注于湖水[10]。其中多箴鱼[11]，其状如儵[12]，其喙如箴[13]，食之无疫疾[14]。

注释：[1]栒状山：指长藏山，今称北长白山，中心在太平岭，这里主要介绍鸡西集镇。
Notes: [1] xun zhuang shan: refers to Changzhang Mountain, known today as the North Changbai Mountains, (Ever white), with its center at Taiping Ling 42° 0′ 20″ N, 128° 3′ 19″ E。
[2] 金玉：指举夷。汉语义为林夷，林口夷。
[2] jin yu (gold jade) refers to the Ju Yi。 It is translated in Chinese as the Lin Yi, Linkou Yi。
[3] 青碧石：指青雅碧氏族，汉语称东鸡氏族，今称鸡西氏族，西是濮语东的音译。
[3] qing bi shi (blue green stone) refers to the Qingyabi tribe, its name implies the East, today known as Jixi tribe. xi （west) a rebus。Xi is the Pu concept for east, reads as xi(west)。

[4]犬，六足：指犬戎的母系氏族。
[4] quan, liu zu (dog, six feet) refers to the Matrilinear tribes of the Dog Rong tribes。
[5] 从从：对移民氏族的称谓。
[5] cong cong (follow follow) a term refers to the migrant tribes。
[6] 鸡而鼠毛：鸡西的俄罗斯人。
[6] ji er shu mao (chicken with rat fur) refers to the Russians at Jixi area，45° 17′ 44.16″ N, 130° 58′ 8.4″ E。
[7] 蚩鼠：指东俄罗斯人。
[7]ci shu (grub rat) refers to the Eastern Russians.ci/chi Pu concept of east。
[8] 大旱：指达罕，即王族、统治氏族。
[8] da han (big draught) refers to the leading tribe, the king branch, ruling branch of the tribe. da 大，达，han 罕，旱，a rebus.
[9] 【氵只】水：指沙石水，今称大石头河。
[9] zhi shui, refers to Shanshishui (sand and stone river), today known as Dashitou River(big stone river)。
[10] 湖水：指虎林水。今称穆棱河。
[10]hu shui (lake river, lake water) refers to Huling (tiger wood) River, known also as Mulin /Muling/Muleng River. lin/ling/leng, close in pronunciation。
[11] 箴鱼：指女真夷。
[11] zhen yu (a kind fish: Hemirhamphus sajori) refers to the Jiuzhen (juzen, nuzhen) tribe 。（刀夷,东夷）
[12]鯈：指太戏靺鞨。
[12] tiao(fish)refers to Taixi Mohe (variants: Malgal, or Mogher, maybe a mispronunciation of the word Mojie) taixi 。
[13] 其喙如箴：指女真支系。
[13] qi hui ru zhen (its mouth is like the zhenfish) refers to the branches of the Juzhen(Nuzhen)。
[14] 无疫疾：指鸡水部落。今称鸡西。
(14) wu ji yi (no pandemic) refers to the Jishui tribes, known today as Jixi, ji 鸡，疾疫，a rebus。

译文：由勒山往南三百里，有座山叫长藏山。山的西面住着林口氏族，东面住着东鸡氏族。有一个氏族，是犬戎的母系氏族，名叫从从，他们自己也这样解释。有一群人，是东鸡镇的俄罗斯族，名叫东俄罗斯人，是那个集镇的统治氏族。沙石水从这里流出，向北流入虎林水。这里住着女真夷，是女真支系的太戏靺鞨，是古老的鸡水部落氏族。

Translation:

Three hundred li southward from Leshan stands Changzangshan。 On its west side live the Jixi tribe, on its east side, the Suifen River tribe。 A tribe is the matrilinear tribe of the Dog Rong people, calling themselves Congcong。 A group of people are the Russians from Jixi, they are the East Russians, the ruling tribe in that town。Shashi River flows out of this mountain, going north into the Hulin River。 The Juzhen people live there, they are the Taixi Mohe, a branch of Juzhen, an ancient Jishui tribal people。

04-01-04 勃垒山

Boleishan

(129,51798E，44,5817N)

又南三百里，曰勃垒之山[1]，无草木[2]，无水[3]。

注释：[1]勃垒山：指胡子山，今称老爷岭。
Notes：[1] bo lei shan: refers to the Huzishan, known today as Laoyeling Mountains。
[2] 无草木：游牧部落地区。
[2] wu cao mu (no grass wood): refers to the nomads' areas。

[3] 无水：指牡丹江部落。无，指部落，水：读绥音， 指牡丹江。
[3] wu shui (no water) refers to the Mudanjiang tribes。Wu: tribes, shui/sui: refers to the Mudanjiang River。

译文：由长藏山往南三百里， 有座山叫老爷岭， 是游牧部落地区， 这里的部落是牡丹江部落。
Translation:
Three hundred li from Changzangshan southward stands the Laoyeling Mountain, a nomad's area, where the Mudanjiang tribes live。

04-01-05 番条山
Fantiaoshan
(129,84816E;42,96845N)

又南三百里，曰番条之山[1]，无草木[2]，多沙[3]。减水[4] 出焉，北流注于海，其中多鳡鱼[5]。

注释：[1]番条山：指汾图山，即东图门山。
Notes:[1] fan tiao shan: refers to Fentushan, the present East Tumen Mountain。East: fen, fan, Pu concept of East, rebus code switch by different Chinese signs。
[2] 无草木：游牧部落地区。
[2] wu cao mu (no grass wood); the nomads' areas。
[3]沙：指外来氏族。
[2] sha(sand) refers to tribes not of local origin but arrived from other places。
[4] 减水：指兰水，今称海兰水。
[4] jian shui (reduce water) refers to Lan River, known today as Hailan River。
[5] 鳡鱼：指高丽夷。
[5] xian yu (salty fish) refers to the Koreans/Gaoli Yi 。

译文：由老爷岭往南三百里，有座山叫汾图山，是游牧部落地区，住着外来氏族。海兰水从这里流出，向北流入大海，这里住着高丽夷。
Translation:
Three hundred li southward from Laoyeling Mountain, stands Fentushan, the land of the nomads。 The outside tribes live here, Hailan River flows out of this mountain, going northward into the sea。 The Koreans live here。

04-01-06 姑儿山
Gu'ershan
(127,88071E; 41,73527N)

又南四百里，曰姑儿之山[1]，其上多漆[2]，其下多桑柘[3]。姑儿之水[4] 出焉，北流注于海，其中多鳡鱼 [5] 。

注释：[1]姑儿山：指鹅山，后称天鹅山，今称望天鹅山。
Notes:[1]gu er shan, refers to Goose Mountain, later on its name changed into Tian'e Mountain(swan mount), today it is known as Wangtian'e Mountain。
[2]漆："漆"的濮语读摩沙，谐音陌舍，借指河畔的氏族。
[2] qi(lacquer)Pu concept is read as Shamo, a rebus to moshe (reverse its order to shemo) refers to the tribes living along the riverbank。
[3] 桑柘：指双岔头氏族。
[3] sang zhe: refers to Shuangchatou tribe。

[4] 姑儿水：指松花江头道水，古称鹅水。
[4]gu er shui: refers to the Toudaoshui River, Songhua River's tributary, its ancient name is E River (goose river) 。
[5] 鳡鱼：指高丽夷。
[5] gan yu (Elopichthys bambusa or yellowcheek carp) refers to the Korean people/Gaoli Yi。

译文：由汾图山往南四百里，有座山叫望天鹅山。山的西面住着河畔氏族，东面住着双岔头氏族。鹅水从这里流出，向北流入大海，这里住着高丽夷。
Translation:
Four hundred li southward from Fentushan stands Wangtian'e Mountain。On its west side live the riverbank tribes, on its east side, the Shuangchatou tribe。E River flows out of here, going north into the sea。 The Koreans/Gaoli Yi live here。

04-01-07 高氏山
Gaoshishan
(126,18439E; 41,12325N)

又南四百里，曰高氏之山[1]，其上多玉[2]，其下多箴石[3]。诸绳之水[4]出焉，东流注于泽[5]，其中多金玉[6]。

注释：[1]高氏山：指通沟山，今吉林省通化市集安城。
Notes： [1] gao shi shan: refers to the Tonggou Mountain, in today's Ji'an county, Tonghua city。 41° 7′ 31.08″ N, 126° 11′ 38.4″ E。
[2]玉：指清河氏族。
[2]yu(jade)refers to the Qinghe tribe, Qinghe, qing river, clear water。
[3] 箴石：指女真氏族。
[3] jian shi/stone, refers to the Juzhen tribe。
[4] 诸绳水：指诸岔沟水，今称通沟河。
[4] zhu sheng shui (various rope water) refers to Zhuchagou River, known today as the Tongguo River。
[5]泽：指鸭绿江。
[5] ze, refers to the Yalu River.
[6] 金玉：指金夷。女真部落在红山文化之前就已称金。
[6] jin yu (gold jade) rebus for Jin tribe, Juzhen tribes address themselves as Jin (kim, gold) before Hongshan Culture came into being。

译文：由望天鹅山往南四百里，有座山叫通沟山。山的西面住着清河氏族，东面住着女真氏族。通沟水从山间流出，向东流入鸭绿江，这里住着金夷。
Translation:
Four hundred li southward from Wangtian'e Mountain, stands the Tonggoushan。 On its west side live the Qinghe tribes, on its east side the Juzhen(nuzhen)tribes。Tonggou River flows out of here, going east to join the Yalu River。 The Jin tribes live there。

04-01-08 岳山
Yueshan
(124,8846E;41,32596N)

又南三百里，曰岳山[1]，其上多桑[2]，其下多樗[3]。泺水[4] 出焉，东流注于泽[5]，其中多金玉[6]。

注释：[1]岳山：指我山，今称本山，在本溪县碱厂镇东侧。主峰老秃顶子。
Notes:[1] yue shan: refers to Woshan, today's Benshan。 It is situated on the east side of the Benxi county's Jian factory; its peak is called Laotudingzi Mountain (ancient bald top) 。

[2]桑：指双河氏族。即本溪与南太子河氏族。
[2] sang, refers to Shuanghe tribe, the Benxi and Nantaizihe Tribes。

[3]櫄：指凉水泉氏族，今称桓仁氏族。
[3] yun: refers to the Liangshuiquan tribes, today known as the Hengren tribes。

[4] 泺水：指普乐水，今称大雅河。
[4] le shui, refers to Pule River, known today as Daya River, Darya, the word for river in Central Asia。

[5]泽：指浑江。
[5] ze, refers to Hun River (muddy water) 。

[6] 金玉：指夹沟、岔沟等山区豁谷氏族。
[6] jin yu (gold jade) refers to the Jiagou tribe, Chagou tribe, those people live along the mountain valley 。

译文：由通沟山往南三百里，有座山叫本山。山的西面住着双河氏族，山的东面住着凉水泉氏族。普乐水从山间流出，向东流入浑江，这里住着山区的豁谷氏族。
Translation：
Three hundred li southward from Tonggoushan stands Benshan。 On its west side live the Shuanghe tribes, on its east the Liangshuiquan tribes。Pule River flows out of the mountains, going east to join the Hun River。The valley tribes live there。

04-01-09 犲山
Chaishan
(124,0981E;40,45823N)

又南三百里，曰犲山[1]。其上无草木[2]，其下多水[3]。其中多堪矜之鱼[4]。有兽焉，其状如夸父而彘毛[5]，其音如呼[6]，见则天下大水[7]。

注释：[1]犲山：指它山，属千山山脉的南麓，今称洼岭。
Notes：[1] cai shan, refers to Ta Mountain, on the south side of the Qianshan Mountains (a thousand mountains), known today as Waling Shan。

[2] 无草木：游牧部落地区。
[2] wu cao mu (having no grass and wood) refers to the land of the nomads。

[3]水：读奢，指凤城氏族。
[3] shui/she refers to Fengcheng tribes. shui/she/feng a rebus。

[4] 堪矜鱼：指华伐夷，濮语读"煦戡"、"戡煦"。
[4] kan yu yu (kanyu fish) refers to Huafa tribe, Pu concept is read as xufa, or faxu。

[5] 夸父而彘毛：指北胡的通古斯外来民。毛，指外来民。
[5] kua fu er zhi mao (father Kua with pig hair) refers to the outsider Tongus tribes who migrated here and becomes the Northern Hu。Mao (hair) refers to outsider migrants.

[6]呼：指东边、东面。这里指东青苔峪。
[6]hu; refers to east side, to the east, here refers to Dongqingtai valley, (east green moss valley) 。

[7] 大水：指达罕氏族。即统治氏族。
[7] da shui (big water) , refers to the ruling tribes。

译文：由本山往南三百里，有座山叫它山。山的西面是游牧部落地区，东面住着凤城氏族。这里还住着华伐夷。有一个氏族，是北胡的通古斯外来民，住在东青苔峪，是那个地方的统治氏族。
Translation:
Three hundred li southward from Benshan stands the Tashan。On its west, the land of the nomads, live the Fengcheng tribes。The Huafa people also live here。Another tribe, the outsider Tongus tribes of the Northern Hu people live in the Dongqingtai valley; they are the ruling class in that area。

04-01-10 独山
Dushan
(130,41876E;51,43934N)

又南三百里，曰独山[1]。其上多金玉[2]，其下多美石 [3] 。末涂之水[4]出焉，而东流注于沔[5]。其中多偹鳙[6]，其状如黄蛇，鱼翼[7]，出入有光[8]，见则其邑大旱[9]。

注释：[1]独山：指图拉纳山，在黑龙江北面的俄罗斯境内，在外兴安岭南面。距离由外兴安岭算起。
Notes:[1] du shan, refers to Tulanashan, now within the Russian territory on the northern part of the Amur River, on the south side of the Xinganling Mountain。Its distance starts from Outer Xinganling Mountain。
[2] 金玉：指沙德临纳夷。
[2] jin yu (gold jade) refers to Shadelinna people。
[3] 美石：指尼曼河氏族。
[3] mei shi (beautiful stone) refers to the Niman River tribes。
[4] 末涂水：指托木河。
[4]mo tu shui: refers to Tomsky River.
[5]沔：指阿穆尔河。
[5] mian; refers to Amur River 。
[6] 偹鳙：指条戎，又称克列人。
[6] tiao yong; refers to Tiao Rong, the Kelie people。
[7] 黄蛇，鱼翼：胡族的哲夷。
[7] huang she (yellow snake) yu yi (fish fins, or wings) refers to the Zhe tribe of the Hu people。
[8] 出如有光：迁居于养鹿镇，今称别洛戈尔斯克。有光：指养鹿。
[8] chu ru you guang (in and out with lights) migrated to Yanglu town， known today as Bylugersky。 You lu: deer keeping。
[9] 大旱：指达罕，即统治氏族。
[9] da han （big draught）; ruling tribe。

译文：由外兴安岭往南三百里，有座山叫图拉纳山。山的西面住着沙德临纳夷，东面住着尼曼河氏族。托木水从山间流出，向东南流入阿穆尔河。河畔住着条戎氏族，是胡族的哲夷，迁居于养鹿镇，是那个集镇的达罕氏族。
Translation:
Three hundred li southward from Outer Xinganling Mountain, stands the Tulanashan。On its west side live the Shadelinna people, on its east side live the Niman River tribes。Tomsky River flows out of this mountain, going southeastward into Amur Rive。On the bank of Amur River live the Tiao Rong tribes, they are the Zhe tribes of the North Hu。They migrated to Yanglu town （Bylugursky）, is the ruling tribe at that town。

04-01-11 泰山
Taishan
(128,90763E；47,7282N)

又南三百里，曰泰山[1]，其上多玉[2]，其下多金[3]。有兽焉，其状如豚而有珠[4]，名曰狪狪[5]，其名自訆。环水[6] 出焉，东流注于江 [7]，其中多水玉[8]。

注释：[1]泰山：指带岭，又称小兴安岭。
Notes:[1] tai shan, refers to Dai Ling, also known as Xiao Xinganling, tai/dai, not distinguishable in Pu concept。
[2]玉：指龙河氏族。
[2]yu(jade) refers to the Long River tribe, Long River (dragon river) 。
[3]金：指上甘岭氏族。
[3] jin(gold)refers to the Shangganling tribe, where during the Korean war, the most famous Shangganling battle took place。
[4] 豚而有珠：指汤旺河的伊春河岔口氏族。
[4] tun er you zhu (pig with pearl) refers to the Hechakou tribe from Yichun, who live along the Tangwang River。
[5] 狪狪：读陀陀，指卡卡氏，又称伊春嘎氏。
[5] tongtong, read in Pu as tuotuo, refers to the Kaka tribe, also known as the Yichunga tribe。
[6] 环水：汤旺河，又称浩良水，简称浩水，谐音环水。
[6] huan shui (circle water) refers to Tangwang River, also known as Haoliangshui River。 It is shortened to Hao River, a rebus to Huan river. Hao/Huan rebus。
[7]江：指松花江。
[7] jiang: refers to the Songhua River。
[8] 水玉：指河滨氏族。水为氏族，玉为河。
[8]shui yu (water jade)refers to the Hebin (riverside)tribes, shui(water)means tribe, yu(jade)means river。

译文：由图拉纳山往南三百里，有座山叫带岭。山的西面住着龙河氏族，东面住着上甘岭氏族。有一个氏族，是汤旺河的伊春河岔口氏族，名叫陀陀，他们也这样称呼自己。浩水从山间流出，向东南流入松花江，河畔住着河滨氏族。
Translation:
Three hundred li southward from Tulanashan, stands Dailingshan。On its wide live the Long River tribes, on its east side, the Shangganling tribes。One tribe, the Tuotuo, as they address themselves thus, is from Tangwang River。They are the Hechakou tribes from Yichun country。Haoshui River flows out from the mountain, going southeastward into Songhua River, along its banks live the Riverside tribes。

04-01-12 竹山
Zhushan
(127,84522E;45,59875N)

又南三百里，曰竹山[1]，錞于江[2]，无草木[3]，多瑶碧[4]。激水[5] 出焉，而东流注于娶檀之水 [6]，其中多茈蠃 [7]。

凡东山经之首，自樕螽之山以至于竹山，凡十二山，三千六百里。其神状皆人身龙首[8]。祠：毛用一犬祈 [9]，聃用鱼 [10]。

注释：[1]竹山：指恩山，读音为竹，濮语的恩字由恒青二字构成，恒青为竹。今称大青山。
Notes:[1] zhu shan (bamboo mountain) refers to Enshan, En in Pu concept read as zhu, written with two signs, one stand for heng (lasting), one stands for qing(green) the two Idiograms combined to make bamboo, which the Daqingshan derived its name: big green mountain。
[2]江：指松花江

[2] jiang(river) refers to Songhua River。

[3] 无草木：游牧部落地区。

[3] wu cao mu (no grass and wood) land of the nomads。

[4] 瑶碧：指大宾氏族，即今宾县氏族。

[4] yao bi, refers to the Dabin tribe, today known as the Binxian tribe。

[5] 激水：指布吉水。布吉指胡子，古人以胡子长来表达延寿。今称延寿水。

[5] ji shui (torrential water) refers to Buji River, in Pu concept, buji refers to beard。 Ancient people think long beard a sign of longevity。The river is known today as Yanshou River, yanshou: add to your ages。

[6] 娶檀水：指庆檀水。娶檀，是沐浴之意。

[6] qu tan shui (marry tan water) refers to Qingtanshui River。Qingtan, Pu concept to refer to taking a bath or shower, or to wash oneself。

[7] 茈羸：指鲰僚，即通古斯人。

[7]ci lei refers to zhi Liao, a term for the Tongus people。

[8] 人身龙首：指定居的牧族的形象。龙首，读勒属，指牧民氏族

[8] ren shen long shou (human body with dragon head), refers to the sedentary herders： long shou (dragon head) a rebus in Pu concept reads as Leshu, refers to pastoralist livelihood。

[9] 毛用一犬祈：用一只角代替祭词。犬，读去，指角。

[9] mao yong yi quan qi(votive offering is one dog in prayer);
Tr: use a horn in place of votive speech, quan(dog)read as qu, a rebus, refers to an animal horn 。

[10] 聃用鱼：读珥用哲，指用铲子掩埋。这里指用铲子将动物的角掩埋。聃指埋。

[10]er yong yu: use fish when pray. In Pu concept reads as er yong zhe, zhe a rebus, fish /shovel, meaning to bury the animal horn using a shovel, er: bury。

译文：由带岭往南三百里，有座山叫恩山，紧挨着松花江，是游牧部落地区，住着大宾氏族。布吉水从山间流出，向东流入庆檀水，河畔住着通古斯人。

Translation:

Three hundred li southward from Dailingshan stands Enshan。Next to the Songhua River is the land of nomads, where the Dabin (big guests) tribe live。Buji River flows out of the mountain, going eastward into Qingtanshui River, along the bank of which live the Tongus tribes。

综观东山第一列山系，自松江山到恩山共计十二座山，延绵三千六百里，这十二座山的山神皆为定居的牧民氏族的形象。祭祀这些山神，用一只角代替祭词，用铲子将其埋入地下。

In sum: Of the first mountain system from Songjiangshan to Enshan, there are 12 mountains covering a distance of 3,600 li。 The mountain deities are in the image of the settled pastoralists。 When making sacrifice to those mountain deities, an animal's horn is used in place of votive speech。 The animal horn is buried underground with a shovel。

东山经第二山系

Book 4 Dongshanjing； chapter 2

04-02-01 空桑山
Kongsangshan
(127,84522E；45,59875N)

东次二经之首，曰空桑之山[1]。北临食水[2]，东望沮吴 [3]，南望沙陵[4]，西望湣泽[5]。有兽焉，其状如牛而虎文[6]，其音如钦[7]，其名曰軨軨[8]，其鸣自訆，见则天下大水[9]。

注释：[1]空桑山：空桑，濮语"嘎韶"的音译，指"锅甑"，今称锅盔山。
Notes：[1] kong sang shan/a rebus with Pu concept ge shao, meaning cooking wok, refers to the Guokui Mountain, whose shape resembles an upside-down wok。

[2] 食水：指松花江。
[2] shi shui, refers to the Songhua River。

[3] 沮吴：指鸡西部落。
[3] ju wu, refers to the Jixi tribes, ju, ji, close in phonetic value, wu: tribe, registered by Chinese glyphs 吴, 武。

[4] 沙陵：梨树镇与穆棱镇合称沙陵。
[4] sha ling: pear tree, and Muleng combined to Shaling。

[5] 湣泽：指牡丹江。
[5] min ze: refers to Mudan River。

[6] 牛而虎文：游牧的乌斯浑支系。虎文，浑的谐音。
[6] niu er hu wen (ox with tiger markings) the wandering pastoralist branch Wusihun tribe。 Hu wen, a rebus, combined into phonetic value, hu, wen hun, hwuen。

[7]钦：指莲。读音扯，谐音钦，今称莲花镇。
[7] qin; refers to lian (lotus)reads as qin/Pu reads as che , known today as Lianhuazhen。

[8] 軨軨：读涅涅，指养鹿氏族。
[8] ling ling, read as Nienie, refers to the Deer herders' tribes。

[9] 大水：指达罕氏族。即统治氏族。
[9] da shui (big water), refers to the ruling tribes, da han,(big Khan)。

译文：东山经第二系列的第一座山，叫锅盔山。这座山北临松花江，东望鸡西部落，南望梨树镇和穆棱镇，西望牡丹江。有一个氏族，是游牧的乌斯浑支系，住在莲花镇，名叫涅涅，他们也这样称呼自己，是那个地区的达罕氏族。
Translations：
Guokuishan is the first one of the second mountain system in the East。 It faces Songhua River on its north, the Jixi tribes on its east。 Looking to its south, there is townships of Lishu (pear tree) and townships of Muleng。 Looking to its west, lies the Mudan River. A pastoralist tribe the Wusihun (Ouse, Oshon) branch live in the town of Lianhua. They call themselves Nienie。They are the ruling tribes in that area。

04-02-02 曹夕山
Caoxishan
(128,3211E; 44,46511N)

又南六百里，曰曹夕之山[1]，其下多穀而无水[2]，多鸟兽[3]。

注释：[1]曹夕山：指秃顶山，又称秃顶子岭。在张广才岭南麓。

Notes: [1] cao xi shan: refers to Tudingshan, also known as the Tudingziling。It is on the south side of Zhangguangcailing Mountains。

[2] 穀而无水：指拉林部落氏族。拉林，濮语读卡举，谐音穀。

[2]gu er wu shui (grain with no water) refers to Lalin tribes。Lalin, Pu concept, reads as Kaju, contracted into kao, gao, gu。

[3] 鸟兽：指河滨氏族。

[3] niao shou (bird beast): refers to the riverside tribes。

译文：由锅盔岭往南六百里，有座山叫秃顶子岭。山的西面住着拉林部落氏族，住着河滨氏族。

Translation:

Six hundred li southward from Guokuiling Mountain, stands the Tulingziling Mountain。On its west side live the Lalin tribe, and the riverside tribes。

04-02-03 峄皋山

Yigaoshan

(126,7713E; 42,536N)

又西南四百里，曰峄皋之山[1]，其上多金玉[2]，其下多白垩[3]。峄皋之水[4] 出焉，东流注于激女之水[5]，其中多蜃珧[6]。

注释：[1]峄皋山：指景城山，景城，今称靖宇县。

[1] yi gao shan; refers to Jingchengshan、Jingcheng is called today Jingyu county。

[2] 金玉：指梁子夷，又称顶子夷。

[2] jin yu (gold jade) refers to Liangzi tribe, also known as Dingzi tribe。 Liangzi and Dingzi, both refers to the mountain top, or ridge, 梁子, 顶子, 岭。

[3] 白垩：指景山镇头道沟氏族。

[3] bai e: refers to Toudaogou tribe, 头道沟: first gully, from Jingshan town。

[4] 峄皋水：指那尔轰河流域。

[4] ji gao shui: refers to narhuun river area:

[5] 激女水：松花江源头的石壁河。激指壁，女指石。

[5] ji nv shui (exciting girl water) refers to the original source water for Songhua River, the Shibi River。 Shi bi (stone wall), shi/stone, a rebus in Pu concept ji/wall, girl/stone。

[6] 蜃珧：指买粮氏，（氏族名）。

[6] shen/chen yao (mirage shellfish) refers to the Mailiang tribe (grain buying) tribe。

译文：由秃顶子岭往西南四百里，有座山叫景城山。山的西面住着顶子夷，东面住着头道沟氏族。那尔轰水从山间流出，向东流入石壁河。这里住着买粮氏族。

Translation:

Four hundred li southwestward from Tudingziling Mountain stands the Jingshan。 On its west side live the Dingzi tribe, on its east side, the Toudaogou tribe。 Narhuun river flows out of this mountain, going eastward into Shibi River。 The Mailiang tribe lives here。

04-02-04 葛山尾

Geshanyi Mountain

(125,27564E; 42,1166N)

又南水行[1]五百里，流沙[2]三百里，至于葛山之尾[3]，无草木[4]，多砥砺[5]。

注释：[1]水行：指沿挥发河行进。
Notes： [1] going by water: march along the Huifahe River。

[2] 流沙：指沿柳河行进，虽然沿水道走，但并不一定通航。
[2] liu sha (moving sands): to move along the Liuhe River。 This does not necessarily mean the waterway is fully navigable。

[3] 葛山尾：指山城南，也称南山城，今辽宁省南山城镇。
[3]ge shan wei (Ge mount tail); refers to Shanchengnan, which is also called Nanshancheng, in today's Nanshancheng township in Liaoning province。

[4] 无草木：游牧部落地区。
[4] wu cao mu (no grass wood); refers to the area where the nomadic tribes are。

[5] 多砥砺：指甸子黎。
[5] duo di li (persistent hard working) refers to the Dianzi Li, a tribe。

译文：由景城山往南沿挥发河行五百里，再沿柳河行三百里，到达南山城，这里是游牧部落地区，住着甸子氏族。
Translation:
Five hundred li southward from Jinchengshan, by water and then for another three hundred li along Liuhe River, one comes to Nanshan town, a land of the nomads。The Dianzi tribe live here。

04-02-05 葛山首
Geshanshou Mountain
(124,08456E; 41,92125N)

又南三百八十里，曰葛山之首[1]，无草木[2]。澧水[3] 出焉，东流注于余泽 [4]，其中多珠鳖鱼[5]，其状如肺而有目[6]，六足有珠[7]，其味酸甘[8]，食之无疠[9]。

注释：[1]葛山首：指西城山，西在濮语中读首，索，萨，今辽宁抚顺县城北山。
Notes: [1]ge shan shou, refers to Xichengshan, xi (west) reads in Pu language as shou, suo, sa, in today's Beishan, Fushun County, Liaoning province。

[2] 无草木：游牧部落地区。
[2]wu cao mu(no gras wood);refers to the land of the nomads。

[3] 澧水：指斟【星戈】水，今称章党水。
[3]li shui: refers to Lishu River, today as Zhangdangshui。in Pu concept: it is read as sha mi she shui。

[4] 余泽：指峪泽，又称萨尔浒。
[4]yu ze: refers to Yu Lake: big water， also known as Saerhu。

[5] 珠鳖鱼：指浊沘夷，又称浑河夷。
[5] zhu bi yu (pearl bi fish) a rebus for zhu bi yi, refers to the Hunhe River Yi, zhu: 珠, zhu 朱; 沘 bi 鳖 bie。

[6] 肺而有目：东部的蒙族。此时期的蒙族指补蒙纠，属东胡苗蒙。
[6] fei er you mu (lungs have eyes) refers to the Mongols in the east。At this time when the book is compiled, Mongolian tribes belong to the Miao meng, a part of Donghu (east Hu) tribal entity and is recorded as Bu Meng Jiu。

[7] 六足有珠：母系的浑河部落。
[7] liu zu you zhu (six feet with pearl) refers to the Hunhe tribes which is a matrilineal organization。

[8] 其味酸甘：古称且维芍嘎，今称东洲。
[8] qi wei suan gan (it tastes sour sweet) its ancient name read in Pu language as :qie wei shao ga, a rebus。 It is known as Dongzhou today。

[9] 食之无疠：古老的斟【星戈】部落氏族。
[9] shi zhi wu li (eaten to cure Diarrhea) refers to the ancient Zhenge tribes。

译文：由南山城往南三百八十里，有座山叫西城山，是游牧部落地区。斟星戈水从山间流出，向东南流入峪泽，这里住着浑河夷，是东部蒙族母系氏族的浑河支系氏族，住在且维芍嘎，是古老的斟戈部落氏族。
Translation:
Three hundred and eighty li southward from Nanshan town, stands the Xichengshan, a nomadic tribal area。Zhenxingge river flows out of the mountain, going southeast into Yuze。 Hunhe Yi lives there, they belong to the Hunhe Yi branch of the East Mongol tribes , a matrilineal organization, living in Qieweishaoga。 They are the ancient Zhenge tribes。
04-02-06 余峨山
Yu'eshan
(122,07372E; 41,136533N)

又南三百八十里，曰余峨之山[1]。其上多梓枏[2]，其下多荆芑[3]。杂余之水[4]出焉，东流注于黄水[5]。有兽焉，其状如菟而鸟喙[6]，鸱目蛇尾[7]，见人则眠[8]，名曰犰狳[9]，其鸣自訆，见则螽蝗为败[10]。

注释：[1]余峨山：指盘锦。盘锦在辽河南岸，故称为溢卧、溢阳。
Notes:[1]yu e shan: refers to Panjin, now the Panjin municipality on the south bank of Liao River, thus the name: yi/river, wo, south, sunny。It is between 40°41′~41°27′N,121°31′~122°28′E。
[2] 梓枏：指太平河氏族。
[2] zi nan2, refers to the Taiping River tribe, Taiping (great peace)
[3] 荆芑：指坝墙子氏族。芑，读己音，意为墙、壁。
[3] jin ji refers to Baqiangzi tribe。 ji: Pu concept for wall。
[4] 杂余水：辽河称为余，外辽河称为杂余。
[4]za yu shui: refers to the Liao River, which is called Yu, Wailiao River is called Zayu: Zayushui, 40° 40′ 9″ N, 122° 8′ 56″ E。
[5] 黄水：指浑河，又称浑江。
[5] hua shui (yellow water) refers to Hun River, also known as Hun Jiang。
[6] 菟而鸟喙：土族的河边支系。
[6] tu er niao hui (rabbit with bird beak)
Tr : Tu tribe's riverside branch。
[7] 鸱目蛇尾：直目人的塞夷。此处因涉及到丝织业，当按月氏塞夷解译。
[7] chi mu she yi (owl eyes with snake tail) refers to the Saka, who are also known as the zhimu people, （people with vertical eyes）。 Here in the context that the silk textile is mentioned, this Saka tribe should be identified as the Yueshi Saka, previously written as rùzh, or ròuzhī。
[8] 见人则眠：是那个集镇的织绸氏族。
[8] jian ren ze mian (fall asleep when seeing people) is the silk industry tribe from that town。
[9] 犰狳：睢(chui)夷，即养蚕夷。
[9] qiu yu (Armadillo): chui yi: refers to the silkworm keepers。
[10] 螽蝗为败：读"则浑溢帕"，指浑江河畔。
[10] zhong huang wei bai: zhonghuang (bush crickets do damage ,) Pu concept reads as: ze hun yi pa,
Tr: the banks of Hun River。

译文：由西城山往西南三百八十里，有座城镇叫溢卧。它的西面住着太平河氏族，东面住着坝墙子氏族。外辽河水从旁边流出，向东南流入浑江河。有一个氏族，是土族的河边支系，是直目人的塞夷，是那个集镇的织绸氏族，名叫睢夷，他们也这样称呼自己，是浑江河畔的氏族。
Translation:
Three hundred and eighty li southwestward from Jiguan Mountain, stands a town called Yiwo。 On its west live the Taiping River tribe, on its east, the Baqiangzi tribe。 Outer Liao River flows past it, going southeast into the Hunjiang River。One tribe, the riverside tribe of the Tu people, is the Shan people from the Zhimu people, who are the silk textile tribes in that town。 They are known as Chui people, and they call themselves thus, they are the tribes along the Hunjiang River。

04-02-07 杜父山
Dufushan
(120,87493E; 40,81261N)

又南三百里，曰杜父之山[1]，无草木[2]，多水[3]。

注释：[1]杜父山：读嗒洪鲁，今谐音称大红螺。原意是指鹰山。
Notes:[1] du fu shan (father du mount) Pu concept: da hong lu, a rebus to da hong luo(big red shell)original meaning: ‘eagle mountain’。
[2] 无草木：游牧部落地区。
[2] wu cao mu (no grass wood) refers to the land of the nomads。
[3]水：指响水河氏族。
[3] shui: refers to the Xiangshui tribe: xiang shui (loud water) 。

译文：由溢卧往南三百里，有座山叫大红螺，是游牧部落地区，住着响水河氏族。
Translation:
Three hundred li southward from Yiwo stands the Dahongluo Mountain, a place for nomads, where the Xiangshuihe tribes live。

04-02-08 耿山
Gengshan
(120,34329E; 40,32813N)

又南三百里，曰耿山[1]，无草木[2]，多水碧[3]，多大蛇[4]。有兽焉，其状如狐而鱼翼[5]，其名曰朱獳[6]，其鸣自訆，见则其国有恐[7]。

注释：[1]耿山：指古山，也称股山。今称高台。
Notes:[1] geng shan: refers to gu(ancient), or gu(share),known today as Gaotaishan(high terrace mount) 。
[2] 无草木：游牧部落地区。
[2] wu cao mu (no grass wood) refers to the land of the nomads。
[3] 耿山：指古山，也称股山。今称高台。
[3] shui bi (water blue) refers to the Suibi tribe, a rebus。
[4] 大蛇：指大肆夷。
[4] da she (big snake) refers to the Dasi Yi。
[5] 狐而鱼翼：东部的哲夷，即东部的渔业氏族。
[5]hu er yu yi (fox with fish fins) refers to the East Zhe people, a fishing tribe from the east。
[6] 朱獳：指六江氏，读浙漏。今称六股河人。

[7] zhu ru (red angry dog) refers to the Liujiang Shi, liujiang/zhelou, a phonetic shift, a rebus 。

[7] 有恐：指补苦，即有夏氏族，属红山文化的主体氏族。

[7] you kong (being afraid) a rebus: you kong reads in Pu language as bu ku, a reference to the You Xia people, they are the major carriers of the Hongshan culture。

译文：由大红螺往南三百里，有座山叫高台山，是游牧部落地区，住着绥沘氏族，住着游牧的大肆夷。有一个氏族，是东部的哲夷，名叫六江氏，他们也这样称呼自己，是那个国家的有夏氏族。

Translation:

Three hundred li southward from Dahongluo mountain, stands the Gaotaishan (high terrace mountain), where the Suibi tribes live。The nomad's tribe, the Dasi Yi also live there。 A tribe known as Zhe tribe is from the east, they are called Liujiang Yi， they also call themselves thus。 They are the country's Youxia(buku) tribe。

04-02-09 卢其山

Luqishan

(119,7561E; 40,0088N)

又南三百里，曰卢其之山[1]，无草木[2]，多沙石[3]。沙水[4] 出焉，南流注于涔水 [5]，其中多鵹鹕[6]，其状如鸳鸯而人足[7]，其鸣自訆，见则其国多土功[8]。

注释：[1]卢其山：指角山。山读卢，角读其，其实介绍山脚的部落，这里后来成为山海关。Notes:[1]lu qi shan: refers to Jiaoshan。Shan reads as Lu, jiao reads as qi, in fact, this is a description of the tribes at the foot of the mountain, a place later became Shanhaiguan Pass。

[2] 无草木：游牧部落地区。

[2] wu cao mu (no grass wood) refers to the land of the nomads。

[3] 沙石：指长河氏族，今称石河氏族。

[3] sha shi (sandstone) refers to the Chang River tribe. Chang(long), known today as Shihe tribes。

[4] 沙水：指长河水，又称石河水。

[4] sha shui: refers to Chang River, also known as Shiheshui (stone water) river。

[5] 涔水：今称辽东湾。

[5] cen shui: refers to Liaodong Wan (Liadong Bay) 。

[6] 鵹鹕：指青胡。

[6] wu hu refers to Qing Hu a tribe。

[7] 鸳鸯而人足：北部的定居支系。

[7] yuanyang er ren zu (water bird Yuanyang with human feet) refers to the settled branches in the North。

[8] 见则其国多土功：那个部落国很贫穷。

[8] jian ze qi guo duo tu gong: (seeing it, the country will start a lot of earth project),

Tr: that tribal state is very poor。

译文：由高台山往南三百里，有座山叫角山，是游牧部落地区，住着石河氏族。石河水从山间流出，向南流入辽东湾。石河河畔住着青胡，是北部的定居支系，他们也这样称呼自己。那个部落国很贫穷。

Translation:

Three hundred li southward from Gaotaishan stands Tuoling (Mountain), a land of the nomads, where the Shihe tribes live。 Chang River flows out of the mountain, going south into Pan River。On the banks of the Pan River, live the settled tribes from north, they call themselves Qing Hu。That country is very poor。

04-02-10 姑射山

Gusheshan

(118,43479E; 39,73084N)

又南三百八十里，曰姑射之山[1]，无草木[2]，多水[3]。

注释：[1]姑射山：读古冶山，指大城山，在今唐山市古冶区。
Notes:[1]gu she shan: Pu concept gu ye shan, refers to Dacheng (big city) Mountain, today's Guye district, Tangshan city。

[2] 无草木：游牧部落地区。
[2] wu cao mu (no grass wood) refers to the land of the nomads。

[3]水：指云氏族，也称睢氏族，分别有黄、习、水三姓。
[3] shui: refers to the Yun tribe, Yun(clouds) is also known as Chui tribe, three surnames come from this tribe; Huang, Xi, Shui。

译文：由陡岭往南三百八十里，有座山叫古冶山，是游牧部落地区，住着云氏族。
Translation:
Three hundred and eighty li southward from Tuling mountain, stands the Guyeshan, a land of the nomads, where the Yun tribes live。

04-02-11 北姑射山
Beigusheshan
(117,1987E; 39,70435N)

又南水行三百里，流沙百里，曰北姑射之山[1]。无草木[2]，多石 [3] 。

注释：[1]北姑射山：读贝古冶山，指津大城，今称天津。津、静、镜都读 bi 音。
Notes:[1] bei gu she shan: read in Pu as bei gu ye shan, refers to Jindacheng, (big river city) today known as Tianjin municipality 。 In Pu concept jin reads as bi。Bi: bei, a rebus, Jin, river port。

[2] 无草木：游牧部落地区。
[2] wu cao mu (no grass wood) refers to the land of the nomads。

[3]石：读砾音，指倪庄、倪黄庄、凝侯庄等带石概念读音的氏族。他们是较早的居民，属游牧氏族。
[3] shi/le, Pu concept Le, refers to stone, here it refers to the village of Ni, Nihuang, and Ninghou。In Pu concept, N/L is not distinguished, here all the village share the Ni syllabary, meaning; stone, they are the earlier residents here, belong to the nomad's tribe。

译文：由古冶水行三百里，旱行百里，有一个地区叫津大城，是游牧部落地区，住着石氏族。
Translation:
Three hundred li following the Guyeshui River, and then one hundred li on land, there stands the big river port city Jindacheng。 This is the land of the nomads, the tribes bearing surname Shi(stone) live here。

04-02-12 南姑射山
Nangusheshan
(116,64419E; 38,70435N)

又南三百里，曰南姑射之山[1]，无草木[2]，多水[3]。

注释：[1]南姑射山：读勒古冶、二姑院，指二大城。因属远古某国的南京，又称召扶。今称大城。

Notes:[1] nan gu she shan; In Pu concept reads Le gu ye, er gu yuan, refers to the Erdacheng, (second big town) 。It used to be the southern capital of certain ancient country, is also known as Zhao Fu, known today as Dacheng, (big city) 。

[2] 无草木：游牧部落地区。

[2] wu cao mu (no grass wood), refers to the land of the nomads。

[3]水：指召扶氏族。扶，在濮语中读携，谐音水。

[3] shui, Pu concept reads as xie, shui/xie/fu a rebus, refers to fu, the Zhaofu tribe。

译文：由津大城往南三百里，是二大城，属游牧部落地区，住着召扶氏族。

Translation:

Three hundred li southward from Jindacheng city, stands Erdacheng city (second big city) 。The Zhaofu tribe lives here。

04-02-13 碧山

Bishan

(116,64419E; 38,70435N)

又南三百里，曰碧山[1]，无草木[2]，多大蛇[3]，多碧[4]、水玉[5]。

注释：[1]碧山：指河边的山，今称泊头。

Notes:[1]bi shan: refers to mountain by the river, known today as Potou, (port head) 。

[2] 无草木：游牧部落地区。

[2] wu cao mu (no grass wood) refers to the land of the nomads。

[3] 大蛇：指大肆夷。

[3] da she (big snake) refers to the Dasi people。

[4]碧：指河滨氏族。

[4]bi(blue) refers to the Riverside tribes。

[5] 水玉：指云夷。

[5] shui yu(water jade) refers to the Yun (clouds)tribes。

译文：由二大城往南三百里，有个地方叫泊头，是游牧部落地区，住着大肆夷、河滨氏族和云夷。

Translation:

Three hundred li southward from Erdacheng, one comes to a place called Potou (port head), the land of the nomads。 The Dasi Yi, Hebin(riverside) tribes and Yun Yi live there。

04-02-14 缑氏山

Houshishan

(116,64999E; 36,93394N)

又南五百里，曰缑氏之山[1]，无草木[2]，多金玉[3]。原水[4] 出焉，东流注于沙泽[6]。

注释：[1]缑氏山：缑氏山，指夏族则柯氏的住地，也称古氏、缑氏。因为是禹的后裔，所以崇拜禹。今称禹城。

Notes: [1] hou shi shan: refers to the residence of the Zeke tribes of the Xia people, also known as the Gu Shi, Hou Shi。 They are the descendants of the legendary Yu, the Xia dynasty founder who is famous for managing the floods。 This place is therefore called the city of Yu。

[2] 无草木：游牧部落地区。

[2] wu cao mu (no grass wood) refers to the land of the nomads。

[3] 金玉：指集镇夷。

[3] jin yu (gold jade) refers to township Yi。

[4] 原水：指救援水，濮语读救援为"徒骇"，今称徒骇河。

[4] yuan shui (original water) In Pu concept, it is called Jiuyuan shui (rescue water), Pu pronunciation is: Tuhai, so the river is known today as Tuhai River。

[6] 沙泽：沙泽：读奢泽，指黄河。

[6] sha ze: Pu concept reads as 'she ze'; she(yellow) here refers to the Yellow River。

译文：由泊头往南五百里，是则柯氏族地区，属游牧部落地区，住着集镇夷。徒骇水从这里流出，向东流入黄河。

Translation:

Five hundred li southward from Potou, is the land of the Zeke tribes, a land of the nomads, where the Jizhen(township)tribes live。 Tuhai River flows out of here, going eastward into the Yellow River。

04-02-15 姑逢山

Gufengshan

(116,76705E; 36,18105N)

又南三百里，曰姑逢之山[1]，无草木[2]，多金玉[3]。有兽焉，其状如狐而有翼[4]，其音如鸿雁[5]，其名曰獙獙[6]，见则天下大旱[7]。

注释：[1]姑逢山：指东城山，今称肥城山，在山东省肥城。

Notes:[1]gu feng shan: refers to Dongcheng (east city) mountain, known today as Feichengshan (fat city mountain) in Feicheng county in Shandong province。

[2] 无草木：游牧部落地区。

[2] wu cao mu (no grass wood): refers to the land of the nomads。

[3] 金玉：指集镇夷。

[3] jin jade (gold jade) refers to township Yi。

[4] 狐而有翼：肥城的羿部落氏族。

[4]hu er you yi (fox with wings), the Yi tribes from Feichengshan。

[5] 鸿雁：指黄叶庄。

[5] hong yan(goose) refers to Huangye (yellow leaves) village,

[6] 獙獙：指背河氏族。背河，濮语读为臂沘，谐音獙獙。

[6]bi bi (a kind of monkey) refers to the Bei River tribes, a rebus, Bei, back, bi, arm, bi, water in Pu language, (arm water) beibei。

[7] 大旱：达罕氏族，统治氏族。

[7] da han (big draught) refers to ruling tribes or clans。

译文：由禹城往南三百里，有座山叫肥城山，是游牧部落地区，住着集镇夷。有一个氏族，是肥城的羿部落氏族，住在黄叶庄，名叫背河氏，是那个地区的统治氏族。

Translation:

Three hundred li from Yu city southward, stands the Feichengshan, a land of the nomads。The Jizhen(township) tribes live there, the Yi (arrow and bow) tribes live there, in the Huangye village, they are known as the Bei River people, they are the ruling tribes of that area。

04-02-16 凫丽山

Fulishan
(127,21702E; 35,50537N)

又南五百里，曰凫丽之山[1]，其上多金玉[2]，其下多箴石[3]。有兽焉，其状如狐而九尾，九首，虎爪[4]，名曰蠪姪[5]，其音如婴儿[6]，是食人[7]。

注释：[1]凫丽山：指沂蒙山， 凫丽，沂蒙在濮语中都指母亲，在山东曲阜东南侧。
Notes:[1] fu li shan: refers to Puyu Mountain, on the southeast side of Qufu county, Shandong province,
[2] 金玉：指济夷。
[2] jin jade, refers to the Ji people。
[3] 箴石：指平邑氏族
[3] jian shi: refers to the Pingyi tribes。
[4] 狐而九尾，九首，虎爪：东部的九夷苗族山区支系。九尾，指九夷；九首，指纠属，即苗族。虎爪，指王族支系。
[4]hu er jiu yi (fox with nine tails) jiu shou (nine heads),hu zhua(tiger claws);
Tr: the branches of the Jiuyi mountain tribes in the east, nine tail, a rebus, meaning nine tribes, jiushou, another rebus, meaning Jiushu, a term for the Miao people, tiger claws a rebus, for the mountainous clans。
[5] 蠪姪：指鲁枝氏，苗族的一个大支系，原籍在山东曲阜地区。迁徙到贵州的鲁枝氏，今称六(lu)枝氏，又称苗。
[5] long zhi(beast) refers to the Luzhi tribe, a major branch of the Miao people。 They originally live in the Qufu area in Shandong province, later migrated to Guizhou province。Today they are bearing the surname of Liu or Lu Shi, as well as Miao。
[6] 婴儿：北面。指曲阜。
[6] yin er (infant), north, refers to Qufu, in Shandong province。
[7] 是食人：是古老的定居氏族。
[7] shi shi ren (yes eat human), refers to the ancient tribes who settled down long ago。

译文：由肥城山往南五百里，有座山叫沂蒙山。山的西面住着济夷，东面住着平邑氏族。有一个氏族，是东部九夷苗族的王族支系，名叫鲁枝氏，住在北面的曲阜，是古老的定居氏族。
Translation:
Five hundred li southward from Feichengshan stands the Yimengshan。 On its west side live the Ji Yi people, on its east side, the Pingyi tribes。 A tribe from the mountain people of the east nine tribes of the Miao, bearing the surname of Luzhi Shi, live in Qufu in the north, they are the ancient tribes who settled down long ago。

04-02-17 碅山
Yinshan
(118,35644E; 35,10207N)

又南五百里，曰碅山[1]，南临碅水[2]，东望湖泽[3]。有兽焉，其状如马，而羊目、四角、牛尾[4]，其音如獆狗[5]，其名曰峳峳[6]。见则其国多狡客[7] 。有鸟焉，其状如凫而鼠尾，善登木 [8] ，其名曰絜钩 [9] ，见则其国多疫[10]。
凡东次二经之首，自空桑山至于碅山，凡十七山，六千六百四十里。其神状皆兽身人面载觡[11] 。其祠，毛用一鸡祈 [12] ，婴 [13] 用一璧瘗。

注释：[1]碅山：指蕑山，即兰山，今临沂市。
Notes:[1] yin shan: refers to jian shan, known as Lanshan, today’s Linyi city。
[2] 碅水：指兰水，今称沂水。

[2] yin shui, refers to Lan River, known today as Yi River。

[3] 湖泽：指虎园，莒南县古称虎园。湖，指园；泽，指虎。

[3]hu ze: refers to Hu Yuan (tiger garden), an ancient name for Junan county。Hu (lake) Pu concept refers to garden, ze, (big water) refers to tiger。

[4] 马而羊目、四角、牛尾：苗族的蚩尤母系僚夷。

[4]ma er yang mu, (horse with sheep eyes) si jiao (four horns) niu yi (ox's tail) 。

Tr: The Lao people of the Chiyou, a Miao matrilineal organization。

[5] 獆狗：指熟城，临沂城的古称谓。濮语以"熟"表示手工业发达的城镇。

[5] gao gou (kind dog) refers to Shucheng, (cooked city), ancient name for Linyi city。 The Pu concept shu(cooked) refers to cities with advanced handcrafts.

[6] 狢狢：蚩尤氏，又称尤尤氏。

[6] you you refer to Chiyou people, also known as Youyou, a legendary figure who was defeated by the Yellow Emperor。

[7] 狡客：指缫丝氏族。

[7] jiao ke; refers to tribes who are silk producers。

[8] 鳧而鼠尾，善登木：东部九夷的明镇苗。善登，指明镇，临沂城的古称谓，又称熟城。

[8] fu er shu yi (water bird with rat tail) shan deng mu (good climbing the trees) 。

Tr: Mingzhen Miao, from the east Jiuyi tribes, shandeng; refers to the Ming town, an ancient name for Linyi, which is also known as Shucheng (cooked town) 。

[9] 絜钩：读契勾，东夏族陈锋部落的濮语称谓。

[9] qi gou: rebus: qi gou, a Pu term for the Chenfeng tribes of Dongxia (East xia) people。

[10] 多疫：读都夷，指古老夷，古老氏族。

[10] duo yi(a lot of pandemics) reads du yi, refers to Gulao yi(people), ancient tribes。

[11] 兽身人面载觡：穿着华丽的定居氏族形象。载觡，指美丽。

[11] shou shen ren mian zai luo:(beast body with human face and hair dresses),

Tr: the settled tribal people who are in gorgeous clothing, zailuo: beautiful.

[12]鸡：指矶，即璧玉。

[12] ji(rooster) refers to jade piece, a ring.

[13]婴：也就是。

[13] yin(infant),

Tr: so, it is。

译文：由沂蒙山往南五百里，有座山叫兰山，这里南临兰水，东望虎园。有一个氏族，是苗族的蚩尤母系僚(lao)夷，住在熟城，名叫尤尤氏。他们是这个国家的缫丝氏族。有一群人，是东部九夷的明镇苗，名叫契勾氏，是契那的古老夷。

综观东山第二列山系，自锅盔山至兰山。共十七座山，延绵六千六百四十里。这些山的山神皆为穿着华丽的定居氏族的形象。祭祀这些山神时，用一璧玉传达祭词，也就是将一块璧玉埋入地下。

Translation:

Five hundred li southward from Yimengshan stands the Lanshan. It borders the Lanshui River on the south side, and overlooks Huyuan to its east。A tribe, a Miao branch from the Chiyou matrilineal people, live in 'shu city, they are called Youyou Shi tribes。They are the silk producer of that country。A group of people, ancient in history of China, is the Mingzhen Miao, they are called Qigou Shi, China's ancient Yi。

In sum: Of the second mountain system, from Guokuishan to Lanshan, there are 17 mountains, covering a distance of 6,640 li。 The mountain deities are in the images of settled residence wearing beautiful clothes 。When offering sacrifice, use a jade piece to communicate the speech, that is, to bury the jade Bi under the ground。

东山经第三山系

Book 4 Dongshanjing； chapter3

04-03-01 尸胡山
Shihushan
(127,32925E; 49,42489N)

又东次三经之首，曰尸胡之山[1]，北望【歹羊】山[2]，其上多金玉[3]，其下多棘[4]。其状如麋而鱼目[5]，名曰婴胡 [6]，其名自訆。

注释：[1]尸胡山：指孙吴山，在小兴安岭北端。
Notes： [1] shi hu shan: refers to Sunwushan, on the North end of the Xiaoxinganling Mountains。 (Lesser Khingan Mountain range in China, 48° 47′ 30″ N, 127° 12′ 30″ E) 。
[2] 【歹羊】山：指西瓦嶷，今称兴安岭；北望，指贝望，即南望。
[2] yang shan: refers to xi wa yi, today known as Xinganling Mountains。Bei wang: north looking, bei, shell, north, Pu concept, shell means south, even it is read as bei(north) registered by Chinese sign for shell。
[3] 金玉：指平度夷。
[3] jin yu (gold jade) refers to Pingdu people。
[4]棘：指腰屯氏族。腰，读音缴，谐音棘。
[4] jin (bushes) refers to Yaotun people。 yao(waist), Pu concept reads as jiao, close to jin, a rebus, y/j, yao--jiao—jin。
[5] 麋而鱼目：王泡子湖的渔民。读为武枝而哲目。麋，指武枝。武枝湖即王泡子。
[5]mi er yu mu (elk with fisheyes) refers to the fishing tribes at Wangpaozi Lake。In Pu language, the text reads as wu zhi er zhe mu, mi refers to wu zhi, thus the Wuzhi Lake, a variant for Wangpaozi Lake。 zhe (fishing) mu(tribe)。
[6] 婴胡：指武湖氏。也称吴湖氏。
[6] yuan hu refers to Wuhu tribe, also known as Wu Lake tribe。

译文：东山第三系列最北端的山，名叫孙吴山，南望兴安岭。山的西面住着平度氏族，东面住着腰屯氏族。有一个氏族，是王泡子湖的渔民，名叫吴湖氏，他们也这样称呼自己。
Translation:
The northmost mountain starting the 3d system is Songwushan。 It looks toward south to the Xinganling Mountains。 On its west live the Pingdu tribe, on its east side the Yaotun tribe。 A tribe called themselves Wuhu people, they are the fishing tribes from the Wangpaozi Lake。

04-03-02 岐山
Qishan
(127,10266; 47,24630N)

又南水行八百里，曰岐山[1]。其木多桃李[2]，其兽多虎 [3] 。

注释：[1]岐山：指平坦的地区，也称平山。今小兴安岭南面的绥化市的努敏河一带。
Notes: [1] qi shan: refers to flat land area, also known as Ping Mountain。 It is around the Numin River area, the Suihua city on the south side of the Lesser Xinganling Mountains。

[2] 桃李：肃慎族和扶余人的各个邑落以圆栅为寨，称为陶篱，谐音桃李或团林。
[2] tao li (peach plum) a rebus for Taoli, which means separating structure between the settlements where the Sushen tribes or the Fuyu tribes live。Those structures are circular, made of tree branches and brushes, and called Taoli, or Tuanlin。

[3]虎：指扶余人。
[3]hu(tiger); refers to Fuyu people. Fuyu: Buyu in Korean language。

译文：由孙吴山往南水行八百里，是平山。那里的检目皆以陶篱为寨，居住的氏族为扶余人。
Translation:
Eight hundred li southward by water from Sunwushan stands Pingshan。 The administration centers are circular fenced villages, its residents are Fuyu people。

04-03-03 诸钩山
Zhugoushan
(126,30852E; 43,86817N)

又南水行七百里，曰诸钩之山[1]，无草木[2]，多沙石[3]。是山也，广员百里，多寐鱼[4]。

注释：[1]诸钩山：指君城山，是肃慎部落的中心区域。今哈尔滨双城地区。
Notes: [1] zhu gou shan (various hooks mount); refers to the Junchengshan (king's city mount), which is the central citadel of the Sushen tribes, today it is called Shuangcheng (double cities) district in Harbin 。45° 23′ 4.2″ N, 126° 20′ 56.4″ E。

[2] 无草木：游牧部落地区。
[2] wu cao mu (no grass wood) refers to the land of the nomads。

[3] 沙石：指松花江氏族。
[3] sha shi (sandstone) refers to the Songhua River tribes。

[4] 寐鱼：指五常夷。寐，濮语数序“五”的读音。
[4] mei yu (sleeping fish) a Pu rebus, Mei/may /five, here refers to the Wuchang (five constant)tribes。wu/mei/may。

译文：由平山往南水行七百里，到达君城山，这里是游牧部落地区，住着松花江氏族。这个地方有百里宽阔，还住着五常夷。
Translation:
Seven hundred li southward by water, one arrives at Junchengshan。On this land of the nomads, the Songhua River tribes live。The area covers one hundred square li, the Wuchang Yi live here。

04-03-04 中父山
Zhongfushan
(126,5679E; 43,86817N)

又南水行七百里，曰中父之山[1]，无草木[2]，多沙[3]。

注释：[1]中父山：指首王山，又称前王山。今吉林市区。

Notes: [1] zhong fu shan (middle father mount) refers to Shouwangshan (first king mount), also known as Qianwangshan (previous king mount) 。Today, it is known as the urban area of Jilin City, in Jilin province。

[2] 无草木：游牧部落地区。

[2] wu cao mu (no grass wood), refers to the land of the nomads。

[3]沙：指松花江氏族。

[3] sha(sand), refers to Songhua River tribes。

译文：由君城山往南水行七百里，有座山叫首王山，是游牧部落地区，住着松花江氏族。

Translation:

Seven hundred li southward by water, from Junchengshan stands Shouwangshan。On this land of the nomads, live the Songhua River tribes。

04-03-05 胡射山

Husheshan

(127,48578E; 42,17088N)

又东水行千里，曰胡射之山[1]，无草木[2]，多沙石[3]。

注释：[1]胡射山：指长白山。胡在此读 wu 音，指白。射读 xie, 指长。

Notes: [1]hu she mounts; refers to Changbai Mountain, a rebus。Pu concept of hu/wu, refers to white, she reads as xie, refers to length。42° 0′ 20″ N, 128° 3′ 19″ E Paektu/Baekdu Mountain in North Korea。

[2] 无草木：游牧部落地区。

[2] wu cao mu (no grass wood); refers to the land of the nomads。

[3] 沙石：指松花江氏族。

[3] sha shi (sandstone) refers to the Songhua River tribes。

译文：由首王山往东水行千里，到达长白山，这里是游牧部落地区，住着松花江氏族。

Translation:

One thousand li by water eastward from Shouwangshan, one arrives at the Changbai Mountain, a nomad's land where the Songhua River tribes live。

04-03-06 孟子山

Mengzishan

(128,29474E; 41,09253N)

又南水行七百里，曰孟子之山[1]。其木多梓桐[2]，多桃李 [3]，其草多菌浦[4]，其兽多麋鹿[5]。是山也，广员百里。其山有水焉，名曰碧阳[6]，其中多鳣鲔[7]。

注释：[1]孟子山：指收马山，今称盖马高原。

Notes:[1] meng zi shan: refers to Shouma Mountain, today known as the Gaima/Kaema Plateau

[2] 其木多梓桐：这里住着开甲胡族。今称甲山胡。

[2] qi mu duo zi tong:(wood mostly Catalpa bungei, commonly known as Manchurian catalpa, is a species of catalpa native to China)

Tr: here live the Kaijiahu people, today known as Jiashan Hu。

[3] 桃李：指团林氏族。团林，也读陶篱，是肃慎族"围寨"的称谓。

[3] tao li (peach plum) refers to the Tuanlin tribe, a Pu rebus for Taoli, a term to refer for the Sushen tribes living structure, the circular fence—weizhai, surrounded village。

[4] 其草多菌浦：住着长津浦游牧民。
[4] qi cao duo jun pu (among the grass, a lot of moss), refers to the nomads at Changjinpu。
[5] 其兽多麋鹿：住着梨寨狩猎氏族。
[5] qi shou duo mi lu (of the beasts, mostly elks] refers to the hunting tribes from Lizhai (pear village) zhai: village, tun, dun。
[6] 碧阳：指大川河。
[6] bi yan: (blue sun}. Refers to the Dachuan River。
[7] 鳣鲔：指咸镜山南面的氏族。
[7] dan you: fish, shan/zhan, sturgeon) refers to the tribes on the south side of the Xianjing Lake (salty mirror lake) 。

译文：由长白山往南水行七百里，有座山叫盖马高原。这里住着甲山胡族，住着团林氏族。这里还住着长津浦游牧民，住着梨寨狩猎氏族。这座山有百里宽广，有大川河发源于这里，河边住着咸镜山南面的氏族。
Translation:
Seven hundred li southward by water, from Changbai Mountain, stands the Gaima highland。 The Jiashan Hu tribes and Tuanlin tribes live here。The nomads of Changjinpu also live there, also the hunting tribes of the Lizhai village。 The mountain is one hundred li wide, Dachuan River flows out of here, on its banks live the tribes on the south side of the Xianjing Mountain。

04-03-07 跂踵山
Qizhongshan
(124,34774E; 40,01866N)

又南水行五百里，曰流沙[1]，行五百里，有山焉，曰跂踵之山[2]，广员二百里，无草木[3]，有大蛇[4]，其上多玉[5]。有水焉，广员四十里皆涌，其名曰深泽[6]，其中多蠵龟[7]。有鱼焉，其状如鲤而六足鸟尾[8]，名曰鮯鮯之鱼[9]，其名自訆。

注释：[1]流沙：指鸭绿江。
Notes:[1] liu sha (flowing sand) refers to the Yalu River。
[2] 跂踵山：指安东山, 今辽宁丹东市。
[2] qi zhong shan (six toes mount), refers to the Andongshan, known today as the Dandong City in Liaoning province。 40° 0′ 2.16″ N, 124° 21′ 15.84″ E
[3] 无草木：游牧部落地区。
[3] wu cao mu (no grass wood) refers to the land of the nomads。
[4] 大蛇：指大集肆。
[4] da she (big snake) refers to a big market town。
[5]玉：指河川氏族。
[5]yu(jade); refers to Hechuan tribes。
[6] 深泽：指沙河。
[6] shen ze (deep water), refers to Sha(sand) River。
[7] 蠵龟：指东渡口氏族。
[7] xi gui (loggerhead sea turtle) refers to Dongdukou tribes。 Xi, a Pu concept of east, registered by Chinese signs; 西, 羲, 且, 契, as in Chi-na, country or place in the east。
[8] 鲤而六足鸟尾：住在青梅岭的僚夷。
[8]li er liu zu niao yi (carp with six feet and bird tail) refers to the Liao people live in the Qingmeiling。
[9] 蛤蛤鱼：指蚕茧夷，即养蚕为业的族群。
[9] ha ha fish(clam) refers to the silkworm keepers—Canjian Yi, they make their living raising silkworms。

译文：由盖马高原往南水行五百里，到达鸭绿江，再水行五百里就到达安东。这里方圆二百里都是游牧部落地区，有一个大集肆，住着河川氏族。有一条河，从河口到源头长四十里，名叫沙河，河畔住着东渡口氏族。有一群僚夷，是住在青梅岭的僚夷，名叫蚕茧夷，他们也这样称呼自己。
Translation:
Five hundred li by water southward from the Gaima Plateau, one comes to Yalujiang River。 A further five hundred li one arrives at Andong, the present Dandong city。The area is about two hundred square li, a land of the nomads。There exists a big market town, the Hechuan tribes live there。 A river, forty li long, from the source to the water mouth, is called Sha River。 On its banks live the Dongdukou tribes。 A group of Liao tribes live in the Qingmeiling Mountain, they call themselves Canjian(cocoon) tribe。

04-03-08 踇隅山
Muyushan
(124,88373E;38,14674N)

又南水行九百里，曰踇隅之山[1]。其上多草木[2]，多金玉 [3]，多赭 [4] 。有兽焉，其状如牛而马尾 [5]，名曰精精 [6]，其鸣自訆。

注释：[1]踇隅山：指瞌睡山。今称梦金浦，在朝鲜黄海南道。
[1]mu yu shan: refers to Keshui (sleepy) Mountain, known today as the Mengjinpu (dream gold port), it is in Huanghai Nandao (yellow sea south circle) in Korea。
[2] 草木：指游牧氏族。
[2] cao mu (grass wood), refers to the nomad's tribe。
[3] 金玉：指金夷，是肃慎族的称谓。
[3] jin yu (gold jade), refers to Jin people, a term for the Sushen tribes。
[4]赭：指渔民。
[4] zhe:(ochre color) refers to fishing people。
[5] 牛而马尾：僚族的苗夷。
[5] niu er ma yi: ox with horse tail: Miao tribes of the Liao people。
[6] 精精：指斤氏族。也称斤斤氏。
[6] jing jing(excellence) refers to the Jin tribe, also known as Jinjin Shi。

译文：由安东往西水行九百里，到达瞌睡山。这里住着游牧氏族，金夷和渔民。有一个氏族，是僚族的苗夷，名叫斤斤氏，他们也这样称呼自己。
Translation:
Nine hundred Li westward by the water from Andong, one arrives at Keshuishan (sleepy mountain) 。 The nomads as well as the Jin tribes and fisherman live there。One tribe belongs to the Miao of the Liao people, they call themselves Jinjin Shi, Jinjin is a surname。

04-03-09 无皋山
Wugaoshan
(127,93807E; 37,33979N)

又南水行五百里，流沙[1]三百里，至于无皋之山[2]，南望幼海[3]，东望榑木[4]，无草木[5]，多风[6]。是山也，广员百里。
凡东次三经之首，自尸胡山至于无皋之山，凡九山，六千九百里。其神状皆人身而羊角[7] 。其祠：用一牡羊 [8]，米用黍。是神也，见则风雨水为败 [9] 。

注释：[1]流沙：指绿江，今称汉江。
Notes: [1] liu sha (flowing sand) refers to the Lv (green)River, today known as Hanjiang, Han River。

[2] 无皋山：指原城，今称原州，在韩国江原道，位于朝鲜半岛的正中心。
[2] wu gao shan: refers to Yuan(original) city, known today as Yuanzhou, situated in Jiangyuan circus (Gangwon-do)/, South Korea, in the center of Korea Peninsula， 37° 30′ 0″ N, 128° 15′ 0″ E 。

[3] 幼海：指庆尚地区。庆、亲都读 you。
[3] you hai (young sea), refers to the Qingshang area (Gyeongsang) 36° 15′ 0″ N, 128° 45′ 0″ E。 In Pu concept, qing(celebrate) qin (kin folks) pronounced as you。

[4] 榑木：指富川检目地区，简称富川地区。
[4] tuan wood (a kind of wood) refers to the Fuchuan (rich river) citadel, known simply as Fuchuan district。

[5] 无草木：游牧部落地区。
[5] wu cao mu (no grass wood) refers to the land of the nomads。

[6]风：指王族。
[6] feng(wind) refers to the ruling clan。

[7] 人身而羊角：东部支系的定居氏族形象。羊角读 chi go 指东部。
[7] ren shen er yang jiao (human body with goat horns) 。
Tr: describe the image of the settled branches of the East tribes, yang jiao (goat horn) a Pu rebus, meaning chi go, refers to the Oriental, the east。

[8] 牡羊：读牡蚩，指玉坠。
[8]mu yang (male sheep) reads as mu chi, refers to jade pendants。

[9] 见则风雨水为败：那个地区的统治氏族的形象。败，指庙宇、偶像。
[9] jian ze feng yu wei bai (seen, the rain and wind cause disaster)
Tr: refers to the image of the ruling clan in that area， bai(defeat) a Pu rebus, refers to temples and idols。

译文：由瞌睡山往南水行五百里，再沿绿江水行三百里，到达原城。这里南望庆尚，东望富川，是游牧部落地区，住着王族氏族。这座山方圆百里。

综观东山第三列山系，北自孙吴山，南至原城，共九座山，延绵六千九百里。这些山的山神都是定居的东部氏族的形象。祭祀这些山神时，用一只玉坠传达祭词，米用黍米。这些神都是那个地区统治氏族的形象。

Translation:
Five hundred li by water southward from Keshuishan, going another three hundred li along the Lv(green)River, one comes to Yuan City。To the city's south, one can see Qingshang, to its east, one can see Fuchuan。This is the land of the nomads。The ruling clan lives here, the mountain covers an area of one hundred li。

In sum: Of the 3rd mountain system in the East, from its northmost Songwushan to its southmost point in Yuan city, there are total of 9 mountains, covering a distance of 6,900 li。 The mountain deities are in the images of the settled tribes from the East, when making offerings to those mountain deities, one jade pendant is offered as a communicator of the speech。Millet is offered in terms of grain。 Those deities are in the images of the local ruling clans。

东山经第四山系

Book 4, Dongshanjing； chapter 4

04-04-01 北号山
Beihaoshan
(129,70107E; 47,01566N)

又东次四经之首，曰北号之山[1]，临于北海。有木焉，其状如杨，赤华[2]，其实如枣而无核[3]，其味酸甘[4]，食之不疟[5]。食水[6] 出焉，而东北流注于海。有兽焉，其状如狼，赤首鼠目 [7]，其音如豚[8]，名曰猲狙[9]，是食人。有鸟焉，其状如鸡而白首[10]，鼠足而虎爪[11]，其名曰鬿雀[12]，亦食人。

注释：[1]北号山：指黑龙江佳木斯的浩良山，今称青黑山。
[1] bei hao shan (north yell mount) refers to the Haoliangshan in Jiamusi city 46°44'N，129 °37'E, Heilongjiang province。The mountain is known as Qingheishan，（green, black mount）。
[2]杨，赤华：南面的桦川氏族。
[2] yang, chi hua:(red willow; poplar; aspen) chi hua (red and beautiful); refers to the Huachuan tribe in the south。
[3] 枣而无核：佳木斯的乌赫氏族。
[3] zao er wu he: (date fruits without stone), refers to the Wuhe tribes in Jiamusi。
[4] 其味酸甘：且维芍嘎，青黑山的远古称谓，也是佳木斯集镇的古称谓。
[4] qi wei suan gan (it tastes sour and sweet) a rebus in Pu concept, reads as qie wei shao ga, an ancient name for Qingheishan (green, black mount), also the old name for Jiamusi township。
[5] 食之不疟：古老的补勒，即古老的游牧氏族。
[5] shi zhi bu nue (eaten no diarrhea) refers to the ancient Bule, an ancient nomad's tribe。
[6] 食水：指松花江。
[6] shi shui (eat water) refers to Songhua River。
[7]狼，赤首鼠目：游牧的犬戎俄罗斯族。
[7] lang(wolf), chi shou shu mu (red head rat eyes) refers to the Russian tribes of the nomads. Dog Rong people。
[8]豚：指汤源。
[8] run (small pig), refers to Tangyuan, 北纬 46°30′至 47°21′, 东经 129°30′至 130°59′。
[9] 猲狙：氏族名，指兴安部落氏族。可称兴纪氏。
[9] jie ju: tribe name: refers to the Xing'an tribes, also refers to tribes bearing surname Xingji。
[10] 鸡而白首：指鸡西的白人氏族。
[10] ji er bai shou (rooster with white head), refers to the white folks from Jixi。
[11] 鼠足而虎爪：俄罗斯族的游牧支系。
[11] shu zu er hu zhua (rat feet but tiger claws) refers to the nomads' tribes of the Russian stock。
[12] 鬿雀：氏族名，指东犬戎。
[12] jin que (jin sparrow) tribal name, refers to the Eastern Dog Rong, (Quanrong)。

译文：东山第四系列最北端的山，叫浩良山，紧邻北海地区。这里有一个管理氏族，是山南的桦川氏族，实际是佳木斯的乌赫氏族，住在且维芍嘎，是古老的游牧氏族。松花江水从这里流过，向东北流入大海。有一个氏族是游牧的犬戎俄罗斯支系，住在汤源，名叫猲狙氏，是古老的居民。有一群人，是鸡西的白人氏族，是俄罗斯族的游牧支系，名叫东犬戎，也是古老的居民。
Translation:
The northmost mountain of the 4th system is called Haoliangshan, boarding the North Sea area。 Here a management tribe, the Huachuan people live on the south side of the mountain, also known as the Wuhe tribe

from Jiamusi。They live in Qieweishaoga, an ancient name for today's Jiamusi city。 They are an ancient nomadic tribe。The Songhua River flows through here and going northeast into the sea。 A Russian branch of the Dog Rong, a nomad's tribe， live in Tangyuan, their name is Jieju Shi, they are very old residents here。 Another group of people is the white Russians from Jixi, they are the nomads branch of the Russian stock, also known as the Eastern Dog Rong, they are also old residents。

04-04-02 旄山
Maoshan
(129,01717E; 45,66162N)

又南三百里，曰旄山[1]，无草木[2]。苍体之水[3] 出焉，而西流注于展水 [4]，其中多鱃[5]，其状如鲤而大首[6]，食者不疣[7]。

注释：[1]旄山：指；亮朱山。属张广才岭北麓。亮朱，读韶旄。
Notes： [1] mao shan: refers to Liangzhu, it belongs to the northern section of the mountain Zhangguangcailing。 Liangzhu in Pu concept reads as Shaomao。
[2] 无草木：游牧部落地区。
[2] wu cao mu (no grass wood) refers to the land of the nomads。
[3] 苍体水：指张广水，包括亮朱河、石头河、黄泥河、驿马河等水系。
[3] cang ti shui (dark body water) refers to the Zhangguanshui River, which collect Liangzhu River, Shitouhe(stone)River, Huangnihe (yellow mud) River and Yimahe (handling horse) River。
[4] 展水：指延展水，又称蚂蜒河。蚂，即展。
[4] zhan shui (spread water) refers to Yanzhanshui River, also known as the Mayan River, ma in Pu concept is to spread。
[5] 鱃鱼：指亮夷。
[5] xiu yu, refers to Liang Yi people。
[6] 鲤而大首：石头河的游牧氏族。鲤，指石头。
[6]li er da shou: (carp with big head), tribes from Shitouhe River, Carp, Li a rebus with Pu concept of Li(stone)。
[7] 食者不疣：古老的北方氏族。疣，同幽，在此指北方。
[7] shi zhe bu you (eaten to stop skin wards)
Tr: ancient northern tribes, You, 幽, 疣 a Pu concept of Northern, a rebus with wards。

译文：由浩良山往南三百里，有座山叫亮朱山，是游牧部落地区。张广水从山间流出，向西流入蚂蜒河，那里住着亮夷，是石头河的游牧氏族，是古老的北方氏族。
Translation:
Three hundred li southward from Haoliangshan stands Liangzhushan, a land of nomads。 Zhangguanshui River flows out of the mountain, going westward into Mayan River。The Liang Yi people live there。An ancient northern tribe, they are the nomads from Shitouhe River。

04-04-03 东始山
Dongshishan
(126,94685E; 44,41285N)

又南三百二十里，曰东始之山[1]，上多苍玉[2]。有木焉，其状如杨而赤理[3]，其汁如血[4]，不实[5]，其名曰芑[6]，可以服马[7]。泚水[8] 出焉，而东北流注于海，其中多美贝 [9]，多茈鱼[10]，其状如鲋，一首而十身[11]，其臭如蘼芜[12]，食之不糟[13]。

注释：[1]东始山：在张广才岭南端的舒兰。东始是氏族名，以此而得山名。
Notes: [1] dong shi shan (east begin mount) which is situated in Shulan, on the south end of the Zhangguangcailing Mountain。 Dongshi, a tribal name, which gives the mountain the name。

[2] 苍玉：指候岭夷，今称猴岭夷。
[2] cang yu (dark jade) refers to the Houling Yi, known today as the Houling (monkey range) Yi。

[3] 杨而赤理：南面的腰红石、南红石氏族。
[3] yang er chi li (polar with red marking): refers to the Yaohongshi tribes and the Nanhongshi tribes to the south。

[4] 其汁如血：指路河支系。血，读奢，指河。
[4] qi zhi ru xue (its juice as blood) refers to the Luhe branches。Xue(blood) reads as She, referring to rivers。

[5] 不实：指氏族。
[5] bu shi (not solid) refers to tribes。

[6]芑：指腰氏，读缴。
[6] ji refers to the Yao Shi people， Yao reads as Jiao。

[7] 可以服马：柯尔克孜的扶余蒙。
[7]ke yi fu ma (can subdue horse) refers to the Kirgiz Fuyumeng people。

[8] 泚水：指徙僚，今称溪浪河。泚，移动之意。
[8]ci shui: refers to Xiliao, which is today's Xilanghe River。Ci, migrating, moving。

[9] 美贝：春十，指满春、永春氏族。
[9] mei bei (beautiful shell): reads as chunshi, (spring ten), refers to the Manchun, Yonchun tribes。

[10] 茈鱼：指移民。
[10]ci yu (moving fish) refers to the migrants。

[11]鲋，一首而十身：东始族的永春支系。鲋一首，指东始族。十身，永春支系。
[11] fu, yi shou er shi shen (fufish, one head ten body): refers to the Yongchun branch of the Dongshi Zu。 Fu yi shou: refers to Dongshi tribe, shishen, refers to the Yongchun branch。

[12] 其臭如蘼芜：是春部落的支系。
[12] qi xiu ru fei wu (its smell like fei wu); which is the branches of the Chun (spring) tribes。

[13] 不糟：手工业氏族。糟，指羆，是蚁族概念，即产业和手工业族群。
[13] bu fei: refers to the handicraft tribes。Fei reads as Pi, a Pu concept for Ants tribes, an epithet for industrial and handicrafts tribes。

译文：由亮朱山往南三百二十里，有座山叫东始山，西面住着候岭氏族。有一个管理氏族，是南面的腰红石、南红石等路河支系氏族，称为腰氏，是柯尔克孜的扶余蒙。溪浪水从这里流出，向东北流入大海。这里还住着永春氏移民，是东始的永春氏，属春部落支系，是古老的手工业氏族。

Translation:

Three hundred and twenty li further south from Liangzhushan stands Dongshishan。On its west live the Houling tribes。A management tribe, the Yaohongshi and the Nanhongshi live to the south, they are the Luhe branches known as the Yaoshi, they belong to the Kirgiz Fuyumeng。 Xilangshui River flows out of here and goes northeast into the Sea。Also living here are the Yongchun migrants, the Yongchun Shi of the Dongshi tribes。 They belong to the branches of the Chun tribes, a very ancient handicrafts tribe。

04-04-04 女烝山

Nuzhengshan

(126,0152E; 43,29887N)

又东南三百里，曰女烝之山[1]。其上无草木[2]， 石膏水 [3] 出焉，而西流注于鬲水[4]。其中多薄鱼[5]，其状如鳣鱼而一目[6]，其音如欧[7]，见则天下大旱[8]。

注释：[1]女烝山：指烟筒山。
Notes: [1] nv zheng shan: refers to the Yantongshan (chimney mount) 。
[2] 无草木：游牧部落地区。
[2] wu cao mu: no grass wood: the nomads' areas。
[3] 石膏水：指梨弯水，今称大梨河。
[3] shi gao shui: refers to the Liwanshui, known today as the Dalihe (big pear water) River。
[4] 鬲水：指清明水，今称饮马河。
[4]ge shui: refers to the Qingmingshui (clear bright water), known as Yinmahe （water horses） River。
[5] 薄鱼：指富夷，读音蚌夷。
[5]bo yu (thin fish); refers to the Fu Yi people, Fu Yi reads as Beng Yi。
[6] 鳣鱼而一目：指游牧支系的伊通部落夷。
[5] tan yu er yi mu (fish with one eye) refers to the Yitong Tribal Yi, of the nomadic branches。
[7]欧：卧的谐音，指南面。
[7] ou: a pun to wo, refers to the south。
[8] 大旱：达罕氏族。
[9] da han (big drought): refers to the Da Khan lineage tribes。

译文：由东始山往东南三百里，有座山叫烟筒山。山的西面是游牧部落地区。梨弯水从山间流出，向西南流入清明河。这里住着富夷，是游牧支系的伊通部落夷，是这个地区的达罕氏族。
Translation:
Three hundred li further southeast from Dongshishan stands Yantongshan。On its west is the nomadic areas。Liwanshui River flows out of the mountains and goes southwest into the Qingming River。 Around this area live the Yitong tribal Yi, of the nomadic branches, they are the Da Khan lineage。

04-04-05 钦山
Qinshan
(125,14265E; 42,88778N)

又南二百里，曰钦山[1]，多金玉无石[2]。师水[3] 出焉，而北流注于皋泽 [4] 。其中多鱃鱼[5]， 多文贝[6]。有兽焉，其状如豚而有牙[7]，其名曰当康[8]，其名自訆，见则天下大穰[9]。

注释：[1]钦山：指欠山。指蒸腾的山，又称烧锅山，今辽源城。
Notes： [1] qin shan: refers to Qianshan, known as steamy mountain, the Shaoguoshan (burn wok hill) , the Liaoyuan city，42° 53′ 16.8″ N, 125° 8′ 38.4″ E。
[2] 金玉无石：指金夷部落氏族。
[2] jin yu wu shi (gold and jade, no stone), refers to the Jin Yi tribal clans。
[3] 师水：指奢咪水，即梨树河。
[3] shi shui (teacher water) refers to Shemishui River, known today as Lishuhe (Pear tree) River。
[4] 皋泽：读共水，指鹿河，今称东辽河。
[4] gao ze: reads as Gong shui, refers to Lu (Deer)River, known today as East Liao River, or Dongliao River。
[5] 鱃鱼：指梨树河氏族。
[5] xiu yu(sturgeon) refers to the Lishuhe (pear tree river) tribes。
[6] 文贝：指渭津河氏族。

[6] wen bei (patterned shell) refers to the Weijinhe tribe。

[7] 豚而有牙：白泉的英俊氏族。白泉，读吐汶。有牙，也读雅优，指漂亮、英俊。

[7] tun er you ya (pig with teeth) refer to the Yinjun tribe from Baiquan (white spring), baiquan, reads in Pu concept as tuwen, youya (having teeth) a rebus with Pu concept as Yayou, meaning handsome, good looking。

[8] 当康：读德酷，指德旺氏。

[8] dang kang: reads in Pu concept as de ku, refers to the Dewang Shi。

[9] 大穰：读达儒，指管理氏族。

[9] da rang: a rebus reads as da ru, meaning controller, manager tribes。

译文：由烟囱山往南二百里，有座山叫烧锅山，住着金夷部落氏族。梨树河水从山间流出，向北流入东辽河。这里住着梨树河夷和渭津河夷。有一个氏族，是白泉的英俊氏族，名叫德旺氏，他们也这样称呼自己，是那个地区的管理氏族。

Translation

Two hundred li southward from Yanconshan stands Shaoguoshan。 The Jin Yi tribe lives there。 Lishushui River flows out of this mountain, going north into Dongliao River。The Lishuhe tribes and the Weijinhe tribes live there。The Yinjun tribe from Baiquan call themselves Dewang tribe, they also thus self-address themselves they are the managerial tribes of that area。

04-04-06 子桐山

Zitongshan

(123,43258E; 41,80501N)

又东南二百里，曰子桐之山[1]。子桐之水[2] 出焉，而西流注于余如之泽[3]。其中多鮹鱼[4]，其状如鱼而鸟翼[5]，出入有光[6]。其音如鸳鸯[7]，见则天下大旱[8]。

注释：[1]子桐山：指甸子山，是沈阳北面的山，实际介绍的是沈阳。

Notes: [1] zi tong shan refers to Dianzishan, on the northside of Shenyang, this segment is a description of Shenyang city。

[2] 子桐水：指甸子水，今称浑河。

[2] zi tong shui: refers to Dianzi River, known today as Hunhe River。

[3] 余如泽：指大龙河，今称辽河。

[3]yu ru ze: refers to Dalong (big dragon) River, today known as Liao River。

[4] 鮹鱼：指大洼渔民。

[4] hua yu (wo fish), refers to the fishing tribes from Dawa, big pond。

[5] 鱼而鸟翼：从事渔业的河滨夷。

[5]yu er niao yi (fish with bird wings) the riverbank tribes who are fishermen。

[6] 出入有光：往来于双河口之间。

[6] chu ru you guan (in and out with lights)

Tr: comes and goes between the two river mouths。

[7] 鸳鸯：指台安。

[7] yuan yan (a pair of water bird) refers to Tai'an county。

[8] 大旱：达罕氏族。

[8] da han (big draught), da khan, ruling tribes。

译文：由烧锅山往东南二百里，有座山叫甸子山。浑河水从山间流出，向西流入辽河。河口处住着大洼渔民，是从事渔业的河滨氏族，往来于双河口，住在台安，是那个地区的达罕氏族。

Translation:

Two hundred li southeast from Shaoguoshan stands the Dianzishan。 Hunhe River flows out of the mountains, going west into Liao River。 At the river mouth, live the Dawa fishing tribes, they are the fishermen from the Hebin tribes, who come and go between the two river mouths。 They live in Tai'an, are the ruling clans in that area。

04-04-07 剡山
Yanshan
(125,53258E; 42,67651N)

又东北二百里，曰剡山[1]，多金玉[2]。有兽焉，其状如彘而人面[3]，黄身而赤尾[4]，其名曰合窳[5]，其音如婴儿[6]。是兽也，食人[7]，亦食虫蛇[8]，见则天下大水[9]。

注释：[1]剡山：指丰山，今吉林省东丰县城。
[1] yan shan: refers to Fengshan, known as Dongfeng county seat city in Jilin province。
[2] 金玉：指集镇夷。
[2] jin yu (gold jade); refers to township people。
[3] 彘而人面：通古斯居民。
[3] zhi er ren mian (wild pig with human face) refers to the Tongus people。
[4] 黄身而赤尾：山区氏族的游牧夷。黄，读洪鲁，指山。
[4] huang shen er chi yi (yellow body with red tail) the nomads from the mountainous tribes, Huang(yellow) reads in Pu Concept as Hong Lu, a term for mountain。
[5] 合窳：指靺鞨夷。
[5] he yu, refers to Mohe tribes。
[6] 婴儿：指北面。
[6] in er(infant) refers to the north。
[7] 食人：古老的居民。
[7] shi ren (eat human), refers to residents with a long history。
[8] 食虫蛇：古老的游牧集肆夷。
[8] shi chong she (eat bug snake) refers to the ancient nomads of the Jizhen(township) people。
[9] 大水：达罕氏族。大，指达罕；水，指氏族。
[9] da shui (big water) refers to ruling big khan tribes, da: da khan, shui/water: tribes。

译文：由甸子山往东北二百里，有座山叫丰山，住着集镇夷。有一个氏族，是通古斯的居民，是山区的游牧夷，名叫靺鞨夷，住在北面。这个氏族，是古老的居民，也是古老的游牧集肆夷，是那个地区的达罕氏族。
Translation:
Two hundred li northeastward from Dianzishan stands Fengshan。The Jizhen Yi people live there。 One Tongus tribe, known as Mohe people, the mountainous nomads also live on the north side of the mountain。They had a long history, are the ancient nomadic Jisi Yi, the ruling Da Khan tribe in that area。

04-04-08 太山
Taishan
(126,74832E; 42,97175N)

又东二百里，曰太山[1]，上多金玉[2]，桢木[3]。有兽焉，其状如牛而白首，一目而蛇尾[4]，其名曰蜚[5]，行水则竭[6]，行草则死[7]，见则天下大疫[8]。钩水[9] 出焉，而北流注于劳水[10]，其中多鱃鱼[11]。
凡东次四经之首，自北号之山至于太山，凡八山，一千七百二十里。

右东经之山志，凡四十六山，万八千八百六十里。

注释：[1]太山：指富太山，在吉林省桦甸市北面。实际往东北向介绍桦甸。
[1] tai shan: refers to Futaishan, on the north side to Huadian city in Jilin province。The direction is in fact northeast, a description of Huadian county。

[2] 金玉：指集镇夷。
[2] jin yu (gold jade) refers to Jizhen people, (township)。

[3] 桢木：指杨姓氏族。
[3] zhen mu refers to the tribe bearing surname Yang。

④牛而白首，一目而蛇尾：河边的摆渡氏族，河畔的塞夷。一目，读溢陌。
[4] niu er bai shou (ox with white head), yi mu er she yi (one eye and with snake tail。
Tr: the Baidu （ferry）tribe on the riverbank, the Saka on the riverbank, yi mu: a Pu concept of yimo(一目), refers to yi/river, mo/bank, a rebus。

[5]蜚：指费氏。汉译为盘氏、漂氏、罗圈氏三大姓。今都有遗存名。
[5] fei; refers to the Fei tribe, in Chinese there are three major surnames: the Pan, the Piao, and the Luoquan, all those surnames remain in the local placenames。

[6] 行水则竭(xie)：指赫哲羲国。
[6] xing shui ze xie, (running water will exhaust) refers to the Hezhe xi nation。

[7] 行草则死：指赫哲氏族。
[7] xing cao ze si;(moving grass die) refers to the Hezhe tribes。

[8] 大疫：指达罕夷。
[8] da yi (big pandemic) refers to the da Khan tribe。

[9] 钩水：指富太沟水，又称富江。
[9] gou shui, (hook water); refers to Futaigoushui River, also known as Fujiang River。

[10] 劳水：指松江。
[10] lao shui (labor water), refers to Song Jiang, the Songjiang River。

[11] 鱃夷：指河渡运输夷。
[11] xiu yi: refers to the tribes who carry river transportation。

译文：从丰山向东行二百里是富太山，山的西边住着集镇夷， 和杨氏族， 有一个氏族，是河边的摆渡氏族，是河畔的集肆夷，名叫费氏，是赫哲羲国的赫哲氏族，是那个地区的达罕夷。富沟水从山间流出，向东流入松江，这里住着河渡运输夷。

综观东山经第四列山系，从浩良山到富太山，共八座山，延绵一千七百二十里。

以上所述东部山系，共计四十六座山，延绵一万八千八百六十里。

Translation:
Two hundred li east from Fengshan stands the Futaishan。On its west side live the Jizhen Yi and tribes bearing surname of Yang。One tribe provide ferry service, they are the Jizhen tribe along the riverbank。They bear the surname of Fei, the Hezhe tribes from the Hezhe xi nation。 They are the ruling tribes, the Da Khan clan。Fugoushui River flows out from the mountain, going east to Song River。 The ferry service tribes live here。

In sum， of the 4th system of mountains in the east, from Haoliangshan to Futaishan, there are total 8 mountains, covering 1,720 li。Adding together, the mountains in the east totals 46, running 18,860 li。

第五卷中山经 (Mountains in the Middle)

中山经第一山系

Book 5 Zhongshanjing; chapter 1

05-01-01 薄山 甘枣山
Boshan   Ganzaoshan
(110,3179E; 34,64051N)

中山经薄山[1] 之首，曰甘枣之山[2]，共水[3]出焉，而西流注于河[4]。其上多杻木[5] 。其下有草 [6]焉，葵本而杏叶 [7] ，黄华而荚实 [8] ，名曰箨 [9] ，可以已懵 [10] 。有兽焉，其状如㹥鼠而文题 [11] ，其名曰難[12]，食之已瘿[13]。

注释：[1]薄山：指条山山脉，在山西蒲州东侧。今称中条山。濮语"条"读薄。
Notes: [1]bo shan (thin mount) refers to the Tiaoshan Mountains, in the east part of Pu Zhou, Shanxi province, known today as the Zhongtiaoshan。In Pu concept tiao is read as bo。

[2] 甘枣山：甘枣读嘎照，指阳山，今风铃渡镇西侯度村。
[2] gan zao shan (sweet dates mount) ganzao read as gazhao, meaning a passage through the mountains, referring Fenglingdu, (wind bell crossing) township。

[3] 共水：指勾水，即候渡水，今称后渡水。濮语读渡为勾。
[3] gong shui (common water) refers to the Goushui, also as Houdushui (duke crossing)， today it is known as the Houdushui (later crossing) River。In Pu concept, du(cross)reads as gou(hook)。

[4]河：指黄河。
[4] he (river) refers to the Yellow River。

[5] 杻木：指言官氏族，今谐音传承为六官寨氏族。
[5] chou mu (a kind of wood to make instruments of torture in ancient times)
Tr: refers to the Yanguan (speech official) tribe, a phonetic rendering to Liuguanzhai tribe。 yanguan/liuguan: yan is shifted to liu phonetically, Liu: six。

[6]草：指游牧民。
[6] cao (grass) a Pu concept for the nomads, a coded term。

[7] 葵本而杏叶：指有夏的恒夷。恒夷，即王族。
[7] kui ben er xing ye (sunflower origin but apricot leaves)
Tr: The Heng Yi of the Youxia nation, Youxia reads as buku, [hengyi] means king tribe。

[8] 黄华而荚实：黄坡寨的姜氏，今称黄洛的姜氏。洛，即寨。
[8] huang hua er jia shi (yellow flower and bean fruits)
Tr: refers to the tribe who bears the surname of Jiang, the Jiang family from the Huangpozhai (yellow slope village), known today as the Jiang family from the Huang Luo。 Luo: village, stronghold or enclosure.

[9]萚：指妥鲁则柯氏，即中央氏。
[9] ze: refers to the Tuoluzeke Shi, also known as the Zhongyang Shi--Center Shi lineage。

[10] 可以已懵：夏国的核心氏族。懵，读梅，指核心。
[10]ke yi yi meng (can cure confusion)
Tr: refers to the core lineages of the Xia Nation。 Meng: reads as Mei, refers to the core, the center。

[11] 椟鼠而文题：洞地的苗族。洞地：指苗族家支的中心。也称度地，有西侯度遗址。
[11] du shu er wen ti (wood panel rat with glyph markings)
Tr: The Dongdi Hmong Miao people。 Dongdi：center of the Miao tribal lineages。 Also known as Dudi, the concept is retained in the name Xihoudu site。

[12]難：指侯氏。
[12] nuó (rat looking animal) refers to the Hou lineage。

[13] 食之已瘿：古老的小侯氏族。瘿，读伊，指小。
[13] shi zhi yi ying(eat it cure swollenness)
Tr: ying: reads as Yi, meaning junior, or smaller, younger, or young。

译文：中山第一列山系是薄山山脉，头一个地方叫阳山。侯渡水从山间流出，向西流入黄河。山的西面住着六官村氏族。东面住着游牧民，是有夏的恒夷，是黄洛的姜氏族，名叫中央氏，是夏国的核心氏族。有一个氏族，是洞地的苗族，名叫侯氏，是古老的小侯夷。

Translation：

The first mountain system in the central area is the Boshan Mountains， heading the 1st mountain system is Shanyakou Mountain。Houdu River flows out of the mountains and flows west into the Yellow River。 On the west side of the mountain, live the Liuguan Village tribes。 On the east side of the mountain live the nomads, the Heng Yi of the Youxia nation。 They are the central lineage of the Xia nation, known as the Zhongyang tribe, the Jiang tribe from Huangluo。 Another tribe is the Hmong Miao people from Dongdi, they are known as the Hou Shi, the ancient Xiaohou Yi。

05-01-02 历儿山
Li'ershan
(110,4307E; 34,6667N)

又东二十里，曰历儿之山[1]。其上多橿[2]，多櫔木 [3]，是木也，方茎而员叶[4]，黄华而毛[5]，其实如楝[6]，服之不忘[7]。

注释：[1]历儿山：今仍称历儿山，在芮城县阳城镇北面。实际介绍阳城镇。
Notes:[1]li er shan: still known today as the Li'er Mountain, situated in the north part of the Yangcheng township, Ruicheng county, Shanxi province, in fact this is a description of the Yangcheng township。
[2]橿：指焦氏族。
[2] jiang: refers to the Jiao tribe, jiang/jiao: close phonetic match。
[3] 櫔木：指任官氏，又称任土目氏族。今称任氏。
[3]li mu refers to the Renguan Shi, also known as the Rentumu tribe, today's people bear the surname of Ren。
[4] 方茎而员叶：统治部落的大氏族。
[4] fang jing er yuan ye (square stems and member leaves)
Tr: refers to the major ruling branch of a large tribe。
[5] 黄华而毛：东历儿山的管理氏族。
[5] huang hua er mao (yellow flower with hair) the management tribe of the East Li'er Mountain。
[6] 其实如楝：实际称为任氏。
[6] qi shi ru jian:(its fruits as jian) they are literally addressed as Ren Shi。
[7] 服之不忘：山区的补华，即山区的华胥氏。
[7] fu zhi bu wang (taken will not forget)
Tr: mountain people, the Bu Hua, refers to the Huaxu Shi from the mountains。

译文：由阳山往东二十里，有座山叫历儿山。山的西面住着焦氏，住着任土目氏族。这个土目氏族，是统治部落的大氏族，是东历儿山的管理氏族，实际称为任氏，是山区的华胥氏族。
Translation：
Twenty li eastwards from Yangshan stands the Li'ershan。 On its west side live the Jiao Shi, and the Rentumu tribe。 This Tumu tribe is the major branch of the ruling tribe, they are the management tribe of the East Li'ershan, addressed as Ren Shi, the Huaxu tribe from the mountains。

05-01-03 渠猪山
Quzhushan
(110,4854E；34,67935N)

又东十五里，曰渠猪之山[1]，其上多竹[2]，渠猪之水出焉，而南流注于河[3]。其中多豪鱼[4]，状如鲔[5]，赤喙尾赤羽 [6]，可以已白癣 [7]。

注释：[1]渠猪山：指角村山。山在阳城镇杜庄北面，这里实际介绍的是杜庄。
Notes： [1] qu zhu shan (ditch pig mount):
Tr: refers to Jiaocunshan (horn village mountain), situated to the north of the Duzhang Village in Yangcheng township. This is a description of Du Village， (Zhuang, Chinese word for village) 。
[2]竹：指角村氏族。竹同猪音，指村。
[2] zhu(bamboo):
Tr: refers to the Jiaocun tribe. Zhu(bamboo)phonetic match to zhu(pig), meaning village。

[3]河：指黄河。
[3] he（river）: refers to the Yellow River。
[4] 豪鱼：指郝夷，属游牧部落的姓氏。
[4] hao yu (big fish) refers to the Hao Yi, a surname of the Nomadic tribes。
[5]鲔：指南，杜庄的古称谓。鲔即渭，东南西北的"汾渭洛武"，对应春夏秋冬的"梅杜苏洗"。
[5] you (you fish)
Tr: you: meaning south, the ancient name for the Du village。 You mean wei，as in Wei River。 In a cardinal system, the four cardinal points east, south, west, north are represented by the fen, wei, luo, wu, the first three being the tributaries of the Yellow River, according to their relative position to the Yellow River, which correspond to the spring, summer, autumn, winter in the four words: Mai, du, su, xi。
[6] 赤喙尾赤羽：游胡夷的游牧支系。
[6] chi hui yi chi yu (red beak tail red feather)
Tr: The Herders branches of the Nomadic Hu tribes。
[7] 可以已白癣：夏国的鲜卑夷。
[7]ke yi yi bai xian (can cure skin white patches)
Tr: refers to the Xianbei people of the Xia nation。

译文：由历儿山往东十五里，有座山叫角村山。山的西面住着角村氏族，角村水从山间流出，向南流入黄河。这里住着郝夷，是南角村游牧胡的游牧支系，是夏国的鲜卑夷。
Translation:
Fifteen li further east from the Li'ershan, stands the Jiaocunshan。 On its west side live the Jiaocun tribe。 The Jiaocunshui River flows out of the mountain and goes south into the Yellow River。The Hao tribe live here, they are the nomadic tribes of the Nanjiaocun nomadic Hu people, the Xianbei people from the Xia nation。

05-01-04 葱聋山
Cunlongshan
(110,66401E; 34,80777N)

又东三十五里，曰葱聋之山[1]，其中多大谷[2]，是多白垩[3]，黑、青、黄垩[4]。

注释：[1]葱聋山：指草坡山。在山西芮城北面的中条山上。
Notes: [1] cong long shan (onion deaf hill) refers to the Caopo (grass slope) Mountain。
[2] 大谷：指塔儿园氏族。
[2] da gu (big grain, or big valley) refers to the Ta'er yuan tribe，(Pagoda Garden)。
[3] 白垩：指大柏峪氏族。
[3] bai e(white clay) refers to the Daboyu tribe, (big poplar valley)
[4]黑、青、黄垩：黑垩，指风伯峪氏族；青垩，指东面的石鹿峪氏族；黄垩，指王官峪氏族。黑读哼音，指风。
[4] hei e" (black clay): the Fengboyu tribe,（wind uncle valley)
Qing e: (green clay): the Shiluyu (stone deer valley) tribe to the east,
Huang e: (yellow clay): the Wangguanyu tribe,
Hei, black, means winds, reads as heng。

译文：由角村山往东三十五里，有座山叫草坡山，住着塔儿园氏族，还住着大柏峪氏族、风伯峪氏族、石鹿峪氏族和王官峪氏族。
Translation:

Thirty-five li further east from the Jiaocunshan stands the Caoposhan。 The Ta'eryuan tribes live here, also living here are the Daboiyu tribe, the Fengboyu tribe, the Shiluyu tribe and the Wangguanyu tribe。

05-01-05 涹山
Woshan
(110,81829E; 34,84666N)

又东十五里，曰涹山[1]，其上多赤铜[2]，其阴多铁[3]。

注释：[1]涹山：指后岭。
Notes： [1] wo shan (soak to soften mount)
Tr: refers to Huolingshan （back ridge mountain）。
[2] 赤铜：指前凹氏族。
[2] chi tong (red copper)； refers to the Qian 'ao (front deep) tribe。
[3]铁：指解州氏族。解，汉语必须读 xie 音，才能对应濮语的 tie 音。
[3] tie(iron) refers to the Xiezhou tribe, the phonetic Chinese is Xie, Pu phonetic value [tie]。

译文：由草坡山往东十五里，称为后岭，山的西面住着前凹氏族，北面住着解州氏族。
Translation:
Fifteen li further east from Caoposhan stands Houlingshan。 On its west side live the Qian'ao tribe, on its north side lives the Xiezhou tribe。

05-01-06 脱扈山
Tuohushan
(111,32413E; 35,14088N)

又东七十里，曰脱扈之山[1]。有草焉，其状如葵叶而赤华[2]，荚实[3]，实如棕荚[4]，名曰植楮[5]，可以已癙[6]，食之不眯[6]。

注释：[1]脱扈山：指中留山。在山西运城市夏县东侧。
Notes： [1] tuo hu shan: refers to the Zhongliushan, to the east side of the Xia County in Yuncheng city, Shanxi province。
[2] 葵叶而赤华：指康家坪山。
[2] kui ye er chi hua (sunflowers leaves and red flowers)
Tr： refers to the Kangjiaping Mountain。
[3] 荚实：指景氏族。
[3] jia shi: refers to the Jing tribe。
[4] 棕荚：指景岭。
[4] zong jia: refers to the Jingling Mountain。
[5] 植楮：指景睢氏。濮语读睢为崔，谐音楮。
[5] zhi zhu: refers to the Jingcui tribe. zhui/cui/zu phonetic match。
[6] 可以已癙：夏国的共工夷。
[6]ke yi yi shu (can cure rat disease)
Tr: refers to the Gonggong people of the Xia nation。
[7] 食之不眯：古老的天人氏族。眯，指天，补眯指天人氏族。
[7] shi zhi bu mi (eat will not squant)

Tr: refers to the ancient Tianren (sky people) tribe, Mi, refers to sky, bu-mi refers to the Sky people who are on the higher land to the west。

译文：由后岭往东七十里，有座山叫中留山。有一个移民氏族，是康家坪山的景氏族，实际住在景岭，名叫景睢氏，是夏国的共工夷，是古老的天人氏族。
Translation:
Seventy li eastwards from the Woshan stands the Zhongliushan。A migrant tribe, the Jing tribe from the Kangjiaping Mountain lives in Jingling Mountain。They are known as the Jingcui people。They are the Gonggong people of the Xia nation, the ancient Tianren tribe。

05-01-07 金星山
Jinxingshan
(111,40962E; 35,12418N)

又东二十里，曰金星之山[1]，多天婴[2]，其状如龙骨[3]，可以已痤[4]。

注释：[1]金星山：指半岭。金，指岭；星，指半。
Notes:[1] jin xing shan (gold star mountain)
Tr: refers to Banling (half ridge) jin: ling/ridge, xing/star/half。
[2] 天婴：指七峪和七草沟氏族。七，读照，又称天照，所以七峪被译为天婴。
[2] tian yin (heavenly infant) refers to the Qiyu tribes and the Qicaogou tribes。 qi(seven) reads zhao, also tianzhao, therefore the Qiyu is transliterated into Tianyin, (heavenly infant) 。
[3] 龙骨：指埝沟氏族。
[3] long gu (dragon bone)
Tr: refers to the Niangou tribe, nian (low banks between the field to retain water) 。
[4] 可以已痤：夏国的照夷。痤，读 zhuo，与照谐音。
[4]ke yi yi zuo (can cure skin illness) a coded term for the Zhao people of the Xia nation。 zhao/zhuo close phonetic match of cuo/zhuo/zhao。

译文：由中留山往东二十里，有座山叫半岭，住着七峪和七草沟氏族，属埝沟支系，是夏国的照夷。
Translation:
Twenty li further east from the Zhongliushan stands the Banling Mountain。 The Qiyu tribes and the Qicaogou tribes live there, they belong to the Niangou branch of the Zhao Yi from the Xia nation。

05-01-08 泰威山
Taiweishan
（111,7433E；35,12418N）

又东七十里，曰泰威之山[1]。其中有谷，曰枭谷[2]，其中多铁[3]。

注释：[1]泰威山：指雷公南岭，今称南岭。
Notes：[1] tai wei shan (big overpower mount) refers to the Leigong (thunder god); nanling (south ridge), known today as the Nanling (south range).
[2] 枭谷：指解国，今称解峪乡。解，读谢，濮语读铁。枭、谢谐音。
[2] xiao gu (owls valley) refers to the xie country, known today as the Xieyu Village， xie; tie, xiao, phonetic match。
[3]铁：指解氏族。
[3] tie(iron) refers to the Xie tribe, xie/tie, Pu concept。

译文：由半岭往东七十里，有座山叫雷公南岭。这里有一个国家，叫解国，住着解姓氏族。
Translation:
Seventy li further east from the Banlingshan stands the Leigongnanling Mountain。 The Xie country, a nation known as Xieguo is situated here。 There live the tribes bearing the surname of Xie。

05-01-09 橿谷山
Jianggushan
(111,88467E; 35,1185N)

又东十五里，曰橿谷之山[1]，其中多赤铜[2]。

注释：[1]橿谷山：指西沟山。在后清河与沇河交汇处的古城镇。
Notes： [1] jiang gu shan (hard wood mount) refers to the Xigoushan （west gully mountain）， where the ancient township stands on the confluence of Houqing River and the Run River。
[2] 赤铜：指坪沿庄氏族。
[2] chi tong (red copper) refers to the Pingyanzhuang tribe， zhuang/village/enclosure。

译文：由雷公南岭往东十五里，有座山叫西沟山，这里住着坪沿庄氏族。
Translation:
Fifteen li further east from the Leigongnanling Mountain, stands the Xigoushan, where the Pingyanzhuan tribes live。

05-01-10 吴林山
Wulinshan
（112,28132E；35,17696N）

又东百二十里，曰吴林之山[1]，其中多葌草[2]。

注释：[1]吴林山：指王屋山。王屋山原称王府山，濮语读府为鬲，谐音林。
Notes:[1] wu lin shan (wu woods mount)
Tr: refers to Wangwushan (wang house mountain), previously known as the Wangfu Mountain。 In Pu concept, fu is read as li, a close phonetic match to lin.li/lin。
[2] 葌草：本指兰姓移民，此处指济源移民，济源切音为葌。
[2] jian cao: refers to the immigrants bearing the surname of Lan, here refers to the Jiyuan migrants。 Jiyuan is phonetically contracted into jian。

译文：由西沟山往东一百二十里，有座山叫王屋山，住着济源移民。
Translation:
One hundred and twenty li further east from the Xigoushan stands the Wangwu Mountain, where the migrants from Jiyuan live。

05-01-11 牛首山
Niushoushan
(112,68595E; 35,19022N)

又北三十里，曰牛首之山[1]。有草焉，名曰鬼草[2]，其叶如葵而赤茎[3]，其秀如禾[4]，服之不忧[5]。劳水[6] 出焉，而西流注于潏水 [7] ，是多飞鱼 [8] ，其状如鲋鱼 [9] ，食之已痔衕 [10] 。

注释：[1]牛首山：指沁河山，因濮语"沁河"的读音像"牛首"，就成了牛首山。
Notes: [1] niu shou shan （ox head mount)
Tr: refers to the Qinheshan。 In Pu concept, Qinghe is a close phonetic match to Niushou, therefore the name of the Mountain in Chinese。

[2] 鬼草：指硬殿氏族，今称硬庄氏族。
[2] gui cao (ghost grass)
Tr: refers to the Yingdian (Solid Hall) tribes, known today as the Yingzhuang (solid village) tribes。

[3] 葵而赤茎：北面的游牧部落氏族。
[3] kui er chi jing (sunflower with red stems)
Tr: the nomadic tribes from the North。

[4] 其秀如禾：实际是牧羊氏族。
[4] qi xiu ru he （its shoots like plants)
Tr: refers to the sheep and goat keeping tribes。

[5] 服之不忧：山区的北部氏族。
[5] fu zhi bu you (taken to calm anxiety)
Tr: the northern tribes from the mountains。

[6] 劳水：指愁沟水。
[6] lao shui (labor water) refers to Chougoushui (sorrow gully) River。

[7] 潏水：指沙石沟水。
[7] jue shui: refers to Shashigou River, Shashigou (sandstone gully) 。

[8] 是多飞鱼：这里住着河东夷。
[8] shi duo fei yu (here many flying fish)
Tr: here lives the Hedong (river east) Yi。

[9] 鲋鱼：指东逯夷。飞、鲋都指东。
[9] fu yu (crucia carps)
Tr: refers to the Donglu YI, fei(fly) fu (crucia carps) Pu concept for east。

[10] 已痔衕：指开阔地、平原地区的氏族，一般都称梓桐或桐梓，这里称紫陵夷。
[10] yi zhi tong refers to the tribes on open land and plains, normally addressed as Zitong or Tongzi, here refers to the Ziling Yi， Ziling (purple mausoleum) Yi。

译文：由王屋山往东北三十里，有座山叫沁河山。有一个游牧氏族，名叫硬庄氏族，属北部游牧部落的支系，实际是牧羊氏族，是山区的北部氏族。愁沟水从山间流出，向东南流入沙沟河，这里住着河东夷，实际是东逯夷，是古老的平原氏族。

Translation:
Thirty li further northeast from Wangwushan stands the Qinheshan。 There is a nomadic tribe named Yingzhuang tribe。 They belong to the northern nomadic branches, a herder's people from the mountains。 Chougoushui River rises from the mountains and goes southeast into the Shagoushui River, where live the Hedong Yi, or the Donglu Yi, known also as the ancient Pingyuan(plain) tribes。

05-01-12 霍山
Huoshan
（113,05693E；35,20996N）

又北四十里，曰霍山[1]，其木多榖[2]。有兽焉，其状如狸，而白尾有鬣[3]，名曰朏朏[4]，养之可以已忧[5]。

注释：[1]霍山：指月山，月读 hu，与霍谐音，这里介绍月山下的聚落，实际往东北方向。
Notes： [1] huo shan: moon mountain, Huo/hu, meaning moon, this is about the settlement at the foot of the Yueshan (Moon mount), in the direction of northeast。
[2]榖：指谷坨和部疙塔氏族。部疙塔，原称部仡。
[2]gu(cereal) refers to the Gutuo tribe and the Gaogada tribe, which was known originally as the Gaoga。 Gaogata, will be read as Gaogada in some areas。 As in Pu language D/T are interchangeable。
[3] 狸而白尾有鬣：山区的丹河牧族。狸，读嶷(lei), 指山区。白尾，读博拉溢，指红河，今称丹河。
[3]li er bai yi you zong: (leopard with white tail and mane)
Tr: refers to the herders from the Dan River。 Li/yi/lei, refers to the mountainous area。 White tail reads as Bolayi, referring to the Red River, known today as the Dan River， Bola/red/dan。
[4] 朏朏(kuku): 指部仡氏，与夏姓同宗。
[4] kuku (moon starts to shine) refers to Gaoga Shi, they bear the same surname as the Xia people。
[5] 养之可以已忧：相同于夏国的北部夷。养，读伊，指同。
[5] yang zhi ke yi yi you (raise it can cure worries) the same as the Northern Yi of the Xia nation, Yang(raise) reads as yi, means the same as。

译文：由沁河山往东北四十里，有座山叫月山，这个管理区住着谷坨和部仡氏族。有一个氏族，是山区的丹河牧族，名叫部仡氏，相同于夏国的北部夷。
Translation:
Forty li further northeast from the Qinheshan stands the Yueshan。 In this management area, live the Gutuo tribe and the Gaoga tribe。One tribe is the herdsman tribe from the Danhe River from the mountains, they are called Kuga tribes, from the same lineage of the northern Yi of the Xia nation。

05-01-13 合谷山
Hegushan
(113,23103E； 35,24246N)

又北五十二里，曰合谷之山[1]，是多薝棘[2]。

注释：[1]合谷山：指焦国山，今焦作市城区。
Notes: [1] he gu shan (close valley mount) 。
Tr: refers to the Jiaoguoshan, in today's Jiaozuo city 's urban areas, Henan province。
[2] 薝棘：指掌部落，即疙角掌部落。薝，指掌；棘，指纪，即部落。
[2] zhan ji(wood), refers to the Zhang tribe, also known as the Gajiaozhang tribe。 Zhan/zhang, jin/ji means tribes。

译文：由月山往东北五十二里，有座山叫焦国山，这里住着疙角掌部落氏族。
Translation:
Fifty-two li further northeast from the Yueshan stands Jiaoguoshan。The Gajiaozhang tribes live there。

05-01-14 阴山
Yinshan
（113,52278E； 35,45059N）

又北三十五里，曰阴山[1]，多砺石、文石[2]。少水[3] 出焉，其中多雕棠 [4]，其叶如榆叶而方 [5]，其实如赤菽[6]，食之已聋[7]。

注释：[1]阴山：指坤山，也称昆山、莽岭。今称王莽岭。实际是往东北方向。
Notes:[1] yin shan (shade mount)
Tr: refers to the Kunshan, also known as Kun Mountain, Mangling。It is known today as the Wangmangling Mountain, in fact going northeast。
[2] 砺石、文石：牛氏、水氏。
[2]li shi, wen shi (whet stone, marked stone)
Tr: Niu Shi, and Shui Shi, two tribes。
[3] 少水：指奢水，即黄水。
[3] shao shui (young water) refers to She shui, meaning yellow water。
[4] 雕棠：指胖(mang)泥，后演变为莽岭。这里指莽岭氏族。
[4] diao tang (carved wood) refers to Mangni, later, the name shifted to Mangling Mountain, here refers to the tribes bearing the name。
[5] 榆叶而方：榆树沟夷的统治氏族。
[5]yu ye er fang (yu leaf square) refers to the ruling tribe of the people in Yushugou 。
[6] 赤菽：指簸箕不铁。赤菽，指簸箕；不，指湾；铁，指解氏族。
[6] chi shu (red grain) refers to Boqibutie: chishu(boqi), bu(wang/bay) tie (xie tribe) 。
[7] 已聋：山区夷。
[7] yi long (cure deafness) refers to the mountain Yi。

译文：由焦国山往东北三十五里，有座山叫坤山，住着牛氏族和水氏族。黄水从山间流出，河畔住着莽岭氏族，属于榆树沟夷的统治氏族，实际是簸箕湾的解氏，是古老的山区夷。
Translation:
Thirty-five li further northeast from Jiaoguoshan stands Kunshan。The Niu Shi and Shui Shi live there。 The Huangshui River rises from the mountains, and along its banks live the Mangling tribes。 They are the ruling branch of the Yushugou YI, in fact, they are the Xie Shi from Boqiwan Bay。 They are the ancient mountain Yi。

05-01-15 鼓镫山
Gudengshan
（114,29186E；35,7502N）

又东北四百里，曰鼓镫之山[1]，多赤铜[2]。有草焉，名曰荣草[3]，其叶如柳[4]，其本如鸡卵[5]，食之已风[6]。

凡薄山之首，自甘枣山至于鼓镫之山，凡十五山，六千六百七十里。历儿，冢也，其祠礼：毛用太牢之具，县以吉玉[7]。其余十三山者，毛用一羊[8]，县婴用桑封[9]，瘗而不糈。桑封者，桑主[10]也，方其下而锐其上，而中穿之加金[11]。

注释：[1]鼓镫山：读勾邓山，指鹤镇山，今称鹤壁。
Notes:[1]gu deng shan (drum stand mount) reads as gou deng mount, refers to the Hezhenshan, today known as Hebi county. he/crane, bi/wall。
[2] 赤铜：指平原氏族。
[2] chi tong (red copper) refers to the plain tribes。
[3] 荣草：指罗氏移民。
[3] rong cao (flourishing grass) refers to the migrants of the Luo tribe。

[4]柳：指僚（lao）族。
[4] liu(willow) a phonetic match to Lao/Liao tribe， liu/lao/liao phonetic match。
[5] 鸡卵：读革哼，指韓羿人。
[5] ji luan (chicken eggs) reads as geheng, refers to the Geyi people。
[6] 已风：指东部夷。
[6] yi feng (stop wind) refers to the Eastern YI, fei /feng, phonetic concept to mean east。
[7] 县以吉玉：敬以璧玉。
[7] xian yi ji yu (devotion with best jade) devote jade Bi in respectful worship。
[8]羊：指瑒（chang）玉，祭祀用的玉。此时期的瑒玉的规格较小，可以用其他玉套加封。
[8] yang(sheep) refers to the chang jade, a jade of votive purpose。At this age, the Chang jade is smaller in size, and can be enveloped in a bigger jade piece。
[9] 县婴用桑封：用信封密闭。县婴，指密闭。
[9] xian ying yong sang feng:
Tr: to be tightly sealed in the jade envelope. Xian ying means to seal tightly。
[10] 桑主：指信封玉，相似于琮。主、诸，指封。
[10] sang zhu (mulberry lord) refers to the seal holding the jade。 It functions as jade zun。 Zhu, as envelope。
[11] 中穿之加金：中空加盖。
[11] zhong chuan zhi jia jin (middle through and add gold)
Tr: it is hallowed in the middle and has a lid。

译文：由坤山往东北四百里，有座山叫鹤镇山，住着平原氏族。有一个移民氏族，名叫罗氏移民，是僚族支系，实际是韓羿人，是古老的东部夷。

综观中山第一列山系，从阳山到鹤镇山，共十五座山，延绵六千六百七十里（九百三十七里）。其中历儿山是宗山，祭祀时用太牢礼，供奉以璧玉。其余十三座山，用一瑒玉供奉，用信封密封、掩埋而不用食物。信封是一种信玉，下方而上尖，中空并加盖。

Translation:

Four hundred li further northeast from the Kunshan stands Hezhenshan。 The plain tribes live there。 One migrant tribe is known as the Luo tribe, they are part of the Lao people, the Geyi people, ancient eastern tribes。

In sum of the first mountain system in the middle part, there are a total of 15 mountains from Yangshan to Hezhenshan, covering a distance of 6,670 li（in fact, only 973 li）。The Li'ershan are the ancestor's mountain。 In sacrificing to the deities, the highest Tailao rite is observed, Bi jade is offered。 The rest of the 13 mountains are given Chang jade as votive objects, sealed tight in a jade envelope, buried underground without food。 The envelope is a trusted jade, the lower end is square, and the upper part is a triangle。 It is hollow inside and with a jade lid。

中山经第二山系

Book5 Zhongshanjing; chapter 2

05-02-01 济山 煇诸山
Jishan Huizhushan

(114,35168E；34,79992N)

中次二经济山之首，曰煇诸之山[1]，其上多桑[2]，其兽多闾麋[3]，其鸟多鹖[4]。

注释：[1]煇诸山：指开封山，濮粤语如今还保持这种读法。实际是指开封县城。
Notes：[1] hui zhu shan: refers to Kaifengshan, still traceable in the Pu, and Yue languages, it is a description of the Kaifeng County seat，Henan province。

[2]桑：指花姓氏族。
[2] sang(berry) refers to the tribes bearing the surname of Hua(flower)。

[3] 闾麋：指楼庄氏族。当地的村落常以洛称谓，指村寨，今谐音称为楼。麋，指庄。
[3]lv mi refers to the Louzhuang tribe. In local dialect, villages are often called Luo, today it is a phonetic to Lou(building), mi: zhuang（enclosure, Hamlet）。

[4]鹖：指牧羊氏族。鹖，同贺，指羊。
[4] he to the herders of sheep or goats, he, a phonetic match, meaning sheep herds。

译文：中部第二列山是济山山系，最东边的一座山叫开封山。山的西边住着花姓氏族，东边住着楼庄氏族，还住着牧羊氏族。
Translation:
The second system is the Jishan in the middle part, with Kaifengshan to its eastmost end。 On the west side of the mountain live the Hua tribe, on its east side live the Louzhuang tribe and the sheepherders' tribes。

05-02-02 发视山
Fashishan
(114,18916E；34,4083N)

又西南二百里，曰发视之山[1]。其山多金玉[2]，其下多砥砺 [3] 。即鱼水 [4] 出焉，而西流注于伊水 [5]。

注释：[1]发视山：指苇肆山，今称尉氏山。指尉氏县城。发，读费，指苇。
Notes: [1] fa shi shan (hair look mount)
Tr： refers to the Weisishan, known today as the Yushishan。It is a description of the Yushi county seat, Fa(hair)reads as fei, refers to the reeds, a close phonetic of fei/fa/yu, shi/si。

[2] 金玉：指要夷。要，通腰，读缴，与金谐音。
[2] jin yu (gold jade) refers to Yao Yi, Yao, 要，腰，jiao 缴，not clearly distinguished in their spelling。 jiao is a phonetic match to the Pu concept of gold (jin, jiao, yao) 。

[3] 砥砺：指河滨夷。砥，读迭，指河滨；砺，通黎，指夷。
[3] di li: refers to the riverside YI, di/die, a Pu concept of riverside。 Li: Yi refers to people。

[4] 即鱼水：指贾鲁河。实际是向东南流，濮语"东"读须音，与西谐音。
[4] ji yu shui (fish water): Jialuhe River, in fact the river goes southeast。 In Pu concept, east is read as xi， a phonetic pun to west in Chinese。

[5] 伊水：今称颖河。
[5] yi shui: today's Yinghe River。

译文：由开封山往西南二百里，有座山叫尉氏山。山的西面住着要氏族，东面住着河滨夷。贾鲁河水从这里流过，向东南流入颖河。
Translation:
Two hundred li further southwest from Kaifengshan stands Yushishan。On its west side live the Yao people, on its east side, live the Riverside Yi。 Jialu River flows through here and goes southeast into Yinghe River。

05-02-03 豪山
Haoshan
（113,77357E；34,38629N）

又西三百里，曰豪山[1]，其上多金玉而无草木[2]。

注释：[1]豪山：指和山，是河南新郑的古称谓，在河南新郑和庄镇。
Notes：[1] hao shan: refers to Heshan, the old name for Xinzheng in Henan province。It is about the Hezhuang township in Xinzheng, Henan province。
[2] 金玉而无草木：郑夷的游牧部落。
[2] jin yu er wu cao mu (gold jade but no grass wood) refers to the nomadic tribes of the Zheng Yi。

译文：由尉氏山往西三百里，有座山叫和山，西边住着郑夷的游牧部落氏族。
Translation:
Three hundred li further west from the Yushishan stands the Heshan。On its west side live the nomadic tribes of the Zheng Yi。

05-02-04 鲜山
Xianshan
(113,3792E；34,53644N)

又西三百里，曰鲜山[1]，多金玉[2]，无草木[3]，鲜水出焉[4]，而北流注于伊水[5]。其中多鸣蛇[6]，其状如蛇而四翼 [7]，其音如磬 [8]，见则其邑大旱 [9]。

注释：[1]鲜山：指新山，在河南新密南面。实际介绍新山北面的新密.
Notes：[1] xian（fresh) shan: refers to the Xin(new)shan, Xinshan is situated to the south of Xinmi, a description of Xinmi to the north of Xinshan, Henan province。
[2] 金玉：指郑夷。
[2] jin yu (gold jade) refers to Zheng Yi。
[3] 无草木：游牧部落氏族。
[3] wu cao mu (no grass wood) refers to the nomadic tribes。
[4] 鲜水: 指新水。
[4] xian shui: refers to today’s Xinshui River。
[5] 伊水：今称颖河。鲜水北流实际上指南流。南读贝，谐音北。
[5] yi shui: refers to today’s Yinghe River。Xian River is flowing to the north。In the Pu concept, south is read as bei, an accidental phonetic match to the Chinese concept of north。
[6] 鸣蛇：指米氏塞夷。
[6] ming she (whistling snake)
Tr: refers to the Saka Yi that bears the surname of Mi。
[7] 蛇而四翼：塞夷的母系氏族。四、六都指母系。
[6] she er si yi(snake with four wings) the matrilineal tribes of the Saka Yi。in the Pu concept, the number 4 and 6 refers to matrilineal structure。
[8]磬：指磬屏，今称青屏。
[7] qing: music stone, refers to Qingping, a close phonetic match to Qingpin（green screen）。
[9] 大旱：指达罕氏族。

[9] da han (big draught) refers to the Khan tribe。

译文：由和山往西三百里，有座山叫新山，住着郑夷的游牧部落氏族。新水从山间流出，向南流入颖河。这里住着米氏塞夷，是塞夷的母系氏族，住在青屏，是这个集镇的达罕氏族。
Translation:
Three hundred li further west from Heshan stands Xinshan。The nomadic tribes of the Zheng YI live here。Xinshui River flows out of the mountain, goes south into the Yinghe River。Here the Saka Yi of the Mi tribe live, they are the matrilineal tribes living in Qingping, they are the Da Khan tribe of that township。

05-02-05 阳山
Yangshan
（113,03206E；34,46401N）

又西三百里，曰阳山[1]，多石[2]，无草木[3]。阳水出焉，而北流注于伊水。其中多化蛇[4]，其状如人面而豺身 [5]，鸟翼而蛇行 [6]，其音如叱呼 [7]，见则其邑大水 [8] 。

注释：[1]阳山：指叱阳山，即嵩山南面的登封县城，简称嵩阳。
Notes： [1] yang shan (sun mount)
Tr: refers to the Chiyangshan, in reference to Dengfeng county seat, south of the Songshan, shortened to Songyang。
[2]石：指独孤氏。今汉语称为石氏，属音译姓氏。
[2] shi(stone) refers to the Gudu（lonely） Shi, today known as Shishi, a phonetic rendering。
[3] 无草木：游牧部落氏族。
[3] wu cao mu (no grass wood) nomadic tribes。
[4] 化蛇：指乌孜别克塞夷。
[4] hua she (change into snake) refers to the Uzbek's Saka Yi。
[5] 人面而豺身：定居的外来氏族。豺，指他，在此表示外来的。
[5] ren mian er chai shen (human face with wolf body)
Tr: the migrant tribes that settled down locally。chai(wolf) refers to other, here means outsider, migrants。
[6] 鸟翼而蛇行：僚族人的打扮，塞夷的习俗。
[6] niao yi er she xing (bird wings but snake movement) dressed like Lao tribe but with the habit of the Saka YI。
[7] 叱呼：指森山，今谐音称嵩山。
[7] chi hu refers to the Senshan, a phonetic match to Songshan。
[8] 大水：指游牧氏族。
[8] da shui (big water) refers to the nomadic tribes。

译文：由新山往西三百里，有座山叫嵩阳山，住着石姓氏族，是游牧部落氏族。阳水从山间流出，向北流入颖河。这里住着乌孜别克塞夷，是定居的外来氏族，僚族人的打扮，塞夷的习俗，住在嵩山，是这个集镇的游牧氏族。
Translation:
Three hundred li westwards from the Xinshan stands Songyangshan。 The Shi tribes live here, they are the nomads。 The Yangshui River flows out of the mountains and goes north into the Ying River。 The Uzbek Saka Yi live here, they are a migrant tribe, dressed like the Lao people but with the habits of the Saka Yi。 They live at the Songshan。 They are the nomadic tribes of this township。

05-02-06 昆吾山
Kunwushan

（112,7441E；34,26558N）

又西二百里，曰昆吾之山[1]，其上多赤铜[2]。有兽焉，其状如彘而有角[3]，其音如号[4]，名曰蠪蚳[5]，食之不眯[6]。

注释：[1]昆吾山：指夏部落的山，今称夏店。
Notes： [1] kun wu shan: refers to the Xia tribal nation's mountain, known today as Xia Dian。
[2] 赤铜：移民区域的氏族。
[2] chi tong (red copper), refers to the tribes residing in the migrants' areas。
[3] 彘而有角：指东部的补苦氏族。
[3] zhi er you jiao (pig with horns) refers to the Buku tribe from the East。
[4]号：指洪哈，意思是张口，夏店的古地名。
[4] hao: hong ha, meaning Zhang Kou, the ancient name for Xia Dian, a Pu concept。
[5] 蠪蚳：指鲁枝氏，苗族的补苦氏族。补苦，即有夏。
[5] long di: refers to the Luzhi Shi, the Hmong Miao 's Buku tribe, Buku means You Xia。
[6] 不眯：指补蒙纠，即苗族。眯，在此指蒙。
[6] bu mi refers to the Bu meng jiu, another name for the Miao tribes。Mi/meng, a phonetic match。

译文：由嵩阳山往西二百里，有座山叫夏部落山，山的西面住着移民区域的氏族。有一个氏族，是东部的补苦氏族，住在张口，名叫鲁枝氏，是古老的苗族。
Translation:
Two hundred li westwards from the Songyangshan, stands the Xiabuluo (Xia tribes) Mountain。 On its west live the tribes in the migrant area。One tribe, the Buku tribe from the east live in Zhangkou, they are called Luzhi Shi, they are the ancient Miao people。

05-02-07 葌山
Jianshan
（112,46923E；34,14921N）

又西百二十里，曰葌山[1]，葌水出焉，而北流注于伊水[2]，其上多金玉[3]，其下多青雄黄[4]。有木焉，其状如棠而赤叶[5]，名曰芒草[6]，可以毒鱼[7]。

注释：[1]葌山：指兰草山。今谐音称为涧山。主要介绍山南的汝阳集镇。
Notes： [1] jian shan: refers to the Lancaoshan (blue grass mountain), known today as Jianshan(brook mount) this is a description of the Ruyang township, to the south of the mountain。
[2] 伊水：指伊川水。今称伊河。
[2] yi shui: refers to the Yichuanshui River, today's Yihe River。
[3] 金玉：指葌夷，即兰村夷
[3] jin yu (gold jade) refers to the Jian Yi, the Lancun Yi-- the Lan village people。
[4] 青雄黄：指东车坊氏族。
[4] qing xiong huang (green male yellow) refers to the Dongchefang (east water mill) tribe。
[5] 棠而赤叶：中心的游牧夷。
[5] tang er chi ye (berry with red leaves) the central nomadic tribes。
[6] 芒草：指苗族移民。
[6] mang cao: refers to the migrants of the Miao people。
[7] 可以毒鱼：有夏国的古老夷。毒，指老。

[7] ke yi du yu (can poison fish) refers to the ancient Yi of the Xia nation, du（poison）: ancient。

译文：由夏部落山往西南一百二十里，有座山叫涧山。涧水从山间流出，向北流入伊河。山的西面住着兰村氏族，东面住着东车坊氏族。有一个管理氏族，是中心的游牧夷，是苗族移民，是有夏国的古老夷。
Translation:
One hundred twenty li further southwest from the Xiabuluo Mountain, stands Jianshan。The Jianshui River flows out of the mountains and goes north into the Yihe River。On the west of the mountain live the Lancun people, on the east side live the Dongchefang people。One tribe is of the managerial tribe, the central nomadic tribe of the Miao migrants。They are the ancient Yi of the Buku /You Xia nation。

05-02-08 独苏山
Dusushan
（111,85719E；34,02276N）

又西一百五十里，曰独苏之山[1]，无草木而多水[2]。

注释：[1]独苏山：指老氏山、旧氏山。在今河南嵩阳县旧县镇。
Notes: [1] du su shan: refers to the Laoshishan（old surname mountain） or the Jiushishan。 It is about the Jiuxian township of Songyang county in Henan province。
[2] 无草木而多水：游牧部落的旧氏的区域。
[2] wu cao mu er duo shui (no grass wood but lot water) refers to the area of the nomadic Jiushi tribe。

译文：由涧山往西一百五十里，有座山叫旧氏山，是游牧部落的旧氏的区域。
Translation:
One hundred and fifty li further west from Jianshan stands Jiushishan。 This is the area of the nomadic Jiushi tribes。

05-02-09 蔓渠山
Manqushan
（111,62391E；33,77896N）

又西二百里，曰蔓渠之山[1]。其上多金[2]，其下多竹箭 [3]，伊水出焉，而东流注于洛 [4] 。有兽焉，其名曰马腹 [5]， 其状如人面而虎身 [6]， 其音如婴儿 [7]， 是食人 [8] 。
凡济山之首，自煇诸之山至于蔓渠之山，凡九山，一千六百七十里。其神皆人面而鸟身[9] 。祠：用毛 [10]， 用一吉玉 [11]， 投 [12] 而不糈。

注释:[1]蔓渠山；指老君山，在河南省栾川城南侧，这里介绍栾川城。蔓渠，指头发花白的长者，这里指老君。
Notes:[1] man qu shan (creep ditch mount)
Tr: refers to the Laojunshan（old man mountain）, to the south of Luanchuan city, Henan province。 This is about the Luanchuan City。Manqu; oldman with flowing long white hair。Here, it means Senior Gentle oldman。
[2]金：指截岭氏族。
[2] jin(gold) refers to the Jieling (cut ridge) tribe。
[3] 竹箭：指朱村氏族。
[3] zhu jian (bamboo arrow) refers to the Zhucun （red village) tribe。
[4] 洛水：指洛河。
[4] luo shui: the Luo River。

[5] 马腹：指莽山濮。
[5]ma fu (horse belly)
Tr： a phonetic match of ma/mang, fu/pu, refers to the Mangshan Pu people。
[6] 人面而虎身：定居的濮族。腹、虎都指濮。
[6] ren mian er hu shen (human face with tiger body)
Tr: refers to the settled Pu tribes, Belly, tiger, a phonetic match to the Pu concept of pu/fu/hu， p/f/h not clearly distinguished。
[7] 婴儿：北面。指北面的赤土店。
[7] ying er (infant)
Tr: refers to the northern part, here refers to the Chitu (red soil) township to the north。
[8] 是食人：是古老的居民。
[8] shi shi ren (yes eat human) refers to the ancient, settled people。
[9] 人面而鸟身：定居的僚族人的形象。
[9] ren mian er niao shen (human face with bird body) the image of settled Lao people。
[10]毛：祭词、闻。
[10] mao(hair) means votive speech, heard 。
[11] 吉玉：指璧玉。
[11] ji yu (best jade) refers to the Jade Bi。
[12]投：指潜，在此指掩埋。
[12] tou(throw)
Tr: to submerge, here means to be buried。

译文：由旧氏山往西二百里，有座山叫老君山。山的西面住着截岭氏族，东面住着朱村氏族。伊河发源于这座山，向东流入洛河。有一个氏族，名叫莽山濮，是定居的濮族，住在北面，是古老的居民。

综观济山山系，从开封山到老君山，共计九座山，延绵一千六百七十里。这九座山的山神皆为定居的僚族人的形象。祭祀这些山神时，只用祭词，用一璧玉传达，将玉掩埋而不用食物。

Translation:
Two hundred li further west from the Jiushishan stands Laojunshan。 On its west side live the Jieling tribe, and on its east side live the Zhucun tribe。 Yihe River rises from this mountain and flows east into the Luo River。 One tribe known as the Mangshan Pu has settled to the north, they are the old township people。

In sum: Of the Ji Mountain system, there are 9 mountains between Kaifengshan to Laojunshan, covering a distance of 1,670 li。 The mountain deities are in the images of the settled Lao people 。 When sacrificing to the mountain deities, votive speech is read, and one piece of jade Bi is used as the message carrier。 The jade is buried, and no food is used。

中山经第三山系

Book 5 Zhongshanjing; chapter 3

05-03-01 萯山 敖岸山

Fushan, Ao'anshan
(111,95259E; 33,63813N)

中次三经萯山[1]之首，曰敖岸之山[2]，其阳多㻬琈之玉[3]，其阴多赭、黄金[4]。神熏池[5]居之。是常出美玉 [6] 。北望河林 [7]，其状如茜如举 [8] 。有兽焉，其状如白鹿而四角 [9]， 名曰夫诸 [10]，见则其邑大水 [11] 。

注释：[1]萯山：指伏牛山山系。
Notes: [1] fu shan: refers to the Funiushan mountains system。 (Funiu Shan, or Mt, Funiushan:33° 39′ 45.36″ N, 111° 47′ 12.12″ E)

[2] 敖岸山：读武恩山，指白水山。今称为白河山。
[2]ao an shan: reads as wu en shan, refers to the Baishuishan (white water mountains), a phonetic match to today's Baiheshan (white river) Mountains 。

[3] 㻬琈玉：白又读吐，㟬琈玉指白马夷。今称白河乡夷。
[3] tu fu yu (a kind of jade) bai/white/tu, tufuyu refers to Baima Yi, (white horse people) known today as the Baihexiang (white river township) Yi。

[4]赭、黄金：指东坪、后岭夷。
[4] zhu, huangjin (ochre, gold) refers to the Dongping Yi, and the Houling Yi。dongping (east flatland) houling (back ridge) Yi。

[5] 神熏池：指井池氏。熏，即陉，指井。
[5] shen xun chi (God incense pond) refers to the Jingchi Shi, jingchi (well pond), xun/jing/jing/water well。

[6] 常出美玉：常出指旁边，美玉指木家。旁边是木家庄。
[6] chang chu mei yu (often come beautiful jade) chang chu (close by) mei yu (Mu family) 。
Tr: close by is the Mujiazhuang village。

[7] 河林：指合林，原读合跟，今称岭南。
[7] he lin (river forest) refers to Helin, previous read as Hegen, today known as Lingnan (ridge south) 。

[8] 如茜如举：指山顶树木成林。茜，读 xi 音，指山峰、山顶；举，指林。
[8]ru xi ru ju (as top as uplift)
Tr: the wood on the mountain top grows into forest。 xi: peak, mountain top, ju: forest。

[9] 白鹿而四角：白山的有夏氏族。四角，读补古，指有夏部落。
[9] bai lu er si jiao (white deer with four horns)
Tr: The Youxia Shi (Buku Shi) from the Bai Mountain。 sijiao (four horns) reads in Pu concepts as Buku, refers to the Youxia tribe。

[10] 夫诸：指苇园氏族。
[10] fu zhu: refers to the Weiyuan (reeds garden) tribes。

[11] 大水：指游牧氏族。
[11] da shui (big water) refers to the nomadic tribes。

译文：中山第三列山系是伏牛山，最西边的山是白河山。山的南面住着白马夷，北面住着东坪氏族和后岭氏族。中部住着井池氏，旁边住着木家庄氏族。从这里北望合林，山顶树木成林。这里有一个氏族，是白云山的有夏氏族，名叫苇园氏，是这个集镇的游牧氏族。
Translation:
The 3rd mountain system in the middle part is the Funiushan with Baiheshan at its west most end。 To its south lives the Baima Yi。 On its north live the Dongping tribe and the Houling tribe。 In the middle part of the mountain lives the Jinchi tribe, and close by it lives the Mujiazhuang tribe。Looking out from here, one can see to

the north the Helin, where trees are extended into forest。One tribe, the Buku Shi from the Baiyunshan, known as the Weiyuan Shi, live here, they are the nomadic tribe from that township。

05-03-02 青要山
Qingyaoshan
（112,05335E；33,13375N）

又东十里，曰青要之山[1]，实惟帝之密都[2]。北望河曲[3]，是多驾鸟[4]。南望墠渚[5]，禹父之所化[6]，是多仆累，蒲卢[7]。魋武罗[8]司之，其状人面而豹文[9]，小腰而白齿，而穿耳以鐻[10]，其鸣如鸣玉[11]。是山也，宜女子[12]。畛水出焉，而北流注于河[13]。其中有鸟焉，名曰鴢鸟[14]，其状如凫，青身而朱目赤尾[15]，食之宜子[16]。有草焉，其状如葌，而方茎黄华赤实[17]，其本如藁本[18]，名曰荀草[19]，服之美人色[20]。

注释：[1]青要山：读池饶山，指龙池山.
Notes: [1] qing yao shan (green want mount) reads as Chiraoshan, refers to the Longchishan (dragon pond mountains) 。

[2] 帝之密都：昳之冥都。昳，指死人。指烧人场。说明远古时期也有火化的习俗。
[2] di zhi mi du (God secret capital)
Tr: die zhi min du: die/dead, die, here refers to the cremation site, a proof that in ancient times, cremation is also practised。

[3] 河曲：读赫去，指宝石角，今称顶宝石村。
[3] he qu: reads as He4 qu4, refers to Baoshijiao (precious stone corner) today known as the Dingbaoshi village: (best-stone village) 。

[4] 驾鸟：读嘉僚（lao），指稻谷田。
[4] jia niao (ride bird) reads as Jialao, refers to the rice fields。

[5] 墠渚：读啥渚，指后院。
[5] sha zhu: back yard。

[6] 禹父之所化：靠山的山区聚落。靠山，今谐音称峰一沟。
[6]yu fu zhi suo hua:(Yu's father 's work)
Tr: the mountain settlements on Kaoshan (leaning mount), today 's Fengyigou area。

[7] 仆累、蒲卢：指僚族、濮民。
[7] pu lei, pu lu: refers to the Lao people and the Pu people。

[8] 魋武罗：指僚部落氏族。
[8] shen wu luo: refers to the Lao tribe and its people。

[9] 人面而豹文：定居的豹子水氏族。
[9] ren mian er bao wen (human face with leopard markings) 。
Tr: refers to the settled people of the Baozishui tribe。 Baozishui (leopard water) 。

[10] 小腰而白齿，而穿耳以鐻：小火焰的白河岔河部落氏族。穿耳，即畛水。穿、畛都读丑，指岔。
[10] xiao yao er bai chi (slim waist and white teeth) er chuan er yi hu (ear piecing with Hu)
Tr: refers to the Baihe; and Chahe tribes at Xiaohuoyan, (small fire flame), chuan er （piecing ears) means Zhenshui (Zhen River) chuan, zhen read in Pu concepts as chou(ugly), which means fork, divert。

[11] 鸣玉：指蒙夷，即苗夷支系。
[11] ming yu(sounding jade) refers to the Meng Yi, the Hmong Miao branches。

[12] 宜女子：也称金山蔓。子读陌音，谐音蔓。
[12] yi nv zi (benefits female) reads Jinshanman (golden mount vines) zi reads as mo, mo/man a phonetic close match。

[13]河：指白河。岔河实际是向南流入白河。
[13] he refers to Baihe (white river), the Chahe River in fact flows to the south into the Baihe River。
[14] 幼鸟：指佑僚。
[14] you niao (baby bird) refers to the You Lao.
[15]鳧，青身而朱目赤尾：东部青沟后院的苗蒙游牧夷。
[15] fu, qing shen er zhu mu chi yi (waterfowl, green body with red eyes red tail) 。
Tr: refers to the nomadic Meng Yi at the east Qinggouhouyuan (green gully back yard) 。
[16] 宜子：读溢陌，指河畔氏族。
[16] yi zi: reads as yi mo, meaning riverbank tribes。
[17]葌，而方茎黄华赤实：葌读纠，指苗族方国的山区游牧氏族。
[17] jian, er fang jing huang hua chi shi (jian, square stem yellow flower red fruits) 。
Tr: jian reads as jiu, refers to the mountain nomadic tribe from the Miao regional nation。
[18] 藁本：读苦樊，指农业氏族。
[18] hao ben reads as kubo, refers to agricultural tribes。
[19] 荀草：读须撮，指东部移民。这里就称须撮，延伸为东部人概念。
[19] xun cao: read as xu cuo, refers to the immigrants from the east, xu/xi/east。 Refers to tribes from east, eastern people。
[20] 服之美人色：马坪门惹舍，今称马市坪。
[20] fu zhi mei ren se (taken will beautify your look)
Tr: refers to the “reshe” at Mapingmen, known today as the Mashiping (horse trading market)， [reshe, a place] 。

译文：由白河山往东十里，有座山叫龙池山，实际是死人的冥都。从这里北望宝石角、稻谷田，南望后院、峰一沟的山区聚落，这些聚落住着僚族濮民。这里是僚部落氏族建立的区域，僚部落是白河岔河的小火焰蒙夷支系。这座山也称金山蔓。岔河水从山间流出，向南流入白河。有一群人，名叫佑僚，是东部青沟后院的苗蒙游牧夷，是古老的河畔氏族。有一群移民，是苗族方国的山区游牧氏族，原本是农业氏族，名叫须撮，是马坪门惹舍人。

Translation:
Ten li eastward from Baiheshan stands Longchishan, which is in fact the capital of the Dead。Looking from here to the north, one sees the Baoshijiao, the rice fields。To the south at the back yard, one sees the settlements by the mountainside at Fengyigou, where the Lao and Pu people took their residence。 This is an area established by the Lao tribe, the Xiaohuoyan branch of the Meng Yi, they belong to the Lao tribe from the Baihe River and the Chahe River。This mountain is also known as the Jinshanman Mountain。Chahe River flows out of the mountain and goes south into the Baihe River。 A group known as the You Lao people, are the nomadic Meng Yi from the east Qinggouhouyuan。 They are the ancient riverbank tribes。Another group of immigrants are the mountain nomad from the Meng 's Miao Fangguo (regional nation) 。Previously they are the settled agricultural people known as Xucuo, from the Mapingmen township。

05-03-03 騩山
Guishan Mountain
（112,13375E；33,70857N）

又东十里，曰騩山[1]，其上有美枣[2]，其阴有琝琈之玉[3]。正回之水[4] 出焉，而北流注于河 [5] 。其中多飞鱼 [6] ，其状如豚而赤文[7] ，服之不畏雷[8]，可以御兵[9]。

注释：[1]騩山：指驴蹄山，简称蹄山，读音果山，谐音騩山。

Notes:[1] gui shan: refers to the Lvtishan (donkey hoof mount) shortened to Tishan，ti/hoof/reads as guo, a phonetic match to gui，gui/guo。

[2] 美枣：指桃花崖氏族。

[2] mei zao (beautiful dates) refers to the Taohua'ai (peach flower cliff) tribe。

[3] 瑀琈玉：指铁伏夷，原意是北关夷。

[3] tuo fu yu (a kind of jade) a phonetic match to Tiefu Yi, meaning North Pass Yi, the Beiguan Yi。

[4] 正回水：指铁伏水，今称铁佛水。伏，指阴。

[4] zheng hui shui: refers to Tiefu River, today known as Tiefoshui River, fu/fo: shady side, the Yin as vs Yang, sunny side。

[5]河：指北汝河。

[5] he: Beiruhe River。

[6] 飞鱼：指伏枝夷，即东坪夷。简称伏夷，谐音飞鱼。

[6] fei yu (flying fish) refers to the Fuzhi Yi, known as the Dongping Yi, shortened to Fu Yi, a phonetic match to feiyu。

[7] 豚而赤文：指车水屯，今称车村。

[7] tun er chi wen:(small pig with red marking) refers to the Cheshui Tun, today's Checun (car village)。

[8] 服之不畏雷：东坪博维黎，今称东城人。黎，指人。

[8] fu zhi bu wei lei (taken will not fear thunder) refers to the Dongcheng (east city) people。Fu, east, dong ping bo wei li, Li, people。

[9] 可以御兵：有夏国的河滨夷。

[9]ke yi yu bing: Buku's Riverside Yi。

译文：由龙池山往东十里，叫驴蹄山，山的西面有桃花崖氏族，北面有铁伏夷。铁伏水从山间流出，向北流入北汝河。河边住着东坪夷，是车水屯的东城人，是有夏国的河滨夷。

Translation:

Ten li eastwards from Longchishan stands Lvtishan。On its west live the Taohua'ai tribe。On its north side live the Tiefu Yi。The Tiefushui River flows out of the mountain and goes north into the Beiruhe River。On the river's banks live the Dongping Yi, they are the east city people from the Cheshui Tun, known as the Buku nation's Hebin (Riverside) Yi。

05-03-04 宜苏山

Yisushan

（112，34172E；33,71906N）

又东四十里，曰宜苏之山[1]。其上多金玉[2]，其下多蔓居之木[3]。滽滽之水[4]出焉，而北流注于河[5]，是多黄贝[6]。

注释：[1]宜苏山：读尼苏山，指石者山，今称石人山。苏，指老者、富翁、有名望的人。

Notes：[1] yi su shan: read as ni su shan, refers to the Shizheshan(stone person mount), today known as Shirenshan (stone human mountain)。Su, a Pu concept referring to a senior, a rich person, a person of fame。

[2] 金玉：指沙岭夷。

[2] jin yu (gold jade) refers to the Shaling Yi, sha(sand) ling(ridge)。

[3] 蔓居木：指苗族部落目夷。

[3] man ju mu refers to the Mu(eyes) Yi of the Miao tribes。

[4] 滽滽水：指龙潭水。龙潭读尧汶，谐音滽滽。

[4] yong yong shui: refers to the Longtanshui (dragon pond) River, long tan read in Pu as raowen, a close phonetic match to yongyong。r/y/w。

[5]河：指沙河。
[5] he refers to the Shahe River: sha/sand。
[6] 黄贝：读伏贝，指东湾。
[6] huang bei (yellow shell) read as fubei, fu/east, bei/bay, east bay: Dongwan。

译文：由驴蹄山往东四十里，有座山叫石人山，西面住着沙岭夷，东面住着苗族部落管理夷，龙潭水从山间流出，向北流入沙河，这里住着东湾氏族。
Translation:
Forty li further east from Lvtishan stands Shirenshan。 On its west live the Shaling Yi, on its east the managerial Yi of the Miao tribe。The Longtanshui River rises from the mountains and goes north into the Shahe River。The Dongwan tribe lives here。

05-03-05 和山
Heshan
（112,7074E；33,68832N）

又东二十里，曰和山[1]。其上无草木而多瑶碧[2] 。实惟河之九都 [3] 。是山也，五曲，九水出焉，合而北流注于河，其中多苍玉 [4] 。吉神泰逢司之 [5] ，其状如人而虎尾 [6] ，是好[7]居于萯山之阳，出入有光[8]。泰逢神动天地气也[9]。
凡萯山之首，自敖岸之山至于和山，凡五山，四百四十里。其祠：泰逢、熏池、武罗[10]皆一牡羊副[11]，婴用吉玉[12]。其二神用一雄鸡[13] 瘗之，糈用稌。

注释：[1]和山：指六羊山。和指羊。同时又称泰山。
Notes:[1] he shan: refers to Liuyangshan (six goats mountain), he means goat, also known as Taishan。
[2] 无草木、多瑶碧：游牧部落、住着老龙河氏族。
[2] wu cao mu (no grass wood), duo yao bi (many yao green) 。
Tr： refers to the nomadic tribe, and the Laolonghe (old dragon river) tribes there。
[3] 河之九都：九条支流汇合之地。
[3] he zhi jiu du (rivers' nine capital) where nine rivers meet。
[4] 苍玉：指羌夷。
[4] cang yu (dark jade) refers to the Qiang Yi。
[5] 吉神泰逢：指计氏族的泰山氏。濮语 "计" 读 tie 音，与 "泰"谐音。
[5] ji shen tai feng (luck god tai feng) refers to the Taishan Shi from the Ji tribes。 In Pu concept, Ji reads as tie, a close phonetic match to tai, tie/tai。
[6] 人而虎尾：定居的胡夷，即游牧夷。
[6] ren er hu yi (human with tiger tail) settled Hu Yi, known as the herders Yi, the nomadic Yi。
[7] 是好：之前，原先。
[7] shi hao: refers to before, or previously。
[8] 出如有光：迁集镇于阴门。有光，读幽光，指阴门、北门。今称下汤镇。
[8] chu ru you guang (when out as light) meaning move their township to Yinmen Gates。 You guang, reads dimmy light, refers to the Yin Gate (north gate), known today as the Lower Tang township—Xiatangzhen。E112 .40°, N33.43°。
[9] 动天地气也：本泰北犬夷。动，指本，原本；天地，读泰狄，指泰北；气也，读犬夷。
[9] doing tian di qi ye (stir the sky earth qi),
Tr: originally the north of Tai's Dog Yi, dong(stir)means original, in the beginning, tiandi (sky earth) a phonetic match to /taidi/tai north, di/north。 Qi: refers to Dog Yi, or Dog Rong。

[10] 泰逢、熏池、武罗：泰山、井池、武僚这些氏族和部落名被用做所在山的山神名。
[10] taifeng, xunchi, wuluo refers to the mountain deities who take their names from the local tribe and people of the Taishan, Jingchi, and Wulao。

[11] 牡羊副：要求用玉坠祭拜。牡，指玉坠；羊读贺，在此指拜；副，指要求。
[11]mu yang fu: need to use jade pendant for sacrificial rite。 Mu: jade pendant, yang/he, here means pray or kneel in devotion, fu/demand。

[12] 吉玉：指璧玉。
[12] ji yu(lucky jade)refers to the jade Bi。

[13] 雄鸡：读珣珏，指软玉。
[13] xiong ji(male chicken)reads xun yu, a kind soft jade, a phonetic match xiong/xun, ji/yu。

译文：由石人山往东二十里，是六羊山。西面是游牧部落，住着老龙河氏族。这里实际是九条支流汇合之地。这座山有五个山峰，有九条支流向北流入沙河，河畔住着羌夷，是泰山氏部落建立的区域。泰山氏是定居的胡夷，原先居住在伏牛山南，后迁集镇于阴门，泰山氏本属泰北的犬夷。

综观伏牛山山系，西自白云山，东至六羊山，共五座山，延绵四百四十里。祭祀泰山、井池、武僚要求用玉坠祭拜，掩埋则用璧玉。其余二山神用软玉掩埋，食物用荞麦饼。

Translation:

Twenty li further east from the Shirenshan, stands the Liuyangshan。 On its west side live the nomads, the Laolonghe tribe。Here, nine rivers meet。 This mountain has five peaks。 Nine tributaries flow northwards into the Shahe River。The Qiang Yi live along the riverbanks, and the Taishan tribes built up the territory。 Taishan Shi are Hu Yi who have settled down。 Previously they lived to the south of the Funiushan, later they moved their towns to Yinmen Gates。The Taishan Shi belongs to the Dog Yi north of Taishan。

In sum, the Funiushan, with Baiyunshan on its west end and Liuyangshan on its east, total five mountains, cover a distance of 440 li。When sacrificing to deities of Taishan, Jingchi and Wulao, jade pendant is used, and jade Bi is buried。 For the other two deities, soft jade buried, and cakes of buckwheat are offered。

中山经第四山系

Book5 Zhongshanjing; chapter4

05-04-01 厘山 鹿蹄山

Lishan Lutishan

（113,52746E；34,75965N）

中次四经厘山之首，曰鹿蹄之山[1]，其上多玉[2]，其下多金[3]。甘水[4] 出焉，北流注于洛 [5]，其中多泠石 [6]。

注释：[1]鹿蹄山：读鲁体山，指上原。在河南郑州须水镇。
[1]lu ti shan (deer hoof mount)

Tr: reads as Lutishan (lu body mount)， a close phonetic match of the names, referring to Shangyuan, in Xushui county, Zhengzhou city in Henan province。

[2]玉：豫陇氏族

[2]yu(jade) refers to Yulong clan。

[3]金：指丁姓氏族，原住在须水镇的东边，今住在北面。

[3] jin(gold)

Tr：refers to the Ding clan, who live to the east of the Xushuizhen, now moved to its north。

[4] 甘水：指孙水，实际为东孙水，今称须水，由东孙水的"须甘汶"简约而来。

[4] gan shui (sweet water)

Tr: refers to Sunshui, or the east Sunshui, known today as the Xushui River, it is a shortened term for Xuganwen, wen: water, river; xu: east。

[5]洛：指贾鲁河。鲁、洛谐音。

[5] luo: refers to Jialu River, lu/luo close phonetic match。

[6] 汵石：指孙氏族。

[6] jin shi: refers to the Sun clan, (sun: not the sol, but grandson)。

译文：中部第四列山系是厘山山脉，最东边是上原。上原的西边住着豫陇氏族，东边住着丁姓氏族。须水从这里流出，向北流入贾鲁河，河边住着孙氏族。

Translation：

The 4th list for the mountains in the middle area is the Lishan Mountains, with Shangyuan as its east most mountain。 To the west of Shangyuan live the Yulong clan, on its east live the Ding clan。 Xushui River flows out of here and goes north into the Jialuhe River, the Sun clan lives along the river。

05-04-02 扶猪山

Fuzhushan

（113,38738E；34,74491N）

西五十里，曰扶猪之山[1]。其上多礝石[2]。有兽焉，其状如貉而人目[3]，其名曰麐[4]。虢水[5]出焉，而北流注于洛[6]，其中多瑌石[7]。

注释：[1]扶猪山：读乌诸山，指官咀山，又称佬倌咀、老官咀。

Notes:[1] fu zhu shan (support pig mount)

Tr: reads as wu zhu shan, refers to Guanzuishan, alternatively known as Laoguanzui, written with different Chinese signs for Lao and guan。

[2] 礝石：指放牧氏族。

[2] ruan shi (nice jade) refers to the sheep or goat's herder's clan。

[3] 貉而人目：佬倌咀的集镇管理氏族。貉，读哈音，指佬。

[3] ha er ren mu (raccoon dog with human eyes)

Tr: it refers to the managerial clan of the Laoguanzui township. luo/ha/raccoon/senior。

[4]麐：指荥氏族。即今荥阳人。

[4] ren（fox like animal），refers to the Xing clan, today's Xingyang people。

[5] 虢水：指西孙水，今称为魏河、傅北河、寨河多个河段，没有统一名称。

[5] guo shui:

Tr: it refers to Xisunshui River, today known as the Weihe River, Fubeihe River, Zhaihe River, without a unified name for different reaches。

[6]洛：指贾鲁河。

[6] luo: refers to Jialuhe River。

[7] 瑌石：放牧氏族。
[7] ruan shi: nice jade, refers to the herders' tribes。

译文：由上原往西五十里，称为佬倌咀，住着放牧氏族。有一个氏族，是佬倌咀的集镇管理氏族，名叫荥氏族。西孙水从这里流出，向北流入贾鲁河，河边住着放牧氏族。
Translation:
Fifty li westwards from Shangyuan there stands the Laoguanzui mountain, where the herdsmen live。 One such tribe is the managerial township tribe, the Xing people。 The Xisunshui River flows out of here and goes north into Jialuhe River。The herder's clan lives along the river 。

05-04-03 釐山
Lishan
（113,1061E；34,6584N）

又西一百二十里，曰釐山[1]，其阳多玉[2]，其阴多蒐[3]。有兽焉，其状如牛。苍身[4]，其音如婴儿[5]，是食人[6]，其名犀渠[7]。滽滽之水[8]出焉，而南流注于伊水[9]。有兽焉，名曰【犭頡】[10]，其状如獳犬而有鳞[11]，其毛如彘鬣[12]。

注释：[1]釐山：读厘山，指青山，今称青龙山。在河南巩义市南侧。
Notes: [1]li shan: refers to Qingshan (green mount), known today as the Qinglongshan (green dragon mount) 。 It is situated to the south of the Gongyi city in Henan province。
[2]玉：指大水氏族。
[2]yu(jade) refers to the Dashui clan, da shui (big water) 。
[3]蒐：读奢，指凤凰台氏族。
[3] sou: reads as she, refers to the Fenghuangtai (phoenix terrace) clan。
[4]牛，苍身：牛苍，读尼采，指候石。牛苍身，指后石河氏族。
[4] niu, cang shen (ox, black body)
Tr: niucang, reads as Nicai, refers to Houshi, Niucangshen: the Houshihe (back stone river) clan。
[5] 婴儿：北面，即巩义城。
[5] ying er (infant)
Tr: it refers to north, the Gongyi city。
[6] 是食人：是古老的居民。
[6] shi shi ren (yes eat human)
Tr: (they) are the ancient residents。
[7] 犀渠：指东郭氏。
[7]si qu (Rhino canal)
Tr: it refers to the Dongguo Shi (east Guo Shi) 。
[8] 滽滽水：指罗河。罗读雍。
[8] yong yong shui (slow flowing water)
Tr: it refers to the Luohe River, in Pu concept, luo is read as yong。
[9] 伊水：指伊洛河。
[9] yi shui: Yiluohe River。
[10] 【犭頡】：指涉氏族。今涉村镇氏族。
[10] jie: refers to the She tribe, she（cross) -- today's Shecunzhen clan。
[11] 獳犬而有鳞：石姓犬戎的定居氏族。氐羌语读石为诺、洛；有鳞，读补令，指定居的氏族。
[11]ru quan er you lin (dog has scales)

Tr: it refers to the settled clans of the Quanrong (dog rong) who bear the surname of Shi(stone), in Diqiang language, stone is read as nuo, luo. You lin (has scales) read as buling, referring to the sedentary clans。

[12] 彘鬣：指种植支系。

[12] zhi lie (pig hard hair)

Tr: it refers to the tribal branches of planters。

译文：由佬倌咀往西一百二十里，有座山叫青龙山，山的南面住着大水氏族，北面住着凤凰台氏族。有一个氏族，是后石河氏族，住在北面，是古老的居民，名叫东郭氏。罗河水从山间流出，向南流入伊洛河。河边有一个氏族，名叫涉氏，是石姓犬戎的定居氏族，属种植支系。

Translation:

One hundred and twenty li westwards from the Laoguanzui stands Qinglongshan。On its south side live the Dashui clan, on its north side live the Fenghuangtai tribe。 One tribe is the Houshihe people, they live in the north, a very ancient people known as the Dongguo Shi。Luo2 River flows out of the mountain and goes south into the Yiluohe River。 Living along the riverbank are the settled Dog Rong (Quanrong) people, with a surname of She。They are the planter's tribe。

05-04-04 箕尾山

Qiweishan

(112,69596E；34,69694N)

又西二百里，曰箕尾之山[1]。多穀[2]，多涂石 [3] 。其上多㻬琈之玉 [4] 。

注释：[1]箕尾山：指再兴山，今称二里头。箕尾，读 ju vei，指第二次兴盛。

Notes: [1] qi wei/yi shan: refers to Zaixingshan。 It is known today as the Erlitou, a famous ancient site, Henan province。 qiwei: reads in Pu concept as juvei, refers to the second revival。

[2]穀：指夏姓氏族。

[2]gu: grain,

Tr: refers to the clans bearing the surname of Gu， in Pu; but it means Xia in Chinese。

[3] 涂石: 指管理氏族

[3] tu shi (smear stone)

Tr： refers to the management clan。

[4] 㻬琈玉：指统治氏族。

[4] tu fu yu: jade, refers to the ruling clan。

译文：由青龙山往西二百里，有个地方叫再兴山，那里住着夏姓氏族，住着管理氏族。西面住着统治氏族。

Translation:

Two hundred li westwards from the Qinglongshan one comes to a place called Zaixingshan。The Gu（xia) clans live there。Also living here is the management clan。 On its west side, lives the ruling clan。

05-04-05 柄山

Bingshan

(112,69596E；34,69694N)

又西二百五十里，曰柄山[1]，其上多玉[2]，其下多铜[3]。滔雕之水[4] 出焉，而北流注于洛[5]。其中多羬羊[6]。有木焉，其状如樗[7]，其叶如桐而荚实[8]，其名曰茇[9]，可以毒鱼 。

注释：[1]柄山：指门山，今称龙门山，在伊河与洛河之间。

Notes:[1] bing shan (handle mount)
Tr: it refers to Menshan (Gate mount) today, it is called Longmenshan (dragon gate mount), located between Yihe River and Luohe River。

[2]玉：指宜阳的锦屏氏族。

[2]yu(jade)
Tr: it refers to the Jinping clan in Yiyang county, Henan province。

[3]铜：指伊河边的窑罐氏族。

[3] tong(copper)
Tr: it refers to the Yaoguan (klin pot) clans by Yihe River。

[4] 滔雕水：指龙门山的上积河，今称上河。

[4] tao diao shui (torrential carve water)
Tr: it refers to the Shangjihe (up collect) River, known today as Shanghe River。

[5]洛：指洛河。

[5] luo: refers to Luohe River。

[6] 羬羊：指东坡氏族。羬读 qio 音，指坡；羊读 ts'i 音，指东。

[6] qio yang (slope goat) refers to the Dongpo (east slope) tribes. yang/ts'i means east。

[7]櫄：指迁徙而来的。

[7] yun (ailanthus altissima, tree of heaven)
Tr: migrants from other places。

[8] 桐而荚实：指上河边的殷氏族。殷在古濮语中读嘉。

[8] tong er jia shi (empress tree with capsuled seeds)
Tr: refers to the Yin tribes on the banks of the Shanghe River。Yin is read as Jia in Proto Pu。

[9]茇：指碗，这里指制碗氏族。

[9] ba(bowl): refers to the clan that produce clay bowls。

[10] 毒鱼：指古老夷。

[10] du yu (poison fish) refers to ancient Yi。

译文：由再兴山往西二百五十里，有座山叫门山，山的西面住着锦屏氏族，东面住着窑罐氏族。上河水从山间流出，向北流入洛河。河边住着东坡氏族。有一支苗族，是迁徙来上河边的殷氏族支系，是夏国的古老夷。

Translation:
Two hundred and fifty li further west from Zaixingshan there stands Menshan。 On its west side live the Jinping clan。 On its east side live the Jiaoguan clan。 Shanghe River rises from the mountain and flows north into Luohe River。The Donghe clan live along the riverbank。 A migrant Miao clan settled down by Shanghe River。They are a branch of the Yin clans of ancient Xia Nation。

05-04-06 白边山
Baibianshan
(111,89259E；34,31869N)

又西二百里，曰白边之山[1]，其上多金玉[2]，其下多青雄黄[3]。

注释：[1]白边山：指贝嘎别，即白果山，今称花果山，属熊耳山东麓。

Notes: [1] bai bian shan (white rim mount)
Tr: reads as beigabie， refers to the Baiguoshan (white fruit mount), known today as Huaguoshan (flower fruit mount)， the east extension of Xiongershan (bear ear mount) 。

[2] 金玉：指涧口夷。

[2] jin yu (gold jade) refers to the Jiankou Yi。

[3] 青雄黄：指阎焦溪氏族，今称焦川氏族。

[3] qing xiong huang (green male yellow) refers to the Yanjiaoxi clan。Today they are known as the Jiaochuan clan。

译文：由门山往西二百里，有座山叫白果山，山的西面住着涧口夷，东面住着阎焦溪氏族。

Translation:

Two hundred li further west from Shimenshan there stands Baiguoshan。On its west live the Jiankou Yi, on its east live the Yanjiaoxi clan。

05-04-07 熊耳山

Xiong'ershan

(111,41572E；34,14142N)

又西二百里，曰熊耳之山[1]，其上多漆[2]，其下多棕[3]。浮濠之水[4] 出焉，而西流注于洛 [5]，其中多水玉[6]，多人鱼[7]。有草焉，其状如苏而赤华[8]，名曰葶苧[9]，可以毒鱼[10]。

注释：[1]熊耳山：今仍然称熊耳山，主峰在河南卢氏县东边。

Notes: [1] xiong er shan (bear ear mount) today the same name stays, its main peak is at the east side of Lushi county, Henan province。

[2]漆；指龙窝，窝的濮语读音 qi，与漆同音。

[2] qi(lacquer)refers to Longwo(dragon den), wo(den): in Pu concept reads qi, a phonetic match to Chinese qi。

[3]棕：指帽缨氏族，又称纵目人。

[3] zong(palm) refers to the Maoying clan, also known as Zongmu(vertical eyes) people, Maoying: cap with tassels。

[4] 浮濠水：指放捋水，今称范里水，流经范里镇。

[4] fu hao shui (float big water)

Tr: refers to the Fanglvshui River, known today as Fanlishui River, flowing through the Fanlizhen。

[5]洛：指洛河。

[5] luo: the Luohe River.

[6] 水玉：读云夷，多指青云族，今称水族，属共工氏支系。

[6] shui yu (water jade), reads as Yun(clouds)Yi, mostly refers to the Qingyun(blue cloud)people, today they are known as Shuizu,(water people),belonging to the Gonggong tribes。

[7] 人鱼：指骨垛村氏族。人，指垛；鱼，指骨。

[7] ren yu (human fish) refers to the Guduocun clan。 ren(human)means duo(pile) yu(fish) means gu(bone)。

[8] 苏而赤华：指北苏村的放羊氏族，来到洛河南岸聚成南苏村和排楼村。

[8]su er chi hua (su with red flow)

Tr: refers to the herders' clan of the Beisu Village, who has settled on the southside of Luo River and grown into two villages--the Nansu village and the Pailou village。

[9] 葶苧：指排楼人，今称河楼人。

[9] ting zhu: refers to the Pailou people known today as the Helou (river tower) people。

[10] 毒鱼：古老夷。

[10] du yu (poison fish) ancient Yi。

译文：由白果山往西二百里，有座山叫熊耳山，山的西面住着龙窝氏族，东面住着纵目氏族。范里水从山间流出，向西流入洛河，河边住着青云夷，住着骨垛村氏族。有一个移民氏族，是来自北苏村的放羊氏族，名叫排楼人，是夏国的古老夷。

Translation:

Two hundred li further west from Baiguoshan, there stands the Xiong'ershan。 On its west side live the Longwo clan, on the east side live the Zongmu clan。 Fanlishui River rises from the mountain and goes west into the Luo River。 On its riverbanks live the Qingyun Yi, and the Guduocun clan。 A migrant people, the herders from the Beisu village are known as Pailou people, they belong to the ancient Xia Nation。

05-04-08 牡山
Mushan
(110,7186E; 34,32453N)

又西三百里，曰牡山[1]。其上多文石[2]，其下多竹箭竹䉋[3]，其兽多㸲牛[4]，羬羊[5]，其鸟多赤鷩[6]。

注释：[1]牡山：读卯山，在濮语中是指猪、朱。今称为朱山，在河南灵宝市朱阳镇。
Notes: [1]mu shan (male mount) reads as mao, in Pu concept means pig, red, today known as the Zhushan (red mount) in Zhuyang township, in Lingbao city, Henan province。
[2] 文石：读卯石，指朱姓氏族。
[2] wen shi (marked stone) read as maoshi, refers to the clans bearing the surname of Zhu。
[3] 竹箭竹䉋：指竹䉋岭的竹䉋氏族。今谐音称走马氏族。
[3] zhu jian zhu mei (bamboo, arrow, bamboo, mei) refers to the Zhumei clan from the Zhumeiling, today known as Zouma tribe, zhumei/zouma are close phonetic matches。
[4] 㸲牛：指琴河氏族，今称前河氏族。
[4] zuo niu (big ox) refers to the Qinhe clan, known today as the Qianhe clan。
[5] 羬羊：指东坡氏族，今谐音称前坡氏族。
[5] qian yang refers to the Dongpo clan, today in a phonetic remake: qianbo clan。
[6] 赤鷩：指运头河氏族，今称董家埝河氏族。
[6] chi bi: refers to the Yuntouhe River clan, known today as the Dongjianianhe clan, (doing family nian river)。

译文：由熊耳山往西三百里，有座山叫朱山，山的西边住着朱姓氏族，东边住着走马氏族。这里的还住着前河氏族、前坡氏族和运头河氏族。
Translation:
Three hundred li further west from Duantouling Mountain stands Zhushan。On the west side of it live the Zhu clan。On its east side live the Zouma clan。Also living here are the clans of Qianhe, Qianbo and Yuntouhe。

05-04-09 讙举山
Huanjushan
(110,21768E; 34,32621N)

又西三百五十里，曰讙举之山[1]。洛水出焉，而东流注于玄扈之水[2]，其中多马肠之物[3]，此二山洛间也[4]。
凡厘山之首，自鹿蹄之山至于玄扈之山，凡九山，千六百七十里。其神状皆人面兽身[5]。其祠之，毛用一白鸡[6]，祈而不糈，以采衣之[7]。

注释：[1]讙举山：指老爷岭，也称洛岭。讙指头人，老爷；举：指岭。
Notes: [1] huan ju shan: refers to the Laoyeling Mountain。 讙 huan refers to head master or chief, Ju: means ling (mountain range)。
[2] 玄扈水：指巡检水。是洛河的支流。

[2] xuan hu shui: xun jian shui, a tributary of Luohe River。

[3] 马肠之物：肠，由腹误译而来。马腹之物，指莽濮部落。

[3]ma chang zhi wu (horse intestines stuff) a mistake in choosing the Chinese graph, chang should be fu(belly) ma fu zhi wu; Mangpu tribe。Fu/Pu, interchangeable。

[4] 此二山洛间也：金堆山是洛岭的主峰。此二，读崔勒，指金堆。间，指姜、主。

[4]ci er shan luo jian ye

Tr: Jinduishan is the main peak of Luoling, ci-er reads as cui le, refers to Jindui (gold pile), jian: means jiang, refers to chieftain, lord。

[5] 人面兽身：定居的氏族的形象。

[5] ren mian er shou shen (human face beast body), the image of the clans who settled down。

[6] 白鸡：指一般的玉。白读玤音。

[6] bai ji(white chicken)refers to the average class jade， bai/bo。

[7] 以采衣之：其他的相同。以采，指其它；衣，指同。

[7] yi cai yi zhi: same as the rest, yicai, rest, yi: same。

译文：由朱山往西三百五十里，有座山叫老爷岭，又称巡检岭、洛岭。洛水从山间流出，向东流入巡检河。河边住着莽濮部落氏族，金堆山是洛岭的主峰。

综观中部第四列山系，东自上原，西至巡检山，共有九座山，延绵一千六百七十里。这些山的山神，都是原住居民的形象。祭祀时，传达祭词用一般的玉，祈祷而不用食物，其他的仪式相同。

Translation:

Three hundred and fifty li further west from Zhushan stands the Laoyeling Mountain。 Its other names are Xunjianling, or Luoling。 Luo River flows out of the mountains and goes east into the Xunjian River。 The Mang Pu clans and tribes live along the river, Jinduishan is the main peak of Luoling。

In sum, the 4th list of the mountains in the middle part starts with Shangyuan in the east and ends with Xunjianshan in the west。 Totalling 9 mountains, the list covers a distance of 1,670 li。 The mountain deities are in the images of the original settlers of the place。 When sacrificing to the mountain deities, a piece of average jade is used, votive speech is not accompanied by food, the rest of the rite is the same。

中山经第五山系

Book 5 Zhongshanjing；chapter 5

05-05-01 薄山 苟床山

Boshan Gouchuangshan

（100,14077E；37,32437N）

中次五经薄山[1]之首，曰苟床之山[2]，无草木[3]，多怪石[4]。

注释：[1]薄山：指博羲山系，这里指博羲部落联盟的山脉，也称包牺氏区域的山脉。

[1]bo shan (thin mount) refers to the Bo Xi mountains of the Boxi tribal confederacy, also known as the Baoxi Shi mountain area。

[2] 苟床山：指刚察山，在青海刚察县。也称尕曲山。

[2] gou chuang shan: refers to Gangcha Mountain, in Gangcha county, Qinghai province。 The mountain is also known as Gaqushan。gangcha/Gaqu, close phonetic match。

[3] 无草木：游牧部落地区。

[3] wu cao mu (no grass wood): nomadic area。

[4] 怪石：指尕曲氏族。怪、尕谐音。也称刚察氏族。

[4] guai shi (strang stone) refers to the Gaqu tribe, guai/ga/gang, close phonetic match , the Gaqu tribe is also known as Gangcha tribe。

译文：中山经第五列山系是博山山脉，最西边的山叫刚察山，是游牧部落地区，住着尕曲氏族。

Translation:

The 5th system of the mountains in the middle area is the Boshan Mountains。 The west most mountain is the Gangchashan where the nomads roam。The Gaqu tribe lives there。

05-05-02 首山

Shoushan

（100,62102E；36,28283N）

东三百里，曰首山[1]，其阴多榖柞[2]，其草多术（zhu）芫[3]，其阳多㻬琈之玉[4]，木多槐[5]。其阴有谷，曰机谷[6]，多䖪鸟[7]，其状如枭而三木，有耳[8]，其音如录[9]，食之已垫[10]。

注释：[1]首山：指共和山，又称日月山。在青海湟源南侧，这里实际介绍的是湟源。

Notes:[1] shou shan (head mount) the Gongheshan also the Riyueshan (sun moon mountain, situated to the south of the Huangyuan county, Qinghai province。 This is descriptive of the Huangyuan county, (source of the Huang River) 。

[2] 古柞：指根照，即大山根氏族。

[2]gu zuo: read as genzhao, refers to the Dashangen (big mountain root) tribe。

[3] 术芫：指岔河氏族。

[3] shu wu: the Chahe River tribe, char/cha/fork

[4] 㻬琈玉：指火焰坡夷。羌语、彝语读火为夺，夺、㻬谐音。

[4] tuo fu yu： refers to the Huoyanpo Yi, In Qiang/Yi language, huo(fire)reads as tuo, duo /tuo a close phonetic match。

[5]槐：指湟水氏族。

[5] huai: Huangshui tribe, huai/huang, close phonetic match。

[6] 机谷：指助国。有互助县的东助国相对应。今称大通。

[6] ji gu; zhu guo, close phonetic remake, corresponding to the Dongzhuguo in Huzhu county。 Dongzhuguo is known today as Datong。

[7] 䖪鸟：指土僚，土族的濮语称谓，今称土族。

[7] tuo niao; refers to Tu lao, a Pu concept, the Tu people,

[8] 枭而三目有耳：大通的外支系牧族。通读 shi, 谐音枭。

[8] xiao er san mu you er（owl with three eyes and have ear)

Tr; Datong tribes outside lineage herders。 Tong/shi/xiao: a phonetic remake。

[9]录：指元树尔。濮语称元为录。

[9]lu(record) refers to Yuanshu'er, yuan, Pu concept of Lu, lu/yuan, same meaning。

[10] 已垫：指坝沟夷，今称土族。垫，即甸，指坝子。坝沟在内蒙古察哈尔南部。
[10] yi dian: refers to the Baigou Yi, today known as the Tujia, Tu people, dian/bazi, a flatland in the mountains。Bagou is situated in the south part of Chaha'er in Inner Mongolia。

译文：由刚察山往东三百里，有座山叫共和山。山的北面住着大山根氏族，住在此地的游牧民是岔河口氏族。山的南面住着火焰坡氏族，管理氏族为湟水氏族。共和山北面有一个国家，叫助国，住着土僚，是大通的外支系牧族，住在元树尔，是古老的坝沟夷。
Translation：
Three hundred li east from Gangchashan stands Gongheshan。 On its north the Dashangen tribe live。 The nomadic tribes living here are the Chahekou tribe。On the south of the mountain, the Huoyanpo tribe live with their management tribe, the Huangshui tribe。 A nation known as Zhu Guo is on the north side of the mountain。They are the Tu Lao, Datong's outside branch living in Yuanshu'er， the ancient Gouba Yi。

05-05-03 县斸山
Xianzhushan
（102,03154E；35,93765N）

又东三百里，曰县斸之山[1]，无草木[2]，多文石[3]。

注释：[1]县斸山：读羲注山，指望尖山、扎尖山。在青海扎尖县。
Notes: [1] xian zhu shan: reads as xi zhu shan; refers to Wangjianshan or Zhajianshan ,situated in Zhajian county, Qinghai province。
[2] 无草木：游牧部落地区。
[2] wu cao mu (no grass wood): nomadic area.
[3] 文石：指马克唐氏族。文读闷，谐音马。
[3] wen shi: refers to the Maketang tribe, wen/ma, close phonetic match。

译文：由共和山往东三百里，有座山叫扎尖山，是游牧部落地区，住着马克唐氏族。
Translation:
Three hundred li eastwards from the Gonghe Mountain， stands the Zhajian Mountain。 This is the nomadic region, the Maketang tribes live there。

05-05-04 葱聋山
Conglongshan
（102,99378E；35,49224N）

又东三百里，曰葱聋之山[1]，无草木[2]，多【广夆】石[3]。

注释：[1]指仓寨山，即霍尔仓香告山。聋，读陇，指寨。在甘肃临夏县城南侧。
Notes: [1] cong long shan (onion deaf mount) refers to the Horcangxianggao Mountain。 Long/deaf, refers to zhaizi (village on the hills) to the south of the Linxia county, Gansu Province。
[2] 无草木：游牧部落地区。
[2] wu cao mu (no grass wood) nomadic area。
[3] 【广夆】石：指巴氏族，即多支巴氏族。多支巴，指历夏人，今称临夏人。
[3] feng shi: refers to the tribes bearing the surname of Ba, Duozhiba, a community of many branches belonging to the Ba, Lixia people, or Linxia people。

译文：由扎尖山往东三百里，有座山叫仓寨山，是游牧部落地区，住着多支巴氏族。
Translation:
Three hundred li eastwards from Zhajianshan stands Cangzhaishan, a nomadic area where the Duozhiba tribes live。

05-05-05 条谷山
Tiaogushan
(103,86418E；35,37416N)

东北五百里，曰条谷之山[1]，其木多槐桐[2]，其草多芍药[3]，虋冬[4]。

注释：: [1]条谷山：指洮国山，在今甘肃临洮县城。
Notes: [1] tiao gu shan (strip vale mount) refers to Taoguo Mountain, in today's Lintao county seat in Gansu province。
[2] 槐桐：指灵洮氏族，今称临洮氏族。
[2] huai tong refers to Lingtao tribes, today known as Lintao tribes。
[3] 芍药：指寻街，今称线街。其草在此指人、人群。
[3] shao yao (peony) refers to Xun Jie（street）， today known as Xian Jie, qi cao (its grass) refers to people, crowds。
[4] 虋冬：指绸衣氏族，即绸衣商贩族群。
[4] men dong refers to silk trade tribes, engaged in trading of silk clothes。

译文：由仓寨山往东北五百里，有座山叫洮国山，那里的管理氏族是灵洮氏族，人群是寻街的绸衣商贩族群。
Translation:
Five hundred li northeast from Cangzhaishan, stands Taoguoshan。 The Lingtao tribes are the management entity, its Xunjie people are engaged in the Silk trading。

05-05-06 超山
Chaoshan
（103,87742E；35,43304N）

又北十里，曰超山[1]，其阴多苍玉[2]，其阳有井[3]，冬有水而夏竭[4]。

注释：[1]超山：指处女川，又称莲儿川、连儿川，今甘肃临洮县十里铺镇。
Notes:[1] chao shan (overtake mount) refers to Chunvchuan(virgin vale river) also known as Lianerchuan (Lotus River), or Lianerchuan(joint river)， in today's Shilipu(ten mile village) township in Lintao county, Gansu province。
[2] 苍玉：指程家铺氏族。
[2] cang yu (dark jade) refers to Chengjiapu tribes。
[3]井：读纪，指部落。竭，也指部落。
[3] jing (water well), reads as ji: meaning tribes, jie: also meaning tribes。
[4] 冬有水而夏竭：指花川坪的夏部落。冬，读堵，指坪；有水，读仰韶，指花川。
[4] dong you shui er xia jie (winter has water, summer dry)
Tr; refers to the Xia tribes at Huachuanping。dong(winter)du, ping, youshui (has water) reads as Yangshao, meaning Huachuan (flower valley) 。

译文：由洮国山往北十里，叫处女川，它的北面住着程家铺氏族，它的南面有一个部落，是花川坪的夏部落。

Translation:
Ten li further north from Taoguoshan is the Chunvchuan River。To its north live the Chengjiapu tribes。 To its south, there is a tribe from Huachuanping, of the Xia tribes。

05-05-07 成侯山
Chenghoushan
（105,19906E；35,70387N）

又东五百里，曰成侯之山[1]，其上多櫄木[2]，其草多芃[3]。

注释：[1]成侯山：指清爽山，读音成侯，今称哼喉山，在甘肃会宁县瞿家所镇西侧。
Notes:[1] cheng hou shan: refers to Qingshuangshan, reads as chenghou, known today as Henghoushan。 In the west side of Dijiasuo Township, Huining county, Gansu Province。
[2] 櫄木：读羲木，指红窑。
[2] xun mu reads as xi mu referring to Hongyao (red kiln) 。
[3]芃：读铺，指陶艺氏族。
[3] fan reads pu, refers to the pottery tribes。

译文：由处女川往东五百里，有座山叫清爽山，山的西面是红窑，住在此地的人群是陶艺族群。
Translation:
Five hundred li eastward from Chunvchuan stands Qingshuangshan。On its west live the Hongyao people, they are the pottery tribes。

05-05-08 朝歌山
Chaogeshan
(105,19906E; 35,85706N)

又东五百里，曰朝歌之山[1]，谷多美垩[2]。

注释：[1]朝歌山又称朝那邑。在今宁夏彭阳县古城镇，在此仍称原名。
Notes:[1] chao ge shan (morning song mount) also known as Chaonayi in today's Guchengzhen, Pengyang county, Ningxia province。The same name lives on。
[2] 美垩：指碱沟卧氏族。卧指山南，山脚下。
[2] mei e: mei(pretty)reads as mo(rich)shares the same meaning with bang, fang, a close phonetic to Peng Peng/fang/bang, refers to the Pengya tribe。

译文：由清爽山往东五百里，有座朝歌山，那个国家住着碱沟卧氏族。
Translation:
Five hundred li eastwards from Qingshuangshan stands Chaogeshan。 In that nation, the Jiangouwo tribe lives。

05-05-09 槐山
Huaishan
(107,75193E; 35,89919N)

又东五百里，曰槐山[1]，谷多金锡[2]。

注释：[1]槐山：指白马铺镇，简称马山，在今甘肃庆阳市白马铺镇。马读音胡，和槐谐音。

Notes [1] huai shan (huai tree)
Tr: refers to Baimapuzhen, shortened to Mashan, in today 's Baimapuzhen, Qingyang city, Gansu province。Ma, reads as Hu, a phonetic pun to Huai。

[2] 金锡：指戴岭氏族，金指岭，锡指捋，戴。

[2] jin xi (gold tin) refers to Dailing tribes, Jin: mountain range, xi: stroke or wear。

译文：由朝歌山往东五百里，有座山叫马山，这个国家住着戴岭氏族。

Translation:

Five hundred li further east from Chaogeshan stands Mashan; in this country live the Dailing tribes live。

05-05-10 历山

Lishan

(107,86581E; 35, 91401N)

又东十里，曰历山[1]，其木多槐[2]，其阳多玉[3]。

注释：[1]历山：指楼山，今称高楼乡。

Notes:[1] li shan: Loushan （building mount） known today as Gaolouxiang (tall building county) 。

[2]槐：指胡同氏族。

[2] huai: refers to the Hutong tribes。

[3]玉：指同，即十字胡同。

[3]yu(jade) meaning: the same as, referring to the Shizihutong (cross lane) 。

译文：由马山往东十里，是楼山，管理氏族为胡同氏族，南面住着十字胡同氏族。

Translation:

Ten li east from Mashan stands Loushan。The manager tribe is the Hutong Shi。 The Shizihutong tribes also live on the south side 。

05-05-11 尸山

Shishan

(107,98268E; 35,88922N)

又东十里，曰尸山[1]，多苍玉[2]，其兽多麋[3]。尸水出焉，南流注于洛水[4]，其中多美玉[5]。

注释：[1]尸山：指视山，也称板桥乡。视指监督，与董同义，尸水即视水，今称县河。

Notes: [1] shi shan (corpse mount) refers to Shishan。Shi: meaning supervise, the same meaning as Dong, know, Shishui is today's Xianhe River。

[2] 苍玉：指塬子夷。今有地名杨家塬子。

[2] cang yu (dark jade) refers to Yuanzi Yi, today a place name Yangjiayuanzi remains。

[3]麋：李姓的濮语读音，这里指李家庄氏族。

[3]mi: Pu concept Li is read as Mi, here refers to the Lijiazhuang tribe。

[4] 洛水：指西河，今称马莲河。

[4] luo shui: Xihe River, today's Malianhe River。

[5] 美玉：指李家沟夷。

[5] mei yu (pretty jade) mei/mi/li, refers to the Lijiagou Yi。

译文：由楼山往东十里，是视山，住着塬子夷，还住着李姓氏族。视水从山间流出，向西南流入马莲河，河边住着李家沟夷。
Translation:
Ten li eastwards from Loushan stands Shishan。The Yuanzi Yi live there, also living here is the tribe bearing the surname of Li。Shashi River flows out of the mountains, goes southwest into Malianhe River。 The Lijiagou Yi live along the river。

05-05-12 良余山
Liangyushan
(108,5288E; 35,82898N)

又东十里，曰良余之山[1]，其上多穀柞，无石[2]。余水[3] 出于其阴，而北流注于河 [4]；汝水[5]出于其阳，而南流注于洛[6]。

注释：[1]良余山：良余读 na yi，指太我山，今指太莪山。
Notes: [1] liang yu shan: liang Yu read as na yi, refers to Taiwoshan, todays' Tai'eshan。
[2] 穀柞无石：指关村部落氏族。
[2] gu zhuo wu shi: the Guancun tribes。
[2] 余水：指莪水。
[3] yu shui; refers to Eshui River。
[4]河：指县河。
[4] he: river, refers to the Xianhe River。
[5] 汝水：指川子水，实际上指北川子水，又称固城河。
[5]ru shui: chuanzishui River, in fact is the Beichuanzishui River, also known as Guchenghe River。
[6]洛：指马莲河。
[6] luo: Malianhe River。

译文：由视山往东十里，是太莪山，它的西面是关村部落氏族。莪水发源于山的北面，向北流入入县河；北川子水发源于山的南面，向南流入马莲河。
Translation:
Ten li east wards from Shishan stands Tai'eshan。The Guancun tribes live to its west。 Eshui River rises out of the north of the mountain and goes north into Xianhe River。Beichuanzishui originates from the south of the mountain and goes south into the Malianhe River。

05-05-13 蛊尾山
Guweishan
（108,5288E；35,82898N）

又东南十里，曰蛊尾之山[1]，多砺石[2]，赤铜[3]。龙余之水[4] 出焉，而东南流注于洛 [5]。

注释：[1]蛊尾山：指固南山，在固城东南侧。
Notes： [1]gu wei shan (poisonous tail mount)
Tr: it refers to Gunanshan (solid south mount) to the southeast side of Gucheng, a local town。
[2] 砺石：指上侍氏族，今称上石庙氏族。
[2]li shi (grinding stone) refers to Shangshi tribes, known today as Shangshimiao tribes。shangshimiao: upper stone temple。

[3] 赤铜：指下侍氏族，今称下石庙氏族。
[3] chi tong (red copper) refers to the Xiashi clan, known today as Xiashimiao tribes。 xiashimiao: lower stone temple。
[4] 龙余水：指僚伊水，即小河子水。
[4] lung yu shui (dragon extra water) refers to Liaoyishui, known also as the Xiaohezishui River。
[5]洛：指洛河，在陕西境内。
[5] luo: refers to Luohe, which is in Shaanxi province。

译文：由太莪山往东南十里，是固南山，那里住着上侍氏族和下侍氏族。小河子水从山间流出，向东南流入洛河。
Translation:
Ten li further southeast from Tai'eshan there stands Gunanshan。 The Shangshi tribes and the Xiashi tribes live there。 Xiaohezishui River flows out of the mountains and goes southeast into the Luohe River。

05-05-14 升山
Sheng Mountain
(109,13287E; 35,89345N)

又东北二十里，曰升山[1]。其木多榖柞棘[2]，其草多藷藇蕙 [3]，多寇脱[4]。黄酸之水[5]出焉，而北流注于河[6]。其中多旋玉[7]。

注释：[1]升山：读蓍山，今称草爬山，实际介绍夏村部落，今称张村驿镇。
Notes: [1] sheng shan (rising mount) reads as Shishan, refers to today's Caopashan, a description of the Xiacun tribes, known now as Zhangcunyi township。
[2] 榖柞棘：指夏村部落。族群有所更迭，只剩遗名下家河。
[2]gu zuo ji refers to the Xiacun tribe, the tribes are different now, the name Xiajiahe remains。
[3] 藷藇蕙：读楚律维，指老鼠沟氏族。
[3] zhu yu hui reads as chu lv wei, refers to the Laoshugou (rat gully) tribes。
[4] 寇脱：指卡桩子氏族，今称卡子沟氏族。
[4] kou tuo: on saddles, refers to the Kazhuangzi tribes, known today as the Kazigou tribes。
[5] 黄酸水：指党河水，黄读音党，黄色读音奢。
[5] huang suan shui (yellow sour water) refers to the Dangheshui River。 huang(yellow) reads as dang, yellow color reads as she。
[6]河：指葫芦河。
[6] he; refers to the Huluhe River。
[7] 旋玉：指猃狁夷，后称匈奴。
[7] xuan yu（turning jade) refers to the Xianyun Yi，later known as the Xiongnu。

译文：由固南山往东北二十里，有座山叫蓍山。那里的管理氏族是夏村部落氏族，人群住着老鼠沟氏族和卡桩子氏族。党河水从山间流出，向北流入葫芦河，河边住着猃狁夷。
Translation:
Twenty li northeast wards from Gunanshan stands Shishan。The manager tribe there is the Xiacun tribes。The people living there are Laoshugou tribes and the Kazhuangzi tribes。 Dangheshui River flows out of the mountains and goes north into Huluh River。 Xianyun Yi lives along the river。

05-05-15 阳虚山
Yangxu Mountain

(109, 38753E; 35,99962N)

又东十二里，曰虚之山[1]，多金[2]，临于玄扈之水[3]。

凡薄山之首，自苟床之山至于阳虚之山，凡十六山（实际 15 山），二千九百八十二里。升山冢也，其祠礼：太牢，婴用吉玉。首山，魋也[4]，其祠用稌、黑牺[5]太牢之具，糵酿[6]；干儛，置鼓[7]；婴用一璧。尸水，合天也[8]，肥牲[9]祠之；用一黑犬[10]于上，用一雌鸡[11]于下，刉一牝羊[12]，献血[13]。婴用吉玉，采之[14]，飨之[15]。

注释 [1]：阳虚之山：指周峁。今称富县县城。阳煦为周，阳煦读成阳虚，是后人理解的变异，今仍称为阳煦山。

Notes:[1] yang xu zhi shan: refers to Zhoumao, today's Fu County seat。 Yangxu means Zhou (the ancient Zhou dynasty), reads as Yangxu, xu: 煦，虚，a mutation by later people。

[2]金：指姬姓氏族。

[2] jin(gold) refers to the tribes bearing the surname of Ji。

[4] 玄扈水：指猃胡水，是洛河富县段的别称。

[4] xuan hu shui: refers to the Xianyunshui River, a different name for part of the Luohe River in Fu County。

[4] 魋也：指轩辕，即首脑山。

[4] shen ye: refers to Xuanyuan, head, the Shounao Mountain。

[5] 黑牺：指赫胥氏。

[5] hei xi (black sacrificial animal) refers to the Hexu Shi。

[6] 糵酿：读量料，指鹿肉。

[6] Nieniang reads as liang liao: refers to deer meat。

[7] 干儛置鼓：勇士列队击鼓。干，读嘎，指勇士，儛。指队伍、列队。

[7] gan wu zhi gu: warriors strike drums in formation。 Gan: ga: warrior. wu: formation。

[8] 合天：赫胥氏的区域。

[8] he tian: area controlled by the Hexu Shi。

[9] 肥牲：指夜晚。

[9] fei sheng (fat animal) refers to night。

[10] 黑犬：指赫胥氏犬戎。

[10] hei quan (black dog) refers to the Hexu Shi Dog Rong。

[11] 雌鸡：指猃狁的游牧部落。

[11]ci ji refers to the Xianyun nomadic tribes。

[12] 刉一牝羊：在同一时候。

[12] kai yi bin yang: at the same time。

[13] 献血：读携糈，指带着食物。

[13] xian xue (donate blood) reads as xiexu, carry food。

[14] 采之：献祭。采，指献、候。

[14] cai zhi: offering in sacrifice, cai: offer, wait。

[15] 飨之：指供奉，给予。飨的濮文是顺时针万字符 "卍"。佛教崇尚施舍，也即此符号。

[15] xiang zhi: offering, give to, the Pu sign for xiang is the clockwise turning cross, the same sign appears in Buddhism for donating, giveaway。

译文：由蓍山往东十二里，是阳煦山，住着姬姓氏族，紧临猃胡河。

综观中山经第五列山系的博（薄）山山脉，从西边的刚察山到东边的阳煦山，共计十六座山（实际只有十五座山），延绵二千九百八十二里。蓍山是东边的宗山，用太牢礼祭祀，用璧玉掩埋。共和山是全山系的首脑山，用荞麦、赫胥氏的太牢礼和鹿肉祭祀；以勇士排列击鼓；用一璧玉掩埋。视水是赫胥氏的区域，在夜晚祭祀；赫胥氏犬戎在西边，猃狁的游牧部落氏族在东边，在同一时候带着食物、掩埋通灵用的璧玉，献祭、供奉。
Translation:
Twelve li eastwards from Shishan stands Yangxushan。The tribes bearing the surname of Ji live there, close to the Xianyunhe River。

In sum: Of the 5th system in the mountains of the middle part, from the westmost Gangchashan to the eastmost Yangxushan, there are a total of 15 mountains, covering a distance of 2,982 li。Shishan is the ancestor's mountain, the highest Tailao rite is observed by burning the Jade Bi。Gongheshan is the head mountain of the whole system, buckwheat, Tailao rite by the Hexu Shi, and deer meat are offered。 Warriors strike their drums in formation。One jade Bi is buried。Gongheshan is the area controlled by the Hexu Shi, they practice rites at night。The Dog rong of Hexue Shi is at the west side。The Xianyun nomadic tribes are on the east side。Choosing a time, both tribes will carry out the sacrificial offering rite with food, Jade Bi as messenger, to be buried。

中山经第六山系

Book 5 Zhongshanjing； chapter 6

05-06-01 缟羝山 平逢山
Gaodishan, Pingfengshan
(112,75034E；34,77624N)

中次六经缟羝山[1]之首，曰平逢之山[2]。南望伊洛，东望穀城之山[3]，无草木，无水[4]，多沙石[5]。有神焉，其状如人而二首[6]，名曰骄虫[7]，是为螫虫[8]，实惟蜂蜜之庐，其祠之，用一雄鸡，禳而勿杀[9]。

注释：[1]缟羝山：指鹤甸山脉。
Notes:[1] gao di shan (white goat mount) refers to the Hedian (crane meadow) Mountain range。
[2] 平逢山：读蚍蜉山，也称邙岭。今为邙岭乡。
[2] ping feng shan (flat sew mount) reads as Pifushan (floating insects and ants mountain), also known as Mangling Mountain。Today it is called Mangling township。
[3] 穀城山：指巩城山。即青龙山。
[3]gu cheng shan (grain town mount) refers to Gongchengshan, also known as Qinglongshan (green dragon mountain) 。
[4] 无草木无水：游牧部落的部落氏族。这里应解读为游牧部落地区。
[4] wu cao mu wu shui (no grass wood no water)
Tr: refers to the nomadic tribes, meaning the territory of the nomads。
[5] 沙石：指外来氏族。
[5] sha shi (sandstone) refers to outside tribes。
[6] 有神焉，人而二首：有一个氏族，是定居的牧族。二首，读勒属，指牧族。
[6] you shen ya, ren er er shou (has god, human with two heads)
Tr: there is a tribe, the settled herders, two heads: reads leshu, refers to the herders。

[7] 骄虫：指北方移民。这里仍用音译表达为缴绰。
[7] jiao chong (proud worms) refers to the northern immigrants, phonetically transliterated as Jiaochao。
[8]螫(shi)虫：指草原移民。
[8] shi chong (sting worm): grassland immigrants。
[9] 蜂蜜之庐：密山（哈密）之民。庐，指民，读音奴。
[9]mi feng zhi lu (hornet honey house)
Tr: refers to Mishan(hami)'s people, Lu means people, reads as nu。
[10] 其祠之，用一雄鸡，禳而勿杀：支系为匈奴部落乌孙戎，即哈萨克族。
[10] qi si zhi (when sacrifice), yong yi xiong ji (use one rooster), xiang er bu sha(pray， not kill)
Tr: its branch belongs to the Wusunrong of the Xiongnu tribes, the Khasaks-- Қазақ / Qazaq / قازاق。

译文：中部第六山系是鹤甸山脉，最东边的地区叫邙岭。那里南望伊河和洛河，东望巩城山，是游牧部落地区，住着外来氏族。有一个氏族，是定居的牧族，名叫缴绰，也是草原移民，实际是密山之民，是匈奴部落的乌孙戎。
Translation：
The 6th mountain system of the middle part is the Hedian Mountain range。Its east most area is the Mangling Mountain。 To its south are the rivers Yihe and Luohe。To its east is the Gongchengshan, a region of the nomads, with outside tribes' settlements。One tribe, a settled herder, known as Jiaochao, a steppe migrant people from Mishan, belongs to the Xiongnu's Wusun Rong。

05-06-02 缟羝山
Gaodishan
(112,62647E；34,81407N)

西十里，曰缟羝之山[1]，无草木[2]，多金玉[3]。

注释：[1]缟羝山：指鹤甸山。在河南孟津县白鹤镇至会盟镇。会盟镇在周之前称白鹤。
Notes: [1] gao di shan (white goat mount)
Tr: refers to the Hedian (crane meadow) mountain。It is between townships of Baihe（white crane) and Huimeng (sign the pack) in Mengjing county， Henan province。Huimeng township is called Baihe before the Zhou dynasty。
[2] 无草木：游牧部落地区。
[2] wu cao mu (no grass wood) refers to the land of the nomads。
[3] 金玉：指贾夷。
[3] jin yu (gold jade) refers to Jia Yi。

译文：由邙岭往西十里，是鹤甸山，是游牧部落地区，住着贾姓氏族。
Translation:
Ten li further west from Manglingshan stands Hedianshan。This is the region of the nomads, where the Jiang tribes live。

05-06-03 瘣山
Guishan
（112,44253E；34,8257N)

又西十里，曰瘣山[1]，其阴多㻬琈之玉[2]，其西有谷，名曰雚谷[3]，其木多柳楮[4]。其中有鸟焉，状如山鸡而长尾[5]，赤如丹火而青喙[6]，名曰鸰【要鸟】[7]，其名自呼，服之不眯[8]。交觞之水[9] 出于其阳，而南流注于洛 [10]；余随之水 [11] 出于其阴，而北流注于榖水[12]。

注释：[1]瑰山：指古岭，今称古庄岭，在孟津县东北侧，实际介绍孟津。
Notes： [1] gui shan: Guling, today's Guzhuang Ling, to the northeast of Mengjing County, a description of Mengjing。

[2] 瑨琈玉：指白滑庄夷，今称滑庄夷。
[2] yun fu yu(jade)
Tr: refers to the Baihuazhuang Yi, known today as the Huazhuang Yi。

[3] 雚谷：孟津县城古称雚国。
[3] huan gu: ancient name for Mengjing county, the Huan Guo。

[4] 柳楮：指瀍河氏族。柳，即流，读劳音，指河；楮、瀍谐音。
[4] liu zhu (willow wood) refers to the Chanhe River tribes。Liu/willow, meaning rio, flowing, reads as Lao/river. zhu/chan, close phonetic match。

[5] 山鸡而长尾：外部落的游牧夷。
[5] shan ji er chang wei (mount chicken with long tail)
Tr: refers to the outsider tribes of the nomadic people。

[6] 赤如丹火而青喙：犬戎牧羊族的东支系。
[6] chi ru dan huo er qing hui (red as cinnabar fire with green beak)
Tr: the east branches of the Dogrong's herders' tribes。

[7]鸰【要鸟】：指朝阳氏族。
[7] ling yao: refers to the Chaoyang (rising sun) tribes。

[8] 不眯：指密山氏族。
[8] bu mi (not squant eyes) refers to the Mishan tribes。

[9] 交觞水：指瀍河水。
[9] jiao shang shui (cross winecups water) refers to Chanhe River。

[10]洛：洛河。
[10] luo: Luohe River

[11] 余随水：指长秋沟水，这里简称为长秋水。
[11]yu sui shui: refers to the Changqiugoushui (long autumn water) River。

[12] 榖水：指古庄河。
[12]gu shui (grain water) refers to the Guzhuanghe River。

译文：由鹤甸山往西十里，有座山叫古岭，山的北面住着滑庄氏族，西面有一个国家，管理氏族为瀍河氏族。这里有一群人，是外部落的犬戎，是犬戎牧羊族的东部支系，名叫朝阳氏，他们自己也这样称呼，是胡族的密山氏族。瀍河水从山的南面流出，向南流入洛河；长秋沟水从山的北面流出，向北流入古庄河。
Translation:
Ten li further west from Hedianshan stands the Gulingshan。 On its north side live the Huazhuang tribes。 On its west there is a nation, its management tribe is the Chanhe tribe。 There lives another group of people, the outsider tribe from the Dogrong。Known as the Chaoyang Shi, they address themselves thus, they are the east branch of herders Dogrong, Hu people from the Mishan tribes。 Chanhe River flows out of the south of the mountain and flows south into Luohe River。 Changqiugou River flows out of the north of the mountain and goes north into the Guzhuang River。

05-06-04 瞻诸山
Zhanzhushan
（111,87526E；34,74661N）

又西三十里，曰瞻诸之山[1]，其阳多金[2]，其阴多文石[3]。谢水[4]出焉，而南流注于洛；少水[5]出其阴，而北流注于穀水[6]。

注释：[1]瞻诸山：指则茹山，意为麻仓山，今义马市城区。茹，读 zhu 音。
Notes:[1] zhan zhu shan (look various mount)
Tr: refers to Zerushan, meaning Macangshan (hemp storage mountain), in today Yima city quarter。 Ru: reads as zhu。
[2]金：指江岭氏族。岭读金音。
[2] jin(gold) refers to the Jiangling tribe。Ling (range) reads as jin。
[3] 文石：石门氏族。
[3] wen shi (marking stone) refers to the Shimen (stone gate) tribes。
[4] 谢水：指谢湾水。
[4] xie shui: refers to the Xiewanshui River。
[5] 少水：指畛水。
[5] shao shui (young river) refers to Zhenshui River。
[6] 穀水：指夏河，黄河仰韶流域的古称谓。
[6]gu shui (grain water) refers to Xiahe River, the ancient name for Yangshao area in the Yellow River catchment。

译文：由古岭往西三十里，有座山叫则茹山，南面住着江岭氏族，北面住着石门氏族。谢湾水从山间流出，向南流入洛河；畛水从北面流出，向北流入夏河。
Translation:
Thirty li further north from Gulingshan stands Zerushan。 The Jiangling tribes live to the south, and the Shimen tribes live to the north。Xiewanshui River rises from the mountains and goes south into the Luohe River。Zhenshui River rises from the north of the mountain and goes north into the Xiahe River。

05-06-05 娄涿山
Louzhuoshan
（111,56796E；34,71462N）

又西三十里，曰娄涿之山[1]，无草木[2]，多金玉[3]。瞻水出于其阳[4]，而东流注于洛；陂水[5]出于其阴，而北流注于穀水[6]，其中多茈石[7]、文石[8]。

注释：[1]娄涿山：指石硖山，今义马市观音堂镇。硖，指山冲，濮语读 zhu 音，与涿谐音。
Notes:[1] lou zhuo shan: refers to Shixiashan, known today as the Guanyintang township in Yima city。 xia/gorge reads as zhu in Pu speech, a close phonetic match to zhuo。
[2] 无草木：游牧部落地区。
[2] wu cao mu (no grass wood) refers to the region of the nomads。
[3] 金玉：指岭上夷。
[3] jin yu (gold jade) refers to the Lingshang Yi。
[4] 瞻水：指昌河。
[4] zhan shui: refers to Changhe River。
[5] 陂水：指涧河，今称涧底河。涧，读 bi 音。
[5]bi shui: refers to Jian River, today it is known as Jiandihe River, jian is read in Pu speech as bi。
[6] 穀水：指夏河，黄河仰韶流域的古称谓。
[6]gu shui (grain water） refers to Xiahe River, the ancient name for the Yangshao region in the Yellow River catchment。

[7] 茈石：指杨厓氏族。
[7]ci shi: refers to the Yangya tribes。
[8] 文石：指南厓氏族，今只遗名东厓。
[8] wen shi: refers to the Nanya tribes, with a relic name found in Dongya。

译文：由则茹山往西三十里，有座山叫石硖山，是游牧部落地区，住着岭上夷。昌水从山的南面流出，向东流入洛河；涧水从山的北面流出，向北流入夏河，河边住着杨厓氏族和南厓氏族。
Translation:
Thirty li further west from Zerushan stands Shixiashan, a region of the nomads。 The Lingshang Yi lives here。The changshui River rises from the south of the mountain and flows east into the Luohe River。 Jianshui River rises from the north of the mountain and flows north into the Xiahe River。The Yangya tribes and the Nanya tribes live along the riverbanks。

05-06-06 白石山
Baishishan
（111,3983E；34,5595N）

又西四十里，曰白石之山[1]。惠水[2] 出于其阳，而南流注于洛，其中多水玉 [3]；涧水 [4] 出于其阴，北流注于穀水 [5]，其中多麋石[6]、栌丹[7]。

注释：[1]白石山：此山名已经汉译，山上有遗存名白石崖村。
Notes： [1] bai shi shan (white stone mount) this is a Chinese translation; a relic name is found in Baishiyan (white stone cliff) village。
[2] 惠水：指浑春河。
[2] hui shui: refers to the Hunchunhe (muddy spring) River。
[3] 水玉：指河滨夷。
[3] shui yu (water jade) refers to the Hebin （riverside) Yi。
[4] 涧水：今称涧河，又称青龙涧河。
[4] jian shui (brook water) known today as Jianhe River, otherwise known as Qinglongjian (green dragon brook) 。
[5] 穀水：指夏河，黄河仰韶流域的古称谓。
[5]gu shui (grain water) refers to Xiahe River, the ancient name for the Yangshao region in Yellow River's catchment。
[6] 麋石：指李姓氏族。
[6]mi shi: refers to the tribes bearing the surname of Li。
[7] 栌丹：指城镇氏族，即三门峡集镇氏族。
[7]lu dan (wax tree) refers to the Chengzhen(township) tribes, also known as the Sanmenxia (three gate gorges) tribes。

译文：由石硖山往西四十里，有座山叫白石山。浑春水从山的南面流出，向南流入洛河，那里住着河滨夷；涧水从山的北面流出，向北流入夏水，那里住着李姓氏族和城镇氏族。
Translation:
Forty li further west from Shixiashan stands Baishishan。Hunchunhe River rises from the south side of the mountain and flows south into the Luohe River。The Hebing Yi lives along the river。 Jianshui River flows from the north of the mountain, and flows north into the Xiashui River, where live the tribes bearing the surname of Li and the tribes of the township。

05-06-07 穀山
Gushan

（110,95165E；34,61176N）

又西五十里，曰穀山[1]，其上多穀，其下多桑[2]。爽水[3] 出焉，而北流注于穀水，其中多碧绿 [4] 。

注释：[1]穀山：指函谷山。在河南灵宝县函谷关镇西南侧。
Notes: [1]gu shan (grain mount) refers to Hanguguan Mountain。 It is located to the southwest of the Hanguguan township in Lingbao county, Henan province。
[2]桑：指凤坪氏族，谐音称稠桑氏族。
[2] sang(mulberry) refers to the Fengping tribes, a phonetic match to Chousang tribes。
[3] 爽水：指雷沟水。雷，读绍音，谐音称爽。
[3] shuang shui (cool water) refers to the Leigoushui River, Lei(thunder) reads as shao, a close phonetic match to shuang。
[4] 碧绿：读沘鲁，指河边氏族。
[4]bi lv (clear green) reads bi lu, refers to riverside tribes。

译文：由白石山往西五十里，有座山叫函谷山。西边住着函谷氏族，东边住着稠桑氏族。雷沟水从山间流出，向东北流入函谷河，那里住着河边氏族。
Translation:
Fifty li further west from Baishishan stands Hangushan。 The Hangu tribes live on the west side。 The Chousang tribes live on the east side。Leigoushui River rises from the mountain, and goes northeast into the Hanguhe River, along its riverbanks live the Hebian tribes。

05-06-08 密山
Mishan
（110,55183E；34,54475BN）

又西七十二里，曰密山[1]，其阳多玉[2]，其阴多铁[3]。豪水[4] 出焉，而南流注于洛 [5] ，其中多旋龟 [6] ，其状鸟首而鳖尾 [7] ，其音如判木 [8] 。无草木。

注释：[1]密山：指眉山，在河南灵宝县故县镇,
Notes: [1]mi shan (secret mount) refers to Meishan (brows mount) , in today's Guxian township, Baoling county, Henan province。
[2]玉：读河滨氏族。河指枣乡河。
[2] yu(jade) refers to the Hebin tribe, He (river) refers to the Zaoxianghe River。
[3]铁：按磨头村氏族。
[3] tie (iron) refers to the Motou Village tribes。
[4] 豪水：读哈水，指芦苔水。芦，读哈音。并且向北流入黄河，汉语翻译为洛，有误。
[4] hao shui (big water) reads as Hashui, meaning the Lutaishui River。 Lu/ha, the river flows north into the Yellow River。The Chinese text has it translated into Luoshui, which is a mistake。
[5]洛：这里指黄河。
[5] luo: refers to the Yellow River。
[6] 旋龟：指轩辕后裔，今称北帝王村氏族。
[6] xuan gui (turning turtle) refers to the descendants of Xuanyuan Shi。Today they are known as the Beidiwangcun (northern emperor village) tribes。
[7] 鸟而鳖尾：僚族的河边夷。
[7] niao er bie yi (bird with turtle tail)

Tr: The Lao/Liao tribes of the riverside, the Hebian Yi。

[8] 判木：读盘陌，指河坎上，今称盘东和盘西。

[8] pan mu (judgement wood) reads as Panmo, meaning on the river curbs。 Today, it is called Pandong (east of Pan) and Panxi (west of Pan) 。

译文：由函谷山往西七十二里，有座山叫眉山，山的南面住着河滨氏族，北面住着磨头村氏族。芦苔水从山间流出，向北流入黄河，河边住着轩辕后裔，是僚族的河边夷，住在河坎上。这里是游牧部落地区。

Translation:

Seventy and two li further west from Hangushan stands Meishan。The Hebin tribes live on the south side of the mountain, and the Motoucun tribes live on the north side of the Mountain。 Lutaishui River rises from the mountains and flows north into the Yellow River。The descendants of Xuanyuan Shi live along the riverbanks, they are the Hebian Yi of the Liao tribes occupying the river curbs。This is the land of the nomads。

05-06-09 长石山

Changshishan

（109,98057E；34,7974N）

又西百里，曰长石之山[1]，无草木，多金玉[2]。其西有谷焉，名曰共谷[3]，多竹[4]。共水出焉，西南流注于洛[5]，其中多鸣石[6]。

注释：[1]长石山：读丘舍山，指坡河山，今称婆合山，在陕西大荔县。

Notes:[1] chang shi shan (long stone mount) reads as Qiusheshan, refers to the Boheshan, known today as Poheshan (mother-in-law harmony mount), in Dali County, Shaanxi province。

[2] 金玉：指邓姓氏族。这里指邓庄夷。

[2] jin yu (gold jade) refers to the Deng tribes, here means Dengzhuang (deng village) Yi。

[3] 共谷：指共国，又称同国，大荔县的古称谓，今陕西大荔县。

[3] gong gu (common vale) refers to the Gong Guo, also known as Tong (same) Guo, an ancient name for today's Dali County in Shaanxi province。

[4]竹：读则，指铁姓氏族。

[4] zhu(bamboo) reads as ze, refers to the tribes bearing the surname of Tie(iron)。

[5]洛：洛河。共水实际向东南流入洛河。

[5] luo: the Luohe River, the Gongshui River takes a southeast course to empty into the Luohe River。

[6] 鸣石：指埝头氏族。埝、粘，读么，谐音鸣。

[6] ming shi (humming stone) refers to the Niantou tribes。Nian (sticky) reads as mo, a close phonetic match to ming(humming)。

译文：由眉山往西一百里，有座山叫坡河山，是游牧部落地区，住着邓庄氏族。山的西面有一个国家，叫荔国，住着铁姓氏族。荔水从那里流出，向东南流入洛河，河边住着埝头氏族。

Translation:

One hundred li further west from Meishan stands the Boheshan, the region of the nomads。 The Dengzhuang tribes live here。On the west of the mountain, there is a country called Liguo nation, the Tie tribes live here。 Lishui River flows out of there and flows southeast into the Luohe River。 The Niantou tribes live along its riverbanks。

05-06-10 傅山

Fushan

（109,18026E；34,74798N）

又西一百四十里，曰傅山[1]，无草木，多瑶碧[2]。厌染之水[3] 出于其阳，而南流注于洛 [4] ，其中多人鱼 [5] 。其西有林 [6]焉，名曰墦冢 [7] 。榖水[8] 出焉，而东流注于洛，其中多珚玉[9]。

注释：[1]傅山：上官山。上官，濮语读鲁乌、立乌，谐音莲湖。濮语乌、湖不分，又演变成富音。今称富平县。
Notes: [1] fu shan (teacher mount) refers to the Shangguanshan (upper official mountain) 。In Pu speech it reads as luwu, or liwu; a close phonetic match to lianhu, (lotus lake) 。In Pu speech, Wu and Hu is not distinguished, and it shifted to Fu, therefore becomes Fuping county。

[2] 瑶碧：指洛瑶碧，即石川河。这里指石川河氏族。
[2] yao bi: refers to Luoyaobi, the Shichuanhe River, here it refers to the Shichuanhe tribes。

[3] 厌染水：指迤惹水，即迤镇水。石川河之阳指北面。
[3] yan ran shui (disgusted dye water) refers to the Yireshui, or the Yizhenshui River, Shiyang River's Yang side refers to the northern side of the river。

[4]洛：指石川河。
[4] luo: refers to the Shichuanhe River。

[5] 人鱼：指集镇夷。这里指迤镇夷。
[5] ren yu(human fish)refers to township people, the Yizhen Yi。

[6]林：指令，即定居点。也称聚落。
[6] lin(forest) meaning Ling(order) refers to settlement, collection of hamlets。

[7] 墦冢：指苇村。今谐音称忽周村。
[7] pan zhong: refers to Wei (reeds) village, today it is phonetically matched into Huzhou Village。 pan/hu, zhong/zhou。

[8] 榖水：指交水，
[8]gu shui: refers to Jiaoshui River。

[9] 珚夷：指石川夷。
[9] yin yi: refers to Shichuan Yi。

译文：由坡合山往西一百四十里，有座山叫上官山，是游牧部落地区，住着石川河氏族。迤镇水发源于北面，向南流入石川河，河边住着迤镇夷。西边有一个聚落，名叫忽周村。交水从那边流出，向东流入石川河，河边住着石川夷。

Translation:

One hundred and forty li further west from Boheshan stands Shangguanshan。 This is the region of the nomads。The Shichuanhe tribes live here。Yizhen River rises from the north and flows south into Shichuanhe River。The Yizhen Yi lives along the riverbanks。 On the west side there is a settlement called Huzhoucun village。Jiaoshui River flows out of there, flows east into the Shichuanhe River。 The Shichuan Yi lives along the riverbanks。

05-06-11 橐山
Tuoshan
（108,9474E；34,897N）

又西五十里，曰橐山[1]，其木多樗[2]，多備木[3]，其阳多金玉[4]，其阴多铁[5]，多萧[6]。橐水[7] 出焉，而北流注于河 [8] 。其中多脩辟之鱼 [9] ，状如黾而白喙 [10] ，其音如鸱 [11] ，食之已白癬 [12] 。

注释：[1]橐山：读棠山，指泥山。在陕西耀州，今谐音称铜川。

Notes: [1] tuo shan (bellow mount) reads as Tangshan, refers to Nishan (mud mount) known today as Tongchuan (copper river in today's Yaozhou, Shaanxi province。

[2]樗：指崔姓氏族。

[2] chu: refers to the tribes bearing the surname of Cui。

[3] 備木：指爷氏土目。今称耀氏土目。

[3] bei mu (backup wood) refers to the Yeshitumu, known today as the Yaoshitumu。

[4] 金玉：指丁沟氏族。

[4] jin yu (gold jade) refers to the Dinggou tribes。

[5]铁：读棠，指泥阳氏族。

[5] tie(iron)meaning tang, refers to the Niyang (mud sun) tribes。

[6]萧：指孝氏族。这个姓氏是赫胥氏的代称，以其夜祭习俗如枭的行为而得名，枭、肖、萧、孝由此而来。

[6] xiao: refers to the Xiao tribes, a surname for Hexu Shi, derived from their ritual habit to sacrifice at night as the owls, Xiao: owl, with different Chinese close phonetic matchings。

[7] 橐水：指泥河水。实际为南流，北应指贝。

[7] tuo shui (bellow water) refers to the Niheshui (mud river) River, it flows south, here bei/shell/south。

[8]河：指孝河，濮语称孝沘、脩沘。

[8] he refers to Xiaohe River, in Pu speech, xiaobi, qiubi， bi—river。

[9] 脩辟鱼：指孝河夷。

[9] qiu bi yu (qiubi fish) refers to the Xiaohe Yi。

[10] 黾而白喙：五台山支系。黾，指五。指耀州的五台山。

[10] min er bai hui (turtle white beak) refers to the Wutaishan (five terrace mount) tribes, min meaning Five as in May, refers to the Wutaishan in Yaozhou。

[11]鴟：指东边。

[11] di (owl) refers to the east。

[12] 食之已白癬：古老的博羲夷。

[12] shi zhi yi bai xian (eat it cures white skinspot)
Tr: the ancient Boxi Yi。

译文：由上官山往西北五十里，有座山叫泥山，那里的管理氏族是崔氏和爷氏，南面住着丁沟氏族，北面住着泥阳氏族和孝氏族。泥河水从山间流出，向南流入孝河。这里住着孝河夷，是五台山支系，住在东边，是古老的博羲夷。

Translation:

Fifty li further northwest from Shangguanshan stands Nishan。 The management tribes bearing the surnames of Cui and Ye。On the south side live the Dinggou tribe。The Niyang tribes and the Xiao tribes live on the north side。Nihe River rises from the mountain, flows south into the Xiaohe River。 Here lives the Xiaohe Yi, a Wutaishan branch, they are on the east side, known as the ancient Boxi Shi。

05-06-12 常烝山
Changzheng
（108,64064E；35,05542N）

又西九十里，常烝之山[1]，无草木，多垩[2]。潐水[3] 出焉，而北流注于河 [4]，其中多苍玉 [5] 。菑水[6]出焉，而北流注于河[7]。

注释：[1]常烝山：指造铁山。常烝，读撮则，指造铁。今称铁王山。

Notes: [1] chang zheng Shan refers to the Zaotieshan (make iron mountain) 。Changzhen in Pu speech reads as zuoze, meaning ironmaking, today it is called Tiewangshan (iron lord mountain) 。

[2] 垩：汶的变音，指甘泉氏族。

[2]e (clay)phonetic shifting from wen, meaning river。 It refers to the Ganquan (sweet spring) tribes。

[3] 潐水：楚水的变音，指凉水。实际向南流，北指贝，表示南方。

[3] jiao shui: phonetic shifting from chu shui, meaning cold water。 It goes into south, bei/shell/south。

[4]河：指清水河氏族。

[4] he(river) refers to the Qingshuihe (clear water) tribes。

[5] 苍玉：读楚夷，指凉水夷。

[5] cang yu (dark jade) meaning Chu Yi, the Liangshui (cold water) Yi。

[6] 菑水：指簸箕水。实际向南流，北指贝。

[6] zi shui: refers to Bojishui River, it goes south in fact, bei/shell/south。

[7]河：指泾河。

[7] he(river): refers to Jinghe River。

译文：由泥山往西北九十里，有座山叫造铁山，是游牧部落地区，住着甘泉氏族。凉水从山间流出，向南流入清水河，河边住着凉水夷。簸箕水从山间流出，向南流入泾河。

Translation:

Ninety li further northwest from Nishan stands Zaotieshan。This is the region of the nomads where the Ganquan tribes live。 Liangshui River flows out of the mountain and goes south into the Qingshui River。 The Liangshui Yi lives along the riverbank。 Pojishui River flows out of the mountain and goes south into Jinghe River。

05-06-13 夸父山

Kuafushan

（108,20209E；35,18568N）

又西九十里，曰夸父之山[1]。其木多椶枏[2]，多竹箭 [3] 。其兽多牿牛 [4] 、羬羊 [5] ，其鸟多鷩 [6] 。其阴多玉[7]，其阳多铁[8]。其北有林焉，名曰桃林[9]，是广员三百里[10]，其中多马[11]。湖水[12]出焉，而北流注于河[13]，其中多珚玉[14]。

注释：[1]夸父山：本应解读为北胡山，但其他相关的叙述中没有游牧和胡的概念，在此按北极解读为北部落山。在陕西彬州市义门镇和北极镇。

Notes: [1] kua fu shan (boasting father mount) it meant Northern Hu Mountain, but since there is no information relating the nomadic herding and Hu tribes, I use the concept Northern tribes' Mountain。 It is in the areas of Yimenzhen and Beijizhen, in Binzhou city, Shaanxi province。

[2] 椶枏：指贵族。

[2] zong nan refers to the noble lineage of the tribes。

[3] 竹箭：指旺京氏族。今称旺安氏族。

[3] zhu jian (bamboo arrow) refers to the Wangjing (strong capital) tribes, known today as the Wangan (strong and peaceful) tribes。

[4] 牿牛：指弥家河氏族。牿，指弥；牛，指河。

[4] zuo niu: refers to the Mijiahe tribes. zuo/mi, niu/river。

[5] 羬羊：指东秦氏族。这个记录说明，早期的秦是在陕甘地区。

[5] zhang yang refers to the east Qin tribes。 This record shows that the early Qin people stayed in today's Shanxi and Gansu provinces。

[6]鷩：读憋，指沟老头氏族。憋，指老。

[6] bie： refers to Goulaotou tribes, bie/lao/old。

[7]玉：指玉子氏族。今称南玉子氏族。

[7]yu: jade refers to the Yuzi tribes, today known as the Nanyuzi (south jade) tribes。

[8]铁：指计氏族。

[8] tie (iron) refers to the Ji tribes。

[9] 桃林：指中府，即政治中心，今称福托，两个概念读音相同。桃，指中，读妥；林，指府。

[9] tao lin (peach grove) refers to center hall, meaning political center, today is called Futuo, tao/peach/center/tuo, lin/fu/hall。

[10] 广原三百里：指北夷的边塞都城。三读 sa，指边、外。

[10] guang yuan san bai li (wide plain 300 li) refers to the frontier stronghold center of the Northern Yi, san: reads as sa, meaning outside, frontier， border。

[11]马：指目，即管理氏族。

[11]ma(horse)means mu, (eyes) a coded concept for management tribes。

[12] 湖水：指师家河水。师读湖音。

[12]hu shui (lake water) refers to Shijiaheshui (teacher family river) shi(teacher)reads hu。

[13]河：指泾河。

[13] he refers to Jinghe River。

[14] 珚玉：指阎夷。

[14] yin yu: refers to Yan Yi, a tribe。

译文：由造铁山往西北九十里，有座山叫北部落山，管理氏族为贵族和旺京氏族。这里还住着弥家河氏族、东秦氏族、沟老头氏族。南面住着南玉子氏族，北面住着计氏族。南面有一个府，名叫中府，是北夷的边塞都城，住着管理氏族。师水从山间流出，向南流入泾河，河边住着阎夷。

Translation:

Ninety li further northwest from Zaotieshan stands Beibuluoshan (northern tribes' Mountain) 。 The management tribes there are the noble lineage and Wangjing。Mijiahe tribes, Dongqin tribes, Goulaotou tribes also live here。On the south side, the Nanyuzi tribes live there, and the Ji tribes live on the north side。There is a Hall in the south, called Zhongfu, a frontier stronghold city of the northern Yi。 Shishui River flows out of the mountains and goes south into the Jinghe River。The Yan Yi lives along the riverbanks。

05-06-14 阳华山

Yanghuashan

（107,37022E；35,33664）

又西九十里，曰阳华之山[1]。其阳多金玉[2]，其阴多青雄黄 [3]，其草多藷藇[4]，多苦辛[5]，其状如橚[6]，其实如瓜[7]，其味酸甘[8]，食之已虐[9]。杨水[10]出焉，而东南流注于洛[11]，其中多人鱼[12]。门水[13]出焉，而东北流注于河[14]，其中多玄𥖨[5]。【纟昔】姑之水[16]出于其阳，而东流注于门水，其上多铜[17]。门水出于河，七百九十里入洛水[18]。

凡缟羝山之首，自平缝之山至于阳华之山，凡十四山，七百九十里。岳在其中[19]，以六月祭之，如诸岳之祠法，则天下安宁。

注释：[1]阳华山：指阳泉山，在甘肃平凉市泾川县城。

Notes: [1] yang hua shan (sunny hua mount) refers to the Yangquanshan (sunny spring mountain), in today's Jingchuan County, Pingliang city, Gansu province。

[2] 金玉：指丁氏族。

[2] jin yu (gold jade) refers to the Ding tribes。

[3] 青雄黄：指东贤氏族，今将东演变为端，称端贤氏族。
[3] qing xiong huang (green male yellow) refers to the Dongxian (east virtue) tribes。 Dong is phonetically shifted to Duan(end)so the Duanxian tribes。

[4] 藷萸：指肃慎夷。
[4] zhu xing: refers to the Sushen Yi.

[5] 苦辛：指古兴氏族，今称嘎仙氏族。汉语指夏兴国氏族。
[5] ku xin (bitter spicy) refers to the Guxing tribe, known today as Gaxian tribe。 In Chinese they are called Xiaxingguo tribes。

[6]櫹：指肃慎族。
[6]su; sushen tribes。

[7]瓜：指古兴氏。
[7] gua(melon); refers to the Guxing Shi。

[8] 其味酸甘：且维索嘎，泾川城的古名。
[8] qi wei suan gan (its taste sour sweet) refers to Qieweisuoga, ancient name for Jingchuan city。

[9] 已虐：指游牧夷。本为狩猎夷，南迁后转为游牧业。
[9] yi nue (cure abuse) refers to Youmu Yi, they are previous hunters and turned into herders after southward migration。

[10] 杨水：指杨家崖水，简称杨水。
[10] yang shui (poplar water) refers to Yangjiayashui, shortened to Yangshui, a river name。

[11]洛：指黑河。氐羌语称黑为纳，谐音洛。
[11] luo: refers to Heihe (black river) in Qiang speech, black is read as Na, a phonetic match to luo, N/L is not clearly distinguished。

[12] 人鱼：指狼儿咀夷。人，是濮语狼的读音。
[12] ren yu (human fish) refers to Langerzui Yi, (wolf mouth) ren(human) meaning wolf in Pu speech。

[13] 门水：泾河的泾川段称门水。
[13] men shui (door water) the Jingchuan part of the Jinghe River is also known as Menshui。

[14]河：指蒲河。
[14] he refers to Pu River。

[15] 玄礵：指盖氏肃慎，又称盖郭氏。
[15] xuan xiao (dark xiao) refers to the Gai Shi's Sushen, also known as the Gaiguo Shi。

[16] 【纟 昔】姑水：指乳川河。今谐音称汭河。
[16] xu gu shui: refers to the Ruchuan (milk river), ru is a phonetic match to nei/nai, today's Nahe River。

[17]铜：指中村氏族，今称同中村氏族。
[17] tong (copper) means Zhongcun tribes, known today as Tongzhongcun tribes。

[18] 洛水：实际指渭河。
[18] luo shui: refers to Weihe River。

[19] 岳在其中：冢在青要山。岳、要都是濮语龙的音译，青要山是则茹部落的祭祀山。
[19] yue zai qi zhong (peak is amidst it)
Tr: The ancestor's burial mount is at Qingyaoshan, yue/yao: Pu speech dragon, Qingyaoshan is the Sacrifice Mount of the Zeru tribes。

译文：由北部落山往西九十里，有座山叫阳泉山。山的南面住着丁姓氏族，北面住着东贤氏族，住着肃慎夷，住着古兴氏，是肃慎的古兴氏，住在且维索嘎，是古老的游牧夷。杨水从山间流出，向南流入黑河，河边住着狼儿咀夷。门水从这里流出，向东北流入蒲河，河边住着盖郭氏。汭水从山的南面流出，向东流入门水，汭水的西边住着同中村氏族。门水汇入蒲河后，经过七百九十里水路汇入渭水。

综观鹤甸山系，从邙岭至阳泉山，共计十四座山，延绵七百九十里。青要山为宗山，在六月祭祀，祭祀方法与其他的宗山相同，是这里山系的大佬。
Translation:
Ninety li further west from Beibuluo Mountain stands Yangquanshan。 On the south of the mountain live the Ding tribes, on its north side live the Dongxian tribes, the Sushen Yi, the Guxing Shi of the Sushen tribes。 Residing in Qieweisuoga, they are the ancient nomadic herders, Yangshui River rises from the mountain and flows south into the Heihe River。 The Langerzui tribes live on the riverbanks。 The Menshui River flows out of here, goes northeast into Puhe River。 The Gaiguo Shi live along the riverbanks。 Naishui River flows out of the south side, goes east into Menshui River。 On the west bank live the Tongzhongcun tribes。 Menshui River joins the Puhe River and meanders for another 790 li to empty into Weihe River。

In sum, there are 14 mountains between Mangling and Yangquanshan。 This Hedianshan system covers a distance of 790 li。 Qingyaoshan is the ancestor's mount, Sacrifice is observed in June。 Its procedure is the same as those in other ancestor' mounts。 It is the lord mount of the system。

中山经第七山系

Book 5 Zhongshanjing; chapter 7

05-07-01 苦山 休与山
Kushan, Xiuyushan
（110,43236E；33,87422N）

中次七经苦山[1]之首，曰休与之山[2]，其上有石[3]焉，名曰帝台之棋[4]，五色而文[5]，其状如鹑卵[6]。帝台之石，所以祷百神者也[7]，服之不蛊[8]。有草焉，其状如蓍[9]，赤叶而本丛生[10]，名曰夙条[11]，可以为簳[12]。

注释：[1]苦山：指夏山。
Notes:[1] ku shan (bitter mount): Xiashan (summer mount) 。
[2] 休与山：指羲庾山。羲指红色，又称丹庾山。今称庾岭。在陕西洛南县莽岭。
[2] xiu yu shan: xi yu shan; xi/red, also known as Danyushan, today it is called Yuling Mountain, in Mangling, Luonan county, Shaanxi province。
[3]石：指氏族。
[3] shi(stone): meaning tribes。
[4] 帝台之棋：北方的犬戎。
[4] di tai zhi qi (God terrace chess)
Tr； the Dogrong from the north。
[5] 五色而文：塞族部落南迁的支系。
[5] wu se er wen (five color and marking)
Tr: the branches of Saka that migrated to the south。
[6] 鹑卵：指移民。读绰鲁，谐音鹑卵。
[6] chun luan (quail eggs)

Tr: immigrants, reads as chuolu, a close phonetic match to chun luan。

[7] 所以祷百神者也：塞夷的景部落支系夷。

[7] suo yi dao bai shen zhe ye (so pray 100 deities) 。

Tr: the Jing tribal branches of Saka Yi。

[8] 服之不蛊：胡族的补苦氏。

[8] fu zhi bu gu (taken will not bedeviled)

Tr: The Buku Shi of the Hu tribes。

[9]蓍：指草原地区。

[9] shi (divine grass) refers to the steppe region。

[10] 赤叶而本丛生：犬戎的农业移民氏族。

[10] chi ye er ben cong sheng (red leaf root tangled grow)

Tr: the agricultural tribes of immigrants of the Dogrong。

[11] 夙条：指麦积氏族。

[11]su tiao: refers to the Maiji tribes。

[12] 可以为簳：夏国的有贡献的氏族，有作为的氏族。

[12]ke yi wei gan（capable of backbone)

Tr: the tribes that contributed greatly to Xia nation, backbone tribes。

译文：中部第七列山系是夏山山脉，最西端的一座山叫庚岭。山的西北面有一个氏族，是北方犬戎塞族部落南迁的支系，是移民氏族，是北方氏族的塞夷景部落支系夷，胡族的补苦氏。有一个移民氏族，是草原犬戎的农业移民氏族，名叫麦积氏，是夏国的有贡献的氏族。

Translation:

The 7th system of the mountains in the middle region is the Xiashan Mountains。Its west most mountain is Gengling Mountain。 On its northwest live a tribe of Dogrong Saka's immigrants who moved down south from the north。They are the branches of the Jing tribes of the Saka Yi from the north, the Buku Shi of the Hu people。Another tribe of immigrants is known as the Maiji Shi, a migrant agricultural tribe of the steppe Dogrong, who contributed greatly to the Xia nation。

05-07-02 鼓钟山

Guzhongshan

（111,07499；33,68784N）

又东三百里，曰鼓钟之山[1]，帝台之所以觞百神也[2]。有草焉，方茎而黄华[3]，员叶而三成[4]，其名曰焉酸[5]，可以为毒[6]。其上多砺[7]，其下多砥 [8] 。

注释：[1]鼓钟山：指耿村山，在河南卢氏县瓦窑沟乡北面。

Notes:[1]gu zhong shan (drum bell mount)

Tr: refers to Gengcunshan, to the north of Wayaogouxiang, Lushi county, Henan province。

[2] 帝台之所以觞百神也：北面是丝绸夷的漂洗氏族之乡。

[2] di tai zhi suo yi shang bai shen ye (God terrace for offer to 100 deities)

Tr: its north is where the Sichou (silk) Yi's washing and dyeing tribes live。

[3] 方茎而黄华：指玉皇岭的山南氏族。方茎指皇岭；黄华，古黄卧，指山南。

[3] fang jing er huang hua (square stem yellow flower)

Tr: refers to the Shannan (mount south) tribes from Yuhuang (jade emperor) Ling。 fangjing: huangling, huanghua: guhuangwo, meaning south of the mountain。

[4] 员叶而三成：颜子河的东边支系。

[4]ye yuan er san cheng (round leaf one third ripe)

Tr: the east branches of the Yanzihe tribes。

[5] 焉酸：读音 yan shao，指莲花氏族。这里的莲同年景的年。

[5] yan suan: yan shao, refers to the Lianhua(lotus) tribes. Lian/nian sound same phonetically。

[6] 为毒：读夷毒，指古老夷。

[6] wei du (as poison) reads: yi du: refers to Gulao Yi, ancient people。

[7]砺：指南泥沟氏族。砺，指泥。

[7]li(stone) refers to Nannigou (south mud gully) tribes。li/ni(mud)。

[8]砥：指戴姓氏族，即刘姓氏族。

[8] di (grind) refers to tribes bearing the surname of Die, aka Liu in Chinese。

译文：由庚岭往东三百里，有座山叫耿村山，北面是丝绸夷的漂洗氏族之乡。有一个游牧氏族，是玉皇岭的山南氏族，是颜子河的东边支系，名叫莲花氏，是夏国的古老夷。耿村的西面住着南泥沟氏族，东面住着刘姓氏族。

Translation:

Three hundred li further east from Gengling Mountain, stands Gengcunshan。To its north is the region of the tribes of Silk Yi, engaging in the washing and dyeing of silks。A nomadic tribe, the Shannan tribe from Yuhuangling Mountain, is from the Yanzihe River。 They are known as the Lianhua Shi, the ancient Yi of the Xia nation。 To its west live the Nannigou tribes, to its east live the tribes bearing the surname Liu。

05-07-03 姑媱山

Guyaoshan

（11153858E；33,50328N）

又东二百里，曰姑媱之山[1]，帝女死焉[2]，其名曰女尸[3]，化为䔄草[4]，其叶胥成[5]，其华黄[6]，其实如菟丘[7]，服之媚于人[8]。

注释：[1]姑媱山：读勾饶山，指军龙山，即军马河与龙潭河之山。在河南西峡县双龙镇北面。

Notes： [1]gu yao shan: reads as Gouraoshan, refers to the Junlongshan (army dragon mountain, which is between Junma (army horse) River and Longtan (dragon pond) River, to the north of Shuanglong (double dragon) township, Xixia county, Henan province。

[2] 帝女死焉：北部是游牧氏族之乡。

[2] di nv si yan (God daughter die)

Tr: the northern part is the land of the nomads。

[3] 女尸：指牧肆，今军马河镇。

[3] nv shi (girl corpse)

Tr: herders township, today's Junmahe (army horse river) township。

[4] 化为䔄草：指山南的龙成街，今双龙镇。化为，指山南；䔄草，指龙成。

[4] hua wei yao cao (become grass)

Tr: refers to the Longcheng (dragon complete) street, today it is known as the Shuanglong (double dragon) township。Huawei: south of mountain, yaocao: longcheng。

[5] 其叶胥成：河街换肆。其叶，指河街；胥成，指换肆。

[5] qi ye chu cheng (its leaf xun complete)

Tr: refers to Hejiehuansi, qiya: river street, xucheng: change city。

[6] 其华黄：南山街。

[6] qi hua huang: refers to Nanshan Street。

[7] 菟丘：换街。

[7] tu qiu: refers to huanjie (change street)

[8] 服之媚于人：马家庄的集镇。
[8] fu zhi mei yu ren (taken, flirting other)
Tr: the townships around Majiazhuang (horse family village) 。

译文：由耿村山往东二百里，有座山叫军龙山，北部是游牧氏族之乡，称为牧肆。山南的龙成街，称为河街换肆、南山街、换街，是马家庄的集镇。
Translation:
Two hundred li further east from Gengcunshan stands Junlongshan。Its north part is the region of the nomads, called Musi (herders township) 。South of the mountain there is the Longcheng street, also known as Hejiehuansi, Nanshanjie, Huanjie, those are the townships in Majiazhuang。

05-07-04 苦山
Kushan
（111,78858E；33,36512N）

又东二十里，曰苦山[1]。有兽焉，名曰山膏[2]，其状如逐[3]。赤如丹火[4]，善詈 [5] 。其上有木焉，名曰黄棘 [6]，黄华而员叶[7]，其实如兰[8]，服之不字[9]。有草焉，员叶而无茎[10]，赤华而不实[11]，名曰无条[12]，服之不瘿[13]。

注释：[1]苦山：指夏山，在河南内乡县夏馆镇。
Notes:[1] ku shan (bitter mount) refers to Xiashan Mountain, in today's Xiaguanzhen, Neixiang county, Henan province。
[2] 山膏：读 sa ga，指撒拉族。
[2] shan gao: reads as sa ga, refers to the Sarla ethnic people。
[3]逐：指幢，即五道幢。
[3] zhu (chase) meaning: chuang, a place name of Wudaochuang。
[4] 赤如丹火：游牧的鞑胡。
[4] chi ru dan huo (red as cinnabar fire) 。
Tr: The Da Hu of the nomads。
[5] 善詈：外来黎。黎，指人、民。
[5] shan yan: outside Li, li means person, people。
[6] 黄棘：指黄靳氏。
[6] huang jing (yellow twig) refers to Huangjin Shi。
[7] 黄华而员叶：又称黄华氏。员叶，指又称。
[7] huang hua er yuan ye (huang flower and round leaves)
Tr： refers to Huanghua Shi, yuanye: means aka. also known as。
[8]兰：指僚族。
[8] lan: refers to Lao tribe。
[9] 服之不字：山区的种植氏族。
[9] fu zhi bu zi (taken not produce child)
Tr: the growers' tribes of the mountains。
[10] 员叶而无茎：也称为靳部落氏族。
[10] yuan ye er wu jin (round leaves without stem)
Tr: is known as Jin tribes。
[11] 赤华而不实：游胡的草原氏族。
[11] chi hua er bu shi (red flower no fruits)
Tr: the nomadic steppe tribes。

[12] 无条：指克列部落氏族。简称武条氏。
[12] wu tiao: refers to the Kelie tribes, shortens to Wutiao Shi。
[13] 服之不瘿：胡族的北方氏族。
[13] fu zhi bu ying (taken will not get big neck)
Tr: the northern tribes of the Hu people。

译文：由军龙山往东二十里，有座山叫夏山。有一个氏族，名叫撒拉族，属五道幢的游牧鞑胡，是外来黎。那里有一个管理氏族，名叫黄棘氏，又称黄华氏，是僚族的山区种植氏族。有一个移民氏族，也称靳部落氏族，是游胡的草原氏族，名叫武条氏，是胡族的北方氏族。
Translation:
Twenty li further east from Junlongshan stands Xiashan。There is a Sarla tribe of outside migrants, belonging to Wudaozhong, of the nomadic Da Hu。There is a management tribe known as Huangjin Shi, aka Huanghua Shi。They are the growers' tribes from the mountains of the Lao people。There is another tribe of immigrants, known as Jing tribe, a Hu steppe nomadic tribe。They are called Wutiao Shi, a northern tribe of the Hu people。

05-07-05 堵山
Dushan
（112,13404E；33,11975N）

又东二十七里，曰堵山[1]，神天愚居之[2]，是多怪风雨[3]。其上有木焉，名曰天楄[4]，方茎而葵状[5]。服者不哩[6] 。

注释：[1]堵山：指平顶山，简称平山，在河南省镇平县北面，赵家湾水库旁。
Notes:[1] du shan (blocked mount) refers to the Pingdingshan, shortened to Pingshan, situated in the north of Zhenping county, beside the Zhaojiawan reservoir in Henan province。
[2] 神天愚居之：响水潭氏族部落。神，指氏族；天愚，读滔溢，指响水。
[2] shen tian yu ju zhi (God sky fool resides)
Tr： refers to the Xiangshuitan (noisy water pond) tribes。shen （God): tribes; tianyu: reads as taoyi, (waves full) meaning Xiangshui (noisy water) 。
[3] 怪风雨：指北苇子夷。
[3] guai feng yu (strange wind rain)
Tr: refers to the Beiweizi (north reeds) Yi。
[4] 天楄：指响濮，响水潭濮。
[4] tian bian: refers to Xiang Pu, aka Xiangshuitan (noisy water pond) Pu 。
[5] 方茎而葵状：平部落的北村氏族。
[5] fang jin er kui zhuang (square stem sunflower shape)
Tr: The Beicun (northern village) people of the Ping tribes。
[6] 服者不哩：平山的濮越人。
[6] fu zhe bu ye (taken will not chock)
Tr: The Pu people and Yue people from Pingshan。

注释：由夏山往东二十七里，有座山叫平山，是响水潭氏族的部落所在地，这里住着北苇子夷。西面有一个管理氏族，是平部落的北村氏族，是平山的濮越人。
Translation:
Twenty-seven li further east from Xiashan, stands the Pingshan, where the Xiangshuitan tribes live。The Beiweizi Yi lives here。To the west side of the mountain, there is a management tribe, the Beicun people from the Ping tribes, they are the Pu and Yue people from Pingshan。

05-07-06 放皋山
Fanggaoshan
（112,53702E；33,00354N）

又东五十二里，曰放皋之山[1]。明水[2] 出焉，南流注于伊水 [3]，其中多苍玉[4]。有木焉，其叶如槐[5]，黄华而不实[6]，其名曰蒙木[7]，服之不惑[8]。有兽焉，其状如蜂[9]，枝尾而反舌[10]，善呼[11]，其名曰文文[12]。

注释：[1]放皋山：指宛城，在河南南阳市城区。
Notes:[1] fang gao shan (release gao mount)
Tr: refers to Wangcheng city, in the city quarter of Nanyang city, Henan province。
[2] 明水：指潦河。古以西、秋为明，称明水。
[2] ming shui (bright water) refers to Liao River。 In ancient vocabulary, west or autumn is described as ming, (bright, clear), thus the Mingshui River。
[3] 伊水：指白河。白俊、清秀、伊是相同的概念。
[3] yi shui (yi water) refers to Baihe River, yi: meaning white, handsome, beautiful。
[4] 苍玉：指褚岗夷。
[4] cang yu (dark jade) refers to the Zhugang Yi。
[5]槐：指贵族支系。
[5] huai (Styphnolobium japonicum) refers to the tribes' noble lineage。
[6] 黄华而不实：黄华氏族。
[6] huang hua er bu shi (yellow flower with no fruits) 。
Tr: refers to the Huanghua tribes。
[7] 蒙木：指苗族土目。
[7] meng mu (cover wood)
Tr； refers to the ranking official below the chieftain in Miao tribes。
[8] 服之不惑：东部的贵族。不惑，读补冯，指贵族。
[8] fu zhi bu huo (taken will not get confused)
Tr: refers to the nobles from the east, bu huo: reads as bu feng, meaning nobles。 h/f not to be distinguished。
[9]蜂：指冯部落。
[9] feng(hornet) refers to the Feng tribes。
[10] 枝尾而反舌：沙河地区的管理氏族。
[10] zhi yi er fan she (branch end reverse tongue)
Tr: the management tribe of Shahe (sand river) region。
[11] 善呼：读巳呼，指独山氏族。
[11] shan hu (good at yell) reads: sihu, refers to the Dushan (lonely mount) tribes。
[12] 文文：指白河氏、白水氏。伊水又称白水，读舞汶，谐音文文。
[12] wen wen (marking marking) refers to the Baiheshi (white water) River, Baishui Shi。 Yishui is also called Baishui, reads as wuwen, wenwen, a phonetic match。

译文：由平山往东五十二里，有座山叫宛城山。潦河水从山间流出，向南流入白河，河边住着褚岗夷。有一个管理氏族，属贵族支系，是黄华氏族，称为苗族土目，是东部的贵族。有一个氏族，是冯部落的沙河地区管理氏族，独山夷，名叫白水氏。
Translation:

Fifty-two li further east from Pingshan stands Wanchengshan。The Liaohe River flows out of the mountain, goes south into the Baihe River。The Zhugang tribe lives along the riverbank。 There is a management tribe, a noble lineage known as Huanghua tribe, is the Miao tribes' Tumu。It is the noble lineage of the east part。 Another tribe is the Sha tribes' management tribe of the Shahe region, they are called Dushan Yi, or Baishui Shi。

05-07-07 大【非/古】山
Dagushan
（112,93683E；33,05544N）

又东五十七里，曰大【非/古】之山[1]，多瑨琈之玉[2]，多麋玉[3]。有兽焉，其状叶如榆[4]，方茎而苍伤[5]，其名曰牛伤[6]，其根苍文[7]，服者不厥[8]，可以御兵[9]。其阳狂水[10] 出焉，西南流注于伊水 [11]，其中多三足龟 [12]，食者无大疾[13]，可以已肿[14]。

注释：[1]大【非/古】山：指泰费山。【非/古】，指费部落。今称泰山。在河南南阳东面的社旗县城。
Notes:[1] da gu shan (big old mount) refers to Taifeishan。 Fei: refers to Fei tribes。 This mountain is known today as the Taishan。It is in Sheqi county, east of Nanyang city, Henan province。

[2] 瑨琈玉：指马桥夷。瑨，指桥；琈，指马。
[2] yun fu yu(jade) refers to the Maqiao (horse bridge) Yi。 Yun/qiao(bridge) fu/horse。

[3] 麋玉：指五庄夷。今称五朝庄夷。
[3]mi yu: refers to Wuzhuang (five village) Yi, known today as Wuchaozhuang Yi。

[4] 其状叶如榆：东赵河之夷。其，在此作东解。
[4] qi zhuang ye ru yu (shape leaves as yu), refers Dongzhuanghe Yi, qi; east。

[5] 方茎而苍伤：费部落的尚舍。费，指卖。尚舍，读且舍，谐音苍伤。今称尚营。
[5] fang jing er cang shang (square stem dark wounds)
Tr: Fei tribe's shangshe(qieshe)a close phonetic match to cangshang, known today as Shangying (shang camp) , Fei: to sell。

[6] 牛伤：指勒舍，即牧族之舍。
[6] niu shang (ox wounds) reads as Leshe, meaning herders camping settlement。

[7] 其根苍文：紧靠尚河。尚河，读且汶，是东赵河的支流。
[7] qi gen cang wen (its root dark marking)
Tr: close to Shanghe River, Shanghe reads as queen, a tributary of Dongzhaohe River。

[8] 服者不厥：费部落的京都。
[8] fu zhe bu que (taken not faint) the capital of Fei tribes.

[9] 御兵：指河滨夷。
[9]yu bing (against army) refers to Hebin (river side) Yi。

[10] 狂水：指夏水，在城北。今称潘河。
[10] kuang shui (crazy water) refers to Xiashui, in Chengbei (city north), the river is known today as Panhe River。

[11] 伊水：指清河，也称河清。在城东侧，今属潘河。
[11] yi shui (yi water) refers to Qinghe River, also known as Heqing River, which is in the east part of the city, it is part of Panhe River.

[12] 三足龟：读奢咀高，指焦家河口。奢咀，指河口；高，是焦的粤濮语读音。
[12] san zu gui (three feet turtle) reads as she zui gao, refers to Jiaojiahekou, (burnt home river mouth) shezui: river month, gao: jiao in Yue and Pu speech。

[13] 食者无大疾：肆部落的游牧氏族。肆，指集市、店，也读赊，是费部落的别称。
[13] shi zhe wu da ji (eaten not have big illness)
Tr: the nomadic branches of Si tribes, si: market town, dian(shop)reads as she, another name for Fei tribes。

[14] 可以已肿：夏国的贵夷，即贵族。
[14]ke yi yi zhong (can cure swollenness)
Tr: noble people of the Xia nation, the noble lineages。

译文：由宛城山往东五十七里，有座山叫泰费山，住着马桥夷，住着五庄夷。有一个游牧氏族，是东赵河费部落的尚舍氏族，名叫勒舍氏，他们依着尚河，是费部落的京都氏族，是夏国的河滨夷。夏水从北面流出，向东南流入清河，这里住着焦家河口氏族，是费部落的游牧氏族，是夏国的贵族。
Translation:
Fifty-seven li further east from Wanchengshan stands Taifeishan。Living here are the tribes of Maqiao (horse bridge) Yi, Wuzhuang (five village) Yi。There is a nomadic tribe, known as Dongzhaohe Fei tribes' Shangshe branch。They live by the Shanghe River, known as the Jingdu branch of the Fei tribes。 They are the Hebin Yi。Xiashui River rises from the north of the mountain, goes southeast into Qinghe River。 The Jiaojiahe tribes live here, they are the nomadic tribes of Fei tribes, a noble lineage of the Xia nation。

05-07-08 半石山
Banshishan
（113,43027E；33,10704N）

又东七十里，曰半石之山[1]。其上有草焉，生而秀[2]，其高丈余[3]，赤叶赤华[4]，华而不实[5]，其名曰嘉荣[6]，服之者不霆[7]。来需之水[8] 出于其阳，而西流注于伊水 [9]，其中多鯩鱼 [10]，黑文 [11]，其状如鲋 [12]，食者不睡 [13]。合水 [14] 出于其阴，而北流注于洛[15]，多螣鱼[16]，状如鳜，居逵[17]，苍文赤尾[18]，食者不痈[19]，可以为瘘[20]。

注释：[1]半石山：读邦舍山，指象河山，实际介绍象河集镇。
Notes： [1] ban shi shan (half stone mount) reads as Bangsheshan, refers to Xiangheshan (elephant river mountain), in fact, a description of the Xianghe township。
[2] 生而秀：建立的王国。秀，读象，指王国、邦国。
[2]: sheng er xiu (birth handsome) kingdom building, xiu: reads as Xiang, meaning kingdom or fiefdoms。
[3] 其高丈余：读契高涿夷，指东史村夷。
[3] qi gao zhang yu (its height meters extra)
Tr: reads as qi gao zhuo yi, meaning Dongshicun (east history village) Yi。
[4] 赤叶赤华：指汇集成的游胡。
[4] chi ye chi hua (red leaf red flower) refers to the collection of nomadic Hu people。
[5] 华而不实：指胡族的埠肆。
[5] hua er bu shi (flowering no fruits)
Tr: the settlements and townships of the Hu tribes。
[6] 嘉荣：指西岗肆。
[6] jia rong (best flourish) refers Xigangsi (west ridge hamlet) 。
[7] 服者不霆：胡族的亳都区域。
[7] fu zhe bu ting (taken no thunder)
Tr: the capital districts known as Bodu (polis), of the Hu tribes。
[8] 来需水：指东流水。
[8] lai xu shui (come need water) refers Dongliushui (east flowing) River。
[9] 伊水：指离水，今称陡河。
[9] yi shui (yi water) refers to Lishui (depart water), known today as the Qianhe River。
[10] 鯩鱼：指菜园夷。鯩，读浓，指菜。

[10] lun yu; refers to Caiyuan (vegetable garden) Yi, Lun reads as non, meaning vegetables。

[11] 黑文：指姜水夷。姜，也称黑。

[11] hei wen (black marking) refers to Jiangshui (black water) River, jiang(black)。

[12]鲋：指东部的。

[12] fu: refers to east part。

[13] 食者不睡：河边氏族。

[13] shi zhe bu shui (taken not sleep)
Tr: refers to Hebian (river side) tribes。

[14] 合水：由两条东西向的小支流汇成，今无名称标注，仍称合水。

[14] he shui (merge water) is created by two small tributaries flowing from east to west。 The Heshui River keeps its name, not shown on map。

[15]洛：指姜水西面的河。由北向南，流经洼张。合水北流，北（贝）指南。

[15] luo: refers to the river west of Jiangshui River, which goes from north to south, via Wazhang. Heshui River goes north, north(bei) means south。

[16] 螣鱼：今已无遗迹，按滕姓氏族称。

[16] teng yu (teng fish): refers to a tribe, without any old trace of the site, now naming it Teng, a surname of a tribe。

[17]鳜，居逵：北部的部落氏族。

[17] que, ju kui: refers to northern tribes。

[18] 苍文赤尾：张洼的游牧夷。张洼，即洼张。

[18] cang wen chi yi (dark marking red tail)
Tr: refers to the nomadic Yi from Zhangwa, also known as Wazhang。

[19] 食者不痈：河边的放牧氏族。痈，读若，指放牧。

[19] shi zhe bu yong (eaten not swell)
Tr: refers to the herding tribes along the river side, yong; reads as ruo, meaning herding。

[20] 可以为瘘：夏国的南僚。

[20]ke yi wei lou (can be infested wounds) refers to the southern Lao tribes of the Xia nation。

译文：由泰费山往东七十里，有座山叫象河山。这里有游牧氏族建立的王国，是东史村夷汇集成的游牧胡的埠肆，名叫西岗肆，是胡族的亳都区域。东流水发源于集肆的南面，向东流入陡河，河边住着菜园夷和姜水夷，是东部的河边氏族。合水从集肆的北面流出，向东南流入西水，河边住着滕姓夷，是北部的部落氏族，是张洼的游牧夷，是河边的放牧氏族，夏国的南僚。

Translation:

Seventy li further east from Taifeishan stands Xiangshan。 This is a kingdom of the nomadic tribes, a settlement of nomadic Hu by the Dongshicun Yi。 The capital of the Hu region is named Xigangsi. Dongliushui rises from the south of the township, and flows eat into Qianhe River。 The Caiyuan Yi and Jiangshui Yi live along the riverbanks, known as the Hebian tribes. Heshui River rises from the north of the capital, goes southeast into Xishui River。 The Teng Yi live by the river, they are the northern tribe, the nomadic Yi from Zhangwa。 They are the herders' tribes by the river, belongs to the southern Lao tribes of the Xia nation。

05-07-09 少室山
Shaoshishan
（113,7875E；33,11416N）

又东五十里，曰少室之山[1]，百草木成囷[2]。其上有木焉，其名曰帝休[3]，叶状如杨[4]，其枝五衢[5]，黄华黑实[6]，服者不怒[7]。其上多玉[8]，其下多铁 [9] 。休水 [10] 出焉，而北流注于洛 [11] ，其中多鯑鱼[12]，状如盩蜼而长距[13]，足白而对[14]，食者无蛊疾[15]，可以御兵[16]。

注释：[1]少室山：花肆山，今称花庄镇。
Notes:[1] shao shi shan (young room mount)
Tr: refers to Huasishan (flower town mount) today's name is Huazhuang (flower village) township。

[2] 百草木成囷：半截楼的蔡丘。蔡丘，指女儿街。半截楼，地名。
[2] bai cao mu cheng qiu (hundred grass wood become piled)
Tr: refers to the Caiqiu (cai mount) at Banjielou (half standing building) caiqiu: refers to Nv'erjie (girls street), Banjielou, a place name。

[3] 帝休：指小花氏。帝休应读刁少，指小花。
[3] di xiu (God rest) refers to the Xiaohua (small flower) Shi, dixiu reads as diaoshao, meaning xiaohua (small flowers) 。

[4] 叶状如杨：读伊嫜额耶，即美女之乡。
[4]ye zhuang ru yang (leaf shape like poplar)
Tr: reads as Yizhong'e-ye: meaning land of beauties。

[5] 其枝五衢：指女儿部落支系，今谐音称五车牛支系。
[5] qi zhi wu chun (its branches five) refers to the Nv'er(daughter) tribes' branches, in phonetic match of Wucheniu/to wuchunnv。

[6] 黄华黑实：指哄哄黑氏，即普者黑氏，意为贤良高贵的氏族。
[6] huang hua hei shi (yellow flower black fruits)
Tr: refers to the Honghonghei Shi, aka Puzhehei Shi, meaning the virtuous, noble tribes。

[7] 服者不怒：统治的母系部落。不怒，读补诺，指女儿部落，也称母系部落。
[7] fu zhe bu nu (taken to cure anger)
Tr: refers to the ruling matriarchal tribes。 bunu (not angry) reads as bu nuo, meaning daughter tribes, also known as the Muxi (mother lineage, matrilinear) tribes。

[8]玉：指河滨氏族。
[8]yu(jade); refers to the Hebin tribes。

[9]铁：指土楼氏族。土按泥读为棠，与铁谐音。
[9] tie(iron)refers to the Tulou (earth house) tribe, tu (dirt, earth) mud reads as tang, a close phonetic match to tie。

[10] 休水：读少水，指花水。向南流。北应指贝。
[10] xiu shui (rest water): reads as shaoshui (young water) the Huashui (flower water) River, which flows south, bei/shell/south。

[11]洛：指汝河。
[11] luo: refers to Ruhe River。

[12] 鯑鱼：指刁夷，即带"小"字的村镇夷，如小和庄、小官庄、小陈庄。
[12] di yu: refers to Diao Yi, the Yi names with a prefix of xiao, such as Yi people of Xiaohezhuang, Xiaoguanzhuang, and Xiaochenzhuang，zhuang(village)。

[13] 螯蛙而长距：花山的分支氏族。螯蛙，花山的氐羌语表达。
[13] zhe zhi er chang ju (long fish long distance)
Tr; the branches of Huashan (flower mount) tribes。Zhezhi means huashan in Diqiang speech。

[14] 足白而对：分走的村镇。分出的村镇。
[14] zu bai er dui (feet white in pair)
Tr: refers to the townships that are divided to establish a separate settlement。

[15] 食者无蛊疾：建立的勾纪部落。勾纪部落，也称部落国。
[15] shi zhe wu gu ji (eaten will no deviled illness)
Tr: to establish Gouji tribes。Gouji tribes are also called tribal nations。

[16] 可以御兵：夏国的河滨夷。

译文：由象河山往东五十里，有个集镇叫花肆，是半截楼的女儿街。那里有个管理中心，名叫小花肆，是美女之乡，是五车牛支系的普者黑氏统治的母系部落。部落的西边住着河滨氏族，东边住着土楼氏族。花水从这里流出，向南流入汝河，河边住着小字夷，是花山的分支氏族分出的村镇建立的勾纪部落，是夏国的河滨夷。

Translation：

Fifty li further east from Xiangheshan stands Huasi township, a place called Nu'er street, at Banjielou。 There exists a management center--Xiaohua town, which is famous for beautiful girls。The township belongs to the matriarchal tribe of Puzhehei Shi, part of the Wuniuche branch。To the tribes west, the Hebin tribes live, to its east the Tulou tribes live。 Huashui River flows out of here and goes south into the Ruhe River。Along the riverbanks live the Yi peoples bearing prefixes of Xiao in their names。 They are a Gouji nation made up of the tribes that divided from Huashan branch's township。 They are the Hebin tribes of the Xia nation。

05-07-10 泰室山

Taishishan

（113,99551E；33,144N）

又东三十里，曰泰室之山[1]。其上有木焉，叶状如梨而赤理[2]，其名曰栯木[3]，服者不妒[4]。有草焉，其状如术(zhu)[5],白华黑实[6]，泽如蘡薁[7]，其名曰䔄草[8]，服之不昧[9]。上多美石[10] 。

注释：[1]泰室山：读堵肆山，指平肆山，今称遂平县城。

Notes:[1] tai shi shan (big room mount)

Tr: reads as du(block)si(town) shan(mount) refers to today's Pingsishan, known as today's county seat of Suiping county, Henan province。

[2] 叶状如梨而赤理：美女乡旁边的移府，今称车府、车站镇。

[2]ye zhuang ru li er chi li (leaves shape like pear with red marking)

Tr: the movable hall by the land of beauties, today it is known as the Chefu (cart hall) or Chezhanzhen (cart station town) 。

[3]栯(yu)木：指离目，即附属管理中心。

[3]yu mu: meaning limu (departure eyes) refers to the subordinate management center。

[4] 服者不妒：东部的平都。不，读亳，指都；妒，指平。

[4] fu zhe bu du (taken cure jealousy)

Tr: Pingdu of east part, bu/bo, capital, du, (flat) ping。

[5]术：读卓，指北方。

[5] shu: reads as zhuo, refers to the north.

[6] 白华而黑实：燕山的贵族。白华，读拜洪，指燕山。

[6] bai hua er hei shi (white flowers with black fruits)

Tr: the nobles of the Yanshan Mountain. Baihua: reads as baihong, meaning Yanshan。

[7] 泽如蘡薁：燕夷的支系。

[7] ze ru ying ao: refers to the Yan Yi's branches。

[8] 䔄草：指燕绰，燕山移民的简称。

[8] yao cao: refers to Yanchao, a shortened address for the Yanshan immigrants。

[9] 服之不昧：东部的河川氏族。

[9] fu zhi bu mei (taken make clear minded)

Tr: refers to the Hechuan tribe from the east。

[10] 美石：指魏氏族。

[10] mei shi (beautiful stone) refers to the tribes bearing the surname of Wei。

译文：由花肆往东三十里，是平肆，这里有一个管理中心，是美女乡旁边的移府，名叫离目，是东部的平都。有一个移民氏族，是北方燕山的贵族燕夷的支系，称为燕绰，是平都东部的河川氏族。西边住着魏氏族。
Translation:
Thirty li further east from Huasi one comes to Pingsi, a management Centre, the movable center by Meinvxiang, named Limu, the Pingdu in the east。Another immigrant tribe is the Yanchao, a noble lineage of Yanyi from Yanshan from the north。It is the Hechuan tribe from the east Pingdu。 On the west live the Wei tribes。

05-07-11 讲山
Jiangshan
（114,02274E；33,38766N）

又北三十里，曰讲山[1]，其上多玉[2]，多柘[3]，多柏[4]。有木焉，名曰帝屋[5]，叶状如椒[6]，反伤赤实[7]，可以御凶[8]。

注释：[1]讲山：指西山，今西平县城。讲，顺序指大，颜色指黑，方位指西。
Notes:[1] jiang shan (speak mount) refers to Xishan (west mount), in today's Xiping county seat. jiang(speak) meaning first, big, refers to black color and west。
[2]玉：指河滨氏族。
[2]yu(jade) refers to Hebin tribes。
[3]柘：指石庄氏族。
[3] zhe: refers to the Shizhuang tribes。
[4]柏：指柏姓氏族。
[4] bai(pine) refers to tribes bearing the surname of Bai。
[5] 帝屋：指北行政中心，北屋。帝指狄，即北。
[5] di wu (emperor house) refers to the northern administration center, Beiwu (northern house) 。 di(emperor)di, north。
[6] 叶状如椒：指美女乡的边缘管区。
[6] ye zhuang ru jiao (leaf shape as pepper)
Tr: the border area management of the Meinuxiang (land of the beautiful girls) 。
[7] 反伤赤实：指游牧氏族的治所。
[7] fan shang chi shi (negative wound red fruits)
Tr: the ruling station of the nomadic tribes。
[8] 御凶：指有熊夷，即华胥夷。这里指华胥夷的管区。
[8]yu xiong (against danger) refers to the Youxiong Yi, another name for Huaxu Yi, here means the regions controlled by the Huaxu Yi。

译文：由平肆往北三十里，有个地方叫西山，这里住着河滨夷，住着石庄氏族，住着柏姓氏族。有一个行政中心，名叫北屋，是美女乡的边缘管区，是游牧氏族的治所，夏国华胥夷的检目。
Translation:
Thirty li further north from Pingsi, there is a place called Xishan, where live the Hebin Yi, the Shizhuang tribes, and tribes bearing the surname of Bai。There is an administration center called Beiwu, a border region controlled by the Meinuxiang township, a township by the nomadic tribes, a city center managed by the Huaxu Yi from the Xia nation。

05-07-12 婴梁山
Yingliangshan

（114,01518E；33,58476N）

又北三十里，曰婴梁之山[1]，上多苍玉[2]，錞于玄石[3]。

注释：[1]婴梁山：指尹河山，今漯河城。尹河，今称为澧河。
Notes:[1] ying liang shan (infant ridge mount) refers to Yinheshan, today's Luohe city。 Yinhe River is called Lihe River now。
[2] 苍玉：指岔河口夷。
[2] cang yu (dark jade) refers to the Chahekou (fork river mouth) Yi。
[3] 玄石：指长河，今称颍河。
[3] xuan shi (dark stone)
Tr: refers to the Changhe River, today is called Yinghe River。

译文：由西山往北三十里，有个集镇叫尹河山，这里住着岔河口氏族，紧挨着颍河。
Translation:
Thirty li further north from the Xishan there is a township called Yinheshan。The Chahekou tribes live here, next to Yinghe River。

05-07-13 浮戏山
Fuxishan
（114,34057E；33,5952N）

又东三十里，曰浮戏之山[1]。有木焉，叶状如樗而赤实[2]，名曰亢木[3]，食之不蛊[4]，汜水出焉，而北流注于河[5]。其东有谷，因名曰蛇谷[6]，上多少辛[7]。

注释：[1]浮戏山：指冯羲山，在漯河市谭庄镇冯村。冯羲指国王。
Notes: [1] fu xi shan (float drama mount)
Tr: refers to Fengxishan in today's Fengcun Village, Tanzhuangzhen, in Luohe city。 fengxi (king, or von) refers to the head of the tribal nation。
[2] 樗而赤实：指母系部落的行政中心。樗，作睢解，指女人、母系。
[2] chun er chi shi (chun with red fruits)
Tr: the administration center of the Matriarchal tribes, chun; reads as zhui, meaning female, woman, mother bloodline。
[3] 亢木：指康目。康，指族群。
[3] keng mu (overexcited wood) refers to kangmu (healthy eyes) kang: tribes。
[4] 不蛊：指夏族，这里指夏族的检目。
[4] bu gu (not bewitched) refers to the Xia tribes, here means their management centers, known as Jianmu (the inspection eyes) 。
[5]河：今称新沽河。
[5] he: today's Xinguhe River。
[6] 蛇古：指河汇国。
[6] she gu (snake ancient) refers to the Hehui (rivers join) nation。
[7] 少辛：指河汇氏族。
[7] shao xin (young bitter) refers to Hehui tribes。

译文：由尹河山往东三十里，有个集镇叫冯羲山，这里有一个检目，是母系部落的行政中心，名叫康目，是古老的夏族的检目。汜水从这里流出，向北流入新沽河。冯羲山的东边有一个国家，名叫河汇国，那里住着河汇氏族。

Translation:

Thirty li further east from Yinheshan, there is a township called Fengxishan, an administration center for the Matrilineage tribes。The center is known as Kangmu, the Jianmu of ancient Xia nation。 The Sishui River rises from here, goes north into the Xinguhe River。 To the east of the township of Fengxishan, there is a country called Hehui nation。The Hehui tribes live there。

05-07-14 少陉山

Shaoxingshan

（114,64233E；33,63654N）

又东四十里，曰少陉之山[1]。有草焉，名曰【艹/冈】草[2]，叶状如葵，而赤茎白华[3]，实如蘡薁[4]，食之不愚[5]。器难之水[6] 出焉，而北流注于役水 [7] 。

注释：[1]少陉山：指河汇山，今河南周口市。

Notes:[1] shao xing shan (young trail mount)

[2] 【艹/冈】草：指孙氏移民。

[2] gang cao (ridge grass) refers to the immigrants bearing the surname of Sun。 (Not to be confused with English word sun(sol)， sun in Chinese means grandson。

[3] 葵而赤茎白华：北方的游牧部落燕胡。

[3] kui er chi jing bai hua (sunflower red stem white flowers)

Tr: refers to the Yan Hu nomadic tribes from the north。

[4] 蘡薁：指燕夷。

[4] ying ao: refers to the Yan Yi。

[5] 不愚：河滨氏族。

[5] bu yu (not stupid) refers to the Hebin tribes。

[6] 器难水：指运河水。这里指贾鲁河水。向南流；北，读贝，指南。

[6] qi nan shui (vessel difficult water) refers to the Yunheshui (canal water) here it refers to Jialu River, which goes south, bei/shell/south。

[7] 役水：指伊水，今称颖河。

[7] yi shui (labor water) refers to Yishui River, today known as the Ying River。

译文：由冯羲山往东四十里，是河汇山。有一个移民氏族，叫孙氏移民，支系为北方游牧部落的燕胡，实际为燕夷，是古老的河滨氏族。贾鲁河水流经这里，向南流入颖河。

Translation:

Forty li further east from Fengxishan township, there stands the Hehui Mountain。There is a tribe of immigrants, known as Sun Shi tribe, a branch of the Yan Hu from the northern nomadic tribes。 This tribe is part of the Yan Yi, the ancient Hebin tribes。The Jialu River flows through here and goes south into the Ying River。

05-07-15 太山

Taishan

（114,76386E；33,60839N）

又东南十里，曰太山[1]。有草焉，名曰梨[2]，其叶状如荻而赤华[3]，可以已疽[4]。太水[5] 出于其阳，而南流注于役水 [6] 。承水 [7] 出于其阴，而东北流注于役水。

注释：[1]太山：指项庄，今称项庄村。在周口东南侧。项，濮读特，谐音太。
Notes: [1] tai shan (great mount) refers to Xiangzhuang, today it is known as the Xiangzhuang Village, located to the southeast side of Zhoukou。Xiang:in Pu speech it is read as te, a phonetic match to tai。

[2]梨：指卑，这里指鲜卑。

[2]li(pear) means bi, refers to the Xianbi people。

[3] 荻而赤华：北方的游牧胡。

[3] di er chi hua (reed flower with red flower) refers to the Hu nomadic tribes from the north。

[4] 已疽：指举夷，即林胡，东胡。

[4] yi jun (cure infestation) refers to Ju(lift) Yi, also known as Linhu, Donghu, the Hu people。

[5] 太水：指项水。

[5] tai shui (big water) refers to the Xiangshui River。

[6] 役水：伊水，今称颍河。

[6] yi shui (labor water) refers to Yishui, known today as Ying River。

[7] 承水：指运河。运、行，读蚩、车，谐音承。

[7] cheng shui (hold water) refers to the Yunhe canal, yun: transport, moving, reads as chi, or che, a close phonetic match to cheng。

译文：由河汇山往东南十里，是项庄。有一个移民氏族，名叫鲜卑氏，是北方的游牧胡，夏国的林胡夷。项水从南面流出，向南流入伊水；运河水从项庄的北面流过，向东南流入伊水。
Translation:
Ten li further southeast from the Hehuishan there stands Xiangzhuang Village。 A tribe of immigrants known as the Xiangbi Shi live here, they are the Hu nomadic from the north, known also as the Linhu Yi of the Xia nation。Xiang River rises from the south and flows south into the Yishui River。 Yunheshui River flows through from the north of Xiangzhuang Village and goes southeast into Yishui River。

05-07-16 末山
Moshan
（114,99941E；33,958N）

又东二十里，曰末山[1]，上多赤金[2]，末水[3]出焉，北流注于役水[4]。

注释：[1]末山：指朱山，中心在朱集北面的冯塘乡。
Notes: [1]mo shan (last mount) refers to the Zhushan (red mountain) 。Its center is at Fengtang Xiang, to the north of Zhuji township。

[2] 赤金：指杨楼氏族。

[2] chi jin (red gold) refers to the Yanglou (poplar building) tribes。

[3] 末水：指朱水。

[3]mo shui (last water) refers to Zhushui River。

[4] 役水：指汲水。

[4] yi shui (labor water) refers to Jishui (fetch water) River。

译文：由项庄往东二十里，是朱山。这里住着杨楼氏族。朱水从这里流出，向北流入汲水。
Translation:
Twenty li further east from Xiangzhuang stands the Zhushan。The Yanglou tribes live here。Zhushui River rises from here and goes north into the Jishui River。

05-07-17 役山

Yishan

（115,20167E；33,64153N）

又东二十五里，曰役山[1]，上多白金[2]，多铁[3]。役水[4] 出焉，北流注于河 [5] 。

注释：[1]役山：指汲山，今称郸城。汲、取，在濮语中都读 yu。

Notes:[1] yi shan (labor mount) refers to Jishan (fetch water mount) today, it is Dancheng。 ji(get) reads in Pu speech as yu。

[2] 白金：指场集氏族。

[2] bai jin (white gold) refers to the Changji tribes， (field market) 。

[3]铁：读投，指前屯氏族。

[3] tie(iron) reads tou, in Pu speech, refers to the Qiantun (front village) tribes。

[4] 役水：指汲水。

[4] yi shui (labor water) refers to the Jishui River。

[5]河：指茨河。

[5] he(river) refers to Cihe River。

译文：由朱山往东二十五里，是汲山，这里住着场集氏族，住着前屯氏族。汲水从这里流出，向北流入茨河。

Translation:

Twenty-five li further east from Zhushan stands Jishan。The Changji tribes, Qiantun tribes live here。 Jishui River rises from here and flows north into the Cihe River。

05-07-18 敏山

Minshan

（115,4892E；33,8599N）

又东三十五里，曰敏山[1]。上有木焉，其状如荆，白华而赤实[2]，名曰蓟柏[3]，服者不寒[4]，其阳多瑀琈之玉[5]。

注释：[1]敏山：指涡山，今鹿邑县城。涡在濮语中读 mie 音，谐音敏。

Notes: [1] min shan (intelligent mount) refers to the Woshan, in today's Luyi (deer hamlet) county seat。 Wo reads as mie in Pu speech, a close phonetic match to the Chinese word Min。

[2]荆，白华而赤实：包牺胡的游牧氏族。荆白，指节并，是包牺氏的称谓。

[2] jin, bai hua er chi shi (twigs white flower red fruits)

Tr: refers to the nomadic tribes of the Baoxi Hu people. Jinbai, jiebing, is the title of Baoxi Shi。

[3] 蓟柏：指节并，是包牺氏的称谓。

[3] ji bai(tree) means Jiebing, a title for the Baoxi Shi。

[4] 不寒：指蚌埠氏。

[4] bu han (not cold) refers to the Bengbu Shi。

[5] 瑀琈玉：指桥口夷。

[5] yun fu yu: refers to Qiaokou (bridge mouth) Yi。

译文：由汲山往东三十五里，有座山叫涡山。那里有一个蒙族，是包牺胡的游牧氏族，名叫节并，是胡族的蚌埠氏。涡山的南面住着桥口夷。

Translation:

Thirty-five li further east from Jishan stands Woshan。 There is a Meng tribe of the Baoxi Hu's nomadic groups, known as Jiebing, aka the Bengbu Shi。On the south side of Woshan, live the Qiaokou Yi。

05-07-19 大騩山
Daguishan
（115,77584E；33,87268N）

又东三十里，曰大騩之山[1]，其阴多铁[2]、美玉[3]、青垩[4]。有草焉，其状如蓍而毛[5]，青华而白实[6]，其名曰【艹/狼】[7]，服之不夭[8]，可以为服病[9]。

凡苦山之首，自休与之山至于大騩之山，凡十有九山，千一百八十四里。其十六神者，皆豕身而人面[10]。其祠：毛牷用一羊羞[11]，婴用一藻玉瘗。苦山、少室山、太室皆冢也，其祠之，太牢之具，婴以吉玉。其神状皆人面而三首[12] 。其余属豕身人面也。

注释：[1]大騩山：指鞑仡山。亳州的古称谓，因是商族人的封地而得名。
Notes:[1] da gui shan: big Gui mount refers to Dageshan, an ancient name for Bozhou, which got this name as the fiefdom of the Shang tribes。

[2]铁：指谯镇氏族。
[2] tie (iron) refers to Qiaozhen tribes。

[3] 美玉：指五里村夷。
[3] mei yu (beautiful jade) refers to the Wulicun (five-mile village) Yi。

[4] 青垩：指驮运部落。青，是濮语 "驮" 的音译。
[4] qing e (green clay) refers to the tribes engaged in transportation by animals. qing(green) is a phonetic match for Pu speech tuo (carry, transport) 。

[5] 有草焉，其状如蓍而毛：指有一群移民，是草原蛮蛮。
[5] you cao yan (has grass alas) qi zhuang ru shi er mao (its shape like divine grass with hair)
Tr: a group of immigrants, they are the Manman from the Steppe。

[6] 青华而白实：驮运的部落氏族。
[6] qing hua er bai shi (green flower and white fruits)
Tr: the tribes engaged in transportation by animals。

[7] 【艹/狼】：指卢氏。
[7]lu: grass wolf, refers to the Lu Shi。

[8] 服之不夭：指胡族的河川氏族。
[8] fu zhi bu yao (taken will not die)
Tr: The Hechuan tribes of the Hu people。

[9] 为服病：属于回鹘。
[9] wei fu bing (to serve overcome illness)
Tr: belongs to the Urghur people。

[10] 豕身而人面：种植氏族的居民形象。
{10] shi shen er ren mian (pig body with human face)
Tr: in the images of agriculture tribes' residents。

[11] 毛牷用一羊羞：用羊尊盛祭食。毛牷，读馍切，指祭食，羊羞，读蚩歇，指羊尊。
[11] mao quan yong yi yang xiu (sacrifice use one ram vessel)
Tr: to hold the sacrificial food in Ram shaped vessels。Maoquan: reads as Moqie, meaning sacrificial food, yangxiu: reads as chixie: meaning ram shaped zun, a kind of utensil。

[12] 人面三首：指定居的王族形象。三首，读韶属，指王族。
[12] ren mian san shou (human face three heads)

Tr: the king house nobles' image of settled tribes。 sanshou (three heads) reads in Pu speech as shaoshu, refers to the king tribe。

译文：由涡山往东三十里，有一个集镇叫鞑仡镇，北面住着谯镇氏族、五里村夷和驮部落氏族。有一群移民，是草原蛮蛮，是运输部落的氏族，名叫卢氏，是胡族的河川氏族，属于夏国的回鹘。
Translation:
Thirty li further east from the Woshan, there is a township called Dagezhen。 To its north live the Qiaozhen tribes, Wulicun Yi and the Tuobuluo tribes。 A group of immigrants are the Manman from the steppe, they are the Lu Shi of the Hechuan tribe of the Hu people and belong to the Urghur of the Xia nation。

综观夏山山系，从庚岭到大陈山，共计十九座山，延绵一千一百八十四里。其中十六座山的山神为定居的种植氏族的形象，祭祀时，用羊尊盛食物，用藻玉掩埋。夏山、花肆、平肆为宗山，祭祀用太牢之礼，用璧掩埋。这三座山的神为定居的王族的形象，其余皆为定居的种植氏族的形象。

In sum, the Xiashan system from Gengling Mountain to Dachenshan has 19 mountains in total。The system covers a distance of 1,184 li。Sixteen mountain deities among them are in the images of settled agricultural tribes。When sacrificing to them, food is offered in ram-shaped vessels, and buried with Zao jade。 The Xiashan, Huasi, Pingsi are the ancestor's mounds。 The rite of sacrifice to them is the Tailao rite, a Bi jade is buried。 The deities of the three mountains mentioned above are in the image of the king lineage of settled tribes。 The rest of the deities are in the images of the agricultural tribes of settled people。

中山经第八山系

Book 5 Zhongshanjing; chapter 8

05-08-01 荆山 景山
Jinshan Jingshan
（109,80248E；32,94227N）

中次八经荆山之首，曰景山[1]，其上多金玉[2]，其木多杼檀[3]。睢水[4] 出焉，东南流注于江 [5]，其中多丹粟 [6]，多文鱼 [7]。

注释：[1]景山：在湖北郧西县景阳乡。实际介绍景阳乡。今称大、小兰乡。
Notes： [1] jing shan (scenic mount)
Tr: it is in Jingyang (scenic sun) Xiang, in Yunxi County, Hubei province。 It is in fact a description of Jingyang Xiang, today it is known as Great Lan district and Lesser Lan district。

[2] 金玉：指景夷。

[2] jin yu (gold jade) refers to Jing Yi。

[3] 杼檀：指花栎巴，今称花栎扒。氐羌语的"花"读照，与杼谐音。

[3] zhu tan refers to Hualiba, known today as Hualipa。Hua(flower)reads as zhao in Diqiang speech, a phonetic match to zhu。

[4] 睢水：指黄龙水。

[4] sui shui: refers to Huanglongshui （yellow dragon water), the Huanglong River。

[5]江：水江，即汉江。

[5] jiang(river) refers to Shuijiang, also known as Hanjiang, Hanjiang River。

[6] 丹粟：指骡马店氏族。

[6] dan su (red millet) refers to the Luomadian (mule donkey horse station) clan。

[7] 文鱼：指官营坡氏族。

[7] wen yu (marking fish) refers to the Guanyingpo (official managed slope) clan。

译文：中部第八列山系叫荆山山系，最西边的一座山叫景山，这里住着景夷，部落叫花栎巴。黄龙水从这里流出，向东南流入汉江，河边住着骡马店氏族，住着官营坡夷。

Translation:

The 8th system of the mountains in the middle region is the Jinshan Mountains, with Jingshan being the westmost。The Jing Yi lives here, their tribe is called Hualiba。The Huanglongshui River flows out of here and goes southeast into Hanjiang River。The Luomadian clan lives along the riverbanks, so does the Guanyingpo Yi。

05-08-02 荆山

Jinshan

（11040596E；32,99288N)

东北百里，曰荆山[1]，其阴多铁[2]，其阳多赤金[3]。其中多犛牛[4]，多虎豹 [5]，其木多松柏 [6]，其草多竹 [7]，多橘櫾[8]。漳水[9]出焉，而东南流注于睢[10]，其中多黄金[11]，多鲛鱼[12]，其兽多闾麋[13]。

注释：[1]荆山：在湖北郧西县北侧，实际介绍郧西县城。

Notes:[1] jin shan (thorn mount): it is located to the north of Yunxi County, Hubei province。 It is in fact a description of Yunxi County。

[2]铁：指土门镇氏族。

[2] tie(iron)refers to the Tumen (earth gate) township clan。

[3] 赤金：赤池涧氏族。

[3] chi jin (red gold) refers to the Chichijian (red pond brook) clan。

[4] 犛牛：指春河氏族。春河，读梅僚，谐音犛牛。

[4] mao niu (Bos grunniens， domestic yak) refers to the Chunhe (spring river) clan。Chunhe， reads as meiliao in Pu speech, is a close match to maoniu。

[5] 虎豹：指阴坡氏族。濮语的阴阳读补伏，补指阳，伏指阴；伏、虎谐音。

[5]hu bao (tiger leopard) refers to the Yinpo (shady slope) clan。Yin and Yang, (shady, sunny) reads as bu fu, bu/yang, fu/yin, fu/hu are close phonetic matchings。

[6] 松柏：指粟巴，即西部落，今称郧西部落。

[6] song bai: refers to Suba, aka Xi(west)tribe, known today as Yunxi tribe。

[7]竹：指北隅氏族。

[7] zhu (bamboo) refers to Beiyu (north corner) clan。

[8] 橘櫾：指龙牌沟氏族。

[8] ju yao (orange) refers to the Longpaigou (dragon card gully) clan。

[9] 漳水：指照水，今称天河。

[9] zhang shui: refers to Zhaoshui River, today’s Tianhe (sky river) River。

[10] 睢水：指汉水。
[10] sui shui: refers to Hanshui River, aka Hanjiang River, or the Han River。
[11] 黄金：指范家岭氏族。
[11] huang jin (yellow gold) refers to the Fanjialing (fan family ridge) clan。
[12] 鲛鱼：指贾姓夷。
[12] jiao yu(fish) refers to Jia Yi。
[13] 闾麋：指阎家沟口氏族。
[13]lv mi， refers to the Yanjiagoukou (yan family gully mouth) clan。

译文：由景山往东北一百里，有座山叫荆山，山的北面住着土门镇氏族，南面住着池涧氏族。中心住着春河氏族，住着阴坡氏族，部落名叫郧西部落，这里还住着北隅游牧民，住着龙牌沟氏族。天河从这里流出，向东南流入汉水，河边住着范家岭氏族，住着贾夷，还住着阎家沟口氏族。
Translation:
One hundred li further northeast from Jingshan stands Jinshan。The Tumenzhen clan lives on its north, the Chijian clan lives on its south。In the middle of it live the Chunhe clan, the Yinpo clan。 The tribe is called Yunxi tribe, with neighbouring nomadic Beiyu herders, and Longpaigou clan。 The Tianhe River flows out of here and goes southeast into Hanshui River。The Fanjialing clan lives along the riverbanks, so does the Jia Yi, and the Yanjiagoukou clan。

05-08-03 骄山
Jiaoshan
（111,19629E；33,01213N）

又东北百五十里，曰骄山[1]，其上多玉[2]，其下多青雘[3]，其木多松柏[4]，多桃枝钩端[5]。神鼉围[6]处之，其状如人面。羊角虎爪 [7]，恒游于睢漳之渊 [8]，出入有光 [9] 。

注释：[1]骄山：指竹山，也称梅塔山，在湖北郧县梅铺镇。濮语称竹为骄、梅塔。
Notes:[1] jiao shan (proud mount) refers to the Zhushan (bamboo mount) which is also called Meitashan (plum tower mount), in today's Meipuzhen, Yun County, Hubei province。 In Pu speech, bamboo is called jiao, meita。
[2]玉：指“家扒”氏族。
[2]yu(jade) refers to the Jiapa clan。
[3] 青雘：指东马黄沟氏族。今称马黄沟氏族。
[3] qing hu (green dyestuff)
Tr: refers to the east Mahuanggou (horse yellow gully) clan, today it is called Mahuanggou clan。
[4] 松柏：指西湾，这里指西湾检目。
[4] song bai (pine) refers to the west bay, the Jianmu (inspection eyes) or the administration center of Xiwan (west bay) 。
[5] 桃枝钩端：滔江部落集镇。
[5] tao zhi gou duan (peach branch hood end)
Tr: refers to the Taojiang tribe's township。taojiang (wave river) 。
[6] 神鼉围：指滔水氏。围，读汶，指水。
[6] shen e wei (holy reptile enclosure)
Tr: refers to the Taoshui Shi。 wei: reads as wen, meaning water。
[7] 人面羊角虎爪：定居的茨沟胡族支系。
[7] ren min yang jiao hu zhua (human face ram horn tiger claws)
Tr: refers to the settled branch of the Cigou Hu tribe。

[8] 恒游于睢漳之渊：迁徙于羲乔之乡，即丹江乔乡。漳渊，指乔迁之乡，简称乔乡。
[8] heng you yu sui zhang zhi yuan (permanent swimming sui zhang pool)
Tr: migrating to the land of Xiqiao, which is Danjiangqiaoxiang。zhang yuan: a place of immigrants, shortened to qiao xiang (migrants district) 。
[9] 出入有光：建立的城镇。
[9] chu ru you guan (out in has lights)
Tr: establish townships。

译文：由郧西山往东北一百五十里，有座山叫竹山。西边住着家扒氏族，东边住着马黄沟氏族。这里的检目叫西湾检目，是滔江部落的集镇。滔水氏族住在这里，他们是定居的茨沟胡族支系，迁徙到丹江乔乡，建立了这个城镇。
Translation
One hundred and fifty li further northeast from Yunxishan stands Zhushan。 The Jiapa clan lives on the west and Mahuanggou clan lives on the east。Here a Jianmu is in place, it is called Xiwan Jianmu, a township of the Taojiang tribe。The Taoshui clan lives here, they are the settled Hu Cigou branch, who migrated to Danjiang migrants' settlement, and built this township。

05-08-04 女几山
Nvjishan
（111,84917E；33,04507N）

又东一百二十里，曰女几之山[1]，其上多玉[2]，其下多黄金[3]，其兽多豹虎[4]，多闾、麋、麖、麂[5]，其鸟多白鷮[6]，多翟[7]，多鸩[8]。

注释：[1]女几山：指勒纪山，即游牧部落山。今称内纪山，内乡山，在河南内乡县城。
Notes: [1] nv ji shan (girl stand mount)
Tr: refers to the Lejishan, aka the nomadic tribe's mount。 It is called Neijishan, as well as Neixiangshan, in Neixiang county, Henan province。
[2]玉：指黄水河氏族。
[2]yu(jade) refers to the Huangshui (yellow water) River clan。
[3] 黄金：指后部落氏族。
[3] huang jin (yellow gold) refers to the Houbuluo (back tribe) clan。
[4] 豹虎：指马湾氏族。读音贝胡。
[4] bao hu (leopard tiger) refers to the Mawan (horse bay) clan, bao hu reads as beihu。
[5] 闾麋麖麂：指靳庄场部落氏族。
[5]lu mi jing ji (deer) refers to the Jinzhuangchangbuluo clan。
[6] 白鷮：指屈湾氏族。白，在此读贝音。
[6] bai qiao (bird) refers to the Quwan (bent bay) clan, bai(white) reads as bei(bay)。
[7]翟：指河滨氏族。翟，在此读迭音。
[7] di（bird) refers to the Hebin clan, di: reads as die。
[8]鸩：在此指郑坑氏族。
[8] zhen(bird) refers to the Zhengkeng clan。

译文：由竹山往东北一百二十里，有座山叫内纪山，西面住着黄水河氏族，东面住着后部落氏族。中部住着马湾氏族，靳庄场部落氏族，屈湾氏族，河滨氏族和郑坑氏族。
Translation:

One hundred and twenty li further northeast from Zhushan stands Neijishan。 The Huangshuihe clan lives on its west, and Houbuluo clan lives on its east。 In the middle part of the region, live the clans of Mawan, Jinzhuanchangbuluo, Quwan, Hebin and Zhengken。

05-08-05 宜诸山
Yizhushan
（112,5904E；32,71117N）

又东北二百里，曰宜诸之山[1]，其上多金玉[2]，其下多青雘[3]。洈水[4] 出焉，而南流注于漳 [5]，其中多白玉 [6] 。

注释：[1]宜诸山：指官村山，今称官庄山，在河南唐河县官庄镇。宜，读 vei 音。
Notes: [1] yi zhu shan: refers to the Guancunshan (official village mountain, known today as the Guanzhuangshan in today's Guanzhuang township, Tanghe County, Henan province。Yi reads as vei.
[2] 金玉：指岳岗氏族。
[2] jin yu (gold jade) refers to the Yuegang (mound ridge) clan。
[3] 青雘：指东何庄氏族。
[3] qing hu (green dyestuff) refers to the Donghezhuang clan。
[4] 洈水：指官庄水。今称涧河。
[4] wei shui: refers to the Guanzhuangshui River, known today as Jianhe River。
[5]漳：指丹江，也称汉江。
[5] zhang: refers to Danjiang River, also known as Hanjiang River。
[6] 白玉：指河湾夷。白读贝，指湾。
[6] bai yu(white jade) refers to the Hewan(river bay)Yi, bai(white)/bei/bay。

译文：由内纪山往东北二百里，有个集镇叫官庄山。西边住着岳岗氏族，东边住着东何庄氏族。官庄水从这里流出，向南流入汉江。河边住着河湾氏族。
Translation:
Two hundred li further northeast from Neijishan stands the township called Guanzhuangshan。 On its west lives the Yuegang clan, on its east, the Donghezhuang clan。Guanzhuangshui River flows out of here and goes south into the Hanjiang River。The Hewan clan lives along the riverbanks。

05-08-06 纶山
Lunshan
（113,67129E；32,18792N）

又东北三百五十里，曰纶山[1]，其木多梓枏[2]，多桃枝[3]，多柤栗橘櫾[4]，其兽多闾麈麢㚟[5]。

注释：[1]纶山：指草山，今湖北随州市草店镇。实际往东南。
Notes： [1] lun shan: refers to Caoshan (grass mount) refers to today's Caodianzhen township in Suizhou city, Hubei province。It goes in fact in a southeast direction。
[2] 梓枏：指枝楼，今称楼子湾。楼，即寨子之意。
[2] zi nan（hard wood) refers to Zhilou, today known as Louziwan, lou (building) means enclosure, stronghold。
[3] 桃枝：指邓子堰氏族。
[3] tao zhi (peach branches) refers to the Dengziyan clan。
[4] 柤栗橘櫾：指下河油村，今称下河油房氏族。

[4] ju li ju yao： refers to the Xiaheyou Village, known today as the Xiaheyoufang clan。 Xiahe: lower river, youfang: oil press house。

[5] 闾麈麢臭：指草堰村氏族。

[5]lv zhu ling zhuo (small animals) refers to the Caoyancun clan。

译文：由官庄山往东南三百五十里，有座山叫草山，检目名叫楼子湾检目。这里住着邓子堰氏族，住着下河油房氏族，还住着草堰村氏族。

Translation:

Three hundred and fifty li further southeast from Guanzhuangshan stands Caoshan。 Its Jianmu is called Louziwan Jianmu (inspection eyes) 。Living in this region are the following clans: the Dengziyan, the Xiaheyoufang, and the Caoyancun。

05-08-07 陆郈山

Luweishan

（114,31543E；31,96904N）

又东北二百里，曰陆郈之山[1]，其上多㻎琈之玉[2]，其下多垩[3]，其木多杻橿[4]。

注释：[1]陆郈山：指涩港山，今河南信阳市灵山镇涩港村。郈，读 gui 音，指港。

Notes:[1]lu gui shan: refers to the Segangshan, known today as the Segangcun, Lingshan township， Xinyang city, Henan province。Gui: meaning river port。

[2] 㻎琈玉：指响塬夷。

[2] yun fu yu(jade) refers to the Xiangyuan Yi。

[3]垩：原指败，这里指垮冲氏族。

[3]e(defeated) refers to the Kuachong (water destroyed) clan。

[4] 杻橿：读陆节，指沙湖。

[4] niu jiang (wood) reads as lujie: meaning sand lake。

译文：由草山往东南二百里，有座山叫涩港山，西面住着响塬氏族，东面住着垮冲氏族，检目称为沙湖检目。

Translation:

Two hundred li further southeast （not northeast） from Caoshan stands a mountain called Segangshan。 On its west side live the Xiangyuan clan, on its east side live the Kuachong clan, its Jianmu is Shahu。

05-08-08 光山

Guangshan

（114,90076E；32,00468N）

又东百三十里，曰光山[1]，其上多碧[2]，其下多木[3]。神计蒙[4] 处之，其状人身而龙首 [5] ，恒游于漳渊 [6] ，出入必有飘风暴雨 [7] 。

注释：[1]光山：指河南光山县县城。

Notes: [1] guang shan (light mount) refers to the county seat of Guangshan， Henan province。

[2]碧：指破楼氏族。破，指逃亡的，跳动的。濮语读 be 音，谐音碧。

[2]bi (clear blue) refers to the Puolou (rundown building） clan, po (run away, jumpy) reads be in Pu speech, a close phonetic match。

[3]木：在此指冯店氏族。冯胡通义，濮语读胡为木。

[3]mu(wood)refers to the Fengdian clan, feng/hu reads as mu in Pu speech。
[4] 神计蒙：指苗族部落氏族。
[4] shen ji meng (God count cover) refers to the tribal branches of Miao ethnic people。
[5] 人身而龙首：定居的僚族。
[5] ren mian er long shou (human body dragon head) refers to the Lao people who settled down。
[6] 漳渊：指乔乡。
[6] zhang yuan (flood pond) refers to communities of immigrants。
[7] 必有飘风暴雨：属于自己统治的部落邑。
[7]bi you piao feng bao yu (must have winds storms) 。
Tr: has tribal settlements ruled by themselves。

译文：由涩港山往东一百三十里，有座山叫光山，山的西面住着破楼氏族，东面住着冯店氏族。苗族部落氏族住在这里，他们是定居的僚族，迁徙到乔乡，建立了属于自己统治的部落邑。
Translation:
One hundred and thirty li further east from Cegangshan stands Guangshan。The Puolou clan lives on the west side of the mountain, the Fengdian clan lives on the east side of the mountain。The Miao tribal branches live here, they are the settled Lao people, migrated here and established and ruled their own communities。

05-08-09 岐山
Qishan
（115,40819E；31,79695N）

又东百五十里，曰岐山[1]，其阳多赤金[2]，其阴多白珉[3]，其上金玉[4]，其下多青雘[5]，其木多樗[6]。神涉鼍处之[7]，其状人身而方面 [8]，三足 [9] 。

注释：[1]岐山：指伤山，后改称商山，今河南商城县城。
Notes:[1] qi shan (different mount) refers to Shangshan (wounded mountain), later changed into Shangshan (merchant mountain), today's Shangcheng county seat， Henan province。
[2] 赤金：指天平岗氏族。
[2] chi jin (red gold) refers to the Tianpinggang clan. tian ping gang (sky balance ridge) 。
[3] 白珉：读贝米，指烟庄氏族。今称烟巴头氏族。
[3] bai min reads as Beimi, refers to the Yanzhuang (smoke village) clan, today it is known as the Yanbatou clan。
[4] 金玉：指薛家岗夷。
[4] jin yu (gold jade) refers to the Xuejiagang Yi。 xue, a surname; jia: home; gang: ridge。
[5] 青雘：指陪山氏族。
[5] qing hu refers to the Peishan (company mount) clan。
[6]樗：指江平子检目。
[6] yun: refers to the Jiangpingzi Jianmu--Jiang(river)ping(flat)zi(son) jianmu (inspection eye, or the administration center) 。
[7] 神涉鼍：指木头河村氏族。简称木村氏。
[7] shen she e (God cross reptile) refers to the Mutouhecun (wood river village) clan, shortened to Mucun (wood village) Shi。
[8] 人身而方面：定居在李湖边的。
[8] ren shen er fang mian (human body with square face)
Tr: settled by the Lihu Lake side。

[9] 三足：指木村。
[9] san zu (three feet) refers to the Mucun (wood village) 。

译文：由光山往东一百五十里，有座山叫商山。山的南面住着天平岗氏族，北面住着烟巴头氏族，西面住着薛家岗夷，东面住着陪山氏族，检目名叫江坪子检目。木头河村氏族住在这里，定居在李湖边的木村。
Translation:
One hundred and fifty li further east from Guangshan stands Shangshan。 The Tianpinggang clan lives on the south side, the Yanbatou clan lives on the north。 The Xuejiagang Yi lives on the west, the Shangshan clan lives on the east。The Jianmu is named Jiangpingzi。The Mutouhecun clan lives in Licun village, by the Lihu Lake。

05-08-10 铜山
Tongshan
（115,91828E；31,84666N）

又东百三十里，曰铜山[1]，其上多金银铁[2]，其木多穀柞柤栗橘櫾[3]，其兽多豹[4]。

注释：[1]铜山：指叶山，意为同山。实际指安徽金寨县叶集镇。
Notes:[1] tong shan (copper mount) refers to Ye(leaf)mount, meaning Tong (same)mountain。 It is in fact a description of Yeji (leaves collect) township, in Jinzhai county, Anhui province。
[2] 金银铁：指丁小台氏族。
[2] jin yi tie (gold silver iron) refers to the Dingxiaotai clan。
[3] 穀柞柤栗橘櫾：殷家园叶集府。栗指富，橘櫾；指叶集，大集。
[3]gu za zu li ju yao: refers to the Yinjiayuan Yeji Hall: Li: rich, Juyao: ye market town, or big market town.
[4]豹：指农业氏族。
[4] bao(leopard) refers to the agriculture tribe。

译文：由商山往东一百三十里，有座山叫叶山，西面住着丁小台氏族，检目名叫殷家园叶集府，住着农业氏族。
Translation:
One hundred and thirty li further east from Shangshan stands a mountain called Yeshan。 On its west lives the Dingxiaotai clan, its Jianmu is called Yinjiayuan-Yeji Hall, settled by the agricultural clans。

05-08-11 美山
Meishan
（116,51559E；31,79001N）

又东北一百里，曰美山[1]，其兽多兕牛[2]，多闾麈[3]，多豕鹿[4]，其上多金[5]，其下多青雘[6]。

注释：[1]美山：指茶棚山，茶，濮语读 mei、mi，彝语读 lu，今安徽六安城北。实际往东。
Notes:[1] mei shan (beauty mount) refers to Chapengshan (tea shed mount) 。 In Pu speech, cha(tea)reads as mei, mi, or lu in Yi speech。 The name refers to the north of Liu'an (six peace) city, Anhui province, in fact going east。
[2] 兕牛：指种稻氏族，在此指犁华塘氏族。
[2]si niu (one horn ox) refers to the rice producing clans, the Lihuatang clan。
[3] 闾麈：指楼村氏族，在此指茶楼村氏族。
[3]lu chen: refers to the Loucun clan, Loucun means the Chaloucun (tea building village) clan。
[4] 豕鹿：指谢塘氏族。
[4] zhu lu (pig deer) refers to the Xietang clan。

[5]金：指沙摊店氏族。
[5] jin(gold) refers to the Shatandian clan。
[6] 青雘：指秦圩氏族。
[6] qing hu (green dyestuff) refers to the Qinxu clan。

译文：由叶山往东北一百里，有座山叫茶棚山，那里住着犁华塘氏族，住着茶楼村氏族，住着谢塘氏族。西边住着沙摊店氏族，东边住着秦圩氏族。
Translation:
One hundred li further northeast from the Yeshan stands Chapengshan。 The Lihuatang clan lives here, also living here are the Chaloucun clan, the Xietang clan。 On the west lives the Shatandian clan, and on the east lives the Qinxu clan。

05-08-12 大尧山
Dayaoshan
（116,87873E；32,07173N）

又东北百里，曰大尧之山[1]，其下多松柏[2]，多梓桑[3]，多机[4]，其草多竹[5]，其兽多虎豹麢臭[6]。

注释：[1]大尧山：读戴耶山，是大刘山的濮语称呼，在今安徽炎刘、双庙、小甸一带。
Notes:[1] da yao shan: reads as Dieyeshan, which is in Pu speech。In Chinese it is Daliushan, in today Anhui province, in regions of Yanliu, Shuangmiao, and Xiaodian。
[2] 松柏：读苏布，指老家园氏族。
[2] song bai(pine) reads as su bu, refers to the Laojiayuan (old family garden) clan。
[3] 梓桑：指二里坪氏族。
[3] zi sang (zi tree and mulberry) refers to the Erliping (two-mile town) clan。
[4]机：指祭田氏族。
[4] ji(device) refers to the Jitian (sacrifice to cultivated land) clan。
[5]竹：指塘咀子氏族。
[5] zhu(bamboo), refers to the Tangzuizi (lowland mouth) clan。
[6] 虎豹麢臭：指东山石坝子氏族。虎豹，指东山；麢臭，指石坪，即石坝子。
[6]hu bao ling chuo (tiger leopard deer rabbit)
Tr: refers to the Dongshan (east mount) Shibazi (stone dam) clan。 hubao: dongshan/east mountain, lingchuo: shiping refers to Shibazi。

译文：由茶棚山往东北一百里，有座山叫大刘山，那里住着老家园氏族，住着二里坪氏族，住着祭田氏族，住着塘咀子氏族，还住着东山石坝子氏族。
Translation:
One hundred li further northeast from the Chapengshan stands Daliushan。 The Laojiayuan clan lives there。Also living there are the following clans: the Erliping, the Jitian, the Tangzuizi, and the Dongshan-shibazi。

05-08-13 灵山
Lingshan
（118,28108E；32,27758N）

又东北三百里，曰灵山[1]，其上多金玉[2]，其下多青雘[3]，其木多桃李梅杏[4]。

注释：[1]灵山：指琅琊山，在安徽滁州东侧。琅琊，即灵芝。

Notes:[1] ling shan (spirit mount) refers to Langxieshan in the east part of Tuzhou, Anhui province. Langxie: aka Lingzhi, an herb。

[2] 金玉：指后岭夷。

[2] jin yu (gold jade) refers to the Houling (back ridge) Yi。

[3] 青䕶：指东湖氏族。

[3] qing hu; east lake clan: clan

[4] 桃李梅杏：指谯楼城头人。梅，读 mu，指城。杏，读 heng，指头人，即首领。

[4] tao li mei xing (peach prunus plum apricot)

Tr: refers to the chieftain of Qiaoloucheng, mei(plum) means city, xing(apricot) reads as heng, meaning clan head, chieftain。

译文：由大刘山往东北三百里，有座山叫琅琊山，西面住着后岭夷，东面住着东湖氏族，检目住着谯楼城的头人。

Translation:

Three hundred li further northeast from Daliushan stands Langxieshan。 The Houling Yi lives on the west side, the Donghu clan lives on the east。 In their Jianmu, the administration center lives the Jiaoloucheng 's chieftain。

05-08-14 龙山

Longshan

（118,56328E；32,50864N）

又东北七十里，曰龙山[1]，上多寓木[2]，其上多碧[3]，其下多赤锡[4]，其草多桃枝钩端[5]。

注释：[1]龙山：龙山是已汉译地名，今安徽省来安县龙山乡。

Notes: [1] long shan (dragon mount) this is a Chinese translation, the mountain is in Longshanxiang (dragon mount district), Lai 'an county, Anhui province。

[2] 寓木：读 yi mo，指河坎。

[2]yu mu (house wood) reads as yimo, refers to the river curbs。

[3]碧：指大背篓氏族，今称大庄子氏族。

[3]bi (clear blue) refers to the Dabeilou (big back basket) clan, known today as the Dazhuangzi (big village) clan。

[4] 赤锡：指涂郢氏族。

[4] chi xi (red tin) refers to the Tuying clan。

[5] 桃枝钩端：指下棚涧边。

[5] tao zhi gou duan (peach branch hook end) refers to the Xiapengjianbian，(low shed brook edge)。

译文：由琅琊山往东北七十里，有座山叫龙山，那里住着河坎氏族，西边住着大庄子氏族，东边住着涂郢氏族，人们住在下棚涧边。

Translation:

Seventy li further northeast from Langyashan stands Longshan。 The Hekan clan lives there。 The Dazhuangzi clan lives on its west, and the Tuying clan lives on the east, people settled by the Xiapengjian Creek。

05-08-15 衡山

Hengshan

（118,83262E；32,45948N）

又东南五十里，曰衡山[1]，其上多寓木榖柞[2]，多黄垩白垩[3]。

注释：[1]衡山：指低海拔的山，今称平山，在南京市六合区马鞍镇北面。
Notes:[1] heng shan (balance mount) refers to the mountain at low sea level, today it is called Pingshan (flat mount), situated to the north of Ma'an (horse saddle) township, in Liuhe district, Nanjing city, Jiangsu province。

[2] 寓木榖柞：指水畔的山根氏族，此处的根只是音译。
[2]yu mu gu za: refers to the Shangen (mount roots) clan by the water, gen is phonetic rendering in Chinese。

[3] 黄垩白垩：指马洼和小洼氏族。小，读 ba 音。
[3] huang e bai e (yellow white clay) refers to the Mawa clan and the Xiaowa clan, xiao reads as ba in Pu speech。

译文：由龙山往东南五十里，有座山叫平山，山的西面住着水畔的山根氏族，住着马洼和小洼氏族。
Translation:
Fifty li further southeast from Longshan stands Pingshan。The Shangen clan by the water lives on the west, and the Mawa clan and Xiaowa clan live on the west too。

05-08-16 石山
Shishan
（119,04465E；32,29436N）

又东南七十里，曰石山[1]，其上多金[2]，其下多青雘[3]，多寓木[4]。

注释：[1]石山：指破山，在南京仪征市西侧。破，濮语读音 she 音，与石同音。
Notes:[1] shi shan (stone mount) refers to Puoshan (broken mount) located to the west side of Yizheng city, Nanjing city, Jiangsu province。Po(broken) reads as She in Pu speech, a close phonetic match to shi(stone)。

[2]金：指横梁氏族。
[2] jin (gold) refers to the Hengliang (horizontal beam) clan。

[3] 青雘：指溪口氏族。溪，指胥浦河。
[3] qing hu refers to the Xikou clan, xi: brook, refers to the Xupuhe River。

[4] 寓木：指江畔氏族。江，即长江，濮语读斜寓。
[4]yu mu refers to the Jiangban clan, Jiang: the Yangtze River, reads as xieyu in Pu speech。

译文：由平山往东南七十里，有座山叫破山，西边住着横梁氏族，东边住着溪口氏族和江畔氏族。
Translation:
Seventy li further southeast from Pingshan stands Puoshan。 The Hengliang clan lives on its west side, and on its east side live the Xikou clan and the Jiangpan clan。

05-08-17 若山
Ruoshan
（118,98671E；31,75655N）

又南百二十里，曰若山[1]，其上多㻬琈之玉[2]，多赭[3]，多邽石[4]，多寓木[5]，多柘[6]。

注释：[1]若山：指仁山，今称大仁山，在南京溧水区北面。
Notes:[1] ruo shan: refers to Renshan (benevolence mount), today known as the Darenshan, to the north of Lishui district of Nanjing city, Jiangsu province。

[2] 㻬琈玉：指安山夷。濮语安、设，读音 t'u。
[2] yun fu yu: refers to the Anshan Yi, In Pu speech, an, she reads as t'u。

[3]赭：指则启，这里指大陈仓夷，是古陈国的下属管理夷。

[3] zhu(ochre) refers to zeqi, meaning: Dachencang Yi, the management Yi under the rule of the ancient Cheng Guo (a nation) 。dachencang (big old silo) 。

[4] 邽石：指港运氏族。

[4] gui shi: water transportation clan, the Gangyun clan。

[5] 寓木：指河坎氏族。

[5]yu mu refers to the Hekan clan。

[6]柘：指柘塘氏族。

[6] Zhe, refers to the Tuotang clan。

译文：由破山往南一百二十里，有座山叫仁山，山的西面住着安山夷，住着大陈仓夷，住着港运氏族，住着河坎氏族和柘塘氏族。

Translation:

One hundred and twenty li further south from Puoshan stands Renshan。 On its west side live the following people: the Anshan Yi, the Dachencang Yi, the Gangyun clan, the Hekan clan and the Tuotang clan。

05-08-18 㲋山

Zhishan

（119,45406E；31,79566N）

又东南一百二十里，曰㲋山[1]，多美石[2]，多柘[3]。

注释：[1]㲋山：指直山，㲋是避汉武帝名讳而更名，今常州市直溪镇，从破山起算距离。

Notes: [1] zhi shan (bore mount) refers to Zhi(straight) Mountain。 Zhi is changed as it is the Name of Hanwu Di, aka today's Zhixi (straight creek) township。 Distance starts from Puoshan。

[2] 美石：指李姓氏族。

[2] mei shi (beautiful stone) refers to the clan bearing the surname of Li。

[3]柘：指柘荡氏族。

[3] zhe: (thorny tree) refers to the Zhedang clan。

译文：由破山往东南一百二十里，有座山叫直山，住着李姓氏族和柘荡氏族。

Translation:

One hundred and twenty li further southeast from Puoshan stands Zhishan。 The Li clan and Tuodang clan live there。

05-08-19 玉山

Yushan

（119,5715E；31,7461N）

又东南一百五十里，曰玉山[1]，其上多金玉[2]，其下多碧[3]、铁[4]，其木多柏[5]。

注释：[1]玉山：指坛山，今常州市金坛区，从破山起算距离。

Notes:[1]yu shan (jade mount) refers to the Tanshan (pot mount) today's Jintan (gold pot) district in Changzhou city。The distance starts from Puoshan。

[2] 金玉：指经夷，即直溪夷。

[2] jin yu (gold jade) refers to the Jing Yi, aka Zhixi Yi。

[3]碧：指元港氏族。

[3]bi: refers to the Yuangang clan。

[4]铁：指东直泡氏族，今称钱资荡氏族。钱资，即东直。
[4] tie(iron) refers to the Dongzhipao clan。 It is known today as the Qianzidang clan, qian(money) zi (capital) dang(waterfront)。qianzi: aka dongzhi (east straight) 。
[5]柏：指下塘桥氏族。
[5] bai: refers to the Xiatangqiao clan。

译文：由破山往东南一百五十里，有座山叫坛山，西边住着直溪夷，东边住着元港氏族，住着东直泡氏族，检目住着下塘桥氏族。
Translation:
One hundred and fifty li further southeast from Puoshan stands Tanshan。 The Zhixi Yi lives on the west。The Yuangang Yi and the Dongzhipao clan live on the east。 At its administration center the Xiatangqiao clan lives。

05-08-20 讙山
Huanshan
（119,42545E；32,18792N)

又东南七十里，曰讙山[1]，其木多檀[2]，多邽石[3]，多白锡[4]。郁水[5] 出于其上，潜于其下，其中多砥砺 [6] 。

注释：[1]讙山：指宝华山东麓的红山，仍称宝华山，今镇江城，从破山起算距离。
Notes:[1] huan shan (noise mount) refers to the Hongshan (red mount) on the east flank of the Baohuashan, the old same name also known today as the Zhenjiang city。 The distance starts from Puoshan。
[2]檀：指指丹徒氏族。
[2] tan (fragrant wood) refers to the Dantu (red followers) clan。
[3] 邽石：指港运氏族。
[3] gui shi: the water port transportation clan, known as the Gangyun clan。
[4] 白锡：指红山氏族。
[4] bai xi (white tin) refers to the Hongshan clan。
[5] 郁水：指斜郁水，即长江。
[5]yu shui (dark water) refers to the Xie(leaning)yu(dark) shui （water）， aka the Yangtze River。
[6] 砥砺：指江心岛氏族。
[6] dili (grinding stone) refers to the Jiang(river) xin(heart) dao(island) clan, who occupies the island in the middle of the river。

译文：由破山往东南七十里，有座山叫宝华山，中心住着丹徒氏族，住着港运氏族，住着红山氏族。长江水从西边向东边流去，江中住着江心岛氏族。
Translation:
Seventy li further southeast from Puoshan stands Baohuashan。In its center live the Dantu clan, the Gangyun clan and the Hongshan clan。 The Yangtze River flows from the west to the east。 In the middle of the river, live the Jiangxindao island clan。

05-08-21 仁举山
Renjushan
（119,44868E；32,78157N)

又东北百五十里，曰仁举之山[1]，其木多穀柞[2]，其阳多赤金[3]，其阴多赭[4]。

注释：[1]仁举山：指双龙山，今江苏高邮市，从破山起算距离。
Notes:[1] ren ju shan (benevolence gesture mount) refers to the Shuang(double)Long(dragon)Mount。 Today it is known as Gaoyou city, Jiangsu province, the distance starts from Puoshan。

[2] 榖柞：指桥村氏族。
[2]gu zuo (grain zuo) refers to the Qiaocun (bridge village) clan。

[3] 赤金：指盐河部落氏族。
[3] chi jin (red gold) refers to the Yanhe (salt river) tribe and their clans。

[4]赭：指绪姓氏族。濮语绪读赭音。
[4] zhe(ochre) refers to the clan bearing the surname of Xu, in Pu speech, it is reads as zhe。

译文：由破山往东北一百五十里，有座山叫双龙山，中心住着桥村氏族，南面住着盐河部落氏族，北面住着绪姓氏族。
Translation:
One hundred fifty li from Puoshan stands Shuanglongshan。In its center lives the Qiaocun clan。 On its south side live the Yanhe tribes and clans。On its north lives the Xu clan。

05-08-22 师每山
Shimeishan
（119,84535E；32,93432N）

又东五十里，曰师每之山[1]，其阳多砥砺[2]，其阴多青雘[3]，其木多柏[4]，多檀[5]，多柘[6]，其草多竹[7]。

注释：[1]师每山：指青苔山，今江苏兴化市。
Notes:[1] shi mei shan (teacher every mount) refers to the Qingtaishan (green moss mount), today it is known as the Xinghua city in Jiangsu province。

[2] 砥砺：指泡子夷。
[2] di li (grinding stone) refers to the Paozi (bubble) Yi。

[3] 青雘：指浸湖氏族，今称乌巾荡氏族。
[3] qing hu (green dyestuff) refers to the Jinhu (soak lake) clan, known today as the Wujindang(black scarf lowland) clan。

[4]柏：指商贩氏族。
[4] bai(poplar) refers to the Shangfan(traders) clan。

[5]檀：指上官河氏族。
[5] tan (fragrant wood) refers to the Shangguan (upper official) River clan。

[6]柘：指仓廪氏族。
[6] zhe: refers to the Cangbing (silo storage) clan。

[7] 其草多竹：绰口荡住着快运氏族。
[7] qi cao duo zhu (its grass plenty bamboo) refers to the Kuaiyun (express delivery)clan who reside in Chuokoudang。

译文：由双龙山往东五十里，有座山叫青苔山，山的南面住着泡子夷，北面住着浸湖氏族。中部住着商贩氏族，住着上官河氏族，住着仓廪氏族。绰口荡住着快运氏族。
Translation:

Fifty li further east from Shuanglongshan stands Qingtaishan。 The Paozi Yi lives on the south side, the Jinhu clan lives on the north side。 The traders' clans occupy the middle region, where the Shangguanhe clan and the Bingcang clan live。In Changkoudang live the Kuaiyun clan。

05-08-23 琴鼓山
Qingushan
（119,96191E；31,81746N）

又东南二百里，曰琴鼓之山[1]，其木多穀柞椒柘[2]，其上多白珉[3]，其下多洗石[4]，其兽多豕鹿[5]，多白犀[6]，其鸟多鸩[7]。

凡荆山之首，自景山至琴鼓之山，凡二十三山，二千八百九十里。其神状皆鸟身而人面[8] 。其祠：用一雄鸡 [9] 祈瘗，用一藻圭 [10] ，糈用稌。骄山冢也，其祠：用羞酒 [11] 少牢祈瘗，婴毛一璧 [12] 。

注释：[1]琴鼓山：指藻溪山，常州的古称谓。琴指溪，鼓指藻。
Notes: [1] qin gu shan (lyre drum mount) refers to the Zaoxishan (moss brook mountain)， the ancient name for Changzhou。 qin(lyre): brook, gu(drum): moss。
[2] 穀柞椒柘：指藻港的巢支系氏族。巢，读 jiao 音。
[2]gu zuo jiao zhe (grain) refers to the Chao(nestle) branch clan from Zaogang。 Chao reads as jiao in Pu speech。
[3] 白珉：指白庄氏族，这里是濮汉混读。
[3] bai min (white min) refers to the Baizhuang （white village) clan。 This name is a mix of Pu and Chinese。
[4] 洗石：指横河氏族，今称横塘河氏族。
[4] xi shi (wash stone) refers to the Henghe clan, known today as the Hengtanghe clan。
[5] 豕鹿：指原住民。
[5] shi lu (pig deer) refers to the local original residents。
[6] 白犀：指经商氏族。
[6] bai xi (white unicorn) refers to the clans engaged in trading。
[7]鸩：指好、漂亮。
[7] zhen(bird): good, beautiful, good looking。
[8] 鸟身人面：僚族居民的形象。
[8] niao shen ren mian (bird body human face) 。
Tr: the image of the residents of Lao tribes。
[9] 雄鸡：指软玉。
[9] xiong ji(male chicken) refers to the soft jade。
[10] 藻圭：玉的形制的一种，是上尖下方的条形玉牌。
[10] zao gui: type of jade, with top triangle and lower square in shape。
[11] 羞酒：指用樽盛酒。
[11] xiu jiu: votive wine held in Zun。
[12] 婴毛一璧：掩埋的信玉用一璧玉。
[12] ying mao yi bi: messenger jade is Bi, to be buried。

译文：由青苔山往东南二百里，有座山叫藻溪山，中心住着藻港的巢支系氏族。山的西面住着白庄氏族，东面住着横河氏族，这里的族群为原住民和经商氏族，这里的人都很漂亮。

综观荆山山系，从景山到藻溪山，共二十三山延绵二千八百九十里。这些山的山神皆为僚族居民的形象。祭祀用一软玉制作的藻圭掩埋，食物用荞麦食品。竹山是宗山，祭祀用樽酒少牢礼，掩埋的信玉要用一璧玉。
Translation:

Two hundred li further southeast from Qingtaishan stands Zaoxishan。 In its center region live the Chao branches of Zaogang clan。 The Baizhuan clan lives on the west of the mountain, the Henghe clan lives on the east side of the mountain。Those tribal people are the local original residents and trader clans。 They are very good -looking folks。
In sum: of the Jingshan system with 23 mountains between Jingshan to Zaoxishan, the distance is a total of 2,890 li。All the mountain deities are in the images of the Lao residents from the settlements。 When sacrificing, a Zaogui of soft jade is buried。 The food is made of buckwheat。Zhushan is the ancestor's mound, the Shaolao rite is observed, using a Zun to offer the wine。 The messenger jade is a piece of Bi, to be buried。

中山经第九山系

Book 5 Zhongshanjing； chapter 9

05-09-01 岷山 女几山
Nvjishan
（102,36317E； 30,81746N）

中次九经岷山[1]之首，曰女几之山[2]，其上多涅[3]，其木多杻橿[4]，其草多菊术（zhu)[5]。洛水[6] 出焉，东流注于江 [7]，其中多雄黄 [8]，其兽多虎豹 [9] 。

注释：[1]岷山：指岷山山脉，南面的大雪山属岷山南脉。
Notes; [1] min shan: refers to the Minshan range, the Daxueshan (big snow mount) belongs to the south part of the Minshan Mountain range。

[2] 女几山：指小金山，女指小，几，指部落，音译为金，今四川小金县。
[2] nv ji shan (girl a few mount) refers to the Xiaojinshan, nv: small, ji: tribe, phonetically rendered into Jin(gold) today is known as Xiaojin county, Sichuan province。

[3]涅：指大金川氏族。
[3] nie (alum stone): refers to the Dajinchuan clan。 Dajinchuan (big gold rivers) 。

[4] 杻橿：指小金关氏族。
[4] niu jiang （oak holm oak）: refers to the Xiaojinguan clan, xiaojinguan (small gold pass) 。

[5] 菊术：指美村氏族。
[5] ju shu (chrysanthemum skill) refers to the Meicun (beauty village) clan。

[6] 洛水：指泸水，是小金川与大金川汇合的水，今称大渡河。
[6] luo shui: refers to Lushui river, after Xiaojinchuan and Dajinchuan join, it is called Daduhe River。

[7]江：指岷江江，属长江支流。
[7] jiang(river) refers to the Minjiang River, a major tributary of the Yangtze River。

[8] 雄黄：指笑山氏族，又称乐山氏族。
[8] xiong huang (male yellow) refers to the Xiaoshan (laugh mount) clan, also known as the Leshan clan, Le, (happy, music) 。

[9] 虎豹：指月弦嘴氏族
[9]hu bao (tiger leopard) refers to the Yuexianzui (moon harp mouth) clan。

译文：中山第九列是岷山山系，最西边的一座山叫金部落山，西边住着大金川氏族，中心住着小金关氏族，住着美村氏族。泸水从这里流出，向东流入岷江，河口处住着乐山氏族，住着月弦嘴氏族。
Translation:
The 9th system of mountains in the middle land is the Minshan Mountains range。The westmost one is called the Jinbuluo Mountain。On its west side lives the Dajinchuan clan。 In the central region live the Xiaojinguan clan, and the Meicun clan。 Lushui River rises from here and goes east into the Minjiang River。On the river mouth, live the Leshan clan and the Yuexuanzui clan。

05-09-02 岷山
Minshan
（103,85306E；31,6812N）

又东北三百里，曰岷山[1]。江水[2] 出焉，东北流注于海，其中多良龟 [3]，多鼍 [4]，其上多金玉 [5]，其下多白珉 [6]，其木多梅棠 [7]，其兽多犀象 [8]，多夔牛 [9]，其鸟多翰、鷩 [10]。

注释：[1]岷山：指岷江山，今四川省茂县县城。
Notes: [1] min shan: refers to the Minjiangshan, known as today's Mao County seat in Sichuan province。
[2] 江水：指岷江，属长江源头之一。
[2] jiang shui: refers to Minjiang River, one of headwaters for Yangtze River。
[3] 良龟：指良渚氏族。
[3] liang gui (good turtle) refers to the Liangzhu clan。
[4]鼍：指蚩尤中国氏族。鼍，指中国，蚩尤联盟最早称中国。
[4] tuo(reptile) refers to the Chiyou China tribal clans。 Tuo; meaning China, aka Zhongguo, the middle country。The Chiyou confederacy is the earliest nation who call themselves China。
[5] 金玉：指得西岭夷。
[5] jin yu (gold jade) refers to the Dexiling (get west ridge) Yi。
[6] 白珉：指岷江部落夷。
[6] bai min (white stone): refers to the Minjiang tribe Yi。
[7] 梅棠：指前敫氏族。
[7] mei tang (plum berry) refers to the Qianjiao clan, qian(front); jiao (flowing time) 。
[8] 犀象：指凤泽夷。今称凤仪镇夷。
[8] xi xiang (unicorn elephant) refers to the Fengze Yi, today known as the Fengyizheng Yi。
[9] 夔牛：指夏河氏族。即甘肃夏河的氏族。
[9] kui niu (huge buffalo): refers to the Xiahe clan, aka the tribal clans from Xiahe, Gansu province。
[10] 翰鷩：指靖州氏族，今称静州氏族。
[10] han bi (high bird) refers to the Jingzhou clan, today known as the Jingzhou (different jing) clan。

译文：由金部落山往东北三百里，有座山叫岷江山。岷江水从那里流出，向东北流入大海，出海口处住着良渚氏族，住着蚩尤中国氏族。岷江山的西边住着得西岭夷，东边住着岷江部落氏族，中心住着前敫氏族，住着凤泽氏族，住着夏河氏族，住着静州氏族。
Translation:
Three hundred li further northeast from the Jinbuluo Mountain stands the Minjiangshan。Minjiang River flows out of there and goes northeast to empty into the sea。 At the river mouth, the Liangzhu people live, also live there are the Chiyou China people。On the west side of the Minjiangshan live the Dexiling Yi。On its east side live the

Minjiang Buluo clans。In the center region live the Qianjiao clan, the Fengze clan, the Xiahe clan and the Jingzhou clan。

05-09-03 崍山
Laishan
（104,73484E；31,77213N）

又东北一百四十里，曰崍山[1]。江水[2] 出焉，东流注大江 [3] 。其阳多黄金 [4]， 其阴多麋麈 [5]， 其木多檀柘 [6]， 其草多薤韭 [7]， 多药、空夺[8]。

注释：[1]崍山：指油山。今四川绵阳市江油县城。
Notes:[1] lai shan (refers to Youshan (oil mount) known today as the Jiangyou county seat in Mianyang city, Sichuan province。

[2] 江水：指涪江水。
[2] jiang shui: refers to the Fujiangshui River。

[3] 大江：指嘉陵江。
[3] da jiang (big river) refers to the Jialingjiang River。

[4] 黄金：指马家冲脊氏族。水北为阳。
[4] huang jin (yellow gold): refers to the Majiachongji (horse family vale ridge) clan, the north of the river is the Yang side。

[5] 麋麈：指沙棠村氏族。水南为阴。
[5]mi chun (elk deer); refers to the Shatangcun clan. South of the river is the Yin side。

[6] 檀柘：指太平村氏族。
[6] tan zhe (sandal wood mulberry): refers to the Taipingcun clan。 Taipingcun: peaceful village。

[7] 薤韭：指谢苗氏族。
[7] fei jiu(leek) refers to the Xiemiao clan。

[8] 药空夺：读月康鞑，指月氏游牧氏族。
[8] yao kong duo (medicine vain grab) reads as Yuekangda, refers to the Less Yuezhi nomadic tribal clans。

译文：由岷江山往东北一百四十里，有座山叫油山。涪江水从山间流出，向东流入岷江。北面住着马家冲脊氏族，南面住着沙棠村氏族，中心住着太平村氏族，住着谢苗移民，住着月氏游牧民。
Translation:
One hundred and forty li further northeast from Minjiangshan stands Youshan。 Fujiangshui River rises from the mountain and goes east into Minjiang River。North of the mountain live the Majiachongji clan。 South of the mountain live the Shatangcun clan。 In the middle region live the Xiemiao immigrants, as well as Yuezhi nomadic herders。

05-09-04 崌山
Jushan
（105,59297E；31,63528N）

又东一百五十里，曰崌山[1]。江水[2] 出焉，东流注于大江 [3]， 其中多怪蛇 [4]， 多鰲鱼 [5]， 其木多楢杻 [6]， 多梅梓 [7]， 其兽多夔牛 [8] 、麢、㚟、犀、兕 [9] 。有鸟焉，状如鸮而赤身白首 [10]， 其名曰穷脂 [11]， 可以御火 [12] 。

注释：[1]崌山：指黄松林山，简称黄林山、林山。在四川广元市剑阁县金仙镇。

Notes:[1] ju shan: refers to the Huangsonglin Mountain, shortened to Huanglinshan, Linshan。 Huang(yellow) song(pine) lin(forest)。It is in the Jinxian township, Jiange county in Guangyuan city, Sichuan province。

[2] 江水：指西江水。

[2] jiang shui: refers to the Xijiangshui River。

[3] 大江：指嘉陵江。

[3] da jiang (big river) refers to Jialingjiang River。

[4] 怪蛇：指双柏村氏族。双，读 gang，谐音怪。

[4] guai she (strange snake) refers to Shuangbaicun clan。shuang(double) reads as gang, a phonetic match to guai。

[5] 鮆鱼：指水碾拐夷。

[5] zhi yu (tough fish); refers to Shuinianguai (water mill limp) Yi。

[6] 楢杻：指涂姓分支氏族。

[6] qiu niu (hard wood oak): refers to the branch clan bearing the surname of Tu。

[7] 梅梓：指仙村氏族。

[7] mei zi (plum hardwood):refers to the Xiancun(fairy village) clan。

[8] 夔牛：指榨油树氏族。

[8] kui niu: (big buffalo) refers to Zhayoushu (oil press tree) clan。

[9] 麢㚟犀兕：指小桥、黄松林、顺村、老青杆氏族。

[9] ling chuo xi si (antelope, hoofed rabbit, rhino unicorn): refers to the clans of Xiaoqiao, Huangsonglin, Shuncun, and Laoqinggan。

[10] 鸮而赤身白首：指东边的苍羲部落氏族。

[10] xiao er chi shen bai shou (owl red body with white head) 。

Tr: refers to the tribal clans on the east side: the Cangxibuluo。

[11] 穷脂：指街坪氏，今称店子坪氏族。

[11] qiong zhi (poor fat) refers to Jieping Shi, today known as the Dianziping clans。

[12] 御火：指念诵氏族，即有文化的氏族。

[12]yu huo: refer Niansun clan, the tribal clans that can recite and read, meaning literate clans。

译文：由油山往东一百五十里，有座山叫林山。西江水从那里流出，向东流入嘉陵江，河边住着双柏村氏族，住着水碾拐夷。中心住着涂姓分支氏族，住着仙村氏族。周围住着小桥村氏族、黄松林氏族、顺村氏族、老青杆氏族。有一群人，是东边的涂姓部落氏族，叫街坪氏，是夏国的念诵氏族。

Translation:

One hundred and fifty li from the Youshan stands Linshan。Xijiangshui River rises from the mountains and goes east into the Jialingjiang River。 On the riverbanks live the Shuangbaishu clan, the Shuinianguai clan。In the middle region live the tribal clan bearing the surname of Tu, as well as Xiancun clan。 In the surrounding regions live the Xiaoqiaocun clan, the Huangsongling clan, the Shuncun clan and the Laoqinggan clan。A group of people, the Tu clan, are known as Jieping Shi, they are the Niansong clan of the Xia nation。

05-09-05 高梁山

Gaoliangshan

（107,10424E；31,56366N）

又东三百里，曰高梁之山[1]，其上多垩[2]，其下多砥砺[3]，其木多桃枝钩端[4]。有草焉，状如葵而赤华[5]，荚实，白柎[6]，可以走马[7]。

注释：[1]高梁山：指蜈蚣山。濮语称蜈蚣为蚣蜈，读音 gonglong,谐音高梁。在四川平昌县城。

Notes:[1] gao liang shan (high beam mount) refers to the Wugong Mountain。 Wugong (Centipedes):in Pu speech reads as gonglong, a close phonetic match to gaoliang。 It is in Pingchang county, Sichuan province。

[2]垩：指牟家湾氏族。

[2]e(clay) refers to the Mojiawan clan。

[3] 砥砺：指石岗坪氏族。

[3] di li (whetstone): refers to the Shigangping clan。

[4] 桃枝钩端：指开平部落集镇氏族。今称平昌氏族。

[4] tao zhi gou duan (peach branch hooked end): refers to the township clan of the Kaiping tribe。 Today it is called the Pingchang clan。

[5] 葵而赤华：北面的游牧濮。

[5] kui er chi hua (sunflowers with red flower); the nomadic Pu people from the north。

[6] 荚实白柎：蒋家坡濮族。

[6] jia shi bai fu (pod with white calyx): refers to the Jiangjiapo Pu people。

[7] 走马：指照苗。即且照苗，都城在合川。

[7] zou ma (walking horse): refers to the Zhao Miao, aka Qiezhao Miao people, their capital is in Hechuan, Sichuan province。

译文：由林山往东三百里，有座山叫蜈蚣山。山的西面住着牟家湾氏族，东面住着石岗坪氏族，中心住着开平部落集镇氏族。有一个游牧氏族，是北面的游牧濮，是蒋家坡濮族，是夏国的且照苗。

Translation:

Three hundred li further east from the Linshan stands Wugongshan。 On the west side of the mountain lives the Mojiawan clan。On the east side live the Shigangping clan。In the middle region live the Kaiping tribe's township clan。A nomadic Pu clan from the north is called the Jiangjiapo Pu, they are the Qiezhao Miao of the Xia nation。

05-09-06 蛇山

Sheshan

（109,51927E；31,40002N）

又东四百里，曰蛇山[1]，其上多栒[2]，多豫樟[3]，其草多嘉荣[4]，少辛[5]。有兽焉，其状如狐而白尾长耳[6]，名曰【犭也】狼[7]，见则国内有兵[8]。

注释：[1]蛇山：指凤山，今重庆市巫溪县凤凰镇。

Notes:[1] she shan (snake mount): refers the Fengshan, which is today's Fenghua township, in Wuxi County in Chongqing city, Sichuan province。

[2]栒：指七星村氏族。栒，指七。

[2] xun(camphor): refers to the Qixing (seven star) clan, xun: seven。

[3] 豫樟：指樟树坪氏族。

[3]yu zhang(asarum): refers to the Zhangshuping clan。

[4] 嘉荣：指贾家塆氏族。

[4] jia rong(grass); refers to the Jiajiatang clan。

[5] 少辛：指兴旺村氏族。

[5] shao xin (young spicy) refers to the Xingwangcun clan. xingwang(prosperity)。

[6] 狐而白尾长耳：濮族的山区游牧夷。狐，指濮；白，指山区；尾长耳，指游牧夷。

[6]hu er bai wei chang er (fox with white tail long ears) 。

Tr： hu(fox)refers to Pu, bai(white) refers to mountainous area, weichang'er (tail long ears) refers to the nomadic Yi。

[7] 【犭也】狼：指私那氏。
[7]ye lang(wolf) refers to the Sina Shi。
[8] 国内有兵：属于中河村的氏族。国内，读果洛，指中心、中村，这里指中河村。
[8] guo nei you bing (state inside has army) refers to the clans belonging to Zhonghe Village。 guonei (inside state) reads as guoluo, meaning center, middle village, here refers to Zhonghe (middle river) Village。

译文：由蜈蚣山往东四百里，有座山叫凤山，它的西面住着七星村氏族，住着樟树坪氏族，住着贾家垧和兴旺村牧民。有一个氏族，是濮族的山区游牧夷，名叫私那氏，属于中河村的氏族。
Translation:
Four hundred li further east from Wugong Mountain stands Fengshan。 On its west side live the clans of Qixingcun village, Zhangshuping, Jiajiashang, and herders of Xingwang village。 Another clan is the Sina Shi, a nomadic Pu Yi from the mountain areas。It belongs to the Zhonghe village clan。

05-09-07 鬲山
Lishan
（112,20191E；31,04649N）

又东五百里，曰鬲山[1]，其阳多金[2]，其阴多白珉[3]。蒲【薨鸟】之水[4]出焉，而东流注于江[5]，其中多白玉[6]。其兽多犀象熊罴[7]，多猿蜼 [8] 。

注释：[1]鬲山：指掇山，今湖北省荆门市城区。
Notes:[1]li shan: refers to Zhuishan, in the city quarter in Jingmen city, Hubei province。
[2]金：指荆门氏族。
[2] jin (gold) refers to the Jingmen clan。
[3] 白珉：指关垱冲氏族。
[3] bai min (white stone): refers to Guandangchong clan。
[4]蒲【薨鸟】水：读 p'u hin 水，指漳沮水。
[4] pu meng shui (pu hin water) refers to Zhangjushui River。
[5]江：指长江。
[5] jiang(river) refers to the Yangtze River。
[6] 白玉：指垱夷，今称当阳夷。
[6] bai yu (white jade) refers to the Dang Yi, today known as the Dangyang Yi。
[7] 犀象熊罴：指鞋堰冲氏族、象山氏族、熊窝子氏族、金鸡庙氏族。
[7] xi xiang xiong pi (unicorn, elephant, bear, bear) refers to the clans of Qieyanchong, Xiangshan, Xiongwozi, Jinjimiao。
[8] 猿蜼：指龙泉氏族。
[8] yuan zhui (ape): refers to Longquan (dragon spring) clan。

译文：由凤山往东五百里，有座山叫掇山，南面住着荆门氏族，北面住着关垱冲氏族。漳沮水从这里流出，向东南流入长江，河边住着当阳夷。集镇中心住着鞋堰冲氏族，住着象山氏族，住着熊窝子氏族，住着金鸡庙氏族，还住着龙泉氏族。
Translation:
Five hundred li further east from Fengshan stands Zhuishan。 On the south side live the Jingmen clan。 To its north live the Guandangchong clan。 Zhangjushui River rises from here and goes southeast into the Yangtze River。On its banks live the Dangyang Yi。In the township center live the following clans: the Xieyanchong clan, the Xiangshan clan, the Xiongwozi clan, the Jinjimiao clan, and the Longquan clan。

05-09-08 隅阳山
Yuyangshan
（113,92513E；30,92243N）

又东三百里，曰隅阳之山[1]，其上多金玉[2]，其下多青雘[3]，其木多桑梓[4]，其草多茈[5]。徐之水[6]出焉，东流注于江 [7]，其中多丹粟 [8]。

注释：[1]隅阳山：指澴水山，今湖北省孝感市城区。阳，读 yo，指澴。
Notes :[1]yu yang shan (corner sunny mount) refers to the Huanshuishan, in today's Xiaogan city quarter in Hubei province。Yang reads as yo, meaning huan。
[2] 金玉：指沙河氏族。
[2] jin yu (gold jade) refers to the Shahe (sand river) clan。
[3] 青雘：指高湖氏族。高，读音 qi，谐音青。高湖，今称王母湖。
[3] qing hu (green malachite): refers to the Gaohu (high lake) clan。 gao(high) reads qi, a close phonetic match to Qing(green)。Gaohu (high lake) is known as the Wangmu (queen mother) Lake。
[4] 桑梓：读 su dzi，指九真氏族，今称九真村氏族。
[4] cangzi (mulberry hardwood): reads as su dzi, refers to the Jiuzhen clan, today known as the Jiuzhencun clan。
[5]茈：指游家湾氏族。
[5]ci(grass): refers to the Youjiawan clan。
[6] 徐水：指献水，今称县河。
[6] xu shui (slow water) refers to Xianshui, known as Xianhe River。
[7]江：指长江。
[7] jiang: refers to Yangtze River。
[8] 丹粟：指刘姓氏族。刘，读音 due，谐音丹。
[8] dan su (red millet): refers to the clan bearing the surname of Liu. Liu reads as due, a close phonetic match to dan。

译文：由掇山往东三百里，有座山叫澴水山，西边住着沙河氏族，东边住着高湖氏族，中心住着九真氏族，住着游家湾移民。献水从这里流出，向东南流入长江，河边住着刘姓氏族。
Translation:
Three hundred li further east from Duoshan stands Huanshuishan。 On its west side live the Shahe clan, on its east side, the Gaohu clan。In its center area live the Jiuzhen clan and the Youjiawan immigrants。 Xianshui River flows out of there and goes southeast into the Yangtze River。Along its riverbanks live the Liu clan。

05-09-09 岐山
Qishan
（115,19202E；30,81969N）

又东二百五十里，曰岐山[1]，其上多白金[2]，其下多铁[3]，其木多梅梓[4]，多杻楢[5]。减水[6] 出焉，东南流注于江 [7]。

注释：[1]岐山：指崎山，今湖北省罗田县大崎镇。
Notes: [1] qi shan: refers to Qishan, refers to today's Daqizhen, in Luotian county in Hubei province。
[2] 白金：指黄泥岗氏族，简称黄岗氏族。
[2] bai jin (white gold) refers to the Huangnigang clan, shortened to Huanggang clan。
[3]铁：指仓下垄氏族。铁，指下。

[3] tie(iron) refers to the Cangxialong clan, tie: down。

[4] 梅梓：指李婆墩氏族，简称李墩氏族。

[4] mei zi (plum catalpa): refers to the Lipodun clan, shortened to Lidun clan。

[5] 杻楢 (oak mulberry)：指过河湾氏族。杻，读 lao，指河；楢，指过。

[5] niu qiu: refers to the Guohewang clan. niu: reads as lao, meaning river, qiu: overtake。

[6] 減水：指桂水，今称五桂河。

[6] jian shui (reduce water) refers to the Guishui, today it is called the Wugui River。

[7]江：指长江，这里将中间汇入的巴水河段列为桂水。实际向西南流。

[7] jiang: refers to the Yangtze River。The compiler has listed the in flowing Bashui as Guishui。 It goes in fact to the southwest。

译文: 由澴水山往东二百五十里，有座山叫崎山，它的西面住着黄泥岗氏族，东面住着仓下垄氏族, 和过河湾氏族，桂水从这里流出，向西南流入长江。

Translation:

Two hundred and fifty li further east from the Huanshuishan stands Qishan。 On its west live the Huangnigang clan。 On its east live the Cangxialong clan。 In the middle region live the Lipodun clan and the Guohewang clan。 Guishui River flows out of here and goes southwest into the Yangtze River。

05-09-10 勾檷山

Goumishan

（116,83329E；30,73282N）

又东三百里，曰勾檷之山[1]，其上多玉[2]，其下多黄金[3]，其木多栎柘[4]，其草多芍药[5]。

注释：[1]勾檷山：读“缴骊山”，指怀宁山。今安徽怀宁县城。

Notes:[1] gou mi shan: reads Jiao li shan, refers to the Huainingshan, today it is known as the Huaining county seat in Anhui province。

[2]玉：指大枫树塘氏族。

[2]yu: refers to the Dafengshutang clan。

[3] 黄金：指黄金水塘氏族。“黄金”在此是音译传承，含义应是指东岭。

[3] huang jin (yellow gold) refers to the Huangjin-shuitang clan。Huangjin is a phonetic rendering of Pu concept, meaning the east ridge: Dongling。

[4] 栎柘：指宁支系氏族，实际应是指令狐支系氏族。

[4]li zhe (chestnut oak, dye mulberry): refers to the Ning branch, in fact that of the Linghu clan。

[5] 芍药：指姚老屋氏族。

[5] shao yao(peony): refers to the Yaolaowu Yao’s old house。

译文：由崎山往东三百里，有座山叫怀宁山，西面住着大枫树塘氏族，东面住着黄金水塘氏族，中心住着宁支系氏族和姚老屋氏族。

Translation:

Three hundred li further east from Qishan stands Huainingshan。 On the west side live the Dafengshutang clan。 On its east side lives the Huangjinshuitang clan。 In the middle region live the Ning branch and the Yaolaowu clan。

05-09-11 风雨山

Fengyushan

（117,48775E；30,65432N）

又东一百五十里，曰风雨之山[1]，其上多白金[2]，其下多石涅[3]，其木多椒椫[4]，多杨[5]。宣余之水[6]出焉，东流注于江，其中多蛇 [7] ，其兽多闾麋 [8] ，多麈豹虎 [9] ，其鸟多白鷮 [10] 。

注释：[1]风雨山：指江阴山，风指阴，雨指江。音译为凤仪山，今安徽池州城。
Notes： [1] feng yu shan (wind rain mount)
Tr: refers to the Jiangyinshan (river shade mountain) 。feng: shade(yin); yu: river(jiang) phonetically rendered into Chinese Fengyishan (phoenix style mount) ， in today's Chizhou city, Anhui province。

[2] 白金：指牙埠氏族，今称百牙氏族。
[2] bai jin (white gold) refers to the Yabu clan, known today as the Baiya (a hundred teeth) clan。

[3] 石涅：指池黎氏族，池读榭音，谐音石。黎在此作大解。
[3] shi nie (stone black) refers to the Chili (pond li) clan, chi reads as xie, a close phonetic match to shi。 Li: means big。

[4] 椒椫：指秀山氏族。
[4] qu shan (hard wood) refers to the Xiushan clan。xiu (good looking) 。

[5]杨：指洋水河氏族。
[5] yang(poplar) refers to the Yangshuihe (big water river) clan。

[6] 宣余水：指长乐水，今称秋浦河。
[6] quan yu shui (declare surplus water) refers to the Changleshui (lasting enjoyment) River， today it is known as Qiupuhe River。

[7]蛇：指池口氏族。
[7] she(snake)refers to the Chikou (pool mouth) clan。

[8] 闾麋：指磨盘庄氏族。
[8]lv mi(deer): refers to the Mopanzhuang (grinding stone village) clan。

[9] 麈豹虎：指孔井房氏族。麈当用儒表达。今称孔井村氏族。
[9] chen bao hu (dust leopard tiger) refers to the Kongjingfang clan。 Chen(dust) should be written with Ru(scholar)。 It is known today as the Kongjingcun (kong well village) clan。

[10] 白鷮：指梅湾氏族。
[10] bai jiao (white mountain bird): refers to the Meiwan (plum bay) clan。

译文：由怀宁山往东一百五十里，有座山叫凤仪山，西面住着百牙氏族，东面住着池黎氏族，中心住着秀山氏族，住着洋水河氏族。长乐水从这里流出，向东北流入长江，河边住着池口氏族，住着磨盘庄氏族，住着孔井房氏族，住着梅湾氏族。
Translation:
One hundred and fifty li further east from Huainingshan stands Fengyishan。 On its west side live the Baiya clan。 On its east side live the Chili clan。 In the center live the Xiushan clan and the Yangshuihe clan。Changleshui River rises from here and goes northeast into the Yangtze River。On the riverbank live the following clans: the Chikou, the Mopangzhuang, the Kongjingfang, and the Meiwan。

05-09-12 玉山
Yushan
（118,19953E；31,07918N）

又东北二百里，曰玉山[1]，其阳多铜[2]，其阴多赤金[3]，其木多豫樟、楢、杻[4]，其兽多豕鹿麢㚟[5]，其鸟多鸩[6]。

注释：[1]玉山：指龙山，今称峨山，峨指蛇，龙、蛇同类。今安徽繁昌县城。

Notes: [1]yu shan (jade mount) refers to the Long(dragon)shan, known today as the Eshan。 E: means snake, dragon and snake fall into the same class of reptiles。It is today's Fanchang county seat, Anhui province。

[2]铜：指铜山冲氏族。铜为音译传承。

[2] tong(copper) refers to the Tongshanchong clan, tong is a phonetic rendering of the Pu concept。

[3] 赤金：指赤岭冲氏族。赤为音译传承。

[3] chi jin (red gold) refers to the Chilingchong clan。Chi is a phonetic rendering of the Pu concept。

[4] 豫樟楢杻：龙山的种稻族。

[4]yu zhang qiu niu (various woods: camphor, oak, holm oak) refers to the rice growing tribes in Longshan。

[5] 豕鹿麢臭：风山的牧民。麢作黎解，指人和民。

[5] shi lu ling chuo (various kinds of animals: pig, deer, antelope, hoofed rabbit): refers to the herders of Fengshan。Ling: reads as li, means people, population。

[6]鸩：指铁姓氏族。

[6] zhen (a kind of bird) refers to the clan bearing the surname of Tie。

译文：由凤仪山往东北二百里，有座山叫龙山，南面住着铜山冲氏族，北面住着赤岭冲氏族。中部住着龙山的种稻族，住着凤山的牧民，住着铁姓氏族。

Translation:

Two hundred li further northeast from Fengyishan stands Longshan。On its south side lives the Tongshanchong clan。 On its north side live the Chilingchong clan。In the middle region live the Longshan rice growing tribes, the Fengshan herders and the clan bearing the surname of Tie。

05-09-13 熊山

Xiongshan

（118,87733E；31,32886N）

又东一百五十里，曰熊山[1]。有穴焉，熊之穴[2]，恒出神人[3]。夏启而冬闭[4]，是穴也，冬启必有兵[5]。其上多白玉[6]，其下多白金[7]。其木多樗柳[8]，其草多寇脱[9]。

注释：[1]熊山：熊是华胥氏的称谓，所以也称为胥山，有河流名为胥水。因是华胥氏的游牧支系，又称游子山。

Notes:[1] xiong shan (bear mount) bear is the title for Huaxu Shi, so the mountain is also called Xushan。 The river is called the Xushui。Since it belongs to the nomadic branch, the mountain is also called Youzishan (wandering people mountain) 。

[2] 熊之穴：华胥氏的国家。今江苏南京市高淳区。

[2] xiong zhi xue (bear's cave) means the country of the Huaxu Shi, today is known as the Gaochun district, Nanjing city, Jiangsu province。

[3] 恒出神人：游人氏的集镇，也称游子氏的集镇。

[3] heng chu shen ren (constant appear godly personage) refers to the township of Youren Shi, or Youzi Shi。Youzi: wandering sons。

[4] 夏启而冬闭：高淳的部落。冬闭，原指氏族支系，在此指部落。

[4] xia qi er dong bi (summer open winter close) refers to the Gaochun tribe。Dong bi means tribal branches, here refers to the tribe。

[5] 冬启必有兵：漆河镇之门。冬启必，读邓漆泚，指漆河镇。

[5] dong qi bi you bing (winter open means soldiering) refers to the Qihezhen's gate。 Dongqibi: reads as dengqibi, refers to the Qihe township。

[6] 白玉：指河埠夷。

[6] bai yu (white jade) refers to the Hebu Yi, he bu: high ground by the river。

[7] 白金：指红岭夷，今称凤岭夷。

[7] bai jin (white gold) refers to the Hongling (red ridge) Yi, today known as the Fengling Yi。

[8] 櫄柳：指淳僚氏族。

[8] yun liu (tree of heaven and willow) refers to the Chunliao clan。

[9] 寇脱：指高唐氏族。

[9] kou tuo (bandit drop) refers to the Gaotang clan。

译文：由龙山往东一百五十里，有座山叫胥山。那里有一个国家，叫华胥之国，是游子氏族的集镇，高淳的部落。这个国家是漆河镇之门。这个部落的西面住着河埠氏族，东面住着凤岭夷，中部住着淳僚氏族和高唐氏族。

Translation:

One hundred and fifty li further east from Longshan stands Xushan。 There is a country called Huaxu nation, a township of the Youzi clan from the Gaochun tribe。 This country stands as the gate of Qihezhen township。On its west side live the Hebu clan, on its east side live the Fengling Yi。 In its middle region live the Chunliao clan and the Gaotang clan。

05-09-14 䰠山

Guishan

（119,49073E；31,42847N）

又东一百四十里，曰䰠山[1]，其阳多美玉赤金[2]，其音多铁[3]，其木多桃枝荆芑[4]。

注释：[1]䰠山：指昆山，读音昆仑。今江苏溧阳县城。

Notes: [1] gui shan: refers to Kunshan, Kunshan reads as Kunlun, refers to today's Liyang county seat, Jiangsu province。

[2] 美玉赤金：指梅燕东岭氏族。

[2] mei yu chi jin (beautiful jade red gold) refers to the Meiyandongling clan。

[3]铁：指胥渚氏族。

[3] tie(iron) refers to the Xuzhu clan。

[4] 桃枝荆芑：指开平集部落氏族，今称平陵集部落氏族。

[4] tao zhi jing ji (peach branch thorn twig) refers to the Kaipingji tribal clan, known today as the Pinglingji tribal clan。

译文：由胥山往东一百四十里，有座山叫昆仑。南面住着梅燕东岭氏族，北面住着胥渚氏族，中部住着平陵集部落氏族。

Translation:

One hundred forty li further east from the Xushan stands a mountain called Kunlun。 On its south side lives the Meiyandongling clan。On its north lives the Xuzhu clan, In the middle region live the Pinglingji tribal clan。

05-09-15 葛山

Geshan

（120,27508E；31,90507N）

又东二百里，曰葛山[1]，其上多赤金[2]，其下多瑊石[3]，其木多柤栗橘櫾楢杻[4]，其兽多麢㚟[5]，其草多嘉荣[6]。

注释：[1]葛山：指澄江山，葛指清澈、明澄，今江苏江阴市澄江区。
Notes:[1]ge shan: refers to the Chengjiangshan。Ge means clear, and clean。 It is today's Chengjiang (clear river) district, in Jiangyi city, Jiangsu province。

[2] 赤金：指运输部落氏族。
[2] chi jin (red gold) refers to the transportation tribal clans。

[3] 瑊石：指管理氏族。
[3] jian shi: the management clans。

[4] 柤栗橘櫾楢杻：固定的底层市民。柤栗，指固定的；橘櫾，指底层；楢杻，指市民。
[4] ju li ju yao qiu niu: (various kinds of wood) the permanent, bottom-level citizens。 Juli: permanent, not changing; juyao: lower level, bottom level, qiu niu: residents of the township。

[5] 麢奠：指浮桥村氏族。
[5] ling chuo: refers to the Fuqiaocun clan。fu(float)qiao(bridge)cun(village)。

[6] 嘉荣：指蒋家村氏族。
[6] jia rong: refers to the Jiangjiacun clan。 jiangjia: family bearing the surname of Jiang。

译文：由昆仑往东二百里，有座山叫澄江山，西面住着运输部落氏族，东面住着管理氏族，中部住着固定的底层市民、周围住着浮桥村氏族和将家村氏族。
Translation：
Two hundred li further east from Kunlun stands Chengjiangshan。The clan engaged in transportation business lives on the west side。The management clan lives on the east side。 In the middle region live the permanent bottom level residents of the townships, and the Fuqiaocun clan and the Jiangjia clan live in the surrounding areas。

05-09-16 贾超山
Jiachaoshan
（120,97876E；32,21636N）

又东一百七十里，曰贾超之山[1]，其阳多黄垩[2]，其阴多美赭[3]，其木多柤栗橘櫾[4]，其中多龙脩[5]。

凡岷山之首，自女几山至于贾超之山，凡十六山，三千五百里。其神状皆马身而龙首[6] 。其祠：毛用一雄鸡瘗。糈用稌。文山 [7] 、勾檷、风雨、騩之山，是皆冢也，其祠之：羞酒[8] ，少牢具，婴毛一吉玉。熊山，席也[9]，其祠：羞酒，太牢具，婴毛一璧。干儛[10]，用兵以禳[11]；祈，璆冕舞[12]。

注释：[1]贾超山：指输港山，今南通市石港镇。贾，读 gu 音，与归谐音，指港。
Notes;[1]gu chao shan: refers to the Shugangshan, in today's Shigangzhen township, Nantong city。Gu: close phonetic match to gui(return) means water port。 shu gang shan (transport port mount) 。

[2] 黄垩：指何部氏族，今已无遗迹。
[2] huang e (yellow clay) refers to Hebu clan, today there is no more trace of their existence。

[3] 美赭：指斜天村氏族，今称屯天河村氏族。
[3] mei zhe (nice ochre) refers to the Xietiancun clan, known today as the Tuntianhecun clan。

[4] 柤栗橘櫾：指坚坝、箕环氏族。
[4] ji su ju yao: (various woods) refers to the Jianba clan and the Qihuan clan。

[5] 龙脩：指蔡家圩氏族。
[5] long xiu: refers to the Caijiaxu clan。

[6] 马身而龙首：指僚族的苗蒙氏族形象。
[6] ma shen er long shou (horse body with dragon head)
Tr: the images of Miaomeng clans of the Lao/Liao tribes。

[7] 文山：指岷山。

[7] wen shan: Minshan。

[8] 羞酒：用羊尊盛酒。

[8] xiu jiu: wine in Ram shape Zhun cup, the rhyton。

[9] 席也：轩辕，指宗山中的轩辕，即最大的宗山。

[9] xi ye (seat) xuan yan: means the mound supreme of all the Zongshan (ancestors' mounds), the biggest mound of all。

[10] 干儛：勇士列队。

[10] gan wu: warriors line up in formation。

[11] 用兵以禳：跳傩祭祀。用兵，读雍比，指跳傩。

[11] yong bing yi xiang (use soldiers to pray) a kind shaman dance for rite, yong bing reads as yongbi, means tiaonuo: Nuo dance。

[12] 璆冕舞：祭礼舞。

[12] liao mian wu: ritual dance。

译文：由澄江山往东一百七十里，有座山叫输港山，南面住着何部氏族，北面住着天村氏族，中心住着坚坝、箕环氏族和蔡家圩氏族。

综观岷山山系，从金部落山到输港山，共十六座山，延绵三千五百里。这些山的山神皆为僚族的苗蒙氏族形象，祭祀的信玉要用软玉掩埋，食物用荞麦食物。岷山、怀宁山、凤仪山、昆仑是宗山，祭祀要用羊樽盛酒和用少牢礼，传信用一吉玉。胥山是最大的宗山，祭祀要用羊樽盛酒和用太牢礼，传信用一璧玉。由勇士列队跳傩祭祀，祈祷时跳祭礼舞。

Translation:

One hundred and seventy li further east from Chengjiangshan stands a mountain called Shugangshan。 To its south live the Hebu clan, to its north the Tiancun clan。 In the middle live the Jianba clan, the Qihuan clan and the Caijiaxu clan。

In sum, the Minshan Mountain system from Jinbuluo Mountain to Shugangshan, hosts 16 mountains covering a distance of 3,500 li。 The mountain deities are all in the images of Miaomeng clans' Liao tribes' people。 The messenger jade is a soft type to be buried。The food is made of buckwheat。 Minshan, Huainingshan, Huainingshan, Fengyishan and Kunlun are the ancestors' mounts, Ritual ram rhytons are used for wines and Shaolao rite is observed。 The messenger jade is a piece of Ji jade。 The Xushan Mountain is the greatest ancestor's mount。Ritual ram rhytons are used for wine and --Rite Dalao is observed。 The messenger jade is Pi。 Warriors dance Nuo dances in formation, and when praying, perform the ritual dances。

中山经第十山系

Book 5 Zhongshanjing; chapter 10

05-10-01 首阳山

Shouyangshan

（108,33612E；33,99279N）

中次十经之首，曰首阳之山[1]，其上多金[2]，无草木[3]。

注释：[1]首阳山：指陕西秦岭首阳山，今陕西户县九焰乡。首即数，指九；阳，指艳。
Notes:[1] shou yang shan (head sunny mount) refers to Shouyangshan of Qinling, Shaanxi province in today's Hu County, Jiuyan district。 Shou: shu, means nine, yang: sunny, bright。
[2]金：指岭上氏族，今称金岭氏族。
[2] jin(gold) refers to the Lingshang clan, known as today's Jinling clan。 Ling: ridge, shang(up)。
[3] 无草木：游牧部落地区。
[3] wu cao mu (no grass wood) refers to the land of the nomads。

译文：中部第十列山系为首阳山系，最东边的山叫首阳山。上面住着金岭氏族，是游牧部落地区。
Translation：
The10th system of mountains in the middle region is called the Shouyangshan mountains system, with Shouyangshan at its east most end。 On the mountains lives the Jinling clan。 This is a region of nomads。

05-10-02 虎尾山
Huweishan
（108,17356E；33,83524N）

又西五十里，曰虎尾之山[1]，其木多椒椐[2]，多封石[3]，其阳多赤金[4]，其阴多铁[5]。

注释：[1]虎尾山：指小王涧山。虎指王；尾，读伊，指小。实际往西南。
Notes:[1]hu yi shan (tiger tail mount) refers to the Xiaowangjian Mountain。 hu(tiger) means king, wei(tail) reads as yi, meaning small, it is in fact in the northwest direction。
[2] 椒椐：指北峁上氏族。
[2] jiao ju (pepper, ju) refers to the Beimaoshan clan。 bei(north)mao (stone mound) shang(up)。
[3] 封石：指王涧氏族。封即冯，指王。
[3] feng shi (seal stone) refers to the Wangjian clan, feng; van, von, refers the king, lord。
[4] 赤金：指东涧沟氏族。
[4] chi jin (red gold) refers to the Dongjiangou clan, dong(east); jian(brook); gou(gully)。
[5]铁：读投音，指前咀子村氏族。
[5] tie(iron) reads as tou, refers to the Qianzuizicun clan。 Qian(front) zuizi(mouth), cun(village)。

译文：由首阳山往西南五十里，有座山名叫小王涧山，那里住着北峁上氏族和王涧氏族，南面住着东涧沟氏族，北面住着前咀子村氏族。
Translation:
Fifty li southwest from Shouyangshan stands the Xiaowangjian Mountain, the Beimaoshang clan and the Wangjian clan live there。 On its south side live the Dongjiangou clan。 On the north side lives the Qianzuizi clan。

05-10-03 繁缋山
Fanguishan
（107,97355E；33,63974N）

又西南五十里，曰繁缋之山[1]，其木多楢杻[2]，其草多枝勾[3]。

注释：[1]繁缋山：指岩铧山，今称天华山。实际介绍山南的长角坝聚落，今称长角坝乡。

Note: [1] fan gui shan: refers to the Yanhuashan, known today as the Tianhuashan Mountain。 In fact, it is a description of the township settlement at the Changjiaoba, south of the mountain。 The place is now called Changjiaoba district。

[2] 楢杻：指龙草坪氏族。杻读 lao 音，即指草。

[2] qiu lao (hard wood oak holm oak): refers to the Longcaoping (dragon grass settlement) clan, lao(grass)。

[3] 枝勾：指苍角氏族，今称长角坝氏族。角，读 go 音，与勾谐音。

[3] zhi gou (branch hook): refers to the Cangjiao (black horn) clan, known today as the Changjiaoba (long horn settlement) clan。jiao(horn) reads as go, a phonetic match to gou(hook)。

译文：由小王涧山往西南五十里，有座山叫岩铧山，那里住着龙草坪氏族，旁边住着长角坝氏族。
Translation:
Fifty li further southwest from the Xiaowangjian Mountain stands Yanhuashan. The Longcaoping clan lives there。The Changjiaoba clan lives nearby。

05-10-04 勇石山
Youshishan
（107,9902E；33,52455N）

又西二十里，曰勇石之山[1]，无草木[2]，多白金[3]，多水[4]。

注释：[1]勇石山：指龙河山。今陕西佛坪县城。
Notes:[1] you shi shan (brave stone mount) refers to the Longheshan (dragon river mountain), in today's Foping county seat, Shaanxi province。

[2] 无草木：游牧部落地区。

[2] wu cao mu (no grass wood) refers to the nomad's region。

[3] 白金：指黄家岭氏族，今称黄家湾氏族。白，读 be 音，指黄。

[3] bai jin (white gold) refers to the Huangjialing clan。Today it is known as the Huangjiawang clan。 bai(white) reads as be(yellow)。

[4]水：指梨房沟氏族。水，读奢音，指梨。

[4] shui(water) refers to the Lifanggou (pear house gully) clan, shui(water)reads as she, meaning Pear。

译文：由天华山往西南二十里，有座山叫龙河山，是游牧部落地区，住着黄家湾氏族，住着梨房沟氏族。
Translation:
Twenty li further southwest from Tianhuashan stands Longheshan。 In this land of the nomads, live the Huangjiawan clan, the Lifangou clan。

05-10-05 复州山
Fuzhoushan
（107,84621E；33,47569N）

又西二十里，曰复州之山[1]，其木多檀[2]，其阳多黄金[3]。有鸟焉，其状如鸮而一足彘尾[4]，其名曰跂踵[5]，见则其国大疫[6]。

注释：[1]复州山：指漂草山。复州，读浮卓，指漂草。
Notes:[1] fu zhou shan: refers to the Piaocaoshan (float grass mountain) 。 Fuzhou reads as fuzhuo, meaning piao cao (float grass) 。

[2]檀：读棠，指栗子坝氏族。

[2] tan (sandal wood): reads as tang, refers to the Liziba clan。

[3] 黄金：指漂草岭氏族。

[3] huang jin (yellow gold) refers to the Piaocaoling clan。

[4] 鸮而一足彘尾：西花村的种植夷。一足，在此指花村。

[4] xiao er yi zhu zhi wei (owl one foot pig tail)

Tr: the grower Yi from the Xihuacun。Yi zhu (one foot) refers to the Huacun, (flower village) 。

[5] 跂踵：在此读丘牂，指杨家院氏族。

[5] qi zhong (fork feet): reads as qiu zhang: refers to the Yangjiayuan clan。

[6] 大疫：指鞑靼夷。

[6] da yi (big epidemic) refers to the Dada (Tartars)Yi。

译文：由龙河山往西南二十里，有座山叫漂草山，中心住着栗子坝氏族，南面住着漂草岭氏族。有一群人，是西花村的种植夷，名叫杨家院氏族，是那个地方的鞑靼夷。

Translation:

Twenty li further southwest from Longheshan stands Piaocaoshan。At its center, live the Liziba clan。 On its south side live the Piaocaoling clan。A group of growers from the Xihuacun is known as the Yangjiayuan clan, they are the Dada Yi of that region。

05-10-06 槠山

Zhushan

（107,73677E；33,32573N）

又西三十里，曰槠山[1]，多寓木[2]，多椒椐[3]，多柘[4]，多垩[5]。

注释：[1]槠山：指星山，也称火星山，今谐音传承为城山和北城山，“北城”是火星的濮语读音。

Notes： [1] zhu shan: refers to the Xingshan (star mountain), also known as the Huoxingshan (fire star or mars mountain), phonetically rendered into Chinese as Chengshan (city mount), and Beichengshan (north city mount) 。Beicheng is the Pu phonetic sound for Huoxing(mars)。

[2] 寓木：指沂蒙氏族，即苗夷。今称苗沟氏族。

[2]yu mu (house wood) refers to the Yimeng clan, aka Miao Yi。They are known today as the Miaogou clan。

[3] 椒椐：指北城氏族，此时期的火星概念已经向北星演变。实际应称火星氏族。

[3] jiao ju (pepper): refers to the Beicheng clan, the name is already shifted from Huoxing to Beixing (northern star), It should be called Huoxing clan。

[4]柘：指岩槽氏族。按谐音应称法则氏族，传承为法槽氏族。

[4] zhe (wood): refers to the Yancao (rock groove) clan, a phonetic exact match should be Faze (rules) clan, now shifted to Facao (rule groove) clan。

[5]垩：指大垭氏族。

[5]e refers to the Daya clan。

译文：由漂草山向西南三十里，有座山叫星山，那里住着苗沟氏族，火星氏族，法槽氏族和大垭氏族。

Translation:

Thirty li further southwest from Piaocaoshan stands Xingshan。The Miaogou clan lives there, so does the Huoxing clan, the Facao clan and the Daya clan。

05-10-07 又原山

Youyuanshan

（107,65488E；33,20845N）

又西二十里，曰又原之山[1]，其阳多青雘[2]，其阴多铁[3]，其鸟多鸜鵒[4]。

注释：[1]又原山：指龙亭山，今陕西洋县龙亭镇。
Notes： [1] you yuan shan (again origin mount) refers to the Longtingshan (dragon pagoda mountain), in today's Longting township, Yang County, Shaanxi province。
[2] 青雘：指园顶山氏族。
[2] qing hu (green malachite): refers to the Yuandingshan (garden top mount) clan。
[3]铁：指万岭氏族。
[3] tie refers to the Wanling (ten thousand range) clan。
[4] 鸜鵒：指齐家坎夷，简称齐夷。
[4] di gu (crested myna) refers to the Qijiakan Yi, shortened to Qi Yi。

译文：由星山往西南二十里，有座山叫龙亭山，南面住着园顶山氏族，北面住着万岭氏族，中部住着齐夷。
Translation:
Twenty li further southwest from Xingshan stands Longtingshan。On its south side lives the Yuandingshan clan。On its north side lives the Wanling clan。 In the middle region lives the Qi Yi。

05-10-08 涿山
Zhuoshan
（107,33345E；33,15226N）

又西五十里，曰涿山[1]，其木多榖柞杻[2]，其阳多㻬琈之玉[3]。

注释：[1]涿山：指望山，又称博望山。濮语读博望为固注、固涿。今陕西城固县城
Notes:[1] zhuo shan: refers to the Wang(lookout)shan, also known as the Bowangshan。In Pu concept bowang reads as Guzhu, or Guzhuo, known today as the Gu County seat in Shaanxi province。
[2] 榖柞杻：指博望僚。榖柞，读固注，指博望。
[2]gu zhuo niu:(mulberry oak holm oak) refers to the Bowang Lao people。Guzhuo: reads as guzhu, refers to Bowang (broad lookout) 。
[3] 㻬琈玉：指白岩夷。
[3] yun fu yu (jade): refers to the Baiyan (white rock) Yi。

译文：由龙亭山往西五十里，有座山叫博望山，中心住着博望僚，南面住着白岩夷。
Translation:
Fifty li further west from Longtingshan stands Bowangshan。At its center live the Bowang Lao, to its south live the Baiyan Yi。

05-10-09 丙山
Bingshan
（107,02655E；33,07064N）

又西七十里，曰丙山[1]，其木多梓檀[2]，多弞杻[3]。

凡首阳山之首，自首阳之山至于丙山，凡九山，二百六十七里。其神皆龙身而人面[4]。其祠之：毛用一雄鸡瘗，糈用五种之糈。楮山也，冢也，其祠之：少牢之具。羞酒祠，婴毛一璧瘗。騩山[5]帝也，其祠羞酒太牢，其合巫祝二人儛，婴一璧。

注释：[1]丙山：指河滨山，今陕西汉中城。
Notes:[1] bing shan: refers to Hebinshan, today's Hanzhong city, Shaanxi province。

[2] 梓檀：指平关氏族。
[2] zi tan (hardwood sandal wood): refers to the Pingguan clan. Ping(flat) guan (gate, pass) 。

[3] 弞杻：指汉僚。持、拿、摘、取皆为弞，也读汉。
[3] han niu (holm oak): refers to the Hanlao people。chi(hold); na(take); zhai(pick) all means han (to get) 。

[4] 龙身人面：指僚族居民的形象。
[4]long shen ren mian(dragon body human face) the images of Lao settlers,

[5] 騩山：指岩铧山。騩是缋的误写。
[5] gui shan: refers to Yanhuashan，Gui a wrong glyph for kui。

译文：由博望山往西七十里，有座山叫河滨山，中心住着平关氏族和汉僚。

综观首阳山系，从首阳之山至于河滨山，共九座山，延绵二百六十七里。这些山的山神皆为僚族居民的形象。祭祀的信玉用一软玉掩埋，食物用五种食物。星山是宗山，祭祀用少牢礼，用羊樽盛酒，信玉用一璧玉掩埋。岩铧山是帝山，祭祀用太牢礼，用羊樽盛酒，由巫、祝二人一起掩埋璧玉。

Translation:

Seventy li further west from Bowangshan stands the Hebinshan。 In the central region live the Pingguan clan and the Han Lao people。

In sum, the Shouyang mountain system from Shouyangshan to Bingshan covers nine mountains and a distance of 267 li。The mountain deities are in the images of local Lao residents。 The messenger jade for the ritual is a piece of soft jade to be buried。Food is from five different kinds。 Xingshan is the Ancestor's Mound, a Shaolao rite is observed。Wines are held in Ram shaped Zun; messenger jade is a piece of Bi to be buried。 Yanhuashan is the God's Mound, use Tailao rite for sacrifice。Wine is served in Ram shaped Zun。Priests Wu and Zhu together bury the Bi jade piece。

中山经第十一山系

Book 5 Zhongshanjing；chapter 11

05-11-01 荆山 翼望山

Jingshan Yiwangshan

（109,87882；31,07452N）

中次十一经荆山之首，曰翼望之山[1]。湍水[2] 出焉，东流注于济 [3]，贶水 [4] 出焉，东南流注于汉 [5]，其中多蛟[6]。其上多松柏[7]，其下多漆梓[8]，其阳多赤金[9]，其阴多珉[10]。

注释：[1]翼望山：指大巫山。实际指巫山县城。
Notes:[1] yi wang shan (wings lookout mount) refers to the Dawushan (big shaman mountain) 。In fact, it is a description of the Wushan county seat, Hubei province。

[2] 湍水：指桐子沟水。
[2] tuan shui (fast moving water) refers to the Tongzigoushui River。

[3] 济水：今称大宁河。
[3] ji shui (rescue water) refers to the Daninghe River。
[4] 觃水：指马鞍沟水，沟口称小下马。
[4] kuang shui: refers to the Ma'angoushui River。 goukou is called xiaoxiama (small off horse) 。
[5] 汉水：指长江。长江称咸滏，咸，读 xian 音，在此被读为汉音了。
[5] han shui: the Yangtze River, which is known in ancient times as Xianyi, xian reads in Chinese as han。
[6]蛟：读照音，指周家坪氏族。
[6] jiao (water snake) reads as zhao, refers to the Zhoujiaping clan。
[7] 松柏：指筲箕岭氏族。
[7] song bai (pine poplar) refers to the Xiaoqi (bamboo basket) ling clan。
[8] 漆梓：指东平氏族。
[8] qi zi (lacquer hardwood): refers to the Dongping clan。
[9] 赤金：指货运场氏族。
[9] chi jin (red gold) refers to the Huoyunchang(warehouse) clan。
[10]珉：指庙湾氏族。
[10] min(stone): refers to the Miaowan (temple bay) clan。

译文：中部第十一列山系是荆山山系，最西端的山叫大巫山。桐子沟水从山间流出，向东流入大宁河；马鞍沟水从山间流出，向东南流入长江，河边住着周家坪氏族。山的西面住着筲箕岭氏族，东面住着东平氏族，南面住着货运场氏族，北面住着庙湾氏族。

Translation:

The 11th mountain system is called the Jingshan system。Its westmost mountain is Dawushan Tongzigoushui River rises from the mountain and goes east into the Daninghe River。 Ma'angoushui River rises from the mountain and goes southeast into the Yangtze River。 The Zhoujiaping clan lives along the riverbanks。On the west side of the mountain lives the Xiaoqiling clan。On the east side of the mountain lives the Dongping clan。On its west side lives the Huoyunchang clan and on its north side lives the Miaowan clan。

05-11-02 朝歌山

Chaogeshan

（110,71333E；30,97895N）

又东南一百五十里，曰朝歌之山[1]，潕水[2]出焉，东南流注于荥[3]，其中多人鱼[4]。其上多梓枏[5]，其兽多麢麋 [6] 。有草 [7]焉，名曰莽草 [8]， 可以毒鱼 [9] 。

注释：[1]朝歌山：指秭归山，在秭归老县城，即今归州镇，所介绍的城镇遗址已沉入长江库区。秭归，指香溪港，简称香港，读音秭归。

Notes:[1] chao ge shan (morning song mount) refers to the Ziguishan, in the old city quarter of the county seat, today known as the Guizhou district。The site mentioned has sunk to the bottom of the Yangtze River Reservoir area。 Zigui refers to Xiangxigang （fragant creek port), shortened to Xianggan。 Xianggang reads in Pu speech as Zigui。

[2] 潕水：指吴家沟水，今称香溪。
[2] wu shui: refers to the Wujigoushui River, today it is called Xiangxi (fragant brook) 。
[3]荥：指长江。
[3] ying: the Yangtze River。
[4] 人鱼：指尹家湾氏族。

[4] ren yu (human fish) refers to the Yinjiawan clan。

[5] 梓枏：指秭归僚。

[5] zi nan (hard wood oak): refers to the Zigui Lao people。

[6] 麢麋：连庄氏族。

[6] ling mi (elk deer) refers to the Lianzhuang clan。

[7]草：在此指专门从事运输的族群。

[7] cao(grass) refers to the clans that specialized in transportation。

[8] 莽草：指江运族群，即长江运输族群。

[8] mang cao (extensive grass) refers to the river transportation clan, aka the Yangtze River shipping clans。

[9] 毒鱼：古老夷。

[9] du yu (poisonous fish) refers to the Gulao (ancient) Yi。

译文：由大巫山往东南一百五十里，有座山叫秭归山。吴家沟水从山间流出，向东南流入长江，河边住着尹家湾夷。山的西面住着秭归僚，住着连庄氏族。有一个专门从事运输业的族群，名叫江运族群，是夏国的古老夷。

Translation:

One hundred and fifty li further southeast from Dawushan stands Ziguishan。 The Wujiagoushui River flows out of the mountain and goes southeast into the Yangtze River。 The Yinjiawan clan lives along the riverbanks。The Zigui Lao lives on the west side of the mountain, so does the Lianjiang clan。 One clan specializing in river transportation is called the Jiangyun clan, they are the ancient Yi from the Xia nation。

05-11-03 帝囷山

Diqunshan

（111,45774E；30,38592N）

又东南二百里，曰帝囷之山[1]，其阳多㻬琈之玉[2]，其阴多铁[3]。帝囷之水[4] 出于其上，潜于其下，多鸣蛇 [5] 。

注释：[1]帝囷山：指拐角山，长江到此形成一个拐角，今湖北省宜都市。

Notes:[1] di jun shan (imperial silo mount) refers to the Guaijiaoshan (corner turn mountain) 。The Yangtze River makes a turn here and forms a corner, referring to today Yidu (fit for capital) city, Hubei province。

[2] 㻬琈玉：龟山夷。

[2] yun fu yu(jade): refers to the Guishan (turtle mount) Yi。

[3]铁：指沙帽山氏族，在长江北岸。帽，读音 tie。

[3] tie(iron) refers to the Shamao (sand cap) clan, on the north bank of Yangtze River。 Mao(cap) reads as tie in Pu speech。

[4] 帝囷水：指拐角水，今仍称长江水。拐角，长江在宜都段的称谓。

[4] di jun shui: refers to the Guaijiao River, known today as the Changjiangshui。Guaijiao refers to Yangtze's section at Yidu。

[5] 鸣蛇：指茶店氏族，今称茶店子氏族。

[5] ming she (singing snake) refers to the Chadian (tea shop) clan, today known as the Chadianzi clan。

译文：由秭归山往东南二百里，有座山叫拐角山，南面住着龟山夷，北面住着沙帽山氏族。长江水从拐角的西边向东边流去，江边住着茶店氏族。

Translation:

Two hundred li further southeast from Ziguishan stands Guaijiaoshan。The Guishan Yi lives on the south side of the mountain, and the Shamaoshan clan lives on the north。The Changjiangshui River flows from the west of the Guaijiao to the east。On the riverbank lives the Chadian clan。

05-11-04 视山
Shishan
（111,7804E；30,17532N）

又东南五十里，曰视山[1]，其上多韭[2]。有井焉，名曰天井[3]，夏有水，冬竭[4]。其上多桑[5]，多美垩金玉 [6] 。

注释：[1]视山：指破河山，因地处破河边而得名，今湖北省松滋县城。有遗名破口、破庙。
Notes:[1] shi shan (look at mount) refers to the Poheshan (broken river mountain) 。It is called today as the Songzi county, in Hubei province, relic names remain such as Pokou (broken pass), Pomiao (broken temple)。
[2]韭：指玉岭氏族。
[2] jiu(leek)refers to the Yuling (jade ridge) clan.
[3] 天井：指恒投部落，简称投部落，读音 t'ei ji。
[3] tian jin (sky well) refers to the Hengtou tribe, shortened to Tou tribe, in Pu speech reads as t'ei ji。
[4] 夏有水冬竭：东部的青云支系部落。水，指青云（lang sui）族，今称水族。
[4] xia you shui dong jie (summer has water winter dry up)
Tr: The Qingyun (green clouds) branch from the East, shui(water) refers to Qingyun in Chinese, which in Pu speech reads Lang sui clan, today they are called Shuizu (water tribes) 。
[5]桑：指外来的。
[5] sang(mulberry) refers to the outsider。
[6] 美垩金玉：指南方部落夷。美垩，读米卧，指天南、南方。
[6] mei e jin yu (beautiful jade clay gold jade)
Tr: refers to the tribal Yi from the south, mei'e: reads as miwo, meaning tian(sky)nan(south), the southern part。

译文：由拐角山往东南五十里，有个地方叫破河山。河的西岸住着玉岭氏族。有一个部落，叫投部落，是东部的青云支系部落。那里还住着外来的南方部落夷。
Translation：
Fifty li further southeast from Guaijiaoshan stands Poheshan。 On its west lives the Yuling clan。 A tribe is called Tou tribe, the Qingyun branch from the east。Also living there is the tribal Yi, outsiders from the south。

05-11-05 前山
Qianshan
（112,90755E；29,81969N）

又东南二百里，曰前山[1]，其木多槠[2]，多柏[3]，其阳多金[4]，其阴多赭[5]。

注释：[1]前山：指圈山，因长江在此地绕圈子而得名。今湖北监利城。
Notes:[1] qian shan: refers to the Quanshan。It derives its name because the Yangtze River turns around here, it is known as Jianli city, Hubei province。
[2]槠：指渔民氏族。
[2] zhu (grey oak): refers to the Fishing clan。
[3]柏：指江湾氏族。
[3] bai(poplar) refers to the Jiangwan (river bay) clan。

[4]金：指顺星村氏族。星，读音 jie，谐音金。
[4] jin (gold) refers to the Shunxingcun clan. xing(star) reads jie, a phonetic match to jin(gold)。
[5]赭：指台子氏族，村名常以台命名。
[5] zhe(ochre) refers to the Taizi (terrace) clan, many villages have [tai]in their names。

译文：由破河山往东南二百里，有座山叫圈山，这里住着渔民氏族和江湾氏族。南面住着顺星村氏族，北面住着台子氏族。
Translation:
Two hundred li southeast from Poheshan stands Quanshan, where the fishing clans and Jiangwan clans live。On its south lives the Shunxingcun tribe, and on its north lives the Taizi clan。

05-11-06 丰山
Fengshan
（114,68866E；29,51594N）

又东南三百里，曰丰山[1]。有兽焉，其状如蝯[2]，赤目，赤喙，黄身[3]，名曰雍和，见则其国大恐[4]。神耕父[5] 处之，常游清泠之渊 [6]，出入有光 [7]，见则其国为败 [8]。有九钟焉 [9]，是知霜鸣 [10]。其上多金 [11]，其下多榖、柞、杻橿 [12]。

注释：[1]丰山：指石马山，简称马山，今湖北通山县九宫山镇。
Notes: [1] feng shan (abundance mount) refers to the Shimashan (stone horse mountain), shortened to Mashan (horse mount) in today's Jiugongshan district, Tongshan county, Hubei province。
[2]蝯：指雍姓氏族。
[2] yuan (monkey like animal) refers to a clan bearing the surname of Yong。
[3] 赤目赤喙黄身：指放马放羊的山区氏族。
[3] chi mu chi hui huang shen (red eyes red beak yellow body)。
Tr: refers to the mountain clans of horse and sheep herders。
[4] 大恐：指游牧氏族。大，指鞑，即游牧；恐，指康，即氏族。
[4] da kong (big fear) refers to the nomadic clans。 da(big) refers to the nomads, kong, reads as kang, meaning tribal clans。
[5] 神耕父：读奢勾畈，指黄陈畈。
[5] shen geng fu (God plough father) reads as Shegoufan: refers to the Huangchenfan。
[6] 清泠之渊：指船埠河。渊，读 ye，指江河。
[6] qing leng zhi yuan (clear cold deep water) refers to the Chuanbuhe River。 Yuan: reads ye, means river。
[7] 出入有光：指交通方便。
[7] chu ru you guan (out in has lights) refers to easy commuting。
[8] 为败：指好客。
[8] wei bai (become defeated) means hospitable。
[9] 九钟焉：指九宫山。焉，读嶷。
[9] jiu zhong yan (nine bell ah) refers Jiugongshan (nine hall mountain), yan: yi。
[10] 知霜鸣：指揽胜之地，即游览圣地。
[10] zhi shuang ming (know frost singing) refers to the place of importance and history, means to travel to holy sites。
[11]金：指老甲乡。甲，读 dze 音，与金谐音。
[11] jin(gold) refers to Laojia district。Jia reads as dze in Pu speech, a phonetic match to Jin。
[12] 榖柞杻橿：指中港村岭。

[12]gu zha niu jiang (grain zuo niu jiang: grain oak hardwood) refers to Zhonggangcunling。

译文：由圈山往东南三百里，有座山叫石马山。有一个氏族，是雍姓的放马放羊的山区氏族，称为雍和氏族，是这个国家的游牧族群，住在黄陈畈，以船埠河为运输，交通方便，这个国家很好客。这里有九宫山，是游览圣地，山的西边是老甲乡，东边中港村岭。
Translation:
Three hundred li further southeast from Quanshan stands Shimashan。 There is a herder's clan from the mountains bearing the surname of Yong, known as Yonghe Yi。This nomadic tribe of the nation live in Huangchenfan, specialized in river port shipping, with easy access。This nation is very hospitable。There is a Jiugongshan, a visitor's hotspot。 On its west there is the Laojia district, on its east side is the Zhonggangcunling。

05-11-07 兔床山
Tuchuangshan
（115,25517E；29,71985N）

又东北八十里，曰兔床之山[1]，其阳多铁[2]，其木多藷薁[3]，其草多鸡榖[4]，其本如鸡卵[5]，其味酸甘[6]，食者利于人[7]。

注释：[1]兔床山：兔床读音 t'e ts'o，指跑运，音译为兔床、太冲，今湖北阳新县木港镇。
Notes: [1] tu chuang shan (rabbit bed mount) tuchuang: reads as t'e ts'o, meaning business in shipping。Phonetically rendered into Chinese matching sounds of tuchuang, taichung, it is today's Muguang town in Yangxin county, Hubei province。

[2]铁：指跑岭冲氏族，音译为铁炉冲氏族，太冲氏族。
[2] tie refers to the Paolingchong clan, phonetically rendered into Tieluchong (iron stove vale) clan or the Taichong clan, tie/tai: phonetic match。

[3] 藷薁：指冲子河氏族。
[3] zhu yu (root vega) refers to the Chongzihe clan。

[4] 鸡榖：指陈部落氏族。
[4] ji gu (chicken grain) refers to the Cheng tribes。

[5] 鸡卵：指冲子部落氏族。
[5] ji luan (chicken egg) refers to the Chongzi tribe。

[6] 其味酸甘：再南面是凤台垭。
[6] qi wei suan gan (its taste sour sweet)
Tr: further south is Fengtaiya。

[7] 食者利于人：运河黎的居住地。人，读 re，指居住地。
[7] shi zhe li yu ren (taken benefits people)
Tr: the settlement location of the Yunhe Li。ren (human in Chinese) reads as re, meaning settlement location。

译文：由石马山往东北八十里，有座山叫跑运港，南面住着跑岭冲氏族，中心住着冲子河氏族；旁边住着陈部落氏族，他们原本是冲子部落氏族。再南面是凤台垭氏族和运河黎的居住地。
Translation:
Eighty li further northeast from Shimashan there is a mountain called Paoyungang。On its south lives the Paolingchong clan。In the middle lives the Chongzihe clan。The Cheng tribe lives in the neighbourhood。Previously they belonged to the Chongzi tribe, Further south is the settlement location for the Fengtaiya tribe and Yunhe Li。

05-11-08 皮山
Pishan
（115,61858E；29,82401N）

又东六十里，曰皮山[1]，多垩[2]，多赭[3]，其木多松柏[4]。

注释：[1]皮山：指半甲山，今江西瑞昌市码头镇。
Notes:[1] pi shan (skin mount) refers to the Banjiashan。It is today's Matou township, Matou（river port)
[2]垩：指湿地氏族。
[2]e(clay) refers to the Shidi clan. Shidi(wetland)。
[3]赭：指渔民。
[3] zhe(ochre)refers to the fishermen。
[4] 松柏：指苏山村氏族。
[4] song bai (pine poplar) refers to the Sushancun clan。

译文：由跑运港往东六十里，有座山叫半甲山，住着湿地氏族和渔民，中心住着苏山村氏族。
Translation:
Sixty li further east from Paoyungang, stands the Banjianshan, where the wetland clan and fishermen clan live。 In the middle region live the Sushancun clan。

05-11-09 瑶碧山
Yaobishan
（115,9899E；29,75684N）

又东六十里，曰瑶碧之山[1]，其木多梓枏[2]，其阴多青雘[3]，其阳多白金[4]。有鸟焉，其状如雉[5]，恒食蜚[6]，名曰鸩[7]。

注释：[1]瑶碧山：读雅泚山，指池河山，今湖北黄梅县小池镇。
Notes:[1] yao bi shan: reads as Ya bi shan, refers to the Chiheshan, today's Xiaochi (small pool) township, Huangmei county, Hubei province。
[2] 梓枏：指梅坝氏族。梓，指坝；枏，读 liu，指梅。
[2] zi nan (hard wood oak); refers to the Meiba clan, zi: flat land between hills(ba), liu(plum)。
[3] 青雘：指依高氏族。青，读 qi，指高；雘，指依、仰仗。
[3] qing hu: (green malachite) refers to the Yigao (depend on high) clan, qing: reads as qi, meaning gao(high), hu: rely, depend。
[4] 白金：指江滨部落氏族。
[4] bai jin (white gold) refers to the Jiangbin tribal clans。
[5]雉：指梅坝的。
[5] zhi:(pheasant): refers to the Meiba area。
[6] 恒食蜚：指统治氏族。
[6] heng shi fei: refers to the ruling, governing clans。
[7]鸩：指荣氏族。
[7] zhen (poisonous bird): refers to the Rong tribe。

译文：由半甲山往东六十里，有座山叫池河山，中心住着梅坝氏族，北面住着依高氏族，南面住着江滨部落氏族。有一群人，是梅坝的统治氏族，叫荣氏族。
Translation:

Sixty li further east from Banjiashan stands Chiheshan。 In the center of it lives the Meiba clan。 The Yigao clan lives in the north, the Jiangbin tribe live on the south。 Another group is the Rong clan, the ruling clan of Meiba area。

05-11-10 支离山
Zhilishan
（116,25014E；29,72815N）

又东四十里，曰支离之山[1]，济水出焉，南流注于汉[2]。有鸟焉，其名曰婴勺[3]，其状如鹊[4]，赤目，赤喙，白身[5]，其尾若勺[6]，其鸣自呼，多㸺牛[7]，多羬羊[8]。

注释：[1]支离山：指石钟山，今江西九江市湖口县城。
Notes: [1] zhi li shan: refers to Shizhongshan (stone bell mountain), today's Hukou county seat in Jiujiang city, Jiangxi province。
[2]汉：指鄱阳湖口，属赣江水系。
[2] han: refers to the mouth of the Boyanghu Lake, which belongs to the Ganjiang River system。
[3] 婴勺：指殷哨，今称大殷村。
[3] ying shao (baby spoon) refers to Yinshao, aka Dayincun Village。
[4]鹊：指南面的。
[4] que(magpie) refers to the south.
[5] 赤目赤喙白身：放马放羊的山区氏族。
[5] chi mu chi hui bai shen (red eyes, red beak white body)
Tr: the mountain tribes and clans engaged in horse and sheep herding。
[6] 其尾若勺：再南是姚哨。
[6] qi wei ruo shao (its tail like spoon) further south is Yaoshao, a place name。
[7] 㸺牛：指扎僚，即农业氏族。
[7] zuo niu(yak) refers to the Zhalao, meaning the agriculture tribes。
[8] 羬羊：读且赤，指东部移民。
[8] chi yang reads as qie chi, refers to the immigrants from the east。

译文：由池河山往东四十里，有座山叫石钟山，济水从山间流出，向南流入湖口。有一群人，名叫殷哨氏族，是南面的放马放羊的山区氏族，再南是姚哨氏族，他们也这样称呼自己。这里还住着农业氏族，住着东部移民。
Translation：
Forty li further east from Chiheshan stands Shizhongshan。 Jishui River flows out of the mountains and goes south into the lake mouth。A group of people known as the Yinshao clan, are herders of horses and sheep from the mountain area in the south。Further south is the Yaoshao clan, they address themselves thus。 One agriculture clan also lives here, as do the immigrants from the east。

05-11-11 祑篚山
Zhidiaoshan
（116,42146E；29,90334N）

又东北五十里，曰祑篚之山[1]，其上多松柏[2]、机柏[3]。

注释：[1]祑篚山：指积水坝山，简称积坝山，今安徽宿松县复兴镇。

Notes:[1] zhi diao shan: refers to the Jishuibashan, shortened to Jibashan, today's Fuxing township in Susong county, Anhui province。

[2] 松柏：指西湾氏族。

[2] song bai (pine poplar) refers to the Xiwan clan。

[3] 机柏：指下湾氏族。

[3] ji bai(pine) refers to the Xiawan clan。

译文：由石钟山往东北五十里，有座山叫积坝山，那里住着西湾氏族和下湾氏族。

Translation:

Fifty li further northeast from Shizhongshan stands Jibashan。 The Xiwan clan and the Xiawan clan live there。

05-11-12 堇理山

Jinlishan

（116,27563E；30,42272N）

又西北一百里，曰堇理之山[1]，其上多松柏[2]，多美梓[3]，其阴多丹雘[4]，多金[5]，其兽多豹虎[6]。有鸟焉，其状如鹊[7]，青身白喙，白目白尾[8]，名曰青耕[9]，可以御疫[10]，其鸣自叫。

注释：[1]堇理山：指湖陵山，今安徽省太湖县老城区。

Notes:[1] jin li shan: refers to the Hulingshan, today it is the old quarter of the Taihu county seat, Anhui province。

[2] 松柏：指松明子，这里指火把山。

[2] song bai (pine poplar) refers to Songmingzi, the pine torch, refers to the Huobashan。

[3] 美梓：指柴火子，这里指火神山。

[3] mei zi(beautiful hardwood) :refers to the firewood, meaning the Huoshenshan, the Fire god mount。

[4] 丹雘：指荡湖。

[4] dan hu (red dyestuff) refers to the Dang Lake。

[5]金：指青岭，又称青岩。

[5] jin (gold) refers to the Qingling (green ridge) also known as Qingyan (green rock) 。

[6] 豹虎：指农业氏族和牧民。

[6] bao hu (leopard tiger) refers to the agricultural clans and herders。

[7]鹊：指南面的。

[7] que(magpie) refers to the south。

[8] 青身白喙，白目白尾：且舍博维集市中心市民。白尾，指市夷，译作市民。

[8] qing shen bai hui (green body white beak), bai mu bai yi (white eyes white tail) 。

Tr: the township center folks of Qieshebowei。 Bai yi： meaning city Yi, here is transliterated as town folks。

[9] 青耕：指凉亭，在此指凉亭村人。

[9] qing geng (green plough) refers to Liangting (cool pavilion) the folks of Liangting Village。

[10] 御疫：指河滨夷。

[10]yu yi: the Hebin Yi, Hebin meaning riverside。

译文：由积坝山往北一百里，有地方叫湖陵山，它的西面是火把山和火神山，北面是荡湖和青岭，这里的氏族是农业氏族和牧民。有一群人，是南面的且舍博维集市中心的市民，叫凉亭村人，是夏国的河滨夷，他们自己也这样说。

Translation：

One hundred li further north from Jibashan stands a place called Hulingshan。 To its west stand the Huobashan and Huoshenshan。To its north is the Dang Lake and Qingling Ridge。 The clans here are engaged in agriculture and animal husbandry。A group of town folks are the people from the Qieshebowei in the south, known as the Liangtingcun people。 They are the Hebin Yi of the Xia nation. They address themselves thus。

05-11-13 依轱山
Yigushan
（116,38761E；30,26692N）

又东南三十里，曰依轱之山[1]，其山多杻橿[2]，多苴[3]。有兽焉，其状如犬，虎爪有甲[4]，其名曰獜[5]，善駚坋[6]，食者不风[7]。

注释：[1]依轱山：指徐桥山，今安徽太湖县徐桥镇。
Notes:[1] yi gu shan: refers to the Xuqiaoshan, today's Xuqiao township, Taihu county, Anhui province。
[2] 杻橿：指种稻米的氏族。
[2] niu jiang (oak holm oak): rice growing clans。
[3]苴：指渡船屋氏族。
[3] ju: Duchuanwu clan; duchuan (crossing boats), wu(house)。
[4]犬，虎爪有甲：东边连湖的少数氏族。
[4] quan, hu zhua you jia (dog, tiger pawn with shield) refers to the minority clans by the Lianhu Lake to the east side。
[5]獜：指水淹地氏族。
[5] lin: refers to the Shuiyandi (water flood earth) tribes。
[6] 善駚坋：指丰屋畈氏族。
[6] shan yang fan refers to the Fengwufan tribes。
[7] 食者不风：古老的王族。
[7] shi zhe bu feng (eaten no wind stroke) ancient King lineage。

译文：由湖陵山往东南三十里，有个地方叫徐桥山，这里住着种稻米的氏族，住着渡船屋氏族。有一个氏族，是东边连湖的少数氏族，名叫水淹地氏族，是丰屋畈的古老王族。
Translation:
Thirty li further southeast from Hulingshan, there is a place called Xuqiaoshan, the rice growing tribe lives here。The Duchuanwu clan also lives here。Another clan is a minority clan from the Lianhu Lake on the east side, they are known as the Shuiyandi clan, the ancient king lineage from Fengwufan area。

05-11-14 即谷山
Jigushan
（116,55574E；30,23071N）

又东南三十五里，曰即谷之山[1]，多美玉[2]，多玄豹[3]，多闾麋[4]，多麢臭[5]。其阳多珉[6]，其阴多青雘 [7] 。

注释：[1]即谷山：指计国山，今安徽望江县长岭镇。
Notes:[1] ji gu shan: refers to Ji guo shan, today's Changling township, Wangjiang county, Anhui province。
[2] 美玉：指茶夷。
[2] mei yu (beautiful jade) refers to the tea clan, the Cha Yi。
[3] 玄豹：指长岭氏族。
[3] quan bao (dark leopard) refers to the Changling (long range) clan。

[4] 闾麋：指湖边庄氏族，今称湖边村氏族。
[4]lv mi(elk): refers to the Hubianzhuang clan, in today's language the Hubiancun clan。
[5] 麢臭：指种菱氏族。
[5] ling chuo (deer and hoofed rabbit): refers to the clans that grow Ling the lotus fruits--Trapa bispinosa Roxb。
[6]珉：指桃园氏族。
[6] min(stone): refers to the Taoyuan （peach garden) clan。
[7] 青雘：指东山氏族。
[7] qing hu (green dyestuff) refers to the Dongshan (east mount) clan。

译文：由徐桥山往东南三十五里，有座山叫计国山，住着茶夷、长岭氏族、湖边村氏族和种菱氏族。南面住着桃园氏族，北面住着东山氏族。
Translation:
Thirty-five li further southeast from the Xuqiaoshan stands a place called Jiguoshan。 The following clans live there, they are the Cha Yi, the Changling clan, the Hubiancun clan and the clan that grows trapa。 To its south live the Taoyuan clan, and to its north live the Dongshan clan。

05-11-15 鸡山
Jishan
（116,6931E；30,12388N）

又东南四十里，曰鸡山[1]，其上多美梓[2]，多桑[3]，其草多韭[4]。

注释：[1]鸡山：指星山，今安徽望江县城区。
Notes:[1] ji shan (chicken mount) refers to Xingshan (star mount), known today as the Wangjiang county city quarter in Anhui province。
[2] 美梓：指望江坝氏族。
[2] mei zi (beautiful hardwood): refers to the Wangjiangba (watch river highland) clan。
[3]桑：读申，指横山氏族。
[3] sang:(mulberry) reads as chen, refers to the Hengshan clan。
[4]韭：指苗族。草，在此指移民。
[4] jiu(leek) refers to the Miao ethnic group。cao(grass)means immigrants。

译文：由计国山往东南四十里，有座山叫星山，这里住着望江坝氏族，住着横山氏族，住着苗族移民。
Translation：
Forty li further southeast from Jiguoshan stands Xingshan。The Wangjiangba clan lives here, the Hengshan clan and the Miao immigrants also live here。

05-11-16 高前山
Gaoqianshan
（117,02446E；30,09684N）

又东南五十里，曰高前之山[1]，其上有水[2]焉，甚寒而清[3]，帝台之浆也[4]，饮之者不心痛[5]。其上有金[6]，其下有赭 [7] 。

注释：[1]高前山：东立山，今称东至山。高，读 gou 音，指立。
Notes:[1] gao qian shan (high front mount) refers to Donglishan (east stand mountain) 。It is called Donglishan。Gao reads as gou, meaning to stand。

[2]水：指氏族。
[2] shui(water) the concept of tribes.
[3] 甚寒而清：指摘云溪，因紧邻云峰山而得名，今称尧渡河。
[3] shen han er qing (very cold therefore clear) refers to the Zhaiyunxi, a brook which gets its name for being close to Yunfengshan (clouds peak), known today as Yaoduhe River。
[4] 帝台之浆也：北面岭乡的。
[4] di tai zhi jiang ye (God terrace liquid) means of the Beimianling （North facing range） village。
[5] 饮之者不心痛：针线专业的内行氏族。
[5] yin zhi zhe bu xin tong (drink it never heart ache) refers to the clans specializing in needle and sewing skills。
[6]金：指云峰岭氏族。
[6] jin(gold) refers to the Yunfengling clan。
[7]赭：指操山氏族。
[7] zhu(ochre) refers to the Caoshan clan。

译文：由星山往东南五十里，有一座山叫东至山。那里有个氏族，是摘云溪北岭乡针线专业的内行氏族。东至山的西边是云峰山氏族，东边是操山氏族。
Translation:
Fifty li further southeast from Xingshan stands Dongzhishan。A clan lives there, they are the skilled needle and sewing crafts people from Beiling by the Zhaiyunxi brook。To the west of Dongzhishan is the Yunfengshan tribe, to the east is the Caoshan tribe。

05-11-17 游戏山
Youxishan
（117,18197E；30,01762N）

又东南三十里，曰游戏之山[1]，多杻橿榖[2]，多玉[3]，多封石[4]。

注释：[1]游戏山：指高而美丽的山，音译为游戏、寓仙、仙寓，实际介绍山西边的洪方乡。
Notes:[1] you xi shan (game play mount) refers to the high and beautiful mountain。 Phonetic close match to Chinese Youxi, Yuxian or Xianyu (fairy adobe) 。 It is a description of Hongfang district in the west of the mountain。
[2] 杻橿榖：指稻米墩氏族，今称白面畈氏族。
[2] niu jiang gu (oak, holm oak grain): refers to the Daomidun (rice silo) clan, known today as the Baimianfan clan。Baimian (white flour) 。
[3]玉：指河滨氏族。
[3]yu(jade): refers to the Hebin clan。
[4] 封石：指黄荆坡氏族。石，读 se 音，指黄。
[4] feng shi (seal stone) refers to the Huangjingpo clan, shi(stone) reads as se, meaning yellow。

译文：由东至山往东南三十里，有座山叫寓仙山，住着白面畈氏族，住着河滨氏族，住着黄荆坡氏族。
Translation:
Thirty li further southeast from Dongzhishan stands Yuxianshan, there live the Baimianfan clan, the Hebin tribe and the Huangjingpo clan。

05-11-18 从山
Congshan
（117,38602E；29,94529N）

又东南三十五里，曰从山[1]，其上多松柏[2]，其下多竹[3]。从水[4] 出于其上，潜于其下，其中多三足鳖，枝尾 [5]，食之无蛊疫 [6] 。

注释：[1]从山：指箬篱山，音译为从山、察山，今安徽祁门县箬坑乡。
Notes:[1] cong shan (follow mount) refers to Ruolishan, phonetically rendered into Congshan, Chashan, today's name is Ruokeng district, Qimen county, Anhui province。
[2] 松柏：指易岭氏族氏族。易，同刈，读音 so。
[2] song bai (pine poplar) refers to Yiling clan, yi: reads as so。
[3]竹：指落渚，即山冲，这里指山冲氏族，今称伦坑氏族。
[3] zhu (bamboo) refers to luozhu (valley), or shan chong, here refers to Shanchong clan, known as the Lunkeng tribe。
[4] 从水：指察水，今称察坑河。
[4] cong shui: refers to Chashui, today as Chakeng River。
[5] 三足鳖枝尾：指外来的土家夷。土家族称比枝康（毕兹卡）。
[5] san zu bie zhi yi (three feet turtle branch tail) refers to the outsider Tujia Yi, also known as Bizhikang. Bizhi, a phonetic match, kang: tribe。
[6] 无蛊疫：指夏部落夷。
[6] wu gu yi (no epidemic) refers to the Xia tribal Yi。

译文：由寓仙山往东南三十五里，有座山叫箬篱山，西面住着易岭氏族，东面住着伦坑氏族。察水从山的西边流出，向东边流去，河边住着外来的土家夷，是古老的夏部落夷。
Translation:
Thirty-five li further southeast from Yuxianshan stands Ruolishan。On its west side lives the Yiling clan. On its east side lives the Lunkeng clan。Chashui River flows out of the west and goes east。Tujia Yi, an outsider group, lives on the riverbank。 They are the ancient tribal Yi of the Xia nation。

05-11-19 婴硜山
Yingyanshan
（117,51234E；29,895N）

又东南三十里，曰婴硜之山[1]，其上多松柏[2]，其下多梓櫄[3]。

注释：[1]婴硜山：指灵锁山，实际介绍山边的灵锁口，简称灵口，今安徽祁县历口镇。
Notes:[1] ying yan shan: lin suo shan (spirit lock mount) in fact a description of place at the mountain edge, Lingsuokou is shortened into Lingkou, today it is called Likouzhen township in Qi county, Anhui province。
[2] 松柏：指灵锁山氏族。
[2] song bai (pine poplar): refers to the Lingsuoshan clan。
[3] 梓櫄：指同类街氏族，今称同铺里氏族。
[3] zi xun:(hardwood xun tree): refers to the Tongleije (same kind street) clan, known today as the Tongpuli (same workshop) clan。

译文：由箬篱山往东南三十里，有座山叫灵锁山，西面住着灵锁山氏族，东面住着同铺里氏族。
Translation:
Thirty li further southeast from Ruolishan, is a mountain called Lingsuoshan。On its west lives the Lingsuoshan clan, on its east lives the Tongpuli clan。

05-11-20 毕山

Bishan
（117,71737E；29,85048N）

又东南三十里，曰毕山[1]，帝苑之水[2]出焉，东北流注于视[3]，其中多水玉[4]，多蛟[5]。其上多㻬琈之玉[6] 。

注释：[1]毕山：指门山，又称祁门山，今安徽祁门县城。
Notes:[1]bi men (finish gate) refer to the Menshan (gate mount) known today as Qimenshan, aka today's Qimen county seat in Anhui province。
[2] 帝苑水：指敞江水，今称阊江水，实际向南流。
[2] di yuan shui (God Garden water) refers to the Changjiangshui, known today as Changjiangshui, flowing to the south。
[3]视：指叹息水，今鄱阳湖叹息洲昌江出口处。昌、阊都是敞的拟音传承。
[3] shi(inspect) refers to the Tanxishui (sigh water) in today's Changjiang's Ust, in Tanxizhou。 Boyang Lake。chang: phonetic matching。
[4] 水玉：指青云夷。
[4] shui yu (water jade) refer to the Qingyun (green clouds) Yi。
[5]蛟：指沟边氏族。
[5] jiao (water dragon) refers to the Goubian clan.
[6] 㻬琈夷：指乾山夷，今称祁山夷。乾、祁都指极大。
[6] yun fu yi: Qianshan Yi, or Qishan Yi, both qian and qi mean biggest。

译文：由灵口山往东南三十里，有座山叫祁门山，阊江水从山间流出，向东南流入叹息水，祁门山住着青云夷，住着沟边氏族，还住着祁山之夷。
Translation:
Thirty li further southeast from Lingkoushan stands the Qimenshan。Changjiang River flows out of the mountain and goes southeast into the Tanxishui River。On the Qimenshan live the Qingyun Yi, the Goubian clan and the Qishan Yi。

05-11-21 乐马山
Lemashan
（117,81309E；29,84411N）

又东南二十里，曰乐马之山[1]。有兽焉，其状如彙[2]，赤如丹火[3]，其名曰【犭戾】[4]，见则其国大疫[5]。

注释：[1]乐马山：指涅冒山，汉语意为金字山，实际往东，今祁门县金字牌镇。
Notes:[1] le ma shan (laugh horse mount) refers to Niemaoshan, its Chinese meaning is Jinzishan(gold word mountain)。It is in fact going east, in today's Jinzipai (gold plaque) township。
[2]彙：指南面的。
[2] hui refers to the south side。
[3] 赤如丹火：游牧的塔山氏族。丹火，指塔山。
[3] chi ru dan huo (red as red fire) refers to the nomadic Tashan (tower mount) tribe, danhuo (red fire): means Tashan。
[4] 【犭戾】：指令狐氏。
[4] lei refers to the Linghu Shi。
[5] 大疫：指塔山夷。

[5] da yi (big epidemic) refers to the Tashan Yi。

译文：由祁门山往东二十里，有座山叫金字山。那里有一个氏族，是南面游牧的塔山氏族，名叫令狐氏，是那个国家的塔山夷。
Translation:
Twenty li further east from Qimenshan stands Jinzishan。There is a clan, the Tashan Shi, a nomadic group from the south side。They are called Linghu Shi, known as the Tashan Yi of that country。

05-11-22 葴山
Zhenshan
（117,97444E；29,83727N）

又东南二十五里，曰葴山[1]。视水[2] 出焉，东南流注于汝水 [3]，其中多人鱼[4]，多蛟[5]，多颉[6]。

注释：[1]葴山：指渔山，又称渔亭山，今安徽省休宁县渔亭镇。渔读 zhe 音，与葴谐音。
Notes: [1] zhen shan: refers to Yushan (fishing mount), also known as the Yutingshan (fishing pavilion mount) 。 It is today's Yuting town, Xiuning county, Anhui province。
[2] 视水：指横水、横江。
[2] shi shui (gaze water） refers to the Hengshui, aka Hengjiang, the Heng River。
[3] 汝水：指虞溪。实际是虞溪汇入横江。
[3]ru shui: refers to Yuxi (yu creek) which runs into Hengjiang。
[4] 人鱼：指集镇夷。
[4] ren yu (human fish) refers to the township Yi, or city folks。
[5]蛟：指沟边氏族。
[5] jiao (big water snake): refers to the Goubian (gully edge) clan。
[6]颉：指工匠氏族。
[6] jie (part of a name): refers to the handicrafts clans。

译文：由金字山往东南二十五里，有座山叫渔亭山，横水从山间流出，向东南流入虞水，这里住着集镇夷，住着沟边氏族，住着工匠氏族。
Translation：
Twenty-five li further southeast from the Jinzishan stands Yutingshan。 Hengshui River flows out of the mountain and goes east into Yushui River。 The Jizhen Yi lives here。 The Goubian clan and the handicrafts clan also live here。

05-11-23 婴山
Yingshan
（118,18258E；29,7823N）

又东四十里，曰婴山[1]，其下多青雘[2]，其上多金玉[3]。

注释：[1]婴山：指息山、休山，实际介绍山南的休宁集镇，今已成为休宁县城。
Notes:[1] jing shan (infant mount) refers to the Xishan, or Xiushan, today's Xiuning township, on the south side of the Mountain。It is the Xiuning county seat。
[2] 青雘：指东山氏族。
[2] qing hu (green dyestuff): refers to the Dongshan (east mount) clan。
[3] 金玉：指漂染夷。金，指染。

[3] jin yu (gold jade) refers to the Piaoran (wash dyeing) Yi。 Jin(gold) means dyeing cloth。

译文：由渔亭山往东四十里，有座山叫休山，东面住着东山氏族，西面住着漂染夷。
Translation:
Forty li further east from Yutingshan stands Xiushan。 Dongshan clan lives on the east, Piaoran Yi lives on the west。

05-11-24 虎首山
Hushoushan
（118,41222E；29,75893N）

又东三十里，曰虎首之山[1]，多苴椆椐[2]。

注释：[1]虎首山：指王族山，今安徽省黄山市王村镇。
Notes: [1]hu shou shan (tiger head mount) refers to the Wangzushan (king tribe mount), is today's Wangcun township in Huangshan city, Anhui province。
[2] 苴椆椐：指庆功岭（氏族），今称瑶岭。
[2] ju chou ju (quince resin tree sturdy bamboo): refers to the Qinggongling (celebrate achievement mount), today known Yaoling。

译文：由休山往东三十里，有座山叫王族山，住着庆功岭氏族。
Translation:
Thirty li further east from Xiushan stands a mountain called Wangzushan。 On the mountain lives the Qinggongling clan。

05-11-25 婴侯山
Yinghoushan
（118,53391E；29,80525N）

又东二十里，曰婴侯之山[1]，其上多封石[2]，其下多赤锡[3]。

注释：[1]婴侯山：指漏口山，又称坑口山，今安徽省黄山市坑口乡。
Notes: [1] ying hou shan (infant prince mount) refers to the Loukoushan, also known as Kengkoushan, is today's Kengkou district, Huangshan City, Anhui province。
[2] 封石：指富贵氏族，音译为芳坑氏族。
[2] feng shi (seal stone) refers to the Fugui (rich and noble) clan, phonetically rendered into the Fangkeng clan。
[3] 赤锡：指薛棠村氏族，今称薛潭村氏族。
[3] chi xi (red tin) refers to the Xuetangcun clan, today is called Xuetancun clan。

译文：由王族山往东二十里，有座山叫坑口山，西边住着芳坑氏族，东边住着薛潭村氏族。
Translation:
Twenty li further east from Wangzushan stands Kengkoushan。 On its west lives the Fangkeng clan。 On its east lives the Xuetancun clan。

05-11-26 大孰山
Dashushan
（118,91847E；29,83582N）

又东五十里，曰大孰之山[1]。杀水[2] 出焉，东北流注于视水 [3]，其中多白垩 [4]。

注释：[1]大孰山：读档素山，指郑族山，今浙江淳安县王阜乡。
Notes:[1] da shu shan: reads as Dangsushan, meaning Zhengzushan, in today's Wangfu district in Chunan county, Zhejiang province。
[2] 杀水：指砂水。实际向南流。
[2] sha shui (murder water) refers to Shashui (sand water) 。 It goes south in fact。
[3] 视水：指胜水，今千岛湖深渡坞水域。
[3] shi shui (gaze water) refers to Shengshui, today's water area in Shenduwu, Qiandao Lake。
[4] 白垩：读摆垩，指潭集氏族。摆指集，垩指潭。
[4] bai e, a phonetic match, refers to the Tanji clan。bai(layout): market town, e(pond)。

译文：由坑口山往东五十里，有座山叫郑族山。砂水从这里流出，向南流入胜水。河边住着潭集氏族。
Translation:
Fifty li further east from Kengkoushan stands Zhengzushan。 Shashui flows out of the mountain and goes south into the Shengshui River。The Tanji clan lives along the riverside。

05-11-27 卑山
Bishan
（119,11933E；29,85132N）

又东四十里，曰卑山[1]，其上多桃李苴梓[2]，多纍[3]。

注释：[1]卑山：指黄泥岭，今淳安县临岐镇。岐，读梓音。
Notes: [1]bi shan（humble mount) refers to the Huangniling (yellow mud ridge) Mountain, in today's Linqi township in Chun 'an county。
[2] 桃李苴梓：指和甫、林岐，即称合浦、临岐。
[2] tao li ju zi (peach plum jun hardwood): refers to Hepu, Linqi, now transliterated in different Chinese signs which share the same phonetic values。
[3]纍：指金坑氏族。
[3] lei(pile) refers to the Jinkeng clan。

译文：由郑族山往东四十里，有座山叫黄泥岭，那里住着合浦、临岐氏族，住着金坑氏族。
Translation:
Forty li further east from the Zhengzushan stands Huangniling Mountain。 The Hebu clan and Linqi clan live there。The Jinkeng clan also lives there。

05-11-28 倚帝山
Yidishan
（119,35789E；29,84868N）

又东三十里，曰倚帝之山[1]，其上多玉[2]，其下多金[3]。有兽焉，状如鼣鼠，白耳白喙[4]，名曰狙如[5]，见则其国有大兵[6]。

注释：[1]倚帝山：指沈家山，实际指山边的久长摆，今称百江镇。
Notes: [1] yi di shan (lean god mount) refers to Shenjiashan, the Jiuchangbai by the foot of the mountain, known as Baijiang (hundred river) town。

[2]玉：指摆水氏族，今称白水氏族。
[2]yu(jade) refers to the Baishui (swing water) clan, today known as the Baishui (white water) clan。
[3]金：读举，指双坞溪氏族。
[3] jin (gold) reads as ju, refers to the Shuangwuxi clan。
[4] 鼣鼠白耳白喙：指久长摆的摆夷，即久长集的市民。
[4] fei shu bai er bai hui (rat white ear white beak) refers to the Jiuchangbai Yi, the township folk of Jiuchangji(long lasting market)。
[5] 狙如：指广饶氏，今称广王氏。
[5] ju ru: refers to Guangrao Shi, known today as Guangwang Shi。
[6] 大兵：指收捐氏族，即收税氏族。
[6] da bing (big soldier) refers to the clan engaged in tax collecting functions, known as the Shoushui (tax collect) clan。

译文：由黄泥岭往东三十里，有座山叫沈家山，西边住着摆水氏族，东边住着双坞溪氏族。有一个氏族，是久长摆的摆夷，名叫广饶，是那个国家的收税氏族。
Translation:
Thirty Li further east from the Huangnilingshan stands Shenjiashan。 On its west side live the Baishui clan. On its east side live the Shuanwuxi clan。 There is a clan known as the Bai Yi from Jiuchangbai, called Guangrao。 They are the tax collecting clan of the nation。

05-11-29 鲵山
Nishan
（119,54027E；28,89828N）

又东三十里，曰鲵山[1]，鲵水[2]出于其上，潜于其下，其中多美垩[3]。其上多金[4]，其下多青雘 [5] 。

注释：[1]鲵山：指姚山，今瑶琳镇。
Notes: [1]ni shan (andrias mount） refers to Yaoshan, today's Yaolinzhen township。
[2] 姚水：指分水。
[2] yao shui: refers to the Fenshui (divide water) River。
[3] 美垩：指桃源氏族。
[3] mei e (beautiful clay) refers to the Taoyuan (peach source) clan。
[4]金：指荷岭氏族。
[4] jin (gold)refers to the Heling (lotus ridge) clan。
[5] 青雘：指东山氏族，今称青山氏族。
[5] qing hu (green dyestuff) refers to the Dongshan（east mount) clan, known today as the Qingshan (green mount) clan。

译文：由沈家山往东三十里，有座山叫姚山，分水从西边流出，向东边流去，河边住着桃源氏族。山的西面住着荷岭氏族，东面住着青山氏族。
Translation:
Thirty li further east from Shenjiashan stands Yaoshan。 Fenshui River flows out from the west side and goes east。 On the riverbanks lives the Taoyuan clan。On the west side of the mountain lives the Heling clan, on the east, lives the Qingshan clan。

05-11-30 雅山
Yashan

（119,66958E；29,98401N）

又东三十里，曰雅山[1]。澧水[2] 出焉，东南流注于视水 [3]，其中多大鱼 [4] 。其上多美桑[5]，其下多苴[6]，多赤金[7]。

注释：[1]雅山：指丫山，实际介绍山脚的胥口镇。
Notes:[1] ya shan (elegant mount) refers to the Yashan, in fact it is a description of Xukou town at the foot of the mountain。

[2] 澧水：指慢流水，今称徐水、胥江。
[2]li shui: refers to the Manliushui (slow flowing water), today it is called Xushui, Xujiang。

[3] 视水：指松溪。
[3] shi shui (gaze water) refers to the Songxi (pine brook)。

[4] 大鱼：指征税夷。
[4] da yu (big fish) refers to the tax collecting Yi。

[5] 美桑：指查弯村氏族，简称查村氏族。
[5] mei sang (beautiful mulberry) refers to the Chawancun clan, shortened to Chacun clan。

[6]苴：指冒山氏族，今谐音称假山头氏族。
[6] ju: refers to the Maoshan clan, in a phonetic rendering, it is called Jiashantou (fake mound top) clan。

[7] 赤金：指金慈村氏族，金慈是音译传承，意为移岭。
[7] chi jin (red gold) refers to the Jincicun (gold kind village) clan, jinci being a phonetic rendering, meaning Yiling (moving range) 。

译文：由姚山往东北三十里，有座山叫丫山。胥水从山间流出，向东南流入松溪。这里住着征税夷。山的西面住着查村氏族，东面住着假山头氏族和金慈村氏族。
Translation:
Thirty li further northeast from Yaoshan stands the Yashan. Xushui River flows out of the mountain and goes southeast into Songxi River。The tax collecting Yi live here。On the west of the mountain live the Chacun clan。On the east of the mountain live the Jiashantou clan and the Jincicun clan。

05-11-31 宣山
Xuanshan
（119,93428E；30,08411N）

又东五十里，曰宣山[1]。沦水[2] 出焉，东南流注于视 [3]，其中多蛟[4]。其上有桑[5]焉，大五十尺[6]，其枝四衢[7]，其叶大尺余[8]，赤理黄华青树[9]，名曰帝女之桑[10]。

注释：[1]宣山：指长山，音译为宣山、贤山，实际介绍贤山东侧的富阳城。
Notes：[1] xun shan (declare mount) refers to Changshan (long mount) phonetically rendered into Xuanshan or Xianshan。This is in fact a description of Fuyang city on the east side of Xianshan Mountain。

[2] 沦水：指山冲水，音译为洛渚水、六谷水，今称白洋溪。
[2] lun shui (ripple water) refers to the Shanchongshui, phonetically rendered into Luozhushui, Liugushui, today known as Baiyangxi River。

[3] 视水：指富春江。
[3] shi shui (gaze water) refers to Fuchunjian (rich spring) River。

[4]蛟：指蒋村氏族。
[4] jiao (water snake) refers to the Jiangcun clan。

[5]桑：指船帮。

[5] sang (mulberry) refers to the shipping guild。

[6] 大五十尺：指运输码头，读达坞施蚩。

[6] da wu shi chi (big five ten chi) refers to the shipping yard, reads as Dawushichi。

[7] 其枝四衢：指久坪街肆。其枝，指久坪；四瞿，读肆丘，指街肆。

[7] qi zhi si qu (its branches four corner) refers to the Jiuping township of street market。 Qizhi: refers to Jiuping, siqu: reads as siqiu, refers to the street market。

[8] 其叶大尺余：指水运码头夷。

[8] qi ye da chi yu (its leaves big chi over) refers to the river shipping port people, known as Shuiyun Matou Yi。

[9] 赤理黄华青树：指小池南山的且舍，即小湖南山的且舍。且舍，古氏族名。

[9] chi li huang hua qing shu (red marking yellow flower green tree)
Tr: refers to the Qieshe clan from the Xiaohunanshan or Xiaochinanshan。 Qieshe, the name of an ancient tribe。

[10] 帝女之桑：指砥砺之帮，即很顽强的群体。

[10] di nv zhi sang (God daughter's mulberry)
Tr: refers to very tough people or enduring community. Dilizhibang, gang of tough people。 Di Li (grinding, tough as nail) 。bang (gang, group) 。

译文：由丫山往东五十里，有座山叫贤山，白洋水从山间流出，向东南流入富春江，河边住着蒋村氏族。西岸有一个船帮，是运输码头久坪街肆的水码头夷，是小湖南山的且舍，称为砥砺之帮。
Translation:
Fifty li further east from Yashan stands Xianshan。 Baiyang River flows out of the mountain and goes southeast into the Fuchunjiang River。 On the riverbank live the Jiangcun clan。There is a boat shipping guild on the west bank, the Shuimatou Yi from the Jiuping town street market at the Shipping yard。 They are the Qieshe people from the Xiaohunanshan, a very tough group known as the Dilizhibang。

05-11-32 衡山
Hengshan
（120,08159E；30,15946N）

又东四十五里，曰衡山[1]，其上青雘[2]，多桑[3]，其鸟多鸜鹆[4]。

注释：[1]衡山：指转塘山，今杭州转塘街道。衡，指转，见彝文字典 156 页。
Notes:[1] heng shan (balance mount) refers to the Zhuantangshan, in today's Zhuangtang street, Hangzhou city, Zhejiang province。 Heng(turning) ref: page 156, Yi Language Dictionary。

[2] 青雘：指马驮氏族，即马帮氏族。

[2] qing hu (green dyestuff) refers to the Horse Packing clan, also known as the Mabang clan。

[3]桑：指船帮氏族。

[3] sang (mulberry): refers to the ship guild, band in control of trading by water, known as the Chuanbang clan。

[4] 鸜鹆：指街城。

[4] ying gu (acridotheres cristatellus)refers to the street market town。

译文：由贤山往东四十五里，有座山叫转塘山，那里住着马驮氏族，住着船帮氏族，还有街城人群。
Translation:
Forty-five li further east from Xianshan stands the Zhuantangshan。The Mabang clan and the Chuanbang clan live there。Also living there are people from the street market town。

05-11-33 丰山
Fengshan

（120,17231E；30,24593N）

又东四十里，曰丰山[1]，其上多封石[2]，多桑[3]，多羊桃[4]，状如桃而方茎[5]，可以为皮张[6]。

注释：[1]丰山：指卖场山，因濮越语吴、封不分，又称吴山，今杭州上城区。
Notes:[1] feng shan (bumper mount) refers to Maichang (sell yard) Mountain。Feng and Wu are not distinguished in Pu and Yue speech, therefore the Fengshan is also known as Wushan, in today's Shangcheng district, Hangzhou, Zhejiang province。

[2] 封石：指商贾氏族。
[2] feng shi (seal stone) refers to the Shanggu clan, shanggu(merchant) clan。

[3]桑：指商会。
[3] sang; refers to the business chamber。

[4] 羊桃：读烊弢，指商铺。
[4] yang tao (goat peach) reads as yangtao, refers to business shops。

[5] 桃而方茎：指集镇的卖场。
[5] tao er fang jing (peach with square stem) refers to the selling yard at the market town。

[6] 为皮张：指商业疆域。为，指卖，皮指手工业、行业。
[6] wei pi zhang (for skin open) refers to the area where trading business is conducted。 wei(selling), pi(handicrafts guilds and branches)。

译文：由转塘山往东四十里，有座山叫卖场山，那里住着商贾氏族，有许多商会，许多商铺，是集镇的卖场，是夏国的商业区。
Translation:
Forty li further east from the Zhuantangshan stands the Maichangshan。A trading and merchant clan lives there, and many trading companies, shops, and selling yards are found there。 This is the business district of the Xia nation。

05-11-34 妪山
Yushan
（120,35642E；30,46634N）

又东七十里，曰妪山[1]，其上多美玉[2]，其下多金[3]，其草多鸡谷[4]。

注释：[1]妪山：指荡湾，今浙江桐乡市崇福镇荡湾村。
Notes:[1]yu shan (old lady mount) refers to Dangwan, in today's Dangwan village, Chongfu county, Tongxiang city, Zhejiang province。

[2] 美玉：指庄湾夷。
[2] mei yu (beautiful jade) refers to the Zhuangwan (village bay) Yi。

[3]金：指漾夷。
[3] jin(gold) refers to the Yang(ripple) Yi。

[4] 鸡谷：指张家凹氏族，简称张凹氏族。濮语凹读 gu 音，汉文写作"谷"或"角"。
[4] ji gu (chicken vale) refers to the Zhangjia'ao clan, shortened to Zhang'ao clan。 Ao reads in Pu speech as gu, phonetically rendered in two different Chinese signs, matching the sound of gu。

译文：由卖场山往东七十里，有个地方叫荡湾，西面住着庄湾氏族，东面住着漾夷，这些人群是张凹氏族。
Translation:

Seventy li further east from Maichangshan there is a place called Dangwan。 On its west side lives the Zhuangwan clan。On its east side lives the Yang Yi。 Both groups belong to the Zhang'ao tribe。

05-11-35 鲜山
Xianshan
（120,5649E；30,62918N）

又东三十里，曰鲜山[1]，其木多楢杻苴[2]，其草多亹冬[3]，其阳多金[4]，其阴多铁[5]。有兽焉，其状如膜大，赤喙[6]，赤目，白尾[7]，见则其邑有火[8]，名曰移即[9]。

注释：[1]鲜山：指凤山，今浙江桐乡市城区。
Notes: [1] xian shan (fresh mount) refers to the Fengshan, in today's city quarter in Tongxiang city, Zhejiang province。
[2] 楢杻苴：指九曲街。
[2] qiu niu ju (various oaks): refers to the Jiuqu (nine turns) street。
[3] 亹冬：指窑工氏族，今称灶家兜氏族。
[3] wei/mei dong (moving winter) refers to the kiln workers' clan, today known as the Zaojiadou clan。
[4]金：读 ji，指日，这里指日山港氏族。
[4] jin(gold) reads as ji, means sun, here refers to the Rishangang clan。
[5]铁：指泡子氏族。
[5] tie(iron) refers to the Paozi clan。
[6] 膜大，赤喙：指窑工支系。
[6]mo da (film big) chi hui (red beak) refers to the Kiln workers clan(yaogong)。
[7] 赤目，白尾：指技艺部落夷。
[7] chi mu, bai yi (red eyes, white tail) refers to the skill and crafts tribal Yi。
[8] 有火：指制镬氏族。
[8] you huo (have fire) refers to the Zhihu clan, the people who make cooking pots。
[9] 移即：指遗兴，意思为传承兴旺的氏族，今称宜兴氏族。
[9] yi ji (drag) refers to Yixing, meaning clans with strong and flourishing offsprings. Today it is known as the Yixing clan。

译文：由荡湾往东三十里，有一个地方叫凤山城，中心住着九曲街氏族，人们称为窑工氏族。凤山的南面住着日山港氏族，北面住着泡子氏族。有一个氏族，是窑工支系的技艺部落夷，是那个地方的制镬氏族，名叫宜兴氏族。
Translation:
Thirty li further east from Dangwan stands a place called Fengshan city。 In its center live the Jiuqujie clan, called by the local people the kiln folks。On the south side of Fengshan live the Rishangang clan。 On the north live the Paozi clan。 A group skillful in kiln technology known as the Jiyibuluo Yi, is a local cooking pot producing people, known as the Yixing clan。

05-11-36 章山
Zhangshan
（120,74918E；30,76196N）

又东三十里，曰章山[1]。其阳多金[2]，其阴多美石 [3] 。皋水 [4] 出焉，东流注于澧水[5]，其中多脆石[6]。

注释：[1]章山：指惋山，意思为一惋地的城，今浙江嘉兴市古城区域。
Notes:[1] zhang shan (chapter mount) refers to Wanshan, meaning a town in a place called Wan, in today's old city quarter, Jiaxing city, Zhejiang province。

[2]金：指泾港氏族，

[2] jin(gold) refers to the Jingang clan。

[3] 美石：指芦席汇氏族。

[3] mei shi (stone): refers to the Luxihui clan (reed mattress collection) 。

[4] 皋水：指环城河。

[4] gao shui: refers to the water ditch surrounding the city。

[5] 澧水：指芦水，今称嘉善河。

[5]li shui: refers to Lushui, known today as Jiashanhe River。

[6] 脆石：指瓶山氏族。

[6] cui shi(breakable stone) refers to the Pingshan(bottle mount) clan。

译文：由由凤山城往东北三十里，有座山叫惋山，南面住着泾港氏族，北面住着芦席汇氏族。环城水从这里流出，向东流入嘉善河，城中住着瓶山氏族。
Translation:
Thirty li further northeast from Fengshancheng stands a mountain called Wanshan。 To its south lives the Jingang clan。 To its north lives the Luxihui clan。 Huanchengshui River flows out of there and goes east into Jiashan River。 The Pingshan clan lives in the city.

05-11-37 大克山
Dakeshan
（120,92713E；30,82937N）

又东二十五里，曰大克之山[1]。其阳多金[2]，其木多榖柞 [3]，无草木[4]。

注释：[1]大克山：指戈收山，演称为嘉善山，今浙江嘉善县城。
Notes:[1] da ke shan: refers to Geshoushan, now phonetically transformed into Jiashashan, in today's Jiashan county, Zhejiang province。

[2]金：指黄泾港氏族。

[2] jin (gold) refers to the Huangjingang clan.

[3] 榖柞：指指渡口氏族。榖，读勾，指渡；柞，指嘴，即口。

[3]gu zuo (grain oak): refers to the Dukou clan, gu(cross): reads as gou, zuo: mouth, river mouth。

[4] 无草木：泊运城，今演称为泊车港。无，读坞，指码头、指泊。

[4] wu cao mu (no grass wood) refers to Poyuncheng, today knowns Pochegang。Wu refers to port or waterfront。

译文：由惋山往东二十五里，有座山叫戈收山。南面住着黄泾港氏族，中心住着渡口氏族和泊运城氏族.
Translation:
Twenty and five li from Wanshan stands Geshoushan。To its south lives the Huangjingang clan。 In its middle lives Dukou clan and the Poyuncheng clan。

05-11-38 区吴山
Ouwushan
（121,21631E；30,93277N）

有东五十里，曰区吴之山[1]。其木[2] 多苴 [2] 。

注释：[1]区吴山：指泖坞山，今上海市松江区泖港镇。
Notes:[1] ou wu shan: refers to Maowushan, in today's Maogang town in Songjiang district, Shanghai Municipality。
[2]苴：指渡口氏族。苴在濮语中是多音字，又读 gou 音，指渡。
[2] ju: refers to the Dukou clan, ju has multiple phonetic values in Pu speech, it reads as gou, meaning crossing。

译文：由戈收山往东五十里，有座山叫泖坞山，中心住着渡口氏族。
Translation:
Fifty li further east from Geshoushan stands the Maowushan。 In its middle lives the Dukou clan。

05-11-39 声匈山
Shengxiongshan
（121,50131E；30,98911N）

又东五十里，曰声匈之山[1]，其木多穀[2]，多玉[3]，上多封石[4]。

注释：[1]声匈山：指金汇山，今上海市奉贤区金汇镇。
Notes:[1] sheng xiong shan: refers to Jinhuishan, today known as the Jinhui town, Fengxian district, Shanghai Municipality。
[2]穀：指顾姓氏族。
[2]gu (grain): refers to the clan bearing the surname of Gu。
[3]玉：指漏下宅氏族，今称楼下宅氏族。
[3]yu(jade) refers to the Louxiazhai clan, known today as the Louxiazhai clan。Lou written in two different Chinese signs。
[4] 封石：读汾姒，指东夏家氏族。
[4] feng shi (seal stone) reads as Fensi, refers to the eastern Xiajia clan。

译文：由泖坞山往东五十里，有座山叫金汇山，中心住着顾姓氏族，住着楼下宅氏族，西面住着东夏家氏族。
Translation:
Fifty li further east from Maowushan stands the Jinhuishan。 In its middle lives the Gu clan, the Louxiazhai clan。 To its west live the Dongxiajia clan。

05-11-40 大騩山
Daguishan
（121,78056E；31,0123N）

又东五十里，曰大騩之山[1]，其阳多赤金 [2]，其阴多砥石 [3]。

注释：[1]大騩山：读 dang go 山，指黄路山，今上海市浦东新区黄路镇。
Notes： [1] dang go shan: refers to the Huanglushan, known to be the Huanglu town in Pudong new district, Shanghai municipality。
[2] 赤金：指奚部落氏族。奚，读音同徒，濮语读 chi 音。
[2] chi jin (red gold) refers to the Tu clan, in Pu speech reads as chi。
[3] 砥石：指埭头氏族。埭，读 di，不读 dai。
[3] di shi(whetstone): refers to the Ditou clan。

译文：由泖坞山往东五十里，有座山叫黄路山，南面住着奚部落氏族，北面住着埭头氏族。
Translation:
Fifty li further east from Maowushan stands Huanglushan。 To its south lives the Xibuluo clan。To its north lives the Ditou clan。

05-11-41 踵臼山
Zhongjiushan
（121,83996E；31,03983N）

又东十里，曰踵臼之山[1]，无草木[2]。

注释：[1]踵臼山：读 zheng ju 山，指老港山，今上海浦东新区老港镇。
Notes: [1] zhengjiu shan in Pu speech, refers to the Laogangshan in today's Pudongxinqu district's Laogang (old port) town, Shanghai Municipality。
[2] 无草木：这里指运输部落。
[2] wu cao mu (no grass wood) refers to the Yunshu (shipping) clan。

译文：由黄路山往东十里，有座山叫老港山，这里住着运输部落。
Translation:
Ten li further east from the Huanglushan stands Laogangshan, where the Yunshu(shipping) clan live。

05-11-42 历石山
Lishishan
（121,83893E；31,3419N）

又东北七十里，曰历石之山[1]，其木多荆芑[2]，其阳多黄金[3]，其阴多砥石[4]。有兽焉，其状如狸而白首虎爪[5]，名曰梁渠[6]，见则其国大兵[7]。

注释：[1]历石山：指横沙山，今长江口横沙岛。
Notes:[1]li shi shan: refer to Hengshashan, today it is called Hengsha Island at the river mouth of the Yangtze River。
[2] 荆芑：指堆沙氏族，也称墩沙氏族。
[2] jing si (jin shrubs): refers to the Duisha (pile sand) clan, also known as Dunsha clan。
[3] 黄金：指海星部落氏族。
[3] huang jin (yellow gold) refers to the Haixing (sea star) clan。
[4] 砥石：指沙圩氏族。
[4] di shi (whetstone): refers to the Shayu (sand formation) clan。
[5] 狸而白首虎爪：横沙摆氏族东支系。
[5]li er bai shou hu zhua (leopard with white head tiger claw)
Tr: the east branch of the Hengshabai clan。
[6] 梁渠：指大渠氏族。
[6] liang qu (beam ditch) refers to the Daqu clan。
[7] 大兵：指河滨氏族。大，读迭，指滨；兵，读沘，指河。
[7] da bing (big soldier) refers to the Hebin clan, da/die refers to riverbank, bing reads as bi, meaning river。

译文：由老港山往东北七十里，有座山叫横沙山，中部住着墩沙氏族，南面住着海星部落氏族，北面住着沙圩氏族。有一个氏族，是横沙摆氏族的东支系，名叫大渠氏族，是那个国家的河滨氏族。
Translation:

Seventy li further northeast from the Laogangshan stands the Hengshashan。 In its middle lives the Dunsha clan。 To its south lives the Xinghai clan。 To its north lives the Shayu clan。 A clan is the east branch of the Hengshabai clan, known as Daqu clan。 They are the Hebin clan of that country。

05-11-43 求山
Qiushan
（121,6463E；30,91584N）

又东南一百里，曰求山[1]。求水出于其上，潜于其下，中有美赭[2]。其木多苴[3]，多簵 [4] 。其阳多金[5]，其阴多铁[6]。

注释：[1]求山：指祭祀山，因供奉神灵，又称为奉山，今上海市浦东新区奉城镇。
Notes:[1] qiu shan (beg mount) the sacrifice mount, called Fengshan because it is on this mountain that rite of deities' worship is observed。 It is known today as Fengcheng town, Pudong new district in Shanghai Municipality。
[2] 中有美赭：指君长由默遮传承。美者，读默（me）遮，指老幺支系。
[2] zhong you mei zhu (in it beautiful ochre)
Tr: the chieftain title is carried on by mozhe, the youngest son, mozhe reads as mezhe, the youngest son branch。
[3]苴：指祝告氏族。
[3] ju: the action to pray and send a message to inform the deities, refers to the Zhugao clan。
[4]簵：指港湾氏族。簵字的濮文由坞字加词缀构成。
[4] mei(bamboo): refers to the Gangwan (port bay) clan。Mei is written in a Pu glyph of port(wu) plus strokes。
[5]金：指墩民。
[5] jin (gold) refers to the people by the dun (dirt sand formation) 。
[6]铁：指河对岸氏族。
[6] tie(iron) refers to the Heduian (opposite bank) clan。

译文：由横沙山往东南一百里，有座山叫奉山，奉水从西边向东边流去，这里的君长由默遮传承，中心住着祝告氏族，住着港湾氏族。奉山的南面住着墩民，北面住着河对岸氏族。
Translation:
One hundred li further southeast from Hengshashan stands Fengshan。 Fengshui River flows from west to east。 The chieftain's title is passed from father to the youngest son, the Mezhe。 In the center lives the Zhugao clan, and the Gangwan clan。To its south lives the Dun folks, to its north lives the people across from the river。

05-11-44 丑阳山
Chouyangshan
（122,45905E；30,72776N）

又东二百里，曰丑阳之山[1]，其上多椆椐[2]。有鸟焉，其状如乌而赤足[3]，名曰鴼鵌[4]，可以御火[5]。

注释：[1]丑阳山：指宫嵊山，今嵊泗列岛嵊泗县城。
Notes： [1] chou yang shan (ugly sun mount) refers to the Gongchengshan, in today's Chengsi county seat in Chengsi Islands。
[2] 椆椐：指宫嵊部落氏族。
[2] chou ju: refers to the Gongcheng clan。
[3] 乌而赤足：船码头的运输支系。
[3] wu er chi zu (bird bare foot) the shipping branch of the water ports。
[4] 鴼鵌：指平涌（chong）氏族。

[4] zhi tu （birds）: refers to the Pingchong clan。

[5] 御火：指海夷。火，读音 hou，指海。

[5]yu huo (court fire); refers to the sea Yi, or the sea people。 huo(fire) reads in Pu speech as hou, meaning sea, (ocean, hou, throat sound) 。

译文：由奉山往东二百里，有座山叫宫嵊山，住着宫嵊部落氏族。那里有一群人，是船码头的运输支系，名叫平涌氏族，是夏国的海夷。

Translation:

Two hundred li further east from Fengshan stands Gongchengshan。 The Gongcheng clan lives here。 A group of people forms the shipping branch at the boat port, known as the Pingchong clan。 They are the Sea Yi from Xia nation。

05-11-45 奥山

Aoshan

（122,64998E；30,81921N）

又东三百里，曰奥山[1]，其上多柏杻橿[2]，其阳多㻞琈之玉[3]。奥水[4] 出焉，东流注于视水 [5] 。

注释：[1]奥山：指绿华岛，华读 or 音，谐音奥。从奉山起算里程。

Notes:[1]ao shan: refers to Lvhua Island, Hua reads as or, a phonetic match to ao, the distance starts from Fengshan。

[2] 柏杻橿：指西停泊场氏族，今西绿华岛氏族。

[2] bai niu jiang: refers to the Xitingbochang (west mooring lot) clan, known today as the Xilvhuadao clan。

[3] 㻞琈玉：指东库山夷。

[3] yun fu yu: refers to the Dongkushan Yi。

[4] 奥水：指泉水。

[4]ao shui: refers to Quanshui (spring water) 。

[5] 视水：指嵊山洋。

[5] shi shui: refers to Shengshanyang, yang: ocean water。

译文：由奉山往东三百里，有座山叫绿华岛，它的西面住着西停泊场氏族，南面住着东库山氏族，那里有泉水从山间流出，向东流入嵊山洋。

Translation:

Three hundred li further east from Fengshan stands a mountain called Lvhuadao。 To its west lives the west Tingpochang clan。To its south lives the Dongkushan clan。 Spring water flows out of the mountains and goes east into Chengshanyang。

05-11-46 服山

Fushan

（122,8146E；30,71732N）

又东三十五里，曰服山[1]，其木多苴[2]，其上多封石[3]，其下多赤锡[4]。

注释：[1]服山：指马鞍列岛。

Notes: [1] fu shan: refers to the Ma'an Islands。

[2]苴：指双帕氏族，即双岸氏族，今称双胖、双盘氏族。

[2] ju: refers to the Shuangpa (double head scarves) clan。Aka the Shuang'an clan。 Today it is called Shuangpang, or Shuangpan。

[3] 封石：指盘氏族，即双盘氏族。

[3] feng shi (seal stone) refers to the Pan clan, also known as the Shuangpan clan。

[4] 赤锡：指工艺制作氏族，即手工业氏族。

[4] chi xi (red tin): refers to the handicraft clan, who are skilled craftsmen。

译文：由绿华山往东南三十五里，有座山叫马鞍列岛，中心住着双帕氏族，西边住着盘氏族，东边住着工艺制作氏族。

Translation:

Thirty-five li further southeast from Lvhuashan stands a mountain called Ma'an Islands。 In its center lives the Shuangpa clan。 To its west lives the Pan clan。 To its east lives the handicrafts clan。

05-11-47 杳山

Miaoshan

（122,29369E；30,43504N）

又东三百里，曰杳山[1]，其上多嘉荣草[2]，多金玉[3]。

注释：[1]杳山：指龙泉山，今称衢山岛，从奉山起算里程。实际往东南。

Notes:[1] miao shan: refers to the Longquanshan (dragon spring) 。 Today it is called Chongshandao。 The distance starts from Fengshan and goes in fact to the southeast。

[2] 嘉荣草：指降央宫氏族，今称羊府殿氏族。草，读 chou 音，指宫殿。

[2] jia rong cao (good flourish grass): refers to the Jiangyanggong clan, known today as the Yangfudian clan. cao(grass) reads as chou, meaning palace。

[3] 金玉：指场镇夷。

[3] jin yu (gold jade) refers to the Changzhen Yi。

译文：由奉山往东南三百里，有座山叫龙泉山，西面住着降央宫氏族，住着场镇夷。

Translation:

Three hundred li further southeast from Fengshan stands Longquanshan。 To its west lives the Jiangyanggong clan, and the Changzhen Yi。

05-11-48 几山

Jishan

（122,10778E；30,01992N）

又东三百五十里，曰几山[1]，其木多楢檀杻[2]，其草多香[3]。有兽焉，其状如彘，黄身白头，白尾[4]，名曰闻【豕粦】[5]，见则天下大风[6]。

凡荆山之首，自翼望之山至于几山，凡四十八山，三千七百三十二里。其神状皆彘身人首[7]。其祠：毛用一雄鸡祈瘗，用一珪，糈用五中之精。禾山[8]，帝也，其祠：太牢之具，羞瘗，倒毛[9]；用一璧，牛无常[10]。堵山[11]、玉山[12]冢也，皆倒祠[13]，羞毛少牢[14]，婴毛吉玉[15]。

注释：[1]几山：指马驮子山，简称驮山，音译为几山、金山，今浙江舟山市本岛，中心在定海区。从奉山算起程实际往东南。

Notes:[1] ji shan: refers to the Matuozi (horse packing) Mountain, shortened to Tuoshan, phonetically rendered into Jishan, Jinshan。 It is today's Zhoushan (boat mountain) city Island, with its center in Dinghai (fix ocean) 。The distance starts from Fengshan, in fact to southeast。

[2] 楢檀杻：指上马街氏族。

[2] qiu tan jiu（oak sandal wood holm oak）: refers to the Shangmajie (amount the horse) clan。

[3]香：指制作氏族，即手工业者。

[3] xiang (fragrant); the manufacture clan, the handicraftsmen。

[4]彘，黄身，白头，白尾：指驮山上的田中央田夷。田，在此读 bo 音，谐音白。

[4] zhi, huang shen, bai tou, bai yi (pig yellow body, white head, white tail)
Tr: refers to the Tianzhongyang Yi at Tuoshan。Tian reads as bo, a phonetic matching to ba(white)。

[5]闻【豕粦】：指泉黎，今称白泉夷，住在白泉镇。

[5] wen lin: refers to Quan (spring) Li(people), today known as Baiquan (white spring) Yi, living in Baiquan town。

[6] 大风：指统治氏族。

[6] da feng (big wind) refers to the governing, ruling clan, the von tribe。

[7] 彘身人首：指农业定居氏族的形象。

[7] shi shen ren shou (pig body human head) the images of the agriculture settlement clans。

[8] 禾山：冯山，音译传承为洪山、禾山。

[8] he shan (shoots mount): refers to Fengshan, phonetically rendered into Hongshan or Heshan。

[9] 羞瘗，倒毛：选择掩埋的神界信玉。羞在此指选择。倒，本指阴界，这里指神界。

[9] xiu ji, dao mao: choose the messenger jade piece to be buried 。 xiu: choose; ben: the Yin realm, the realm of the dead, here refers to the realm of deities。

[10] 牛无常：祈祷五常神。牛：指祈。五常，杭州冯山五常乡，冯山山神供奉在五常乡，故称五常神。

[10] niu wu chang: pray to the Wuchang God. niu: pray, wuchang: a district called Wuchang, in Fengshan, Hangzhou, Zhejiang province。The mountain deities of Fengshan takes its residence in Wuchang district, therefore the name of the deity。

[11] 堵山：坑口山，音译传承为堵山。

[11] du shan (block mount) refers to Kengkoushan, phonetically rendered into Dushan。

[12] 玉山：寓仙山的简称。

[12]yu shan (jade mount) short name for Yuxianshan (housing fairy mountain) 。

[13] 倒祠：指阴祭，这里指与神界沟通的方式，

[13] dao si: refers to the rite of sacrifice to the deities in the Yin realm。 Here it talks about the way of communicating with deities and God。

[14] 羞毛少牢：按少牢礼选择信玉。

[14] xiu mao shao lao: choose messenger jade according to the procedure of Shaolao ritual。

[15] 婴毛吉玉：掩埋传信的吉玉。

[15] ying mao ji yu: bury the Goodluck charm messenger jade。

译文：由奉山往东南三百五十里，有座山叫驮山，中心住着上马街氏族，人群为手工业者。有一个氏族，是驮山上的田中央田夷，名叫泉黎，是那个地方的统治氏族。

Translation:
Three hundred and fifty li further southeast from Fengshan stands the mountain called Tuoshan。 In the middle lives the Shangmajie clan, a group of handicrafts men。Another clan from the Tuoshan is the Tianzhongyang Yi。Their name is Quan Li。They are the ruling clan of that nation。

综观中部第十一列山系荆山山系，从大巫山到驮山，共四十八座山，延绵三千七百三十二里。这些山的山神皆为农业定居氏族的形象。祭祀这些山神，信玉用一软玉掩埋，用一珪，食物用五种精制食物。冯山是

帝山，祭祀用太牢礼，选择传往神界信的玉，用一璧玉祈祷五常神。坑口山、寓仙山是宗山，与神界沟通选用少牢礼的信玉，掩埋传信的吉玉。

In sum, the Jingshan system of the mountains in the middle between Dawushan and Tuoshan, covers 48 mountains with a total distance of 3,732 li。 All the mountain deities are in the images of settled agriculture clans。 When sacrificing to those deities, a Gui piece of soft jade is buried as messenger。 Food is made of five different kinds of grain。 Fengshan is the Di Mount, to it, Tailao rite is observed。A piece of Bi jade is chosen as messenger to beg the blessing of Wuchang God。 Kengkoushan and Yuxianshan are the ancestors' mounts。 A piece of messenger jade is chosen in a Shaolao ritual and buried as a communication good luck charm。

中山经第十二山系

Book 5 Zhongshanjing; Chapter 12

05-12-01 洞庭山 篇遇山

Dongtingshan Pianyushan
（106,29828E；31,26816N）

中次十二经洞庭山[1]之首，曰篇遇之山[2]，无草木[3]，多黄金[4]。

注释：[1]洞庭山：指平坦山，以湖北建始县平坦山为标志。
Notes: [1] dong ting shan: refers to Pingtanshan (flat mount), a landmark for Jianshi county, Hubei province。
[2] 篇遇山：指仪邑山。仪，读 pi 音，今四川省仪陇县城。
[2] pian yu shan: refers to Yiyishan, first Yi reads as pi, known today as the Yilong county seat in Sichuan province。
[3] 无草木：游牧部落地区。
[3] wu cao mu (no grass wood) refers to the nomadic region。
[4] 黄金：山区部落氏族。
[4] huang jin (yellow gold) refers to the mountain area clans and tribes。

译文：中部第十二列山系是平坦山系，最西端的山叫仪邑山，是游牧部落地区，住着山区部落氏族。
Translation:
The 12th list of the mountains in the middle region is the Pingtanshan Mountains。 With Yiyishan at its west most end, this region is a nomadic tribe's territory。 The mountainous tribes and clans live here。

05-12-02 云山

Yunshan
（106,56462E；31,07628N）

又东南五十里，曰云山[1]，无草木[2]，有桂竹[3]，甚伤人必死[4]，其上多黄金[5]，其下多璆琈之玉[6]。

注释：[1]云山：指营山。今四川营山县城。
Notes:[1] yun shan (clouds mount) refers to Yingshan (camp mount) in today's Yingshan county, Sichuan province。
[2] 无草木：游牧部落地区。

[2] wu cao mu (no grass wood) refers to the nomadic territory。

[3] 桂竹：指城北肆，今称北观肆。

[3] gui zhu (cassia and bamboo) refers to the Chengbeisi (city north market) today known as Beiguansi (north watch town) 。

[4] 甚伤人必死：朗池镇所属的集肆。甚伤人，读申榭惹，指朗池镇；必，指属；死，指肆。

[4] shen shang ren bi si (very hurting person must die) the township belongs to Langchizhen district。Shenshangren: reads as Shenxiere, refers to the town of Langchi。 bi(belong) si (small town) 。

[5] 黄金：指岭上氏族，这里指翠屏村氏族。

[5] huang jin (yellow gold) refers to the Lingshang clan, aka Cuipingcun clan。

[6] 瑨琈玉：指白家山夷。

[6] yun fu yu (yunfu jade): refers to the Baijiashan Yi, (white family mount people) 。

译文：由仪邑山往东南五十里，有座山叫营山，是游牧部落地区。有一个北观肆，是朗池镇所属的集肆。集镇的西面住着翠屏村氏族，东面住着白家山氏族。

Translation:

Fifty li further southeast from Yiyishan stands Yingshan。 This is the territory of nomadic tribes。 A township is called Beiguansi, belonging to the Langchizhen。 To its west lives the Cuipingcun clan。To its east lives the Baijiashan clan。

05-12-03 龟山

Guishan

（107,28E；31,06059N）

又东南一百三十里，曰龟山[1]，其木多穀柞椆椐[2]，其上多金[3]，其下多青雄黄[4]，多扶竹[5]。

注释：[1]龟山：指渡山。龟，读 gou 音，指渡，今四川达州渡市镇。

Notes:[1] gui shan (turtle mount) refers to Dushan。 Gui reads as gou, meaning cross, in today's Dazhoudu township, Sichuan province。

[2] 穀柞椆椐：指渡村白藉氏族。椆椐，指白藉。

[2]gu zuo chou ju（mulberry oak wood bamboo）: refers to the Baiji clan from Ducun (crossing village), chouju: baiji（white lineage) 。

[3]金：指岭上氏族。

[3] jin(gold) refers to the Lingshang clan（range up)。

[4] 青雄黄：指溪峡口氏族。

[4] qing xiong huang (green male yellow) refers to the Xixiakou clan。

[5] 扶竹：指盘村氏族，今称金盘村氏族。扶，指盘。

[5] fu zhu (hold bamboo): refers to the Pancun clan, today known as the Jinpan (gold plate)cun clan. fu: plate. pan, f/p interchangeable。

译文：由营山往东一百三十里，有座山叫渡山，中心住着渡村白藉氏族，西面住着岭上氏族，东面住着溪峡口氏族，住着盘村氏族。

Translation:

One hundred and thirty li from Yingshan stands Dushan。 In its middle area live the Baiji clan from Ducun。 To its west lives the Lingshang clan。 To its east lives the Xixiakou clan and the Pancun clan。

05-12-04 丙山

Bingshan

（107,86428E；31,08808N）

又东七十里，曰丙山[1]，多筀竹[2]，多黄金[3]、铜铁[4]，无木[5]。

注释：[1]丙山：指峨门山，简称门山、峨城，今达州开江区。峨，读音 hou。
Notes:[1] bing shan: refers to Emenshan, shortened to Menshan or Echeng, known today as Kaijiang district, Dazhou, e, reads as hou。

[2] 筀竹：指桂村氏族。
[2] gui zhu(bamboo): refers to the Guicun clan。

[3] 黄金：指峨岭氏族。峨岭，今称万花岭。
[3] huang jin (yellow gold) refers to the Eling clan, Eling known today as Wanhualing (10000 flower ridge) 。

[4] 铜铁：指坝子氏族。
[4] tong tie (copper iron) refers to the Bazi clan。

[5] 无木：指部落中心。
[5] wu mu (no wood) refers to the tribal center。

译文：由渡山往东七十里，有座山叫门山，住着桂村氏族，住着峨岭氏族和坝子氏族，是部落中心。
Translation:
Seventy li further east from Dushan stands Menshan。 Living in these regions are the Guicun clan, Eling clan and Bazi clan。 This is the tribal center。

05-12-05 风伯山
Fengboshan
（108,34809E；30,83883N）

又东南五十里，曰风伯[1]之山，其上多金玉[2]，其下多痠石[3]、文石[4]，多铁[5]。其木多柳杻檀楮[6] 。其东有林焉，曰莽浮之林 [7] ，美木鸟兽 [8] 。

注释：[1]风伯山：读斛伯，指斛山。今重庆万州区万斛城。斛是多音字，也读 jin。
Notes:[1] feng bo shan (wind uncle mount) reads as Hubo, hu also reads jin, refers to Hushan, today it is known as Wanhu city, in Wanzhou district, Chongqing city, Sichuan province。

[2] 金玉：指千家岭夷。
[2] jin yu (gold jade) refers to the Qianjialing (thousand family range) Yi。

[3] 痠石：指沙河村。
[3] suan shi (weak stone) refers to the Shahe Village。

[4] 文石：指流水村。
[4] wen shi (marked stone): refers to the Liushuicun (flowing water village) 。

[5]铁：指救兵村氏族。
[5] tie(iron) refers to the Jiubingcun clan。 Jiubingcun (save soldier village) 。

[6] 柳杻檀楮：指岔河旗村氏族，今称插旗村氏族。
[6] liu niu tan zhu (willow, oak, sandal wood, holm oak): refers to the Chaheqicun clan, known today as the Chaqicun (raise flag village) clan。

[7] 莽浮林：指密山府，在万州的长江东岸。
[7] mang fu lin (wide floating forest) refers to the Mishanfu, on the east bank of the Yangtze River at Wanzhou city, Sichuan province。 fu: an ancient Chinese administrative unit。

[8] 美木鸟兽：指密蒙僚族。美木、密蒙都是指娘，密蒙僚族即娘僚族。

[8] mei mu niao shou (pretty tree bird beast) refers to the Mimeng Liao people。 Meimu, Mimeng, are both close phonetic matches to Ma(niang/mother), Mimenglao is also known as Nianglao。Mi, ma, mei, mu, niang, share the same meaning Mother, phonetically shifting.

译文：由门山往东南五十里，有座山叫斛山，西面住着千家岭氏族，东面住着沙河村氏族、流水村氏族和救兵村氏族。中心住着岔河旗村氏族。东边有一个府，是密山府，是密蒙僚族的治府。
Translation:
Fifty li further southeast from Menshan stands Hushan。 To its west lives the Qianjialing clan。 To its east live the Shahecun clan, Liushuicun clan, and Jiubingcun clan。In its center lives the Chaheqicun clan。 To its east side there is a governing center, it is called Mishanfu。 This is the governing center of the Mimeng Liao people。

05-12-06 夫夫山
Fufushan
（109,46401E；31,01876N）

又东一百五十里，曰夫夫之山[1]，其上多黄金[2]，其下多青雄黄[3]，其木多桑楮[4]，其草多竹、鸡鼓[5]。神于兒居之[6]，其状人身而身操两蛇 [7]，常游于江渊 [8]，出入有光[9]。

注释：[1]夫夫山：指复堡山，后称鱼复，再后称奉节，今重庆市奉节县城。
Notes:[1] fu fu shan (male male mount) refers to the Fubaoshan, later known as Yufu and Fengjie。It is today's Fengjie county seat in Chongqing city, Sichuan province。
[2] 黄金：指复部落。
[2] huang jin (yellow gold) refers to the Fu tribe。
[3] 青雄黄：东穴山，后称夔门。
[3] qing xiong huang (green male yellow) refers to the Dongxueshan (east cave mount) later known as Kuimen。
[4] 桑楮：指江湾。
[4] sang zhu (mulberry wood):refers to the Jiangwan(river bay)。
[5] 竹鸡鼓：指虎牙村，今谐音称竹枝街。
[5] zhu ji gu (bamboo chicken drum) refers to the Huyacun (tiger teeth village), known today as Zhuzhijie (bamboo stick street) 。
[6] 神于兒居之：指长江的部落支系。
[6] shen yu er ju zhi (God yuer occupies it) refers to the tribal clans and branches along the Yangtze River。
[7] 人身而操两蛇：重要的运河肆。
[7] ren shen er cao liang she (human body holding two snakes) important river shipping and crossing townships。
[8] 常游于江渊：蚩尤的乔夷。
[7] chang you yu jiang yuan (often swim in the river deep) refers to the Qiao Yi branch of Chi You the great hero。
[9] 出入有光：建立之城。出入，指建树、建立。
[9] chu ru you guan (out in, have lights) State building city。

译文：由斛山往东一百五十里，有座山叫复堡山，西面住着复堡部落氏族，东面住着东穴山氏族，中心住着江湾氏族，虎牙村氏族。这里是长江的部落支系，是蚩尤的迁徙夷建立之城。
Translation:
One hundred and fifty li further east from Zhenshan there stands Fubaoshan。 To its west lives the Fubao tribal clan, to its east lives the Dongxueshan clan, and in the middle, lives the Jiangwang clan, the Huyacun clan。 This is the territory of tribal clans along the Yangtze River, is the founding city of the migrant Yi of Chiyou the great hero。

05-12-07 洞庭山
Dongtingshan
（109,7262E；30,60128N）

又东南一百二十里，曰洞庭之山[1]，其上多黄金[2]，其下多银铁[3]，其木多柤梨橘櫾[4]，其草多葌、蘼芜、芍药、芎藭[5]。帝之二女[6] 居之，是常游于江渊 [7] 。澧沅之风 [8] ，交潇湘之渊[9] ，是在九江之间[10]，出入必以飘风暴雨[11]，是多怪神[12]，状如人而载蛇[13]，左右手操蛇[14]，多怪鸟[15]。

注释：[1]洞庭山：指平坦山，今湖北恩施州建始城。
Note: [1] dong ting shan (cave yard mount) refers to the Pingtanshan, in today's Jianshi city, Enshizhou, Hubei Province。

[2] 黄金：指火石岭氏族。
[2] huang jin (yellow gold) refers to the Huoshiling (fire stone ridge) clan。

[3] 银铁：指菜园子村氏族。
[3] yin tie (silver iron) refers to the Caiyuanzicun clan:(vegetable garden village) 。

[4] 柤梨橘櫾：指纠黎蚩尤。
[4] ju li ju yao (quince, pear, oranges): refers to the Jiu Li Chi You。

[5]葌、蘼芜、芍药、芎藭：指建庄部落茨川象街。
[5] jian, miwu, shaoyao, gongqiong(chinese flowers and herbs) refers to the Jianzhuang tribes' Cichuanxiang Street。

[6] 帝之二女居之：叠枝阿黎部落支系，指刘姓人部落支系。
[6] di zhi er nv ju zhi (Di's two daughters live here)
Tr: Diezhi- Ali tribal branch of the Liu tribes。

[7] 常游于江渊：蚩尤的疆域。
[7] chang you yu jiang yuan (often swim in river deep) the territory of Chi You, the great Hero。

[8] 澧沅之风：定居胭脂山。澧，指定居；胭脂山，今称红土坪。
[8]li yuan zhi feng (high-brow style)
Tr: settle in Yanzhishan. li(settle), yanzhishan known today as Hongtuping (red clay ping) 。

[9] 交潇湘之渊：成割据之域。交，读 gao 音；潇湘，指割据。
[9] jiao xiao xiang zhi yuan (meet at Xiaoxiang water's deep)
Tr: becomes a self-armed governing territory。 jiao(gao) xiaoxiang (illegitimate separation and self-governing) 。

[10] 九江之间：读纠疆之纪，这里指苗疆区域。
[10] jiu jiang zhi jian (amidst nine rivers) reads as Jiujiangzhiji, which refers to the Miao controlled territories。

[11] 出入必以飘风暴雨：建立属于自己统治的部落邑。出入，指建立；必以，指属于；飘，指自己；风，指统治；暴雨，指部落邑。
[11] chu ru bi yii piao feng bao yu (out in must ride blowing winds and downpour rain)
Tr: establish the tribal cities and townships that belong to and controlled by their own chieftains。 Chu ru: establish； biyi: belong, piao; self, feng: rule； baoyu: tribal settlements townships and cities。

[12] 怪神：指专业氏族。
[12] guai shen (strange deities) refers to the clans with special skills。

[13] 人而载蛇：集镇的手工业氏族。载，读 zhe 音，是罴的苗语读音。
[13] ren er zai she (human but carry snakes) the handicrafts clans of the townships。 Zai: zhe, the Miao speech of Pi。

[14] 左右手操蛇：渚雍族的迁徙氏族。渚雍即良渚。
[14] zuo you shou cao she (left right hands hold snakes)
Tr: the emigrated clans of the Zhuyong tribes。 Zhuyong are also known as Liangzhu。

[15] 多怪鸟：指笃古僚，即银匠。

[15] duo guai niao (many strange birds) refers to the Dugu Liao, meaning the silversmiths。

译文：由复堡山往东南一百二十里，有座山叫平坦山，西面住着火石岭氏族，东面住着菜园子村氏族，中心住着纠黎蚩尤，住着建庄部落茨川象街氏族。这里是刘姓人部落支系蚩尤的疆域，他们定居胭脂山，成就割据之域，在苗疆的区域，建立属于自己部落邑。这里还住着专业的氏族，是集镇的手工业氏族，是良渚的迁徙氏族的银匠。
Translation:
One hundred and twenty li further southeast from Fubaoshan stands Pingtanshan。 To its west lives the Huoshiling clan。 To its east lives the Caiyuanzicun clan。 In the middle lives the Jiuli Chi You, as well as the Cichuanxiangjie clan of the Jianzhuang tribe。 This is the territory of the Chi You branch of the tribes bearing the surname of Liu。 They settled in Yanzhishan, successfully became self-governing, and built towns and cities controlled by themselves in this Miao territory。Also living here are the clans with special skills, they are the township handicrafts clans, the silversmiths who have migrated from Liangzhu in the East。

05-12-08 暴山
Baoshan
（110,67393E；30,19967N）

又东南一百八十里，曰暴山[1]，其木多棕枏荆芑[2]竹箭䉋菌[3]，其上多黄金[4]，其下多文石铁[5]，其兽多麋鹿【鹿旨】就[6]。

注释：[1]暴山：指宝山，今称宝塔坡。今湖北宜昌五峰县城。
Notes:[1] bao shan (violence mount): refers to Baoshan (treasure mount)， today it is known as the Baotapo(treasure pagoda slope）,in Wufeng(five peaks) county, Yichang ,Hubei province。
[2] 棕枏荆芑：指僮僚场部落。即布依族部落。
[2] zong nan jin si (palm oak thorny twigs): refers to the Dongliaochang clan, known also as the Buyi ethnic tribes。
[3] 竹箭䉋菌：诸李五峰氏族。
[3] zhu jian mei jun (bamboo shoots mushroom): refers to the various Liwufeng clan, (li five peaks)。
[4] 黄金：指马鬃岭氏族。
[4] huang jin (yellow gold) refers to the Mazongling (horse mane ridge) clan。
[5] 文石铁：指五峰肆营氏族。
[5] wen shi tie (glyph stone iron) refers to the Wufengsiying (five peaks town camp) clan。
[6] 麋鹿【鹿旨】就：指香姑苗。香姑，今称香沟。
[6]mi lu zhi jiu (elk deer stay): refers to the Xianggumiao (fragrant aunt Miao), xianggu known as Xianggou (fragrant gully) 。

译文：由平坦山往东南一百八十里，有座山叫宝山，中心住着僮僚场部落诸李五峰氏族，西面住着马鬃岭氏族，东面住着五峰肆营氏族。这里还住着香姑苗。
Translation:
One hundred and eighty li further southeast from Pingtanshan stands a mountain called Baoshan。 In the middle of it live the various clans bearing the surname of Li Wufeng, from the Tongliaochang tribes。 To its west lives the Mazongling clan。 To its east lives the Wufengsiying clan。 The Xianggu Miao people also live here。

05-12-09 即公山
Jigongshan
（111,37996E；29,58439N）

又东南二百里，曰即公之山[1]，其上多黄金[2]，其下多㻬琈之玉[3]，其木多柳杻檀桑[4]。有兽焉，其状如龟，而白身赤首[5]，名曰蛫[6]，是可以御火[7]。

注释：[1]即公山：指壁门山，今称石门山。今湖南常德市石门县城。
Notes: [1] ji gong shan (thus male mount) refers to the Bimeshan (cliff gate mountain), known today as the Shimenshan (stone gate mountain), in today's Shimen county, Changde city, Hunan province。

[2] 黄金：指界山氏族。
[2] huang jin (yellow gold) refers to the Jieshan (border mount) clan。

[3] 㻬琈玉：指平山夷，今称坪山夷。
[3] yun fu yu(jade) refers to Pingshan (flat mount) Yi, known today as the Pingshan Yi. ping written in different Chinese signs。

[4] 柳杻檀桑：指岔河潭湾氏族。这里的潭，是接近汉语的苗契语。
[4] liu niu tan cang (willow, oak, sandalwood, mulberry): refers to the Chahe (fork river) Tanwan(pond bay)clan, the word Tan, is a Miao Qi concept。It is closer to Chinese。

[5] 龟而白身赤首：竹编专业的手艺氏族。白身，读 bushe，指竹类的。
[5] gui er bai shen chi shou (turtle with white body red head)
Tr: refers to the handicraft's clan engaged in bamboo stripe weaving business。Baishen (white body) reads as bushe, meaning of the bamboo。

[6]蛫：指归姓氏族。归姓，得姓于做事专业。
[6] gui(kind of turtle) refers to the clan bearing the surname of Gui(return), the name means they are specialized in their skills。

[7] 可以御火：夏国的传承氏族。这里指竹编传承氏族。御火，指传送。
[7]ke yi yu huo (able to protect from fire)
Tr: Xia nation's Chuancheng clans who inherited the skills of bamboo strip weaving。 Yuhuo: pass the skills down to the later generations。

译文；由宝山往东南二百里，有座山叫石门山，西边住着界山氏族，东边住着平山夷，中心住着岔河潭湾氏族。有一个氏族，是竹编专业的手艺氏族，叫归姓氏族，是夏国的竹编传承氏族。
Translation:
Two hundred li further southeast from Baoshan stands Shimenshan。 To its west live the Jieshan clan。 To its east lives the Pingshan Yi。The Chahetanwan clan lives in the middle region。 A clan, a skilled bamboo weaving specialist group of the Xia nation, bears the surname of Gui。 They carry on the bamboo weaving skill and pass it down。

05-12-10 尧山
Yaoshan
（112,17005E；29,41105N）

又东南一百五十九里，曰尧山[1]，其阴多黄垩[2]，其阳多黄金[3]，其木多荆芑柳檀[4]，其草多藷藇术[5]。

注释：[1]尧山：指诸夭之山，简称夭山。诸夭，指低地。今湖南常德市安乡县城。
Notes:[1] yao shan: refers to the Zhuyaoshan, shortened to Yaoshan。 Zhuyao means lowland, in today's Anxiang county, Changde city, Hunan province。

[2] 黄垩：指垸部落氏族。
[2] huang e(yellow clay) refers to the Wan tribal clans。

[3] 黄金：指垸岭洲氏族，今称长岭洲氏族。

[3] huang jin (yellow gold) refers to the Wanglingzhou clan, known today as the Changlingzhou clan。

[4] 荆芑柳檀：指清溪河族。

[4] jing si liu tan (thorny twigs willow sandalwood): refers to the Qingxihe (clear creek river)tribe。

[5] 藷藇术：指诸夭族，即低地氏族。

[5] zhu yu shu (various herbs): refers to the Zhuyao tribe, the tribes that occupy the low land。

译文：由石门山往东南一百五十九里，有座山叫夭山，北面住着垸部落氏族，南面住着垸岭洲氏族，中心住着清溪河族，住着低地族移民。

Translation:

One hundred fifty and nine li further southeast from Shimenshan stands a mountain called Yaoshan。To its north live the Wanbuluo clan。 To its south live the Wanlingzhou clan。 In its center lives the Qingxihe clan, as well as the immigrants of the Didi tribes。

05-12-11 江浮山

Jiangfushan

（112,75433E；29,04763N）

又东南一百里，曰江浮之山[1]，其上多银砥砺[2]，无草木[3]，其兽多豖鹿[4]。

注释：[1]江浮山：指苗语的右手山，今译为资年山，在湖南常德沅江市阳罗镇。

Notes:[1] jiang fu shan (river float mount) in Miao speech, it means Youshou (right hand mount) Mountain。It is translated into Zinianshan, in today's Yangluo town, Changde's Yuanjiang city, Hunan province。

[2] 银砥砺：指阴箩黎，今称阳罗黎。水北为阳，银读阴，指水之阳。

[2] yin di li (silver grinding stone)

Tr: refers to Yinluo Li, known today as Yangluo Li。 North of water is the Yang side, yin reads as yin, meaning the sunny side of the water。

[3] 无草木：指运输部落中心。

[3] wu cao mu (no grass wood) refers to the center of Transportation tribes。

[4] 豖鹿：指运输民。豖读施，指运输；鹿读鲁，指民。

[4] zhu lu (pig deer) refers to the Folks of transportation。 Zhu reads shi in Pu speech, meaning shipping, Lu(deer) means people, folk, volk。

译文：由夭山往东南一百里，有座山叫资年山，那里住着阳罗黎，是运输部落中心，氏族为运输民。

Translation:

One hundred li further southeast from Yaoshan stands Zinianshan。 The Yangluo Li lives there, they constitute the center of transportation tribes, their clans are folks of shipping and packing 。

05-12-12 真陵山

Zhenlingshan

（113,68189E；29,02197N）

又东二百里，曰真陵之山[1]，其上多黄金[2]，其下多玉[3]，其木多榖柞柳杻[4]，其草多荣草[5]。

注释：[1]真陵山：指板市山，也称板江山。今湖南岳阳市平江县板江乡。

Notes:[1] zhen ling shan (true ridge mount) refers to the Banshishan, known today as Banjiangshan, in today's Banjiangxiang in Pingjiang county, Yueyang city, Hunan province。

[2] 黄金：指卜巫场氏族，简称巫场。今称卜屋场氏族。

[2] huang jin (yellow gold) refers to the Puwuchang clan, shortened to Wuchang (witch field) today known as Puwuchang clan。wu: in different Chinese signs。

[3]玉：指河滨氏族。

[3]yu(jade) refers to the Hebin clan。

[4] 榖柞柳杻：指板江河支系氏族。

[4]gu zuo liu niu (grain oak willow wood): refers to the Banjianghe branch clan。

[5] 荣草：指罗姓移民。

[5] rong cao (lush grass) refers to the immigrants bearing the surname of Luo。

译文：由资年山往东二百里，有座山叫板市山，西面住着巫场氏族，东面住着河滨氏族，中心住着板江河支系氏族，住着罗姓移民。

Translation:

Two hundred li further east from Zinianshan stands Banshishan。 To its west lives the Wuchang clan。 To its east lives the Hebing clan。 The Banjianghe branch clan lives in the middle。 The immigrants bearing the surname Luo also live there。

05-12-13 阳帝山

Yangdishan

（114,24402E；29,00478N）

又东一百二十里，曰阳帝之山[1]，多美铜[2]，其木多橿杻檿楮[3]，其兽多麢麝[4]。

注释：[1]阳帝山：指杨泆山，又称渣津山。查姓即杨姓，泆、津都指河畔。今江西修水县渣津镇。

Notes:[1] yang di shan (sunny di mount) refers to Yangdieshan, also known as the Zhajinshan。 Surname cha/zha is Yang in Chinese。 Die/yi and Jing both refer to riverbanks, in today's Zhajin town in Xiushui county, Jiangxi Province。

[2] 美铜：指店前村氏族。

[2] mei tong (beautiful copper): refers to the Dianqiancun clan。

[3] 橿杻檿楮：指渣津大村氏族。

[3] jiang niu yan zhu (oak wood): refers to the Chajindacun clan。

[4] 麢麝：指长潭村氏族。

[4] ling she (a kind deer): refers to the Changtancun clan。changtan: long pond。

译文：由板市山往东一百二十里，有座山叫杨泆山，住着店前村氏族，中心住着渣津大村氏族，住着长潭村氏族。

Translation:

One hundred and twenty li further east from Banshishan stands Yangyishan。 The Dianqiancun clan lives there。 Living in the center are the Chajindacun clan and the Changtancun clan。

05-12-14 柴桑山

Chaisangshan

（113,93909E；28,7118N）

又南九十里，曰柴桑之山[1]，其上多银[2]，其下多碧[3]，多泠石赭[4]，其木多柳芑楮桑[5]。其兽多麋鹿[6]，多白蛇飞蛇 [7] 。

注释：[1]柴桑山：指姑湾山，也称咪噜湾山。谐音称长寿，今湖南平江县长寿镇。

Notes:[1] chai sang shan (firewood mulberry mount) refers to Guwanshan。 It also reads as Miluwan Mountain, a close phonetic rendering into Changshou(longevity), in today's Changshou town, Pingjiang county, Hunan province。

[2]银：指泥坑氏族。

[2] yin(silver) refers to the Nikeng(mudhole) clan。

[3]碧：读河畔氏族。

[3]bi: refers to the Hepan (riverbanks) clan。

[4] 泠石赭：指量肆村氏族。量肆即商肆。

[4] ling shi zhe (stone ocher): refers to the Liangsicun clan。 liangsi: meaning Shangsi, market town。

[5] 柳芑楮桑：指堧溪渚湾氏族。

[5] liu si zhu sang (willow twig wood mulberry); refers to the Ruanxizhuwan clan。

[6] 麋鹿：读咪噜，指姑湾氏族。

[6]mi lu (elk deer) reads as milu, referring to the Guwan clan。

[7] 白蛇飞蛇：摆肆、卖肆。

[7] bai she fei she (white snake flying snake): baisi, maisi: meaning sell yard。

译文：由杨泆山往南九十里，有座山叫姑湾山，西面住着泥坑氏族，东面住着河畔氏族，住着量肆氏族。中心住着的堧溪渚湾氏族，主要是姑湾的摆肆、卖肆氏族。

Translation:

Ninety li further south from the Yangyishan stands Guwanshan。 To its west lives the Nikeng clan。 To its east lives the Hepan clan and the Liangsi clan。 In the middle lives the Ruanxizhuwan clan。 Of them the major clans are the Baisi and Maisi from Guwan。

05-12-15 荣余山

Rongyushan

（115,07388E；28,68053N）

又东二百三十里，曰荣余之山[1]。其上多铜[2]，其下多银 [3] 。其木多柳芑 [4]，其虫多怪蛇怪虫 [5] 。

凡洞庭山之首，自篇遇之山至于荣余之山，凡十五山，二千八百里。其神状皆鸟身而龙首[6] 。其祠：毛一雄鸡，一牝豚刉 [7]，糈用稌。凡夫夫之山，即公之山，尧山，阳帝之山，皆冢也，其祠皆肆瘗 [8]，祈用酒，毛用少牢，婴毛一吉玉。洞庭、荣余之山神也[9]，其祠：皆肆瘗，祈酒太牢，祠婴用圭璧十五[10]，五采惠之[11]。

右中经之山志，大凡百九十七山，二万一千三百七十一里。

大凡天下名山五千三百七十，居也，大凡六万四千五十六里。

禹曰：天下名山经，五千三百七十山，六万四千五十六里，居地也。言其《五臧》[12]，盖其余小山甚众，不足记云。天地之东西二万八千里，南北二万六千里，出水之山者八千里，受水者八千里，出铜之山四百六十七，出铁之山三千六百九十。此天地之所分壤树谷[13]也，戈矛之所发也，刀鎩之所起也，能者有余，拙者不足。封于太山 [14]，禅于梁父 [15]，七十二家，得失之数，皆在此内，是谓国用。

右《五臧山经》五篇，大凡一万五千五百三字。

注释：[1]荣余山：指罗峒山，又称罗市山。今江西奉新县罗市镇。

Notes:[1] rong yu shan: refers to Luoyushan, also known as Luoshishan, in today's Luoshi town in Fengxin county, Jiangxi province。

[2]铜：指黄泥山氏族。

[2] tong(copper) refers to the Huangnishan clan。

[3]银：指泽下氏族。

[3] yin(silver) refers to the Zexia clan。

[4] 柳芑：指潦溪氏族。今称南潦河氏族。
[4] liu si (willow) refers to the Liaoxi clan, today the clan is known as Nanliao (south flood river)。
[5] 怪蛇怪虫：指黄冈墩移民。
[5] guai she guai chong (strange snake strange worm) refers to the immigrants of Huanggangdun。
[6] 鸟身而龙首：农业氏族的僚族形象。
[6] niao shen er long shou (bird body with dragon head)
Tr: the image of Lao tribes of the agricultural people。
[7] 牝豚刉：指珠白玉。这里的珠白是指一种河玉白。
[7] pin tun ge (female river fish open): refers to the Pearl white jade, pearl white means river jade white。
[8]肆：远古时期专供书写用的麻布，也称可称作纸。氏丝为纸。这里指写祭词的肆。
[8]si: the hemp cloth order made for ancient scribers to write on, which can be called the early paper。 In Chinese the glyph of paper is written with parts standing for shi and silk。 Here it refers to the Si for writing prayers。
[9] 神也：指大神，大山神。
[9] shen ye(spirit) refers to the supreme spirit, the supreme deity of big mountains。
[10] 十五：读祀武，指祭祀财神，这些山的山神，实际是财神。五，指买家，也称财神。
[10] shi wu (ten five), read as siwu, refers to the rite of sacrificing to the god of wealth。 The mountain deities are money god。 wu(five)； refers to buyer, also called as Caishen (wealth god) 。
[11] 五采惠之：指买卖兴隆。惠，读韦音，指卖。
[11] wu cai hui zhi: business booms, hui/wei, meaning sell。
[12] 五臧：指东、西、南、北、中五大疆域，臧指疆。
[12] wu zang: refers to five areas of east, west, south, north and middle。zang(treasure) means area。
[13] 分壤树谷：指分疆立国。
[13] fen rang shu gu (divide land plant grain)
Tr: divide territories and build nations。
[14] 太山：指山东泰山。
[14] tai shan: refers to the Taishan in Shandong province。
[15] 梁父：梁父山在山东新泰县徂徕镇，梁父应读立胡，指福山。立，指福；胡，指山。又称地坛。
[15] liang fu (liang father): refers to the Liangfushan, in Julai town, Xintai county in Shandong province。 Liangfu should be read as Lifu and refers to Fushan。 Li/fu, Hu: mount, Liangfu means earth altar。

译文：由姑湾山往东二百三十里，有个地方叫罗嵎山，西面住着黄泥山氏族，东面住着泽下氏族。中心住着潦溪氏族，住着黄冈墩移民。

综观中部第十二列平坦山山系，从仪邑山到罗嵎山，共计十五座山，延绵二千八百里。山神皆为农业的僚族人的形象。祭祀信玉用软玉，用珠白玉，食物用荞麦食物。复堡山、石门山、夭山、杨泆山，都是宗山，祭祀要写祭词掩埋，用酒祈祷，信玉用少牢礼，掩埋一吉玉。平坦、罗隅的神是大神，祭祀要写祭词掩埋，祈酒用太牢礼，用圭和璧祭祀埋给财神，祈求买卖兴隆。
Translation:
Two hundred and thirty li further east from Guwanshan stands Luoyushan。 To its west lives the Huangnishan clan。 To its east lives the Zexia clan。 In the middle lives the Liaoxi clan and the Huanggangdun immigrants。

In sum, the Pingtanshan list records 15 mountains from Yiyishan to Luoyushan, covering a total distance of 2,800 li。 The mountain deities are in the images of the agricultural Liao tribes。When sacrificing to them, the messenger jade is soft jade, and pearl white jade。 Foods are made of buckwheat。Fubaoshan, Shimenshan, Yaoshan and Yangyishan are ancestors' burial mounds。When sacrificing at these mountains, prayers are written on the hemp cloth, and buried。 Wines are used in votive rites。 Messenger jade is buried in Shaolao rite, one piece of good luck jade is buried。The deities of Pingtanshan and Luoyushan are supreme ones。When sacrificing to them, prayers are written down and buried with votive wine rites of Tailao, Gui jade and Bi jade are buried for the God of Wealth, in the hope of being blessed with booming business of buying and selling。

上述中山十二列山，共计一百九十七山，二万一千三百七十一里。
所有天下名山，共五千三百七十座，可居住的有六万四千五十六里。
Of the 12 mountain lists of the middle area, a total of 197 mountains are covered with a total distance of 21,371 li。Of all the famous mountains under heaven, there are a total of 5,730 mountains, with 64,056 li available for human occupation。

大禹说：天下名山，五千三百七十座，六万四千五十六里，可以居住。称为《五疆》，其它小山太多，不必记录。天地东西长二万八千里，南北长二万六千里，出水之山有八千里，受水之山有八千里，出铜之山有四百六十七里，出铁之山三千六百九十里。这些是分疆立国、发生刀兵杀伐的原因，先进强悍的民族就得到充足的物产资源，落后柔弱的民族，物资就会贫乏。那些去泰山和梁父山封禅的七十二家，兴衰得失皆因为这个原因。事关国家的战略。
上述《五疆山经》五篇，总共一万五千五百零三字。
Yu the great comments: Of the famous mountains under heaven, there are a total of 5,370 of them, with 64,056 li available for human occupation, known as Wuzang。 The rest are small mountains, numerous and not worth recording。The distance under the sky is 28,000 li east to west, and 26,000 li south to north。 The mountains where rivers rise, total 8,000 li, and those mountains that receive waters total 8,000 li。 467 mountains turn out copper; 3,690 mountains turn out iron。 This is the reason why territories are divided, different nations are formed, wars to kill started。 The strong nations are with abundant resources, and the weak and backward nations always suffer from shortage。 The 72 nations who go to Taishan and Liangfushan to get mandates to their rules experience gains and losses, they thrive or fail for the same reason。 This is a vital strategy for state building。

Of the above-mentioned five books of mountains, 15,503 words are written down。

第六卷 海外南经 (Haiwai Region: the South)

Book 6 Haiwainanjing

06-01 结胸国

Jiexiong Guo

（103,71898E；27,33638N）

海外自西南陬至东南陬者[1]。

结胸国[2]在其西南，其为人结胸[3]。

注释：[1]陬：指角、角落。海外指近海的、离中原较近的。

Notes:[1] zou: refers to the corner, where two cardinal lines meet。 Haiwai (sea out): closer to the center, closer to the center plain（zhongyuan）。

[2] 结胸国：指宰赫国，在云南昭通地区。濮语读为宰拜赫国，简称宰赫，音译为结胸。宰赫，也读者黑、者恒，者海，指交易之市。如今有者海、者黑等地名遗存。

[2] jie xiong guo (tie breast country) refers to Zaihe Guo, in Shaotong district， Yunnan province。 In Pu speech it is read Zaibaihe Guo, shortened to Zaihe, phonetically rendered into Chinese as Jiexiong。 Zaihe, also reads as zhehei, zheheng, zhehai, meaning trading town。 Its relic names can still be found in place names such as Zhehai, Zhehei。

[3] 其为人结胸：指定都于宰拜赫嘎，即今昭通城。

[3] qi wei ren jie xiong (as person his chest tied)

Tr: having their capital setup in Zaibaihega, known today as Shaotong city。

译文：海外南经从西南角记述到东南角。

宰赫国在西南，定都于宰拜赫嘎。

Translation:

Chapter Haiwainanjing starts from southwest corner to southeast corner。 Zaihe Guo is in the southwest, with its capital city in Zaibaihega。

06-02 南山
Nanshan
（103,30006E；26,41518N）

南山[1]在其东南。自此山来[2]，虫为蛇 [3]，蛇号为鱼 [4]。一曰南山在结胸东南。

注释：[1]南山：指郎舍，即夜郎部落。在云南东川会泽地区。实际在宰赫国的南面。
Notes:[1] nan shan (south mount) refers to Langshe, the Yelang tribe。It is in Huize district， Dongchuan，Yunnan province。In fact, it is to the south of Zaihe Guo。

[2] 自此山来：指知痴夜舍僚。知痴夜是夜郎开国君主僰雅蒙的先祖，传三十一代至僰雅蒙时才建立了夜郎部落，又过三代后才东扩建立了大夜郎国。这里记录的是未东扩之前的夜郎部落。
[2] zi ci shan lai (up here mount come) refers to the Zhichiye Sheliao。Zhichiye is the ancestor of Boyameng, the founder of the Yelang Kingdom。 The title passed 31 generations to Boyameng, when the tribal confederacy was established。 After another three generations of expanding eastward, the Great Yelang Kingdom was established。 This description is about the Yelang tribe before their eastward expansion。

[3] 虫为蛇：建立部落。
[3] chong wei she (worm be snake)
Tr: set up their tribe。

[4] 蛇号为鱼：部落号为益。即益那、夜郎。
[4] she hao wei yu (snake title is fish) tribal name is Yi, Yina, Yelang。

译文：郎舍在东南面，是知痴夜舍僚建立的部落，部落号为夜郎。又说郎舍在宰赫国东南。
Translation：
Langshe lies to the southeast, a tribe set up by the Zhichiye Sheliao。 The tribal title is Yelang。 Also, Langshe is said to lie to the southeast of Zaihe Guo。

06-03 比翼鸟
Biyi’niao
（105,77046E；26,66358N）

比翼鸟[1]在其东，其为鸟青、赤[2]，两鸟比翼[3]。一曰在南山东。

注释：[1]比翼鸟：指大元国，历史误传为鳖国。比翼，指大元。鸟读“那”音，指国。
Notes:[1]bi yi niao (wing to wing bird) refers to Dayuan Guo, is mistakenly called Bie Guo。 Bie (big turtle), biyi (wing to wing) refers to Dayuan, niao(bird) reads as na, meaning Guo (country, nation) 。

[2] 其为鸟青、赤：此国区域为莲江、应江流域。莲江即牂牱江（今北盘江）；应江即今乌江（有遗存名印江）。
[2] qi wei niao qing chi (as birds green, red)
Tr: this country’s territory is the Lianjiang River and Yingjiang River area。 Lianjiang:(lotus river) is also called Zangke River， today known as the Beipan River。Yingjiang is known today as Wujiang River, a relic name Yinjiang has survived。

[3] 两鸟比翼：国都在大元，今贵州省织金县老城区。
[3] liang niao bi yi(two birds wing to wing)its national capital is in Dayuan, in today’s old city quarter of Zhijin county, Guizhou province。

译文：大元国在东面，其国为莲江、应江流域，都城建在大元。又说，大元国在夜郎部落的东面。

Translation:
Dayuan nation is in the east。 Its territory covers the Lianjiang River and Yinjiang River areas, with its capital in Dayuan。 In another word, Dayuan nation lies east to the Yelang tribe。

06-04 羽民国
Yumin Guo
（107,77917E；26,98994N）

羽民国[1]在其东南，其为人长头[2]，身生羽[3]。一曰在比翼鸟东南，其为人长颊[4]。

注释：[1]羽民国：指沂蒙国。苗族大迁徙进入贵州后，仍按原籍部落名建国。
Notes:[1]yu min guo (feather folk country) refers to the Yimeng Guo (previously in Shandong province)。 After the big migration of the Miao people into Guizhou, they kept their old tribal name for the new country in new territory。
[2] 其为人长头：定都于奢堵。长头读奢堵，指黄平。
[2] qi wei ren chang tou (as person his head long)
Tr: made his capital at Shedu。 Chang tou (long head) reads as Shedu in Pu speech, refers to Huangping (yellow flat) 。
[3] 身生羽：指奢施溢帕，即今杉木河畔。
[3] shen sheng yu (body grow feather) reads as Sheshiyipa, in today's Shanmu River banks。
[4] 长颊：指奢贾，即黄洼。
[4] chang xia (long cheek) refers to Shejia, meaning Huang wa (yellow swamp) 。

译文：沂蒙国在东南面，定都于黄平，在杉木河畔。又说，沂蒙国在大元国的东南面，定都城在黄洼。
Translation:
Yimeng Guo is in the southeast part, with its capital in Huangping, by the Shanmu River。 Also, it is said that Yimeng Guo lies to the southeast of the Dayuan country, with its capital in Huangwa。

06-05 二八神
Erbashen
（111,60015E；26,45404N）

有神人[1]二八[2]，连臂，为帝司夜于此野[3]。在羽民东。其为小人颊赤肩[4]，尽十六人[5]。

注释：[1]神人：指集肆。
Notes： [1] shen ren (God man) refers to township。
[2] 二八：读勒巴，指刺绣。二八神。
[2]er ba (two eight) reads as Leba， refers to embroidery。Erbashen: a town famous for its needle work。
[3] 连臂为帝司夜于此野：连江北端潇水河之乡。
[3] lian bi wei di si ye yu ci ye (arm in arm for God keep night watch in this wilderness)
Tr: Lianjiang River's north end, the Xiaoshuihe district。
[4] 小人颊赤肩：部落名，潇惹贾且纪。今称永州。
[4] xiao ren xia chi jian (small person cheek red shoulder)
Tr: a tribal name: Xiaorejiaqieji, today known as Yongzhou, Hunan province。
[5] 尽十六人：尽出娘惹。十，读 bei，指出；六人，读娘惹，即有修养的女孩。
[5] jing shi liu ren (altogether 16 person)
Tr: reads as jin chu niang re: shi: reads as bei (bring out) liu ren: niangre, well cultivated young girls。

译文：有一个集肆，叫勒巴肆，是连江北端潇水河之乡，在沂蒙国的东面，建镇于永州部落，尽出娘惹。
Translation:
There is a market town called Leba town, the district of Xiaoshui River at the north end of Lianjiang。 It is to the east of Yimeng Guo, its capital city is where the Yongzhou tribe stay, famous for their well cultivated girls。

06-06 毕方鸟
Bifangniao
（113,03082E；25,79536N）

毕方鸟[1]在其东，青水[2]西，其鸟人面一脚[3]。一曰在二八神东。

注释：[1]毕方鸟：指贝濮国，有两层含义，一是指十濮僚部落联盟国，一是指南方濮僚国。有遗名为十都。
Notes: [1]bi fang niao (finish square bird) refers to the Beipu Guo。 Its meaning is twofolds: 1. refers to the tribal confederacy of ten Pu-Lao tribes。 2.refers to the Pu-lao Guo in the south。 A relic name Shidu (ten city) has survived。
[2] 青水：指东江。
[2] qing shui (green water) refers to the Dongjiang River。
[3] 人面一脚：管理地在郴州。一脚，郴州的濮语音译。
[3] ren mian yi jiao (human face one foot)
Tr: its management center is in Binzhou。 yijiao (one foot) is the phonetic rendering of the Pu speech for Binzhou。

译文：贝濮国在东面，在东江的西面，管理地在郴州。又说，贝濮国在勒巴肆的东面。
Translation:
Beipu Guo lies in the east, to the west of Dongjiang River, with its management center in Binzhou。 It is also said that Beipu Guo lies to the east of Leba township。

06-07 讙头国
Huantou Guo
（113,43168E；24,94457N）

讙头国[1]在其南，其为人人面有翼[2]，鸟喙[3]，方捕鱼[4]。一曰在毕方东。或曰讙朱国[5]。

注释：[1]讙头国：指桂头国。濮语读桂为惠，谐音讙。在广东乳源县桂头镇，其国包括乳源县。
Notes:[1] huan tou guo; refers to Guitou Guo。In Pu speech, gui is read as hui, a close phonetic match to huan。It is in today's Guitou town, Ruyuan county, Guangdong province。 Its country includes Ruyuan county。
[2] 人面有翼：桂头镇古称龙门河。龙门之河读为人面有翼，今称桂头镇。
[2] ren mian you yi (human face has wings) refers to Guitouzhen, its ancient name is Loongmen (dragon gate) River。 Loongmen zhi he (dragon gate river) reads Renmianyouyi。Today, it is called Guitou town。
[3] 鸟喙：僚族支系。
[3] niao hui (bird beak) refers to Lao tribal branch。
[4] 方捕鱼：指山区濮夷。
[4] fang pu yu (just catch fish) refers to the Pu Yi from the mountainous areas。
[5] 讙朱国：指桂村国、桂寨国。
[5] huan zhu guo (noise red country) refers to the Guicun Guo, or the Guizhai Guo。

译文：桂头国在南面，建都于龙门河，是僚族支系的山区濮夷。又说，桂头国在濮国的东面，或称桂寨国。
Translation:

Guitou Guo is in the south, with its capital in Loongmen River area。They are the Pu branch of the Pu Yi from the mountains。 It is also said that the Guitou Guo is to the east of Pu Guo, or it is also called Guizhai Guo。

06-08 厌火国
Yanhuo Guo
（113,59044E；24,80076N）

厌火国[1]在其国南，兽身黑色[2]。生火出其口中[3] 。一曰在讙朱东。

注释：[1]厌火国：指乐和国。今称乐合。濮语读“乐”为 ye，都城在广东韶关。
Notes:[1] yan huo guo (tired of fire country) refers to Yuehuo Guo, known today as Yuehe。 In Pu speech, le reads as ye, capital is in Shaoguan city, Guangdong province。
[2] 兽身黑色：韶氏族的贵族部落国。
[2] shou shen hei se (beast body black) refers to the noble tribe of the Shao people。
[3] 生火出其口中：部落中心建于合园。此处的火读薨，指中心。口中，指口园，音意混译为合园，今乐园镇。
[3] sheng huo chu qi kou zhong (raw fire out of its mouth)
Tr: the tribal center is set up in Heyuan。Huo(fire) reads as hong, meaning center。 Kouyuan is a rendering of name by phonetic as well as semantic matching。 It is today's Leyuan town。

译文：乐合国在南面，是韶氏族的贵族部落国。建部落中心于合园。又说，乐合国在桂寨的东面。
Translation:
Yuehe Guo is in the south, a noble tribal country of the Shao Shi。 They set up their tribal center in Heyuan。 It is also said that Yuehe Guo lies to the east of Guizhai village。

06-09 三株树
Sanzhushu
（113,13648E；27,8288N）

三株树[1]在厌火北，生赤水上[2]，其为树如柏[3]，叶皆为珠[4]。一曰其数若慧[5] 。

注释：[1]三株树：指外来族群居住的部落，简称外驻部落。三，读啥，指外；树，苗族人称部落支系为栋树。今湖南株洲。
Notes:[1] san zhu shu (three trees) refers to the tribes that are made up of immigrates of outside people, shortened to station tribes。 san(three) reads as sha, meaning outsider。shu(tree) a Miao term for tribal branches。Those branches are call Dongshu, also refers to Zhuzhou, in today's Hunan province。
[2] 生赤水上：建在湘江边。湘江属长江水系，故也称赤水。
[2] sheng chi shui shan (born on the red river) set up their settlements on the banks of Xiangjiang River。 Xiangjiang River, being part of the Yangtze River, is also known as Chishui (red river) 。
[3]柏：读僰音，指农业氏族。
[3]bo (poplar) reads as Bo, refers to the agricultural tribes。
[4] 叶皆为珠：人们皆依水而居。为，在此作汶解，指水。
[4]ye jie wei zhu (leaves are pearls)
Tr: people choose to build their settlements by the water。 Wei; wen, meaning water。
[5]慧：读 ve 音，指越。即越人的迁徙族群。
[5] hui (wise) reads as ve, refers to the Yue tribes, meaning the migrant tribes of the Yue people。

译文：外驻部落在乐合部落的北面，建在湘江边，这个部落是农业氏族部落，人们皆依水而居。又说，这个部落是越部落。
Translation:
Outsider tribes live to the north of Yuehe clan, along the Xiangjiang River。 This tribe makes their living in agriculture, living by the water。 It is also said that this tribe belongs to the Yue people。

06-10 三苗国
Sanmiao Guo
（112,93414E；28,22546N）

三苗国[1]在赤水东，其为人相随[2]。曰三毛国[3] 。

注释：[1]三苗国：指奢陌国，即河坎上的国家，在今湖南长沙市。
Notes:[1] san miao guo (three sprouts nation)
Tr: refers to Shemo Guo, meaning country on the riverbanks rising grounds。It is in today's Changsha city, Hunan province。
[2] 相随：指湘塞，即湘店、湘肆。
[2] xiang sui(following) refers to Xiangsai, Xiangdian, or Xiangsi, sai, dian, si all refer to settlement such as village or to town。
[3] 三毛：读奢陌，指河坎。
[3] san mao (three hair) reads as Shemo, meaning Hekan, riverbanks, higher ground。

译文：奢陌国在湘江的东面，这个国家建都在湘肆。又说这个国家叫河坎国。
Translation:
Shemo Guo lies to the east of Xiangjiang River。This country set up its capital in Xiangsi。 It is also said that this country is also called Hekan Guo。

06-11 载国
Die Guo
（113,63072E；28,14183N）

载国[1]在其东，其为人黄[2]，能操弓射蛇[3]。一曰载国在三毛东。

注释：[1]载(die)国：指刘姓氏族的国家，今湖南浏阳。苗语读刘为载。
Notes:[1] die guo: refers to the nation bearing the surname of Liu, known today as Liuyang, in Hunan province。In Miao speech, Liu as a family name is read as Die。
[2]黄：读侯，指关口之口，今湖南浏阳县城。
[2] huang (yellow) reads as Hou, meaning pass gate, refers to the Liuyang county seat, Hunan province。
[3] 能操弓射蛇：原是照门的谢夷。山东半岛的古称为照门。
[3] neng cao gong she she (can use a bow to shoot a snake)
Tr: They are previously the Xie Yi from Zhaomen (shine gate) 。Zhaomen is the ancient name for the Shandong Peninsula。

译文：刘国在长沙国的东面，建集镇在关口，原是山东照门的谢夷。又说，刘国在奢陌国的东面。
Translation:

Liu Guo is to the east of Changsha Guo, with its township at Guankou。They are originally the Xie Yi immigrants from Shandong Zhaomen。It is also said that the Liu Guo lies to the east of Shemo Guo。

06-12 贯胸国
Guanxiong Guo
（115,89133E；28,67751N）

贯胸国[1]在其东，其为人胸有窍[2]。一曰在䖍国东。

注释：[1]贯胸国：指灌湘国，今江西南昌。
Notes： [1] guan xiong guo (through chest nation)
Tr: refers to Guanxiang Guo, in today's Nanchang city, Jiangxi province。
[2] 胸有窍：指洪城。
[2] xiong you qiao (chest has hole) refers to Hongcheng (flood city) 。

译文：灌湘国在东边，建都在洪城。又说，灌湘国在刘国的东边。
Translation:
Guanxiang Guo is in the east, with its capital in Hongcheng。It is also said that Guanxiang Guo is to the east of Liu Guo。
06-13 交胫国
Jiaojing Guo
（117,06302E；28,70955N）

交胫国[1]在其东，其为人交胫[2]。一曰在穿胸[3]东。

注释：[1]交胫国：交，读勾音，指陈集国。在江西万年县陈营镇。
Notes:[1] jiao jing guo (cross leg nation) jiao(cross) reads as gou, refers to the Chenji Guo, in today's Chenyingzhen, Wannian county, Jiangxi province。
[2] 交胫：指陈集。
[2] jiao ji(cross legs): refers to Chenji(Chen Market); chen, a family name。
[3] 穿胸：指灌湘国。
[3] chuang xiong (pierce chest) refers to Guanxiang Guo。

译文：陈集国在东面，建都在陈集。又说，陈集国在灌湘国的东边。
Translation:
Chenji Guo is in the east, with its capital in Chenji。 It is also said that Chenji Guo lies to the east of Guanxiang Guo。

06-14 不死民
Busimin
（117,95712E；28,43291N）

不死民[1]在其东，其为人黑色[2]，寿不死[3]。一曰在穿胸东。

注释：[1]不死民：指茅山庄，又称茅岭庄，今江西上饶。
Notes:[1] bu si min (never die folk) refers to the Maoshanzhuang, aka Maolingzhuang, in today's Shangrao city, Jiangxi province。
[2] 黑色：这里指信江边。

[2] hei se (black color) refers to the banks of Xinjiang River。

[3] 寿不死：指前茅山，这里指前茅山部落。

[3] shou bu si (longevity does not die) refers to the Qianmaoshan, here meant the Qianmaoshan tribe。

译文：茅山庄在东面，建镇在信江边，是前茅山部落。又说，茅山庄在灌湘国的东边。

Translation

Maoshanzhuang is in the east, with their township by the Xinjiang River, they are the Qianmaoshan tribe。 It is also said that the Maoshanzhuang lies to the east of Guanxiang Guo。

06-15 岐舌国

Qishe Guo

（118,87265E；28,95905N）

岐舌国[1]在其东。一曰在不死民东。

注释：[1]岐舌国：指衢肆国，今浙江衢州市城区。

Notes:[1] qi she guo (fork tongue nation) refers to the Qusi Guo, in today's city quarter of Quzhou city, Zhejiang province。

译文：衢肆国在东面。又说在茅岭庄的东面。

Translation:

Qusi Guo is in the east。It is also said that it is to the east of Maolingzhuang。

06-16 昆仑墟

Kunlunxiu

（119,6445E；29,08372N）

昆仑墟[1]在其东，墟四方[2]。一曰在岐舌东，为墟四方。

注释：[1]昆仑墟：指岭东部落与婺罗部落争肆堡的地方，简称为岭罗争，今称金华。昆，由岭演变而来，岭，读金音；仑由罗演变而来，罗又演变为诺，指女。后来演变为金星与婺女星争地盘的神话。

Notes: [1] kun lun xu: a town stronghold which becomes the battleground for Lingdong tribe and Maoluo tribe。The incident is coded as Lingluozheng, (the place of conflict) in today's Jinhua city, Zhejiang province。 Kun means ling(ridge), ling reads as Jin。Lun has gone through a few sound and meaning changes into luo, nuo（female), niu(female)。Later this motif gives rise to a fable story in which the Jinxing and Maoniu engaged in a land grab conflict。

[2] 墟四方：指争肆堡，也称争市场。商业竞争使这里繁华起来。墟，读斜，指争。四方，指肆堡。

[2] xu si fang (hallow four areas): refers to the fights for the townships, also known as fights for markets。Commerce has given the place a chance to prosper。Xu reads as xie, meaning fight for, sifang; market township。

译文：岭罗争在东面，争市场。又说岭罗争在衢肆的东面，是为争市场发展起来的集肆。

Translation:

Lingluozheng is in the east, engaged in fights for markets。 It is also said that Lingluozheng lies to the east of Qusi, which is a township as the result of competition。

06-17 羿与凿齿战

Yiyuzaochizhan
（120,12691E; 29,5504N）

羿[1]与凿齿[2]战于寿华之野[3]，羿射杀之[4]。在昆仑墟东。羿持弓矢[5]，凿齿持盾[6]。一曰戈[7] 。

注释：[1]羿：指义部落，今称义乌。
Notes [1] yi, refers to the Yi tribe, known today as Yiwu city, Zhejiang province。
[2] 凿齿：指诸暨部落，今称诸暨。
[2] zao chi (chisel tooth) refers to the Ji tribe, today known as Zhuji。
[3] 寿华之野：指安华乡，读音 so wo ye。
[3] shou hua zhi ye (longevity flower land) refers to the Anhuaxiang, reads as so wo ye 。
[4] 射杀之：远遁而去。
[4] she sha zhi (shoot kill it) left for a faraway place。
[5] 持弓矢：指迁到江肆。
[5] zhi gong shi (holding bow and arrow)
Tr: move to a place called Jiangsi, town by the river。
[6] 持盾：指迁到浦阳镇。
[6] chi dun (holding shield) moved to Puyang township。
[7]戈：指城。

译文：义乌与诸暨战于安华之乡，义乌远遁而去，到了岭罗争的东面。义乌迁到江肆，诸暨迁到浦阳镇。又说诸暨迁到浦阳城。
Translation:
Yiwu and Zhuji fought in the land of Anhua。Yiwu left for a faraway place, to the east of Lingluozheng。 Yiwu moved to Jiangsi, Zhuji moved to Puyang。 It is also said that Zhuji moved to Puyang city。

06-18 三首国
Sanshou Guo
（120,58719E; 29,99621N）

三首国[1]在其东，其为人一身三首[2]，一曰在凿齿东。

注释：[1]三首国：读萨苏国，指富庶之国，今称绍兴。
Notes:[1] san shou guo (three heads nation) reads as Sasu Guo, refers to the rich country in today's Shaoxing, Zhejiang province。
[2] 一身三首：大肆萨苏，今称绍兴大市。一，读耶音。
[2] yi shen san shou (one body three heads)
Tr: the big township Sasu, known as today's Shaoxing big city, yi(one) reads as ye。

译文：绍兴国在东面，建都于大肆绍兴。又说，绍兴国在诸暨的东面。
Translation:
Shaoxing Guo is in the east, with its capital city in Dasishaoxing。 It is also said that Shaoxing Guo is to the east of Zhuji。

06-19 周饶国
Zhourao Guo
（121,14016E; 30,04851N）

周饶国[1]在其东，其为人短小，冠带[2]。一曰焦侥国在三首东。

注释：[1]周饶国：指放蜂国，也称吁咽、焦侥，今称余姚。后传为防风氏国。
Notes:[1] zhou rao guo: refers to Fangfengguo (release hornets nation) also known as Yuyan, Jiaorao, known as today's Yuyao, later the name became Fangfeng Shi Guo, (protect against winds nation) 。
[2] 短小冠带：指秀镇云门。今古名已失传。
[2] duan xiao guan dai (short, small cap belt)
Tr: refers to the Xiuzhenyunmen。Its ancient name is lost。

译文：放蜂国在东面，建都于秀镇云门。又说，放蜂国在绍兴国的东面。
Translation:
Fangfeng Guo is in the east, with its capital in Xiuzhenyunmen。 It is also said that the Fangfeng Guo lies to the east of Shaoxing Guo。

06-20 长臂国
Changbi Guo
（121,5487E；29,87307N）

长臂国[1]在其东，捕鱼水中[2]，两手各操一鱼[3]。一曰在焦侥东，捕鱼海中。

注释：[1]长臂国：读俦沘国，指岔河之国。在浙江宁波城。
Notes:[1] chang bi guo (long arm nation) reads as Shoubi Guo referring to the country on the river fork, known as the Chahe Guo, in today's Ningbo city, Zhejiang province。
[2] 捕鱼水中：捕鱼水中与捕鱼海中，皆指濮夷贵族。
[2] pu yu shui zhong (fishing in the water) both puyushuizhong, and puyuhaizhong (fishing in the sea) refer to the noble lineages of Pu Yi.
[3] 两手各操一鱼：首都俦城之夷。
[3] liang shou ge cao yi yu (two hands each holds a fish)
Tr: capital city's Shoucheng Yi。

译文：岔河国在东面，这里的氏族是濮夷的贵族，是首都岔城之夷。又说，岔河国在照饶国的东面，居民是濮夷的贵族。
Translation:
Chahe Guo is in the east。The tribes here are the Pu noble lineages, the capital Chacheng Yi。 It is also said that Chahe Guo lies to the east of Zhaorao Guo。 Its residents are the noble Pu lineages。

06-21 狄山离朱、视肉
Dishanlizhu，shirou
（121,40004E；30,08199N）

狄山[1]，帝尧葬于阳[2]，帝喾葬于阴[3]。爰有熊、罴、文虎、蜼、豹、离朱、视肉[4]；吁咽、文王[5]皆葬其所。一曰汤山[6] 。一曰爰有熊、罴、文虎、蜼、豹、离朱、【丘鸟】久 [7] 、视肉、虖交 [8] 。其范林方三百里[9]。

注释：[1]狄山：指北山，在宁波北面。
Notes:[1] di shan: refers to the North Mountain, to the north of Ningbo city, Zhejiang province。

[2] 帝尧葬于阳：周饶国的疆域在南面。
[2] di yao zang yu yang (di yao is buried in the sunny side)
Tr: the territory of Zhourao Guo is in the south。
[3] 帝喾葬于阴：考僚的疆域在北面。今称慈溪。
[3] di ku zang yu yin (di ku is buried in the shade side)
Tr: Kao Liao's territory is in the north, called Cixi today。
[4]熊、罴、文虎、蜼、豹、离朱、视肉：指逍林、老塘、洋浦、普惠、四塘、掌起、伏龙等村落。
[4] xiong(bear)； pi(bear)； wenhu (marked tiger)； wei(long-tailed monkey)； bao(leopard)； lizhu (leave red)；shirou(gaze meat) refers to the following villages: Xiaolin, Laotang, Yangpu, Puhui, Sitang, Zhangqi, Fuloong,etc。
[5] 吁咽、文王：指余咽、玉皇山，属焦侥的村落。
[5]yu yan, wen wang refers to Yuyan, Yuhuangshan, villages belonging to the Jiaorao。
[6] 汤山：指田螺山。狄山又称田螺山。
[6] tang shan (hot water mount) refers to the Tianluoshan。 Dishan is known otherwise as Tianluoshan。 Tianluo: freshwater snails。
[7] 【丘鸟】久：指裘村。
[7] qiu jiu: refers to Qiucun (fur village) 。
[8] 虖交：指附城。交，读勾音。
[8]hu gou: refers to Fucheng, jiao/gou, (city)。
[9] 范林方三百里：治府在湖荪京城。俦沘国的京城称为湖荪亳里。今有遗名叫荪湖。
[9] fan lin fang san bai li (model forest area 300 li)
Tr: the capital is Huxiu city。Choubi Guo's capital city is called Huxunboli。A relic name Xunhu has survived。

译文：北山，周饶的疆域在南面，考僚的疆域在北面。还有逍林、老塘、洋浦、普惠、四塘、掌起、伏龙，有余咽、玉皇山等村落的疆域都在那里。又说叫田螺山，有逍林、老塘、洋浦、普惠、四塘、掌起、裘村、伏龙、附城等村落，治府在湖荪京城。
Translation:
Beishan and Zhourao 's area are in the south, Kaoliao's area in the north。Also existing here are the territories of the following villages: Xiaolin, Laotang, Yangpu, Puhui, Sitang, Zhangqi, Fuloong, as well as Yuyan and Yuhuangshan。It is also said that the place is also called Tianluoshan, with the following villages of Xiaoling, Laotang, Yangpu, Puhui, Sitang, Zhangqi, Qiucun, Fuloong and Fucheng。 Its administration center is in Huxun city。

06-22 南祝融
Nanzhurong
（119,99028E；30,39278N）

南祝融[1]，兽身人面[2]，乘两龙[3]。

注释：[1]南祝融：读良渚雍，指良渚川。本条因正文没有"方"字，所以不是南方祝融。
Notes: [1] nan zhu rong (south pray melt)
Tr: reads as Liangzhuyun, refers to Liangzhuchuan。 No 'fang' is used, so it is not explained as Zhurong in the South。
[2] 兽身人面：读收萨惹米，指富饶的居住地。
[2] shou shen ren mian (beast body human face)
Tr: reads as Shousaremi, means very affluent and rich settlements。
[3] 乘两龙：读扯两僚，指凭借着两稻而著名。两稻，指海姆双稻，今称河姆双稻，即河姆籼稻与河姆粳稻。
[3] cheng liang loong (ride two dragons)

Tr: reads Che liang liao, meaning being famous for two kinds of rice, liangdao (two species of rice), known as Haimu rice, or Hemu rice, the Xian rice grown in dry fields, and the Jing rice (Oryza sativa) also known as Asian rice。

译文：良渚地区是富饶的居住地，凭借着两稻而著名。
Translation:
Liangzhu area is a very rich and affluent homestead, with great fame of being the land of two kinds of rice。

第七卷海外西经 (Haiwai Region: the West)

Book 7, Haiwaixijing

07-01 灭蒙鸟
Miemengniao
（102,26748E；27,8832N）

海外自西南陬至西北陬者。
灭蒙鸟[1]在结胸国北，为鸟青，赤尾[2]。

注释：[1]灭蒙鸟：指妈妈国、娘国，今娘演变为凉，即凉山国。在四川凉山州。
Notes： [1] mie meng niao (destroy cover bird)
Tr: refers to Mama Nation, Mother nation, ma/niang is now phonetically shifted into liang (cool), therefore the Liangshan Nation, in today's Liangshan Zhou, Sichuan province。 Liangshan (cool mount) 。
[2] 为鸟青赤尾：为良邛池峪，即建都在邛池峪，今称西昌。
[2] wei niao qing chi yi (as bird, green and red tail)
Tr: reads as: wei liang qiong chi yu, --establish capital at Qiong Chi Yu, today's Xichang county。

译文：从海外西南角记述到西北角。
娘国在宰赫国的北面，建都在邛池峪。
Translation:
The narrative starts from Haiwai 's southwest corner, moves to northwest corner。The Niang Nation is situated to the north of Zaihe Nation, with its capital in Qiongchiyu。

07-02 夏后启
Xiahouqi
（103,2618E；29,23063N）

大运山[1]高三百仞，在灭蒙鸟北。

大乐之野[2]，夏后启于[3]此儛九代[4]，乘两龙[5]，云盖三层[6]，左手操翳，右手操环，佩玉璜[7]。在大运山北。一曰大遗之野[8]。

注释：[1]大运山：指大伊山，即峨眉山。又称峨眉洪所。
Notes;[1] da yun shan (big luck mount)
Tr: refers to the Dayishan, today's Emeishan。It is also called Emei hong suo。

[2] 大乐之野：指峨眉之乡。
[2] da le zhi ye (big fun outskirt)
Tr: refers to Emei land。

[3] 夏后启于：指所洪脚夷，即峨边夷。
[3] xia hou qi yu (summer prince initiate from): refers to Suo hong jiao Yi, also known as Ebian Yi。

[4] 此儛九代：人名，蚩武举第，指维护功勋的人。举第，指铜帽、功勋。
[4]ci wu jiu dai (this dance nine generation)
Tr: a title, chiwu ju di: refers to the heroes who uphold militant achievements。Ju di: means bronze crown, cap, in reference to achievements in military missions。

[5] 乘两龙：在两河口，也称双河口。
[5] cheng liang loong (ride two dragons)
Tr: at the conjunction where two rivers meet, also known as Shuang He Kou (mouth of two rivers) 。

[6] 云盖三层：在清河坪，今称铜河坝。
[6] yun gai san ceng (clouds cover three layers)
Tr: at Qinghe (clear water) Ping (town), today known as Tongheba --Copper River Dam。

[7] 左手操翳，右手操环，佩玉璜：一边从事渔业，一边从事畜牧业和农业。
[7] zuo shou cao yi (left hand hold feather Yi)； you shou cao huan (right hand hold Huan jade)， pei yu huang (wear Huang jade) 。
Tr: is engaged in fishing on one hand， and in animal husbandry, and agriculture on another hand。

[8] 大遗之乡：指大河之乡。实际在峨眉山的南面，北应是指贝，即南面。
[8] da yi zhi xiang (big remain place)
Tr: refers to the land of the big river, in fact it is referring to the south side of the Emeishan。 Bei: north, a phonetic match with bei(shell), which in Pu concept means south。

译文：峨眉山高三百仞，在娘国的北面。 峨眉之乡是峨边夷蚩武举第的支系的所在地，处于两河口，他们在清河坪一边从事渔业，一边从事畜牧业和农业。峨眉之乡在峨眉山南面， 又说在大河之乡。
Translation：
Emeishan is as high as three hundred Ren, it is to the north of the Mama Nation。The land of Emei is inhabited by the branch of Ebian Yi's Chiwujudi。 Occupying the confluence of two rivers, the tribes are engaged, at Qinghe Ping, in fishing on one hand；animal husbandry and agriculture on the other hand。 The land of Emei is situated to the south of the Emeishan and is also said that it is in the land of the Big River。

07-03 三身国
Sanshen Guo
（102,99858E；29,98567N）

三身国[1]在夏后启北，一首而三身[2]。

注释：[1]三身国：读奢堵国，指凤坪国，在四川雅安。奢原意指凤，后来按鸡译为雅。
Notes: [1] san shen guo (three body nation)

Tr: reads as she du guo, refers to Fengping Guo, today's Ya'an in Sichuan province。She/phoenix, also transliterated as chicken, therefore, Ya。

[2] 一首而三身：雅族的凤坪国。

[2] yi shou er san shen (one head three body)

Tr: Ya tribes' Fengping Nation。

译文：凤坪国在峨边的北面，是雅族的凤坪国。

Translation:

Fengping Nation is to the north of Ebian, which is Ya tribes' Fengping Nation。

07-04 一臂国

Yibi Guo

（102,2053E；31,90603N）

一臂国[1]在其北，一臂[2]，一目[3]，一鼻孔[4]。有黄马虎文[5]，一目而一手 [6] 。

注释：[1]一臂国：指大金川国，今四川阿坝州府。

Notes：[1] yi bi guo (one arm nation)

Tr: Dajinchuan (big golden river) guo, known today as the county seat of Aba Zhou in Sichuan province。

[2] 一臂：大金川（包括麻尔曲河）。

[2] yi bi (one arm)

Tr: big jin chuan (big golden river) including Marqu River。

[3] 一目：指梭磨河。

[3] yi mu (one eye) refers to the Suomo River。

[4] 一鼻孔：指杜柯河。孔、洞，濮语读 du。

[4] yi bi kong (one nostril) refers to the duke River, in Pu concept, hole, opening, reads as du。

[5] 黄马虎文：指马尔山、岷山氏族。

[5] huang ma hu wen (yellow horse tiger marking)

Tr: refers to the Marshan tribes and the Minshan tribes。

[6] 一目一手：梭磨河边的大氏族。

[6] yi mu yi shou (one eye one hand)

Tr: refers to the major tribes along the banks of the Suomo River。

译文：大金川国在【凤坪国】的北面，那里有大金川氏族，梭磨河氏族和杜柯河氏族。那里还有马尔山、岷山氏族，是梭磨河边的大氏族。

Translation：

The Dajinchuan Nation is situated to the North of the Fengping Nation， where the Dajinchuan tribe live, also living there are the Suomo River tribes and the Duke River tribes。 There are also the Marshan tribes and Minshan tribes 。They are the major tribes along the banks of the Suomo River。

07-05 奇肱国

Qigong Guo

（99,99276E；31,62303N）

奇肱之国[1]在其北[2]，其人一臂三目[3]，有阴有阳[4]，乘文马[5]。有鸟焉，两头，赤黄色，在其旁[6]。

注释：[1]奇肱国：指孜肱国，即孜门国，汉语称肱孜或甘孜，今四川甘孜县城。

Notes: [1] qi gong guo (strange upper arm nation)
Tr: refers to the Zigong Nation, also known as the Zimen Guo。 In Chinese, it is called Gongzi or Ganzi, known today as the Ganzi county in Sichuan province。

[2]北：实际在大金川国的西南面，因北、贝同音而混淆。

[2] bei(north) in fact it is to the southwest of the Dajinchuan Nation。 bei/shell(south), not to be confused with bei: a chinese concept for north。

[3] 一臂三目：雅江边的高地上。一读雅；三读啥，指边。

[3] yi bi san mu (one arm three eyes)
Tr: refers to the high ground along the Yajiang River。yi (one)is read as Ya, three reads as sha(what), refers to the borderline。

[4] 有阴有阳：分南、北两个聚居区。

[4] you yin you yang (have shade have shine)
Tr: refers to the two settlements, one in the northern part and one in the southern part 。

[5] 乘文马：座落在水岸边。文马，指汶陌，也称溢陌。

[5] cheng wen ma (ride patterned horse)
Tr: is situated along the waterfront。 Wenma: wenmo, also as yimo, wen, yi: both refer to water, river。

[6] 两头，赤黄色，在其旁：利吐东山的沙鲁里支系青濮。两头赤黄，指利吐东山；色在，指沙鲁里支系；其旁，指青濮。利吐，今称白利。

[6] liang tou, (two heads), chi huang se (red, yellow color), zai qi pang (by its side)
Tr: litudongshan 's Shaluli's branch's qingpu (green Pu) 。liang-tou-chi-huang: refers to Litudongshan (litu east mountain), sezai: refers to the Shaluli branch; qipang: refers to the Qingpu, litu: known today as Baili: tu/bai(white)。

译文：甘孜国在大金川国的西南面，集镇建在雅江边的高地上，分南北两个聚居区，座落于水岸边。有一群人，是利吐东山的沙鲁里支系的青濮族。

Translation:
Ganzi Nation is situated to the southwest of the Dajinchuan Nation。 Its township is located on the higher ground by the Yajiang River。Sitting along the riverbanks, one of the settlements is in the northern part, and the other one is on the southern part。A group of people from the Shaluli branch of the Litudongshan are the Qingpu ethnic group。

Ganzi Nation: today's Garzê Tibetan Autonomous Prefecture (Tibetan: དཀར་མཛེས་བོད་རིགས་རང་སྐྱོང་ཁུལ་, THL Kardzé Börik Rangkyongkhül; Chinese: 甘孜藏族自治州; pinyin: Gānzī Zàngzú Zìzhìzhōu) also known as Ganzi。

07-06 形天与帝争神
Xingtianyudizhengshen
（100,3305E；32,30297N）

形天与帝至此争神[1]，帝断其首[2]，葬之常羊之山[3]。乃以乳为目[4]，以脐为口 [5]，操干戚以舞 [6] 。

注释：[1]形天与帝至此争神：色达北端的嘎琼扎赛，今已更名为姑扎村。

Notes:[1] xingtian yu di zhici zheng shen (Xingtian and Di here fight for the Holy title),
Tr: refers to the Gaqiongzhasai, to the North of Seda （Sêrtar，also: gser rda rdzong, Sêrtar County or Serthar County）, today it is renamed as Guzha Village。

[2] 帝断其首：北端的氏族。

[2] di duan qi shou (God broke his head from the neck)
Tr: Northern side tribes。

[3] 葬之常羊之山：座落于长雅山。

[3] zang zhi changyang zhi shan (buried on the Changyang Mountain)

Tr: it is situated on the Changyashan， changya (long elegant) 。

[4] 乃以乳为目：他们以乳为粮。

[4] nai yi ru wei mu (use nipples as eyes)

Tr: they live on dairy products。

[5] 以脐为口：以牛角为杯子。

[5] yi qi wei kou (use navel as mouth)

Tr: use Bull horns as drinking cups。

[6] 操干戚以舞：是长须干玛曲流域的部落。

[6] cao ganqi yi wu (dance with weapons)

Tr: they are the tribes from the Maqu River (Maqu Zong, or rma chu rdzong) region at Changxugan。

译文：色达北端的嘎琼扎赛，是北端的氏族部落，座落于长雅山。他们以乳为粮，以牛角为杯子，是长须干玛曲流域的部落。

Translation:

Gaqiongzhasai on the northern end of Seda is a tribe from the Northern end。They are situated on the Changyashan。 They live on dairy products and use bull horns as drinking cups。 They are tribes from the Maqu River region from the Changxugan。

07-07 女祭女戚

Niu Ji and Niu Qi

（100,23813E；34,47771N。102,07684E；33,99755N）

女祭女戚[1]在其北，居两水间[2]，戚操鱼䱇[3]，祭操俎[4]。

注释：[1]女祭女戚：指玛沁部落和玛曲部落。即今青海的玛沁县城和瑪曲县城。

[1]: nv ji nv qi (female ji， female qi)

Tr: refers to the Maqin tribe and the Maqu tribe, today's Maqin county and Maqu county in Qinghai province。

[2] 居两水间：坐落于黄河的两岸。

[2] ju liang shui jian (situated between two rivers)

Tr: situated on both banks of the Yellow River。

[3] 戚操鱼䱇：玛曲在河的下游。

[3] qi cao yu shan (qi holds Shan fish) Maqu is at the lower reach of the river。

[4] 祭操俎：瑪沁在上游。俎，读举，指上游。

[4] ji cao ju (ji holds chopping board) Maqin is at the upper reach of the river。Ju: raise, upper reach of the river 。

译文：玛沁部落和玛曲部落在其北面，座落于黄河的两岸，玛曲部落座落于黄河（此段）的下游，玛沁部落座落于黄河（此段）的上游。

Translation

Maqin tribe and Maqu tribe are located to the north, along both banks of the Yellow River。 Maqu tribe is situated on the lower reach of the river, Maqin tribe is on the upper reach of the river。

07-08 鸂鸟【詹鸟】鸟

Ciniao Zhanniao

（100,57791E；34,47771N。101,43049E；36,0466N）

鸂鸟[1]【詹鸟】鸟[2]，其色青黄[3]，所经国亡[4]。在女祭北，鸂鸟人面。居山上[5] 。一曰维鸟，青鸟[6]， 黄鸟所集 [7] 。

注释：[1]鶬鸟：指同德。濮语称河为僚，苗语称河为德。
Notes： [1]ci niao (ci bird)
Tr: refers to Tongde, Pu concept for river is Lao, Miao concept for river is De。

[2] 【詹鸟】鸟：指贵德。【詹鸟】，读詹音，与表示"贵"的"傯"谐音。
[2] zhan niao (zong bird),
Tr: refers to Guide, in Pu concept, zhan, a phonetic match to Zong, (gui)。

[3] 其色青黄：贵德水清，同德水黄。
[3] qi se qing huang (its color green and yellow) the water in Guide is clear, the water in Tongde is yellow。

[4] 所经国亡：数纪国的部落，即共工国的部落。
[4] suo jin guo wang (where water flows nations die)
Tr: refers to the Shuji Nation's tribes, also known as Gonggong confederacy 's tribes。

[5] 鶬鸟人面居山上：同德的集镇在山上。
[5]ci niao ren mian ju shan shang (ci bird human face lives on the hill)
Tr: Tongde's townships are located on the hills。

[6] 维鸟、青鸟：指南河，东河。
[6] wei niao, qing niao (wei bird, green bird)
Tr: the southern river, and the eastern river-- Nanhe, Donghe。

[7] 黄鸟所集：黄河边的部落。
[7] huang niao suo ji (yellow birds collect here)
Tr: refers to the tribes along the Yellow River。

译文：同德部落和贵德部落以水得名，贵德的水清，同德的水黄，他们都是共工国的部落。他们在玛沁部落的北面，同德的集镇在山上。又说同德部落和贵德部落叫南河部落与东河部落，是黄河边的部落 。
Translation：
Tongde tribes and Guide tribes derive their names from the river。 Guide has clear water, while Tongde has yellow water。Both belong to the Gonggong Nation。They are located to the north of Maqin tribes。 The townships of Tongde are on the hills。 It is also said that the Tongde tribes and Guide tribes are also known as Nanhe tribes and Donghe tribes。 They are the tribes along the banks of the Yellow River。

07-09 丈夫国
Zhangfu Guo
（100,13793E；37,3282N）

丈夫国[1]在维鸟北，其为人衣冠带剑[2]。

注释：[1]丈夫国：指折山国。刚察山，又称折夷刚德山，简称折山，读为折胡，谐音丈夫。
Notes： [1] zhang fu guo (husband nation)
Tr: refers to Zheshan Nation, also known as Gangchashan, Zheyigangde Mountain, shortened to Zheshan。Zheshan reads as Zhehu, a phonetic match to zhangfu (husband)。

[2] 衣冠带剑：指折夷刚德纪，即折夷刚德部落。今称刚察。有遗名折夷果东。
[2] yi guan dai jian (wear cap and sword)
Tr: refers to Zhe yi gang de ji, the Zhe yi gang de tribe, known today as Gangcha county。A relic place name is Zheyiguodong。

译文：折山国在南河部落的北面，定都在折夷刚德部落所在地。
Translation：

Zheshan Guo is on the northern part of the Nanhe tribe, its capital is where Zheyigangde tribes live。

07-10 女丑之尸
Niuchouzhishi
(100,16218E; 39,15205N)

女丑之尸[1]，生而十日炙杀之[2]。在丈夫北。以其右手鄣其面[3]。十日居上[4]，女丑居山上 [5] 。

注释：[1]女丑之尸：指临泽之肆。泽读策音，与丑谐音。
Notes: [1] nv chou zhi shi (lady ugly's corpse)
Tr: refers to the town over water, Linze town, ze: reads as ce, a close phonetic match to chou(ugly)
[2] 生而十日炙杀之：建于羌惹之外的集肆。十日，读羌惹，今称张掖。杀，指外。
[2] sheng er shi ri jiu sha zhi (born ten days burn to death)
Tr: the townships established outside Qiangre。 Shiri: (ten days) reads as Qiangre, known as today's Zhangye。sha (burn to death) refers to outside, beyond。 Zhangye, formerly Romanized as Changyeh, or Kanchow, is a prefecture-level city in central Gansu province in PRC。
[3] 以其右手鄣其面：是由裕固族管理那个地方。
[3] yi qi you shou zhang qi mian (use its left hand to cover her face)
Tr: refers to the place managed by the Yugu (Urghur) ethnic tribes。
[4] 十日居上：羌惹在北面，
[4] shi ri ju shang (ten suns on top) 。
Tr: Qiangre is to its north。
[5] 女丑居山上：临泽肆在北面的北面。山，在此读啥，指外面。
[5] niu chou ju shan shang (lady Ugly lives on the hill)
Tr: Linze town is further north from the northern part。 shan(hill) reads as sha, refers to outside, beyond。

译文：临泽之肆，是建于张掖之外的集肆。它在折山国的北面。是由裕固族管理那个地方。张掖在北面，临泽在北面的北面。
Translation:
Linze town is a market township established outside Zhangye。 It is to the north of Zheshan Nation。 It is a place managed by the Yugu ethnic group。 Zhangye is in the north, and Linze is further to the north。

07-11 巫咸国
Wuxian Guo
（98,51037E; 39,74462N）

巫咸国[1]在女丑北，右手操青蛇[2]，左手操赤蛇[3]。在登葆山[4]，群巫所上下也 [5] 。

注释：[1]巫咸国：指久部落国，今根据"久"谐音称为酒泉。
Notes: [1] wu xian guo (witch salty nation)
Tr: refers to the Jiu tribes' Nation。Jiu(longlasting) a phonetic match to Jiu(wine), known today as the Jiuquan (wine spring) city。
[2] 右手操青蛇：东边是东肆，今称东洞。
[2] you shou cao qing she (right hand holds green snake)
Tr: on the east side is the Dongsi (east town) today known as Dongdong (east hole) 。
[3] 左手操赤蛇：西边是草肆，今称嘉峪关。
[3] zuo shou cao chi she (left hand holds red snake)

Tr: on the west side is the Caosi (grass town), known today as Jiayuguan city (Jiayu Pass) in Gansu province。

[4] 登葆山：指登葆山隘口，又称葆登道，今称白登道。

[4] deng bao shan (climb bao hill)

Tr: refers to the Dengbaoshan Pass, also known as the Dengbaodao, today's Baidengdao。

[5] 群巫所上下也：关内关外的部落人群都要从这里经过。

[5] qun wu sou shang xia ye (the witches go up and down here)

Tr: tribal peoples within or beyond the Pass must go through here。

译文：酒泉部落国在临泽北面，国的东边是东肆，西边是草肆。其国在葆登山隘口，关里关外的部落人群都要从这里经过。

Translation:

Jiuquan tribal state is located on the north of Linze。On its east side is Dongsi， on its west side is Caosi。 This tribal nation is located at where the Baodengdao Pass is, and all the tribal peoples within or beyond the pass must go through here。

07-12 并封国

Bingfeng Guo

（98,90102E；39,97924N）

并封国[1]在巫咸东，其状如彘[2]，前后皆有首[3]，黑[4]。

注释：[1]并封国：指泚汾国。即东河国。泚汾，今称北大河。

Notes: [1] bing feng guo (parallel close state):

Tr: refers to the Bifen Guo, also known as the Donghe Guo（east river nation）。Bifen: today' s Beidahe, the northern big river。

[2]彘：指农业氏族。

[2] zhi (wild pig) refers to the agriculture tribes。

[3] 前后皆有首：前后皆，指东塔部落，今称金塔；有首，指氏族。

[3] qian hou jie you shou (front back have heads), qian-hou-jie: refers to the Dongta (east tower) tribe, Dongta is known today as Jinta (golden tower), you shou (have heads) meaning tribes。

[4]黑：指赫胥氏，即哈萨克族。

[4] hei(black) refers to the Hexu Shi, also known as the Kazakh tribes。

译文：东河国在酒泉部落的东面，属农业部落国，是东塔部落的氏族，是哈萨克族。

Translation:

Donghe state is located to the east of the Jiuquan tribe。They are the agriculture tribes, belonging to the Dongta tribes, they are the Kazakh people。

07-13 女子国

Niuzi Guo

（97,04527E；40,29179N）

女子国[1]在巫咸北，两女子居[2]，水周之[3]。一曰居一门[4]中。

注释：[1]女子国：指勒枝国，濮语读勒疏国，今称疏勒。

Notes: [1] niu zi guo (females nation)

Tr: refers to Lezhi Nation。 In Pu concept it reads as Leshu Guo, known today as Shule county, the ancient Shule Kingdom。

[2] 两女子居：有两个勒疏部落，一个是玉门，一个是瓜州。

[2] liang niu zi ju (two girls live)

Tr: two Shule tribes, one is Yumen (jade gate) tribe, one is Guazhou (melon zhou) tribe。

[3] 水周之：疏勒河水照顾着他们。

[3] shui zhou zhi (water surrounds them)

Tr: The Shulehe River's water nurtures them 。

[4] 居一门中：玉门部落是宗主部落。

[4] ju yi men zhong （live within one gate)

Tr: The Yumen (jade gate) tribe is the leading one。

译文：疏勒国在酒泉部落国的北面，有两个疏勒部落，一个是玉门，一个是瓜州，疏勒河水照顾着他们。又说，玉门部落是宗主部落。

Translation:

The Shule nation is located to the north of the Juquan tribal nation。 There are two Shule tribes, one is the Yumen tribe, the other is the Guazhou tribe。 The water from the Shulehe River takes care of those tribes。It is said that the Yumen tribe is the leading one。

07-14 轩辕国

Xuanyuan Guo

（93,50291E；42,83603N）

轩辕国[1]在此穷山之际[2]，其不寿者八百岁[3]，在女子国北。人面蛇身[4]，尾交首上 [5] 。

注释：[1]轩辕国：指匈夷国，在新疆哈密地区。

Notes: xuanyuan guo (cartshaft nation)

Tr: refers to the Xiong Yi nation, in today's Hami region in Xinjiang。

[2] 此穷山之际：东博尔羌山的部落。

[2] ci qiong shan zhi ji (this poor hill 's time)

Tr: refers to the tribes from the east Bolqiang Mountains。

[3] 其不寿者八百岁：氏族支系为巴里坤部落氏族。八百，指巴里坤部落。岁，指氏族。

[3] qi bu shou zhe ba bai sui (its short-lived reach 800 years old)

Tr: its branches are the Balikun tribes。 babai (800) refers to the Balikun tribes。 sui(year) means tribes。

[4] 人面蛇身：是塞族居民。

[4] ren mian she shen (human face snake body)

Tr: residents are from the Saka tribes。

[5] 尾交首上：管理着塞上地区。尾交，读珥检，指管理。

[5] wei jiao shou shang (tail touch overhead)

Tr: manage the region of Saishang, weijiao (tail touch) reads as erjian, a close phonetic match, meaning management。

译文：匈夷国支系是东博尔羌山的部落支系，其氏族为巴里坤部落氏族，在疏勒国的北面。他们是塞族居民，管理着塞上地区。

Translation:

The branches of the Xiong Yi nation are the east Bolqiang Mountain tribes。 They belong to the Balikun, to the north of Shule nation。 They are the Saka people, managing the areas of Saishang。

07-15 穷山
Qiongshan
（93,01177E；43,59971N）

穷山[1]在其北，不敢西射[2]，畏轩辕之丘。在轩辕国北，其丘方[3]。四蛇相绕[4] 。

注释：[1]穷山：指博尔羌山。
Notes: [1] qiong shan (poor hill) refers to Bolqiang Mountain。
[2] 不敢西射：博格山的东面。西射（ye），指东面。
[2] bu gan xi she (dare not west shoot)
Tr: the east side of the Bog Mountain。Xi she (west shoot) reads as xi ye, refers to east side。
[3] 其丘方：是博尔羌部落统治区。方，指冯，即统治。
[3] qi qiu fang (its hill square)
Tr: is the area controlled by the Bolqiang tribes, fang(square) means van, von, meaning rule, control。
[4] 四蛇相绕：四个塞族部落治理着这个地方。四蛇，指巴里坤、博尔羌吉、大红柳峡和下涝坝四个支系。
[4]si she xiang rao (four snakes surround)
Tr: four Saka tribes control this area。Si she (four snakes) refers to the tribal branches of Balikun (Barköl), Bo' erqiangji, Dahongliuxia (big red willow gorge), and Xialaoba（lower flooded dam）。

译文：博尔羌山在北面，在博格达山东面，南面是匈夷城。在匈夷国的北面，是博尔羌部落统治区，有四个塞族支系治理着这个地方。
Translation:
Bo'erqiang Mountain is to the north, on the east side of the Bogeda Mountain。 Xiong Yi city is to its south。 To the north of the Xiong Yi nation, is the territory ruled by the Bo'erqiang tribes, which is managed by the four Saka branches 。

07-16 诸夭之野
Zhuwozhiye
（86,86638E；47,70377N）

此诸夭之野[1]，鸾鸟自歌[2]，凤鸟自舞[3]；凤凰卵，民食之[4]；甘露，民饮之[5]，所欲自从也[6]。百兽相与群居[7] 。在四蛇北。其人两手操卵食之 [8] ，两鸟居前导之 [9] 。

注释：[1]诸夭之野：指准葛尔之乡。
Notes： zhu wo zhi ye (all wo 's land)
Tr: refers to the Zhungar region。 (jegün ɣar) Dzungar Khanate, Zunghar Khanate。
[2] 鸾鸟自歌：西部人的城镇。
[2] luan niao zi ge (luan bird self-sings)
Tr: refers to the townships of the western tribes。
[3] 凤鸟自舞：东部人的部落。
[3] feng niao zi wu (phoenix self-dances)
Tr: refers to the tribes of the eastern people。
[4] 凤凰卵，民食之：东部人是原住民。食，指始，即原；民，读米，指住。
[4] feng huang luan (phoenix's eggs), min shi zhi (people eat them)

Tr: the people from the east are the original residents。shi (food, eat) a phonetic match to shi(beginning), which means original, min(people) reads as mi (rice), meaning reside 。

[5] 甘露，民饮之：外来民住在北面。甘，读嘎，指外。露，读鲁，指民。

[5] gan lu (sweet dew), min yin zhi (people drink it)

Tr: outside immigrants live in the northern parts。Gan:/gar/outside, lu:/dew/people。

[6] 所欲自从也：是斋桑夷东迁之乡。

[6] suo yu zi cong ye (desire itself follows)

Tr: is the settlements for the Zaysan Yi's east moving tribes。

[7] 百兽相与群居：在布尔斯王河建立部落。

[7] bai shou xiang yu qun ju (hundred beasts live in groups)

Tr: establish tribal settlements along the Bulswang River。

[8] 其人两手操卵食之：定都于乃施吉木，今称布尔津。

[8] qi ren liang shou cao luan shi zhi (such person two hands hold eggs and eat them)

Tr: chose to establish its capital in Naishijimu, which is known today as Burqin county。

[9] 两鸟居前导之：都城部落是浅堵支系，今称冲乎尔支系。

[9] liang niao ju qian dao zhi (two birds in front lead the rest)

Tr: the tribes that settled at the capital are the Qiandu branch, known today as the Chonghur branch。

译文：在准葛尔之乡，有西部人的城镇，东部人的部落；东部人是原住民；外来民住在北面，北面是斋桑夷东迁之乡，人们在布尔斯王河建立部落，定都在乃施吉木，都城氏族是冲乎尔支系，在四塞族部落的北面。

Translation:

In the land of Zhungar, there are townships of the western people, as well as townships of the eastern people。People from the east are the original residents, outside immigrants live to the north, they are the settlements for migrant tribes from the Zaysan Yi。 People set up settlements along the Burswang River, with capital at Naishijimu。The tribal people who take residence at the capital are the Chonghuer branches, to the north beyond the areas controlled by the four Saka tribes。

07-17 龙鱼陵居

Loongyulingju

（83,76935E；53,35502N）

龙鱼陵居[1]在其北，状如狸[2]。一曰鰕[3] 。即有神圣 [4] 乘此 [5] 以行九野。一曰鳖鱼 [6] 在夭野北，其为鱼，也如鲤 [7] 。

注释：[1]龙鱼陵居：指鄂沘瑙尔部落，在鄂沘的源头。鄂沘，即鄂毕河。华夏称鳄为龙，鄂沘就称为龙溢，称鄂沘瑙尔部落为龙溢瑙纪，谐音龙鱼陵居。今称巴尔瑙尔。

Notes: [1]: loong yu ling ju (dragon fish live over)

Tr: refers to the Ob Nuur tribes, close to the headwater of Ob River。 Obi, another name for Ob River。 In ancient Sino language, reptile is called dragon, Obi, is called Lung/loong (dragon) yi(river), Obi nuur tribes are called Lungyi nuurji, a close phonetic match to Loong yu ling ju, today it is known as Barnaul city in Russia。

[2]狸：指尼塞族。

[2]li(leopard) refers to Nisai tribe。

[3]鰕：指罗刹族，即俄罗斯族。

[3] xia (shrimp) refers to Luosha tribes, also known as the Russ tribe。

[4] 神圣：指氏族人群。

[4] shen sheng (holy highly) refers to tribal peoples。

[5] 乘此：指从这里。
[5] cheng ci (ride this) meaning starts from here。
[6] 鳖鱼：指鄂毕河，简称毕溢，谐音鳖鱼。
[6] bie yu (turtle fish)
Tr: refers to the Ob River, simply biyi, a close phonetic match to Bieyu (turtle fish)
[7] 其为鱼，也为鲤：既为河，也为交通线。
[7] qi wei yu, ye wei li (it is fish, it is carp)
Tr: it is a river, as well as a transportation line。

译文：鄂沘瑙尔部落在准噶尔之乡的北面，氏族是尼塞族。也有说是罗刹族。各部落的氏族人群都从这里行走九乡。又说鄂沘在准葛尔的北面，既为河，也是交通线路。
Translation:
The Obnuur tribes are situated to the north side of Zhungar land, the tribes are the Nisai ethnic group, some say they are the Luosha ethnic group。 People from all the tribes travel to other places from here。 It is also said that Obi is to the north of Zungar。 It is a river, and a line of transportation too。

07-18 白民国
Baimin Guo
（82,89615E；54,98324N）

白民之国[1]在龙鱼北，白身被发[2]。有乘黄[3]，其状如狐 [4]，其背有角[5]，乘之寿二千岁[6]。

注释：[1]白民国：指伯利亚国，在新西伯利亚。民，读米，指地方；利亚，指地方。
Notes: [1] bai min guo (white folks' country)
Tr: refers to the Bolia nation in today's Novosibirlia。 Min: reads as Mi /place, lia/place。
[2] 白身被发：指伯利亚河岸。
[2] bai shen bei fa (white body cover hair)
Tr: the Bolia Riverbanks。
[3] 乘黄：指骆驼。
[3] cheng huang (ride yellow) refers to camels。
[4]狐：指马。濮语读马为胡。
[4] hu(fox) refers to horse, Pu concept for Horse is read as Hu。
[5]角：指驼峰。
[5] jiao(horn) refers to camel hump。
[6] 乘之寿二千岁：乘着它可到达托木斯克。寿二，读施勒，指到达；千岁，读托克，指托木斯克。
[6] cheng zhi shou er qian sui (ride it lives up to 2000 years old)
Tr: shou er: reads as shile, meaning arrive, qiansui (1000 years old) reads as tuoke, refers to Tomsk。

译文：伯利亚国在鄂沘瑙尔国的北面，在伯利亚河岸边。那里有骆驼，形状像马，背上有驼峰，乘着它可以到达托木斯克。
Translation:
Bolia nation is to the north of Obnuur nation by the banks of Bolia River。There are camels, looking like horses but with humps on the back, one can travel to Tomsk by riding the camels。

07-19 肃慎国
Sushen Guo
（86,0134E；56,08482N）

肃慎之国[1]在白民北。有树名曰雄常[2]，先入伐帝 [3]，于此取之 [4] 。

注释：[1]肃慎国：指苏真斯克国。全称"安热罗苏真斯克"。
Notes: [1] su shen guo: refers to Sudzhensk, full name now is Anzhero-Sudzhensk。
[2] 雄常：氏族名，应是指匈奴游牧民。雄，指匈奴；常，指游牧。
[2] xiong chang (male constant) : tribe name for nomads of the Xiongnu。 xiong(male) refers to the Xiongnu, chang(constant) refers to a nomadic way of life。
[3] 先入伐帝：安热罗河北岸。先入，读恩惹，指安热罗河；伐帝，读法狄，指北岸。
[3] xian ru fa di (enter first kill di)
Tr: the north bank of the Anzhero River。 Xian ru (enter first) reads as enre: refers to the Anzhero river; fadi (kill di) reads as fadi, refers to the northern bank。
[4] 于此取之：河边的茨克氏族支系。
[4]yu ci qu zhi (from here get it)
Tr: The Ciq tribal branches by the riverbanks。

译文：苏真斯克国在伯利亚国的北面。那里有个氏族名叫匈奴游牧民，住在安热罗河北岸，是河边的茨克氏族支系。
Translation:
Sudzhensk nation is located to the north of Bolia nation。A Xiongnu nomadic tribe lives there, on the northern bank of the Anzhero River, known as the Ciq tribal branches by the river。

07-20 长股国
Changgu Guo
（73,39624E；61,25406N）

长股之国[1]在雄常北，披发[2]。一曰长脚[3] 。

注释：[1]长股国：指斜尔古国，今称苏尔古特。
Notes: chang gu guo (long leg nation)
Tr: refers to the Xiergu nation, today is known as Surgut。
[2] 披发：指河岸边。
Tr: pi fa (loose hair)
Tr: refers to the riverbanks。
[3] 长脚：指下瓦尔国，全称 "下瓦尔托夫斯克" 。
[3] chang jiao (long feet)
Tr: refers to the Lower Var country, known today as Nizhnevartovsk。

译文：斜尔古国在匈奴游牧民国的北面，在河岸边。又说叫下瓦尔国。
Translation:
Surgut country is located to the north of the Xiongnu nomadic country。 It is on the riverbanks, also known as the Lower Var country。

07-21 西方蓐收
Xifangrushou
（30,33816E；59,95843N）

西方蓐收[1]，左耳有蛇[2]，乘两龙[3]。

注释：[1]西方蓐收：西面是罗刹国，今乌拉尔山以西地区，是古俄罗斯的疆域。
Notes: [1] xi fang ru shou (west part harvest)
Tr: on the west part is the Russ country, in today's west side of the Ural Mountain, which is the area of the ancient Russ。

[2] 左耳有蛇：是著名的国家。左耳，读卓尔，指著名的；蛇，在此指羲，即国家。罗刹实际读洛羲。
[2] zuo er you she (left ear has snake)
Tr: it is a famous country: zuoer (left ear) reads as zhuoer, meaning famous。she(snake) here means xi/nation/state/country。Luosha reads as luoxi, all means Russ。

[3] 乘两龙：有两条河养育着这个国家，一条是伏尔加河，一条是顿河。乘，凭借，依靠。
[3] cheng liang loong (ride two dragons)
Tr: two rivers nurture this country, one is the Volga River, the other is the Don River。
cheng/ride: rely on, supporting。

译文：西面是罗刹国，是著名的国家。有两条河养育着这个国家，一条是伏尔加河，一条是顿河。
Translation:
On the west side (of Ural Mountains) is the Luosha Guo， a famous country。 Two rivers are nurturing this country, one is the Volga River, the other is the Don River。

第八卷海外北经 (Haiwai Region: the North)

Book 8 Haiwaibeijing

08-01 无啓国
Wuqi Guo
（87,61246E；43,79137N）

海外自西北陬至东北陬者[1]。
无啓之国[2]在长股东[3]，为人无啓[4]。

注释：[1]海外自西北陬至东北陬者：从海外西北角记述到东北角。
Notes: [1] haiwai starts from northwest corner to northeast corner。
Tr: the narrative starts from Haiwai's northwest corner to northeast corner。
[2] 无啓国：指乌鲁木克齐国，意为蜘蛛城，简称乌齐国。在新疆乌鲁木齐。
[2] wu qi guo: refers to the Ulumuqi Guo, the Spider city, simplified to Wuqi Guo, in today's Ulumuqi in Xinjiang。
[3] 在长股东：长股国在乌鲁木齐北面的俄罗斯境内，此处的长股应是指乌鲁木齐西面的昌城，今称昌吉。
[3] zai chang gu dong (at long thigh east)
Tr: Changgu Guo is situated to the north of Ulumuqi in the present Russian territory。 It refers to the Chang city to the west of Ulumuqi, it is known today as Changji, Xingjiang。
[4] 为人无啓：定都于乌鲁木克齐。
[4] wei ren wu qi: decides to set up its capital in Ulumuqi。

译文：从海外内西北角记述到东北角。
乌鲁木克齐国在昌吉的东面，定都于乌鲁木克齐。
Translation:
It starts from the Haiwai northwest corner to northeast corner。 Ulumukeqi Guo is to the east of Changji, with its capital in Ulumukeqi, today 's Ulumuqi, Xinjiang。

08-02 钟山烛阴
Zhongshanzhuyin
（89,58648E；44,01425N）

钟山之神[1]，名曰烛阴[2]，视为昼[3]，瞑为夜[4]，吹为冬，呼为夏[5]，不饮，不食，不息[6]，息为风[7]。身长千里[8] 。在无晵东。其为物，人面，蛇身，赤色 [9] ，居钟山下。

注释：[1]钟山之神：指天山的氏族。
Notes:[1] zhong shan zhi shen (bell mount gods)
Tr: refers to the Tianshan (sky mount) tribes。
[2] 烛阴：指草原氏族。
[2] zhu yin (candle shade)
Tr: refers to the steppe tribes, or the grassland tribes。
[3] 视为昼：烛指草。昼是烛的变写，视是蓍的变写。
[3] shi wei zhou (look as daytime) zhou(daytime) is transliterated from zhu(candle) shi(look) is transliterated from Shi (divine grass) 。
[4] 瞑为夜：阴指原。夜是阴的变写；瞑是米，指地，即原。
[4] min wei ye (close eyes as night)
Tr: yin(shade) refers to plain, Ye(night) transliterated from Yin(shade), Min (close eyes) a close phonetic rendering of mi。 Mi a term for locale-- plain, land, region。
[5] 吹为冬，呼为夏：这两句是将吹呼与冬夏肢解了。吹呼，指草原胡，冬夏，指国家。
[5] chui wei dong (blowing is winter) hu wei xia (inhale is summer),
Tr： The sentence is split into two parts, the original sentence should be: chui hu, dongxia。 Chuihu (blow and inhale) refers to the steppe Hu people。dongxia (winter and summer) refers to the term of a country or nation。
[6] 不饮，不食，不息：指大月氏，塞族和匈奴。
[6] bu yin, bu shi, bu xi (no drink, no food, no rest)
Tr: bu: tribe, yin(drink)refers to the Yuezhi, shi(food) refers to the Saka, xi(rest) refers to the Xiongnu, using the technique of phonetic matching to create a narrative。
[7] 息为风：匈奴为王族。
[7] xi wei feng (rest is wind)
Tr: The Xiongnu tribes are the king lineages。
[8] 身长千里：指游牧的东部黎。长，指游牧；千里，读且黎，即东部黎。
[8] shen chang qian li (body long 1000 li)
Tr: the nomadic Dongbu Li (Li people from the east), chang(long): nomadic, qianli (1000 li) reads as Qieli, meaning the eastern Li。 Li a Pu concept for people。
[9] 其为物，人面，蛇身赤色：部落居民是塞族游牧氏族。
[9] qi wei wu, (it as thing), ren mian (human face), she shen chi se (snake body red color)
Tr: the tribal settlers belong to the nomadic Saka tribes。

译文：天山的氏族名叫草原氏族，烛指草，阴指原，是国家的草原胡，他们是大月氏、塞族和匈奴，匈奴为王族。他们是游牧的东部黎，部落居民是塞族游牧氏族，住在天山下。
Translation:
The Tianshan Mountain tribes are known as the steppe tribes。 Zhu means grass, Yin means steppe。 They are the nation's steppe Hu, the Dayuezhi, the Saka, and the Xiongnu。 Xiongnu is the king lineage。 They are the eastern Li of the nomads。 The tribal settlers are the Saka nomadic tribes living by the foot of Tianshan Mountain。

08-03 一目国
Yimu Guo
（94,68793E；43,25092N）

一目国[1]在其东，一目中其面而居[2]，一曰有手足[3]。

注释：[1]一目国：指伊吾国。目，在此读乌音，乌、吾同音。
Notes:[1] yi mu guo (one eye country) refers to the Yiwu Guo。Mu(eye) reads as wu, a phonetic match to u。 In Chinese it means 1. Bird, 2. I, or me。
[2] 一目中其面而居：伊吾山地区的国家。伊吾是裕固族部落的简称。
[2] yi mu zhong qi mian er ju (one eye in face to live)
Tr: a country in Yiwu Mountain areas。Yiwu is the shortened form for Yugu people。
[3] 有手足：裕固族支系。"有手"读"裕属"，是裕固族的简称。
[3] you shou zu (has hands feet)
Tr: the branches of Yugu tribes。 You shou (has hands) reads as yushu, shortened form for Yugu tribes。

译文：伊吾国在东面，是伊吾山地区的国家，又说是裕固族支系的国家。
Translation:
Yiwu Guo lies to the east, it is a country in Yiwu Mountain areas。 It is also said that it is a country of the Yugu branches。

08-04 柔利国
Rouli Guo
（97,28165E；42,95215N）

柔利国[1]在一目国东，为人一手一足[2]，反膝[3]，曲足居上[4]。一云留利[5] 之国，人足反折 [6] 。

注释：[1]柔利国：指大狼国，因山形像一只狼而得名，在甘肃省玉门市大一明镇北端的中蒙边境上，集镇在蒙古国内，今称为大狼山、大甲山，蒙古国开辟为大甲戈壁国家公园。柔指狼，利指大。
Notes: [1] rou li guo (soft interest nation)
Tr: refers to the Dalang (big wolf) country for the form of mountain resembles a wolf。It is around Chinese and Mongolian border 's northern end, where the Dayiming (big one bright) town is situated in Yumen (jade gate) city, Gansu province。The township is in Mongolia。 It is known today as Dalangshan, (big wolf mount), Dajiashan, Dajia Govi, a national park developed by the Mongolia government。 rou(soft) means wolf, li (interest) means big。
[2] 一手一足：指大爪大嘴。
[2] yi shou yi zu (one hand one foot) refers to big claw and big beak。
[3] 反膝：指岩脚。
[3] fan xi (backward knee) refers to the foot of the rock。
[4] 曲足居上：指喉结林边。
[4] qu zhu ju shang (twist feet stay atop) refers to Houjielinbian。
[5] 留利：指大虎。
[5] liu li (keep benefit) means big tiger。
[6] 人足反折：定村落在仓岩。
[6] ren zu fan zhe (human feet reverse broken)
Tr; decide to set up homestead by the Cangyan (silo rock) 。

译文：大狼国在伊吾国的东面，定集镇在大爪大嘴岩脚的喉结林边。又说叫大虎国，定村落在仓岩。

Translation:
Dalang Guo lies to the east of Yiwu Guo。They decide to build townships by the Houjielinbian, at the Dazhuadazui Rock's feet。 It is also said that it is called Dahu Guo, with its settlements decided at the Cangyan。

08-05 共工之臣相柳氏
Gonggong zhichen xiangliushi
（101,0603E；41,95286N）

共工之臣曰相柳氏[1]，九首，以食于九山[2]。相柳之所抵[3]，厥为泽谿 [4] 。禹杀相柳[5]，其血腥[6]，不可以树五谷种[7]。禹厥之，三仞三沮[8]，乃以为众帝之台[9]。在昆仑之北，柔利之东。相柳者[10]，九首人面[11]，蛇身而青[12]。不敢北射[13]，畏共工之台[14]。台在其东[15]。台四方[16]，隅有一蛇，虎色[17]，首冲南方[18]。

注释：[1]共工之臣相柳氏：索额苏吉的沼泽河肆。今称额济纳。
Notes:[1] gonggong zhi chen xiang liu shi (gonggong's aide willow): the Zhaoze River township of Suoesuji, today's Ejin or Ejina。

[2] 九首以食于九山：是索族建立的索部落。山，在此指部落。
[2] jiu shou yi shi yu jiu shan (nine heads to eat food from nine mounds) 。
Tr: The Suo people form a Suo tribe。shan(mount) means tribes。

[3] 相柳之所抵：沼泽河旁边的坝子。
[3] xiang liu zhi suo di (aide willow to go against)
Tr: The Bazi by the swamps, river, and lakes。

[4] 厥为泽谿：皆为湿地。
[4] que wei ze yu (it is deep water valley) all around are wet land。

[5] 禹杀相柳：水进入沼泽河，
[5]yu sha xiang liu (yu kills aide willow)
Tr: the water runs into the Zhaoze River。

[6] 其血腥：成为沼泽。
[6] qi xue xing (its blood smells): become swamps 。

[7] 不可以树五谷种：补苦氏用它来种五谷。补苦氏，是周族的祖先，属东胡族。
[7] bu keyi shu wu gu zhong (can't plant five grains)
Tr: Buku Shi plants five grains at this place。 Buku Shi, the ancestors of Zhou people, belong to the East Hu (Donghu)。

[8] 禹厥之，三仞三沮：水养育了索额苏吉。
[8]yu que zhi, san ren san ju:(yu dig it, three times through, three times block) water nurtures Suoesuji。

[9] 乃以为众帝之台：勒伊维尚德区域。
[9] nai yi wei zhong di zhi tai (thus make it gods' terrace)
Tr: refers to the area of Leyiweishangde。

[10] 相柳者：沼泽河支系。
[10] xiang liu zhe (aide willow): the Zhaozhehe (swamp river) branches。

[11] 九首人面：索族居民。有说是共工氏，有说是乌孙氏。但下一句强调是塞族的东部氏族，就为乌孙氏。
11] jiu shou ren mian (nine heads human face) refers to the Suo people。There is a conflicting narrative about what tribes they belong to, either the Gonggong Shi, or the Wusun Shi。 Since the next sentence lays emphasis on Saka's eastern tribes, then the Suo people are the Wusun Shi。

[12] 蛇身而青：塞族的东部氏族。

[12] she shen er qing (snake body also green)
Tr: the eastern tribes of the Saka people。

[13] 不敢北射：宝格山的北面。即巴彦宝都格的北面。射，读耶，指阴。

[13] bu gan bei she (dare not shoot north)
Tr: the north side of Baoge Mountain, refers to the north of Bayan Baoduge。 she(shoot) reads as ye, meaning Yin (shade)north。

[14] 畏共工之台：为索额苏吉的管理区。

[14] wei gonggong zhi tai (fear the Gonggong terrace)
Tr: meaning the management territory by Suoesuji。

[15] 台在其东：管理着部落。东，读栋，指部落。

[15] tai zai qi dong (terrace its east)
Tr: managing the tribes。 dong (as dong4,) refers to tribes。

[16] 台四方：管理着四方。

[16] tai si fang (terrace four sides)
Tr: managing the four sides。

[17] 隅有一蛇，虎色：边境上有一个氏族，是游牧族。

[17]yu you yi she, hu se (corner has one snake, tiger color)
Tr: One tribe is at the border; it is a nomadic tribe。

[18] 首冲南方：照看着南方，守卫着南方。

[18] shou chong nan fang (head towards south)
Tr: watch out for the south, safeguard the south。

译文：索额苏吉的沼泽河肆，是索族建立的索部落。沼泽河旁边的坝子，皆为湿地。水进入沼泽河，成为沼泽，补苦氏用它来种五谷。水养育了索额苏吉、勒伊维尚德区域。在昆仑的北面，在狼山国的东面。沼泽河支系氏族，是乌孙族居民，是塞族的东部夷。在包格山的北面，为索额苏吉的管理区，管理着部落，管理着四方。边境上有一个氏族，是游牧族，守卫着南方。

Translation:

The Zhaozehe township by Suoesuji is built by the tribes of Suo people。 The Bazi along the Zhaozehe River are wetlands。 Water runs into the Zhaozehe River, creating swamps。 Buku Shi grows five grains on it。The water nurtures Suoesuji and Leyiweishangde region。 To the north of Kunlun, to the east of Langshan (wolf mount) Guo, live the Zhaozehe branches, the Wusun people of the eastern Yi of Saka。 To the north of Baoge Mountain is the territory managed by Suoesuji, which manages the tribes and the four sides of the territories。 On the border there is a tribe, a nomadic one, who keeps watch for the south。

08-06 深目国
Shenmu Guo
（105,70933E；38,83884N）

深目国[1]在其东，为人举一手一目[2]。在共工台东。

注释：[1]深目国：指善目国。目，指管理中心。今称阿拉善盟。在内蒙古自治区西部。

Notes:[1] shen mu guo (deep eye country) refers to the Shanmu （kind eyes）Guo。 Mu(eye) meaning management center。 It refers to the Alxi Banner, in the west part of Inner Mongolia Autonomous region。

[2] 举一手一目：林夷族之目，即林胡族的中心。

[2] ju yi shou yi mu (raise one hand one eye)
Tr: the management centre of the Linyi people, also known as the Lin Hu people。

译文：善目国在东面，定都于林胡族的中心，在索额苏吉的东面。
Translation:
Shanmu Guo is in the east, with its capital city at the centre of the Lin Hu people, it is to the east of Suoesuji。

08-07 无肠国
Wuchang Guo
（106,82038E；39,68389N）

无肠之国[1]在深目东，其为人长而无肠[2]。

注释：[1]无肠国：指乌桑国。因地处黄河的内湾边，故称为桑。在内蒙古乌海市。
Notes: [1] wu chang guo (no guts country)
Tr: refers to Wusang (black berry nation) since it is located to the inner curve of the Yellow River, it is called sang, in Wuhai city, Inner Mongolia。
[2] 长而无肠：黄河的乌桑，今称海勃湾。长，指长河，黄河的别称。
[2] chang er wu chang (long without guts)
Tr: refers to the Wusang, known as Haibo Bay by the Yellow River, Chang (long) means long river, another name for the Yellow River。

译文：乌桑国在善目国的东面，定都于黄河岸边的乌桑。
Translation:
Wusang Country lies to the east side of Shanmu Country, with its capital in Wusang along the banks of the Yellow River。

08-08 聶耳国
Nie'er Guo
（107,4199E；40,75559N）

聶耳之国[1]在无肠国东，使两文虎[2]，为人两手聶其耳[3]。县居海水中[4]，及水所出如奇物 [5] 。两虎在其东 [6] 。

注释：[1]聶耳国：指淖尔国。淖尔指沼泽。这里指巴颜淖尔。
Notes: [1] nie er guo （whisper ear guo）: refers to Nuur Guo, Nuur means swamps, here refers to Bayan Nuur。
[2] 使两文虎：统治着两个水边的胡族部落。
[2] shi liang wen hu (handle two marked tigers)
Tr: controls two Hu tribes who are located along the water。
[3] 两手聶其耳：定都于淖尔。
[3] liang shou nie qi er (two hands whisper ears)
Tr: decide to have their capital city at Nuur。
[4] 县居海水中：黄河部落杭族的农业区域。海水，指杭族；中，指农业区域。
[4] xian ju hai shui zhong (hanging in sea water)
Tr: refers to the agricultural regions of the Yellow River tribes' Hang branch。
Haishui (sea water) refers to the Hang branch, zhong (in, middle) refers to the agricultural regions。
[5] 及水所出如奇物：乌加尔水所出灌溉着谷物。奇物，指穄物。穄，读奇音。
[5] ji shui suo chu ru qi wu (things out water strange stuff)
Tr: Wujiaer River provides water irrigating the grains。Qiwu: refers to grains, ji reads as qi。
[6] 两虎在其东："两虎" 指 "良浮"，今称包头。

[6] liang hu zai qi dong (two tigers in its east)
Tr: liang hu (two tigers) means Liangfu, known today as Baotou city。

译文：淖尔国在乌桑国的东面，统治着两个水边的胡族部落，定都于巴彦淖尔，是黄河部落杭族的农业区域。乌加尔水所出灌溉着谷物。良浮国在它的东面。
Translation:
The Nuur Guo is located to the east of Wusang Guo。 It controls two Hu tribes by the water, with capital in Bayan Nuur, an agricultural region of the Hang branch of the Yellow River tribes。 Wujiaer River provides water to irrigate the grains。 The Liangfu Guo is to its east。

08-09 夸父与日逐走
Kuafuyurizuozou
（112,57711E；40,8937N）

夸父与日逐走[1]，入日[2]，渴欲得饮[3]，饮于河渭[4]，河渭不足[5]，北饮大泽[6]。未至，道渴而死[7]。弃其杖[8] 。化为邓林 [9] 。

注释：[1]夸父与日逐走：北胡的集镇卓资。
Notes:[1] kuafu yu ri zhuo zou (kuafu sun compete walking)
Tr: the township named Zhuozi (**Chotze)**, set up by the Beihu (northern Hu people) 。
[2] 入日：是一个管理的集镇。
[2]ru ri (into sun) is a township of administration。
[3] 渴欲得饮：位于岱水的北面。渴，指位。欲得，指溢岱。
[3]ke yu de yin (thirst wish get drink)
Tr: located to the north of Daishui River。ke(thirst) meaning located, yude (wish get) a phonetic rendering of Yidai, Dai River。yi: water, river in Pu concept。
[4] 饮于河渭：在阴山南。于河，读阴洪，指阴山。
[4] yin yu he wei (drink from river wei)
Tr: located to the south of Yinshan Mountain, yuhe: reads as yinhong, a phonetic rendering of Yishan Mountain。 Hong(flood): means mountain。
[5] 河渭不足：南面的氏族。不足，读补则，即氏族支系。
[5] he wei bu zu (river wei not enough)
Tr: the tribes to the south, bu zu (not enough) refers to Buze, meaning tribal branches。
[6] 北饮大泽：巴颜鞑支系。
[6] bei yin da ze (north drink deep water)
Tr: Bayan Da branch。
[7]未至，道渴而死：南方疆域的托克氏。
[7] wei zhi (not reaching), dao ke er si (road thirst die)
Tr: The Tuoke Shi from the southern regions。
[8] 弃其杖：迁到东部疆域。
[8] qi qi zhang (throw away its walking stick)
Tr: move to the eastern regions。
[9] 化为邓林：开辟为镇府。邓林，指镇府。也称政府。
[9] hua wei deng lin (become deng woods)
Tr: developed into a township centre。Denglin: means township hall, known as government。

译文：北胡的集镇卓资，是一个管理的集镇，位于岱水的北面，阴山的南面。南面的氏族是巴颜鞑支系在南部疆域的托克氏，他们迁到东部疆域，将卓资开辟为政府。
Translation:
Bei Hu's township Zhuozi is an administration centre。 It is located to the north of Daishui River, south of Yinshan。 To its south lives the Tuoke Shi from the south region, a Bayan Da branch。 They moved to the eastern part and developed Zhuozi township as their government seat。

08-10 博父国
Bofu Guo
（111,19174E；40,27707N）

博父国[1]在聶耳东，其为人大[2]，右手操青蛇[3]，左手操黄蛇[4]。邓林在其东[5]，二树木 [6] 。一曰博父 [7] 。

注释：[1]博父国：指巴颜胡国。
Notes: [1]bo fu guo (profound father nation) refers to the Bayan Hu country。
[2]大：指拐城，今内蒙古托克托县城。
[2] da(big) refers to Guaicheng, today's Tuoketuo county seat in Inner Mongolia。
[3] 右手操青蛇：东边统治着东胡氏族。
[3] you shou cao qing she (right hand holds a green snake)
Tr: it controls the Dong Hu tribe in the east。
[4] 左手操黄蛇：西边统治着乌孙氏族。
[4] zuo shou cao huang she (left hand holds a yellow snake)
Tr: It controls the Wusun tribe in the west。
[5] 邓林：指卓资政府。
[5] deng lin (deng woods) refers to the Zhuozi government。
[6] 二树木：第二次建的政治中心。
[6]er shu mu (second tree wood)
Tr: a political centre set up for the second time。
[7] 一曰博父：又说叫北胡国。
[7] yi yue bo fu (one speaks profound father)
Tr: it is said that it is called Beihu Guo (north Hu nation) 。

译文：巴颜胡国在聶耳国的东面，建集镇在拐城，东边统治着东胡氏族，西边统治着乌孙氏族。现在的政府在东面，是第二次建的政治中心。又说叫北胡国。
Translation:
The Bayan Hu nation is to the east of Nie'er Guo, with its township at Guaicheng。It controls the Dong Hu tribes in the east and controls the Wusun tribes in the west。Its present government is in the east, a political center set up for the second time。 It is also said to be called Bei Hu Guo。

08-11 禹所积石山
Yusuojishishan
（109,746E；39,57561N）

禹所积石之山[1]在其东，河水所入[2]。

注释：[1]禹所积石山：指伊索金霍洛地区，今称伊金霍洛旗。在内蒙古鄂尔多斯市。实际在北胡国的南面。

Notes:[1]yu suo ji shi shan (yu pile up rock mount)
Tr: refers to the Yisuojinholuo region, known today as the Ejin Horo Banner, also known as Ejin Horo Qi or Yijinhuoluo County, is a banner in Ordos City in southwestern Inner Mongolia, China。108°58′-110°25′E，38°56′-39°49′N。 It actually lies to the south of Bei Hu Guo。

[2] 河水所入：指牧羊氏族居住的地方。
[2] he shui suo ru (river water rush in)
Tr: the sheep herders tribe's settlements。

译文：伊金霍洛山在北胡国的南面，是牧羊氏族居住的地区。
Translation:
Yijinhuoluoshan is to the south of Bei Hu Guo, a land of sheep herders' settlements。

08-12 拘缨国
Juying Guo
（111,2356E；39,86548N）

拘缨之国[1]在其东，一手把缨[2]。一曰利缨之国[3] 。

注释：[1]拘缨国：读诸夭国，指低地国，今内蒙古准格尔旗。
Notes:[1] ju ying guo (holds ribbons country)
Tr: reads as Zhuwo Guo, meaning lowland country, refers to today's Zhunger Banner, Inner Mongolia。

[2] 一手把缨：氏族为巴颜氏。
[2] yi shou ba yin (one hand holds ribbons)
Tr: tribes belong to the Bayan Shi。

[3] 利缨：指低山。
[3]li ying (benefit ribbons) refers to the Dishan Guo (low hill country) 。

译文：低地国在伊金霍洛山的东面，氏族为巴颜氏。又说叫低山之国。
Translation:
Didi Guo is to the east of Yijinhuoluoshan。Its tribes belong to the Bayan Shi。It is said that Didi Guo is also called Dishan Guo。

08-13 寻木
Xunmu
（111,49878E；39,44263N）

寻木长千里[1]，在拘缨南，生河上西北[2]。

注释：[1]寻木长千里：寻木指偏关。千里，读芊黎，意为偏关，今山西偏关县城。
Notes:[1] xun mu chang qian li (search wood long 1000 li)
Tr: xun mu means Pianguan (side gate), qianli reads qianli meaning side gate。It is today's Pianguan county in Shanxi province。

[2] 生河上西北：建在黄河边的东山。西，读须，指东；北，读博，指山。
[2] sheng he shang xi bei (live river's northwest)
Tr: stands on the Dongshan (east mount) by the Yellow River。 Xi: reads as xu, meaning east, bei reads as bo, meaning mountain。

译文：寻木指偏关，在准格尔南面，建在黄河边的东山上。
Translation:
Xunmu means Pianguan, it lies to the south of Dzungar, set up on Dongshan by the Yellow River。

08-14 跂踵国
Zhizhong Guo
（113,3022E；40,09356N）

跂踵国[1]在拘缨东，其为人大[2]，两足亦大[3]。一曰大踵[4]。

注释：[1]跂踵国(raised heels nation)：指平关国。濮语的跂、扯、堵都指“平”，跂、扯同时指“代”。
Notes:[1] zhi zhong guo: refers to Pingguan Guo。In Pu concepts: zhi, che, du all share the meaning of flat, zhi, che also mean Dai（represent）。
[2] 其为人大：建集镇于平关。大，读音 dai，指代，指平。
[2] qi wei ren da (as person is big)
Tr: establish township at Pingguan。Da: reads as dai, meaning dai /ping （flat）。
[3] 两足亦大：都城也在平关，后称平城，今山西大同。
[3] liang zu yi da (two feet also big)
Tr: its capital city is at Pingguan, later known as Pingcheng city, today it is called Datong city, Shanxi province。
[4] 大踵：指代关，也就是平关。
[4] da zhong (big ankle)
Tr: refers to Daiguan, also known as Pingguan, guan (pass gate, checkpoint)

译文：平关国在准格尔东面，建集镇于平关，都城也在平关。又说叫代关。
Translation:
Pingguan Guo lies to the east of Dzungar, with its township at Pingguan。 Its capital city is also at Pingguan, which is also called Daiguan。

08-15 欧丝之野
Ousizhiye
（114,63059E；4025761N）

欧丝之野[1]在大踵东，一女子[2]跪据[3]树欧丝[4]。

注释：[1]欧丝之野：指化稍之乡。今河北省阳原县化稍营镇。
Notes ;[1] ou si zhi ye （ou silk countryside)
Tr: refers to the area of Huashao, in today's Huashaoying Township, Yangyuan county, Hebei province。
[2] 一女子：耶律支系。
[2] yi nv zi (one female) refers to the Yelv branch。
[3] 跪据：北方部落。
[3] gui ju (kneel down) refers to the northern tribes。
[4] 树欧丝：建立化稍集镇。在此仍称化稍营。
[4] shu ou si (tree ou silk): set up the Huashao township, here the name Huashaoying (ying; camp) is kept。

译文：化稍之乡在平关国的东面，是耶律支系的北方部落建立的化稍营。
Translation:
Huashao area is to the east of Pingguan Guo, Huashaoying is set up by Yelv branch of the Northern tribes。

08-16 三桑无枝
Sansangwuzhi
（116,4045E；39,90733N）

三桑无枝[1]，在欧丝东，其木长百仞[2]，无枝[3]。

注释：[1]三桑无枝：富饶的昌部落。
Notes: [1] san sang wu zhi (three mulberry no branch)
Tr: the rich and affluent Chang tribe。
[2] 其木长百仞：这个检目是昌部落的集镇。百，读巴音，指部落；仞，读惹音，指集镇。
[2] qi mu chang bai ren (its trunk long 100 ren)
Tr: this Jianmu is the township of Chang tribes。bai(hundred) reads as ba, meaning tribes。 Ren: reads as re, meaning township。
[3] 无枝：指昌部落，北平的远古称谓，今北京城。无，指部落；枝，指发展、昌盛。
[3] wu zhi (no branch)
Tr: refers to the Chang tribes, an ancient name for Beiping, today known as Beijing。 Wu: means tribe, zhi: development, prosper。

译文：富饶的昌部落，在化稍营的东面，这个检目是昌部落的集镇，称为无枝。
Translation:
The rich and affluent Chang tribes lie to the east of Huashaoying。 This Jianmu is the township of the Chang tribe, named Wuzhi。

08-17 平丘
Pingqiu
（118,17443E；40,7693N）

平丘[1]在三桑东。爰有遗玉[2]、青鸟[3]、视肉[4]、杨柳[5]、甘柤[6]、甘华[7]，百果所生[8]。有两山夹上谷[9]，二大丘居中[10]，名曰平丘。

注释：[1]平丘：指板城，分为上板城和下板城两部分，代表滦河地区，今称承德地区。
Note:[1] ping qiu (flat mound) refers to Bancheng, including the Shangban, and Xiaban, (upper bancheng, lower bancheng), representing the Luan River area, today called Chengde district。
[2] 遗玉：指水泉，今称水泉镇。
[2] yi yu (lost jade) refers to Shuiquan (water spring) known today as the Shuiquan township。
[3] 青鸟：东河，今称东营子。
[3] qing niao (green bird) refers to Donghe (east river) known today as the Dongyingzi (east camp) 。
[4] 视肉：指龙须门，今称龙须门镇。
[4] shi rou (gaze meat) refer to Longxumen (dragon whisker gate), known today as Longxumen Township。
[5] 杨柳：指大柳河部落，今称大营子镇。
[5] yang liu (poplar and willow) refers to the Daliuhe (big willow river) tribes, known today as the township of Dayingzi (big camp) 。
[6] 甘柤：指甲山，今称甲山镇。
[6] gan ju (sweet wood): refers to Jiashan, known today as the Jiashan township。
[7] 甘华：指化皮部落，今称化皮溜子镇。
[7] gan hua (sweet flower): refers to the Huapi tribes, known today as the township of Huapiliuzi。

[8] 百果所生：建有很多部落国。
[8] bai guo suo sheng (hundred fruits thus grow)
Tr: many tribal nations came into being。

[9] 有两山夹上谷：是滦河流域的国家。两山，读滦奢，指滦河；夹上，读颉苏，指经过，在此作流域解。
[9] you liang shan jia shang gu (two hills pinch up vale)
Tr: is the country in Luanhe River region。 Liangshan (two mount) reads as luanshe, meaning Luanhe River。 Jiashan: reads as jisu, meaning passing through, here refers to river catchment。

[10] 二大丘居中：指上板城和下板城居中间。
[10]er da qiu ju zhong (two big mounds in middle)
Tr: The Shangban city and Xiaban city are in the middle。

译文：板城在昌部落的东面。那里有水泉、青河、龙须门、大柳河、甲山、化皮等，是多个部落建立的国家，是滦河流域的国家，有两大城镇居中间，称为板城。
Translation:
Bancheng city lies to the east of the Chang tribes。 It is a nation of townships developed by many tribes, such as the townships of Shuiquan, Qinghe, Longxumen, Daliuhe, Jiashan and Huapi。 It is a nation of the Luanhe River region, with two big towns in the middle, known as Bancheng。

08-18 范林
Fanlin
（118,96994E；42,27223N）

范林[1]，方三百里[2]，在三桑东，洲环其下[3]。

注释：[1]范林：读法能，指红岩，即赤峰，这里指赤峰国，在内蒙古赤峰市，是红山文化的中心，在北平的东北面。
Notes: [1] fan lin: reads as fa neng, refers to red rock--Chifeng (red cliff), the Chifeng Guo, in today's Chifeng city, Inner Mongolia, the centre of Hongshan Culture, in the northeast side of Beiping (Beijing)。

[2] 方三百里：京都在宝丰山下。方三，指宝丰山，百里读亳里，指京都
[2] fang san bei li (area 300 li)
Tr: capital is at the foot of Baofengshan。Fang san refers to Baofengshan。 baili (hundred li) reads as boli, refers to Poli, the capital city。

[3] 洲环其下：意为照恒其须，指称王东方。
[3] zhou huan qi xia (continent surround under it) reads as Zhaohengqixu: meaning lord over the east, is the king of the east。

译文：赤峰国，京都在宝丰山下，在北平的东北面，称王东方。
Translation:
Chifeng Guo has its capital city at the foot of Baofengshan。 It is to the northeast of Beiping, a kingdom lording over east。

08-19 务隅山
Wuyushan
（121,60206E；41,59782N）

务隅之山[1]，帝颛顼葬于阳[2]，九嫔葬于阴[3]，一曰有熊、罴、文虎、离朱、【丘鸟】久、视肉[4]。

注释：[1]务隅山：指濮夷山，后音变为巫医山（南方的武夷山也是如此）。在辽宁省锦州市北面。南至锦州市，北至阜新市。今称医巫闾山。
Notes:[1] wu yu shan: refers to Pu Yi Mountain, later phonetically rendered into Wuyishan (as in the case of Wuyishan in the south) 。 It is in the north of Jinzhou city, Liaoning province。Its south end reaches Jinzhou city, its north end reaches Fuxin city。Today it is known as Yiwulvshan。

[2] 帝颛顼葬于阳：北照羲的疆域在山的南面。
[2] di zhuanxu zang yu yang (God zhuanxu buried in the sunny side)
Tr: The Beizhaoxi has its territory in the south of the mountain。

[3] 九嫔葬于阴：九濮的疆域在山的北面。濮，可读 pu 音，也可读 fu 音，今称阜新。
[3] jiu pin zang yu yin (nine ladies buried in the shady side)
Tr: the Nine Pu has their territory in the north side of the mountain。Pu also reads as fu, known today as Fuxin city, Liaoning province。

[4]熊、罴、文虎、离朱、【丘鸟】久、视肉：指九道岭、清河门、卧凤山、凌渚，东梁和龙湾等村落。
[4] xiong(bear), pi(bear), wenhu (marked tiger), lizhu (leave red), qiu jiu (qiubird long), shirou (gaze meat)
Tr: refers to the following villages as Jiudaoling, Qinghemen, Wofengshan, Lingzhu, Dongliang and Loongwan。

译文：巫医山地区，北照羲的疆域在南面，九濮的疆域在北面。又说，有九道岭、清河门、卧凤山、凌渚、东梁、和龙湾等村落氏族在那里居住。
Translation:
In the Wuyishan region, the territory of Beizhaoxi is to the south, and Jiupu's territory is in the north。 It is also said that tribal villagers live in the following places: Jiudaoling, Qinghemen, Wofengshan, Lingzhu, Dongliang, and Loongwan。

08-20 北海诸兽
beihaizhushou
（122,19E~124,33E；38,76N~43,19N）

北海内有诸兽[1]，其状如马[2]，名曰騊駼[3]。有兽焉，其名曰駮[4]，状如白马，锯牙[5]，食虎豹[6]。有素兽焉[7]，状如马，名曰蛩蛩 [8] 。有青兽 [9]焉，状如虎 [9]，名曰罗罗 [11]。

注释：[1]北海内有诸兽：北海内有诸氏族。北海内指钜燕地区。
Notes:[1] bei hai nei you zhu shou (North Sea within many beasts)
Tr: many countries bearing different family names in the Beihainei region, which is also known as the Juyan region。

[2]马：指东胡族。
[2]ma(horse) refers to the Donghu, east Hu tribes。

[3] 騊駼：指吐谷氏，是东胡的支系。
[3] tao yu: refers to the Tuyu Shi, a branch of the Dong Hu tribes。

[4]駮：指巴颜氏。
[4] jiao: refers to Bayan Shi。

[5] 白马，锯牙：巴颜蒙的钜燕氏族。
[5] bai ma, ju ya (white horse saw teeth)
Tr: refers to the Juyan Shi of the Bayan Meng tribes。

[6] 食虎豹：从事游牧和农业两种劳动。
[6] shi hu bao (eat tiger leopard)
Tr: engaged in two kinds of labor, the nomadic herding and the agriculture。

[7] 素兽：指狩猎氏族。

[7]su shou (plain beast) refers to the hunter tribes。

[8] 蛩蛩：指移民支系的氏族，读羌羌更恰当。

[8] zhezhe: refers to the tribes of immigrants, Qiangqian is a better transliteration。

[9] 青兽：指犬戎族。

[9] qing shou (green beasts) refers to the Dogrong tribes。

[10]虎：指胡族。

[10]hu (tiger) refers to the Hu people。

[11] 罗罗：一般指黑虎支系，这里指来自西部的氏族。

[11] luoluo: generally, the term refers to the Heihu (black tiger) branch, here it refers to the tribes coming from the west。

译文：北海外有氏族，是东胡族，名叫吐谷。有一个氏族，名叫巴颜氏，是巴颜蒙的钜燕氏族，从事游牧业和农业两种劳动。有一个狩猎氏族，服饰像胡族，名叫羌羌氏。有一个犬戎族，是游牧氏族，名叫罗罗。

Translation:

In the so called Haiwai North region, there are the Dong Hu tribes bearing the family name of Tuyu。 A tribe named Bayan, is the Juyan Shi branch, engaged in herding and agriculture。 Another hunting tribe is dressed as Hu, with a name Qiangqiang Shi。 There is also the Dogrong, a nomadic tribe called Luoluo。

08-21 北方禺彊

Beifangyuqiang

（121,3E~126,3E；43,8N~47,8N）

北方禺彊[1]，人面鸟身[2]，珥两青蛇，践两青蛇[3]。

注释：[1]北方禺彊：钜燕北面的松嫩平原是扶余疆域。禺彊，指扶余疆域。

Notes:[1] bei fang yu qiang: refers to the Songnon Plain to the north of Juyan, a territory of Fuyu, which is known as Yuqiang。

[2] 人面鸟身：定居的僚族。

[2] ren mian niao shen (human face bird body)

Tr: the Liao people who are settled down。

[3] 珥两青蛇，践两青蛇：这是一种分章拆句表达，实际指珥践四夷，即管理着四周之夷。

[3]er liang qing she, jian liang qing she (earlop wearing two green snakes, stepping on two green snakes), This should be combined into: erjian si yi, (manage four snakes) meaning managing the Yi people all around in that region。

译文：再往北是扶余的疆域，定居的僚族管理着四周之夷。

Translation:

Further north is the territory of Fuyu, where the Liao settlers' tribes manage the various Yi peoples around the nation。

第九卷海外东经 (Haiwai Region: the East)

Book 9 Haiwaidongjing

09-01瑳丘
Chaqiu
（120,58506E；31,37549N）

海外自东南陬至东北陬者。

瑳丘[1]，爰有遗玉[2]、青马[3]、视肉[4]、杨柳[5]、甘柤[6]、甘华[7]。甘果所生[8]，在东海。两山夹丘[9]，上有树木 [10] 。一曰嗟丘。一曰百果所在 [11]，在尧葬 [12]东。

注释：[1]瑳丘：指丝街，在姑苏城北门外，当时还没有姑苏城。
Notes: [1] cha qiu; refers to the Sijie (silk street), the street is located to the north of the city gate of Gusu Cheng(township), at that time then the Gusu city was not built yet。

[2] 遗玉：指姑水，今称十字洋河，这里指姑水氏族。
[2] yi yu(left-behind jade): refers to the Gushui or Gu River， known today as the Shiziyanghe River (cross big water river)。 Here Yiyu is a term for the Gushui tribe。

[3] 青马：指青苔氏族，今称青台氏族。
[3] qing ma (green horse) refers to the Qingtai (green moss) tribe, known today as Qingtai(green terrace)tribe。

[4] 视肉：读始柔，指元和塘氏族。
[4] shi rou (gaze meat) reads as shi rou (begin soft) refers to the Yuanhetang tribe。

[5] 杨柳：读雅柳，指虎丘。
[5] yang liu (poplar willow) reads as Yaliu (elegant willow) refers to the place Huqiu (tiger mound) 。

[6] 甘柤：指后村。甘，读 ga 音，指后。
[6] gan ju: refers to Houcun (back village) gan: reads as ga, meaning in the back。

[7] 甘华：指后湖。

[7] gan hua: refers to Houhu (back lake) 。

[8] 甘果所生：夏后氏建立的国家。

[8] gan guo suo sheng (sweet fruits thus grow)
Tr: refer to the countries built by Xiahou Shi。

[9] 两山夹丘：久街为都城。两山，指都城；夹丘，即槎丘。

[9] liang shan jia qiu (two hills pinch mound)
Tr: Jiujie is the capital。Liangshan (two hills) means the capital city。 Jiaqiu; is Chaqiu， (qia/chia/jia: all possible phonetic renderings) 。

[10] 上有树木：那里有纺织检目。树木，也读苏目，指管理纺织的机构。

[10] shang you shu mu (upon it has trees)
Tr: there is the managing office--Jianmu for textile productions。 Shumu(trees) also reads as sumu, a term for the organizations which manage the textile industry。

[11] 百果所在：指黄桥纺仓。

[11] bai guo suo zai (hundred fruits store here)
Tr: refers to the storages or offices that handle textile products at Huangqiao (yellow bridge) 。

[12] 尧葬：指大阳山。山可读照，谐音葬。

[12] yao zang (Yao burial) refers to the Dayangshan (big sun mount) 。shan also reads as zhao, a phonetic match for zang(burial)。

译文：从海内的东南角记述到东北角。

丝街，所属氏族有姑水氏族、青苔氏族、元和塘氏族、后村氏族、后湖氏族，是夏后氏建立的国家，在东海地区，以丝街为都城，那里有纺织管理中心。也有说叫丝城，也有说叫黄桥纺仓，在大阳山的东面。

Translation:
This chapter starts from the southeast corner of Hainei to the northeast corner of Hainei。 Sijie is a state built by Xiahou Shi。 It has the following tribes: the Gushui tribe, the Qingtai tribe, the Houcun tribe, and the Houhu tribe。The state is in the region called Donghai (east sea), with Sijie as its capital city。 There is a management centre for the textile industry。It is also said the capital city is called Sicheng (silk city), or alternatively called Huangqiao Fangcang (weaving storage) 。 It is located to the east of Dayangshan。

09-02 大人国
Daren Guo
（119,91232E；32,45475N）

大人国[1]在其北，为人大[2]，坐而削船[3]。一曰在【长差】丘北。

注释：[1]大人国：指泰惹国，今称泰州，在江苏省泰州市及北部地区。

Notes:[1] da ren guo (big man country) refers to Taire Guo, known today as Taizhou, in the present Taizhou city and the northern areas in Jiangsu province。

[2] 为人大：定都于泰惹。

[2] wei ren da (as person big)
Tr: designates Taire as their capital city。

[3] 坐而削船：后又转到宿迁。削船，指宿迁市。

[3] zuo er xiao chuan (sit to chop boat)
Tr: later moved to Suqian, xiaochuan (chop boat) refers to Suqian city in today’s Jiangsu province。

译文：泰惹国在北面，定都于泰惹，后又转到宿迁。又说，泰惹国在丝街的北面。

Translation:

Taire Guo is in the northern region; its designated capital is in Taire。 Taire Guo later moved to Suqian。 It is also said that Taire Guo is located to the north of Sijie (silk street) 。

09-03 奢比尸
Shebishi
（119,2412E；34,28897N）

奢比之尸[1]在其北，兽身，人面，大耳[2]，珥两青蛇[3]。一曰肝榆之尸[4] 在大人北。

注释：[1]奢比尸：指奢沘肆，即黄河肆，在废黄河岸边的灌云。
Notes:[1] she bi shi: refers to Shebisi， meaning Huanghesi (yellow river town) it is Guanyun by the deserted Yellow River banks。
[2] 兽身，人面，大耳：氏族为定居的泰惹国氏族。
[2] shou shen, ren mian, da er (beast body, human face, big ear)
Tr: its tribes are the settled people of the Taire Guo。
[3] 珥两青蛇：管理着两个街肆。
[3]er liang qing she (ear two green snakes)
Tr: managing two street townships。
[4] 肝榆尸：奢沘肆又称灌云肆，谐音肝榆尸。
[4] gan yu shi (liver elm corpse)
Tr: refers to the Shebisi, also known as Guanyun si, a phonetic match to ganyushi。

译文：黄河肆在北面，氏族是定居的泰惹国氏族，管理着两个街肆。又说灌云肆在泰惹的北面。
Translation:
Huanghe Si is in the north, the settled people are the tribes of the Taire Guo。 They manage two street market towns。 It is also said that Guanyun Si is located to the north of Taire。

09-04 君子国
Junzi Guo
（117,67749E；36,22736N）

君子国[1]在其北，衣冠带剑[2]，食兽[3]，使二大虎在旁[4]，其人好让不争[5]。有薰华草[6]，朝生夕死[7]。一曰在肝榆之尸北。

注释：[1]君子国：指契那国。君子读纪枝、具枝、与契那同意。图腾为“金乌负日过山图”。
Notes:[1] jun zi guo (gentlemen's country) refers to the China Guo。
Junzi reads as jizhi, juzhi, with the same meaning as China。Its totem is the Picto-script of 【Jin wu fu ri guo shan tu】: golden bird carrying sun on its back, flying over the mountains。
[2] 衣冠带剑：指沂蒙岱纪，即沂蒙支系部落国。岱，在濮语中指树、栋、支系。
[2] yi guan dai jian (dress cap with sword)
Tr: refers to the Yimengdaiji, the tribal nation of Yimeng people。 Dai, a Pu speech term, meaning tree, trunk, branches。
[3] 食兽：古老的氏族部落。
[3] shi shou (eat beast) meaning ancient tribes。
[4] 使二大虎在旁：建在莱达芜江畔。莱达芜江，又称牧汶江，今称牟汶河。莱达芜，今称莱芜。
[4] shi er da hu zai pang (command two big tigers by the side)

Tr: it is built by the riverbank of Laidawujiang。 Laidawujiang is known as Muwenjiang, or Mowenhe as the river's name today, Laidawu: today's Laiwu city, Shandong province。

[5] 其人好让不争：这个集镇的统治氏族是苗族。好让，读冯儒，指统治；不争，读补纠，指苗族。

[5] qi ren hao rang bu zheng (its people accommodating, not confronting)

Tr: the ruling tribe of this town is the Miao people。 haorang(accommodating) reads as fengru, meaning rule over, buzheng (not confronting) reads as bujiu, a term for the Miao people。

[6] 有薰华草：沂煦山移民。今称沂蒙山移民。临煦南面的沂蒙山，古称沂煦山。

[6] you xun hua cao (has perfumed flower grass)

Tr: the immigrants from Yixushan, today they are called the immigrants from Yimengshan。Yimengshan lies to the south of Linxu, the mountain's ancient name is Yixunshan。

[7] 朝生夕死：指照舍羲氏，即且舍氏。

[7] zhao sheng xi si (morning born, evening die)

Tr: refers to the Zhaoshexi Shi, also known as Qieshe Shi。

译文：契那国在北面，是沂蒙支系部落国，是古老的氏族部落，建在莱达芜江畔，集镇的统治氏族是苗族，是沂蒙山移民的且舍氏。又说，契那国在灌云肆的北面。

Translation:

The China Guo is in the north, a tribal nation of Yimeng people。 They are very ancient tribes, with the capital city built at the riverbank of Laidawujiang。 The ruling class of the town is from the Miao people, who are the immigrants from Yimengshan, known as the Qieshe Shi。 It is also said that the China Guo is located to the north of Guanyun Si。

09-05 虹虹

Honghong

（117,33915E；38,37175N）

虹虹[1]在其北，各有两首[2]。一曰在君子北。

注释：[1]虹虹：指黄骅肆。

Notes: [1] hong hong (rainbow rainbow)

Tr： refers to Huanghua Si。 huang hua (yellow horse) 。

[2] 各有两首：孤尤国的首都。有遗存名为孤东。

[2]ge you liang shou (each has two heads)

Tr: Guyou Guo's capital city。 A relic named Gudong survives。

译文：黄骅肆在北面，是孤尤国的首都。又说，黄骅肆在契那国的北面。

Translation:

Huanghua Si is located to the north。 It is the capital city of Guyou Guo。It is also said that Huanghua Si is located to the north of China Guo。

09-06 朝阳之谷神天吴

Chaoyangzhigushen tianwu

（117,19212E；39,12951N）

朝阳之谷[1]，神曰天吴[2]，是为水伯[3]。在虹虹北两水间[4] 。其为兽也，八首人面，八足八尾 [5] ，皆青黄 [6] 。

注释：[1]朝阳之谷：指朝阳国。
Notes： [1] chao yang zhi gu (morning sun valley)
Tr: refers to the Chaoyang Guo。

[2] 神曰天吴：集肆叫天坞，今称天津。
[2] shen yue tian wu (God name sky wu)
Tr: the township is called Tianwu, today it is called Tianjin。

[3] 是为水伯：这里是水码头。
[3] shi wei shui bo (it is water god)
Tr: this is a river port。

[4] 两水间：指永定河与海河地区。
[4] liang shui jian (between two rivers)
Tr: refers to the area of Yongdinghe River and Haihe River。

[5] 八首人面，八足八尾：芝饶族居民，饶族饶夷。
[5]ba shou ren mian (eight heads human face), ba zu ba yi (eight feet eight tails)
Tr: refers to the residents of Zhirao tribes, known as Rao tribes, or Rao people。

[6] 皆青黄：皆为东胡氏族。
[6] jie qing huang (all green, yellow)
Tr: all the tribes belong to the Donghu people, Donghu: east hu tribes。

译文：朝阳国的集肆叫天坞，这里是水码头。在黄骅肆北面的永定河与海河地区。这里的氏族是芝饶族居民，是饶族饶夷，皆为东胡氏族。
Translation:
The township of Chaoyang Guo is called Tianwu, a river port。 It is situated between Yongdinghe River and Haihe River， to the north of Huanghua Si。The residents are Zhirao tribe settlers, known as Rao tribe, or Rao Yi, part of the Donghu tribes。

09-07 青丘九尾狐
Qingqiujiuweihu
（118,17753E；39,63388N）

青丘国[1]在其北，其狐四足九尾[2]。一曰在朝阳北。

注释：[1]青丘国：指城街国，又称城山国，因大城山而得名，今河北唐山市城区。
Notes： [1] qing qiu guo (green mound country)
Tr: refers to the Chengjie Guo， also known as Chengshan Guo。 It derived its name from Dachengshan, it is in today's Tangshan city urban quarters in Hebei province。

[2] 其狐四足九尾：那里的游牧氏族是古老的缴夷。
[2] qi hu si zu jiu wei (its fox four feet nine tails)
Tr: the nomadic tribes there are the ancient Jiao Yi。

译文：城街国在北面，那里的游牧氏族是古老的缴夷。又说城街国在朝阳国的北面。
Translation：
Chengjie Guo is in the north, the nomadic tribes there are the ancient Jiao Yi。 It is also said that Chengjie Guo is situated to the north of Chaoyang Guo。

09-08 帝命竖亥步
Dimingshuhaibu

（119,9417E；40,81852N）

帝命竖亥步[1]，自东极至于西极，五亿十选九千八百步[2]。竖亥右手把算[3]，左手指丘北 [4] 。一曰禹令竖亥。一曰五亿十万 [5] 九千八百步 [6] 。

注释：[1]帝命竖亥步：北地的松黑山。帝命，狄米，指北地；竖亥步，指松岭、黑山山脉。
Notes： [1] di ming shu hai bu (God order shuhai to measure with his foot)
Tr: refers to the Songheishan in Beidi (northern land)。Diming reads as dimi, meaning northern land。 Shuhaibu: refers to Songling (pine range) and Heishan Mountains (black mountain range) 。
[2] 五亿十选九千八百步：五溢十峰九坳口八部落山。
[2] wu yi (five 100 million) shi xuan (ten elect) jiu qian ba bai bu (9800 paces)
Tr: meaning five rivers, ten peaks, nine valleys and eight tribal mountains。
[3] 竖亥右手把算：松黑山北面是巴数。巴数，指九濮部落地区。翁牛特刻文有记载。
[3] shu hai you shou ba suan (shuhai's right hand do the numbers)
Tr: to the north of Songheishan there is Bashu。Bashu is the region of the Jiupu (nine Pu) tribes。 Bashu is recorded on the rock inscription at Ongniud Banner (pinyin: Wēngniútè Qí), a banner of eastern Inner Mongolia, People's Republic of China。
[4] 左手指丘北：南面是角山。丘北，读去博， 指角山。
[4] zuo shou zhi qiu bei (left hand points to the north of mound)
Tr: to the south stands the Jiaoshan (corner mount) 。qiubei: reads as qubo, meaning Jiaoshan。
[5]万：指门。
[5] wan (ten thousand)
Tr: means gate, door。
[6] 八百步：第一个八百步指八部落山，第二个八百步指八票阜。
[6]ba bai bu (eight hundred feet)
Tr: refers to 1. Babuluoshan: eight tribe mountains。
2. To a place called Bapiaofu (Eight ticket town) 。

译文：北地的松黑山，从东北至西南，共有五条河流、十座山峰，九个坳口和八个部落。松黑山的东北端是巴数地区，西南端是角山，人们又说那是北蔺地区的松黑山，又说有五河十门九坳八票阜。
Translation:
The Songheishan in Beidi, running from northeast to southwest, hosts five rivers, ten mountain peaks, nine valleys and eight tribes。 The northeast end of Songheishan is the Bashu territory。 Jiaoshan stands to the southwest end。It is also said that is the Songheishan in the Beilin region, it hosts five rivers, ten gates, nine valleys and a place called Bapiaofu。

09-09 黑齿国
Heichi Guo
（123,43176E；41,80543N）

黑齿国[1]在其北，为人黑[2]，食稻啖蛇[3]，一赤一青[4]，在其旁[5]。一曰在竖亥北，为人黑首[6]，食稻使蛇[7]，其一蛇赤[8]。

注释：[1]黑齿国：指浑丘国。沈阳地区的古称谓，因属浑河流域而得名。
Notes:[1] hei chi guo (black teeth country) refers to the Hunqiu Guo, the ancient name for Shenyang region。It derives its name from being in the Hunhe River basin。
[2] 为人黑：定都于浑丘。沈阳城，古称浑丘。

[2] wei ren hei (for human black)
Tr: make Hunqiu its capital。The present Shenyang city, its ancient name is Hunqiu (muddy mount) 。

[3] 食稻啖蛇：从此诞生了集肆。食，指始，从此；稻啖，指诞生；蛇，指集肆。

[3] shi dao dan she (eat rice eat snake)
Tr: from then the township came into being。shi(eat) meaning beginning, from then on。 Dao dan (rice eat) came into being, she(snake) township。

[4] 一赤一青：有一个于红肆，有一个东肆。

[4] yi chi yi qing (one red one green)
Tr: there are two townships: one is Yuhong Si, one is Dong Si。

[5] 在其旁：在都城旁边。

[5] zai qi pang (by its side)
Tr: by the side of the capital city。

[6] 为人黑首：定都浑河。首，在此读蛇，指河。

[6] wei ren hei shou (as human black head)
Tr: designates Hunhe River area as the site for the capital。Shou(head) reads as she(snake) meaning river。

[7] 食稻使蛇：始生市肆。

[7] shi dao shi she (eat rice handle snake)
Tr: this is the start for township and city building。

[8] 其一蛇赤：其中有一个集肆叫红肆。

[8] qi yi she chi(one snake is red)
Tr: one of the townships is called Hong Si (red town) 。

译文：浑丘国在北面，定都于浑丘，从此诞生了集肆，有一个叫于红肆，一个叫东肆，在都城的旁边。又说浑丘国在松黑山北面，定都浑河边，始生市肆，其中一肆叫红肆。

Translation:
Hunqiu Guo lies in the north, with its capital at Hunqiu, thus the township came into being。 There are the townships; one is called Yuhong Si, one is called Dong Si, by the capital。 It is also said that Hunqiu Guo lies to the north of Songheishan, and their designated capital is by the Hunhe River。They started city building。 One of the townships is called Hong Si。

09-10 汤谷十日
Tanggushiri
（123,72327E；42,99917N）

下有汤谷[2]，汤谷上有扶桑[3]，十日所浴[4]，在黑齿北。居水中，有大木[5]，九日居下枝[6]，一日居上枝[7]。

注释：[1]汤谷十日：指通江十惹，分别为：通江口、两家子、四大家子、金家镇、照苏台（今称七家子）、曲家店、八面城、老四平、梨树、十家堡。

Notes:[1] tang gu shi ri (hotwater valley ten suns)
Tr: refers to the following ten townships on the Tongjiang River:
Tongjiangkou, Liangjiazi, Sidajiazi, Jinjiazhen, Zhaosutai (today’s Qijiazi), Qujiadian, Bamiancheng, Laosiping, Lishu, and Shijiabao。

[2] 下有汤谷：在东方有一条通江，今称照苏台河。

[2] xia you tang gu(below is Hotwater valley)
Tr: in the east, there is a river called Tongjiang, known today as the Zhaosutai River。

[3] 汤谷上有扶桑：通江边的疆域。扶桑，指疆域。

[3] tang gu shang you fu sang(hotwater valley up has Fusang)
Tr: refers to the regions along the Tongjiang River。 Fusang: means territory, region。

[4] 十日所浴：是十镇部落开辟。所浴，指开辟。
[4] shi ri suo yu (ten suns thus bath)
Tr: the territory is developed by the Shizhen tribe (ten towns tribe) 。 suoyu (thus bath) meaning develop, build。

[5] 居水中，有大木：照苏台是游牧部落的检目。
[5] ju shui zhong (stay in water) you da mu (has big tree)
Tr: Zhaosutai is the Jianmu(centre) of the nomadic tribes。

[6] 九日居下枝：九个集镇住在河畔的东面。
[6] jiu ri ju xia zhi (nine suns stay on the lower branches)
Tr: nine townships are located to the east side of the riverbank。

[7] 一日居上枝：一个集镇住在河畔的西面。
[7] yi ri ju shang zhi (one sun stay on top branch)
Tr: one township is located to the west side of the riverbank。

译文：在东方有一条通江，通江边的疆域，是十镇部落开辟，在浑丘国的北面。照苏台是游牧部落的检目，有九个集镇座落在河畔的东面，一个集镇座落在河畔的西面。

Translation:

There is a river called Tongjiang in the east。 The territory along the river is developed by ten townships, to the north of Hunqiu Guo。 Zhaosutai is the centre of nomadic tribes。 Nine townships are located to the east of the riverbank, one township is located to the west side of the riverbank。

09-11 雨师妾
Yushiqi
（125,30446E；43,34216N）

雨师妾[1]在其北。其为人黑，两手各操一蛇[2]，左耳有青蛇[3]，右耳有赤蛇[4]。一曰在十日北，为人黑身人面[5]，各操一龟[6]。

注释：[1]雨师妾：读伊施纪，指伊通部落。
Notes : [1]yu shi qi (Rain lord concubine)
Tr: reads as Yishiji, a phonetic rendering, refers to the Yitong tribes。

[2] 其为人黑，两手各操一蛇：定都于哈达岭下，首都在古绰河肆。各操一，指古绰溢，意为流动很汹涌的河，后称伊通河。
[2] qi wei ren hei, liang shou ge cao yi she (as person black, two hands holding one snake in each hand)
Tr: designates its capital city at the foot of Hadaling Mountains。The capital is at Guchuohe Si。 gecaoyi; reads as guchaoyi, meaning a river with torrential waves, later it is known as the Yitong River。

[3] 左耳有青蛇：左边有东肆。
[3] zuo er you qing she (left ear has green snake)
Tr: to the left side there is Dong Si (east town) 。

[4] 右耳有赤蛇：右边有通肆。这里是按照左东右西表达。赤，指移动，在此作通解。
[4] you er you chi she (right ear has red snake)
Tr: to the right side there is the Tong Si。Here the cardinal direction is expressed as left /east, right/west。 chi(red) means moving, (through, across) 。

[5] 为人黑身人面：定都于哈达岭下的集镇。
[5] wei ren hei shen ren mian (as person black body human face)
Tr: designates the capital township at the foot of Hadaling Mountain。

[6] 各操一龟：古绰河的北面。
[6]ge cao yi gui (each holds a turtle)
Tr: to the north of Guchaohe River。

译文：伊通部落在北面，定都与哈达岭下，首都在古绰河肆，河的左岸有一个东肆，右岸有一个通肆。又说在十镇的北面，定都于哈达岭下的集镇，在古绰河的北岸。
Translation:
Yitong tribe is in the north, designating their capital at the foot of the Hadaling Mountains, with their capital city at Guchaohe Si。There is a Dong Si at the left bank of the river, and a Tong Si at the right bank of the river。It is also said that the capital is located to the north of Shizhen。 Designating their centre at the foot of Hadaling Mountains, the capital townships are located to the north of the riverbank of Guchaohe River。

09-12 玄股国
Xuangu Guo
（125,33599E；43,9167N）

玄股国在其北[1]，其为人衣鱼食驱[2]，使两鸟夹之[3]。一曰在雨师妾北。

注释：[1]玄股国：指长城国，又称宽城国，今称长春宽城区。
Notes;[1] xuan gu guo (dark thigh country)
Tr: refers to the Changcheng (long wall) Guo, also called Kuancheng (wide city country) Guo, today known as Kuancheng district, Changchun (lasting spring), Jilin province。
[2] 其为人衣鱼食驱：定都于伊通河畔的奢岭旁。衣鱼，指伊溢，伊通河；食驱，指奢角、奢岭。奢，即长。
[2] qi wei ren yi yu shi qu (as person wear fish eat chase)
Tr: designates their capital by Sheling by the Yitong River。 Yiyu (wear fish) reads as Yiyi-Yitong River。 Shiqu (eat chase) refers to Shejiao, or Sheling Mountain, she means long。
[3] 使两鸟夹之：从事并管理渔业和农业两种职业。
[3] shi liang niao jia zhi (make two birds squeeze from both sides)
Tr: engaged in and manages two kinds of production--fishing and agriculture。

译文：长城国在北面，定都于伊通河畔的奢岭旁，从事并管理着渔业和农业两种职业。又说长城国在伊通国北面。
Translation:
The Changcheng Guo is in the north, the capital is located by Sheling Mountain by the Yitong River。 The country is engaged in and manages two kinds of production: fishing, and agriculture。 It is also said that the Changcheng Guo is located to the north of Yitong Guo。

09-13 毛民国
Maomin Guo
（126,64251E；45,75759N）

毛民国[1]在其北，为人身生毛[2]。一曰在玄股北。

注释：[1]毛民国：读陌米国，指河岸边的国家，这里指松花江畔的国家。
Notes： [1] mao min guo (hairy folk country)

Tr: reads as Momi Guo, meaning the country by the riverbank, here refers to the countries by the Songhuajiang River。

[2] 为人身生毛：定都于松花江畔。身生毛，读松蛇陌，指松花江畔，今称哈尔滨。

[2] wei ren shen sheng mao (as person body grow hair)
Tr; designates their capital by the Songhuajiang River。 Shen sheng mao (body grows hair) reads as song she mo, refers to the Songhuajiang riverbank, known today as Harbin city, Heilongjiang province。

译文：陌米国在北面，定都于松花江畔。又说陌米国在长道国北面。
Translation:
Momi Guo is located to the north, with the capital city by the Songhuajiang River。 It is said that the Momi Guo is located to the north of Changdao Guo。

09-14 劳民国
Laomin Guo
（127,52691E；50,29088N）

劳民国[1]在其北，其为人黑[2]。或曰教民[3] 。一曰在毛民北，为人面目首足尽黑 [4] 。

注释：[1]劳民国：指沼泽地的国家。劳民，即淖尔米，指沼泽地。
Notes：[1] lao min guo (labor folk country)
Tr: refers to the countries in the swampy land。Laomin (labor folk): nuur region, Naoermi, means swamps。

[2] 其为人黑：定都于黑河。

[2] qi ren wei hei (as person black)
Tr: decides to build a capital by the Heihe (black river) River。

[3] 教民：读诸米，指低地，也称张米、张地。

[3] jiao min (teach folk)
Tr: reads as Zhumi, refers to the lowland, also transliterated as Zhangmi, or Zhangdi, mi, di: region。

[4] 为人面目首足尽黑：定都于母系的狩猎氏族部落的黑河。面目，指娘，母系；首足，指氏族；尽，读纪，指部落。

[4] wei ren mian mu shou zu jin hei (as human face eye head feet all black)
Tr: decides to build the capital by the Heihe River which is the territory of the matrilineal hunting tribes。 Mian mu (face eye) means Mother, matriarch; shou zu (head foot) refers to tribes, jin (all) reads ji, meaning tribes。

译文：沼泽国在北面，定都于黑河, 又称低地国。又说沼泽国在陌米国的北面，定都于母系的狩猎氏族部落的黑河。
Translation:
Zhaoze Guo, the swamp country, is located to the north, with the capital by the Heihe River, called Didi Guo--low land country。It is also said that the Zhaoze Guo is to the north of Momi Guo, its capital is by the Heihe River where the matrilineal nomadic tribes live。

09-15 东方句芒
Dongfangjumang
（129,12E~144,84E；46,87N~55,34N）

东方句芒[1]，鸟身人面[2]，乘[3]两龙[4]。

注释：[1]东方句芒：东方，指沼泽国的东方，要站在黑河对岸的张地淖尔的位置向东看，中心点在伯力；句芒，指基姆族。主要生活在两江下游至出海口地区。基姆族群分为三大族群，即句芒族群、倭基姆族群（日本族群）、爱斯基姆族群（北极族群）。倭，指南部，不是指矮。

Notes: [1] dong fang ju mang:(east land jumang)

Tr: dongfang (east land) refers to the east of Zhaoze Guo。 One needs to look east from the Zhangdi Nuur on the opposite bank of Heihe River, with the centre at Boli (Khabarovsk in Russia) 。 Jumang: refers to Kimu people 。 Living mainly around the river mouth area where two rivers enter the sea, Jimu people are divided into three groups, the Jumang, the Wojimu (Japanese) and Eskimos （Esquimaux) people (the Beiji--north pole group) wo: refers to the south, not to the concept of short stature as people are led to believe。

[2] 鸟身人面：是僚族居民。

[2] niao shen ren mian (bird body human face)

Tr: refers to the Liao tribal residents。

[3]乘：指集中在, 世代居住在。

[3] cheng (ride) meaning; centered at, concentrate in。

Tr: people for generations have lived in this place。

[4] 两龙：指两江下游，即松花江与黑龙江下游至出海口地区。

[4] liang loong (two dragons) refers to the area between the lower reaches of the Songhuajiang River and Heilongjiang River to where the two rivers enter the sea。

译文：沼泽国的东面是基姆族的生活地区，他们是僚族居民，集中在松花江和黑龙江两江下游至出海口地段。

Translation：

To the east of Zhaoze Guo is the area where Jimu people live。 They are the Liao people, who are centered in the areas between the lower reaches of Songhuajiang River and Heloongjiang River to where the two rivers enter the sea。

第十卷 海内南经 (Hainei Region: the South)

Book 10 Haineinanjing

10-01 瓯居海中
Oujuhaizhong
（116,7E~121,3E；24,3N~28.4N）

海内东南陬以西者[1]。
瓯居海中[2]。闽在海中[3]，其西北有山。一曰闽中山 [4] 在海中。

注释：[1]海内东南陬以西者：从海外东南角记述到西南角。海内，实际指海外。
Notes：[1] hai nei dong nan zuo yi xi zhe (sea within east south corner to west)
Tr: description of regions of Hainei starts from southeast corner to southwest corner。 Hainei (sea within) refers to the region further away from the centre, it is rather the land further beyond the concept of sea, Haiwai, a term which is not about the waterbody per se, but regions beyond the center region。

[2] 瓯居海中：瓯，指东瓯，古代浙江南部和温州地区；海中，指沿海地区。东瓯在沿海地区。后来的海中是检目行政单位，包括江苏、浙江和福建省。
[2] ou ju hai zhong (pot stay sea middle)
Tr: Ou refers to Dong 'ou, (east Ou) an ancient name for region covering the south part of present Zhejiang province and Wenzhou。 hai zhong (sea middle) refers to the coastal regions。Dong 'ou is in the coastal region。 Hai zhong, (sea middle) later became an administration centre, which supervises provinces of Jiangsu, Zhejiang, and Fujian。

[3] 闽在海中：闽，福建古称七闽；七闽在沿海地区。
[3] min zai hai zhong (min is sea middle)
Tr: min refers to Fujian province. In ancient times, the region of Fujian was called Qimin (seven min), Qimin is in the coastal regions。

[4] 闽中山：指七闽地区。

[4] min zhong shan (min middle mountain) refers to the region of Qimin。

译文：从海外东南角记述到西南角。
东瓯在沿海地区。七闽在沿海地区，它的西北面为山区。又说七闽地区属东南沿海地区。
Translation:
The description starts from Haiwai southeast corner to southwest corner。Dong'ou is in the coastal region。Qimin is in the coastal region。 Its northwest part is mountainous。 It is also said that the Qimin region belongs to the southeast coastal areas。

10-02 三天子鄣山
Santianzizhang Mountain
（119,26311E；28,48184N）

三天子鄣山[1]在闽西北。一曰在海中。

注释：[1]三天子鄣山：指福建西北部浙江境内的九龙山，有松阳、遂昌、遂昌大柘三个山间平地，被称为三妥柘堵山，谐音称为三天子都山或三天子鄣山，同时也称为柘岭或柘岱。
Notes:[1] san tian zi zhang shan (three sky son block mount)
Tr: refers to the three flat lands between three mountains in the northwest part of Fujian, and Zhejiang。 The three flat lands are flanked by Jiuloong (nine dragon) Mountain。 The three flatlands are called respectively Songyang, Suichang, and Suichangdazhe。The three flatlands are also called Santuozhidu Mountain, which is phonetically rendered into Santianzidushan or Santianzizhangshan, which are also called Zheling or Zhedai。

译文：三天子鄣山在闽西北。又说三天子鄣山在沿海地区。
Translation:
Santianzizhang Mountain is in the northwest of Min。 It is also said that the Santianzizhang Mountain is in the coastal areas。

10-03 桂林八树
Guilinbashu
（117,1693E；27,13604N）

桂林[1]八树[2]在番隅[3]东。

注释：[1]桂林：指杉岭南端的桂林乡，属福建邵武市。
Notes: [1] gui lin (Osmanthus fragrans grove)
Tr: refers to the Guilin town in the south end of Shanling (pine range), it belongs to the Shaowu city, Fujian province。

[2] 八树：读音"饶舍"，指八个氏族支系，今称为八个行政村，分别为：惠林、桂林、槎口、下岚、盖竹、横坑、余山和大岭。为便于表达，按八舍解读。
[2]ba shu (eight trees) it reads as raoshe, rao(eight)
Tr: rao she refers to the eight tribal branches, in today's term, they are called administrative villages; they are Huilin, Guilin, Chakou, Xialan, Gaizhu, Hengkeng, Yushan and Daling。 For the sake of narration, bashu is termed as bashe。 She: in Chinese means house, compartments。

[3] 番隅：指西溪。又称番溢。
[3] pan yu (pan corner) refers to the Xixi (west creek) also known as Panyi。

译文：桂林八舍在西溪的东面。
Translation:
Guilin Bashe lies to the east of Xixi。

10-04 伯虑国
Bolv Guo
（116,64008E；27,56886N）

伯虑国[1]、离耳国[2]、雕题国[3]、北朐国[4]皆在郁水[5]南。郁水出湘陵南海[6] 。一曰相虑 [7] 。

注释：[1]伯虑国：读贝略国，指南城。
Notes：[1]bo lv guo (uncle worry nation)
Tr: reads as beilue guo; meaning Nancheng (south town) 。
[2] 离耳国：读黎流国，指黎川。
[2]li er guo (leave ear nation)
Tr: reads as liliu guo, refers to Lichuan, a place name。
[3] 雕题国：读妥体国，指广昌。
[3] diao ti guo (carving sentence nation)
Tr: reads tuo ti guo， refers to Guangchang, a place name。
[4] 北朐国：读贝盱国，指南丰。
[4] bei qu guo: reads as bei xu guo, refers to Nanfeng。
[5] 郁水：指盱江。
[5]yu shui: refers to the Xujiang River。
[6] 湘陵南海：江西古称灌湘和湘陵，南部地区则称湘陵南海。
[6] xiang ling nan hai; the ancient name for Jiangxi province is Guanxiang or Xiangling。 Its southern part region is called Xianglingnanhai。
[7] 相虑：湘陵的谐音。
[7] xiang lv: a phonetic match to Xiangling。

译文：南城国、黎川国、广昌国、南丰国皆在盱江南部地区。盱江发源于湘陵的南部。又说此四国在湘陵南部。
Translation:
Nancheng Guo, Lichuan Guo, Guangchang Guo and Nanfeng Guo are all located in the southern part of Xujiang River。 Xujiang River rises from the south of Xiangling。 It is also said that those four countries lie in the southern part of Xiangling。

10-05 枭阳国
Xiaoyang Guo
（114,9151E；27,039N）

枭阳国[1]在北朐之西。其为人人面长唇[2]，黑身有毛 [3]，反踵 [4]，见人笑亦笑[5]；左手操管[6]。

注释：[1]枭阳国：指峡阳国。在江西省峡山南面，今称吉安县。相邻的赣江古称峡溢、峡江。
Notes:[1] xiao yang guo (owl sun country) refers to Xiayang Guo。 It lies to the south of Xiashan Mountain in Jiangxi province。 It is known as Ji'an county。 The Ganjiang River nearby is known in ancient times as Xiayi, as well as Xiajiang。
[2] 人面长唇：指草禾场集镇。

[2] ren mian chang chun (human face long lips)
Tr: refers to the Caohechang (grass plants field) township。

[3] 黑身有毛：王族是有苗，即苗族。

[3] hei shen you mao (black body with hair)
Tr: their king tribe is the Miao, now known as the Miao ethnic people。

[4] 反踵：善于管理。

[4] fan zhong (backward heels) good at administrative functions。

[5] 见人笑亦笑：这个集镇与峡江相邻。

[5] jian ren xiao yi xiao (see human laugh therefore laugh)
Tr: this township neighbours to the Xiajiang River。

[6] 左手操管：在峡江的西面建立的城镇。左手，在此指西面。

[6] zuo shou cao guan (left hand holds tube)
Tr: establishes township to the west of Xiajiang River。Zuo shou: left hand, meaning west。

译文：峡阳国在南丰国的西面，定都于草禾场集镇，王族为苗族，是善于治理的氏族。这个集镇与峡江相邻，是在峡江的西岸建立的城镇。
Translation:
Xiayang Guo lies to the west of Nanfeng Guo, with its capital in Caohechang town。 Its king tribe is the Miao tribe, very capable of administrative functions。This township is close by the Xiajiang River, established on its west bank。

10-06 兕
Si
（113,04065E；25,80055N）

兕[1]在舜葬[2]东，湘水南。其状如牛[3]，苍黑 [4]，一角 [5] 。

注释：[1]兕：指苏城，又称郴州。在湖南郴州市。
Notes:[1]si（rhinoceros): refers to Sucheng, known today as Binzhou, in today's Binzhou city, Hunan province。

[2] 舜葬：指纹身氏族的疆域。

[2] shun zang (shun burial): refers to the territory of tribes who tattoo their bodies。

[3]牛：指僚族。

[3] niu (ox) refers to Lao/Liao tribes。

[4] 苍黑：指郴恒，贝濮僚国的王都，称为郴恒。

[4] cang hei (deep black) refers to Binheng, the king tribes' capital of Beipulao Guo。The capital is called Binheng。

[5]角：读郭，指城。

[5] jiao(horn) reads as guo, refers to the city。

译文：苏城在纹身氏族疆域的东面，在湘水的南面，是僚族的郴恒之城。
Translation:
Sucheng city is to the east of Wenshen tribes, south of Xiangshui River。 It is the Binheng, capital of the Lao tribes。

10-07 苍梧山
Cangwushan
（111,98804E；25,34963N）

苍梧之山[1]，帝舜葬于阳[2]，帝丹朱葬于阴[3]。

注释：[1]苍梧山：指九嶷山。
Notes:[1] cang wu shan (dark straight trunk mount) refers to Jiuyishan。

[2] 帝舜葬于阳：纹身氏族的疆域在南面。
[2] di shun zang yu yang (di shun buried in sunny side) : the Wenshen （tattoo tribes) live to the south of it 。

[3] 帝丹朱葬于阴：诸苗氏族的疆域在北面。丹，是濮文“大”的谐音。大，读朵音，指落后的，大弓为夷，即落后的支系为夷，这是汉语的造字定义，由此，诸苗被称为大诸，谐音丹朱。
[3] di danzhu zang yu yin (di danzhu buried in shady side)
Tr: various Miao tribes' territories lie to the north。 Dan； Pu concept of da(great), a phonetic match to duo(backward)。 Chinese sign Yi is a compound sign with da and bow, big bow means Yi, and backwards; people are called Yi, this is the logic behind the Chinese construction of the word of Yi。 Therefore, the various Miao tribes are called dazhu, a phonetic match to Danzhu。

译文：九嶷山，纹身氏族的疆域在南面，诸苗氏族的疆域在北面。
Translation:
There is the Jiuyishan, with Wenshen tribes' territory to its south, and various Miao tribes' territory to its north。

10-08 泛林
Fanlin
（111,27661E；24,81748N）

泛林[1]，方三百里[2]。在狌狌[3]东。

注释：[1]泛林：指天府，今谐音传承为天丰、富川，在广西富川县城。
Notes:[1] fan lin: refers to Tianfu （sky hall) , its phonetic match can be found in Tianfeng, Fuchuan, in present Fuchuan county, Guangxi province。

[2] 方三百里：天丰部落的都城。方三，指天丰；百里，读亳里，指都城。
[2] fang san bai li (area 300 li)
Tr: refers to the capital city of Tianfeng tribe。 Fang san: refers to Tianfeng, baili, reads as boli (poli) meaning capital city, poli。

[3] 狌狌：读生生。这里指奢肆，即阳朔。
[3] shengsheng: reads shengsheng, refers to Shesi, today known as Yangshuo city, Guangxi province。

译文：天府，天丰部落的都城，在奢肆的东面。
Translation:
Tianfu is the capital city for the Tianfeng tribe。It lies to the east of Shesi。

10-09 狌狌知人名
Shengshengzhirenming
（110,49373E；24,7766N）

狌狌知人名[1]，其为首如豕而人面[2]，在舜葬[3]西。

注释：[1]狌狌知人名：指凤鸣坪集镇，今广西桂林市阳朔县阳朔镇。
Notes： [1] sheng sheng zhi ren ming (monkey knowns human name)
Tr: refers to the township of Fengmingping (phoenix singing town), is today's Yangshuo town in Yangshuo county, Guilin city, Guangxi province。

[2] 豕而人面：集肆的居民。

[2] shi er ren mian (pig with human face) the residents of townships。

[3] 舜葬：指纹身氏族疆域。

[3] shun zang (shun buried) refers to the territory of Wenshen （tattooing ） tribes。

译文：凤鸣坪集镇，那里的氏族是集肆居民，在纹身氏族疆域的东面。

Translation:

There is Fengmingping township, where the tribal residents are the township folks。 The township lies to the east of the Wenshen tribes' territory。

10-10 犀牛

Xiniu

（109,40952E；24,33518N）

狌狌西北[1]有犀牛[2]，其状如牛而黑[3]。

注释：[1]狌狌西北：指奢肆西南。北，读贝音，指南。

Notes:[1] shengsheng xi bei (monkey west north): southwest of Shesi。 Bei reads as bei(shell) meaning south。

[2] 犀牛：读肆僚，指僚肆，即河边的集肆。今谐音传承为柳肆、柳州。

[2] xi niu (rhinoceros) reads as Siliao, a reversed word order to Liaosi (Laosi), meaning the townships along the riverside。 Its relic name survived in Liusi, Liuzhou。

[3] 牛而黑：指柳部落的王城。牛而黑，读柳而恒。

[3] niu er hei (ox also black) refers to the king's town of the Liu tribe。Niu er hei reads as liu er heng, a close phonetic match。

译文：奢肆的西南面有僚肆，是河边部落的王城。

Translation:

To the southwest of Shesi, there is the Liaosi, a king's town of the tribes along the riverside。

10-11 夏后启之臣孟涂

Xiahouqizhichen mengtu

（108,08683E；24,68741N）

夏后启之臣[1]曰孟涂[2]，是司神于巴[3]。人请讼于孟涂之所[4]，其衣有血者乃执之 [5] 。是请生[6]，居山上[7]，在丹山西[8]。丹山在丹阳南，丹阳居属也[9]。

注释：[1]夏后启之臣：长河池的部落。臣，读纪，指部落。

Notes： [1] xia hou qi zhi chen (summer back start 's official)

Tr: refers to the Changhechi (long river pool) tribe, chen(official)reads as ji, refers to tribes。

[2] 孟涂：指毛吐部落。

[2] meng tu: refers to Maotu tribe, mengtu and maotu are close phonetic matches。

[3] 是司神于巴：建在金城江畔。今河池市城区。

[3] shi si shen yu ba （supervise deity at ba)

Tr: establish settlement along the riverbanks of Jincheng (gold city) 。It is in today's Hechi city's urban quarters。

[4] 人请讼于孟涂：定检署在毛吐。

[4] ren qin song yu meng tu (person ask judgement from meng tu)

[4] decides to establish their administration center at Maotu。

[5] 其衣有血者乃执之：这里的氏族是有池部落的拉沙氏。
[5] qi yi you xue zhe nai zhi zhi (its cloth blood stain punish)
Tr: the tribal branches living here are the Lasha Shi from Youchi tribes。
[6] 是请生：建检舍。
[6] shi qing shen (ask to let live)
Tr: set up checking posts, meaning set up administrative center。
[7] 居山上：在河的西岸。山，读舍，在此指河。
[7] ju shan shang (living mount up)
Tr: is on the west bank of the river, shan(mount) reads as she, meaning river。
[8] 在丹山西：在丹舍的东面。山，读舍，在此指部落。
[8] zai dan shan xi (at dan mount west), xi means east。
Tr: to the east of Danshe, shan: reads she, meaning tribes。
[9] 丹阳居属也：丹阳部落所属之乡。今广西南丹。
[9] dan yang ju shu ye (dan sunny reside belong thus)
Tr: the land the Danyang tribes occupy, in today's Nandan, Guangxi province。

译文：长河池的部落叫毛吐部落，建在金城江畔，定检署在毛吐所。这里的氏族是有池部落的拉沙氏，建检舍在河的西岸，在丹舍的东面。丹舍在丹阳的南面，是丹阳部落之乡。
Translation:
The tribes from Changhechi area are called Maotu tribes。 Their settlements are built along the banks of Jincheng River, with their administration center at Maotu suo。 The tribal branches are the Lasha Shi from the Youchi tribes, set up their administration center on the west bank of the river, east of Danshe。 Danshe is in the south of Danyang, which is the land of Danyang tribes。

10-12 窫窳龙首
Yayulongshou
（109,22697E；23,7342N）

窫窳龙首[1]，居弱水中[2]，在狌狌知人名之西，其状如龙首[3]，食人[4]。

注释：[1]窫窳龙首：指大河龙族。大河，指红水河。
Notes： [1] ya yu loong shou (ya yu dragon head)
Tr: refers to the Daheloongzu (big river dragon tribe) 。Dahe: Hongshuihe (red river water) 。
[2] 弱水：指龙水，又称古瓦水。古瓦为龙。弱水地区，今称为广西来宾城。
[2] ruo shui (weak water) refers to Loongshui (dragon water) also known as the Guwashui。guwa: means loong, the dragon, referring to Ruoshui area, in today Laibin city， Guangxi province。
[3] 龙首：指古瓦氏族，是最早称龙的氏族。
[3] loong shou (dragon head) refers to the Guwa tribe, the earliest tribe who named themselves Guwa, the tribes of dragons。
[4] 食人：古老的集镇氏族。
[4] shi ren (eat human) : ancient township people。

译文：大河龙族，住在古瓦水地区，在凤鸣坪地区的西南面，是龙族古老的集镇氏族。
Translation:
The Daheloongzu (big river dragon tribe) lives in the Guwa River area, to the southwest of Fengmingping region。They are the ancient township tribes of the Loong (dragon) people。

10-13 建木
Jianmu
（107,99423E；23,73643N）

有木[1]，其状如牛，引之有皮[2]，若缨，黄蛇[3]。其叶如罗，其实如栾[4]，其木若蓲[5]，其名曰建木。在窫窳西弱水上[6] 。

注释：[1]木：指管理中心，也称建木、检目。
Notes： [1] mu (tree) refers to the administration center, also known as Jianmu, with different Chinese signs in close phonetic matching。
[2] 牛引之有皮：红河的大元河段。牛引，指大河，即红河；有皮，读耶比，指大元。
[2] niu yin zhi you pi (ox pull it has skin)
Tr: The Dayuan River part of the Honghe (red River) River。 Niuyin: means big river, the Honghe。 Youpi: reads as yebi, meaning dayuan。
[3] 若缨黄蛇：叫大化肆。
[3] ruo ying huang she (as rope yellow snake)
Tr: refers to the Dahuasi township。
[4] 其叶如罗，其实如栾：指骆越的绣部落支系氏族。
[4] qi ye ru luo, (its leaves like luo) qi shi ru luan (its fruits like Luan fruits) 。
Tr: this refers to the Xiu tribe's branch of Luoyue。
[5]蓲：读瓯，指内桑。
[5] ou refers to Neisang, a place name。
[6] 在弱水上：在古瓦河的西面。
[6] zai ruo shui shang (on weak water)
Tr: on the west bank of Guwa River。

译文：有一个管理中心，在红河的大元河段河岸边，叫大化肆。氏族支系是骆越的绣部落支系氏族，管理中心在内桑，名叫建木，在红水河流域古瓦河地区的西面。
Translation:
There is an administration center, on the Dayuan River's bank。 The Dayuan River is part of the Honghe River, the centre is called Dahua township。The tribal branch is the Xiu clan of the Luoyue tribes, with its administration center at Neisang, known as a Jianmu。 The Jianmu is on the west side of the Guwa River region of the Hongshui River catchment。

10-14 氐人国
Diren Guo
（107,65833E；23,97551N）

氐人国[1]在建木西，其为人人面而鱼身[2]。

注释：[1]氐人国：指堵惹国，后称都阳国，都阳镇。在广西大化县都阳镇。
Notes: [1] di ren guo (di people country)
Tr: refers to the Dure Guo, later known as Duyang Guo or Duyang town, in today's Duyang town, Dahua county, Guangxi province。
[2] 人面而鱼身：勉箐山下的丰江边，人面，指勉箐；鱼身，指丰江。
[2] ren mian er yu shen (human face with fish body)

Tr: refers to the riverbanks of Fengjiang River by the foot of Mianqingshan。 Renmian (human face) refers to Mianqing; yushen (fish body) refers to the Fengjiang River。

译文：都阳国在建木的西面，定都于陇敏的同泽。
Translation:
Duyang Guo is situated to the west side of Jianmu, with its capital in Tongze, Longmin。

10-15 巴蛇食象
Basheshixiang
（106,61698E；23,89774N）

巴蛇食象[1]，三岁而出其骨[2]，君子服之[3]，无心腹之疾[4]。其为蛇青黄赤黑[5]，一曰黑蛇青首 [6]，在犀牛西 [7] 。

注释：[1]巴蛇食象：指博涩部落建立王国。巴蛇，指博涩，濮文意为阳圩东南，今广西百色。象，指王、王国。
Notes:[1]ba she shi xiang (ba snake eat elephant)
Tr: refers to the kingdom established by Bose tribe。 Bashe: bose, a Pu concept meaning southeast of Sunny side, which is known today as Baise, Guangxi province。 Xiang: elephant, refers to king, and kingdom。
[2] 三岁而出其骨：三年而成其国。
[2] san sui er chu qi gu (three years since put out its bones)
Tr: it took them three years to build this country。
[3] 君子服之：棘枝冯纪。国名叫棘枝王国，即南方王国。
[3] jun zi fu zhi (gentleman bow to it)
Tr: reads as ji zhi feng ji: the kingdom's name is jin zhi wang guo, kingdom of the thorny branches, meaning the kingdom of the south。
[4] 无心腹之疾：读汝喜胡之纪，指迎龙山的部落国。
[4] wu xin fu zhi ji (no heart and belly illness)
Tr: reads as ru xi hu zhi ji: refers to the tribal kingdom of Yingloongshan (receiving the dragon mount) 。
[5] 其为蛇青黄赤黑：下属分舍为青黄赤黑四舍。
[5] qi wei she qing huang chi hei (its snakes green, yellow, red, black)
Tr: its branches are arranged each under a different color; the Qingshe, Huangshe, Chishe, and Heishe。
[6] 黑蛇青首：黑舍排在第一。
[6] hei she qing shou (black snake green head)
Tr: The Heishe ranks number one。
[7] 犀牛：指左江与红河，在此指左江。
[7] xi niu(rhinoceros) refers to Zuojiang (left river)and Honghe (red river), here refers to Zuojiang。

译文：博涩建国，三年才成其国，叫棘枝王国，是迎龙山的部落国。下属划分为青黄赤黑四舍，黑舍排在第一。在左江的西面。
Translation:
Bose builds a kingdom; it takes them three years to accomplish it。 The kingdom is called Jinzhiwangguo, a tribal kingdom of the Yingloongshan。 Its tribal branches are arranged under four color-houses of green, yellow, red, and black。 The Heishe-black house ranks No. 1。 It is situated to the west of Zuojiang River。

10-16 旄马
Maoma

（105,09649E；24,49178N）

旄马[1]，其状如马，四节有毛[2]，在巴蛇西北，高山[3]南。

注释[1]旄马：指毛南苗，今称毛南族，毛马部落，今称西林，在广西西林市。
Notes:[1] mao ma (hairy horse) refers to the Maonan Miao, known today as Maonan ethnic people, the Maoma tribe。It is called Xilin, in today's Xilin city, Guangxi province。

[2]马，四节有毛：苗族支系的驮娘江部落的苗族。驮娘江部落，谐音传承为八达镇，在西林市城区。
[2]ma, si jie you mao (horse, four section has hair)
Tr: refers to the Tuoniangjiang tribe of the Miao people。 Tuoniangjiang tribes are transliterated into Badazhen, in today's Xilin city's urban quarter。

[3] 高山：读耿山，今称隆林。林读耿、举，此处读耿，谐音高。今广西隆林县城。
[3] gao shan (high mount) reads as Gengshan, known today as Lunglin。Lin reads as geng or ju, Here the sound geng is a phonetic match to Chinese gao。 It is today's Lunglin county seat, Guangxi province。

译文：毛南苗，是苗族的驮娘江部落苗族，在百舍的西面，隆林的南面。
Translation:
Maonan Miao is part of the Tuoniangjiang tribe, to the west of Baishe, south of Lunglin。

10-17 匈奴开题之国
（103,76536E；24,53093N。103,99387E；24,82615N。103,42164E；24,40938N）

匈奴[1]、开题之国[2]、列人之国[3]并在西北。

注释：[1]匈奴：指煦泸国，也称泸煦国。今云南泸西县。
Notes:[1] xiong nu refers to the Xunlu Guo, also known as Luxun Guo, in today's Luxi county, Yunnan province。

[2] 开题国：指丝宗国，今云南师宗县。
[1] kai ti guo (open question country) refers to the Sizong (silk master) Guo, in today's Shizong County, Yunnan province。

[3] 列人国：指勒惹国，今云南弥勒县。这个记录证明，弥勒县的名称形成远早于佛教文化的传入，而我们却在忘记自己的文化资源，并被外来文化所取代。
[3] lie ren guo (rank person country) refers to Lere Guo, in today's Mile County, Yunnan province。 This record shows that the Mile County as a place name occurred far earlier than the introduction of Buddhism into China。We, as Chinese, seem to have forgotten our history and replaced it with a foreign one。

译文：煦泸国、丝宗国、勒惹国都在毛南苗部落的西北面。
Translation:
Xulu Guo, Sizong Guo and Lere Guo are all situated to the northwest of Maonan Miao tribes。

第十一卷 海内西经 (Hainei Region: the West)

Book 11 Haineixijing

11-01 危与贰负杀窫窳
Weiyuerfu sha yayu
(103,30006E；26,41518N)

海内西南陬以【西】北者。

贰负之臣[1]曰危[2]，危与贰负杀窫窳[3]。帝乃梏[4] 之疏属之山 [5]， 桎其右足 [6]， 反缚两手与发[7]，系之山上木[8]。在开题西北。

注释：[1]贰负之臣：诺洪鲁的部落。诺洪鲁，山脉名，指乌蒙山，西侧主峰牛山，今称黎山。臣，读纪音，指部落。

Notes: [1]er fu zhi chen (two negative's minister)

Tr: Nuohonglu tribes。Nuohonglu: mountain name, today's Wumengshan。Its west peak is Niu(bull) Mount, known today as Lishan。 chen(minister) reads in Pu Concept as Ji, meaning tribes。

[2]危：指会泽部落。

[2] wei(danger) refers to the Huize tribes。hui/wei, phonetically close。

[3] 贰负杀窫窳：诺洪鲁的大河边。

[3]er fu sha ya yu (two negatives kill Yayu)

Tr: refers to the banks of big river along the Nuohonglu。

[4] 帝乃梏：武僰固育育的第十一代后裔蒂乃苦。

[4] di nai ku (God is locked up)

Tr: refers to Dinaiku, the 11th generation descendent of Patriarch Guyuyu of the Wubo tribes。

[5] 疏属之山：直系后裔的根据地。

[5] shu shu zhi shan (distant belong mount)

Tr: the base area of the direct lineage of the tribes。

[6] 桎其右足：知痴夜，又称樊雅夜，樊雅蒙之父。足，指支系。

[6] zhi qi you zu (lock his left foot)

Tr: Zhichiye, also known as Boyaye, is the father of Boyameng。zu(foot) means branches of the tribe。

[7] 反缚两手与发：开拓都城于大岩。大岩，今称金钟山。

[7] fan fu liang shou yu fa (back tying two hands and hair)

Tr: blaze trails and establish the capital city at Dayan （big rock） which is known today as Jinzhongshan (golden bell mountain) 。

[8] 系之山上木：建立了河边的管理中心。山上，读奢啥，指河边。

[8] xi zhi shan shang mu (tying the Mount Wood)

Tr: has established the management centre along the riverbank。 shanshang, (uphill) reads as shesha, meaning riverbanks。

译文：从海内西南角记述到西北角。

诺洪鲁的部落，叫会泽部落，会泽部落在诺洪鲁的大河边。蒂乃苦的直系后裔知痴夜支系开拓都城于大岩，建立了大河边的管理中心。在师宗的西北面。

Translation

The narrative is from the southwest corner of Hainei to the northwest corner。Nuohonglu tribes, also known as Huize tribes, live along the riverbanks at the Nuohonglu Mountains。 Dinaiku, the 11th generation descendent of Zhichiye has established the capital city at Dayan, which functions as the management center along the riverbanks。It is located to the northwest of Shizong, today's Shizong county。

11-02 大泽

Daze

（104,64231E；28,75833N）

大泽方百里[1]，群鸟所生及所解[2]。在雁门北[3] 。

注释：[1]大泽方百里：宜宾王国的都城。大泽，指耶泚，即金沙江，传承为宜宾。方，读冯，指王国；百里，读毫里，指京城、都城。

Notes:[1] da ze fang bai li (big marsh area 100 li)

Tr: Yibin Kingdom's capital。 daze (big marsh) refers to the Yebi, also known as Jinsha (golden sands) River。 The name's sound Yebi has shifted a little to Yibin。 fang (square, area), reads as von, van, meaning kingdom。Baili (100 li), reads as boli, meaning Poli, capital city。Poli/boli not distinguished in ancient times。

[2] 群鸟所生及所解：许多僚族的发源地和出发地。

[2] qun niao suo sheng ji suo jie (group birds thus live thus scatter)

Tr: this is the homeland of many Lao/Liao tribes, and from here they set off to other places。

[3] 雁门北：指盐门南面。北，在此指南。盐门，今称自贡，贡也指门。

[3] yan men bei (goose gate north)

Tr: the south side of Yanmen (salt gate) 。 bei(north) means nan(south) in Pu concept。 Yanmen (salt gate) is known today as Zigong(self-tribute) 。 gong(tribute), also means gate。

译文：宜宾王国的都城，是许多僚族的发源地和出发地。在盐门的南面。

Translation:

The capital city of Yibin Kingdom is the homeland of many Lao tribes, who also set off from here to other places。It is located to the south of Yanmen。

11-03 雁门山
Yanmen Mountain
（104,77817E；29,33939N）

雁门山[1]，雁出其间[2]。在高柳北[3] 。

注释：[1]雁门山：指盐门所，今称自贡。
Notes： [1] yan men shan (goose gate mount) 。
Tr: refers to Yanmen Suo, salt gate, known today as Zigong city in Sichuan province。
[2] 雁出其间：盐出产于这里。
[2] yan chu qi jian (goose fly out here)
Tr: salt is harvested here。
[3] 在高柳北：高柳，指里江、内江，今称内江。北，指南。
[3] zai gao liu bei (at high willow north)
Tr: gao liu (high willow) refers to Lijiang (inner river), Neijiang (in river), today's Neijiang River。 bei(north) means nan(south) in Pu concept。

译文：盐门所，盐出产于这里。在内江的南面。
Translation:
This is Yanmen Suo, a place where salt is produced。 It is located to the south of Neijiang River。

11-04 高柳
Gaoliu
（105,06611E；29,58642N）

高柳[1]在代北[2]。

注释：[1]高柳：指内江，原读音果僚，谐音高柳。
Notes： [1] gao liu (high willow)
Tr: refers to Neijiang, originally reads as guoliao, a close phonetic match to Gaoliu。
[2] 代北：代，指堵，意为平川，又称资，今称资阳。北，指南。
[2] dai bei (replace north)
Tr: dai(block), means flat land, also known as zi, today's Ziyang city, Sichuan province。bei(north) meaning nan(south)。

译文：内江在资阳的南面。
Translation:
Neijiang is located to the south of Ziyang。

11-05 后稷之葬
Hou-yi-zhi-zang
（104,65164E；30,12192N）

后稷之葬[1]，山水环之[2]。在氐国西[3] 。

注释：[1]后稷之葬：后稷，指候接，四川资阳的古称谓。之葬，指平坦的疆域，也称资疆。
Notes: [1] hou ji zhi zang (houji 's burial)

Tr: hou ji: meaning hou jie (prince receive), an ancient name for Ziyang in Sichuan。Zhi zang, (its burial) means flat land area, also called Zijiang (zi's area) 。

[2] 山水环之：指龙泉山和沱江环绕着。

[2] shan shui huan zhi (mount water surround it)

Tr: loongquan (dragon spring) mount and Tuojiang River surround it。

[3] 氐国：指堵国，今丹山镇，在资阳的东面，在此以丹国解读。

[3] di guo: refers to Du Guo, today's Danshan (red mount) township, which is located to the east of Ziyang。 Here Danshan is known as Dan country。

译文：候接资疆这个山水环绕美丽的地方，在丹国的西面。

Translation:

Houjiezijiang, a beautiful place surrounded by mountains and rivers, is located to the west of Dan country。

11-06 流黄酆氏国

Liu-huang feng-shi-guo

（103,83415E；30,04234N）

流黄酆氏之国[1]，中方三百里[2]；有涂四方[3]，中有山[4]。在后稷葬西。

注释：[1]流黄酆氏国：指眉山堡氏族之国。

Notes:[1] liu huang feng shi guo (flow yellow feng shi country)

Tr: refers to the Meishanbao (eyebrows mount castle) country。

[2] 中方三百里：是眉部落王国的都城。

[2] zhong fang san bai li (center square 300 li)

Tr: is the capital city of the Mei tribal kingdom。

[3] 有涂四方：有四个管理区。分别为彭山、仁寿、青神、丹棱。

[3] you tu si fang (has mires four place)

Tr: has four management districts, the Pengshan area, the Renshou area, the Qingshen area and the Danling area。

[4] 中有山：并设有治所。

[4] zhong you shan (among it mount)

Tr: also, with the center of management。

译文：眉山堡氏族之国，是眉部落王国的都城；有四个管理区，并设有治所,在候接资疆的西面。

Translation:

Meishanbao tribal Kingdom is where the tribal capital is located。 It has four management districts。 It also has a management center。 It is located to the west of Houjiezijiang。

11-07 流沙

Liusha

（103,51536E；30,58678N）

流沙[1]出钟山[2]，西行又南行昆仑之墟[3]，西南入海，黑水之山[4]。

注释：[1]流沙：读 lao xie，音译为流沙、流斜、斜江，指长河，在今四川崇州市大邑县。

Notes:[1] liu sha (flow sands)

Tr: reads as Lao xie, phonetically rendered in Chinese as Liusha, Liuxie, Xiejiang, which means Long River, in today's Dayi County, Chongzhou city, Sichuan province。

[2] 钟山：指雾钟山，简称钟山，今称雾中山。
[2] zhong shan (bell mount)
Tr: refers to Wuzhong (misty bell) Mountain, shortened to Zhongshan, today known as Wuzhong (mist in) Mountain, a mountain in the mist。

[3] 昆仑之墟：指正山口。正山，读音 k'o lu，谐音昆仑。实际向东南。
[3] kun lun zhi xu (kun lun's shallow)
Tr: refers to Zhengshankou (centered mount gap) zhengshan: reads as K'o lu, a close phonetic match to Kunlun。 It is in fact to the southeast direction。

[4] 西南入海，黑水之山：转向东南流入大海， 是长江的水源之一。
[4] xi nan ru hai (west south enter sea), hei shui zhi shan (black water 's mount)
Tr: it turns southeast and empty into sea。 It is one of the headwaters of the Yangtze River。

译文：斜江发源于雾中山，东行又南行至正山口，又转向东南流入大海，是长江的水源之一。
Translation:
Xiejiang rises from Wuzhong Mountain。It flows east and then turns south up to Zhengshankou。 It then turns southeast to empty into the sea。 It is one of the headwaters of the Yangtze River。

11-08 东胡
Donghu
(103,5637E；30,90664N)

东胡[1]在大泽东[2]。

注释：[1]东胡：读朵胡，指丈人山，今称青城山。山边的江称为朵江，音译为都江。
Notes: [1] dong hu reads as duo hu, refers to the Zhangren Mountain, known today as the Qingcheng (green city) Mountain。 The river flowing by the mountain is Duo Jiang, phonetically rendered into Dujiang River。

[2] 大泽：指青城后山的泰安镇，今称水磨古镇。
[2] da ze (big marsh)
Tr: refers to the Tai'an township at the Qingchenghou Mountain。The township is known today as the Shuimoguzhen (watermill old town) 。

译文：丈人山在泰安镇的东面。
Translation:
Zhangren Mountain is situated to the east of the Tai'an township。

11-09 夷人
Yiren
（103,58493E；31,47751N）

夷人[1]在东胡东。

注释：[1]夷人：读溢惹，指河边的集镇，今称汶川。实际在丈人山的东北面。
Notes: [1] yi ren: reads as Yire, refers to the townships along the river, it is known today as Wenchuan。 It is in fact located to the northeast of Zhangren Mountain。

译文：汶川在丈人山的东面。
Translation:

Wenchuan is located to the east of Zhangren Mountain。

11-10 貊国
Mo Guo
（103,85393E；31,68597N）

貊国[1]在汉水[2]东北。地近于燕[3]，灭之 [4] 。

注释：[1]貊国：指茂国，今四川省茂县。
Notes: [1]mo guo: refers to Mao Guo, today's Mao County in Sichuan Province。
[2] 汉水：指夏水，读音则柯淖，今称扎谷脑，同时是汶川镇的别称。
[2] han shui (xia river)
Tr: refers to Xia River, pronounced as Zekenao, known today as Zhagunao, another name for the township of Wenchuan。
[3] 地近于燕：在礼数乡，今称凤仪镇。地，指在。
[3] di jin yu yan (place close to Yan)
Tr: in Lishuxiang, known today as Fengyizhen。Di: location。
[4] 灭之：指坪台，今称坪头寨。
[4] mie zhi (destroy it)
Tr: refers to Pingtai, known today as Pingtouzhai village。

译文：茂国在夏水东北，在礼数乡坪头寨。
Translation:
Mao Guo is located to the northeast of Xiashui River， which is today's Pingtouzhai village, Lishuxiang。

11-11 孟鸟
Meng Niao
（103,6008E；32,64751N）

孟鸟[1]在貊国东北。其鸟文赤、黄、青，东乡[2]。

注释：[1]孟鸟：指岷江源，今四川省松潘县。实际在茂县北面。
Notes： [1] meng niao: refers to the headwaters of Minjiang River, today's Songpan county, in Sichuan province, in fact, to the north of Mao County。
[2] 其鸟文赤、黄、青东乡：河源由羊洞河、川主河、曲其格曲汇成。鸟文，指河源；东乡，指汇在一起，是倒装句。
[2] qi niao wen chi, huang、 qing dong xiang (its bird marking red, yellow, green east village)
Tr: River's headwaters are Yangdonghe River, Chuanzhu River, Quqigequ River。 niaowen (bird marking) meaning source water。 dongxiang (east village) means join。 This sentence is in a reversed word order than the Chinese style。

译文：岷江源在茂国的北面。河源由羊洞河、川主河、曲其格曲汇成。
Translation:
Minjiangyuan is to the north of Mao country。Its headwaters are Yangdonghe River, Chuanzhuhe River and Quqigequ River joining in。

11-12 海内昆仑墟

Hai-nei-kun-lun-xu
（93,5533E；35,71969N）

海内昆仑墟[1]，在西北，帝之下都[2]，昆仑之墟，方八百里，高万仞。上有木禾[3]，长五寻 [4]，大五围 [5] 。面有九井，以玉为槛 [6] 。面有九门 [7]，门有开明兽守之 [8]，百神所在 [9] 。在八隅之岩 [10]，赤水之际 [11]，非仁羿莫能上冈之岩[12]。

注释：[1]昆仑墟：指昆仑山口。海内，指比海外远的地方，实际指海外。
Notes: [1] kun lun xu: refers to Kunlunshankou, （mouth of Kunlun Mountain）。Hainei (sea within): actually, refers to localities further removed from the proper China, in this contact, it is even further than Haiwai (beyond sea), hai has two meanings, water body as sea and ocean, or landmass areas which is not a body of water。

[2] 西北帝之下都：唐古拉山的东麓。西北帝，读曦鳖抵，指彤老剌，即唐古拉。
[2] xi bei di zhi xia du (west north di's lower capital)
Tr: the east side of Tanggula Mountains。Xibeidi: reads as xibidi, refers to Tonglaola, another phonetic rendering of Tanggula。

[3] 上有木禾：那里有扎曲。扎曲，古称木禾河。
[3] shang you mu he (up has wood plant)
Tr: there is the Zhaqu River, its ancient name is Muhe River。

[4] 长五寻：楚玛须河。五，读梅音，与玛谐音。
[4] chang wu xun (long as five xun)
Tr: refers to the Machu River。Wu (five) reads as may, a close phonetic match to Ma。

[5] 大五围：达玛维河，今称通天河。
[5] da wu wei (big five wei)
Tr: the Damawei River, known today as the Tongtian (reach sky) River。

[6] 面有九井，以玉为槛：山上有无数的源泉，是由冰融化而成。
[6] mian you jiu jing (face has nine wells), yi yu wei lan(jade as rails and handles)
Tr: there are countless springs on the mountains, from the melting ice。

[7] 面有九门：上面有许多通道。
[7] mian you jiu men (face has nine gates)
Tr: there are many passageways。

[8] 有开明兽守之：有丝绸族通过。这里的丝绸族是指丝绸贩运氏族。
[8] you kai ming shou shou zhi (has open bright beasts guard it)
Tr: silk tribes go through here; silk tribes refer to the tribes engaged in trade and transportation of silk products。

[9] 百神所在：到达巴斯蜀纪。
[9] bai shen suo zai (hundred deities are here)
Tr: travelling to Basishuji。

[10] 赤水之纪：且舍的部落。
[10] chi shui zhi ji (red water this record)
Tr: The Qieshe tribes。

[11] 非仁羿莫能上冈之岩：从事织绸的能沽之乡。非仁，指专门；羿莫，指织绸；能冈，指能沽洛略；岩，指乡。
[11] fei ren yi mo neng shang gang zhi yan (not virtue yi not can up cliff 's rock)
Tr: refers to the Nenggu area that is engaged in silk production。 Feiren: specialize; yimo: weaving silk; nenggang: nengguluolui; yan: locale, xiang: township。

译文：海外昆仑山口，在唐古拉山东麓，属昆仑山脉的东部，方圆八百里，高万仞。那里有木禾河、楚玛须河、达玛维河。上面有无数的源泉，是由冰融化而成。上面有许多通道，有丝绸(贩运)族从那里通过，到达巴斯蜀纪、且舍部落和专门从事织绸的能沽之乡。
Translation:
Haiwai Kunlunshankou is located to the east side of the Tanggula Mountains, an east stretch of the Kunlun Mountains。 It commands 800 li wide and stands as high as ten thousand ren。 There are Muhe River, Chumaxu River, Damawei River。 There are countless springs bubbling out as a result of the melting ice。 There are many passageways。The Silk trade tribes go through there to reach Basi-shuji, Qieshe tribes, and the Nenggu township which specializes in silk production。

11-13 赤水
Chishui
（97,38499E； 32,82766N~104,63339E； 28,76544N）

赤水[1]出东南隅[2]，以行其东北[3]，西南流入南海[4]，在厌火东[5]。

注释：[1]赤水：指金沙江，原读音澈澈那液，简称赤水。
Notes: [1] chi shui (red water)
Tr: refers to the Jinsha (gold sands) River。 Original language reads as Cheche-naye, shortened to Chishui (red water), or the Chishui River。
[2] 东南隅：昆仑墟的东南隅。
[2] dong nan yu (east south corner)
Tr: Kunlun Xu's southeast corner。
[3] 以行其东北：指至凤足河转向东北流。以行其，指凤足河，今称鸡足河或枯木河。
[3] yi xing qi dong bei (thus goes its northeast)
Tr: travels to Fengzu (phoenix foot) River and then turns to flow northeast。 yixingqi: Fengzu River, known today as the Jizu (chicken feet) River, or the Kumu (dead wood) River。
[4] 西南流入南海：指又转向东南流入大海，这里的"南海"是指大海。
[4] xi nan liu ru nan hai (southwest flows into South Sea)
Tr: turns to southeast into the sea。The so-called Nanhai (south sea) refers to the big sea。
[4] 在厌火东：指乐和国东面。
[4] zai yan huo dong (at yan fire east)
Tr: east of Lehe country。

译文：金沙江发源于昆仑山的东南隅，流至凤足河转向东北流去，又转向东南流入大海，出海口在乐和国的东面。
Translation:
Jinshajiang River rises from the southeast of the Kunlun Mountains and flows up to Fengzu River and then turns to flow northeast。It then turns southeast to empty itself into the sea。 The river mouth is at the east of the Lehe country。

11-14 河水
Heshui
（97,77007； 35,0845N~119,25315E； 37,8213N）

河水[1]出东北隅，以行其北，西南又入勃海[2]，又出海外[3]，即西而北，入禹所导积石山[4]。

注释：[1]河水：指黄河。
Notes: he shui: refers to the Yellow River。

[2] 勃海：指红原至诺尔盖地区。
[2]bo hai: refers to the area between Hongyuan and Nuorgai。

[3] 又出海外：指又折返离去。
[3] you chu hai wai (again it goes away beyond)
Tr: then it turns back and flows away。

[4] 禹所导积石山：指大禹疏导的陕西与山西交界的黄河段，即兴门至佳川河段。
[4]yu suo dao jishishan (Yu channeled the pile stone mountain)
Tr: refers to the water project to channel the Yellow River course between Xingmen and Jiachuan along the Shaanxi and Shanxi border line。

译文；黄河发源于昆仑山的东北隅，从北向南进入诺尔盖地区，又折返离去，向西又转向北，再向南进入大禹疏导的河段。（以后再折向东北流入大海。）
Translation:
The Yellow River rises from the northeast corner of the Kunlun Mountains。 It flows from north to south to the Nourgai area, and then turns away towards west and then turns north, and again to south into the area where Yu the great channeled the river course， (afterwards, it goes northeast into the sea) 。

11-15 洋水
Yangshui
（98,0273E；33,39977N~101,80351E；26,60223N）

洋水[1]，黑水[2]出西北隅[3]，以东，东行，又东北，南入海，羽民南[4]。

注释：[1]洋水：指雅砻江。
Notes: [1] yang shui: refers to the Yalong River.

[2] 黑水：指泥曲河，又称兴水河，至雅江县与雅砻江汇合。
[2] hei shui (black water)
Tr: refers to the Niqu (mud twist) River, also known as the Xingshui River。 Xingshui River flows up to Yajiang county to join the Yalong River。

[3] 西北隅：指东南隅，即发源于白鹤山。
[3] xi bei yu (west north corner)
Tr: refers to the southeast corner, where the river rises from the Baihe (white crane) Mountain。

[4] 羽民南：山东沂蒙山及苏北地区，古称沂蒙地区，长江的出海口在沂蒙南。
[4]yu min nan (feather people south)
Tr: refers to Yimeng region in today's Shandong and northern Jiangsu。In ancient times this region is known as Yimeng。The Yangtze River enters the sea south of Yimeng。

译文：雅砻江、泥曲河发源于白鹤山，向东南行，又向东北，从东南面流入大海，从沂蒙地区的南面。
Translation:
Yalong River and Niqu River rise from the Baihe Mountain and flow southeast and then northeast。 The rivers empty into the sea south of Yimeng region, from the southeast。

11-16 弱水
Ruoshui
（100,38916E；33,61452N~103,7666E；29,54499N）

（102,81164E；30,38278N~103,71716E；29,55335N）

弱水[1]、青水[2]，出西南隅[3]，以东，又北，又西南，过毕方东[4]。

注释：[1]弱水：濮语马可河的意译，下游为大渡河，发源于巴颜喀拉山。马可指不旺。
Notes: [1] ruo shui (weak water)
Tr: in Pu concept it refers to the Ma-ke River, its lower reach is the Dadu (big crossing) River, with its source from the Bayan Kara Mountains。Ma-ke means not very strong。

[2] 青水：指青衣江，发源于夹金山脉的四姑娘山。
[2] qing shui (green water)
Tr: refers to the Qingyi (green dress) River, it rises from the Siguniang (four girls) Mountain of the Jiajinshan Range。

[3] 西南隅：指东南隅。
[3] xi nan yu (west south corner)
Tr: it refers to the southeast corner。

[4] 毕方东：指贝濮国的东面，今湖南地区的东面。
[4]bi fang dong (end place east)
Tr: refers to the east side of Beipu country, in today's east part of Hunan province。

译文：大渡河、青衣江发源于昆仑墟的东南面，向东，又向北，又向东南，流向贝濮国的东面。
Translation:
The Dadu River and Qingyi River rise from the southeast of Kunlun Xu。 Then running first east, and then north, and then southeast, the rivers flow past the east part of the Beipu country。

11-17 开明兽
Kaimingshou
（104,0657E；30,6625N）

昆仑南渊深三百仞[1]。开明兽身[2] 大类虎而九首 [3]， 皆人面 [4]， 东向立昆仑上 [5] 。

注释：[1]昆仑南渊深三百仞：昆仑南乡富饶的部落集镇区。
Notes: [1] kun lun nan yuan (kunlun's south cham) shen san bai ren (deep as 300 fathom)
Tr: Prosperous and rich, Kunlun Nanxiang is where tribal townships are located。

[2] 开明兽身：丝绸氏族。早期部落为三星堆大月氏陀尼部落，著名的君长名叫知那那。后期为小月氏开明部落，著名的君长名叫格杰杰。实际上是德阳与成都分治。开明氏族对君长的称呼叫阻摩，谐音纵目，君长塑像也以纵目表达阻摩。
[2] kai ming shou shen (open bright beast body)
Tr: refers to the Silk tribes。In its earlier period, the tribes belonged to the greater Yuezhi's Tuoni tribes from the Sanxingdui (three stars pile) 。 Its most famous chieftain is Zhinana。In its later period, it refers to the less Yuezhi tribes。Its most famous chieftain is Gejiejie。 It is separately managed by Deyang and Chengdu as their centers of administration。Kaiming tribes call their chieftains Zumo, a phonetic matching to Zongmu (vertical eyes), thus the iconic statue of their chieftain with vertical eyes to represent the idiom of the title of Chieftains。

[3] 大类虎而九首：游牧胡的共工氏族。共工国最早建于青海。
[3] da lei hu er jiu shou (big type tiger with nine heads)
Tr: refers to the Gonggong tribes who are the nomadic Hu people。 Gonggong first established their kingdom in Qinghai。

[4] 皆人面：皆织绸。
[4] jie ren mian (all human faces)

Tr: everybody is engaged in weaving silk。

[5] 东向立昆仑上：国家建于昆仑旁边。东向，栋羲，指国家。

[5] dong xiang li kunlun shang (east towards stand kunlun up)

Tr: its kingdom is established close by the Kunlun。Dong xiang: country, state, nation。

译文：昆仑南乡富饶的部落集镇区，是丝绸氏族游牧胡的共工氏族地区，人们皆织绸，这个族群的国家最早建于昆仑旁边。

Translation:

The tribal township district of Kunlun Nanxiang is rich and prosperous。 It is the area where the Gonggong nomadic Hu's silk weaving tribes live。In this area, everybody is engaged in weaving silk。 This tribal group first established their kingdom by the Kunlun Mountains。

11-18 开明西凤凰

Kaimingxi fenghuang

（103,29585E；30,58141N）

开明西有凤凰[1]、鸾鸟[2]，皆戴蛇[3]践蛇[4]，膺有赤蛇[5]。

注释：[1]凤凰：指灌口（今都江堰市）氏族。

Notes:[1] fenghuang (phoenix): refers to Guankou (today's Dujiangyan city) tribes。

[2] 鸾鸟：指西河氏族。

[2] luanniao (west bird) refers to Xihe tribes。Xihe (west river) 。

[3] 戴蛇：指丹巴氏族。

[3] daishe (wear snake) refers to Danba tribes。

[4] 践蛇：指夹金氏族。

[4] jianshe (step on snakes) refers to Jiajin tribes。

[5] 膺有赤蛇：住在且舍地区。

[5] ying you chishe (bosom has red snake) living in the Qieshe area。

译文：丝绸族的西面有灌口氏族，有西河氏族，皆是丹巴氏族和夹金氏族，住在且舍地区。

Translation:

To the west of Sichou (silk) tribes, there are the Guankou tribes and Xihe tribes。 They all belong to the Danba tribes and Jiajin tribes, living in Qieshe area。

11-19 开明北不死树

Kai-ming-bei-bu-si-shu

（97,00952E；32,99993N。100,24337E；34,47287N）

开明北有视肉、珠树、文玉树、玗琪树、不死树[1]。凤凰、鸾鸟皆戴瞂[2]。又有离朱、木禾、柏树、甘水、圣木曼兑[3]，一曰挺木牙交[4]。

注释：[1]视肉、珠树、文玉树、不死树：指玉树地区的集镇扎多、治多、玉树、曲麻莱。

Notes: [1] shirou (gaze meat)； zhushu (pearl tree)； wenyushu (marking jade tree)； busishu (never die tree): refers to the townships of Zhaduo, Zhiduo, Yushu, and Qumalai in the Yushu area。

[2] 凤凰、鸾鸟皆戴瞂：胡族和西部僚皆择水而居。戴瞂，指择水。

[2] feng huang, (phoenix) luan niao jie dai fa (west bird all wear shields)

Tr: The Hu tribes and western Lao tribes all prefer to live by the water。Daifa: prefer water。

[3] 离朱、木禾、柏树、甘水、圣木曼兑：指瑪沁地区的集镇久治、玛沁、班玛树、甘德、玛多。圣木，指面部彩绘的族群，即赭面蒙。
[3] lizhu (leave red); muhe (wood plant); baishu (poplar tree)； ganshui (sweet water); shengmu mandui (holy wood easy mix)
Tr: refers to the townships of Jiuzhi, Maqin, Banmashu, Gande, Maduo。 Shengmu --holy wood refers to the tribes who tattooed their faces with multiple colors, also known as the Zhemianmeng (ochre powder tattoo) 。
[4] 挺木牙交：指万神之城，实际指众多氏族之城。
[4] ting mu ya jiao (support wood teeth crossing)
Tr: refers to the city of Thousand Deities, meaning city of many tribes。

译文：丝绸族的北面有扎多、治多、玉树、曲麻莱集镇。有胡族和西部僚，皆择水而居。又有久治、玛沁、班玛树、甘德和瑪多集镇，又说玛多叫万神之城。
Translation:
To its north, the silk tribes have as neighbors the townships of Zhaduo, Zhiduo, Yushu, Qumalai。 The Hu tribes and western Lao tribes prefer to live by the water。 Also living here are the townships of Jiuzhi, Maqin, Banmashu, Gande and Maduo。The township of Maduo is also known as the city of Ten Thousand deities。

11-20 开明东诸巫夹窫窳之尸
Kai-ming-dong-zhu-wu-jia-yayu-zhi-shi
（106,15332E；33,32827N~106,58548E；29,56908N）

开明东有巫彭、巫抵、巫阳、巫履、巫凡、巫相[1]，夹窫窳之尸[2]，皆操不死药以距之[3]。窫窳者，蛇身人面[4]，贰负臣所杀也[5]。

注释：[1]巫彭、巫抵、巫阳、巫履、巫凡、巫相：指嘉陵江边的彭部落（今彭城镇）、氐部落（今略阳县）、阳部落（今阳平关镇）、苍溪部落（今阆中）、果部落（今南充）、汇部落（今合川）。
Notes: [1] wupeng (shaman peng); wudi (shaman di)； wuyang (shaman yang)； wu lu(shaman lu);wufan(shaman fan)； wuxiang(shaman xiang):
Tr: refers to the tribes that live along the Jialing River: Peng tribe: today's Pengcheng Township, Di tribes: today's Lueyang county, Yang tribes: today's Yangpingguan township, Cangxi tribes: today's Liangzhong, Guo tribes: today's Nanchong city, Hui tribes: today's Hechuan city。
[2] 夹窫窳之尸：借助大河的便利。这里的大河是指嘉陵江。
[2] jia yayu zhi shi (carry Yayu's corpse)
Tr: take advantage of the great river's water way。The big river is the Jialing River。
[3] 皆操不死之药以距：皆建埠肆之要津以盘踞。
[3] jie cao busi zhiyao yi ju (all use never die recipe to distance)
Tr: all set up high ground strongholds at strategic points。
[4] 窫窳者，蛇身人面：大河支系的氏族，都是种植氏族的居民。蛇，在此作种植解。
[4] yayu zhe (so-called Yayu), she shen ren mian (snake body human face)
Tr: the tribes of the Dahe (big river) branch, all of them are planters' tribal residents。 Snake is a coded shorthand for planting。
[5] 贰负臣所杀也：这里指能沽国之外的氏族，有蚌氏、有月氏、也有僚族。也，指夷。
[5]er fu chen suo sha ye (two negative officials kill thus)
Tr: refers to the Nenggu country's neighbouring tribes, such as the Bang Shi, the Yueshi, as well as the Lao /Liao Shi, the Chinese sign ye, a phonetic match for Yi, meaning people。

译文：丝绸氏族区域的东面有彭部落、氐部落、阳部落、苍溪部落、果部落、汇部落僚族部落，借助大河的便利，皆建埠肆之要津以盘踞。大河支系的氏族，都是种植氏族的居民，是能沽国之外的氏族。
Translation:
To its east, the Silk tribes' region has as neighbors the various tribes such as: the Peng, the Di, the Yang, the Cangxi, the Guo, the Hui of the Lao/Liao 。Taking advantages of the big river's water course, the tribes set up strongholds at higher ground's strategic points。 The tribes of the Dahe branch are all the residents of the planting tribes, they are not part of the Nenggu country。

11-21 服常树上三头人
Fu chang shu shang san tou ren
（109,46401E；31,01876N）

服常树[1]，其上有三头人[2]，伺琅玕树[3]。

注释：[1]服常树：指奉节部落氏族地区。服，指复堡，常指查，即部落。
Notes: [1] fu chang shu (dress constant tree)
Tr: refers to the area of the Fengjie tribes。 Fu: fubao, chang: cha, meaning tribes。
[2] 三头人：奢投惹，指凤坪镇。苗族人称坪、平为 da，音译为投。
[2] san tou ren (three heads man)
Tr: reads as she-tou-re, refers to Fengping township。In the Miao language, ping is read as da， transliterated as tou(throw), a phonetic rendering into Chinese。
[3] 伺琅玕树：夏国苗族。伺琅，指姒那，即夏国；玕树，指嘎属，即苗族。
[3]si lang gan shu (cares for Langgan tree) refers to the Miao tribes of the Xia Nation。 Silang: reads as sina/Xia nation; ganshu: gashu, Miao tribes。

译文：复堡部落氏族地区，那里有个集镇叫凤坪镇，那里的氏族是夏国的苗族。
Translation:
In the area of the Fubao tribes, there is a township called Fengping Zhen, where the Miao tribes of the Xia State live。

11-22 开明南树鸟
Kaimingna Shuniao
(104,64231E；28,75833N)

开明南有树鸟[1]，六首[2]；蛟[3]、蝮[4]、蛇[5]、蜼[6]、豹[7]、鸟秩树[8]，于表池树木[9]，诵鸟[10]，鶽视肉[11]。

注释：[1]树鸟：树，指九，树鸟指九僚。
[1] Shuniao (tree bird): tree: shu, means nine, tree bird (Shuniao) refers to Jiu Lao。
[2] 六首：读洛苏，指城者。
[2] liu shou (six heads) reads as luosu, meaning chengzhe (township)。
[3]蛟：指邛崃。
[3] jiao (big snake) refers to qionglai, a place name。
[4]蝮：指濮江，今蒲江县。
[4] fu(snake) refers to Pujiang, today's Pujiang county。
[5]蛇：指青神，今青神县。
[5] she (snake) refers to Qingshen (green god), today's Qingshen county。

[6]雔：指惹擞，今仁寿县。
[6] zhui: refers to Resou, today's Renshou county。
[7]豹：指宝飞，意为山间盆地。
[7] bao(puma) refer to Baofei, meaning basins surrounded by mountains。
[8] 鸟秩树：指迎接树，今资阳市。
[8] niao zhi shu (bird order tree) refers to Yingjieshu (welcome tree) today's Ziyang city。
[9] 于表池树木：宜宾运输城。
[9]yu biaochi shu mu (at surface pond plant tree); refers to Yibin transportation city。
[10] 诵鸟：读索诺，指起雾城，今泸州市。
[10] song niao (reciting bird) reads as suonuo, refers to misty city(qiwucheng), today's Luzhou city。
[11] 鶽视肉：指叙肆惹，今叙永县。
[11] zhui shirou (eagle watch meat) refers to Xusire, today's Xuyong County。

译文：丝绸族的南面有九僚城者(城镇)：有邛崃、濮江、青神、惹擞、宝飞、迎接树、宜宾运输城、起雾城、叙肆惹。
Translation:
To the south of the silk tribes, there are nine cities by the Pulao: they are Qionglai, Pujiang, Qingshen, Resou, Baofei, Yingjieshu, Yibin transportation city, Qiwucheng city and Xusire。

第十二卷海内北经(Hainei Region: the North)

Book 12 Haineibeijing

12-01 蛇巫山上操杯人
shewushan-shang-caobeiren
（35,47232E；28,72305N）

海内西北陬以东者。

蛇巫之山[1]，上有人[2]操柸而东向立[3]。一曰龟山[4] 。

注释：[1]蛇巫山：指塞利部落山，在土尔其开塞利地区。
Notes： [1] she wu shan (snake witch mount)
Tr: refers to the Saili (Seri) tribe mountain, in today's Kayseri city, the seat of Kayseri province, in Central Anatolia, Turkey。

[2] 上有人：那里有个集镇，指开塞利城。
[2] shang you ren (up there has human)
Tr: there is a township, the Kayseri town。

[3] 操柸而东向立：是游牧部落建立的国家。操柸，读撮邦，指游牧部落；东向，读栋羲，指国家。
[3] cao bei er dong xiang li (holding cup face east stand)

Tr: a country set up by nomadic tribes。 caobei (holding cup) reads cuobang, refers to the nomadic tribe, dongxiang (east facing) reads as Dongxi, meaning country or nation。

[4] 龟山：指开塞利山。

[4] gui shan (turtle mount) refers to the Kayseri Mountain。

译文：从海外西北角记述到东北角。

开塞利部落山，那里有一个集镇，是游牧部落建立的国家。又说叫开塞利山。

Translation:

The description starts from the northwest corner to the northeast corner in the area known as Haiwai。There is a township where the Kayseri tribes gather, a country established by the nomadic tribes。 The tribal country is also called Kayseri Mountain。

12-02 西王母

Xiwangmu

（37,01041E；39,74841N）

西王母[1]梯几而戴胜杖[2]。其南[3] 有三青鸟 [4]，为西王母取食 [5]，在昆仑墟 [6]北。

注释：[1]西王母：这里的西王母指锡瓦斯高原，在土尔其中部。

Notes:[1] xi wang mu (west queen mother)

Tr: west queen mother is a coded term for Sivas's plateau in the middle of Turkey。

[2] 梯几而戴胜杖：万际的储水疆域。梯几，指万际的、宽广的；戴，读德，指水；胜，指储。

[2] ti ji er dai sheng zhang (stairs and wear victory stick)

Tr: immense capacity of water supply region。Tiji: broad, wide, Dai reads as de， meaning water, sheng(victory) meaning capacity of water supply。

[3] 其南：作那里解，不作南解。

[3] qi nan (its south) refers to out there, not referring in the south。nan: na, there, a place。Na， nan, close phonetic matching, but different in meaning。

[4] 三青鸟：指幼发拉底河、底格里斯河、克孜勒河三条河流。

[4] san qing niao (three green birds) referring to the Euphrates River, the Tigris River and the Kizilirmak， (Kizilir River) 。

[5] 取食：指起始、发源于。

[5] qu shi (get food) meaning, the rivers rise, originate。

[6] 昆仑墟：这里的昆仑墟指开塞利山。

[6] kunlun xu (kunlun mount) refers to the Kayseri Mountain。

译文：锡瓦斯高原是很宽广的储水疆域。那里有幼发拉底河、底格里斯河、克孜勒河三条河流发源于锡瓦斯高原，在开塞利山的北面。

Translation:

Sivas Plateau is a vast and broad region with a great capacity for water supply。The Euphrates, the Tigris and Kizilirmak all rise from the Plateau which stands to the north of the Kayseri Mountain。

12-03 大行伯

Daxingbo

（51,38327E；35,69136N）

有人曰大行伯[1]，把戈[2]，其东有犬封国[3]。贰负之尸[4] 在大行伯东。

注释：[1]大行伯：指德黑兰，在今伊朗境内。
Notes:[1] da xing bo (big walking lord) refers to Tehran in Iran。
[2] 把戈：读博贾歌，指都城。
[2]ba ge (holding weapon) reads as Bojiage(bogage)meaning capital city。
[3] 犬封国：指班迪突厥斯坦山国。
[3] quan feng guo (dog von country) refers to the Bandi Turkistan Mountain Country。
[4] 贰负之尸：指阿富汗之肆。
[4]er fu zhi shi (two carry corpses) refers to townships in Afghanistan。

译文：有个集镇叫德黑兰，是都城，它的东面有班迪突厥斯坦山国。阿富汗的集肆也在德黑兰的东面。
Translation:
There is a township called Tehran, the capital city。To its east stands the Bandi-Turkistan Mountain country。 The townships in Afghanistan too lie to the east of Tehran。

12-04 犬封国
Quanfeng Guo
（63,13295E；34,98691N）

犬封国[1]曰犬戎国，状如犬。有一女子[2]，方跪进杯食 [3] 。有文马 [4] ，缟身朱鬣 [5] ，目若黄金，名曰吉量 [6] ，乘之寿千岁 [7] 。

注释：[1]犬封国：指班迪突厥斯坦山国。
Notes: [1] quan feng guo (dog von country) refers to the Bandi Turkistan Mountain Country。
[2] 女子：指瑙孜堡。
[2] nv zi (a female) refers to the Naozibao: today is known as Qala-e-Naw in Afghanistan。
[3] 方跪进杯食：统治着北边部落的氏族。方，读冯，指统治；跪，指北边；进杯，读纪邦，指部落。
[3] fang gui jin bei shi (kneel eat cup food)
Tr; rule the northern tribes。fang (von, rule, ruler)， gui(kneel) refers to northern part, jinbai (in cup) reads as jibang， refers to tribes。
[4] 文马：指大宛马。
[4] wen ma (markings horse) refers to the Dayuan Horse, also known as the Ferghana horse。
[5] 缟身朱鬣：白身红鬃。
[5] gao shen zhu lie (white body red mane)
Tr: white horse with red mane。
[6] 吉量：指汗血。
[6] ji liang (lucky measure) refers to sweat blood, refers to the horse。
[7] 乘之寿千岁：乘着它可以日行千里。寿，指通过、行进。
[7] cheng zhi shou qian sui (ride it lives up to 1000 years)
Tr: riding the horse for a thousand li a day。 shou (long life) meaning cover or ride for the distance。

译文：犬封国又叫犬戎国，是犬戎族的国家。那里有一个集镇叫瑙孜堡，统治着北面的部落氏族。那里有宛马，白身红鬃，目若黄金，名叫汗血马，乘着它可以日行千里。
Translation:
Quanfeng Guo is also known as Quanrong Guo, (dog rong country) 。There is a township called Qala-e- Naw, which controls the tribes in the north。 The north is the land of Ferghana horses, with white bodies and red

manes, eyes like shining gold。It is called Hanxue Ma (sweat blood horse) 。This horse can carry you to travel one thousand li a day。

12-05 鬼国
Gui Guo
（58,39784E；37,93698N）

鬼国[1]在贰负之尸北，为物人面而一目[2]。一曰贰负神在其东，为物人面蛇身[3]。

注释：[1]鬼国：指北国，即土库曼斯坦。
Notes [1] gui guo (ghost country) refers to Bei Guo --Northern country: Turkmenistan 。
[2] 为物人面而一目：国家的管理集镇叫雅什哈巴顿检目。为物原是指部落，在此指国。
[2] wei wu ren mian er yi mu (as stuff human face with one eye)
Tr: this country's administration center is at a township Jianmu called Yashihabadon。 Wei wu (as stuff) previously refers to tribe, now refers to country。
[3] 蛇身：谢拉赫斯。
[3] she shen (snake body) refers to the city of Serakhs (Sarakhs, Saraxs) 。

译文：北国在阿富汗之肆的北面，国家的管理集镇叫雅什哈巴顿检目。又说阿富汗氏族在它的东面，北国定部落集镇在谢拉赫斯。
Translation：
Bei Guo is to the north of Afghanistan's townships。The country's administration center is in the town of Yashihabadun Jianmu。 It is also said that Afghanistan tribes are located to its east。 The Bei Guo makes the township of Serakhs its tribal country's capital。

12-06 蜪犬
Taoquan
（68,7855E；38,56267N）

蜪犬[1]如犬，青[2]，食人从首始[3]。

注释：[1]蜪犬：指塔吉克犬戎。
Notes: [1] tao quan (baby grasshopper worm dog) refers to Tajik Dog rong。 tao/tajik, close phonetic match。
[2]青：指多数民族。
[2] qing (green) refers to the majority ethnic groups。
[3] 食人从首始：古老的草原塞族。食人，指古老的；从，指草原；首始，指塞族。
[3] shi ren cong shou shi (eat human start from head)
Tr: the ancient steppe Saka people。 shiren (eat human) meaning ancient。cong (from) means steppe or grassland, shoushi (head start) refers to the Saka people。

译文：塔吉克犬戎，是犬戎的多数民族，是古老的草原塞族。
Translation:
The Tajik Dog Rong people are the majority group of the Quanrong (dog rong) 。 They are the ancient steppe Saka people。

12-07 穷奇
Qiongqi

（75,29527E；42,85091N）

穷奇[1]，状如虎，有翼[2]，食人从首始。所食被发[3] 。在蜪犬北。

注释：[1]穷奇：指乔犬，即高大的犬戎，又称吉尔吉斯犬戎。
Notes:[1] qiong qi (poor strange) refers to the Qiao Quan (big dog or huge wolf) meaning the Quanrong (dog rong) people who are famous for being tall and strong。 They are also known as the Kyrgyz Quan Rong。

[2]虎，有翼：游牧族的支系。
[2]hu, you yi (tiger, with wings)
Tr: the branches of the nomadic tribes。

[3] 所食被发：圣城在比什河畔，这里指中心城托克马克。发，指岩，这里指河畔。
[3] suo shi bei fa (its food cover hair)
Tr: The holy city is on the bank of the Bish River。The center city is Tokamak。 fa(hair) means Rock, here it refers to riverbank。

译文：穷奇是游牧族的支系，是古老的草原塞族，圣城在比什河畔，在塔吉克犬戎的北面。
Translation:
Qiongqi is a branch of the nomadic tribes, the ancient steppe Saka people。 The holy city is on the bank of Bish River, to the north of Tajik Dog Rong tribes。

12-08 帝尧台
Diyaotai
（81,32178E；43,9188N）

帝尧台[1]、帝喾台[2]、帝丹朱台[3]、帝舜台[4]，各二台[5]，台四方[6]，在昆仑[7]东北。

注释：[1]帝尧台：指北幼水地区，今称伊犁河地区。台，指区域。帝，指北部。
Notes:[1] di yao tai (God Yao's terrace) refers to the Beiyoushui (north young water) area, in today's Ili River basin。 tai(terrace) means region, area。Di: north。

[2] 帝喾台：指塔尔迪库尔干地区。
[2] di ku tai (God Ku's terrace) refers to the area of Tardi Kurgan (Талдықорған, Taldykurgan (Kazakh: Талдықорған, romanized: Taldyqorǵan, Taldıqorğan), known as Taldy-Kurgan。

[3] 帝丹朱台：指奎屯诸区。
[3] di danzhu tai (God Danzhu's terrace) refers to the various townships in Kuitun area。

[4] 帝舜台：指乌孙地区，今称塔城。
[4] di shun tai (God Shun's terrace) refers to the Wusun area, known today as Tacheng, Xinjiang。

[5] 各二台：指江布尔地区。
[5]ge er tai (each two terrace) refers to the Jiangbuer region (Jambyl Region (Kazakh: Жамбыл облысы, romanized: Jambyl oblysy, جامبىل وبلىسى) is a region of Kazakhstan。 Its capital is Taraz。)

[6] 台四方：指博乐地区。四方，读 bo lo。
[6] tai si fang (terrace four area) refers to the Bole region。si fang reads as bo lo (蒙古语：ᠪᠣᠷᠣᠲᠠᠯ᠎ᠠ ᠬᠣᠲᠠ，中蒙胡都木文转写：Borotal_ɑ xota；托忒蒙古语：ᠪᠣᠷᠣᠲᠠᠯᠠ ᠬᠣᠲᠣ，中蒙托忒文转写：Borotala xoto，中蒙通用转写：Ḃórótala ẋótó；维吾尔语：بۆرتالا，拉丁维文：Börtala）

[7] 昆仑：指南天山。
[7] kunlun: refers to the South Tianshan, or the Nantianshan Mountain。

译文：北幼水地区、迪库尔干、奎屯诸区、乌孙地区、江布尔、博乐地区，在南天山的东北面。

Translation:
The following regions and places are located to the northeast side of South Tianshan Mountains: the Beiyoushui, Taldykurgan, Kuitun, Wusun, Jambyl and Bolo。

12-09 大蜂
Dafeng
（88,33243E；43,80208N）

大蜂[1]，其状如螽[2]。朱蛾[3]，其状如蛾 [4] 。

注释：[1]大蜂：指博格达山。蜂，是山"冯"的谐音。
Notes: [1] da feng (big hornet) refers to the Bogeda Mountain。 Feng （hornet）a phonetic match to feng (von, in German) which means mountain。
[2]螽：指钟山，即天山。
[2] zhong(worms) phonetic match to zhong(bell) means Tianshan, the sky mountain。
[3] 朱蛾：指准葛尔。
[3] zhu e (red moth) zhu/dzun, a phonetic match, means Dzungar。
[4]蛾：指盆地。
[4]e (moth) means basin。

译文：博格达山，实际就是天山；准葛尔，实际就是盆地。
Translation:
Bogeda Mountain in fact means Tianshan, Dzungar means basin。

12-10 蟜
Qiao
（81,87128E；41,79658N）

蟜[1]，其为人虎文[2]，胫有晵[3]。在穷奇东。一曰状如人[4]，昆仑墟北所有[5]。

注释：[1]蟜：读桥音，指拜部落，在今拜城至库车一带。
Notes:[1] qiao （insect）: refers to the Bai tribe, in today's area between Baicheng and Kuche, Xinjiang。
[2] 其为人虎文：定都于弱水。虎文，原读音伊马克，指弱水，是木扎尔河的支流。
[2] qi wei ren hu wen（as person have tiger marks)
Tr: have their capital on the Ruoshui River。 Huwen reads as Yimak, referring to Ruoshui, a tributary of Muzhar River。
[3] 胫有晵：国名叫有拜。
[3] jing you qi (leg has calf)
Tr: the name of the nation is Youbai。
[4]人：指惹氏。一个擅长于制造兵器的氏族。
[4] ren(person) refers to the Re Shi, a tribe famous for producing weapons。
[5] 昆仑墟北所有：南天山东北面的氏族。
[5] kun lun xu bei suo you (kunlunxu north all have)
Tr: the tribes on the northeast side of the Nantianshan Mountains。

译文：拜氏族，定都于弱水，国名叫有拜。在穷奇的东面。又说是惹氏族，是南天山东北面的氏族。
Translation:

The Bai tribe, with their capital at Ruoshui River, is called Youbai Guo。 It is located to the east of Qiongqi。 It is also said that the tribe is Re tribe, living on the northeast side of the Nantianshan Mountain。

12-11 闒非
Tafei
（89,18513E；42,95152N）

闒非[1]，人面而兽身[2]，青色[3]。

注释：[1]闒非：指吐鲁番氏族。
Notes： [1] ta fei: refers to the Tulufan (Turpan) tribe。
[2] 人面而兽身：定居的氏族。
[2] ren mian er shou shen (human face with beast body)
Tr: the settled tribes, the sedentary settlers of tribes。
[3] 青色：指祁善氏，又称鄯善氏。
[3] qing se (green color) refers to the Qishan Shi, also known as the Shanshan Shi。

译文：吐鲁番氏族，是定居的氏族，是祁善氏。
Translation:
The Turpan tribes are settled down people, known also as the Qishan Shi。

12-12 据比尸
Jubishi
（106,28752E；36,00786N）

据比之尸[1]，其为人折颈被发[2]，无一手[3]。

注释：[1]据比尸：清水河肆，今称固原。据比，读泾泚，指清水河。
Notes: [1] ju bi shi: refers to Qingshui River township, today it is known as Guyuan city in Ningxia province。Jubi: reads as jingbi, refers to the Qingshui (clear water) River。
[2] 其为人折颈被发：座落于清水河畔。其为人，指设定集镇、坐落；折，指在；颈被，指泾泚；发，指岩、岸、河畔。
[2] qi wei ren zhe jing pei fa (as person breakneck, cover hair)
Tr: it is situated on the bank of Qingshui River。 Qi wei ren: refers to deciding the location of township。 zhe (break) means at, jingbei (neck cover) refers to the river Clearwater, a phonetic match to jingbi。 fa(hair) refers to rock, bank, riverside。
[3] 无一手：指裕固族的部落。无，指部落；一手，指裕固属。
[3] wu yi shou (no one hand) refers to the tribes of Yugu ethnic people。 wu(no) means tribe, yishou(one hand) a phonetic match to Yugu Shu， shu, tribes。

译文：清水河肆，座落于清水河畔，是裕固族的部落。
Translation:
The Qingshuihe township is situated on the bank of the Qingshui River。 It is a township of the Yugu tribes。

12-13 环狗
Huangou
（107,30891E；36,57002N）

环狗[1]，其为人兽首人身[2]，一曰蝟[3]，状如狗，黄色[4]。

注释：[1]环狗：指环部落国，在今甘肃庆阳市环县。狗，指勾纪，部落国的称谓。
Notes： [1] huan gou (surround dog) refers to the Huan tribe country, in today's Huan county, Qingyang city, Gansu province。 gou(dog)means gouji, a Pu term for tribal country。
[2] 兽首人身：指所水惹舍，是环县县城的古称谓，又称洪德惹舍，与所水惹舍含义相同。
[2] shou shou ren shen (beast head human body)
Tr; refers to the place: Suoshuireshe, an ancient name for the county seat of Huanxian county。 It is also known as Hongdereshe, another name for Suoshuireshe。
[3]蝟：指华池。
[3] wei: refers to Huachi (flower pool)
[4] 黄色：指洪德惹舍。
[4] huang se (yellow color) refers to Hongdereshe。

译文：环部落国，定都于所水惹舍，又称为华池，实际是环固国的所水惹舍，后称为洪德惹舍。
Translation:
The Huan tribal state has its capital city in Suoshuireshe。 The capital is also known as Huachi, of the Huangu Guo。 It is later called Hongdereshe。

12-14 袜
Mie
（109,32882E；36,86389N）

袜[1]，其为物，人身黑首[2]从目[3]。

注释：[1]袜：读绵（mie），指克绵氏族，即丝绸族。
Notes: [1] wa (stocking) reads as mie, refers to the Kemian tribes--the silk weaving tribes。
[2] 人身黑首：惹舍的王族。惹舍，集镇名，这里指陕西安塞。
[2] ren shen hei shou (human body black head)
Tr: the king lineage of Reshe, a term standing for township。 Here it refers to Ansai in Shaanxi province。 Ansai: fort with family name of An。
[3] 从目：读纵目，氏族名，指头饰帽缨和留额发髻的氏族。
[3] cong mu (follow eyes) reads as zongmu (vertical eyes) it is the name of a tribe。The tribe is known for wearing caps with tassels and hair knots over their foreheads。

译文：丝绸氏族，是安塞部落的王族，是纵目人。
Translation:
Silk tribe is the king lineage of the Ansai tribes, the Zongmu people。

12-15 戎
Rong
（110,2632E；37,50189N）

戎[1]。其为人，人首三角[2]。

注释：[1]戎：指戎部落。

Notes:[1] rong (warring) refers to the Rong tribes。

[2] 人首三角：指定水绥城。角，读郭音，指城。今称绥德，在陕西绥德县。德，指水。

[2] ren shou san jiao (human head three horns)

Tr: refers to the Dingshuisuicheng city, today it is known as Suide。jiao(horn) reads as guo, meaning town, city, in today's Suide county, Shaanxi province。 De; means water, river。

译文：戎部落，定都于定水绥城。

Translation:

The Rong tribe has its capital city in Dingshuisuicheng。

12-16 林氏国驺吾

Linshiguo zouwu

（109,73103E；38,28388N）

林氏国[1]有珍兽[2]，大若虎[3]，五采毕具[4]，尾长于身[5]，名曰驺吾[6]，乘之日[7]行千里[8]。

注释：[1]林氏国：指古上国，后称上郡，今称榆林。

Notes:[1] lin shi guo: refers to Gushang Guo, later known as Shang Jun， today's name is Yulin 。

[2] 珍兽：指支系氏族。

[2] zhen shou (precious beast) meaning branches of a clan。

[3] 大若虎：指游牧的胡族。

[3] da ruo hu (big as tiger) refers to the nomadic Hu people。

[4] 五采毕具：属东北的部落。五采，指东北。

[4] wu cai bi ju (five color all contain) refers to the tribes from Northeast。 Wucai: (five color) refers to Northeast。

[5] 尾长于身：南迁至黄河边。尾长：指南迁，于身：读溢奢，指黄河。

[5] yi chang yu shen (tail longer than body)

Tr: migrated southward to the riverbanks of Yellow River。 Weichang (tail long): migrates southward; Yushen: reads as Yishe, refers to Yellow River。

[6] 驺吾：指周部落氏族，简称周族。周，濮语读照。

[6] zou wu: refers to the Zhou tribes, shortened to Zhouzu。 Zhou, in Pu speech reads as zhao。

[7] 乘之日：指发展于，日，读曰，同濮语的“于“。

[7] cheng zhi ri（ride its date） developed from, ri reads as yue, the same as yu in Pu speech。

[8] 行千里：指横山东部地区。

[8] xing/heng qian li (travel 1000 li) reads as Hengqieli， refers to the east part of Hengshan。

译文：古上国的支系， 游牧胡， 原属东北的部落，南迁到黄河边，名叫周部落。周部落发展于横山东部地区。

Translation：

A branch of Gushang Guo, a nomadic Hu, previously belonging to the tribes in Northeast, migrated southward to the riverbanks of Yellow River, their name is Zhou tribes。Zhou tribes developed from the east part of Hengshan。

12-17 昆仑墟南汜林
Kunlunxu Nansilin
（110,49323E；38,84271N）

昆仑墟南所[1]，有汜林[2]方三百里[3]。

注释：[1]昆仑墟南所：指窟野河的南部地区。
Notes： [1] kunlunxue nansuo: refers to the south part of Kuyehe River。
[2] 汜林：指神府，今称神木。有的版本写为氾，氾不能译为神，只有汜能译为神。
[2]si lin: refers to Shenfu, known today as Shenmu (holy beam) some texts show a similar Chinese sign 氾, but it can't be translated into shen。
[3] 方三百里：藩王的都城。
[3] fang san bai li (area three hundred li)
Tr: the capital city of a frontier kingdom。

译文：在窟野河南部地区，有一个集镇叫神木，是藩王的都城。
Translation:
In the south part of Kuye River, there is a township called Shenmu。 It is the capital city of a frontier kingdom。

12-18 从极之渊冰夷
Congjizhiyuanbingyi
（112,56111E；37,87316N）

从极之渊[1]深三百仞[2]，维冰夷[3]恒都焉，冰夷人面[4]，乘两龙[5]，一曰忠极[6]之渊。

注释：[1]从极之渊：指尖草之乡，在山西省太原市城区。
Note： [1] cong ji zhi yuan refers to the land of the Jiancao (sharp grass blades) in today's Taiyuan city's urban quarter, Shanxi province。
[2] 深三百仞：读叟萨巴惹，指富饶的部落集镇。
[2] shen san bai ren (deep 3 hundred fathom) reads as Sousabare, meaning the affluent township of tribes。

[3] 冰夷：指太原部落。冰夷，读博原，以十字太阳"博"的读音命名。
[3] bing yi (ice people) refer to the Taiyuan tribes。 bingyi (ice people) reads as Boyuan。 Bo being the cross sign representing the sun, which is read as bo。 Bo--bing, phonetic match。

[4] 冰夷人面：太原居民。
[4] bing yi ren mian (ice people human face) refers to the citizens of Taiyuan city。

[5] 乘两龙：从事两种以上的劳动，指游牧业和农业，或手工业和农业。
[5] cheng liang loong (ride two dragons) meaning: engaged in two or more kinds of production labor, such as herding and agriculture, or handicrafts and agriculture。

[6] 忠极：指雀尖。
[6] zhong ji refers to Que jian, (magpie tip) 。

译文：尖草之乡是富饶的部落集镇，是太原部落的恒都，太原居民从事两种以上的劳动。又说，叫雀尖之乡。

Translation:
The land of Jiancao is an affluent township of the Taiyuan tribes。 It is also their permanent capital; citizens of this city are engaged in two or more kinds of labor。 It is also said that this place is also called Quejianzhixiang。

12-19 阳汙山
Yangxu Mountain
（113,88666E；39,27488N）

阳汙山[1]，河[2]出其中；凌门山[3]，河出其中。

注释：[1]阳汙山：指横崖山，濮语读横崖为阳乌，在山西繁峙县横涧乡，是滹沱河北支流的源头。
Notes:[1] yang xu shan: refers to the Hengyan Mountain。 In Pu speech, Hengyan (horizontal rock cliff) is read as Yangwo (sun bird) 。It is in the Hengjian (horizontal creek) xiang, which is the headwater for the north branch of Hutuo River。

[2]河：指滹沱河。
[2] he refers to Hutuo River。

[3] 凌门山：指五台山，濮语读五台为戾梅，谐音凌门，在山西五台县，是滹沱河南支流的源头。
[3] ling men shan: refers to the Shimen (stone gate) Mountain。 In Pu speech, shi(stone) reads as Li, a phonetic match to linmen。 It is in the Wutai（five terrace） county， Shanxi province。It is the headwater for the south branch of Hutuo River。

译文：横崖山，滹沱河北支流发源于这里；五台山，滹沱河南支流发源于这里。

Translation:
Hengyan Mountain is where the north branch of Hutuo River rises。 Wutaishan is where the south branch of Hutuo River rises。

12-20 王子夜尸
Wangziyeshi
（116,39785E；39,9N）

王子夜之尸[1]，两手[2]、两股[3]、胸[4]、首[5]、齿[6]，皆断异处[7]。

注释：[1]王子夜尸：读无枝耶肆，指昌部落大肆，此表述是大范围介绍，各个部落国定都的地点不同，有多个大肆。

Notes:[1] wang zi ye shi (prince night corpse) reads Wuzhiyesi, refers to the big township of the Chang tribe。Here it is the general area where various tribal states each have their respective capitals。

[2] 两手：指速剌部落，属医巫闾地区的氏族部落。

[2] liang shou (two hands) refers to the Sula tribe, which belongs to the tribal state of Yiwulv area。

[3] 两股：指古剌部落，即补苦氏部落，属红山地区的东胡。

[3] liang gu (two thighs) refers to the Gula tribe, also known as the Buku Shi tribe。 They belong to the Dong Hu people from Hongshan area。

[4]胸：指匈奴部落。

[4] xiong(chest) refers to the Xiongnu tribes。

[5]首：指肃慎部落。

[5] shou(head) refers to the Sushen tribe。

[6]齿：指古契丹部落。

[6] chi(teeth) refers to the ancient Qidan (kit daan, Khitan people) tribes。

[7] 皆断异处：都曾经定都于此。

[7] jie duan yi chu (all break apart) meaning all the above-mentioned nations have set up capitals in this location。

译文：昌部落大肆，速剌、古剌、匈奴、肃慎、契等部落，都曾定都于此。

Translation:

There is the big capital city of the Chang tribes。The various tribal nations such as Sula, Gula, Xiongnu, Sushen and Qidan all chose to build their capitals in this location。

12-21 宵明、烛光

Xiaoming zhuguang

（121,61365E；38,91545N。122,12451E；37,5259N）

舜妻[1]登比[2]氏生[3]宵明[4]、烛光[5]，处河大泽[6]，二女之灵[7]能照此所百里[8]。一曰登北氏[9]。

注释：[1]舜妻：辽河古称通溪，濮语读为"输期"，谐音舜妻。

Notes:[1] shun qi (shun's wife) refers to Liaohe River, whose ancient name is Tongqi。 Tongqi reads in Pu speech as shuqi, a phonetic match to shunqi。

[2] 登比：黄河，濮语读为档泚，传承变音为德泚，谐音登比。档，指黄色。

[2] deng bi: the Yellow River， in Pu speech reads as dangbi, transmitted as debi, a phonetic match to dengbi；dang, de, deng, all means yellow color。

[3] 氏生：指出口处。

[3] shi sheng: outlet of river, or water。

[4] 宵明：读啥门，指外门，是辽东半岛的别称。

[4] xiao ming（night bright), reads as shamen, referring to Waimen (outer door) another name for the Liaodong Peninsula。

[5] 烛光：读照拱，指天门，是山东半岛的别称。

[5] zhu guang:(candlelight) reads as Zhaogong, referring to Tianmen (sky gate) another name for the Shandong Peninsula。

[6] 大泽：指渤海。

[6] da ze (big zee) refers to the Bohai Sea。

[7] 二女之灵：二流之篱，指两条河流的大门。

[7]er nv zhi ling (two girls' spirits) reads as er liu zhi li (two rio 'fence) meaning the gate for two rivers。

[8] 能照此所百里：能护卫着这个海域数百里。

[8] neng zhao ci suo bai li (can shine this place 100 li)
Tr: can protect this coastal area up to a few hundred square miles。

[9] 登北氏：黄河门神。

[9] deng bei shi (climb north shi) meaning: the Gate God of Yellow River。

译文：辽河、黄河出口处的外门和照门，地处河外的渤海，两河之门能护卫着这个海域数百里。又称为黄河门神。

Translation：

The river mouths of the Liao River as well as the Yellow River are known as the Out Gate--the Waimen, and the Shine Gate--the Zhaomen。The two gates are located where the rivers empty into Bohai Sea。 These two gates of Rivers provide protection to the coastal areas up to a few hundred miles。 They are also called the Gate God for the Yellow River。

第十三卷 海内东经 (Hainei Region : the East)

Book 13 Haineidongjing

13-01 钜燕
Juyan
（122,99449E；41,11231N）

海内东北陬以南者。
钜燕[1]在东北陬。

注释：[1]钜燕：全称钜燕那，是东北著名的部落国之一。
Notes： [1] ju yan: full name is Juyanna, a famous tribal state in Northeast part of Eurasia。

译文：从海外东北角向南描述。
钜燕在海内的东北角。
Translation:
The text starts from the northeast corner going south。 Juyan is in the northeast corner of Hainei。

13-02 盖国
Gai Guo
（122,36544E；40,40002N）

盖国[1]在钜燕[2]南，倭[3]北。倭属燕。

注释：[1]盖国：指盖汝米那，今称盖州，在辽宁盖州市。
Notes:[1] gai guo； refers to Gairumina, today it is known as Gaizhou, in Gaizhou city, Liaoning province。
[2] 钜燕：辽宁鞍山市以及北面地区，古称燕国。
[2] ju yan: refers to the area in today's Anshan and the area to Anshan's north. It is called Yan Guo in ancient times。
[3]倭：指吴姑，今属大连。古时属燕国。
[3] wo refers to Wugu， in today's Dalian。It belongs to Yan Guo in ancient times。

译文：盖国位于钜燕国的南面，在吴姑的北面。吴姑国臣属于燕国。

Translation:
Gai Guo is located to the south of Juyan Guo, to the north of Wugu Guo。Wugu Guo is subjected to Yan Guo。

13-03 国在流沙中者
Guozailiushazhongzhe
（126,18466E；41,1232N。125,36241E；41,26526N）

国在流沙[1]中者埻端[2]、玺唤[3]，在昆仑墟[4]东南。一曰海内之郡[5]，不为郡县 [6]，在流沙中。

注释：[1]流沙：读 lang she，指绿江，后称鸭绿江。中，指北岸。
Notes: [1] liu sha (moving sands) reads as lang she, refers to the Lvjiang River, later known as the Yalv River, zhong, meaning northern bank。
[2] 埻端：指丸都，今称集安。
[2] chun duan: refers to Wandu, known today as Ji'an city。
[3] 玺唤：又读玄浑、玄桓，浑江的远古称谓，这里实际指玄桓集镇，后称玄菟、桓州，今为桓仁县城。
[3] xi hua, also reads as Xuanhun, xuanheng, the ancient name for Hunjiang River。 It in fact describes the Xuanheng township, which is later called Xuantu, or Hengzhou。Today it is called Hengren country。
[4] 昆仑墟：古时，较高的山都称为昆仑。这里指龙岗山。
[4] kunlunxu: a generic term for mountains of relatively height。It refers to the Loonggang Mountain, Loonggang (dragon ridge) 。
[5]郡：读纪，指部落。
[5] jun(province) reads as ji, meaning tribe。
[6] 不为郡县：是重要的码头部落。不，指是；为郡码头部落；县，重要的。
[6] bu wei jun xian (not be province county)
Tr: is an important port tribe。bu(no)means is, wei jun (as province) meaning port tribe， xian(county) important。

译文：在鸭绿江北岸的国家有丸都、玄桓，在龙岗山的东南面。又说是海内东北角的部落，是重要的码头部落，在鸭绿江边。
Translation:
The states on the north bank of Yalu River are Wandu, and Xuanheng, to the southeast of Loonggang Mountain。It is also said that the tribes in the northeast corner of Hainei is an important port tribe, by the Yalu River。

13-04 国在流沙外者
Guozailiushawaizhe
（127,7813E；41,4231N。124,95344E；40,45029N）
（126,6439E；412,45798。127,12987E；40,97667N）

国在流沙外者，大夏[1]、竖沙[2]、居繇[3]、月支[4]之国。

注释：[1]大夏：读那沙，指大河，今朝鲜龙河镇。
Notes： [1] da xia: reads as nasha, meaning big river, today's Loonghe Zhen in Korean。
[2] 竖沙：指丰饶水，今朝鲜朔州竖棚镇。
[2] shu sha: refers to Fengraoshui, or Fengrao River, today's Shupeng Zhen in Suozhou, Korea。
[3] 居繇：指朝鲜的芝城，今称慈城。
[3] ju yao: refers to Korea's Zhicheng, known today as Cicheng。
[4] 月支：指朝鲜的狼林。

[4] yue zhi: refers to Langlin (wolf forest) in Korea。

译文：在鸭绿江南岸的国家有龙河、竖棚、慈城、狼林之国。
Translation:
Located along the south bank of the Yalu River are the following nations： Loonghe, Shupeng, Cicheng, Langlin。

13-05 西胡白玉山
Xihubaiyushan
（129,21524E；41,71342N）

西胡白玉山[1]在大夏[2]东，苍梧[3]在白玉山西南，皆在流沙[4]西，昆仑墟[5]东南。昆仑山[6] 在西胡西。皆在西北 [7] 。

注释：[1]西胡白玉山：指朝鲜的东山摩天岭。
Notes:[1] xi hu bai yu shan (west Hu white jade mount)
Tr: refers to Korea's Dongshan (east mountain) Motianling (touch sky mountains) 。
[2] 大夏：指龙河。
[2] da xia (big summer) refers to the Loonghe (dragon water) River。
[3] 苍梧：指朝鲜的长白部落，今称惠山。
[3] cang wu: refers to the Changbai (lasting white) tribe, known today as Huishan (benefit mount) 。
[4] 流沙西：指鸭绿江东。
[4] liu sha xi (moving sands west)
Tr: to the east side of the Yalu River。
[5] 昆仑墟：这里指长白山。
[5] kunlunxu (kunlun mound) refers to the Changbai Mountains。
[6] 昆仑山：指镜面山，今称咸镜山。
[6] kunlunshan: refers to Jingmian (mirror face mount), known today as the Xianjing (salt mirror mount) Mountain。
[7] 皆在西北：指皆在长白山的东北面。
[7] jie zai xi bei (all locate west north)
Tr: all located to the northeast of the Changbai (lasting white) Mountain。

译文：东山摩天岭在龙河的东面，长白部落在摩天岭的西南面，皆在鸭绿江的东面，在长白山的东南面。咸镜山在摩天岭的东面，皆在长白山的东北面。
Translation:
The Dongshan Motianling Mountain is located to the east of Loonghe River。The Changbai tribe is located to the southwest of Motianling Mountains, all to the east of the Yalu River and to the southeast of the Changbai Mountains。 Xianjing Mountain is to the east of Motianling Mountain, all to the northeast of the Changbai Mountains。

13-06 朝鲜
Korea(chaoxian)
（12437783E~129,46724E；33,24099N~40,33346N）

朝鲜在列阳[1]东，海北山[2]南。列阳属燕。

注释：[1]列阳：即连阳，今称丹东。
Notes:[1] lie yang (file sunny) e.g., Lieyang, today known as Dandong。

[2] 海北山：指咸镜山。镜是北的濮语音译。
[2] hai bei shan (sea north mount) refers to Xianjing Mountain。 Jing(mirror) a phonetic notation of Pu concept for north。

译文：朝鲜在连阳的东面，在咸镜山的南面。连阳属燕国。
Translation:
Korea is to the east of Lianyang, to the south of Xianjing Mountain。 Lianyang belongs to the Yan Guo (swallow country) 。

13-07 列姑射
Liegushe
（133,90572E；34,67331N）

列姑射[1]在海河洲[2]中。

注释：[1]列姑射：指冈山列岛，今日本国。
Notes： [1] lie gu she refers to Gangshanliedao (Okayama archipelago) today's Japanese Archipelago。
[2] 河洲：读哼洲，指弹丸陆地、小陆地。
[2] he zhou； reads as Hengzhou, refers to tiny island or small sized land。

译文：冈山列岛在大海中的小陆地上。
Translation:
Okayama Archipelago is on a small piece of land in the sea。

13-08 射姑国
Shegu Guo
（131,6652E；32,58327N）

射姑国[1]在海中，属列姑射[2]。西南，山环之。

注释：[1]射姑国：指延冈国。
Notes:[1] she gu guo: refers to the Yangang Guo。
[2] 属列姑射：属冈山列岛的九州岛。
[2] shu liegushe: belong to the Kyushu Island, part of the Okayama Archipelago。

译文：延冈国在海中，属冈山列岛的九州岛，是西南岛国，周围都是山。
Translation:
Yangang Guo is in the sea, belonging to the Kyushu Island , Okayama Archipelago。 It is an island country to the southwest, surrounded by mountains on four sides。

13-09 大蟹
Daxie
（129,49162E；28,37932N）

大蟹[1]在海中。

注释：[1]大蟹：指大喜，即大岛和喜界岛。大岛，濮语读为“奄美屿”，属琉球国。

Notes:[1] da xie (big crab) refers to Daxi, e.g., Dadao (Amami Ōshima Great Island) and Xijiedao (Kikaijima Island) 。In Pu speech, Dadao is read as Yanmeiyu, belonging to Ryukyu Kingdom。

译文：大岛和喜界岛在海中。
Translation:
Dadao and Xijiedao are in the middle of the sea。

13-10 陵鱼
Lingyu
（127,79944E；26,28422N）

陵鱼人面[1]，手足[2]，鱼身[3]，在海中。

注释：[1]陵鱼人面：指中心屿居民。中心屿，今称那霸屿，在琉球国的中部。
Notes：[1] ling yu ren mian (ling fish human face)
Tr: refers to the residents in Zhongxinyu (centre island) known today as Nabayu (Naha city in Okinawa), in the middle section of the Ryukyu Kingdom。
[2] 手足：指姒族，即夏族，是江苏宿迁骆马湖迁徙到琉球群岛的夏族。
[2] shou zu (hand feet): kins, relatives,
Tr: refers to the Sizu, e.g., Xia zu, the Xia people who migrated from Luoma Lake in today's Suqian city, Jiangsu province to the Ryukyu archipelago。
[3] 鱼身：指渔业氏族。
[3]yu shen (fish body)
Tr: the fishing tribes。

译文：中心屿的居民，是夏族的渔业氏族，住在海岛上。
Translation:
The residents in Zhongxinyu are the fishing tribe of Xia people, they live on the pelages。

13-11 大鯾
Dabian
（124,15829E；24,37531N）

大鯾[1]居海中。

注释：[1]大鯾：指大鯾列岛，包括宫古岛、多良间岛、东鯾岛（今石垣岛）、小鯾岛、西鯾岛、与那国岛 Yonaguni-jima 等。鯾，读 bio 音，指鱼。
Notes: [1] da bian(bio/fish): refers to the islands of Dabian Archipelago: it includes the Gonggu Island (Miyako-jima), the Duoliangjian Island (Tarama-jima) , Dongbio Island (Ishigaki jima), Xiaobio Island (small fish island) and Yunaguo Island (Yonaguni-jima) among the other islands。

译文：大鯾列岛在海中。
Translation:
The Dabio Islands are in the middle of the sea。

13-12 明组邑
Mingzuyi
（120,67305E；24,14745N）

明组邑[1]居海中。

注释：[1]明组邑：指台湾岛，原称妈祖屿，读音灭组邑，谐音明组邑。
Notes:[1] ming zu yi (bright group settlements)
Tr: refers to Taiwan Island, its original name is Mazuyu, a phonetic match to the Pu speech Miezuyi, rendered into Mingzuyi。

译文：妈祖屿在海中。
Translation:
Mazuyu is in the middle of the sea。

13-13 蓬莱山
Penglai Mountain
（120,89964E；16,60139N）

蓬莱山[1]在海中。

注释：[1]蓬莱山：指帕拉山，即菲律宾北部的中科迪勒拉山和马德雷山。
Notes:[1] peng lai shan: refers to Palashan, e.g.， the Central Cordillera and Sierra Madre 。

译文：帕拉山在海中。
Translation:
Palashan Mountain is in the middle of the sea。

13-14 大人之市
Darenzhishi
（125,45274E；7,19003N）

大人之市[1]在海中。

注释：[1]大人市：指菲律宾的南部重镇达沃，古称达惹，谐音大人。
Notes:[1] da ren shi (big person city)
Tr: refers to the important city in southern Philipine: Dawo city, e.g., its ancient name is Dare, a phonetic match to Chinese Daren (big person) 。

译文：达沃市在海岛上。
Translation：
Dawo city is on the island。

13-15 琅琊台
Langyatai
（119,91406E；35,6418N）

琅琊台[1]在勃海[2]，琅琊之东。其北有山[3]，一曰海间 [4] 。

注释：[1]琅琊台：原意指灵的芝，“台”指集、芝，并非台地，实际介绍山东狼牙山南面的台东和台西集。古称灵的芝，今称灵芝，所以解读时再加一个“集”字才通顺。

Notes:[1] lang ya tai refers to Lingdezhi, (a legendary herb lingzhi) 。 Tai: in Pu speech means ji(township), it is not to be confused with the Chinese concept of Tai(terrace)。It describes Taidongji and the Taixiji to the south of Langyashan (wolf teeth mount) in Shandong province。 The herb is called in ancient times Lingdezhi, known today as Lingzhi。When translating the term, a classifier: ji(township) needs to be added to make sense of the concept。

[2] 勃海间：勃，读 be, 指黄。勃海间，指黄海缴、黄海边。

[2]bo hai jian: bo reads as be, meaning yellow。 The term Bohaijian refers to Huanghaijiao, Huanghaibian, the coastal area of Yellow Sea。

[3]山：因介绍海边的是灵芝集肆，所以描述其北有山。

[3] shan: the term shan means the Lingzhi township by the sea, shan /mountain is to the north of it。

[4] 海间：指海州的北面。间，读缴，在此指北面。

[4] hai jian: refers to the north of Haizhou。 Jian: reads as jiao, here means north。

译文：灵芝集在黄海边，在灵芝府的东面，北面有山。又说在海州的北面。

Translation:

Lingzhiji is by the Yellow Sea, to the east of Lingzhifu city, to its north there is a mount。It is said that Lingzhiji town is to the north of Haizhou。

13-16 都州

Duzhou

（119,19617E；34,60562N）

都州[1]在海中[2]，一曰郁州。

注释：[1]都州：指云州，云读待，谐音都。今江苏连云港。

Notes:[1] du zhou: refers to Yunzhou, yun(clouds) reads as dai, close phonetic match to Chinese concept du。 It is today's Lianyungan Port, Jiangsu province。

[2] 海中：苏北地区古称海州，在海州地区的集镇称为在海中。

[2] hai zhong (sea middle) : the northern part of Jiangsu is known as Subei region, or Haizhou in ancient times。All the townships in this area are described as in the Haizhong region。

译文：云州在海中，又说称为郁州。

Translation:

Yunzhou is Haizhong。It is also said that Yunzhou is also called Yuzhou。

13-17 雷泽中雷神

Leizezhognleishen

（118,27409E；33,952N）

雷泽[1]中有雷神[2]，龙身而人头[3]，鼓其腹[4]。在吴西[5] 。

注释：[1]雷泽：指骆马湖地区，在江苏宿迁市。

Notes: [1] lei ze (thunder zee) refers to the Luomahu area, in Suqian city, Jiangsu province。

[2] 雷神：指骆肆，即宿迁城。

[2] lei shen (thunder lord) refers to Luosi，e.g.， today's Suqian city。

[3] 龙身而人头：僚族的政治中心。

[3] loong shen er ren tou (dragon body and human head)

Tr: the political centre of the Liao/Lao people。

[4] 鼓其腹：东夏的王城。鼓其，指东夏国。腹，指王，这里指王城。
[4]gu qi fu (drum it belly)
Tr: the king capital of the Dongxia state/East Xia State。 Guqi; means Dongxia state。 Fu(belly) means king, referring to the king city。
[5] 吴西：吴，指契乌部落国，后称吴国。西，指东面。
[5] wu xi: wu refers to the Qiwu tribal state, later known as Wu Guo。xi(west) means east。

译文：骆马湖地区有一个骆肆，是僚族的政治中心，是东夏国的王城，在吴国的东面。
Translation:
There is a Luosi township in the Luomahu Lake area。It is the political centre of the Liao people。 It is the king city of East Xia State, to the east of Wu Guo。

13-18 韩雁
Hanyan
（119,0255E；33,59666N）

韩雁[1]在海中[2]，在都州南。

注释：[1]韩雁：指淮安，雁读 an 音。
Notes:[1] han yan: refers to Huai'an city。 Yan: reads as an。
[2] 海中：指海州地区。
[2] hai zhong (in the middle of sea)
Tr: refers to the Haizhou area。

译文：淮安在海州地区，在云州的南面。
Translation:
Huai'an is in the Haizhou area, to the south of Yunzhou。

13-19 始鸠
Shijiu
（120,97879E；32,21641N）

始鸠[1]在海中[2]，辕厉[3]南。

注释：[1]始鸠：指施港，也称司港、丝港，意为通港，在此仍以施港解读。
Notes:[1] shi jiu: refers to Shi gang (operate port) e.g., sigang (supervise port) si gang (silk port) a generic term is Tonggang（path port）。 Here the term Shigang (operate port) is kept in the explanation。
[2] 海中：指海州地区。
[2] hai zhong (zee in) refers to the Haizhou area (zee regions) 。
[3] 辕厉：读 rue li，意为龙岗，今称如皋。
[3] yuan li: reads as rue li, meaning Loonggang (dragon port) today it is called Rugao。

译文：施港在海州地区，在如皋的南面。
Translation:
Shigang is in the Haizhou area, to the south of Rugao。

13-20 会稽山
Huijishan
（120,6409E；29,68764N）

会稽山[1]在大楚[2]南。

注释：[1]会稽山：南具区山。南具区，濮语读为会稽。会，读维音，并不是指计功开会。
Notes:[1] hui ji shan: Nanjuqu Mountain。 In Pu speech Nanjuqu reads as weiji。 Wei: meaning south。 The term is often misinterpreted as having a celebration of achievements。

[2] 大楚：指具区大泽，古称具区，今称太湖。区，读欧音。
[2] da chu: refers to Ju'ou-Daze (the big deep zee) known today as Taihu Lake。 qu (区） reads as ou。The lake's ancient name is Ju'ou。

译文：南具区山，在具区的南面。
Translation：
Nanjuou Mountain is to the south of Ju'ou, (the Taihu Lake) 。

第十四卷 大荒东经 (The Great Wilderness: the East)

Book 14 Dahuadongjing

14-01 少昊之国
Shaohaozhiguo
（122,05637E; 37,19775N）

东海之外大壑[1]，少昊[2]之国。少昊孺帝颛项于此[3]，弃其琴瑟 [4] 。有甘山者 [5]，甘水出焉 [6]，生甘渊 [7] 。

注释：[1]大壑：指泰山国，今称昆嵛山国，都城在文登城。濮语称泰山为泰洪、泰博。
Notes: [1] da he、huo (big chams)
Tr: refers to Taishan Guo, today it is called Kunyushan Guo。Its capital is Wendeng City。 In Pu speech, Taishan is read as Taihong, or Taibo (洪，博为山）Hong and bo, Pu concept as mountain。

[2] 少昊：指海边，少昊之国，指海边的国家。在此仍按少昊表达。
[2] shao hao: meaning seaside, coastal。Shaohaozhiguo means the coastal states。 Here the term Shaohao is kept。

[3] 孺帝颛项于此：管理的照羲东部区域。孺、儒，指管理、治理。
[3]ru di zhuanxu yu ci (the scholar god Zhuanxu is here),
Tr: managing the Zhaoxi eastern territory。Ru:(scholar) means management, administration。

[4] 弃其琴瑟：称为且舍。
[4] qi qi qin se (discard its lyre and music wares)
Tr: it is called Queshe (a tribe branch title) 。

[5] 有甘山者：是苗山支系。
[5] you gan shan zhe (has sweet mount)
Tr: refers to the Miaoshan branch。

[6] 甘水出焉：苗族的发源地。
[6] gan shui chu yan (sweet water rises)
Tr: the homeland where the Miao ethnic people originate。

[7] 生甘渊：是苗族诞生之乡。

[7] sheng gan yuan (begets sweet deep-water)
Tr: the birthplace of the Miao ethnic people。

译文：东海之外的泰山国，是少昊之国，是少昊管理的照羲东部区域，称为且舍，是苗山支系的苗族的发源地，是苗族诞生之乡。
Translation:
The Taishan Guo located in the land beyond the Donghai area, is known also as the Shaohao Guo。 It is the Zhaoxi eastern territory managed by Shaohao, known as Qieshe。 It is the birthplace of the Miaoshan branch, the birthplace of the Miao ethnic people。

14-02 甘山
Ganshan
（121,75704E；37,27368N）

有甘山者[1]，甘水出焉[2]，生甘渊[3]。

注释：[1]有甘山者：有一个苗山，指昆嵛山。
Notes: [1] you gan shan zhe (has sweet mount)
Tr: there is Miaoshan, e.g., Kunyu Mountain。
[2] 甘水出焉：是苗族的发源地。
[2] gan shui chu yan (sweet water rises)
Tr: the birthplace of the Miao ethnic people。
[3] 生甘渊：是苗族诞生之乡。
[3] sheng gan yuan (born sweet deep-water)
Tr: the birthplace of Miao people。

译文：有一座苗山，是苗族的发源地，是苗族诞生之乡。
Translation:
There is a Miaoshan Mountain, the Miao people's homeland, the birthplace of the Miao ethnic people。

14-03 皮母地丘
Pimudiqiu
（120,46789E；36,38849N）

大荒东南隅有山，名皮母地[1]丘[2]。

注释：[1]皮母地：指制绸业。
Notes;[1] pi mu di (skin mother place)
Tr: refers to the silk production。
[2]丘：指城、街肆。皮母地丘，指制绸业之城。今称即墨城。
[2] qiu(mound)
Tr: refers to township, market street。 Pimudiqiu means the city of silk, e.g., today's Jimo city in Shandong province。

译文：大地的东南面有一个地方，叫制绸业之城。
Translation:
There is a place in the southeast in the land called Silk city。

14-04 大言山
Dayanshan
（120,6314E；36,18342N）

东海之外，大荒之中，有山名曰大言[1]，日月所出。

注释：[1]大言：又称大延山、大任山、那罗延、崂山。今称崂山。
Notes:[1] da yan:(big speech)
Tr: refers to the various names: Dayanshan, the Darenshan, Naluoyan, or Laoshan。 Today it is called Laoshan, the Lao Mountain。

译文：东海外的大地中有座山，名叫崂山，是太阳和月亮升起的地方。
Translation:
There is a mountain in the land beyond the Donghai, which is called Laoshan。 This is where the Sun and Moon rise from。

14-05 大人国大人市
Daren Guo Darenshi
（118,08489E；36,35981N）

有波谷山[1]者，有大人[2]之国，有大人之市，名曰大人之堂[3]。有一大人踆其上[4]，张其两耳 [5] 。

注释：[1]波谷山：指博崮山，今称博山、鲁山。
Notes:[1]bo gu shan (wave valley mount)
Tr: refers to the Bogu Mountain, known as Boshan, or Lushan。
[2] 大人：读达惹，指落后的。
[2] da ren (big person)
Tr: reads as Dare, meaning backward, falling behind。
[3] 大人之堂：指开拓落后的集肆，简称迟拓肆。
[3] da ren zhi tang (big person's hall)
Tr: meaning to develop the townships that have fallen behind。 The concept is expressed as Chi tuo si (late developed town) 。
[4] 大人踆其上：落后的部落在上面，由此得名迟上部落，在今淄博市博山区池上镇。
[4] da ren qun qi shan (big person squad above)
Tr: the backward tribes are above (north)therefore they are called Chishang (late above) tribe。 It is today's Chishang township in Boshan district, Zibo city, Shandong province。
[5] 张其两耳：是安迟国的首府。
[5] zhang qi liang er (prick its two ears)
Tr: it is the capital of Anchi Guo。

译文：东海外地区有一个落后的国家，叫安迟国。那里有一个落后的集肆叫迟拓肆，有一个落后的部落叫迟上部落，是安迟国的首府。
Translation:
There is a country in the land beyond Donghai, which is slow in developing and is known as the Anchi Guo。 There is Chituo Si, a slow developing township, the capital of Anchi Guo。 The backward tribe is called the Chishang tribe。

14-06 小人国靖人
Xiaorenguojingren
（118,54282E；36,51408N）

有小人国[1]，名靖人[2]。

注释：[1]小人国：指朐惹国，今山东临朐县。
Notes： [1] xiao ren guo (tiny people country)
Tr: refers to Jure Guo, in today's Linju County, Shandong province。
[2] 靖人：指先进的集镇，先进的国家。
[2] jing ren: refers to the more advanced townships or countries。

译文：有一个国家叫朐惹国，是一个先进的国家。
Translation:
There is a country called Jure Guo。 It is an advanced nation。

14-07 犁䰠尸
Lilingshi
（118,47463E；36,68434N）

有神[1]，人面兽身[2]，名曰犁䰠之尸[3]。

注释：[1]神：在此指集肆。
Notes: [1] shen (God, or spirit)
Tr: here shen means township, or Jisi, or Si。
[2] 人面兽身：织绸族的集肆。
{2] ren main shou shen (human face beast body)
Tr: refers to the townships of Silk tribes。
[3] 犁䰠尸：指青府肆，后称青州肆。
[3]li ling shi (plough spirit corpse)
Tr: refers to the Qingfu Si, later known as the Qingzhou（green province） Si（township）。

译文：有一个集肆，是织绸族的集肆，名叫青州肆。
Translation：
There is a township, a Si of the Silk tribe, known as the Qingzhou Si。

14-08 蒍国
Wei Guo
（117,02061E；36,66782N）

有潏山[1]，杨水[2]出焉。有蒍国[3]，黍食[4]。使四鸟[5]：虎、豹、熊、罴[6]。

注释：[1]潏山：读橘山，指济山。
Notes:[1] jue (yu)shan (fast flow water mount): reads as Jushan, refers to Jishan。
[2] 杨水：指羊水，出海口称羊口，实际应读豁口，羊读 huo 音。

[2] yang shui (poplar water) refers to Yangshui (goat river) , the river mouth where the water empties into the sea is termed as Yangkou, which reads as Huokou, Goat(yang)should be read as Huo, in Pu speech。

[3] 蔿国：指澖蔿国，今称济南。蔿，即维，指南。

[3] wei guo: as Yuwei Guo, today known as Jinan city, capital of Shandong province。 Wei means south。

[4] 黍食：氏族为原住民。

[4] shu shi (millet food)

Tr: the tribes are the original residents。

[5] 四鸟：指四种劳动。

[5]si niao (four birds)

Tr: four kinds of labor。

[6]虎、豹、熊、罴：指牧业、农业、狩猎业、手工业。

[6]hu, bao, xiong, pi (tiger, leopard, bear, pi-bear)

Tr: refers to husbandry, agriculture, hunting and handicrafts。

译文：有一个地方叫济山，羊水从那里流向渤海。那里有一个国家叫济南国，氏族是原住民，从事四种劳动，即牧业、农业、狩猎业、手工业。

Translation:

There is a place called Jishan。Yangshui flows into Bohai Sea from there。There is a country called Jinan Guo。Its residents are original tribal people, engaged in four kinds of labor production: husbandry, agriculture, hunting, and handicrafts。

14-09 合虚山

Hexushan

（117,4984E；38,1405N）

大荒之中，有山名曰合虚[1]，日月所出。

注释：[1]合虚：指海兴。在河北海兴。

Notes:[1] he xu (close emptiness)

Tr: refers to Haixing (sea boom), in today's Haixing city in Hebei province。

译文：东海的大地中，有一个地方叫海兴，太阳和月亮最先从那里升起。

Translation:

In the land of Donghai there is a place called Haixing, from there the sun and moon first rise。

14-10 中容国

Zhongrong Guo

（115,8718E；39,05016N）

有中容之国[1]。帝俊[2] 生中容，中容人食兽 [3]，木实 [4]，使四鸟：豹、虎、熊、罴。

注释：[1]中容国：今河北容城。

Notes： [1] zhong rong guo (middle contain country)

Tr: today's Rongcheng city, Hebei province。

[2] 帝俊：北方部落。

[2] di jun (God handsome)

Tr: the northern tribes。

[3] 中容人食兽：中容镇氏族是古老的氏族。
[3] zhong rong ren shi shou (zhong rong people eat beast) 。
Tr: the tribes at Zhongrong Zhen are the ancient tribes。
[4] 木实：指慕容氏。
[4]mu shi (wood fruit)
Tr: refers to the tribal lineage of Murong Shi。

译文：大地中有一个国家叫中容国。北方部落建起了中容集镇，中容集镇氏族是古老的氏族，叫慕容氏，从事四种劳动，农业、牧业、狩猎业和手工业。
Translation:
In the middle of the land there is a country called Zhongrong Guo。 The northern tribes build the Zhongrong townships。 The Zhongrong Township tribes are very ancient tribes, known as Murong Shi。 They are engaged in the four kinds of labor production: husbandry, agriculture, hunting and handicrafts。

14-11 君子国
Junzi Guo
（116,30943E；39,43787N）

有东口[1]之山，有君子之国[2]，其人衣冠带剑[3]。

注释：[1]东口：指邓口，即镇守的关口。
Notes:[1] dong kou (east pass)
Tr: refers to Deng kou, the pass fort-town guarded by soldiers。
[2] 君子国：指很平的国度，在河北固安。"固"，指门。
[2] jun zi guo （gentleman country)
Tr: refers to the country on very flat land, e.g., Gu'an (reinforced peace) city in Hebei province。
[3] 其人衣冠带剑：名叫水门邓纪，邓，濮语'镇'的音译，纪指部落国。
[3] yi guan dai jian (this person clothes cap with sword)
Tr: refers to the Deng tribe at Shuimen (water gate) 。 Deng, Pu speech for town, Ji for tribal nation。

译文：有一个镇守关口的地方，是一个很平坦的国家，名叫水门邓纪。
Translation:
There is a place where Pass is being guarded, this is a country of very flat land, known as Shuimendengji。

14-12 司幽国
Siyou Guo
（116,05591E；39,6172N）

有司幽之国[1]。帝俊生晏龙[2]，晏龙生司幽 [3]，司幽生思士，不妻；思女，不夫 [4][5] 。食黍，食兽[6]，是使四鸟 [7] 。

注释：[1]司幽国：指幽燕国。
Notes： [1]si you guo (manage dim nation)
Tr: refers to the Youyan Guo (dim swallow country) 。
[2] 帝俊生晏龙：北方部落养育、分出了燕僚氏族。
[2] di jun sheng yan long (God handsome begets the Yan dragon)
Tr: the northern tribes develop and a Yanlao tribe branched out from the mother tribe。

[3] 晏龙生司幽：燕僚氏族建立了一个司幽国。
[3] yan long sheng si you (Yan dragon begets si you)
Tr: The Yanliao tribe set up a Siyou Guo。
[4] 思士、思女：指青年男女。
[4]si shi si nv (miss man, miss woman)
Tr: refers to the young men and young women。
[5] 不妻、不夫：指实行走婚制，不建立家庭，属于母系社会。
[5] bu qi、bu fu (no wife, no husband)
Tr: practice the so-called walking marriage system, do not organize families, and keep on the matriarchal system。
[6] 食黍、食兽：以古老的方式传承氏族。
[6] shi shu, shi shou (eat milliet, eat beast)
Tr: carry on the tribal existence in ancient ways。
[7] 使四鸟：从事四种劳动。
[7] shi si niao: engaged in four kinds of labor production。

译文：燕山南部地区有一个国家，叫司幽国。北方的部落中有燕僚氏族，燕僚氏族建立了司幽国。司幽国的青年男女不嫁不娶，实行走婚制，以古老的方式传承氏族。他们从事四种劳动。
Translation:
In the southern part of Yanshan, there is a country called Siyou Guo。 Of the northern tribes there is the Yanlao tribe。 The Yanlao tribes become the Siyou Guo。 In this country, young men and young women do not get married。 They practice the so-called walking-partnership system, carrying on their tribal existence in the ancient way。 They are engaged in the four kinds of labor production。

14-13 明星山
Mingxingshan
（116,70868E；40,58595N。116,84498E；40,69778N）

有大阿山[1]者。
大荒中有山，名曰明星[2]，日月所出。

注释：[1]大阿山：指云蒙山，在北京市密云区。大阿，读待卧，指云蒙。
Notes;[1] da a shan： refers to the Yunmengshan (cloud cover mount) 。 It is in today's Miyun district, in Beijing city。 Da 'a, which reads as daiwo, refers to Yunmeng。
[2] 明星山：指迎锋山，今称迎风山，在云蒙山的东北侧。
[2] ming xing shan (bright star mount)
Tr: refers to the Yingfengshan (welcome sword tip mount) known today as the Yingfengshan (welcome wind) Mountain, to the northeast of Yunmengshan。

译文：有一个叫云蒙山的地方，紧挨着一座山叫迎风山，人们常能看到太阳和月亮从山后升起。
Translation:
There is a place called Yunmengshan, next to a mountain called Yingfengshan。People often can see the sun and moon rise from behind the mountain。

14-14 白民国
Baimin Guo
（117,96511E；40,18772N）

有白民之国[1]。帝俊生帝鸿[2]，帝鸿生白民 [3]，白民销姓 [4]，黍食 [5]，使四鸟：虎、豹、熊、罴。

注释：[1]白民国：指博米国，即兴化国，在河北遵化县城。博，指化；民，指兴。
Notes:[1] bai min guo (white folk country)
Tr: refers to Bomi Guo, e.g., Xinghua Guo in today's Zunhua county seat, Hebei province。Bo means Hua, (cultivate), min means xing(boom)。
[2] 帝俊生帝鸿：北方的部落分支出北胡。
[2] di jun sheng di hong (God handsome begets God Hong)
Tr: part of the northern tribes branches out to form Beihu, the northern Hu people。
[3] 帝鸿生白民：北胡分支出兴化氏族。
[3] di hong sheng bai min (God Hong begets white folk)
Tr: part of the northern Hu branches out to form the Xinghua tribe。
[4] 白民销姓：兴化氏族为萧姓，是古契丹姓氏。
[4] bai min xiao xin (white folk cancel surname)
Tr: The Xinghua tribe bears the surname of Xiao, an ancient family name of Qidan people。
[5] 黍食：古老的氏族。
[5] shu shi (millet eat)
Tr: ancient tribes。

译文：有一个兴化之国。北方的部落中分支出了北胡，北胡分支出了兴化氏族。兴化氏族为萧姓，是古老的氏族。他们从事四种劳动：牧业、农业、狩猎业和手工业。
Translation:
There is a Xinghua nation。From the northern tribes, the Beihu tribes branch out。From the Beihu tribes, the Xinghua tribes branched out。The Xinghua tribes bear the family name of Xiao。 They are an ancient tribe, engaged in four kinds of labor production: husbandry, agriculture, hunting, and handicrafts。

14-15 青丘国
Qingqiu Guo
（118,17753E；39,63388N）

青丘之国[1]，有狐[2]，九尾[3]。

注释：[1]青丘国：指城街国，又称城山国，今河北唐山市。
Notes:[1] qing qiu guo (green mound country) refers to the Chengjie (city street) country， also known as the Chengshan Guo in today's Tangshan city, Hebei province。
[2] 有狐：是游牧民族的国家。
[2] you hu (has fox)
Tr: is a state of nomadic tribes.
[3] 九尾：指缴夷，属赤峰缴胡联盟国之夷。
[3] jiu yi (nine tails)
Tr: refers to the Jiao Yi， belonging to the Jiao Hu confederacy in Chifeng city。

译文：大城山国，是游牧氏族的国家，氏族叫缴夷。
Translation：
There is the Dachengshan Guo, a state of nomadic tribes, its people are called Jiao Yi。

14-16 柔仆民

Roupumin
（121,12887E；41,11637N）

有柔仆民[1]，是维嬴土之国[2]。

注释：[1]柔仆民：指辽濮地，今辽宁锦州地区。柔，指亮，后演变为辽。
Notes :[1] rou pu min (soft servant folk)
Tr: refers to the Liao Pu territory, in today's Jinzhou district, Liaoning province。 rou(soft) bright, later shifting into liao from Liang(bright) and then into Liao, the Liaoning province。

[2] 是为嬴土之国：是医巫部落联盟管理的国家。土，濮文写作白，指管理。
[2] shi wei ying tu zhi guo (thus is the winner earth country)
Tr: is a state managed by the tribal confederacy of Yiwu tribes。 Tu: in Pu script is written as bai(white) meaning manage。

译文：有一个辽濮之地，是医巫部联盟落管理的国家。
Translation:
There is a place called the land of Liao Pu, a state managed by the tribal confederacy of Yiwu tribes。

14-17 黑齿国
Heichi Guo
（123,43176E；41,80543N）

有黑齿之国[1]。帝俊生黑齿，姜姓[2]，黍食[3]，使四鸟[4]。

注释：[1]黑齿国：指浑丘国，今沈阳地区。
Notes:[1] hei chi guo (black teeth country)
Tr: refers to the Hunqiu Guo, in today's Shenyang region, Liaoning province。

[2] 姜姓：指王族，这里仍按姜姓表述。
[2] jiang xin: refers to the king lineage, here the family name Jiang is kept。

[3] 黍食：古老的氏族。
[3] shu shi (milliet eat): refers to the ancient tribes。

[4] 使四鸟：从事四种劳动。
[4] shi si niao: engaged in four kinds of labor。

译文：有一个国家叫浑丘国。北方的部落建立了浑丘国，浑丘国的氏族是姜姓氏族，是古老的氏族，从事四种劳动。
Tranlation:
There is a country called Hunqiu Guo。 The northern tribes established the Hunqiu Guo, whose tribes bear the family name of Jiang。They are ancient tribes, engaged in four kinds of labor。

14-18 天吴
Tianwu
（125,32432E；43,90164N）

有夏州之国[1]。有盖余之国[2] 。有神人 [3] 。八首人面 [4] ， 虎身十尾 [5], 名曰天吴 [6] 。

注释：[1]夏州国：指长州国，即长春。

Notes: [1] xia zhou guo (summer province country)
Tr: refers to the Changzhou (long province) country, e.g., Changchun (Lasting spring) city, Jilin province。

[2] 盖余国：指吉夷国。

[2] gai yu guo (cover extra country) refers to the Jiyi (lucky chaps' country) 。

[3] 神人：指肆镇。

[3] shen ren (holy person)
Tr: refers to the township: the Si and Zhen。

[4] 八首人面：指芝饶族聚居地。

[4]ba shou ren mian (eight heads human face)
Tr: refers to the settlements of Zhirao tribes。

[5] 虎身十尾：胡族的石韦。

[5]hu shen shi wei (tiger body ten tails)
Tr: The Shiwei people of the Hu tribes。

[6] 天吴：指宽城部落。

[6] tian wu (sky wu)
Tr: refers to the Kuancheng (wide city) tribe。

译文：大地的东北边有一个长州国，是吉夷之国。那个肆镇，是芝饶族的聚居地，是石韦胡族部落，称为宽城部落。

Translation:
In the northeast rim of the land there is Changzhou Guo, the country of the Jiyi。Their township is the settlements of the Zhirao tribes, who belong to the Hu people of the Shiwei。It is called the Kuancheng tribe。

14-19 鞠陵于天山
Julingyutianshan
（126,56767E；43,42777E）

大荒之中，有山名曰鞠陵于天[1]、东极[2]、离瞀[3]，日月所出。名曰折丹[4]，东方曰折，来风曰俊[5]，处东极以出入风 [6] 。

注释：[1]鞠陵于天：指鞠陵伊通山，今称哈达岭。
Notes: ju ling yu tian refers to Juling Yitong Mountain, it is known as Hadaling Mountain。

[2] 东极：指老爷岭。

[2] doing ji (east pole) refers to Laoyeling (grand old man ridge) mountain。

[3] 离瞀：指张广才岭。上述为吉林东部三山在夏商时期的古称谓。

[3]li mao: refers to Zhangguangcailing Mountain, the old names in the Xia and Shang times for the three mountains mentioned above in eastern Jilin province。

[4] 折丹：指丹江，又称牡丹江。

[4] zhe dan: refers to Danjiang River, also known as Mudanjiang River。

[5] 来风曰俊：来风指山里人，俊指镜泊，山里人称牡丹江为镜泊江。

[5] lai feng yue jun (come wind names handsome)
Tr: laifeng: people from the mountains, jun: refers to Jingpo (mirror lake)， the mountain people call the Mudanjiang River as Jingpojiang River。

[6] 出入风：指童子峰。

[6] chu ru feng (out in wind)
Tr: refers to Tongzi feng (baby kids peak) 。

译文：大地东北角有山名叫吉林伊通山、东极山、离瞀山，太阳和月亮从山的东面升起。这里有条江名叫牡丹江，东边的人称它为牡丹江，山里人称它为镜泊江，发源于老东极山的童子峰。
Translation:
In the northeast corner of the land there are mountains called Jilinyitongshan, Dongjishan, Limaoshan。 Sun and moon rise from the east of the mountains。 There is a river called Mudanjiang River。 People from the east call it Mudanjiang。 People from the mountains call it Jingpojiang。This river rises from the Tongzifeng of the Laodongji Mountain。

14-20 禺虢、禺京
Yuhao, Yujing
（131,94282E；43,80154N。130,96674E；45,29532N）

东海之渚中，有神[1]，人面鸟身[2]，珥两黄蛇，践两黄蛇[3]，名曰禺虢[4]。黄帝生禺虢[4]，禺虢生禺京 [6] 。禺京处北海 [7] ，禺虢处东海 [8] ，是为海神 [9] 。

注释：[1]神：指氏族。
Notes:[1] shen (deity): refers to tribes。
[2] 人面鸟身：定居河边的氏族。也称河边的定居氏族。
[2] ren mian niao shen (human face bird body)
Tr: refers to the tribes living by the riverbanks, also known as the settled tribe by the river。
[3] 珥两黄蛇、践两黄蛇：管理着双河地区的胡族。双河只是河流名，并没有两条。
[3]er liang huang she, jian liang huang she (earlop two yellow snakes, step two yellow snakes)
Tr: managing the Hu tribes by the Shuanghe region。Shuanghe is a river name, shuanghe does not mean two rivers, shuanghe is the name of just one river。
[4] 禺虢：指双河，在海参崴地区。
[4]yu hao: refers to Shuanghe, in Haishenwai region, today known as Vladivostok, Russia 。
[5] 黄帝生禺虢：北方的游牧民建立了双河部落。
[5] huang di sheng yu hao (yellow emperor begets Yuhao)
Tr: the northern nomads establish Shuanghe tribes。
[6] 禺京：穆棱河及下游的乌苏里江，在古代统称鸡溪，濮语读为溢鸡，谐音禺京。鸡溪部落不一定是珲春河部落所建，“禺虢生禺京”是造神的附会。
[6]yu jing: refers to Mulinghe and its lower branch the Wusuli River。Wusuli River was called in ancient times Jixi, in Pu speech it reads Yiji, a phonetic match to Yujing。The Jixi tribes were not necessarily established by Hunchunhe tribes。 Yuhao sheng Yujing is a fictional creation。
[7] 禺京处北海：鸡溪部落在北面。
[7]yu jing chu Beihai (Yujing is in North Sea)
Tr: Jixi tribe is located to the north。
[8] 禺虢处东海：双河部落在东面。
[8] yuhao chu Donghai (yuhao is in East Sea)
Tr: Shuanghe tribe is in the east。
[9] 是为海神：也就是海参崴地区。
[9] shi wei hai shen (thus is sea lord)
Tr: this is the Haishenwai region (Vladivostok）。

译文：在东海低地的地区，有一个氏族是河边的定居氏族，管理着双河地区的游牧民族，名叫双河部落。北方的游牧民族建立了双河部落，又建立了鸡溪部落。鸡溪部落在北面，双河部落在东面。双河部落实际就是海参崴地区。

Translation:
In the lowland of Donghai, there is a tribe which has settled by the river。 Managing the nomadic tribes in Shuanghe region, the tribe is called Shuanghe tribe。 The northern nomads established the Shuanghe tribe, and the Jixi tribe。Jixi tribe is in the north, Shuanghe tribe is in the east。 Shuanghe tribes in fact occupy the Haishenwai region。

14-21 玄股国
Xuangu Guo
（130,93207E；45,81609N）

有招摇山[1]，融水[2]出焉。有国曰玄股[3]，黍食 [4]，使四鸟。

注释：[1]招摇山：指七台山。今称北长白山。
Notes:[1] zhao yao shan (wave shake mount)
Tr: refers to the Qitai (seven terrace) Mountain， e.g., known today as Northern Changbai Mountain。
[2] 融水：指倭肯河，又称七台河。
[2] rong shui (melting water) refers to Woken River, also known as the Qitai River。
[3] 玄股国：指兴勾国，今称新兴区，在七台河。此处的玄股国不是海外东经所述的玄股国。
[3] xuan gu guo (dark thigh country)
Tr: refers to Xinggou Guo, known today as Xinxing (new boom) district in Qitaihe district。It is not to be confused with the Xuangu Guo in Haiwaidongjing。
[4] 黍食：古老的氏族。
[4] shu shi (millet eat)
Tr: ancient tribes。

译文：东北大地中有座山叫七台山，融水发源于这座山的西北麓。这里有一个国家叫兴勾，住着古老的氏族，从事着四种劳动。
Translation:
In the land of northeast region, there is a mountain called Qitaishan。Rongshui River rises from the northwest part of the mountain。There is a country called Xinggou。An ancient tribe lives there and is engaged in four kinds of production labour。

14-22 有易潜出
Youyiqianchu
（132,04151E；47,25081N）

有困民国[1]，勾姓而食[2]。有人曰王亥[3]， 两手操鸟 [4]， 方食其头 [5] 。王亥托于有易，河伯仆牛 [6] 。有易杀王亥取仆牛 [7]， 河念有易 [8]， 有易潜出 [9]， 为国于兽 [10]， 方食之 [11]， 名曰摇民 [12] 。帝舜生戏 [13]， 戏生摇民 [14] 。

注释：[1]困民国：指富强的国家。指友谊部落被迫迁徙后变成了富强之国。
Notes:[1] kun min guo (frustrated folk country)
Tr: refers to the powerful and rich country。It describes the Youyi tribe who was forced to migrate and became a very powerful and rich state。
[2] 勾姓而食：指勾羲的氏族。勾羲、勾尔沘、戈汝米那，应属远古的东北补苦氏族。
[2] gou xing er shi (gou as family name and eat)

Tr: refers to the Gouxi tribes。Gouxi, Gouerbi, Gerumina refers to the Buku tribes in northeast regions in ancient times。

[3] 有人曰王亥：有个集镇叫乌赫，今称双鸭山镇，在黑龙江省双鸭山市。

[3] you ren yue wang hai (has person called wang hai)
Tr: there is a township called Wuhe, known today as the Shuangyashan (double ducks mount) town, in Shuangya city, Heilongjiang province。

[4] 两手操鸟：是移民氏族的都城。

[4] liang shou cao niao (two hands handle birds)
Tr: refers to the capital city of the tribes of immigrants。

[5] 方食其头：统治着原住民的区域。

[5] fang shi qi tou (just eat its head)
Tr: rule the territory of the local original residents。

[6] 王亥托于有易，河伯仆牛：乌赫部落想将统治区域拓宽到友谊、宝山等仆挠河流域。

[6] wang hai tuo yu you yi, he bo bu niu (wang hai hires himself out to Lord of river to herd the cattle)
Tr: The Wuhe tribe wish to extend their control to cover the Burao River area where the Youyi and Baoshan tribes stay。

[7] 有易杀王亥取仆牛：友谊部落旁边的乌赫部落想攻占仆挠河流域的消息。

[7] you yi sha wang hai qu bu niu (You yi kill wanghai get Bu cattle)
Tr: refers to the news that the Youyi tribe's neighbour Wuhe tribe wish to take control of Burao River territory。

[8] 河念有易：宝山部落及时通知了友谊部落。河，指河伯，即宝山部落。

[8] he nian you yi (river read you yi)
Tr: the news is immediately passed to Youyi tribe by the Baoshan tribe, which is termed as He (river, or lord of river)。He (river) means Hebo (river duke), refers to the Baoshan tribe。

[9] 有易潜出：友谊部落提前转移。"潜出"，指向东迁移。友谊，音译词，指昌盛。

[9] you yi qian chu (youyi tribe sneak out)
Tr: Youyi tribe made quick move to escape, Qianchu (sneak out) means move to the east, Youyi(friendship) phonetic rendering of Pu speech, meaning prosper。

[10] 为国于兽：立国于富锦地区。

[10] wei guo yu shou (set up country where beasts are)
Tr: establish their state in Fujin region, Liaoning province。

[11] 方食之：治理着那里。

[11] fang shi zhi (thus eat it)
Tr: manage that region。

[12] 摇民：指绕米。即富饶之地。今称富锦。

[12] yao min (shake folk)
Tr: refers to Raomi, meaning land of abundance, known today as Fujin city, Liaoning province。

[13] 帝舜生戏：北边的松花江造就了温馨的疆域。

[13] dishun sheng xi (God Shun begets Drama)
Tr: The Songhuajiang River from the north gives birth to this warm and feel-at-home territory。

[14] 戏生摇民：温馨的疆域成就了饶米之国。

[14] xi sheng yao min (drama begets shake folk)
Tr: the warm feel-at-home territory makes the Raomi country possible。

译文：在七台山的北面，有一个富强之国，是勾羲氏族建立的国家。有一个集镇叫乌赫，是移民氏族的都城，统治着原住民的区域。乌赫部落想将统治区域拓宽到宝山、友谊等仆挠河流域。友谊地区旁边的乌赫部落想攻占仆挠河流域的消息，被宝山部落及时通知了友谊部落，友谊部落提前转移，建国于富锦地区，治理着那里，取名叫饶米国。北方的松花江造就了温馨的疆域，温馨的疆域成就了饶米国。

Translation:
To the north of Qitaishan, there is a rich and powerful country, a state built by the Gouxi tribes。 A township called Wuhe, a migrant city, rules over the territory of the residents。 The Wuhe tribe wishes to extend their control of territory over to the Purao River basin where the Baoshan tribe and Youyi tribe occupy。This news of the Wuhe tribe's intention to attack and occupy the Purao River area is passed by the Baoshan tribe to the Youyi tribe。 The Youyi tribe made immediate steps to move the tribes out and establish their state in Fujin area。They rule that new area and call it Raomi Guo。The Songhuajiang River in the north creates a warm and feel-at-home region, this region completes the Raomi Guo。

14-23 女丑、大蟹
Nvchou, Daxie
（134,3043E；46,44151N）

海内[1]有两人[2]，名曰女丑[2]。女丑有大蟹[4] 。

注释：[1]海内：指海外地区。
Notes:[1] hai nei (sea within) refers to the further out areas from the centre of China。
[2] 两人：指重镇。两，指良，即主要的，中心的。
[2] liang ren (two persons)
Tr: refers to important townships。 liang(two) means better, major, central in Pu speech。
[3] 女丑：指内切。今称卢切戈尔斯克。
[3] nv chou (girl ugly)
Tr: refers to a place called Neiqie, a shortened name for Luchegorsk, in present day Russia。
[4] 大蟹：读大湘，指大沼泽，也称大湖。
[4] da xie (big crab) reads as da xiang, meaning big zee, big lake。

译文：在东海外海参崴的北边，有一个重要的集镇，叫内切。内切有一个大湖。
Translation:
In the northern part of Haishenwai (*Vladivostok*) in Donghaiwai region, there is a very important township called Neiqie。There is a big lake in Neiqie。

14-24 孽摇頵羝山与汤谷扶木
Nieyaojundishan and Tanggufumu
（137,02257E；50,5425N）

大荒之中，有山名孽摇頵羝[1]。上有扶木[2]， 柱三百里 [3]， 其叶如芥 [4] 。有谷曰温源谷 [5] 。汤谷上有扶木 [6]， 一日方至，一日方出 [7]， 皆载于乌 [8] 。

注释：[1]孽摇頵羝：烈奥万丹山东面的坝子叫孽摇頵羝，意为霜剑之甸。
Notes： [1] nie yao jun di (evil shake jun goat)
Tr: refers to the place (bazi) east of Lieaowandan Mountain。Its meaning is the meadow of frosty sword。
[2] 上有扶木：那里有一个统治中心。统治中心的名称也叫孽摇頵羝，今称共青城。
[2] shang you fu mu (above there is hold wood)
Tr: there is a controlling centre, also named Nieyaojundi, today known as Komsomolsk-na-Amure。
[3] 柱三百里：指外族的都城。
[3]zhu san bai li (column 300 li)
Tr: refers to the capital city of foreign tribes or of outsider people。

[4] 其叶如芥：支系为基姆族。
[4] qi ye ru jie (its leaves like mustard seeds) its branches are the Kimu people。
[5] 有谷曰温源谷：有国家叫乌溢国，即乌苏里河国。
[5] you gu yue wen yuan gu (has valley name warm water source valley)
Tr: there is a country called Wuyi Guo, e.g., Wusulihe (Ussuri River) Guo。
[6] 汤谷上有扶木：中心国外还有治所。
[6] tang gu shang you fu mu (hotwater valley up has fumu) fumu: Fu wood。
Tr: besides the center of state, there are other management offices。
[7] 方至、方出：指比金、伯力。汉语按比进、伯离译为方至、方出。
[7] fang zhi, fang chu (just arrive, just leave)
Tr: refers to Bijin, and Boli。Bijin is today's Bikin, Boli is today's Khabarovsk/ the names are transliterated into Chinese signs of Fangzhi, and Fangchu。
[8] 皆载于乌：皆座落于乌苏里江畔。
[8] jie zai yu wu （all carried by bird)
Tr: all those townships are located on the bank of Ussuri River。

译文：在大地中有个地方叫孽摇頵羝，那里有一个统治中心，是外族的都城，氏族支系为基姆族。国家的名称叫乌溢国。中心国外还有治所，一个集镇叫比金，一个集镇叫伯力，都座落于乌苏里江畔。
Translation:
In the middle of land there is a place called Nieyaojundi。 There is an administration centre there, which is the capital city of outsider tribes。The tribes belong to the Jimu people。 The name of the state is Wuyi nation。Beside the central state, there are other controlling centers, one is Bikin, one is Boli, both centers are located on the banks of Ussuri River。

14-25 奢比尸
Shebishi
（136,49517E；52,42251N）

有神[1]，人面，大耳，兽身[2]，珥两青蛇[3]，名奢比尸[4]。

注释：[1]有神：有一个氏族。
Notes:[1] you shen (has deity): there is a clan。
[2] 人面，大耳，兽身：定居的游牧氏族。
[2] ren mian (human face), da er (big ears), shou shen (beasts' body)
Tr. Refers to the nomadic clans that have settled down。
[3] 珥两青蛇：管理着东边的两个集肆区域，即奥西片科肆与红亚尔肆。
[3] er liang qing she (earlop two green snakes)
Tr. Manage two market townships district in the east, Osipenko and Krasny Yar。
[4] 奢比尸：指奥西片科氏。
[4] she bi shi (luxurious compare corpse)
Tr. Refers to Osipenko Shi。

译文：有一个氏族，是定居的游牧氏族，管理着东边的两个集肆区域，名叫奥西片科。Translation:
There is a settled nomadic tribe, in control of the territory of two townships in the east。 The name of the tribe is Osipenko。

14-26 五彩鸟相乡弃沙
Wucainiaoxiangxiangqisha
（140,20216E; 53,54295N）

有五彩之鸟[1]，相乡弃沙[2]，惟帝俊下友[3]。帝下两坛[4]，彩鸟是司 [5] 。

注释：[1]五彩鸟：指奇利亚部落。五，指部落；彩鸟，指奇利亚。
Notes: [1] wu cai niao (five color bird)
Tr: refers to the Qilia tribe。wu(five)meaning tribe。 cainiao (color bird) a phonetic rendering of Kiria。
[2] 相乡弃沙：指尚塔尔群岛。小的岛屿称沙。
[2] xiang xiang qi sha: refers to the Shantar Islands located off the northwestern shore of the Sea of Okhotsk east of Uda Gulf and north of Academy Bay。 Small islands are termed Sha（sand) in Pu concept。
[3] 帝俊下友：北方部落的东部属地。帝，指北；下，指东。
[3] di jun xia you (God handsome lower friend)
Tr: the eastern territory of the Northern tribes。 Di (God)meaning north, xia(lower) meaning east。
[4] 帝下两坛：东北边的两个区域。
[4] di xia liang tan (God lower two terrace)
Tr: the two districts in the northeast part。
[5] 彩鸟是司：奇利亚部落管理的地方。
[5] cai niao shi si (color bird is supervising)
Tr: the territory managed by the Kirian tribes。

译文：有一个奇利亚部落和尚塔尔群岛，是北方部落国东边的属地。东北边的两个区域，是奇利亚部落管理的地方。
Translation:
There is a Kirian tribe and the Shantar Islands, the territories controlled by the northern tribes in the east。 The two districts in the northeast part are the territory managed by the Kirian tribes。

14-27 猗天苏门山
Yitiansumenshan
（135,56656E; 62,65301N）

大荒之中，有山名叫猗天苏门[1]，日月所生。有壎民国[2] 。

注释：[1]猗天苏门：读溢丹苏木，指恒的勾，今汉德加。溢丹，指阿尔丹河；苏木，指管理中心、集镇。溢丹苏木山，指外兴安岭。今称斯塔洛夫山。
Notes: [1]yi tian su men: reads as yi dan su mu。The phrase refers to Hengdigou, known today as Khandyga, a close phonetic rendering with Chinese signs。Yidan, refers to the Aldan River, right tributary of the Lena River in the Sakha Republic in Eastern Siberia。 sumu(sum) refers to the administration centre or the township。Yidansumushan refers to the Waixinganling Mountains, known today as the Stanovoy Range (Russian: Станово́й хребе́т, Stanovoy khrebet; simplified Chinese: 外兴安岭; traditional Chinese: 外興安嶺; pinyin: Wài Xīng'ān Lǐng) also known as Sükebayatur and Sükhbaatar in Mongolian, Stanovoy Mountains, or Outer Khingan Range。
[2] 壎民国：指湿地国、沼泽地国，地图标注为 Saydy。
[2] xun min guo (xun folk country)
Tr: refers to the wetland country, the swamp country。 The term Saydy is used in the map, which is very likely a phonetic rendering of shidi (wet land) 。

译文：东北大地中有座山，叫溢丹苏木山，是太阳和月亮升起的地方。那里有个国家叫湿地国。
Translation:
In the middle of northeast land there is a mountain range called Yidansumu Mountain。 It is from here that the sun and moon rise。There is a country called Shidi Guo (wetland country) 。

14-28 壑明俊疾山
Huomingjunjishan
（171,15737E；61,95458N）

有綦山[1]。又有摇山[2] 。有䰝山 [3]， 又有门户山 [4]， 又有盛山 [5] 。又有待山 [6] 。有五彩之鸟 [7] 。东荒之中，有山名曰壑明俊疾 [8]， 日月所出。有中容之国 [9] 。

注释：[1]綦山：指切尔斯基山。
Notes:[1] ji shan: refers to the Chersky Range。 (Gora Cherskogo)
[2] 摇山：指雅布洛夫山。
[2] yao shan: refers to the Yablonoi Mountains in today's Transbaikal in Russia。
[3] 䰝山：指中部山，又称堪察加半岛。
[3] zeng shan: refers to Zhongbushan (middle part mountain) known today as the Kamchatka Peninsula in Russian Far East。
[4] 门户山：指穆霍莫尔山，又称楚科奇山。
[4] men hu shan (door hallway mount)
Tr: refers to the Mohuomore Mountain, e.g., Chukotskoye Nagorye (Chukot Range, Chukotka Mountains) 。
[5] 盛山：指萨哈林山，又称库页岛。
[5] sheng shan: refers to Sakhalin Mountains, also known as Sakhalin Island in Russia, *pinyin: Kùyè dǎo; lit. 'island of the Ainu') or "Kuye Fiyaka"* 。
[6] 待山：指塔洛夫卡山，又称科里亚克山。
[6] dai shan: refers to the Taluofuka Mountain, e.g., Koryaksky Volcano or Koryakskaya Sopka in Russia。
[7] 五彩鸟：指东方的部落。
[7] wu cai niao (five color bird)
Tr: the tribes in the east。
[8] 壑明俊疾山：读壑穆俊纪山，指海岸卡拉金部落山，今称科里亚克山。
[8] huo ming jun ji shan: refers to the Huomujunjishan, e.g., Kharajin tribe Mountain by the coast, known today as Koryak Mountain (Koryaksky mountain) 。
[9] 中容国：指美丽之国。即烈奥万丹国，又称乌溢国。
[9] zhong rong guo: the country of the beautiful, e.g., Lieaowandan Guo， also called Wuyi Guo。

译文：在须伯利亚，有切尔斯基山，有雅布洛夫山，有中部山，有穆霍莫尔山，有萨哈林山，有塔洛夫山，有东方的部落。 在东部地区，有座山叫海岸美丽之国山，是日月升起的地方。有美丽之国。
Translation：
In the land of Siberia, there are the Chernsky Mountain, Yabuluov Mountain, the Zhongbu Mountain, the Muhuomo'er Mountain, the Sakhalin Mountain, the Tarov Mountain and the tribes from the East。
In the eastern region, there is a mountain known as the beautiful mountain country along the coast, where the sun and the moon rise。There is a country of beautiful land。

14-29 三青马、三骓
Sanqingma, sanzhui.

（粮食类，无需标注坐标）kinds of grains no location is needed。

东北海外，又有三青马[1]、三骓[2]、甘华[3]。爰有遗玉[4] 、三青鸟 [5] 、三骓、视肉 [6] 、甘华、甘柤 [7] 。百谷所在。

注释：[1]三青马：指外穄馍，即黑麦。
Notes:[1] san qing ma (three green horses) refers to Waijimo: e.g., black wheat。
[2] 三骓：外穄、奢穄，即黄米。
[2] san zhui (three horse): waiji, sheji, e.g., yellow millet。
[3] 甘华：读嘎华，指小麦。
[3] gan hua (sweet flower) reads as gahua, referring to wheat。
[4] 遗玉：指水芋，即芋头。
[4] yi yu (drop jade) refers to water taro, e.g., taro。
[5] 三青鸟：指老麦、青稞、外青麦。
[5] san qing niao (three green grain) refers to Laomai (old wheat), qingke(buckwheat), waiqingmai (a kind of wheat) 。
[6] 视肉：读厶挠，指稻谷。
[6] shi rou (gaze meat) reads as sirao, referring to rice。
[7] 甘柤：一种散穗的麦类，也称燕麦。
[7] gan ju (sweet grain) a kind of wheat with loose kernels, also known as oats。

译文：东北海外地区，有黑麦、黄米、小麦，又说有芋头、老麦、黄米、稻谷、小麦、燕麦等谷物，是百谷生长的好地方。
Translation:
In the land of northeast Haiwai, there are black wheat, yellow millet, wheat, as well as taro, old wheat, yellow millet, rice, wheat, oats。 This is a good place for one hundred kinds of grain to grow。

14-30 女和月母国
Nvheyuemu Guo
（173,24818E；66,50574N）

有女和月母之国[1]。有人名曰鵷[2]，北方曰鵷，来风曰【犭炎】[3]，是处东极隅，以止日月 [4]，使无相间出没 [5]，司其短长 [6] 。

注释：[1]女和月母国：指穆霍高原国，今称穆霍莫尔国。女读 me 音；月母，指高原。
Notes: [1] nv he yue mu guo (girl and moon mother country)
Tr: refers to the Muhuo Plateau country, known today as the Muhuomo'er Guo, nv(girl) reads as me, yuemu (moon mother) a term in Pu speech as Gaoyuan, upland or plateau。
[2]鵷：读汶，指奥莫隆，即水岸的村庄。
[2] wan, reads as wen, refers to Aomolong, meaning: the villages by the water。
[3] 【犭炎】：指溢，水岸，即奥莫隆。
[3] yan: reads as Yi, meaning water bank, e.g., Aomolong （Omolon）。
[4] 以止日月：指伊孜诺耶，今称穆霍莫尔诺耶。伊孜，指水源；诺耶，即淖尔。
[4] yi zhi ri yue (to stop sun moon) refers to Yizinuoye, known today as Muhuomo'ernuoye。 Yizi: water source, Nuoye (nuur, naor, a body of water) 。
[5] 使无相间出没："使无"，建立部落；"相间"，指称王；"出没"，指楚科奇高原。
[5] shi wu xiang jian chu mo (make no fail rise setting)

Tr: shi wu; form tribes, xiang jian: be the lord over others, chu mo: the Chukot plateau。

[6] 司其短长：统治着各个城镇。"短长"，即邓丘，指城镇。

[6]si qi duan chang (order its short, long)

Tr: rule over all and each of the townships。Duanchang (short, long) refers to the Dengqiu, meaning townships。

译文：东北角有一个国家叫穆霍莫尔国。有一个集镇部落叫奥莫隆，山里人称为溢莫隆，这个部落迁到东边的伊孜诺耶，建立穆霍莫尔国，称雄于楚科奇高原，统治着各个城镇。

Translation:

In the northeast corner there is a country called Muhuomore Guo。 There is a township tribe called Aomolong (Omolon)。 The mountain people call it Yimolong。 This tribe migrated to Yizinuoye in the east and established Muhuomo'er Guo, lording over the Chukqi Highland, controlling all the townships。 (The Chukotka Mountains (Russian: Чукотское нагорье) or Chukotka Upland (Чукотская горная страна)

14-31 应龙杀蚩尤与夸父

Yinglong-sha-chiyou-yu-kuafu

（127,35749E；70,68402N）

大荒东北隅中，有山名曰凶犁土丘[1]。应龙处南极[2]，杀蚩尤与夸父，不得复上 [3]，故下数旱 [4] 。旱而为应龙之状 [5]，乃得大雨 [6] 。

注释：[1]凶犁土丘：指丘休尔地区。

Notes: [1] xiong li tu qiu (danger plough earth mound)

Tr: refers to the Qiuxiuer region。

[2] 应龙处南极：部落名，指伊勒楚那纪。

[2] yinglong chu nan ji (ying dragon stay south pole)

Tr: a tribe name: Yilechunaji。

[3] 杀蚩尤与夸父，不得复上：外迁入的北胡的巴塔迈支系。

[3] sha chi you yu kua fu (kill chiyou and Kuanfu) bu de fu shan (can't return)

Tr: refers to the Batamai branch of the northern Hu people who migrated here。

[4] 故下数旱：甘斯萨赫支系。

[4]gu xia shu han (therefore release a few droughts)

Tr: refers to the Gansisahe branch。

[5] 旱而为应龙之状：霍尔维伊勒支系。

[5] han er wei ying long zhi zhuang (drought thus be yinglong look)

Tr: refers to the Hurweiyile branch。

[6] 乃得大雨：游牧的鞑夷。

[6] nai de da yu (thus got big rain)

Tr: the nomadic Da/Dar Yi。

译文：在大地东北角的丘休尔地区，有一个部落国叫伊勒楚那纪。那里的氏族是外迁入的北胡的巴塔迈支系、甘斯萨赫支系、霍尔维伊勒支系，是游牧的鞑夷。

Translation:

In the northeast corner of the land there is the Qiuxiur region。 There is a tribal state called Yilechunaji。 The tribes there are the Northern Hu's migrant Batamai branch, Gansisahe branch, Hurweiyile branch。 They are the nomadic Da/Dar Yi。

14-32 东海夔牛

Donghaikuiniu
（127,79944E；26,28442N）

东海中有流波山[1]，入海七千里。其上有兽，状如牛，苍身而无角[2]，一足[3]，出入水则必风雨[4]，其光如日月[5]，其声如雷[6]，其名曰夔[7]。黄帝得之，以其皮为鼓[8]，撅以雷兽之骨[9]，声闻五百里[10]，以威天下。

注释：[1]流波山：指琉球群岛。
Notes:[1] liu po shan (flow wave mount) refers to the Ryukyu Islands。
[2]牛，苍身而无角：僚族在夏草的夏部落支系。苍身，指夏草，又称宿迁；无角，读武鼓，指夏部落。
[2] niu, cang shen er wu jiao (ox, dark body but no horns)
Tr: the Liao people's Xia tribes' branches in Xiacao。 cangshen (dark body): refers to Xiacao, also known as Suqian。wujiao (no horns) reads as wugu, referring to the Xia tribes。
[3] 一足：指大氏族。
[3] yi zu (one foot) refers to the major tribal branch。
[4] 出入水则必风雨：迁子支系于统属地。
[4] chu ru shui ze bi feng yu (out in water must make storm)
Tr: move the branches to the controlled territory。
[5] 其光如日月：让族人管理着移居地。光，指族人；日，指居住；月，指越。
[5] qi guang ru ri yue (its light like sun and moon)
Tr: let tribal folks manage the land they migrated to。 guang(light) means own tribal people, ri(sun) means to reside; yue(moon) means going across。
[6] 其声如雷：声名显赫。
[6] qi sheng ru lei (its sound as thunder) its reputation is as loud as thunder。
[7]夔：指夏僚。夔牛也指夏僚。
[7] kui (a kind ox) refers to the Xiao Liao, Kuiniu means the Xialao people。
[8] 其皮为鼓：其祖为夏族。
[8] qi pi wei gu (its skin make drum)
Tr: its ancestors belong to the Xia ethnic people。
[9] 撅以雷兽之骨：祖籍为骆马湖支系的夏族。
[9] jue yi lei shou zhi gu (dig with thunder beast's bone)
Tr: its origin be traced back to the Xia tribe from the Luoma Lake branch。
[10] 声闻五百里：表彰于部落和京城。
[10] sheng wen wu bai li (sound heard five hundred li) 。
Tr: Praise of their achievement is spread throughout the tribes and the capital city。

译文：东海中有一个琉球群岛，离海岸有七千里，那里的氏族是僚族在夏草的夏部落的大氏族。他们迁子支系于统属地，让族人管理着移居地，声名显赫，他们的氏族名称叫夏僚。黄帝得知这个情况，以他们的祖先是祖籍在骆马湖的夏部落的支系，在各个部落以及京城表彰他们，以威天下。
Translation:
In the East Sea there is a group of islands called Ryukyu Islands。 It is 7000 li away from the seacoast。 The tribes on the islands are the Liao people's Xia tribes who had migrated from Xiacao to the islands。 They moved their branches to the territory, and let tribal people manage the settlements。 They become famous, and their tribal name is Xialao。 Huangdi heard of this news and praised their achievement citing that their ancestors are the Xia people, their birthplace is at Luoma Lake 。Huangdi's praise is spread far and wide throughout all the tribes and the capital city to show to the world his state power。

第十五卷大荒南经 （The Great Wilderness: the South）

Book 15 Dahuangnanjing

15-01 跊踢、双双
Chuti、Shuangshuang
（108,9056E；25,753N，111,6109E；26,42357N）

南海之外，赤水[1]之西，流沙之东[2]，有兽，左右有首[3]，名曰跊踢[4]。有三青鸟[5] 相并，名曰双双[6] 。

注释：[1]赤水指湘江。湘江属长江水系，故称赤水。
Notes: [1] refers to Xiangjiang River, which is part of the Yangtze River system, therefore also known as Chishui (Red River) 。

[2] 流沙：读腊舍，指红水河。
[2] liu sha (flowing sands) reads as Lashe, refers to the Hongshuihe (red water) River。

[3] 左右有首：指招瑶之族，即过山瑶。
[3] zuo you you shou (left right has heads) refers to the Zhaoyao tribes, also known as Guoshan (cross hills) Yao people。

[4] 跊踢：读苏体，指九万大山氏族。
[4] chu ti reads as suti, refers to the Jiuwandashan (ninety thousand big mountains) tribes。

[5] 三青鸟：三个东部的僚族。指毛南、么佬和苗族。
[5] san qing niao (three green birds) refers to the three eastern Lao tribes。 They are the Maonan, Yaolao and Miao。

[6] 双双：指舜舜氏族，即纹身氏族。
[6] shuang shuang (twin twin) refers to the Shunshun tribes, famous for tattooing their bodies。

译文：在南海外的大地中，在湘江的西面，在红水河的东面，有一个氏族是过山瑶支系，名叫九万大山氏族。与九万大山氏族相邻的，有三个东部的僚族，他们是刺绣和纹身的氏族。
Translation:

In the land of Nanhaiwai, in the west part of Xiangjiang River, to the east part of Hongshuihe River, there lives the Guoshanyao, called Jiuwandashan tribe。 It has three neighbours of eastern Lao tribes。 They are the triibes practicing embroidery and tattooing。

15-02 苍梧之野
Cangwuzhiye
（112,10267E; 23,75711N）

有阿山者[1]。南海之中，有汜天之山[2]，赤水穷焉[3]，赤水之东有苍梧之野[4]，舜与叔钧之所葬也[5]。爰有文贝[6]、离俞[7]、【丘鸟】久[8]、鹰[9]、贾[10]、委维[11]、熊、罴、象、虎、豹、狼、视肉[12]。

注释：[1]阿山者：指大阿山支系，即岭南支系。大阿，读歹卧，指岭南。
Notes:[1] a 'shan: refers to the Da'ashan branch。 It is also known as the Lingnan (ridge south) branch。 Da'a: reads as dai wo, refers to the south of ridge。
[2] 汜天山：指数歹山，数歹，即九岭。今称九嶷山。
[2]si tian shan [rising water sky mount)
Tr: refers to Shudaishan。 Shudai means Nine ridge, known today as Jiuyishan。
[3] 赤水穷焉：湘江的源头。
[3] chi shui qiong yan （red water dry out)
Tr: refers to the headwater of Xiangjiang River。
[4] 苍梧之野：指苍部落之乡。这里指九嶷山地区。
[4] cang wu zhi ye (dark straight wood land) refers to the land of the Cang tribes。 It refers to the Jiuyishan area。
[5] 舜与叔钧之所葬也：纹身的九嶷部落的疆域。叔钧，读数纪，指九嶷部落。
[5] shun yu shu yun zhi suo zang ye:(shun and shuyun buried here)
Tr: the territory of tattooing people from Jiuyi tribes。 Shuyun: reads as shuji, refers to the Jiuyi tribe。
[6] 文贝：指贝江部落。
[6] wen bei (marked shell) refers to the Beijiang tribes。
[7] 离俞：指宁远部落。
[7]li yu: refers to the Ningyuan tribes。
[8] 【丘鸟】久：指蓝山部落，原读且照部落。
[8] qiu jiu: refers to the Lanshan (blue mount) tribes, previously read as Qiezhao tribes。
[9]鹰：指英水部落。
[9] ying（eagle) refers to the Yingshui tribe。
[10]贾：指道部落。
[10] jia: refers to the Dao tribes。
[11] 委维：指江华部落。
[11] wei wei: refers to the Jianghua tribes。
[12]熊、罴、象、虎、豹、狼、视肉：指狩猎业、手工业、制漆业、牧业、农业、种麻业、种稻业。泛指各行各业。
[12] xiong(bear), pi(bear), xiang(elephant), hu(tiger), bao(leopard), lang(wolf), shirou (gaze meat) refers to the professions of hunting, handicrafts, lacquer making, husbandry, agriculture, hemp growing, rice growing, a figurative way to refer to all kinds of specialized labour in production, manufactures, industry。

译文：有岭南支系的氏族。在南方地区，有座九嶷山，是湘江的源头，湘江的东面是苍部落之乡，是纹身的九嶷部落的疆域。那里有贝江部落、宁远部落、蓝山部落、英水部落、道部落、江华部落氏族，从事着各行各业的劳动。
Translation：
There are the branches from the Lingnan tribes。 In the land of southern regions, there is the Jiuyishan, where the headwater for Xiangjiang River rises。 To the east of the river lies the land of the Cangwu tribes, the territory of the tattooing branches from the Jiuyi tribes。 The following tribes live there: the Beijiang, the Ningyuan, the Lanshan, the Yingshui, the Dao, the Jianghua。 They are engaged in all kinds of labour and profession。

15-03 黑水玄蛇
Heishuixuanshe
（113,29223E；25,85476N）

有荣山[1]，荣水[2]出焉。黑水[3] 之南，有玄蛇 [4]，食麈 [5] 。

注释：[1]荣山：指雍山，汉语称为罗围山，今称天鹅山，在湖南郴州资兴市。
Notes; [1] rong shan: refers to the Yongshan, in Chinese it is called Luoweishan, known today as the Tian'eshan (mount swan) in Zixing city, Binzhou, Hunan province。
[2] 荣水：指罗围河，今称山河。
[2] rong shui: refers to Luoweihe River, today it is known as Shanhe River (mount river) 。
[3] 黑水：指湘江。湘，读 hang 音，与黑谐音。
[3] hei shui (black water) refers to the Xiangjiang River, xiang reads as hang, close phonetic to hei (black)。
[4] 玄蛇：指东河，又称东江。
[4] xuan she (black snake) refers to the Donghe (east river), also known as the Dongjiang。
[5] 食麈：指通航。
[5] shi chen (eat dust) meaning the river is navigable, and water transportation provided。

译文：有一座山叫罗围山，罗围水发源于这里。湘江的南部，有一条东江，通航。
Translation:
There is a mountain called Luoweishan。 Luoweishui River rises out of here。 In the south part of the Xiangjiang River, there is the Dongjiang where river navigation and transportation are carried out。

15-04 巫山黄鸟
Wushanhuangniao
（114,16663E；26,02009N）

有巫山[1]者，西有黄鸟[2]。帝药、八斋[3]。黄鸟于巫山，司此玄蛇[4]。

注释：[1]巫山：指沤山，今称诸广山。
Notes:[1] wu shan (witch mount) refers to Oushan, known today as Zhuguangshan。
[2] 黄鸟：指沤河，又称沤水。
[2] huang niao (yellow bird) refers to Ouhe River, or Oushui River。
[3] 帝药、八斋：北面有八面山。
[3] di yao, (God medicine) ba zhai (eight restrains)
Tr: to its north, there is the Bamianshan (eight-sided mountain) 。
[4] 司此玄蛇：流入东江。
[4]si ci xuan she (govern this black snake)

Tr: flows into Dongjiang River。

译文：有一座山叫沤山，它的西面有一条河叫沤水。北面有八面山。沤水从沤山流向东江。
Translation:
There is a mountain called Oushan。 To its west there is a river called Oushui。 To its north, there is the Bamianshan。 Oushui River flows out of Oushan and goes into Dongjiang River。

15-05 三身国
Sanshen Guo
（114,28962E；26,74716N）

大荒之中，有不庭之山[1]，荣水[2]穷焉。有人三身[3]，帝俊妻娥皇 [4]，生此三身之国 [5]，姚姓，黍食 [6]，使四鸟。有渊四方 [7]，四隅皆达，北属黑水，南属大荒。北方名曰少和之渊 [8]，南方名曰从渊 [9]，舜之所浴也 [10]。

注释：[1]不庭山：指万山，今称万洋山。
Notes:[1] bu ting shan (no hall mount)
Tr: refers to Wanshan, known today as Wanyangshan (10000 oceans mount)。
[2] 荣水：指灕水。
[2] rong shui: refers to the Lishui River。
[3] 有人三身：有惹厦堵，有一个集镇叫厦坪。
[3] you ren san shen (has human three body)
Tr: reads as you re sha du, a phonetic rendering, meaning there is a township called Shaping。
[4] 帝俊妻娥皇：北面的碧溪湖。
[4] di jun qi e huang (di handsome marry girl queen E)
Tr: refers to the Bixi (green brook) lake to the north。
[5] 生此三身之国：建此厦堵之国，建此厦坪之国。
[5] sheng ci san shen zhi guo (born this three bodies country)
Tr: has established this Shadu nation, or this Shaping nation。
[6] 姚姓，黍食：是苗瑶的古老氏族。
[6] yao xin, shu shi (surname yao, millet eat)
Tr. Refers to the ancient clans of the Miao and Yao。
[7] 有渊四方：有四方乡。
[7] you yuan si fang (has deep water four corner)
Tr: has townships all around, in four corners。
[8] 少和之渊：指年彤之乡。
[8] shao he zhi yuan (young peace deep water) refers to the land of Niantong。
[9] 从渊：指拿乡。从，指持、拿。
[9] cong yuan (follow pond): refers to Naxiang, cong, means hold or take in hands。
[10] 舜之所浴也：指纹身氏族之乡。
[10] shun zhi suo yu ye (shun bathing place) refers to the land of tribes who tattoo their bodies。

译文：在南方地区，有一座山叫万洋山，灕水发源于这座山。这里有一个集镇叫厦坪，是北面的碧溪湖部落建立的厦坪国，是古老的苗瑶氏族的生活地，他们从事着四种劳动。这里有四方乡村，四处相通，北属黑水，南属大荒，北面属年彤之乡，南面是拿乡，是纹身氏族之乡。
Translation:

In the southern area, there is a mountain called Wanyangshan。 The Lishui River rises from this mountain。 There is a township called Shaping, the Shaping Guo established by the Bixihu tribes from the north。 The place is the land of the ancient Yao Miao tribes。 They are engaged in four kinds of labor。 This is a place open to neighbouring countryside in four corners, to its north the Heishui, to its south the Dahuang。 The north belongs to the Niantong land, to the south is Naxiang, the land of the tattooing tribes。

15-06 季禺国、羽民国、卵民国
Jiyu Guo, Yumin Guo, Luanmin Guo
（114,03923E；27,63371N。114,3877E；27,79274N。114,61693E；27,38275N）

又有成山[1]，甘水[2]穷焉。有季禺之国[3]，颛顼之子 [4]，食黍 [5] 。有羽民之国 [6]，其民皆生毛羽 [7] 。有卵民之国 [8]，其民皆生卵 [9] 。

注释：[1]成山：指卢山，今称武功山。
Notes:[1] cheng shan: refers to Lushan, today known as Wugongshan。
[2] 甘水：指赣江。
[2] gan shui (sweet water) refers to the Ganjiang River。
[3] 季禺国：指芦溪国。
[3] jiyu guo: refers to Luxi Guo, (reed creek nation) 。
[4] 颛顼之子：指萍国的支系。颛顼，读藻羲，指萍国。
[4] zhuanxu zhi zi (Zhuanxu's son): refers to the Pingguo branch。Zhuangxu reads as zaoxi, meaning Ping Guo。
[5] 食黍：古老氏族。
[5] shi shu (eat millet): ancient tribes。
[6] 羽民国：指宜春国。春，读音 mei，谐音民。
[6]yu min guo (feather people nation) refers to Yichun Guo, chun (spring season) reads as mei, (may in English), a close phonetic match to min。
[7] 其民皆生毛羽：其民皆是苗夷。
[7] qi min jie sheng mao yu (its people all grow hair feather)
Tr: its people are all Miao Yi。
[8] 卵民国：指寮地国。今江西吉安市安福县，有遗存名寮塘。
[8] luan min guo (egg people nation) refers to Liaodi Guo, in today's Anfu county, Ji'an city, Jiangxi province, a relic name Liaotang survives。
[9] 其民皆生卵：其民皆是僚族。
[9] qi min jie sheng luan (all its people lay eggs)
Tr: all its people are Liao/Lao people。

译文：南方地区有座山叫武功山，是赣江的源头之一。那里有一个芦溪国，是萍国支系的古老氏族；有一个宜春国，那里的氏族皆为苗夷；有一个寮米国，那里的氏族皆为僚族。
Translation：
In the southern region there is a mountain called Wugongshan, the headwater of Ganjiang rises from here。The country called Luxi Guo is one of the ancient tribes of Ping Guo。 There is a Yichun Guo, its people are Miao tribes。Another country is the Laomi Guo, its people are Lao tribes。

15-07 不姜山
Bujiangshan
（114,57566E；29,36491N）

大荒之中，有不姜之山，黑水穷焉[1]，又有贾山，汔水[2]出焉。又有言山[3] 。又有登备山 [4] 。有䴔䴔之山 [5] 。又有蒲山，澧水 [6] 出焉。又有隗山，其西有丹，其东有玉 [7] 。又南有山，漂水 [8] 出焉。有尾山 [9]，有翠山 [10] 。

注释：[1]不姜山，黑水穷焉：指幕阜山脉，山的东麓到了长江边。
Notes: [1] bu jiang shan (no ginger mount)， hei shui qiong yi (black water dries)
Tr: refers to the Mufushan, its east stretch reaches the Yangtze River。

[2] 贾山，汔水：贾山，指通道山，简称通山，是幕阜山主峰；汔水，指修水。

[2] jia shan, qi shui: refers to the Tongdaoshan, shortened to Tongshan, which is the peak of Mufushan。 Qi shui: refers to Xiushui River。

[3] 言山：指梅山。言读音 niu，梅读音 liu，二者谐音。

[3] yan shan (speech mount) refers to Meishan, yan reads as niu, mei reads as liu, a close phonetic match, N/L not distinguished。

[4] 登备山：指连云山。

[4] deng bei shan (climb prepare mount） refers to Lianyunshan (linking clouds mount) 。

[5] 䴔䴔山：指洛霄山，今称罗霄山。

[5] jia jia shan (indifferent mount) refers to the Luoxiaoshan, known today as the Luoxiaoshan。 (Luo: 洛，罗) 。

[6] 蒲山，澧水：蒲山，指濮山，今称复山，今江西修水县复原乡；澧水，指漫江。

[6] pu shan (reeds mount) li shui: Li River
Tr: refers to Pushan, known today as Fushan, in today 's Fuyuan district, Xiushui county, Jiangxi province。 Lishui River, refers to Manjiang River。

[7] 隗山，其西有丹，其东有玉：隗山，指官山，在江西宜丰县黄岗乡；丹，指灯盏窝氏族；玉，指龙潭氏族。

[7] wei shan (big mount) qi xi you dan (its west has cinnabar), qi dong you yu (its east has jade)
Notes: refers to the Guanshan in Huanggang (yellow ridge) district, Yifeng county, Jiangxi province。 Dan(cinnabar) refers to the Dengzhanwo tribe, Yu, (jade) refers to the Loongtan (dragon pond) tribes。

[8] 有山：指七宝山，因 '宝'与古汉语的 '有'读音相近，被汉译为 '有山'。

[8] you shan (has hills)
Tr. Refers to the Qibaoshan (seven treasure mount), bao and you phonetically close in Classical Chinese, therefore, transliterated as Bo (you), therefore, the Youshan。

[9] 漂水：指牛膀水，读音渌撇溢，今称渌水，发源于湖南浏阳东侧的七宝山。

[9] piao shui (floating water) refers to Niupangshui (ox hoof water)
Tr: it reads as lu pie yi, known today as Lvshui River, rising from Qibaoshan to the east side of Liuyang county in Hunan province。

[10] 尾山：指武陵岩，属九岭山北麓。

[10] wei shan (tail mount) refers to Wulingyan Mountain, part of the north section of Jiulingshan。

[11] 翠山：指庐山。

[11] cui shan (green mount) refers to Lushan。

译文：南方大地中有幕阜山脉，山的东麓到了长江边，又有通山，是修水的源头；又有梅山，又有连云山，有洛霄山；又有复山，漫江水从这里流出；又有官山，山的西面有灯盏窝氏族，东面有龙潭氏族。再往南还有山，渌水从这里流出。有武陵岩，有庐山。

Translation

In the southern land, there is the Mufu Mountain range, its east end reaching the Yangtze River。 There is also Tongshan, where the Xiushui River rises。 There are also the Mountains of Meishan, Liangyunshan, Luoxiaoshan and as well as Fushan。 Manjiang River flows out of here。 There is also the Guanshan。 The Dengzhanwo tribes live in the west of the mountain and the Loongtan tribes live in the east of the mountain。 Further south, there are more mountains and the Lvshui River rises from here, the mountains being Wulingyan, and Lushan。

15-08 盈民国
Yingmin Guo
（117,21772E；29,34606N）

有盈民之国[1]，於姓，黍食[2]。又有人方食木叶[3] 。

注释：[1]盈民国：指水地国，古称溢米国，今江西浮梁县城。
Notes:[1] ying min guo (full people nation)
Tr: refers to Shuidi Guo, shuidi (water earth), its ancient name is Yimi Guo, in today's Fuliang county, Jiangxi province。
[2] 於姓，黍食：因水而形成私稻氏族。於姓，指水形成。黍食，倒装句，私稻族。
[2]yu xing, shushi (surname Yu, millet eat)
Tr: refers to the tribes who invented wetland rice growing because of their location in the wet land。 Yuxing: water leads to the formation of this agriculture tribe。 Sushi, a reversed word order from the Chinese, meaning Sidao tribes, Sidao: rice。
[3] 有人方食木叶：有个集镇是禾杆岭的大检目。方食，指稻杆、禾杆；木叶，指大检目。
[3] you ren fang shi mu ye (someone just eat wood leaf)
Tr: this township is the big Jianmu (administration centre) of the Heganling Mountain。 Fang shi: refers to the stems of rice, plants stick; muye: refers to the big Jianmu。

译文：在大地中有一个水地国，因水而形成私稻氏族，那里有一个集镇，是禾杆岭的大检目。
Translation:
In the land of earth there is a Shuidi Guo, where water has led to the formation of Sidao tribes。 There is a township, which is the administration center of Hegangling Mountain。

15-09 不死国
Busi Guo
（117,95712E；28,43291N）

有不死之国，阿姓[1]，甘木是食[2]。

注释：[1]不死国，阿姓：指茅山国，以茅山而得名，在今江西上饶。
Notes:[1] bu si guo (never die nation)
Tr: refers to the family bearing the surname of Ah。 This refers to the Maoshan Guo, named after the Maoshan, in today's Shangrao city, Jiangxi province。
[2] 甘木是食：是苗族人建立的国家。甘木是，读嘎蒙氏，指苗族人。
[2] gan mu shi shi (sweet wood is food)
Tr: this is a country built up by the Miao people。 Ganmushi: reads as Gamengshi, referring to the Miao people。

译文：有一个茅山国，以茅山得名，是苗族人建立的国家。
Translation:
There is a Maoshan Guo, which got its name after Maoshan。 This is a nation built by the Miao people。

15-10 去痓山

Quzhishan
（114,4926E；24,36926N）

大荒之中有山，名曰去痓[1]。南极果[2]，北不成 [3]，去痓果。

注释：[1]去痓：指广东南岭的连平山，那里有一个连平县，古称去痓国。
Notes:[1] qu zhi (rid of cramps)
Tr: refers to the Lianpingshan, part of the Nanling range in Guangdong, there is a Lianping county, its ancient name is Quzhi Guo。
[2] 南极果：指大吉国，今江西赣州市全南县大吉山镇。
[2] nan ji guo (south pole fruits)
Tr: refers to the Daji Guo, in today's Dajishan town, in Quannan county, Ganzhou city, Jiangxi province。
[3] 北不成：指广东韶关市翁源县城，古称贝布城。
[3] bei bu cheng (north not work)
Tr: refers to the Wengyuan county, Shaoguan city, Guangdong province。 Its ancient name is Beibucheng, a phonetic match。

译文：在南方大地中有座山，叫连平山。那里有三个相邻的部落：大吉国、贝布城、连平国。巫师们将这三个部落名连起来成为一句咒语，用以祈祷平安，读为："南极果，北不成，去痓果"。
Translation:
In the land of the south there is a mountain called Lianpingshan。 There are a group of three neighbouring tribes: the Daji Guo, the Beibucheng, the Lianping Guo。 Priests have created a charm with the three names praying for good luck。 It reads as: nanjiguo, beibucheng, quzhiguo。

15-11 不廷胡余
Butinghuyu
（113,9139E；22,03619N）

南海渚中，有神，人面[1]，珥两青蛇，践两赤蛇[2]，曰不廷胡余[3]。

注释：[1]有神、人面：有氏族居民。
Notes:[1] you shen, ren mian (has God, human face)
Tr: there live tribal residents。
[2] 珥两青蛇，践两赤蛇：古时香港、澳门都属万山群岛区域，东边的九龙、香港为东部氏族，西边的氹仔、横琴为西部氏族，管理这些氏族，称珥践四夷。
[2]er liang qing she, jian liang chi she (ear lop two green snake, step two red snake)
Tr: in ancient times, Hong Kong, Macau belong to the Wanshan islands area。 The people in Jiulong and Hongkong belong to the eastern tribes, people in Dangzai, Hengqin belong to the western tribes。 Management of those tribes are figuratively described as Erjian four yi。
[3] 不廷胡余：指万山群岛，在广东珠江出海口外的南海中。不廷，指万山；胡余，读濮屿，指群岛。
[3] bu ting hu yu: refers to Wanshan Islands, in the south sea beyond the Pearl River's mouth, in Guangdong province。 Bu ting: refers to the ten thousand islands, meaning Wanshanqundao。 Hu yu: reads as Pu yu, meaning group of islands。

译文：在南海渚中，有一个定居的氏族，管理着四周的水上夷民，叫万山群岛氏族。
Translation:

In the south sea area, there is a tribe of settled people。 They manage the inhabitants on the islands in the sea。 They are the Wanshanqundao tribes。

15-12 因因乎
Yinyinhu
（114,69626E；23,73428N）

有神名曰因因乎[1]，南方曰因乎，夸风曰乎民[2]，处南极[3]以出入风[4]。

注释：[1]因因乎：濮族的一个支系，叫雍雍濮、罗濮。
Notes： [1] yin yin hu
Tr. refers to a Pu branch called Yongyong Pu, or Luo Pu。
[2] 夸风曰乎民：北山的人称为濮民。
[2] kua feng yue hu min (boast wind say Hu min)
Tr: people from Beishan (northern mount) are called Pu Min(people)。
[3] 南极：指僚纪，这里泛指岭南僚族部落地区。
[3] nan ji (south pole) refers to Liaoji(laoji) a generic term for the areas occupied by the Lao tribes from Lingnan。
[4] 出入风：罗浮山古称游龙山。"游龙"，濮语读绰惹，谐音"出入"。
[4] chu ru feng (out in wind) Luofushan is called Youlongshan in ancient times。 Youlong (swimming dragon) in Pu speech reads as chuore, a phonetic match to Chinese speech churu。

译文：有一个氏族叫雍雍濮，南方称为罗濮，北山的人称为濮民，住在僚族部落的游龙山地区。
Translation:
There is a tribe called Yongyong Pu, in the southern land, it is called Luo Pu。 The people living in the Beishan are called Pu people, they live in the Youlongshan area where the Liao tribes occupy。

15-13 季釐国
Jixi Guo
（116,36995E；2355281N）

有襄山[1]。又有重阴山[2] 。有人食兽 [3] ，曰季釐 [4] 。帝俊生季釐 [5] ，故曰季釐之国。有缗渊 [6] 。少昊 [7] 生倍伐 [8] ，倍伐降处缗渊。有水四方，名曰俊坛 [9] 。

注释：[1]襄山：指广东丰顺县。
Notes:[1] xiang shan: refers to the Fengshun county， Guangdong province。
[2] 重阴山：指广东潮州。
[2] chong yin shan (double shades mount) refers to Chaozhou, Guangdong province。
[3] 人食兽：定居的古老氏族。
[3] ren shi shou (man eats beast) refer to the settled ancient tribes。
[4] 季釐：读揭羲，指揭羲国，今称揭阳。
[4] ji xi or jiexi: refers to the Jiexi Guo in today's Jieyang county。
[5] 帝俊生季釐：帝俊，在此指句甸，及大坝子。大坝子养育了揭羲氏族。
[5] di jun sheng jie xi: dijun： judian, dabazi, a term for big space, big space nurtures the Jiexi tribes。
[6] 缗渊：指南澳海域。
[6] min yuan (rope deep pond) refers to the Nan'aohai area。
[7] 少昊：指海上。

[7] shao hao: on the sea。
[8] 倍伐：指南澳岛。
[8] bei fa (double invade) refers to Nanaodao Island。
[9] 俊坛：指最好的拜海的神坛。
[9] jun tan (handsome altar) the best altar for Sea worshipping。

译文：在丰顺和潮州之间，有一个定居的古老氏族，叫揭羲氏。平阳大坝养育了揭羲氏族，揭羲氏族建立了揭羲国。那里有一个南澳海域，海上有一个南澳岛，南澳岛座落于南澳海。南澳岛四周都是水，因此成为最好的祭拜大海的地方。
Translation:
Between Fengshun and Chaozhou, there is an ancient tribe who are settlers of the area。 They are known as the Jiexi Shi。 The Pingyang Daba raised and nurtured the tribe, which grew into the Jiexi Guo。 There is a Nan 'ao coastal area, a Nan'ao island in the sea。 The Nan'ao Island is situated in the Nan'ao sea。 The Nan'ao Island is surrounded on its four sides by water, therefore becomes the best place for sea worshipping。

15-14 臷民国
Diemin Guo
（115,36612E；22,77768N）

有臷民之国[1]。帝舜生无淫[2]，降臷出 [3]，是谓巫臷民 [4]。巫臷民朌姓，食谷 [5]，不绩不经，服也 [6]；不稼不穑，食也 [7]。爰歌舞之鸟 [8]，鸾自歌，凤自舞 [9]。爰有百兽，相群爰处 [10]。百谷所聚 [11]。

注释：[1]臷民国：指平地之国。
Notes:[1] die min guo: refers to the flat land country。
[2] 帝舜生无淫：汕尾坝子养育了雍部落。帝舜，指甸汕。无淫，指雍部落。
[2] di shun sheng wu yin: Shanwei Bazi gives birth to the Yong tribe。 Dishun: dian shan, (a place name) 。 Wu yin: refers to Yong tribe。
[3] 降臷出：读姜臷处，指管理着坝子区域。
[3] jiang die chu: reads as Jiang die chu, means management of the Bazi areas。
[4] 巫臷民：指坝子部落。
[4] wu die min refers to the Bazi tribe。
[5] 朌姓食谷：海姓的古老国家。
[5] fen /ban reads as ju, the nation bearing surname of Hai(sea)。
[6] 不绩不经，服也：补绩补经是制衣氏族。
[6] bu ji bu jing, fu ye: (no weave, no thread) cloth: Buji and Bujing are tribes engaged in textile and clothing production。
[7] 不稼不穑，食也：补稼补穑是种植氏族。
[7] bu jia bu qiang, shi ye (no grow, no till, can eat) Bujia and Buqiang are tribes engaged in growing and planting。
[8] 歌舞之鸟：城镇和部落的人们。
[8]ge wu zhi niao (singing dancing birds) refers to the township and tribal people。
[9] 鸾自歌，凤自舞：不论是西部的城镇，还是东部的部落。
[9] luan zi ge, feng zi wu (luanbird self-sings， phoenix self-dances) the townships in the west and the tribes in the east。
[10] 爰有百兽，相群爰处：所有氏族都和谐相处。
[10] yuan you bai shou, xiang qun yuan chu (thus 100 beasts, groups live close by) 。

Tr: all the tribes are co-existing in peace。

[11] 百谷所聚：是国家团结的象征。

[11] bai gu suo ju (100 grain gather) is the symbol for unity in the nation。

译文：【南方地区】有一个平地之国。汕尾坝子养育了雍部落氏族，他们管理着坝子地区，称为坝子部落。坝子部落是海姓的古老国家，补绩补经，是制衣氏族，补稼补穑是种植氏族。这里的城镇和部落人群，不论是西部的城镇，还是东部的部落，所有氏族都和谐相处。这是国家团结的象征。

Translation:

There is a flat land country in the south。 The Shanwaibazi is where the Yong tribe thrive。 They manage the Bazi areas, known as Bazi tribe。 Bazi tribe is an ancient country bearing the surname of Hai。 Buji tribe and Bujing tribe are clothing producing people。 The Bujia tribe and Buqian tribe are food growing people。 The township and tribal people, regardless of where they live, whether they are the townships in the west, or the tribes in the east, all the tribes live in harmony。 This is a sign of unity in the country。

15-15 融天山

Rongtianshan

（114,83924E；22,72104N）

大荒之中，有山，名曰融天[1]，海水南入焉。

注释[1]融天：是涌铁的音译，指一个叫涌的地区，今称铁涌（cong），在广东大亚湾。

[1] rong tian（melt sky）: the phonetic rendering of Yongtie, a place called Yong。 Today it is known as Tiecong, in the Daya Bay in Guangdong province。

译文：在南方，有一个地方名叫涌铁，是进出海的南入口。

Translation:

In the south， there is a place called Congtie, the south point to go to the sea or come back to land。

15-16 羿杀凿齿

Yishazaochi

（114,42069E；23,11308N）

有人曰凿齿[1]，羿杀之[2]。

注释：[1]凿齿：读照炽，广东惠州的古称谓，指太阳的恩惠。

Notes:[1] zao chi (chisel tooth) reads as zhao zhi (shine hot) the old name for Huizhou, in Guangdong province。 Hui means the blessings by the sun。

[2] 羿杀之：在此指圩沙地区。圩，在此读于，谐音羿。

[2] yi sha zhi: refers to the Yusha area. Yu; phonetic match to yi。

译文：有一个集镇叫照炽，在圩沙地区。

Translation:

There is a township called Zhaozhi, which is in the Yusha area。

15-17 蜮民国

Yumin Guo

（113,67336E；22,8149N）

有蜮山者[1]，有蜮民之国[2]，桑姓，黍食，射蜮是食[3]。有人方扜弓[4] 射黄蛇 [5]， 名曰蜮人 [6] 。

注释：[1]蜮山者：指河边的地方。这里指珠江口。
Notes:[1]yu shan zhe (from Yushan): refers to the river side areas。 Here it refers to the river mouth of Pearl River。
[2] 蜮民之国：指溢陌之国，即河岸边的国家。
[2]yu min zhi guo (Yu people country): refers to the Yimo Guo, meaning countries along the riverbanks。
[3] 桑姓黍食，射蜮是食：河湾的古老氏族；桑指河湾；射蜮是食，指以水上运输为业。
[3] sang xing shu shi (surname Sang, corn eat) she yu shi shi (shoot Yu is food)
Tr: refers to the ancient tribe by the river bay。 Sang: bay, she yu shi shi: make a living by providing river transportation。
[4] 有人方扜弓：有个集镇叫虎门。方扜，切韵为虎，实际指东水。方扜弓，指东水门。
[4] you ren fang yu gong (has person play bow): there is a township called Humen (tiger gate), fangyu: phonetic combination of F and u into fu、fu /hu, meaning east water, fangyugong; dong shui men, (east water gate) 。
[5] 射黄蛇：指沙维肆，即南沙肆。
[5] she huang she (shoot yellow snake) refers to Shawei town, also known as Nanshansi, (south sand town) 。
[6] 蜮人：指蜮惹，即水边的集镇。
[6]yu ren: reads as yure, refers to the township by the river。

译文：在珠江口，有一个水岸之国，那里住着河湾的古老氏族，他们以水上运输为业。那里有集镇叫虎门、南沙肆，是水边的集镇。
Translation:
There is a riverside country by the Pearl River mouth。 The ancient bay tribes live there。 They make a living by providing water transportation。 There is a township called Humen（tiger gate）, there is also the Nanshasi。 It is a riverside town。

15-18 宋山枫木
Songshanfengmu
（113,83899E；22,90622N）

有宋山者[1]，有赤蛇[2]，名曰育蛇[3]，有木生山上[4]，名曰枫木[5]。枫木，蚩尤所弃其桎梏[6]，是为枫木。

注释：[1]宋山：指松山，今称大岭，在虎门镇东侧。
Notes:[1] song shan: refers to Song (pine mount) today it is known as Daling, on the east side of Humen town。
[2] 赤蛇：指东边的聚落。
[2] chi she (red snake)
Tr: the settlements on the east side。
[3] 育蛇：指大舍，即大的聚落。
[3]yu she (raise snake) refers to a big settlement。
[4] 有木生山上：有一个管理中心建在那里。
[4] you mu sheng shan shang (a tree grows on mountain) where a management centre is setup there。
[5] 枫木：指敷目，意为东边的检目。
[5] feng mu (maple tree) refers to Fumu; Fumu means the administration centre on the east side。
[6] 蚩尤所弃其桎梏：地址在濂溪东边的平凹地带。
[6] chiyou suo qi qi zhiku (chieftain Chiyou discarded his locks and chains)
Tr: its location is in the flat shallow area to the east of Lianxi River。

译文：有一个松山，山的东边有一个聚落，名叫大舍，有一个检目建在那里，名叫敷目。之所以称敷目，是因为地址在濂溪东边的平凹地带，所以称为敷目。
Translation:
There is a Songshan。 On its east side there is a settlement called Dashe (big house) 。 There is an administration centre set up there, it is called Fumu。 The reason it is so called is because the centre is located on the flat shallow to the east of Liangxi River。

15-19 相状尸
Zuzhuangshi
（113,24832E；23,1147N）

有人方齿[1]虎尾[2]，名曰相状之尸[3]。

注释：[1]方齿：读 fu ci，指王此、统治着、雄踞。
Notes:[1] fang chi (square teeth) reads as fu ci, meaning the king in this place, a ruling class, in control of, lording over others。
[2] 虎尾：指东南。
[2]hu wei (tiger tail) refers to the southeast。
[3] 相状之尸：指广疆之肆，今广州肆。相，指广。
[3] zu zhuang zhi shi: refers to the Guangjiangsi （township of wide regions）, today it is known as Guangzhou city。 Zu means broad and wide。

译文：有一个集镇统治着东南地区，名叫广疆肆。
Translation:
There is a township that controls the southeast areas, its name is Guangjiangsi。

15-20 焦侥国
Jiaorao Guo
（113,29478E；22,80627N）

有小人[1]，名曰焦侥国[2]，几姓[3]，嘉谷是食[4]。

注释：[1]小人：指顺惹，又称顺邓，今称顺德。
Notes:[1] xiao ren (small people) refers to Shunre, or Shundeng, today known as Shunde (a place name) 。
[2] 焦侥国：指沙河国。
[2] jiao rao guo: refers to Shahe Guo。 (Sand river country)
[3] 几姓：读瑾，指丁姓氏族，又称陈姓氏族。这几个姓氏的濮文都为“口”，应是同源关系。
[3] ji xing (ji surname) reads as jin, surname as Ding or Chen。 In Pu script, those signs share a form referring to a mouth, very possible of the same root sign。
[4] 嘉谷是食：沙国的古老氏族，实际指沙河国的古老氏族。
[4] jia gu sh shi (nice grain to eat) the ancient tribe of Shaguo, in fact it refers to the ancient tribe of Shahe Guo。

译文：有一个顺德镇，名叫沙河国，是丁姓氏族国家，丁姓氏族是沙河国的古老氏族。
Translation:
There is a Shunde town, called Shahe Guo, bearing the surname of Ding, the ancient tribe of Shahe Guo。

15-21 禹攻云雨
Yugongyunyu
（113,08316E；22,5793N）

大荒之中，有山名歼涂之山[1]，青水[2]穷焉。有云雨之山[3]，有木名曰栾 [4] 。禹攻云雨 [5] 。有赤石焉生栾 [6]，黄木，赤枝，青叶 [7]，群帝焉取药 [8] 。

注释：[1]歼涂山：指顺中山，又称秀中山。今称中山市，在广东中山。
Notes:[1] xiu tu shan: refers to Shunzhongshan, Xiuzhongshan, today known as Zhongshan city, in Guangdong province。
[2] 青水：指西江，属珠江流域西水系。
[2] qing shui (green water) refers to Xijiang (west river), part of the west river system of Pearl River basin。
[3] 云雨山：指大泽山。
[3] yun yu shan (clouds rain mount) refers to Daze Mountain。 (Daze: big water)
[4] 有木名栾：有管理中心，名叫沙朗。沙朗，意为商号。
[4] you mu ming luan (a tree named luan) there is a management centre, its name is Shalang, a business company name。
[5] 禹攻云雨：指江门大泽。这里泛指江门的大江边。
[5]yu gong yun yu (Yu attack clouds rain) refers to the Jiangmendaze, meaning the big riverbanks of the Jiangmen area in general。
[6] 有赤石焉生栾：有移民氏族建的商号。
[6] you chi shi yan sheng luan (has red stone begets Luan):
Tr: there are business shops established by the migrant tribes。
[7] 黄木、赤枝、青叶：指会木（今称新会）、沙堆、莲溪。
[7] huang mu, chizhi, qingye (yellow wood, red branches, green leaves)
Tr: refers to Huimu, today known as Xinhui； Shadui, and Liangxi。
[8] 群帝焉取药：这些集镇都是越人的街肆。
[8] qun di yan qu yao (gods get medicine)
Tr: all these townships are the street markets run by the Yue people。

译文：在南方地区，有个地方叫秀中山，是西江的尽头。那里有大泽镇，有管理中心，名叫沙朗。在江门的大江边，有许多移民氏族建立的商号：会木、沙堆、莲溪，这些集镇都是越人建的街肆。
Translation:
In the regions of Southern areas， there is a place called Xiuzhongshan, the end of Xijiang River。 There is Dazezhen, a management centre known as Shalang。 Along the riverbanks at Jiangmen, there are a few business shops set up by the migrant tribes: such as the Huimu, the Shadui, the Lianxi, all those business towns are built and run by the Yue people。

15-22 有国曰颛顼
Youguoyuezhuanxu
（110,222E~112,762E；20,94N~22,443N）

有国曰颛顼[1]，生伯服，食黍[2]。有鼬姓之国[3] 。有苕山 [4] 。又有宗山 [5] 。又有姓山 [6]，又有壑山 [7] 。又有陈山 [8]，又有东州山 [9] 。又有白水山 [10]，白水出焉生白渊 [11]，昆吾之师所治也 [12] 。

注释：[1]颛顼：指照羲，意为很温暖的地区。
Notes： [1] zhuanxu: a phonetic rendering of zhaoxi。 Zhaoxi means very warm places。

[2] 生伯服，食黍：养育了百濮古老氏族。
[2] sheng bo fu，shi shu (begets Bofu, eat corn): has nurtured the ancient Hundred Pu tribes--the Bai Pu tribes。
[3] 鼬姓之国：腰兴之国，指云浮市。
[3] you xing zhi guo: a phonetic rendering of Yaoxing Guo, refers to the Yunfu city。
[4] 苕山：指台山，即江门市。
[4] tiao shan: refers to Taishan, known today as Jiangmen city。
[5] 宗山：指照山，即阳江地区。
[5] zong shan: a phonetic rendering of Zhaoshan, in today's Yangjiang district。
[6] 姓山：指信宜山，今信宜地区。
[6] xing shan: refers to Xinyishan, in today's Xinyi district。
[7] 壑山：指化山，今化州地区。
[7] huo shan: Hua shan in today's Huazhou district。
[8] 陈州山：指赤坎部落，今赤坎、湛江地区。
[8] chen zhou shan: refers to the Chikan tribe。It is today's Chikan, Zhanjiang regions。
[9] 东州山：指东海岛。
[9] dong zhou shan: refers to Donghaidao (east sea island)。
[10] 白水山：指雷水山，今雷州地区。
[10] bai shui shan (white water mount） refers to the Leishuishan (thunder water mount), in today's Leizhou district。
[11] 白渊：指雷州湾。
[11] bai yuan （white deep）refers to Leizhou Bay。 Lei(thunder); zhou(district); wan(bay)。
[12] 昆吾之师所治也：昆吾，读凯巫，指南方部落。师，指氏族。南方部落氏族所治之乡。
[12] kun wu zhi shi suo zhi ye (kunwu teacher rules it)
Tr' kunwu reads as Kaiwu, refers to the southern tribes。 shi(teacher) means tribes。 This is the land run by the southern tribes。

译文：【在南海地区，】有热带的国家，养育了百濮古老氏族。有腰兴之国，有台山，有照山，有信宜山，有化山，有赤坎部落，有东海岛，有雷水山，雷水流出后形成雷州湾，是南方部落氏族治所之乡。
Translation:
In the south sea areas, there are the tropical countries, which nurtured the ancient Hundred Pu tribes。 There are the of Yaoxing Guo, Taishan, Zhaoshan, Xinyishan, Huashan, Chikan tribes, Donghaidao, and Leishuishan。 Leishui River rises and forms the Leizhou Bay, a land run by the southern tribes。

15-23 张弘国
Zhanghong Guo
（109,70904E；21,02233N）

有人名曰张弘[1]，在海上捕鱼[2]。海中有张弘之国，食鱼[3]，使四鸟。

注释：[1]张弘：指江洪镇，在广东雷州半岛西侧。
Notes: [1] zhang hong: refers to the Jianghong township, located in the west side of Leizhou Peninsula , Guangdong province。
[2] 海上捕鱼：指海边的濮夷。
[2] hai shang bu yu (fishing on the sea) the Pu Yi on the coastal areas。
[3] 食鱼：古老的哲氏族，即渔业氏族。
[3] shi yu (eat fish) the ancient Zhe tribes, meaning the fishing tribes。

译文：有一个集镇叫江洪，是海边濮夷的集镇。又说，南海中有一个江洪之国，住着古老的渔业氏族，从事四种劳动。
Translation:
There is a township called Jianghong, run by the Pu Yi in the coastal areas。 It is also said, that in the middle of South Sea, there is a Jianghong country。 The ancient fishing tribes live there, engaged in the four kinds of labour production。

15-24 驩头国
Huantou Guo
（109,19933E；21,66218N）

有人焉，鸟喙，有翼[1]，方捕鱼于海[2]。大荒之中，有人名曰驩头[3]。鲧妻士敬[4]，士敬子曰炎融[5]，生驩头。驩头人面鸟喙，有翼，食海中鱼[6]，杖翼而行[7]。维宜芑苣[8]，穋杨是食[9]。有驩头之国。

注释：[1]有人，鸟喙，有翼：有一个集镇，是南流江瑶夷的集镇。鸟喙，指南流江。
Notes:[1] you ren, niao hui, you yi (a person, bird beak, has wings)
Tr: there is a township, the settlement by the Yao Yi from Nanliujiang River。 Niaohui (bird beak) refers to the Nanliujiang (south run river)。
[2] 方捕鱼于海：统治渔民于南海地区。捕，同补，指族群
[2] fang bu yu yu hai (thus fishing on the sea)
Tr: control fishing tribes in the south sea area。bu(catch) a phonetic match to Bu (patch up) meaning tribes。
[3] 驩头：指土目的铺子，演称为合浦，今广西北海市合浦县城。
[3] huan tou: refers to the shops of local market centre。 It is transformed into today's Hepu, in today 's Hepu county, Beihai city, Guangxi province。
[4] 鲧妻士敬：指双溪河部落。鲧，读 gang，指双。
[4] gun qi shi jing (gun's wife shijing) refers to the Shuangxihe tribes。 Gun: reads as gang, meaning double, or in Chinese Shuang (a pair)。
[5] 士敬子曰炎融：双溪河部落支系的大合氏。(这里有重复的语句。)
[5] shi jing zi yue yan rong:(shijing'son flame melt)
Tr: refers to the Dahe Shi of the Shuagnxihe tribe, (repetition of sentences occur)
[6] 食海中鱼：古老的海上渔民。
[6] shi hai zhong yu (eat sea fish)
Tr: the ancient sea fishermen people。
[7] 杖翼而行：以渔为业。杖，读则，指渔。行，在此指业。
[7] zhang yi er xing (carry stick wings to move)
Tr: depends on fishing for a living。zhang (walking stick) reads as ze, meaning fishing。 xing (walk or move) meaning business, way of life。
[8] 维宜芑苣：南流江的换市。芑苣，读 qi ts'e，指换市。
[8] wei yi si chen: Nanliujiang's trading market, Qi ts'e: means trade market。
[9] 穋杨是食：读洛雅施始，指古老的流通之城。
[9] liao yang shi shi: reads as Luo ya shi shi。
Tr: refers to the ancient city of exchange and circulation。

译文：有一个集镇，是僚族支系瑶夷的集镇，统治渔民于南海地区。在南海地区，有一个城镇叫合浦。双溪河部落的支系叫大合，建了合浦城。合浦居民是南流江的瑶夷，是古老的海上渔民，以渔为业。南流江的换市，是古老的流通之城，称为合浦之国。
Translation:
There is a township of the Liao tribe's Yao Yi branch, who controls the fishing communities in the South Sea area。In the South Sea region, there is a township called Hepu。The branch from the Shuangxihe tribes is called Dahe, who built the Hepu city。 The citizens of Hepu are the Yao Yi from Nanliujiang。 They are a very ancient fishing people, making a living by fishing in the sea。The Huanshi, an ancient exchange and circulation centre of Nanliujiang, is called Hepu Guo。

15-25 岳山
Yueshan
（109,46257E；22,45777N）

帝尧、帝喾、帝舜[1]葬于岳山[2]。爰有文贝、离俞、【丘鸟】久、鹰贾、延维、视肉[3]、熊、罴、虎、豹[4]；朱木、赤枝、青华、玄实[5]。有申山者[6] 。

注释：[1]帝尧、帝喾、帝舜：指广西罗阳山的集镇浦北、福旺、北神。
Notes:[1] di rao, di ku, di shun (three mythical figures)
Tr: refers to the townships of Pubei, Fuwang, and Beishen in Luoyang Mountain, Guangxi province。
[2] 岳山：指罗阳山。岳，读雍音，指罗。
[2] yue shan: refers to Luoyang Mountain。Yue: reads as yong, refers to Luo。
[3] 文贝、离俞、【丘鸟】久、鹰贾、延维、视肉：指伯劳河、小江、久隆街、旧州、武利河、神流河。
[3] wen bei (marked shell), li yu (leave Yu), niao jiu (bird lasting), ying jia (eagle jia), yan wei(expand dimension), shi rou(gaze meat)
Tr: refers to Bolao River, Xiaojiang River, Jiulong street, Jiuzhou, Wuli River and Shenliu River。
[4]熊、罴、虎、豹：指四业濮僚。
[4] xiong, pi, hu, bao (bear bear tiger leopard)
Tr: refers to the Pu Lao people who are engaged in four kinds of business。
[5] 朱木、赤枝、青华、玄实：指那蒙、钦州、青塘、那丽。
[5] zhu mu (red wood), chi zhi (red branch), qing hua (green flowers), xuan shi (black fruits)
Tr: refers to places of Nameng, Qinzhou, Qingtang and Nali。
[6] 申山者：指通鱼山，今称铜鱼山。这里指铜鱼山部落。
[6] shen shan zhe: refers to the Tongyushan (through fish mount) today it is known as the Tongyushan (copper fish mount) 。 Here it refers to the Tongyushan tribes。

译文：浦北、福旺、北神部落的疆域在罗阳山。那里还有伯劳河、小江、久隆街、旧州、武利河、神流河等集镇，有四业濮僚，还有较大的城镇那蒙、钦州、青塘、那丽，还有铜鱼山部落。
Translation:
The territory of Pubei tribes, Fuwang tribes, Beishen tribes are in the Luoyangshan area。 Other townships also exist there, such as the townships of Bolaohe, Xiaojiang, Jiulongjie, Jiuzhou, Wulihe, and Shenliuhe。 The Pu people living there are engaged in four kinds of labour production。 Other bigger townships are Nameng, Qingzhou, Qingtang, and Nali。 Also living there is the Tongyushan tribes。

15-26 天台高山
Tiantaigaoshan
（108,62663E；21,96534N）

大荒之中，有山名曰天台高山[1]，海水入焉[2]。

注释：[1]天台高山：指上下蒌园，是钦州的古称谓。天，读 ti，指下；台，读 ta，指上。
Notes： [1] tian tai gao shan (sky terrace high mount)
Tr: refers to the Shangxialouyuan (up down lou garden), an ancient name for Qinzhou。 tian(sky)reads as ti, meaning lower, tai reads as ta, meaning upper。
[2] 海水入焉：是海边的港湾。
[2] hai shui ru yan (sea water rush in)
Tr: a bay port by the sea。

译文：在南海海边，有个地方叫上下蒌园，是海边的港湾。
Translation:
There is a place called Shangxialouyuan, by the South Sea coast, a coastal bay port。

15-27 羲和生日
Xiheshengri
（108,35566E；21,76213N）

东南海之外，甘水[1]之间，有羲和之国[2]，有女子名曰羲和[3]，方日浴于甘渊[4]。羲和者，帝俊之妻[5]，生十日[6]。

注释：[1]甘水：指苗岭江。今称茅岭江。
Notes: [1] gan shui (sweet water)
Tr: refers to Miaolingjiang River. It is known as Maolingjiang River today。
[2] 羲和之国：指东海国。今广西钦州。
[2] xi he zhi guo (xihe's country)
Tr: refers to the Donghai Guo, today's Qinzhou city, Guangxi province。
[3] 有女子名曰羲和：指龙平，又称龙门港、东海、防镇。
[3] you nv zi ming yue xi he (a girl named Xihe)
Tr: refers to Longping, a place also known as Longmen port, Donghai, Fangzhen。
[4] 方日浴于甘渊：防镇座落于钦州湾。甘渊，因为苗岭江出口而得名。今称钦州湾。
[4] fang ri yu gan yuan (just day bathing in sweet deep)
Tr: fangzhen is in Qingzhou Bay. Ganyuan (sweet deep) derives its name being the river outlet of Miaolingjiang River。 The place is called Qinzhou Bay。
[5] 帝俊之妻：指台浸部落。
[5] di jun zhi qi (di jun's wife)
Tr: refers to the Taijin tribe。
[6] 生十日：建立的博惹。十日，读博惹，指都城。
[6] sheng shi ri (give birth to ten suns)
Tr: establishes Bore， townships or capital cities or towns。 shiri (ten suns or ten days) reads as bo re, meaning capital cities。

译文：在东南海之滨，茅岭江的出口处，有东海之国，有一个龙平镇，又叫东海镇，防镇。防镇座落于钦州湾。东海镇是台浸部落支系建立的都城。
Translation:

On the coastal areas of southeast sea, at the river mouth of Maolingjiang River, there is a Donghai country。 A township is called Donghaizhen, or Fangzhen。 Fangzhen is in Qingzhou Bay。 Donghaizhen is the capital city built by the Taijin tribal branches。

15-28 盖犹山
Gaiyoushan
（109,76875E；19,24867N）

有盖犹之山[1]者，其上有甘柤[2]，枝干皆赤[3]，黄叶，白华，黑实[4]。东又有甘华 [5] ，枝干皆赤，黄叶。有青马，有赤马，名曰三骓 [6] 。有视肉 [7] 。

注释：[1]盖犹山：指苗瑶山，今称海南岛。盖，读嘎，指苗。
Notes:[1] gai you shan: refers to the Miaoyao Mountain, today is known as Hainan Island。 Gai reads as ga, referring to the Miao ethnicity。
[2] 甘柤 (sweet wood)：读嘎举，指苗部落。
[2] gan ju: reads as gaju, refers to the Miao tribes。
[3] 枝干皆赤：枝干，指著名的、突出的，英勇的。皆赤，指部落。
[3] zhi gan jie chi (branches all red)
Tr: zhi gan: famous, outstanding, brave。 Jie chi: tribes。
[4] 黄叶、白华、黑实：指大岭、穷崖（今称琼崖）、那罗（指大疍）部落。
[4] huang ye (yellow leaves) bai hua (white flower) hei shi (black fruits)
Tr: refers to the Daling, Qiuyan, Naluo(dadan) tribes。
[5] 甘华：指苗部落。
[5] gan hua (sweet flower): refers to the Miao tribes。
[6] 青马、赤马，名曰三骓：青苗、红苗，称为外住苗。
[6] qing ma, chi ma (green horse, red horse) ming yue san zui (named three horses)
Tr: refers to the Qing Miao, Hong Miao, they are the outside living Miao。
[7] 视肉：指厶饶，即稻谷。
[7]si rou (gaze meat) refers to Sirao, meaning rice。

译文：南海海中有苗瑶山，上面有苗部落，是著名的部落，有大岭、穷崖、和那罗部落。东部又有苗部落，是英勇的大黄岭蚩尤部落，那里有青苗、红苗，称为外住苗。那里的粮食为稻谷。
Translation:
There is a Miaoyao Mountain in the south sea。 The Miao tribes live there, they are the tribes of Daling, Qiongyan, and Naluo。 In the east part, there are also Miao tribes。 The famous tribe is the legendary glorious Chiyou tribes from Dahuangling。 Also living there are the Qing Miao and Hong Miao。 They are the outside resident Miao。 The food grain there is rice。

15-29 小人菌人
Xiaorenjunren
（110,32969E；20,02699N）

有小人[1]，名曰菌人[2]。

注释：[1]小人：指秀惹，今称海口市。
Notes:[1] xiao ren(small people) refers to Xiure, today's Haikou city, Hainan Island。
[2] 菌人：读群惹，群，通琼，即琼惹，今称琼山区。

[2] jun ren (mushroom people) reads as qunre, known today as Qiushan district。

译文：苗瑶山的北端有一个集镇，叫秀惹，又称琼惹。
Translation:
At the Miaoyao Mountain's north end, a township called Xiure is located, it is also known as the Qiongre。

15-30 南类山
Nanleishan
（109,16597E；18,3708N）

有南类之山[1]。爰有遗玉[2]，青马 [3]，三骓 [4]，视肉 [5] 、甘华 [6] 。百谷所在。

注释：[1]南类山：指大疍山。濮语读为"疍大"，读音 na lei，是崖州的古称谓。
Notes:[1] nan lei shan (south type mount) refers to the Dadan Mountain。 In Pu concept and speech, Danda (reversed word order) reads as na lei, which is the ancient name for Yanzhou。
[2] 遗玉：指芋头。
[2] yi yu (drop jade) refers to taro。
[3] 青马：指青芒。
[3] qing ma (green horse) refers to green plants。
[4] 三骓：指外穄。
[4] san zhui:(three color horse) refers to the waiji grain。
[5] 视肉：指稻谷。
[5] shi rou (gaze meat) refers to rice。
[6] 甘华：指小麦。
[6] gan hua (sweet flower) refers to xiaomai(wheat)。

译文：苗瑶山的南端，叫大疍山，那里有芋头、青芒、外穄、稻谷、小麦等食物，是百谷所生之地。
Translation:
To the south end of Miaoyaoshan stands Dadanshan。The grains growing there are taro, qingmang, waiji, rice and wheat。This is a place where one hundred kinds of grain species grow。

第十六卷 大荒西经 (The Great Wilderness: the West)

Book 16, Dahuangxijing

16-01 女娲之肠
Nvwazhichang
（109,21314E；34,36934N）

有神十人[1]，名曰女娲之肠[2]，化为神[3]，处栗广之野[4]；横道而处[5]。

注释：[1]有神十人：有一个京都的集肆。十，读博，指十字太阳概念，也指京都地区。神，指肆。
Notes [1] you shen shi ren (have deities ten person)
Tr: a market township in the capital, shi(ten)reads as bo, a Pu concept for sun cross, also refers to the capital area。shen(deity/God) means township, shen/si, close phonetic matching。

[2] 女娲之肠：指骊华之场，在陕西西安市临潼区骊门乡，今华清池北面。
[2] nv wa zhi chang (girl wa's guts)
Tr: refers to the Field of Lihua, in today's Limen Xiang, Lintong district, Xi'an city, Shaanxi province, north of Huaqingchi，(a famous hot spring)。

[3] 化为神：华南肆，今临潼老城区，称为骊华之场。
[3] hua wei shen (change into deity)
Tr: refers to Huanansi or Huanan township, today's Lintong city's old quarter, formerly called Lihua's field, (Lihuazhichang), wei/nan/south。

[4] 处栗广之野：座落于骊门之乡。
[4] chu li guang zhi ye (locate in li- wide wilderness)
Tr: is in the land of the Limen (Li gate)。

[5] 横道而处：恒都之处。恒都，指姜寨。
[5] heng dao er chu (horizontal way to stay)
Tr: refers to Hengdu (lasting capital) otherwise known as Jiangzhai, the Jiang Stronghold。

译文：有一个京都的集肆，名叫骊华之场——华南肆，座落于骊门之乡，恒都之处。

Translation:
There is a market township in the capital, called Lihua's Field, the Huanansi, or Huanan township。 It is situated in the land of Limen, a place where Hengdu, the Lasting capital is。

16-02 西周国
Xizhou Guo
（111,067E; 39,02832N）

有西周之国，姬姓，食谷[1]。有人方耕[2]，名曰叔均 [3] 。帝俊生后稷 [4]，稷降以百谷 [5] 。稷之弟曰台玺 [6]，生叔均 [7] 。叔均是代其父及稷播百谷 [8]，始作耕 [9] 。有赤国妻氏 [10] 。有双山 [11] 。

注释：[1]姬姓，食谷：姬姓的古老国家,在陕西最北端。
Notes: [1] ji xing, shi gu (surname Ji, eat grain)
Tr: refers to the ancient country bearing the surname of Ji, located in the northernmost part of Shaanxi province。
[2] 有人方耕：有一个集镇叫府谷。
[2] you ren fang geng (have person just plow)
Tr: there is a township called Fugu, a close phonetic match to fang geng。
[3] 名曰叔均：是叔均部落。
[3] ming yue shu jun (name is uncle even)
Tr: refers to the tribes of Shujun。
[4] 帝俊生后稷：北方地区有一个海则部落。陕西府谷至今有海则庙遗存。
[4] di jun sheng hou ji (di handsome begets hou ji)
Tr: up north there is a Haize tribe, a relic name is the Haize Temple, still found today in Fugu County, Shaanxi province。
[5] 稷降以百谷：海则是姜嫄地区的部落国。
[5] ji jian yi bai gu (ji shower down hundred grain)
Tr: Haize is a tribal country at the Jiangyuan region。
[6] 稷之弟曰台玺：海则的北面是台玺部落。弟，指狄，即北面。
[6] ji zhi di yue tai xi (ji's brother is terrace seal)
Tr: to the north of Haize is the Taixi tribe。di(brother) means Di, north， northern。
[7] 生叔均：酋长是叔均。
[7] sheng shu jun (begets uncle even)
Tr: the tribe's chieftain is Shu Jun。
[8] 叔均代其父及稷播百谷：叔均创立台玺并兼并了海则部落国。
[8] shu jun dai qi fu ji ji bo bai gu (shujun on behalf of his father and Ji to sow hundred grain)
Tr: Shujun establishes the Taixi tribe and annexes the Haize tribal country。
[9] 始作耕：开始建立国家。耕，读勾，指部落国。
[9] shi zuo geng (start to cultivate)
Tr: starts state building。geng (cultivate, plow) reads as Gou (hook), meaning tribal country。
[10] 赤国妻氏：游牧国犬戎氏族。
[10] chi guo qi shi (red state wife lineage)
Tr: the nomadic country of the Dog Rong tribes。
[11] 双山：指双山部落。
[11] shuang shan (twin mounts) refers to the Shuangshan tribes。

译文：有一个西周之国，是姬姓的古老国家。有一个叫府谷的集镇，那里是叔均的部落。北方地区有一个海则部落，海则部落是姜嫄地区的部落国。海则的北面是台玺部落，酋长是叔均。叔均创立了台玺并兼并了海则部落国，开始建立国家，包括有游牧国的犬戎氏族，有双山氏族。
Translation:
There is a country called Xizhou, an ancient one bearing the surname of Ji。There is a township called Gufu, a settlement of the Shu Jun tribes。 Up in the north, there is a region where the Haize tribes occupy, the Haize tribes are the tribal country of the Jiangyuan area。 To the north of Haize live the Taixi tribes, their chieftain is Shu Jun。Shu Jun established Taixi and annexed Haize tribal country。Shu Jun started state building, which includes the nomadic Dog rong tribe and the tribes of the Shuangshan Shi。

16-03 长胫国
Changjing Guo
（106,20219E；37,9902N）

西北海外，赤水之东，有长胫之国[1]。

注释：[1]长胫国：指通场国，今称利通，在宁夏吴中市。长，读绰，指迁移，疏通；胫，指场镇。
Notes: [1] chang jing guo (long thigh country)
Tr: refers to Tongchang country, known today as Litong, in Wuzhong city, Ningxia province。chang(long) reads as chuo, meaning moving from place to place, go through, jing(thigh) meaning township。

译文：在西北海外，黄河的东岸，有一个通场之国。
Translation:
In the area of northwest Haiwai region, on the east bank of the Yellow River, there is a Tongchang Nation。

16-04 盖山国
Gaishan Guo
（105,40373E；37,88614N）

有盖山之国[1]。有树[2]，赤皮枝干，青叶 [3]，名曰朱木 [4] 。

注释：[1]盖山国：中卫市，古称嘎勒赛汉国，在宁夏中卫市。
Notes: [1] gai shan guo (cover mount country)
Tr: refers to Zhongwei city, in ancient times it is known as Galesai Khanate, located in the Zhongwei(mid-guard) city, Ningxia province。

[2] 有树：有一个管理中心。
[2] you shu (have tree)
Tr: has an administration center。

[3] 赤皮枝干青叶：黄河旁边犬戎的中心。
[3] chi pi zhi gan qing ye (red bark branch dry green leaf)
Tr: refers to the center of Dog Rong tribes by the banks of Yellow River。

[4] 朱木：读偬昧，偬卫，今称中卫。
[4] zhu mu (red wood)
Tr: reads as zongmei, zongwei, a close phonetic rendering into zhongwei。

译文：有一个嘎勒赛汉国。有一个管理中心，是黄河边的犬戎的中心，名叫中卫。
Translation:

There is a Khanate -Galesai。 There is a center of administration set up by the Dog Rong along the Yellow River, known as Zhongwei。

16-05 柜格松
Guigesong
（105,18997E；37,51196N）

西海之外，大荒之中，有方山者[1]，上有青树[2]，曰柜格松[3]。日月所入也[4] 。

注释：[1]方山者：指部落统治区。
Notes:[1] fang shan zhe (square mount)
Tr: the area controlled by the tribes。
[2] 青树：指东胡族的建目。
[2] qing shu (green tree)
Tr: the tribal center of the Donghu (east Hu) tribes。
[3] 柜格松：指沙坡头，在宁夏中卫市。柜格，读音 ji ge，指沙帽、沙坡；松，指笼头。
[3] gui ge song refers to Shapotou, in today's Zhongwei city, Ningxia province, Guige, reads as ji ge, meaning shamao (sand cap) or sand dune, song(harness)。
[4] 日月所入也：柔然族治理之乡。
[4] ri yue suo ru ye (sun moon go through here)
Tr: the land managed by the Rouran （Juan Juan） tribes。

译文：在西海外的大地中，有一个部落统治区，那里有东胡的检目，叫沙坡头，是柔然族治理之乡。
Translation:
In the land beyond the West Haiwai, there is a region managed by tribal people。 It is the center of the Donghu people, which is called Shapotou, a land managed by the Rouran tribes。

16-06 白氏国
Baishi Guo
（104,17261E；36,54143N）

有大泽之长山[1]。有白氏之国[2] 。

注释：[1]大泽长山：指莲池山，在甘肃省白银市城区的北面。
Notes：[1] da ze chang shan (big water long mount)
Tr: refers to the Lianchishan (lotus pond mountain), in today's north of Baiyin (white silver) city, Gansu province。
[2] 白氏之国：指白肆，今称白银市。
[2] bai shi zhi guo (white shi surname country)
Tr: refers to White Si (city, market town) today's Baiyin city。

译文：在沙坡头的西面，有一座莲池山，那里有一个白肆之国。
Translation:
Located to the west of Shapotou, there is the Lianchishan, where the Baisi Nation resides。

16-07 先民国
Xianmin Guo
（103,83881E；36,05389N）

西北海之外，赤水之西，有先民之国[1]，食谷，使四鸟。

注释：[1]先民：甘肃兰州，古称金地，读音斜米、先民，治所在金城，今兰州市城关区。
Notes: [1] xian min (early folk)
Tr: refers to today's Lanzhou in Gansu province, its ancient name is Jindi (gold land)， reads as xiemi, a close phonetic match to xianmin。 Its center is in Jincheng, today's Chengguan (city pass) district, Lanzhou city, Gansu province。

译文：在西北海之外，在黄河的西部地区，有一个金地之国，是一个古老的国家。这里的氏族从事四种劳动。
Translation:
In the land beyond the northwest wilderness, in the western part of the Yellow River catchment, there is an ancient country-- a land of gold。 The tribal residents are engaged in four different ways of labor production。

16-08 夏耕尸
Xiagengshi
（103,61995E；36,10054N）

有人无首[1]，操戈盾立[2]，名曰夏耕之尸[3]。故成汤[4] 伐夏桀于章山 [5]，克之，斩耕厥前 [6] 。耕既立 [7]，无首，走厥咎，乃降于巫山 [8] 。

注释：[1]有人无首：有一个北方氏族的集镇。
Notes: [1] you ren wu shou (somebody without head)
Tr: a township of the northern tribes。
[2] 操戈盾立：绰歌当的治府，今谐音称为陈官当。
[2] cao ge dun li (with sword shield standing)
Tr: the administration center of Chuogedang, known today as Chenguandang, a close phonetic match。
[3] 夏耕尸：指金门肆，今谐音称为西固肆、西固区，在甘肃兰州。
[3] xia geng shi (summer plough corpse)
Tr: refers to Jinmensi, now Xiagengshi is rendered through phonetic matching to Xigusi, or xiguqu, in today's Lanzhou city, Gansu province。
[4] 故成汤：绰歌当的变写。
[4]gu cheng tang (therefore become hot water)
Tr: another rendering of Chuogedang, through phonetic match。
[5] 伐夏桀于章山：统治金门部落的疆域。
[5] fa xia jie yu zhang shan (attack xia jie at zhang mount)
Tr: in control of the area held by the Jinmen (gold gate) tribes。
[6] 克之，斩耕厥前：指连接丝绸之路的门纪关关口。
[6]ke zhi, zhan geng jue qian (overcome, kill gen in front of)
Tr: refers to the path, or passage gate connecting the Silk Road。 The gate is Menjiguan。
[7] 耕既立：指门纪关，今称水洞门。
[7] geng ji li (gen thus stand)
Tr: refers to Menjiguan Pass, known today as the Shuidongmen (water cave gate) 。
[8] 无首，走厥咎，乃降于巫山：北方氏族边关统领贾氏的驻地。走厥咎，指边关统；乃降，指贾氏；巫山，指驻地。
[8] wu shou (no head), zou que jiu (walk to wrong), nai jiang yu wu shan (therefore surrender to Shamen Mount)

Tr: refers to the controlled area by Jia Shi who is the chieftain of the northern tribes guarding frontier。 Zou que jiu: commander of the frontier。naijiang; Jia Shi the chieftain, wushan: their station garrison。

译文：有一个北方的氏族集镇，是绰歌当的治府，名叫金门肆，是绰歌当统治金门部落的疆域，是连接丝绸之路的门纪关关口，门纪关是北方氏族边关统领贾氏的驻地。
Translation:
There is a township of the northern tribes, the commander center of Chuogedang, which is called Jinmen Si。 It is the region of Jinmen tribes controlled by Chuogedang, the passage gate that connects the silk road。 The gate is called Menjiguan Pass, which is the garrison station of Chieftain Jia, whose tribes are guarding the northern frontier。

16-09 淑士国
Shushi Guo
（100,62182E；36,27507N）

有国名曰淑士[1]。颛顼之子[2] 。

注释：[1]淑士国：读数羲，指青海共和地区。汉语称共和、共工。
Notes: [1] shu shi guo (gentleman country)
Tr: reads as shu xi, refers to the Gonghe area in Qinghai province。 In Chinese, it is called Gonghe or Gonggong。
[2] 颛顼之子：颛顼指贤德，贤德指长水，长水就是黄河。颛顼之子，即黄河边的部落。
[2] zhuan xu zhi zi (virtu's children)
Tr: zhuan xu means virtuous, a coded term for long water, which is the Yellow River。 Zhuanxuzhizi: refers to the tribes along the Yellow River。

译文：有一个部落国，名叫数羲，是黄河边的部落国。
Translation：
There is a tribal nation called Shuxi, made up of tribes along the Yellow River。

16-10 不周负子山
Buzhoufuzi Mountain
（94,18509E；37,35545N）

西北海之外，大荒之隅，有山而不合[1]，名曰不周负子[2]，有两黄兽守之[3]。有水曰寒暑之水[4] 。水西有湿山 [5] ，水东有幕山 [6] ，有禹攻共工国山 [7] 。

注释：[1]有山而不合：有一个叫灶火湖的地方。不合，指贝湖。即灶火湖。
Notes:[1] you shan er bu he (has mount not together)
Tr: a place known as Zaohuo（hearth fire) Lake。 buhe(beihu) bu/bei, he/hu, means Zaohuo Lake。
[2] 不周负子：指灶火湖盆地。不，读贝，指火。今称柴达木盆地。
[2] bu zhou fu zi (not round negative child) refers to Zaohuo Lake basin, bu/bei/fire, today is known as the Chaidamu Basin (Tibetan: tshwa vdam gshong) 。
[3] 有两黄兽守之：属最大的咸水湖盆地。两黄，读良湖，指首湖；兽守，读shui shei，指咸水；之，指盆地。
[3] you liang huang shou shou zhi (two yellow beasts guard it)
Tr: stands as the biggest saltwater lake basin。lianghuang: two yellow (fine lake, means top lake) shou shou (beasts guard) reads as shui shei, meaning salty water, zhi: basin。

[4] 寒暑之水：哈鲁苏河与素梭河，简称哈素之水，谐音寒暑之水。
[4] han shu zhi shui (cold hot water)
Tr: refers to Halusu River and Susuo River, jointly known as Hasuzhishui, phonetically rendered into Hanshuzhishui。
[5] 湿山：指夏日哈山。
[5] shi shan (wet mount) refers to Xiariha Mountain。
[6] 幕山：指牦牛山。
[6]mu shan (canopy mount) refers to Maoniu(yak)Mountain。
[7] 禹攻共工国山：指伊科布拉格山，今称布青山。
[7]yu gong gonggong guo shan (Yu attack the Gonggong country's mountain)
Tr: refers to Yikebulag Mountain, known today as the Buqing Mountain。

译文：在西北海外的大地之间，有一个叫灶火湖的地方，称为灶火湖盆地，是最大的咸水湖盆地。有哈鲁苏河与素梭河水流入其中。湖水的西面有夏日哈山，东面有牦牛山和伊科布拉格山。
Translation:
In the land of Northwest Haiwai, there is a place called Zaohuo Lake, also known as the Zaohuo Lake Basin。 It is the biggest saltwater lake basin。 Two rivers, the Halusu and the Susuo, flow into it。 To its west there is the Xiariha Mountain。 To its east are the Maoniu (Yak) Mountain and the Yikebulag Mountain。

16-11 北狄国
Beidi Guo
（103,13906E；36,97125N）

有北狄[1]之国。黄帝[2] 之孙 [3] 曰始均 [4]，始均生北狄。
有芒山，有桂山、有摇山，其上有人，号曰太子长琴[5]。颛顼生老童[6]，老童生祝融 [7]，祝融生太子长琴，是处摇山，始作乐风 [8]。

注释：[1]北狄：北，在此读博，指山；狄，指北。北狄，即北山。
Notes: [1] bei di (north di)
Tr: bei: reads as bo, meaning mountain, di: refers to the north, therefore beidi, beishan (north mountain) 。
[2] 黄帝：指北山。
{2] huang di (yellow Emperor) meaning Beishan (north mountain) 。
[3]孙：指氏族。
[3] sun(grandson) refers to tribes, lineages。
[4] 始均：指草原部落氏族。
[4] shi yun (beginning even) refers to the steppe tribes。
[5] 太子长琴：指天祝草沁。
[5] tai zi chang qin (prince long lyre)
Tr: refers to the Tianzhucaoqin (a steppe township) 。
[6] 颛顼生老童：黄河边形成了中央氏的僚族，
[6] zhuan xu sheng lao tong (virtuous begets old child)
Tr: The Lao tribes become Zhongyang(central) Shi confederacy by the Yellow River。
[7] 老童生祝融：中央氏僚族分支出了草原氏族。
[7] lao tong sheng zhu rong (old child begets pray warm)
Tr: The Zhongyang Lao tribal confederacy has the steppe tribes branching out。
[7] 始作乐风：开始建立了游牧王国。乐，读勒，指游牧；风，读冯，指王国。
[7] shi zuo yue feng (start make music wind)

Tr: yue (music） reads as le, a phonetic match to Pu concept of nomads。feng(wind)reads as von, van, meaning Kingdom。

Tr; start to build up nomadic kingdom。 yue/le: nomadic; feng/wind: von, van: kingdom。

译文：有一个北山之国。北山的氏族，叫草原部落氏族，草原部落氏族建立了北山国。 有芒山、桂山、摇山，那里有个集镇，叫天祝草沁。黄河边的中央氏僚族的一个分支变成了草原氏族，草原氏族建立了天祝草沁，座落于摇山，从此开始建立游牧王国。

Translation:

There is a Beishan Kingdom。 Its tribes are steppe nomadic people。 The steppe tribes established a Beishan State。 There are Mangshan, Guishan, Yaoshan, and a township called Tianzhucaoqin。The Lao tribe, a branch of Zhongyang Shi by the Yellow River banks became steppe tribe, and this steppe tribe established the Tianzhucaoqin。It is in Yaoshan。 From then on, a kingdom of steppe nomads is being built。

16-12 五彩鸟三名

Wucainiaosanming

(102,89851E；37,47173N)

有五彩鸟三名[1]：一曰皇鸟[2]，一曰鸾鸟[3]，一曰凤鸟[4]。

注释：[1]五彩鸟三名：祁连部落的河流有三条。五彩，指祁连部落，今称古浪县；

Notes;[1] wu cai niao san ming (five color birds three name)

Tr: where the Qilian tribes are, there are three rivers。 wucai: refers to the Qilian tribes, in today’s Gulang (ancient waves) county。

[2] 皇鸟：指哈溪河，又称黄羊河。

[2] huang niao (king bird)

Tr: refers to Haxi River, known otherwise as Huangyang (yellow goat) River。

[3] 鸾鸟：指柳条河，又称古浪河。

[3] luan niao (phoenix bird)

Tr: refers to the Liutiao (willow branch) River, otherwise known as Gulang River。

[4] 凤鸟：指凤河，后称鸡冠河、萱麻河。

[4] feng niao (phoenix bird)

Tr: refers to Feng River, later known as Jiguan (chicken crown) River, Xuanma (xuan hemp) River。

译文：发源于祁连部落山的河流有三条，一条是哈溪河，一条是柳条河，一条是凤河。

Translation：

Three rivers originate from Qilianbuluo Mountain, one is Haxihe River, one is Liutiaohe River, one is Fenghe River。

16-13 吴回

Wuhui

（102,63658E；37,92805N）

有人名曰吴回[1]，奇左[2]，是无右臂[3]。

注释：[1]吴回：指武威。

Notes: [1] wu hui (wu return)

Tr: refers to Wuwei, a city in Gansu province。

[2] 奇左：座落在。

[2] qi zuo (strange left)
Tr: it is located at,

[3] 是无右臂：石武羊河，今称石羊河。

[3] shi wu you bi (is no right arm)
Tr; refers to the Shiwuyang (stone warlike goat) River, known today as the Shiyanghe (stone goat) River。

译文：有一个集镇名叫武威，座落在石羊河边。
Translation:
There is a township named Wuwei, it is located by the Shiyanghe River。

16-14 狂鸟
Kuang Niao
(100,46375E; 38,9433822N)

有五彩之鸟[1]，有冠[2]，名曰狂鸟[3]。

注释：[1]五彩鸟：指祁连部落的国家。
Notes: [1] wu cai niao (five color bird)
Tr: refers to the nation of Qilian tribes。

[2] 有冠：指裕固族之国。

[2] you guan (has crown)
Tr: refers to the nation of Urghur tribes。

[3] 狂鸟：指北河国，今甘肃省张掖市。北河，即黑河的古称谓。

[3] kuang niao (crazy bird)
Tr: refers to Beihe (north river) country, in today's Zhangye city, Gansu province。 Beihe, an ancient name for Heihe (black river) River。

译文：有一个祁连部落的国家，是裕固族之国，称为北河国。
Translation:
There is a nation of Qilian tribes, the Urghur tribal country, which is also known as the Beihe country。

16-15 灵山十巫
Lingshanshiwu
（98,49549E；39,75029N）

有灵山[1]，巫咸、巫即、巫朌、巫彭、巫姑、巫真、巫礼、巫抵、巫谢、巫罗[2]十巫，从此升降[3]，百药爰在[4]。

注释：[1]灵山：指篱山，即关山口，又称葆登山口，在甘肃酒泉。
Notes: [1] ling shan (ghost mount)
Tr: refers to Lishan (fence mount) also known as Guanshankou (shut mount pass), another name is Baodengshankou, a mountain pass located in Jiuquan city, Gansu province。

[2] 巫咸、巫即、巫朌、巫彭、巫姑、巫真、巫礼、巫抵、巫谢、巫罗：指酒泉、芨芨、板滩、并封、高台、勒者、临泽、河坝、河东、石包城十个部落。

[2] shaman xian, shaman ji, shaman pan, shaman peng, shaman gu, shaman zhen, shaman li, shaman di, shaman xie, shaman luo:
Tr: refers to the ten tribes: Jiuquan, Jiji, Bantan, Bingfeng, Gaotai, Lezhe, Linze, Heba, Hedong, Shibaocheng。

[3] 从此升降：从这里进出。
[3] cong ci sheng jiang (go up and down through here)
Tr: passing through, in and out from here。
[4] 百药爰在：是国家的大关卡。
[4] bai yao yuan zi (hundred medicine are here)
Tr: is a major passage gate of the country。

译文：在西北地区有一个关山口，有酒泉、芨芨、板滩、并封、高台、勒者、临泽、河坝、河东、石包城十个部落人群从这里进出，是国家的大关卡。
Translation:
There is a passage gate in the Northwest region。 The people from ten tribes such as Jiuquan, Jiji, Bantan, Bingfeng, Gaotai, Lezhe, Linze, Heba, Hedong, and Shibaocheng go through here。 This is a major passage gate of the nation。

16-16 丰沮玉门山
FengjuYumenshan
（97,04967E；40,29078N）

大荒之中，有山名曰丰沮玉门[1]，日月所入[2]。

注释：[1]丰沮玉门：指玉门王国。丰沮，读冯纪，指王国。
Notes: [1[feng ju yu men (bumper sad jade gate)
Tr: refers to the Yumen Kingdom， fengju: reads as fengji, meaning Kingdom。
[2] 日月所入：是游牧氏族的集镇。此处因未提到东胡，不能按柔然解读。
[2] ri yue suo ru (sun moon enter here)
Tr: refers to the townships of the nomads。Since Donghu is not mentioned, the nomads are not part of the Rouran。

译文：西北大地中，有个地方名叫玉门王国，是游牧氏族的集镇。
Translation：
In the land of the northwest region, there is a place where the Yumen Kingdom resides, it is a township of the nomadic tribes。

16-17 有虫状如菟
Youchongzhuangrutu
（95,77714E；40,52701N）

有虫状[1]如菟[2]，胸以后者[3]裸不见[4]，青如猨状[5]。

注释：[1]有虫状：有一个游牧的疆域。指瓜州、敦煌、肃北、阿克塞一带。
Notes: [1] you chong zhuan (has worm form)
Tr: there is a region of the nomads， which refers to areas of Guazhou, Dunhuang, Northern Gansu, and Aksai。
[2] 如菟：指管理区。
[2]ru tu:(like tu) refers to administration district。
[3] 胸以后者：匈夷王族支系。
[3] xiong yi hou zhe (that behind the chest)
Tr: the royal lineage of the Xiong Yi。
[4] 裸不见：指罗布纪，即罗布部落。

[4] luo bu jian (naked don't see)
Tr: refers to Luobuji, also known as the Luobu tribes。

[5] 青如猨状：东部的疆域。

[5] qing ru yuan zhuan (green as monkey form)
Tr: refers to the territory of eastern region。

译文：有一个游牧疆域的管理区，是匈夷国的罗布部落在东部的疆域。
Translation:
There is an administration district of the nomadic country, which is the eastern part of the Luobu tribe of the Xiong Yi country。

16-18 沃民沃野
Wominwoye
（93,51203E；42,81821N）

西有王母之山[1]，壑山[2]，海山[3]。有沃民之国[4]，沃民是处沃之野，凤鸟之卵是食 [5]，甘露是饮 [6] 。凡其所欲，其味尽存 [7] 。爰有甘华、甘柤、白柳、视肉、三骓 [8] 、璇瑰、瑶碧、百木、琅玕、白丹、青丹 [9] 、多银铁 [10] 。鸾凤自歌，凤鸟自舞 [11] ，爰有百兽，相群是处 [12] ，是为沃之野 [13] 。

注释：[1]王母之山：指很高的山。
Notes:[1] wang mu zhi shan (queen mother's mountain)
Tr: refers to very high mountains。

[2] 壑山：指托木尔提山。

[2] huo shan (gap mount) refers to the Tomurti Mountain。

[3] 海山：大黑山。

[3] hai shan (sea mount) refers to the Dahei (big black) Mountain。

[4] 沃民之国：指哈密国。沃，指好，译音与哈谐音。

[4] wo min zhi guo (fertile people's country)
Tr: Hami country, wo means good, wo/hao/ha, close phonetic rendering into Chinese。

[5] 凤鸟之卵是食：东边的人是原住民。

[5] feng niao zhi luan shi shi (phoenix's eggs are food)
Tr: people in the east are the original residents。

[6] 甘露是饮：外来民在北面。

[6] gan lu shi yin (sweet dew is drink)
Tr: immigrants are living in the north。

[7] 凡其所欲，其味尽存：统治着这里的夷民和犬戎部落的草原民。

[7] fan qi suo yu, (whatever it desires), qi wei jin cun (its flavor is fully retained)
Tr: [the Xiongnu] control the Yi people and the steppe nomads of the Dogrong tribes。

[8] 甘华、甘柤、白柳、视肉、三骓：指小麦、小米、山芋、稻谷、外穄。

[8] gan hua, gan zu, bai liu, shi rou, san zhui:
Tr: wheat, millet, potato, rice, wai ji

[9] 璇瑰、瑶碧、百木、琅玕、白丹、青丹：指棉花、葡萄、盘桃、苎麻、白提、青提。

[9] quankui(cotton)、yaobi(grapes)、 baimu (pan peach) 、langgan(zhu hemp)、 baiti (big white grapes) 、qingti (green big grapes) 。

[10] 多银铁：北方系列的农作物。银，指北方；铁，指系列。

[10] duo yin tie (much silver iron)
Tr: the various species of plants from the north。 silver(northern) iron (spectrum of plants) 。

[11] 鸾凤自歌，凤鸟自舞：西部牧民的城镇，东部人的部落。
[11] luanfeng zi ge (Luan birds self-sing) fengniao zi wu (feng birds self-dance)
Tr: means the township of the western nomadic herdsman, the tribes of the eastern people。

[12] 爰有百兽，相群是处：所有部落氏族和谐相处。
[12] yuan you bai shou (there are hundred beasts), xiang qun shi chu (groups to coexist)
Tr: all the tribes are in peaceful coexistence。

[13] 是为沃之野：这里是很好的家乡。
[13] shi wei wo zhi ye (thus is fertile land)
Tr: this is really a good place for homeland。

译文：在西北地区有很高的山，有托木尔提山、大黑山，有哈密国。哈密是个好地方，东边的人群是原住民，外来民族在北面。哈密王族统治着这里的夷民和犬戎部落的草原民。这里有小麦、小米、山芋、稻谷和外穄；又有棉花、葡萄、盘桃、苎麻、白提、青提等多种农作物。西部牧民的城镇和东部人群的部落，所有部落氏族都和谐相处。这里是美好的家乡。

Translation:

In the Northwest region, there are very high mountains, the Tomurti, the Daheishan, and the Hami country。Hami is a good place, the local original residents are in the east part, the immigrants are in the north。 The King lineage of the Hami Nation controls the Yi people and the steppe people of the Dog Rong tribes。 There grows wheat, millet, potato, rice and waiji; also available are the agricultural products such as cotton, grapes, Pan peach, Zhuhemp, White grapes and green grapes。

16-19 三青鸟

Sanqingniao

（89,18872E；42,95156N）

有三青鸟[1]，赤兽黑目[2]，一名曰大鵹[3]，一名曰少鵹[4]，一名曰青鸟[5]。

注释：[1]三青鸟：指吐鲁番青河流域的三个远古集镇。远古时期以托克逊为中心，所以称为青鸟的集镇。青鸟，指青河。
Notes: [1] san qing niao (three green birds)
Tr: refers to the three ancient townships along the Qinghe River area in Tulufan。 The ancient center is Tuokexun (Toxsun), therefore it is called the township of green birds。 Green bird is a transliteration of Pu concept green river, niao/liao(river)。

[2] 赤首黑目：犬戎族的恒目，即管理中心。
[2] chi shou hei mu (red head black eyes)
Tr: refers to the Hengmu--administration center of Dogrong tribes。

[3] 大鵹：妥尼的变音，吐鲁番远古时期称妥尼，即中青城。
[3] da li (big li-bird) phonetic shifted notation of Tuoni, an ancient name for Tulufan (Turpan），also known as Zhongqing city。

[4] 少鵹：指鄯善镇。鵹，指蔺、府。因远古时的政治结构较松散，读为镇恰当一些。
[4] shao li (young Li-bird） refers to Shanshanzhen, Li /fu/administrative unit; in ancient times, it is rather loosely connected political unit, a more proper term should be Zhen: township。

[5] 青鸟：又称青汶、青河，后称托克逊。有遗名琼外合帕。
[5] qing niao (green bird) also termed qingwen, qinghe, niao/wen/he: all meaning river。 Qing niao, otherwise known as Tuokexun (Toxsun)，a relic name of Qunwaihepa survives 。

译文：有三个青河地区的集镇，是犬戎族的管理恒目，一个叫中青城，一个叫鄯善，一个叫青河。
Translation:
There are three townships in the Qinghe area。 They are administrative centers managed by Dogrong tribes. They are Zhongqing city, Shanshan and Qinghe。

16-20 轩辕台
Xuanyuantai
（86,56638E；42,05793N）

有轩辕之台[1]，射者[2]不敢西向射[3]，畏轩辕之台[4]。

注释：[1]轩辕台：匈夷的区域。台，读妥，指区域。
Notes: [1] xuan yuan tai refers to Xiong Yi's region, tai reads as tuo, meaning region。
[2] 射者：指焉耆。汉译者为造神话，故意将耆改为者。
[2] she zhe: Yan qi (Qarasheher, Yanqi), transliterated by Chinese scribe, substituting zhe to qi, to fit for the myth。
[3] 不敢西向射：博嘎羲湘耶，指博嘎羲湖之乡。今称博斯腾湖。
[3] bu gan xiang xi she (dare not west towards shoot)
Tr: bo-ga-xi-xiang-ye, refers to land of Bogaxi Lake, today's Boston Lake。
[4] 畏轩辕之台：南匈夷地区。畏，即渭，指南。
[4] wei xuanyuan zhi tai (fear cartshaft terrace)
Tr: southern Xiong Yi's territory, wei(fear) means wei/south。

译文：有一个匈夷地区，是焉耆博嘎羲湖之乡，是南匈夷地区。
Translation:
There is a territory of the Xiong Yi, the Yanqi Bogaxi Lake area。It is the land of the Nan(south) Xiong Yi。

16-21 石夷
Shiyi
（86,06388E；44,30143N）

有人名曰石夷[1]，来风曰韦[2]，出西北隅以司日月之长短[3]。

注释：[1]石夷：指斯溢，以玛纳斯河而得名。今称石河子。
Notes: [1] shi yi: si yi, derives its name from the Manas River, known today as Shihezi。
[2] 来风曰韦：牧民称为斯汶、石韦。
[2] lai feng yue wei (come winds called wei)
Tr: herdsman called it Siwen, or Shiwei。
[3] 司日月之长短：接待游牧迁徙之休整。日月，读勒鞑，指游牧；长，读绰，指迁徙；短，指休整。
[3]si ri yue zhi chang duan (control sun moon long short)
Tr: receive and provide service to the nomads when they move to different grazing ground。 riyue (sun moon) reads leda: nomadic way, chang(long) reads as chuo, meaning migrant, duan(short) temporary stayover between different grazing camps。

译文：有一个集镇叫石河子，牧民称为石韦，座落于西北角，负责游牧迁徙休整的接待。
Translation:
There is a township called Shihezi。 The herdsmen call it Shiwei。 It is in the northwest corner。 It is a place where the nomads receive service between their trips to different grazing grounds。

16-22 龙山
Longshan
（82,07391E；44,90472N）

大荒之中，有龙山[1]，日月所[2]入。有三泽水，名曰三淖[3]，昆吾之所食也[4]。

注释：[1]龙山：指阿拉套山，指新疆博乐地区。
Notes: [1] long shan (dragon mount) refers to Alatau, today's Bole district，Xinjiang。
[2] 日月所入：游牧民族管理的地方。
[2] ri yue suo ru (sun moon here enter)
Tr: the places managed by the nomadic tribes。
[3] 三淖：指阿拉湖、艾比湖、赛里木湖。
[3] san nao: (three nuurs) refers to the three lakes: the Ala, the Aybi, the Sailimu。
[4] 昆吾之所食：昆吾，指高山的雪水，吾，指雪；所食，流入形成。
[4] kunwu zhi suo shi (kunwu's food)
Tr: kunwu: melting snow from the high mountains。Wu: snow； suoshi: made by water flowing through。

译文：在大地中，有阿拉套山，是游牧民族管理的地方。那里有三个湖泊，称为三淖，是高山的雪水流入而形成的。
Translation:
In the land where the Alatau mountain stands, the nomadic tribes manage it。 There are three lakes called Sanao (three nuurs), created by the melting snow running down from the high mountains。

16-23 女丑尸
Niuchoushi
（81,32086E；43,92183N）

有人衣青[1]，以袂蔽面[2]，名曰女丑之尸[3]。

注释：[1]衣青：指伊沁，即今新疆伊犁草原。
Notes: [1] yi qing (wear green)
Tr: refers to Yiqin, today's Yili grassland, in Xinjiang。
[2] 以袂蔽面：伊梅沘陌，指伊梅河畔。伊梅河，今称伊犁河。
[2] yi mei bi mian (use dress cover face)
Tr: reads as Yi-mei-bi-mo: Riverbanks of Yimei River, Yimei River is known today as the Yili (Ili) River。
[3] 女丑之尸：犁查之肆，即犁部落肆。今称伊犁。
[3] nv chou zhi shi (girl ugly's corpse)
Tr: Licha township, meaning the township of the Li tribes, today's Ili city。

译文：有一个伊犁草原的集镇，座落于伊梅河畔，名叫犁查肆。
Translation:
There is a township at the Ili grassland。 It is located by the banks of Yimei River, its name is Licha township。

16-24 女子国
Nvzi Guo
（82,50297E；43,78768N）

有女子国[1]。

注释：[1]女子国：指玉兹地区。今称巩留和尼勒克。玉兹，越濮语读为女子，在新疆伊犁巩留县和尼勒克县。
Notes: [1] nv zi guo (girls' country)
Tr: Yuzi region, known today as Gongliu and Nileke (Nilka, Nilqa) 。Yuzi reads in Yue and Pu speech as Nvzi, it is in today's Gongliu county and Nileke county in Xinjiang。

译文：在犁查肆的东面，有一个玉兹国。
Translation:
To the east of Licha town, there is the Yuzi (Zhuzi) nation。

16-25 桃山
Taoshan
（80,12533E；42,045N）

有桃山[1]。有寅山[2] 。有桂山 [3] 。有于土山 [4] 。

注释：[1]桃山：指托木尔山，在新疆阿克苏。
Notes:[1] tao shan (peach mount) refers to Tomur Mountain, in Aksu, Xinjiang。
[2] 寅山：指木扎尔山，今称汗腾格里峰，在阿克苏。
[2] wang shan: refers to Muzar Mountain, known today as Hantengri Peak, in Aksu。
[3] 桂山：指库尔干山，在阿克苏。
[3] gui shan: refers to Kurgan Mountain in Aksu。
[4] 于土山：指英阿瓦提山，在阿克苏。
[4]yu tu shan: refers to Ying'awati Mountain in Aksu。

译文：在阿克苏地区，有托木尔山，有木扎尔山，有库尔干山，有英阿瓦提山。
Translation:
In Aksu region, there are Tomur Mountain, Muzar Mountain, Kurgan Mountain and Ying'awati Mountain。

16-26 丈夫国
Zhangfu Guo
（80,24038E；41,27102N）

有丈夫之国[1]。

注释：[1]丈夫国：阿克苏，古称温宿国。"温宿"在濮语中是指丈夫。
Notes:[1] zhangfu guo (husband country) refers to Aksu, known in ancient times as Wensu country。 In Pu concept wensu means husband。

译文：有一个国家，名叫温宿国。
Translation:
There is a country known as the Husband country, or the Wensu country。

16-27 弇州山鸣鸟

Yanzhoushan Mingniao
（75,98958E；39,46733N）

有弇州之山[1]，五彩之[2]鸟仰天[3]，名曰鸣鸟[4]。爰有百乐歌儛之风[5] 。

注释：[1]弇州之山：指月氏之所，即新疆喀什地区。
Notes: yanzhou zhi shan (yanzhou mount)
Tr: refers to the land of the Yuezhi people, the Kash region in Xinjiang。
[2] 五彩之：指乌恰部落的。
[2] wu cai zhi (five color it)
Tr: of the Wuqia tribes。wucai/wuqia, close phonetic match。
[3] 鸟仰天：指阿克陶人。
[3] niao yang tian (bird turn towards sky)
Tr: The Arktau people 。
[4] 鸣鸟：指天山人，即南天山人，也称米僚。米、鸣，是濮语天的音译。
[4] ming niao (singing bird) refers to the Tianshan folks, the tribal people from the southern Tianshan, the tribes also known as Miliao, mi/ming: Pu concept for sky, a close phonetic rendering。
[5] 百乐歌儛之风：游牧部落城邦的统治。百乐，指游牧部落；歌，指城；儛，本指队伍，这里做邦解。
[5] bai le ge wu zhi feng (hundred music song dance the wind)
Tr: controlled by the city state run by the nomadic tribes。 baile; refers to the nomads, ge/sing, or song a Pu concept for city, wu/dance: teams here mean townships teamed up into state。

译文：有一个月氏地区，那里住着乌恰部落的阿克陶人，称为天山人。他们隶属于游牧部落城邦的统治。
Translation：
There is a region run by the Yuezhi, where the Aktau people from the Wuqia tribes live。 They are also known as Tianshan people， the people from the Tianshan Mountains。 They belong to the city-state run by the nomadic tribes。

16-28 轩辕国
Xuanyuan Guo
（73,24992E；39,72729N）

有轩辕之国[1]。江山之南[2] 栖为吉 [3] 。不寿者 [4] 乃八百岁 [5] 。

注释：[1]轩辕国：指萨雷耶国，今萨雷塔什城。
Notes:[1] xuan yuan guo (cart shaft country)
Tr: refers to the Sarleye country, in today's Sarlitash City。
[2] 江山之南：指天山南面的，实际是南天山南面的。
[2] jiang shan zhi nan (river mount 's south)
Tr: refers to the south part of Tianshan Mountain, in fact the south side of the southern Tianshan, the Nan Tianshan。
[3] 栖为吉：指小集市部落国。栖为，指小集市。
[3] qi wei ji(nestle is luck）
Tr: refers to the country of small market towns。 Qiwei; bazaar。
[4] 不寿者：氏族支系。
[4] bu shou zhe (not long-lived people)

Tr: refers to tribal branches。

[5] 乃八百岁：这句话有两层含义，一是指游牧部落的山区氏族；一是指刺绣部落的氏族。根据当地不谈刺绣的情况，选择前者。

[5] nai ba bai sui (thus 800 years old)

Tr: this sentence has double meanings: one refers to the tribes from the mountains of the nomadic areas。The other refers to the tribes engaged in embroidery。 Since embroidery is not mentioned here, the first explanation is chosen。

译文：有一个萨雷耶国，是南天山南面的小集市部落国，这里的氏族是游牧部落的山区氏族。

Translation:

There is a Saleiye country, a state of small market towns in the southern part of the Nan Tianshan。Those tribes are the mountain nomadic tribal people。

16-29 西海神弇兹

Xihaishenyanzi

西海陼中，有神[1]，人面鸟身[2]，珥两青蛇，践两青蛇[3]，名曰弇兹[4]。

注释：[1]神：指氏族。

Notes: [1] shen(deity) refers to tribes。

[2] 人面鸟身：指定居的草原氏族。鸟，读“老”音，在此作草解。

[2] ren mian niao shen (human face bird body)

Tr: refers to the tribes of settled steppe people。

[3] 珥两青蛇，践两青蛇：指珥践四夷，即管理着四周的族群。

[3]er liang qing she (wear in ears two green snakes), jian liang qing she (tread on two green snakes): er-jian four snakes, manage people from surrounding regions。

[4] 弇兹：指月氏氏族。

[4] yanzi: the Yuezhi tribes。

译文：在西海陼中，有一个氏族，是定居的草原氏族，管理着四周的族群，名叫月氏。

Translation:

Amid Xihai, the west region, there is a tribe, a settled steppe people, managing the surrounding tribes。 This tribe is known as Yuezhi。

16-30 黄姬尸、比翼鸟、天犬

Huangjishi, biyiniao, tianquan

（107,35828E；29,71746N~111,05042E；30,82534N）

有巫山[1]者。有壑山[2]者。有金门之山 [3] ，有人名曰黄姬之尸 [4] 。有比翼之鸟 [5] 。有白鸟 [6] ，青翼，黄尾，玄喙 [7] 。有赤犬，名曰天犬 [8] ，其所下者有兵 [9] 。

注释：[1]巫山：今仍称巫山。

Notes:[1] wu shan: shaman mount, the name is still in use。

[2] 壑山：指观面山，在长江三峡北岸。

[2] huo shan (gap mount)

Tr: refers to the Guanmian (see face) Mountain, on the northern bank of the three gorges area on the Yangtze River。

[3] 金门山：今称金缸山，在长江三峡南岸秭归县茅坪镇。门，濮语读攻，谐音缸。

[3] jin men shan (golden gate mount)

Tr: today known as the Jingang Mountain。 It is at Maoping Zhen, Zigui county, south bank of Yangzte's three gorge。 men(gate) read as gong, close to gang phonetically。

[4] 黄姖尸：指万斛（jin）肆。今称万州。

[4] huang ji shi: refers to wan jin si, today's Wanzhou, Sichuan province。

[5] 比翼鸟：指大元河，今称乌江河。

[5]bi yi niao (wing to wing bird) refers to the Dayuan River, today's Wujiang River。

[6] 白鸟：指白龙江，今称小江。

{6] bai niao (white bird) refers to Bailoong (white dragon) River, today known as the Xiaojiang (small river) 。

[7] 青翼、黄尾、玄喙：指汇成白龙江的三条支流。称为东河、巫南河，长沙河。长沙河，今称普里河。

[7] qing yi (green wings) huang yi (yellow tail), xuan hui (black beak)

Tr: refers to the three rivers that join to form the Bailongjiang River。 They are the Donghe River, the Wunan River, and the Changsha River。 Changsha River is known today as Puli River。

[8] 赤犬，天犬：赤犬，指移民的城镇；天犬，指天城。

[8] chi quan (red dog), tian quan (sky dog)

Tr: refers to the townships of immigrants。 Tian quan: means Tiancheng, (sky city) 。

[9] 其所下者有兵："所下者"，指长江三峡；"有兵"，指隶属。全句为：这些都是长江三峡的区域。

[9] qi suo xia zhe you bing (its subjects has army)

Tr: suo xia zhe: three gorges of the Yangtze River。 You bing, belong to。 The whole sentence is translated as, all those areas located in the Yangtze River's three gorges area。

译文：这里有巫山、观面山、金门山。有万斛肆，有乌江河，有小江，有东河、巫南河、长沙河。有一个移民的城镇，名叫天城。这些都是长江三峡的区域。

Translation:

There are the Wushan, the Guanmianshan, and the Jinmenshan。 There are also the Wanjinsi township, the Wujiang River, the Xiaojiang River, the Donghe River, the Wunan River, and the Changsha River。 There is the township of immigrants, known as Tiancheng city。These are the three gorges region of the Yangtze River。

16-31 屏蓬

Pingpeng

（107,50428E；31,21311N）

有兽，左右有首[1]，名曰屏蓬[2]。

注释：[1]左右有首：指州江流域的氏族，范围较宽。州江，今称州河，在四川达州境内。

Notes:[1] zuo you you shou (left right has head)

Tr: refers to the tribes around the Zhoujiang catchment。 Its area is rather wide。 Zhoujiang is known today as Zhouhe River, in Dazhou, Sichuan province。

[2] 屏蓬：读妣（pi）彭，指彭祖氏族，今称土家族。

[2] ping peng (screen canopy) reads as pi peng, refers to the tribes of Pengzu, known today as the Tujia ethnic people。

译文：有一个氏族，是州江的氏族，名叫彭祖氏族。

Translation:

There is a tribe known as the tribe from Zhoujiang, its name is the Pengzu tribe。

16-32 鏖鳌钜山
Luanaojushan
（106,63166E；30,45852N）

大荒之中，有山名曰鏖鳌钜山[1]，日月所入[2]。

注释：[1]鏖鳌钜山：指华安广山，后称广安。
Notes：[1] lun ao ju shan: refers to Hua'anguang Mountain, later known as Guang'an。
[2] 日月所入：是游牧部落统治的地区。
[2] ri yue suo ru (sun moon enter here)
Tr: refers to the territory controlled by the nomadic tribes。

译文：大地之中，有一个地方叫华安广山，是游牧部落统治的地区。
Translation:
Amid land, there is a place called Hua'anguang Mountain, the territory controlled by the nomadic tribes。

16-33 孟翼之攻颛顼之池
Mengyi zhi gong zhuanxu zhi chi
（106,27604E；29,97212N）

有池[1]，名曰孟翼之攻[2]颛顼[3]之池。

注释：[1]池：指城、城池。
Notes: [1] chi(pool) refers to township or strongholds。
[2] 孟翼之攻：指蒙渝之门。蒙，指涪江；渝，指嘉陵江。蒙渝之门是嘉陵江与涪江的会合口。
[2] meng yi zhi gong (meng wings attacks) refers to the Mengyu 's gate。 Meng refers to Fujiang River, Yu refers to Jiangling River。 The so-called Mengyuzhimen (gate) is where Jiangling River and Fujiang River meet。
[3] 颛顼：指照羲，巴国在苗蒙统治时期的国名。照羲城，今称合川，在重庆市合川区。
[3] zhuanxu: zhaoxi, the country name of Ba during the Miao tribes'rule。 Zhaoxi city, is today's Hechuan, in Chongqing city, Sichuan province。

译文：有一个城池，名叫蒙渝之门，照羲之城。
Translation：
There is a city named Menyu Gate, also known as Zhaoxi city。

16-34 常羲生月
Changxi sheng yue
（105,96806E；31,58132N）

有女子[1]方浴月[2]。帝俊妻[3] 常羲 [4]，生月十有二 [5]，此始浴之 [6] 。

注释：[1]女子：指阆竺，今称阆中，"阆"是苍的濮语读音，在四川阆中。

Notes: [1] nv zi(female) refers to Langzhu, today's Langzhong, Lang, a Pu concept of Cang, in Langzhong, Sichuan province。

[2] 方浴月：统治着月氏氏族。月，指月氏氏族。

[2] fang yu yue (just bath moon)

Tr: in control of the Yuezhi tribes。 Yue(moon) refers to the Yuezhi tribes。

[3] 帝俊妻：指北方的部落。

[3] di jun qi (God handsome wife)

Tr: refers to the tribes from the north。

[4] 常羲：指賨羲部落，后演称为苍溪部落，治所在阆竺。

[4] chang xi: refers to Congxi tribes, later shifted phonetically into Cangxi (dark stream) tribe, with its center at Langzhu。

[5] 生月十有二：发展为十二个支系。

[5] sheng yue shi you er (begets moon ten and two)

Tr: developed into twelve tribal branches。

[6] 此始浴之：从此开始管理他们。浴，读儒，指治理、管理。

[6]ci shi yu zhi (now start bath them)

Tr: from this point on, starts to rule them, Yu/ru: rule, manage, administrate。

译文：有一个阆竺管理的月氏部落地区。北方的苍溪部落发展为十二个支系，从此开始管理着他们。

Translation:

There is a region of the Yuezhi tribes managed by Langzhu。 The Cangxi tribes from the North grow into twelve branches and start to manage them。

16-35 青鳶黄鷔

Qing wen huang ao

（104,77877E；31,89069N~105,86577E；30,18216N）

有玄丹之山[1]。有五色之鸟[2]，人面有发 [3] 。爰有青鳶、黄鷔、青鸟、黄鸟 [4]，其所集者其国亡 [5] 。

注释：[1]玄丹之山：河镇之所，指河岸边的集镇部落。

Notes: [1] xuan dan zhi shan (black cinnabar mount)

Tr: riverside townships area, refers to the township tribes along the riverbanks。

[2] 五色之鸟：指安河之僚，今称涪江之僚。

[2] wu se zhi niao (five color birds)

Tr: refers to the Lao tribes at Anhe River, known today as Lao tribes of Fujiang River。

[3] 人面有发：定居于河岸边。

[3] ren mian you fa (human face has hair)

Tr: settlements by the riverbanks。

[4] 青鳶、黄鷔、青鸟、黄鸟：指郪江僚，凯江僚，梓江僚、琼江僚等涪江支流的僚族。凯江又称南水，读音卧汶；梓江又称东江，读音青鸟；琼江又称白马河，读音胡鸟。

[4] qing wen, huang ao (green bird, yellow bird)

Tr: refers to Qijiang Lao tribe, Kaijiang Lao tribe, Zijiang Lao tribes and Qiongjiang Lao tribes, they are， among other Lao tribes，branches living by the Peijiang River。 Kaijiang: nanshui (south river), reads as Wo-wen; Zijiang: dongjiang (east river) reads as Qingniao; Qiongjiang: also known as Baima(white horse) river, reads as Huniao。

[5] 其所集者其国亡：集中起来像一条巨龙。国亡，读古瓦，指龙。

[5] qi suo ji zhe qi guo wang (when gather, the kingdom dies)

Tr: those tribes collect along the river, as if becoming a great dragon。 Guowang (kingdom die) reads as Guwa, a Pu concept of dragon, (long, lung, lao) 。

译文：有河岸边的集镇部落，那里有涪江之僚定居于河岸边，还有郪江僚、凯江僚、梓江僚、琼江僚等涪江支流的僚族，集中起来像一条巨龙。
Translation:
There are many riverside tribes along the river。 The Fujiang Lao tribe settled by the river。 Other Lao tribes are Qijiang Lao, Kaijiang Lao, Zijiang Lao and Qiongjiang Lao, among other Lao tribes, by the Fujiang river branches。 They collect along the big river like a great dragon。

16-36 日月山
Riyue Mountain
（104,0659E；30,65851N~104,39496E；31,12655N）

大荒之中，有山名曰日月山[1]，天枢也[2]。吴姬天门[3]，日月所入 [4] 。有神，人面无臂 [5]， 两足反属于头 [6] 。山名曰虚 [7] 。颛顼生老童 [8]， 老童生重黎 [9]， 帝令重献上天 [10]， 令黎卬下地 [11] 。下地是生噎 [12]， 处于西极，以行日月星辰之行次 [13] 。

注释：[1]日月山：在此指织乡之所，即四川成都、德阳平原。
Notes: [1] ri yue shan (sun moon mount)
Tr: it refers to the land where silk is produced, in today's Chengdu city and Deyang Plain in Sichuan province。
[2] 天枢也：天枢之乡。枢，指织机；天枢之乡，比喻织绸业发达之乡。
[2] tian shu ye (sky shuttle) land of sky shuttle (weaving machine)
Shu: shuttle and weaving machine, figurative saying for advanced silk weaving industry。
[3] 吴姬天门：广元部落的天门，今称剑门。吴，指部落；姬，指广。
[3] wu ji tian men (state wu's queen sky gate)
Tr: the geonym for Guangyuan tribe: sky gate, today known as Jian(sword)gate。 Wu/tribes, ji/wide and long。
[4] 日月所入：织乡的治理区。
[4] ri yue suo ru(sun moon enter here)
Tr: the territories managed by tribes of silk weaving business。
[5] 有神，人面无臂：有一个氏族定居于绵远河边。无臂，即无沘，指远河，今称绵远河，是涪江的上游河段。
[5] you shen, ren mian wu bi (has deity human face no arm)
Tr: a tribe settled by the Mianyuan River。 wubi (no arm) refers to Yuan(faraway)River, known as today's Mianyuan River, the upper reach of Fujiang River。
[6] 两足反属于头：都城王族之境。
[6] liang zu fan shu yu tou (two feet back on top of head)
Tr: this is the territory belonging to the city-state's royal tribes。
[7] 山名曰虚：部落国名叫蜀的羲，也称叔德羲，指制作丝绸的国家，今四川德阳市。
[7] shan ming yue xu (mount name is shallow)
Tr: the name of the tribal state is Xi, in fact the whole name is Shudexi, refers to the state engaged in silk production。 It is today's Deyang city in Sichuan province。
[8] 颛顼生老童：大自然养育了劳动者。
[8] zhuangxu sheng laotong (virtu begets oldchild)
Tr: nature nurtures the working laborer tribes。
[9] 老童生重黎：劳动者分支出游牧民和种植民。
[9] laotong sheng chongli (oldchild begets double li)

Tr: Labourers become two specialized groups, the herders, and the planters。

[10] 帝令重献上天：北蔺的游牧部落在高寒地区。

[10] di ling chong xian shang tian (God order chongxian up to heaven)

Tr: the nomadic herder's tribes of Beilin(northern) roam the high and cold areas。

[11] 令黎卬下地：南蔺的种植部落在低凹的热带。

[11] ling liyin xia di (order liyin down earth)

Tr: Nanlin(southern)'s planter tribes occupy the tropical lowland。

[12] 下地是生噎：低地的地区又分支出织绸氏族。

[12] xia di sh sheng ye (low land is begetting ye)

Tr: in the lowland areas, some tribes have got into the silk producing industry。

[13] 出于西极，以行日月星辰之行次：迁至东边，以行织乡先进的蚕业。次，读崔，指蚕。

[13] chu yu xi ji (out from west pole), yi xing riyuexingchen zhi xingci (thus order the movement of sun moon stars)

Tr: they migrated to the east to promote their advanced silk industry based on mulberry leaves。ci/order, reads as cui, refers to mulberry leaves silkworms。

译文：在大地中，有个地方名叫织绸之乡，被喻为天枢之乡。从北面南下。过了广元部落的天门，就进入了织乡的辖区。有一个统治氏族，定居于涪江都城王族之境，部落国的名称叫蜀的羲。大自然养育了劳动者，劳动者分支出游牧民和种植民，北蔺的游牧民住在高寒地区，南蔺的种植民住在低凹的热带。低地的地区又分支出织绸氏族，他们迁至东边，以行织乡先进的蚕业。

Translation:

In the middle of earth, there is the land of silk making tribes, known as the Heavenly Shuttle city。From north going down south, one passes the Skygate: Tianmen of the Guangyuan tribes, to enter the territory managed by the Silk making tribes。 The controlling tribe of this territory settled by the Fujiang River, the territory of the city royal lineages。 Its name is Shudexi。 Mother nature has given birth to labor tribes, and labor tribes grow into tribes specializing in planting and in herds keeping。 The north nomads live in the high and cold areas。 The south planters live in lowland tropical areas。 Some tribes from lowlands have developed into silk making tribes。 The silk making tribes moved to the east, to further promote their silkworm farming industry。

16-37 天虞

Tianyu

（104,39496E；31,12655N）

有人反臂[1]，名曰天虞[2]。

注释：[1]有人反臂：有一个隶属王族的集镇。反臂：读冯毕，指王属。

Notes：[1] you ren fan bi (has one back arm)

Tr: a township belongs to the royal tribe。 fanbi (back arm) reads as fengbi, meaning royal lineage。

[2] 天虞：指旌阳镇。旌阳，古称旌川，濮语读为 to ye，谐音天虞，今四川德阳城。

[2] tian yu (sky yu)

Tr: today's Jinyang town, Jinyang (banner sun) known in ancient times as Jinchuan, in Pu concept it reads as to ye, a close phonetic rendering to tianyu。 It is today's Deyang city in Sichuan province。

译文：有一个隶属王族的集镇，名叫旌川镇。

Translation:

There is a township under the supervision of the royal tribe。The name of the township is Jinchuan township。

16-38 大荒山

Dahuang Shan
（103,33421E；29,522N）

大荒之中，有山，名曰大荒之山[1]。

注释：[1]大荒山：指达洪鲁，汉译为皇木山。今称峨眉山。
Notes：[1] da huang shan (big wilderness mount)
Tr: refers to Dahonglu: transliterated into Chinese as Huangmu (royal wood) Mountain, known today as the E'mei Mountain。

译文：大地之中，有座山叫达洪之山。
Translation:
In the middle of the earth, there is a mountain called Dahong Mountain。

16-39 夏后开
Xianhoukai
（103,2618E；29,23063N）

西南海之外，赤水之南，流沙之西[1]，有人珥两青蛇，乘两龙[2]，名曰夏后开[3]。开上三嫔于天[4]，得《九辩》与《九歌》以下 [5] 。此天穆之野 [6] ，高二千仞 [7] ，开焉得始歌《九招》[8] 。

注释：[1]流沙之西：指流沙之东。流沙指金沙江，属长江上游。
Notes: liu sha zhi xi (flowing sand to west)
Tr: refers to Liusha's east, Liusha, another name for Jinsha River, which forms the upper reach of the Yangtze River。

[2] 珥两青蛇，乘两龙：在两河口管理着两河边的氐族。两河口，今峨边县城。
[2]er liang qing she, cheng liang loong (ears wear two green snakes, ride two dragons)
Tr: refers to the tribes that manage the tribal affairs at the Lianghekou（two river mouth),in today's Ebian Yi Autonomous County , a county of Sichuan province。

[3] 夏后开：指所洪启，即峨边。
[3] xia hou kai (summer back open) refers to Suohongqi, also known as Ebian。

[4] 三嫔于天：指设置金河支系。三嫔，读 she bi，指金河；天，读音 t'e，指设置。
[4] san pin yu tian (three females in sky)
Tr: set up the Jinhe (gold river) branches。 Sanpin: reads as she bi, refers to Jinhe。 Tian (sky) reads as t'e, meaning to set up a structure。

[5]得《九辩》与《九歌》以下：治理共和与五渡于东。九辩，读音 shu be，指共和；九歌，原是伍勾，指盟渡，因盟与共有近义，被改为《九歌》创造神话，今称五渡镇。
[5]de jiu bian yu jiu ge yi xia (get nine counterpoints and nine songs and below)
Tr: manage the Gonghe country and Wudu country in the east。Jiubian, reads as shu be, meaning Gonghe。 jiuge: wugou, meaning united crossings, meng, and common are close in meaning, and is transliterated into Nine songs to create a mythical narrative。 The place in point is known today as Wudu (five crossing) town。

[6] 此天穆之野：指码头之乡。天穆，即天坞，指码头。
[6]ci tian mu zhi ye (this sky endless land)
Tr: refers to river ports。 Tianmu: tian wu, meaning ports.

[7] 高二千仞：读郭勒丘惹，指河流集镇地区。
[7] gao er qian ren (high 2000 fathom)
Tr: reads as guo-le-qiu-re: meaning the riverfront townships。

[8] 开焉得始歌《九招》：所洪启部落维护着通渡的数个村落。焉得，指庇佑治理，即维护；九招，读数卓，指数个村落。始歌。即施勾，指通渡，也可以理解为通航。
[8] kai yan de shi ge jiuzhao (start to sing nine summons)
Tr: Suohongqi tribes maintain control of the many villages whom the river front ports service。 Yande: protection and management, maintenance。Jiuzhao: reads as shuzhuo， meaning a few villages。Shige means Shigou, refers to crossing, ferry service, and can be understood as water transportation。

译文：在西南海之外，在黄河源头的南面，金沙江的东面，有一个集镇在两河口管理着两河边的氏族，叫所洪启部落。所洪启部落在西面设置金河的村寨，又在东面治理着共和与五渡码头之乡、河流集镇区域，维护着通渡的数个村落。
Translation:
Beyond Xinanhai, to the south of the headwaters of Yellow River, and to the east of Jinsha River， a township manages the tribes along the two rivers at the Lianghekou, it is called Suohongqi。 Suohongqi tribes set up villages at Jinhe River to its west, and to it east, manages the areas of Gonghe and Wudu ports, townships by the riversides and maintain the many villages using water transportations。

16-40 偏句、常羊山
Pianju Changyangshan
（101,74208E；28,30698N。102,37586E；28,72871N）

有大巫山[1]。有金之山[2] 。西南，大荒之中隅，有偏句 [3] 、常羊之山 [4] 。

注释：[1]大巫山：指大雪山。巫，指雪。
Notes: [1] da wu shan (big shaman mount) refers to Daxueshan (great snow) mountains, Wu: snow。
[2] 金之山：指牦牛岭，又称金山，在凉山州冕宁县，是大雪山的南端。
[2] jin zhi shan (gold mount) refers to the Maoniu(yak) ling(range), known today as Jinshan (gold mountain) 。It is the south extension of the Daxueshan Mountain。
[3] 偏句山：指屏锦山，今称锦屏山，在西昌地区。
[3] pian ju shan (sideway sentence mount)
Tr: refers to Pinjinshan (screen colorful mount) known as today's Jinping Mountain in Xichang district。
[4] 常羊山：指小相岭，在西昌地区。
[4] chang yang shan (constant goat mount) refers to the Xiaoxiangling Mountain, in Xichang district。

译文：那里有大雪山，有金山。在西南大地之中，有屏锦山，有小相岭。
Translation:
There is the Daxueshan, the Jinshan。In the land of southwest, there is the Pinjinshan and the Xiaoxiangling Mountain。

16-41 互人国
Huren Guo
（102,26675E；27,89203N）

有互人之国[1]。炎帝之孙名曰[2] 灵恝 [3] ，灵恝生互人 [4] ，是能上下于天 [5] 。

注释：[1]互人国：指马镇国。马，读胡，谐音互。马镇，西昌的古称谓，有遗名马道镇。

Notes： [1]hu ren guo (mutual people country) refers to Mazhen country。 Ma: reads as Hu, a phonetic match to hu4(mutual)。Mazhen (horse town), the ancient name for Xichang, its relic name still retained in Madaozhen (horse trail town) 。

[2] 炎帝之孙名曰：指大凉山地区的。

[2] yandi zhi sun ming yue (yan di's grandson name is)

Tr: refers to the area of the Daliangshan Mountains。

[3] 灵恝：指良贾，即首府。

[3] ling jia (spirit undisturbed)

Tr: a phonetic match to liang jia (best merchant)， meaning the capital city。

[4] 灵恝生互人：良贾建立了马镇。

[4] ling jia sheng hu ren (spirit undisturbed begets mutual person)

Tr: The capital city established Mazhen, the Horse town。

[5] 是能上下于天：这里是能素的广阔之境。能素，今称彝族；上下，读妥体，指千万、广阔。

[5] shi neng shang xia yu tian (therefore can go up down through sky)

Tr: here is the endless territory of the Nengsu tribes, Nengsu being Yi tribes, shangxia, reads as tuoti, meaning thousand upon thousand, long and wide。

译文：有马镇之国。大凉山地区的良贾，建立了马镇，这里是能素的广阔之境。

Translation:

There is a Mazhen country。 The capital city in Daliangshan Mountain set up the Mazhen。 This is the open country for the Nengsu Yi people。

16-42 鱼妇

Yufu

（102,54102E；27,37851N）

有鱼偏枯[1]，名曰鱼妇[2]。颛顼死即复苏[3] 。风道北来 [4] ，天乃大水泉 [5] ，蛇乃化为鱼 [6] ，是为鱼妇。颛顼死即复苏。

注释：[1]鱼偏枯：指蒲口夷，今称普格彝。

Notes: yu pian ku (fish half dry)

Tr: refers to Pukou Yi, today known as Puge Yi。

[2] 鱼妇：指荫胡，曾被译为鱼凫，属小月氏氏族。

[2]yu fu (fish wife)

Tr: refers to Yinhu, also transliterated into Yufu, they belong to the Lesser Yuezhi tribes。

[3] 颛顼死即复苏：照羲菩纪的胡族。照羲，指新疆北天山地区。菩纪，指草原部落。

[3] zhuan xu si ji fu su (Virtue die at once come alive)

Tr: refers to the Hu tribes of the Zhaoxishiji, Zhaoxi: the norther Tianshan area in Xinjiang。 Sheji refers to the steppe tribes。

[4] 风道北来：统治螺髻山地区。北来，读博螺，指螺髻山。

[4] feng dao bei lai (wind way north come)

Tr: in control of Luoji (shell hairdo) Mountain area。 Beilai: bo luo, refers to luojishan。

[5] 天乃大水泉：指云雾河鞑族犬戎，今称黑河彝族。

[5] tian nai da shui quan (sky thus big water spring)

Tr: The Dogrong tribes of Dar people from Yunwu (clous mist) River, known today as the Yi people from the Heihe (black water) River。

[6] 蛇乃化为鱼：塞族演变为荫。荫，三星堆文为一大十字套四小十字。

[6] she nai hua wei yu (snake become fish)
Tr: the Saka people became Yin, the sign for Yin appears in Sanxingdui (three-star pile) with one small cross on each of the big cross's four corners。

译文：有普格夷，称为荫胡，是照羲著纪胡族，统治螺髻山地区的云雾河鞑族犬戎，由塞族演变为荫，称为荫胡，实际是照羲著纪胡族。
Translation:
There are the Puge Yi people, also known as Yinhu, the Hu tribes of Zhaoxisheji, also known as the Dar Dogrong tribes from Yunwu River who are in control of the Luoji Mountain territory。 They are previous Sakas, later become Yinhu。 Known as Yinhu, they are in fact the Hu people from Zhaoxisheji。

16-43鸀鸟
Shuniao
（101,50699E；29,00106N）

有青鸟[1]，身黄[2]、赤足、六首[3]，名曰鸀鸟[4]。

注释：[1]青鸟：在此指犬戎。
Notes:[1] qing niao (green bird) here refers to the Dogrong tribes。
[2] 身黄：指胡族。
[2] shen huang (body yellow) refers to the Hu tribes。
[3] 赤足、六首：游牧的母系氏族。
[3] chi zu(bare feet) liu shou(six heads)
Tr: the matrilineal tribes of the nomads。
[4] 鸀鸟：指数僚，即九河氏族，在今康定九龙县。
[4] shu niao (shu bird) shu lao, refers to the Jiuhe (nine river) tribes, in today's Jiulong county in Kangding district, Qinghai province。

译文：有犬戎胡族，是游牧的母系氏族，称为九河氏族。
Translation:
There are the Dogrong Hu tribes, they are a matrilineal nomadic group, also known as the Jiuhe tribes。

16-44 三面一臂人
Sanmianyibiren
（101,07994E；29,39395N）

有人焉三面[1]，是颛顼之子[2]。三面一臂[3]，三面之人不死[4]。是谓大荒之野[5]。

注释：[1]三面：指沙绒濮，在四川雅江县波斯河镇和普沙绒镇。
Notes: [1] san mian (three faces)
Tr: refers to the Sharong Pu people, in Bosihe town and Pusharong town in Yajiang county, Sichuan province。
[2] 颛顼之子：指长河边的集镇，这里指雅砻江边的集镇。
[2] zhuanxu zhi zi (virtu's son)
Tr: the townships along the Changhe River。 It refers to the townships by the Yalongjiang River。
[3] 三面一臂：雅江边的沙绵氏族。
[3] san mian yi bi (three faces one arm) the Shamian tribes by the Yajiang River。
[4] 不死：指波斯河镇。

[4] bu si (not die) refers to the Bosihe township.

[5] 大荒之野：指大雪山之乡。

[5] da huang zhi ye (big wilderness) refers to the land of Daxueshan (big snow mountains)

译文：有一个沙绒濮的集镇，是长江流域的集镇。在雅江边住着沙绒氏族，沙绒氏族的集镇叫波斯河镇，称为大雪山之乡。

Translation:

There is a township of the Sharong Pu people, a township in the Yangtze River's catchment。The Sharong tribes live by the Yajiang River, their township is called Posihe township, also known as the land of big snow mountains--Daxueshan zhixiang。

16-45 一臂民

Yibimin

（101,01534E；30,03215N）

有一臂民[1]。

注释：[1]一臂民：指雅江地区，今雅江县城。

Notes: [1] yi bi min (one arm folk)

Tr: refers to the Yajiang area, in today's Yajiang county。

译文：有雅江这个地区。

Translation:

There is a place known as Yajiang。

16-46 昆仑西王母

Kunlun xiwangmu

（92,44287E；34,21468N）

西海之南，流沙之滨，赤水之后，黑水[1]之前，有大山，名曰昆仑之丘[2]。有神，人面虎身，有文有尾[3]，皆白，处之[4]。其下有弱水之渊环之[5]，其外有炎火之山，投物辄然 [6] 。有人戴胜 [7] ，虎齿 [8] ，有豹尾，穴处 [9] ，名曰西王母 [10] 。此山万物尽有 [11] 。

注释：[1]赤水、黑水：指黄河、长江。西海之南指大地西部。

Note:[1] chi shui, hei shui (red water, black water) refers to the Yellow River, the Yangtze River。Xihaizhinan（Xihai 'south） refers to the west land 。

[2] 昆仑之丘：指昆仑山，也称唐古拉山。

[2] kun lun zhi qiu (kun lun Mount)

Tr: Kunlun Mountains, also known as the Tanggula Mountains。

[3] 有神，人面虎身，有文有尾：有一个氏族，是定居的胡族，依鄂茸夷。依鄂茸，指斯依鄂茸陇巴。

[3] you shen (have God), ren mian hu shen (human face tiger body) you when you yi (have markings have tails)

Tr: there is a tribe, they are the Hu people who settled down, known as Yierong Yi。Yierong, refers to si-yi-e-rong-long-ba。

[4] 皆白，出之：出自白马部落支系。

[4] jie bai, chu zhi (all white, out it)

Tr: they are branches from the Baima (white horse) tribes。

[5] 其下有弱水之渊环之：东边有弱水之乡的恒投支系。

[5] qi xia you ruo shui zhi yuan huan zhi (under it has weak water surround it)
Tr: to its east side there is the Hengtou branch from the Ruoshui area。

[6] 其外有炎火之山，投物辄然：南面有雅壑砻恒投部落农业集镇区。其外，指其南。投物，指恒投部落。

[6] qi wai you yan huo zhi shan, tou wu zhe ran:(outside it has flame mount, throw things in catch fire)
Tr: to its south are the agricultural townships of the Hengtou tribe from the Yahuolong。

[7] 有人戴胜：有个集镇叫多尔丘索。

[7] you ren dai shen (has person wear victory)
Tr: a township is called Duo'erqiusuo。

[8] 虎齿：指游牧地区。

[8]hu chi (tiger teeth) refers to the nomadic territory。

[9] 有豹尾，穴处：有山夷，山间很冷。

[9] you bao yi (has leopard tail), xue chu (cave dwelling)
Tr: there are the mountain tribes, it is very cold in the mountains。

[10] 西王母：指雪域高原。

[10] xi wang mu (west queen mother) refers to the Snow plateau。

[11] 此山万物尽有：山上只有金矿、玉石、冰雪和野生动物，说万物尽有只是一个美丽的遐想。

[11]ci shan wan wu jin hou (this mount everything it has)
Tr: this is a mythical statement to say on the snowy mountains, there is everything。 In fact, there are only gold mines, jade deposit, snow and ice and wild animals。

译文：在大地西部的流沙河地区，在黄河源头的后面，长江源头的前面，有大山名叫昆仑山。那里有个氏族，是定居的依鄂茸夷，出自白马支系。东面有弱水之乡的恒投支系，南面是雅砻恒投部落农业集镇区。昆仑山有一个集镇叫多尔丘索，是游牧地区，有山夷，山间很冷，称为雪域高原。此山万物尽有。

Translation:

In the territory south to the Liusha River in the west land, behind the headwaters of the Yellow River， in front of the headwaters of the Yangtze River, there stands the big mountain range, the Kunlun Mountains。 There is a tribe, the settled Yierong Yi from the Baima tribes。 To the east, there are the Hengtou tribes from the land of the Ruoshui River, to the south, the Yalong Hengtou tribes' agricultural townships。 There is a township called Duo'erqiusuo by the Kunlun Mountains, a nomadic area, where live the mountain tribes。 It is very cold up the mountains which boast of having everything you can name。

16-47 常阳山

Changyangshan

（93,08128E；33,69234N）

大荒之中，有山名曰常阳之山[1]，日月所入[2]。

注释：[1]常阳之山：指恰日升山。旁边是多尔丘索部落。

Notes:[1] chang yang zhi shan (often goat mount) refers to Qiarisheng Mountain, the Duo'erqiusuo tribe is by the mountain。

[2] 日月所入：游牧部落管理区。

[2] ri yue suo ru (sun moon enter here)
Tr: the territory managed by the nomads。

译文：大地之中，有座山叫恰日升山，是游牧部落管理区。

Translation:

In the middle of land, there is the Qiarisheng Mountain, an area controlled by the nomadic tribes。

16-48 女祭、女薎
Niu ji niu meng
（92,78431E；34,37235N。95,12015E；33,67139N）

有寒荒之国。有二人女祭[1] 、女薎 [2] 。

注释：[1]女祭：在此指陇琼吉，即茶措村。
Notes: [1] nv ji refers to Longqiongji, also known as Chacuo township。
[2] 女薎：在此指龙莫弄。
[2] nv mie; refers to Longmonon township 。

译文：那里有寒荒之国，叫楚玛须国。有两个集镇，一个叫陇琼吉，一个叫龙莫弄。
Translation:
There is the country of cold and wilderness, it is called Chumaxu。 There are two townships, one is Longqiongji, the other is Longmeonon。

16-49 寿麻国
Shouma Guo
（95,79897E；34,12702N）

有寿麻之国[1]。南岳娶[2] 州山女，名曰虔 [3] 。女虔生季格 [4] ，季格生寿麻。寿麻正立无景 [5] ，疾呼无响 [6] 。爰有大暑 [7] ，不可以往 [8] 。

注释：[1]寿麻国：指曲麻莱，古称寿麻国，又称不死国、不死药。
Notes： [1] shou ma guo (longevity hemp country)
Tr: refers to a place called Qumalai, its ancient name is Shouma Guo, also known as Busi (never die) guo, or Busiyao (die not medicine) 。
[2] 南岳娶：指通天曲，即通天河。
[2] nan yue qi (south mount receive bride)
Tr: refers to the Tongtianqu (reach sky), today's Tongtianhe River。
[3] 州山女虔：指草山麻沁氏族。
[3] zhou shan nv qian (zhou mount girl qian)
Tr: refers to the grass mountain's Maqin tribes。
[4] 女虔生季格：麻沁氏族建立部落。
[4] nv qian sheng ji ge (girl qian deliver ji ge)
Tr: Maqin tribes organized themselves into tribal confederacy。
[5] 季格生寿麻，寿麻正立无景：部落又发展成寿麻国，叫寿麻当陇部落国。
[5] ji ge sheng shou ma (ji ge begets longevity hemp), shou ma zheng li wu jing (longevity hemp stand straight cast no shadow)
Tr: tribes developed into Shouma country, is called Shouma Danglong tribal state。
[6] 疾呼无响：国家统治着北羌。
[6]ji hu wu xiang (quick yell no echo)
Tr: state rules the Northern Qiang。
[7] 爰有大暑：又统治着鞑属族。
[7] yuan you da shu (thus has big heat)

Tr: rules as well the nomadic Dardars (Tartars)。

[8] 不可以往: 补苦的部落。

[8] bu ke yi wang (can't go)

Tr: The Buku tribes。

译文：有一个寿麻国。通天河的草山麻沁氏族，建立了部落，部落发展成为寿麻国，叫寿麻当陇部落国，统治着北羌的氏族，还统治着鞑族和补苦的部落。

Translation:

There is country called Shouma， the Caoshan Maqin people from the Tongtianhe River organized themselves into tribes, and then into Shouma tribal state。 Its full name is Shouma Danglong tribal state。They rule the Qiang tribe from the north。 They also rule the Dar tribes and Buku tribes。

第十七卷大荒北经 (The Great Wilderness: the North)

Book 17 Dahuangbeijing

17-01 附禺山
Fuyushan
（124,82138E；45,11422N）

东北海之外，大荒之中，河水之间[1]，附禺之山[2]，帝颛顼与九嫔葬焉[3]。爰有【丘鸟】久、文贝、离俞、鸾鸟、凤鸟、大物、小物[4]。有青鸟、琅鸟、玄鸟、黄鸟、虎、豹、熊、罴、黄蛇、视肉、璿瑰、瑶碧[5]，皆出卫于山[6]。丘方员三百里，丘南帝俊竹林在焉[7]，大可为舟[8]。竹南有赤泽水，名曰封渊[9]。有三桑无枝[10] 。丘西有沈渊 [11] ，颛项所浴 [12] 。

注释：[1]河水之间：指松花江与嫩江的交汇处。
Notes:[1] he shui zhi jian (river water in between)
Tr: refers to the confluence of Songhua River and Nenjiang River。

[2] 附禺山：指扶余部落，即前郭尔罗斯，今松原。前郭尔，应读投郭尔，指松花江。

[2] fu yu shan: refers to the Fuyu tribe, also known as the Qian Gorlos, in today's Songyuan。 Qian Gorlos should be read as Tou-guo-er, (gol,) it means the Songhua River。

[3] 帝颛顼与九嫔葬焉：北方照羲与九濮部落的疆域。九濮部落，称为巴数，红山文化刻文有记载。

[3] di zhuanxu yu jiu pin zang yan (di zhuanxu and his nine wives buried here)
Tr: this is the land of Zhaoxi tribe and Jiupu tribes in the north。 Jiupu (nine Pu) is called Bashu, which is reserved in the rock carving in Hongshan (red mountain) culture。

[4] 【丘鸟】久、文贝、离俞、鸾鸟、凤鸟、大物、小物：指城镇居民、河埠居民、种植民、西部僚、东部僚、游牧民和狩猎氏族。

[4] qiu jiu (qiu bird remain): city dwellers。
Wen bei (marking shell): settlers along the riversides。
Liyu (leave yu): plant growers。
Luanniao (luan bird): west Liao people。
Fengniao (phoenix): east Liao people。
Dawu (big stuff): nomadics。

Xiaowu (small stuff): hunting tribes。

[5] 青鸟、琅鸟、玄鸟、黄鸟、虎、豹、熊、罴、黄蛇、视肉、璿瑰、瑶碧：指吉拉人、嫩江人、松江人、东浪河人、牧民、农民、猎人、手工业者、扶余人、私粟人、松城人、幼河人，今已无遗名。

[5] qingniao (green bird): Jila people
Langniao(bird): Nenjiang people
Xuanniao (black bird): Songjiang people
huangniao (yellow bird): Donglanghe River people
Hu(tiger): herders
Bao(leopard): peasants
Xiong(bear): hunters
Pi(bear): handicraftsman
Huangshe (yellow snake): Fuyu people
Shirou (gaze meat): Cereal growers
Xuan gui (xuan jade) Songcheng people
Yaobi (green jade) Youhe River people。 Their traces are not available anymore。

[6] 皆出卫于山：皆陪伴过这个地方。

[6] jie chu wei yu shan (all out guard this mount) all the above-mentioned peoples have kept accompaniment of this place。

[7] 丘方员三百里，丘南帝俊竹林在焉：城为扶余所的亳里；城南的江北是祚耶的墓园，在富达、富康、常保三村的交汇处。亳里指京都，帝俊竹林指江北墓园，在焉指祚耶。

[7]: qiu fang yuan san bai li (mound area 300 li)
Qiu nan di jun zhu lin zai yan (mound south di's bamboo grove stand)
Tr: the city is the capital of Fuyusuo, Jiangbei to the south of the city is the tomb garden of Zuoye, which is situated in the place where three villages of Fuda, Fukang and Changbao meet。 baili (hundred li): poli, refers to the capital city。 Dijunzhulin: refers to Beifang (the north), here is referring to the north of the river, where the Tomb Garden is located。 Zaiyan: refers to Zuoye。

[8] 大可为舟：游牧可汗的冥府。舟，指冥府。

[8] da ke wei zhou:(big as a boat)
Tr: The Hall of the Dead for the nomadic Khan, zhou(boat) the dead realm, Hall of the Dead。

[9] 赤泽水，名曰封渊：移土形成的水泡，称赤泽水；封渊即扶泡子，今称富康泡。

[9] chi ze shui (red zee water)
Ming yue feng yuan (name is seal deep)
Tr: the water-filled location created by moving dirt, which is called Chizeshui。 Fengyuan (sealed deep) also known as Fupaozi (hold bubble) is called today as Fukangpao。

[10] 三桑无枝：指富饶的平原。

[10] san sang wu zhi (three mulberry without branches)
Tr: refers to the rich and affluent plain。

[11] 沈渊：沈，读音 cheng，查干湖的“查”的变音。

[11] shen yuan;(shen deep) shen is read as cheng, a phonetic shift of cha(white), as in the name of Chagan Lake。

[12] 颛顼所浴：著名的冬季渔场，颛顼，读 zhe xi，指冬季渔场；所浴，指著名的。

[12] zhuan xu suo yu (Di zhuanxu bath here) zhuan xu: reads zhe xi, meaning winter fishing ground。 Suo yu (bath here) meaning famous, well-known。

译文：在东北海之外的大地中，松花江与嫩江交汇的地方，有一个扶余部落的地区，是照羲与九濮部落的疆域。那里有城镇居民、河埠居民、种植民、西部僚、东部僚、游牧民和狩猎氏族。有吉拉人、嫩江人、松江人、东浪河人、牧民、农民、猎人、手工业者、扶余人、私粟人、松城人、幼河人，皆陪伴着这个地方。城镇为扶余所的亳里。城南的江对岸是扶余部落祚耶的墓园，是游牧可汗的冥府。墓园南面有移土泡子，名叫扶渊。还有富饶的平原。城西有沈渊，是著名的冬季渔场。
Translation:
In the land beyond the Northeast Hai, in a place where the Songhua River and the Nenjiang River meet, there is the territory of Fuyu tribes， occupied by the tribes of Zhaoxi, and Jiupu。 In this territory there are the city dwellers, settlers along the riverbanks, plant grows, Lao people from the west, Lao people from the east， nomadic tribes, hunters。 The people of Jila, Nenjiang, Songjiang, Donglanghe, herders, peasants, hunters, handicraftsman, Fuyu, Sisu, Songcheng and Youhe have all kept companionship to this place。 The city is the Poli, capital of Fuyusuo。 Opposite the riverbank in the south of the city is the tomb garden of the Zuoye Khan of the Fuyu tribes, a Hall of the Dead for the nomadic Khan。 To the south of the Tomb Garden there is a Tupaozi, called Fuyuan。 There is also the fertile plain。 To the west of the city, there is Shenyuan, the famous winter fishing ground。

17-02 胡不与国
Hubuyu Guo
（125,08314E；45,52205N）

有胡不与国[1]，烈姓[2]，黍食[3]。

注释：[1]胡不与国：指马蹬泡之国，今黑龙江省肇源县。
Notes:[1]hu bu yu guo (hu not to country) refers to the Madengpao Guo, in today’s Zhaoyuan county, Heilongjiang province。
[2] 烈姓：指从事游牧业的。
[2] lie xing (family name Lie) refers to the nomadic way of living。
[3] 黍食：指古老氏族。
[3] shu shi (millet food) refers to the ancient tribes。

译文：北边有一个马蹬泡之国，是从事游牧业的古老氏族国家。
Translation:
In the northern land there is a Madengpao Guo, an ancient nomadic nation。

17-03 肃慎国
Sushen Guo
（122,07614E；46,07444N）

大荒之中，有山名曰不咸[1]，有肃慎氏之国[2]。有蜚蛭，四翼[3]。有虫[4]，兽首蛇身 [5]，名曰琴虫 [6] 。

注释：[1]不咸：读博兴，指大兴安岭。
Notes： [1] bu xian (not salty) reads as boxing, refers to the Daxinganling Mountain。
[2] 肃慎国：指以狩猎为主的国家，今乌兰浩特。
[2]su shen guo: refers to the hunters’ country, in today’s Wulan Haotet (Ulanhot (Mongolian: ᠤᠯᠠᠭᠠᠨᠬᠣᠲᠠ; Chinese: 乌兰浩特), formerly known as Wangin Süm, alternatively Wang-un Süme, Ulaɣanqota (Red City) in Classical Mongolian。
[3] 蜚蛭，四翼：指管理着四周的夷民。
[3] pei zhi(insects) si yi (four wings)
Tr: managing the local Yi people living around the place。
[4]虫：指游牧民。
[4] chong (worm) refers to nomadic people。

[5] 兽首蛇身：指输通河氏，今称洮儿河。
[5] shou shou she shen (beast heads snake body)
Tr: refers to Shutonghe Shi people, Shutonghe River is known today as Tao'er River。
[6] 琴虫：指科尔沁游牧民。
[6] qin chong (lyre worm) refers to the Kerqin nomadic people。 Kerqin: Horqin grassland， Kerqin Steppe。

译文：在西面的大地中，有一座山叫大兴安岭，那里有一个肃慎国，管理着四周的夷民。有一个游牧氏族，是输通河氏，称为科尔沁游牧民。
Translation:
In the land to the west, there is a mountain range called Daxinganling。 There is a Sushen Country, it manages all the local people。 There is a nomadic tribe, the Shutong River people, known as the nomadic people from the Kerqin steppe。

17-04 大人国
Daren Guo
（125,34105E；46,41109N）

有人名曰大人[1]。有大人之国[2]，釐姓，黍食 [3] 。有大青蛇 [4]，黄头，食麈 [5] 。

注释：[1]大人：指大惹，应是今安达。
Notes:[1] da ren (big man) refers to Da Re, is today's Anda city, in Heilongjiang province。
[2] 大人之国：指达惹国。
[2] da ren zhi guo (big man nation): refers to Dare Guo。
[3] 釐姓，黍食：指游牧的古老氏族。釐读勒音。
[3] le xing (family name le) shu shi (millet eat)
Tr: refers to the ancient nomadic tribes。 Li: reads as Le, meaning nomadic。
[4] 大青蛇：指大庆肆。
[4] da qing she (big green snake)
Tr: refers to Daqingsi, township of Daqing (big celebration town) 。
[5] 黄头，食麈：指王都根据地。
[5] huang tou（yellow head) shi chen (eat dirt) 。
Tr: the base of King's capital, king: khan。

译文：有一个集镇叫达惹，那里有一个达惹国，是古老的游牧氏族的国家。那里有一个大庆肆，是王都的根据地。
Translation:
There is a township called Dare, which is the Dare Guo, a very ancient country of the nomadic tribes。 There is a Daqing township, which is the base for the king's capital 。

17-05 鲧攻程州山
Gungongchengzhoushan
（123,95698E；47,34151N）

有榆山[1]，有鲧攻程州[2]之山。

注释：[1]榆山：指扎龙山地区。榆，龙 rue 的变音。
Notes:[1]yu shan: refers to Zhalongshan region。 Yu; a transmuted phonetic sign for Rue: dragon。

[2] 鲧攻程州：指奎门盐仓，今齐齐哈尔地区。奎门，即北门；陈州，楚则的变音。
[2] gun gong cheng zhou (God Gun attack Cheng zhou)
Tr: refers to the Kuimen Salt silo, known today as the Qiqihaer region。 Kuimen, Beimen, (north gate) 。chenzhou, a phonetic shifting from chuze。

译文：有一个扎龙山地区，那里有一个叫奎门盐仓的地方。
Translation:
There is a Zhalongshan region, in that region there is a place called Kuimen salt silo。

17-06 先民山槃木
xianminshanpanmu
（128,84083E；47,72672N）

大荒之中，有山名曰衡天[1]。有先民之山[2]，有槃木千里 [3] 。

注释：[1]衡天山：指万桐山，今称万猪山，在小兴安岭伊春河畔。
Notes:[1] heng tian shan: refers to Wantong Mountain, known today as Wangzhu (10000 pigs) Mountain。 It is by the bank of Yichun River, in Xiaoxinganling Mountains。
[2] 先民之山：指小兴安岭地区。
[2] xian min zhi shan: refers to the Xiaoxinganling Mountains。
[3] 槃木千里：指河畔的建目且里。建目，指管理中心；且里，指城镇。实际指伊春。
[3] pan mu qian li (tangled wood 1000 li) refers to the administration center by the riverbank, which is called Jianmu, qianli (1000 li) reads as Qieli, meaning city or towns, here it refers to Yichun。

译文：在东北大地中，有座山叫万桐山，是小兴安岭地区，那里有河岸边的管理城镇。
Translation:
In the land of northeast region, there is a mountain called Wantong Mountain。 This is the Xiaoxinganling region, with riverside administration townships。

17-07 叔歜国
Shuchu Guo
（127,32509E；49,42302N）

有叔歜国[1]，颛顼之子，黍食[2]，使四鸟：虎、豹、熊、罴[3]。有黑虫如熊状[4]，名曰猎猎 [5] 。

注释：[1]叔歜国：指孙楚部落，简称孙吴，今黑龙江孙吴县。
Note:[1] shu chu guo: refers to the Sunchu tribe, shortened to Sunwu, in today's Sunwu county, Heilongjiang province。
[2] 颛顼之子，黍食：长河支系的古老氏族。长河，指孙河。
[2] zhuanxu zhi zi, shu shi (God zhuanxu's son, millet eat) 。
Tr: the ancient tribe 's Changhe (long river) branch。 chang he (long river) refers to Sunhe River。
[3] 使四鸟，虎、豹、熊、罴：从事四种劳动，牧、农、猎、手工业。
[3] shi si niao, hu bao xiong pi (use four birds tiger, leopard, bear, pi) 。
Tr: are engaged in the four kinds of labour: herding, agriculture, hunting and handicrafts。
[4] 黑虫如熊状：黑河移民的狩猎氏族。
[4] hei chong ru xiong zhuang (black worm as bear form) 。
Tr: the hunting tribes of migrant people from Heihe。

[5] 猎猎：指那拉氏。黑河的那拉氏，称为溢黑那拉氏，今称叶赫那拉氏。
[5] lielie: refers to the family name of Nala。 (Yehe Nara hala), the Nara Shi from Heihe (black river), in Pu speech it is called Yihei (black river) nara hala: Yihei has been shifted to Yehe。

译文：有一个孙吴国，那里住着孙河的古老氏族，他们从事四种劳动：牧业、农业、狩猎业和手工业。那里有黑河移民的狩猎氏族，名叫那拉氏。
Translation:
There is a Wusun Guo, the ancient tribe from Sunhe River lives there, engaged in four kinds of production labour: herding, agriculture, hunting and handicrafts。 There is also a hunting tribe that migrated from the Heihe River, with the family name of Nara Shi。

17-08 北齐国
Beiqi Guo
（126,1983E；48,51436N）

有北齐之国[1]，姜姓[2]，使虎豹熊罴[3]。

注释：[1]北齐国：贝池国，即温暖的池子之国，今称五大连池。
Notes： [1] bei qi guo: refers to Beichi Guo, meaning the country with warm ponds, known today as the Wudalianchi (five big connected warm pools) 。
[2] 姜姓：老黑山氏族。姜，指黑色。
[2] jiang xing (family name jiang)
Tr: refers to the Laoheishan tribe (old black mountain) 。 jiang: black color。
[3] 使虎豹熊罴：从事牧、农、猎、手工业四种劳动。
[3] shi hu bao xiong pi (use tiger leopard xiong pi)
Tr: engaged in four kinds of production labour: herding, agriculture, hunting, and handicrafts。

译文：有一个贝池国，住着老黑山氏族，从事牧、农、猎、手工业四种劳动。
Translation:
There is a Beichi Guo, the Laoheishan tribe live there, engaged in four kinds of production labour: husbandry, agriculture, hunting, and handicrafts。

17-09 先槛大逢山、禹所积石山
Xianjiandafengshan, Yusuojishishan
（128,47702E；49,58023N。128,65103E；49,62199N）

大荒之中，有山，名曰先槛大逢之山[1]，河济所入[2]，海北注焉。其西有山，名曰禹所积石[3]。

注释：[1]先槛大逢山：指逊克鞑胡镇，今称逊克。
Notes:[1] xian jian da feng shan (early thresh big meet mount)
Tr: refers to the Xunke Dahu town, known today as Xunke county in Heilongjiang province。
[2] 河济所入：黑龙江从这里流过。
[2] he ji suo ru (river water come here)
Tr: the Heilongjiang (Amur River) River flows through here。
[3] 禹所积石：指伊索季斯克，今称波亚尔科沃。
[3]yu suo ji shi (Yu piled stone)
Tr: Yisuojisike (Yisurjisk), known today as Поярковский сельсовет。

译文：东北大地中有一个地方，叫逊克鞑胡镇，黑龙江从这里流过，向东北流入北海。逊克鞑胡的西边有一个集镇，名叫伊索季斯克。
Translation:
In the land of Northeast there is a township called Xunke Dahuzhen。 The Heilongjiang River flows through here and goes northeast into the North Sea。 There is a township to the west of the Xunke Dahu, known as Yisuojisk。

17-10 始州国
Shizhou Guo
（126,95944E；47,45922N）

有阳山者[1]。有顺山者[2]，顺水 [3] 出焉。有始州之国 [4]，有丹山 [5] 。

注释：[1]阳山：指通肯河西侧的乾丰山。
Notes: [1] yang shan (sun mount) refers to the Qianfeng Mountain to the west side of Tongken River。
[2] 顺山：指通肯河源头的顺楞山。
[2] shun shan (smooth mount): refers to the headwater mount of Tongken River, the Shunleng Mountain。
[3] 顺水：指通肯河。濮语读通为苏、顺。
[3] shun shui (smooth water) refers to the Tongken River。In Pu speech, tong (through, smooth) reads as su, as shun。
[4] 始州国：指苏尔沁咀子，简称苏咀，谐音始州，后称海伦市，在大、小兴安岭的结合部地区。
[4] shi zhou guo (begin province country)
Tr: refers to the Surqinzuizi: shortened to Suzui, a phonetic rendering into Shizhou。 It is later known as Hailun City。 It is located where the Daxinganling and the Xiaoxinganling meet。
[5] 丹山：指丹羲山，意为平顶山，在小兴安岭西南部边缘。
[5] dan shan (red mount) refers to Danxishan, meaning Pingdingshan, a mountain having a flat top。 It is located to the southwest rim of the Xiaoxinganling Mountain。

译文：在大兴安岭与小兴安岭的结合部，有一座阳山，有一座顺山，通肯河发源于顺山。那里有一个国家，叫苏尔沁咀子。再往东边，还有一座平顶山。
Translation:
In where the Daxinganling and the Xiaoxinganling meet, there is a mountain called Yangshan, and a mountain called Shunshan。 The Tongken River rises from the Shunshan。 There is a country called Surqinzuizi。Further to the east, there is a mountain called Pingdingshan。

17-11 大泽
Daze
（松花江）

有大泽[1]方千里[2]，群鸟所解[3]。

注释：[1]大泽：指大江，这里指松花江。
Notes:[1] da ze (big zee) refers to the big river, the Songhuajiang River。
[2] 方千里：统属千里。
[2] fang qian li (area 1000 li) its territory thousand li wide and long。
[3] 群鸟所解：会集所有的支流。
[3] qun niao suo jie (flock birds thus dissolve) 。

Tr: gather all the tributaries 。

译文：有一条大江统属千里，汇集所有的支流。
Translation:
There is a big river that commands thousand li areas long and wide, collecting all the tributaries。

17-12 毛民国
Maomin Guo
（126,64251E；45,75759N）

有毛民之国[1]，依姓，食黍，使四鸟[2]。禹生均国[3]，均国生役采 [4]，役采生修鞈 [5]，修鞈杀绰人 [6] 。帝念之 [7]，潜之为国 [8]，是为毛民。

注释：[1]毛民国：毛，指溢陌，即河岸，毛民国读陌米国，指河岸地区之国，今哈尔滨。
Notes:[1] mao min guo (hairy man country)
Tr: mao (hair) refers to Yimuo, meaning riverbank； maominguo: reads as Momiguo, meaning country built along the riverbank。 It is called Harbin, the capital city of Heilongjiang province。

[2] 依姓，食黍，使四鸟：河边的古老氏族，从事四种劳动。依，指溢，即河边。
[2] yi xing shi shu, shi si niao (family name Yi, eat millet, use four birds)
Tr: the ancient tribe by the riverbank, engaged in four kinds of labour。 Yi(lean) a phonetic match to Yi(water) meaning riverbank。

[3] 禹生均国：大河形成了部落国家。
[3]yu sheng yun guo (Yu begets even country)
Tr: the big river creates tribal states。

[4] 均国生役采：部落国养育了水边的游牧氏族。役，指溢，即水边；采读驰，指游动。
[4] yun guo sheng yi cai (even country begets yi cai)
Tr: tribal states create nomadic tribes by the riverside。 Yi(employ) a phonetic match to Yi, meaning by the water。 Cai reads as Chi, meaning roaming around, nomadic。

[5] 役采生修鞈：水边的游牧氏族分支出住房氏族。修鞈，指宿房、住房。
[5] yi cai sheng xiu ge (yicai begets repair breastpiece) 。
Tr: the nomadic tribe by the river creates Housing tribes。Xiu ge: lodge, house。

[6] 修鞈杀绰人：住房氏族另外建立集镇。杀，指外；绰，指建、造；人，指惹、集镇。
[6] xiu ge sha chuo ren (repair breastpiece kill chuo person)
Tr: The Housing tribes create other townships。 sha(kill) meaning out, outside。 Chuo: build, construct, ren: re, township， Poli。

[7] 帝念之：北临大江。
[7] di nian zhi (God remember it)
Tr: overlook to the north at the big river。

[8] 潜为之国：游牧部落南面的国家。
[8] qian wei zhi guo (submerge be the country)
Tr: the countries to the south of the nomadic tribes。

译文：有一个河岸边的国家，住着河边的古老氏族，从事四种劳动。大河流域形成了部落国，部落国养育了游牧氏族，游牧氏族分支出了住房氏族，住房氏族另外建立集镇，北临大江，是游牧部落南面的国家，称为陌米国。
Translation:

There is a country by the riverbank, an ancient tribe by the river。 It is engaged in four kinds of labour。 The big river catchment creates tribal states。 Tribal states create nomadic tribes。 Nomadic tribes branch out to form a housing tribe。 Housing tribe built another township, overlooking the big river to its north。 This country is to the south of the nomadic tribes。 This country is called Momi Guo。

17-13 儋耳国
Daner Guo
（129,28263E；47,13678N）

有儋耳之国[1]，任姓[2]，禺号子，食谷[3]。北海之渚中，有神，人面鸟身[4]，珥两青蛇，践两赤蛇[5]，名曰禺强[6]。

注释：[1]儋耳国：指带岭国，今黑龙江省伊春市南岔县。
Notes:[1] dan er guo (carry ear country)
Tr: refers to the Dailing Guo, in today's Nancha county, Yichun city, Heilongjiang province。
[2] 任姓：氏族名与地名相同，称为任姓。
[2] ren xing: the tribe bears the same name as the place name: ren: called Renxing tribe。
[3] 禺号子，食谷：浩良河支系的古老国家。
[3]yu hao zi, shi gu (yuhaozi eat grain)
Tr: the ancient nation of the Haoliang River branch。
[4] 有神，人面鸟身：有一个氏族，是定居的僚族。
[4] you shen, ren mian niao shen (a god, human face bird body)
Tr: there is a tribe, the settled tribe of Lao people。
[5] 珥两青蛇，践两赤蛇：管理着周边四个支流的氏族，东面是朱拉比拉河氏族、亮子河氏族，西面是大青川氏族、西岔河氏族。
[5]er liang qing she, jian liang chi she:(earlopped two green snakes, step on two red snakes)
Tr: manage the tribes along the four tributaries。 To the east is the Zhulabilahe tribe, the Liangzihe tribe, and to the west is the Daqingchuan tribe and the Xichahe tribe。 All the names are derived from the rivers they live by。
[6] 禺强：指翠河氏族。禺强，读溢翠，今称永翠河。
[6]yu qiang: refers to the Cuihe tribes。 Yuqiang reads as Yicui, known today as the Yongcui River (forever jade-green water) 。

译文：有一个带岭国，是带岭氏族在浩良河支系的古老国家。在北海渚中，有一个氏族，是定居的僚族，管理着周边四个支流的氏族，名叫翠河氏。
Translation:
There is a country called Dailing Guo, an ancient country of the Haoliang River branch, part of the Dailing tribes。 In the land of Northern territory, there is a tribe, the settled tribe of the Lao people。 It manages the four tribes along the four river tributaries。 This manager tribe is called Cuihe Shi。

17-14 北极天柜山
Beijitianguishan
（177,02218E；68,1378N）

大荒之中，有山名叫北极天柜[1]，海水北注焉[2]。有神九首，人面鸟身[3]，名曰九凤[4]。又有神衔蛇操蛇[5]，其状虎首人身 [6]，四蹄长肘 [7]，名曰彊良 [8]。

注释：[1]北极天柜山：指楚科奇山，在须伯利亚东北端。天柜（ju），指部落区域。

Notes:[1] bei ji tian gui shan (north pole sky chest mount)
Tr: refers to the Chukeqi Mountain (Chukotsky), located to the northeast tip of Siberia, tiangui: (sky chest) reads as Tianju, means the territory of the tribes。

[2] 海水北注焉：北极海岸之乡。

[2] hai shui bei zhu yan (zee water north rush in)
Tr: the land of Northmost sea coast (north pole coastal land).

[3] 九首人面鸟身：楚族定居的僚族。九首指楚族，即楚科奇族。

[3] jiu shou ren mian niao shen (nine heads human face bird body)
Tr: The Lao tribes 's settlers called Chuzu, Jiushou (nine heads) refers to the Chu people, aka the Chukotzi ethnic group。

[4] 九凤：指楚胡，即楚科奇胡。

[4] jiu feng (nine phoenix) refers to the Chu Hu people, also known as the Chukotzi Hu。

[5] 衔蛇操蛇：指赛伊草原夷。蛇，在此读夷音。

[5] xian she cao she (pick up snake with teeth, and play the snake)
Tr: refers to the Yi people from the Saiyi steppe。 she(snake) reads as Yi, a phonetic match。

[6] 虎首人身：定居的胡族。

[6]hu shou ren shen (tiger head human body)
Tr: sedentary Hu people。

[7] 四蹄长肘：指斯特列尔恰移民。

[7]si ti chang zhou (four hooves long elbow)
Tr: refers to the Strelka immigrants。（斯特列尔卡：俄语：Стрелка，罗马化：*Strelka*）

[8] 彊良：读“恰黎”，指斯特列尔恰人。

[8] jiang liang; reads as Qiali, refers to the Strelka immigrants。 Simplified as Qiali, (qia/ka) 。

译文：大地之中有座山，名叫楚科奇山，是北极海岸之乡。那里有楚族定居的僚族，名叫楚胡。还有一个氏族是赛伊草原夷，是定居的胡族，是斯特列尔恰移民，名叫恰黎。
Translation:
In the middle of land, there is a mountain called Chukotzi, the land of Northmost coast。 There are the Lao people of settled Chu Hu。 There is another tribe known as the Yi people from Saiyi steppe。 They are also the settled Hu people, immigrants from Strelka, known also simply as Qia Li。

17-15 夸父追日
Kuafuzhuiri
（112,57711E；40,8937N）

大荒之中，有山名曰成都载天[1]。有人珥两黄蛇，把两黄蛇[2]，名曰夸父[3]。后土生信，信生夸父[4]。夸父不量力，欲追日景[5]，逮之于禺谷[6]。将饮河而不足也，将走大泽[7]，未至，死于此[8]。应龙已杀蚩尤，又杀夸父[9]，乃去南方处之[10]，故南方多雨[11]。

注释：[1]成都载天：卓资，又称绰堵，谐音成都。载天，读辄提，指管理区。也可译为察哈尔草原。
Notes:[1] cheng du zai tian (cheng city carry sky)
Tr: refers to Zhuozi, also as Chuodu, a phonetic match to Chengdu。 zaitian (carry sky) reads as Zheti, a phonetic match, meaning managed territory, here can also be interpreted as the Chahar Steppe。

[2] 有人珥两黄蛇，把两黄蛇：有一个集镇管理着四周的胡族。

[2] you ren er liang huang she (someone earlopped two yellow snakes) ba liang huang she (handle two yellow snakes) 。
Tr: there is a township managing the Hu people in and around the territory。

[3] 夸父：指北胡国。
[3] kua fu (boast father) refers to the Beihu Guo (northern Hu country) 。
[4] 后土生信，信生夸父：浩特部落发展到兴旺时期，建立了北胡国。
[4] hou tu sheng xin (back earth begets credible) xin sheng kua fu (credible begets boast father)
Tr: Hot tribe developed to its most powerful stage and established a Beihu Guo。
[5] 夸父不量力，欲追日景：北胡草原人逐日而居。不量力，指补僚黎；僚读老，指草。
[5] kua fu bu liang li, yu zhui ri jing (boast father overestimates his strength, wishes to chase sun image)
Tr: the steppe people of Northern Hu chose their settlement following the sun。 buliangli (overestimate his strength) reads bu liao li。 Liao; reads as lao, meaning grass, hereby grassland or steppe。 Bulaoli, tribe name。
[6] 逮之于禺谷：读鞑之于溢谷，指游牧于有水草的地方。
[6] dai zhi yu yu gu (catch it at Yu valley)
Tr: reads as da zhi yu yi gu, herding at places with water and grass.
[7] 将饮河而不足，将走大泽：管理着荫凉湖边的氏族，管理着王族的巴颜鞑支系。
[7] jiang yi he er bu zu, jiang zou da ze (will drink the river, river dried, wish to walk to the big zee)
Tr: manage the tribes of Yinliang Lake, manage the Bayan Da branch, which is the king lineage。
[8] 未至，死于此：南方疆域的草原游牧民。未至，指渭枝，即南部疆域。
[8] wei zhi, si yu ci (did not arrive, died here)
Tr: the steppe nomadic in the southern territory。 weizhi (did not arrive) refers to weizhi, meaning the southern part of the territory。
[9] 应龙杀蚩尤，又杀夸父：燕僚入侵蚩尤地区，又入侵北胡地区。燕僚，指黄帝集团。
[9] ying long sha chiyou, you sha kuafu (answer dragon kill Chiyou, then kill Boast father)
Tr: the Yan Lao invaded the territory of Chiyou, and then invaded the Beihu area。 Yanliao: refers to the Huangdi confederacy, the Yellow Emperor's contingency。
[10] 乃去南方处之：驱逐僚濮于荆楚。乃去，指放牧、驱赶。
[10] nai qu nan fang chu zhi (therefore went to the south stay)
Tr: exiled the Liao of the Pu to the Jingchu area (today's Hubei province) 。 Nai qu: meaning exile, or chase out, to send them off 。
[11] 故南方多雨：只留下了僚濮的夏族。故南方，读古僚濮；多雨，只余，只留下。
[11]gu nan fang duo yu (thus south lot rain)
Tr: only allow the Liao of Pu tribes of Xia to remain。Gu nan fang (thus south area) reads as gu liao pu, (xia liao pu) duo yu (lot rain) only left to remain, only let stay。

译文：大地之中，有一个地方名叫卓资管理区。那里有一个集镇，管理着四周的胡族，名叫北胡国。浩特部落发展到兴旺时期，建立了北胡国。北胡国的草原人逐日而居，游牧于有水草的地方。他们管理着荫凉湖边的氏族，管理着王族的巴颜鞑支系，管理着南部疆域的草原游牧民。燕僚入侵蚩尤地区，又入侵北胡地区，驱逐僚濮于荆楚，只留下了僚濮的夏族。
Translation:
In the land of earth, there is a place called Zhuozi management territory。 There existed a township managing the Hu people over the territory。 The township is known as the Beihu Guo。 The Hot tribe established the Beihu Guo after they thrived and grew。 The steppe people of Beihu Guo follow the sun in choosing their settlement, and roam at the places that have water and grass。 They manage the tribes around the Yinliang Lake, and manage the King lineage of Bayan branch, as well the steppe herders in the southern territory。 The Yanliao group invaded the Chiyou territory and the Beihu territory。 Only the Lao people of Pu of the Xia were allowed to remain where they were, and the rest were chased out and exiled to the place known as Jingchu。

17-16 无肠国
Wuchang Guo

（106,82038E；39,68389N）

又有无肠国[1]，是任姓[2]。无继，食鱼[3]。

注释：[1]无肠国：指乌桑国，因地处黄河的内湾边，故称为桑，今内蒙古乌海市。
Notes:[1] wu chang guo (no guts country)
Tr: refers to the Wusang Guo。Due to its location at the in curve of the Yellow River, it is called Sang, in today Wuhai (dark zee) city, Inner Mongolia。

[2] 是任姓：氏族就叫乌桑。
[2] shi ren xing (family name is Ren)
Tr: the tribe bears the family name of Ren, is called Wusang tribes。

[3] 无继，食鱼：北方部落的古老氏族。
[3] wu ji, shi yu (no inheritance, eat fish)
Tr: the ancient branch of Northern tribes。

译文：有一个乌桑国，氏族就叫乌桑，那里的氏族是北方部落的古老氏族。
Translation:
There is a Wusang Guo, its tribes are called Wusang。 They are the ancient branch of Northern tribes。

17-17 共工臣相繇
Gonggongchenxiangyao
（101,0603E；41,95286N）

共工臣名曰相繇[1]，九首蛇身，自环[2]，食于九土[3]。其所歍所尼，即为源泽[4]，不辛乃苦[5]，百兽莫能处[6]。禹湮洪水，杀相繇，其血腥臭[7]，不可生谷[8]；其地多水，不可居也[9]。禹湮之，三仞三沮，乃以为池[10]，群帝是因以为台[11]。在昆仑北。

注释：[1]共工臣名曰相繇：指索额苏吉地区的幼泽，今内蒙古额济纳地区的弱水。
Notes:[1] gonggong chen ming yue xiang yao (gonggong's aide name Yao)
Tr: refers to the Youze (young zee) in Suoesuji area。 It is the Ruoshui River in today's Ejina region, Inner Mongolia。
Ruoshui:(Heihe River): Ruo Shui (Chinese: 弱水; lit. 'weak river'), also Etsin Gol or Ruo He or Ejin River。

[2] 九首蛇身，自环：弱水的塞上地区的居延海。
[2] jiu shou she shen (nine heads snake body), zi huan(self-circle)
Tr: refers to Juyanhai (Juyan Lake basin), the Saishang area where the Ruoshui River flows。

[3] 食于九土：发源于祁连山。
[3] shi yu jiu tu (eat from nine land)
Tr: the river originates from the Qilian Mountain。

[4] 其所歍所尼，即为源泽：远道而来，成为水源的渠道。
[4] qi suo qian suo ni, ji wei yuan ze (its vomit, its ni, is its origin)
Tr: the water comes from afar, creates channels for source water。

[5] 不辛乃苦：指补苦氏。
[5] bu xin nai ku (not spicy, but bitter)
Tr: refers to the tribe of Buku Shi。

[6] 百兽莫能处：农业馍僚之地。
[6] bai shou mo neng chu (hundred beasts can't live in peace)
Tr: the agricultural Molao people occupy this land。

[7] 禹湮洪水，杀相繇，其血腥臭：水从山里进入弱水河，形成沼泽。

[7]yu yan hongshui, (Yu controls flood), sha xiang yao (kill aide Yao) qi xue xing chou (its blood stink)
Tr: water flows to the Ruo River through the mountains, and this creates swamps。

[8] 不可生谷：补苦氏族用以种谷。

[8] bu ke sheng gu (cannot grow grain)
Tr: The Buku tribe make use of swamps for growing grains。

[9] 其地多水，不可居也：水最多的地方是补苦氏的居延海。

[9] qi di duo shui, bu ke ju ye (its place plenty water, can't live in)
Tr: the place that receives the most water is Juyan Lake where the Buku tribe occupy。

[10] 禹湮之，三仞三沮，乃以为池：水养育了索额苏吉等勒伊维尚德部落的城镇居民。

[10]yu yan zhi, san ren san ju, nai yi wei chi:
(Yu stops it, three times dig[ren] three times dam [ju], thus make a pool)
Tr: water provides livelihood to the township dwellers of the Suoesuji's tribes。 They are part of the Leyiweishangde tribal group。

[11] 群帝是因以为台：这里是勒伊维尚德部落的政治中心。群帝，指这里。

[11] qun di sh yin yi wei tai (multiple gods make it a terrace)
Tr: this is the political center of the Leyiweishangde tribes。 Qundi: means here, this place。

译文：索额苏吉地区的幼泽，弱水的塞上地区的居延海，发源于祁连山。祁连山雪水远道而来，成为水源的唯一渠道，这里是补苦氏农业馍僚的区域。水从山里进入弱水河，形成沼泽，补苦氏族用以种谷；水最多的地方是补苦氏的居延海。水养育了索额苏吉等勒伊维尚德部落的城镇居民，这里是勒伊维尚德部落的政治中心，在昆仑山的北面。

Translation:
The Youze in Suoesuji area is also known as the Juyan Lake at Saishang area（northern border） where the Ruoshui River flows。 Juyan Lake has its headwater in Qilian Mountain。 The snow water from the Qilian Mountain comes from afar and is the only water channel from its source。 This is the territory of the agriculture tribes of Buku Shi。Water goes through the mountains before entering the Ruoshui River and creates swamps。 The Buku tribes make use of the water to grow grains。 The place with the most abundance of water is the Juyan Lake where the Buku tribes occupy。 Water provides livelihood for the Suoesuji branch's township dwellers of Leyiweishangde tribes。 This place is the political centre of the Leyiweishangde tribe, to the north of Kunlun Mountain。

17-18 岳山寻竹
Yueshanxunzhu
（97,28165E；42,95215N）

有岳之山[1]。寻竹生焉[2]。

注释：[1]岳山：指大狼山。在甘肃西北端。

Notes:[1] yue shan (big mount)
Tr: refers to the Dalangshan (big wolf mount) in the northwest end of Gansu province。

[2] 寻竹生焉：因狩猎老虎而形成的家乡。

[2] xun zhu sheng yan (search bamboo grows)
Tr: the homeland comes into being because the tribes are hunting tigers here。

译文：有一个大狼山，是因狩猎老虎而形成的家乡。

Translation:
There is a Dalang Mountain, the homeland for the tribes who hunt tigers。

17-19 不句山
Bugoushan
（89,58648E；44,01425N）

大荒之中，有山名曰不句[1]，海水入焉[2]。

注释：[1]不句山：读不勾山，指博格达山。
Notes:[1] bu gou shan (no hook mount)
Tr: refers to the Bogeda Mountain, also written as Bogdashan。
[2] 海水入焉：海水，指赫胥氏，今称哈萨克族。入焉，指治理的家乡。
[2] hai shui ru yan (sea water enter)
Tr: haishui refers to Hexu Shi, known today as the Kazakhs (also spelled Kazaks, Qazaqs; Kazakh: singular: Қазақ, Qazaq, [qɑˈzɑq], plural: Қазақтар, Qazaqtar,) an ethnic people. Ru yan, (enter) means homeland being managed。

译文：大地之中，有座山名叫博格达山，是赫胥氏治理的家乡。
Translation:
In the land, there is mountain called Bogda, the homeland managed by the Hexu Shi。

17-20 黄帝女妭
Huangdinvba
（86,56638E；42,05973N）

有系昆之山者，有共工之台，射者不敢北乡[1]。有人衣青衣，名曰黄帝女妭[2]。蚩尤作兵伐黄帝[3]，黄帝乃令应龙攻之冀州之野[4]。应龙畜水，蚩尤请风伯雨师[5]，纵大风雨[6]。黄帝乃下天女曰妭，雨止[7]，逐杀蚩尤。妭不得复上[8]，所居不雨[9]。叔均言之帝[10]，后置之赤水之北[11]。叔均乃为田祖[12]。妭时亡之[13]，所欲逐之者，令曰："神北行"，先除水道[14]，决通沟渎[15]。

注释：[1]共工之台，射者不敢北乡：指共和地区，焉耆博嘎羲湖之乡。今博斯腾湖地区。
Notes: [1] gonggong zhi tai (gonggong's terrace), she zhe bu gan bei xiang (shooter dare not north land)
Tr: refers to the Gonghe region, the land of Yanqibogaxi Lake, today it is known as the Bosten Lake region。 (Yanqi Hui Autonomous County (Uyghur: Qarasheher, Karashahr)
[2] 有人衣青衣，名曰黄帝女妭：有一个集镇叫焉耆邑，又称为北和的牧区农业部落。
[2] you ren yi qing yi (has person wears green dress) ming yue huangdi nvba (name yellow emperor's nvba)
Tr: there is a township called Yanqi Yi, also called the agricultural tribe in the nomadic region of Beihe。
[3] 蚩尤作兵伐黄帝：草原天河边的北和。
[3] Chiyou zuo bing fa huangdi (Chiyou send army attack Huangdi)
Tr: The Beihe, Tianhe river area of the steppe。
[4] 黄帝乃令应龙攻之冀州之野：北和牧王焉犁巩的部落之乡。焉犁巩，指小月氏。
[4] huangdi nai ling yinglong gong zhi jizhou zhi ye(Huangdi orders Yingloong to attack the land of Jizhou)
Tr: the homeland of the Yanligong, the nomadic king of Beihe。 Yanligong : xiao yueshi (lesser Yuezhi)
[5] 应龙畜水，蚩尤请风伯雨师：乌拉斯河、草原沁的开都河都流入这里。
[5] yinglong xu shui (Ying dragon store water) Chiyou qing fengbo yushi (Chiyou invites Wind uncle and Rain teacher)
Tr: Wulas River and grassland Kaidu River all flow here。
[6] 纵大风雨：指形成水泡子，这里指形成湖水。
[6] zong da feng yu (release big storm)

Tr: creates big water holes, meaning lake is formed。

[7] 黄帝乃下天女曰妭，雨止：北和王带领特乌鲁之农业氏族——焉孜氏，也称月氏氏。

[7] huangdi nai xia tiannu yue ba (Huangdi send sky girl Ba) yu zhi (rain stops)
Tr: The Beihe Khan leads the Tewulu agricultural tribes--Yanzi Shi, also known as the Yuezhi Shi。

[8] 逐杀蚩尤，妭不得复上：进入草原农业氏族的湖边地区。

[8] zhuo sha chiyou (chase and kill Chiyou), ba bu de fu shang (girl Ba cannot return),
Tr: enter the lakeside regions of the steppe agricultural tribes。

[9] 所居不雨：和硕、和静、博湖、焉耆四个乡镇。

[9] suo ju bu yu (the residence no rain)
Tr: refers to the four county townships of Heshuo, Hejing, Bohu and Yanqi。

[10] 叔均言之帝：和硕、和静在北面。

[10] shu jun yan zhi di (shujun talk to God)
Tr: the township of Heshuo and Hejing are in the north。

[11] 后置之赤水之北：博湖、焉耆族在南面。后置，指博海、博湖；赤水，指焉耆族。北，读贝，指南。

[11] hou zhi zhi chishui zhi bei(late station it red water north)
Tr: The tribes of Bohu, Yanqi are to the south。 Houzhi: refers to Bohai, or Bohu (bo lake), chishui (red water) refers to Yanqi people。 Bei(north) reads as bei, meaning south。

[12] 叔均乃为田祖：和硕、和静区域为农业基地。

[12] shuyun nai wei tian zu(shuyun becomes field lord)
Tr: the territories of Heshuo and Hejing are bases for agriculture。

[13] 妭时亡之：种稻于平野。

[13]ba shi wang zhi (girl Ba time die it)
Tr: growing rice on the flat plain。

[14] 所欲逐者，令曰："神北行！"先除水道：苏夷雀河是王国通向南部沼泽的通道。苏夷雀，即孔雀。

[14] suo yu zhuo zhe (wish to chase those out), ling yu:" shen bei xing" ;(command: god north go_
Xian chu shui dao (first clear water channel)
Tr: Suyique River is the channel for the kingdom to access the swampland in the south。 Suyique: Kongque, (peafowl or peacock) 。

[15] 决通沟渎：是盐碱国度。

[15] jue tong gou du (clear ditches and channels)
Tr: the country of saline soil。

译文：大地中有系昆山，有共和的焉耆博斯腾湖之乡。有一个集镇叫焉耆邑，称为北和的牧区农业部落，是草原天河边的北和牧王焉犁巩的部落之乡。乌拉斯河、草原沁的开都河都流入这里，形成湖水。北和王带领特乌鲁之农业氏族——月氏氏，进入草原农业氏族的湖边地区，建立和硕、和静、博湖、焉耆四个乡镇。和硕、和静在北面，博湖、焉耆氏族在南面。和硕、和静为农业基地，种稻谷于平野。苏夷雀河是王国通向南部沼泽的通道，那里是盐碱地区。

Translation:

On the land there is the Xikun Mountain, the land of Yanqi Bosten Lake of the Gonghe country。 There is a township called Yanqi city, known as the agricultural tribes in Beihe's nomadic region。 This territory is the land of Yanligong tribe under the nomadic king of Beihe, which is located by the Tianhe River on the steppe。 Both Wulasi River and Kaidou River from the steppe flow and gather here to form lake。 The Khan of Beihe took the Tewulu agriculture tribe-- the Yuezhi with him and entered the lake side regions of the agriculture tribes of the steppe。 The Khan built four townships, the Heshuo, the Hejing, the Bohu and the Yanqi。 Both Heshuo and Hejing are in the north, while Bohu and Yanqi are in the south。 The Heshou and Hejing territories are agricultural bases, growing rice over the plain。 The Suyique River is the waterway for the kingdom to access the swamplands in the south。 The land in the south has saline soil。

17-21 深目民国
Shenmumin Guo
（86,06388E；44,30143N）

有人方食鱼[1]，名曰深目民之国[2]，朌姓，食鱼[3]。

注释：[1]有人方食鱼：有个集镇管理着瑪纳斯河地区。
Notes: [1] you ren fang shi yu (someone just ate fish)
Tr: there is a township that manages the region of Manas River。
[2] 深目民之国：瑪纳斯河畔之国。指石河子市。深目，读奢陌，指河畔。
[2] shen mu min zhi guo (deep set eyes country)
Tr: the country by the riverbank of Manas River, referring to the Shihezi (stone river) city。 Shenmu (deep set eyes) reads as shemo, meaning riverbank or river side。
[3] 朌姓，食鱼：河畔的古老氏族。
[3] pan xing, shi yu (family name Pan, eat fish)
Tr: refers to the ancient tribe along the riverbanks。

译文：有一个集镇管理着瑪纳斯河地区，名叫河畔之国。这里住着河畔的古老氏族。
Translation:
There is a township managing the region of Manas River。 It is called Hepan(riverside) country。 An ancient riverbank tribe lives there。

17-22 赤水女子献
Chishui nuzi xian
（81,32086E；43,92183N）

有钟山者[1]。有女子衣青衣[2]，名曰赤水女子献 [3] 。

注释：[1]钟山者：指南天山支系。
Notes:[1] zhong shan zhe (of bell mount) refers to the tribal branches at Southern Tianshan Mountains。
[2] 女子衣青衣：指玉兹夷和伊沁夷，在新疆伊犁地区。
[2] nv zi yi qing yi (girl wears green dress)
Tr: refers to the two Yi peoples of Yuzi and Yiqin, in today's Ili area, Xinjiang province。
[3] 赤水女子献：指犬戎族的玉兹国。
[3] chisui nvzi xian (red river girl xian)
Tr: refers to the Yuzi country of the Quanrong (dog rong) tribes。

译文：这里有南天山支系氏族，有玉兹氏族和伊沁夷，国名叫犬戎族的玉兹羲。
Translation:
There are the Branches of Southern Tianshan tribes, they are the Yuzi tribe and Yiqin Yi。 Their country is called Yuzixi of the Dogrong people。

17-23 犬戎（赤兽戎宣王尸）
Quanrong (chishourong xuanwang shi)
（79,4635E；43,5366N）

大荒之中，有山名曰融父山[1]，顺水入焉[2]。有人名曰犬戎[3] 。黄帝生苗龙 [4]， 苗龙生融吾 [5]， 融吾生弄明 [6]， 弄明生白犬 [7]， 白犬生牝牡 [8]， 是为犬戎，肉食 [9] 。有赤兽，马状无首 [10]， 名曰戎宣王尸 [11] 。

注释：[1]融父山：戎胡地区，指哈萨克地区。
Notes:[1] rong fu shan (melt father mount)
Tr: refers to the Rong Hu territory, the Kasakh territory。
[2] 顺水入焉：乌孙氏族统治之乡。
[2] shun shui ru yan (smooth water in)
Tr: the territory controlled by the Wusun tribes。
[3] 有人名曰犬戎：所有的集镇都是犬戎族的集镇。
[3] you ren ming yue quan rong (someone named dog rong)
Tr: all the townships belong to the Quanrong tribes (the Dogrong tribes) 。
[4] 黄帝生苗龙：北胡地区形成了缅奴。
[4] huangdi sheng miao long (Huangdi begets Miao dragon)
Tr: The Beihu territory form the country of Miannu。
[5] 苗龙生融吾：缅奴建立了戎部落。
[5] miao loong sheng rong wu (Miao dragon begets Rongwu)
Tr: Miannu set up the Rong tribes。
[6] 融吾生弄明：戎部落中又分支出西部缅。
[6] rongwu sheng nong ming (rongwu begets nongming)
Tr: from the Rong tribes, a branch of western Mian is created。
[7] 弄明生白犬：西部缅中又分支出白犬戎。
[7] nongming sheng bai quan (nongming begets white dog)
Tr: from the western Mian, a branch of Baiquanrong (white dog rong) is created。
[8] 白犬生牝牡：白犬戎开始争雄。
[8] bai quan sheng pinmu (white dog begets female and male)
Tr: the white dog rong are fighting among themselves for control。
[9] 是为犬戎肉食：这就是犬戎相残。
[9] shi wei quan rong rou shi (thus dog rong meat eat)
Tr: this is how the Quanrong tribes fight among themselves。
[10] 有赤兽，马状无首：有一个游牧氏族，是春贾部落氏族。马状，读梅贾，指春贾。
[10] you chi shou, ma zhuang wu shou (a red beast, horse look no head)
Tr: there is a nomadic tribe, called Chunjia。 Mazhuang; reads mayjia, ma/may/spring, thus the name of the tribe is Chun（spring) jia。
[11] 戎宣王尸：指戎羲乌肆。即戎国的部落集肆。
[11] rong xuan wang shi (rong declare king corpse)
Tr: refers to the Rongxiwu Shi, the township of tribes of the Rong state。

译文：西部大地中，有个地方是戎胡地区，是乌孙氏族统治之乡，所有的集镇都是犬戎族的集镇。北胡地区形成了缅奴，缅奴建立了犬戎部落，犬戎部落中又分支出西部缅，西部缅中又分支出白犬戎，白犬戎开始争雄，这就是犬戎相残。还有一个游牧氏族，是春贾部落氏族，称为戎羲乌氏。
Translation:
In the land of west territory, there is Rong Hu's territory, the homeland of tribes ruled by the Wusun tribes。 All the townships belong to the Quanrong tribes。 The Miannu is formed in the North Hu territory。 The Miannu set up the Quanrong tribes。 It is from the Quanrong tribes that the western Mian branches out。 It is from the

Western Mian, the white Quanrong branches out。 The white Quanrong fight among themselves for control, this is the internal fighting。 There is another nomadic tribe known as Chunjia, called Rongxiwu Shi。

17-24 齐州山
Qizhoushan
（65,48395E；44,84923N）

有山名曰齐州之山[1]，君山[2]，鬵山[3]，鲜野山[4]，鱼山[5]。

注释：[1]齐州山：指克孜勒奥尔达部落，在哈萨克斯坦锡尔河流域。
Notes:[1]qi zhou shan: refers to the Kyzylorda tribes in the catchment of Syr Darya (Jaxartes，Old Persian name Yakhsha Arta ("True Pearl")。
[2]君山：指肯套部落，在锡尔河流域。
[2]jun shan(gentleman mount) refers to the Kentau tribes in Syr Darya catchment。
[3]鬵山：指奇伊利部落，在锡尔河流域。
[3]ji shan: refers to the Qiyili tribes in Syr Darya catchment。
[4]鲜野山：指希姆肯特部落，在锡尔河流域。
[4]xian ye shan(fresh wild mount)
Tr: refers to the Shymkent (Şymkent, known until 1993 as Chimkent; Russian: Чимкент, romanized: Čimkent) tribes in Syr Darya catchment。
[5]鱼山：指塔拉兹部落，在锡尔河流域。
[5]yu shan(fish mount)
Tr: refers to the Taraz tribes in Syr Darya catchment。

译文：在锡尔河流域，有克孜勒奥尔达部落，有肯套部落，有奇伊利部落，有希姆肯特部落，有塔拉兹部落。
Translation:
In the catchment area of Syr Darya, there are the following tribes, the Kyzylorda , the Kentau, the Qiyili , the Shymkent and the Taraz。

17-25 一目人
Yimuren
（69,46099E；56,10872N）

有人一目[1]，当面中生[2]，一曰威姓[3]，少昊之子，食黍[4]。

注释：[1]有人一目：有一个集镇叫伊希姆，在俄罗斯境内。
Notes:[1]you ren yi mu(person one eye)
Tr: there is a township called Ishim, now in Russia。
[2]当面中生：坦缅贵族建造。
[2]dang mian zhong sheng(appear in the face)
Tr: is built by the noble branch of Tanmien。
[3]威姓：南面的氏族。
[3]wei xing (family name wei)
Tr: the tribes in the south。
[4]少昊之子，食黍：绍尔坦胡支系的古老氏族。

[4]shao gao zhi zi(Shaohao's son), shi shu(eat millets)
Tr: the ancient tribe branch of the Shaortan Hu people。

译文：有一个集镇叫伊希姆，是坦缅贵族建造的集镇。又说是南面的绍尔坦胡支系的古老氏族所建。
Translation:
There is a township called Ishm, built by the noble branch of Tanmien 。 It is also said that the township is built by the ancient tribe of Shaortan Hu people in the south。

17-26 继无民
Jiwumin
（83,8454E；49,71617N）

有继无民[1]，继无民任姓[2]，无骨子[3]，食气鱼[4]。

注释：[1]继无民：指乌斯季卡缅地区。
Notes:[1] ji wu min (inherit no folk)
Tr: refers to the region of Ustkamian。 (Öskemen， Oskemen (Kazakh: Өскемен, romanized: Óskemen) or Ust-Kamenogorsk (Russian: Усть-Каменогóрск) 。
[2] 继无民任姓：指斯基泰部落氏族。
[2] ji wu min ren xing (jiwumin family name ren)
Tr: refers to the Scythians (/ˈsɪθiən, ˈsɪð-/; from Greek Σκύθης, Σκύθοι), also known as Scyth, Saka, Sakae, Iskuzai, or Askuzai。
[3] 无骨子：北国支系。
[3] wu gu zi (no bones)
Tr: the northern country branch。
[4] 食气鱼：古老的犬戎夷。
[4] shi qi yu (eat air fish)
Tr: the ancient Quanrong Yi, also known as the Dog Rong。

译文：有一个乌斯季卡缅地区，住着斯基泰部落氏族，是北国支系古老的犬戎夷。
Translation:
There is a region called Ustkamian, the Scythians live there。They are the ancient Quanrong of the northern countries。

17-27 中輻国
Zhongbian Guo
（78,38212E；49,01779N）

西北海外，流沙[1]之东，有国名曰中輻[2]，颛顼之子，食黍[3]。

注释：[1]流沙：指哈萨克的萨雷耶西阿特劳沙漠。
Notes:[1] liu sha (flowing sand)
Tr: refers to the Saryesik-Atyrau Desert, Kazakhstan。
[2] 中輻国：指塔尔迪库尔干国。
[2] zhong bian guo: refers to Taldi Kurgan Guo。
[3] 颛顼之子，食黍：指萨雷耶西支系的古老氏族。

[3] zhuanxu zhi zi， shi shu (zhuangxi 's son, eat millet)
Tr: refers to the ancient tribe of Saryesik tribes。

译文：在西北海外，萨雷耶西克阿特劳沙漠的东面，有一个国家叫塔尔迪库尔干国，住着萨雷耶西支系的古老氏族。
Translation:
In the northwest land, east of the Saryesik-Atyrau Desert, there is a country called Taldi Kurgan Guo, the ancient branch of the Saryesik tribe lives here。

17-28 犬戎国
Quanrong Guo
（71,44486E；51,15221N）

有国名曰赖丘[1]。有犬戎国。有神，人面兽身[2]，名曰犬戎。

注释：[1]赖丘：指淖尔丘，又称赖丘、阿斯塔纳，今称努尔苏丹。今仍按赖丘表述。
Notes:[1] lai qiu: refers to Nuur mount, also Laiqiu, Astana, known today as Nuur Sutan。 The description keeps the place name of Laiqiu。
[2] 有神，人面兽身：氏族是定居的塞族。
[2] you shen, ren mian shou shen (has God, human face beast body)
Tr: the tribes are settled Saka people。

译文：有一个国家叫赖丘，那里是犬戎国，氏族是定居的塞族，称为犬戎。
Translation:
There is a country called Laiqiu, it is the Quanrong state。 Its tribes are the settled Sakas, known as the Quanrong (dog rong) 。

17-29 苗民
Miaomin
（73,76244E；43,60557N）

西北海外，黑水之北，有人有翼[1]，名曰苗民[2]。颛顼生驩头[3]，驩头生苗民 [4]，苗民釐姓，食肉 [5] 。有山名曰章山 [6] 。

注释：[1]黑水之北，有人有翼：在纳伦河的北面，有一个繁荣的集镇。有翼，指繁荣。
Notes: [1] hei shui zhi bei, you ren you yi (black water's north, has person has wings)
Tr: to the north of Nalun River（Naryn River), there is a boom township。 you yi: boom, thriving。
[2] 苗民：读么米，指中心，因是楚河国的统治中心而得名，今称楚城。
[2] miao min reads as Momi, meaning centre, becoming well known for being the control centre of the Chuhe Guo (the Chu River country) 。The centre is known today as Chu city。
[3] 颛顼生驩头：楚河边建起了一个恒都。恒都，指都城。
[3] zhuanxu sheng huan tou: the capital city is built on the riverbank of the Chu River。 Hengdu: capital city。
[4] 驩头生苗民：恒都建在中心。
[4] huantou sheng miaomin: Hengdu is built where the centre is。
[5] 苗民釐姓，食肉：中心的草原氏族是古老的月氏氏族。釐姓，在此读耆氏，指草原氏族。
[5] miao min qi xing，shi rou (miao people surname qi, eat meat)
Tr: the steppe tribe in the centre is the ancient Yuezhi Shi。qi xing: qi shi, meaning steppe tribes。

[6] 章山：指天山，实际指南天山。
[6] zhang shan: refers to the Tianshan, the Southern Tianshan Mountains。

译文：在西北海外，纳伦河的北面，有一个繁荣的集镇，名叫中心。楚河上建起了恒都，恒都建在楚河盆地中心，中心的草原氏族是古老的月氏氏族。那里有座山，名叫天山。
Translation:
In the land beyond the northwest Hai, to the north of Naryn River, there is a boom town, called Zhongxin(centre)。The capital city is built on the Chu River banks, in the middle of Chu River's basin。 The tribe in the centre is the ancient steppe Yuezhi Shi。There is a mountain called Tianshan Mountain。

17-30 洞野山
Dongye Mountain
（68,7552E；38,58454N）

大荒之中，有衡石山[1]、九阴山[2]、洞野之山[3]，上有赤树[4]，青叶赤华[5]，名曰若木[6]。

注释：[1]衡石山：指罕肆山，即萨马尔罕。
Notes:[1] heng shi shan: refers to Khansishan, known today as Samarkand。
[2] 九阴山：指杨吉尤尔，是塔什干的古称谓。
[2] jiu yin shan (nine shade mount)
Tr: refers to the Yangjiyour, an ancient name for Tashkent。
[3] 洞野山：指杜墅别，今称杜尚别。
[3] dong ye shan (hole wild mount) refers to Dushubie, known today as Dushanbe, capital of Tajikistan。
[4] 赤树：指卡桑赛，即长岗，这里指长岗之城。
[4] chi shu (red tree)
Tr: refers to Kasangsai， meaning Changgang （long range), the city of Changgang。 It is written as Kosonsoy (Uzbek pronunciation: [kɒsɒnsɒj]; Tajik and Uzbek Cyrillic: Косонсой) also spelled as Kasansay (Russian: Касансай) or simply, Kasan, (ancient Kathan) is a town in Uzbekistan。
[5] 青叶赤华：指奇尔奇胡。
[5] qing ye chi hua (green leaves red flower)
Tr: refers to Qirq Hu people。
[6] 若木：音译为纳曼，指纳曼干，即若木城。
[6] ruo mu (ruo wood)
Tr: phonetically transcribed as Naman, also known as Namangan, the phonetic shifting is Ruomu /Nuomu/Naman 。

译文：在西北海大地中，有一个罕肆，有一个杨吉尤尔肆，有一个杜墅别，还有一个长岗之城，是奇尔奇胡的城镇，名叫纳曼干。
translation：
In the land of Northwest Hai, there is Khan city, Yangjiyour city, Dushanbe， and a Changgang city。 The Changgang is the city built by the Qirq Hu people。 The city is known today as Namangan。

17-31 牛黎国
Niuli Guo
（60,63137E；41,55192N）

有牛黎之国[1]。有人无骨[2]，儋耳之子 [3] 。

注释：[1]牛黎国：乌兹别克斯坦的阿姆河，古称鲁尼河、沘鲁尼，鲁尼河流域的国家称为鲁尼国，谐音牛黎国。

Notes： [1] niu li guo: (ox people country) refers to the Amu Darya in Uzbekistan, its ancient name is Lunihe, Biluni。 The country along the Luni River is called Luni Guo, a phonetic match is Niuli Guo。

[2] 有人无骨：有一个集镇叫乌尔根奇。

[2] you ren wu gu (has person no bone)

Tr: there is a township called Urgench, Urgench (Uzbek: Urganch, Урганч, ئۇرگەنچ; Persian: گرگانج, Gorgånch/Gorgānč/Gorgânc) is a city in western Uzbekistan。

[3] 儋耳之子：图尔特人的管理中心。子，读儒，指管理。

[3] zhan er zhi zi (zhan ear's son)

Tr: the management centre of Turt people。 zi(son) reads as Ru, meaning to manage or to administrate。

译文：在大月氏的北面，有一个鲁尼河边的国家，有一个集镇叫乌尔根奇，是图尔特人的管理中心。

Translation:

To the north of Greater Yuezhi Shi, there is a country by the river Luni。 There is a township called Urgench, the management centre of Turt people。

17-32 章尾山烛龙

Zhangweishan

（73,7378E；41,05043N）

西北海之外，赤水之北，有章尾山[1]。有神，人面蛇身而赤[2]，直目正乘[3]，其瞑乃晦，其视乃明[4]，不食不寝不息[5]，风雨是谒[6]。是烛九阴，是谓烛龙[7]。

注释：[1]章尾山：指天山南山，即南天山，在喷池河的北面。

Notes:[1] zhang wei shan (chapter end mount)

Tr: refers to the Southern Tianshan, also known as Tianshan's South Mountain, to the north of Panj River。

[2] 有神，人面蛇身而赤：有氏族，是定居的塞族犬戎。

[2] you shen, ren mian she shen er chi (has God, human face snake body and red)

Tr: there are tribal people, the settled Quanrong of the Saka people。

[3] 直目正乘：指直目人的支系氏族，当属小月氏氏族，包括塔吉克和吉尔吉斯氏族。

[3] zhi mu zheng cheng (vertical eyes straight ride)

Tr: refers to the branch of Zhimuren, belonging to the Lesser Yuezhi clan, including the Tajiks and Kyrgyz tribes。

[4] 其瞑乃晦，其视乃明：这个地方是宝贵的游牧草场之地。晦，指宝贵；视，指草场。

[4] qi ming nai hui, qi shi nai ming (when shut its eyes, it is dark, when open its eyes, it sees light)

Tr: this is a precious steppe grazing ground for the nomads, Hui(dark)precious, shi(see) grassland。

[5] 不食不寝不息：指补私氏，犬戎族，匈奴。

[5] bu shi bu qin bu xi (not eat, not sleep, not rest)

Tr: refers to the Busi Shi, Quanrong tribe and the Xiongnu。

[6] 风雨是谒：都曾统治过这个地区。谒，指家乡，在此作地区解。

[6] feng yu shi jie(wind rain thus visit)

Tr: (those tribes) all have taken control of this place。 jie(visit) homeland, here means region。

[7] 是烛九阴，是谓烛龙：这里是天山草原，又称为草山。

[7] shi zhu jiu yin (is candle nine shade), shi wei zhu loong (is so called candle dragon)

Tr: this is the Tianshan steppe， also called Caoshan (grass mountain) 。

译文：在西北海之外，喷池河的北面，有一个南天山山脉。这里的氏族是直目人支系。这个地方是宝贵的游牧草场之地，补私氏、犬戎族、匈奴都曾统治过这里。这里是天山草原，又称为草山。

Translation:

In the land beyond the northwest Hai, to the north of Panj River, there is a mountain range called the Southern Tianshan Mountains。 The tribes here are the branches of Zhimu people。 This place is a precious steppe grassland for the nomads。 The Busi tribes, the Quanrong tribes, and the Xiongnu all have taken control of this place。 This is the Tianshan grassland, also called grass mountains。

第十八卷海内经（Hainei Regions）

Book 18 Haineijing

18-01 鬿市
Huoshi
（77,98612E；45,24859N）

西海之内，流沙[1]之中，有国名曰鬿市[2]。

注释：[1]流沙：指萨雷耶西阿特劳沙漠，简称劳沙、流沙。
Notes:[1] liu sha (flowing sands)
Tr: refers to the Saryesik-Atyrau Desert。Atyrau desert is shortened to Laosha (Rausha) e.g., liusha。
[2] 鬿市：指乌什国，今称乌什托别。
[2] huo shi: refers to Wush Guo, today known as Ush-tobe or Ush-tyube。

译文：西海内的劳沙地区，有一个国家叫乌什国。
Translation：
In the land of west Hainei 's Laosha region, there is a Wush Guo。

18-02 汜叶
Siye
（73,76244E；43,60551N）

西海之内，流沙之西[1]，有国名曰汜叶[2]。

注释：[1]流沙之西：指阿特劳沙漠的西面，实际是西南面。
Notes:[1] liu sha zhi xi(flowing sand west)
Tr: refers to the west side of Atyrau Desert。 It is in fact to the southwest。

[2] 汜叶：指奢液，意为长河，今称楚河，以奢液流域扩展形成的国家叫奢液国。
[2]si ye (return water leaves)
Tr: refers to Sheye, meaning Long River, e.g., Chu River。The territory extended from the Sheye drainage area and became a country called Sheye Guo(nation)。

译文：在西海之内，劳沙的西南面，有一个国家叫奢液国。
Translation:
In the land beyond Xihai, to the southwest of Laosha, there is a country called Sheye Guo。

18-03 鸟山
Niaoshan
（64,26252E；49,02001N）

流沙之西，有鸟山[1]者，三水[2]出焉。爰有黄金、璿瑰、丹货、银铁[3]，皆流于此中[4]。又有淮山[5]，好水 [6] 出焉。

注释：[1]鸟山：指哈萨克斯坦的乌勒套山。流沙之西，是指阿特劳沙漠的西面。
Notes:[1] niao shan (bird mount) refers to the ULetau Mountain in Kazakhstan。 Liu sha zhi xi (west of flowing sands) refers to the west of Atyrau Desert。
[2] 三水：指图尔盖河、兹班河、奇伊利河。
[2] san shui (three waters) refers to the three rivers: the Turgai, Ziban, Qiyili。
[3] 黄金、璿瑰、丹货、银铁：指兹班、阿克沙拉、拉赫梅特、吕孜鲁伊四个集镇的氏族。
[3] huangjin (yellow gold) 、 yongkui (precious stones) 、danhuo (cinnabar products) 、 yintie (silver iron) refers to the following township tribes: Zipan, Arkshala, Lahemeite, and Lyzluyi。
[4] 皆流于此中：皆定居于这里。
[4] jie liu yu ci zhong (all flow into this)
Tr: all build settlements in this place。
[5] 淮山：乌勒套山北部区域称北山，读'武山'，濮语 w/h 不分，武谐音淮。
[5] huai shan: the northern part of Uletau Mountains。 Huaishan reads as Wushan, in Pu speech, w and h are not distinguished。wu and hui are phonetically close。
[6] 好水：伊希姆河的南支流，称沃姆水。濮语'南'与'好'同音。
[6] hao shui (good water) refers to the south tributary of Ishim River, the tributary is called Omo River。 In Pu speech, nan(south) and hao(good) are homophones。

译文：在阿特劳沙漠的西面，有一座乌勒套山，有三条河流发源于这里。又有兹班、阿克沙拉、拉赫梅特、和吕孜鲁伊等集镇氏族定居在这里。这里还有武山，沃姆水发源于这里。
Translation:
To the west of the Atyrau desert, there is a mountain called Uletau。 Three rivers rise from this mountain, and the tribes of Zipan, Arkshala, Lahemeit, and Lyzluyi have their settlements townships here。 Also the Wushan, Omo River rise from here。

18-04 韩流生帝颛顼
HanliushengdiZhuanxu
（65,50042E；44,84812N）

流沙之东[1]，黑水之西[2]，有朝云之国[3]，司彘之国[4]。黄帝妻雷祖[5]，生昌意 [6] 。昌意降处若水 [7]，生韩流 [8] 。韩流擢首 [9]，谨耳 [10]，人面 [11]，豕喙 [12]，麟身 [13]，渠股 [14]，豚止 [15]，娶淖子曰阿女 [16]，生帝颛顼 [17] 。

注释：[1]流沙之东：实际指萨雷沙丘陵的西面。
Notes： [1] liu sha zhi dong (flowing sands east)
Tr: in fact, it is referring to a place west of the Sarysha Hills。
[2] 黑水之西：实际指咸海之东。
[2] hei shui zhi xi (black water west)
Tr: in fact, refers to the east side of Aral Sea。
[3] 朝云之国：指草原之国。
[3] zhao yun zhi guo (morning clouds country)
Tr: refers to the steppe nation。
[4] 司彘之国：指种植之国。
[4]si zhi zhi guo (supervise pig country)
Tr: refers to the planter nation。
[5] 黄帝妻雷祖：北山脚的游牧区。
[5] huang di qi lei zu (yellow emperor wife thunder ancestress)
Tr: refers to the steppe nomadic territory at the foot of Northern hills，(Beishanjiao)。
[6] 生昌意：形成了一条楚河。昌意，指楚溢，即楚河。
[6] sheng chang yi (begets changyi)
Tr: forms a river called Chu, changyi: chu yi(river), the Chu Darya。
[7] 昌意降处若水：楚河的西面是弱水。弱水又称奇伊利河。
[7] chang yi jiang chu ruo shui (changyi descends to weak water)
Tr: to the west of Chu River, there is the Ruoshui (weak water), which is also known as the Qiyili River。
[8] 生韩流：汇入锡尔河。
[8] sheng han liu (begets Han rio)
Tr: joins the Syr Darya。
[9] 韩流擢首：锡尔河流域的游牧氏族集镇。
[9] han liu di shou (han rio wash head)
Tr: refers to the nomadic tribal townships in the drainage areas of Syr Darya。
[10] 谨耳：克孜勒奥尔达。
[10] jin er (careful ear) refers to Kyzylorda。
[11] 人面：指热米，即热孜卡孜甘。
[11] ren mian (human face): refers to Remi, (hot rice) is known now as Zhezqazghan (杰兹卡兹甘)。
[12] 豕喙：指萨特帕耶夫。
[12] zhi hui (pig snout) refers to today's city of Satbayev (Kazakh: Сәтбаев, romanized: Sátbaev) 。
[13] 麟身：扎林斯克。
[13] lin shen (scaled body)
Tr: refers to today's Zarinsk。
[14] 渠股：奇伊利甘。
[14] qu gu (canal share)
Tr: refers to Qiyiligan (kylygan)
[15] 豚止：突厥斯坦。
[15] tun zhi (baby pig stop) refers to Turkistan。
[16] 娶淖子曰阿女：塔拉兹的阿雷西。
[16] qu nao zi yue a nv (marry naozi named a girl)

Tr: refers to Taraz' Alyci。

[17] 生帝颛顼：皆建在锡尔河边。

[17] sheng di zhuanxu (begets di zhuangxu)
Tr: all the townships are built along the riverbanks of Syr Darya。

译文：在萨雷沙的西面，咸海的东面，有草原之国，有种植之国。北山脚的游牧区有一条楚河，楚河向西汇入弱水后再汇入了锡尔河。锡尔河的游牧氏族集镇，有克孜勒奥尔达、热孜卡孜甘、萨特帕耶夫、扎林斯克、奇伊利甘、突厥斯坦、塔拉兹的阿雷西，这些集镇皆建在锡尔河边。

Translation:
To the west of Sarysha, to the east of the Aral Sea, there is the steppe nation, the grower's nation。 At the foot of the Northern mountains of nomadic territory, the river Chu forms。 Its west is the Ruoshui， flowing into the Syr Darya。 The townships by the nomadic tribes along the Syr Darya are the Kyzylorda, Zhezikazigan, Satpajev, Zhalinsk, Qiyilygan, Turkistan, Alyci of Taraz。 All those townships are built along riverbanks of the Syr Darya。

18-05 不死山
Busishan
（59,3513E；45,14299N）

流沙之东[1]，黑水之间[2]，有山名曰不死之山[3]。

注释：[1]流沙：这里指咸海东岸的卡拉库姆沙漠，咸海在其西面。
Notes:[1] liu sha (flowing sands)
Tr: it refers to the Karakum Desert to the east coast of Aral Sea。The sea is to the west of the desert。

[2] 黑水：指咸海。

[2] hei shui (black water) refers to the Aral Sea。

[3] 不死山：指复活岛。

[3] bu si shan (never die mount)
Tr: refers to the Fuhuodao (resurrection island) 。

译文：在卡拉库姆沙漠的西面，在咸海中间，有一座山叫复活岛。

Translation:
To the west of Karakum desert, in the middle of Aral Sea, there is a mountain called Fuhuo Island。

18-06 肇山柏高
Zhaoshanbogao
（71,39286E；42,89967N）

华山青水之东[1]，有山名曰肇山[2]。有人名曰柏高[3]，柏高上下于此 [4]， 至于天 [5] 。

注释：[1]华山青水之东：指活山楚水之东，即复活岛与楚河的东面。
Notes:[1] hua shan qing shui zhi dong (flower mount green water east)
Tr: the Huo(alive) mountain and Chu river's east side: the east side of Fuhuodao Mountain and the Chu River。

[2]肇（shao）山：指别肇兹，即肇兹山，今标注为别萨兹。别，指山。

[2] shao shan: refers to the Bieshaozi, e.g., Shaozishan, today labelled as Biesazi。 bie: mountain in Pu speech， as in Dabieshan （大别山）in China。

[3] 柏高：指摆鬲，即鬲昆人的场镇，在今塔拉兹地区。

[3]bo gao (poplar tall) refers to Baige: the township and grazing land of Gekun people, in today's Taraz region。

[4] 上下于此：妥体于敕，即游牧区域。
[4] shang xia yu ci (up down from here) reads as tuo ti yu she: meaning the nomadic region。
[5] 至于天：指塔拉兹，即塔河平原。兹、至都指平原；于天、塔拉都指塔河。
[5] zhi yu tian (up to sky)
Tr: refers to the Taraz region e.g., Tahe (ta river) plain。 Zi, zhi all means plain。 Yutian, Tara both refer to the Tahe, Ta River。

译文：在复活岛与楚河的东边，有一座山叫肇兹山，山边有一个集镇叫摆鬲，摆鬲坐落于游牧区域的塔河平原。
Translation:
To the east of Fuhuodao and Chu River, there is a mountain called Shaozi Mountain。 By the mountain side, there is a township called Baige, it is in the Tahe plain。 The plain is the nomadic region。

18-07 都广之野
Duguangzhiye
（75,29472E；44,84858N）

西南黑水[1]之间，有都广之野[2]，后稷葬焉[3]。爰有膏菽、膏稻、膏黍、膏稷[4]、百谷自生[5]，冬夏播琴[6]。鸾鸟自歌，凤鸟自儛，灵寿实华[7]，草木所聚[8]。爰有百兽，相群爰处[9]。此草也，冬夏不死[10]。

注释：[1]西南黑水：指锡尔河和纳伦河。西南，读锡潦，指锡尔河。
Notes:[1] xi nan hei shui (black water) refers to the Syr Darya and the Naryn River (Kara Darya) 。xinan reads as Xiliao, referring to the Syr Darya。
[2] 都广之野：指吉尔吉斯之乡。吉尔吉斯，指广而又广，简称都广。
[2] du guang zhi ye (both wide broad wildness)
Tr: refers to Kyrgyz land, Kyrgyz (Kirghizia): very wide and broad, shortened to duguang。
[3] 后稷葬焉：读哈纪藏原，指月亮氏族的疆域。
[3] hou yi zang yan (God Houyi burial) reads as Hajizangyuan, refers to the territory of the moon tribes, moon(yueliang)。
[4] 膏菽、膏稻、膏黍、膏稷：指拉拉勾纪、柳克特勾纪、扎苏勾纪、卡吉勾纪。
[4] gaoshu, gaodao, gaoshu, gaoyi (gao: cream) shu(grain)dao(rice) shu(millet)yi(cereal)
Tr: refers to the four Gouji (tribe) the Lala Gouji, Lyuket Gouji, Zhasu Gouji, and Kaji Gouji。
[5] 百谷自生：许多自然形成的部落。
[5] bai gu zi shen (hundred grains grow by themselves)
Tr: many tribes have formed naturally。
[6] 冬夏播琴：国家联盟。
[6] dong xia bo qin (winter summer broadcast lyre)
Tr: the confederation of nations。
[7] 灵寿实华：指黎族胡族，即种植民和牧民。
[7] ling shou shi hua (spirit longevity fruit flower)
Tr: refers to the Li people and the Hu people。 The Li people are the growers, the Hu people are the herders。
[8] 草木所聚：人们相聚在一起。
[8] cao mu suo ju (grass wood thus gather)
Tr: people collect and gather。
[9] 爰有百兽，相群爰处：所有氏族，和谐相处。
[9] yuan you bai shou (thus hundred beast) xiang qun yuan chu (groups to live side by side)

Tr: all the tribes are living in harmony。

[10] 此草也，东夏不死：此草也，指吉尔吉斯草原；冬夏不死，是国家的草山。不死，读博著，指草山。
[10]ci cao ye, dong xia bu si (this grass, east summer does not die)
Tr: ci cao ye (this grass) refers to the Kyrgyz steppe, dong xia bu si (winter summer not die) means Nation's steppe, busi (not die) reads as boshi, refers to grass hills。

译文：在锡尔河和纳伦河之间的地区，有吉尔吉斯之乡，是月亮氏族的疆域。这里有拉拉勾纪、柳克特勾纪、扎苏勾纪、卡吉勾纪等许多自然形成的部落，不论是西部的城镇还是东部的部落，不论是种植民还是牧民，所有氏族都和谐相处。吉尔吉斯草原，是国家的草山。
Translation:
In the land between the Syr Darya and the Naryn Darya to the southwest of Aral Sea, there is the Land of Kyrgyz, the territory of the Moon tribes。 There are the Gouji of Lala, Lyuket, Zhasu, Kaji, among other naturally formed tribes。 Both the tribal towns in the east and in the west, whether they are growers or herders, all the tribes and their people are living in harmony。 The Kyrgyz steppe is the grass hills of the nation。

18-08 若木
Ruomu
（71,64035E；41,00757N）

南海之外，黑水[1]青水[2]之间，有木名曰若木[3]，若水[4]出焉。

注释：[1]黑水：指纳伦河，在吉尔吉斯斯坦。南海之外应是指西南海之外。
Notes: [1] hei shui (black water) refers to the Naryn River in Kyrgyzstan。Beyond South Sea, refers to the area beyond the west Nanhai (south sea)。

[2] 青水：指锡尔河。青、锡都是指东。
[2] qing shui (green water)
Tr: refers to the Syr Darya, both qing and Syr means east。

[3] 若木：指纳曼干城。若木指纳曼，干，是城（歌）的音译，在乌兹别克斯坦。
[3] ruo mu: (like wood)
Tr: refers to the Namangan city, ruomu refers to Naman, gan is the phonetic rendering of the concept of city (ge; as in Chinese song: ge), it is in Uzbekistan。

[4] 若水：指月氏氏族。
[4] ruo shui (like water) refers to the Yuezhi or Yueshi Shizu (tribes)。

译文：在西南海之外的纳伦河与锡尔河的连接处，有一个管理中心，叫纳曼干，是月氏氏族居住之乡。
Translation:
In the land where the Naryn River and the Syr River meet in the southwest Haiwai area, there is an administration center called Namangan。 Namangan is the land where reside the Yuezhi tribes, the tribes of the moon。

18-09 灵山蝡蛇
Lingshanruanshe
（72,80446E；40,53431N）

有禺中之国[1]。有列襄之国[2] 。有灵山 [3] ，有赤蛇生木上 [4] ，名曰蝡蛇 [5] 。

注释：[1]禺中国：指水寨国，又读奥卡国，在吉尔吉斯奥卡河流域。

Notes:[1]yu zhong guo: refers to the Shui zhai Guo (water ford country) reads as Aoka Guo, in the Aoka River drainage areas in Kyrgyzstan。

[2] 列襄国：指湿地边的国家。列，指邻；襄，同湘，指湿地。

[2] lie xiang guo: refers to the countries along the rim of the wetland regions。

Tr: Lie/file, meaning neighbour, xiang; as Xiang in Chinese, meaning wetland。

[3] 灵山：指阿赖山、外阿赖山。

[3] ling shan (spirit mount) refers to Alai Mountain and trans-Alai (Alay) mountains。

[4] 有赤蛇生木上：有游牧氏族建立的外检目。上，读音 sha，指外。

[4] you chi she sheng mu shang:(has red snake grow on wood)

Tr: there is the Waijianmu, outlying administration centre, built by the nomadic tribes。 Shang, on, or above, reads as sha, meaning beyond, outside, outlying。

[5] 蝡蛇：指奥什。

[5] ruan she (worm snake) refers to Osh city。

译文：有一个水寨国，是湿地边的国家，那里有阿赖山，有一个游牧氏族建立的外检目，名叫奥什。

Translation:

There is Shuizhai Guo, a country by the wetland。 There is the Alay Mountain, where an outlying administration centre is built by the nomadic tribes。 This Waijianmu is called Osh.

18-10 盐长国鸟氏

Yanchangguoniaoshi

（73,29775E；40,77165N）

有盐长之国[1]。有人焉，鸟首[2]，名曰鸟氏[3]。

注释：[1]盐长国：指察江国，在吉尔吉斯贾拉拉巴德地区的察江流域。

Notes: [1] yan chang guo (salt long country)

Tr: it refers to Chajiang Guo (search river country) in the Chajiang catchment in Jalalabad region in Kirgizia。Jalal-Abad Region, also known as Jalalabat (Kyrgyz: Жалалабат облусу), is a region (oblast) of Kyrgyzstan。

[2] 鸟首：指小月氏的鸟俗氏，又称乌兹氏。

[2] niao shou (bird head)

Tr: refers to the Niaosu Shi (bird tradition) of the Lesser Yuezhi Shi, also known as Wuzi Shi。

[3] 鸟氏：指乌兹根。鸟禽类在濮语中读乌。

[3] niao shi (bird as family name) refers to Uzgen。 In Pu speech, birds are called Wu。

译文：有一个察江国，那里有一个集镇，是鸟俗氏的集镇，名叫乌兹根。

Translation:

There is a Chajiang Guo, and in that country there is a township。 The township is built by the Niaosu Shi, the township is known as Uzgen。

18-11 九丘建木

Jiuqiujianmu

有九丘[1]，以水络之：名曰陶唐之丘[2]、有叔得之丘[3]、孟盈之丘[4]、昆吾之丘[5]，黑白之丘[6]、赤望之丘[7]、参卫之丘[8]、武夫之丘[9]、神民之丘[10]。有木，青叶紫茎，玄华黄实，名曰建木[11]，百仞无枝[12]，有九欘，下有九枸[13]，其实如麻，其叶如芒[14]。大皞爰过[15]，黄帝所为。

注释：[1]九丘：黄帝统一华夏时划分的九个大区。
Notes: [1] jiu qiu (nine mounds)
Tr: refers to the Nine major divisions created by Huangdi (Yellow Emperor) when he unified the Hua nations and Xia nations。

[2] 陶唐丘：管理区域为陕西、山西、河北南部，治所在山西太原。
[2] tao tang Qiu refers to Taotang region with its regional centre in Taiyuan city in today's Shanxi province controlling Shaanxi, Shanxi and the southern part of Hebei province。

[3] 叔得丘：指三星堆地区，治所在德阳。叔得，原文三留，读音叔得，今称三星堆。
[3] shu de qiu: refers to Sanxingdui (three-star pile) region with its regional centre at Deyang, today's Sichuan province。 Shude, original Pu script is Sanliu, reads as Shude, today known as Sanxingdui (three-star pile) 。

[4] 孟盈丘：山东苏北徽州地区，治所在青州。
[4] meng ying qiu: refers to the Shandong area and Huizhou region in Northern Jiangsu, with its regional centre in Qingzhou, today's Shandong province。

[5] 昆吾丘：河南地区与安徽西部与南部地区，治所在偃师。
[5] kun wu qiu: refers to Henan and the west and south parts of Anhui, with its regional centre in Yanshi, in today's Luoyang, Henan province。

[6] 黑白丘：辽宁巫医山地区，治所在北镇。
[6] hei bai qiu: (black, white mound) refers to the Liaoning Wuyishan region, with its regional centre at Beizhen (northern township) 。

[7] 赤望丘：江西、苏南、浙江北部地区，治所在苏州黄桥。
[7] chi wang qiu (red watch mound) refers to the regions of Jiangxi, southern part of Jiangsu, northern part of Zhejiang province, with their capital centre in Huangqiao (yellow bridge) in Suzhou city， in today's Jiangsu province。

[8] 参卫丘：东瓯、七闽地区，治所在温州。
[8] can wei qiu (join guard mound) refers to Dong'ou, and Qimin (Fujian) regions with its centre in Wenzhou in today's Zhejiang province。

[9] 武夫丘：指北胡地区，治所在卓资。
[9] qu fu qiu (warlike male mound) refers to the Bei Hu region, with its centre in Zhuozi。

[10] 神民丘：甘肃、青海地区，治所在兰州。
[10] shen min qiu (God folk mound) refers to Gansu and Qinghai region with centre in Lanzhou, in today's Gansu province。

[11] 有木，青叶紫茎，玄华黄实，名曰建木：有行政中心，负责管理百姓和部落国，执行王事，称为检目。检，实际读音为 jie，指理。
[11] you mu, qing ye zi jing (has wood, green leaf purple stem); xuan hua huang shi, ming yue jian mu (dark flower yellow fruits,) Its name is erect or inspect wood, jie/manage。
Tr: there is an administration centre handling the management of its people and branch nations and carrying out king's orders。 This function centre is called Jianmu。Jian reads as jie, meaning to manage。 jian, jie phonetically close。

[12] 百仞无枝：联盟政府在昌部落（今北京）。
[12] bai ren wu zhi (hundred ren no branch) ren: unit of length。
Tr: the confederacy 's government is located where the Chang tribes are, which is today's Beijing。

[13] 有九欘，下有九枸：行政建制为九欘九枸。
[13] you jiu shu, xia you jiu gou (has nine division, and each division further divide into nine gou)
Tr: the administrative system is constituted with nine divisions and each division is further divided into nine sub-divisions。

[14] 其实如麻，其叶如芒：再下分就如麻如芒。
[14] qi shi ru ma, (its fruits like threads), qi ye ru mang (its leaves like needles)

Tr: further dividing the kingdom make it as hemp threads and needles on the stem。

[15] 大皞爰过，黄帝所为：浩瀚的大国，是黄帝所创立。

[15] da hao yuan guo (big hao thus pass) huang di suo wei (Yellow Emperor did it)

Tr: the immense nation is founded by Huangdi (the yellow emperor) 。

译文：华夏有九大行政区，以河流相连接，称为陶唐、叔得、孟盈、昆吾、黑白、赤望、参卫、武夫、神民之丘。各大区都有行政中心，负责管理百姓和部落国，负责执行王事，称为检目。联盟政府在昌部落，行政建制为九大区，各大区下设九个部落，各部落又下设氏族聚落，氏族聚落又下分各支系族群，管理建制细分如麻如芒。如此浩瀚的大国，是黄帝所创立。

Translation:

Huaxia has nine major administrative divisions, linked by rivers。 They are called mounds, the nine mounds are: Taotang, Shude, Mengyin, Kunwu, Heibai, Chiwang, Canwei, Wufu, and Shenmin。 Each mound has its own administrative centers, managing its people and tribal nation, carrying out king's orders。 This function is called Jianmu。 The government of the Confederacy is at the Chang tribal residence。 The administration system is constituted of nine divisions。 And under each division, there are nine tribes to each division。 Under each tribe, there are tribal settlements。 Under the tribal settlement there are branches。 The administration system is so detailed as plants with fibers and needles on its stems。 Such an immense country was founded by Huangdi。

18-12 窫窳、猩猩

Yayu, Xingxing

（103,76299E；29,55572N）

有窫窳，龙首[1]，是食人[2]。有青首，人面[3]，名曰猩猩[4]。

注释：[1]窫窳龙首：指大河僚族，在四川乐山市。

Notes: [1] ya yu long shou (yayu dragon head)

Tr: refers to the Dahelao （big river Lao） people in Leshan city, Sichuan province。

[2] 是食人：是古老的居民。

[2] shi shi ren (is eat human)

Tr: the ancient inhabitants。

[3] 青首人面：穿青衣氏族居民。

[3] qing shou ren mian (green head human face)

Tr: the tribal inhabitants wearing blue colored clothes。

[4] 猩猩：青衣江，又称迎江、迎溪。濮语读迎溪为喜溪，谐音猩猩。

[4] xing xing (ape) refers to Qingyijiang (blue clothes river) which is also known as Yingjiang, Yingxi。 In Pu speech it is read as Xixi, xixi, a phonetic match to xingxing。

译文：这里有大河僚族，是古老的居民。有穿青衣的氏族居民，名叫迎江氏。

Translation:

There are the Dahe Lao tribes, they are ancient inhabitants。 There are the tribal inhabitants who wear blue clothes, called Yingjiang Shi。

18-13 巴国

Ba Guo

（106,27604E；29,97212N）

西南有巴国。大皞[1] 生咸鸟 [2]， 咸鸟生乘釐 [3]， 乘釐生后照 [4]， 后照是始为巴人 [5] 。

注释：[1]大暤：指大自然。
Notes:[1] da hao: refers to mother nature。

[2] 咸鸟：指长江。
[2] xian niao (salty bird) refers to the Yangtze River。

[3] 乘釐：指擅长于撑船的人群。
[3] cheng li (ride luck)
Tr: the groups of people who are skillful in operating boats。

[4] 后照：指后照羲国，是蚩尤族群西迁后建立的国家。
[4] hou zhao (later shine) refers to the Houzhaoxi Guo, a nation founded by the Chiyou tribes after their westward migration。

[5] 是始为巴人：开始建立巴国的集镇。巴国，指河畔之国。
[5] shi shi wei ba ren (is begin be ba person)
Tr: start to build the townships of Ba Guo。 Ba Guo means nations by the riverside。

译文：西南地区有一个巴国，大自然形成了长江，长江边产生了会撑船的人群，撑船人群的生活区形成了后照羲国，后照羲国开始建立起巴国的集镇。
Translation:
In the land of southwest there is Ba Guo。 Mother nature gives birth to the Yangtze River, Yangtze River brings forth people who are skillful in operating boats。 The skillful boatpeople build their region into a Houzhaoxi Guo, Houzhaoxi Guo starts to build the townships of Ba Guo。

18-14 流黄辛氏国
Liuhuangxingshi Guo
（106,75888E；31,85686N）

有国名曰流黄辛氏[1]，其域中方三百里[2]，其出是尘土[3]。有巴遂山[4]，渑水出焉 [5] 。

注释：[1]流黄辛氏国：指南江巴肆国。彝濮语读巴为辛。
Notes:[1] liu huang xin shi guo(rio yellow spicy surname country)
Tr: refers to the Nanjiang (the south river) Basi Guo。 In Yi speech, ba is read as xin。

[2] 中方三百里：中方三，指摇铃舍、擂鼓舍，是巴中的古称谓；百里，读毫里，指都城。
[2] zhong fang san bai li:(middle area three hundred li)
Tr: zhong fang san refers to the Yaoling (ring bell) House, or Leigu(drumming) House。 House reads as she。 Both names are the ancient names for Bazhong (middle Ba), baili (hundred li) reads as boli, meaning poli, capital city, urban centre。

[3] 其出是尘土：这个地方是賨人管辖。其出，指这个地方。
[3] qi chu shi chen tu (it out is dirt)
Tr: this place is managed by Cong people。 Qichu: this place。

[4] 巴遂山：指大巴山。
[4]ba sui shan: refers to the Dabashan。

[5] 渑水出焉：前江流域之乡。
[5] mian shui chu yan: refers to the Qianjiang River drainage area。

译文：有一个国家名叫南江巴肆国，这个地域的都城在擂鼓舍，这个地方是賨人的辖区，它的东面是大巴山，是前江流域之乡。
Translation:

There is a country called Nanjiangbasi Guo。 This region's capital is Leigu She (share, shire) 。 This place is managed by the Cong people。 Dabashan is to its east, the land of Qianjiang area。

18-15 朱卷国
Zhujuan Guo
（115,89134E；28,67752N）

又有朱卷之国[1]。有黑蛇[2]，青首 [3]，食象 [4] 。

注释：[1]朱卷：江西南昌，古称朱建。
Notes:[1]zhu juan (red curl)
Tr: refers to Nanchang, Jiangxi province, its ancient name is Zhujian, a close phonetic match。
[2] 黑蛇：指黑舍，濮族支系的称谓；黑舍为贵族。
[2] hei she (black snake)
Tr: refers to black she (house), a term for the noble lineage of the Pu people。 Black House means noble lineage。
[3] 青首：这里指青云濮。
[3] qing shou (blue head) refers to the Qingyun (blue clouds) Pu people。
[4] 食象：建立的国家。
[4] shi xiang (eat elephant)
Tr: nations or states which are built。

译文：又有一个朱建国，是黑舍的青云濮建立的国家。
Translation:
There is a Zhujian Guo, a nation built by the Heishe noble lineage of the Qingyun Pu tribes。

18-16 赣巨人
Ganjuren
（114,9151E；27,039N）

南方有赣巨人[1]，人面长臂[2]，黑身有毛[3]，反踵[4]，见人笑亦笑[5]，因即逃也[6]。

注释：[1]赣巨人：指赣吉镇，今老吉安县城。
Notes:[1] gan ju ren (gan giant) refers to Ganjizhen, in today's old quarter of Ji'an county, Jiangxi province。
[2] 人面长臂：座落于草禾河边。长臂，读绰泚，指草禾河。
[2] ren mian chang bi (human face long arms)
Tr: is located by the banks of Caohe River (grass plants river) 。changbi (long arm) refers to the Chuobi, the Caohe River。
[3] 黑身有毛：贵族为苗族。
[3] hei shen you mao (black body with hair)
Tr: its noble lineage is the Miao tribe。
[4] 反踵：善于管理。
[4] fan zhong (backward ankles)
Tr: good at management。
[5] 见人笑亦笑：这个集镇紧邻峡江。
[5] jian ren xiao yi xiao (see people laugh then laugh)
Tr: this township is very close to the Xiajiang River。
[5] 因即逃也：所以是一个吉祥之境的家乡。即，指吉；逃，读妥，指境；也，指乡。

[5] yin ji tao ye (cause is runaway)
Tr: therefore, is a homeland of good luck region。 Ji: good luck, Tao reads as tuo, land, ye: homeland。

译文：南方有一个赣吉镇，座落于草禾河边，贵族为苗族，善于管理。这个集镇紧邻峡江，所以是一个吉祥之境的家乡。
Translation:
There is a Ganji Zhen in the south, next to the Caohe River, its noble lineage is the Miao tribes, very skillful managers。 This township is next to Xiajiang River; therefore, it is the homestead with good luck。

18-17 黑人
Heiren
（114,512E；26,31322N）

又有黑人[1]，虎首鸟足[2]，两手持蛇[3]，方啖之[4]。

注释：[1]黑人：指禾镇，今称遂川，在江西遂川。
Notes:[1] hei ren (black person)
Tr: refers to Hezhen, today it is known as Suichuan, Jiangxi province。
[2] 虎首鸟足：濮族的僚支系。
[2]hu shou niao zu (tiger head bird feet)
Tr: The Lao branch of Pu people。
[3] 两手持蛇：建都于岔河口。
[3] liang shou chi che (two hands hold snakes)
Tr: establish their capital by Chahekou (fork river mouth) 。
[4] 方啖之：是王族的集镇。
[4] fang dan zhi (just eat it)
Tr: is a township of the king branch。

译文：又有一个禾镇，是濮族的僚支系建都于岔河口而形成的集镇，是王族的集镇。
Translation:
There is Hezhen, a township built by the Lao branch of the Pu people at the river month of Chahe River。 It is a township by the king branch。

18-18 嬴民、封豕
Yingmin、fengshi
（117,21772E；29,34606N）

有嬴民[1]，鸟足[2]，有封豕[3]。

注释：[1]嬴民：读溢米，指水地，今称浮梁。
Notes:[1] ying min reads as yi mi, refers to Shuidi (watery land), known today as Fuliang。
[2] 鸟足：指僚族，这里指僚族部落。
[2] niao zu (bird feet) refers to the Lao people, the Lao tribes。
[3] 封豕：指稻杆，今称禾杆，是水地的中心、检目。
[3] feng shi (seal pig)
Tr: meaning rice stems, today it is called Hegan (shoot stem), refers to the centre (jianmu) in Shuidi (watery land) 。

译文：有一个地方叫水地，是僚族部落，那里有禾杆检目。
Translation:
There is a place called Shuidi, the settlements of Lao tribes, they have a management centre there called Hegan Jianmu。

18-19 苗民神延维
MiaominshenYanwei
（117,85873E；29,25849N）

有人曰苗民[1]。有神焉，人首蛇身[2]，长如辕[3]，左右有首[4]，衣紫衣[5]，冠旃冠[6]，名曰延维[7]，人主得而飨食之[8]，伯天下[9]。

注释：[1]苗民：在此指敄米，即河岸之地，今江西婺源县。敄，读 mou 音。
Notes:[1] miao min (miao people)
Tr: reads as mou mi, meaning riverbank areas, in today's Maoyuan county, Jiangxi province。
[2] 人首蛇身：定居的种植氏族。
[2] ren shou she shen (human head snake body) settled growers' tribes。
[3] 长如辕：指丛村河，今称北河。
[3] chang ru yuan （long as cartshaft) refers to Congcun River, today known as Beihe (north river) 。
[4] 左右有首：指慕口氏族，今称思口氏族。
[4] zuo you you shou (left right has heads) referring to the Mukou tribe, today known as Sikou tribe。
[5] 衣紫衣：指段莘水，今称东河。紫衣，濮语段莘的音译。
[5] yi zi yi (wear purple dress) refers to the Duanxinshui, known today as Donghe (east river), ziyi(purple dress) a phonetic rendering of Pu concept of Duanxin。
[6] 冠旃冠：指蒋镇岗氏族，今称蒋村岗氏族。
[6] guan dan guan (wear red crown) refers to the Jiangzhengang tribe, known today as the Jiangcungang tribes。
[7] 延维：延山南面的氏族称延维氏。
[7] yan wei: the tribes living to the south of Yanshan is known as Yanwei Shi。
[8] 人主得而飨食之：定中心集镇在香肆坪。主，指基地，这里指中心。
[8] ren zhu de er xiang shi zhi (folk lord got to eat it)
Tr: designates its centre township at Xiangsiping。 zhu: base, here refers to centre。
[9] 伯天下：下香边，今婺源县城。下香，指下香坑口。伯，指方位、边。
[9]bo tian xia (lord sky under)
Tr: xia xiang bian (under fragrant rim) today's Maoyuan county seat。 Xiaxiang: Xiaxiangkengkou, a place name, bo(lord) refers to locality, by the rim, outlying。

译文：有一个集镇叫敄米。这里的氏族，是定居的种植氏族。丛村河住着思口氏族，段莘水住着蒋镇岗氏族，他们统称为延维氏族。中心集镇定在香肆坪的下香边。
Translation:
There is a township called Moumi。 The tribes living here are the settled growers' tribes。 The Sikou tribes live by Congcun River。 The Jiangzhengang tribes live by the Duanxin River。 The people here are known as the Yanwei tribes, with their centre township at Xiaxiangbian in Xiangsiping。

18-20 鸾鸟、凤鸟
Luanniao、 Fengniao
（富春江流域）
Fuchunjiang River drainage areas

有鸾鸟自歌，凤鸟自舞[1]。凤鸟首文曰德[2]，翼文曰顺 [3]，膺文曰仁[4]，背文曰义[5]，见则天下和[6]。

注释：[1]有鸾鸟自歌，凤鸟自舞：有西河的城镇，东河的部落。
Notes:[1] you luanniao zi ge, fengniao zi wu (luan sings feng dances)
Tr: there are the townships in Xihe (west river) and tribes in Donghe (east river) 。
[2] 首文曰德：第一条河叫建德河，今称新安江。
[2] shou wen yue de (head marking says virtue) first river is called Jiande River, known today as Xin'anjiang River。
[3] 翼文曰顺：第二条河叫顺河，今称衢江。
[3] yi wen yue shun (wing marking says obedient) second river is called Shun River, known today as Qujiang River。
[4] 膺文曰仁：第三条河叫龙溪，音读音为 rue，被译作仁，今称分水溪。
[4] yin wen yue ren (arm marking says benevolence) third river is called Longxi, long(dragon) reads as rue, a close phonetic rendering into Chinese concept of Ren: benevolence， today it is called Fenshuixi River (parting water creek)
[5] 背文曰义：第四条河叫武义江。
[5] bei wen yue yi (back marking says ren) forth river is called Wuyijiang River。
[6] 见则天下和：那里四通八达，犹如一体。描述的是富春江流域。
[6] jian ze tianxia he (seen peace under heaven)
Tr: there the waterway network links ways everywhere, as a whole body, this is a description of the Fuchunjiang River region。

译文：有西河的城镇，东河的部落。东河地区第一条河是建德河，第二条河是顺河，第三条河是龙溪，第四条河是武义江，那里四通八达，犹如一体。
Translation:
There is the Xihe township and Donghe tribes。 In the Hedong region, the first river is Jiande River, the second river is Shun River, the third river is Longxi, the fourth river is Wuyijiang。In this land, the waterways link everywhere as a big body of network。

18-21【山/困】狗、孔鸟
Kungou 、kongniao
（119,64542E；29,08014N）

又有青兽如菟[1]，名曰【山/困】狗[2]。有翠鸟[3] 。有孔鸟 [4] 。

注释：[1]青首如菟：指赤松山的管理区，在浙江金华市。
Notes: qing shou ru tu (green head like grass)
Tr: refers to the managed region in Chisongshan, in today's Jinhua city, Zhejiang province。
[2] 【山/困】狗：指金城，即金华城。
[2] kun gou: refers to Jincheng (gold city) e.g., today's Jinhua city。
[3] 翠鸟：指富春江。
[3] cui niao (green bird) refers to the Fuchunjiang River。
[4] 孔鸟：指北界河。
[4] kong niao (kong bird) refers to the Beijie River。 Beijie (north border)

译文：有赤松山的管理区，名叫金华城，那里有富春江与北界河。
Translation:

There is a management region in Chisongshan, which is called Jinhua city。 There are the Fuchunjiang River and Beijie River。

18-22 三天子都山
Santianzidushan
（119,26311E；28,48184N）

南海之内，有衡山，有菌山，有桂山[1]。有山名三天子都山[2]。

注释：[1]衡山、菌山、桂山：指常山、江郎山、九龙山。
Notes:[1] hengshan, junshan, kuishan: refer to Changshan, Jianglangshan, Jiulongshan。
[2] 三天子都山；指福建西北部浙江境内九龙山，有松阳，遂昌，遂昌大柘三个山间平地，被称为三妥柘堵山，谐音为三天子都山，同时也称为柘岭或柘岱。
[2] san tian zi du shan (three sky prince capital mount) refers to Jiulongshan at the northwest of Fujian province and Zhejiang province, there are three flat lands Songyang, Suichang and Suichangdazhe; among the mountains known as the Santuozhedu Mountain, a phonetic punning to Santianzidu Mountain。 It is also known as Zheling or Zhedai。

译文:南海地区，有常山、江郎山、九龙山，九龙山又称三妥柘堵山。
Translation:
In the land of Naihai region, there are three mountains: the Changshan, the Jianglangshan and the Jiulongshan, Jiulongshan is also called Santuozhedu Mountain。

18-23 苍梧丘
Cangwuqiu
（111,98804E；25,34963N）

南方苍梧之丘，苍梧之渊[1]，其中有九嶷山，舜之所葬[2]，在长沙零陵界中。

注释：[1]苍梧之渊：指苍梧之乡。
Notes:[1] cang wu zhi yuan refers to the land of Cangwu (wu: a kind of straight wood)。
[2] 舜之所葬：纹身、刺绣氏族的疆域。
[2] shun zhi suo zang (God Shun burial)
Tr: the territory of Wenshen tribes and Cixiu tribes。 Wenshen(tattoo)， Cixiu
(Embroidery needle work)。

译文：南方苍梧地区，苍梧之乡，那里有九嶷山，是纹身、刺绣氏族的疆域，在长沙零陵境内。
Translation:
In the Cangwu region, the land of dark Wu tree in the south, there is the Jiuyi Mountains。 It is the territory of the Wenshen tribes and the Cixiu tribes, in present day Lingling in Changsha city, Hunan province。

18-24 朝鲜、天毒

东海之内，北海之隅，有国名曰朝鲜，天毒[1]，其人水居[2]，偎人爱之[3]。

注释：[1]天毒：日本岛的古称谓。
Notes :[1] tian du (sky poison) ancient Name for Japan。

[2] 其人水居：东瀛族的部落国。其人水，指东瀛族；居，指部落国。
[2] qi ren shui ju (its people water live)
Tr: the tribal nation of Dongying tribes。 Qirenshui: refers to the Dongying tribe, ju: means nation of tribes。
[3] 偎人爱之：指倭基姆地区，即日本列岛。爱之，读阿之，指地区。
[3] wei ren ai zhi (snuggle person love it)
Tr: refers to the Wojimu region, e.g., Japanese Islands。 Aizhi (love it) reads azhi, meaning regions。

译文：在东北海外的北海一角，有一个国家叫朝鲜；还有一个国家叫天毒，是东瀛族的部落国，是倭基姆地区。
Translation:
In the corner of North Sea in the northeast Haiwai, there is a country called Korea。 There is another country called Tiandu。 It is a tribal nation by the Dongying tribes。 This is the Wojimu region。

18-25 蛇山、翳鸟
Sheshan、Yiniao

北海之内，有蛇山[1]者，蛇水出焉，东流入于海[2]，有五彩之鸟[3]，飞蔽一乡[4]，名曰翳鸟[5]。又有不距之山[6]，巧倕葬于西 [7] 。

注释：[1]蛇山：指色楞格山。
Notes:[1] she shan (snake mount) refers to the Selenge Mountain。
[2]海：指贝加尔湖。
[2] hai(sea) the Baikal Lake。
[3] 五彩之鸟：指五岔之河。彩，读音 chou，指岔。
[3] wu cai zhi niao (five color bird)
Tr: refers to the Wucha River, cai reads chou, meaning fork。
[4] 飞蔽一乡：贯穿全境。
[4] fei bi yi xiang (fly over one village)
Tr: going through the whole territory。
[5] 翳鸟：指叶尼塞河。
[5] yi niao: refers to the Yenisei River。
[6] 不距之山：指雅布洛诺夫山，简称布纪山。
[6] bu ju zhi shan (no distance mount) refers to the Yablonovy Mountains in Siberia, in Transbaikal in Russia, the name is shortened to Buji Mountain。
[7] 巧倕葬于西：赤塔城的疆域在东面。巧倕在此指赤塔。西，指东。
[7] qiao chui zang yu xi (clever chui buried to the west)
Tr: Chita city's territory is in the east。 Qiaochui: Chita （red pagoda）， xi: means east。

译文：在北海外，有一座色楞格山，色楞格河发源于这座山，向东流入贝加尔湖。有一条五岔之河，贯穿全境，称为叶尼塞河。有雅布洛诺夫山，赤塔城的疆域在它的东面。
Translation:
In the land beyond Beihaiwai, there is a mountain called Selenge Mountain。 The Selenge River rises from the mountain and flows east into the Baikal Lake。There is a river with five forks called Wucha River。 It flows throughout the whole territory; the name of the river is Yenisei。 There is also the Yablonovy Mountain。 The territory of Chita city is to the east of it。

18-26 相顾之尸

Xiangguzhishi
（100,71883E；46,19569N）

北海内，有反缚盗械[1]，带戈常倍[2]之佐，名曰相顾之尸[3]。

注释：[1]反缚盗械：指冯胡妥羲，外蒙部落国的名称。
Notes:[1] fan fu dao xie (back tie steal weapon)
Tr: refers to the Fenghutuoxi, a name for the tribal nation in Outer Mongolia。
[2] 带戈常倍：指戈壁阿尔泰山。
[2] dai ge chang bei (wear sword often double)
Tr: refers to the Govi Altai Mountains。
[3] 相顾之尸：指洪戈尔肆。
{3] xiang gu zhi shi (both look corpse)
Tr: refers to the Khonger township。

译文：在北海外，有一个叫冯胡妥羲的国家，在戈壁阿尔泰山旁边，都城称为洪戈尔肆。
Translation:
In the land of Beihaiwai, there is a country called Fenghutuoxi。 It is located next to Govi Altai Mountains， its capital city is called Khonger。

18-27 伯夷父
Boyifu
（113,37362E；49,24433N）

伯夷父生西岳[1]，西岳生先龙[2]，先龙是始生氐羌[3]，氐羌乞姓[4]。

注释：[1]伯夷父生西岳：巴颜湖形成了聚落。西岳读希略，指聚落。
Notes： [1]bo yi fu sheng xi yue (boyifu begets west mound)
Tr: Around Bayan Lake area settlements formed。 Xiyue reads xilue, meaning settlements。
[2] 西岳生先龙：聚落产生了国家。
[2] xi yue sheng xian long (west mount begets early dragon)
Tr: settlements developed into country or nation。
[3] 先龙是始生氐羌：国家最早由氐羌建立。
[3] xian long shi shi sheng di qiang (early dragon start begetting Diqiang)
Tr: countries, nations were first set up by Di Qiang tribes。
[4] 氐羌乞姓：氐羌属犬戎族。
[4] di qiang qi xin (diqiang beg family name)
Tr: Di Qiang people belong to the Quanrong people (dog rong tribes) 。

译文：巴颜湖形成了聚落，聚落产生了国家，国家最早由氐羌建立，氐羌属犬戎族。
Translation:
The Bayan Lake attracts settlements。 Settlements develop into country。 Country is first set up by the Diqiang tribes。Di Qiang people belong to the Quanrong, the Dog Rong tribes。

18-28 幽都山、大幽国
Youdushan, Dayouguo
（121,06513E；50,99581N）

北海之内，有山，名曰幽都之山[1]，黑水[2]出焉。其上有玄鸟[3]、玄蛇[4]、玄豹[5]、玄虎[6]、玄狐蓬尾[7]。有大玄之山[8]。有玄丘之民[9]。有大幽之国[10]。有赤胫之国[11]。

注释：[1]幽都山：指耳朵山，濮语读帝都。大兴安岭西北麓。
Notes: [1] you du shan (shady poli mount) refers to Erduoshan (ear mount), in Pu concept it is read as Didu(emperor capital)， referring to the northwest part of Daxinganling Mountain。
[2] 黑水：指额尔古纳河。
[2] hei shui (black water) refers to the Ergune River (the Argun river)。
[3] 玄鸟：达斡尔族。玄鸟，指鹰，读达。
[3] xuan niao (dark bird) the Daur tribe （pinyin: Dáwò'ěr zú) are a Mongolic-speaking East Asian ethnic group in Northeast China。 Xuan niao means eagle, in Pu concept reads as Da。
[4] 玄蛇：鄂温克族。玄蛇，指长河，读乌汶克。
[4] xuan she (dark snake) refers to the Ewenke tribe 。Xuanshe: long river, in Pu speech reads wuwenke。
[5] 玄豹：鄂伦春族。玄豹，指高山，读乌姆隆。
[5] xuan bao (dark leopard)
Tr: refers to the Oroqen (Oroonco, Oronqo) people。Xuanbao: refers to high mountains, in Pu speech reads as Wumulong。
[6] 玄虎：东胡族。
[6] xuan hu (dark tiger) the Donghu (east hu) people。
[7] 玄狐蓬尾：指以大兴安岭命名的锡伯族。
[7] xuan hu peng wei (dark fox hairy tail)
Tr: refers to the Xibo people who derived their name from the Daxinganling Mountains。
[8] 大玄之山：指大兴安岭。
[8] da xuan zhi shan (big dark mount) refers to the Daxinganling Mountains。
[9] 玄丘之民：指根河地区。玄丘，读 she qie，指根河，也谐音西尼契。
[9] xuan qiu zhi min (dark mound folks)
Tr: refers to the Genhe region。 Xuanqiu reads as she qie, referring to Genhe, a phonetic match to Xiniqi。
[10] 大幽之国：指得尔布尔国，今称根河市。
[10] da you zhi guo (big dark country) refers to the Derbur Guo, known today as Genhe city。
[11] 赤胫之国：指游牧部落国，又称西尼契部落国。
[11] chi jing zhi guo (red leg country)
Tr: refers to the nomadic state, also known as Xiniqi tribal country。

译文：北海之外，有一座山叫耳朵山，额尔古纳河发源于这座山。这个地区有达斡尔族、鄂温克族、鄂伦春族、东胡族、还有锡伯族。这里是大兴安岭的根河地区。有得尔布尔之国，有西尼契部落国。
Translation:
In the land of northern Haiwai, there is a mountain called Erduo Mountain。 Erguna River rises from this mountain。 In this region there are the Darwo tribe, Ewenke tribe, Oronqi tribe, Donghu tribe and Xibo tribe。This is the Genhe region at Daxinganling Mountains。 The Derbur country and the Xiniqi tribal country are here。

18-29 钉灵国
Dingling Guo
（128,1353E；51,37848N）

有钉灵之国[1]，其民从膝已下[2]有毛[3]，马蹄善走[4]。

注释：[1]钉灵国：指德内国,即斯沃博德内。
Notes:[1] ding ling guo (nail clever country) refers to Dena Guo, also known as Svobodny (Russian: Свобóдный) is a town in Amur Oblast, Russia, located on the right bank of the Zeya River, 167 kilometers (104 mi) north of Blagoveshchensk, the administrative center of the oblast。

[2] 从膝已下：指从捷溢东边的，即结雅河的东边。
[2] cong qi ji xia (from knee down)
Tr: from the east of Jieyi。 Jieyi is known today as Zeya River。

[3] 有毛：读溢陌，指河岸之国。
[3] you mao (has fur)
Tr: refers to Yimo, meaning the countries along the riverbank, the He'an country。

[4] 马蹄善走：指江域驮运。
[4]ma ti shan zou (horse hoof best walk)
Tr: the transportation operations over the river regions。

译文：有一个德内国，那里是从捷溢东边的河岸之国，是一个以江河流域驮运而兴起的国家。
Translation:
There is Dene Guo, a riverbank country to the east side of the Zeya River。 It is a country that benefited from water transportation in that region。

18-30 伯陵生鼓、延、殳
Boling sheng Gu Yan Yi

炎帝之孙伯陵[1]，伯陵同[2]吴权之妻[3]阿女缘妇[4]，缘妇孕三年[5]，是生鼓、延、殳[6]。始为侯[7]，鼓、延是始为钟，为乐风 [8] 。

注释：[1]炎帝之孙伯陵：北方的西伯陵，指北方的贝加尔湖的西边。
Notes:[1] yan di zhi sun boling (God yan grandson boling)
Tr: The Xiboling area in the north, referring to the west part of Baikal Lake in the north。

[2] 伯陵同：读伯陵妥，指贝加尔湖地区。
[2]bo ling tong reads as bolingtuo, referring to the Baikal Lake region。

[3] 吴权之妻：指乌斯季犬戎。
[3] wu quan zhi qi (wu quan's wife) refers to the Ust（usji） Dogrong tribes。

[4] 阿女缘妇：指奥尔耶胡。
[4] a nv yuan fu (girl A woman)
Tr: refers to the Aorye Hu people。

[5] 缘妇孕三年：耶胡统治萨彦岭地区。
[5] yuan fu yun san nian (yuan wife pregnant three years)
Tr: The Ye Hu people are in control of the Sayanling region。

[6] 是生鼓、延、殳：在这里建立了库兹涅茨克、伊尔库茨克、苏真斯克三个城镇。鼓、延都是指巴尔虎氏族。"虎"读"古"音。
[6] shi sheng gu, yan, shu (thus give birth to drum, delay, weapon)
Tr: at this region, three townships are set up, they are the township of Kuznetsk (Russian: Кузнéцк), Irkutsk, and Sudzhensk。 Both Gu and Yan refer to the Barhu tribe。 Hu(tiger) reads as gu。

[7] 始为侯：苏真斯克为侯国。
[7] shi wei hou (start to become Hou count)
Tr: The Sudzhensk is a prince country。

[8]鼓、延是始为钟、为乐风：库兹涅茨克、伊尔库茨克为王城，为游牧王国。
[8]gu yan shi shi wei zhong, wei yue feng (drum, delay start to bell, music wind)
Tr: Kuznetsk and Irkutsk are king cities, are nomadic kingdoms。

译文：北方贝加尔湖西部地区的乌斯季犬戎奥尔耶胡，统治着萨彦岭地区，在那里建立了库兹涅茨克、伊尔库茨克、苏真斯克三个城镇，苏真斯克为侯国，库兹涅茨克、伊尔库茨克为王城，为游牧王国。
Translation:
The Ust Dogrong Aorye Hu people from the west side of Baikal Lake in the north are in control of the Sayanling region。Three townships are built up there, they are Kutsnetsk, Irkutsk, and Sudzhensk。 The Sudzhensk is the prince country, Kutsnetsk and Irkutsk are the king cities, theirs are the nomadic kingdoms。

18-31 鲧
Gun

黄帝[1]生骆明[2]，骆明生白马[3]，白马是为鲧[4]。

注释：[1]黄帝：在此指氐胡。
Notes: [1] huangdi (yellow emperor)
Tr: it refers to Di Hu。
[2] 骆明：指西部地区。
[2] luo ming: refers to the west region。
[3] 白马：氐羌的部落名，有白日巴马、白日窝马等。
[3] bai ma （white horse)
Tr: the tribal names of Di Qiang tribes, such as Bairibama, Bairiwoma。
[4]鲧：指昆仑奴。
[4] gun refers to the Kunlun-nu。

译文：氐胡来源于西部地区，西部的氐羌氐族，有白马、白日巴马、白日窝马等部落，统称为昆仑奴。
Translation:
The Di Hu people originated from the west。 The Di Qiang tribes from the west are the Baima group, such as the Bairibama, Bairiwoma, they are generally known as the Kunlun-nu。

18-32 番禺、奚仲
Fanyu 、Xizhong

帝俊[1]生禺号[2]，禺号生淫梁[3]，淫梁生番禺[4]，是始为舟。番禺生奚仲[5]，奚仲生吉光 [6]，吉光是始以木为车 [7] 。

注释：[1]帝俊：在此指大自然。
Notes:[1] di jun (God handsome) here refers to mother nature。
[2] 禺号：指海洋。
[2]yu hao: refers to oceans and seas。
[3] 淫梁：指大河。
[3] yin liang: big rivers。
[4] 番禺：指河畔氏族。
[4] fan yu: riverbank tribes。

[5] 奚仲：指贤明的人。
[5] xi zhong: refers to wise man。
[6] 吉光：指太阳智慧。
[6] ji guang (lucky light) refers to the Sun's wisdom.
[7]车：以太阳之圆移动的器物称为车，最初读"吉"音，是用太阳的读音来表达。
[7] che(car) a kind rolling device imitating a sun disk is called Che(car), its original sound is Ji。 ki, chi, which stands for the phonetic value of sun in Pu speech。

译文：大自然形成了海洋，又形成了大河，大河边聚集了河畔氏族，他们开始发明了一种碗形的器物，以碗的濮语读音命名为笠，后来又称为舟。在发明了笠之后，河畔氏族中有贤明之人，受到了太阳智慧的启发，便用木头做成形如太阳光芒四射的圆，并且像太阳一样可以移动的器物，人们便以太阳的濮语读音将这种器物命名为"車"，"車"即且，指太阳。
Translation:
Mother Nature creates oceans and seas, which create big rivers。 Riverside tribes collected and settled by the big rivers。 They created a kind of bowl-shaped device。 The device is called: Li in Pu speech for bowl, and later called zhou(boat)。 After the invention of Li, the wise man of the riverbank tribes, enlightened by the wisdom of the sun, created a circular shape with wood, resembling the rays of the sun, which can roll and move like the sun。 Thus, people name the device Che which is the Pu speech for sun。 Che is a car, e.g., Qie, as well as the sun。

18-33 般
Ban

少皞生般[1]，般是始为弓矢。

注释：[1]般：指工匠头领。相当于工程师。由布、恩二字拼成。布，指师；恩，指头。
Notes:[1] ban: the headmaster of handicrafts guild。 The headmaster can be compared to the engineers today。 The script for Ban, the headmaster, is a compound of two parts, bu and en, bu， as teacher, en, as head。

译文：少皞部落中最早产生了工匠头，工匠头最早发明了弓箭。
Translation:
It is first in the Shaohao tribes that the headmaster of handicrafts comes into being。 The headmaster is the first engineer who created the bow and arrows。

18-34
帝俊赐羿彤弓素矰
Dijunciyi tonggong suzeng

帝俊[1]赐羿彤弓[2]素矰[3]，以扶下国[4]，羿是始去恤下地之百艰[5]。

注释：[1]帝俊：大地中。
Notes: [1] di jun (God handsome): on earth, on the land。
[2] 赐羿彤弓：指蚩尤中国。
[2]ci yi tong gong (bestow Yi red bow)
Tr: refers to Chiyou's China。
[3] 素矰：指九夷支系。
[3]su zeng: refers to the nine branches of Yi 。
[4] 以扶下国：指大伏羲国。

[4] yi fu xia guo (hold lower country)
Tr: refers to the Dafuxi Guo。

[5] 羿是始去恤下地之百艰：尤最早开创东方的首脑之国。百艰，读博贾，指首脑。
[5] yi sh shi qu xue xia di zhi bai jian (Yi starts to relieve the hundred difficulties of its subordinates)
Tr: the chieftain Chiyou is the first to take the title of King in the east。 baijian (hundred difficulties) meaning bojia, the head of state or kingdom， shounao (head and brain) 。

译文：在大地之中，有一个蚩尤中国的九夷支系，称为大伏羲国。蚩尤最早开创了东方的首脑之国。
Translation:
In the middle of land, there is a Chiyou China composed of nine Yi, which is known as Dafuxi Guo。 Chiyou is the first one to create， in the East, a nation with a head of the state。

18-35 晏龙
Yanlong
（121,76312E；37,26963N）

帝俊生晏龙[1]，晏龙是为琴瑟[2]。

注释：[1]晏龙：指昆嵛山，简称嵛山，读音嵛陇，谐音晏龙。
Notes： [1] yan long: refers to Kunyu Mountain, shortened to Yushan, reads as Yulong, a phonetic match to Yanlong。

[2] 琴瑟：指且舍。
[2] qin se: refers to Qieshe, a place name 。

译文：大自然形成了昆嵛山，昆嵛山就是且舍地区。
Translation:
Mother Nature created the Kunyu Mountain。 The Kunyu Mountain is also known as the Qieshe region。

18-36 帝俊八子
Dijunbazi

帝俊有子八人[1]，是始为歌舞[2]。

注释：[1]帝俊有子八人：北方有芝饶惹。帝俊，在此指北方；子八人，读芝饶惹。
Notes:[1] di jun you zi ba ren (God handsome has eight sons)
Tr: in the northern region, there is a Zhiraore。 Dijun： refers to the north, zibaren: eight sons: a region called Zhiraore。

[2] 是始为歌舞：是最早的北方城镇。指赤峰古城，是芝饶石韦蒙羲的都城。
[2] shi shi wei ge wu (thus start singing and dancing)
Tr: this is the earliest township in the north, known as Chifeng (red cliff), which is the capital city of the Shiweimengxi of the Zhirao area。

译文：北方有一个集镇叫芝饶惹，是最早的北方城镇。
Translation:
There is a township in the north called Zhiraore, the earliest township in the north。

18-37 巧倕、叔均

（111,06552E；39,25102N）

帝俊生三身[1]，三身生义均[2]，义均是始为巧倕[3]，是始作下民百巧[4]。后稷是播百谷[5]。稷之孙曰叔均[6]，是始作牛耕[7]。大比赤阴[8]，是始为国。禹、鲧是始布土[9]，均定九州[10]。

注释：[1]三身：指较平缓的地区。
Notes: [1] san shen (three body) refers to the relatively flat land。
[2] 义均：指水边部落。
[2] yi jun: refers to the waterside tribes。
[3] 巧倕：指穄氏族，代指种粮氏族。
[3] qiao chui: refers to the Ji tribe, a term for the grain growing tribes。
[4] 下民百巧：指国家种粮部落。百巧，读巴穄。
[4] xia min bai qiao: refers to the nation's tribes that grow grains。
[5] 播百谷：农业部落国。
[5]bo bai gu (grow hundred grains): agricultural tribal nations。
[6] 稷之孙曰叔均：海则之肆的叔均。
[6] shu zhi song yue shu jun (shun's grandson name shujun) refers to Haizesi's Shujun。
[7] 是始作牛耕：最早建立河边之国。牛耕，指河边之国。
[7] shi shi zuo niu geng (thus start ox plow) the earliest nation by the riverside。Niugeng: countries by the riverbanks。
[8] 大比赤阴：读档沘澈溢，指清水河镇，是叔均兼并`海则部落前的部落名和集镇名。
[8] da bi chi yin reads as dangbicheyi, referring to the Qingshuihe Zhen, a tribal name and township name known before Shuyun annexed the Haize tribe。
[9]禹、鲧是始布土：窟野河是最早征服的地区，称为博吐。
[9]yu, gun shi shi bu tu (yu and gun thus spread soil)
Tr: Kuye River area is the first region to be conquered。 It is called Botu。
[10] 均定九州：叔均将它定为叔周。
[10] jun ding jiu zhou (jun divides nine provinces)
Tr: Shujun decided to name it Shuzhou。

译文：大自然形成了较平缓的地区，又产生了河边的部落。河边的部落最早形成粮食氏族，最早形成了国家的种粮部落。海则部落是农业部落国。海则之肆的叔均最早建立河边的城镇，叫清水河镇，是最早建立的国家联盟。窟野河是叔均最早征服的地区，并将其定为叔周。
Translation:
Mother Nature creates relatively flat lands and tribes created along the riverbanks。The riverbank tribes become the earliest grain growing tribes, the earliest tribes to produce grain for the state。 Haize tribe is an agricultural tribal nation。Shuyun from Haize Si built the earliest township by the river, which is called the Qingshuihe Zhen。Qingshuihe Zhen is the earliest union of nations。 Kuye River region is Shuyun's earliest conquest, which he named Shuzhou。

18-38 炎帝之孙

炎帝之妻[1]，赤水之子听訞生炎居[2]，炎居生节并[3]，节并生戏器[4]，戏器生祝融[5]。祝融降处江水，生共工[6]。共工生术器[7]，术器首方颠[8]，是复土穰[9]，以处江水[10]。共工生后土[11]，后土生噎鸣[12]，噎鸣生岁十有二[13]。

注释：[1]炎帝之妻：大地中的犬戎。
Notes： [1] yan di zhi qi (God yan's wife)
Tr: The Quanrong (dog rong) of the land。

[2] 赤水之子听訞生炎居：黄河支系的大庭氏建立了大部落联盟。听訞，指大庭氏；炎居，指大部落联盟。
[2] chi shui zhi zi ting wo sheng yan ju (red river's son listen to wo begets yan ju)
Tr: The Dating Shi from the Yellow River branch established a big tribal confederacy。 Tingwo: Dating shi (big hall meeting) yan ju: big confederacy of tribes。

[3] 焉居生节并：大部落联盟叫吉博，也称博羲、包牺。
[3] yan ju sheng jie bing (yanju begets Bingjie)
Tr: the big tribal confederacy is called Jibo, also known as Boxi, or Baoxi。

[4] 节并生戏器：吉博中有煦犬戎。也称华胥犬戎。
[4] jie bing sheng xi qi (jiebing begets xiqi) Jibo includes Xu Dogrong, which is also known as Huaxu Dogrong (quan rong) 。

[5] 戏器生祝融：煦犬戎分支出草原氏族。
[5] xi qi sheng zhu rong (xiqi begets zhurong)
Tr: the Xu Dogrong branches out to form the steppe tribes。

[6] 祝融降处江水，生共工：草原氏族得势辉煌，分支出共工氏。
[6] zhu rong jiang chu jiang shui, sheng Gonggong (zhurong descended to Jiangshui, begets Gonggong)
Tr: the steppe tribes become very powerful and branches out to form the Gonggong Shi。

[7] 共工生术器：共工氏分支出蜀犬戎。
[7] Gong gong sheng shu qi (gonggong begets shuqi)
Tr: gonggong Shi branches out to form the Shuquanrong (the Shu dog rong) 。

[8] 术器首方颠：蜀犬戎族统治的能沽平原。颠，指甸、平原。
[8] shu qi shou fang dian: the Dogrong of Shu controls the Nenggu plain。dian (top）refers to Dian, the flat land and the plain。

[9] 是复土穰：成为濮族地区的王。穰，指龙，代指王。
[9] shi fu tu xiang: thus become the lord or king of the territory of the Pu people, xiang: dragon, a term for lord or king。

[10] 以处江水：再度辉煌。
[10] yi chu jiang shui (thus stay in river）
Tr： become glorious and powerful again。

[11] 共工生后土：共工后裔的恒投氏。
[11] gonggong sheng hou tu (gonggong begets Houtu)
Tr: The Descendants of Gonggong are called Hengtou Shi。

[12] 后土生噎鸣：恒投氏形成了织绸氏族。
[12] houtu sheng yiming (Houtu begets Yiming) Hengtou Shi form the silk producing tribes。

[13] 噎鸣生岁十有二：织绸氏族分支成十二个支系，就是十二个月亮氏族，被喻为常羲生月。
[13] yi ming sheng sui you shi er (yiming begets year with 12 months)
Tr: the silk tribes branched out into 12 lineages, known as the 12 moon tribes。 The fact is narrated as Changxi gives birth to 12 moons。

译文：大地中的犬戎，黄河支系的大庭氏建立了大部落联盟，称为博羲联盟。博羲联盟中的华胥犬戎的草原氏族，在辉煌时期分支出了共工氏。共工氏分支出的蜀犬戎，因统治着能沽平原，成为濮族地区的王而再度辉煌。共工氏的后裔恒投氏在能沽平原形成了织绸氏族，并分支为十二个支系。
Translation:

The Quanrong (dogrong) of the land, the Dating Shi of the Yellow River branch, established a big tribal confederacy, known as the Boxi confederacy。 Of this Boxi confederacy, a branch called Huaxu Dogrong from the steppe creates the Gonggong Shi during its most glorious and powerful period。 From the Gonggong Shi branches out the Shu Quanrong。 It has taken control of the Nenggu plain, thus creating a second period of glorious and powerful stage。 The Gonggong Shi's descendants Hengtou Shi formed the silk producing tribes in Nenggu Plain and divided the group into 12 branches。

18-39 鲧窃息壤
Gunqiexirang
（110,31322E；38,56515N）

洪水滔天[1]。鲧窃帝之息壤以堙洪水[2]，不待帝命 [3] 。帝令祝融 [3] 杀鲧于羽郊 [5] 。鲧复生禹 [6] 。帝乃命禹卒布土 [7] 以定九州 [8] 。

注释：[1]洪水滔天：胡族饕餮，即胡族侵蚀夏土。
Notes:[1] hong shui tao tian (floods rise to sky)
Tr: The Hu people （taotie） invaded the land of the Xia nation。
[2] 鲧窃帝之息壤以堙洪水：夏启北上攻杀以战胡族。息壤，指攻杀；堙，指战。
[2] gun qie di zhi xi rang yi yan hong shui (gun steal god's settling soil to stop the flood)
Tr: Xiaqi went to the north to attack and conquer the Hu people. xirang (settling soil), attack and kill; yan; to fight against。
[3] 不待帝命：布兵于北地。待，指兵；帝命，狄米，指北地。
[3] bu dai di ming (not wait for God order)
Tr: position army in the north. dai(wait)means army, diming (god's order) reads as dimi, meaning northern territory。
[4] 帝令祝融：北蔺的草原氏族。
[4] di ling zhu rong (di order zhurong)
Tr: the steppe tribes from Beilin (northern regions) 。
[5] 杀鲧于羽郊：入侵夏的羽召。羽召，指北朝歌，即北王城，又称圣城，读音石峁（mu）。
[5] sha yun yu yu jiao (kill gun at feather suburb)
Tr: invading Xia's territory known as Yuzhao。 Yuzhao is Beichaoge, the Beiwang cheng (Northern King's city), also known as Holy city, reads as Shimu (shimao)。
[6] 鲧复生禹：夏王收复了羽召。鲧复，指夏王；禹，指羽召。
[6] gun fu sheng yu (Gun again begets Yu)
Tr. Xia king reclaimed the city Yuzhao。 Gunfu; refers to the Xiawang, king of the Xia nation, Yu; refers to Yuzhao, the Holy city。
[7] 帝乃命禹布土：北地羽召管理区。
[7] di nai ming yu bu tu (God order Yu spread earth)
Tr: northern territory is controlled by Yuzhao。
[8] 以定九州：定给叔周。九，读"数"音，是"叔"的谐音。
[8] yi ding jiu zhou (thus decide nine provinces)
Tr: designated the city to Shuzhou's control。 jiu(nine) reads shu, a phonetic match to shu in Pu speech。

译文：胡族侵蚀夏土，夏启北上攻杀以战胡族，布兵于北地。北蔺的草原氏族入侵夏的羽召，夏王收复了羽召，将北地羽召管理区定给叔周部落管理。
Translation:

Hu people invaded the territory of Xia nation。 Qi, Xia's King commanded his force to go to the north to attack the Hu and positioned his army in the north。 The steppe tribes of Beilin invaded the holy city Yuzhao, and the king of Xia reclaimed the city of Yuzhao and entrusted this northern administration city to the care of Shuzhou tribes。

Feb. 28,2024

附录：线路图

山海经山经线路图

Maps of Mountains

一、　　南山经线路图：1、2、3：mountains in the south

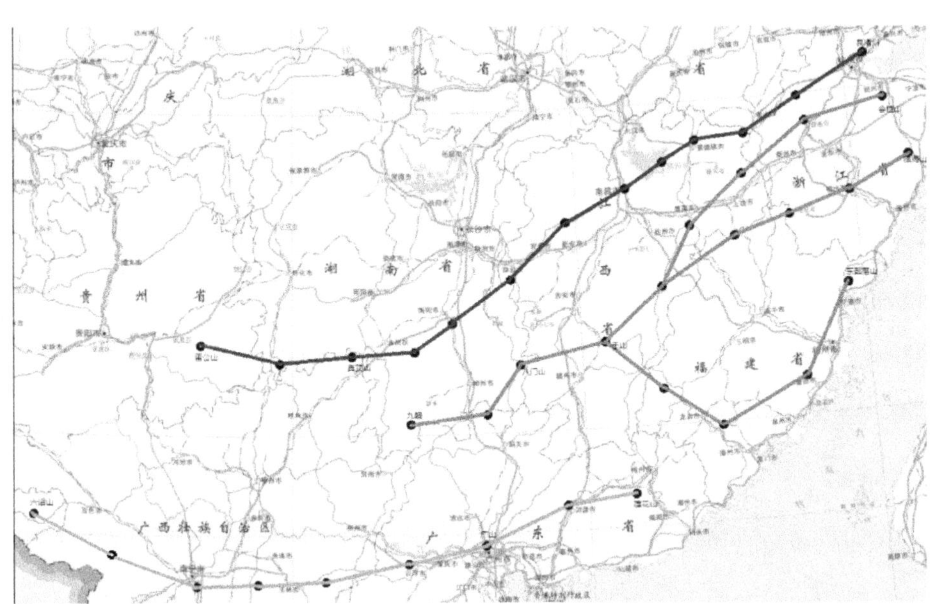

南山经顺序为绿、红、深红

二、西山经线路图 1、2：mountains in the west

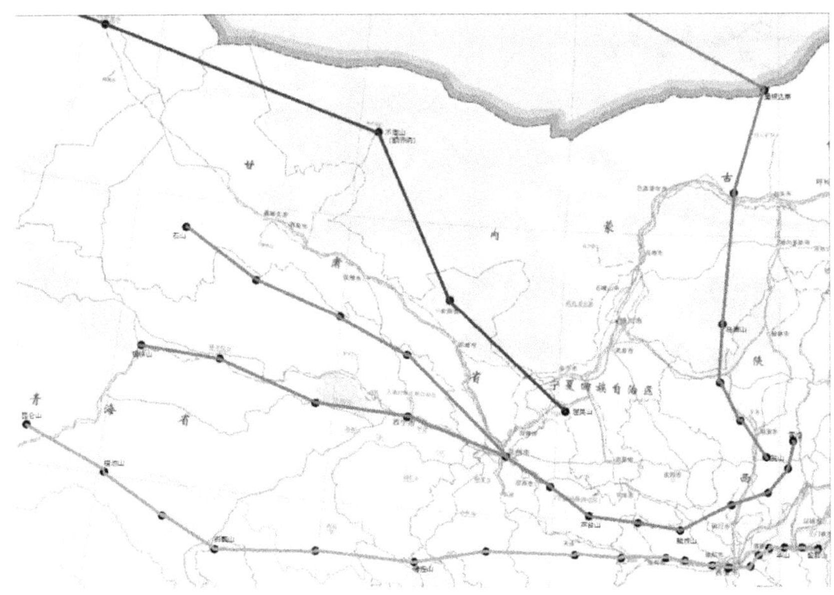

西山经图 1：　1、2、3、4 经顺序为绿、红、深红、紫

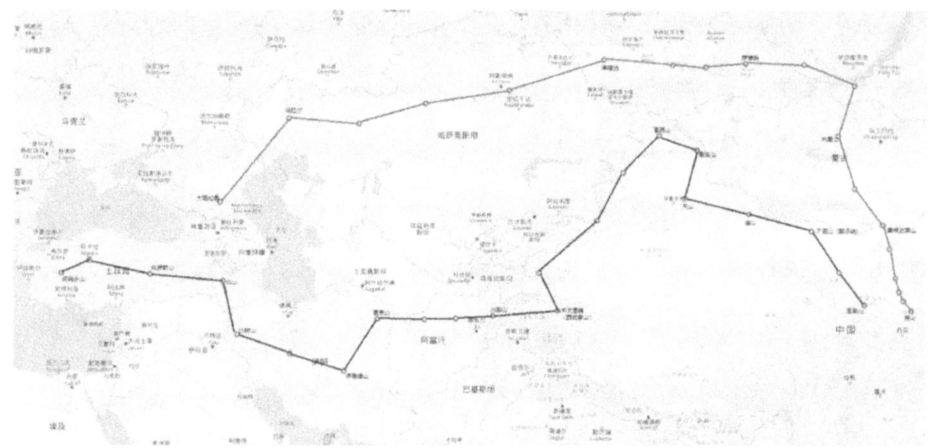

西山经图 2. 3、4 经顺序为深红、紫

三、北山经线路图 1、2：mountains in the north

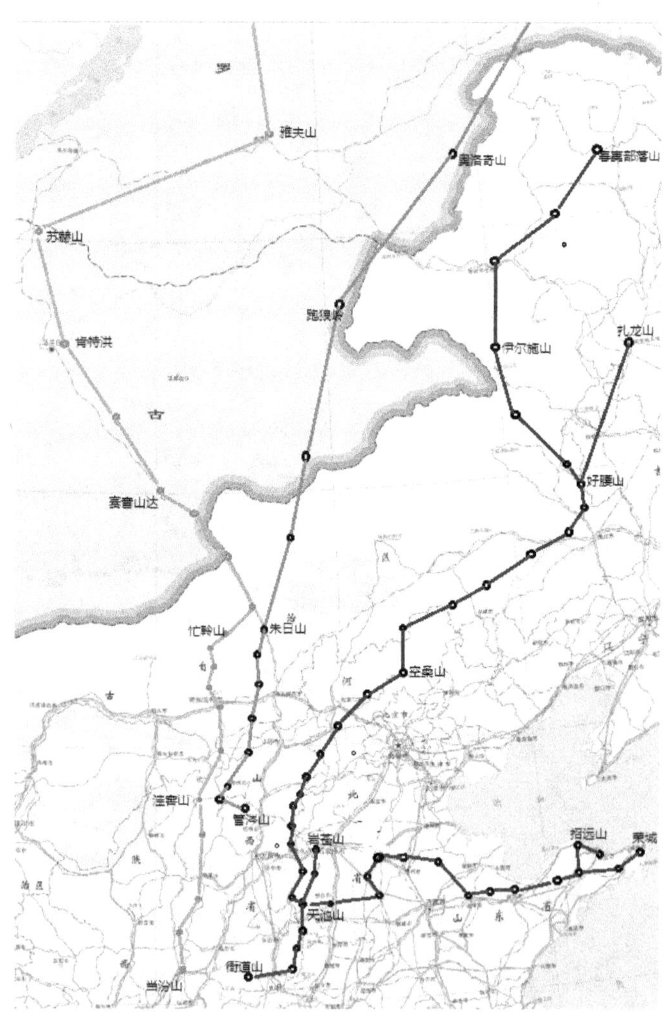

北山经图 1. 1、2、3 经顺序为绿、红、深红

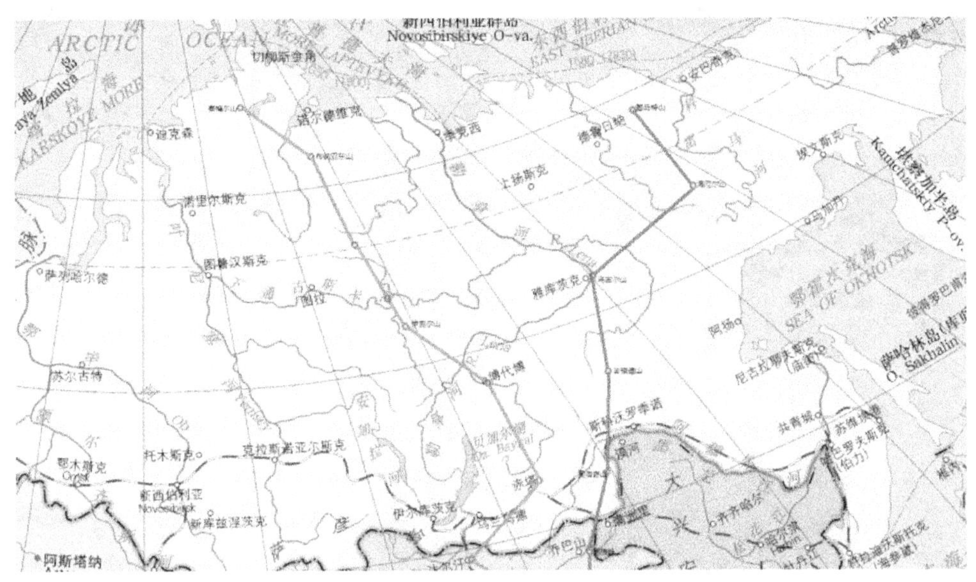

北山经图 2. 1、2 经顺序为绿、红

四、东山经线路图：mountains in the east

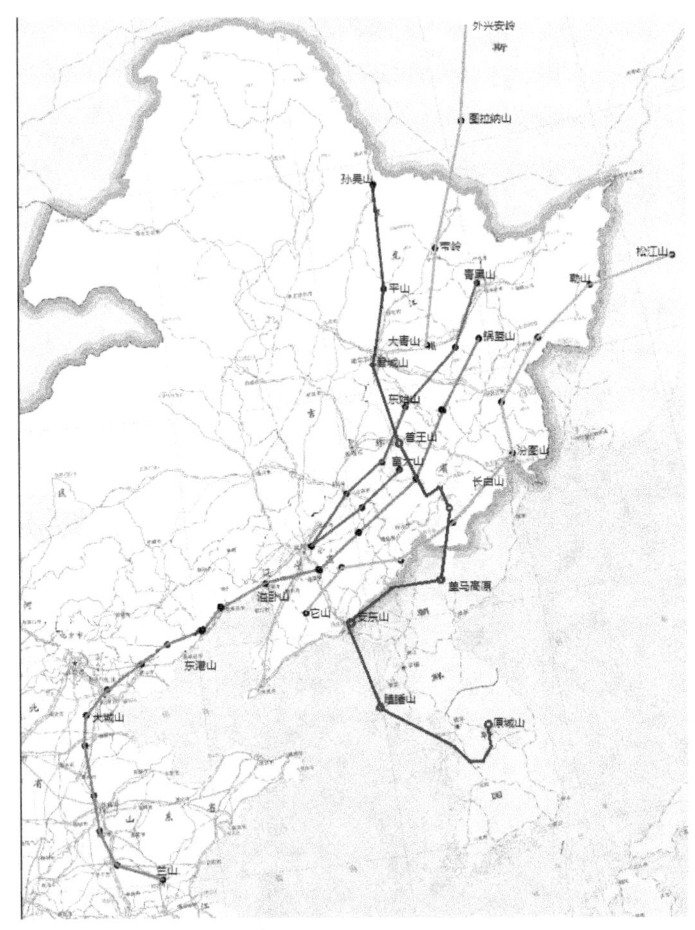

东山经顺序为绿、红、深红、紫

五、中山经线路图：mountains in the middle

（一）1、2、3、4 经：

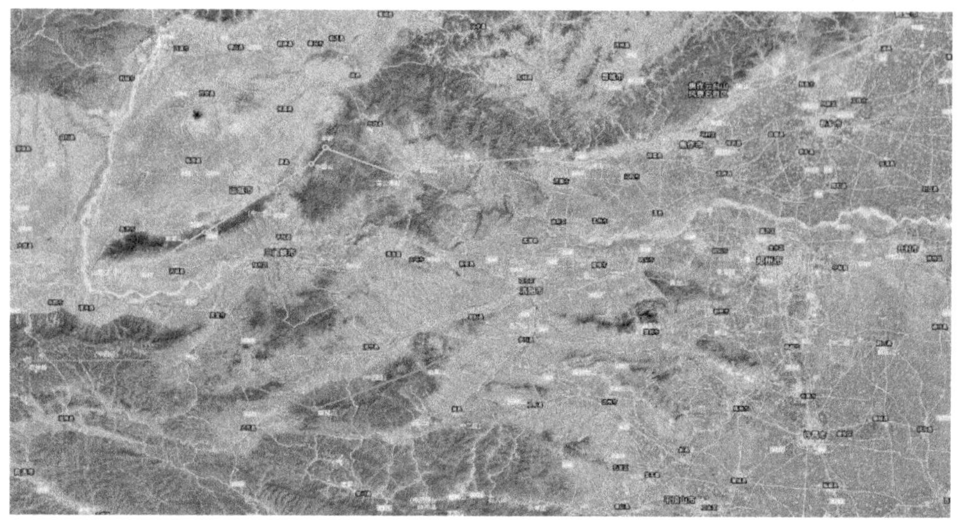

1、2、3、4 经顺序为绿、红、深红、紫

（二）5、9、10 经：

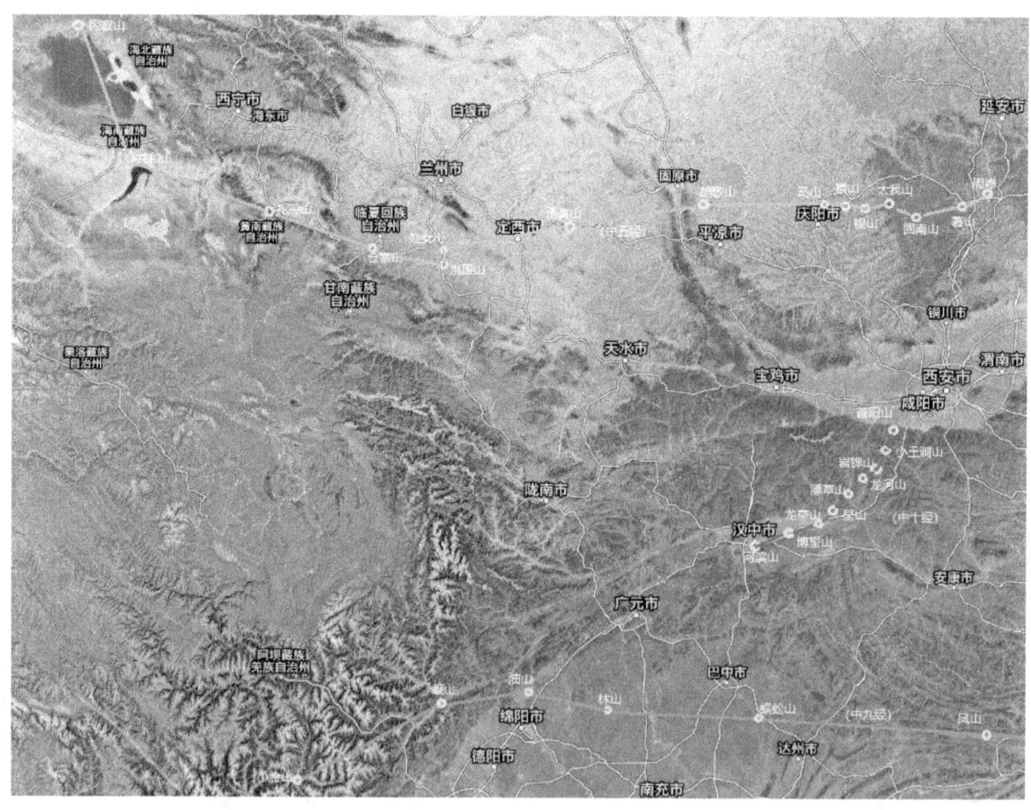

5、9、10 经顺序为绿、红、深红

（三）6、7、12 经：

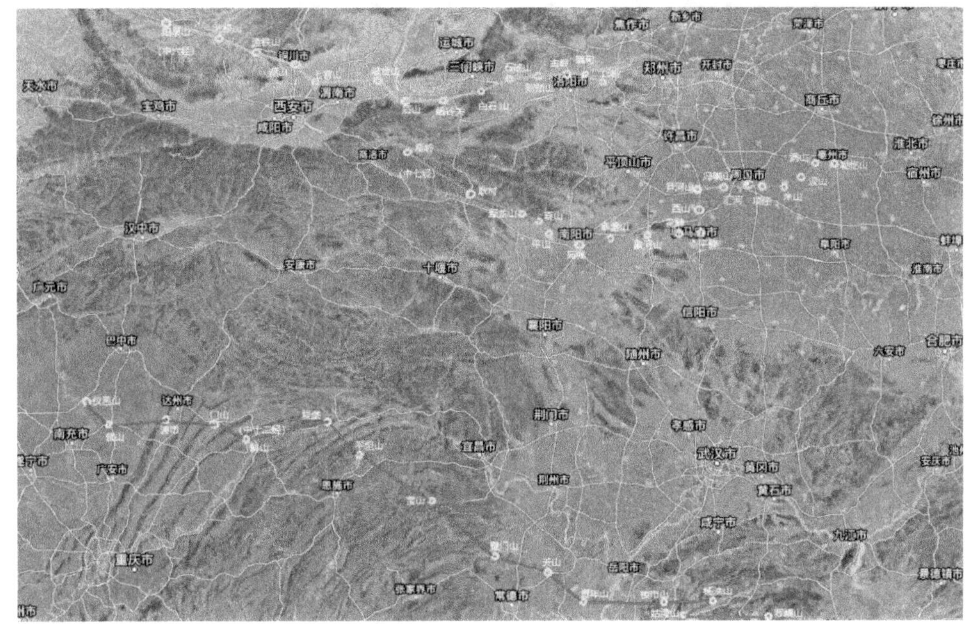

6、7、12 经顺序为绿、红、深红

（四）8、9、11 经：

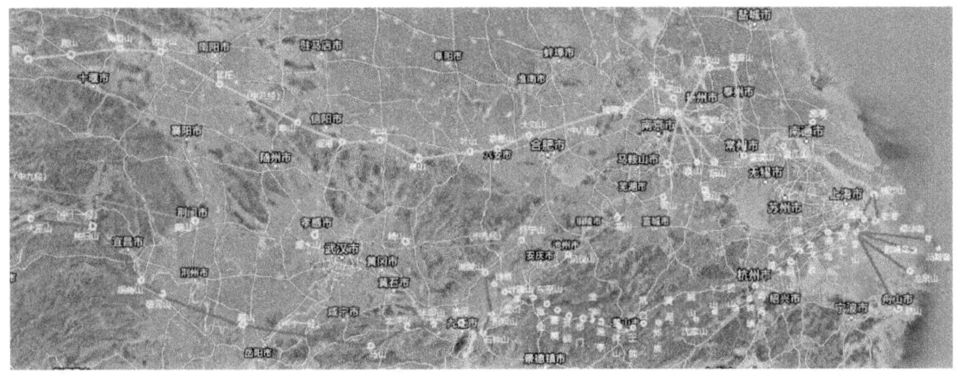

8、9、11 经顺序为绿、红、深红

山海经海经线路图

Shanhaijing Maps of Haiwai and Hainei

一、海外南经：south region of Haiwai

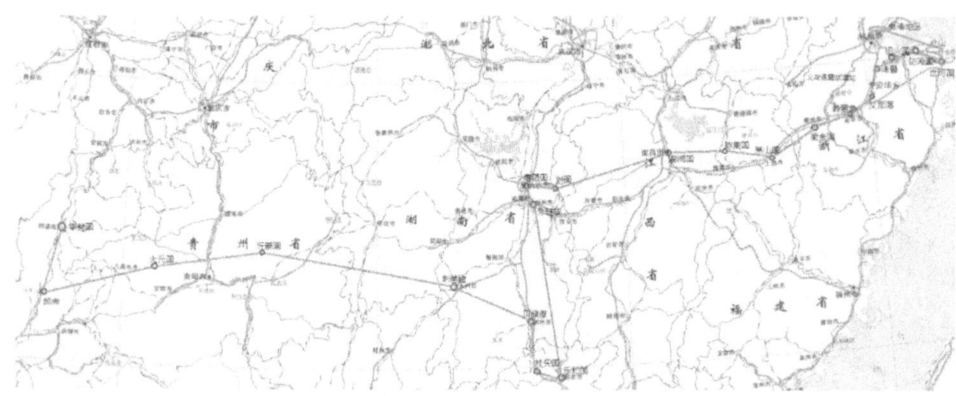

二、海外西经：west region of Haiwai

三、海外北经：north region of Haiwai

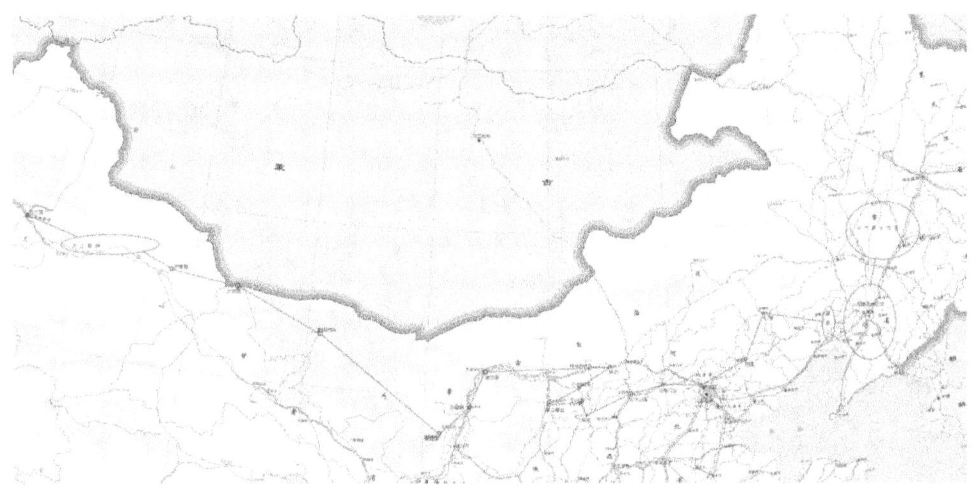

四、海外东经：east region of Haiwai

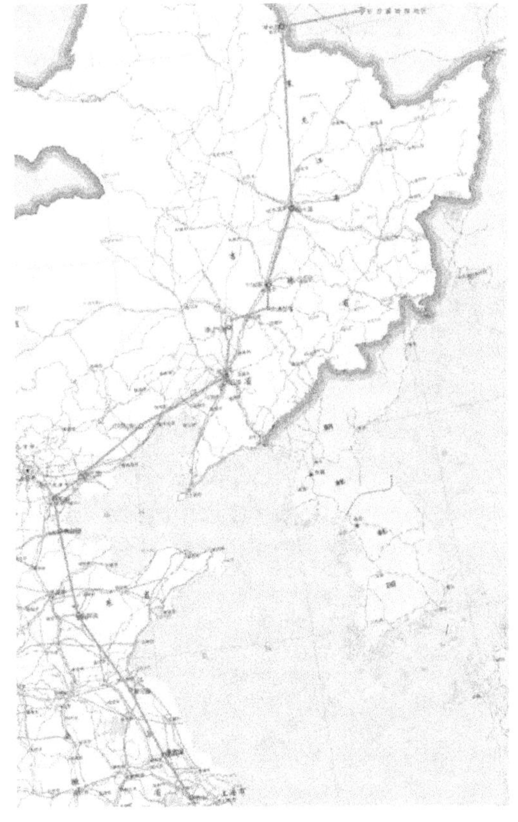

五、海内南经：south region of Hainei

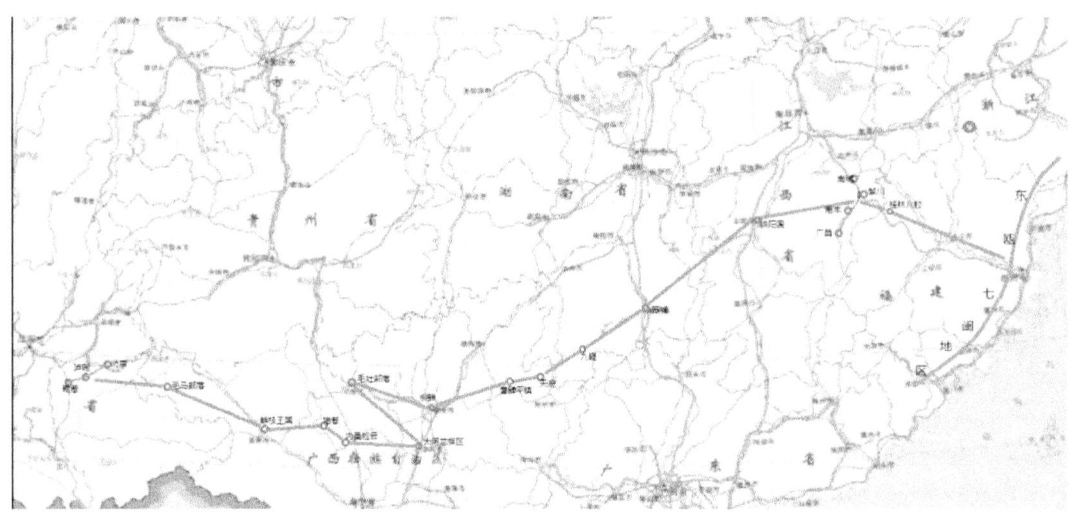

六、海内西经：west region of Hainei

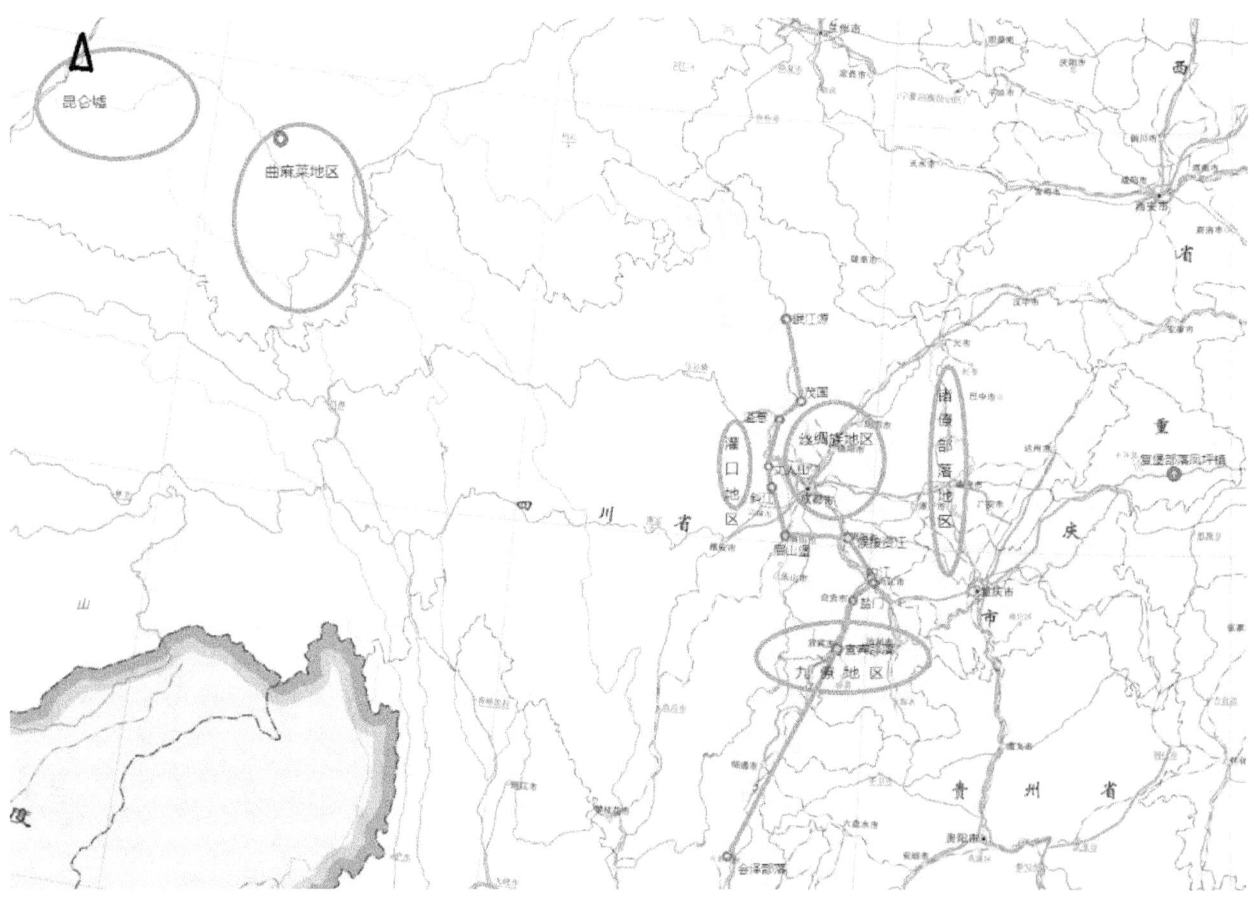

七、海内北经：north region of Hainei

八、海内东经：east region of Hainei

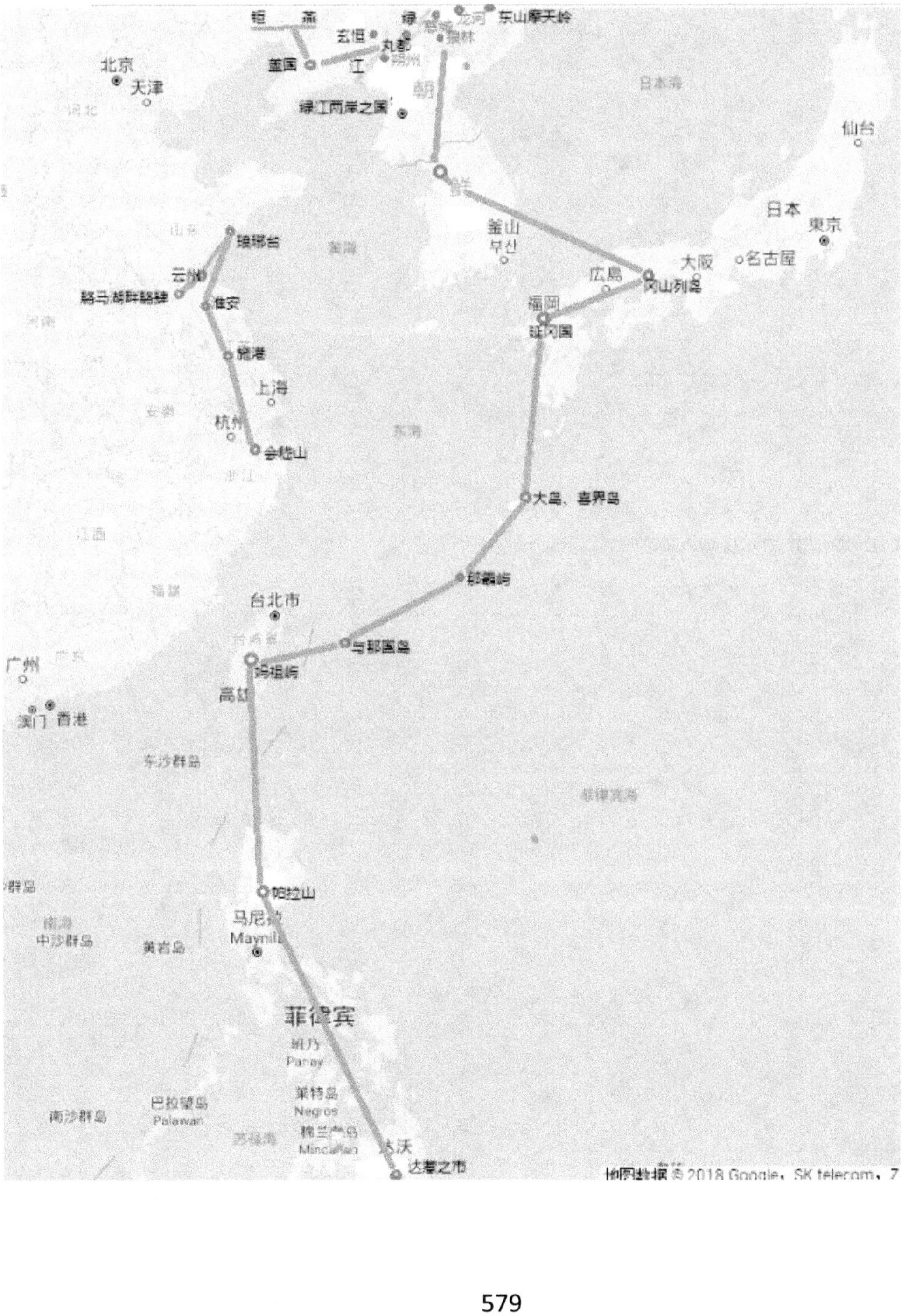

山海经大荒经线路图

Maps of Great Wilderness

一、大荒南经：south region of great wilderness

二、大荒西经：west region of great wilderness

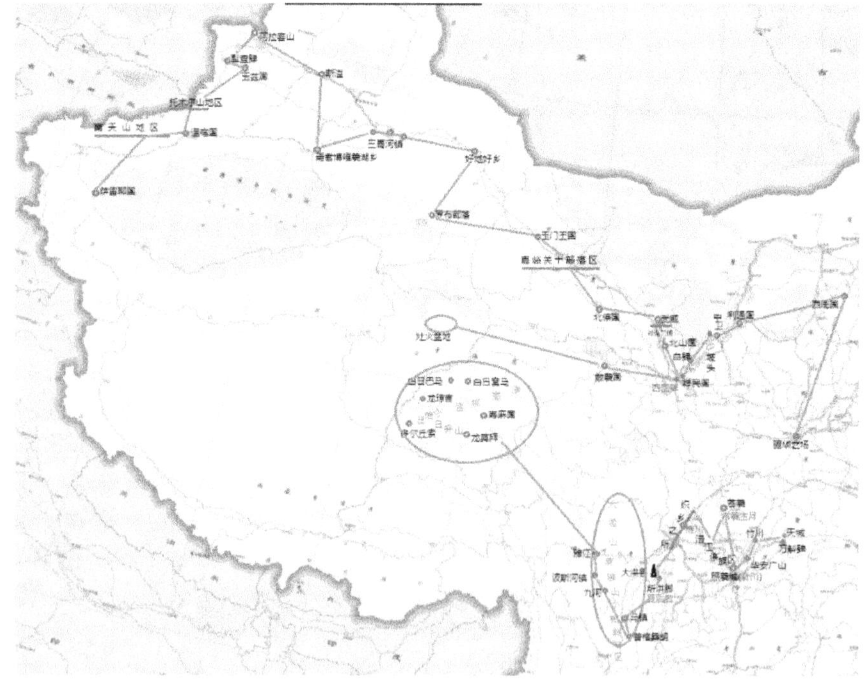

三、大荒北经（1、2）： north region of great wilderness

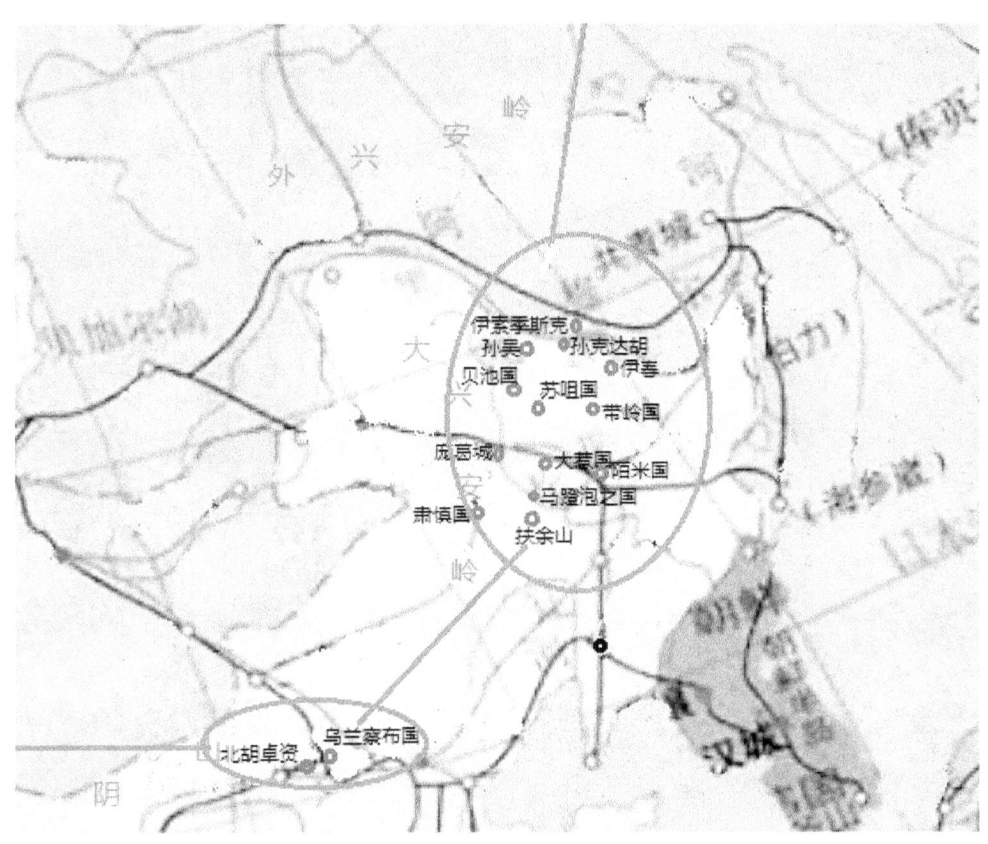

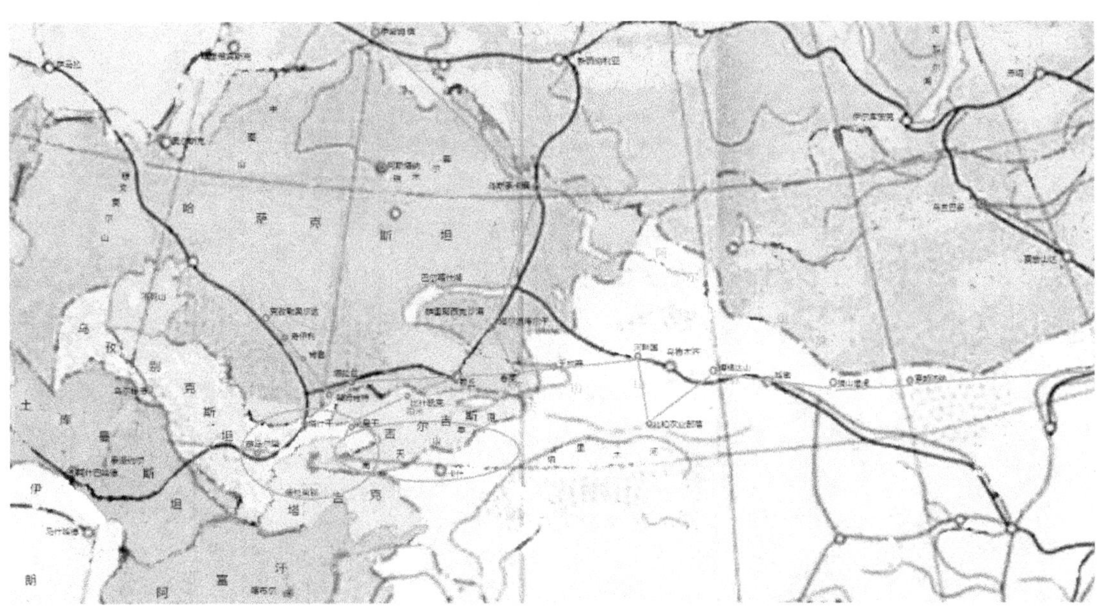

四、大荒东经：east region of great wilderness

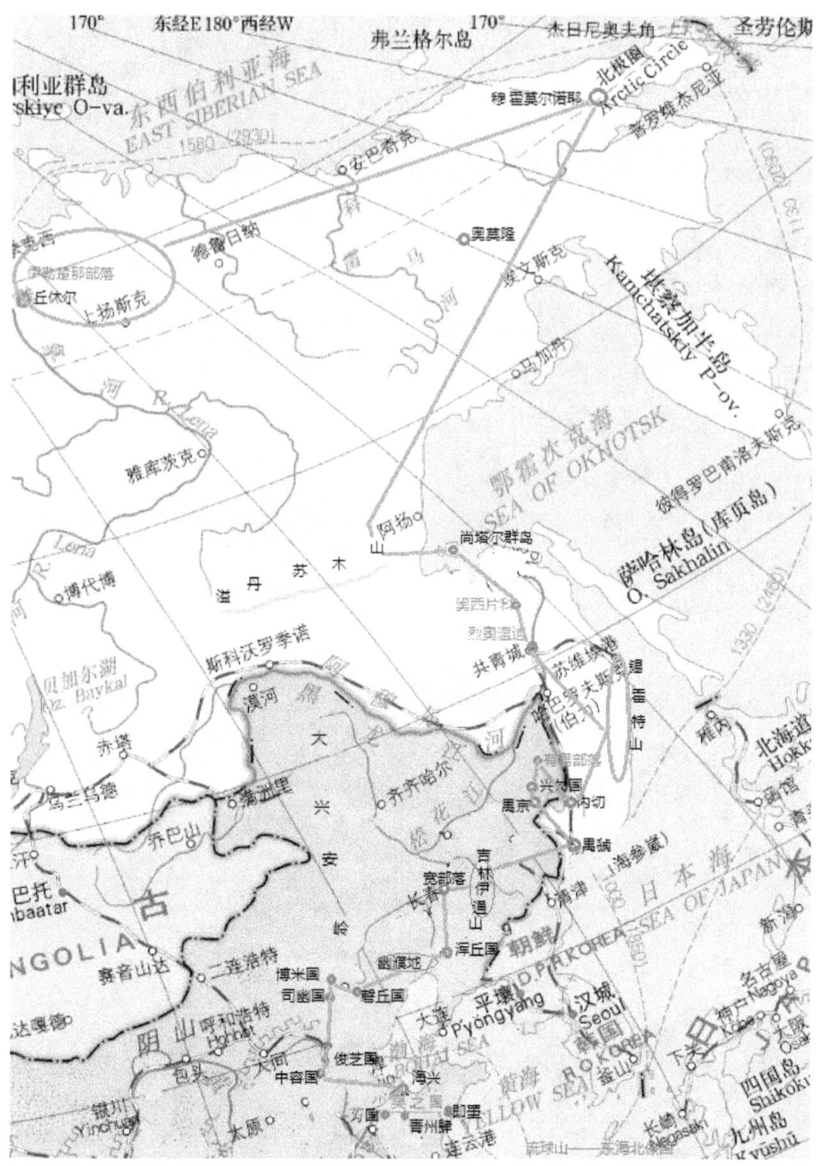